Who Was Who in America
Index
1607-1993

Biographical Titles Currently Published by Marquis Who's Who

Who's Who in America
Who's Who in America derivatives:
  Who's Who in America Junior & Senior High School Version
  Geographic/Professional Index
  Who's Who in America Classroom Project Book
Who Was Who in America
  Historical Volume (1607-1896)
  Volume I (1897-1942)
  Volume II (1943-1950)
  Volume III (1951-1960)
  Volume IV (1961-1968)
  Volume V (1969-1973)
  Volume VI (1974-1976)
  Volume VII (1977-1981)
  Volume VIII (1982-1985)
  Volume IX (1985-1989)
  Volume X (1989-1993)
  Index Volume (1607-1993)
Who's Who in the World
Who's Who in the East
Who's Who in the Midwest
Who's Who in the South and Southwest
Who's Who in the West
Who's Who in Advertising
Who's Who in American Education
Who's Who in American Law
Who's Who in American Nursing
Who's Who of American Women
Who's Who of Emerging Leaders in America
Who's Who in Entertainment
Who's Who in Finance and Industry
Who's Who in Religion
Who's Who in Science and Engineering
Index to Who's Who Books
The Official American Board of Medical Specialties
  Directory of Board Certified Medical Specialists

Who Was Who in America ®
with World Notables

Index
1993
Volumes I-X and Historical Volume

MARQUIS
Who's Who

A Reed Reference Publishing Company
121 Chanlon Road
New Providence, New Jersey 07974 U.S.A.

Sandra S. Barnes—Publisher
Peter E. Simon—Senior Vice President, Database Publishing
Leigh Yuster—Associate Publisher
Paul Canning—Editorial Director
Frederick Marks—Senior Managing Editor
Harriet Tiger—Senior Editor

Library of Congress Catalog Card Number 81–84493
International Standard Book Numbers 0–8379–0221–5

CÜI1
91649

Manufactured in the United States of America

Introduction

This Index to *Who Was Who in America* lists biographees
found in the Historical Volume (1607-1896) and in volumes
I through X (1897-1993). The Index includes the names
of approximately 122,000 deceased biographees whose
personal and career data came from the following publi-
cations: *Who's Who in America, Who's Who in the East,
Who's Who in the Midwest, Who's Who in the South and
Southwest, Who's Who in the West, Who's Who in American
Law, Who's Who of American Women, Who's Who in
Entertainment, Who's Who in Finance and Industry, Who's Who
in Religion, Who's Who in Science and Engineering,* and
Who's Who in the World. Addition of date of death and place of
interment completes the sketches in *Who Was Who in America.*

The Index lists biographees alphabetically by surname.
The number following each name indicates the volume in
which the biographical sketch is found. An asterisk (*)
denotes that more than one such name is listed in the
volume indicated. H found after a name refers to the
Historical Volume.

Alphabetical Practices

Names are arranged alphabetically according to the surnames, and under identical surnames according to the first given name. If both surname and first given name are identical, names are arranged alphabetically according to the second given name.

Surnames beginning with De, Des, Du, however capitalized or spaced, are recorded with the prefix preceding the surname and arranged alphabetically under the letter D.

Surnames beginning with Mac and Mc are arranged alphabetically under M.

Surnames beginning with Saint or St. appear after names that begin Sains, and are arranged according to the second part of the name, e.g. St. Clair before Saint Dennis.

Surnames beginning with Van, Von or von are arranged alphabetically under letter V.

Compound hyphenated surnames are arranged according to the first member of the compound. Compound unhyphenated surnames are treated as hyphenated names.

Many hyphenated Arabic names begin Al–, El–, or al–. These names are alphabetized according to each biographee's designation of last name. Thus Al–Bahar, Mohammed may be listed either under Al–or under Bahar, depending on the preference of the listee.

Parentheses used in connection with a name indicate which part of the full name is usually deleted in common usage. Hence Abbott, W(illiam) Lewis indicates that the usual form of the given name is W. Lewis. In such a case, the parentheses are ignored in alphabetizing and the name would be arranged as Abbott, William Lewis. However, if the name is recorded Abbott, (William) Lewis, signifying that the entire name William is not commonly used, the alphabetizing would be arranged as though the name were Abbott, Lewis. If an entire middle or last name is enclosed in parentheses, that portion of the name is used in the alphabetical arrangement. Hence Abbott, William (Lewis) would be arranged as Abbott, William Lewis.

Index

Name		Name		Name		Name		Name	
AIRD, Alexander N.	3	ALBERTS, Joseph Ortan	4	ALDEN, Harold L.	8	ALDRICH, Sherwood	1	ALEXANDER, Hattie	5
AIREY, Charles Theodore	1	ALBERTS, Abraham	4	ALDEN, Henry Mills	1	ALDRICH, Thomas Bailey	1	Elizabeth	
AIREY, John	4	Horace		ALDEN, Herbert Watson	3	ALDRICH, Truman	1	ALEXANDER, Henry Clay	5
AIREY, Richard	4	ALBERTSON, Charles	3	ALDEN, Ichabod	H	Heminway		ALEXANDER, Henry	1
AIRHART, John C.	5	Carroll		ALDEN, Isabella	1	ALDRICH, William	H	Martyn	
AISHTON, Richard Henry	2	ALBERTSON, George	1	MacDonald		ALDRICH, William	1	ALEXANDER, Henry	3
AITCHISON, Clyde Bruce	4	Roger		ALDEN, James	H	Farrington		Martyn	
AITCHISON, John Young	1	ALBERTSON, J. Mark	4	ALDEN, John	H	ALDRICH, William Sleeper	4	ALEXANDER, Henry	H
AITCHISON, Robert J.	4	ALBERTSON, Jack	8	ALDEN, John	1	ALDRICH, William	4	Porteous	
AITKEN, David D.	4	ALBERTSON, James	4	ALDEN, John B.	1	Truman		ALEXANDER, Herbert G.	1
AITKEN, Peter		Herbert		ALDEN, Joseph	H	ALDRICH, Winthrop	6	B.	
AITKEN, Robert	H	ALBERTSON, Nathaniel	H	ALDEN, Raymond		Williams		ALEXANDER, Herbert M.	9
AITKEN, Robert Grant	3	ALBERTSON, Ralph	3	MacDonald		ALDRIDGE, Clayson	2	ALEXANDER, Hooper	1
AITKEN, Robert Ingersoll	2	ALBERTY, Harold	5	ALDEN, Timothy	H	Wheeler		ALEXANDER, Hubbard	3
AITKEN, Webster	7	(Bernard)		ALDEN, William Clinton	4	ALDRIDGE, Frederick	7	Foster	
AITKEN, Webster	8	ALBERY, Bronson James	1	ALDEN, William	1	Ferdinand		ALEXANDER, James	H
AITKEN, William Inglis	10	ALBERY, Faxon Franklin	4	Livingston		ALDRIDGE, George	4	ALEXANDER, James, Jr.	H
AKAR, John J.	6	Duane		ALDEN, William Tracy	3	Washington		ALEXANDER, James F.	1
AKE, Russell Everett	1	ALBIG, John William	4	ALDER, Byron	3	ALDRIDGE, Ira Frederick	H	ALEXANDER, James	2
AKED, Charles Frederic	1	ALBIG, Reed Harrison	4	ALDER, Kurt	3	ALDRIDGE, Walter Hull	3	Patterson	
AKELEY, Carl Ethan	1	ALBIN, Harold Cornelius	8	ALDERMAN, Edward	4	ALDRIN, Edwin Eugene	10	ALEXANDER, James	1
AKELEY, Healy Cady	1	ALBING, Otto Frederick	1	Sinclair		ALDUNATE, Don	1	Strange	
AKELEY, Lewis Ellsworth	4	ALBION, James Francis	4	ALDERMAN, Edwin	1	Santiago		ALEXANDER, James	H
AKELEY, Mary L. Jobe	4	ALBION, Robert	8	Anderson		ALEMANY, Jose Sadoc	H	Waddel	
AKERBERG, Herbert	4	Greenhalgh		ALDERMAN, Frank	6	ALENCASTRE, Stephen	2	ALEXANDER, James	1
Vestner		ALBJERG, Victor L.	9	ALDERMAN, Grover		Peter		Waddell	
AKERMAN, Alexander	2	ALBRAND, Martha (Mrs.	8	Henry		ALERDING, Herman	1	ALEXANDER, James	5
AKERMAN, Amos Tappan	H	Sydney J. Lamon)		ALDERMAN, Louis	9	Joseph		Wadell, II	
AKERMAN, John D.	5	ALBRECHT, Arthur Emil	9	Cleveland, Jr.		ALESHIRE, Arthur	1	ALEXANDER, James	8
AKERS, Anthony Boyce	7	ALBRECHT, George Jacob	7	ALDERMAN, Rhenas	6	William		Wendell	
AKERS, Benjamin Paul	H	ALBRECHT, Ralph	10	Hoffard		ALESHIRE, Edward	4	ALEXANDER, Jerome	3
AKERS, Elizabeth	1	Gerhart		ALDERMAN, William	4	ALESHIRE, James	1	ALEXANDER, John	H
AKERS, Floyd Desoto	7	ALBRECHT, Richard	7	Elijah		Buchanan		ALEXANDER, John	3
AKERS, Lewis Robeson	6	George		ALDERMANN, Lewis R.	5	ALESSANDRI-PALMA,	5	ALEXANDER, John	4
AKERS, Milburn Peter	5	ALBRECHT, William	8	ALDERSON, Victor Clifton	2	Arturo		Brevard	
AKERS, Oscar Perry	5	A(lbert)		ALDERSON, Wroe	4	ALESSANDRO, Victor	7	ALEXANDER, John	10
AKERS, Samuel Luttrell	7	ALBRECHT-CARRIÉ,	7	ALDINGTON, Richard	4	Nicholas		Davis, Sr.	
AKERS, Sheldon		René		ALDIS, Arthur Taylor	1	ALESSANDRONI, Eugene	8	ALEXANDER, John E.	4
Buckingham		ALBREN, Edward Joseph	6	ALDIS, Dorothy Keeley	4	Victor		ALEXANDER, John Frank	10
AKERS, Susan Grey	9	ALBRIGHT, Adam Emory	3	ALDIS, Graham	4	ALESSANDRONI, Walter	4	ALEXANDER, John	7
AKERS, Thomas Peter	H	ALBRIGHT, Arthur	9	ALDIS, Mary Reynolds	2	Edwin		Gordon	
AKERSON, George	1	S(tanley)		ALDIS, Owen Franklin	1	ALEXANDER, Abraham	H	ALEXANDER, John Heald	10
Edward		ALBRIGHT, Charles	H	ALDRED, John Edward	2	ALEXANDER, Adam	H	ALEXANDER, John Henry	H
AKERSON, George	7	ALBRIGHT, Charles	6	ALDREDGE, George N.	7	ALEXANDER, Adam	1	ALEXANDER, John L.	1
Edward, Jr.		Clinton		ALDREY Y MONTOLIO,	1	Rankin		ALEXANDER, John	3
AKHARAJ	4	ALBRIGHT, Charles Edgar	2	Pedro de		ALEXANDER, Albert	4	MacMillan	
VARADHARA, Phya		ALBRIGHT, Charles		ALDRICH, Anne Reeve	H	Victor		ALEXANDER, John	3
AKIN, Charles Vivian	8	Jefferson		ALDRICH, Auretta Roys	4	ALEXANDER, Albert	7	Romich	
AKIN, John	4	ALBRIGHT, Edward	1	ALDRICH, Bess Streeter	3	Victor (Viscount		ALEXANDER, John White	1
AKIN, Margaret Catherine	6	ALBRIGHT, Edwin	1	ALDRICH, Charles	1	Alexander of		ALEXANDER, Joseph	H
Rouse (Mrs. Austin		ALBRIGHT, E(dwin) Roy	8	ALDRICH, Charles	2	Hillsborough)		Addison	
Franklin Akin)		ALBRIGHT, Frank	1	Anderson		ALEXANDER, Archibald	7	ALEXANDER, Joshua W.	1
AKIN, Spencer Ball	6	Herman		ALDRICH, Charles Henry	1	Stevens		ALEXANDER, Julian	3
AKIN, Theron	1	ALBRIGHT, Fuller	5	ALDRICH, Charles John	5	ALEXANDER, Armstead	H	Power	
AKIN, Thomas Russell	2	ALBRIGHT, Guy Harry	5	ALDRICH, Charles	6	Milton		ALEXANDER, Leigh	2
AKINS, Zoe	3	ALBRIGHT, Horace	9	Spaulding		ALEXANDER, Arvin J.	8	ALEXANDER, Leroy	7
AKOLT, John Patrick, Jr.	7	Madden		ALDRICH, Chester Hardy	1	ALEXANDER, Barton	H	Montgomery	
ALA, Hussein	4	ALBRIGHT, Ivan	8	ALDRICH, Chester Holmes	1	Stone		ALEXANDER, Lester	3
ALABASTER, Francis	3	ALBRIGHT, Jacob	H	ALDRICH, Chilson	2	ALEXANDER, Ben	2	Fisher	
Asbury		ALBRIGHT, Jacob	5	Darragh		ALEXANDER, Benjamin	4	ALEXANDER, Louis	10
ALAJALOV, Constantin	9	Dissinger		ALDRICH, Clyde Frank	8	Carter		ALEXANDER, Lyle	8
ALANSON, Bertram	3	ALBRIGHT, John Joseph	1	ALDRICH, Cyrus	H	ALEXANDER, Charles	5	Thomas	
Edward		ALBRIGHT, Malvin Marr	8	ALDRICH, Daniel Gaskill,	10	Beatty		ALEXANDER, M. Moss	3
ALARCON, Hernando	H	ALBRIGHT, Penrose	8	Jr.		ALEXANDER, Charles	1	ALEXANDER, Magnus	1
ALBACH, George H.	4	Strong		ALDRICH, Darragh	4	McCallon		Washington	
ALBANI, Emma	H	ALBRIGHT, Percy R.	1	ALDRICH, Donald	4	ALEXANDER, Charles	9	ALEXANDER, Maitland	1
ALBANI, Emma	4	ALBRIGHT, Raymond	4	Bradshaw		P(aul)		ALEXANDER, Mark	H
ALBARDA, Horatius	4	Wolf		ALDRICH, Edgar	1	ALEXANDER, Charles	1	ALEXANDER, Minnie	5
ALBAUGH, George	5	ALBRIGHT, Robert	6	ALDRICH, Edward	3	Tripler		(Rebecca)	
Sylvanus		Choate		Burgess		ALEXANDER, Charlton	1	ALEXANDER, Moses	1
ALBAUGH, John W.	1	ALBRIGHT, William	5	ALDRICH, George Ames	1	ALEXANDER, Christine	6	ALEXANDER, Nathaniel	H
ALBEE, Edward F.	1	Foxwell		ALDRICH, George	7	ALEXANDER, Clyde C.	4	ALEXANDER, Norman	7
ALBEE, Ernest	1	ALBRITTON, Claude	10	Davenport		ALEXANDER, Clyde H.	6	Dale	
ALBEE, Fred Houdlett	2	Carroll, Jr.		ALDRICH, Henry Clay	1	ALEXANDER, Cosmo	H	ALEXANDER, Oakey	2
ALBEE, Grace Arnold	9	ALBRITTON, Errett	9	ALDRICH, Henry Ray	9	ALEXANDER, Dealva	1	Logan	
ALBEE, John	1	C(yril)		ALDRICH, Herbert	4	Stanwood		ALEXANDER, Park	9
ALBEE, Percy F.	3	ALBRIZIO, Humbert	5	Lincoln		ALEXANDER, Donald	3	Jacobus	
ALBER, David O.	5	ALBRO, Addis	1	ALDRICH, James	H	ALEXANDER, Douglas	2	ALEXANDER, Paul Julius	7
ALBER, Louis John	4	ALBRO, Mrs. Curtis		ALDRICH, James Thomas	8	ALEXANDER, Eben	1	ALEXANDER, Paul W.	4
ALBERDING, Charles	10	Sanford		ALDRICH, John Abram	7	ALEXANDER, Eben Roy	7	ALEXANDER, Raymond	6
Howard		ALCIATORE, Roy Louis	5	ALDRICH, John Gladding	3	ALEXANDER, Edward	2	Pace	
ALBERS, George	5	ALCOCK, Nathaniel	3	ALDRICH, John Gladding	5	Albert		ALEXANDER, Robert	H
ALBERS, Henri	4	Graham		ALDRICH, John Merton	5	ALEXANDER, Edward	1	ALEXANDER, Robert	1
ALBERS, Homer	2	ALCORN, Douglas Earle	5	ALDRICH, Kildroy Philip	5	Porter		ALEXANDER, Robert C.	1
ALBERS, Josef	7	ALCORN, Howard Wells	10	ALDRICH, Leander	4	ALEXANDER, Evan		ALEXANDER, Roger	
ALBERS, Joseph H.	4	ALCORN, Hugh Mead	3	Jefferson		Shelby		Gordon	
ALBERS, William Henry	3	ALCORN, Hugh Meade, Jr.	10	ALDRICH, Louis	1	ALEXANDER, Francesca	1	ALEXANDER, Samuel	H
ALBERT, A(braham)	5	ALCORN, James Floyd	2	ALDRICH, Louise Banister	6	ALEXANDER, Francis	H	Davies	
Adrian		ALCORN, James Lusk	H	(Mrs. Truman Aldrich)		ALEXANDER, Franz	4	ALEXANDER, Samuel	5
ALBERT, Allen Diehl	1	ALCORN, Paul	9	ALDRICH, Loyal Blaine	4	ALEXANDER, Frederick	5	Nathan	
ALBERT, Allen Diehl, Jr.	5	ALCORN, Roy Anvil	6	ALDRICH, Lynn Ellis	6	ALEXANDER, George	1	ALEXANDER, Stephen	H
ALBERT, Aristides	4	ALCOTT, Amos Bronson	H	ALDRICH, Malcolm Pratt	5	ALEXANDER, George F.	2	ALEXANDER,	8
Elphonso Peter		ALCOTT, Carroll Duard	4	ALDRICH, Mary Jane	1	ALEXANDER, George	8	Summerfield S.	
ALBERT, Calvin Dodge	5	ALCOTT, John	9	ALDRICH, Mildred	1	Milton		ALEXANDER, Suydenham	1
ALBERT, Charles Elwood	7	ALCOTT, Louisa May	H	ALDRICH, Morton Arnold	3	ALEXANDER, George	8	B.	
ALBERT, Charles Stanley	1	ALDEN, Bertram F.	1	ALDRICH, Nelson	1	Murrell		ALEXANDER, Taliaferro	1
ALBERT, Charles Sumner	1	ALDEN, Carlos Coolidge	4	Wilmarth		ALEXANDER, Gordon	7	ALEXANDER, Thomas	5
ALBERT, Clifford Edmund	4	ALDEN, Carroll Storrs	1	ALDRICH, Nelson	9	(Edward)		(Richard)	
ALBERT, Edward John	7	ALDEN, Charles Henry	1	Wilmarth		ALEXANDER, Grace	5	ALEXANDER, Truman	2
ALBERT, Elma Gates	3	ALDEN, Charles Henry	4	ALDRICH, Orlando W.	4	ALEXANDER, Gross	1	Hudson	
ALBERT, Ernest	2	ALDEN, Mrs. Cynthia May	1	ALDRICH, Perley Dunn	1	ALEXANDER, Harold	5	ALEXANDER, Vance J.	4
ALBERT, Henry	5	Westover		ALDRICH, Richard	1	David		ALEXANDER, Wallace	1
ALBERT, John	8	ALDEN, Ebenezer	H	ALDRICH, Richard S.	1	ALEXANDER, Harry	9	McKinney	
ALBERT, Brother Sylvester	4	ALDEN, Edith Jarvis	7	ALDRICH, Richard S.	2	Louis		ALEXANDER, W(alter)	10
ALBERT, William Julian	H	ALDEN, Edward S.	3	ALDRICH, Richard	9	ALEXANDER, Hartley	1	Boyd	
ALBERTO, Alvaro	8	ALDEN, Ezra Hyde	2	Stoddard		Burr		ALEXANDER, Walter R.	3
ALBERTS, Irwin N.	10	ALDEN, George Henry	4	ALDRICH, Robert	8			ALEXANDER, Wilford S.	3

ALEXANDER, Will Winton 3
ALEXANDER, Sir William 3
ALEXANDER, William H
ALEXANDER, William 1
ALEXANDER, William Albert 2
ALEXANDER, William Dewitt 1
ALEXANDER, William Henry 5
ALEXANDER, William Leidy 1
ALEXANDER, William McFaddin 3
ALEXANDER, William Patterson 10
ALEXANDER, William Valentine 5
ALEXANDER, Willis Walter 9
ALEXANDERSON, Ernst Frederik Werner 6
ALEXION, John Coulon 9
ALEXIS, Algert Daniel 4
ALEXOPOULOS, Constantine John 9
ALEXY, Janko 5
ALEY, Robert Judson 1
ALFANGE, Dean 10
ALFANO, Vincenzo 1
ALFARO, Colon Eloy 5
ALFARO, Ricardo Joaquin 5
ALFARO, Ricardo Joaquin 7
ALFARO, Victor Ricardo 6
ALFFREDSON, Bernard V(ictor) 5
ALFOLDI, Andrew 8
ALFONCE, Jean H
ALFONTE, James R. 7
ALFORD, Andrew 10
ALFORD, Julius Caesar H
ALFORD, Leon Pratt 1
ALFORD, Leon Pratt 2
ALFORD, Mrs. Nell 3
ALFORD, Newell Gilder 9
ALFORD, Theodore Crandall 2
ALFORD, William Hays 4
ALFRED, Frank H. 4
ALFREY, Turner, Jr. 8
ALFRIEND, Edward Morrisson 4
ALFRIEND, John Samuel 10
ALGER, Cyrus H
ALGER, Frederick M., Jr. 1
ALGER, George William 4
ALGER, Horatio, Jr. 1
ALGER, John Lincoln 4
ALGER, Mary Donlon (Mrs. Martin J. Alger) 7
ALGER, Philip Langdon 7
ALGER, Philip Rounseville 1
ALGER, Russell Alexander 1
ALGER, William Rounseville 1
ALGREN, Nelson 7
ALI, Anwar 6
ALI, Asaf 8
ALI, Mohammed 4
ALIG, Cornelius O., Jr. 8
ALI KHAN, Liaquat 8
ALINSKY, Saul David* 5
ALIOTO, Robert Franklyn 9
ALISON, Francis H
ALKEN, George David 8
ALKER, George, Jr. 10
ALLABEN, Fred Roland 8
ALLAIRE, James Peter 4
ALLAIRE, William Herbert 1
ALLAN, Chilton H
ALLAN, Denison Maurice 6
ALLAN, Frank Nathaniel 7
ALLAN, John H
ALLAN, John J. 4
ALLAN, Rupert Mortimer, Jr. 10
ALLAN, Thomas A. 9
ALLARD, John S. 4
ALLARDICE, Robert Edgar 1
ALLAWAY, Howard 7
ALLCUT, Edgar Alfred 8
ALLDERDICE, Norman Perry 4
ALLDREDGE, Eugene 3
ALLDREDGE, J. Haden 4
ALLEBAUGH, Frank Irving 8
ALLEE, James Frank 1
ALLEE, John Gage 9
ALLEE, Marjorie Hill 2
ALLEE, Warder Clyde 3
ALLEFONSCE, Jean H
ALLEGRO, John Marco 9
ALLEMAN, Gellert 2

ALLEMAN, G(ellert) S(pencer) 8
ALLEMAN, Herbert Christian 3
ALLEMANG, Herbert John 4
ALLEN, Abel Leighton 1
ALLEN, Addison 4
ALLEN, Albert Charles 7
ALLEN, Alexander John 5
ALLEN, Alexander Viets Griswold 1
ALLEN, Alfred 2
ALLEN, Alfred Gaither 1
ALLEN, Alfred Reginald 1
ALLEN, Amos Lawrence 1
ALLEN, Andrew H
ALLEN, Andrew Aniel 4
ALLEN, Andrew Hussey 1
ALLEN, Andrew Jackson H
ALLEN, Andrews 1
ALLEN, Anthony Benezet H
ALLEN, Arch Turner 1
ALLEN, Arthur Augustus 4
ALLEN, Arthur Edgar 8
ALLEN, Arthur Francis 2
ALLEN, Arthur Moulton 3
ALLEN, Arthur Watts 4
ALLEN, Arthur Wilburn 3
ALLEN, Austin Fletcher 9
ALLEN, Austin Oscar 5
ALLEN, Ben (William Benjamin) Holker 9
ALLEN, Benjamin 1
ALLEN, Benjamin 3
ALLEN, Benjamin Franklin 5
ALLEN, Benjamin Leach 1
ALLEN, Bennet Mills 4
ALLEN, Beulah Ream 10
ALLEN, Beverly Sprague 1
ALLEN, Burrell Clinton 7
ALLEN, Byron Gilchrist 9
ALLEN, Calvin Francis 2
ALLEN, Carlos Eben 3
ALLEN, Charles H
ALLEN, Charles 1
ALLEN, Charles Claffin 1
ALLEN, Charles Claflin 6
ALLEN, Charles Curtis 3
ALLEN, Charles Dexter 1
ALLEN, Charles Edward 1
ALLEN, Charles Elmer 3
ALLEN, Charles Herbert 1
ALLEN, Charles Julius 1
ALLEN, Charles Lucius 1
ALLEN, Charles Metcalf 3
ALLEN, Charles Morse 2
ALLEN, Charles Ricketson 1
ALLEN, Charles Warrenne 1
ALLEN, Chester Arthur 4
ALLEN, Claxton Edmonds 1
ALLEN, Clay 5
ALLEN, Clifford Robertson 7
ALLEN, Clinton L. 4
ALLEN, Courtney 5
ALLEN, Crombie 2
ALLEN, Cuthbert Edward 7
ALLEN, David 10
ALLEN, David Oliver H
ALLEN, Devere 3
ALLEN, Don B. 4
ALLEN, Don Cameron 5
ALLEN, Dudley Peter 1
ALLEN, Duff S. 6
ALLEN, Edgar 2
ALLEN, Edgar van Nuys 5
ALLEN, Edmund Thompson 1
ALLEN, Edward Archibald 4
ALLEN, Edward Bartlett 4
ALLEN, Edward Ellis 3
ALLEN, Edward Frank 7
ALLEN, Edward Jones 10
ALLEN, Edward Mortimer 4
ALLEN, Edward Normand 5
ALLEN, Edward Patrick 1
ALLEN, Edward Switzer 8
ALLEN, Edward Tyson 1
ALLEN, Edward Weber 7
ALLEN, Edwin Brown 6
ALLEN, Edwin Madison 2
ALLEN, Edwin West 1
ALLEN, Eliot Dinsmore 5
ALLEN, Elisha Hunt H
ALLEN, Emil William, Jr. 7
ALLEN, Eric William 2
ALLEN, Ernest Bourner 1
ALLEN, Ethan H
ALLEN, Ethan 1
ALLEN, Eugene Thomas 4
ALLEN, Ezra Griffen 3
ALLEN, F. Sturges 1
ALLEN, Florence Ellinwood 4
ALLEN, Frances H
ALLEN, Francis Henry 4
ALLEN, Francis Richmond 1

ALLEN, Francis V. 7
ALLEN, Frank 2
ALLEN, Frank Bigelow 3
ALLEN, Frank Emmett 7
ALLEN, Frank G. 3
ALLEN, Frank Leonard 7
ALLEN, Frank Philip, Jr. 1
ALLEN, Frank Waller 6
ALLEN, Fred 3
ALLEN, Fred Harold, Jr. 9
ALLEN, Fred Hovey 1
ALLEN, Fred William 6
ALLEN, Frederic De Forest H
ALLEN, Frederic Winthrop 7
ALLEN, Frederick 7
ALLEN, Frederick Baylies 1
ALLEN, Frederick H. 8
ALLEN, Frederick Henry 4
ALLEN, Frederick Hobbes 1
ALLEN, Frederick Innes 1
ALLEN, Frederick James 1
ALLEN, Frederick Lewis 3
ALLEN, Frederick Madison 6
ALLEN, Freeman Harlow 2
ALLEN, Gardner Weld 2
ALLEN, Geo A., Jr. 1
ALLEN, George 10
ALLEN, George H
ALLEN, George Edward 5
ALLEN, George Garland 4
ALLEN, George Henry 3
ALLEN, George Venable 6
ALLEN, George Walton 6
ALLEN, George Washington 1
ALLEN, George Whiting 1
ALLEN, Glover Morrill 2
ALLEN, Gordon 5
ALLEN, Gordon Forrest 6
ALLEN, Gracie 1
ALLEN, Grant 4
ALLEN, Grosvenor Noyes 3
ALLEN, Guy Fletcher 4
ALLEN, Hamilton Ford 4
ALLEN, Hans 1
ALLEN, Harland Hill* 8
ALLEN, Harold Byron 2
ALLEN, Harris Campbell 5
ALLEN, Harrison H
ALLEN, Harry Julian 7
ALLEN, Heman* H
ALLEN, Henry, Jr. 4
ALLEN, Henry Butler 4
ALLEN, Henry Crosby 5
ALLEN, Henry D. 4
ALLEN, Henry Ellsha 4
ALLEN, Henry Justin 2
ALLEN, Henry Tureman 1
ALLEN, Henry Watkins H
ALLEN, Herbert 10
ALLEN, Hope Emily 4
ALLEN, Horace Eugene 5
ALLEN, Horace Newton 1
ALLEN, Horatio H
ALLEN, Howard Cameron 4
ALLEN, Hubert A. 2
ALLEN, Ida Bailey 6
ALLEN, Ira H
ALLEN, Ira Wilder 1
ALLEN, Irving Ross 8
ALLEN, Irwin 10
ALLEN, J. Weston 1
ALLEN, James 1
ALLEN, James Browning 7
ALLEN, James E. 4
ALLEN, James Edward 2
ALLEN, James Edward, Jr. 5
ALLEN, James Henry 3
ALLEN, James Lane 1
ALLEN, James Norman 7
ALLEN, James R. 10
ALLEN, James Seddon 7
ALLEN, James Sircom 8
ALLEN, James Stewart 7
ALLEN, James Turney 2
ALLEN, Jean Malven (Mrs. Frederick H. Allen) 6
ALLEN, Jeremiah Mervin H
ALLEN, Joel Asaph 1
ALLEN, John* H
ALLEN, John Alpheus 6
ALLEN, John Beard 1
ALLEN, John Clayton 3
ALLEN, John Denby 4
ALLEN, John Eliot 2
ALLEN, John F. H
ALLEN, John James 1
ALLEN, John Johnson 4
ALLEN, John Kermott 3
ALLEN, John Mills 1
ALLEN, John Rex 5
ALLEN, John Robert 4
ALLEN, John Stevenson 4
ALLEN, John Stuart 8
ALLEN, John Wesley 1
ALLEN, John Weston 2

ALLEN, John William H
ALLEN, Joseph H
ALLEN, Joseph Dana 4
ALLEN, J(oseph) Garrott 10
ALLEN, Joseph Henry H
ALLEN, Joseph Holmes 5
ALLEN, Judson H
ALLEN, Julian 4
ALLEN, Junius 4
ALLEN, Katherine Yarnell 10
ALLEN, Kenneth 1
ALLEN, Laurence Edmund (Larry) 6
ALLEN, Leo Elwood 5
ALLEN, Leon Menard 1
ALLEN, Leroy 2
ALLEN, Lewis Falley 8
ALLEN, Lewis George 2
ALLEN, Linton E. 8
ALLEN, Louis J. 1
ALLEN, Lucy Ellis 2
ALLEN, Lyman Whitney 1
ALLEN, M. Marshall 3
ALLEN, Mrs. Marian Boyd 4
ALLEN, Martha Meir 1
ALLEN, Maryland 1
ALLEN, Milton Irving 4
ALLEN, Morse Shepard 8
ALLEN, Nat Burtis 2
ALLEN, Nathan H
ALLEN, Nathaniel H
ALLEN, Nellie Burnham 5
ALLEN, Paul H
ALLEN, Paul James 7
ALLEN, Paul S. 4
ALLEN, Perry S. 1
ALLEN, Philip H
ALLEN, Philip Loring 1
ALLEN, Philip Ray 4
ALLEN, Philip Schuyler 3
ALLEN, Ralph 4
ALLEN, Ralph Clayton 4
ALLEN, Ray 1
ALLEN, Raymond Bernard 9
ALLEN, Richard H
ALLEN, Richard Day 2
ALLEN, Richard Frazer 3
ALLEN, Richard Lamb H
ALLEN, Riley Harris 4
ALLEN, Robert* H
ALLEN, Robert Chester 8
ALLEN, Robert Day 5
ALLEN, Robert E. Lee 4
ALLEN, Robert Emmet 9
ALLEN, Robert Gray 4
ALLEN, Robert H. 4
ALLEN, Robert I. 4
ALLEN, Robert L. 8
ALLEN, Robert McDowell 6
ALLEN, Robert Porter 4
ALLEN, Robert Sharon 7
ALLEN, Roderick Random 5
ALLEN, Roger 9
ALLEN, Roger Williams 10
ALLEN, Rolland Craten H
ALLEN, Roy O., Jr. 10
ALLEN, Russell Morton 4
ALLEN, Ruth Alice 8
ALLEN, Samuel Clesson H
ALLEN, Samuel Edward 1
ALLEN, Samuel G. 3
ALLEN, Samuel James McIntosh 5
ALLEN, Sherman 2
ALLEN, Sidney J. 1
ALLEN, Stephen Haley 1
ALLEN, Sturges 3
ALLEN, Thomas H
ALLEN, Thomas 1
ALLEN, Thomas Grant 4
ALLEN, Thomas M. 1
ALLEN, Thomas Oscar 10
ALLEN, Thomas Stinson 2
ALLEN, Timothy Field 1
ALLEN, Viola 2
ALLEN, Walter H
ALLEN, Walter Alfred 7
ALLEN, Walter Barth 3
ALLEN, Walter Cleveland 4
ALLEN, Ward P. 7
ALLEN, Warren Dwight 7
ALLEN, William* H
ALLEN, William Fitch 1
ALLEN, William Francis H
ALLEN, William Franklin 1
ALLEN, William Frederick 1
ALLEN, William H., Jr. 2
ALLEN, William Henry* H
ALLEN, William Hervey 4
ALLEN, William Joshua 1
ALLEN, William M. 9
ALLEN, William Orville 1
ALLEN, William Ray 3
ALLEN, William Reynolds 1
ALLEN, William Sims 3
ALLEN, William Vincent 1
ALLEN, Willis H

ALLEN, Willis Boyd 1
ALLEN, Wilmar Mason 3
ALLEN, Wyeth 5
ALLEN, Zachariah H
ALLENDOERFER, Carl Barnett 6
ALLENDOERFER, Carl W. 3
ALLENSON, Hazel Sandiford 6
ALLER, Curtis Cosmos, Jr 8
ALLER, Howard Lewis 3
ALLERTON, Isaac H
ALLERTON, Samuel Waters 1
ALLERUP, Paul Richard 6
ALLEY, Calvin Lane 5
ALLEY, Charles Edwin (C. Ed) 5
ALLEY, James Burke 8
ALLEY, James Pinckney 1
ALLEY, John Bassett H
ALLEY, Norman Williams 7
ALLEY, Rayford W. 6
ALLEZ, George Clare 3
ALLGOOD, Clarence William 10
ALLGOOD, Dwight Maurice 5
ALLGOOD, Miles Clayton 6
ALLIBOXE, Samuel Austin H
ALLIN, Arthur 1
ALLIN, Bushrod Warren 5
ALLIN, Cephas Daniel 1
ALLIN, George Litchfield 5
ALLIN, George R. 6
ALLIN, Roger 3
ALLINE, Henry H
ALLING, Arthur Nathaniel 2
ALLING, Asa Alling 1
ALLING, Harold Lattimore 4
ALLING, John Wesley 1
ALLING, Joseph Tilden 1
ALLING, Paul Humiston 2
ALLINGTON, Homer C. Emery 4
ALLINSON, Anne Crosby 1
ALLINSON, Francis Greenleaf 1
ALLIOT, Hector 1
ALLIS, Edward Phelps 1
ALLIS, Edward Phelps, Jr. 4
ALLIS, James Ashton 6
ALLIS, Louis 3
ALLIS, Oscar Huntington 1
ALLIS, Oswald Thompson 5
ALLISON, B. R. 10
ALLISON, Everett E. 9
ALLISON, Fran 10
ALLISON, Fred 6
ALLISON, George Boggs 7
ALLISON, Irl 10
ALLISON, James, Jr. H
ALLISON, James Boyd 4
ALLISON, James Edward 5
ALLISON, James Nicholls 1
ALLISON, James Richard 8
ALLISON, John 4
ALLISON, John H(oward) 7
ALLISON, John Maudgridge Snowden 2
ALLISON, John P. 4
ALLISON, Nathaniel 1
ALLISON, Noah Dwight 5
ALLISON, Richard H
ALLISON, Robert H
ALLISON, Robert Burns 6
ALLISON, Samuel King 4
ALLISON, Stanley Frederick 9
ALLISON, William Boyd 1
ALLISON, William Henry 1
ALLISON, William Henry 2
ALLMAN, David Bacharach 5
ALLMAN, George Dudley 7
ALLMAN, Heyman B. 8
ALLMAN, Justin Paul 5
ALLMAN, Leslie Coover 4
ALLMOND, Marcus Blakey 4
ALLOTT, Gordon Llewellyn 9
ALLOUEZ, Claude Jean H
ALLOWAY, R(upert) Brooke 8
ALLPORT, Fayette Ward 3
ALLPORT, Floyd Henry 8
ALLPORT, Frank 1
ALLPORT, Gordon Willard 4
ALLPORT, Gordon Willard 5
ALLPORT, Hamilton 8
ALLRED, Evan Leigh 10
ALLRED, James V. 3
ALLRED, Oran H(enderson) 9

ALLRICH, Robert William 9
ALLSMAN, Paul T. 10
ALLSOPP, Clinton Bonfield 4
ALLSOPP, Frederick William 2
ALLSTON, Robert Francis Withers H
ALLSTON, Washington 10
ALLTON, James Miller (Tom) 6
ALLTOP, James Howard 9
ALLWARDT, Henry Augustus 1
ALLWORK, Eleanor Bloom (Mrs. Ronald Allwork) 5
ALLYN, Arden Lacey 4
ALLYN, Arthur Cecil 4
ALLYN, Arthur Cecil 8
ALLYN, Harriett May 3
ALLYN, Richard 8
ALLYN, Robert H
ALLYN, Stanley Charles 5
ALMACK, John C. 3
AL-MAKTUM, Sheikh Rashid ibn Said (Sheikh Rashid bin Said Al-Maktum)* 10
ALMAND, Claude Marion 3
ALMENDROS, Nestor 10
ALMERT, Harold 5
ALMIRALL, Lloyd Vincent 9
ALMON, Edward Berton 1
ALMOND, James Edward 3
ALMOND, James Lindsay, Jr. 9
ALMOND, Nina 4
ALMSTEDT, Hermann Benjamin 5
ALMY, Frederic 1
ALMY, Gerald Marks 7
ALMY, John Jay H
ALMY, Robert Forbes 5
ALONSO, Amado 3
ALOTT, William Andrus 4
ALPER, Jonathan Louis 10
ALPERN, Anne X. 7
ALPERS, William Charles 1
ALPERT, George 10
ALPERT, Harry 7
ALPHONSA, Mother H
ALPHONSA, Mother 4
ALPHONSUS, Brother 7
ALRICH, Samuel Nelson 1
AL-SAID, Nuri 8
ALSAKER, Elwood Cecil 10
ALSBERG, C. Lucas 1
ALSCHULER, Alfred S. 1
ALSCHULER, Benjamin Philip
ALSCHULER, Jacob Edward 7
ALSCHULER, Samuel 1
ALSDORF, James William 10
ALSEVER, John B. 7
ALSOP, George H
ALSOP, John H
ALSOP, Joseph Wright 3
ALSOP, Joseph Wright, Jr. 10
ALSOP, Reese Fell 7
ALSOP, Richard H
ALSOP, Stewart Johonnot Oliver 6
ALSPACH, Russell King 7
ALSTON, Angus Sorensen 6
ALSTON, Charles Henry 7
ALSTON, George L. 4
ALSTON, Joseph H
ALSTON, Lemuel James H
ALSTON, Philip Henry 6
ALSTON, Philip Henry, Jr. 9
ALSTON, Robert Cotten 1
ALSTON, Walter Emmons 8
ALSTON, William Jeffreys H
ALSTON, Willis H
ALSTORK, John Wesley 1
ALT, Howard Lang 5
ALTE, Visconde de 3
ALTEMEIER, William Arthur 8
ALTER, David H
ALTER, Dinsmore 5
ALTER, George Elias 1
ALTER, Karl Joseph 7
ALTER, Lucien Weaver Scott 4
ALTER, Nicholas M(ark) 1
ALTER, Wilbur McClure 6
ALTERMAN, Zipora Stephania Balaban 6
ALTFILLISCH, Charles 9
ALTGELD, John Peter 1
ALTGLASS, Max Mayer 3
ALTHAM, John H
ALTHAUS, Edward 4
ALTHAUS, John Carl 9

ALTHAUSER, Norman Ray 4
ALTHER, Joseph G. 6
ALTHERR, Alfred 5
ALTHOFF, Henry 2
ALTHOUSE, Harry Witman 1
ALTHOUSE, Howell Halberstadt 5
ALTHOUSE, Paul Marcks 5
ALTHOUSE, Paul Shearer 3
ALTMAIER, Clinton John 3
ALTMAN, Benjamin H
ALTMAN, Benjamin 4
ALTMAN, Julian Allen 6
ALTMAN, Oscar Louis 5
ALTMEYER, Arthur Joseph 5
ALTON, Alfred Edward 5
ALTON, Charles De Lancey 4
ALTON, John Taylor 7
ALTON, Robert M(Intie) 8
ALTROCCHI, Julia Cooley (Mrs. Rudolph Altrocchi) 6
ALTROCCHI, Rudolph 3
ALTSCHUL, Frank 7
ALTSCHUL, Helen G. (Mrs. Frank Altschul) 8
ALTSCHULER, Modest 5
ALTSHELER, Joseph Alexander 1
ALTUS, William David 5
ALTVATER, H. Hugh 3
ALVARADO, Juan Bautista H
ALVAREZ, Alejandro 5
ALVAREZ, Luis W. 9
ALVAREZ, Vidaurre Antonio 8
ALVAREZ, Walter Clement 7
ALVAREZ-TOSTADO, Claudio 7
ALVERSON, Claude B. 1
ALVES, Charles Stebbins 4
ALVES, Henry F(red) 5
ALVEY, Richard Henry 1
ALVORD, Benjamin H
ALVORD, Benjamin 1
ALVORD, Clarence Walworth 10
ALVORD, Corydon Alexis H
ALVORD, Elisworth Chapman 4
ALVORD, Henry Elijah 1
ALVORD, Idress Head (Mrs. Clarence W. Alvord) 5
ALVORD, James Church H
ALVORD, James Church 4
ALVORD, John Watson 2
ALVORD, Katharine Sprague 5
ALWARD, Herbert Vaughan 6
ALWAY, Frederick James 5
ALWAY, Robert Hamilton 10
ALWOOD, Olin Good 3
ALWOOD, William Bradford 1
ALWORTH, Royal D. 4
ALWYNE, Horace 6
ALYEA, Edwin Pascal 8
ALY KHAN, Shah 4
ALZADO, Lyle Martin 10
AMADAS, Phillip H
AMADO, Gilberto 8
AMAR, Henri 1
AMAT, Thaddeus H
AMATEIS, Edmond Romulus 8
AMATEIS, Louis 1
AMATEIS, Louis 4
AMATO, Pasquale 2
AMAYA, Mario Anthony 7
AMAZEEN, Edward Sutherland 7
AMBAUEN, Andrew Joseph 4
AMBERG, Emil 2
AMBERG, Harold Vincent 4
AMBERG, Julius H. 3
AMBERG, Raymond Michael 10
AMBERG, Richard Hiller 4
AMBERG, Samuel 5
AMBERSON, J(ames) Burns
AMBLER, Benjamin Mason 1
AMBLER, Charles Henry 3
AMBLER, Chase P. 4
AMBLER, Frank Rhoades 4
AMBLER, James Markham H
Marshall
AMBLER, James Murray 4
AMBLER, Mason Gaither 4
AMBLER, Sara Ellmaker 4

AMBRIDGE, D. W. 7
AMBROSE, Arthur Warren 3
AMBROSE, Luther Martin 7
AMBROSE, Paul 4
AMBRUSTER, Howard Watson
AMBRUSTER, Watson 1
AMDUR, Isadore 5
AMEEL, Donald Jules 7
AMELI, Howard Wilmurt 6
AMELIA H
AMEN, Harlan Page 1
AMEN, John Harlan 3
AMEND, Bernhard Gottwald 3
AMEND, Edward Bernard 1
AMENT, James E. 1
AMERASINGHE, Hamilton Shirley Adjutor
AMERMAN, Lemuel H
AMERMAN, Ralph Alonzo 1
AMES, Adelbert, Jr. 3
AMES, Butler 3
AMES, Charles Bismark 1
AMES, Charles Gordon 1
AMES, Charles Wilberforce 1
AMES, Edgar 2
AMES, Edward Elbridge 3
AMES, Edward Raymond H
AMES, Edward Scribner 3
AMES, Eleanor Kirk 1
AMES, Elizabeth 7
AMES, Ezra H
AMES, Fisher H
AMES, Fisher 4
AMES, Frederick Lothrop H
AMES, Harold Taylor 8
AMES, Harry Clifton 8
AMES, Herman Vandenburg 1
AMES, Hobart 2
AMES, James Barr H
AMES, James Barr 1
AMES, James Barr 4
AMES, James Tyler H
AMES, Jesse Hazer 3
AMES, John Dawes 9
AMES, John Griffith 1
AMES, John Griffith 3
AMES, John Lincoln 4
AMES, John Ormsbee 1
AMES, Joseph Alexander H
AMES, Joseph Bushnell 1
AMES, Joseph Sweetman 2
AMES, Knowlton Lyman 1
AMES, Lewis Darwin 5
AMES, Louis Annin 3
AMES, Mary Lesley 1
AMES, Nathan Peabody H
AMES, Norman Bruce 4
AMES, Oakes H
AMES, Oakes 3
AMES, Oliver* H
AMES, Oliver 1
AMES, Robert Barbour 9
AMES, Robert Parker Marr 4
AMES, Samuel H
AMES, Susie M(ay) 5
AMES, Van Meter 9
AMES, Walter Irving 7
AMES, William 1
AMES, William Lafayette 3
AMES, Winthrop 1
AMEY, Harry Burton 1
AMEZAGA, Juan Jose 3
AMHERST, Jeffery H
AMICK, Erwin Hamer, Jr. 5
AMIDON, Beulah 3
AMIDON, Charles Fremont 1
AMIDON, Samuel Barker 1
AMIGER, William Thomas 1
AMINO, Leo 10
AMIOKA, Shiro 9
AMIS, Edward Stephen 9
AMMANN, Othmar Hermann 4
AMMAR, Abbas Moustafa 6
AMMEN, Daniel H
AMMEN, Jacob H
AMMEN, Samuel Zenas 4
AMMIDON, Hoyt 9
AMMIDOWN, Edward Holmes 4
AMMONS, Elias Milton 1
AMMONS, Eugene (Gene) 7
AMMONS, Teller 5
AMORY, Arthur 1
AMORY, Charles Walter 1
AMORY, Harcourt 5
AMORY, John James 1
AMORY, Robert 5
AMORY, Robert 5
AMORY, Robert, Jr. 10
AMORY, Thomas H
AMORY, William 3
AMOS, Frank R. 4

AMOS, Franklyn Boothroyd 7
AMOS, John Beverly 10
AMOS, John Ellis 9
AMOS, Thyrsa Wealhtheow 1
AMOS, William Frederick 5
AMOSS, Harold L. 3
AMRAM, Philip Werner 10
AMRINE, William Frederick
AMSBARY, Frank C., Jr. 4
AMSBARY, Wallace Bruce 3
AMSLER, Henry Moore 6
AMSTER, Nathan Leonard 1
AMSTUZ, John O. 5
AMWEG, Frederick James 1
AMY, Ernest Francis 7
AMY, Ernest Valentine 7
AMYOT, Louis Joseph 5
ANAGNOS, Julia Romana Howe H
ANAGNOS, Michael H
ANAGNOS, Michael 4
ANAST, James Louis 5
ANASTASSY 5
ANCENEY, Charles L. 1
ANCERL, Karel 6
ANDERBERG, Edward Clarence 10
ANDEREGG, Frederick 1
ANDERES, Robert L. 3
ANDERL, Stephen 10
ANDERLEDY, Anthony Maria H
ANDERMAN, William 4
ANDERS, James Meschter 1
ANDERS, John Daniel H
ANDERS, Paul R. 4
ANDERS, Thomas Jefferson 1
ANDERSEN, Albert M. 3
ANDERSEN, Andreas Storrs 6
ANDERSEN, Arthur Edward 2
ANDERSEN, Arthur Olaf 3
ANDERSEN, Bjorn 5
ANDERSEN, Christian Schmidt 1
ANDERSEN, Fred C. 7
ANDERSEN, Hendrik Christian 1
ANDERSEN, Hendrik Christian 2
ANDERSEN, James Roy 2
ANDERSEN, John Dlbos 4
ANDERSEN, Joyce Marilyn Off (Mrs. Chester W. Andersen) 1
ANDERSEN, Martin 9
ANDERSON, Abraham Archibald 1
ANDERSON, Abraham Archibald 2
ANDERSON, Ada Woodruff 4
ANDERSON, Adolph Gustof 7
ANDERSON, Alan Ross 6
ANDERSON, Albert 1
ANDERSON, Albert Barnes 1
ANDERSON, Alden 2
ANDERSON, Alexander H
ANDERSON, Alexander Outlaw H
ANDERSON, Alexander Pierce 2
ANDERSON, Alvin George 6
ANDERSON, Amabel A. 1
ANDERSON, Amos Carey 5
ANDERSON, Andrew Freeman 1
ANDERSON, Andrew Runni 3
ANDERSON, Andrew Work 2
ANDERSON, Anton Bennett 6
ANDERSON, Arch W. 1
ANDERSON, Archibald Watson 4
ANDERSON, Arnold Stuart 10
ANDERSON, Arthur Julius 6
ANDERSON, Arthur Marvin 4
ANDERSON, Asher 1
ANDERSON, Axel Gordon 6
ANDERSON, Axel Henry 2
ANDERSON, Benjamin McAlester 2
ANDERSON, Carl C. 1
ANDERSON, Carl David 10
ANDERSON, Carl Harold 6
ANDERSON, Carl Magnus 5

ANDERSON, Carl Thomas 2
ANDERSON, Carlotta Adele 3
ANDERSON, Chandler Parsons 1
ANDERSON, Charles Albert 4
ANDERSON, Charles Alfred 10
ANDERSON, Charles Arner 9
ANDERSON, Charles Arnold 10
ANDERSON, Charles Burroughs 9
ANDERSON, Charles Hardin 5
ANDERSON, Charles Joseph 6
ANDERSON, Charles Loftus Grant 5
ANDERSON, Charles Palmerston 1
ANDERSON, Charles S. 8
ANDERSON, Clifford Le Conte 1
ANDERSON, Clinton Presba 6
ANDERSON, Clinton Presba 7
ANDERSON, Cortland Edwin, Jr. 9
ANDERSON, David Allen 5
ANDERSON, Dewey 10
ANDERSON, Dice Robins 2
ANDERSON, Dillon 6
ANDERSON, Donald Brown 3
ANDERSON, Douglas Smith 3
ANDERSON, Dwight 3
ANDERSON, Dwight 4
ANDERSON, Earl W. 4
ANDERSON, Edgar 5
ANDERSON, Edward 1
ANDERSON, Edward Delmar 3
ANDERSON, Edward Lee 5
ANDERSON, Edward Lowell 1
ANDERSON, Edward Wharton 2
ANDERSON, Edwin Alexander 1
ANDERSON, Edwin Hatfield 2
ANDERSON, Edwin John 9
ANDERSON, Elam Jonathan 2
ANDERSON, Elbert Ellery 1
ANDERSON, Elbridge R. 2
ANDERSON, Elizabeth Preston 4
ANDERSON, Elsie Grace 5
ANDERSON, Erica 7
ANDERSON, Ernest 3
ANDERSON, Ernest Gustave 9
ANDERSON, Ernest LeRoy 10
ANDERSON, Ernest W. 7
ANDERSON, Esther L. 5
ANDERSON, Eugene Newton 8
ANDERSON, Eva Greenslit 6
(Mrs. Leonard O. Anderson)
ANDERSON, F. Paul 1
ANDERSON, Florence 9
ANDERSON, Florence Mary Bennett (Mrs. Louis Francis Anderson) 7
ANDERSON, Forrest Howard 10
ANDERSON, Francis Maurice 7
ANDERSON, Frank 3
ANDERSON, Frank Bartow 1
ANDERSON, Frank Leonard 1
ANDERSON, Frank Maley 6
ANDERSON, Frederick 8
ANDERSON, Frederick Irving 2
ANDERSON, Frederick L. 5
ANDERSON, Frederick Lincoln 4
ANDERSON, Frederick William 8
ANDERSON, Galusha 1
ANDERSON, Gaylord West 5
ANDERSON, George 5
ANDERSON, George A. 5
ANDERSON, George Alburtus H

Name	
ANDERSON, George Edward	5
ANDERSON, George Everett	1
ANDERSON, George K.	7
ANDERSON, George LaVerne	6
ANDERSON, George Lucius	1
ANDERSON, George Minor	3
ANDERSON, George Smith	1
ANDERSON, George Thomas	H
ANDERSON, George Walter	10
ANDERSON, George Weston	1
ANDERSON, George Wood	5
ANDERSON, Grace Merle	10
ANDERSON, Harald	7
ANDERSON, Harold	5
ANDERSON, Harold Durbin	3
ANDERSON, Harold H.	9
ANDERSON, Harold H(omer)	10
ANDERSON, Harold MacDonald	1
ANDERSON, Harold V.	4
ANDERSON, Harold V(ictor)	8
ANDERSON, Harrison Ray	7
ANDERSON, Harry Bennett	1
ANDERSON, Harry Loy	7
ANDERSON, Harry Pierce	8
ANDERSON, Harry Reuben	1
ANDERSON, Harry William	3
ANDERSON, Helen Natalie Johnson	4
ANDERSON, Henry Clay	1
ANDERSON, Henry Hill	H
ANDERSON, Henry James	H
ANDERSON, Henry Tompkins	H
ANDERSON, Henry Watkins	3
ANDERSON, Henry William	1
ANDERSON, Herbert L.	9
ANDERSON, Herbert Walfred	9
ANDERSON, Homer Willard	7
ANDERSON, Howard B.	4
ANDERSON, Howard Clevenger	10
ANDERSON, Howard Richmond	7
ANDERSON, Hugh Johnston	H
ANDERSON, Hugo A.	8
ANDERSON, Isaac	H
ANDERSON, Isabel	2
ANDERSON, Ivan Delos	10
ANDERSON, J. Blaine	10
ANDERSON, J. Joseph	9
ANDERSON, Jack Z.	7
ANDERSON, Jacob Nelson	4
ANDERSON, James Arthur	4
ANDERSON, James Cuyler	5
ANDERSON, James Howard	5
ANDERSON, James Nesbitt	2
ANDERSON, James Patton	H
ANDERSON, James R.	H
ANDERSON, James Richard	7
ANDERSON, J(efferson) Randolph	5
ANDERSON, Jeremy R.	8
ANDERSON, Jesse Thomas	9
ANDERSON, John	H
ANDERSON, John	1
ANDERSON, John*	3
ANDERSON, John	9
ANDERSON, John Albert	4
ANDERSON, John Alexander	H
ANDERSON, John August	3
ANDERSON, John Benjamin	3
ANDERSON, John B(enjamin)	7
ANDERSON, John Crawford	1
ANDERSON, John Edward	2
ANDERSON, John Edward	4
ANDERSON, John F.	3
ANDERSON, John Francis	1
ANDERSON, John George	2
ANDERSON, John Hargis	2
ANDERSON, John Jacob	1
ANDERSON, John Murray	3
ANDERSON, John Quincy	6
ANDERSON, John Will	4
ANDERSON, John William	5
ANDERSON, John W(illiam)	6
ANDERSON, Joseph	H
ANDERSON, Joseph	1
ANDERSON, Joseph Gaudentius	1
ANDERSON, Joseph Halstead	H
ANDERSON, Joseph James	9
ANDERSON, Joseph Paul	7
ANDERSON, Joseph Reid	H
ANDERSON, Joseph Starr	3
ANDERSON, Josiah McNair	H
ANDERSON, Karl	3
ANDERSON, Karl Leopold	5
ANDERSON, Kenneth Eugene	9
ANDERSON, Larz	1
ANDERSON, Lee	5
ANDERSON, Lee William	6
ANDERSON, Leroy	6
ANDERSON, Leroy Dean	4
ANDERSON, Lewis Calvin	7
ANDERSON, Lewis Flint	1
ANDERSON, Louis Francis	3
ANDERSON, Martha Fort (Mrs. Frank Hartley Anderson)	7
ANDERSON, Martin	4
ANDERSON, Martin Brewer	H
ANDERSON, Mary	H
ANDERSON, Mary*	4
ANDERSON, Mary Mortlock (Mrs. Walter Anderson)	5
ANDERSON, Maxwell	3
ANDERSON, Melville Best	1
ANDERSON, Merle Hampton	5
ANDERSON, Neal Larkin	1
ANDERSON, Nels Ehlert	8
ANDERSON, Nelson Paul	3
ANDERSON, Newton Mitchell	4
ANDERSON, Nils	4
ANDERSON, Oscar V.	5
ANDERSON, Paul B.	8
ANDERSON, Paul F.	9
ANDERSON, Paul Lewis	3
ANDERSON, Paul N(athaniel)	10
ANDERSON, Paul N(athaniel)	5
ANDERSON, Paul Vernon	5
ANDERSON, Paul Y.	1
ANDERSON, Peirce	4
ANDERSON, R. T.	4
ANDERSON, Ralph J.	4
ANDERSON, Rasmus Bjorn	1
ANDERSON, Richard Clough	H
ANDERSON, Richard Clough, Jr.	H
ANDERSON, Richard Heron	H
ANDERSON, Richard James	5
ANDERSON, Robert	H
ANDERSON, Robert Alexander	10
ANDERSON, Robert Bernard	9
ANDERSON, Robert Bernerd	10
ANDERSON, Robert Campbell	3
ANDERSON, Robert Cletus	9
ANDERSON, Robert Earle	4
ANDERSON, Robert Edward, Jr.	5
ANDERSON, Robert Gordon	3
ANDERSON, Robert Hargis	4
ANDERSON, Robert Nelson	7
ANDERSON, Robert Palmer	3
ANDERSON, Robert van Vleck	2
ANDERSON, Rose	4
ANDERSON, Rose Gustava	7
ANDERSON, Roy Martin	7
ANDERSON, Roy Nels	6
ANDERSON, Rudolph John	4
ANDERSON, Rudolph Martin	4
ANDERSON, Rufus	H
ANDERSON, Samuel	H
ANDERSON, Samuel Wagner	4
ANDERSON, Sherwood	1
ANDERSON, Sigurd	10
ANDERSON, Simeon H.	H
ANDERSON, Sophie	H
ANDERSON, Stewart Wise	9
ANDERSON, Stonewall	1
ANDERSON, Sydney	2
ANDERSON, Theodore W(ilbur)	8
ANDERSON, Thomas Davis	1
ANDERSON, Thomas F(oxen)	10
ANDERSON, Thomas H.	1
ANDERSON, Thomas Joel, Jr.	4
ANDERSON, Thomas Leighton	10
ANDERSON, Thomas Lilbourne	H
ANDERSON, Thomas McArthur	1
ANDERSON, Totton James	10
ANDERSON, Troyer Steele	2
ANDERSON, Victor E.	4
ANDERSON, Victor Emanuel	4
ANDERSON, Victor Vance	4
ANDERSON, W. C.	1
ANDERSON, Wallace Ludwig	9
ANDERSON, Walter	H
ANDERSON, Walter Alexander	4
ANDERSON, Walter Stratton	7
ANDERSON, Walter Stratton, Jr.	7
ANDERSON, Walter Williams	6
ANDERSON, Wells Foster	3
ANDERSON, Wendell W.	3
ANDERSON, Willaim	6
ANDERSON, William	H
ANDERSON, William	7
ANDERSON, William A.	1
ANDERSON, William A.	3
ANDERSON, William Allison	2
ANDERSON, William Banks	7
ANDERSON, William Beverly	5
ANDERSON, William Brennan	1
ANDERSON, William Clayton	H
ANDERSON, William D.	3
ANDERSON, William Downs	5
ANDERSON, William Dozier	5
ANDERSON, William Ernest	9
ANDERSON, William Evan	8
ANDERSON, William Franklin	2
ANDERSON, William Gilbert	2
ANDERSON, William Hamilton	3
ANDERSON, William Harry	4
ANDERSON, William Henry	1
ANDERSON, William Joseph, Jr.	4
ANDERSON, William Ketcham	2
ANDERSON, William Madison	1
ANDERSON, William Otis	9
ANDERSON, William Otto	4
ANDERSON, William Thomas	2
ANDERSON, William Thompson	4
ANDERSON, William Wallace	H
ANDERSON, Winslow	1
ANDERSON, Winslow Samuel	2
ANDERSSON, Alfred Oscar	3
ANDERTON, Stephen Philbin	1
ANDERVONT, Howard B(ancroft)	7
ANDES, John Wilbur	9
ANDRADE, Cipriano	1
ANDRAS, Robert Knight	8
ANDRE, Floyd	5
ANDRE, John	H
ANDRE, Louis	H
ANDREA, Frank A. D.	4
ANDREASEN, Milian Lauritz	5
ANDREEN, Gustav Albert	1
ANDREJEVIC, Milet	10
ANDRESEN, Albert Frederick Ruger	4
ANDRESEN, August Herman	3
ANDRESS, James Mace	1
ANDRESS, James Mace	2
ANDRESS, Robert Joseph	4
ANDRETTA, S. A.	4
ANDREW, A. Piatt	1
ANDREW, C. E.	7
ANDREW, Edwin Lee	6
ANDREW, Hardage L.	3
ANDREW, Harriet White Fisher	1
ANDREW, Henry Hersey	1
ANDREW, James Osgood	H
ANDREW, John Albion	H
ANDREW, John Forrester	H
ANDREW, Joseph Atkins	5
ANDREW, Joseph Atkins	7
ANDREW, Samuel	8
ANDREW, Seymour Lansing	8
ANDREW, Warren	8
ANDREWES, Christopher Howard	9
ANDREWES, Sir William (Gerrard)	6
ANDREWS, Addison Fletcher	1
ANDREWS, Adolphus	2
ANDREWS, Albert H., Jr.	9
ANDREWS, Alexander Boyd	1
ANDREWS, Alexander Boyd	2
ANDREWS, Alexander Speer	5
ANDREWS, Ambrose	H
ANDREWS, Annulet	2
ANDREWS, Arthur Leonard	1
ANDREWS, Avery Delano	3
ANDREWS, Bert	3
ANDREWS, Carl Willis, Jr.	7
ANDREWS, Charles	H
ANDREWS, Charles	1
ANDREWS, Charles Bartlett	1
ANDREWS, Charles Cecil	4
ANDREWS, Charles Edgar, Jr.	3
ANDREWS, Charles Henry	2
ANDREWS, Charles McLean	2
ANDREWS, Charles Oscar	2
ANDREWS, Charles Oscar, Jr.	5
ANDREWS, Charlton	6
ANDREWS, Chauncey Hummason	H
ANDREWS, Christopher Columbus	1
ANDREWS, Clarence Edward	1
ANDREWS, Clarence L.	5
ANDREWS, Clayton Farrington	4
ANDREWS, Clement Walker	1
ANDREWS, Clifford Martin	7
ANDREWS, Columbus	7
ANDREWS, Daniel Marshall	1
ANDREWS, Donald Hatch	6
ANDREWS, E. Benjamin	1
ANDREWS, E. Wyllys	1
ANDREWS, Edmund	1
ANDREWS, Edward Gayer	1
ANDREWS, Edwin Carlos	3
ANDREWS, Eliphalet Frazer	1
ANDREWS, Eliza Frances	1
ANDREWS, Elmer Frank	4
ANDREWS, Elmore Lynnwood	9
ANDREWS, Emmet Charles	8
ANDREWS, Ethan Allen	4
ANDREWS, Eugene Plumb	4
ANDREWS, Evangeline Walker	4
ANDREWS, F. Emerson	7
ANDREWS, Fannie Fern	3
ANDREWS, Fletcher Reed	9
ANDREWS, Fonnie Jackson	9
ANDREWS, Frances M.	7
ANDREWS, Frank	1
ANDREWS, Frank L.	4
ANDREWS, Frank Maxwell	2
ANDREWS, Frank Mills	2
ANDREWS, Frank Taylor	1
ANDREWS, Garnett	1
ANDREWS, Garnett	2
ANDREWS, George	1
ANDREWS, George Clinton	9
ANDREWS, George Leonard	H
ANDREWS, George Leonard	1
ANDREWS, George Lippitt	1
ANDREWS, George Pierce	1
ANDREWS, George Rex	H
ANDREWS, George Whitfield	1
ANDREWS, George William	5
ANDREWS, Gwendolen Foulke	4
ANDREWS, Harry Eugene	1
ANDREWS, Herbert Marston	1
ANDREWS, Hiram Bertrand	4
ANDREWS, Horace Ellsworth	1
ANDREWS, Irene Osgood (Mrs. John B. Andrews)	5
ANDREWS, Israel Dewolf	H
ANDREWS, Israel Ward	H
ANDREWS, J. Floyd	9
ANDREWS, J. Warren	1
ANDREWS, James Dewitt	1
ANDREWS, James Frederick	7
ANDREWS, James Newton	7
ANDREWS, James Parkhill	2
ANDREWS, Jesse	4
ANDREWS, John	H
ANDREWS, John	3
ANDREWS, John Bertram	2
ANDREWS, John Newman	1
ANDREWS, John Tuttle	H
ANDREWS, John Williams	6
ANDREWS, Joseph	H
ANDREWS, Joseph C(hurch)	7
ANDREWS, Julia Lincoln Ray	4
ANDREWS, Justin M.	4
ANDREWS, Landaff Watson	H
ANDREWS, Launcelot	1
ANDREWS, Leila Edna	5
ANDREWS, Leland Stanford	5
ANDREWS, Lewis Whiting	4
ANDREWS, Lincoln Clark	3
ANDREWS, Lorin	H
ANDREWS, Lorrin	H
ANDREWS, Marie Scherer	6
ANDREWS, Marietta Minnigerode	1
ANDREWS, Marshall	6
ANDREWS, Martin Register	1
ANDREWS, Mary Raymond Shipman	1
ANDREWS, Matthew Page	2
ANDREWS, Matthew Thomas	1
ANDREWS, M(aurice) Nell	10
ANDREWS, Newton Lloyd	1
ANDREWS, Paul Shipman	1
ANDREWS, Philip	2
ANDREWS, Robert Christie	4
ANDREWS, Robert Day	1
ANDREWS, Robert Macon	5
ANDREWS, Robert Robbins	1
ANDREWS, Roger Merccin	3
ANDREWS, Roland Franklyn	1
ANDREWS, Roy Chapman	2
ANDREWS, Samuel George	H
ANDREWS, Samuel James	1
ANDREWS, Schofield	5
ANDREWS, Sherlock James	H
ANDREWS, Sidney	H
ANDREWS, Sidney Francis	1
ANDREWS, Steffan	3
ANDREWS, Stephen Pearl	1
ANDREWS, T. Coleman	8
ANDREWS, T. Wingate	1
ANDREWS, Thelma	10
ANDREWS, Thomas G.	4

ANDREWS, Thomas Galphin 2
ANDREWS, Timothy Patrick H
ANDREWS, Vernon Daniel 1
ANDREWS, W. Earle 4
ANDREWS, Walter Gresham 2
ANDREWS, Walter Pemberton 1
ANDREWS, Wayne 9
ANDREWS, Wilfred Leslie 3
ANDREWS, William E. 5
ANDREWS, William Given 1
ANDREWS, William Loring 1
ANDREWS, William Noble 5
ANDREWS, William Page 1
ANDREWS, William Shankland 1
ANDREWS, William Symes 1
ANDREWS, William Watson H
ANDRIC, Ivo 6
ANDRIEU, Mathuren Arthur H
ANDROS, Sir Edmund H
ANDRUS, Carlton Leverett 8
ANDRUS, Clift 5
ANDRUS, Edwin Cowles 7
ANDRUS, Elwin A. 8
ANDRUS, John Emory 1
ANDRUS, Valle Steele 8
ANDRUSS, E. Van Arsdale 1
ANDRY, E. Robert 7
ANDRY, E. Robert 8
ANDUZE-FARIS, Gustave 9
ANFUSO, Victor L. 4
ANGAS, W. Mack 4
ANGEL, Benjamin Franklin H
ANGEL, Franz 6
ANGEL, John 4
ANGEL, J(ohn) Lawrence 9
ANGEL, William G. H
ANGELA, Mother H
ANGELESCO, Constantin 2
ANGELI, Pier (Anna Marie Pierangeli) 5
ANGELIQUE, Mother Mary 7
ANGELL, Alexis Caswell 1
ANGELL, Donald Kinney 7
ANGELL, Emmett Dunn 6
ANGELL, Ernest 5
ANGELL, Frank 1
ANGELL, George Thorndike 1
ANGELL, Henry Clay 1
ANGELL, Israel H
ANGELL, James Burrill 1
ANGELL, James Rowland 2
ANGELL, James Waterhouse 10
ANGELL, James Waterhouse 9
ANGELL, Joseph Kinnicutt H
ANGELL, L(isbeth) Gertrude 5
ANGELL, Martin Fuller 1
ANGELL, Montgomery B. 3
ANGELL, Norman (Ralph Norman Angell Lane) 5
ANGELL, Sir Norman 4
ANGELL, Philip Harold 9
ANGELL, Robert Cooley 8
ANGELL, Robert Henderson 1
ANGELL, Walter Foster 1
ANGELL, William Gorham H
ANGELL, William Robert 2
ANGELLOTI, Frank M. 1
ANGER, Sister Mary Alacoque 5
ANGERS, Eugène-réal 7
ANGERSTEIN, Thomas Chester 7
ANGERT, Eugene Henry 1
ANGEVINE, Daniel Murray 8
ANGEVINE, Jay B(ernard) 5
ANGIER, Roswell Parker 2
ANGIER, Walter Eugene 1
ANGLAND, Emmett Cyril 5
ANGLE, Edward Hartley 1
ANGLE, Edward John 1
ANGLE, George Keyser 1
ANGLE, Glenn D(ale) 5
ANGLE, Jay Warren 3
ANGLE, Paul McClelland 6
ANGLE, Wesley Motley 4
ANGLE, Wesley Motley 7
ANGLEMAN, Sydney Winfield 5
ANGLIN, Margaret (Mary) 5
ANGLY, Edward 3
ANGOFF, Charles 7
ANGOOD, Sidney Bernard 5
ANGRIST, Alfred Alvin 8
ANGSTMAN, Albert Henry 8
ANGULO, Charles 9
ANHEUSER, Eberhard 4
ANIGSTEIN, Ludwik 7
ANISFELD, Boris 6
ANJARIA, Jashwantrai Jayantilal 5
ANKCORN, Charles M. 3
ANKENBRANDT, Francis L. 7
ANKENEY, John Sites 2
ANKENY, John D'Art 2
ANKENY, Levi 1
ANNADOWN, Ruth Vivian 5
ANNAND, Percy Nicol 3
ANOFF, Isador Samuel 9
ANOKHIN, Petr Kusmich 6
ANSBERRY, Timothy Thomas 2
ANSCHUTZ, Karl H
ANSEL, Martin Frederick 4
ANSELL, Samuel Tilden 5
ANSERMET, Ernest Alexandre 5
ANSHEN, S. Robert 5
ANSHUTZ, Edward Pollock 1
ANSHUTZ, Thomas Pollock 1
ANSLEY, Clarke Fisher 1
ANSLINGER, Harry Jacob 6
ANSLOW, Gladys Amelia 5
ANSLOW, W. Parker, Jr. 4
ANSON, Adrian Constantine H
ANSON, Adrian Constantine 4
ANSORGE, Martin Charles 4
ANSPACH, Brooke Melancthon 5
ANSPACH, Charles Leroy 10
ANSPACH, Charles Leroy 7
ANSPACHER, Louis Kaufman 2
ANSPRENGER, Aloys George 6
ANSTADT, Henry 1
ANSTED, Harry Bidwell 3
ANSTICE, Henry 1
ANTES, Henry H
ANTES, John H
ANTEVS, Ernst Valdemar 8
ANTHEIL, George 3
ANTHON, Charles H
ANTHON, Charles Edward H
ANTHON, John H
ANTHONY, Sister H
ANTHONY, Alfred Williams 1
ANTHONY, Andrew Varick Stout 1
ANTHONY, Ann 4
ANTHONY, Ann 7
ANTHONY, Arthur Cox 3
ANTHONY, Benjamin Harris 1
ANTHONY, Brayman William 4
ANTHONY, Carl 8
ANTHONY, Charles R. 7
ANTHONY, Daniel Read 1
ANTHONY, Daniel Read, Jr. 1
ANTHONY, Donald Elliot 6
ANTHONY, Earle C. 4
ANTHONY, Edward 5
ANTHONY, Ernest Lee 4
ANTHONY, Ernest Lee 8
ANTHONY, Gardner Chace 1
ANTHONY, George Tobey H
ANTHONY, Graham Hudson 9
ANTHONY, Harold Elmer 8
ANTHONY, Henry Bowen H
ANTHONY, John Gould H
ANTHONY, Joseph Biles H
ANTHONY, Joseph Garner 8
ANTHONY, Katharine Susan 4
ANTHONY, Katharine Susan 5
ANTHONY, Lovick Pierce 5
ANTHONY, Luther B. 3
ANTHONY, Norman (Hume) 5
ANTHONY, Roy David 7
ANTHONY, Susan Brownell 1
ANTHONY, William Arnold 1
ANTIN, Mary (Mary Antin Grabau) 6
ANTISDALE, Louis Marlin 1
ANTISDEL, Clarence Baumes 2
ANTOINE, Josephine Louise 5
ANTOINE, Pere H
ANTON, John J. 8
ANTON, Mark 5
ANTON, Nicholas Guy 10
ANTON, Roberta Charlotte Weiss (Mrs. Aaron Anton) 6
ANTONIA, Sister 2
ANTONIEWICZ, Wlodzimierz 6
ANTOON, A(lfred) J(oseph) 10
ANTRIM, Doron Kemp 4
ANTRIM, Elbert Manly 7
ANTRIM, Ernest Irving 3
ANTRIM, Eugene Marion 3
ANTRIM, Minna Thomas 4
ANTROBUS, John H
ANTROBUS, John 4
ANUNDSEN, Brynild 1
ANZA, Juan Bautista de H
ANZALONE, Joseph James 8
AOKI, Viscount Siuzo 4
APES, William H
APGAR, Austin Craig 1
APGAR, Virginia 6
APLIN, Henry Harrison 4
APONTE, Gonzalo Enrique 7
APOSTLE, Hippocrates George 10
APP, Frank 4
APPEL, Benjamin 7
APPEL, Daniel Frederick 1
APPEL, George F(rederick) Baer 5
APPEL, James Ziegler 8
APPEL, John Wilberforce, Jr. 2
APPEL, Joseph Herbert 2
APPEL, Kenneth Ellmaker 10
APPEL, Leon Howard 6
APPEL, Monte 5
APPEL, Monte 8
APPEL, Theodore 1
APPEL, Theodore Burton 1
APPELT, Frank R. 1
APPENZELLAR, Paul 3
APPENZELLER, Alice Rebecca 3
APPENZELLER, Henry Gerhard H
APPERLY, Frank Longstaff 8
APPLBAUM, Karl 6
APPLE, Andrew Thomas Geiger 1
APPLE, Henry Harbaugh 2
APPLE, Joseph Henry 2
APPLE, Thomas Gilmore H
APPLE, William Shoulden 8
APPLEBY, Frank 1
APPLEBY, Stewart 8
APPLEBY, Thomas Henry Montague Villiers 4
APPLEBY, Troy Wilson 2
APPLEBY, William Remsen 1
APPLEGARTH, Margaret Tyson 7
APPLEGATE, Albert Angelo 8
APPLEGATE, Frank G. 1
APPLEGATE, H. W. 1
APPLEGATE, Irvamae Vincent 5
APPLEGATE, Jesse H
APPLEGATE, John Stilwell 1
APPLEGATE, Kenneth Pomeroy 8
APPLEGATE, Paul Ray 4
APPLEMAN, Charles Orville 4
APPLEMAN, John Alan 8
APPLESEED, Johnny H
APPLETON, Charles W. 2
APPLETON, Daniel H
APPLETON, Daniel 1
APPLETON, Donald 10
APPLETON, Edward Victor 4
APPLETON, Floyd 3
APPLETON, Francis Henry 1
APPLETON, Francis Randall 1
APPLETON, Francis Randall 6
APPLETON, Harold Donald 8
APPLETON, James H
APPLETON, Jesse H
APPLETON, John* H
APPLETON, John Adams 4
APPLETON, John Howard 1
APPLETON, L. Estelle 1
APPLETON, Nathan H
APPLETON, Nathaniel Walker H
APPLETON, Samuel H
APPLETON, Thomas Gold H
APPLETON, William H
APPLETON, William Channing 5
APPLETON, William Henry H
APPLETON, William Henry 1
APPLETON, William Hyde 3
APPLETON, William Sumner 2
APPLETON, William Worthen 1
APTHORP, William Foster 4
ARAKI, Eikichi 3
ARAMANY, Mohamed Abdelal 9
ARAMBURU, Pedro Eugenio 5
ARAND, Louis A. 9
ARANETA, Gregorio 1
ARANNA, Oswaldo 3
ARANOW, Henry, Jr. 9
ARANT, Herschel Whitfield 1
ARANYOS, Alexander Sandor 9
ARBEELY, Abraham Joseph 4
ARBEIT, Arnold Arvin 7
ARBOGAST, Zollie O., Jr. 10
ARBUCKLE, Charles Nathaniel 3
ARBUCKLE, Ernest Comings 9
ARBUCKLE, Howard Bell 2
ARBUCKLE, John 1
ARBUCKLE, John D. 4
ARBUCKLE, John William 7
ARBUCKLE, MacLyn 1
ARBUCKLE, Matthew H
ARBUCKLE, Roscoe Conkling 1
ARBUS Diane 5
ARBUTHNOT, Charles Criswell 4
ARBUTHNOT, Charles Criswell 5
ARBUTHNOT, May Hill (Mrs. Charles C. Arbuthnot) 5
ARBUTHNOT, Thomas Shaw 5
ARBUTHNOT, Wilson S. 1
ARCAYA, Pedro Manuel 5
ARCE, Jose 5
ARCHAMBAULT, A. Margaretta 3
ARCHBALD, James Vi 1
ARCHBALD, Robert Wodrow 1
ARCHBOLD, John Dustin 1
ARCHBOLD, Richard 7
ARCHDALE, John H
ARCHER, Allen Thurman 4
ARCHER, Arthur Ward 7
ARCHER, Belle 1
ARCHER, Branch Tanner H
ARCHER, Clifford Paul 5
ARCHER, Franklin Morse 2
ARCHER, Franklin Morse, Jr. 8
ARCHER, Frederic 1
ARCHER, Gleason Leonard 4
ARCHER, Hiram John 7
ARCHER, James J. H
ARCHER, Jerome Walter 8
ARCHER, John H
ARCHER, John Clark 3
ARCHER, John Dale 9
ARCHER, Julian Lawrence 4
ARCHER, Laird 9
ARCHER, Peter 4
ARCHER, Ralph Curtis 3
ARCHER, Raymond LeRoy 8
ARCHER, Shreve MacLaren 2
ARCHER, Stevenson* H
ARCHER, Thomas P. 2
ARCHER, William Segar H
ARCHIBALD, Andrew Webster 1
ARCHIBALD, Arnold Adams 7
ARCHIBALD, Frank C. 1
ARCHIBALD, Fred Irwin 7
ARCHIBALD, Mrs. George 1
ARCHIBALD, James Francis Jewell 5
ARCHIBALD, Maynard Brown 3
ARCHIBALD, Raymond Clare 3
ARCHIE, William Councill 7
ARCHIPENKO, Alexander 4
ARCOMANO, Joseph Peter 10
ARCTOWSKA, Adrian Jane 5
ARCTOWSKI, Henryk 3
ARDEN, Edwin Hunter Pendleton 1
ARDEN, Elizabeth 4
ARDEN, Eve (Eunice Guedens)* 10
ARDERY, Julia Hoge Spencer 8
ARDERY, William Breckenridge 4
ARDISON, Robert Joseph 4
ARDREY, Robert 7
AREF, Abdul Salam 5
AREL, Bulent 10
ARENALES CATALAN, Emilio 5
ARENBERG, Albert Lee 5
AREND, Harry O. 4
ARENDS, Leslie Cornelius 8
ARENDT, Hannah 6
ARENDT, Morton 5
ARENS, Egmont 4
ARENS, Franz Xavier 1
ARENS, Henry 5
ARENS, Richard 5
ARENSBERG, Walter Conrad 3
ARENTS, Albert 4
ARENTS, Chester Abbo 9
ARENTS, George 4
ARENTZ, Frederic C. H. 4
AREY, Hawthorne 5
AREY, Leslie Brainerd 9
AREY, Melvin Franklin 1
ARGALL, Philip 1
ARGALL, Samuel H
ARGETSINGER, J. C. 3
ARGUELLO, Jose Dario H
ARGUELLO, Leonardo 2
ARGUELLO, Luis Antonio H
ARGYLE, William Robertson 4
ARIES, Leon Judah 8
ARIETI, Silvano 9
ARJONA, Jaime Homero 4
ARKELL, Bartlett 2
ARKELL, William Clark 4
ARKELL, William J. 1
ARKUSH, Arthur Spencer 7
ARKUSH, Ralph Montgomery 4
ARKWRIGHT, George Alfred 5
ARKWRIGHT, Preston Stanley 2
ARLEN, Harold 9
ARLEN, Michael 3
ARLING, Leonard Swenson 8
ARLISS, George 2
ARLT, Gustave Otto 10
ARMAS, Carlos Castillo 3
ARMBRECHT, William Henry 2
ARMBRISTER, Victor Stradley 4
ARMBRUSTER, Adolph Henry 3
ARMBRUSTER, Christian Herman 8
ARMBRUSTER, Christian Herman 9
ARMBRUSTER, John Philip 8
ARMENTANO, Anthony John 9
ARMENTROUT, James Sylvester 8
ARMENTROUT, Winfield Dockery 8
ARMES, William Dallam 4
ARMISTEAD, George H
ARMISTEAD, George H(arrison), Jr. 9
ARMISTEAD, Henry Beauford 3
ARMISTEAD, Henry Marshall 3
ARMISTEAD, Jesse Warren 3
ARMISTEAD, Lewis Addison H
ARMISTEAD, Parkes 10
ARMITAGE, Albert T. 5
ARMITAGE, Merle 6
ARMITAGE, Paul 2
ARMITAGE, Robert Ernest 10
ARMOR, James Burton 10
ARMOR, Mrs. Mary Elizabeth Harris 4
ARMOUR, A. Watson 3

ASHE, David I(rving) 9
ASHE, Edmund Marion 5
ASHE, Edward Joseph 5
ASHE, George B(amford) 5
ASHE, John H
ASHE, John Baptista* H
ASHE, Samuel H
ASHE, Samuel A'Court 1
ASHE, Thomas Samuel H
ASHE, William Francis, Jr. 4
ASHE, William Shepperd H
ASHER, Eugene Leon 10
ASHFORD, Bailey Kelly 1
ASHFORD, Emma Louise 1
ASHFORD, Mahlon 3
ASHFORTH, Albert C. 10
ASHHURST, Astley Paston Cooper 1
ASHHURST, John 1
ASHHURST, John, Jr. 1
ASHHURST, Richard Lewis 1
ASHKIN, Julius 8
ASHLEY, Barnas Freeman 4
ASHLEY, Charles Sumner 1
ASHLEY, Chester H
ASHLEY, Clarence Degrand 1
ASHLEY, Clifford Warren 2
ASHLEY, Daniel W. 2
ASHLEY, Delos Rodeyn H
ASHLEY, Edward 1
ASHLEY, Frederick William 3
ASHLEY, George Hall 3
ASHLEY, Henry H
ASHLEY, James Mitchell H
ASHLEY, John Pritchard 1
ASHLEY, Maurice C. 4
ASHLEY, Ossian D. 1
ASHLEY, Paul Pritchard 7
ASHLEY, Richard Chace 8
ASHLEY, Roscoe Lewis 4
ASHLEY, William Henry H
ASHMAN, James Ernest 6
ASHMEAD, Isaac H
ASHMEAD, John, Jr. 10
ASHMEAD, William Harris 1
ASHMORE, Frank Leon 6
ASHMORE, Jack Pearce, Jr. 7
ASHMORE, James 7
ASHMORE, John Durant H
ASHMORE, Otis 4
ASHMORE, Robert Thomas 10
ASHMORE, Sidney Gillespie 1
ASHMORE, William H
ASHMORE, William 4
ASHMUN, Eli Porter H
ASHMUN, George H
ASHMUN, George Coates 1
ASHMUN, Jehudi H
ASHMUN, Margaret Eliza 1
ASHTON, Albert A. 6
ASHTON, Eve 4
ASHTON, Frederick (William Mallandaine) 6
ASHTON, Henry Rusling 5
ASHTON, John H
ASHTON, John 4
ASHTON, John William 5
ASHTON, Joseph Hubley 1
ASHTON, Leonard C. 8
ASHTON, Linwood E. 8
ASHTON, Raymond J. 6
ASHTON, Samuel Collier 9
ASHTON, William 4
ASHTON, William Easterly 1
ASHTON, Winifred 4
ASHURST, Henry Fountain 4
ASHWORTH, Hattie Tiller (Mrs. Eugene Marvin Ashworth) 5
ASHWORTH, John H. 2
ASHWORTH, Robert Archibald 3
ASHWORTH, Walter C. 4
ASIMOV, Isaac 10
ASKENSTEDT, Fritz Conrad 2
ASKEW, Ralph Kirk 6
ASKEW, Sarah Byrd 2
ASKEW, Thyrza Simonton 3
ASKEY, Edwin Vincent 6
ASKIN, Robert J. 4
ASKREN, William David 4
ASKWITH, Herbert 8
ASNES, Marvin Arthur 10
ASPEGREN, John 1
ASPER, Joel Funk H
ASPINALL, Joseph 1
ASPINALL, Richard 6
ASPINALL, Wayne Norviel 8
ASPINWALL, Clarence Aikin 4
ASPINWALL, Glenn William 5
ASPINWALL, J. Lawrence 4
ASPINWALL, Thomas 1
ASPINWALL, William H
ASPINWALL, William Billings 3
ASPINWALL, William Henry H
ASPLUND, Rupert Franz 3
ASPLUNDH, E. T. 6
ASPLUNDH, Lester 9
ASQUITH, Anthony 5
ASSMUTH, Joseph 3
ASSUM, Arthur Louis 6
ASTAIRE, Fred 9
ASTAUROV, Boris Lvovich 6
ASTIN, Allen Varley 8
ASTMAN, Joseph Gustav 9
ASTON, Anthony H
ASTON, James 4
ASTON, Ralph 1
ASTON, Richard Douglas 5
ASTOR, Viscountess 4
ASTOR, John Jacob* H
ASTOR, John Jacob 1
ASTOR, Mary Lucille Langhanke 9
ASTOR, Vincent 3
ASTOR, William Backhouse H
ASTOR, William Waldorf 1
ASTOR OF HEVER, Baron (John Jacob Astor) 5
ASTOR OF HEVER, Baron (John Jacob Astor) 7
ASTROM, Axel Leonard 7
ASTURIAS, Miguel Angel 6
ASWELL, Edward C. 3
ASWELL, James Benjamin 1
ATCHESON, George, Jr. 2
ATCHISON, David Rice H
ATCHISON, Thomas Cunningham 1
ATCHLEY, Dana Winslow 8
ATEN, Fred N. 3
ATHA, Joseph Samuel 10
ATHEARN, Fred Goodrich 3
ATHEARN, Walter Scott 1
ATHENAGORAS, His All Holines 5
ATHERTON, Charles Gordon H
ATHERTON, Charles Humphrey H
ATHERTON, Edwin Newton 2
ATHERTON, Frank Cooke 2
ATHERTON, George W. 1
ATHERTON, Gertrude Franklin 2
ATHERTON, Gibson H
ATHERTON, Henry Francis 2
ATHERTON, James Peyton, Jr. 9
ATHERTON, John C. 3
ATHERTON, Joseph Ballard 4
ATHERTON, Joshua H
ATHERTON, Louis M. 3
ATHERTON, Percy Lee 2
ATHERTON, Ray 3
ATHERTON, Thomas Henry 7
ATHERTON, Warren Hendry 7
ATKESON, Clarence Lee Conner 6
ATKESON, Floyd Warnick 3
ATKESON, Thomas Clark 1
ATKESON, Thomas Conner 7
ATKESON, William Oscar 2
ATKIELSKI, Roman R. 5
ATKIN, Isaac Cubitt Raymond 3
ATKINS, Albert Henry 3
ATKINS, Arthur 4
ATKINS, Arthur Kennedy 6
ATKINS, Charles Duke 4
ATKINS, Craig Starbuck 10
ATKINS, Edwin F. 1
ATKINS, Frank Douglas, Jr. 8
ATKINS, George Tyng 2
ATKINS, George Washington Ely 4
ATKINS, Harry T. 1
ATKINS, Harry Thomas 5
ATKINS, Henry Hornby 5
ATKINS, James 1
ATKINS, Jearum H
ATKINS, John De Witt Clinton 1
ATKINS, Joseph Alexander 6
ATKINS, Joseph Preston 6
ATKINS, Mrs. Louise Allen 3
ATKINS, Oliver Ollie F. 7
ATKINS, Paul Moody 7
ATKINS, Paul Sidney 7
ATKINS, Smith Dykins 1
ATKINS, Thomas Lee 10
ATKINS, Willard Earl 5
ATKINSON, Albert Algernon 5
ATKINSON, Arcibald H
ATKINSON, Arthur John 10
ATKINSON, Arthur Kimmins 4
ATKINSON, Benjamin Searcy 3
ATKINSON, Carroll Holloway 9
ATKINSON, Charles Edwin 4
ATKINSON, Charles Harry 10
ATKINSON, Charles R. 5
ATKINSON, Christopher Joseph 1
ATKINSON, Donald Taylor 3
ATKINSON, Edward 1
ATKINSON, Eleanor 2
ATKINSON, Fred Washington 4
ATKINSON, Frederick Griswold 10
ATKINSON, Geoffrey 4
ATKINSON, George Francis 1
ATKINSON, George Henry H
ATKINSON, George Herring 7
ATKINSON, George Wesley 1
ATKINSON, Guy F. 5
ATKINSON, Harry Hunt 5
ATKINSON, Henry H
ATKINSON, Henry Avery 3
ATKINSON, Henry Morrell 1
ATKINSON, Herbert Spencer 3
ATKINSON, Herschel C. 4
ATKINSON, Hugh Craig 9
ATKINSON, Isaac Edmondson 1
ATKINSON, J. Robert 4
ATKINSON, John H
ATKINSON, John Bradshaw 4
ATKINSON, Joseph Story 5
ATKINSON, Justin Brooks 8
ATKINSON, Louis Evans 1
ATKINSON, Ralph 2
ATKINSON, Ralph Waldo 4
ATKINSON, Samuel C. 2
ATKINSON, Spencer Roane 7
ATKINSON, Thomas H
ATKINSON, Thomas Edgar 4
ATKINSON, Thomas Wilson 1
ATKINSON, Walter Sydney 7
ATKINSON, William Biddle 4
ATKINSON, William Brockliss 4
ATKINSON, William E. 1
ATKINSON, William Elrie 1
ATKINSON, William Sackston 1
ATKINSON, William Walker 1
ATKINSON, William Yates H
ATKINSON, William Yates 1
ATKINSON, William Yates 3
ATKINSON, Wilmer 1
ATKYNS, (Willie) Lee, (Jr.) 9
ATLASS, H. Leslie 4
ATLEE, John Light H
ATLEE, John Light 3
ATLEE, Samuel John H
ATLEE, Washington Lemuel H
ATTEBERY, Olin Moody 3
ATTERBERG, Kurt Magnus 9
ATTERBURY, Anson Phelps 1
ATTERBURY, Grosvenor 3
ATTERBURY, William Wallace 1
ATTERIDGE, Harold Richard 1
ATTERIDGE, Harold Richard 2
ATTLEE, Earl 4
ATTRIDGE, Richard 4
ATTUCKS, Crispus H
ATTWILL, Henry Converse 1
ATTWOOD, Frederic 5
ATTWOOD, James Albert 10
ATTWOOD, Stephen S. 4
ATTWOOD, Stephen S(tanley) 10
ATTWOOD, William 10
ATWATER, Caleb H
ATWATER, David Hay 2
ATWATER, Edward Perrin 5
ATWATER, Francis 1
ATWATER, George Parkin 1
ATWATER, Helen Woodard 2
ATWATER, Henry G. 3
ATWATER, John Wilbur 4
ATWATER, Lyman Hotchkiss H
ATWATER, Mary Meigs 3
ATWATER, Reginald Myers 3
ATWATER, Richard Mead 1
ATWATER, Wilbur Olin 1
ATWATER, William Cutler 1
ATWELL, Charles Beach 1
ATWELL, William Hawley 4
ATWILL, Douglass Henry 4
ATWILL, Edward Robert 1
ATWILL, Lionel 2
ATWILL, William 1
ATWOOD, Albert William 6
ATWOOD, Arthur R. 3
ATWOOD, Charles B. H
ATWOOD, Charles Edwin 1
ATWOOD, David H
ATWOOD, Edward Leland 5
ATWOOD, Edward Vincent 7
ATWOOD, Edward Wilson 10
ATWOOD, Edwin Byron 1
ATWOOD, Elmer Bugg 3
ATWOOD, Felix 6
ATWOOD, Frank Ely 2
ATWOOD, Frank J(arvis) 7
ATWOOD, Frederick H. 9
ATWOOD, George Edward 4
ATWOOD, Harrison 3
ATWOOD, Harry 1
ATWOOD, Henry 3
ATWOOD, Hinckley Gardner 2
ATWOOD, Isaac Morgan 1
ATWOOD, James Arthur 2
ATWOOD, Jesse H
ATWOOD, John Harrison 1
ATWOOD, John Murray 3
ATWOOD, Julius Walter 2
ATWOOD, Lemuel True 1
ATWOOD, Millard V. 1
ATWOOD, Millard V. 2
ATWOOD, Oscar 1
ATWOOD, Roy Franklin 4
ATWOOD, Wallace Walter 2
ATWOOD, William 10
AUB, Joseph Charles 6
AUBERT, Lloyd Lees 5
AUBREY, Edwin Ewart 3
AUBREY, Henry George 5
AUBREY, James Thomas 4
AUBREY, John Edmond 5
AUBREY, William 1
AUCH, John F. 4
AUCHINCLOSS, Charles C. 4
AUCHINCLOSS, Gordon 2
AUCHINCLOSS, Hugh D. 7
AUCHINCLOSS, James Coats 7
AUCHINCLOSS, John Winthrop 1
AUCHINCLOSS, William Stuart 1
AUCHMUTY, Richard Tylden H
AUCHMUTY, Robert* H
AUCHMUTY, Samuel H
AUCHTER, Eugene Curtis 3
AUCOCK, Arthur Morgan 5
AUD, Guy 4
AUDEN, Wystan Hugh 6
AUDRIETH, Ludwig Frederick 4
AUDSLEY, George Ashdown 4
AUDUBON, John James H
AUDUBON, John Woodhouse H
AUDUBON, Victor Gifford H
AUDY, Jack Ralph 6
AUER, Edward Daniel 7
AUER, Harry Anton 6
AUER, Johannes A. C. Fagginger 7
AUER, John 2
AUER, Joseph Lawrence 4
AUER, Leopold 1
AUERBACH, Beatrice Fox 5
AUERBACH, Beatrice Fox 8
AUERBACH, Erich 3
AUERBACH, Frank Ludwig 4
AUERBACH, Herbert S. 2
AUERBACH, Joseph S. 2
AUERBACH-LEVY, William 4
AUF DER HEIDE, Oscar Louis 2
AUGELLI, Anthony Thomas 9
AUGENBLICK, Robert Lee 7
AUGENSTEIN, Leroy George 5
AUGER, Charles L. 1
AUGHINBAUGH, William Edmund 1
AUGSPURGER, Owen Beal 5
AUGUR, Christopher Columbus H
AUGUR, Hezekiah H
AUGUR, Jacob Arnold 1
AUGUR, Margaret Avery 7
AUGUST, Harry Wirt 5
AUGUSTINE, Harry Hamill 4
AUGUSTINE, Sister Mary 10
AUGUSTINE, W(alter) O(rr) 8
AUGUSTINE, William Franklin 2
AUGUSTUS, Ellsworth Hunt 4
AUGUSTUS, John H
AUGUSTYN, Godfrey William 2
AULD, George P. 4
AULD, John Maxwell 4
AULICK, Amos Lindsey 7
AULT, Bromwell 5
AULT, James Percy 1
AULT, Nelson Allen 4
AULT, Otto Thurman 3
AULT, Warren Ortman 9
AULTMAN, Dwight Edward 1
AUMAN, Orrin W. 3
AUMAN, Russell Frank 5
AUMAN, William 1
AURAND, Samuel Herbert 4
AURBACH, Gerald Donald 10
AURELL, Alvin Karl 4
AURELL, George Emanuel 5
AURIN, Fritz Love 9
AURINGER, Obadiah Cyrus 1
AURIOL, Vincent 4
AURTHUR, Robert Alan 7
AUSE, Orval Hope 6
AUSE, Orval Hope 7
AUSLEY, Charles Saxon 6
AUSTAD, Mark Evans 9
AUSTELL, Adelaide Roberts 6
AUSTELL, Alfred H
AUSTEN, Benjamin H
AUSTEN, Peter Townsend 1
AUSTIN, Albert E. 1
AUSTIN, Albert E. 2
AUSTIN, Allan Stewart 8
AUSTIN, Archibald H
AUSTIN, Benjamin Fish 4
AUSTIN, Bernard Lige 7
AUSTIN, Calvin 1
AUSTIN, Charles Burgess 6
AUSTIN, Clem C. 7
AUSTIN, Clyde Bernard 4
AUSTIN, Cyrus Brooks 1
AUSTIN, David H
AUSTIN, Dwight Bertram 3
AUSTIN, Edward Thompson 6
AUSTIN, Edwin Charles 8
AUSTIN, Ennis Raymond 3
AUSTIN, Eugene Munger 4
AUSTIN, Francis Marion 1
AUSTIN, Frank Stearns 7
AUSTIN, Fred Thaddeus 1
AUSTIN, Frederick Carleton 1
AUSTIN, George Curtis 4
AUSTIN, Henry H
AUSTIN, Henry 4
AUSTIN, Herbert Douglas 5
AUSTIN, Howard 4
AUSTIN, Howard Albert, Jr. 5
AUSTIN, Isabella McHugh 1
AUSTIN, James Harold 3
AUSTIN, James Trecothick H
AUSTIN, Jane Goodwin H
AUSTIN, John Corneby Wilson 5
AUSTIN, John Langshaw 4
AUSTIN, John Osborne 1
AUSTIN, John Paul 9

AUSTIN, John Turnell 5
AUSTIN, Jonathan Loring H
AUSTIN, Kenneth Ralph 9
AUSTIN, Leonard S. 1
AUSTIN, Lloyd Lewis 5
AUSTIN, Louis Winslow 1
AUSTIN, Mary 1
AUSTIN, Moses H
AUSTIN, Oscar Phelps 1
AUSTIN, Richard Bevan 7
AUSTIN, Richard Loper 2
AUSTIN, Richard Wilson 1
AUSTIN, Samuel H
AUSTIN, Samuel Yates 5
AUSTIN, Stephen Fuller H
AUSTIN, T. Louis, Jr. 8
AUSTIN, Warren Robinson 4
AUSTIN, Wilbert John 1
AUSTIN, William H
AUSTIN, William Lacy 3
AUSTIN, William Lane 2
AUSTIN, William Liseter 1
AUSTIN-BALL, Thomas 5
AUSTRIAN, Alfred S. 1
AUSTRIAN, Carl Joseph 5
AUSTRIAN, Charles Robert 3
AUSTRINS, Emilija Pone (Mrs. Peteris Austrins) 6
AUSUBEL, Herman 7
AUTEN, James Ernest 2
AUTHIER, George Francis 5
AUTORI, Franco 10
AUXIER, George Washington 7
AVANCENA, Ramon 5
AVELLANUS, Arcadius 1
AVENT, Joseph Emory 3
AVERBACH, Albert 6
AVERELL, William Woods H
AVERETT, Elliott 8
AVERETT, Thomas Hamlet H
AVERILL, George G. 3
AVERILL, Glenn Mark 1
AVERILL, John H. 5
AVERILL, John Thomas H
AVERILL, Lawrence Augustus 9
AVERITT, George Alfred 5
AVERS, Henry Godfrey 2
AVERY, Alphonso Calhoun 4
AVERY, Benjamin Parke H
AVERY, Catherine Hitchcock Tilden 1
AVERY, Christopher Lester 3
AVERY, Clarence Willard 2
AVERY, Coleman 1
AVERY, Cyrus Stevens 5
AVERY, Daniel H
AVERY, Delos 4
AVERY, Elroy McKendree 1
AVERY, George C. 1
AVERY, George True 2
AVERY, Henry Ogden H
AVERY, Isaac Wheeler H
AVERY, Isaac Wheeler 1
AVERY, John* H
AVERY, John 1
AVERY, John 4
AVERY, Johnston 5
AVERY, Milton 4
AVERY, Moses Nathan 2
AVERY, Nathan Prentice 2
AVERY, Oswald Theodore 3
AVERY, Rachel Foster 1
AVERY, Ray Longfellow 7
AVERY, Robert 1
AVERY, Samuel 1
AVERY, Samuel Putnam 1
AVERY, Sewell Lee 4
AVERY, Susan Look 1
AVERY, Thomas Burt 4
AVERY, William Tecumsah H
AVERY, William Turner 8
AVERY, William Waightstill H
AVERY, Willis Frank 6
AVES, Dreda 2
AVES, Henry Damerel 1
AVILDSEN, Clarence 4
AVINOAM, Reuben 6
AVINOFF, Andrew 2
AVIS, John Boyd 2
AVIS, Samuel Brashear 1
AVITABILE, Salvatore 3
AVNET, Lester Francis 5
AVNSOE, Thorkild 3
AVON, Earl of (Sir Robert Anthony Eden) 7
AVRAM, Mois H(erban) 6
AVRUTICK, Abraham Noah 8
AWALT, Francis Gloyd 10
AWL, William MacLay H
AXE, Emerson Wirt 4
AXE, Leonard Henry 7
AXE, Ruth Houghton 4
AXEEN, Marina Esther 8
AXEL, Hans H
AXEL, Peter 8
AXELRAD, Jacob 8
AXELRAD, Sidney 6
AXELRAD, Sidney 7
AXELROD, Haim Izchak 5
AXELROD, James J. 8
AXELROD, Leonard Richardson 6
AXELSON, Charles Frederic 5
AXELSON, Charles Frederic 7
AXELSON, John S. 8
AXFORD, Hiram William 8
AXLINE, George Andrew 1
AXMAN, Laurence Henry 9
AXSON, Stockton 1
AXTELL, Decatur 1
AXTELL, Edwin Rodarmel 1
AXTELL, Frances Cleveland 4
AXTELL, Harold Lucius 3
AXTELL, John Thomas 1
AXTELL, Samuel Beach H
AXTELLE, George Edward 6
AXTHELM, Pete 10
AXTON, John Thomas 1
AYALA, Juan Manuel de H
AYALA Y AYALA, Rafael 9
AYARS, George W(ashington) 5
AYCOCK, Charles Brantley 1
AYCOCK, Ezra Kenneth 10
AYCOCK, William Lloyd 8
AYCRIGG, John Bancker H
AYDELOTT, James Howard 4
AYDELOTTE, Dora 5
AYDELOTTE, Frank 3
AYDLETT, Edwin Ferebee 1
AYER, Sir Alfred Jules 10
AYER, Benjamin F. 1
AYER, Charles Fanning 3
AYER, Charles Frederick 5
AYER, Clarence Walter 1
AYER, Edward Everett 1
AYER, F. Wayland 1
AYER, Franklin Deming 4
AYER, Fred Carleton 6
AYER, Frederic Eugene 5
AYER, Frederick 1
AYER, Frederick Fanning 1
AYER, Harriet Hubbard 1
AYER, James Bourne 4
AYER, James Cook H
AYER, John 4
AYER, Joseph Cullen 2
AYER, Nathaniel Farwell 6
AYER, Richard Small H
AYER, Winslow B. 4
AYERS, Allan Farrell 4
AYERS, Clarence Edwin 5
AYERS, Edward Everett 4
AYERS, Fred Wesley 4
AYERS, Harry Mell 4
AYERS, Howard 1
AYERS, Joseph Burton 6
AYERS, Lemuel 3
AYERS, Lorenz Kneedler 9
AYERS, Roy E. 3
AYERS, Rufus Adolphus 4
AYERS, William P(endergast) 6
AYETA, Francisco de H
AYLER, Albert 5
AYLESWORTH, Barton Orville 1
AYLESWORTH, Merlin Hall 3
AYLING, Charles Lincoln 5
AYLLON, Lucas Vasquez De H
AYLSWORTH, Leon Emmons 5
AYLSWORTH, Nicholas John 4
AYLSWORTH, William Prince 1
AYLWIN, John Cushing H
AYMAR, Gordon Christian 10
AYME, Louis Henri 1
AYME, Marcel 4
AYNESWORTH, Kenneth Hazen 2
AYRE, Henry Glenn 10
AYRES, Albert Douglass 2
AYRES, Anne H
AYRES, Atlee Bernard 5
AYRES, Brown 1
AYRES, Burt Wilmot 5
AYRES, Edward 1
AYRES, Eugene Edmond 1
AYRES, Frank C. 3
AYRES, Franklin Herman 4
AYRES, George Frederic 1
AYRES, Harry Morgan 2
AYRES, Joseph Gerrish 1
AYRES, Leonard Porter 2
AYRES, Louis 2
AYRES, Martha Oathout 8
AYRES, Milan Church 1
AYRES, Milan Valentine 5
AYRES, Philip Wheelock 5
AYRES, Quincy Claude 4
AYRES, Romeyn Beck H
AYRES, Samuel Gardiner 2
AYRES, Samuel Loring Percival 1
AYRES, Stephen Cooper 1
AYRES, Steven Beckwith 1
AYRES, Thomas A. H
AYRES, William Augustus 3
AYRES, William Leake 7
AYUB KHAN, Mohammed 6
AZAD, Abul Kalam Maulana 3
AZARIAS, Brother H
AZCARATE Y FLOREZ, Pablo De 5
AZEVEDO, Philadelpho 3
AZUELA, Mariano 5
AZUOLA, Eduardo 3

B

BAAB, Otto J. 3
BAADE, Walter 4
BAAR, Arnold R. 3
BAAR, Emil N. 9
BAASDEVANT, Pierre Jules 4
BABASINIAN, V. S. 1
BABB, Clement Edwin 1
BABB, Cyrus Cates 1
BABB, Howard Selden 7
BABB, James Elisha 1
BABB, James T(inkham) 5
BABB, Jervis Jefferis 8
BABB, Max Wellington 2
BABB, Washington Irving 1
BABBIDGE, Homer Daniels, Jr. 8
BABBITT, Benjamin Talbot H
BABBITT, Charles James 4
BABBITT, Dean 9
BABBITT, Edwin Burr 1
BABBITT, Edwin Dwight 4
BABBITT, Elijah H
BABBITT, Eugene Howard 4
BABBITT, Frank Cole 1
BABBITT, George Franklin 4
BABBITT, Irving 1
BABBITT, Isaac H
BABBITT, Juliette M. 3
BABBITT, Kurnal R. 1
BABBITT, Lawrence Sprague 1
BABBOTT, Frank Lusk 1
BABBS, Arthur Vergil 4
BABBS, Charles Frederick 6
BABCOCK, Albert 4
BABCOCK, Alfred H
BABCOCK, Allen 5
BABCOCK, Bernie 5
BABCOCK, Birton E. 1
BABCOCK, Bruce L(anders) 8
BABCOCK, Charles 1
BABCOCK, Charles Dwight, Jr. 9
BABCOCK, Charles Henry 1
BABCOCK, Charles Henry 4
BABCOCK, Charles Henry 5
BABCOCK, Conrad Stanton 7
BABCOCK, Earle Brownell 1
BABCOCK, Earle Jay 1
BABCOCK, Edward Vose 2
BABCOCK, Ernest Brown 3
BABCOCK, F. Huntington 7
BABCOCK, Franklin 7
BABCOCK, Frederic 7
BABCOCK, George Herman H
BABCOCK, Harold Delos 5
BABCOCK, Harriet 3
BABCOCK, Harry Allan 4
BABCOCK, Havilah 4
BABCOCK, Howard Edward 3
BABCOCK, Irving Brown 4
BABCOCK, James Chester 6
BABCOCK, James Francis H
BABCOCK, James Woods 1
BABCOCK, John Brazer, III 8
BABCOCK, John Breckinridge 1
BABCOCK, John Pease 4
BABCOCK, Joseph Weeks 1
BABCOCK, Kendric Charles 1
BABCOCK, Leander H
BABCOCK, Louis Locke 5
BABCOCK, Maltbie Davenport H
BABCOCK, Orville Elias H
BABCOCK, Pervin Lathrop 9
BABCOCK, Richard Earle 3
BABCOCK, Robert Hall 1
BABCOCK, Robert Shillingford 9
BABCOCK, Robert Weston 4
BABCOCK, Rodney Whittemore 8
BABCOCK, Samuel Denison 1
BABCOCK, Samuel Gavitt 2
BABCOCK, Stephen Moulton 1
BABCOCK, Warren La Verne 2
BABCOCK, Washington Irving 1
BABCOCK, William H
BABCOCK, William Henry 1
BABCOCK, William Waterman 4
BABCOCK, William Wayne 5
BABCOCK, Winnifred Eaton (Onoto Watanna) 6
BABER, Alice 8
BABER, Carroll Preston 7
BABER, George W. 5
BABER, Ray Erwin 4
BABIN, Hosea John 4
BABIN, Victor 5
BABINGTON, Suren H. 7
BABKA, John Joseph 7
BABLER, Bernard Joseph 6
BABLER, Jacob L. 2
BABSON, Arthur Clifford 8
BABSON, Herman 1
BABSON, Paul Talbot 5
BABSON, Roger Ward 4
BABST, Earl D. 4
BACCALONI, Salvatore 5
BACH, Harry 6
BACH, Oscar Bruno 3
BACH, Ralph Edward 5
BACH, Ralph Edward 7
BACH, Richard F. 4
BACH, Thomas Cumming 4
BACHARACH, Eric William 5
BACHARACH, Isaac 3
BACHAUER, Gina 7
BACHE, Alexander Dallas H
BACHE, Benjamin Franklin H
BACHE, Dallas 1
BACHE, Franklin H
BACHE, Harold L. 5
BACHE, Jules Semon 2
BACHE, Leopold Semon 1
BACHE, Louise Franklin 2
BACHE, Rene 4
BACHE, Richard H
BACHE, Theophylact H
BACHE, William H
BACHELDER, John Badger H
BACHELDER, Nahum Josiah 1
BACHELLER, Irving Addison 2
BACHELLER, Joseph Henry 1
BACHEM, Albert 3
BACHER, Otto Henry 1
BACHE-WIIG, Jens 6
BACHKE, Halvard Huitfeldt 3
BACHMAN, Absalom Pierre 4
BACHMAN, Allan Earnshaw 5
BACHMAN, Frank Puterbaugh 1
BACHMAN, George William 8
BACHMAN, Ingeborg 6
BACHMAN, John H
BACHMAN, Jonathan Waverly 1
BACHMAN, Nathan 1
BACHMAN, Nathan Lynn 1
BACHMAN, Paul Stanton 3
BACHMAN, Robert Abraham 5
BACHMAN, Walter Crawford 10
BACHMAN, William Francis 7
BACHMANN, Raphael Otto 5
BACHMANN, Werner Emmanuel 3
BACHMEYER, Arthur Charles 3
BACHNER, Lester R. 7
BACHOUR, Rafic Jibrail 6
BACHRACH, Bradford K. 10
BACHRACH, Louis Fabian 4
BACHRACH, Walter Keyser 4
BACIGALUPI, James Augustus 3
BACIGALUPI, Tadini 4
BACK, Ernest Adna 6
BACK, George Irving 5
BACKER, George 6
BACKES, John H. 1
BACKHAUS, Wilhelm 5
BACKMAN, Gustave Pollard 9
BACKMAN, Jules 8
BACKMAN, Kenneth B. 4
BACKSTRAND, Clifford J. 5
BACKSTROM, Lathrop Gustaf 10
BACKUS, August Charles 3
BACKUS, Azel H
BACKUS, Cecil Franklin 7
BACKUS, Edward Wellington 1
BACKUS, Edwin Burdette 3
BACKUS, Isaac H
BACKUS, Jim (James Gilmore Backus) 10
BACKUS, Louise Burton Laidlaw (Mrs. Dana Converse Backus) 6
BACKUS, Manson Franklin 1
BACKUS, Samuel Woolsey 4
BACKUS, Standish 2
BACKUS, Truman Jay 1
BACKUS, Wilson Marvin 2
BACOATS, J. Alvin 4
BACON, Albert Williamson 1
BACON, Albion Fellows 1
BACON, Alexander Samuel 1
BACON, Alice Mabel 1
BACON, Augustus Octavius 1
BACON, Benjamin Wisner 1
BACON, Charles Sumner 2
BACON, Clara Latimer 2
BACON, Clarence Everett 8
BACON, David H
BACON, David William H
BACON, Delia Salter H
BACON, Edgar Mayhew 1
BACON, Edward Alsted 10
BACON, Edward Payson 1
BACON, Edward Rathbone 1
BACON, Edwin Munroe 1
BACON, Edwin Munroe 2
BACON, Ernst 10
BACON, Ezekiel H
BACON, Francis 10
BACON, Francis 1
BACON, Francis Leonard 3
BACON, Francis R. 4
BACON, Frank 1
BACON, Frank Rogers 2
BACON, Gaspar Griswold 2
BACON, George Andrew 1
BACON, George Morgan 5
BACON, George P. 1
BACON, George Wood 3
BACON, Henry 1
BACON, J. Raymond 10
BACON, John H
BACON, John Baptiste Ford 9
BACON, John Harwood 5
BACON, John Mosby 1
BACON, John Watson 1
BACON, Josephine Dodge Daskam 5
BACON, Leonard H
BACON, Leonard 3
BACON, Leonard Woolsey 1
BACON, Mary Elizabeth (Mrs. Philip Bacon) 6
BACON, Mary Schell Hoke (Dolores Marbourg) 5
BACON, Nathaniel H
BACON, Peggy 9
BACON, Raymond Foss 3
BACON, Robert 1
BACON, Robert Low 1
BACON, Robert Stillwell 5
BACON, Selden 2
BACON, Thomas H
BACON, Walter W. 4
BACON, William Johnson H
BACON, William Stevens 3
BACON, William Thompson 7
BADAWI PASHA, Abdel Hamid 4
BADDELEY, Hermione 9
BADE, William Frederic 1
BADEAU, Adam H
BADENBERGER, Henry 4
BADER, Jesse Moren 4

BADER, Ralph Hedrick 1
BADER, Richard George 6
BADERTSCHER, J(acob) A.
BADGER, Charles Johnston 1
BADGER, Dewitt Clinton 4
BADGER, Erastus Beethoven 7
BADGER, George Edmund H
BADGER, George Henry 4
BADGER, James Golvin
BADGER, Joseph* H
BADGER, Luther H
BADGER, Oscar Charles 1
BADGER, Oscar Charles 3
BADGER, Philip Owen 5
BADGER, Richard McLean 10
BADGER, Theodore Learnard 7
BADGER, Walter Irving 1
BADGER, Walter Irving, Jr. 9
BADGER, Walter Lucius 3
BADGLEY, Maxwell Forrest 5
BADGLEY, Sidney Rose 1
BADIN, Stephen Theodore H
BADING, Gerhard Adolph 2
BADLEY, Brenton Thoburn 2
BADSKEY, Lorin Justin 9
BADT, Harry Asher 7
BADT, Milton B. 4
BAEHR, Carl Adolph 4
BAEHR, George 7
BAEHR, Max Joseph 1
BAEHR, William Alfred 2
BAEHR, William Frederick Otto 5
BAEKELAND, Celine 3
BAEKELAND, George 4
BAEKELAND, Leo Hendrik 2
BAENSCH, Emil 3
BAENSCH, Willy E. 5
BAEPLER, Walter A. 3
BAER, Arthur A. 6
BAER, Benjamin Franklin 10
BAER, Francis Shaw 10
BAER, George, Jr. H
BAER, George Frederick 1
BAER, Jean Hitchcock 6
BAER, John M(iller) 5
BAER, John M(iller) 7
BAER, John Willis 1
BAER, Joseph Augustus 6
BAER, Joseph Louis 3
BAER, Libbie C. 4
BAER, Rexford Levering 8
BAER, Sidney R. 3
BAER, Townsend W. 1
BAER, William Bush 3
BAER, William Jacob 1
BAERG, Gerhard 8
BAERG, William J. 7
BAERWALD, Paul 5
BAETJER, Anna Medora 8
BAETJER, Edwin G. 1
BAETJER, Frederick Henry 1
BAETJER, Howard 2
BAEZ, Cecilio 4
BAEZA, Marco A. 4
BAGAR, Robert 3
BAGBY, Albert Morris 1
BAGBY, Arthur Pendleton H
BAGBY, George Franklin 4
BAGBY, George Poindexter 1
BAGBY, George William H
BAGBY, John Courts 1
BAGBY, John Hampden Chamberlayne 1
BAGBY, William Buck 4
BAGDATOPOULOS, William Spencer 5
BAGG, Lyman Hotchkiss 1
BAGG, Rufus Mather 5
BAGGARLY, Franklin Clyde 8
BAGGER, Henry Horneman 4
BAGGETT, Samuel Graves 4
BAGGS, Arthur Eugene 2
BAGGS, Mae Lacy 1
BAGGS, William Calhoun 5
BAGHDIGIAN, Bagdasar Krikor 8
BAGLEY, Charles Leland 5
BAGLEY, Clarence Booth 1
BAGLEY, David Worth 4
BAGLEY, William Chandler 2
BAGLEY, Willis Gaylord Clark 2
BAGNELL, Robert 3
BAGNOLD, Enid (Lady Jones) 7
BAGOT, Sir Charles H

BAGSTAD, Anna Emilia 5
BAGSTER-COLLINS, Elijah William 5
BAGWELL, Paul D(ouglas) 6
BAHL, F. J. 7
BAHL, William Edgar 3
BAHMER, Robert H. 10
BAHN, Chester Bert 4
BAHNSON, Agnew Hunter 4
BAHR, Emory J. 4
BAHR, Walter Julien 6
BAHRENBURG, Louis P. H. 1
BAIER, Victor 1
BAIL, Philip Milo 10
BAILEY, Albert David 7
BAILEY, Albert Edward 5
BAILEY, Alexander Hamilton H
BAILEY, Alfred Halsey 7
BAILEY, Alfred Marshall 7
BAILEY, Alice Ward 4
BAILEY, Ann H
BAILEY, Anna Warner H
BAILEY, Arthur Low 1
BAILEY, Arthur Scott Franklin 5
BAILEY, Benjamin 2
BAILEY, Bert Heald 1
BAILEY, Bertha 1
BAILEY, Calvin Weston 5
BAILEY, Carl Edward 2
BAILEY, Carlos A(ugustus) 8
BAILEY, Cassius Mercer 1
BAILEY, Charles Franklin 3
BAILEY, Charles Justin 2
BAILEY, Charles Langdon 1
BAILEY, Charles Olin 1
BAILEY, Charles Reuben 1
BAILEY, Charles William 4
BAILEY, Clarence Mitchell 1
BAILEY, Cleveland Monroe 9
BAILEY, Clyde H. 8
BAILEY, Consuelo Northrop 7
BAILEY, David Jackson H
BAILEY, E. Stillman 1
BAILEY, Ebenezer H
BAILEY, Edd Hamilton 9
BAILEY, Edgar Henry Summerfield 1
BAILEY, Edward H
BAILEY, Edward Monroe 2
BAILEY, Elijah Prentiss 1
BAILEY, Elwood Tewksbury 7
BAILEY, Ervin George 4
BAILEY, Everett Hoskins 1
BAILEY, Florence Augusta Merriam 2
BAILEY, Francis H
BAILEY, Frank 3
BAILEY, Frank Harvey 1
BAILEY, Frank Moye 4
BAILEY, Fred Oliver 4
BAILEY, Frederick Eugene, Jr. 10
BAILEY, Frederick Randolph 1
BAILEY, Gamaliel H
BAILEY, George Davis 4
BAILEY, George Gilbert 10
BAILEY, George Washington 1
BAILEY, George Wicks 1
BAILEY, George William 7
BAILEY, Gilbert Ellis 1
BAILEY, Goldsmith Fox H
BAILEY, Guy Winfred 1
BAILEY, Hannah Johnston 1
BAILEY, Harold Harris 6
BAILEY, Harold Wood 6
BAILEY, Harry Louis 4
BAILEY, Harry Paul 7
BAILEY, Henry Turner 1
BAILEY, Hollis Russell 1
BAILEY, Irving Widmer 4
BAILEY, Ivon Arthur 4
BAILEY, Jack Blendon 10
BAILEY, Jacob H
BAILEY, Jacob Whitman H
BAILEY, James Anthony 1
BAILEY, James Edmund H
BAILEY, James Garfield 1
BAILEY, James Montgomery 1
BAILEY, Jennings 4
BAILEY, Jeremiah H
BAILEY, Jessie Emerson 6
BAILEY, John H
BAILEY, John Hays 5
BAILEY, John Moran 6
BAILEY, John Mosher 1
BAILEY, John Ora 3
BAILEY, John Wendell 4
BAILEY, Joseph* H
BAILEY, Joseph T. H

BAILEY, Joseph Weldon 1
BAILEY, Joseph Weldon, Jr. 2
BAILEY, Josiah William 2
BAILEY, Leonard Henry 4
BAILEY, Lewis W. 6
BAILEY, Liberty Hyde 3
BAILEY, Loring Woart 1
BAILEY, Louis Jonathan 4
BAILEY, Lydia R. H
BAILEY, Margaret Emerson 3
BAILEY, Mark, Jr. 4
BAILEY, Mercer Silas 1
BAILEY, Mervyn J. 3
BAILEY, Milus Kendrick 4
BAILEY, Morton 3
BAILEY, Morton Shelley 1
BAILEY, Nathan Lynch 7
BAILEY, Pearce 4
BAILEY, Pearce 7
BAILEY, Pearl 10
BAILEY, Percival 6
BAILEY, Ralph Edward 4
BAILEY, Ralph Emerson 6
BAILEY, Ray W. 3
BAILEY, Richard Paul 7
BAILEY, Roger 8
BAILEY, Rufus William H
BAILEY, Solon Irving 1
BAILEY, Steele 4
BAILEY, Stephen Kemp 8
BAILEY, Temple 3
BAILEY, Theodore Mead 4
BAILEY, Theodorus* H
BAILEY, Thomas Andrew 8
BAILEY, Thomas David 10
BAILEY, Thomas L. 2
BAILEY, Thomas Pearce 2
BAILEY, Vernon 2
BAILEY, Vernon Howe 3
BAILEY, Warren Grant 7
BAILEY, Warren Worth 1
BAILEY, William Arthur 5
BAILEY, William Bacon 3
BAILEY, William John 10
BAILEY, William Louis 7
BAILEY, William Stuart 7
BAILEY, William Whitman 1
BAILEY, William Whitman 4
BAILEY, Willis J. 1
BAILHACHE, Preston Heath 1
BAILIE, Alexander Joseph 8
BAILIE, Earle 1
BAILIE, Virginia 1
BAILIE, William 1
BAILIE, William Lamdin 1
BAILIET, John Mason 8
BAILLARGEON, Cebert 7
BAILLIE, Archie Fraser 3
BAILLIE, Hugh 1
BAILLIE, John 4
BAILLOT, Edouard Paul 4
BAILLY, Edward Cashman 7
BAILLY, Joseph Alexis 1
BAILLY-BLANCHARD, Arthur 1
BAILOR, Edwin Maurice 5
BAILY, Alfred William 4
BAILY, Elisha Ingram 1
BAILY, Harold James 4
BAILY, Joshua L. 1
BAIN, Charles Wesley 1
BAIN, Edgar Collins 5
BAIN, Ferdinand R. 2
BAIN, Fred B. 5
BAIN, George Grantham 4
BAIN, George Luke Scobie H
BAIN, George Washington 1
BAIN, George William 10
BAIN, Harry Foster 2
BAIN, Jarvis Johnson 6
BAIN, Read 9
BAIN, Robert Edward Mather 1
BAIN, William James 10
BAINBRIDGE, Alexander Gilbert 1
BAINBRIDGE, Charles Newton 8
BAINBRIDGE, John 10
BAINBRIDGE, Lucy Seaman 1
BAINBRIDGE, William H
BAINBRIDGE, William Seaman 2
BAINER, Roy 10
BAINES, Edward Richards 5
BAINES-MILLER, Minnie Willis 1
BAINTER, Fay Okell 5
BAINTON, Roland Herbert 8
BAIONE, Luke A. 9
BAIRD, Absalom 1
BAIRD, Albert Craig 7

BAIRD, Alexander Kennedy 8
BAIRD, Andrew D. 1
BAIRD, Andrew McClung 4
BAIRD, Bruce 4
BAIRD, Cameron 4
BAIRD, Charles Washington H
BAIRD, Cora 5
BAIRD, David 1
BAIRD, David, Jr. 3
BAIRD, David W. E. 6
BAIRD, Edward Rouzie 2
BAIRD, Edwin 7
BAIRD, Flave Saunders 8
BAIRD, Frank Burkett 9
BAIRD, Frederick H. 9
BAIRD, Frederick Rogers 1
BAIRD, George Washington 1
BAIRD, George William 1
BAIRD, H.B. 8
BAIRD, Henry Carey 1
BAIRD, Henry Martyn 1
BAIRD, Henry W. 4
BAIRD, Henry Welles, III 9
BAIRD, James 3
BAIRD, Jean Katherine 1
BAIRD, John L. 4
BAIRD, John Wallace 1
BAIRD, Joseph Edward 2
BAIRD, Julian Braden 9
BAIRD, Julian William 1
BAIRD, Louise 5
BAIRD, Lucius Olmsted 2
BAIRD, Matthew H
BAIRD, Phil C. 1
BAIRD, Raleigh William 9
BAIRD, Richard F. 1
BAIRD, Robert H
BAIRD, Robert W. 5
BAIRD, Samuel John H
BAIRD, Spencer Fullerton H
BAIRD, Spencer Lawrence 8
BAIRD, Thomas H. 8
BAIRD, Walter Scott 8
BAIRD, Warner Green 7
BAIRD, William Britton 9
BAIRD, William Cameron (Bil Baird) 9
BAIRD, William Jesse 3
BAIRD, William Raimond 1
BAITER, Richard Englis 5
BAITS, Vera Burridge 4
BAITSELL, George Alfred 7
BAITY, George Perry 4
BAITY, Herman Glenn 6
BAITY, James L. 5
BAJPAI, Sir Girja Shankar 3
BAKELESS, John (Edwin) 1
BAKENHUS, Reuben Edwin 4
BAKER, A. B. 9
BAKER, A. George 4
BAKER, Abijah Richardson H
BAKER, Albert 2
BAKER, Albert C. 1
BAKER, Albert Rufus 1
BAKER, Albert Zachary 8
BAKER, Alfred Brittin 1
BAKER, Alfred Landon 1
BAKER, Alfred Zantzinger 5
BAKER, Alton Fletcher 4
BAKER, Alton Wesley 10
BAKER, Archibald Eachern 1
BAKER, Arthur Josiah Mountford 3
BAKER, Arthur Latham 1
BAKER, Arthur Mulford 1
BAKER, Asa George 1
BAKER, Asher Carter 1
BAKER, Benedict J. 2
BAKER, Benjamin Franklin H
BAKER, Benjamin Webb 5
BAKER, Benton 8
BAKER, Bernard Nadal 1
BAKER, Bertha Kunz 2
BAKER, Bertha Kunz 5
BAKER, Bruce Alexander 5
BAKER, Bryant 5
BAKER, Burke 5
BAKER, Burton Lowell 7
BAKER, Caleb H
BAKER, Carlos Heard 9
BAKER, Charles Fuller 1
BAKER, Charles Henry H
BAKER, Charles Hinckley 1
BAKER, Charles Samuel 1
BAKER, Charles Whiting 1
BAKER, Charles William 1
BAKER, Chauncey Brooke 1
BAKER, Chet 9
BAKER, Claude Milem 5
BAKER, Cora Warman 5
BAKER, Cornelia 1
BAKER, Crosby Fred 3

BAKER, Crowdus 8
BAKER, Daniel H
BAKER, Daniel Clifton 6
BAKER, Darius 1
BAKER, David 4
BAKER, David Dudrow 3
BAKER, David Floyd 5
BAKER, D(avid) Gordon 7
BAKER, David Jewett H
BAKER, Dorothy 5
BAKER, Earl Dewey 5
BAKER, Earle A. 3
BAKER, Edgar Campbell 6
BAKER, Edgar Park 7
BAKER, Edgar Robey 5
BAKER, Edna Dean 3
BAKER, E(dward) Carleton 7
BAKER, Edward Dickinson H
BAKER, Edwin George 4
BAKER, Edwin Lathrop 7
BAKER, Elbert H. 1
BAKER, Elizabeth Bradford Faulkner 5
BAKER, Elizabeth Bradford Faulkner 7
BAKER, Elizabeth Gowdy 1
BAKER, Ellis Crain 2
BAKER, Elsie 7
BAKER, Emilie Kip (Addoms) (Mrs. Franklin Thomas Baker) 5
BAKER, Eric Wilfred 6
BAKER, Ernest Hamlin 6
BAKER, Everett G. 9
BAKER, Everett Moore 3
BAKER, Ezra H
BAKER, Ezra Flavius 5
BAKER, Ezra Henry 4
BAKER, Francis Asbury H
BAKER, Francis Elisha 1
BAKER, Frank* 1
BAKER, Frank Collins 1
BAKER, Frank E. 5
BAKER, Frank Kline 5
BAKER, Frank S. 4
BAKER, Franklin, Jr. 5
BAKER, Franklin Thomas 2
BAKER, Frederick Cecil 4
BAKER, Frederick Sherman 7
BAKER, Frederick Storrs 4
BAKER, Frederick Van Vliet 5
BAKER, George 6
BAKER, George Augustus H
BAKER, George Augustus 4
BAKER, George Barr 2
BAKER, George Bramwell 1
BAKER, George Claude 6
BAKER, George Danielson 1
BAKER, George Fisher* 1
BAKER, George Hall 1
BAKER, George Holbrook H
BAKER, George Holbrook 4
BAKER, George L. 4
BAKER, George Merrick 6
BAKER, George Pierce 1
BAKER, George Randolph 1
BAKER, George Randolph 2
BAKER, George Theodore 4
BAKER, George Titus 1
BAKER, Gertrude 10
BAKER, Gladden Whetstone 6
BAKER, Gordon Harrington 4
BAKER, Harold Bruss 5
BAKER, Harold Griffith 3
BAKER, Harold Wallace 8
BAKER, Harriette Newell Woods H
BAKER, Harry B. 3
BAKER, Harvey Almy 1
BAKER, Harvey Humphrey 1
BAKER, Henry 7
BAKER, Henry Dunster 1
BAKER, Henry Meredith 7
BAKER, Henry Moore 1
BAKER, Henry Moore 4
BAKER, Henry Scott 7
BAKER, Herbert 1
BAKER, Herbert Abram 1
BAKER, Herbert Howard 8
BAKER, Herbert Madison 6
BAKER, Herman Marcus 1
BAKER, Hollis 4
BAKER, Holmes Davenport 3
BAKER, Horace 4
BAKER, Horace Burrington 8
BAKER, Horace Forbes 3
BAKER, Howard H. 4
BAKER, Hugh Benton 4
BAKER, Hugh Potter 1
BAKER, Ira Osborn 1
BAKER, Isaac Post 1
BAKER, Ivan Franklin 7

BAKER, J. Thompson 1
BAKER, James H
BAKER, James Addison 1
BAKER, James Addison, Jr. 9
BAKER, James Andrew 6
BAKER, James Barnes 1
BAKER, James Chamberlain 6
BAKER, James Heaton 1
BAKER, James Hutchins 1
BAKER, James Marion 1
BAKER, James Norment 2
BAKER, Jehu 1
BAKER, Joanna 8
BAKER, John H
BAKER, John Austin 8
BAKER, John Daniel 4
BAKER, John Earl 3
BAKER, John Harris 1
BAKER, John Hopkinson 6
BAKER, John Stewart 1
BAKER, John W. 7
BAKER, Joseph Dill 1
BAKER, Joseph Richardson 2
BAKER, Josephine 6
BAKER, Josephine Turck 4
BAKER, Julia Wetherill 4
BAKER, Karle Wilson 4
BAKER, La Fayette Curry H
BAKER, Lawrence Simons 1
BAKER, Leonard Joel 1
BAKER, Leonard Stanley 8
BAKER, Leonard Theodore 3
BAKER, Lewis 1
BAKER, Lucien 1
BAKER, Lucius K. 1
BAKER, Marcus 1
BAKER, Marjorie Montgomery Ward 3
BAKER, Martha Susan 1
BAKER, Mary Francis 5
BAKER, Melvin Houston 7
BAKER, Michael, Jr. 7
BAKER, Milton G. 10
BAKER, Milton Grafly 7
BAKER, Morton 6
BAKER, Moses Nelson 4
BAKER, Murray M. 4
BAKER, Murray M. 4
BAKER, Naaman Rimmon 1
BAKER, Newman Freese 1
BAKER, Newton Diehl 1
BAKER, Oliver Edwin 2
BAKER, Orlando Harrison 1
BAKER, Osmon Cleander H
BAKER, Osmyn 1
BAKER, Page M. 1
BAKER, Peter Carpenter H
BAKER, Phil 4
BAKER, Purley A. 1
BAKER, Ralph Jackson 4
BAKER, Ray Palmer 7
BAKER, Ray Stannard 2
BAKER, Raymond T. 1
BAKER, Remember H
BAKER, Rex Gavin 9
BAKER, Richard Terrill 8
BAKER, Robert 1
BAKER, Robert Calhoun 7
BAKER, Robert Homes 1
BAKER, Roland Morris 4
BAKER, Rollo C. 8
BAKER, Ross Allen 1
BAKER, Roy Newsom 5
BAKER, Russell 7
BAKER, Russell Montez 7
BAKER, S. Josephine 2
BAKER, S. Orville 7
BAKER, Sam A. 1
BAKER, Samuel Garland 6
BAKER, Sarah Schoonmaker 1
BAKER, Simon Strousse 1
BAKER, Smith 1
BAKER, Stannard Luther 8
BAKER, Stephen H
BAKER, Stephen 2
BAKER, Tarkington 1
BAKER, Thomas Rakestraw 1
BAKER, Thomas Stockham 1
BAKER, Virginia 4
BAKER, W. Browne 5
BAKER, Wakefield 9
BAKER, Wakefield, Jr. 8
BAKER, Walter Browne 1
BAKER, Walter Cummings 10
BAKER, Walter Cummings 5
BAKER, Walter David 8
BAKER, Walter Hudson 2
BAKER, Walter Ransom Gail 4
BAKER, Warren Lowe 9
BAKER, Wilder DuPuy 6
BAKER, William Avery 8
BAKER, William B. 1

BAKER, William C. 9
BAKER, William Clyde, Jr. 4
BAKER, William Edgar 1
BAKER, William Emery 8
BAKER, William Gideon, Jr. 2
BAKER, William Henry 1
BAKER, William Jesse 3
BAKER, William L. 1
BAKER, William Mumford H
BAKER, William Pimm 1
BAKER, William Reginald 6
BAKER, William Taylor 1
BAKER, William W. 4
BAKER, Woolford Bales 9
BAKETEL, H. Sheridan 3
BAKETEL, Oliver Sherman 1
BAKEWELL, Charles Montague 3
BAKEWELL, Donald Campbell 3
BAKEWELL, Paul 4
BAKHMETEFF, Boris Alexander 3
BAKHMETEFF, George 1
BAKHSHI, Chulam Mohammad 5
BAKKE, Arthur Lawrence 7
BAKKE, Clarence L. 7
BAKKE, E. Wight 5
BAKKE, Oscar 8
BAKKEN, Clarence John 5
BAKKEN, Herman Ernst 4
BAKKUM, Glenn A(lmer) 9
BAKLANOFF, Georges 1
BAKST, Henry Jacob 5
BAKULEV, Aleksander Nikolaevitch 8
BAKWIN, Harry 6
BAKWIN, Ruth Morris 9
BALABAN, Abraham Joseph 4
BALABAN, Barney 5
BALABAN, Emanuel 5
BALABAN, John 3
BALAGOT, Reuben Castillo 9
BALAKIAN, Nona Hilda 10
BALAMUTH, William 8
BALANCHINE, George 8
BALASSA, Bela 10
BALASSA, Leslie Ladislaus 10
BALASSONE, Francis Salvatore 6
BALATKA, Hans H
BALBACH, Edward 4
BALBOA, Vasco Nunez de H
BALCH, Allan Christopher 2
BALCH, Edwin Swift 1
BALCH, Emily Greene 4
BALCH, Ernest Berkeley 1
BALCH, Franklin Greene 3
BALCH, George Beall 1
BALCH, Glenn O. 10
BALCH, Richard Herrocks 8
BALCH, Thomas Willing 1
BALCH, William Monroe 2
BALCHEN, Bernt 6
BALCOM, Max Fenton 4
BALD, J. Dorsey H
BALD, Robert Cecil 4
BALDANZI, George 5
BALDENSPERGER, Fernand 5
BALDERSTON, C. Canby 7
BALDERSTON, John Lloyd 3
BALDERSTON, Katharine Canby 7
BALDERSTON, Lydia Ray 3
BALDERSTON, William 8
BALDES, Edward James 6
BALDES, Raymond Charles 5
BALDINGER, Albert Henry 5
BALDINGER, Lawrence H. 5
BALDOCK, Robert Hugh 8
BALDOMIR, Alfredo 2
BALDRIDGE, C(yrus) Le Roy 9
BALDRIDGE, Edgar Earl 7
BALDRIDGE, H. Clarence 2
BALDRIDGE, Howard Hammond 1
BALDRIDGE, Kenneth Ferguson 5
BALDRIDGE, Kenneth Ferguson 7
BALDRIDGE, Thomas Jackson 4
BALDRIGE, Malcolm 9
BALDUF, Emery Winfield 7
BALDWIN, A. Stuart 1
BALDWIN, Abel Seymour 4
BALDWIN, Abraham H

BALDWIN, Abram Martin 1
BALDWIN, Albertus 4
Hutchinson
BALDWIN, Alexander 3
Richards
BALDWIN, Alice Mary 4
BALDWIN, Arthur Charles 3
BALDWIN, Arthur 5
Douglas
BALDWIN, Arthur J. 1
BALDWIN, Asa Columbus 2
BALDWIN, Asa Fred 4
BALDWIN, Benjamin 1
James
BALDWIN, Benjamin 2
James
BALDWIN, Billy 8
BALDWIN, Bird Thomas 1
BALDWIN, Calvin Benham 6
BALDWIN, Charles Jacobs 4
BALDWIN, Charles Sears 1
BALDWIN, Clarke Edward 3
BALDWIN, Daniel Pratt 1
BALDWIN, Donald R. 7
BALDWIN, Edward 5
Chauncey
BALDWIN, Edward J. H
BALDWIN, Edward 2
Robinson
BALDWIN, Elbert Francis 1
BALDWIN, Elihu H
Whittlesey
BALDWIN, Ernest J. 8
BALDWIN, Evelyn Briggs 1
BALDWIN, F. Spencer 4
BALDWIN, Faith 7
BALDWIN, Francis Everett 3
BALDWIN, Francis Marsh 3
BALDWIN, Frank A. 3
BALDWIN, Frank Bruce, 7
Jr.
BALDWIN, Frank Cecil 7
BALDWIN, Frank Conger 2
BALDWIN, Frank Dwight 1
BALDWIN, Frank F. 4
BALDWIN, Geoffrey P. 3
BALDWIN, George Colfax 1
BALDWIN, George 1
Johnson
BALDWIN, Hadley 3
BALDWIN, Hanson 10
Weightman
BALDWIN, Harmon Allen 1
BALDWIN, Harry Streett 3
BALDWIN, Henry H
BALDWIN, Henry 1
Alexander
BALDWIN, Henry 2
de Forest
BALDWIN, Henry Perrine 4
BALDWIN, Henry Porter H
BALDWIN, Horace Strow 8
BALDWIN, Howard C. 4
BALDWIN, Jack Norman 10
BALDWIN, James 1
BALDWIN, James 3
BALDWIN, James Fairchild 1
BALDWIN, James Fosdick 5
BALDWIN, James Fowler H
BALDWIN, James H. 1
BALDWIN, James Hewitt 5
BALDWIN, James Mark 1
BALDWIN, Jane North 5
BALDWIN, Jesse A. 1
BALDWIN, John* H
BALDWIN, John Brown H
BALDWIN, John Denison H
BALDWIN, John Finley, Jr. 4
BALDWIN, John Thomas 6
BALDWIN, John William 7
BALDWIN, Joseph Clark 3
BALDWIN, Joseph Clark, 1
Jr.
BALDWIN, Joseph Glover 1
BALDWIN, Laverne 5
BALDWIN, Lawrence 5
(Counsell) Martin
BALDWIN, Le Roy Wilbur 1
Warrington
BALDWIN, Lewis 2
BALDWIN, Loammi H
BALDWIN, Loammi, Jr. H
BALDWIN, Maitland 5
BALDWIN, Marshall 6
Whithed
BALDWIN, Martin 3
Mortimer
BALDWIN, Matthias 1
William
BALDWIN, Minor Coe 4
BALDWIN, Neilson Abeel 1
BALDWIN, Nellie 4
Elizabeth
BALDWIN, Noyes H
BALDWIN, Oliver Hazard 5
Perry

BALDWIN, Onias Barber 7
BALDWIN, Paul Clay 10
BALDWIN, Percy Mallet 7
BALDWIN, Ralph Lyman 5
BALDWIN, Raymond Earl 9
BALDWIN, Raymond 5
Peacock
BALDWIN, Robert Chester 9
BALDWIN, Robert James 5
BALDWIN, R(obert) 7
J(ames)
BALDWIN, Roger Nash 8
BALDWIN, Roger Sherman H
BALDWIN, Roger Sherman 1
BALDWIN, Roland Dennis 3
BALDWIN, Samuel 4
Atkinson
BALDWIN, Samuel 1
Prentiss
BALDWIN, Sherman 5
BALDWIN, Simeon 1
BALDWIN, Simeon Eben 1
BALDWIN, Sylvanus H
BALDWIN, Theodore 1
Anderson
BALDWIN, Theron 1
BALDWIN, Thomas Scott 1
BALDWIN, Thomas 8
Whitfield
BALDWIN, Vincent John 7
BALDWIN, Wesley 1
Manning
BALDWIN, Wilbur 1
McIntosh
BALDWIN, William H
Alpheus
BALDWIN, William 3
Ayer 2
BALDWIN, William 1
Delevan
BALDWIN, William 1
Edward
BALDWIN, William 5
Edward
BALDWIN, William Henry 1
BALDWIN, William 7
H(enry)
BALDWIN, William Henry, 1
Jr.
BALDWIN, William James 1
BALDWIN, William Lester 4
BALDWIN, William Wright 2
BALDY, Christopher 4
BALDY, Edward Vincent 1
BALDY, John Montgomery 2
BALE, William Freer 8
BALENCIAGA, Cristobal 5
BALES, James Anthony 4
BALESTIER, Charles H
Wolcott
BALEWA, Alhaji Abubaker 4
Tafawa
BALFOUR, Donald Church 4
BALFOUR, Lloyd G. 8
BALFOUR, Maxwell W. 7
BALFOUR OF 4
BURLEIGH, Lord
BALINT, Dennis Martin 4
BALK, Eugene Norman 8
BALK, Robert 3
BALKE, Clarence William 2
BALKEN, Edward Duff 4
BALL, A. Brayton 1
BALL, Alice Worthington 1
BALL, Caroline Peddle 4
BALL, Charles Backus 1
BALL, C(harles) Olin 10
BALL, Charles Thomas 4
BALL, Duard Daniel 9
BALL, Edward H
BALL, Elmer Darwin 2
BALL, Ephraim H
BALL, Eric Glendinning 7
BALL, Farlin Q. 1
BALL, Francis Kingsley 2
BALL, Frank Clayton 1
BALL, Frank Harvey 4
BALL, Fred Lincoln 8
BALL, Fred Samuel 1
BALL, Frederick Joseph 4
BALL, George Alexander 2
BALL, George Harvey 1
BALL, Gordon Reginald 6
BALL, Helen Elizabeth 6
Voellmig
BALL, Henry Price 3
BALL, Herbert Morton 7
BALL, Herman Frederick 4
BALL, James Moores 1
BALL, John Dudley, Jr. 4
BALL, John Rice 3
BALL, John Willis 7
BALL, L. Heisler 1
BALL, Louise Charlotte 4
BALL, Lucille 10
BALL, Max W. 3
BALL, Michael Valentine 2

BALL, Munger T(homas) 9
BALL, Norman T(ower) 5
BALL, Oscar Melville 2
BALL, Otho Fisher 3
BALL, Raymond Nathaniel 4
BALL, Robert Bruce 6
BALL, Robert Hamilton 5
BALL, Robert Lee 5
BALL, Robert Pearl 7
BALL, Syndey Hobart 2
BALL, Thomas 1
BALL, Thomas Henry 2
BALL, Thomas Raymond 2
BALL, Vaughn Charles 9
BALL, William 10
BALL, William David 5
BALL, William David 7
BALL, William Lee H
BALL, William Sherman 2
BALL, Willis Watts 5
BALL, Willis Manville 2
BALLAGH, James Curtis 2
BALLAINE, Francis 4
Knight
BALLANTINE, Arthur 4
Atwood
BALLANTINE, Edward 5
BALLANTINE, George W. 9
Winthrop
BALLANTINE, Henry 3
BALLANTINE, John H. 7
BALLANTINE, Joseph 5
William
BALLANTINE, Joseph 8
William
BALLANTINE, Stuart 2
BALLANTINE, William 1
Gay
BALLANTYNE, John 2
BALLARD, Aaron Edward 1
BALLARD, Addison 1
BALLARD, Bland Williams H
BALLARD, Charles 4
William
BALLARD, Edward 10
Goodwin
BALLARD, Edward 1
Lathrop
BALLARD, Ellis Ames 1
BALLARD, Ernest 3
Schwefel
BALLARD, Frederic 4
Lyman
BALLARD, Harlan Hoge 1
BALLARD, Harold Edwin 10
BALLARD, James Franklin 1
BALLARD, John Henry 7
BALLARD, Lloyd Vernor 8
BALLARD, Nathaniel 3
Harrison
BALLARD, Russell Henry 1
BALLARD, Russell Ward 7
BALLARD, S. Thruston 4
BALLARD, Sam M. 4
BALLARD, Sumner 2
BALLARD, W.C., Jr. 3
BALLENGER, Edgar 5
Garrison
BALLENGER, George 1
Walter
BALLENGER, Howard C. 4
BALLENGER, Howard C. 4
BALLENGER, William Lee 7
BALLENGER, William 1
Lincoln
BALLENGER, William 3
Sylvester
BALLENTINE, George 5
Andrew
BALLENTINE, John 5
Jennings
BALLER, Stuart Taylor 6
BALLER, Warren Robert 9
BALLIET, Thomas M. 2
BALLIN, Hugo 3
BALLIN, Max 1
BALLINGER, Charles L. 6
BALLINGER, John H. 6
BALLINGER, Richard 1
Achilles
BALLINGER, Robert 6
Irving
BALLMAN, Donald Karl 10
BALLMANN, Martin 1
BALLOCH, Edward Arthur 2
BALLOTTI, Geno Arthur 8
BALLOU, Adin Augustus 1
BALLOU, Charles 1
Clarendon
BALLOU, Frank 3
Washington
BALLOU, Hosea H
BALLOU, Hosea, II H
BALLOU, Hosea Starr 2
BALLOU, Levi Herbert 3
BALLOU, Maturin Murray H
BALLOU, Paul Holton 10

BALLOU, Sidney 1
BALLOU, William Hosea 2
BALLS, Arnold Kent 9
BALLUDER, Erwin 7
BALLY, Louis Henry 5
BALMAIN, Pierre 8
BALMANNO, Charles 1
  Gorden
BALMER, Edwin 3
BALMER, Frank Everett 3
BALMER, Thomas 3
BALMER, Thomas James 10
BALOUGH, Charles 4
BALOUGH, Charles 7
BALSAM, Aldo R. 4
BALSLEY, Irol Whitmore 10
BALTER, Robert Brandon 1
BALTES, Peter Joseph H
BALTIMORE, baron 1st H
BALTIMORE, baron 1st H
BALTIMORE, lord 1st H
BALTIMORE, lord 2d H
BALTIMORE, baron 3d H
BALTZ, William N. 4
BALTZELL, Maude Day 4
BALTZELL, Robert C. 3
BALTZELL, Winton James 1
BALTZLY, Alexander 9
BALTZLY, Oliver Daniel 5
BALUTIS, Bronius Kasimir 6
BALYEAT, Ray Morton 3
BALZ, Albert George 3
  Adam
BALZAR, Frederick 1
  Bennett
BAMBERGER, Bernard 8
  Jacob
BAMBERGER, Clarence 7
BAMBERGER, Ernest 3
BAMBERGER, Fritz 9
BAMBERGER, Louis 2
BAMBERGER, Ralph 5
BAMBERGER, Simon 1
BAMBOROUGH, William 8
BAMBOSCHEK, Giuseppe 5
BAMFORD, Mary Ellen 5
BANAY, Ralph Steven 5
BANCROFT, Aaron H
BANCROFT, Cecil 1
  Franklin Patch
BANCROFT, Charles Grey 3
BANCROFT, Charles 1
  Parker
BANCROFT, Edgar 1
  Addison
BANCROFT, Edward H
BANCROFT, Francis 3
  Sydney
BANCROFT, Frederic 2
BANCROFT, George H
BANCROFT, Harding 10
  Foster
BANCROFT, Howland 4
BANCROFT, Hubert Howe 1
BANCROFT, Hugh 1
BANCROFT, J. Sellers 1
BANCROFT, Jessie 4
  Hubbell
BANCROFT, Joseph 1
BANCROFT, Levi Horace 3
BANCROFT, Milton H. 2
BANCROFT, Philip 1
BANCROFT, Theodore 9
  Alfonso
BANCROFT, Thomas 5
  Moore
BANCROFT, Wilder 3
  Dwight
BANCROFT, William 1
  Amos
BANCROFT, William H. 1
BANCROFT, William 1
  Poole
BAND, Charles Shaw 5
BANDARANAIKE, 3
  Solomon West Ridgeway
  Dias
BANDELIER, Aldolph 1
  Francis Alphonse
BANDHOLTZ, Harry Hill 1
BANDLER, Clarence G. 3
BANDMANN, Daniel 1
  Edward
BANDY, Orville Lee 6
BANDY, William Thomas, 10
  Jr.
BANE, Frank 8
BANE, John Curry, Jr. 7
BANE, Juliet Lita 5
BANEN, David Merton 9
BANFIELD, Armine 8
  Frederick
BANFIELD, Richard 4
  Wallace
BANFIELD, Thomas Harry 3
BANG, Frederik Barry 8
BANGHAM, Ralph 1
  Vandervort

BANGS, Clare William 8
  Hobart
BANGS, Francis Nehemiah H
BANGS, Francis Reginald 1
BANGS, George Archer 3
BANGS, Isaac Sparrow 1
BANGS, J. Edward 4
BANGS, John Kendrick 1
BANGS, John R. 4
BANGS, L. Bolton 1
BANGS, Nathan 1
BANGS, Outram 1
BANGS, Tracy R. 4
BANGSBERG, Harry 4
  Frederick
BANISTER, John* H
BANISTER, John Robert 7
BANISTER, Marion Glass 3
BANISTER, William 4
  Brodnax
BANISTER, Zilpah Grant H
BANK, Arnold 1
BANK, Carl C. 8
BANK, Theodore Paul, Jr. 9
BANKER, Howard James 2
BANKER, Oscar H. 7
BANKER, Walter 6
BANKHEAD, Henry 5
  McAuley
BANKHEAD, Johm Hollis 1
BANKHEAD, John Hollis 5
BANKHEAD, Tallulah 5
  Brockman
BANKHEAD, William 1
  Brockman
BANKS, A.A. 3
BANKS, Alexander French 2
BANKS, Alexander 4
  Robinson
BANKS, Aloysius Burton 4
BANKS, Charles Eugene 1
BANKS, E.S. 3
BANKS, Edgar James 3
BANKS, Edwin Melvin 9
BANKS, Elizabeth 1
BANKS, Frank Arthur 3
BANKS, George B. 4
BANKS, Harry Pickands 3
BANKS, James Jones 3
BANKS, John H
BANKS, John Henry 1
BANKS, John Wallace 3
BANKS, Linn H
BANKS, Louis Albert 1
BANKS, Nathan 3
BANKS, Nathanial Prentiss 1
BANKS, Robert Louis 10
BANKS, Talcott Miner 8
BANKS, Theodore H. 1
BANKS, Virginia 9
BANKS, William Nathaniel 4
BANKS, William Venoid 9
BANKSON, Russell Arden 4
BANKSON, Virgil Lee 4
BANNARD, Otto Tremont 1
BANNARD, William 9
  Newell, III
BANNEKER, Benjamin H
BANNER, Franklin 10
  Coleman
BANNER, John 5
BANNER, Peter 1
BANNERMAN, Arthur 6
  Marling
BANNERMAN, Charles S. 7
BANNERMAN, Harold 7
  MacColl
BANNERMAN, Robin 9
  Mowat
BANNEROT, Frederick 8
  George, Jr.
BANNING, Ephraim 1
BANNING, Henry H
  Blackstone
BANNING, Kendall 2
BANNING, Margaret 8
  Culkin
BANNING, Pierson 1
  Worrall
BANNING, William 6
  Vaughn
BANNISTER, Edward M. 4
BANNISTER, Harry Ray 4
BANNISTER, Henry 4
  Martyn
BANNISTER, Lemuel 7
BANNISTER, Lucius Ward 3
BANNISTER, Nathaniel H
  Harrington
BANNISTER, Robert 6
  James
BANNON, Henry Towne 3
BANNON, John Francis 6
BANNON, John Joseph 6
BANNOW, Rudolph F. 4
BANOV, Leon 6
BANSER, Henry P. 8

BANTA, Arthur Mangun 2
BANTA, George, Jr. 7
BANTA, N.Moore 1
BANTA, Parke Monroe 5
BANTEL, Edward 5
  Christian Henry
BANTHIN, John Frederick 9
BANTLE, Louis A. 7
BANVARD, John H
BANVARD, Joseph H
BANZHAF, Clayton Harris 10
BANZHAF, Henry Leo 3
BAPST, John H
BAPST, Robert Thomas 3
BARA, Theda 1
BARACH, Alvan Leroy 7
BARACH, Frederica Pisek 3
BARACH, Joseph H. 3
BARACK, Louis Barry 5
BARAGWANATH, John 1
  Gordon
BARAKAT, Mohammad 6
  Zaki Taha Ibrahim
BARANOV, Alexander H
  Andrevich
BARAZA, Frederic 4
BARBA, Charles Elmer 5
BARBA, Philip S(tanley) 10
BARBE, Waitman 5
BARBEAU, Andre 9
BARBEE, David Rankin 3
BARBEE, Hugh Arthur 3
BARBEE, James Thomas 4
BARBEE, William 4
  Randolph
BARBELIN, Felix Joseph H
BARBER, Amzi Lorenzo 1
BARBER, Azro Lucien 9
BARBER, Charles Newell 3
BARBER, Charles Williams 2
BARBER, Daniel 3
BARBER, Donn 1
BARBER, Edward John 3
BARBER, Edwin Atlee 1
BARBER, Francis H
BARBER, George Garfield 1
BARBER, George Holcomb 1
BARBER, Gershom Morse 1
BARBER, Henry A., Jr. 3
BARBER, Henry Hervey 3
BARBER, Herbert Goodell 3
BARBER, H(oratio) 5
BARBER, Joel Allen 1
BARBER, John Edwin 7
BARBER, John Warner 1
BARBER, Joseph 8
BARBER, Levi 1
BARBER, Mary I. 4
BARBER, Milton Augustus 1
BARBER, Muriel V. (Mrs. 6
  J.S. Barber)
BARBER, Noyes H
BARBER, Ohio Columbus 1
BARBER, Orion Metcalf 1
BARBER, Raymond 3
  Jenness
BARBER, Red (Walter 10
  Lanier Barber)*
BARBER, Samuel 7
BARBER, Sidman I(ra) 5
BARBER, Virgil 1
BARBER, William A. 2
BARBER, William Harley 6
BARBER, William Henry 4
BARBEY, Daniel Edward 5
BARBEY, John Edward 5
BARBIROLLI, Sir John 5
BARBORKA, Clifford 5
  Joseph
BARBOT, Louis J. H
BARBOUR, Mrs. Anna 1
  Maynard
BARBOUR, Clarence 1
  Augustus
BARBOUR, Clifford 7
  Edward
BARBOUR, Erwin Hinckly 5
BARBOUR, Frank 3
  Alexander
BARBOUR, George 8
  B(rown)
BARBOUR, George 1
  Harrison
BARBOUR, Henry 2
  Ellsworth
BARBOUR, Henry Gray 5
BARBOUR, Henry Merlin 4
BARBOUR, James H
BARBOUR, James Joseph 4
BARBOUR, John Carlyle 4
BARBOUR, John 1
  Humphrey
BARBOUR, John S. 6
BARBOUR, John Strode H
BARBOUR, John Strode, H
  Jr.
BARBOUR, Lola Diehl 4

BARBOUR, Lucien H
BARBOUR, Oliver Lorenzo H
BARBOUR, Percy E. 2
BARBOUR, Philip Foster 2
BARBOUR, Philip H
  Pendleton
BARBOUR, Ralph Henry 2
BARBOUR, Robert 7
BARBOUR, Thomas 2
BARBOUR, Thomas 1
  Seymour
BARBOUR, W. Warren 2
BARBOUR, Walworth 8
BARBOUR, William 1
BARBOUR, William 4
  Rinehart
BARBOUR, William Tefft 3
BARCELLA, Ernest 6
  Lawrence
BARCHFIELD, Andrew 1
  Jackson
BARCK, Carl 4
BARCLAY, Bertram 3
  Donald
BARCLAY, Charles 1
  Frederick
BARCLAY, Charles James 1
BARCLAY, David H
BARCLAY, George A. 4
BARCLAY, Hartley Wade 7
BARCLAY, James Edward 4
BARCLAY, Lorne Webster 7
BARCLAY, McClelland 2
BARCLAY, McKee 5
BARCLAY, Robert 4
BARCLAY, Robert 9
  Hamilton
BARCLAY, Shepard 1
BARCLAY, Thomas H
BARCLAY, Thomas Swain 9
BARCLAY, Wade 5
  Crawford
BARCLAY, William 4
  Franklin
BARCLAY, William 3
  Kennedy, Jr.
BARCUS, James Samuel 5
BARCUS, John M. 1
BARCUS, Norman 5
BARD, A.T. 3
BARD, Albert Sprague 5
BARD, Cephas L. 1
BARD, David H
BARD, Guy Kurtz 3
BARD, Harry 7
BARD, Harry Erwin 3
BARD, John H
BARD, Philip 7
BARD, Ralph A. 6
BARD, Ralph A. 7
BARD, Roy Emerson 3
BARD, Samuel H
BARD, Sara Foresman 5
BARD, Thomas Robert 1
BARD, William H
BARDEEN, Charles Russell 1
BARDEEN, Charles Valde 1
BARDEEN, Charles 1
  William
BARDEEN, John 10
BARDEL, William 1
BARDEN, Graham Arthur 4
BARDEN, Horace George 5
BARDEN, Roderick 6
  Dudley
BARDES, Paul Metzner 8
BARDES, Paul Metzner 9
BARDGETT, Edward 5
  Russell
BARDIN, James C(ook) 8
BARDO, August John 6
BARDO, Clinton Lloyd 9
BARDON, Thomas 1
BARDON, Thomas 4
BARDWELL, Richard 8
  W(oleben)
BARDWELL, Rodney 3
  Jewett
BARDWELL, Winfield 2
  William
BARFF, Stafford Edward 7
  Douglas
BARFIELD, Thomas 10
  Harwell
BARGEN, J.Arnold 7
BARGER, Floyd 6
BARGER, Harold 10
BARGER, Harry S. 5
BARGER, Herman H. 9
BARGER, Milton Sanford 1
BARGER, Samuel F. 4
BARGER, Thomas Charles 9
BARGERON, Carlisle 1
BARGHOORN, Elso 8
  Sterrenberg
BARGMANN, Valentine 10
BARHAM, Charles 3

BARHAM, Frank Forrest 3
BARHAM, John A. 4
BARIL, Ofier L(udger) 10
BARING, Alexander H
BARING, Maurice 5
BARING, Walter Stephan 6
BARING, Walter Stephan 7
BARINGER, Richard E. 7
BARIT, A. Edward 8
BARJA, Cesar 3
BARK, John Daly H
BARKALOW, Frederick 8
  Schenck, Jr.
BARKAN, Adolf 1
BARKAN, Alexander Elias 10
BARKAN, Hans 7
BARKAN, Otto 3
BARKDULL, Charles J. 3
BARKDULL, Howard L. 4
BARKE, (James) Allen 10
BARKER, Albert Smith 1
BARKER, Albert Winslow 2
BARKER, Benjamin H
  Fordyce
BARKER, B(urrill) 6
  Devereux
BARKER, Burt Brown 6
BARKER, Carl 9
BARKER, Charles Whitney 1
  Tillinghast
BARKER, Clare Wright 4
BARKER, Creighton 9
BARKER, David 4
BARKER, David, Jr. H
BARKER, David R. H
BARKER, Ellen Blackmar 5
  (Ellen Blackmar Maxwell)
BARKER, Elsa 3
BARKER, Ernest Franklin 1
BARKER, Franklin Davis 1
BARKER, Frederick 2
  William
BARKER, George 1
BARKER, George 1
  Frederick
BARKER, George 10
  Granville
BARKER, George John 8
BARKER, Harold Richard 4
BARKER, Harry 6
BARKER, Helen Morton 1
BARKER, Henry Ames 1
BARKER, Henry Stites 1
BARKER, Howard Hines 1
BARKER, Jacob H
BARKER, James L(ouis) 6
BARKER, James Madison 1
BARKER, James Madison 5
BARKER, James Nelson 1
BARKER, James William H
BARKER, Jeremiah H
BARKER, John, Jr. 5
BARKER, John Marshall 1
BARKER, John Tull 3
BARKER, Joseph H
BARKER, Joseph Warren 6
BARKER, Joseph Warren 7
BARKER, Josiah 1
BARKER, LeBaron R. 6
BARKER, Lebaron R., Jr. 1
BARKER, Leslie Paxton 10
BARKER, Lewellys 2
  Franklin
BARKER, Lillian Marion 5
BARKER, M. Herbert 2
BARKER, Nelson W(aite) 1
BARKER, Prelate Demick 5
BARKER, Ralph 5
  Hollenback
BARKER, Ralph Malcolm 3
BARKER, Ray W. 8
BARKER, Reginald 2
  Charles
BARKER, Reginald 2
  Charles
BARKER, Robert Whitney 9
BARKER, Samuel Haydock 5
BARKER, Theodore 4
  Gaillard
BARKER, W. Gardner 10
BARKER, Walter R. 1
BARKER, Wendell Phillips 1
BARKER, Wharton 1
BARKER, William J. 7
BARKER, William Judson 7
BARKER, William Morris 1
BARKEY, Patrick Terrence 9
BARKHORN, Henry 2
  Charles
BARKLEY, Alben William 3
BARKLEY, Frederick R. 9
BARKLEY, Henry L. 1
BARKLEY, James 1
  Morrison
BARKLEY, Jane Rucker 4
BARKLEY, William Elliot 2

BARROW, Frances Elizabeth Mease H
BARROW, Pope 1
BARROW, Roscoe Lindley 7
BARROW, Washington H
BARROWS, Anna 3
BARROWS, Arthur Stanhope 4
BARROWS, Charles Clifford 1
BARROWS, Charles Henry 1
BARROWS, C(harles) Storrs 9
BARROWS, Chester Willard 1
BARROWS, David Prescott 5
BARROWS, Edwin Armington 2
BARROWS, Harlan H. 4
BARROWS, Harold Kilbrith 3
BARROWS, Isabel Chapin 1
BARROWS, John Chester 4
BARROWS, John Henry 1
BARROWS, John Otis 1
BARROWS, Lewis Orin 4
BARROWS, Lucius D(welley) 7
BARROWS, Marjorie 8
BARROWS, Morton 4
BARROWS, Nathaniel Albert 2
BARROWS, Nathaniel Haven 3
BARROWS, Raymond H. 3
BARROWS, Robert Brewster 7
BARROWS, Samuel June 1
BARROWS, Stanley Hill 2
BARROWS, Thomas Nichols 4
BARROWS, Wayne Groves 6
BARROWS, William Morton 2
BARROWS, William Stanley 1
BARRUS, Clara 1
BARRUS, George Hale 1
BARRY, Clinton Rogers 7
BARRY, David C. 8
BARRY, David Sheldon 1
BARRY, David W. 8
BARRY, Edward Buttevant 1
BARRY, Etheldred Breeze 5
BARRY, Fred, Jr. 7
BARRY, Frederick Lehrle 4
BARRY, Henry W. H
BARRY, Herbert 2
BARRY, Jack 8
BARRY, James Henry 1
BARRY, James Milne 8
BARRY, John* H
BARRY, John 7
BARRY, John Daniel 2
BARRY, John G(erald) 7
BARRY, John H. 3
BARRY, John Stewart H
BARRY, Joseph Gayle Hurd 1
BARRY, Leland Clifford 4
BARRY, Maggie W. 4
BARRY, Maurice Joseph 6
BARRY, Patrick H
BARRY, Patrick 1
BARRY, Peter 5
BARRY, Philip 2
BARRY, Robert Raymond 9
BARRY, Thomas Henry 1
BARRY, Walter R. 4
BARRY, William Bernard 2
BARRY, William Farquhar H
BARRY, William Taylor H
BARRY, William Taylor Sullivan H
BARRYMORE, Ethel 3
BARRYMORE, Georgiana Emma Drew H
BARRYMORE, John 2
BARRYMORE, Lionel 3
BARRYMORE, Maurice 1
BARSANTI, Olinto Mark 5
BARSE, George Randolph, Jr. 1
BARSKY, Arthur Joseph 8
BARSS, John Edmund 5
BARSTOW, Edith 3
BARSTOW, Edwin Ormond 5
BARSTOW, Frank Quarles 1
BARSTOW, Gamaliel Henry H
BARSTOW, George Eames 1
BARSTOW, Gideon H
BARSTOW, John Lester 1
BARSTOW, Richard 7
BARSTOW, Robbins Wolcott 4
BARSTOW, William Augustus H
BARSTOW, William Slocum 2
BARTCH, George Washington 1
BARTEL, William Edwin 3
BARTELL, Floyd Earl 4
BARTELL, Gerald Aaron 10
BARTELMEZ, George William 7
BARTELS, Vernon C. 3
BARTELT, Edward F. 3
BARTEMEIER, Lee H(enry) 10
BARTH, Alan 7
BARTH, Carl G. 1
BARTH, Charles H. 1
BARTH, Charles H., Jr. 2
BARTH, Earl E. 10
BARTH, Ernest 10
BARTH, George Bittman 5
BARTH, Karl 5
BARTH, Lester George 7
BARTH, Theodore H. 4
BARTH, Theodore Nott 4
BARTH, William George 4
BARTHBERGER, Charles H
BARTHEL, Oliver Edward 5
BARTHELME, Donald 10
BARTHELMESS, Richard 4
BARTHES, Roland 7
BARTHOLD, Robert M. 6
BARTHOLDT, Richard 1
BARTHOLF, John Charles Palmer 5
BARTHOLOMAY, Anthony Francis 6
BARTHOLOME, Peter William 10
BARTHOLOMEH, George Kellam 4
BARTHOLOMEW, Abram Glenni 1
BARTHOLOMEW, Allen R. 1
BARTHOLOMEW, Charles L. 2
BARTHOLOMEW, Edward Fry 2
BARTHOLOMEW, Edward Sheffield H
BARTHOLOMEW, Frank H. 8
BARTHOLOMEW, Harland 9
BARTHOLOMEW, J.M. 1
BARTHOLOMEW, Pliny Webster 1
BARTHOLOMEW, Rudolph A. 5
BARTHOLOMEW, Tracy 3
BARTHOLOMEW, Truman C. H
BARTHOLOMEW, William Henry 2
BARTHOLOMEW, William Newton H
BARTHOLOW, Roberts 1
BARTINE, Horace F. 4
BARTKY, Aldolph John 6
BARTKY, Walter 3
BARTLE, H(arold) Roe 6
BARTLEMAN, Richard Milne 4
BARTLESON, John H
BARTLET, William H
BARTLETT, Adolphus Clay 1
BARTLETT, Albert Leroy 1
BARTLETT, Alden Eugene 5
BARTLETT, Alice Elinor 4
BARTLETT, Alice Hunt (Mrs. William Allen Bartlett) 5
BARTLETT, Allan Charles 5
BARTLETT, Arthur Charles 4
BARTLETT, Bailey H
BARTLETT, Boyd Wheeler 4
BARTLETT, Sir Charles John 3
BARTLETT, Charles Lafayette 1
BARTLETT, Charles Ward 1
BARTLETT, Charles William 4
BARTLETT, Clarence 3
BARTLETT, Claude Jackson 8
BARTLETT, Craig Scott 4
BARTLETT, Dana Webster 4
BARTLETT, Dewey Follett 7
BARTLETT, Edgar Elliott 1
BARTLETT, Edmund Morgan 4
BARTLETT, Edward Everett, Jr. 4
BARTLETT, Edward Lewis 5
BARTLETT, Edward Randolph 3
BARTLETT, Edward Theodore 1
BARTLETT, Edwin Julius 1
BARTLETT, Edwin Rice 3
BARTLETT, Elisha H
BARTLETT, Ford 7
BARTLETT, Frank Leslie 4
BARTLETT, Frank W. 4
BARTLETT, Franklin 1
BARTLETT, Frederic Clay 3
BARTLETT, Frederic Huntington 2
BARTLETT, Frederic Pearson 5
BARTLETT, Frederick Bethune 1
BARTLETT, Frederick Orin 5
BARTLETT, Gene Ebert 10
BARTLETT, George A. 5
BARTLETT, George Griffiths 5
BARTLETT, George True 2
BARTLETT, Harley Harris 4
BARTLETT, Homer Lyman 4
BARTLETT, Homer Newton 4
BARTLETT, Ichabod H
BARTLETT, J. Gardner 1
BARTLETT, John 1
BARTLETT, John Frank 5
BARTLETT, John Henry 3
BARTLETT, John Pomeroy 2
BARTLETT, John Russell H
BARTLETT, John Russell 1
BARTLETT, John S. 1
BARTLETT, John Sherren H
BARTLETT, John Thomas 2
BARTLETT, John W. 4
BARTLETT, Joseph H
BARTLETT, Joseph Warren 4
BARTLETT, Josiah H
BARTLETT, Josiah, Jr. H
BARTLETT, Louis 5
BARTLETT, Lynn Mahlon 5
BARTLETT, Maitland 2
BARTLETT, Margaret Abbott 3
BARTLETT, Murray 2
BARTLETT, Paul Dana 4
BARTLETT, Paul Wayland 1
BARTLETT, Robert Abram 2
BARTLETT, Ruhl Jacob 10
BARTLETT, Samuel Colcord H
BARTLETT, Thomas, Jr. H
BARTLETT, Walter Manny 5
BARTLETT, Willard 1
BARTLETT, William Henry H
BARTLETT, William Henry 1
BARTLEY, Donald 5
BARTLEY, Elias Hudson 1
BARTLEY, Mordecai H
BARTLEY, Nalbro 8
BARTLEY, S. Howard 9
BARTMAN, Russell C(lyde) 6
BARTOK, Bela H
BARTOK, Bela 4
BARTOL, Cyrus Augustus H
BARTOL, Cyrus Augustus 1
BARTOL, George E. 1
BARTOL, George E, III 10
BARTOL, John Washburn 5
BARTON, Alan Raymond 10
BARTON, Andrew H
BARTON, Arthur Gipson 7
BARTON, Arthur James 2
BARTON, Benjamin Smith H
BARTON, Bruce 4
BARTON, Carlyle 4
BARTON, Charles Harmon 1
BARTON, Charles William 3
BARTON, Clara 1
BARTON, David H
BARTON, Donald Clinton 1
BARTON, Edmund Mills 4
BARTON, Enos M. 1
BARTON, Francis Brown 5
BARTON, George 1
BARTON, George Aaron 2
BARTON, George Arthur 7
BARTON, George Hunt 1
BARTON, George Samuel Horace 7
BARTON, Helen 9
BARTON, Henry Askew 8
BARTON, Jackson Mounce 9
BARTON, James H
BARTON, James Levi 1
BARTON, James Moore 1
BARTON, James Richard 8
BARTON, John Kennedy 1
BARTON, John Rhea H
BARTON, John Wynne 1
BARTON, Joseph Wesley 6
BARTON, Lela Viola 5
BARTON, LeRoy 8
BARTON, Levi Elder 5
BARTON, Olive Roberts 3
BARTON, Philip Price 4
BARTON, Ralph 1
BARTON, Ralph Martin 2
BARTON, Randolph 4
BARTON, Richard Walker H
BARTON, Robert McKinney 1
BARTON, Robert T. 1
BARTON, Robert Thomas, Jr. 7
BARTON, Roger 7
BARTON, Samuel H
BARTON, Samuel Marx 1
BARTON, Silas Reynolds 1
BARTON, Stephen Emory 4
BARTON, Thomas Frank, Sr. 9
BARTON, Thomas Harry 4
BARTON, Thomas Pennant H
BARTON, Walter Elbert 7
BARTON, Wilfred Mason 1
BARTON, William H
BARTON, William Edward 5
BARTON, William Eleazar 1
BARTON, William Henry, Jr. 2
BARTON, William Paul Crillon H
BARTOW, Charles K. 3
BARTOW, Edward 3
BARTOW, Francis Dwight 2
BARTOW, Harry Edwards 5
BARTRAM, John H
BARTRAM, William H
BARTSCH, Edward 4
BARTSCH, Paul 4
BARTTER, Frederic Crosby 8
BARUCH, Bernard Mannes 4
BARUCH, Dorothy Walter 4
BARUCH, Emanuel de Marnay 1
BARUCH, Herman Benjamin 3
BARUCH, Simon 1
BARUCH, Sydney Norton 3
BARUH, Joseph Y. 4
BARUS, Annie Howes 5
BARUS, Carl 1
BARUS, Maxwell 8
BARUTH, Ralph Howard 2
BARWELL-WALKER, Francis John 6
BARZINI, Luigi 5
BARZINI, Luigi 8
BARZMAN, Ben Frank 10
BARZYNSKI, Joseph E. 5
BARZYNSKI, Vincent H
BASALDELLA, Mirko 5
BASCH, Antonin 5
BASCOM, Florence 2
BASCOM, Henry Bidleman H
BASCOM, John 1
BASDEVANT, Jules 5
BASE, Daniel 1
BASEHART, Richard 9
BASH, Louis Hermann 3
BASHEV, Ivan Hristov 5
BASHFORD, Coles H
BASHFORD, Herbert 1
BASHFORD, James Whitford 1
BASHIR, Antony 4
BASHORE, Harry William 5
BASHORE, Harvey Brown 1
BASIE, William 8
BASILE, Anthony Robert 6
BASING, Charles 4
BASINGER, William S. 3
BASKERVILL, Charles Read 1
BASKERVILL, William Malone 3
BASKERVILLE, Charles 10
BASKERVILLE, Charles 1
BASKERVILLE, Jack H. 7
BASKETT, James Newton 1
BASKETTE, Gideon Hicks 1
BASKIN, Robert N. 5
BASQUIN, Olin Hanson 2
BASS, Charles Cassedy 5
BASS, Edgar Wales 1
BASS, Edward H
BASS, Elizabeth 3
BASS, Frederic Herbert 3
BASS, George Arthur 4
BASS, George Arthur 5
BASS, Ivan Ernest 4
BASS, John Foster 1
BASS, John Meredith 1
BASS, Joseph Parker 1
BASS, Leo 3
BASS, Lyman Kidder H
BASS, Lyman Metcalfe 3
BASS, Ray Spurgeon 3
BASS, Robert Perkins 4
BASS, Sam H
BASS, Stirling Wesley 8
BASS, Ula Lehentz 4
BASS, William Capers H
BASSE, Jeremiah H
BASSET, Norman Leslie 1
BASSET, William Rupert 3
BASSETT, Adelaide Florence 4
BASSETT, Austin Bradley 1
BASSETT, Basil Blaine 7
BASSETT, Ben 9
BASSETT, Burwell H
BASSETT, Carolyn Fassett 8
BASSETT, Carroll Phillips 3
BASSETT, Charles A., II 4
BASSETT, Charles Nebeker 2
BASSETT, Claude Oscar 7
BASSETT, Ebenezer Don Carlos 1
BASSETT, Edward Murray 2
BASSETT, George Jarvis 3
BASSETT, Harry Hood 10
BASSETT, Harry Winfred 5
BASSETT, J. D., Jr. 4
BASSETT, James Elias 7
BASSETT, John 3
BASSETT, John David, Sr. 4
BASSETT, John Spencer 1
BASSETT, Lee Emerson 5
BASSETT, Louis D. 6
BASSETT, Neal 3
BASSETT, Richard H
BASSETT, Royal 4
BASSETT, Samuel Eliot 1
BASSETT, Sara Ware 5
BASSETT, Thomas J. 4
BASSETT, W.M. 4
BASSETT, Wallace 7
BASSETT, William Austin 1
BASSETT, William Hastings 1
BASSFORD, Homer S. 1
BASSFORD, Horace Richardson 3
BASSI, Amadeo 5
BASSICH, J(oseph) B(eauregard) 7
BASSILL, John E. 3
BASSLER, Anthony 3
BASSLER, Ray Smith 6
BASSO, Hamilton 4
BASTEDO, Frank Lindsay 9
BASTEDO, Paul Henry 3
BASTEDO, Philip 9
BASTIAN, Robert Owen 5
BASTIAN, Walter Maximillian 6
BASTIANINI, Ettore 4
BASTIEN, Ralph Henry 8
BASTIN, Edson Sunderland 3
BASTION, Joseph Edward 7
BASYE, Paul Edmond 10
BASYN, Thomas 4
BATCH, John Martin 8
BATCHELDER, Ann 3
BATCHELDER, Charles Clarence 2
BATCHELDER, Charles Foster 3
BATCHELDER, Edward Trumbull 3
BATCHELDER, Ernest Allen 5
BATCHELDER, Frank Charles 1
BATCHELDER, Howard Timothy 8
BATCHELDER, John Putnam H
BATCHELDER, Loren Harrison 4
BATCHELDER, Nathaniel Horton 3
BATCHELDER, Richard N. 1
BATCHELDER, Roger 2
BATCHELDER, Samuel H
BATCHELDER, Wallace 1
BATCHELLER, George Clinton 1
BATCHELLER, George Sherman 1
BATCHELLER, Hiland Garfield 4

BATCHELLER, Tryphosa 3
Bates
BATCHELLER, Willis 7
Tryon
BATCHELOR, Clarence 7
Daniel
BATCHELOR, George 1
BATCHELOR, Horace 4
BATCHELOR, James 5
Madison
BATCHELOR, Leon 7
Dexter
BATDORF, Grant David 3
BATE, William Brimage 1
BATEMAN, Alan Mara 5
BATEMAN, Charles 1
Heisler
BATEMAN, E. Allen 4
BATEMAN, Ephraim H
BATEMAN, Frank B(race) 10
BATEMAN, George Cecil 3
BATEMAN, George F. 2
BATEMAN, George 5
Monroe
BATEMAN, Harry 3
BATEMAN, Herbert D. 3
BATEMAN, John 3
BATEMAN, John H. 3
BATEMAN, Newton H
BATEMAN, Robert 2
Johnston
BATEMAN, Sidney Frances H
Cowell
BATEN, Anderson Edith 1
BATEN, Anderson Monroe 2
BATES, Albert Carlos 5
BATES, Albert H. 1
BATES, Alexander Berry 1
BATES, Alfred Elliott 1
BATES, Arlo 1
BATES, Arthur Laban 1
BATES, Barnabas H
BATES, Blanche 1
BATES, Blanche 2
BATES, Charles Austin 4
BATES, Charlotte Fiske 1
BATES, Claude Ellsworth 9
BATES, Clement 1
BATES, Clinton Owen H
BATES, Daniel Moore H
BATES, David Stanhope 1
BATES, E.D. 4
BATES, Edward 1
BATES, Emma Frances 1
Duncan
BATES, Ernest Sutherland 1
BATES, Floyd Elton 8
BATES, Francis Oliver H
BATES, Frederick H
BATES, Frederick 3
BATES, George Andrew 1
BATES, George Dennis 1
BATES, George Handy H
BATES, George Handy 4
BATES, George Hubert 5
BATES, George Joseph 2
BATES, George W. 1
BATES, G(eorge) Wallace 9
BATES, George Williams 1
BATES, Harriet Hegar 6
BATES, Harriet Leonora H
Vose
BATES, Harry C. 5
BATES, Harry Cole 2
BATES, Henry Clay 1
BATES, Henry George 9
BATES, Henry Liberty 4
BATES, Henry Moore 2
BATES, Herbert 1
BATES, Herbert Ernest 6
BATES, Isaac Chapman 1
BATES, J. W., Sr. 9
BATES, James 4
BATES, James L. 1
BATES, James Woodson H
BATES, Jefferson Blakey 1
BATES, John H
BATES, John Coalter 1
BATES, John Lewis 2
BATES, John Loren 10
BATES, Josephine White 5
(Mrs. Lindon Wallace
Bates)
BATES, Joshua H
BATES, Katharine Lee 1
BATES, Legare 7
BATES, Lewis Elon 6
BATES, Lindon, Jr. 1
BATES, Lindon Wallace 1
BATES, Margret Holmes 3
BATES, Marston 6
BATES, Mary Elizabeth 4
BATES, Merle Banker 7
BATES, Miner Lee 1
BATES, Onward 1
BATES, Oric 1
BATES, Phaon Hilborn 6

BATES, Putnam Asbury 5
BATES, Richard Waller 6
BATES, Robert L(ee) 7
BATES, Samuel Penniman 1
BATES, Sanford 5
BATES, Stuart Jeffery 8
BATES, Theodore Cornelius 1
BATES, Theodore Lewis 5
BATES, Vyrl Raymond 5
BATES, Walter H
BATES, Walter Irving 1
BATES, William Albert 4
BATES, William 8
Bartholemew
BATES, William H. 5
BATES, William Nickerson 2
BATES, William Oscar 5
BATES, William Wallace 1
BATH, Albert Alcus 5
BATHON, Wingrove 5
BATHRICK, Ellsworth R. 1
BATISTA Y ZALDIVAR, 5
Fulgencio
BATJER, Lawrence Paul 4
BATLLE BERRES, Luis 4
BATMAN, Levi Gordon 5
BATOR, Paul Michael 9
BATOR, Peter Anthony 9
BATRUS, Frederick 7
Edward
BATSCHELET, Clarence 8
Edmund
BATSON, David William 4
BATSON, William Howard 3
BATT, George Kenneth 9
BATT, William Loren 4
BATTCOCK, Gregory E. 8
BATTELL, Joseph 1
BATTELLS, Sarah M. E. 3
BATTEN, Charles Edward 4
BATTEN, Harry Albert 4
BATTEN, John Henry, III 9
BATTEN, Joseph Minton 3
BATTEN, Loring Woart 3
BATTEN, Percy Haight 4
BATTEN, Samuel Zane 1
BATTENHOUSE, Henry 4
Martin
BATTERSHALL, Fletcher 4
Williams
BATTERSHALL, Walton 1
Wesley
BATTERSON, Hermon 1
Griswold
BATTERSON, James 1
Goodwin
BATTEY, George 8
Magruder, Jr.
BATTEY, Paul Leon 9
BATTEY, Robert H
BATTIN, Charles Reginald 3
BATTIN, Charles Thomas 4
BATTLE, Archibald John 1
BATTLE, Burrill Bunn 1
BATTLE, Cullen Andrews 1
BATTLE, George Gordon 2
BATTLE, Henry Wilson 5
BATTLE, Herbert 1
Bemerton
BATTLE, Hyman Llewellyn 5
BATTLE, John S(tewart) 1
BATTLE, John Thomas 1
Johnson
BATTLE, Kemp Davis 6
BATTLE, Kemp Plummer* 1
BATTLE, Richard Henry 1
BATTLE, S. Westray 1
BATTLE, Thomas Hall 1
BATTLE, William Horn H
BATTLE, William James 1
BATTLEY, Joseph F. 5
BATTS, Arthur Alanson 1
BATTS, Robert Lynn 1
BATTS, William Oscar 6
BATTSON, Leigh 9
McMaster
BA U, (Agga Maha Thiri 8
Thudhamma)
BAUCUM, A. W. 5
BAUDER, Frederick 7
William
BAUDER, Reginald I. 4
BAUDOIN, Michael H
BAUDOUX, Msgr. Maurice 4
BAUER, Augustus H
BAUER, Benjamin 7
Baumzweiger
BAUER, Benjamin F. 4
BAUER, Charles Christian 3
BAUER, Clyde Max 7
BAUER, Dale Robert 10
BAUER, Edmond S. 8
BAUER, Eugene Casper 3
BAUER, Frank Stanley 8
BAUER, Franz Karl 6
BAUER, Franz Karl 7
BAUER, Frederick Charles 7

BAUER, George Neander 5
BAUER, H(ans) G(ustav) 5
BAUER, Harold 3
BAUER, Harry Charles 7
BAUER, Harry John 3
BAUER, Johannes Henrik 4
BAUER, L. A. 5
BAUER, Leland Mason 5
BAUER, Louis Hopewell 5
BAUER, Marion Eugenie 3
BAUER, Ralph S. 1
BAUER, Ralph Stanley 3
BAUER, Raymond 7
Augustine
BAUER, Royal D(aniel 8
M(ichael)
BAUER, Walter 3
BAUER, Walter E(mil) 10
BAUER, Walter Herman 5
BAUER, William Charles 5
BAUER, William Hans 4
BAUER, William Waldo 4
BAUERS, Eloi 9
BAUGH, Albert Croll 7
BAUGHER, A. Charles 4
BAUGHER, Henry Louis H
BAUGHER, Norman J. 5
BAUGHMAN, Cortlandt 1
Chesterfield
BAUGHMAN, Harry 9
Fridley
BAUGHMAN, James 7
Stanley
BAUGHMAN, L. Victor 1
BAUGHMAN, Lyle 4
Lynden
BAUGHMAN, Roland 4
BAUHOF, Rudolf 10
BAUKE, Joseph Padur 6
BAUKHAGE, Hilmar 6
Robert
BAUM, Dwight James 1
BAUM, Ellis Conrad 4
BAUM, Frank George 1
BAUM, Harry 3
BAUM, Harry A. 8
BAUM, Harvey A. 3
BAUM, Henry Mason 4
BAUM, Isidor 4
BAUM, John Harry 8
BAUM, L. Frank 1
BAUM, Mary Helen 6
BAUM, Maurice 4
BAUM, Morton J. 4
BAUM, Paull Franklin 1
BAUM, Vicki 4
BAUM, Walter Emerson 3
BAUM, William Miller, Jr. 1
BAUMAN, Edward H
BAUMAN, Helen Wood 9
BAUMAN, Val Samuel 4
BAUMANN, Frederick 8
L(lewellyn)
BAUMANN, Frieda 9
BAUMANN, Gustave 6
BAUMANN, Rudolf 5
BAUMBERGER, James 4
Percy
BAUME, James Simpson 1
BAUMEISTER, Theodore 7
BAUMER, Bertha 4
BAUMER, Franklin L. 10
BAUMERT, Andrew, Jr. 7
BAUMES, Caleb Howard 1
BAUMGARDNER, Evelyn 6
Julia Groves (Mrs.
Charles Ernst
Baumgardner)
BAUMGARDT, B. R. 1
BAUMGARTEN, Gustav 1
BAUMGARTMER, 5
William Jacob
BAUMGARTNER, 6
Apollinaris
BAUMGARTNER, 6
Josephine Mae
BAUMGARTNER, Leona 10
BAUMGARTNER, Warren 4
William
BAUR, Bertha 1
BAUR, Bertha E. 3
BAUR, Bertha E. 4
BAUR, Clara 1
BAUR, John Ireland Howe 9
BAUSCH, Carl Louis 8
BAUSCH, Edward 2
BAUSCH, John Jacob 1
BAUSCH, William 2
BAUSLIN, David Henry 1
BAUSMAN, Benjamin 1
BAUSMAN, Frederick 1
BAUSMAN, J. W. B. 1
BAVOR, Herbert John 7
BAWDEN, Samuel Day 2
BAWDEN, William Thomas 5
BAXENDALE, Esther 4
Minerva

BAXLEY, Henry Willis H
BAXTER, Anne 9
BAXTER, Batsell 3
BAXTER, Batsell Barrett 8
BAXTER, Bruce Richard 2
BAXTER, Clarence 1
Hughson
BAXTER, Dow Vawter 4
BAXTER, Earl Hayes 5
BAXTER, Edmund 1
Dillabunty
BAXTER, Edmund Francis 4
BAXTER, Elisha H
BAXTER, Frank Condie 8
BAXTER, George Edwin 4
BAXTER, Gregory Paul 5
BAXTER, H. R. 4
BAXTER, Henry H
BAXTER, Hubert Eugene 8
BAXTER, Irving Franklin 1
BAXTER, James Phinney 1
BAXTER, James Phinney 6
BAXTER, James Phinney, 10
III
BAXTER, Jere 1
BAXTER, John H
BAXTER, John Babington 2
MacAulay
BAXTER, John Kirkman 7
BAXTER, John Lincoln 8
BAXTER, Lionel David 3
MacKenzie
BAXTER, Norman 3
Washington
BAXTER, Percival Proctor 5
BAXTER, Portus H
BAXTER, Richard Reeve 7
BAXTER, Samuel Newman, 8
Jr.
BAXTER, Samuel Serson 8
BAXTER, Sylvester 1
BAXTER, Warner 3
BAXTER, William H
BAXTER, William Joseph 5
BAY, Charles A. 7
BAY, Charles Ulrick 3
BAY, Howard 9
BAY, Jens Christian 4
BAY, William Van Ness H
BAYAR, (Mahmut) Celal 7
BAYARD, Alexis Irénée 9
Dupont
BAYARD, Edwin Stanton 3
BAYARD, Fairfax 5
BAYARD, James Asheton* 1
BAYARD, John Bubenheim H
BAYARD, Nicholas H
BAYARD, Richard Henry H
BAYARD, Samuel H
BAYARD, Thomas Francis H
BAYARD, Thomas Francis 2
BAYARD, William H
BAYDUR, Huseyin Ragip 3
BAYER, Herbert 1
BAYER, Lloyd Felch 3
BAYLES, Edwin Atkinson 5
BAYLES, George James 1
BAYLES, James Copper 4
BAYLES, Theodore Floyd 7
BAYLESS, Herman 7
Armstrong
BAYLESS, James Leavell 8
BAYLESS, William Silver 1
BAYLEY, Edward Bancroft 5
BAYLEY, Francis Reed 5
BAYLEY, Frank Sawyer 3
BAYLEY, Frank Tappan 1
BAYLEY, James Roosevelt H
BAYLEY, Richard H
BAYLEY, Warner Baldwin 1
BAYLEY, William Shirley 1
BAYLIES, Edmund Lincoln 1
BAYLIES, Edwin 4
BAYLIES, Francis H
BAYLIES, Walter Cabot 1
BAYLIES, William H
BAYLIS, Adelaide Brooks 7
BAYLIS, Charles Augustus 7
BAYLIS, Charles T. 5
BAYLIS, Robert Nelson 1
BAYLISS, Alfred 1
BAYLISS, Charles William 4
BAYLISS, Clara Kern 4
BAYLISS, Major William 1
BAYLOR, Adelaide Steele 1
BAYLOR, Frances H
Courtenay
BAYLOR, Frances 4
Courtenay
BAYLOR, George H
BAYLOR, Hugh Murray 10
BAYLOR, James Bowen 1
BAYLOR, John Roy 3

BAYLOR, Robert Emmett H
Bledsoe
BAYLOR, William Henry 5
BAYLY, Thomas H
BAYLY, Thomas Henry H
BAYLY, Thomas Monteagle H
BAYMA, Joseph H
BAYNE, Howard 3
BAYNE, Howard Randolph 1
BAYNE, Hugh Aiken 3
BAYNE, Reed Taft 3
BAYNE, Samuel Gamble 1
BAYNE, Stephen Fielding 6
BAYNE, Thomas McKee H
BAYNE, William 3
BAYNE-JONES, Stanhope 5
BAYNES, Ernest Harold 1
BAYNES, John 1
BAYNHAM, William H
BAYOL, Edgar Sansom 5
BAYS, Karl Dean 10
BAYS, Alfred William 3
BAYUK, Samuel 3
BAZETT, Henry Cuthbert 3
BAZIN, Germain Rene 10
Michel
BAZIN, John Stephen 4
BAZIOTES, William 4
BAZZONI, Charles Blizard 7
BEA, Augustin Cardinal 5
BEACH, Albert Isaac 1
BEACH, Alfred Ely 1
BEACH, Amy Marcy 2
Cheney
BEACH, Arthur Grandville 1
BEACH, Charles Fisk* 1
BEACH, Charles Lewis 1
BEACH, Chester 3
BEACH, Daniel 1
BEACH, Daniel Magee 2
BEACH, David Nelson 1
BEACH, Earl Edward 6
BEACH, Edward Latimer 4
BEACH, Francis Asbury 4
BEACH, Frank Ambrose 9
BEACH, Frederick 1
Converse
BEACH, George Corwin, 2
Jr.
BEACH, Goodwin 7
Batterson
BEACH, Harlan Page 1
BEACH, Harrison L. 4
BEACH, Harry Prescott 2
BEACH, Henry Harris 1
Aubrey
BEACH, John Kimberly 1
BEACH, John Newton 4
BEACH, Joseph Warren 3
BEACH, Joseph Watson 8
BEACH, King D. 3
BEACH, Lansing Hoskins 2
BEACH, Lewis H
BEACH, Miles 1
BEACH, Moses Sperry 4
BEACH, Moses Yale 4
BEACH, P. Goff 8
BEACH, R. Clyde 3
BEACH, Rex Ellingwood 2
BEACH, S. Judd 3
BEACH, Seth Curtis 4
BEACH, Spencer Ambrose 1
BEACH, Stanley Yale 5
BEACH, Stewart (Taft) 2
BEACH, Sylvester 1
Woodbridge
BEACH, Walter Greenwood 4
BEACH, William Augustus H
BEACH, William Dorrance 4
BEACH, William Harrison 4
BEACH, William 1
Mulholland
BEACH,.William 2
Mulholland
BEACH, Wooster H
BEACHAM, Joseph, Jr. 3
BEACHAM, Woodard 4
Davis
BEACHER, Lawrence 9
Lester
BEACHLEY, Charles E. 3
BEACHLEY, Ralph 5
Gregory
BEACOM, Thomas H. 3
BEACOM, Thomas H. 4
BEADLE, Chauncey Delos 5
BEADLE, Erastus Flavel H
BEADLE, George Wells 10
BEADLE, Robert Cameron 7
BEADLE, William Henry 4
Harrison
BEAGLE, Charles 9
Wellington
BEAHAN, John M. 9
BEAHAN, Willard 1
BEAHM, William 4
McKinley

BELLINGER, John 1
Bellinger
BELLINGER, John Dooley 10
BELLINGER, Joseph H
BELLINGER, Martha 5
Fletcher
BELLINGER, Patrick 4
Niesen Lynch
BELLINGER, William 2
Whaley
BELLINGHAM, Richard H
BELLINO, Carmine 10
Salvatore
BELLIS, Leon Robert 5
BELLMAN, Lawrence 5
Stevens
BELLMAN, Russell 6
BELLOC, Hilaire 3
BELLOMONT, 1st earl H
BELLOT, Hugh Hale 9
BELLOWS, Albert Fitch H
BELLOWS, George Wesley
BELLOWS, Henry Adams 5
BELLOWS, Henry Whitney H
BELLOWS, Howard Perry 1
BELLOWS, Johnson 2
McClure
BELLOWS, Robert 3
Peabody
BELLPORT, Bernard Philip 10
BELMONT, Alan Harnden 7
BELMONT, Alva E. Smith 4
BELMONT, August H
BELMONT, August 1
BELMONT, Morgan 3
BELMONT, Mrs. O.H.P.
BELMONT, Oliver Hazard 1
Perry
BELMONT, Perry 2
BELNAP, LaMonte Judson 6
BELO, Alfred H. 1
BELO, Alfred Horatio 1
BELSER, James Edwin H
BELSTERLING, Charles 3
Starne
BELT, Benjamin Carleton 4
BELT, Harry H. 3
BELT, William Bradley 5
Tyler
BELTZ, LeRoy Duane 9
BELTZ, William Ray 6
BELUSHI, John 8
BELVISO, Thomas Henry 4
BELYAYEV, Pavel 5
Ivanovich
BELZ, Mrs. Henry 6
(Dorothy Pershall Belz)
BEMAN, Nathan Sidney H
Smith
BEMAN, Solon Spencer 1
BEMAN, Wooster 1
Woodruff
BEMB, Walter J(acob) 7
BEMELMANS, Ludwig 4
BEMENT, Alburto 4
BEMENT, Alon 3
BEMENT, Caleb N. H
BEMENT, Clarence Edwin 1
BEMENT, Dorothy 8
Montgomery
BEMENT, Howard 1
BEMIS, Albert Farwell 1
BEMIS, Edward Webster 1
BEMIS, George H
BEMIS, Harold Medberry 5
BEMIS, James 10
R(osborough)
BEMIS, Judson Stephen 1
BEMIS, Samuel Flag 6
BEMIS, Thomas Frederick 6
BEMIS, William May 7
BEMISS, Samuel Merrifield 4
BENADE, Arthur Henry 9
BENADE, James Arthur H
BENARD, Henri Jean 4
Emile
BENBOW, Charles Frank 7
BENBRIDGE, Henry H
BENBROOK, Edward 4
Antony
BENCHER, Walter Seaman 7
BENCHLEY, Mrs. Belle 7
Jennings
BENCHLEY, Nathaniel 8
Goddard
BENCHLEY, Robert 2
Charles
BENCHOFF, Howard 3
Johnston
BENCHOFF, Robert 5
J(ohnston)
BENCKENSTEIN, Leonard 4
Julius
BENCKER, Ralph 7
B(uckley)
BENDA, Harry Jindrich 5

BENDA, Wladyslaw 2
Theodor
BENDELARI, Arthur 6
Enrico
BENDELARI, George 1
BENDER, Albert Maurice 1
BENDER, Eric J. 4
BENDER, George H. 4
BENDER, Harold H. 3
BENDER, Jack I. 5
BENDER, John Frederick 6
BENDER, Lauretta 9
BENDER, Melvin T. 5
BENDER, Morris B. 8
BENDER, Myron Lee 9
BENDER, Prosper 4
BENDER, Ralph Edward 10
BENDER, Walter 5
BENDER, Wilbur H. 1
BENDER, Wilbur Joseph 5
BENDETSEN, Karl Robin 10
BENDICH, Aaron 7
BENDINER, Alfred 4
BENDIRE, Charles E. H
BENDIX, Ella Crosby 5
(Mrs. Ella Crosby Bendix)
BENDIX, Max 2
BENDIX, Vincent 2
BENDIX, William 4
BENECKE, Adelbert 4
Oswald
BENEDEK, Martin Henry 7
BENEDETTO, Francis 8
Aristide
BENEDICT, A.L. 4
BENEDICT, Alfred 1
Barnum
BENEDICT, Andrew Bell 3
BENEDICT, Anne 4
BENEDICT, Asa Gardiner 4
BENEDICT, C. Harry 4
Keith
BENEDICT, Cleveland 4
BENEDICT, Cooper 5
Procter
BENEDICT, Crystal 6
Eastman
BENEDICT, Daniel Norris 7
BENEDICT, David H
BENEDICT, Elias 4
Cornelius
BENEDICT, Erastus H
Cornelius
BENEDICT, Francis Gano 3
BENEDICT, Frank Lee 1
BENEDICT, George 1
Grenville
BENEDICT, George Wyllys 5
BENEDICT, Harris Miller 1
BENEDICT, Harry E. 1
BENEDICT, Harry Yandell 1
BENEDICT, Henry Harper 1
BENEDICT, James Everard 2
BENEDICT, Jay Leland 3
BENEDICT, Lorenzo 1
BENEDICT, Murray Reed 9
BENEDICT, Ralph C. 4
BENEDICT, Robert Dewey 1
BENEDICT, Russell 1
BENEDICT, Ruth Fulton 2
BENEDICT, Samuel Durlin 5
BENEDICT, Samuel 1
Ravaud
BENEDICT, Stanley R. 1
BENEDICT, Wayland 1
Richardson
BENEDICT, Wayne 5
Leclaire
BENEDICT, William 7
Lemuel
BENEDICT, William 1
Leonard
BENEDIKTSSON, Bjarnl 5
BENEDUM, Micheal Late 3
BENEDUM, Paul Gregory 1
BENEKER, Gerrit Albertus 1
BENES, Eduard 2
BENESCH, Alfred 1
Abraham
BENET, Christie 3
BENET, Laura 7
BENET, Laurence Vincent 2
BENET, Stephen Vincent 2
BENET, Walker 4
BENET, William Rose 2
BENETAR, David L. 9
BENETATOS, Demetrios 7
BENEVENTANO, Thomas 9
Carmine
BENEZET, Anthony H
BENEZET, Louis Paul 4
BENFIELD, William 9
Avery, Jr.
BENGEL, Lawrence Woods 7
BENGOUGH, Elisa 1
Armstrong
BENGTSON, Nels August 6

BENGTZ, Ture 7
BEN-GURION, David 6
BENHAM, Allen Rogers 6
BENHAM, Andrew Ellicott 1
Kennedy
BENHAM, Henry H
Washington
BENHAM, John Samuel 4
BENINGTON, Arthur 1
BENINGTON, George 4
Arthur
BENIOFF, Hugo 4
BENIOFF, Hugo 5
BENITEZ, Francisco 8
BENITZ, William Logan 3
BENJAMIN, A. Cornelius 5
BENJAMIN, Adam, Jr. 8
BENJAMIN, Anna 1
Northend
BENJAMIN, Asher H
BENJAMIN, Burton 9
Richard
BENJAMIN, Charles Henry 1
BENJAMIN, David Joel* 4
BENJAMIN, Dowling 4
BENJAMIN, Edward B. 7
BENJAMIN, Eugene S. 2
BENJAMIN, George 1
Hillard
BENJAMIN, Gilbert 2
Giddings
BENJAMIN, Harold 10
(Raymond Wayne)
BENJAMIN, John Forbes H
BENJAMIN, Judah Philip H
BENJAMIN, Louis 1
BENJAMIN, Marcus 1
BENJAMIN, Nathan H
BENJAMIN, Park H
BENJAMIN, Park 1
BENJAMIN, Ralph James 8
BENJAMIN, Raphael 1
BENJAMIN, Raymond 3
BENJAMIN, Reuben 1
Moore
BENJAMIN, Richard 7
Newton
BENJAMIN, Robert M. 4
BENJAMIN, Robert S. 7
BENJAMIN, Samuel 1
Greene Wheeler
BENKEN, Eugene Edwin 6
BENMOSCHE, M. 3
BENN, Ben 8
BENNARD, George 5
BENNER, Nolan Paul 10
BENNER, Philip H
BENNER, Raymond Calvin 5
BENNER, Walter Meredith 5
BENNER, Winthrop 7
Webster
BENNERS, Augustus 1
BENNESON, Cora Agnes 1
BENNET, A.A. H
BENNET, Benjamin H
BENNET, Robert Ames 3
BENNET, Sanford Fillmore 1
BENNET, Walter Mills 1
BENNET, William Stiles 5
BENNETT, Albert Arnold 4
BENNETT, Albert Dwight 4
BENNETT, Alfred Allen 4
BENNETT, Alfred S. 1
BENNETT, Alonzo 8
BENNETT, Andrew Carl 2
BENNETT, Andrew Carl 1
BENNETT, Archibald 3
Synica
BENNETT, Arthur 2
Ellsworth
BENNETT, Arthur 5
Ellsworth
BENNETT, Arthur Lawton 6
BENNETT, Belle H. 1
BENNETT, Bertram 7
Whitcomb
BENNETT, Burton 1
Ellsworth
BENNETT, Caleb Prew H
BENNETT, Carrol 7
Mortimer
BENNETT, Charles 1
Andrew Armstrong
BENNETT, Charles Edwin 1
BENNETT, Charles 1
Goodwin
BENNETT, Charles Henry 1
BENNETT, Charles 1
Washington
BENNETT, Charles Wilbur 5
BENNETT, Clarence Edwin 10
BENNETT, Clarence F. 5
BENNETT, Claude 1
Nathaniel
BENNETT, Constance 4
BENNETT, David Smith H

BENNETT, De Robigne H
Mortimer
BENNETT, Donald 5
Menzies
BENNETT, Dorothea 10
BENNETT, Earl Willard 6
BENNETT, Edmund Hatch H
BENNETT, Edward 3
BENNETT, Edward Brown 1
BENNETT, Edward 3
Herbert
BENNETT, Edward L. 8
BENNETT, Elbert G. 3
BENNETT, Elmer Frank 10
BENNETT, Emerson · 1
BENNETT, Eugene Dunlap 5
BENNETT, Frank Marion 3
BENNETT, Frank 4
Woodrow
BENNETT, George Allen 3
BENNETT, George Kettner 6
BENNETT, Granville G. 1
BENNETT, Harriet 5
BENNETT, Harry 10
BENNETT, Harry Jackson 8
BENNETT, Hendley Stone H
BENNETT, Henry 2
BENNETT, Henry Eastman 2
BENNETT, Henry Garland 3
BENNETT, Henry 1
Holcomb
BENNETT, Henry William 1
BENNETT, Hiram 7
Rockwell
BENNETT, Horace Wilson 2
BENNETT, Howard Clifton 8
BENNETT, Howard 6
Franklin
BENNETT, Hugh 4
Hammond
BENNETT, Ida Dandridge 1
BENNETT, Ira Elbert 3
BENNETT, Irving T. 3
BENNETT, Ivan Loveridge, 10
Jr.
BENNETT, James Eugene 4
BENNETT, James Gordon H
BENNETT, James Gordon 1
BENNETT, James Murrell 6
BENNETT, James 1
O'Donnell
BENNETT, James Van 7
Benschoten
BENNETT, James William, 5
Jr.
BENNETT, Jesse Lee 1
BENNETT, Joan 10
BENNETT, John 3
BENNETT, John Bonifas 4
BENNETT, John Charles 7
BENNETT, John Foster 1
BENNETT, John George 3
BENNETT, John James 4
BENNETT, John Newton 3
BENNETT, John William 4
BENNETT, Johnstone 1
BENNETT, Joseph Bentley 3
BENNETT, Josiah Whitney 10
BENNETT, Lawrence 5
BENNETT, Louis H
BENNETT, Louis L. 2
BENNETT, Louis Lowell 10
BENNETT, Louis Winston 3
BENNETT, M. Katharine 1
Jones
BENNETT, Maillard 6
BENNETT, May Friend 4
BENNETT, Melba Berry 5
(Mrs. Frank Henry
Bennett)
BENNETT, Michael John 2
BENNETT, Nathaniel H
BENNETT, Newcomb 7
Benjamin, Jr.
BENNETT, Orval 8
BENNETT, Philip Allen 4
BENNETT, Ralph Culver 3
BENNETT, Rawson 5
BENNETT, Reginald Victor 7
BENNETT, Richard 2
BENNETT, Richard Heber 6
BENNETT, Robert Henry 7
BENNETT, Robert Root 1
BENNETT, Robert Russell 10
BENNETT, Robert William 7
BENNETT, Roy Coleman 8
BENNETT, Russell 1
Hoadley
BENNETT, Samuel Crocker 1
BENNETT, Thomas F. 8
BENNETT, Thomas Gray 1
BENNETT, Thomas H
Warren
BENNETT, Victor 7
A(lexander)
BENNETT, Victor Wilson 3
BENNETT, Walter Harper 4

BENNETT, Wells Ira 8
BENNETT, Wendell C. 3
BENNETT, Willard 9
Harrison
BENNETT, William 7
Andrew Cecil
BENNETT, William Hunter 8
BENNETT, William James H
BENNETT, William Lyon 4
BENNETT, William Rainey 5
BENNETT, W(illiam) 5
R(eece)
BENNETT, William Wirt 1
BENNETT, William Zebina 1
BENNETT, James 1
Mitchell
BENNING, Bernhard 6
BENNING, Henry A. 4
BENNING, Henry Lewis 5
BENNION, Adam Samuel 3
BENNION, Howard Sharp 8
BENNION, Hugh Clark 8
BENNION, Milton 5
BENNION, Samuel Otis 5
BENNITT, George Stephen 1
BENNITT, Rudolph 3
BENNS, F(rank) Lee 8
BENNY, Allan 2
BENNY, Jack (stage name 6
of Benjamin Kubelsky)
BENOIST, Jean-Marie Jules 10
BENOIT, Emile 7
BENOIT, Richard Charles, 8
Jr.
BENOIT-LEVY, Jean 3
BENOLIEL, Solomon D. 1
BENRIMO, Joseph Henry 1
McAlpin
BENSEL, Francis Scott 6
BENSEL, James Berry H
BENSEL, John A. 1
BENSINGER, Benjamin 1
Edward
BENSINGER, Benjamin 7
Edward
BENSINGER, C.G. 4
BENSLEY, Robert Russell 3
BENSON, Alfred Washburn 1
BENSON, Allan L. 1
BENSON, Barry T. 10
BENSON, Blackwood 4
Ketcham
BENSON, Carl H
BENSON, Carl Frederick 4
BENSON, Carville 1
Dickinson
BENSON, Charles Emile 4
BENSON, Egbert H
BENSON, Einar William 4
BENSON, Elizabeth English 6
BENSON, Emanuel Mervyn 5
BENSON, Eugene 4
BENSON, Frank Weston 3
BENSON, Frank 1
Williamson
BENSON, Franklin Thomas 1
BENSON, George A. 3
BENSON, George Edward 5
BENSON, George Stuart 10
BENSON, Henry Kreitzer 5
BENSON, Henry Lamdin 1
BENSON, Henry Perkins 1
BENSON, Herbert Allen 8
BENSON, Howard Hartwell 8
James
BENSON, John 4
BENSON, John Cabot 8
BENSON, John Edward 8
BENSON, John Joseph 8
BENSON, Lawrence Kern 4
BENSON, Louis Fitzgerald 1
BENSON, Lucille 8
BENSON, Oscar Algot 9
BENSON, Oscar Herman 3
BENSON, Philip Adolphus 2
BENSON, R. Dale 4
BENSON, Ramsey 4
BENSON, Reuel A. 3
BENSON, Robert Dale 9
BENSON, Robert Dix 1
BENSON, Robert Green 8
BENSON, Robert Louis 6
BENSON, Sally 5
BENSON, Samuel Page H
BENSON, Simon 4
BENSON, Stuart 2
BENSON, Wilbur Earle 5
BENSON, William 7
Archibald
BENSON, William August 4
BENSON, William Clarence 7
BENSON, William 1
Shepherd
BENSTEAD, Horace 9
Melville
BENSWANGER, William 5
Edward

BENT, Bruce Roger 8
BENT, Charles H
BENT, Erling Sundt 3
BENT, Josiah H
BENT, Michael James 7
BENT, Myron Hammond 1
BENT, Quincy 3
BENT, Samuel Arthur 1
BENT, Silas H
BENT, Silas 2
BENT, Willard Osborn 8
BENT, William H
BENT, William Woodworth 7
BENTE, Frederick 1
BENTER, Charles 8
BENTHALL, Michael Pickersgill 6
BENTHIN, Howard Arthur 5
BENTLEY, Alvin Morell 5
BENTLEY, Arthur 2
BENTLEY, Arthur F. 3
BENTLEY, Charles Edwin 1
BENTLEY, Charles Eugene 1
BENTLEY, Charles Harvey 1
BENTLEY, Charles Staughton 4
BENTLEY, Claude 10
BENTLEY, Clavin Pardee 4
BENTLEY, Cyril Edmund 3
BENTLEY, Edwin 4
BENTLEY, F(ranklin) L(ee) 8
BENTLEY, Gordon Mansir 3
BENTLEY, Harry Clark 5
BENTLEY, Henry 1
BENTLEY, Irene 1
BENTLEY, Jerome Harold 4
BENTLEY, John Edward 4
BENTLEY, Julian 4
BENTLEY, Madison 3
BENTLEY, Max 8
BENTLEY, Percy Jardine 4
BENTLEY, Richard 5
BENTLEY, Robert Irving 1
BENTLEY, Walter E. 4
BENTLEY, William H
BENTLEY, William Burdelle 3
BENTLEY, William Frederick 1
BENTLEY, Wilson Alwyn 1
BENTON, Alva Hartley 2
BENTON, Angelo Ames 1
BENTON, Arthur B. 1
BENTON, Charles, Jr. 7
BENTON, Charles Swan H
BENTON, Charles William 1
BENTON, Corning 7
BENTON, Edward Lamar 7
BENTON, Elbert Jay 2
BENTON, Elma Hixson 2
BENTON, Frank 4
BENTON, George Alden 1
BENTON, George Young 8
BENTON, Glenn Harrison 8
BENTON, Guy Potter 1
BENTON, Jacob H
BENTON, James Gilchrist H
BENTON, James Webb 2
BENTON, Jay Rogers 3
BENTON, Joel 1
BENTON, John Edwin 2
BENTON, John Frederic 9
BENTON, John Keith 3
BENTON, John Robert 1
BENTON, Joseph George 7
BENTON, Josiah Henry 1
BENTON, Lemuel H
BENTON, Maecenas E. 4
BENTON, Margaret Peake 6
BENTON, Mary Lathrop 3
BENTON, Ralph 7
BENTON, Rita 6
BENTON, Stephen Olin 1
BENTON, Thomas Hart* H
BENTON, Thomas Hart 6
BENTON, William 5
BENTONELLI, Joseph 6
BENTONELLI, Joseph (Joseph Horace Benton) 7
BENTSUR, Shmuel 6
BENTZ, Charles William 8
BENY, Wilfred Roy 8
BENYAURD, William H. H. 1
BENZ, Alexander Otto 6
BENZ, Francis E. 3
BENZ, Harry Edward 4
BENZ, John Stephen 7
BENZ, Margaret Gilbert (Mrs. Luke L. Benz) 5
BENZE, C. Theodore 1
BENZEL, Charles Frederick, Sr. 5
BENZENBERG, George Henry 1
BENZIGER, August 3
BENZINGER, Frederic 4
BEN-ZION 9
BEN-ZVI, Izhak 4
BERANGER, Clara 3
BERBERIAN, Cathy 8
BERCH, Samuel Harry 3
BERCHTOLD, William Edward 8
BERCKEMEYER, Fernando 8
BERCKMANS, Bruce 5
BERCOVICI, Konrad 4
BERDAN, John 3
BERDANIER, Paul Frederick 4
BERDIE, Ralph Freimuth 6
BERDYAEV, Nickolai Alexadrovich 4
BEREDAY, George Zygmunt Fijalkowski 8
BERENDSEN, Carl August 8
BERENGER, Victor Henry 3
BERENS, Anthony F(rancis) 7
BERENS, Conrad 4
BERENSEN, Bertram Melvin 9
BERENSON, Bernard 3
BERESFORD, Harry 2
BERESFORD, Hobart 8
BERESFORD, John Percival 9
BERESFORD, Richard H
BERETTA, King John 2
BEREZOWSKY, Nicolai 3
BERG, Alban 4
BERG, Albert Ashton 3
BERG, Charles I. 1
BERG, David Eric 8
BERG, Douglas Spearman 5
BERG, Ernst Julius 1
BERG, George Olaf 1
BERG, Gertrude 4
BERG, Irving Husted 1
BERG, J. Frederic 3
BERG, John Daniel 2
BERG, Joseph Frederic H
BERG, Kaj 5
BERG, Louis 5
BERG, Royal Howard 4
BERG, Walter Gilman 1
BERG, William Henry 1
BERGAN, Gerald T. 5
BERGANTZ, Joseph Arthur 7
BERGAUST, Erik 7
BERGE, Edward 1
BERGE, Irenee 1
BERGE, Wendell 3
BERGEL, Egon Ernest 5
BERGEMANN, Gustav Ernst 5
BERGEN, Edgar (John) 7
BERGEN, Fanny Dickerson 4
BERGEN, James J. 1
BERGEN, John Tallmadge 2
BERGEN, John Teunis H
BERGEN, Joseph Young 4
BERGEN, Julius 9
BERGEN, Teunis Garret H
BERGEN, Thomas Joseph 10
BERGEN, Tunis G. 1
BERGEN, Van Brunt 1
BERGEN, William Benjamin 9
BERGENDOFF, Ruben Nathaniel 7
BERGENGREN, Roy Frederick 3
BERGER, Aldolph 4
BERGER, Anita Louise Fremault (Mrs. Henry Berger) 6
BERGER, Augustin 4
BERGER, C.A. 4
BERGER, Calvin Michael 1
BERGER, Charles L. 2
BERGER, Evelyn Miller 10
BERGER, George Bart 1
BERGER, George William 6
BERGER, Lowe 4
BERGER, Maurice Wibert 5
BERGER, Meyer 3
BERGER, Morroe 7
BERGER, Morroe 8
BERGER, Nathan Hale 8
BERGER, Samuel D(avid) 7
BERGER, Victor L. 1
BERGER, Vilheim 7
BERGERMAN, Melbourne 6
BERGERON, Victor J. 8
BERGERON, Wilbur Lee 8
BERGEY, David Hendricks 1
BERGFELD, Albert Joseph 7
BERGH, Albert Ellery 4
BERGH, Arthur 4
BERGH, Christian H
BERGH, Henry H
BERGH, Lillie D'Angelo 5
BERGH, Louis De Coppet 1
BERGH, Louis O. 3
BERGHERM, Charles Russell 4
BERGHOF, Herbert 10
BERGHOFF, Robert S. 4
BERGHOLZ, Leo Allen 4
BERGIDA, Jerome Jacob 6
BERGIN, Alfred 2
BERGIN, Charles Kniese 4
BERGIN, John William 2
BERGLAND, John McFarland 6
BERGLER, Edmund 4
BERGLUND, Abraham 2
BERGLUND, Everett Rudolph 6
BERGMAN, Bernard Aaron 7
BERGMAN, Bernard Aaron 8
BERGMAN, Edwin Alfred 9
BERGMAN, Elmer Otto 9
BERGMAN, Henry Dale 7
BERGMAN, Ingrid 8
BERGMAN, Jules 9
BERGMAN, Walter James 5
BERGMANN, Carl H
BERGMANN, Werner 3
BERGQUIST, J.Victor 1
BERGQUIST, Stanard Gustaf 3
BERGREN, Gustav Walter 9
BERGSAKER, Anders Johannessen 3
BERGSON, Henri H
BERGSON, Henri 4
BERGSON, Henri Louis 2
BERGSON, Herbert Augustus 7
BERGSTRAND, Karl Johan Hilding 7
BERGSTROM, George Edwin 5
BERGSTROM, Nathan Hough 10
BERGTOLD, William Harry 1
BERGWALL, Evan Harold 7
BERING, Frank West 4
BERING, Vitus Jonassen H
BERINGER, George M. 1
BERINGER, Milton S. 4
BERITASHVILI, Ivane 6
BERK, Viola Greenhut 7
BERKE, Mark 6
BERKELEY, Busby (William Berkeley Enos) 6
BERKELEY, Busby (William Berkeley Enos) 7
BERKELEY, James Percival 6
BERKELEY, John H
BERKELEY, Norborne H
BERKELEY, Norborne 4
BERKELEY, Randolph Carter 3
BERKELEY, Sir William H
BERKELEY, William Nathaniel 1
BERKENMEYER, Wilhelm Christoph H
BERKEY, Benjamin 8
BERKEY, Charles Peter 3
BERKEY, Peter 3
BERKEY, Russell Stanley 8
BERKINSHAW, Richard Coulton 9
BERKLEY, Claude Wellington 4
BERKLEY, Henry Johns 1
BERKMAN, Alexander H
BERKMAN, Alexander 4
BERKMAN, Anton Hilmer 6
BERKMAN, David Mayo 7
BERKMAN, Irving Jay 9
BERKNER, Lloyd Viel 4
BERKO, Stephan 10
BERKOWITZ, Abram 5
BERKOWITZ, David Sandler 8
BERKOWITZ, Henry 1
BERKOWITZ, Mortimer 4
BERKOWITZ, Walter J. 4
BERKSON, Maurice 6
BERKSON, Seymour 3
BERL, Ernst 2
BERL, Eugene Ennalls 3
BERLA, Julian Emerson 6
BERLACK, Harris 5
BERLAGE, Hendrik Petrus 5
BERLE, Adolf Augustus 4
BERLE, Adolf Augustus 5
BERLIN, Alfred Franklin 1
BERLIN, Don R. 10
BERLIN, Ellin 9
BERLIN, Harold Robert 4
BERLIN, Irving 10
BERLIN, Richard E. 9
BERLIN, Theodore H. 4
BERLINER, Emile 1
BERLINER, Henry Adler 5
BERMAN, Benjamin Frank 4
BERMAN, Edgar Frank 9
BERMAN, Emile Zola 9
BERMAN, Eugene 5
BERMAN, Louis 2
BERMAN, Louis Keva 9
BERMAN, Morris 2
BERMAN, Morton Mayer 9
BERMAN, Myron Philip 7
BERMAN, Oscar 3
BERMAN, Philip Grossman 5
BERMANN, Isidor Samuel Leopold 4
BERMINGHAM, Arthur THomas 5
BERMUDEZ, Edouard Edmund H
BERN, Howard Leonard 7
BERN, Paul 1
BERNADOTTE FOLKE, Count 2
BERNADOU, John Baptiste 1
BERNAL, Ignacio 10
BERNARD, Dallas Gerald Mercer 8
BERNARD, Florence Scott (Mrs. Ebbert Louis Bernard) 8
BERNARD, Frances Fenton 3
BERNARD, Sir Francis H
BERNARD, Frank Basil 5
BERNARD, Frederic Horton 7
BERNARD, Hugh John 8
BERNARD, Hugh Robertson 5
BERNARD, John H
BERNARD, Joseph Alphonsus 6
BERNARD, Lawrence Joseph 5
BERNARD, Luther Lee 3
BERNARD, Merrill 3
BERNARD, Sam 1
BERNARD, Simon H
BERNARD, Victor Ferdinand 4
BERNARD, William Bayle H
BERNARDI, Herschel 9
BERNARDI, Theodore C. 10
BERNARDIN, Joseph Mariotte 4
BERNARDY, Amy Allemand 6
BERNAT, Eugene 10
BERNATOWICZ, Albert John 5
BERNAYS, Augustus Charles 1
BERNBACH, William 8
BERNBAUM, Ernest 3
BERNDT, Alvin Harold 8
BERNDT, Rexer 10
BERNE, Eric Lennard 5
BERNE-ALLEN, Allan 5
BERNECKER, Edward M. 3
BERNEKER, Louis Frederick 1
BERNER, Harry M. 3
BERNER, Norman Arthur 10
BERNER, T. Roland 10
BERNERS, Edgar Hubert 10
BERNET, John J. 1
BERNET KEMPERS, Karel Phillipus 6
BERNHARD, Alva Douglas 3
BERNHARD, Arnold 9
BERNHARD, Dorothy Lehman 5
BERNHARD, John Helenus 7
BERNHARD, Joseph 3
BERNHARD, Richard J. 4
BERNHARD, William 5
BERNHARDT, Sarah 1
BERNHARDT, Wilhelm 1
BERNHEIM, Bertram Moses 3
BERNHEIM, Elinor Kridel (Leonard H. Bernheim) 10
BERNHEIM, Emile 9
BERNHEIM, Oscar Frederick 4
BERNHEIMER, Charles L. 2
BERNHEIMER, Charles Seligman 5
BERNHISEL, John Milton H
BERNIE, Ben 2
BERNIER, Paul 4
BERNINGHAUS, Oscar Edmund 3
BERNO, Jack Charles 6
BERNSTEIN, Allne 3
BERNSTEIN, Charles 2
BERNSTEIN, David 10
BERNSTEIN, David 2
BERNSTEIN, Harold Joseph 9
BERNSTEIN, Herman 1
BERNSTEIN, Jacob Lawrence 5
BERNSTEIN, Joel 7
BERNSTEIN, Leonard 10
BERNSTEIN, Louis 1
BERNSTEIN, Louis 4
BERNSTEIN, Marver Hillel 10
BERNSTEIN, Paul Murray 10
BERNSTEIN, Richard Barry 10
BERNSTEIN, Theodore Menline 7
BERNSTROFF, Count Johann 1
BERNSTROM, Victor 1
BERNTON, Harry Saul 7
BEROL, Alfred C. 6
BEROLZHEIMER, Edwin Michael 2
BEROUJON, Claude H
BERRES, Albert Julius 5
BERRESFORD, Arthur William 1
BERRETH, Herbert Raymond 6
BERREY, Rhodes Clay 6
BERREY, Ruth Robertson 6
BERRI, William 1
BERRIDGE, William Arthur 10
BERRIEN, Cornelius Roach 5
BERRIEN, Frank Dunn 3
BERRIEN, John MacPherson H
BERRIGAN, Edmund Joseph Michael, Jr. 8
BERRIGAN, Thomas Joseph 5
BERRY, Albert Edgar 1
BERRY, Albert Gleaves 1
BERRY, Albert Seaton 1
BERRY, Cecil Ralph 5
BERRY, Charles Harold 4
BERRY, Charles Scott 6
BERRY, Charles White 3
BERRY, Edward Wilber 2
BERRY, Edward Willard 5
BERRY, Edwin Carlos (Bill) 9
BERRY, Frank 5
BERRY, Frank Allen 4
BERRY, Frank B(rown) 7
BERRY, Frank John 8
BERRY, Franklin Haywood 7
BERRY, George Leonard 2
BERRY, George Packer 9
BERRY, George Ricker 2
BERRY, George Titus 3
BERRY, Gilbert Milo 1
BERRY, Gordon Lockwood 1
BERRY, Harold Haile 4
BERRY, Harold Lee 4
BERRY, Hiram Gregory H
BERRY, Howard 3
BERRY, Jack 8
BERRY, James Berthold 6
BERRY, James Edward 4
BERRY, James Henderson 1
BERRY, James Lampton 7
BERRY, J(ames) Raymond 9
BERRY, John H
BERRY, John Cutting 4
BERRY, Joseph Flintoft 1
BERRY, Joseph Francis 6
BERRY, Kearie Lee 4
BERRY, Keehn W. 8
BERRY, Levette Joe 9
BERRY, Lillian Gay 5
BERRY, Llyod Eason 7
BERRY, Loren Murphy 7
BERRY, Mark Perrin Lowrey 6
BERRY, Martha McChesney 2
BERRY, Mervin Albert 6
BERRY, Nathaniel Springer H
BERRY, NIXON T. 6
BERRY, Raymond H. 9
BERRY, Raymond Hirst 5
BERRY, Richard Chisholm 10
BERRY, Robert Mallory 1
BERRY, Robert W. 4
BERRY, Thomas 3
BERRY, Wallace 2

BERRY, Walter Van Rensselaer 1
BERRY, Ward Leonard 4
BERRY, Wilbur Fisk 4
BERRY, William 7
BERRY, William Franklin 1
BERRY, William H. 4
BERRY, William H. 5
BERRYHILL, Walter Reece 7
BERRYMAN, Clifford Kennedy 2
BERRYMAN, James Thomas 5
BERRYMAN, Jerome Woods 1
BERRYMAN, John 5
BERRYMAN, John Brondgeest 2
BERRYMAN, Robert Benton 7
BERRYMAN, W.A. 3
BERSELL, Petrus Olof Immanuel 5
BERSELL, Petrus Olof Immanuel 7
BERSTED, Alfred 5
BERTALANFFY, Ludwig von 6
BERTHEAU, Cesar Jordan 10
BERTHIAUME, Paul Wilfred 8
BERTHIAUME-DUTREM-BLAY, Angelina 7
BERTHOLF, Ellsworth Price 1
BERTKE, Eldridge Melvin 8
BERTOIA, Harry 7
BERTOLET, William S(chaeffer) 5
BERTOLETTE, Norman B(oone) 9
BERTRAM, Helen (Lulu May Burt) 5
BERTRAM, James 1
BERTRAM, John H
BERTRAM, John Elwood 9
BERTRAND, Charles Edward 7
BERTRAND, Ernest 3
BERTRANDIAS, Victor Emile 4
BERTRON, Samuel R. 3
BERTRON, Samuel Reading 1
BERTSCH, Howard 5
BERUH, Joseph 10
BERWALD, William 4
BERWIN, Franklin 6
BERWIND, Edward Julius 1
BESANT, Alvin William Kenway 8
BESEMER, Howard Burhans 1
BESHLIN, Earl Hanley 5
BESLER, William George 2
BESLEY, Fred Wilson 5
BESLEY, Frederic Atwood 2
BESLEY, Harold Joslyn 7
BESOSA, Harry Felipe 6
BESS, Demaree Caughey 4
BESS, Elmer Allen 5
BESS, Gordon Clark 10
BESSE, Arthur 3
BESSE, Harry William 7
BESSELL, William Weston, Jr. 7
BESSEY, Charles Edwin 1
BESSEY, Ernst Athearn 3
BESSEY, Roy Frederic 8
BESSIN, Hyman 7
BESSIRE, Dale Philip 7
BESSON, Harlan 2
BESSON, Waldemar Max 5
BEST, Alfred M. 3
BEST, Allen Charles 8
BEST, Charles Herbert 7
BEST, Clarence L. 3
BEST, Ernest Maurice 4
BEST, George Newton 1
BEST, Gertrude Delprat 2
BEST, Gordon 7
BEST, Harry 5
BEST, Henry Riley 1
BEST, Howard Richard 3
BEST, James Irvin 4
BEST, James MacLeod 5
BEST, John Carter 8
BEST, John G(arvin) 5
BEST, John Stevens 10
BEST, Marshall Ayres 8
BEST, Nolan Rice 1
BEST, William 3
BEST, William Hall 4
BEST, William Newton 8
BEST, William Parker 1
BESTIC, John Brereton 5
BESTON, Henry 5
BESTOR, Arthur Eugene 2
BESTOR, Paul 4
BESTROM, Leonard L. 5
BETELLE, James O. 6
BETETA, Ramon 4
BETH, Hilary Raymond 4
BETHEA, Jack 1
BETHEA, James Albertus 8
BETHEA, Oscar Walter 6
BETHEA, Solomon Hicks 1
BETHEL, George Emmett 1
BETHEL, John P. 3
BETHEL, Lawrence L. 4
BETHELL, Frank Hartsuff 3
BETHELL, Frank Hopkins 5
BETHELL, Union Noble 1
BETHKE, Robert Harder 9
BETHKE, William 4
BETHUNE, George Washington H
BETHUNE, Lauchlin H
BETHUNE, Louise 1
BETHUNE, Marion H
BETHUNE, Mary McLeod 3
BETJEMAN, John 8
BETO, George John 10
BETTELHEIM, Bruno 10
BETTELHEIM, Edwin Summer J. 3
BETTEN, Cornelius 5
BETTEN, Francis Salesius 2
BETTENBENDER, John I. 9
BETTENDORF, Joseph William 1
BETTENDORF, William Peter H
BETTENDORF, William Peter 4
BETTERIDGE, Walter Robert 1
BETTERS, Paul V. 3
BETTI, Ugo 4
BETTIS, Valerie 8
BETTLE, Griscom 8
BETTMAN, Alfred 2
BETTMAN, Gilbert 2
BETTMANN, Bernhard 1
BETTON, Silas H
BETTONEY, Wilfred Estey 8
BETTS, Albert Deems 4
BETTS, B. Frank 1
BETTS, Charles Henry 1
BETTS, Charles Julius 8
BETTS, Craven Langstroth 1
BETTS, Edgar Hayes 3
BETTS, Edward C. 2
BETTS, Emmett Albert 9
BETTS, Frederic H. 1
BETTS, Frederick A. 4
BETTS, Frederick William 1
BETTS, George Herbert 1
BETTS, George Whitefield, Jr. 3
BETTS, Isaac Franklin 10
BETTS, James A. 1
BETTS, Louis 4
BETTS, Philander, III 2
BETTS, Robert Budd 10
BETTS, Rome Abel 6
BETTS, Samuel Rossiter H
BETTS, Thaddeus H
BETTS, William James 4
BETTY, Frank F. 6
BETZ, Carl 7
BETZ, Robert Milton 5
BETZNER, Jean 8
BEUGLER, Edwin James 5
BEUKEMA, Herman 4
BEUKEMA, John Charles 9
BEURY, Charles E. 3
BEUTEL, Albert Phillip 5
BEUTEL, Frederick Keating 8
BEUTENMULLER, William 1
BEUVE-MERY, Hubert 10
BEVAN, Arthur Charles 8
BEVAN, Arthur Dean 2
BEVAN, Charles Frederick 5
BEVAN, Guy Theodore Molesworth 8
BEVAN, Laurence A. 4
BEVAN, Lynne J. 3
BEVAN, Ralph Hervey 6
BEVAN, Thomas Horatio 1
BEVAN, W. Lloyd 1
BEVEN, John Lansing 2
BEVEN, Thomas D. 10
BEVERIDGE, Albert Jeremiah 1
BEVERIDGE, Andrew Bennie 5
BEVERIDGE, Frank Stanley 3
BEVERIDGE, George David, Jr. 9
BEVERIDGE, Hugh Raymond 4
BEVERIDGE, John Harrie 1
BEVERIDGE, John Lourie 1
BEVERIDGE, Kuhne 5
BEVERIDGE, Thomas Robinson 7
BEVERIDGE, Lord William Henry 4
BEVERLY, Robert H
BEVERSDORF, Samuel Thomas 7
BEVIER, Isabel 2
BEVIER, Louis 1
BEVILACQUA, Joseph A. 10
BEVIN, Ernest 3
BEVIN, Newton Philo 7
BEVIS, Howard Landis 5
BEVIS, Joseph C. 10
BEWER, Julius August 3
BEWKES, Eugene Garrett 10
BEWLEY, Anthony H
BEWLEY, Edwin Elmore 2
BEWLEY, Loyal Vivian 10
BEWLEY, Luther Boone 5
BEXELL, John Andrew 2
BEYCHOK, Sherman 9
BEYE, Howard Lombard 1
BEYE, William 1
BEYEA, Herbert Writer 5
BEYEN, Johan Willem 7
BEYER, Clara Mortenson 9
BEYER, Frederick Charles 4
BEYER, George Eugene 4
BEYER, Gustav 4
BEYER, Henry Gustav 1
BEYER, Otto Sternoff 2
BEYER, Samuel Walker 1
BEYERS, Henry Wendell 1
BEYL, John Lewis 4
BEYMER, William Gilmore 6
BEZANSON, Osborne 4
BEZANSON, Philip Thomas 6
BEZAZIAN, Paul D. 10
BEZIAT, Andre 1
BHABHA, Homi Jehangir 4
BHAKTIVEDANTA, Abhay Charanaravinda (Swami Prabhupada) 7
BHARATI, Agehananda 10
BHARUCHA-REID, Albert Turner 8
BHATIA, Avadh Behari 8
BIANCHI, João A(ntonio) De 7
BIANCHI, Julio Domingo 3
BIANCHI, Martha Dickinson 2
BIANCHI-BANDINELLI, Ranuccio 6
BIANCO, Margery Williams (Mrs. Francesco Bianco) 6
BIANCOLLI, Louis 10
BIARD, Pierre H
BIAS, Randolph 3
BIBB, George Motier H
BIBB, Thomas William 7
BIBB, William Wyatt H
BIBBY, James Harry 5
BIBERMAN, Herbert J. 5
BIBERMAN, Jacob M. 7
BIBIGHAUS, Thomas Marshal H
BIBLE, Alan 9
BIBLE, Frank William 1
BIBLE, George Albert 3
BIBLER, Lester David 8
BICKEL, Alexander Mordecai 6
BICKEL, Karl August 5
BICKEL, Karl August 7
BICKEL, Shlomo 5
BICKEL, William Forman 8
BICKEL, William Harold 8
BICKELHAUPT, Carroll Owen 3
BICKELHAUPT, George Bernard 5
BICKERDYKE, Mary Ann Ball H
BICKERMAN, Elias Joseph 8
BICKET, James Pratt 1
BICKETT, Fanny Neal Yarborough 3
BICKETT, Thomas Walter 1
BICKFORD, Faith 7
BICKFORD, George Percival 10
BICKFORD, John Van Buren 10
BICKFORD, Thomas 1
BICKFORD, Walter Mansur 1
BICKHAM, Thomas Marion, Jr. 9
BICKHAM, Warren Stone 1
BICKING, Ada Elizabeth 3
BICKLE, Edward William 4
BICKLE, John Marcher 9
BICKLEY, George Harvey 1
BICKLEY, Howard Lee 2
BICKMORE, Albert Smith 1
BICKMORE, Lee Smith 9
BICKNELL, Bennet H
BICKNELL, Frank Alfred 2
BICKNELL, Frank Martin 1
BICKNELL, George Augustus H
BICKNELL, George Augustus 1
BICKNELL, John W. 7
BICKNELL, Lewis Williams 3
BICKNELL, Thomas Williams 1
BICKNELL, Warren 6
BICKNELL, Warren Moses 1
BICKNELL, William Harry Warren 4
BICKS, Alexander 4
BICKSLER, W. Scott 1
BICNKELL, Ernest Percy 1
BIDDINGER, Noble Lycester 5
BIDDISON, Pascal McDonald 7
BIDDLE, A.J. Drexel 4
BIDDLE, Alexander 5
BIDDLE, Andrew Porter 2
BIDDLE, Anthony Joseph Drexel 2
BIDDLE, Arney Sylvenus 1
BIDDLE, Charles J. 5
BIDDLE, Charles John H
BIDDLE, Clement H
BIDDLE, Clement Miller, Sr. 5
BIDDLE, Edward H
BIDDLE, Edward William 1
BIDDLE, Francis 5
BIDDLE, Francis 7
BIDDLE, George 6
BIDDLE, Henry Chalmers 1
BIDDLE, Horace P. 1
BIDDLE, James H
BIDDLE, James 1
BIDDLE, James Stokes 1
BIDDLE, John H
BIDDLE, John 1
BIDDLE, John Hunter 7
BIDDLE, Nicholas* H
BIDDLE, Nicholas 1
BIDDLE, Richard H
BIDDLE, Theodore William 9
BIDDLE, Ward Gray 2
BIDDLE, William Baxter 1
BIDDLE, William Phillips 1
BIDEZ, Earle Felton 10
BIDGOOD, Lee 7
BIDLACK, Benjamin Alden H
BIDWELL, Abel Trood 7
BIDWELL, Annie Ellicott Kennedy 1
BIDWELL, Barnabas H
BIDWELL, Charles Clarence 4
BIDWELL, Daniel Doane 1
BIDWELL, Edwin Curtis 1
BIDWELL, George Rogers 4
BIDWELL, John H
BIDWELL, Marshall Spring H
BIDWELL, Marshall Spring 4
BIDWELL, Percy Wells 5
BIDWELL, Seth Roland 8
BIDWELL, Walter Hilliard H
BIEBEL, Franklin Matthews 4
BIEBER, Charles L. 4
BIEBER, Ralph Paul 8
BIEBER, Sidney 5
BIEDERBICK, Henry 1
BIEDERMANN, August Julius 4
BIEDERWOLF, William Edward 1
BIEFELD, Paul Alfred 4
BIEGLER, Philip Sheridan 2
BIELASKI, Alexander Bruce 4
BIELASKI, Fred 7
BIELER, Andre (Charles Bieler) 10
BIEMESDERFER, Daniel L(uke) 10
BIEMILLER, Andrew John 8
BIEN, Julius 1
BIEN, Morris 1
BIENFANG, Ralph David 7
BIENSTOCK, Abraham Lawrence 8
BIENSTOCK, David Paul 6
BIENVENU, Rene Joseph 8
BIENVILLE, sieur de H
BIER, William Christian 7
BIERBAUM, Christopher Henry 2
BIERBOWER, Austin 1
BIERCE, Ambrose 4
BIERCE, Ambrose Gwinett H
BIERD, William Grant 2
BIERER, Andrew Gordon Curtin, Jr. 3
BIERER, Andrew Gregg Curtin 3
BIERER, John M(ichael) 8
BIERI, Bernhard Henry 5
BIERKOE, George Olaf 10
BIERMANN, Fred 7
BIERRING, Walter Lawrence 4
BIERS, Howard 4
BIERSTADT, Albert 1
BIERWIRTH, F(rederick) W(illiam) 8
BIERWIRTH, John E. 7
BIERY, John Carlton 8
BIESECKER, Frederick Winters 1
BIESER, Irvin Gruen 10
BIESTERFELD, Chester H. 3
BIFFLE, Leslie L. 4
BIGARD, Albany Barney Leon 7
BIGART, Homer 10
BIGELOW, Abijah H
BIGELOW, Albert Francis 6
BIGELOW, Archibald Pierce 3
BIGELOW, Bruce MacMillan 3
BIGELOW, Charles C. 3
BIGELOW, Daniel Folger H
BIGELOW, Daniel Folger 4
BIGELOW, Edith Evelyn 4
BIGELOW, Edward Fuller 1
BIGELOW, Erastus Brigham H
BIGELOW, Florence 3
BIGELOW, Francis Hill 1
BIGELOW, Frank Hagar 1
BIGELOW, Frank Hoffnagel 1
BIGELOW, Frederic Russell 2
BIGELOW, Frederick Southgate 3
BIGELOW, George Hoyt 1
BIGELOW, Harriet Williams 1
BIGELOW, Harry Augustus 2
BIGELOW, Henry Bryant 4
BIGELOW, Henry Forbes 1
BIGELOW, Henry Jacob H
BIGELOW, Herbert Seely 3
BIGELOW, Jacob H
BIGELOW, John* 1
BIGELOW, John Milton 4
BIGELOW, John Ogden 6
BIGELOW, Karl Worth 7
BIGELOW, Lewis H
BIGELOW, Marshall Train 1
BIGELOW, Mason Huntington 5
BIGELOW, Maurice Alpheus 3
BIGELOW, Melville Madison 1
BIGELOW, Poultney 3
BIGELOW, Prescott 1
BIGELOW, Robert Mansfield 5
BIGELOW, Robert Payne 3
BIGELOW, Samuel Lawrence 2
BIGELOW, Willard Dell 1
BIGELOW, William Frederick 4
BIGELOW, William Sturgis 1
BIGGAR, Edward Samuel 9
BIGGAR, Frank 6
BIGGAR, Hamilton Fisk 1
BIGGAR, Oliver Mowat 2
BIGGE, George Edmund 8
BIGGER, Frederick 4
BIGGER, Isaac Alexander 3
BIGGER, Robert Rush 4
BIGGERS, Earl Derr 1
BIGGERS, George Clinton 4
BIGGERS, John David 6
BIGGIN, Frederic Child 2
BIGGS, Albert Welburne 1
BIGGS, Asa H
BIGGS, Benjamin T. 1
BIGGS, Benjamin Thomas H
BIGGS, David Clifton 1

BIGGS, Edward George 7
Power
BIGGS, Hermann Michael 1
BIGGS, J. Crawford 3
BIGGS, J William 4
BIGGS, John, Jr. 8
BIGGS, Kate Britt (Mrs. 6
Furnam Kenneth Biggs)
BIGGS, Robert Wilder
BIGGS, Walter 4
BIGGS, William Richardson 6
BIGHAM, Madge Alford 4
BIGHAM, Truman C. 3
BIGLER, Henry William H
BIGLER, John H
BIGLER, John Adolph 4
BIGLER, Regina Marie 4
BIGLER, William H
BIGLER, William H. 4
BIGLEY, George Arthur 10
BIGLOW, Lucius Horatio 4
BIGNELL, Effie Molt 4
BIJUR, Nathan 1
BIKLE, Henry Wolf 1
BIKLE, Philip Melanchthon 1
BIKRAM, Tribhubana Bir 3
BILBO, Theodore Gilmore 2
BILBY, George N. 1
BILBY, Ralph Mansfield 8
BILBY, Ralph Willard 9
BILDER, Nathaniel 6
BILDERSEE, Adele 5
BILDERSEE, Barnett 8
BILES, George Phineas 1
BILGRAM, Hugo 1
BILL, Alfred Hoyt 4
BILL, Earl Gordon 2
BILL, Edward Lyman 1
BILL, Harry Leon 6
BILL, John G. 3
BILL, Ledyard 1
BILL, Nathan D. 4
BILL, Raymond 3
BILLADO, Francis William 4
BILLANY, Harry Hilton 4
BILLER, George, Jr. 1
BILLHARDT, Fred A. 5
BILLHEIMER, Albert 7
BILLIKOPF, Jacob 3
BILLINGHURST, Benson 1
Dillon
BILLINGHURST, Charles H
BILLINGS, Charles Ethan 4
BILLINGS, Cornelius 1
Kingsley Garrison
BILLINGS, Dorothy Baker 9
BILLINGS, Edmund 1
BILLINGS, Edward Everett 1
BILLINGS, Frank 1
BILLINGS, Frank Seaver 4
BILLINGS, Franklin Swift 1
BILLINGS, Frederic 5
Church
BILLINGS, Frederick H
BILLINGS, Frederick 5
Horatio
BILLINGS, George Herrick 1
BILLINGS, J(ohn) Harland 5
BILLINGS, John Shaw 1
BILLINGS, John Shaw 6
BILLINGS, Josh H
BILLINGS, Luther Guiteau 1
BILLINGS, Stephen 5
Ellsworth
BILLINGS, Thomas Henry 6
BILLINGS, W. Chester 1
BILLINGS, William H
BILLINGS, William 10
Howard
BILLINGSLEA, Charles 10
BILLINGSLEY, Allen 3
Loren
BILLINGSLEY, John 7
Dabney
BILLINGSLEY, Paul 4
BILLINGSLEY, Paul 8
Raymond
BILLINGSLEY, Sherman 4
BILLINGSLEY, William 4
Newton
BILLINGTON, Ray Allen 7
BILLMAN, Carl 6
BILLNER, Karl Paul 4
BILLOCK, George 6
D(onald)
BILLOW, Clayton Oscar 2
BILLS, Benjamin Franklin 9
BILLS, Hubert Leo 4
BILLSON, William Weldon 1
BILLUPS, Richard 6
Alphonzo
BILLY THE KID H
BILMANIS, Alfred 2
BILOTTI, Anton 4
BILTZ, John Fredric 6
BILTZ, Norman Henry 6
BIMEL, Frederick B. 7

BIMELER, Joseph Michael H
BIMSON, Lloyd A. 4
BINCH, Wilfred Reese 5
BINDER, Carroll 3
BINDER, Rudolph Michael 3
BINDERUP, Charles 3
Gustav
BINDRA, Dalbir 8
BINES, Thomas H
BINFORD, Jessie Florence 4
BINFORD, Lloyd Tilghman 3
BINFORD, Raymond 5
BINFORD, Thomas Howell 6
BINFORD, Thomas Peter 9
BING, Karl Roger 7
BING, R. H. 9
BINGAY, James Sclater 7
BINGAY, Malcolm Wallace 3
BINGER, Carl A.L. 7
BINGER, Walter D(avid) 1
BINGHAM, Albert Young 6
BINGHAM, Amelia 4
BINGHAM, Anne Willing H
BINGHAM, Barry 9
BINGHAM, Caleb 1
BINGHAM, Curtis Harry 10
BINGHAM, David Judson 4
BINGHAM, Edward 4
Franklin
BINGHAM, Eugene Cook 2
BINGHAM, Florence 4
Cornell
BINGHAM, George Caleb H
BINGHAM, George 5
Hutchins
BINGHAM, Gonzalez 4
Sidney
BINGHAM, Guy Morse 5
BINGHAM, Harry H
BINGHAM, Henry 1
Harrison
BINGHAM, Herbert 4
MacKay
BINGHAM, Hiram H
BINGHAM, Hiram 1
BINGHAM, Hiram 3
BINGHAM, James Lyman 7
BINGHAM, Joel Foote 1
BINGHAM, John Armor H
BINGHAM, Jonathan 9
Brewster
BINGHAM, Joseph Walter 6
BINGHAM, Kinsley Scott 1
BINGHAM, Millicent Todd 5
(Mrs. Walter V. Bingham)
BINGHAM, Norman 3
Williams
BINGHAM, Ralph 1
BINGHAM, Robert 1
BINGHAM, Robert 8
BINGHAM, Robert Fry 2
BINGHAM, Robert Worth 1
BINGHAM, Sidney Hedley 7
BINGHAM, Stillman 1
BINGHAM, Theodore 1
Alfred
BINGHAM, Theodore 6
Clifton
BINGHAM, Walter Van 3
Dyke
BINGHAM, Wheelock 5
Hayward
BINGHAM, William* H
BINGHAM, William, II 3
BINGHAM, William J. 5
BINGHAM, William 1
Theodore
BINGHAM, Woodbridge 9
BINING, Arthur Cecil 3
BIN ISHAK, Inche Yusoff 5
BINKERD, Robert 7
Studebaker
BINKLEY, Almond 5
M(adison)
BINKLEY, Christian 1
Kreider
BINKLEY, James Samuel 8
BINKLEY, James Samuel 9
BINKLEY, Robert Cedric 1
BINKLEY, Wilfred 4
Ellsworth
BINKLEY, William 5
Campbell
BINNEY, Amos H
BINNEY, Arthur 1
BINNEY, Arthur Fremont 7
BINNEY, Charles Chauncey 1
BINNEY, Edwin 1
BINNEY, Horace H
BINNEY, John 1
BINNICKER, Richard 5
Johnson
BINNIE, John Fairbairn 1
BINNION, Randolph 1
BINNS, Archie 5
BINNS, Charles Fergus 1
BINNS, Jack 3

BINNS, James Hazlett 9
BINNS, John H
BINNS, John Alexander H
BINNS, Joseph Patterson 7
BINNS, Walter Pope H
BIN-NUN, Dov 5
BINSSE, Louis Francis de 4
Paul
BINSTED, Norman Spencer 4
BINYON, Robert Laurence 2
BINZ, Leo 7
BINZEN, Frederick William 8
BIOLETTI, Frederic 4
Theodore
BIOSSAT, Bruce 6
BIOW, Milton H. 6
BIPPUS, Rupert Frederick 3
BIRCH, Albert Francis 10
BIRCH, Alexander 6
Clitherall
BIRCH, David Robert 5
BIRCH, Frank Victor 6
BIRCH, Raymond Russell 6
BIRCH, Reginald Bathurst 2
BIRCH, Stephen 1
BIRCH, T. Bruce 1
BIRCH, Thomas H
BIRCH, Thomas Howard 4
BIRCH, William Russell H
BIRCHARD, Clarence C. 4
BIRCHARD, Glen Robbins 4
BIRCKHEAD, Hugh 1
BIRCKHEAD, Oliver W. 4
BIRD, Abraham Calvin 4
BIRD, Angus Eugene 8
BIRD, Anna Child 4
BIRD, Anna Pennock 5
BIRD, Arthur 3
BIRD, Charles 1
BIRD, Charles 3
BIRD, Charles Sumner 1
BIRD, Eugene Hunt 8
BIRD, Francis Wesley 7
BIRD, Frederic Mayer 1
BIRD, George Emerson 1
BIRD, Hobart Stanley 4
BIRD, J(ames) Malcolm 7
BIRD, James Pyper 3
BIRD, John 4
BIRD, John E. 1
BIRD, Paul Percy 5
BIRD, Philip Smead 2
BIRD, Reginald William 3
BIRD, Remsen Du Bois 5
BIRD, Richard Ely 6
BIRD, Robert Montgomery H
BIRD, Robert Montgomery 1
BIRD, Robert Montgomery 7
BIRD, Viggo Edward 7
BIRD, Wallace Samuel 5
BIRD, William C. 9
BIRD, William Ernest 8
BIRD, William Russell 10
BIRD, Winfield Austin 4
Scott
BIRD-MALEY, Rose Anna 7
BIRDSALL, Benjamin P. 1
BIRDSALL, Carl A. 3
BIRDSALL, Guy Henry 7
BIRDSALL, James H
BIRDSALL, Samuel H
BIRDSALL, William W. 1
BIRDSEYE, Clarence 3
BIRDSEYE, Claude Hale 1
BIRDSEYE, Victory H
BIRDSONG, H(enry) E(llis) 3
BIRDWELL, Alton William 3
BIRDZELL, Luther Earle 6
BIRGE, Edward Asahel 3
BIRGE, Edward Bailey 3
BIRGE, Henry Warner 4
BIRGE, Julius 3
BIRGE, Raymond Thayer 7
BIRK, Newman Peter 4
BIRKBECK, Morris H
BIRKE, William D. 4
BIRKENHAUER, 8
Frederick Waller
BIRKENMEYER, Carl 5
Bruce
BIRKENSTEIN, Lillian 10
Ray
BIRKHAHN, N. Steven 9
BIRKHAUG, Konrad Elias 9
BIRKHEAD, Claude Vivian 3
BIRKHEAD, Leon Milton 3
BIRKHIMER, William 1
Edward
BIRKHOFF, George David 2
BIRKINBINE, John 1
BIRKMIRE, William 5
Harvey
BIRMINGHAM, Frederic 8
Alexander
BIRMINGHAM, Henry 1
Patrick
BIRNBAUM, Martin 5

BIRNBAUM, Nathan 6
BIRNBAUM, Nathan 7
BIRNBAUM, Stephen 10
Norman
BIRNEY, Arthur Alexis 1
BIRNEY, David Bell H
BIRNEY, Hoffman 3
BIRNEY, James H
BIRNEY, James Gillespie 1
BIRNEY, Lauress J. 1
BIRNEY, William 1
BIRNEY, William 1
Verplanck
BIRNIE, Rogers 2
BIRNIE, Upton, Jr. 3
BIRNKRANT, Michael 4
Charles
BIRNKRANT, Norman 8
Howard
BIRO, Robert Henry, Jr. 7
BIRR, Herman Theodore 4
BIRREN, Faber (Gregor 9
Lang)
BIRREN, Joseph P. 1
BIRTHRIGHT, William C. 8
BIRTLEY, Robert Lewis 3
BIRTWELL, Charles 1
Wesley
BISBEE, Eldon 4
BISBEE, Frank Doan 4
BISBEE, Frederick Adelbert 1
BISBEE, Horatio 4
BISBEE, Joseph Bartlett 4
BISBEE, Marvin Davis 1
BISBEE, Spaulding 3
BISBEE, William Henry 2
BISBING, Henry 1
Singlewood
BISCH, Louis Edward 5
BISCH, Louis Edward 7
BISCHOFF, Elmer 10
BISCHOFF, Henry, Jr. 1
BISCOE, Alvin B. 4
BISCOE, Howard Morton 3
BISCOE, Thomas Dwight 3
BISEY, Sunker Abaji 1
BISGYER, Maurice 6
BISHOP, Abraham H
BISHOP, Arthur Giles 2
BISHOP, Arthur Vaughan 3
BISHOP, Avard Longley 1
BISHOP, Bruce Clay 5
BISHOP, Cecil William 4
(Runt)
BISHOP, Charles Alvord 1
BISHOP, Charles McTeyire 2
BISHOP, Charles Reed 1
BISHOP, Charles Reed 4
BISHOP, Curtis Vance 4
BISHOP, Daniel Sanborn 1
BISHOP, David Horace 5
BISHOP, Donald Francis 10
BISHOP, Eben Faxon 2
BISHOP, Edwin Whitney 1
BISHOP, Elias B. 1
BISHOP, Elizabeth 7
BISHOP, Emily Montague 1
BISHOP, Ernest Simons 1
BISHOP, Eugene Lindsay 4
BISHOP, Everett L. 4
BISHOP, Farnham 1
BISHOP, Frederic Lendall 2
BISHOP, Geo(rge) Lee 5
BISHOP, George Sayles 1
BISHOP, George Taylor 1
BISHOP, George Wesley, Jr. 7
BISHOP, Harry Gore 1
BISHOP, Heber Reginald 1
BISHOP, Henry Alfred 1
BISHOP, Hewlett Ryder 4
BISHOP, Hubert Keeney 5
BISHOP, Inez Shannon 6
BISHOP, Irving Prescott 4
BISHOP, Isabel (Mrs. 9
Harold G. Wolff)
BISHOP, James H
BISHOP, James 1
BISHOP, James Robert 3
Thoburn
BISHOP, Jim 9
BISHOP, Joel Prentiss H
BISHOP, John H. 10
BISHOP, John Michael 8
BISHOP, John Peale 2
BISHOP, Jon Remsen 4
BISHOP, Joseph Bucklin 1
BISHOP, Joseph Warren, Jr. 8
BISHOP, Judson Wade 4
BISHOP, Mrs. L. Brackett 4
BISHOP, Louis Faugeres 1
BISHOP, Morian Hoover 10
BISHOP, Morris Gilbert 6
BISHOP, Nathan 4
BISHOP, Percy Poe 4
BISHOP, Phanuel H
BISHOP, Robert 10
BISHOP, Robert H. 4

BISHOP, Robert Hamilton H
BISHOP, Roswell P. 4
BISHOP, Samuel A. 5
BISHOP, Samuel Henry 1
BISHOP, Sereno Edwards 1
BISHOP, Seth Scott 1
BISHOP, William Darius 1
BISHOP, William Henry 1
BISHOP, William Samuel 2
BISHOP, William Warner 3
BISHOP, William Warner, 9
Jr.
BISHOPP, Fred Corry 5
BISKUP, George Joseph 7
BISPHAM, David Scull 1
BISPHAM, George Tucker 1
BISPLINGHOFF, 8
Raymond Lewis
BISSELL, Arthur Douglas 1
BISSELL, Betty Chapman 9
BISSELL, Charles Spencer 5
BISSELL, Clayton 5
Lawrence
BISSELL, Cushman Brewer 9
BISSELL, Dougal 1
BISSELL, E. Perot 2
BISSELL, Edwin Cone H
BISSELL, French Rayburn 1
BISSELL, George Henry H
BISSELL, George Welton 4
BISSELL, Goerge Edwin 1
BISSELL, Herbert Porter 1
BISSELL, Hezekiah 1
BISSELL, Hillary Rarden 6
(Mrs. Wadsworth Bissell)
BISSELL, Howard 1
BISSELL, Jean Galloway 10
BISSELL, John Henry 1
BISSELL, John William 4
BISSELL, Louis G. 7
BISSELL, Mary Taylor 5
BISSELL, Patrick 9
BISSELL, Pelham St 2
George
BISSELL, Pelham St. 8
George, III
BISSELL, Richard 7
BISSELL, Richard Mervin 1
BISSELL, Walter Henry 1
BISSELL, William 1
Grosvenor
BISSELL, William Henry H
BISSELL, Wilson Shannon 1
BISSELLE, Hulbert T. 4
BISSET, Andrew G(ustave) 6
BISSET, George 6
BISSETT, Clark Prescott 1
BISSHOPP, Kenneth 6
Edward
BISSHOPP, Kenneth 7
Edward
BISSIER, Julius 4
BISSIKUMMER, Charles 4
Hills
BISSON, Wheelock 9
Alexander
BISSONNETTE, T. Hume 3
BISSOT, Francois Marie H
BISSOT, Baptiste Jean H
BISTLINE, Francis M. 5
BITKER, Bruno Voltaire 8
BITNER, Harry Murray 4
BITNER, Lynn Nevin 9
BITTER, Francis 4
BITTER, Karl Theodore 1
Francis
BITTING, William 1
Coleman
BITTINGER, Charles 6
BITTINGER, John 1
Lawrence
BITTINGER, Lucy Forney 4
BITTLEMAN, Arnold 9
BITTNER, John Joseph 4
BITTNER, Van Amburg 2
BITTNER, Walton S(imon) 7
BITZER, Charles W. 9
BIXBY, Ammi Leander 1
BIXBY, Anna Pierce Hobbs H
BIXBY, Augustus Rufus 4
BIXBY, Edson Kingman 1
BIXBY, Harold McMillian 4
BIXBY, Harold McMillan 8
BIXBY, Horace Ezra H
BIXBY, Horace Ezra 4
BIXBY, James Thompson 1
BIXBY, Kenneth Roberts 5
BIXBY, R. Burdell 10
BIXBY, Tams 1
BIXBY, Walter Edwin 6
BIXBY, William Herbert 1
BIXBY, William Keeney 1
BIXLER, Edmond P. 5
BIXLER, Edward Clinton 5
BIXLER, James Wilson 2
BIXLER, Julius Seelye 8
BIZE, Louis A. 5

BLANCHARD, Arthur Horace 5
BLANCHARD, Charles Albert 1
BLANCHARD, Clarence John 4
BLANCHARD, Clyde Insley 8
BLANCHARD, Ferdinand Quincy 5
BLANCHARD, Frank Leroy 1
BLANCHARD, Frederic Thomas 2
BLANCHARD, George Roberts 1
BLANCHARD, George Washington 7
BLANCHARD, Grace 2
BLANCHARD, Harold Hooper 5
BLANCHARD, Harold M. 4
BLANCHARD, Henry 1
BLANCHARD, Henry G. 7
BLANCHARD, James Armstrong 1
BLANCHARD, John H
BLANCHARD, Jonathan* H
BLANCHARD, Lafayette Randall 5
BLANCHARD, Lucy Mansfield 1
BLANCHARD, Murray 5
BLANCHARD, Nathan Weston 1
BLANCHARD, Newton Crain 1
BLANCHARD, Ozro Seth 3
BLANCHARD, Ralph Harris 10
BLANCHARD, Ralph Harris 5
BLANCHARD, Ralph Harrub 6
BLANCHARD, Raoul 5
BLANCHARD, Robert Wesley 7
BLANCHARD, Rufus 5
BLANCHARD, Thomas H
BLANCHARD, William H. 4
BLANCHARD, William Martin 2
BLANCHET, Antoine Albert 7
BLANCHET, Clement Theophilus 4
BLANCHET, Francois Norbert H
BLANCHET, John Baptiste 3
BLANCHETTE, Romeo Roy 8
BLANCHFIELD, Florence A. 7
BLANCK, Jacob Nathaniel 6
BLANCKE, Leo Mulford 4
BLANCKE, William Henry 3
BLANCKE, Wilton Wendell 5
BLANCO, Jose G. 6
BLANCO-FOMBONA, Rufino 5
BLAND, Henry Meade 1
BLAND, John Randolph 1
BLAND, Oscar E. 3
BLAND, Pascal Brooke 1
BLAND, Richard H
BLAND, Richard Howard 4
BLAND, Richard Parks 1
BLAND, Schuyler Otis 1
BLAND, Theodorick H
BLAND, Thomas 1
BLAND, William Thomas 1
BLANDEN, Charles Granger 1
BLANDFORD, John Bennett, Jr. 5
BLANDIN, Amos Noyes, Jr. 8
BLANDIN, Charles Kenneth 3
BLANDING, Albert Hazen 5
BLANDING, Don 3
BLANDING, Sarah Gibson 8
BLANDY, William Henry Purnell 3
BLANEY, Dwight 2
BLANEY, Henry R. 4
BLANEY, Isabella Williams H
BLANEY, William Osgood 1
BLANK, Abe H. 6
BLANK, Samuel 10
BLANK, Samuel Allan 6
BLANK, Sheldon Haas 9
BLANKENAGEL, John Charles 7
BLANKENBUEHLER, John H. 4

BLANKENBURG, Lucretia Longshore 2
BLANKENBURG, Rudolph 1
BLANKENHORN, Marion Arthur 3
BLANKINSHIP, Leslie Charles 6
BLANKS, Robert Franklin 3
BLANN, John Edward 6
BLANNING, Wendell Yeager 8
BLANSHARD, Brand 9
BLANSHARD, Paul 7
BLANTON, Annie Webb 2
BLANTON, John Diell 1
BLANTON, Joseph Philip 3
BLANTON, Lindsay Hughes 1
BLANTON, Smiley 4
BLANTON, Thomas Lindsay 3
BLANTON, Wyndham Bolling 4
BLASDEL, Henry Goode H
BLASH, Rudolph F. 3
BLASHFIELD, Albert Dodd 1
BLASHFIELD, Edwin Howland 1
BLASIER, Robert Dalton 9
BLASINGAME, R(alph) U(pshaw) 7
BLATCH, Harriet Stanton 3
BLATCHFORD, Charles Hammond
BLATCHFORD, Eliphalet Wickes
BLATCHFORD, Richard Milford H
BLATCHFORD, Richard Milford 1
BLATCHFORD, Samuel H
BLATCHLEY, Willis Stanley 1
BLATMAN, Saul 8
BLATNIK, John A. 10
BLATT, Burton 8
BLATT, Solomon 8
BLATT, William M(osher) 5
BLATTEIS, Simon Risefeld 5
BLATTENBERGER, Raymond 5
BLAU, Henry Hess 7
BLAU, Max Friedrich 1
BLAUCH, Lloyd E. 6
BLAUER, William E. 3
BLAUG, Seymour Morton 7
BLAUSTEIN, Jacob 5
BLAUSTEIN, Louis 1
BLAUSTEIN, Morton K. 10
BLAUVELT, Bradford 5
BLAUVELT, Charles F. 1
BLAUVELT, Lillian Evans 2
BLAUVELT, Martin Post 1
BLAUVELT, Mary Taylor 5
BLAVATSKY, Helena Petrovna Hahn H
BLAXTER, Henry Vaughan 2
BLAYLOCK, Louis 1
BLAYNEY, James Roy 7
BLAYNEY, John McClusky 1
BLAYNEY, Lindsey 6
BLAYNEY, T(homas) Lindsey
BLAZER, Paul Garrett 4
BLAZER, Rexford Sydney 6
BLEAKLEY, William Francis 5
BLEAKLEY, William Francis 7
BLEASE, Coleman Livingston 1
BLEASE, Coleman Livingston 2
BLECKER, Michael John 10
BLECKLEY, Logan E. 1
BLECKWENN, William Jefferson 4
BLEDSOE, Albert Taylor H
BLEDSOE, Benjamin Franklin 1
BLEDSOE, Jesse
BLEDSOE, Samuel Thomas 1
BLEE, Harry Harmon 8
BLEECKER, Ann Eliza H
BLEECKER, Harmanus
BLEECKER, John Van Benthuysen 1
BLEGEN, Carl William 5
BLEIBTREU, Jacob 7
BLEICH, Clements Harry 7
BLEICH, Hans Heinrich 8
BLEICHER, Clarence E. 3
BLEICKEN, Gerhard David 8

BLEININGER, Albert Victor 2
BLEITZ, Donald Louis 9
BLENDER, Dorothea Klotz 5
BLENDINGER, Fred L. 1
BLENK, James Hubert 1
BLENKINSOP, Peter H
BLENKO, Walter John 7
BLENNER, Carle John 3
BLENNERHASSETT, Harman H
BLESH, Abraham Lincoln 1
BLESH, Rudi (Rudolph Pickett) 9
BLESSE, Frederick Arthur 3
BLESSING, Edgar M. 5
BLESSING, George Frederick 1
BLESSING, Lewis Greene 4
BLESSING, Richard Allen 8
BLESSING, Riley Andrew 5
BLETHEN, Alden Joseph 1
BLETHEN, Clarence Brettun 2
BLETHEN, Frank Alden 5
BLETHEN, William Kingsley 4
BLETTNER, Edward Frederick 9
BLEWER, Clarence Frederick 5
BLEWETT, Ben 1
BLEWETT, William E., Jr. 4
BLEWITT, Thomas Hugh 8
BLEYER, Herman 3
BLEYER, J. Mount 1
BLEYER, Willard Grosvenor 1
BLICHFELDT, Emil Harry 5
BLICHFELDT, Hans Frederik 2
BLICKENSDERFER, Joseph Patrick 4
BLICKENSDERFER, Robert 4
BLIEM, Milton Jacob 4
BLIGHT, Reynold E. 3
BLIM, Miles G. 6
BLINKEN, Maurice Henry 9
BLINKS, Lawrence Rogers 10
BLINN, Charles Payson 6
BLINN, Clarence J. 7
BLINN, Holbrook 1
BLINN, Keith Wayne 10
BLINN, Randolph 2
BLISH, Morris Joslin 8
BLISS, A. Richard, Jr. 1
BLISS, Aaron Thomas 1
BLISS, Anthony Addison 10
BLISS, Arthur 6
BLISS, Charles Bemis 4
BLISS, Chester Ittner 7
BLISS, Collins Pechin 2
BLISS, Cornelius Newton 1
BLISS, Cornelius Newton 2
BLISS, D. Spencer 3
BLISS, Daniel 1
BLISS, Don Alfonso 4
BLISS, Don C. 4
BLISS, Dorothy Elizabeth 9
BLISS, Edwin Elisha 1
BLISS, Edwin Munsell 1
BLISS, Eliakim Raymond 1
BLISS, Eliphalet Williams 1
BLISS, Elmer Jared 2
BLISS, Eugene Frederick 4
BLISS, Francis Walter 8
BLISS, Frederick Jones 1
BLISS, George* H
BLISS, George Laurence 5
BLISS, George William 7
BLISS, George Yemens 5
BLISS, Gilbert Ames 3
BLISS, Harding 5
BLISS, Harry Hayner 5
BLISS, Henry Evelyn 5
BLISS, Howard Sweetser 1
BLISS, James Harris 3
BLISS, John Carlton 3
BLISS, Jonathan H
BLISS, Leslie Edgar 8
BLISS, Louis Denton 5
BLISS, Louis G. 5
BLISS, Malcolm Andrews 1
BLISS, Mildred 6
BLISS, Paul Southworth 1
BLISS, Philemon H
BLISS, Philip Elijah H
BLISS, Phillip Paul H
BLISS, Porter Cornelius H
BLISS, Ralph Kenneth 5
BLISS, Ray Charles 8
BLISS, Raymond Whitcomb 5
BLISS, Robert Pratt 4
BLISS, Robert Woods 4
BLISS, Tasker Howard 1

BLISS, Walter Phelps 1
BLISS, William 1
BLISS, William Carpenter 5
BLISS, William Dwight Porter 1
BLISS, William Henry 1
BLISS, William J. 5
BLISS, William Julian Albert 1
BLISS, William Lancer 6
BLISS, William Root 1
BLISS, Zenas Randall 1
BLISS, Zenas Work 3
BLITZ, Anne Dudley 3
BLITZ, Antonio H
BLITZSTEIN, Marc 4
BLIVEN, Bruce 7
BLIXEN-FINECKE, Karen Christentze 4
BLIZZARD, Reese 4
BLIZZARD, Warren Lale 4
BLOCH, Albert 4
BLOCH, Alexander 1
BLOCH, Bernard 4
BLOCH, Charles Julian 6
BLOCH, Claud Charles 4
BLOCH, Ernest 3
BLOCH, Felix 8
BLOCH, Henry Simon 9
BLOCH, Herbert Aaron 4
BLOCH, Herman Samuel 10
BLOCH, Jesse A. 3
BLOCH, Julius 4
BLOCH, Louis 3
BLOCH, Monroe Percy 5
BLOCH, Ray E. 10
BLOCH, Robert Gustav 6
BLOCK, Adolph 7
BLOCK, Adriaen H
BLOCK, Edward 4
BLOCK, Henry David 7
BLOCK, Herman Bernhardt 4
BLOCK, Irving Alexander 9
BLOCK, Karl Morgan 3
BLOCK, Leigh B(loom) 9
BLOCK, Leopold E. 3
BLOCK, Louis James 1
BLOCK, Marvin Avram 10
BLOCK, Melvin A. 4
BLOCK, Paul 1
BLOCK, Paul, Jr. 9
BLOCK, Philip D., Jr. 7
BLOCK, Philip Dee 2
BLOCK, Ralph 6
BLOCK, Rudolph 1
BLOCK, Samuel Westheimer 5
BLOCKER, Dan 5
BLOCKER, Daniel James 3
BLOCKER, Truman Graves, Jr. 9
BLOCKER, William Preston 2
BLOCKLINGER, Gottfried 1
BLOCKSOM, Augustus Perry 1
BLODGET, Lorin 1
BLODGETT, Benjamin Colman 4
BLODGETT, Francis Branch 5
BLODGETT, Frank Dickinson 5
BLODGETT, Henry Williams 1
BLODGETT, Hugh Carlton 4
BLODGETT, Isaac N. 1
BLODGETT, John Taggart 1
BLODGETT, John Wood 3
BLODGETT, Katharine Burr 7
BLODGETT, Mabel Louise Fuller 3
BLODGETT, Ralph Hamilton 10
BLODGETT, Rufus 1
BLODGETT, Samuel* H
BLODGETT, Thomas Harper 4
BLODGETT, Thurston P(ond)
BLODGETT, Wells Howard
BLOEDE, Gertrude 1
BLOEDE, Victor Gustave 1
BLOEDEL, Julius Harold 5
BLOEDORN, Fernando Germane 6
BLOEDORN, Walter Andrew 7
BLOIS, Marsden Scott 4
BLOIS, Marsden Scott 9
BLOM, Frans 4
BLOMGREN, Carl August 4
BLOMMERS, Paul J. 7
BLOMQUIST, Edwin Oscar 4

BLOMQUIST, Hugo Leander 4
BLONDEL, Jacob D. H
BLONDELL, Joan 7
BLOOD, Charles H. 4
BLOOD, Henry Ames 1
BLOOD, Henry Hooper 2
BLOOD, Howard Earl 7
BLOOD, Robert McCutchins 3
BLOOD, Robert Oscar 6
BLOOD, Robert Oscar 8
BLOOD, William Henry, Jr. 1
BLOODGOOD, Clare Sutton 1
BLOODGOOD, Delavan 1
BLOODGOOD, Joseph Colt
BLOODGOOD, Wheeler Peckham 1
BLOODWORTH, Andrew Dunn Franklin 3
BLOODWORTH, James Nelson 8
BLOODWORTH, Timothy H
BLOOM, Allan 10
BLOOM, Charles James 2
BLOOM, Edgar Selden 3
BLOOM, Isaac H
BLOOM, Julius 8
BLOOM, Max Samuel 8
BLOOM, Melvin Harold 4
BLOOM, Sol 2
BLOOM, W. Knighton 1
BLOOMBERG, Maxwell 5
BLOOMER, Amelia Jenks H
BLOOMER, Edgar Nelson 4
BLOOMER, Millard J. 6
BLOOMER, Millard J. 5
BLOOMFIELD, Arthur Collier
BLOOMFIELD, Arthur L. 4
BLOOMFIELD, Daniel 4
BLOOMFIELD, Joseph H
BLOOMFIELD, Leonard 2
BLOOMFIELD, Maurice 1
BLOOMFIELD, Meyer 1
BLOOMFIELD, Mike B. 7
BLOOMFIELD, Morton Wilfred 9
BLOOMGARDEN, Kermit 7
BLOOMHARDT, Paul Frederick 8
BLOOMINGDALE, Alfred S. 8
BLOOMINGDALE, Charles 2
BLOOMINGDALE, Emanuel Watson 1
BLOOMINGDALE, Samuel Joseph 5
BLOOMQUIST, Howard Richard 8
BLOOMSTEIN, Max, Jr. 4
BLOOR, Alfred Janson 1
BLOOR, Walter Ray 4
BLOSS, James Ramsdell 3
BLOSSOM, Francis 5
BLOSSOM, George W., Jr. 4
BLOSSOM, Harold Hill 1
BLOSSOM, Henry Martyn, Jr. 1
BLOSSOM, Robert Alden 6
BLOUGH, Carman George 10
BLOUGH, Earl 5
BLOUGH, Elijah Robert 6
BLOUGH, Roger M. 9
BLOUGH, Sanford P. 5
BLOUNT, Charles, Jr. 10
BLOUNT, George Dexter 6
BLOUNT, Henry Fitch 4
BLOUNT, James Henderson 1
BLOUNT, Roy A. 6
BLOUNT, Roy Eugene 5
BLOUNT, Thomas H
BLOUNT, William H
BLOUNT, William Alexander 1
BLOUNT, William Grainger H
BLOUNT, Willie H
BLOUSTEIN, Edward J. 10
BLOW, Allmand M. 2
BLOW, Henry Taylor H
BLOWERS, Sampson Salter H
BLOXHAM, William D. 1
BLUCHER, Franz 3
BLUE, Burdette 2
BLUE, Frederick Omar 1
BLUE, John Howard 5
BLUE, Rupert 2
BLUE, Victor 1
BLUEMEL, Clifford 7
BLUETT, John Joseph 4
BLUFORD, Ferdinand Douglas 3

BLUGERMAN, Lee N. (Leonid) 5
BLUHDORN, Charles G. 8
BLUM, Alex Aladar 8
BLUM, Anna Ottillia 8
BLUM, Bernard 7
BLUM, Daniel 4
BLUM, Edward Charles 2
BLUM, E(dward) H(oward) 7
BLUM, Elias 6
BLUM, Harold F. 7
BLUM, Harry 5
BLUM, Harry H. 4
BLUM, Leon 2
BLUM, Robert 8
BLUM, Robert Frederick 1
BLUM, Samuel J. 3
BLUM, Stella 8
BLUM, Virgil Clarence 10
BLUM, William 5
BLUMBERG, Henry 7
BLUMBERG, Hyman 5
BLUMBERG, Nathan J. 4
BLUME, Clinton Willis 6
BLUME, Fred H. 5
BLUME, Peter 10
BLUMENBERG, Marc A. 1
BLUMENFELD, M. Joseph 9
BLUMENFELD, Ralph David
BLUMENFIELD, Samuel M. 5
BLUMENSCHEIN, Ernest L. 4
BLUMENSCHEIN, Mary Shepard Greene 3
BLUMENSCHEIN, William Leonard 1
BLUMENSCHINE, Leonard G. 5
BLUMENTHAL, Andre 10
BLUMENTHAL, George 1
BLUMENTHAL, Gustave Adolph 1
BLUMENTHAL, Sidney 10
BLUMENTHAL, Sidney 2
BLUMER, G. Alder 1
BLUMER, George 4
BLUMEYER, Arthur Adolphus 3
BLUMGART, Herrman L(udwig) 10
BLUMGART, Herrman Ludwig 7
BLUN, Henry 1
BLUNT, Edmund March H
BLUNT, George William H
BLUNT, Hugh Francis 5
BLUNT, James Gillpatrick H
BLUNT, John Ellsworth 1
BLUNT, John S. H
BLUNT, Katharine 3
BLUNT, Matthew M. 1
BLUNT, Stanhope English 1
BLUSTEIN, Herman 6
BLY, Eleanor Schooley 5
BLY, John Marius 2
BLY, Nelly H
BLY, Nelly 4
BLY, Robert Stewart 3
BLYDE, Lewis J(ohn) N(ewberry) 5
BLYDEN, Larry (Ivan Lawrence Blieden) 6
BLYDENBURGH, Charles Edward 1
BLYLEY, Katherine Gillette 4
BLYNN, Lloyd Ross 5
BLYTH, Charles R. 3
BLYTHE, David Gilmour H
BLYTHE, Joseph L. 3
BLYTHE, Joseph William 1
BLYTHE, Samuel George 2
BLYTHE, Stuart Oakes 8
BLYTHIN, Edward 3
BLYTHIN, Robert 4
BOAK, Arthur Edward Romilly 4
BOAK, Thomas Isaac Slack 8
BOAL, Arthur McClure 5
BOAL, Pierre de Lagarde 4
BOARDMAN, Albert Barnes 1
BOARDMAN, Charles Willis
BOARDMAN, Charles 3
BOARDMAN, Elijah H
BOARDMAN, Eugene Powers 9
BOARDMAN, Francis 7
BOARDMAN, George Dana 1
BOARDMAN, George Henry 5
BOARDMAN, George Nye 5
BOARDMAN, Harold Sherburne 5

BOARDMAN, Harry Clow 3
BOARDMAN, Harry L. 4
BOARDMAN, Henry Augustus H
BOARDMAN, Henry Bradford 1
BOARDMAN, Mabel Thorp 2
BOARDMAN, Paul Lawrence 6
BOARDMAN, Samuel Lane 1
BOARDMAN, Samuel Ward 1
BOARDMAN, Thomas Danforth H
BOARDMAN, W. Wade 8
BOARDMAN, Waldo Elias 4
BOARDMAN, William Bradford
BOARDMAN, William Henry 1
BOARDMAN, William Kilbourne 7
BOARDMAN, William Whiting H
BOARMAN, Aleck 3
BOARTS, Robert Marsh 4
BOAS, Emil Leopold 3
BOAS, Ernst Philip 3
BOAS, Franz 2
BOAS, George 7
BOAS, Robert Sanford 10
BOAST, Warren Benefield 10
BOATMAN, Conway 8
BOATNER, Charles Knox 2
BOATNER, Victor Vincent 2
BOATRIGHT, Byron B. 3
BOATRIGHT, Mody Coggin H
BOATRIGHT, William Louis 1
BOATWRIGHT, Frederic William 3
BOATWRIGHT, Gertrude Floyd Harris 5
BOATWRIGHT, James, III 9
BOATWRIGHT, Purvis James, Jr. 10
BOATWRIGHT, Walter Putney 7
BOAZ, Hiram Abiff 4
BOAZ, Hiram Abiff 5
BOBB, Byron Arthur 5
BOBB, Clyde S. 3
BOBB, Earl Victor 3
BOBBITT, Archie Newton 10
BOBBITT, Franklin 3
BOBBITT, Joseph Matthew 6
BOBBITT, Mary Lavinia Reed (Mrs. Vernon L. Bobbitt)
BOBBITT, Robert Lee 8
BOBBS, William Conrad 9
BOBER, Harry 9
BOBER, Mandell Morton 5
BOBER, Sam Henry 5
BOBLETER, Lowell Stanley 7
BOBRINSKOY, George Vladimir 5
BOBROVNIKOFF, Nicholas Theodore 10
BOBST, Elmer H. 7
BOCHER, Main Rousseau (Mainbocher) 7
BOCHER, Maxime 1
BOCHNER, Salomon 8
BOCK, Arlie Vernon 5
BOCK, Harold Pattendon 5
BOCK, Otto 2
BOCK, Robert M. 10
BOCKEE, Abraham 3
BOCKES, Thomas Willis 7
BOCKHOFF, Harry W 10
BOCKIUS, George Hamlin 7
BOCKLET, Charles J. 7
BOCKMAN, Marcus Olaus 2
BOCKUS, Charles E. 1
BOCKUS, Henry L. 10
BOCKUS, Henry L. 8
BOCOCK, Clarence Edgar 1
BOCOCK, John Holmes 5
BOCOCK, Thomas S. H
BOCOCK, Willis Henry 4
BOCQUERAZ, Leon Edward 6
BODANSKY, Meyer 1
BODANSKY, Oscar 7
BODANZKY, Artur 2
BODDE, John R. 5
BODDINGTON, Ernest Fearby 3
BODDIS, George 4
BODDY, E. Manchester 4
BODDY, William Henry 1
BODE, Albert William 4
BODE, Boyd Henry 3

BODE, Dietrich Adam 8
BODE, Frederick 1
BODE, Hendrik Wade 9
BODECKER, Carl Friedrich Wilhelm 4
BODELL, David Eugene 5
BODELL, Joseph James 3
BODEMER, Charles William 9
BODEN, Andrew H
BODEN, Reynold Blomerley 4
BODEN, Robert Francis 9
BODENHAFER, Walter Blaine 8
BODENHAMER, Osee Lee 1
BODENHEIM, Maxwell 4
BODENSIECK, Julius H(enry) 9
BODENSTEIN, Dietrich H. F. A. 8
BODENWEIN, Theodore 1
BODER, Bartlett 5
BODER, David Pablo 4
BODFISH, Morton 4
BODIAN, David 10
BODINE, A(ldine) Aubrey 5
BODINE, Alfred Van Sant 4
BODINE, James Morrison 1
BODINE, Joseph Hall 3
BODINE, Joseph Lamb 3
BODINE, Roy L. 6
BODINE, Samuel Louis 3
BODINE, Samuel Taylor 1
BODINE, William Budd 3
BODINE, William Warden 3
BODINE, William Warden, Jr. 8
BODKIN, Henry Grattan 7
BODLE, Charles H
BODLEY, Ronald Victor Courtenay 9
BODLEY, Temple 1
BODMAN, Ernest James 3
BODMAN, Henry Edward 4
BODMAN, Henry Taylor 9
BODMER, Karl H
BODMER, Walter 6
BODY, Charles William Edmund 1
BODY, Ralph C. 6
BOE, Archie R. 9
BOE, Jason Douglas 10
BOE, Lars Wilhelm 2
BOECKEL, Florence Brewer (Mrs. Richard Martin Boeckel) 7
BOECKEL, Richard Martin 9
BOECKLIN, Roland 5
BOEGNER, Marc 5
BOEHLER, Peter H
BOEHM, Edward Marshall 5
BOEHM, Henry H
BOEHM, John Philip H
BOEHM, Karl 8
BOEHM, Martin H
BOEHME, Ernest Adolph 4
BOEHMER, Florence Elise 4
BOEHMER, Max 1
BOEING, William Edward 3
BOELEN, Jacob H
BOELTER, Llewellyn Michael Kraus 4
BOER, Benjamin C. 8
BOER, Germain Boniface 8
BOERICKE, Garth Wilkinson 5
BOERKER, Richard Hans Douai 8
BOERNSTEIN, Ralph A(ugustus) 5
BOERUM, Simon H
BOESCHENSTEIN, Charles 3
BOESCHENSTEIN, Harold 5
BOESEL, Frank Tilden 4
BOETTCHER, Arthur Henry 7
BOETTCHER, Charles 2
BOETTCHER, Charles, II 4
BOETTCHER, Claude Kedzie 3
BOETTGER, Theodore 6
BOETTIGER, John 3
BOEYE, John Franklin 4
BOEYNAEMS, Libert Hubert John Louis 3
BOFINGER, D. T. 2
BOGAN, Louise 5
BOGAN, R. A. L. 3
BOGAN, William Joseph 1
BOGARDUS, Emory Stephen 6
BOGARDUS, Emory Stephen 7
BOGARDUS, Everardus H
BOGARDUS, James H

BOGART, Ernest Ludlow 3
BOGART, Humphrey Deforest 3
BOGART, John 1
BOGART, Neil 8
BOGART, Paul Nebeker 5
BOGART, Walter Thompson 5
BOGART, William Henry H
BOGARTE, Martin Bruce 7
BOGARTE, Martin Eugene 4
BOGEN, Emil 4
BOGEN, Jules Irwin 4
BOGER, Glen Alvin 5
BOGER, Robert Forrester 5
BOGER, Roy Garland 1
BOGERT, Edward Strong 1
BOGERT, George Gleason 7
BOGERT, George H. 2
BOGERT, John Lyman 8
BOGERT, Marston Taylor 4
BOGERT, Walter Lawrence 5
BOGGESS, Arthur Clinton 1
BOGGS, A. Maris (Anita Uarda Maris Boggs) 8
BOGGS, Carroll Curtis 1
BOGGS, Charles Stuart H
BOGGS, Earl Huffner 5
BOGGS, Frank Cranstoun 5
BOGGS, Frank M. 1
BOGGS, Gilbert Hillhouse 1
BOGGS, Lillburn W. H
BOGGS, Marion A. 10
BOGGS, Robert 4
BOGGS, S. Whittemore 3
BOGGS, Sara E. 3
BOGGS, Thomas Hale 5
BOGGS, Thomas Richmond 1
BOGGS, Wade Hamilton 7
BOGGS, William Brenton H
BOGGS, William Ellison 1
BOGGS, William Robertson 1
BOGIE, Mord M. 3
BOGLE, Henry Charles 9
BOGLE, James H
BOGLE, Robert Boyd 1
BOGLE, Sarah Comly Norris 1
BOGLE, Thomas Ashford 1
BOGLE, Walter Scott 1
BOGOSIAN, Ares George 1
BOGOSLOVSKY, Boris Basil 4
BOGUE, Harold J. 4
BOGUE, Jesse Parker 3
BOGUE, Morton Griswold 1
BOGUE, Virgil Gay 1
BOGUSLAWSKI, Molssaye 2
BOGY, Lewis Vital H
BOHACHEVSKY, Constantine 4
BOHAN, Merwin Lee 6
BOHAN, Merwin Lee 5
BOHAN, Peter Thomas 5
BOHANNON, Eugene William 3
BOHANNON, William Everette 1
BOHART, Philip Harris 4
BOHEN, Frederick Owen 6
BOHLEN, Charles Eustis 6
BOHLEN, Diedrich A. H
BOHLEN, Francis Hermann 2
BOHLEN, Joe Merl 10
BOHLER, John Frederick 7
BOHLMAN, Herbert William 5
BOHLMANN, Henry Frederic Theodore 4
BOHM, Karl 8
BOHM, Max 3
BOHMAN, George Vroom 10
BOHMBACH, Stanton Monroe 5
BOHN, Charles B. 3
BOHN, Donald George 5
BOHN, Ernest John 6
BOHN, Ernest John 6
BOHN, Frank 6
BOHN, Frank Probasco 4
BOHN, Gebhard C. 6
BOHN, J(acob) Lloyd 10
BOHN, John J. 8
BOHN, William Frederick 2
BOHR, Frank 5
BOHR, Niels Henrik David 7
BOHROD, Aaron 10
BOHSTEDT, Gustav H
BOHUNE, Lawrence H
BOICE, James Young 4
BOIES, Henry Martyn 1
BOIES, Horace 1
BOIES, Lawrence Randall 9
BOIES, William Artemas 1
BOIES, William Dayton 1

BOIFEUILLET, John Theodore 1
BOILEAU, Philip 1
BOISE, Otis Bardwell 1
BOISOT, Emile Kellogg 4
BOISOT, Louis 1
BOISSEVAIN, Charles Hercules 2
BOISSEVAIN, Inez Milholland 1
BOIVIN, Bernard 9
BOJANOWSKI, Jerzy 8
BOJER, Johan 3
BOK, Bart Jan 8
BOK, Cary William 5
BOK, Curtis 4
BOK, Edward William 1
BOKAT, George 6
BOKEE, David Alexander H
BOKER, George Henry H
BOKHARI, Ahmed Shah 3
BOKOR, Margit 3
BOLAND, Edward R. A. 9
BOLAND, Francis Joseph 4
BOLAND, Frank Kells 3
BOLAND, George Bernard 6
BOLAND, John J. 3
BOLAND, John Peter 5
BOLAND, Mary 4
BOLAND, Patrick J. 2
BOLAND, Thomas Aloysius 10
BOLD, Harold C. 9
BOLDEN, Charles H
BOLDEN, Charles 4
BOLDREY, Edwin Barkley 10
BOLDT, George C. 1
BOLDT, George Hugo 4
BOLDT, Hermann Johannes 2
BOLDUAN, Charles Frederick 3
BOLE, Benjamin Patterson 1
BOLE, William McLure 1
BOLEND, Floyd Jackson 1
BOLES, C. E. 8
BOLES, Edgar Howard 2
BOLES, Ewing Thomas 10
BOLES, H(enry) Leo 5
BOLES, John 5
BOLES, Russell Sage 9
BOLET, Jorge 10
BOLGER, Henry Joseph 4
BOLGER, Ray 9
BOLGER, William Frederick 10
BOLIN, Harvey Wesley 7
BOLIN, Rolf Ling 6
BOLINGER, Dwight Lemerton 10
BOLIVAR, Simon H
BOLL, Charles Louis 8
BÖLL, Heinrich 8
BOLL, Jacob H
BOLLAN, William H
BOLLAY, William 8
BOLLENBACHER, Paul E(dward) 1
BOLLENGIER, Albert Emile 6
BOLLENS, John Constantinus 1
BOLLER, Alfred Pancoast 1
BOLLES, Albert Sidney 1
BOLLES, Blair 10
BOLLES, Edwin Cortlandt 1
BOLLES, Frank H
BOLLES, Frank Crandall 1
BOLLES, Stephen 1
BOLLES, Thomas Darley 7
BOLLING, Alexander Russell 4
BOLLING, George Melville 5
BOLLING, Raynal Cawthorne 1
BOLLING, Richard 10
BOLLINGER, James Wills 3
BOLLMAN, Justus Erich H
BOLLMEIER, Emil Wayne 10
BOLOTOV, Ivan Il'ich H
BOLOTOWSKY, Ilya 8
BOLSTAD, Milo Myrum 6
BOLSTER, Calvin Mathews 10
BOLSTER, Stanley Marshall 5
BOLSTER, Wilfred 2
BOLSTER, William Wheeler 4
BOLT, Richard Arthur 4
BOLTE, William John 4
BOLTEN, Joseph Stirling 8
BOLTON, Abby 1
BOLTON, Benjamin Meade 1
BOLTON, Charles Edward 1
BOLTON, Charles Houston 1
BOLTON, Charles Knowles 3
BOLTON, Chester Castle 1
BOLTON, Elmer Keiser 5
BOLTON, Ethel 3

BOLTON, Frances Payne 7
BOLTON, Frederick Elmer 5
BOLTON, Frederick Rolshoven 10
BOLTON, Guy 8
BOLTON, Henry Carrington 1
BOLTON, Herbert Eugene 5
BOLTON, J. Gray 1
BOLTON, James Calderwood 7
BOLTON, John H
BOLTON, (John) Whitney (French) 5
BOLTON, Margaret 3
BOLTON, Paul H. 4
BOLTON, Reginald Pelham 2
BOLTON, Sarah Knowles 1
BOLTON, Sarah Tittle Barrett H
BOLTON, T. Coulston 8
BOLTON, Thaddeus Lincoln 2
BOLTON, Theodore 8
BOLTON, William E(rnest) 9
BOLTON, William Jay H
BOLTON, William Jordan 1
BOLTON, William P. 7
BOLTWOOD, Bertram Borden 1
BOLTWOOD, Edward 1
BOLTZIUS, Johann Martin H
BOLZ, Sanford Hegleman 10
BOLZA, Oskar 4
BOMANN, George Atkins 5
BOMAR, Edward Earle 3
BOMAR, Paul Vernon 1
BOMAR, William Purinton 7
BOMAR, William Purinton 8
BOMBERGER, John Henry Augustus H
BOMBERGER, Louden Lane 4
BOMFORD, George H
BOMMARITO, Peter 10
BOMPIANI, Sophia Van Matre 4
BOMZE, Henry Daniel 6
BOMZER, Herbert Wallace 9
BONACCOLTO, Girolamo 6
BONACUM, Thomas 1
BONAFEDE, Vincent Ignatius 8
BONAPARTE, Charles Joseph 1
BONAPARTE, Charles Lucien H
BONAPARTE, Charlotte Julie H
BONAPARTE, Elizabeth Patterson H
BONAPARTE, Jerome Napoleon H
BONAPARTE, Louis Napoleon H
BONAPARTE, Napoleon H
BONAR, John Stanley 7
BONARD, Louis H
BONASCHI, Alberto Cinzio 3
BONBRIGHT, William Prescott 4
BONCHER, Hector Peter 6
BONCI, Alessandro 5
BOND, A. Russell 1
BOND, Ahva J. C. 5
BOND, Albert Richmond 2
BOND, Alfred M. 7
BOND, Bernard Q. 1
BOND, Beverly Waugh 6
BOND, Carrie Jacobs 2
BOND, Carroll Taney 2
BOND, Charles Grosvenor 5
BOND, Charles Sumner 3
BOND, Chauncey David 7
BOND, Daniel Carl 7
BOND, Donald Frederic 9
BOND, Douglas Danford 7
BOND, Drew (Frederic) 5
BOND, Earl Danford 6
BOND, Edward Johnson 1
BOND, Edwin Austin 1
BOND, Edwin E. 4
BOND, Elizabeth Powell 3
BOND, Elsie M(urdoch) 7
BOND, Ford 4
BOND, Frank 1
BOND, Frank Stuart 1
BOND, George Hopkins 3
BOND, George Hopkins 6
BOND, George Meade 1
BOND, George Phillips H
BOND, George William 9
BOND, H. Wheeler 4
BOND, Henry 1
BOND, Henry Whitelaw 1
BOND, Hiram E. 9
BOND, Horace Mann 5
BOND, Hugh Lennox, Jr. 1
BOND, Hugh Lenox H
BOND, James Clarence 8
BOND, James Leslie 5
BOND, John Reed 10
BOND, Johnny (Cyrus W.) 7
BOND, Joseph Francis 10
BOND, Lester L. 1
BOND, Maurice Chester 10
BOND, Nelson L. 6
BOND, Oliver James 1
BOND, Otto Ferdinand 7
BOND, Perry A(very) 6
BOND, Raymond T. 8
BOND, Reford 3
BOND, Richard H
BOND, Richard Guy 9
BOND, Richmond Pugh 7
BOND, Robert McGehee 9
BOND, Shadrach H
BOND, Sirus Orestes 3
BOND, Thomas H
BOND, Thomas Burke 6
BOND, Thomas Emerson 2
BOND, Thomas Jackson 8
BOND, Walter Huntington 6
BOND, Willard Faroe 5
BOND, William Cranch H
BOND, William Key H
BOND, William Scott 3
BOND, Young Hance 4
BONDS, Archibald 5
BONDS, Margaret 6
BONDURANT, Alexander Lee 1
BONDURANT, Eugene Dubose 5
BONDURANT, Herbert W(illiam) 9
BONDURANT, William Walton 4
BONDY, Philip Lederer 10
BONDY, Robert Earl 10
BONDY, William 4
BONE, Alfred Rufus, Jr. 5
BONE, Homer Truett 5
BONE, Robert Gehlmann 10
BONE, Scott Cardelle 1
BONE, Winstead Paine 2
BONEBRAKE, Peter Oren 4
BONEHILL, Ralph 1
BONELL, Benjamin Walter 5
BONER, Charles Paul 7
BONER, John Henry 1
BONESTEEL, Charles Hartwell 4
BONESTEEL, Verne C. 4
BONESTEEL, Verne Clinton 8
BONFIELD, George R. H
BONFIG, Henry Carl 4
BONFILS, Frederick Gilmer H
BONFILS, Frederick Gilmer 4
BONFILS, Helen G. 5
BONGARTZ, Roy 10
BONGGREN, Olof Jakob 4
BONGIOVANNI, Alfred Marius 9
BONHAM, John Henry 7
BONHAM, Kenneth Arlington 5
BONHAM, Milledge Lipscomb 2
BONHAM, Milledge Louis, Jr. 1
BONHAM, Milledge Luke H
BONI, Albert 8
BONIFACE, Mother Mary 4
BONIFIELD, Charles Lybrand 1
BONILLA, Charles Francis 9
BONILLAS, Ygnacio 2
BONINE, Chesleigh Arthur 8
BONISTEEL, Roscoe Osmond 8
BONNAR, John Duncan 1
BONNELL, Henry Houston 1
BONNELL, Hettie Hazlett 10
BONNELL, John Sutherland 10
BONNER, Albert Sydney 2
BONNER, Arthur 3
BONNER, Campbell 5
BONNER, Charles 4
BONNER, David Findley 3
BONNER, David Mahlon 4
BONNER, Emmett Peyton 6
BONNER, Eugene (MacDonald) 8
BONNER, Francis A. 3
BONNER, Geraldine 1
BONNER, Griffith 1
BONNER, Herbert Covington 4
BONNER, Hugh 1
BONNER, James Bernard 1
BONNER, John H
BONNER, John Joseph 2
BONNER, John Woodrow 5
BONNER, Joseph Claybaugh 4
BONNER, Mary Graham 6
BONNER, Paul Hyde 5
BONNER, Robert 1
BONNER, Robert Johnson 2
BONNER, Sherwood H
BONNER, Tom Wilkerson 4
BONNER, Walter D. 3
BONNER, Willard Hallam 7
BONNET, Frank Henry 4
BONNET, Henri 8
BONNETT, Leland Brewer 8
BONNEVILLE, Benjamin Louis Eulalie de H
BONNEY, Charles Carroll 1
BONNEY, Herbert Staats, Jr. 8
BONNEY, Sherman Grant 2
BONNEY, Wilbert Lowth 5
BONNEY, William H. H
BONNHEIM, Albert 1
BONNIE, Robert Palen 8
BONNIER, Ake 7
BONNY, John Bruce 7
BONNYMAN, Alexander 3
BONOMO, Alfred J. 3
BONOMO, Joe 7
BONRIGHT, Daniel 1
BONSAL, Stephen 3
BONSALL, Amos 1
BONSALL, Edward Horne 1
BONSALL, Elizabeth Hubbard 1
BONSALL, William Hartshorn 1
BONSER, Frederick Gordon 1
BONSER, Thomas A. 1
BONTE, George Willard 2
BONTECOU, Daniel 1
BONTECOU, Reed Brockway 1
BONTEMPS, Arna Wendell 5
BONVIN, Ludwig 1
BONWILL, William Gibson Arlington 1
BONYNGE, Robert William 1
BONZANO, John 1
BOOCOCK, Cornelius Brett 6
BOOCOCK, Philip Milledoler Brett 6
BOODELL, Thomas J. 5
BOODIN, John Elof 3
BOODY, Azariah H
BOODY, Bertha M. 3
BOODY, David Augustus 1
BOOG, Carle Michel 5
BOOGHER, Elbert Willis Griffin 6
BOOHER, Charles F. 1
BOOHER, Edward E. 10
BOOK, Dorothy L. 3
BOOK, George Milton 1
BOOK, William Frederick 1
BOOK, William Henry 2
BOOKBINDER, Jack 10
BOOKER, George Edward 3
BOOKER, George William H
BOOKER, Henry George 10
BOOKER, Joseph Albert 1
BOOKER, Russell Everett 7
BOOKER, William David 1
BOOKHOLT, William John 9
BOOKMAN, Clarence Monroe 7
BOOKSTAVER, Henry Weller 1
BOOKWALTER, Alfred Guitner 1
BOOKWALTER, Charles A. 4
BOOKWALTER, John W. 4
BOOKWALTER, Lewis 4
BOOLE, Ella Alexander 3
BOOMER, George Ellsworth 4
BOOMER, George O(wens) 8
BOOMER, Lucius Messenger 2
BOOMER, Robert Deforest 4
BOOMHOUR, J. Gregory 4
BOOMSLITER, Paul Colgan 10
BOON, Henry George 3
BOON, Ratliff H
BOONE, Andrew Rechmond H
BOONE, Arthur Upshaw 5
BOONE, Charles Theodore 1
BOONE, Daniel H
BOONE, Daniel 2
BOONE, Henry Burnham 5
BOONE, James Buford, Sr. 8
BOONE, Joel Thompson 6
BOONE, John Lee 1
BOONE, Joseph Prince 4
BOONE, Richard Allen 7
BOONE, Richard Gause 1
BOONE, Thomas H
BOONE, William Cooke 9
BOONE, William Judson 1
BOORAEM, John Van Vorst 1
BOORAEM, Robert Elmer 1
BOORD, Cecil Ernest 5
BOORKMAN, Charles John 8
BOORMAN, James H
BOOS, Ludwig Charles 3
BOOS, William Frederick 6
BOOSKTAVER, Alexander 10
BOOTE, Ward E. 4
BOOTH, Agnes 1
BOOTH, Ballington 1
BOOTH, Ballington 2
BOOTH, Bradford Allen 5
BOOTH, Charles Arthur 5
BOOTH, Charles Brandon 6
BOOTH, Charles Gordon 2
BOOTH, Christopher Henry Hudson 1
BOOTH, Clarence Moore 5
BOOTH, Edwin Prince 5
BOOTH, Edwin Thomas H
BOOTH, Evangeline Cory 3
BOOTH, Ewing E. 2
BOOTH, Fenton Whitlock 2
BOOTH, Frank Walworth 4
BOOTH, Franklin 5
BOOTH, George E. 7
BOOTH, George Francis 3
BOOTH, George Gough 2
BOOTH, Harold Simmons 3
BOOTH, Henry Kendall 2
BOOTH, Henry Matthias 1
BOOTH, Henry Scripps 10
BOOTH, Hiram Evans 1
BOOTH, Isaac Walter 5
BOOTH, James Curtis H
BOOTH, John Edward 8
BOOTH, John Henry 4
BOOTH, John Wilkes H
BOOTH, Junius Brutus H
BOOTH, Louis Wineera 6
BOOTH, Mary Ann Allard 1
BOOTH, Mary Louise H
BOOTH, Maud Ballington 2
BOOTH, Newell Snow 5
BOOTH, Newton H
BOOTH, Ralph Douglas 4
BOOTH, Ralph Harman 1
BOOTH, Robert Asbury 2
BOOTH, Robert Edmond 10
BOOTH, Robert Highman 5
BOOTH, Robert Plues 4
BOOTH, Robert Russell 1
BOOTH, Samuel Babcock 1
BOOTH, Thomas Butler 1
BOOTH, Walter H
BOOTH, Warren S. 9
BOOTH, Wilbur Franklin 4
BOOTH, William Edward 6
BOOTH, William Stone 1
BOOTH, William Wallace 9
BOOTH, Willis H. 3
BOOTHBY, Everett J. 6
BOOTHBY, Ralph Edwin 8
BOOTHBY, Walter Meredith 3
BOOTHE, Gardner Lloyd 5
BOOTHE, Viva Belle 10
BOOTHROYD, Samuel Latimer 5
BOOTH TUCKER, Emma Moss 1
BOOTH TUCKER, Frederick St George de Lautour 3
BOOTON, John Roller 7
BOOTT, Kirk H
BOOZ, Donald Robert 8
BOOZ, Edwin George 3
BOPE, Henry P. 4
BOPP, Karl Richard 7
BORAAS, Julius 3
BORAH, Leo Arthur 4
BORAH, Wayne G. 4
BORAH, William Edgar 1
BORBER, William 3
BORCH, Gaston 5
BORCHARD, Edwin 3
BORCHARDT, Albert Hugo 4
BORCHARDT, Selma Munter 5
BORCHERS, Charles Martin 5
BORCHERS, Robert Harley 9
BORDALLO, Ricardo Jerome 10
BORDEAUX, Le Pecq Andree 6
BORDEN, Bertram Harold 4
BORDEN, C. Seymour 3
BORDEN, Daniel Carey 4
BORDEN, Daniel Leray 5
BORDEN, Gail H
BORDEN, George Pennington 1
BORDEN, Henry 10
BORDEN, Howard Seymour 5
BORDEN, John 4
BORDEN, Lizzie Andrew H
BORDEN, Lizzie Andrew 4
BORDEN, Mary (Mary Borden Spears) 5
BORDEN, Mary (Mary Borden Spears) 7
BORDEN, Nathaniel Briggs H
BORDEN, Richard H
BORDEN, Sam Wheatley 6
BORDEN, Simeon H
BORDEN, Spencer 3
BORDEN, William A. 8
BORDEN, William Alanson 1
BORDEN, William Cline 2
BORDEN, William Silvers 5
BORDENAVE, Enrique 8
BORDERS, Joseph H. 4
BORDERS, M. W. 4
BORDET, Jules 4
BORDEWICH, Henry 1
BORDLEY, John Beale* H
BORDNER, Harvey Albert 5
BORDWELL, Walter 1
BORE, Jean Etienne H
BOREING, Vincent 1
BORELLA, Victor 6
BOREMAN, Arthur Ingram H
BOREMAN, Herbert Stephenson 8
BOREMAN, Jacob Smith 4
BORER, Harold Peter 7
BORG, Alvin Andrew 6
BORG, Carl Oscar 2
BORG, Donald Gowen 6
BORG, George William 3
BORGER, Edward M. 3
BORGER, Hugh Donald 5
BORGERHOFF, Elbert Benton Op'teynde 5
BORGERHOFF, Joseph Leopold 4
BORGES, Jorgo Luis 9
BORGESE, G. A. 3
BORGESS, Casper Henry H
BORGLUM, Gutzon 1
BORGLUM, James Lincoln de la Mothe 9
BORGLUM, Solon Hannibal 1
BORGMAN, Albert Stephens 3
BORGMANN, Dmitri Alfred 9
BORGMEYER, Ernest 6
BORGQUIST, Erasmus Swan 6
BORGSTROM, Georg Arne 10
BORHEGYI, Stephan Francis De 5
BORI, Lucrezia 4
BORIE, Adolph Edward H
BORIE, Adolphe 1
BORIE, Charles Louis 2
BORING, Edwin Garrigues 5
BORING, Omen Konn 7
BORING, William Alciphron 1
BORKLAND, Ernest Waldermar, Jr. 9
BORLAND, Andrew Allen 6
BORLAND, Barbara Dodge (Hal Borland) 10
BORLAND, Charles, Jr. H
BORLAND, Chauncey Blair 5
BORLAND, Hal (Harold Glen) 7
BORLAND, Mand Rives 7
BORLAND, Solon H
BORLAND, Wilfred P. 4
BORLAND, William Patterson 1
BORMAN, Abraham 6
BORN, Max 5
BORN, Max 7
BORNE, John E. 1
BORNE, Mortimer 9
BORNEMANN, Alfred Henry 10
BORNEMEIER, Walter Carl 8

BORNHOLDT, Wallace John 6
BORNSTEIN, Sol 4
BORNSTEIN, Yetta Libby Frieden (Mrs. Harry Bornstein) 5
BOROVSKY, Maxwell Philip 4
BOROWSKI, Felix 3
BORSODI, Ralph 8
BORST, Guernsey J. 3
BORST, Henry Vroman 1
BORST, Peter I. H
BORTHWICK, Harry Alfred 6
BORTHWICK, John David H
BORTIN, David 8
BORTMAN, Mark 4
BORTON, Elon G. 6
BORTREE, Leo Williams 7
BORTZ, Edward LeRoy 10
BORTZ, Edward Leroy 5
BORWELL, Robert Crane 9
BORZAGE, Frank 4
BOSCH, Herbert Michael 4
BOSCHEN, Frederick Wegener 2
BOSE, Emil 1
BOSETTI, Joseph 3
BOSHER, Kate Lee Langley 1
BOSHER, Lewis Crenshaw 1
BOSHES, Benjamin 8
BOSKOWITZ, George W. 1
BOSKOWSKY, Willy 10
BOSLAUGH, Paul E. 4
BOSLEY, Frederick Andrew 2
BOSLEY, Harold Augustus 6
BOSLEY, William Bradford 5
BOSMAN, David 1
BOSS, Andrew 2
BOSS, Benjamin 5
BOSS, Charles Frederick, Jr. 8
BOSS, Edwin August 9
BOSS, Henry M. 5
BOSS, John Linscom, Jr. H
BOSS, Lewis 1
BOSS, Louis Joseph 6
BOSS, Wallace LaMont 8
BOSS, William 4
BOSSANGE, Edward Raymond 2
BOSSARD, Guido 1
BOSSARD, James Herbert Siward 3
BOSSART, Karel Jan 6
BOSSHART, John Henry 7
BOSSIDY, John Collins 1
BOSSIER, Pierre Evariste John Baptiste H
BOSSOM, Alfred Charles 4
BOST, Ralph Walton 3
BOST, Thomas Creasy 7
BOSTOCK, Edward Crary 4
BOSTON, Charles Anderson 1
BOSTON, Joseph H. 3
BOSTON, L. Napoleon 1
BOSTON, Orlan William 9
BOSTROM, Wollmar Filip 3
BOSTWICK, Arthur Elmore 2
BOSTWICK, Charles Dibble 1
BOSTWICK, Charles Francis 1
BOSTWICK, Frank Matteson 2
BOSTWICK, Harry Rice 1
BOSTWICK, Lucius Allyn 1
BOSTWICK, Roy Grier 2
BOSUSTOW, Stephen 8
BOSWELL, Charles Martin 1
BOSWELL, Clay Carlton 6
BOSWELL, Elmer E. 9
BOSWELL, Grover Cleveland 1
BOSWELL, Guy Thomas 9
BOSWELL, Ira Matthews 2
BOSWELL, Lorin Albert 1
BOSWELL, Peyton, Jr. 3
BOSWORTH, Arthur Harding 3
BOSWORTH, Benjamin Miller 1
BOSWORTH, Charles Wilder 5
BOSWORTH, Edward Increase 1
BOSWORTH, Edwin Carpenter 5
BOSWORTH, Francke Huntington, Jr. 2
BOSWORTH, Frederic Manning 8
BOSWORTH, Hobart Van Zandt 2

BOSWORTH, Robert Graham 3
BOSWORTH, Welles 4
BOTEIN, Bernard 6
BOTELER, Alexander Robinson H
BOTETOURT, 1st baron H
BOTHE, Walther 3
BOTHNE, Gisle 1
BOTKE, Jesse Arms 6
BOTKIN, Alexander Campbell 1
BOTKIN, Benjamin Albert 6
BOTKIN, Harold Mitchell 5
BOTKIN, Henry 8
BOTKIN, Jeremiah Dunham 1
BOTSFORD, Elmer Francis 1
BOTSFORD, Florence Hudson 5
BOTSFORD, George Willis 1
BOTSFORD, Stephen Blakeslee 4
BOTT, Herbert Joseph 4
BOTTA, Anne Lynch H
BOTTA, Rico 8
BOTTA, Vincenzo H
BOTTHOF, Walter E. 5
BOTTINEAU, Pierre H
BOTTOLFSEN, C. A. 4
BOTTOM, Raymond Blanton 3
BOTTOME, Harry Howard 4
BOTTOME, Margaret 1
BOTTOME, Phyllis 4
BOTTOMLEY, Allen W. T. 1
BOTTOMLEY, John Taylor 1
BOTTOMLEY, William Lawrence 3
BOTTOMLY, Raymond Victor, Sr. 4
BOTTORFF, Charles Russell 8
BOTTORFF, Orville Oris 7
BOTTORFF, Robert Ingram 7
BOTTS, Charles Tyler H
BOTTS, Clarence Milton 4
BOTTS, Hugh Pearce 4
BOTTS, John Minor H
BOUATTOURA, Tewfik 5
BOUCHE, Louis 10
BOUCHER, Anthony (Pseudonym For William Anthony Parker) 5
BOUCHER, Carl Opdycke 6
BOUCHER, Chauncey Samuel 3
BOUCHER, Chauncey Watson 1
BOUCHER, Horace Edward H
BOUCHER, Horace Edward 4
BOUCHER, Israel Edmond 7
BOUCHER, Jerome H. P. 7
BOUCHER, Jonathan 8
BOUCHER, Paul Robert 8
BOUCHER, Roger 7
BOUCICAULT, Dion H
BOUCICAULT, Dion G. H
BOUCICAULT, Ruth Baldwin Holt (Mrs. Aubrey Boucicault) 5
BOUCK, Francis Eugene 1
BOUCK, Joseph H
BOUCK, William C. H
BOUCKE, Ewald Augustus 5
BOUCKE, O. Fred 1
BOUDE, Thomas H
BOUDEMAN, Dallas 4
BOUDEMAN, Robert Meier 6
BOUDET, Dominic W. H
BOUDET, Nicholas Vincent H
BOUDIN, Leonard B. 10
BOUDIN, Louis B. 3
BOUDINOT, Elias* H
BOUDINOT, Elias Cornelius 1
BOUDINOT, Jane J. 5
BOUDINOT, Truman Everett 2
BOUDLEAUX, Bryant 9
BOUDREAU, Frank George 7
BOUDREAU, James Clayton 1
BOUFFARD, Paul Henri 10
BOUGHNER, Leroy John 6
BOUGHTON, Alice Caroline (Mrs. Arthur B. Schaffner) 1
BOUGHTON, George Henry H

BOUGHTON, George Henry 1
BOUGHTON, Martha Arnold 1
BOUGHTON, Walter Leroy 9
BOUGHTON, Willis 2
BOUGUEREAU, Elizabeth Gardner 4
BOUHUYS, Arend 7
BOUILLON, Lincoln 5
BOULANGER, Nadia Juliette 7
BOULDIN, James Wood H
BOULDIN, Thomas Tyler H
BOULDIN, Virgil 5
BOULIGNY, Dominique 1
BOULIGNY, John Edward H
BOULT, Sir Adrian Cedric 8
BOULT, William Thomas 2
BOULTER, Howard Thornton 3
BOULTER, Thornton 3
BOULTON, Laura Craytor 7
BOULTON, Payne Augustin 4
BOULWARE, Lemuel Ricketts 10
BOUMEDIENNE, Houari 7
BOUNETHEAU, Henry Brintell H
BOUQUET, Henry H
BOUQUILLON, Thomas 1
BOURAS, Harry 10
BOURDEAUX, Robert Montgomery 7
BOURDIER, Lillian Blanche (Mrs. James Bourdier) 6
BOURGADE, Peter 1
BOURGEOIS, Lionel John, Sr. 4
BOURGET, Maurice 7
BOURGMONT, sieur de H
BOURGOINE, Joseph John 3
BOURKE, John Gregory H
BOURKE-WHITE, Margaret 5
BOURLAND, Albert Pike 1
BOURLAND, Benjamin Parsons 2
BOURLAND, Caroline Brown 5
BOURN, Augustus Osborn 1
BOURNE, Benjamin H
BOURNE, Edward Gaylord 1
BOURNE, Edward Walter 7
BOURNE, Frank Augustus 1
BOURNE, Frank Card 8
BOURNE, Frederick Gilbert 1
BOURNE, Geoffrey Howard 9
BOURNE, George H
BOURNE, Granville Harman 8
BOURNE, Henry Eldridge 2
BOURNE, Jonathan, Jr. 1
BOURNE, Nehemiah H
BOURNE, Philip Walley 10
BOURNE, Randolph 1
BOURNE, Shearjashub H
BOURQUIN, George M. 3
BOURSKAYA, Ina 3
BOUSCAREN, Louis Frederic Gustave 1
BOUSCAREN, Louis H. G. 4
BOUSFIELD, Edward Lloyd 7
BOUSFIELD, Midian Othello 2
BOUSH, Clifford Joseph 1
BOUSLOG, John Samuel 8
BOUTELL, Clarence Burley (Clip) 9
BOUTELL, Henry Sherman 1
BOUTELL, Hugh G. 8
BOUTELLE, Charles Addison 1
BOUTELLE, De Witt Clinton H
BOUTELLE, Richard Schley 4
BOUTON, Archibald Lewis 2
BOUTON, Burrett Beebe 4
BOUTON, Charles Leonard 1
BOUTON, Edward Henry 4
BOUTON, Emily St. John 5
BOUTON, John Bell 1
BOUTON, Nathaniel 4
BOUTON, Rosa 4
BOUTON, S(tephen) Miles 5
BOUTWELL, George Sewall 1
BOUTWELL, John M(ason) 5
BOUTWELL, Paul Winslow 5
BOUTWELL, William Rowe 4

BOUVE, Clement Lincoln 2
BOUVE, Pauline Carrington 1
BOUVET, Jeanne Marie 4
BOUVET, Marie Marguerite 1
BOUVIER, John H
BOUVIER, John Andre, Jr. 10
BOUVIER, Maurice 5
BOUWSMA, Oets Kolk 7
BOVAIRD, Davis D(outhett) 10
BOVARD, Charles Lincoln 1
BOVARD, Freeman Daily 1
BOVARD, George Finley 1
BOVARD, James Moorhead 8
BOVARD, John Freeman 6
BOVARD, Warren Bradley 1
BOVARD, William Sherman 1
BOVE, Charles Frederick 8
BOVEE, Christian Nestell 1
BOVEE, J. Wesley 1
BOVEE, Matthias Jacob H
BOVENIZER, George Wallace 4
BOVET, Daniel 10
BOVEY, Charles Cranton 3
BOVEY, Edmund Charles 10
BOVIE, William T. 3
BOVING, Adam Giede 5
BOVING, Charle B(rasee) 5
BOW, Frank Townsend 5
BOW, Jonathan Gaines 4
BOW, Kathy O'Connor 9
BOW, Warren E. 2
BOWATER, Sir Eric Vansittart 4
BOWDEN, A. Bruce 8
BOWDEN, Aberdeen Orlando 2
BOWDEN, Burnham 9
BOWDEN, Garfield Arthur 2
BOWDEN, George Edwin 4
BOWDEN, John H
BOWDEN, Laurens Reeve 2
BOWDEN, Lemuel Jackson H
BOWDEN, Nicholls White 8
BOWDEN, Ray B. 8
BOWDEN, Robert John 7
BOWDEN, Witt 7
BOWDERN, Thomas Stephen 9
BOWDEY, George H(all) 7
BOWDITCH, Charles Pickering 1
BOWDITCH, Ebenezer Francis 10
BOWDITCH, Henry Ingersoll H
BOWDITCH, Henry Pickering 1
BOWDITCH, Nathaniel H
BOWDITCH, Richard Lyon 3
BOWDITCH, Vincent Yardley 1
BOWDLE, Stanley Eyre 4
BOWDOIN, George E. 3
BOWDOIN, George Sullivan 1
BOWDOIN, James* H
BOWDOIN, William Goodrich 4
BOWDON, Franklin Welsh H
BOWE, Augustine J. 4
BOWEN, Abel H
BOWEN, Albert E. 3
BOWEN, Arthur John 5
BOWEN, Asa Bosworth 3
BOWEN, Benjamin Lester 1
BOWEN, Catherine Drinker 6
BOWEN, Cawthon Asbury 7
BOWEN, Charles Corbin 9
BOWEN, Charles Francis 8
BOWEN, Charles Parnell, Jr. 8
BOWEN, Christopher H
BOWEN, Clarence Winthrop 1
BOWEN, Clayton Raymond 1
BOWEN, Daniel H
BOWEN, Earl 1
BOWEN, Edwin Winfield 3
BOWEN, Elizabeth Dorothea Cole 8
BOWEN, Ezra 2
BOWEN, Francis H
BOWEN, Frank Sayles, Jr. 7
BOWEN, George H
BOWEN, Harold Gardiner 4
BOWEN, Harold Linwood 7
BOWEN, Harry 4
BOWEN, Henry Chandler H
BOWEN, Herbert Wolcott 1
BOWEN, Howard Rothmann 10
BOWEN, Ira Sprague 5
BOWEN, Ivan 3

BOWEN, J(ean) Donald 10
BOWEN, John C. 3
BOWEN, John Campbell 5
BOWEN, John Clyde 7
BOWEN, John Henry H
BOWEN, John Templeton 1
BOWEN, John Wesley Edward 4
BOWEN, Joseph Henry 4
BOWEN, Kenneth Blount 8
BOWEN, Lem Warner 1
BOWEN, Louise de Koven 3
BOWEN, Marcellus 1
BOWEN, Norman Levi 3
BOWEN, Ray Preston 7
BOWEN, Raymond Brower 8
BOWEN, Rees Tate H
BOWEN, Reuben Dean 1
BOWEN, Richard LeBaron 6
BOWEN, Thomas M. 1
BOWEN, Wilbur Pardon 1
BOWEN, William 1
BOWEN, William Abraham 1
BOWEN, William Miller 1
BOWER, Adelaide Howell 4
BOWER, Alexander 3
BOWER, Bertha Muzzy 1
BOWER, George Hoyle 4
BOWER, Gustavus Miller H
BOWER, Joseph Augustus 4
BOWER, Lucy Scott 1
BOWER, Raymond G. 4
BOWERMAN, George Franklin 4
BOWERMAN, Guy Emerson 2
BOWERS, Albert 10
BOWERS, Alphonzo Benjamin 1
BOWERS, Claude G. 3
BOWERS, Eaton Jackson 4
BOWERS, Edgar 4
BOWERS, Edison Louis 5
BOWERS, Edward Augustus 4
BOWERS, Elizabeth Crocker H
BOWERS, Elsworth 6
BOWERS, Fredson Thayer 10
BOWERS, George Meade 1
BOWERS, Harold C. 8
BOWERS, Henry Francis 1
BOWERS, Henry Smith 1
BOWERS, Herbert Edmund 1
BOWERS, John Hugh 1
BOWERS, John Myer H
BOWERS, Lamont Montgomery 1
BOWERS, Larkin Bruce 1
BOWERS, Lloyd Wheaton 1
BOWERS, Raymond 7
BOWERS, Renzo Dee 7
BOWERS, Robert Graves 5
BOWERS, Robert Hood 1
BOWERS, Theodore Shelton H
BOWERS, Thomas Wilson 2
BOWERS, Walter Abraham 6
BOWERS, William Gray 2
BOWERSOCK, Donald Curtis 3
BOWERSOCK, Justin Dewitt 1
BOWES, Major Edward 2
BOWES, Frank B. 1
BOWES, Joseph 4
BOWES, Theodore F. 4
BOWES, Theodore F. 5
BOWIE, Clifford Pinckney 3
BOWIE, Edward Hall 2
BOWIE, James H
BOWIE, Oden H
BOWIE, Richard Johns H
BOWIE, Robert H
BOWIE, Sydney Johnston 1
BOWIE, Thomas Fielder H
BOWIE, Walter H
BOWIE, Walter Russell 5
BOWIE, William 1
BOWKER, Horace 3
BOWKER, Richard Rogers 1
BOWLBY, Harry Laity 4
BOWLBY, Joel Morgan 3
BOWLBY, Samuel Fisher 7
BOWLEN, John James 4
BOWLER, Edmond Wesley 4
BOWLER, Henry Reginald 8
BOWLER, James B. 3
BOWLER, John Pollard 4
BOWLER, John William 1
BOWLER, Metcalf H
BOWLER, William Howard 4
BOWLES, Aubrey Russell, Jr. 8
BOWLES, Charles 3
BOWLES, Charles Phillips 4
BOWLES, Chester 9

BOWLES, Edward Lindley	10	BOWSER, Edward Albert	1	
BOWLES, Ella Shannon	7	BOWSFIELD, Colvin C.	1	
(Mrs. Archie Raimond Bowles)		BOWYER, John Marshall	1	
BOWLES, Elliott A.	3	BOWYER, John Wilson	5	

BOWLES, Edward Lindley 10
BOWLES, Ella Shannon 7
(Mrs. Archie Raimond Bowles)
BOWLES, Elliott A. 3
BOWLES, Francis Tiffany 1
BOWLES, Frank Hamilton 6
BOWLES, Gilbert 5
BOWLES, Heloise 7
BOWLES, Henry Leland 4
BOWLES, John Davis 7
BOWLES, Lester Llewellyn 7
BOWLES, Luanna Jane 9
BOWLES, Oliver 3
BOWLES, Phillip Ernest 1
BOWLES, Pinckney Downie 1
BOWLES, Samuel H
BOWLES, Samuel 1
BOWLES, Samuel, II H
BOWLES, Sherman Hoar 3
BOWLES, William H
Augustus
BOWLEY, Albert Jesse 2
BOWLEY, Arthur Lyon 5
BOWLIN, Jamer Butler H
BOWLIN, William Ray 6
BOWLING, Edgar Simeon 3
BOWLING, Jack Frank 7
BOWLING, William 2
Bismarck
BOWMAN, A. Smith 7
BOWMAN, Albert Chase 1
BOWMAN, Alpheus Henry 1
BOWMAN, Charles Calvin 1
BOWMAN, Charles Grimes 1
BOWMAN, Charles Henry 5
BOWMAN, Clellan Asbury 1
BOWMAN, Crete Dillon 5
(Mrs. John W. Boman)
BOWMAN, Earl Cassatt 7
BOWMAN, Edward J. 1
BOWMAN, Edward Morris 1
BOWMAN, Frank
Llewellyn
BOWMAN, Frank Otto 3
BOWMAN, George Arvene 7
BOWMAN, George Ernest 1
BOWMAN, George Lynn 3
BOWMAN, George T. 3
BOWMAN, Grover Chester 7
BOWMAN, Gus Karl 6
BOWMAN, Harold 4
Leonard
BOWMAN, Harold Martin 2
BOWMAN, Harry Lake 4
BOWMAN, Harry Samuel 6
BOWMAN, Howard 5
H(iestand)
BOWMAN, Isaiah* 2
BOWMAN, James H
BOWMAN, James Clinton 5
BOWMAN, James Cloyd 4
BOWMAN, James Schenck 8
BOWMAN, John Brady 1
BOWMAN, John Bryan H
BOWMAN, John Calvin 1
BOWMAN, John Fife 6
BOWMAN, John Gabbert 4
BOWMAN, John McEntee 1
BOWMAN, John R. 4
BOWMAN, John Wick 10
BOWMAN, Joseph Merrell, 5
Jr.
BOWMAN, Karl Murdock 5
BOWMAN, Le Roy 8
Edward
BOWMAN, Lloyd David 4
BOWMAN, Milo Jesse 3
BOWMAN, Paul Haynes 8
BOWMAN, Raymond 1
Albert
BOWMAN, Robert A. 1
BOWMAN, Robert Jay 3
BOWMAN, Roland Claude 1
BOWMAN, Rufus David 3
BOWMAN, Samuel Henry, 1
Jr.
BOWMAN, Thomas*
BOWMAN, Wesley 10
Ellsworth
BOWMAN, Willard Eugene 8
BOWMAN, William C. 7
BOWMER, Angus 7
Livingston
BOWN, Ralph 5
BOWNE, Borden Parker 1
BOWNE, John H
BOWNE, Obadiah H
BOWNE, Samuel Smith H
BOWNE, William Rainear 6
BOWNOCKER, John 1
Adams
BOWRA, Cecil Maurice 5
BOWRING, Eva 1
BOWRON, Arthur John, Jr. 4
BOWRON, Fletcher 5
BOWRON, James 1

BOWSER, Edward Albert 1
BOWSFIELD, Colvin C. 1
BOWYER, John Marshall 1
BOWYER, John Wilson 5
BOX, John Calvin 5
BOXER, Harold Horton 6
BOXLEY, Calvin Peyton 5
BOYAJIAN, Setrak Krikor 5
BOYCE, Carroll Wilson 9
BOYCE, Charles Meredith 5
BOYCE, Charles Prevost 3
BOYCE, Earnest 9
BOYCE, Frank Gordon 9
BOYCE, Fred Grayson, Jr. 4
BOYCE, Heyward E. 3
BOYCE, James 1
BOYCE, James Petigru H
BOYCE, John H
BOYCE, John Shaw 8
BOYCE, Sir Leslie 3
BOYCE, William A. 6
BOYCE, William D. 2
BOYCE, William George 10
BOYCE, William H. 1
BOYCE, William Waters 5
BOYD, A. Hunter 1
BOYD, Adam H
BOYD, Alan Wilson 9
BOYD, Albert 7
BOYD, Alexander H
BOYD, Alfred 5
BOYD, Augusto Samuel 3
BOYD, Belle H
BOYD, Bernard Henry 6
BOYD, Bernard Henry 7
BOYD, Charles Alexander 8
BOYD, Charles Arthur 6
BOYD, Charles Morgan 3
BOYD, Charles Parker 8
BOYD, Chester Eugene 9
BOYD, Colin MacNicol 4
BOYD, D. Knickerbacker 2
BOYD, Darrell Sully 5
BOYD, David French H
BOYD, David Milton 10
BOYD, David Preston 10
BOYD, David Ross 1
BOYD, Donald Lewis 4
BOYD, Drexell Allen 9
BOYD, Edwin Forrest 5
BOYD, Elise Stephens 10
BOYD, Ellen Wright 4
BOYD, Ernest 2
BOYD, Everett Marion 3
BOYD, Fiske 6
BOYD, Francis R(aymond) 4
BOYD, George Adams 5
BOYD, George H. 4
BOYD, George Washington 1
BOYD, Harold Buhalts 8
BOYD, Harry Burton 5
BOYD, Harry Hutcheson 5
BOYD, Henry W., Jr. 3
BOYD, Homer Leon 7
BOYD, Hugh Newell 7
BOYD, James 1
BOYD, James 2
BOYD, James 9
BOYD, James Churchill 5
BOYD, James E. 1
BOYD, James Edmund 1
BOYD, James Ellsworth 3
BOYD, James Harrington 2
BOYD, James Oscar 2
BOYD, James P. 1
BOYD, John Frank 3
BOYD, John Hardgrove 1
BOYD, John Huggins H
BOYD, John Parker H
BOYD, Joseph Milton 4
BOYD, Julian Parks 7
BOYD, Linn John 8
BOYD, Louise Arner 5
BOYD, Lynn H
BOYD, Mark Frederick 9
BOYD, Mary Brown 5
Sumner (Mrs. Mark Boyd)
BOYD, Myron Fenton 7
BOYD, P. M. 8
BOYD, Paul Prentice 5
BOYD, Ralph E. 5
BOYD, Ralph Gates 5
BOYD, Richard Moody 8
BOYD, Robert 5
BOYD, Robert Osborne 7
BOYD, Robert Stewart 8
BOYD, Sempronius H
Hamilton
BOYD, Thomas 1
BOYD, Thomas Alexander H
BOYD, Thomas Alvin 8
BOYD, Thomas Duckett 4
BOYD, Thomas Henry 8
BOYD, Thomas M. 1
BOYD, Thomas Munford 9
BOYD, William 2

BOYD, William (Hopalong 5
Cassidy)
BOYD, William Clouser 8
BOYD, William H. 2
BOYD, William Kenneth 1
BOYD, William Robert 3
BOYD, William Robert 4
BOYD, William Rufus, Jr. 3
BOYD, William Sprott 3
BOYD, William Waddell 2
BOYD, William Young 1
BOYD-CARPENTER 6
BOYDEN, Alan Arthur 10
BOYDEN, Albert 3
BOYDEN, Albert Augustus 1
BOYDEN, Albert Gardner 1
BOYDEN, Arthur Clarke 1
BOYDEN, Edward Allen 7
BOYDEN, Elbridge H
BOYDEN, Frank Learoyd 5
BOYDEN, Guy Lee 3
BOYDEN, Nathaniel H
BOYDEN, Roger Talbot 8
BOYDEN, Roland William 1
BOYDEN, Seth 1
BOYDEN, Uriah Atherton 3
BOYDEN, Willard Newhall 10
BOYDEN, William Cowper 1
BOYDEN, William Cowper 4
BOYE, Martin H. 1
BOYER, Benjamin Franklin 8
BOYER, Benjamin Markley 3
BOYER, C. Valentine 6
BOYER, Charles 7
BOYER, Charles Clinton 3
BOYER, Emanuel Roth 1
BOYER, Francis 4
BOYER, J. U. 8
BOYER, John F. 1
BOYER, Joseph 1
BOYER, Lewis Leonard 3
BOYER, Pearce Fowler 3
BOYER, Willis Boothe 6
BOYES, Kurwin Robert 3
BOYESEN, Hjalmar Hjorth H
BOYKIN, Frank William 5
BOYKIN, Garland Lester 4
BOYKIN, James Chambers 1
BOYKIN, Lester Ernest 7
BOYKIN, Richard Manning 6
BOYKIN, Samuel Francis 3
BOYLAN, Grace Duffie 1
BOYLAN, J. Richard 9
BOYLAN, John J. 1
BOYLAN, John J. 3
BOYLAN, John Patrick 4
BOYLAN, Murtha Joseph 3
BOYLAN, Richard Joseph 4
BOYLAN, Robert P. 4
BOYLAN, William A. 1
BOYLE, Albert Clarence 6
BOYLE, Andrew Joseph 6
BOYLE, Ashby Douglas 4
BOYLE, Charles A. 3
BOYLE, Charles Edmund H
BOYLE, Emmet D. 1
BOYLE, Ferdinand Thomas
Lee
BOYLE, Ferdinand Thomas 4
Lee
BOYLE, Francis Dennis 7
BOYLE, Harold Vincent
(Hal)
BOYLE, Hugh Charles 3
BOYLE, James 1
BOYLE, James Ernest 1
BOYLE, Jeremiah Tilford H
BOYLE, John H
BOYLE, John J. 1
BOYLE, John S. 1
BOYLE, Leo Martin 5
BOYLE, Murat 4
BOYLE, Robert William 9
BOYLE, Thomas H
BOYLE, Thomas Newton 4
BOYLE, Virginia Frazer 1
BOYLE, W. H. Wray 4
BOYLE, Walter Fabien 3
BOYLE, Wilbur Fisk 5
BOYLE, William Anthony 8
BOYLE, William Marshall, 4
Jr.
BOYLEN, Matthew James 5
BOYLES, Aubrey 6
BOYLES, Emerson 6
R(ichard)
BOYLES, George Robert 8
BOYLON, Francis Oscar 5
BOYLSTON, Zabdiel H
BOYNE, Edwin McKinley 10
BOYNTON, Arthur Jerome 1
BOYNTON, Ben Lynn 6
BOYNTON, Charles Albert 5
BOYNTON, Charles 1
Augustus

BOYNTON, Charles H
Brandon
BOYNTON, Charles Homer 5
BOYNTON, Charles 1
Hudson
BOYNTON, Charles 1
Theodore
BOYNTON, Edward H
Carlisle
BOYNTON, Edward Young 4
BOYNTON, Frank David 1
BOYNTON, George Mills 1
BOYNTON, George Rufus 2
BOYNTON, Henry Van 1
Ness
BOYNTON, Henry Walcott 5
BOYNTON, James 1
Stoddard
BOYNTON, Melbourne 2
Parker
BOYNTON, Morrison 3
Russell
BOYNTON, Nathan Smith 1
BOYNTON, Nehemiah 1
BOYNTON, Paul L. 3
BOYNTON, Percy Holmes 2
BOYNTON, Ray Scepter 7
BOYNTON, Richard 4
Wilson
BOYNTON, Thomas 2
Jefferson
BOYNTON, William Pingry 3
BOYSEN JENSEN, Peter 4
BOYSEN, Neil 3
BOZA, Hector 8
BOZELL, Harold Veatch 5
BOZELL, Leo B. 2
BOZEMAN, John M. H
BOZMAN, John Leeds H
BOZORTH, Richard Milton 8
BRAASCH, William 6
Frederick
BRABSON, Reese Bowen H
BRACE, Charles Loring H
BRACE, Charles Loring 1
BRACE, Clayton H. 9
BRACE, Dewitt Bristol 1
BRACE, Donald Clifford 3
BRACE, Gerald Warner 7
BRACE, John Pierce H
BRACE, Jonathan H
BRACE, Lloyd D. 5
BRACE, Richard Munthe 7
BRACE, Theodore 4
BRACELAND, Francis 9
James
BRACELEN, Charles 2
Michael
BRACH, Edwin J. 4
BRACH, Emil J. 2
BRACH, Frank Vincent 5
BRACKEN, Aaron Francis 8
BRACKEN, Archie Kay 7
BRACKEN, Clio Hirton 5
BRACKEN, Edward P. 1
BRACKEN, Henry Martyn 1
BRACKEN, James Lucas 8
BRACKEN, John 5
BRACKEN, John Robert 9
BRACKEN, Stanley 4
BRACKENRIDGE, 4
Alexander
BRACKENRIDGE, Henry H
Marie
BRACKENRIDGE, Hugh H
Henry
BRACKENRIDGE, 1
William Algernon
BRACKENRIDGE, H
William D.
BRACKER, Milton 4
BRACKETT, Anna 1
Callender
BRACKETT, Byron Briggs 1
BRACKETT, Charles 1
Albert
BRACKETT, Cyrus Fogg 1
BRACKETT, Dexter 1
BRACKETT, Elliott Gray 2
BRACKETT, E(lmer) 5
E(ugene)
BRACKETT, Frank 5
Parkhurst
BRACKETT, Gustavus 1
Benson
BRACKETT, Haven 5
Darling
BRACKETT, J. Raymond 1
BRACKETT, Jeffery 4
Richardson
BRACKETT, John Quincy 1
Adams
BRACKETT, Ledru Joshua 5
BRACKETT, Richard 4
Newman
BRACKETT, Walter M. 1

BRACKETT, William 2
Oliver
BRACKMAN, Robert 7
BRACQ, Jean Charlemagne 1
BRACY, Carl Cluster 7
BRADBURN, James 7
Rupert
BRADBURY, Albert 1
Williams
BRADBURY, George H
BRADBURY, Howard 4
William
BRADBURY, James Ware H
BRADBURY, Joseph P. 1
BRADBURY, Robert Hart 2
BRADBURY, Samuel 2
BRADBURY, Theophilus H
BRADBURY, William 4
BRADBURY, William H
Batchelder
BRADBURY, William 1
Frothingham
BRADBURY, Woodman 1
BRADDOCK, Daniel 7
McCoy
BRADDOCK, Edward H
BRADDOCK, Robert 5
Louis
BRADDY, Haldeen 8
BRADEN, Arthur 6
BRADEN, Charles Samuel 9
BRADEN, George Walter 6
BRADEN, J. Noble 3
BRADEN, James Andrew 3
BRADEN, John 1
BRADEN, Samuel Ray 8
BRADEN, Spruille 7
BRADEN, Waldo W. 10
BRADEN, William 2
BRADFIELD, George 6
Herndon
BRADFIELD, Richard 10
BRADFIELD, William D. 4
BRADFORD, Royal Bird 1
BRADFORD, Alexander H
Warfield
BRADFORD, Allen H
BRADFORD, Allen H
Alexander
BRADFORD, Amory 1
Howe
BRADFORD, Andrew H
BRADFORD, Augustus H
Williamson
BRADFORD, Charles 1
BRADFORD, Edward 1
Anthony
BRADFORD, Edward H
Green
BRADFORD, Edward 1
Green
BRADFORD, Edward 1
Hickling
BRADFORD, Ernest Smith 4
BRADFORD, Eugene 8
Francis
BRADFORD, Fancis Scott 4
BRADFORD, Gamaliel* 1
BRADFORD, George 2
Henry
BRADFORD, Gerard 3
BRADFORD, Harry E. 6
BRADFORD, James 8
Cowdon
BRADFORD, John H
BRADFORD, John Ewing 1
BRADFORD, Joseph H
BRADFORD, Joseph 3
Nelson
BRADFORD, Karl 5
Slaughter
BRADFORD, Karl 8
Slaughter
BRADFORD, Lindsay 3
BRADFORD, Ralph 9
BRADFORD, R(ichard) 10
Knox
BRADFORD, Roark 2
BRADFORD, Robert D. 5
BRADFORD, Robert Fiske 5
BRADFORD, Saxton 4
BRADFORD, Taul H
BRADFORD, Thomas 1
BRADFORD, Thomas
Lindsley
BRADFORD, William* H
BRADFORD, William 4
Brooks
BRADFORD, William 8
Leslie
BRADFORD, William 9
Parkinson
BRADFUTE, Oscar Edwin 1
BRADISH, Alvah H
BRADISH, Luther H
BRADLEE, Arthur Tisdale 5
BRADLEE, Caleb Davis H

BRASLAU, Sophie 1
BRASOL, Boris 4
BRASSERT, Herman 5
Alexander
BRASTED, Alva Jennings 5
BRASTED, Fred 1
BRASTED, Robert Crocker 9
BRASTOW, Lewis 1
Orsmond
BRASWELL, James Craig 4
BRATBY, John R.A. 10
BRATENAHL, George 1
Carl Fitch
BRATNEY, John Frederick 6
BRATT, Elmer Clark 9
BRATT, Floyd Clarence 9
BRATTAIN, Walter Houser 9
BRATTLE, Thomas H
BRATTLE, William H
BRATTON, John H
BRATTON, John Walter 4
BRATTON, Leslie Emmett 3
BRATTON, Robert H
Franklin
BRATTON, Sam Gilbert 4
BRATTON, Samuel Tilden 1
BRATTON, Theodore 2
Dubose
BRATTON, Walter Andrew 2
BRAU, Charles Frederick 6
BRAUCHER, Frank 5
BRAUCHER, Howard S. 2
BRAUCHER, Robert 8
BRAUDE, Abraham Isaac 9
BRAUDE, Jacob Morton 10
BRAUDE, Jacob Morton 5
BRAUER, Alfred 4
BRAUER, Alfred T(heodor) 9
BRAUER, George R. 1
BRAUER, John Charles 5
BRAUER, Richard 7
Dagobert
BRAUFF, Herbert D. 3
BRAULICK, Edward 8
Joseph
BRAUN, Armin Charles 9
John
BRAUN, Arthur E. 6
BRAUN, Carl Franklin 3
BRAUN, Gaius A. 7
BRAUN, John F. 1
BRAUN, Maurice 2
BRAUN, Robert 3
BRAUN, Theodore William 8
BRAUN, Werner 5
BRAUNE, Gustave Maurice 1
BRAUNER, Julius 6
Frederick
BRAUNER, Olaf Martinius 2
BRAUNSCHWEIGER, 6
Walter J.
BRAUSE, Edward 4
BRAUTIGAN, Richard 8
BRAWLEY, Benjamin 1
BRAWLEY, Frank 4
BRAWLEY, Paul Holm 9
BRAWLEY, William H. 3
BRAWNER, James Paul 8
BRAXTON, A. Caperton 2
BRAXTON, Carter H
BRAXTON, Elliott Muse H
BRAY, Charles I. 3
BRAY, Everett Newton 7
BRAY, Frank Chapin 2
BRAY, Harold Bryan 5
BRAY, Henry Truro 1
BRAY, John Leighton 3
BRAY, John P. 1
BRAY, John Randolph 4
BRAY, Patrick Albert 4
BRAY, Richard Marvin 3
BRAY, Robert Stuart 6
BRAY, Stephen 6
BRAY, Thomas H
BRAY, Thomas Joseph 1
BRAY, William Crowell 4
BRAY, William L. 3
BRAYMAN, Harold 9
BRAYMAN, Mason H
BRAYMER, Daniel Harvey 1
BRAYTON, Aaron Martin 2
BRAYTON, Alembert 1
Winthrop
BRAYTON, Charles Ray 1
BRAYTON, Dean Fleming 7
BRAYTON, Israel 5
BRAYTON, William Daniel H
BRAZEAU, Theodore 5
Walter
BRAZELTON, Frank 10
Alexander
BRAZELTON, William 1
Buchanan
BRAZER, Clarence Wilson 3
BRAZER, John H
BRAZIER, Carl Edward 7

BRAZIER, Miss Marion 1
Howard
BRCIN, John David 8
BREADON, Sam 2
BREADY, Charles J. 5
BREAN, Herbert 6
BREARLEY, Harry Chase 6
BREARLEY, William 1
Henry
BREASTED, James Henry 1
BREATHED, John William 9
BREATHITT, James 4
BREAUX, Joseph A. 1
BREAZEALE, Hopkins 7
Payne
BREAZEALE, Phanor 3
BREBNER, John Bartlet 3
BRECHER, Edward Moritz 10
BRECHER, Gerhard Adolf 9
BRECHER, Samuel 8
BRECHT, Arnold 7
BRECHT, Bertoit Eugen 4
Friedrich
BRECHT, Bertolt Eugen H
Friedrich
BRECHT, Robert Paul 5
BRECK, Daniel H
BRECK, Edward 1
BRECK, George William 1
BRECK, Henry C(ushman) 10
BRECK, James Lloyd H
BRECK, John H. 4
BRECK, Joseph 1
BRECK, Samuel 8
BRECK, Samuel 1
BRECKENRIDGE, Clifton 1
Rodes
BRECKENRIDGE, Hugh 1
Henry
BRECKENRIDGE, James H
BRECKENRIDGE, James 8
Douglas
BRECKENRIDGE, James 4
Miller
BRECKENRIDGE, John H
BRECKENRIDGE, John 4
C.
BRECKENRIDGE, Lester 3
Paige
BRECKENRIDGE, Ralph 1
W.
BRECKINRIDGE, Aida de 4
Acosta
BRECKINRIDGE, Desha 1
BRECKINRIDGE, Henry 4
BRECKINRIDGE, James 2
Carson
BRECKINRIDGE, James H
Douglas
BRECKINRIDGE, H
Jefferson
BRECKINRIDGE, John 7
Bayne
BRECKINRIDGE, John 1
Cabell
BRECKINRIDGE, Joseph 1
Cabell
BRECKINRIDGE, 1
Madeline McDowell
BRECKINRIDGE, Mary 4
BRECKINRIDGE, 2
Sophonisba Preston
BRECKINRIDGE, William 1
Campbell Preston
BRECKINRIDGE, William 1
Lewis
BRECKNER, Elmer 8
Leander
BRECKONS, Robert W. 1
BREDELL, Harold Holmes 8
BREDELL, Harold Holmes 9
BREDER, Charles Marcus, 8
Jr.
BREDIN, R. Sloan 1
BREDVOLD, Louis 8
Ignatius
BREECE, Charles Albert 7
BREECH, Ernest Robert 7
BREED, Charles Blaney 3
BREED, Charles Henry 3
BREED, David Riddle 1
BREED, Dwight Payson 1
BREED, Ebenezer H
BREED, Frances 9
BREED, James McVickar 7
BREED, Mary Bidwell 6
BREED, R. E. 1
BREED, Robert Stanley 3
BREED, William Constable 3
BREED, William Constable, 6
Jr.
BREEDEN, Edward 10
Lebbaeus, Jr.
BREEDEN, Harvey Oscar 4
BREEDING, Earle Griffith 8

BREEDING, Glenn 5
Edward
BREEDIS, Charles 7
BREEN, Aloysius Andrew 3
BREEN, John William 8
BREEN, Joseph Ignatius 4
BREEN, Joseph Sylvester 9
BREEN, Leonard Zachary 7
BREEN, Patrick H
BREEN, Robert A. 3
BREEN, William John, Jr. 5
BREEN, William P. 1
BREENE, Frank Thomas 1
BREER, Carl 7
BREES, Herbert Jay 5
BREESE, Burtis Burr 1
BREESE, Edmund 1
BREESE, Randolph Kidder H
BREESE, Sidney H
BREESE, William Llywelyn 3
BREESKIN, Adelyn 9
Dohme
BREG, W. Roy 3
BREGY, Francis Amedee 1
BREGY, Katherine Marie 4
Cornelia
BREHAN, Marquis de H
BREHM, Cloide Everett 5
BREHM, John S. 2
BREHM, Marie Caroline 1
BREIDENBAUGH, H
Edward Swoyer
BREIDENTHAL, John W. 1
BREIDENTHAL, John W. 5
BREIDENTHAL, Maurice 4
L.
BREIDENTHAL, Maurice 5
Lauren, Jr.
BREIDENTHAL, Willard 4
J.
BREIL, Joseph Carl 1
BREISACH, Paul 3
BREISACHER, Leo M. D. 4
BREIT, Gregory 8
BREITEL, Charles D. 10
BREITENBACH, Edward 6
Victor
BREITENSTEIN, Jean Sala 9
BREITHAUPT, Louis 4
Orville
BREITHUT, Frederick 3
Ernest
BREITUNG, Charles 3
Adelbert
BREITUNG, Edward H
BREITUNG, Edward 1
Nicklas
BREITWIESER, Joseph 3
Valentine
BREL, Jacques 7
BRELSFORD, Charles 4
Henry
BRELSFORD, Millard 2
BREM, Thomas Hamilton 10
BREM, Walter Vernon 1
BREMER, Adolf 3
BREMER, Edith Terry 8
BREMER, George A. 3
BREMER, John Lewis 3
BREMER, Otto 3
BREMNER, George 1
Hampton
BREMNER, John Burton 9
BREMNER, William 1
Hepburn
BRENAN, Ralph Betts 7
BRENDEL, Otto Johannes 6
BRENDLER, Charles 4
BRENDLINGER, Margaret 5
Robinson
BRENEMAN, Abram 1
Adam
BRENEMAN, Gerald 10
Myers
BRENEMAN, William 10
Raymond
BRENGLE, Francis H
BRENGLE, Henry Gaw 2
BRENIZER, Addison 7
Gorgas
BRENKE, William Charles 5
BRENN, Harry Allen 4
BRENNAN, Alfred 4
Laurens
BRENNAN, Andrew James 3
BRENNAN, Donald 7
George
BRENNAN, Edward James 3
BRENNAN, Edward 7
Thomas
BRENNAN, Edward 8
Thomas
BRENNAN, Frederick 4
Hazlitt
BRENNAN, George E. 1
BRENNAN, George M. 3
BRENNAN, Gerald Leo 4

BRENNAN, James Dowd 1
BRENNAN, John Aloysius, 7
Jr.
BRENNAN, John Francis 3
BRENNAN, Joseph 9
Cantwell
BRENNAN, Martin Adlai 1
BRENNAN, Martin S. 1
BRENNAN, Robert 6
BRENNAN, Thomas 4
Francis
BRENNAN, Vincent M. 1
BRENNAN, Walter 8
Andrew
BRENNAN, William Henry 4
BRENNECKE, Cornelius 3
G.
BRENNECKE, Ernest 5
BRENNECKE, Henry 4
BRENNEMANN, Joseph 2
BRENNER, Clarence Dietz 7
BRENNER, Daniel 7
BRENNER, Edward John 10
BRENNER, James Emmet 8
BRENNER, John L. 4
BRENNER, Mortimer 5
BRENNER, Otto 5
BRENNER, Robert 9
BRENNER, Ruth Marie 6
(Mrs. Chester T.
Mellinger)
BRENNER, Victor David 1
BRENON, Herbert 3
BRENT, Charles Henry 1
BRENT, Frank Pierce 4
BRENT, Henry Johnson H
BRENT, Joseph Lancaster 1
BRENT, Margaret H
BRENT, Meade Stith 6
BRENT, Richard H
BRENT, Theodore 3
BRENT, William Leigh H
BRENTANO, Arthur 2
BRENTANO, Lorenz H
BRENTANO, Lowell 3
BRENTANO, Theodore 1
BRENTON, Charles 1
Richmond
BRENTON, Clyde Edward 1
BRENTON, Cranston 1
BRENTON, Samuel 4
BRENTON, Woodward 5
Harold
BRERETON, Lewis Hyde 4
BRERETON, William 8
Denny, Jr.
BRES, Edward Sedley 5
BRESCHARD H
BRESCIANI-TURRONI, 7
Constantino
BRESKY, Otto 6
BRESLER, Emanuel 8
Harold
BRESLICH, Arthur Louis 1
BRESLICH, Ernst Rudolph 5
BRESLIN, George 10
M(ontgomery)
BRESLIN, James H. 1
BRESNAHAN, Thomas F. 5
BRESNAHAN, William H. 4
BRESS, David Gerald 7
BRESSLER, Raymond G., 4
Jr.
BRESSLER, Raymond 2
George
BRESTELL, Rudolph Emile 5
BRETALL, Robert Walter 7
BRETHERTON, Sidney 1
Elliott
BRETHORST, Alice 6
Beatrice
BRETON, Andre 4
BRETON, Ruth 4
BRETSCHGER, Max E. 1
BRETT, Agnes Baldwin 3
BRETT, Alden Chase 5
BRETT, Axel 3
BRETT, Dorothy 7
BRETT, George Howard 1
BRETT, George Platt 1
BRETT, Homer 5
BRETT, Lloyd M. 1
BRETT, Philip Milledoler 4
BRETT, Rutherford 3
BRETT, Sereno E. 3
BRETT, William Howard 1
BRETT, William Pierce 4
BRETZ, J Harlem 7
BRETZ, Julian Pleasant 3
BREUER, Bessie 6
BREUER, Carl A. 6
BREUER, Henry Joseph 4
BREUER, Louis Henry 4
BREUER, Marcel Lajos 8
BREUNINGER, Lewis 1
Talmage
BREVARD, Joseph H

BREVOORT, James Carson H
BREVOORT, James 1
Renwick
BREW, John Otis 9
BREWBAKER, Cassie Leta 6
(Mrs. William Styne
Brewbaker)
BREWBAKER, Charles 5
Warren
BREWER, Abraham T. 1
BREWER, Arthur Allen 6
BREWER, Basil 6
BREWER, Basil 7
BREWER, Carlos 7
BREWER, Charles H
BREWER, Charles Edward 3
BREWER, Charles S. 1
BREWER, Clara Tagg 1
BREWER, D. Chauncey 1
BREWER, David Josiah 1
BREWER, Earl Leroy 2
BREWER, Edward Eugene 10
BREWER, Edward Vere 6
BREWER, Francis Beattie 1
BREWER, F(rancis) Thrall 6
BREWER, Franklin Nourse 1
BREWER, George 1
BREWER, George Emerson 1
BREWER, George St P. H
BREWER, Hugh Graham 4
BREWER, James Arthur 3
BREWER, John Bruce 4
BREWER, John Hyatt 1
BREWER, John Marks 3
BREWER, John Withrow 8
BREWER, John Withrow 9
BREWER, Leigh Richmond 1
BREWER, Leo 4
BREWER, Luther Albertus 1
BREWER, Mark Spencer 1
BREWER, Nicholas 2
Richard
BREWER, Norman, Jr. 7
(Craig)
BREWER, Oby T. 5
BREWER, Richard 7
Frederick, Jr.
BREWER, Robert Du Bois 2
BREWER, Robert Paine 1
BREWER, Thomas Mayo H
BREWER, Wayne Burdette 7
BREWER, William A., Jr. 4
BREWER, William Henry 1
BREWER, Willis 5
BREWER, Wilma Denell 9
BREWSTER, Albert 3
Vincent
BREWSTER, Andre Walker 2
BREWSTER, Benjamin 1
BREWSTER, Benjamin H
Harris
BREWSTER, Benjamin 4
Harris
BREWSTER, Benjamin 1
Harris, Jr.
BREWSTER, Chauncey 1
Bunce
BREWSTER, David Lukens 2
BREWSTER, David P. H
BREWSTER, Edward 1
Lester
BREWSTER, Edwin 3
Tenney
BREWSTER, Elisha Hume 2
BREWSTER, Ellis Wethrell 9
BREWSTER, Ethel 2
Hampson
BREWSTER, Eugene 1
Valentine
BREWSTER, Few 3
BREWSTER, Frances 4
Stanton
BREWSTER, Frederick H
Carroll
BREWSTER, George 2
Thomas
BREWSTER, George 1
Washington Wales
BREWSTER, Henry Colvin 1
BREWSTER, James H
BREWSTER, James 7
BREWSTER, James Henry 1
BREWSTER, James Henry, 7
Jr.
BREWSTER, Kingman 7
BREWSTER, Kingman 9
BREWSTER, Leo 7
BREWSTER, Osmyn H
BREWSTER, Owen 4
BREWSTER, Ray Quincy 9
BREWSTER, Raymond 5
BREWSTER, Reginald R. 2
BREWSTER, Sardius 1
Mason
BREWSTER, Stanley 8
Farrar

BREWSTER, Walter Stanton — 3
BREWSTER, William — H
BREWSTER, William — 1
BREWSTER, William Nesbitt — 1
BREWSTER, William Roe — 4
BREWSTER, William Tenney — 4
BREWTON, Charles Sidney — 7
BREWTON, John E. — 10
BREYER, Frank Gottlob — 9
BREYER, Henry W., Jr. — 5
BREYFOGEL, Sylvanus Charles — 1
BREZING, Herman — 2
BRIAN, Donald — 2
BRICE, Ashbel Green — 10
BRICE, Calvin Stewart — H
BRICE, Charles Rufus — 4
BRICE, Fanny — 3
BRICE, John A. — 2
BRICHER, Alfred Thompson — 3
BRICK, Abraham Lincoln — 1
BRICK, Alyea M. — 4
BRICK, Nicholas William — 1
BRICKELL, Henry Herschel — 3
BRICKELL, Robert Coman — 1
BRICKELL, William David — 4
BRICKEN, Carl Ernest — 5
BRICKER, Edwin Dyson — 4
BRICKER, Garland Armor — 6
BRICKER, George W(alter) — 1
BRICKER, John William — 9
BRICKER, Luther Otterbein — 2
BRICKER, Mead L. — 4
BRICKLEY, Bartholomew A. — 3
BRICKMAN, William Wolfgang — 9
BRICKNER, Barnett Robert — 3
BRICKNER, Walter M. — 1
BRICKWEDDE, Ferdinand Graft — 10
BRIDAHAM, Lester — 7
BRIDE, William Witthaft — 1
BRIDENBAUGH, Carl — 10
BRIDGE, Ann (Lady O'Malley) — 6
BRIDGE, Gerard — 5
BRIDGE, James Howard — 1
BRIDGE, Norman — 1
BRIDGER, Grover Leon — 7
BRIDGER, James — H
BRIDGERS, Robert Rufus — 4
BRIDGES, Calvin Blackman — 1
BRIDGES, Charles Higbee — 2
BRIDGES, Charles Scott — 4
BRIDGES, Edson Lowell — 4
BRIDGES, Fidelia — 1
BRIDGES, George Washington — H
BRIDGES, Harry (Alfred Renton Bridges) — 10
BRIDGES, Hedley Francis Gregory — 2
BRIDGES, Horace James — 3
BRIDGES, James Robertson — 1
BRIDGES, Jesse B. — 1
BRIDGES, Milton Arlanden — 1
BRIDGES, Robert* — H
BRIDGES, Robert — 1
BRIDGES, Ronald — 4
BRIDGES, S. Russell — 4
BRIDGES, Samuel Augustus — H
BRIDGES, Styles — 4
BRIDGES, Thomas Henry — 4
BRIDGES, Thomas Reed — 7
BRIDGES, William Andrew — 8
BRIDGES, Willson Orton — 4
BRIDGHAM, Frank Nelson — 8
BRIDGMAN, Charles Simmons — 7
BRIDGMAN, Elijah Coleman — H
BRIDGMAN, Frederic Arthur — 1
BRIDGMAN, George Henry — 4
BRIDGMAN, George Herbert — 4
BRIDGMAN, Grenville Temple — 3
BRIDGMAN, Helen Bartlett (Mrs. Herbert L. Bridgman) — 5
BRIDGMAN, Herbert Lawrence — 1

BRIDGMAN, Howard Allen — 1
BRIDGMAN, Laura Dewey — H
BRIDGMAN, Lewis Jesse — 1
BRIDGMAN, Olga Louise — 6
BRIDGMAN, Percy Williams — 4
BRIDGMAN, Raymond Landon — 1
BRIDGWATER, William — 4
BRIDPORT, Hugh — H
BRIEFS, Goetz A(ntony) — 6
BRIEN, William Given — 4
BRIER, Ernest — 3
BRIER, John Crowe — 8
BRIER, Royce — 6
BRIER, Warren Judson — 5
BRIERLEY, Wilfrid Gordon — 1
BRIERLY, James Leslie — 6
BRIERTON, John — H
BRIESEN, Arthur von — 1
BRIETZKE, June Oneson (Mrs. Charles H. Brietzke) — 7
BRIGANCE, W. Norwood — 3
BRIGGLE, Charles Guy — 7
BRIGGS, Arthur Hyslop — 1
BRIGGS, Asa Gilbert — 2
BRIGGS, Austin Eugene — 6
BRIGGS, Charles — H
BRIGGS, Charles Augustus — 1
BRIGGS, Charles Frederick — H
BRIGGS, Charles S. — 4
BRIGGS, Charles William — 7
BRIGGS, Charles William — 8
BRIGGS, Clare A. — 1
BRIGGS, Clay Stone — 1
BRIGGS, Corona Hibbard — 4
BRIGGS, Edward Cornelius — 1
BRIGGS, Elizabeth Darling — 3
BRIGGS, Ellis O. — 6
BRIGGS, Ellis Ormsbee — 7
BRIGGS, Ernest — 8
BRIGGS, Eugene Stephen — 8
BRIGGS, Frank Alonzo — 3
BRIGGS, Frank Obadiah — 1
BRIGGS, Frank P. — 10
BRIGGS, Frank Richmond — 5
BRIGGS, Frederic Melancthon — 3
BRIGGS, George — H
BRIGGS, George Ernest — 6
BRIGGS, George Isaac — 2
BRIGGS, George Nathaniel — 3
BRIGGS, George Nixon — H
BRIGGS, George Waverley — 3
BRIGGS, George Weston — 4
BRIGGS, Gordon Dobson — 3
BRIGGS, Henry Birdice — 1
BRIGGS, Henry Harrison — 4
BRIGGS, Herbert Whittaker — 10
BRIGGS, J. Emmons — 1
BRIGGS, John De Quedville — 4
BRIGGS, John Ely — 3
BRIGGS, John Gurney, Jr. — 10
BRIGGS, Joseph Hamilton — 1
BRIGGS, L. Vernon — 1
BRIGGS, Leon Eugene — 4
BRIGGS, Lloyd Arnold — 8
BRIGGS, Lucia Russell — 3
BRIGGS, Lyman James — 4
BRIGGS, Marvin James — 9
BRIGGS, Mitchell Pirie — 9
BRIGGS, Raymond Westcott — 1
BRIGGS, Robert Aldrich — 4
BRIGGS, Robert William — 4
BRIGGS, Roger Thomas — 9
BRIGGS, Roswell Emmons — 4
BRIGGS, Le Baron Russell — 1
BRIGGS, Stephen Albro — 4
BRIGGS, Stephen Foster — 7
BRIGGS, Thomas Henry — 5
BRIGGS, Thomas Roland — 3
BRIGGS, Walter Owen — 3
BRIGGS, Walter Owen, Jr. — 4
BRIGGS, Warren Richard — 2
BRIGGS, William Harlowe — 1
BRIGHAM, Albert Perry — 1
BRIGHAM, Amariah — H
BRIGHAM, Arthur Amber — 1
BRIGHAM, Carl Campbell — 2
BRIGHAM, Clarence Saunders — 4
BRIGHAM, Claude Ernest — 6
BRIGHAM, Dwight Stillman — 4
BRIGHAM, Elbert Sidney — 4
BRIGHAM, Elijah — H
BRIGHAM, Francis Gorham — 7
BRIGHAM, Gertrude Richardson (Viktor Flambeau) — 5

BRIGHAM, Harold Frederick — 5
BRIGHAM, Henry Randolph — 4
BRIGHAM, Johnson — 1
BRIGHAM, Joseph Henry — 1
BRIGHAM, L. Ward — 4
BRIGHAM, Lewis Alexander — H
BRIGHAM, Mary Ann — H
BRIGHAM, Nat Maynard — 1
BRIGHAM, Richard Douglas — 3
BRIGHAM, Sarah Jeannette — 1
BRIGHAM, William Erastus — 1
BRIGHAM, William Tufts — 1
BRIGHT, Alfred Harris — 1
BRIGHT, David Edward — 4
BRIGHT, Edward — H
BRIGHT, James Wilson — 1
BRIGHT, Jesse David — H
BRIGHT, John — 2
BRIGHT, J(oseph) S(hirley) — 6
BRIGHT, Louis Victor — 1
BRIGHT, Marshal Huntington — 1
BRIGHT EYES — H
BRIGHTLY, Frank Frederick — 4
BRIGHTLY, Frederick Charles — H
BRIGHTMAN, Alvin Collins — 1
BRIGHTMAN, Edgar Sheffield — 3
BRIGHTMAN, Harold Wan — 8
BRIGHTMAN, Harold Warren — 9
BRIGHTMAN, Horace Irving — 1
BRIGHTMAN, Horace Irving — 2
BRIGMAN, Bennett Mattingly — 1
BRILES, Charles Walter — 5
BRILL, Abraham Arden — 2
BRILL, George MacKenzie — 5
BRILL, George Reiter — 5
BRILL, Harvey Clayton — 5
BRILL, Hascal Russel — 3
BRILL, Henry — 10
BRILL, Joseph Eugene — 6
BRILL, Leonardo — 7
BRILL, Nathan Edwin — 1
BRILL, William Hascal — 1
BRILLANT, Jules Andre — 8
BRILLHART, David H. — 1
BRILLOUIN, Leon N(icholas) — 8
BRIM, Kenneth Milliken — 6
BRIM, Orville Gilbert — 7
BRIMHALL, George Henry — 1
BRIMSON, Alice W. S. — 7
BRIMSON, William George — 1
BRIN, Fanny Fligelman — 7
BRINCKE, William Draper — H
BRINCKERHOFF, Arthur Freeman — 4
BRINCKERHOFF, Charles M. — 9
BRINCKERHOFF, Henry Morton — 2
BRIND, Charles Albert — 1
BRIND, Sir Patrick — 4
BRINDLEY, George Valter — 1
BRINDLEY, John Edwin — 6
BRINDLEY, Paul — 3
BRINEY, Paul Wallace — 6
BRINEY, Russell — 4
BRINGHURST, John Henry — 7
BRINGHURST, Robert Porter — 1
BRINIG, Myron — 10
BRININSTOOL, Earl Alonzo — 3
BRINK, Carol Ryrie — 6
BRINK, Charles Bernard — 6
BRINK, Francis G. — 4
BRINK, Gilbert Nicholas — 1
BRINK, Joseph Andrew, Jr. — 7
BRINK, Raymond Woodard — 8
BRINK, Rodney Liddell — 6
BRINK, Royal Alexander — 9
BRINKEN, Carl Ernest — 5
BRINKER, Howard Rasmus — 4
BRINKER, John Henry — 10
BRINKER, Josiah Henry — 1
BRINKERHOFF, Henry Roelif — H
BRINKERHOFF, Jacob — H

BRINKERHOFF, Robert Moore — 3
BRINKERHOFF, Roeliff — 1
BRINKLEY, Homer Lee — 8
BRINKLEY, Sterling G(ardner) — 7
BRINKMAN, Oscar H. — 5
BRINKMAN, William Augustus — 1
BRINKWORTH, John J. — 8
BRINLEY, Charles A. — 4
BRINLEY, Charles Edward — 6
BRINLEY, Daniel Putnam — 1
BRINLEY, Katherine Gordon Sanger — 4
BRINSER, Harry Lerch — 2
BRINSMADE, John Chaplin — 1
BRINSMADE, Robert Bruce — 1
BRINSMADE, William Barrett — 4
BRINSON, Samuel Mitchell — 1
BRINSTAD, Charles William — 2
BRINTON, Anna — 8
BRINTON, Christian — 1
BRINTON, Daniel Garrison — 1
BRINTON, Howard Haines — 7
BRINTON, Howard T. — 4
BRINTON, Jasper Yeates — 6
BRINTON, John Hill — 1
BRINTON, Paul Henry Mallett-prevost — 4
BRINTON, Willard Cope — 1
BRISBANE, Albert — H
BRISBANE, Arthur — 1
BRISBIN, Clarence Franklin — 5
BRISBIN, James S. — H
BRISBIN, John — H
BRISBINE, Annie M'Iver — 4
BRISCO, Norris Arthur — 2
BRISCOE, Birdsall Parmenas — 5
BRISCOE, Herman T. — 4
BRISCOE, John Parran — 1
BRISCOE, Robert Pearce — 5
BRISCOE, William Alexander — 1
BRISKIN, Samuel Jacob — 5
BRISSENDEN, Paul Frederick — 6
BRISSON, Frederick — 8
BRIST, George Louis — 6
BRISTED, Charles Astor — H
BRISTED, John — H
BRISTER, Charles James — 3
BRISTER, John Willard — 1
BRISTOL, Arthur E. — 3
BRISTOL, Arthur Leroy — 2
BRISTOL, Augusta Cooper — 1
BRISTOL, Benjamin Hiel — 9
BRISTOL, Charles Lawrence — 1
BRISTOL, Edward Newell — 2
BRISTOL, Frank Milton — 1
BRISTOL, George Prentiss — 4
BRISTOL, Henry P. — 3
BRISTOL, John Bunyan — 1
BRISTOL, John Isaac Devoe — 1
BRISTOL, Lee Hastings — 4
BRISTOL, Lee Hastings, Jr. — 7
BRISTOL, Leverett Dale — 3
BRISTOL, Mark Lambert — 1
BRISTOL, Rexford Allyn — 9
BRISTOL, Theodore Louis — 7
BRISTOL, William Henry — 1
BRISTOW, Algernon Thomas — 1
BRISTOW, Benjamin Helm — H
BRISTOW, Francis Marion — H
BRISTOW, George F. — 4
BRISTOW, George Frederick — H
BRISTOW, George Washington — 4
BRISTOW, Gwen — 7
BRISTOW, Joseph Little — 2
BRISTOW, Louis Judson — 5
BRITAIN, Kenneth Edward — 7
BRITAN, Halbert Hains — 3
BRITSCH, Carl Conrad — 7
BRITT, James J. — 1
BRITT, Laurence Vincent — 7
BRITT, Steuart Henderson — 7
BRITT, Walter Stratton — 1
BRITTAIN, Carlo Bonaparte — 1
BRITTAIN, Charles Mercer — 1
BRITTAIN, Frank Smith — 1
BRITTAIN, Joseph I. — 1
BRITTAIN, Marion Luther — 3
BRITTAN, Belle — H
BRITTEN, Clarence R. — 7

BRITTEN, Edward Benjamin — 7
BRITTEN, Edwin Franklin, Jr. — 4
BRITTEN, Flora Phelps Harley — 4
BRITTEN, Fred Albert — 2
BRITTEN, Fred Ernest — 4
BRITTIN, Lewis Hotchkiss — 5
BRITTINGHAM, Thomas Evans — 1
BRITTINGHAM, Thomas Evans, Jr. — 4
BRITTON, Alexander Thompson — 1
BRITTON, Edgar C. — 4
BRITTON, Edward Elms — 1
BRITTON, Elizabeth Gertrude — 1
BRITTON, Frank Hamilton — 1
BRITTON, Frederick O. — 1
BRITTON, John Alexander — 1
BRITTON, Mason — 6
BRITTON, Nathaniel Lord — 1
BRITTON, Ralph Burton — 7
BRITTON, William Everett — 9
BRITTON, Wilton Everett — 1
BRIXEY, John Clark — 10
BRIZGYS, Vincentas — 10
BRIZZOLARA, Ralph Dominic — 5
BROADBENT, James Thomas — 5
BROADBENT, Sam Robert — 7
BROADDUS, Bower — 3
BROADFOOT, Grover L. — 4
BROADHEAD, Garland Carr — 1
BROADHEAD, James Overton — H
BROADHURST, Edward T. — 3
BROADHURST, Edwin Borden — 4
BROADHURST, George H. — 3
BROADHURST, Jean — 3
BROADLEY, Sir Herbert — 9
BROADUS, John Albert — H
BROADWATER, J. A. B. — 3
BROADY, K(nute) O(scar) — 10
BROCE, Thomas Edward — 9
BROCH, Hermann Joseph — 4
BROCK, Charles Robert — 1
BROCK, Charles William Penn — 1
BROCK, Clifford Edward — 3
BROCK, Elmer Leslie — 3
BROCK, George William — 2
BROCK, Henry Irving — 5
BROCK, James Ellison — 4
BROCK, Larry — 5
BROCK, Loring Stewart — 5
BROCK, Pope Furman — 8
BROCK, Robert Alonzo — 1
BROCK, Sidney Gorham — 4
BROCK, Thomas Sleeper — 5
BROCK, Ventress Nolan — 4
BROCK, William Elihu — 7
BROCK, William Emerson — 3
BROCK, William Emerson, Jr. — 1
BROCK, William Megrue — 7
BROCKEL, Harry Charles — 8
BROCKELBANK, William John — 10
BROCKENBROUGH, William Henry — H
BROCKETT, Linus Pierpont — H
BROCKEY, Harold — 10
BROCKHAGEN, Carl Homer — 1
BROCKIE, Arthur H. — 2
BROCKLESBY, John — H
BROCKMAN, Earl Hugo — 9
BROCKMAN, Fletcher Sims — 1
BROCKSON, Franklin — 4
BROCKWAY, Albert Leverett — 1
BROCKWAY, Fred John — 1
BROCKWAY, George A. — 5
BROCKWAY, Hobart Mortimer — 1
BROCKWAY, Howard — 3
BROCKWAY, John Hall — H
BROCKWAY, Lawrence Olin — 7
BROCKWAY, Louis Newell — 7
BROCKWAY, Zebulon Reed — 1
BROD, Ruth Hagy — 7
BRODA, Frederick Martin — 7
BRODBECK, Andrew R. — 1
BRODBECK, May — 8

BRODE, Charles Geiger 4
BRODE, Howard Stidham 4
BRODE, Robert B. 9
BRODE, Wallace Reed 6
BRODEK, Charles Adrian 2
BRODERICK, Bonaventure 2
  Finnbarr
BRODERICK, Carroll 5
  Joseph
BRODERICK, Case 3
BRODERICK, David H
  Colbreth
BRODERICK, Henry 6
BRODERICK, Henry 7
BRODERICK, James 8
  Joseph
BRODERICK, John P. 6
BRODERICK, John T. 4
BRODERICK, Joseph A. 3
BRODERICK, William 4
  Stephen
BRODERS, Albert 4
  Compton
BRODESSER, Roman 4
  Adolph
BRODEUR, Arthur 8
  Gilchrist
BRODEUR, Clarence 1
  Arthur
BRODHEAD, Daniel H
BRODHEAD, George 5
  Livingston
BRODHEAD, George 4
  Milton
BRODHEAD, J. Davis 1
BRODHEAD, John Curtis H
BRODHEAD, John H
  Romeyn
BRODHEAD, Jonn H
BRODHEAD, Richard H
BRODIE, Alexander 1
  Oswald
BRODIE, Allan Gibson 6
BRODIE, Andrew Melrose 4
BRODIE, Arnold Frank 8
BRODIE, Bernard 4
BRODIE, Bernard Beryl 9
BRODIE, Donald M. 6
BRODIE, Edward Everett 4
BRODIE, Fawn McKay 7
BRODIE, Gandy 6
BRODIE, Gandy 7
BRODIE, Israel B. 4
BRODIE, Renton 8
  Kirkwood
BRODNEY, Spencer 6
BRODRICK, Lynn 3
  Rosegrant
BRODRICK, Richard 1
  Godfrey
BRODSHAUG, Melvin 9
BRODSKY, Nathan 6
BRODSKY, Nathan 7
BRODSKY, Paul 5
BRODY, Clark Louis 4
BRODY, Daniel Anthony 6
BRODY, Joseph Isaac 4
BRODY, Samuel 3
BRODY, Samuel Mandell 10
BROEDEL, Max 1
BROEDEL, Max 2
BROEK, Jan Otto Marius 6
BROEK, John Yonker 5
BROEKMAN, David 3
  Hendrines
BROEMAN, Charles 8
  William
BROENING, William 3
  Frederick
BROERSMA, Sybrand 9
BROGAN, Albert Perley 8
BROGAN, Sir Denis 6
  William
BROGAN, Francis Albert 5
BROGAN, James M. 5
BROGAN, Thomas J. 4
BROGDEN, Wilfred John 6
BROGDEN, Wilfred John 7
BROGDEN, Willis James 1
BROGGINI, Adrian Joseph 8
BROGHAMER, George P. 6
BROGLIE, Duc de 4
BROIDA, Dan 4
BROIDA, Herbert Philip 7
BROIDY, Edward William 3
BROKAMP, Frank William 4
BROKAW, Charles 1
  Livingston
BROKAW, Howard Crosby 3
BROKENBURR, Robert 7
  Lee
BROKENSHIRE, Charles 3
  Digory
BROKENSHIRE, Norman 4
BROKENSHIRE, William 4
  Samuel, Jr.
BROKMEYER, Henry C. H

BROKMEYER, Henry C. 4
BROMAGE, Arthur 7
  Watson
BROMBERG, Ben George 8
BROMBERG, Frederick 1
  George
BROMER, Edward 3
  Sheppard
BROMER, Ralph Shepherd 3
BROMFIELD, Donald 10
  Coleman
BROMFIELD, John H
BROMFIELD, Louis 3
BROMILOW, Frank 6
BROMLEY, Bruce 7
BROMLEY, Charles 5
  Dunham
BROMLEY, Charles 8
  Vinson, Jr.
BROMMAGE, Claude 7
  Stilson
BROMWELL, Charles 1
  Summers
BROMWELL, Jacob Henry 4
BRONDEL, John B. 1
BRONFENBRENNER, 3
  Jacques Jacob
BRONFMAN, Allan 10
BRONFMAN, Samuel 5
BRONK, Detlev W. 6
BRONK, Detlev W. 7
BRONK, Isabelle 2
BRONK, Mitchell 3
BRONLEM, Isaac Hill H
BRONNER, Augusta Fox 6
  (Mrs. William Healy)
BRONNER, Edmond D. 1
BRONNER, Harry 1
BRONOWSKI, Jacob 6
BRONSON, Bennet 3
BRONSON, Charles Eli 4
BRONSON, David H
BRONSON, Dillon 2
BRONSON, Francis 4
  Woolsey
BRONSON, Harrison 2
  Arthur
BRONSON, Henry H
BRONSON, Isaac Hopkins H
BRONSON, Patricia Ann 10
BRONSON, Roy A. 7
BRONSON, Samuel 1
  Lathrop
BRONSON, Solon Cary 1
BRONSON, Thomas 3
  Bertrand
BRONSON, Walter 1
  Cochrane
BRONSON, William 5
  Howard
BRONSON, William 4
  Sherlock
BROOK, Alexander 7
BROOK, Charles Henry 4
BROOK, Clive 6
BROOKE, Ben C. 5
BROOKE, Flavius Lionel 1
BROOKE, Francis Key 1
BROOKE, Francis H
  Taliaferro
BROOKE, Franklin 4
  Ellsworth
BROOKE, James J. 6
BROOKE, John Mercer 1
BROOKE, John Rutter 1
BROOKE, Mary Myrtle 5
BROOKE, Richard Norris 1
BROOKE, St George 1
  Tucker
BROOKE, Thomas Preston 4
BROOKE, Tucker 2
BROOKE, Walter H
BROOKE, William 4
  Ellsworth
BROOKE, William 5
  Ellsworth
BROOKEBOROUGH, 6
  Viscount (Brooke)
BROOKER, Charles 1
  Frederick
BROOKER, John William 3
BROOKE-RAWLE, 1
  William
BROOKES, John St Clair, 4
  Jr.
BROOKES, Samuel H
  Marsdon
BROOKFIELD, Dutton 8
BROOKHART, Smith W. 2
BROOKINGS, Robert 1
  Somers
BROOKINGS, Walter 3
  Dubois
BROOKINGS, Walter 4
  Dubois
BROOKINS, Homer De 3
  Wilton

BROOKMAN, Herman 9
BROOKS, Alfred Hulse 1
BROOKS, Alfred Mansfield 5
BROOKS, Allerton Frank 3
BROOKS, Alonzo Beecher 4
BROOKS, Anson Strong 1
BROOKS, Arbie Leroy 3
BROOKS, Arthur H
BROOKS, Arthur Alford 2
BROOKS, Arthur Thomas 2
BROOKS, Arthur Wolfort 2
BROOKS, Benjamin 4
  Talbott
BROOKS, Bryant Butler 2
BROOKS, Burrow Penn 7
BROOKS, C. Wayland 3
BROOKS, Chandler 10
  McCuskey
BROOKS, Charles H
BROOKS, Charles Alvin 1
BROOKS, Charles Edward 1
BROOKS, Charles F. 3
BROOKS, Charles Hayward 5
BROOKS, Charles Stephen 1
BROOKS, Charles Timothy H
BROOKS, Christopher 1
  Parkinson
BROOKS, Clarence Richard 3
BROOKS, Clyde 7
BROOKS, David H
BROOKS, Douglas 8
  Walworth
BROOKS, Edward 1
BROOKS, Edward Hale 7
BROOKS, Edward Pennell 10
BROOKS, Edward 3
  Schroeder
BROOKS, Edwin B. 4
BROOKS, Elbridge Streeter 1
BROOKS, Erastus 5
BROOKS, Ernest, Jr. 9
BROOKS, Eugene Clyde 2
BROOKS, Florence 4
BROOKS, Forrest Edmund 8
BROOKS, Frank Hilliard 1
BROOKS, Frank Pickering 10
BROOKS, Frank Wilks 1
BROOKS, Franklin Eli 1
BROOKS, Fred Emerson 1
BROOKS, Frederick A. 5
BROOKS, George Merrick 1
BROOKS, George Sprague 4
BROOKS, George H
  Washington
BROOKS, George William 8
BROOKS, Geraldine 5
BROOKS, Harlow 1
BROOKS, Harry Sayer 3
BROOKS, Henry Luesing 5
BROOKS, Henry S. 1
BROOKS, Henry Turner 4
BROOKS, J. Wilton 1
BROOKS, Jabez 1
BROOKS, James 10
BROOKS, James H
BROOKS, James Byron 1
BROOKS, James Gordon 4
BROOKS, Jesse Wendell 1
BROOKS, John H
BROOKS, John B. 4
BROOKS, John G(aunt) 5
BROOKS, John Graham 1
BROOKS, John Pascal 4
BROOKS, John Wood 9
BROOKS, Joseph Hudson 3
BROOKS, Joshua Loring 2
BROOKS, Joshua Twing 7
BROOKS, Laurance 5
  Waddill
BROOKS, Laverne W. 5
BROOKS, Lawrence 9
  Graham
BROOKS, Lee M(arshall) 4
BROOKS, Leon Richard 4
BROOKS, Maria Gowen H
BROOKS, Mary Willard 3
BROOKS, Micah H
BROOKS, Morgan 2
BROOKS, Ned 5
BROOKS, Neil 5
BROOKS, Noah 1
BROOKS, Olin L. 4
BROOKS, Overton 4
BROOKS, Paul David 3
BROOKS, Peter Anthony 2
BROOKS, Peter Chardon H
BROOKS, Philip Coolidge 7
BROOKS, Phillips 5
BROOKS, Phillips 6
BROOKS, Phillips Moore 5
BROOKS, Preston Smith H
BROOKS, Ralph Gilmour 5
BROOKS, Raymond 2
  Cummings
BROOKS, Richard 10
BROOKS, Richard E. 1
BROOKS, Robert Angus 7

BROOKS, Robert Blemker 4
BROOKS, Robert Clarkson 1
BROOKS, Robert Mary 2
BROOKS, Robert Nathaniel 3
BROOKS, Robert Preston 6
BROOKS, Robert Romano 10
  Ravi
BROOKS, Robert William 10
BROOKS, Rodney Joseph 3
BROOKS, Roelif 6
  Hasbrouck
BROOKS, Samuel Palmer 1
BROOKS, Sarah Warner 1
BROOKS, Stewart 2
BROOKS, Stratton Duluth 2
BROOKS, Summer Cushing 5
BROOKS, Thomas Benton 1
BROOKS, Thomas Dudley 7
BROOKS, Van Wyck 4
BROOKS, Victor Lee 1
BROOKS, Walter Rollin 3
BROOKS, Wendell Stanton 4
BROOKS, Whitney Lawton 7
BROOKS, Wiley Glen 7
BROOKS, William Benthall 1
BROOKS, William E. 5
BROOKS, William F. 6
BROOKS, William Keith 1
BROOKS, William Myron 5
BROOKS, William Penn 1
BROOKS, William Robert 1
BROOKS, William Thomas H
  Harbaugh
BROOKS, Winfield Sears 4
BROOKSHER, William 6
  Riley
BROOKSHIRE, Elijah 1
  Voorhees
BROOM, Jacob H
BROOM, James Madison H
BROOMALL, John Martin H
BROOME, Edwin Cornelius 3
BROOME, Harvey 4
BROOME, Harvey 5
BROOME, Isaac 1
BROOME, John Parran 8
BROOME, Robert Edwin 4
BROOMELL, I. Norman 1
BROOMFIELD, John 2
  Calvin
BROONZY, William Lee 1
  Conley
BROPHY, C. Gerald 3
BROPHY, Daniel Francis 4
BROPHY, Ellen Amelia 1
BROPHY, Frank Cullen 7
BROPHY, Gerald B. 7
BROPHY, James Edward 9
BROPHY, James John 10
BROPHY, John 7
BROPHY, Thomas D'Arcy 1
BROPHY, Truman William 1
BROPHY, William Henry 1
BROREIN, Carl D. 6
BROREIN, William G. 1
BROSE, Louis D. 1
BROSIO, Manlio 7
BROSIUS, Marriott 1
BROSMAN, Paul William 3
BROSMITH, William 1
BROSNAHAN, Patrick 3
  Edward
BROSNAHAN, Timothy 1
BROSNAN, Dennis William 8
BROSNAN, John F(rancis) 8
BROSNAN, Thomas Joseph 8
BROSS, Ernest 1
BROSS, John Adams 10
BROSS, William H
BROSSARD, Edgar 7
  Bernard
BROSSART, Ferdinand 4
BROSSARD, Alfred J. 1
BROTEMARKLE, Robert 9
  Archibald
BROTHER, Doran Palmer 4
BROTHERTON, Alice 1
  Williams
BROUGH, John H
BROUGH, Kenneth James 9
BROUGH, William 4
BROUGHAM, John H
BROUGHAM, Royal H
BROUGHER, J. Whitcomb 5
BROUGHER, J(ames) 5
  Whitcomb
BROUGHER, William E. 8
BROUGHTON, Carrie 1
  Loungee
BROUGHTON, Charles 3
  Elmer
BROUGHTON, Charles 6
  Frederic
BROUGHTON, Donald 8
  Beddoes
BROUGHTON, Joseph 2
  Melville

BROUGHTON, Leonard 1
  Gaston
BROUGHTON, Leslie 5
  Nathan
BROUGHTON, Levin 2
  Bowland
BROUGHTON, William R. H
BROUGHTON, William S. 3
BROUILLETTE, J(oseph) 7
  W(alter), Sr.
BROUILLETTE, T. Gilbert 5
BROULLIRE, John Merlin 5
BROUN, Heywood 1
BROUN, Maurice 7
BROUN, William Le Roy 1
BROUNOFF, Platon 1
BROUSE, Arthur H. 7
BROUSE, Edwin Walter 4
BROUSSARD, Edwin 1
  Sidney
BROUSSARD, James 2
  Francis
BROUSSARD, Robert F. 1
BROUSSEAU, Kate 1
BROUWER, Dirk 4
BROUWER, Luitzen 4
  Egbertus Jan
BROWARD, Napoleon 1
  Bonaparte
BROWDER, Basil David 3
BROWDER, Earl (Russel) 5
BROWER, Alfred Smith 5
BROWER, Alonzo Blaine 7
BROWER, Charles 8
  Hendrickson
BROWER, Daniel 6
BROWER, Daniel Roberts 1
BROWER, Harriette Moore 1
BROWER, Horace W. 9
BROWER, Jacob 1
  Vradenberg
BROWER, Reuben Arthur 6
BROWER, Robert Clark 10
BROWER, Walter Scott 4
BROWER, William 1
  Leverich
BROWERE, Albertus D. O. H
BROWERE, John Henri H
  Isaac
BROWN, A. Curtis 2
BROWN, A. Luther 3
BROWN, A. Page H
BROWN, Aaron Switzer 5
BROWN, Aaron Venable H
BROWN, Abbie Farwell 1
BROWN, Abner Wolcott 8
BROWN, Abram English 1
BROWN, Addison 1
BROWN, Alanson Charles 7
BROWN, Alanson David 1
BROWN, Albert Edmund 4
BROWN, Albert Frederic 4
BROWN, Albert Gallatin H
BROWN, Albert Oscar 1
BROWN, Albert Sidney 5
BROWN, Alexander H
BROWN, Alexander 1
BROWN, Alexander 2
BROWN, Alexander 4
  Cushing
BROWN, Alexander 1
  Ephraim
BROWN, Alfred Hodgdon 5
BROWN, Alfred Seely 5
BROWN, Alice 2
BROWN, Alice Cooke 6
BROWN, Allen Van 2
  Vechten
BROWN, Allen Webster 10
BROWN, Allyn Larrabee 2
BROWN, Alvin (Mccreary) 5
BROWN, Amanda 1
  Elizabeth
BROWN, Ames 2
BROWN, Ames Thorndike 4
BROWN, Amos Peaslee 1
BROWN, Ann Mary 5
  Marothy (Mrs. Ernest M.
  Brown)
BROWN, Anson H
BROWN, Archer 1
BROWN, Archibald 3
  Manning
BROWN, Arlo Ayres 4
BROWN, Armstead 4
BROWN, Arthur 10
BROWN, Arthur 1
BROWN, Arthur, Jr. 3
BROWN, Arthur Charles 2
  Lewis
BROWN, Arthur Edward 1
BROWN, Arthur Erwin 1
BROWN, Arthur 10
  Huntingdon
BROWN, Arthur Judson* 4
BROWN, Arthur Lewis 1
BROWN, Arthur Morton 3

BROWN, Arthur Voorhees 2
BROWN, Arthur William 4
BROWN, Arthur Winton 3
BROWN, Arvin Harrington, 7
  Jr.
BROWN, Ashmun Norris 2
BROWN, Barnum 4
BROWN, Baxter Lamont 3
BROWN, Bedford H
BROWN, Ben Hill, Jr. 10
BROWN, Benjamin H
BROWN, Benjamin 2
  Beuhring
BROWN, Benjamin 1
  Chambers
BROWN, Benjamin Gratz H
BROWN, Benjamin Henry 3
BROWN, B(enjamin) 7
  Warren
BROWN, Bernard 3
BROWN, Bolton 1
BROWN, Brendan F. 10
BROWN, Brian 6
BROWN, Bruce K. 7
BROWN, Buford Mason 4
BROWN, Burdette 5
  Boardman
BROWN, C. Foster, Jr. 4
BROWN, C. Henry 1
BROWN, Calvin Luther 1
BROWN, Calvin Smith 2
BROWN, Carey Herbert 7
BROWN, Carleton 1
BROWN, Caxton 3
BROWN, Cecil 9
BROWN, Cecil Kenneth 9
BROWN, Charles H
BROWN, Charles Allen 1
BROWN, Charles Brockden H
BROWN, Charles C. 8
BROWN, Charles Carroll 1
BROWN, Charles Edward 2
BROWN, Charles Francis 1
BROWN, Charles H. 1
BROWN, Charles Harvey 3
BROWN, Charles Ira 1
BROWN, Charles Irwin 1
BROWN, Charles Leonard 4
BROWN, Charles Reynolds 3
BROWN, Charles Rufus 1
BROWN, Charles Sumner 1
BROWN, Charles Walter 1
BROWN, Charles William 1
BROWN, Charles Wilson 5
BROWN, Charlotte H
  Emerson
BROWN, Charlotte 3
  Harding
BROWN, Chester Melville 8
BROWN, Clarence J. 4
BROWN, Clarence 3
  Montgomery
BROWN, Clyde 1
BROWN, Colvin W. 3
BROWN, Courtney C. 10
BROWN, Cyrus Jay 5
BROWN, Cyrus Perrin 3
BROWN, D. J. 3
BROWN, Daniel L(ucius) 9
BROWN, Daniel Russell 1
BROWN, David Abraham 5
BROWN, David Chester 2
BROWN, David E. 8
BROWN, David Paul H
BROWN, Demarchus 1
  Clariton
BROWN, Demetra Vaka 2
BROWN, Donald C. 3
BROWN, Donald Erwin 9
BROWN, Donald Lamont 1
BROWN, Donald Lee 4
BROWN, Donaldson 4
BROWN, Douglass Vincent 9
BROWN, Downing P. 3
BROWN, Dudley 6
  B(radstreet) W(illiams)
BROWN, Earl Theodore 3
BROWN, Earle Godfrey 4
BROWN, Ebenezer H
BROWN, Edgar 5
BROWN, Edgar Allan 9
BROWN, Edith 1
BROWN, Edith Petrie 9
BROWN, Edmund, Jr. 8
BROWN, Edmund 8
  Randolph
BROWN, Edna Adelaide 2
BROWN, Edward Eagle 3
BROWN, Edward Fisher 6
BROWN, Edward James 10
BROWN, Edward Killoran 3
BROWN, Edward Lee 4
BROWN, Edward McLain, 9
  Jr.
BROWN, Edward Miles 1
BROWN, Edward Norphlet 3

BROWN, Edward Osgood 1
BROWN, Edward Scott 2
BROWN, Edward Vail 5
  Lapham
BROWN, Edwin Hacker 1
BROWN, Edwin Perkins 1
BROWN, Edwin Pierce 5
BROWN, Edwin Putnam 1
BROWN, Edwy Rolfe 1
BROWN, Eli Huston, III 7
BROWN, Eli Huston, Jr. 2
BROWN, Elias H
BROWN, Eliphalet M., Jr. H
BROWN, Elliott Wilber 1
BROWN, Elmer 5
BROWN, Elmer Ellsworth 1
BROWN, Elon Rouse 4
BROWN, Elzear Joseph 5
BROWN, Emily Clark 7
BROWN, Emma Elizabeth 4
BROWN, Enoch 4
BROWN, Eric Gore 4
BROWN, Ernest G(ay) 6
BROWN, Ernest William 1
BROWN, Estelle Aubrey 3
BROWN, Esther Lucile 10
BROWN, Ethan Allen H
BROWN, Everett Chase 1
BROWN, Everett Ernest 8
BROWN, Everett J. 2
BROWN, F. E. 3
BROWN, F. E. 4
BROWN, Fay (Cluff) 6
BROWN, Fayette 1
BROWN, Fayette 3
BROWN, Felix Harry 3
BROWN, Fletcher 3
BROWN, Foster Sargent 8
BROWN, Foster Vincent 4
BROWN, Francis H
BROWN, Francis 1
BROWN, Francis Cabell 4
BROWN, Francis Henry 1
BROWN, Francis James 1
BROWN, Francis Shunk 1
BROWN, Frank 1
BROWN, Frank Arthur, Jr. 8
BROWN, Frank Chilton 3
BROWN, Frank Chouteau 2
BROWN, Frank Clyde 2
BROWN, Frank Edward 9
BROWN, Frank Llewellyn 1
BROWN, Frank Xavier 5
BROWN, Franklin Q. 3
BROWN, Franklin Stewart 1
BROWN, Fred 6
BROWN, Fred Comings 3
BROWN, Fred Herbert 3
BROWN, Frederic Kenyon 1
BROWN, Frederic L. 6
BROWN, Frederick Anson 1
BROWN, Frederick 7
  Fernando
BROWN, Frederick Harvey 1
BROWN, Frederick Nathan, 7
  Jr.
BROWN, Frederick Ronald 6
BROWN, Frederick 5
  Walworth
BROWN, Frederick William 4
BROWN, Frederick 1
  Winfield
BROWN, Fredric 5
BROWN, George* H
BROWN, George 1
BROWN, George (Alfred) 8
BROWN, George Francis 1
BROWN, George Garvin 5
BROWN, George Granger 3
BROWN, George H. 1
BROWN, George Harold 9
BROWN, George Houston H
BROWN, George Lincoln 3
BROWN, George Loring H
BROWN, George M. 1
BROWN, George Marion 2
BROWN, George Newland 4
BROWN, George Pliny 1
BROWN, George Rothwell 4
BROWN, George Rowland, 5
  III
BROWN, George Rufus 8
BROWN, George Samson 2
BROWN, George Scratchley 7
BROWN, George Stewart 1
BROWN, George Stewart 2
BROWN, George Stewart 3
BROWN, George Tiden 4
BROWN, George Van 2
  Ingen
BROWN, George W. 1
BROWN, George Warren 1
BROWN, George 4
  Washington
BROWN, George William H
BROWN, George William 2
BROWN, George Woodford 5

BROWN, Gertrude Foster 4
BROWN, Gilmor 3
BROWN, Glen David 3
BROWN, Glenn 1
BROWN, Goold H
BROWN, Grace Marn 4
BROWN, H. Emmett 10
BROWN, H. Martin 1
BROWN, H. Templeton 8
BROWN, Harlan Craig 8
BROWN, Harold Eugene 6
BROWN, Harold Haven 1
BROWN, Harrison Scott 9
BROWN, Harry Alvin 1
BROWN, Harry B. 4
BROWN, Harry Fletcher 2
BROWN, Harry Gunnison 6
BROWN, Harry Joe 5
BROWN, Harry Lowrance 4
BROWN, Harry Peter 9
  McNab, Jr.
BROWN, Harry Sanford 2
BROWN, Harry Winfield 2
BROWN, Harvey H., Jr. 3
BROWN, Helen Dawes 1
BROWN, Helen Gilman 2
BROWN, Henry B. 1
BROWN, Henry Bascom 1
BROWN, Henry Bedinger 7
  Rust
BROWN, Henry Billings 1
BROWN, Henry Collins 4
BROWN, Henry Daniels 5
BROWN, Henry Harrison 4
BROWN, Henry Kirke H
BROWN, Henry Matthias 5
BROWN, Henry Seabury 9
BROWN, Henry Seymour 4
BROWN, Herbert Daniel 4
BROWN, Herbert Daniel 5
BROWN, Herbert J. 2
BROWN, Herman 4
BROWN, Hilton Ultimus 3
BROWN, Hiram Chellis 4
BROWN, Hiram Staunton 4
BROWN, Holcombe James 3
BROWN, Homer Caffee 3
BROWN, Homer S. 7
BROWN, Horace 1
  Manchester
BROWN, Howard Benner 4
BROWN, Howard Junior 6
BROWN, Howard 1
  Nicholson
BROWN, Hugh 6
  Auchincloss
BROWN, Hugh 7
  Auchincloss
BROWN, Hugh B. 6
BROWN, Hugh Elmer 3
BROWN, Hugh Henry 1
BROWN, Hugh S. 4
BROWN, Irving H(enry) 8
BROWN, Irving Joseph 9
BROWN, Isaac Eddy 1
BROWN, Isaac Van H
  Arsdale
BROWN, Ivor John 6
  Carnegie
BROWN, J. Appleton 1
BROWN, J. Calvin 10
BROWN, J. Hammond 3
BROWN, J. Hay 1
BROWN, J. Stanley 1
BROWN, J. Thompson 3
BROWN, J. Vallance 1
BROWN, Jacob Jennings H
BROWN, James* 1
BROWN, James* 1
BROWN, James B. 5
BROWN, James Barrett 5
BROWN, James Dorsey, Jr. 3
BROWN, J(ames) Douglas 9
BROWN, James Elwyn, Jr. 4
BROWN, James F. 1
BROWN, James F. 8
BROWN, James Grady 8
BROWN, James Greenlief 3
BROWN, James Henry 4
BROWN, James R. 1
BROWN, James Raphael, 8
  Jr.
BROWN, James Salisbury H
BROWN, James Sproat 3
BROWN, James Thomas 3
BROWN, James Vincent 3
BROWN, James Wilson 9
BROWN, James Wright 3
BROWN, James Wright, Jr. 5
BROWN, Jeremiah 1
BROWN, Jo Baily 7
BROWN, Joe Evan 5
BROWN, Joel Bascom 5
BROWN, John* H
BROWN, John A. H
BROWN, John Albert 2
BROWN, John Anthony 7

BROWN, John Bernis 5
BROWN, John C. 1
BROWN, John Calvin H
BROWN, John Carter H
BROWN, John Crosby 1
BROWN, John Elward 3
BROWN, John Franklin 1
BROWN, John George 1
BROWN, John Griest 2
BROWN, John Hamilton 4
BROWN, John Henry H
BROWN, John Herbert, Jr. 4
BROWN, John Howard 1
BROWN, John Jacob 2
BROWN, John MacKenzie 3
BROWN, John Marshall 1
BROWN, John Mifflin H
BROWN, John Newton H
BROWN, John Nicholas 7
BROWN, John Pinkney 1
BROWN, John Porter H
BROWN, John Richard 1
BROWN, John W. H
BROWN, John William 7
BROWN, John Young* 1
BROWN, Joseph H
BROWN, Joseph 6
BROWN, Joseph 8
BROWN, Joseph Alleine 5
BROWN, Joseph Clifton 2
BROWN, Joseph Eckford 3
BROWN, Joseph Emerson H
BROWN, Joseph Gill 1
BROWN, Joseph M. 1
BROWN, Joseph Real 4
BROWN, Joseph Rogers H
BROWN, Josiah 9
BROWN, Julius L. 1
BROWN, Junius Calvin 5
BROWN, Justus Morris 1
BROWN, Karl 10
BROWN, Kate Louise 1
BROWN, Katharine 1
  Holland
BROWN, Kenneth 4
BROWN, Kenneth Harold 8
BROWN, Kenneth Rent 3
BROWN, Larue (Herman) 7
BROWN, Larue (Herman) 5
BROWN, Lathrop 3
BROWN, Lawrason 1
BROWN, Lee Henry 8
BROWN, Leigh A. 3
BROWN, Leo Cyril 7
BROWN, Leslie Edwin 10
BROWN, Levant Frederick 4
BROWN, Lew 3
BROWN, Lewis H. 3
BROWN, Lindsey 8
BROWN, Lloyd Arnold 4
BROWN, Lloyd Davidson 3
BROWN, Louis M(yron) 5
BROWN, Louise Fargo 3
BROWN, Lucius 1
BROWN, Lucius Polk 1
BROWN, Lucy Hall 1
BROWN, Lyle 8
BROWN, Lyndon Osmond 4
BROWN, Lytle 3
BROWN, M. McClellan 1
BROWN, Manuel Nicholas 5
BROWN, Margaret 9
  Christina
BROWN, Margaret Wise 3
BROWN, Mark 8
BROWN, Mark A. 5
BROWN, Marshall 4
BROWN, Marshall Stewart 2
BROWN, Martin Parks 10
BROWN, M(ary) Belle 5
BROWN, Mather H
BROWN, Matthew L. 8
BROWN, Maxine 5
  McFadden (Mrs. Jack T.
  Brown)
BROWN, May Belleville 1
BROWN, Melford Losee 8
BROWN, Milton H
BROWN, Milton Fleming 9
BROWN, Milton Wilbert 5
BROWN, Montreville Jay 6
BROWN, Montreville Jay 7
BROWN, Moreau Delano 7
BROWN, Morris H
BROWN, Moses* H
BROWN, Moses True 1
BROWN, Nathaniel Smith 1
BROWN, Neal 1
BROWN, Neill Smith H
BROWN, Nelson 1
  Courtlandt
BROWN, Nestor Melloy 8
BROWN, Nicholas* H
BROWN, Norriw 3
BROWN, Obadiah H
BROWN, Olympia 1
BROWN, Orville Harry 2

BROWN, Orvon Graff 4
BROWN, Oswald Eugene 1
BROWN, Owen Clarence 5
BROWN, Owsley 3
BROWN, Parke 2
BROWN, Paul 10
BROWN, Paul 4
BROWN, Paul Goodwin 2
BROWN, Paul Howard 10
BROWN, Paul Marvin, Jr. 8
BROWN, Paul Winthrop 1
BROWN, Pembroke 7
  Holcomb
BROWN, Percy 3
BROWN, Percy A. 4
BROWN, Percy Edgar 1
BROWN, Percy W. 3
BROWN, Philip Bransfield 8
BROWN, Philip E. 1
BROWN, Philip Greely 1
BROWN, Philip King 1
BROWN, Philip King 2
BROWN, Philip Marshall 4
BROWN, Phoebe Hinsdale H
BROWN, Prentiss Marsh 6
BROWN, Preston 2
BROWN, R. Lewis 2
BROWN, Ralph Hall 2
BROWN, Ralph Manning, 9
  Jr.
BROWN, Ray 2
BROWN, Ray Andrews 5
BROWN, Ray Everett 6
BROWN, Raymond Dwight 3
BROWN, Reed McClellan 8
BROWN, Revelle Wilson 7
BROWN, Rex Ivan 9
BROWN, Rexwald 1
BROWN, Reynolds Driver 5
BROWN, Rezeau Blanchard 1
BROWN, Rhett Delford 10
  (Harriett Brown)
BROWN, Richard Evan 6
BROWN, Richard Fargo 7
BROWN, Richard Parke 7
BROWN, Robert H
BROWN, Robert Abner 1
BROWN, Robert Alexander 1
BROWN, Robert Alfred 8
BROWN, Robert Arthur, 5
  Jr.
BROWN, Robert Burns 1
BROWN, Robert Carlton 7
  (Bob Brown)
BROWN, Robert Clarence, 8
  Jr.
BROWN, Robert Coleman 9
BROWN, Robert Elliott 1
BROWN, Robert Frederick 5
BROWN, Robert K. 2
BROWN, Robert Marshall 1
BROWN, Robert Rankins 1
BROWN, Robert Sater 2
BROWN, Robert Woodrow 6
BROWN, Robert Young 1
BROWN, Rollo Walter 3
BROWN, Rome G. 1
BROWN, Ronald Frederick 2
BROWN, Ensign Roscoe
  Conkling
BROWN, Roy 3
BROWN, Roy Howard 6
BROWN, Rufus Everson 3
BROWN, Ruth Mowry 1
BROWN, Samuel H
BROWN, Samuel Alburtus 3
BROWN, Samuel Gilman H
BROWN, Samuel Horton, 1
  Jr.
BROWN, Samuel Robbins H
BROWN, Sanborn C(onner) 8
BROWN, Sanford Miller 1
BROWN, Sanger 1
BROWN, Selden Stanley 1
BROWN, Seth W. 4
BROWN, Sevellon 3
BROWN, Sevellon Ledyard 3
BROWN, Simon H
BROWN, S(impson) Leroy 6
BROWN, Solyman H
BROWN, Spencer Wharton 7
BROWN, Stanely L. 4
BROWN, Stanley Doty 7
BROWN, Stanley Doty 7
BROWN, Sterling Wade 9
BROWN, Stimson Joseph 1
BROWN, Sydney Barlow 3
BROWN, Sydney 3
  MacGillvary
BROWN, Sylvanus H
BROWN, T. Dawson 9
BROWN, Thaddeus Harold 8
BROWN, Thatcher M. 3
BROWN, Theodore Dana 8
BROWN, Theodore Henry 6
BROWN, Theophilus 7
BROWN, Theron 1

BROWN, Theron Adelbert 4
BROWN, Thoburn Kaye 8
BROWN, Thomas Allston 4
BROWN, Thomas Cook 4
BROWN, Thomas Edwin 4
BROWN, Thomas F. 4
BROWN, Thomas Jefferson 1
BROWN, Thomas 10
McPherson
BROWN, Thomas 3
Richardson
BROWN, Timothy 8
BROWN, Titus H
BROWN, Travis Walter 9
BROWN, Vandyke H
BROWN, Volney Mason 6
BROWN, W. Cabell 1
BROWN, W. Kennedy 4
BROWN, W. Shelburne 7
BROWN, Wade Hampton 2
BROWN, Wade R. 4
BROWN, Waldron Post 1
BROWN, Wallace Elias 1
BROWN, Wallace Winthrop 4
BROWN, Walter Folger 1
BROWN, Walter Folger 5
BROWN, Walter Franklin 3
BROWN, Walter Harold, 9
Jr.
BROWN, Walter L. 6
BROWN, Walter Lewis 1
BROWN, Warner 9
BROWN, Warwick Thomas 4
BROWN, Webster Everett 4
BROWN, Wilbur Vincent 1
BROWN, Willard Cowles 7
BROWN, Willard Dayton 5
BROWN, William* H
BROWN, William H
BROWN, William Adams 2
BROWN, William Adams, 3
Jr.
BROWN, William Atwell, 5
Jr.
BROWN, William Averell 3
BROWN, William C. 1
BROWN, William C. 4
BROWN, William Carey 1
BROWN, William Channing 5
BROWN, William Edward 1
BROWN, William F. 10
BROWN, William Fuller, 8
Jr.
BROWN, William G., Jr. 1
BROWN, William Garl, Jr. H
BROWN, William Garrott 4
BROWN, William Gay H
BROWN, William George 1
BROWN, William Henry H
BROWN, William Henry* 1
BROWN, William Hill 1
BROWN, William Horace 1
BROWN, William Hughey H
BROWN, William John H
BROWN, William Lacy 10
BROWN, William Lee 1
BROWN, W(illiam) L(ee) 5
Lyons
BROWN, William Liston 1
BROWN, William 1
Montgomery
BROWN, W(illiam) 6
Norman
BROWN, W(illiam) 7
Norman
BROWN, William O. 3
BROWN, William Perry 2
BROWN, William 7
Robertson
BROWN, William Russell 8
BROWN, William Thayer 1
BROWN, William Thurston 4
BROWN, William Wallace 1
BROWN, William Wells H
BROWN, Wilson 1
BROWN, Winthrop Gilman 9
BROWN, Wood 8
BROWN, Wrisley 2
BROWN, Wylie 4
BROWN, Wyourn D. 7
BROWN, Zaidee 5
BROWNE, Aldis Birdsey 1
BROWNE, Alfred David 6
BROWNE, Arthur Wesley 2
BROWNE, Belmore 3
BROWNE, Benjamin H
Frederick
BROWNE, Benjamin 7
Patterson
BROWNE, Bennet Bernard 1
BROWNE, Beverly 6
F(ielding)
BROWNE, Byron 4
BROWNE, Causten 1
BROWNE, Charles 2
BROWNE, Charles Albert 2
BROWNE, Charles Farrar H

BROWNE, Charles Francis 1
BROWNE, Daniel Jay H
BROWNE, Dik 10
BROWNE, Dudley 9
BROWNE, Duncan Hodge 3
BROWNE, Edward Everts 2
BROWNE, Edward 3
Tankard
BROWNE, Francis Cedric 9
BROWNE, Francis Fisher 1
BROWNE, Frederick 4
William
BROWNE, George Elmer 2
BROWNE, George Henry 1
BROWNE, George H
Huntington
BROWNE, George Israel 3
BROWNE, George Waldo 1
BROWNE, Harry C. 3
BROWNE, Harry L. 9
BROWNE, Herbert 2
Wheildon Cotton
BROWNE, Irving H
BROWNE, J. Lewis 1
BROWNE, Jefferson Beale 1
BROWNE, John H
BROWNE, John Barton 8
BROWNE, John Ross H
BROWNE, Junius Henri H
BROWNE, Lewis 2
BROWNE, Lewis Allen 1
BROWNE, Louis Edgar 3
BROWNE, Margaret 5
Fitzhugh
BROWNE, Margaret 7
Fitzhugh
BROWNE, Maurice 3
BROWNE, Nina Eliza 4
BROWNE, Page 5
BROWNE, Porter Emerson 1
BROWNE, Ralph Cowan 3
BROWNE, Rhodes 1
BROWNE, Robert Bell 4
BROWNE, Robert H. 4
BROWNE, Roger J. 6
BROWNE, Rollin 6
BROWNE, Secor Delahay 9
BROWNE, Thomas H
BROWNE, Thomas Henry H
Bayly
BROWNE, Thomas H
McLelland
BROWNE, Waldo Ralph 3
BROWNE, Walter Lyman 7
BROWNE, William H
BROWNE, William Hand 1
BROWNE, William 1
Hardcastle
BROWNELL, Amanda 8
Benjamin Hall (Mrs. John
Angell Brownell)
BROWNELL, Atherton 1
BROWNELL, Baker 4
Ludlow
BROWNELL, Clarence 1
Ludlow
BROWNELL, Eleanor 5
Olivia
BROWNELL, Emery 4
Albert
BROWNELL, Francis 3
Herbert
BROWNELL, George 8
Abbott
BROWNELL, George 1
Francis
BROWNELL, George 1
Griffin
BROWNELL, Harry 1
Franklin
BROWNELL, Harry Gault 4
BROWNELL, Henry H
Howard
BROWNELL, Jane Louise 1
BROWNELL, Kenneth C. 3
BROWNELL, Roy Edmund 7
BROWNELL, Samuel 10
Miller
BROWNELL, Silas B. 4
BROWNELL, Thomas 1
Church
BROWNELL, Walter A. 1
BROWNELL, William 7
Arthur
BROWNELL, William 1
Crary
BROWNING, Arthur 6
Montcalm
BROWNING, Charles 1
Clifton
BROWNING, Charles 1
Henry
BROWNING, Eliza Gordon 5
BROWNING, Frank 10
Milton
BROWNING, George 2
Landon
BROWNING, Gordon 7

BROWNING, Grace 3
BROWNING, Iben 10
BROWNING, John Hull 1
BROWNING, John M. 1
BROWNING, Matthew 1
Sandefur
BROWNING, McPherson 3
BROWNING, Miles 3
BROWNING, Nolan 8
BROWNING, Orville H
Hickman
BROWNING, Philip 1
Embury
BROWNING, Ralph 4
Rushton
BROWNING, Robert 5
Turner
BROWNING, Webster E. 2
BROWNING, William 1
BROWNING, William Hull 4
BROWNING, William J. 1
BROWNLEE, Frederick 4
Leslie
BROWNLEE, James F. 4
BROWNLEE, James 4
Leaman
BROWNLEE, Oswald 9
Harvey
BROWNLEE, Richard 10
Smith
BROWNLEE, William 7
Allen
BROWNLEE, William H
Craig
BROWNLOW, Louis 4
BROWNLOW, Walter 1
Preston
BROWNLOW, William H
Gannaway
BROWNRIGG, Dorothy 6
Ruth Akin (Mrs. Robert
Charles Brownrigg)
BROWNSCOMBE, Jennie 1
BROWNSON, Carleton 2
Lewis
BROWNSON, Charles 9
Bruce
BROWNSON, Henry 4
Francis
BROWNSON, James Irwin 1
BROWNSON, Marcus 1
Acheson
BROWNSON, Mary Wilson 5
BROWNSON, Nathan 1
BROWNSON, Orestes H
Augustus
BROWNSON, Truman 4
Gaylord
BROWNSON, Willard 1
Herbert
BROY, Charles Clinton 2
BROYDE, Isaac 4
BROYHILL, James Edgar 1
BROYLES, Joseph Warren 2
BRUBACHER, Abram 1
Royer
BRUBACHER, John Seller 10
BRUBACK, Theodore 4
BRUBAKER, Albert 4
Philson
BRUBAKER, Howard 3
BRUCE, Alexander 4
Campbell
BRUCE, Alexander Douglas 1
BRUCE, Andrew Alexander 1
BRUCE, Andrew Davis 5
BRUCE, Archibald 1
BRUCE, Blanche Kelso H
BRUCE, Bryson 7
BRUCE, Charles Arthur 4
BRUCE, Charles Morelle 1
BRUCE, David K. E. 7
BRUCE, Donald Cogley 5
BRUCE, Dwight Hall 1
BRUCE, Edward 2
BRUCE, E(dwin) L(awson), 8
Jr.
BRUCE, Eugene Sewell 1
BRUCE, Frank M., Sr. 2
BRUCE, Frank M., Sr. 3
BRUCE, George H
BRUCE, Gustav Marius 6
BRUCE, H. Duane 4
BRUCE, Harold Lawton 1
BRUCE, Harold Rozelle 1
BRUCE, Harry William, Jr. 9
BRUCE, Helm H
BRUCE, H(enry) 5
Addington (Bayley)
BRUCE, Henry William 2
BRUCE, Homer Lindsey 8
BRUCE, Horatio 1
Washington
BRUCE, Howard 4
BRUCE, Imon Elba 9
BRUCE, Jackson Martin 4
BRUCE, James 7

BRUCE, James Deacon 2
BRUCE, James Douglas 1
BRUCE, James Latimer 6
BRUCE, James William 8
BRUCE, John 1
BRUCE, John Edgar 3
BRUCE, John Edward 4
BRUCE, John Eldridge 1
BRUCE, John Markey 7
BRUCE, Lenny 4
BRUCE, Logan Lithgow 5
BRUCE, Louis Rooks 10
BRUCE, Matthew Linn 1
BRUCE, Philip Alexander 1
BRUCE, Phineas H
BRUCE, Robert H
BRUCE, Robert Glenn 2
BRUCE, Robert Watson 8
BRUCE, Roscoe Conkling 6
BRUCE, Saunders Dewees 1
BRUCE, Wallace 1
BRUCE, William Cabell 2
BRUCE, William Conrad 1
BRUCE, William George 2
BRUCE, William Henry, Jr. 9
BRUCE, William Herschel 2
BRUCE, William Paterson 1
BRUCE OF 4
MELBOURNE, Viscount
BRUCH, Hilde 8
BRUCHHAUSEN, Walter 7
BRUCKER, Herbert 7
BRUCKER, Joseph 4
BRUCKER, Wilber 5
M(arion)
BRUCKNER, Aloys L. 4
BRUCKNER, Henry 1
BRUCKNER, Jacob 5
Herbert
BRUDNO, Ezra Selig 6
BRUECKMANN, John 4
George
BRUECKNER, Leo John 4
BRUECKNER, Leo John 8
BRUEGGEMAN, Bessie 1
Parker
BRUEGGER, John 4
BRUEGING, Edward 6
H(enry)
BRUENING, Heinrich 5
BRUENING, Heinrich 7
BRUENING, William 4
Ferdinand
BRUENNER, Adolph F. 8
BRUERE, Henry 3
BRUERE, Robert Walter 5
BRUES, Charles Thomas 3
BRUESTLE, George 1
Matthew
BRUETSCH, Walter L. 10
BRUFF, Joseph H
Goldsborough
BRUFF, Lawrence 1
Laurenson
BRUGGMANN, Charles 4
BRUGLER, Frank Russell 9
BRUGMAN, Francis 7
Albert
BRUHL, Gustav H
BRUHN, Carl 5
BRUHN, Erik Belton Evers 9
BRUHN, Wilhelm L. 3
BRUHN, Wilhelm L. 4
BRUINS, John H. 3
BRULE, Etienne H
BRUMAGIM, Robert 6
Smith
BRUMBAUGH, Aaron 8
John
BRUMBAUGH, Clement 1
BRUMBAUGH, David 7
Emmert
BRUMBAUGH, G. Edwin 8
BRUMBAUGH, Gaius 5
Marcus
BRUMBAUGH, Granville 10
Martin
BRUMBAUGH, I. Harvey 1
BRUMBAUGH, Martin 1
Grove
BRUMBAUGH, Roy 3
Talmage
BRUMBY, Frank 5
Hardeman
BRUMBY, Richard Trapier H
BRUMBY, Thomas Mason 1
BRUMIDI, Constantino H
BRUMLEY, Albert Edward 7
BRUMLEY, Albert Edward 8
BRUMLEY, Benjamin Basil 1
BRUMLEY, Corwin H. 7
BRUMLEY, Daniel Joseph 1
BRUMLEY, Oscar Victor 2
BRUMM, Charles Napoleon 3
BRUMM, George Franklin 1
BRUMM, John Lewis 3
BRUMMITT, Dan Brearley 1

BRUMMITT, Dennis G. 1
BRUN, Antoine Edmond 7
BRUN, Constantin 2
BRUN, Edmond Antoine 10
BRUNAUER, Esther 3
Caukin
BRUNCKEN, Ernest 4
BRUNDAGE, Albert 1
Harrison
BRUNDAGE, Avery 6
BRUNDAGE, Charles 5
Edwin
BRUNDAGE, Edward 1
Jackson
BRUNDAGE, John Denton 10
BRUNDAGE, Percival 7
Flack
BRUNDAGE, William 1
Milton
BRUNDIDGE, Oscar Dean 3
BRUNDIDGE, Stephen, Jr. 4
BRUNE, Adolf Gerhard
BRUNE, Frederick W. 5
BRUNER, Henry Lane 2
BRUNER, Herbert Bascom 6
BRUNER, James Dowden 4
BRUNER, Lawrence 1
BRUNER, Raymond 5
Alphonse
BRUNER, Weston 4
BRUNER, William Evans 5
BRUNER, William Wallace 10
BRUNET, Meade 9
BRUNET, Michel 9
BRUNIA, William Frans 5
BRUNIE, Henry C. 8
BRUNING, Walter Henry 6
BRUNINGS, Karl John 9
BRUNIS, Georg (George 6
Brunies)
BRUNKER, Albert Ridgley 3
BRUNNER, Arnold 1
William
BRUNNER, David B. 1
BRUNNER, Edmund de 6
Schweinitz
BRUNNER, Henry George 4
BRUNNER, John 1
BRUNNER, John Hamilton 4
BRUNNER, Karl 10
BRUNNER, Nicholaus H
Joseph
BRUNNER, William F. 4
BRUNNIER, Henry J. 7
BRUNNOW, Rudolph 1
Ernest
BRUNO, Angelo J. 10
BRUNO, Frank J. 3
BRUNO, Guido (Pen 7
Names Maude Martin
And Mildred Meeker)
BRUNO, Harry A. 7
BRUNOT, Harney Felix 4
BRUNS, Franklin Richard, 7
Jr.
BRUNS, Friedrich 6
BRUNS, Henry Dickson 1
BRUNS, Henry Frederick 2
BRUNS, Thomas Nelson 4
Carter
BRUNSCHWIG, Alexander 5
BRUNSCHWIG, Roger E. 5
BRUNSDALE, C(larence) 9
Norman
BRUNSON, James Edwin 4
BRUNSON, May Augusta 5
BRUNSON, William Reeder 10
BRUNSTETTER, Roscoe 8
BRUNSTING, Louis Albert 7
BRUNSWICK, Mark 5
BRUNSWIG, Lucien 2
Napoleon
BRUNTON, David William 1
BRUNTON, Frederic 7
Kemble
BRUSH, Alvin G. 4
BRUSH, Charles Francis 1
BRUSH, Daniel Harmon 1
BRUSH, Edward Nathaniel 1
BRUSH, Florence 4
BRUSH, Frank Spencer 1
BRUSH, Frederic (Louis) 5
BRUSH, George de Forest 1
BRUSH, George Jarvis 1
BRUSH, George 1
Washington
BRUSH, Henry H
BRUSH, Henry Raymond 1
BRUSH, Howard Grafton 5
BRUSH, Jacob Henry 1
BRUSH, Katharine 3
BRUSH, Louis Herbert 1
BRUSH, Matthew 1
Chauncey
BRUSH, Murray Peabody 5
BRUSH, Rapp 8
BRUSH, Robert Murray 8

BRUSH, William Whitlock 5
BRUSHINGHAM, John 1
  Patrick
BRUSIE, Charles Frederick 4
BRUSKE, Augustus 4
  Fredrich
BRUSKI, George 9
BRUSON, Herman 7
  Alexander
BRUSSEL-SMITH, Bernard 10
BRUST, Peter 2
BRUTE DE REMUR, H
  Simon William Gabriel
BRUTON, John Fletcher 5
BRUTON, Paul Wesley 9
BRUYN, Andrew De Witt H
BRUYN, Charles Dewitt 3
BRYAN, Adolphus Jerome 3
BRYAN, Albert V(ickers) 8
BRYAN, Albert Vickers 9
BRYAN, Alvin Wesley 7
BRYAN, Arthur Evan 9
BRYAN, Beauregard 4
BRYAN, Benjamin 1
  Chambers
BRYAN, Charles Page 1
BRYAN, Charles W., Jr. 4
BRYAN, Charles Wayland 2
BRYAN, Claude S. 3
BRYAN, Curtis France 10
BRYAN, Daniel Bunyan 4
BRYAN, Edward Payson 1
BRYAN, Elmer Burritt 1
BRYAN, Enoch Albert 2
BRYAN, Enoch Albert 1
BRYAN, Ernest Rowlett 3
BRYAN, Frederick Carlos 1
BRYAN, Frederick Van 7
  Pelt
BRYAN, George H
BRYAN, George 1
BRYAN, George Sands 2
BRYAN, George Sloan 7
BRYAN, Guy Morrison 1
BRYAN, Henry Francis 3
BRYAN, Henry H. H
BRYAN, Henry Lewis 1
BRYAN, Henry 4
  Ravenscroft
BRYAN, Jack Yeaman 9
BRYAN, Jacob Franklin, 8
  III
BRYAN, James Wesley 3
BRYAN, James William 3
BRYAN, John Buckley 7
BRYAN, John Edward 8
BRYAN, John Heritage H
BRYAN, John P. Kennedy 1
BRYAN, John Stewart 2
BRYAN, Joseph H
BRYAN, Joseph Hammond 4
BRYAN, Joseph Hunter H
BRYAN, Joseph Roberts 1
BRYAN, Julien 6
BRYAN, Kirk 3
BRYAN, L. R., Jr. 3
BRYAN, Leslie Aulls 5
BRYAN, Lewis Randolph 1
BRYAN, Louis Allen 4
BRYAN, Malcolm Honroe 4
BRYAN, Mary Edwards 1
BRYAN, Nathan 4
BRYAN, Nathan Philemon 1
BRYAN, Oscar Eugene 9
BRYAN, O(val) N(elson) 6
BRYAN, Paul E(asterling) 7
BRYAN, Ralph 8
BRYAN, Robert Coalter 1
BRYAN, Sheldon Martin 5
BRYAN, Shepard 6
BRYAN, Thomas Barbour 1
BRYAN, W. S. Plumer 1
BRYAN, Wilhelmus 10
  B(ogart), Jr.
BRYAN, William Alanson 2
BRYAN, William James 1
BRYAN, Mrs. William 1
  Jennings
BRYAN, William Jennings 1
BRYAN, William Lowe 3
BRYAN, William Shepard, 1
  Jr.
BRYAN, Winfred Francis 5
BRYAN, Worcester Allen 1
BRYAN, Wright 8
BRYAN-JONES, Noel D. 6
BRYANS, Henry Bussell 5
BRYANS, William 4
  Alexander, III
BRYANS, William 6
  Remington
BRYANT, Anna Burnham 5
BRYANT, Arthur Peyton 1
BRYANT, Daniel 6
  Pennington
BRYANT, Daniel 7
  Pennington

BRYANT, David E. 1
BRYANT, De Witt Clinton 4
BRYANT, Donald H. 6
BRYANT, Edgar Reeve 1
BRYANT, Edward Kendall 10
BRYANT, Edwin Eustace 1
BRYANT, Eliot H. 3
BRYANT, Emmons 6
BRYANT, Ernest Albert 1
BRYANT, Eugene 5
BRYANT, Floyd Sherman 4
BRYANT, Frank Augustus 1
BRYANT, Frederick 2
  Howard
BRYANT, George Archie 4
BRYANT, Gridley H
BRYANT, Harold W. 8
BRYANT, Henry H
BRYANT, Henry Edward 5
  Cowan
BRYANT, Henry Grier 1
BRYANT, John H. 1
BRYANT, John Howard 1
BRYANT, John Myron 7
BRYANT, Joseph Decatur 1
BRYANT, Lorinda Munson 1
  Griswold
BRYANT, Louise Stevens 3
BRYANT, Paul William 8
BRYANT, Ralph Clement 1
BRYANT, Randolph 3
BRYANT, Reece 10
  L(awrence)
BRYANT, Samuel 6
  Hollinger
BRYANT, Samuel Wood 4
BRYANT, Sara Cone 5
BRYANT, Thomas Wallace 1
BRYANT, Victor Silas 1
BRYANT, W. Sohier 3
BRYANT, Waldo Calvin 1
BRYANT, William Cullen H
BRYANT, William Cullen 1
  McKendree
BRYCE, James 1
BRYCE, Lloyd 1
BRYCE, Robert Alexander 4
BRYCE, Ronald 1
BRYCE, Wilson Bartlett 6
BRYDEN, William 5
BRYN, Helmer Halvorsen 3
BRYNE, Andrew H
BRYNE, Edward H
BRYNE, John H
BRYNE, Richard H
BRYNE, William H
BRYNGELSON, Bryno 9
BRYNILDSSEN, Yngvar 7
BRYNNER, Yul 9
BRYSON, Charles Lee 2
BRYSON, Charles William 1
BRYSON, Gladys 3
BRYSON, John Paul 1
BRYSON, Joseph 3
  Montgomery
BRYSON, Joseph Raleigh 3
BRYSON, Lyman 3
BRYSON, Olive Flora 5
BRYSON, Robert Hamilton 4
BRYSON, Robert Hassey 1
BUBB, Henry Agnew 10
BUBB, Henry Clay 4
BUBB, John Wilson 1
BUBER, Martin 4
BUBIER, Robert Harvey 7
BUCH, Joseph Godfrey 2
BUCHANAN, Andrew H
BUCHANAN, Andrew 1
  Hays
BUCHANAN, Archibald C. 7
BUCHANAN, Arthur 1
  Stillingfleet
BUCHANAN, Benjamin 1
  Franklin
BUCHANAN, Daniel 3
  Houston
BUCHANAN, David H. 5
BUCHANAN, Douglas N. 8
BUCHANAN, Edwin 8
BUCHANAN, Ella 3
BUCHANAN, Frank 1
BUCHANAN, Frank 3
BUCHANAN, Franklin H
  Sidney
BUCHANAN, George 4
BUCHANAN, George 1
  Edward
BUCHANAN, Herbert 6
  Earle
BUCHANAN, Hugh H
BUCHANAN, James H
BUCHANAN, James 1
  Anderson
BUCHANAN, James 7
  Herman
BUCHANAN, James Isaac 1
BUCHANAN, James L. 3

BUCHANAN, James P. 1
BUCHANAN, James 1
  Shannon
BUCHANAN, James 3
  William
BUCHANAN, Jesse Everett 9
BUCHANAN, John H
BUCHANAN, John 1
  Alexander
BUCHANAN, John Jenkins 1
BUCHANAN, John Lee 4
BUCHANAN, John 10
  Murdoch
BUCHANAN, John P. 3
BUCHANAN, Joseph H
BUCHANAN, Joseph Boyd 8
BUCHANAN, Joseph Ray 4
BUCHANAN, Joseph Ray 4
BUCHANAN, Joseph 1
  Rodes
BUCHANAN, Kenneth 4
BUCHANAN, Kenneth B. 3
BUCHANAN, Leonard 3
  Brown
BUCHANAN, Malcolm 1
  Griswold
BUCHANAN, M(arion) 7
  L(ynn)
BUCHANAN, Norman 3
  Sharpe
BUCHANAN, Oswald C. 4
BUCHANAN, Roberdeau 1
BUCHANAN, Robert H
  Christie
BUCHANAN, Robert Earle 7
BUCHANAN, Scott 5
BUCHANAN, T. Drysdale 1
BUCHANAN, Thomas 4
BUCHANAN, Thomas C. 3
BUCHANAN, Thompson 1
BUCHANAN, Mrs. Vera 3
  Daerr
BUCHANAN, W. C. 5
BUCHANAN, Walter 1
  Duncan
BUCHANAN, Wiley 9
  Thomas, Jr.
BUCHANAN, William 3
  Asbury
BUCHANAN, William 1
  Insco
BUCHBINDER, Jacob 3
  Richter
BUCHEN, Walther 4
BUCHER, August Johannes 1
BUCHER, Charles 9
  Augustus
BUCHER, George Heisler 8
BUCHER, John Calvin 2
BUCHER, John Conrad* H
BUCHER, John Emery 5
BUCHER, Oliver Boone 4
BUCHER, Walter H. 8
BUCHER, William Henry 4
BUCHHEISTER, Carl 9
  William
BUCHHOLZ, Heinrich 3
  Ewald
BUCHHOLZ, John 3
  Theodore
BUCHHOLZ, Ludwig 1
  Wilhelm
BUCHHOLZ, William 1
BUCHIN, Irving D. 10
BUCHLER, Justus 10
BUCHMAN, Frank N. D. 4
BUCHNER, Edward 1
  Franklin
BUCHOLTZ, Carl 7
BUCHSER, Frank H
BUCHTA, J. Williams 4
BUCHTEL, Henry 1
  Augustus
BUCHTEL, John Richards H
BUCK, Albert Henry 1
BUCK, Alfred Eliab 1
BUCK, Arthur Eugene 3
BUCK, Beaumont 3
  Bonaparte
BUCK, Benjamin F. 1
BUCK, C. Douglas 4
BUCK, Carl Darling 3
BUCK, Carl E. 3
BUCK, Cassius M. 4
BUCK, Charles Henry 6
BUCK, Charles Neville 1
BUCK, Charles William 1
BUCK, Clarence Frank 2
BUCK, Clayton Douglass 4
BUCK, Clifford Howard 9
BUCK, Daniel 1
BUCK, Daniel 1
BUCK, Daniel Azro Ashley H
BUCK, Dudley 1
BUCK, Ellsworth Brewer 5
BUCK, Ernest Ferguson 6

BUCK, Eugene Edward 7
  (Gene Buck)
BUCK, Florence 1
BUCK, Foster 5
BUCK, Frank 2
BUCK, Frank E(ugene) 8
BUCK, Frank Henry 1
BUCK, Frank Henry 2
BUCK, George H. 7
BUCK, George MacHan 1
BUCK, George Sturges 1
BUCK, Gertrude 1
BUCK, Gurdon H
BUCK, Harold Winthrop 3
BUCK, Harry Lambert 4
BUCK, Henry William 4
BUCK, Jirah Dewey 1
BUCK, John Lossing 6
BUCK, John Ransom 4
BUCK, Leffert Lefferts 1
BUCK, Norman Sydney 4
BUCK, Oscar MacMillan 1
BUCK, Paul Herman 7
BUCK, Pearl Sydenstricker 5
  (Mrs. Richard J. Walsh)
BUCK, Peter Henry 3
BUCK, Phillip Earl 2
BUCK, Philo Melvin 3
BUCK, Philo Melvin, Jr. 3
BUCK, Raymond Elliott 5
BUCK, Richard Sutton 3
BUCK, Samuel Jay 1
BUCK, Solon Justus 4
BUCK, Walter Albert 3
BUCK, Walter E. 5
BUCK, Walter Hooper 4
BUCK, William Bradford 6
BUCKALEW, Charles H. 1
BUCKBEE, Anna 4
BUCKBEE, John T. 1
BUCKELEY, Peter H
BUCKENDALE, L. Ray 3
BUCKHAM, James 1
BUCKHAM, John Wright 2
BUCKHAM, Matthew 1
  Henry
BUCKHOUT, Isaac Craig H
BUCKINGHAM, Burdette 5
  Ross
BUCKINGHAM, Charles 1
  Luman
BUCKINGHAM, David 5
  Eastburn
BUCKINGHAM, Earle 8
BUCKINGHAM, Edgar 1
BUCKINGHAM, Edward 5
  Taylor
BUCKINGHAM, George 1
  Tracy
BUCKINGHAM, Joseph 1
  Tinker
BUCKINGHAM, Norman 1
  S.
BUCKINGHAM, 6
  Theophilus Nash
BUCKINGHAM, Walter, 4
  Jr.
BUCKINGHAM, William 1
  Alfred
BUCKISCH, Walter G. M. 8
BUCKLAND, Albert 3
  William James
BUCKLAND, Charles 1
  Clark
BUCKLAND, Cyrus H
BUCKLAND, Edward 3
  Grant
BUCKLAND, Ralph H
  Pomeroy
BUCKLAND, William 1
BUCKLE, John Franklin 3
BUCKLER, Leslie Hepburn 8
BUCKLER, Richard 3
  Thompson
BUCKLER, Thomas H
  Hepburn
BUCKLER, William Earl 10
BUCKLER, William 3
  Hepburn
BUCKLEY, Albert Coulson 1
BUCKLEY, Alfred 8
BUCKLEY, Charles A. 4
BUCKLEY, Edmund 4
BUCKLEY, Edwin M. 3
BUCKLEY, Emerson 10
BUCKLEY, Ernest 1
  Robertson
BUCKLEY, Frank Michael 8
BUCKLEY, George Wright 4
BUCKLEY, Harry D. 3
BUCKLEY, Homer John 6
BUCKLEY, James Monroe 1
BUCKLEY, James R. 5
BUCKLEY, James V. 3
BUCKLEY, Jere D. 4
BUCKLEY, John 7
BUCKLEY, John Beecher 9

BUCKLEY, John Peter 2
BUCKLEY, John Raymond 9
BUCKLEY, John William 8
BUCKLEY, Joseph 8
BUCKLEY, Leo Jerome 3
BUCKLEY, May 5
BUCKLEY, Oliver 3
  Ellsworth
BUCKLEY, Samuel H
  Botsford
BUCKLEY, Tim 6
BUCKLEY, Warren 9
  Bowman
BUCKLIN, Edward C. 1
BUCKLIN, George 5
  Augustus
BUCKLIN, James C. H
BUCKLIN, James W. 1
BUCKLIN, Walter Stanley 4
BUCKMAN, C. B. 3
BUCKMAN, Harry Oliver 4
BUCKMAN, Henry 5
  Holland, II
BUCKMASTER, Leland 4
  Stanford
BUCKMINSTER, Joseph H
  Stevens
BUCKNAM, Ransford D. 1
BUCKNELL, Howard, Jr. 5
BUCKNELL, William H
BUCKNER, Albert Gallatin 4
BUCKNER, Alexander H
BUCKNER, Aylett Hawes H
BUCKNER, Aylette H
BUCKNER, Chester Arthur 3
BUCKNER, David Ernest 3
BUCKNER, E. C. 4
BUCKNER, Emory Roy 1
BUCKNER, G(arrett) 7
  Davis
BUCKNER, George 8
  Walker, Jr.
BUCKNER, George 4
  Washington
BUCKNER, Mortimer 2
  Norton
BUCKNER, Richard Aylett H
BUCKNER, Simon Bolivar 1
BUCKNER, Simon Bolivar, 2
  Jr.
BUCKNER, Thomas 2
  Aylette
BUCKNER, Walker 1
BUCKNER, Walter 3
  Coleman
BUCKS, William Henry 4
BUCKSTONE, John B. H
BUCKWALTER, Tracy V. 2
BUCKY, Gustav 7
BUCKY, Philip Barnett 3
BUCOVE, Bernard 6
BUDA, Joseph 5
BUDD, Britton Ihrie 4
BUDD, Charles Henry 3
BUDD, Charles Jay 1
BUDD, Edward G. 2
BUDD, Edward G., Jr. 4
BUDD, Henry 5
BUDD, James Herbert 1
BUDD, John M. 5
BUDD, Nathan P. 5
BUDD, Ralph 8
BUDD, Thomas Allibone 8
BUDDINGTON, Arthur 7
  Francis
BUDDY, Charles F. 4
BUDENZ, Louis Francis 3
BUDER, Gustavus 3
  Adolphus
BUDGE, Alfred 3
BUDGE, David Clare 2
BUDGE, Ross A. 5
BUDGE, Walter Lyttleton 4
BUDGETT, Sidney Payne 4
BUDINA, Adolph Otto 6
BUDINGER, John Michael 4
BUDINGTON, Robert 3
  Allyn
BUDLONG, Frederick 3
  Grandy
BUDROW, Lester Rusk 5
BUDRYS, Jonas 8
BUECHE, Arthur Maynard 9
BUEDING, Ernest 9
BUEHL, Louis Harry, III 9
BUEHLER, Albert Carl 7
BUEHLER, Alfred Grether 5
BUEHLER, Calvin A. 10
BUEHLER, Henry Andrew 2
BUEHLER, Huber Gray 1
BUEHLER, William 1
  Emmett
BUEHLER, William George 1
BUEHNER, Carl William 6
BUEHR, Karl Albert 3
BUEHRER, Theophil 6
  Frederic

BUEHRIG, Edward Henry 9
BUEHRING, Paul Henry 3
BUEHRMAN, Peter A. 4
BUEK, Charles Welles 9
BUEK, Gustave Herman 1
BUEL, Alexander Woodruff H
BUEL, Clarence Clough
BUEL, James William 1
BUEL, Jesse H
BUEL, Walker Showers 3
BUELL, Abel H
BUELL, Alexander Hamilton H
BUELL, Augustus C. 1
BUELL, Caroline Brown 1
BUELL, Charles Edward 1
BUELL, Don Carlos H
BUELL, Ellen Louise 8
BUELL, Eugene F(ranklin) 9
BUELL, Marcus Darius 1
BUELL, Murray F. 6
BUELL, Raymond Leslie 2
BUELL, Robert Catlin, Jr. 5
BUELL, Robert Lewis 4
BUELL, Wayne Herbert 8
BUENGER, Theodore 2
BUENTING, Otto Wilhelm 1
BUERKI, Robin Carl 9
BUESCHING, Charles Henry 4
BUESS, Charles Merlyn 7
BUESSER, Frederick G. 5
BUETOW, Herbert P(aul) 5
BUFF, Conrad 7
BUFF, Mary Marsh 8
BUFFALO CHILD LONG LANCE 1
BUFFETT, Howard 4
BUFFINGTON, Adelbert Rinaldo 1
BUFFINGTON, Albert Franklin 8
BUFFINGTON, Eugene Jackson 1
BUFFINGTON, Francis Stephan 10
BUFFINGTON, Joseph H
BUFFINGTON, Joseph 2
BUFFINTON, James H
BUFFINTON, Merrill 4
BUFFORD, John H. H
BUFFUM, Arnold H
BUFFUM, Burt C. 4
BUFFUM, Douglas Labaree 4
BUFFUM, George Tower 8
BUFFUM, Hugh Straight 3
BUFFUM, Joseph, Jr. H
BUFFUM, Robert Earle 1
BUFORD, Abraham* H
BUFORD, Charles Homer 4
BUFORD, Elizabeth Burgess 4
BUFORD, John H
BUFORD, Lawrence B. 6
BUFORD, Napoleon Bonaparte H
BUFORD, Rivers Henderson 6
BUGAN, Thomas Gregory 3
BUGAS, John Stephen 8
BUGBEE, Benjamin C. 2
BUGBEE, Henry Greenwood 2
BUGBEE, Lester Gladstone 1
BUGBEE, Lucius Hatfield 2
BUGBEE, Percy Isaac 3
BUGG, Benjamin Lamar 5
BUGG, Lelia Hardin 1
BUGG, Robert Malone H
BUGGE, Sven Brun 2
BUGGELLI, Blanche Swett (Mowry) 5
BUGNIAZET, G. M. 3
BUHL, Arthur Hiram 1
BUHL, Lawrence D. 3
BUHLER, Charlotte 6
BUHLER, Curt Ferdinand 8
BUHLER, John Embich 7
BUHRMAN, Parker Wilson 7
BUICK, James McNair 1
BUIE, Louis Arthur 6
BUISSERET STEENBECQUE DE BLAREGHIEN, Count Conrad de 4
BUIST, Archibald Johnston 2
BUIST, George Alexander 1
BUIST, George L. 4
BUIST, George Lamb 1
BUIST, Harold J. 3
BUIST, Henry 2
BUIST, John Somers 3
BUKOFZER, Manfred F. 3
BUKOWSKI, Arthur F. 10
BUKOWSKI, Peter Ivan 2
BULAND, George Leonard 7
BULEY, Hilton Clifford 9

BULEY, R. Carlyle 5
BULFINCH, Charles H
BULFINCH, Thomas H
BULGAKOW, Michael Afanasievich 4
BULGANIN, Nikolai Aleksandrovich 6
BULKELEY, Harry Clough 2
BULKELEY, Max M. 7
BULKELEY, Morgan Gardner
BULKELEY, William E. A. 3
BULKLEY, Edwin Muhlenberg, Jr. 7
BULKLEY, Frank 1
BULKLEY, George Grant 1
BULKLEY, Harry Conant 2
BULKLEY, John Williams H
BULKLEY, L. Duncan 1
BULKLEY, Robert Johns 4
BULKLEY, William Francis H
BULL, Alfred Castleman 5
BULL, Carroll Gideon 1
BULL, Charles Livingston 1
BULL, Charles Stedman 1
BULL, Daniel F. 7
BULL, Dorothy 1
BULL, E. Myron H
BULL, Ephraim Wales H
BULL, Ernest M. 1
BULL, Frank Kellogg 1
BULL, George Mairs 2
BULL, Henry Bolivar 8
BULL, James Henry 1
BULL, John* H
BULL, Ludlow 3
BULL, Mason 8
BULL, Melville 1
BULL, Sara Chapman 1
BULL, Storm 1
BULL, William* H
BULL, William Lanman 1
BULL, William Lyle 9
BULL, William Rutledge 6
BULL, William Tillinghast 1
BULLA, Charles Dehaven 1
BULLA, Robert Nelson 1
BULLARD, Arthur 4
BULLARD, Daniel R. 5
BULLARD, Edward Clarke 5
BULLARD, Edward Crisp 7
BULLARD, Edward Payson, Jr. 5
BULLARD, Ernest Luther 1
BULLARD, F. Lauriston 3
BULLARD, Frank Dearborn 1
BULLARD, Frederic Field 1
BULLARD, Henry Adams H
BULLARD, James Atkins 3
BULLARD, Otis A. H
BULLARD, Ralph Hadley 4
BULLARD, Robert Felton 5
BULLARD, Robert Lee 2
BULLARD, Sellar 7
BULLARD, Stanley Hale 1
BULLARD, Washington Irving 2
BULLARD, William Hannum Grubb 1
BULLARD, William Norton 1
BULLARD, Willis Clare 8
BULLEN, Adelaide Kendall (Kenneth Sutherlan Bullen) 10
BULLEN, Keith Edward 7
BULLEN, Percy Sutherland 5
BULLENE, Egbert Frank 2
BULLIET, Clarence Joseph 3
BULLINGTON, John P. 2
BULLIS, Harold Edmund 8
BULLIS, Harry Amos 4
BULLIS, John Lapham 1
BULLITT, Alexander Scott H
BULLITT, Dorothy Stimson 9
BULLITT, Henry Massie H
BULLITT, John C. 1
BULLITT, John C. 9
BULLITT, John Marshall 9
BULLITT, Orville Horwitz 7
BULLITT, Scott 1
BULLITT, Thomas W. 1
BULLITT, William Christian 3
BULLITT, William Marshall 3
BULLOCH, Archibald H
BULLOCH, Joseph Gaston Baillie 4
BULLOCH, William Bellinger H
BULLOCK, A. George 1
BULLOCK, Alexander Hamilton H

BULLOCK, Alexander Hamilton 4
BULLOCK, Calvin 2
BULLOCK, Chandler 5
BULLOCK, Charles Jesse H
BULLOCK, Harry Elmer 3
BULLOCK, Henry Morton 8
BULLOCK, James Dunwoody H
BULLOCK, John Rice 7
BULLOCK, Marie Leontine (Marie Leontine Graves) 9
BULLOCK, Motier Acklin 1
BULLOCK, Stephen H
BULLOCK, Theodore 3
BULLOCK, Thomas Seaman 4
BULLOCK, William A. H
BULLOCK, Wingfield H
BULLOWA, Jesse G. M. 2
BULMAN, Joel Noel Thompson 5
BULMAN, Olivier Meredith Boone 6
BULOVA, Arde 1
BULOW, William John 3
BULTMAN, Fritz 8
BULWINKLE, Alfred Lee 3
BUMBY, Horace Abrum 8
BUMBY, John Harold 6
BUMGARDNER, Albert Orin 9
BUMGARDNER, Helen Ayers 6
BUMGARNER, Ray Quincy 5
BUMP, Boardman 9
BUMP, Charles Weathers 1
BUMP, Milan Raynard 1
BUMPOUS, E. T. 4
BUMPUS, Hermon Carey 2
BUMPUS, Hermon Carey, Jr. 9
BUMSTEAD, Charles W. 5
BUMSTEAD, Freeman Josiah H
BUMSTEAD, Henry Andrews 1
BUMSTEAD, Horace 1
BUNCE, Allen Hamilton 4
BUNCE, Arthur C. 3
BUNCE, Edgar F. 6
BUNCE, Frances Marvin 1
BUNCE, J. Oscar 4
BUNCE, Oliver Bell H
BUNCE, W. Gedney 1
BUNCH, Samuel H
BUNCHE, Ralph Johnson H
BUNDEL, Charles Michael 1
BUNDESEN, Herman Niels 4
BUNDESEN, Russell 7
BUNDLIE, Gerhard 4
BUNDY, Edwin S. 4
BUNDY, Harvey Hollister 4
BUNDY, Hezekiah Sanford 1
BUNDY, John Elwood 1
BUNDY, Jonas Mills H
BUNDY, Omar 1
BUNDY, Solomon H
BUNDY, Walter Ernest 8
BUNDY, William Edgar 1
BUNEY, Virgil Dan 7
BUNGE, Helen Lathrop 5
BUNGER, William Boone 9
BUNIM, Joseph J. 4
BUNIN, Ivan Alekseevich 3
BUNKER, Alonzo 1
BUNKER, Arthur H. 4
BUNKER, Charles C. 6
BUNKER, Charles Waite Orville 3
BUNKER, Ellsworth 8
BUNKER, Frank Forest 1
BUNKER, George M. 9
BUNKER, Harry Surfus 4
BUNKER, John Wymond Miller 7
BUNKLEY, Joel William 5
BUNKLEY, Joel William, Jr. 5
BUNN, Charles 4
BUNN, Charles Wilson 1
BUNN, Clinton Orrin 1
BUNN, Edward Bernard 5
BUNN, Edward Schaible 1
BUNN, George Lincoln 1
BUNN, George Wallace, Jr. 1
BUNN, Henry Gaston 1
BUNN, Howard Stolpp 4
BUNN, Jacob 1
BUNN, Paul Axtell 5
BUNN, Romanzo 1
BUNN, William Hall 4
BUNNELL, Charles Ernest 3
BUNNELL, Edward Horace 1
BUNNELL, Sterling Haight 5

BUNNELLE, Robert Ellsworth 10
BUNNER, Henry Cuyler H
BUNNER, Rudolph H
BUNNEY, William E. 10
BUNSHAFT, Gordon 10
BUNTEN, William Andrew 7
BUNTING, Charles Henry 5
BUNTING, George Avery 3
BUNTING, Guy J. 1
BUNTING, Martha 1
BUNTING, Russell Welford 4
BUNTLINE, Ned H
BUNTS, Frank Emory 1
BUNZELL, Herbert Horace 4
BUONO, Victor Charles 9
BURBA, Edwin Hess 5
BURBA, George Francis 1
BURBAGE, William Henry 4
BURBANK, Elbridge Ayer 2
BURBANK, Harold Hitchings 3
BURBANK, James Brattle 1
BURBANK, Luther 1
BURBANK, Mortimer Lincoln 3
BURBANK, Reginald 8
BURBANK, Wilbur Swett 6
BURBIDGE, Frederick 4
BURBIDGE, Sir Richard Grant Woodman 4
BURBRIDGE, Stephen Gano H
BURCH, Albert 5
BURCH, Angelus Teague 4
BURCH, Charles Bell 3
BURCH, Charles Newell 1
BURCH, Charles Sumner 1
BURCH, Dean 10
BURCH, Edward Parris 2
BURCH, Ernest Ward 1
BURCH, Francis Boucher 9
BURCH, Frank Earl 5
BURCH, George Bosworth 6
BURCH, George E. 9
BURCH, Guy Irving 3
BURCH, Henry Reed 5
BURCH, H(ubert) Wendel 5
BURCH, John Chilton H
BURCH, Lowell R. 5
BURCH, Lucius Edward 4
BURCH, Newton Dexter 1
BURCH, Rousseau Angelus 3
BURCH, Thomas Granville 3
BURCHAM, Lester Arthur 9
BURCHAM, Paul Baker 8
BURCHAM, William David 7
BURCHARD, Edward Lawyer 2
BURCHARD, Ernest Francis 1
BURCHARD, Horatio Chapin 1
BURCHARD, John Ely 6
BURCHARD, John Ely 7
BURCHARD, Samuel Dickinson 1
BURCHARD, Waldo Wadsworth 9
BURCHETT, George Jerome 4
BURCHFIELD, A.H.J. 1
BURCHFIELD, Albert Horne 4
BURCHFIELD, Charles Ephraim 4
BURCHILL, George Percival 8
BURCHILL, Thomas F. 3
BURCHKARDT, Charles Jacob 6
BURCK, Jacob 8
BURCKHALTER, Charles 1
BURCKHALTER, Frank Lucien 1
BURD, George H
BURD, George Eli 1
BURD, Henry Alfred 9
BURDELL, Edwin Sharp 7
BURDELL, William Frederick 2
BURDEN, Harry P. 5
BURDEN, Henry H
BURDEN, James Abercrombie* 1
BURDEN, Oliver D. 1
BURDEN, William Armistead Moale 8
BURDEN, William Douglas 7
BURDETT, Allen Mitchell, Jr. 7
BURDETT, Everett Watson 1
BURDETT, Fred Hartshorn 1
BURDETT, George Albert 4
BURDETT, Herbert C. H
BURDETT, Samuel Swinfin 1
BURDETT, William Carter 2

BURDETTE, Clara Bradley (Mrs. Robert J. Burdette) 5
BURDETTE, Franklin L. 6
BURDETTE, Robert Jones 1
BURDGE, Franklin 1
BURDGE, Howard Griffith 3
BURDICK, Alfred Stephen 1
BURDICK, Charles Baker 3
BURDICK, Charles Kellogg 1
BURDICK, Charles Kellogg 2
BURDICK, Charles Lalor 10
BURDICK, Charles Williams 1
BURDICK, Clark 2
BURDICK, Clinton De Witt
BURDICK, Dean Lanphere 8
BURDICK, Donald Langworthy 5
BURDICK, Eugene L. 4
BURDICK, Francis Marion 1
BURDICK, Harold Ormond 6
BURDICK, Joel Wakeman 1
BURDICK, Quentin Northrop 10
BURDICK, Raymond T(erry) 8
BURDICK, Usher L. 4
BURDICK, Willard Delure 3
BURDICK, William Livesey 3
BURDINE, William M. 8
BUREAU, E.A. 1
BURES, Charles Edwin 6
BURFORD, Archie Dean 2
BURFORD, Bernard Boyd 4
BURFORD, Cyrus Edgar 5
BURFORD, John Henry 1
BURG, Alfred William 3
BURGAN, John 3
BURGE, Flippen D. 2
BURGE, J.H. Hobart 1
BURGEE, Clyde Elmore 3
BURGEE, Joseph Zeno 3
BURGER, John D. 2
BURGER, Kathryn Reynolds 3
BURGER, Othmar Joseph 9
BURGER, Owen Francis 1
BURGER, Rudolph E. 7
BURGER, William Henry 4
BURGER, William Henry 1
BURGERS, J. M. 8
BURGES, Dempsey H
BURGES, Richard Fenner 2
BURGES, Tristam H
BURGESS, William Henry 2
BURGESS, Albert Franklin 3
BURGESS, Alexander Frederick 2
BURGESS, Charles McFetridge 5
BURGESS, Cora Louise Turney 4
BURGESS, Edward H
BURGESS, Edward Sanford 1
BURGESS, Edwin Haines 1
BURGESS, Elizabeth Chamberlain 2
BURGESS, Ellis Beaver 2
BURGESS, Ernest Watson 4
BURGESS, Frank H. 1
BURGESS, Frederick 1
BURGESS, Gaven D. 1
BURGESS, Gelett 3
BURGESS, George 1
BURGESS, George Farmer 1
BURGESS, George Heckman 3
BURGESS, George Kimball 1
BURGESS, George Van Trump 7
BURGESS, Harold Dempster 10
BURGESS, Harry 1
BURGESS, Ida Josephine 1
BURGESS, John Albert 5
BURGESS, John William 1
BURGESS, Kenneth Farwell 4
BURGESS, Magnus Mallory 10
BURGESS, May Ayres 3
BURGESS, Merrill Charles 7
BURGESS, Perry 5
BURGESS, Philip 5
BURGESS, Rembert Bennett 1
BURGESS, Robert Wilbur 5
BURGESS, Robert Wilbur 8
BURGESS, Roy Howard, Jr. 3
BURGESS, Ruth Payne Jewett 1

BURGESS, Mrs. Samuel 5
  Rostron
BURGESS, Theodore 1
  Chalon
BURGESS, Theodore 4
  Herbert
BURGESS, Thomas M. 4
BURGESS, Thornton 4
  Waldo
BURGESS, Warren 7
  Randolph
BURGESS, William* 1
BURGESS, William Starling 2
BURGEVINE, Henry H
  Andrea
BURGHALTER, Daniel 2
BURGIN, Henry T. 5
BURGIN, Samuel H.C. 5
BURGIN, William Garner 5
BURGIN, William Olin 2
BURGISS, William 4
BURGISS, William Wesley 3
BURGOON, Norman 9
  Aaron, Jr.
BURGOYNE, John H
BURGREEN, David 7
BURGSTAHLER, Herbert 7
  John
BURHOP, William Charles 7
BURHOP, William Henry 4
BURK, Dean 9
BURK, Frederic Lister 1
BURK, Henry 1
BURK, Jesse Young 1
BURK, Joseph Edwill 2
BURK, W. Herbert 1
BURKARD, Ralph 9
  Frederick
BURKAT, Leonard 10
BURKE, Aedanus H
BURKE, Andrew H. 4
BURKE, Arthur Devries 3
BURKE, B. Ellen 4
BURKE, Billie 5
BURKE, Charles Henry 2
BURKE, Charles St H
  Thomas
BURKE, Daniel 5
BURKE, Daniel Webster 1
BURKE, Edmund* 4
BURKE, Edmund 5
BURKE, Edmund Whitney 4
BURKE, Edward M. 4
BURKE, Edward Nolan 7
BURKE, Edward Raymond 5
BURKE, Edward Timothy 1
BURKE, Ellen Coolidge 6
BURKE, Ellen Coolidge 7
BURKE, Eugene Paul 4
BURKE, George James 3
BURKE, Harold P. 8
BURKE, Haslett Platt 3
BURKE, James A. 8
BURKE, James Francis 1
BURKE, James Owen 4
BURKE, James Vincent, Jr. 8
BURKE, Jeremiah Edmund 1
BURKE, Joe 10
BURKE, John 1
BURKE, John Edmund 4
BURKE, John Garrett 10
BURKE, John J. 1
BURKE, John Miles 10
BURKE, John P. 4
BURKE, John Stephen 4
BURKE, John Woolfolk 3
BURKE, Joseph A. 4
BURKE, Joseph Henry 1
BURKE, Kendall Edwards 2
BURKE, Lloyd Hudson 9
BURKE, Maurice Francis 1
BURKE, Melville 7
BURKE, Michael E. 3
BURKE, Milo Darwin 4
BURKE, N. Charles 4
BURKE, Patrick H. 3
BURKE, Raymond H. 6
BURKE, Robert Belle 1
BURKE, Robert Emmet 1
BURKE, Stephen Patrick 2
BURKE, Stevenson 1
BURKE, Thomas H
BURKE, Thomas 1
BURKE, Thomas A. 5
BURKE, Thomas Francis 10
BURKE, Thomas Henry 3
BURKE, Thomas John M. 1
BURKE, Thomas Joseph 4
BURKE, Thomas Martin 1
  Aloysius
BURKE, Timothy Farrar 4
BURKE, Victor 8
BURKE, Vincent C. 5
BURKE, Vincent John 6
BURKE, Webster H. 3
BURKE, William J. 1

BURKET, Harlan 3
  Fessenden
BURKET, Jacob F. 1
BURKETT, Charles 4
  William
BURKETT, Charles 5
  William
BURKETT, Elmer Jacob 1
BURKHALTER, Edward 1
  Read
BURKHALTER, Everett 6
  Glen
BURKHALTER, Frank 6
  Elisha
BURKHALTER, George 7
  Lewis
BURKHALTER, John 5
  Thomas
BURKHARD, Samuel 7
BURKHARDT, Samuel, Jr. 1
BURKHARDT, Wilbur 1
  Neil
BURKHART, Harvey 2
  Jacob
BURKHART, Roy Abram 4
BURKHART, Samuel 6
  Ellsworth
BURKHART, Summers 1
BURKHART, William H. 7
BURKHEAD, Margaret 6
  Bristow
BURKHOLDER, Charles 4
  Harvey
BURKHOLDER, Charles 5
  Irvine
BURKHOLDER, Paul 5
  Rufus
BURKLEY, George 10
  Gregory
BURKLIN, Robert 4
  Reyburn
BURKLUND, Carl Edwin 4
BURKS, Jesse Desmaux 4
BURKS, Martin Parks 1
BURLAGE, Henry 1
  Matthew
BURLEIGH, Cecil 7
BURLEIGH, Charles H
  Calistus
BURLEIGH, Clarence 1
BURLEIGH, Clarence 1
  Blendon
BURLEIGH, Edwin Chick 1
BURLEIGH, George 1
  Shepard
BURLEIGH, George 1
  William
BURLEIGH, Harry T. 2
BURLEIGH, John Holmes H
BURLEIGH, May Halsey 4
  Miller
BURLEIGH, Nathaniel 5
  George
BURLEIGH, Sydney 1
  Richmond
BURLEIGH, Walter H
  Atwood
BURLEIGH, William H
BURLEIGH, William H
  Henry
BURLESON, Albert Sidney 1
BURLESON, Edward H
BURLESON, Elizabeth 7
  (Mrs. Gamewell David
  Burleson)
BURLESON, Hugh Latimer 1
BURLESON, Omar 10
BURLESON, Rufus 1
  Columbus
BURLEW, Ebert Keiser 2
BURLEY, Clarence 1
  Augustus
BURLEY, William V. 8
BURLIN, Natalie Curtis 1
BURLIN, Paul 5
BURLING, Albert E. 4
BURLING, Edward H
BURLING, Edward 5
  Burnham
BURLING, (Fred) Temple 6
BURLINGAME, Anson H
BURLINGAME, C. 3
  Charles
BURLINGAME, Edward 1
  Livermore
BURLINGAME, Eugene 1
  Watson
BURLINGAME, Leonas 5
  Lancelot
BURLINGAME, Leroy J. 4
BURLINGAME, Luther D. 1
BURLINGAME, Roger 4
BURLINGHAM, Aaron 1
  Hale
BURLINGHAM, Charles 7
BURLINGHAM, Charles 3
  C.

BURLINGHAM, Mrs. 7
  Grace Semple
BURLINGHAM, Louis 2
  Herbert
BURLIUK, David 4
  Davidovich
BURMA, John Harmon 1
BURMAN, Ben Lucien 8
BURMEISTER, Richard 4
BURMESTER, Harry 7
  Frederick
BURMESTER, Henry 7
  Finch
BURN, Belle Sumner 5
  Angier
BURN, Harry Thomas 7
BURNAM, Anthony 7
  Rollins
BURNAM, Curtis Field 2
BURNAM, John Miller 1
BURNAM, Joseph 7
  E(dward)
BURNAP, George 7
BURNAP, George H
  Washington
BURNELL, Barker 1
BURNELL, Edward John 3
BURNELL, Edward John, 4
  Jr.
BURNELL, Max Ronald 3
BURNELL, Nathaniel 7
  Alanson
BURNES, Alonzo D. 1
BURNES, James Alton 7
BURNES, James Nelson H
BURNES, Matthews James 4
BURNET, Dana 8
BURNET, David 7
BURNET, David H
  Gouverneur
BURNET, Duncan 5
BURNET, Frank 9
  MacFarlane
BURNET, Jacob H
BURNET, W. Everit H
BURNET, William* H
BURNETT, Charles 1
BURNETT, Charles Henry 1
BURNETT, Charles Hoyt 5
BURNETT, Charles Hugh, 5
  Jr.
BURNETT, Charles 2
  Theodore
BURNETT, Chester Arthur 7
  (Howlin' Wolf)
BURNETT, Cordas Chris 6
BURNETT, Dana 4
BURNETT, Edgar Albert 1
BURNETT, Edmund Cody 2
BURNETT, Edwin Clark 1
BURNETT, Frances 1
  Hodgson
BURNETT, George Henry 1
BURNETT, George Jackson 5
BURNETT, Hamilton 10
  S(ands)
BURNETT, Henry H
  Cornelius
BURNETT, Henry 1
  Lawrence
BURNETT, Jesse 5
  McGarrity
BURNETT, John Lawson 1
BURNETT, John Torrey 1
BURNETT, Joseph H
BURNETT, Joseph 1
  Herndon
BURNETT, Leo 5
BURNETT, Leo 6
BURNETT, Paul Moreton 2
BURNETT, Peter 1
  Hardeman
BURNETT, Robert M. 1
BURNETT, Rogers 4
  Levering
BURNETT, Swan Moses 1
BURNETT, Whit 5
BURNETT, William Riley 8
BURNETTE, Nancy Everitt 10
BURNETTE, Wells Dewey 6
BURNHAM, Alan 3
BURNHAM, Alfred Avery H
BURNHAM, Charles 4
  Edwin
BURNHAM, Clara Louise 1
BURNHAM, Claude 1
  George
BURNHAM, Daniel 1
  Hudson
BURNHAM, Daniel 4
  Hudson
BURNHAM, E(noch) Lewis 5
BURNHAM, Frederic 1
  Lynden
BURNHAM, Frederick 5
  E(dwin)

BURNHAM, Frederick 2
  Russell
BURNHAM, Frederick 5
  William
BURNHAM, George 1
BURNHAM, George, Jr. 1
BURNHAM, Henry Eben 1
BURNHAM, Hubert 5
BURNHAM, James 9
BURNHAM, John Bird 1
BURNHAM, Joseph 7
  Andrew
BURNHAM, Michael 1
BURNHAM, Ralph W. 1
BURNHAM, Roger Noble 4
BURNHAM, Sherburne 1
  Wesley
BURNHAM, Silas Henry 1
BURNHAM, Smith 2
BURNHAM, Sylvester 1
BURNHAM, Walter Henry 5
BURNHAM, Wilbur 8
  Herbert
BURNHAM, William 1
  Henry
BURNHAM, William 1
  Power
BURNIGHT, Ralph 6
  Fletcher
BURNITE, Caroline 5
BURNQUIST, Joseph 4
  Alfred Arner
BURNS, Allen Tibbals 3
BURNS, Andrew J. 3
BURNS, Anna Letitia 5
BURNS, Anthony H
BURNS, Arthur Edward 9
BURNS, Arthur F. 9
BURNS, Beryl Iles 8
BURNS, Bob 3
BURNS, Charles Wesley 1
BURNS, Clyde Edwin 4
BURNS, Cornelius F. 1
BURNS, Daniel M. 4
BURNS, Daniel Matthew 8
BURNS, David 5
BURNS, Dean Carl 7
BURNS, Dennis Francis 3
BURNS, Donald Bruce 6
BURNS, Edward H. 3
BURNS, Edward McNall 3
BURNS, Elmer Ellsworth 3
BURNS, Eveline M(abel) 1
BURNS, Francis Highlands 1
BURNS, Frank 2
BURNS, George Plumer 3
BURNS, Hendry Stuart 5
  MacKenzie
BURNS, Henry B. 4
BURNS, Herbert 3
  Deschamps
BURNS, Howard Fletcher 5
BURNS, James Aloysius 1
BURNS, James Austin 1
BURNS, James Francis 10
BURNS, James Henry 7
BURNS, James J. 1
BURNS, James Matthew 7
BURNS, John Anthony 6
BURNS, John Horne 4
BURNS, John Joseph 3
BURNS, John Lawrence 10
BURNS, Joseph H
BURNS, Kevin 3
BURNS, Lawrence 9
BURNS, Lee 3
BURNS, Louis Henry 1
BURNS, Matthew D. 4
BURNS, Matthew James 8
BURNS, Melvin P. 1
BURNS, Michael Anthony 1
BURNS, Murray Edwin 6
BURNS, Otway H
BURNS, Owen McIntosh 3
BURNS, P.P. 1
BURNS, Raymond Joseph 7
BURNS, Robert H
BURNS, Robert Edward 5
BURNS, Robert Emmett 5
BURNS, Robert Homer 7
BURNS, Robert M(artin) 8
BURNS, Robert Whitney 8
BURNS, Sir Alan 8
BURNS, Vincent Godfrey 7
BURNS, Vincent Leo 9
BURNS, Walter Noble 1
BURNS, W(illiam) Haydon 1
BURNS, William Henry 1
BURNS, William John 1
BURNS, William Joseph 7
BURNSIDE, Ambrose H
  Everett
BURNSIDE, Cameron 7
BURNSIDE, Thomas H
BURNSTAN, Rowland 7
BURNTVEDT, Thorvald 8
  Olsen

BURPEE, Charles Winslow 4
BURPEE, David 7
BURPEE, David 8
BURPEE, George William 4
BURPEE, Lucien Francis 1
BURPEE, W. Atlee 1
BURPEE, William Partridge 4
BURQUE, Henri Alphonse 2
BURR, Aaron* H
BURR, Albert George 1
BURR, Alexander George 3
BURR, Alfred Edmund H
BURR, Allston 2
BURR, Anna Robeson 1
BURR, Borden 3
BURR, C.B. 1
BURR, Charles Walts 3
BURR, David Anthony 9
BURR, Donald David 10
BURR, Edward 3
BURR, Enoch Fitch 1
BURR, Eugene Wyllys 4
BURR, Freeman F. 5
BURR, George Elbert 1
BURR, George Howard 1
BURR, George Hutchinson 4
BURR, George Lincoln 1
BURR, George L(indsley) 5
BURR, George Washington 1
BURR, Hanford Montrose 4
BURR, Henry Turner 5
BURR, Hudson C. 3
BURR, Hugh Chamberlin 8
BURR, I. Tucker 4
BURR, Joseph Arthur 4
BURR, Karl Edward 2
BURR, Leslie L. 1
BURR, Nelson Beardsley 1
BURR, Samuel Engle, Jr. 9
BURR, Theodosia H
BURR, William Henry 1
BURR, William Hubert 1
BURR, William P. 1
BURR, William Wesley 4
BURRAGE, Albert 1
  Cameron
BURRAGE, Champlin 5
BURRAGE, Charles Dana 1
BURRAGE, Dwight 1
  Grafton
BURRAGE, Guy Hamilton 3
BURRAGE, Henry 1
  Sweetser
BURRAGE, Walter Lincoln 1
BURRALL, William Porter H
BURRELL, Berkeley 7
  Graham
BURRELL, Claude 1
  Adelbert
BURRELL, David De 5
  Forest
BURRELL, David James 1
BURRELL, Edward Parker 1
BURRELL, Frederick 1
  Augustus Muhlenberg
BURRELL, George Arthur 3
BURRELL, George W. 5
BURRELL, H. Cayford 1
BURRELL, Herbert Leslie 1
BURRELL, John Angus 1
BURRELL, Joseph Dunn 1
BURRELL, Loomis 7
BURRILL, Alexander H
  Mansfield
BURRILL, Harvey D. 1
BURRILL, James H
BURRILL, Stanley Stinton 3
BURRILL, Thomas 1
  Jonathan
BURRINGTON, George H
BURRINGTON, Howard 4
  Rice
BURRIS, Benjamin J. 1
BURRIS, Joseph Jennings 1
BURRIS, Quincy Guy 5
BURRIS, William Paxton 2
BURRISS, Stanley William 7
BURRITT, Bailey Barton 3
BURRITT, Eldon Grant 1
BURRITT, Elihu H
BURRITT, Henry W. 4
BURRITT, Maurice Chase 7
BURROUGH, Edmund 4
  Weldmann
BURROUGHS, Bryson 1
BURROUGHS, Charles 4
  Franklin
BURROUGHS, Clyde 7
  Huntley
BURROUGHS, Edgar Rice 3
BURROUGHS, Edith 1
  Woodman
BURROUGHS, Edmund 8
BURROUGHS, Prince 2
  Emmanuel

BURROUGHS, George 1
Stockton
BURROUGHS, George W. 3
BURROUGHS, Harry 2
Ernest
BURROUGHS, John 1
BURROUGHS, John Curtis H
BURROUGHS, Jonothan 4
Edington
BURROUGHS, Marie 4
BURROUGHS, Sherman 1
Everett
BURROUGHS, Silas H
Mainville
BURROUGHS, Walter 10
Laughlin
BURROUGHS, Wilbur 7
Greeley
BURROUGHS, W(illiam) 5
Dwight
BURROUGHS, William H
Seward
BURROW, James Randall 1
BURROW, Joel Randall 1
BURROW, Trigant 3
BURROW, William Fite, Sr. 10
BURROWES, Alexander J. 1
BURROWES, Alonzo 1
Moore
BURROWES, Arthur 5
Victor
BURROWES, Edward 1
Thomas
BURROWES, Hillier 8
M(cClure)
BURROWES, Katherine 1
BURROWES, Peter Edward 1
BURROWES, Thomas 6
BURROWES, Thomas H
Henry
BURROWS, Abe 1
BURROWS, Charles Robert 9
BURROWS, Charles 1
William
BURROWS, Daniel H
BURROWS, Daniel Chapel 5
BURROWS, Frederick 4
Nelson
BURROWS, J(ames) Austin 7
BURROWS, Julius C. 1
BURROWS, Lansing 1
BURROWS, Lorenzo H
BURROWS, Mark 4
BURROWS, Millar 7
BURROWS, Montrose 2
Thomas
BURROWS, Robert Jay 2
BURROWS, Warren Booth 3
BURROWS, William H
BURROWS, William 1
BURROWS, William 3
Russell
BURRUD, William James 10
BURRUS, John Perry 1
BURRUS, John T. 1
BURRUSS, Julian Ashby 2
BURRY, George W. 4
BURRY, William 1
BURSE, Walter Morrill 5
BURSK, Edward Collins 10
BURSLEY, Herbert Sidney 1
BURSLEY, Joseph Aldrich 3
BURSON, George Allen, Jr. 7
BURSUM, Holm O. 1
BURT, Alfred LeRoy 8
BURT, Alonzo 1
BURT, Andrew Sheridan 1
BURT, Armistead H
BURT, Arthur Hartwell 9
BURT, Austin 5
BURT, Charles Kennedy H
BURT, Charles Morrison 4
BURT, Clayton Raymond 3
BURT, David Allan 2
BURT, Edward Angus 1
BURT, Frank 4
BURT, Frank Henry 2
BURT, Frederic Percy 4
BURT, George Haskell 4
BURT, Glenn Brigham 6
BURT, Henry Jackson 1
BURT, Horace Greeley 1
BURT, John H
BURT, Joseph Bell 5
BURT, Katharine Newlin 7
BURT, Laura 1
BURT, Mary Elizabeth 1
BURT, Richard Lafayette 7
BURT, Russell Jeffords 7
BURT, Silas Wright 1
BURT, Stephen Smith 1
BURT, Struthers 3
BURT, Thomas Gregory 1
BURT, Wayne Vincent 10
BURT, Wilbur F. 8
BURT, William 1
BURT, William Austin H

BURTIN, Will 5
BURTIS, Arthur 1
BURTNER, Charles Allen 7
BURTNESS, Harold 7
William
BURTNESS, Olger B. 4
BURTNESS, Thorstein 8
Warren
BURTON, Alfred Edgar 1
BURTON, Andrew Mizell 4
BURTON, Asa H
BURTON, Charles Emerson 1
BURTON, Charles 1
Germman
BURTON, Charles Luther 4
BURTON, Charles Pierce 4
BURTON, Charles Wesley 10
BURTON, Clarence 8
G(odber)
BURTON, Clarence Monroe 1
BURTON, Edgar Gordon 5
BURTON, Edward Francis 4
BURTON, Ernest Dewitt 1
BURTON, Frank 7
BURTON, Frederick 1
Russell
BURTON, George Dexter 1
BURTON, George Hall 1
BURTON, George William 4
BURTON, Harold Hitz 4
BURTON, Harry B. 8
BURTON, Harry Edward 2
BURTON, Harry Edwin 2
BURTON, Harry Payne 7
BURTON, Hazen James 1
BURTON, Henry Fairfield 1
BURTON, Hiram Rodney 3
BURTON, Hutchings H
Gordon
BURTON, James 1
BURTON, Jean 3
BURTON, Joe Wright 7
BURTON, John Flack 7
BURTON, Joseph Ashby 9
BURTON, Joseph Ralph 1
BURTON, Laurence 5
V(reeland)
BURTON, Laurence 8
V(reeland)
BURTON, Lewis William 1
BURTON, Malcolm King 9
BURTON, Marion Leroy 1
BURTON, Myron Garfield 1
BURTON, Nathaniel H
Judson
BURTON, Oliver Milton 3
BURTON, Phillip 8
BURTON, Richard 1
BURTON, Richard 8
BURTON, Robert H
BURTON, Robert Allen 5
BURTON, Robert Mitchell 1
BURTON, Scott 10
BURTON, Spence 6
BURTON, Theodore Elijah 1
BURTON, Virgil Lee 5
BURTON, Warren H
BURTON, William H
BURTON, William Evans H
BURTON, William Henry 4
BURTON, William Meriam 7
BURTON-OPITZ, Russell 3
BURTS, Charles Elford 1
BURTT, Edwin Arthur 9
BURTT, Everett Johnson 10
BURTT, Harold Ernest 8
BURTT, Wilson Bryant 3
BURWELL, Armistead 1
BURWELL, Arthur Warner 2
BURWELL, Benjamin 1
Franklin
BURWELL, Charles Sidney 4
BURWELL, Harvey S. 8
BURWELL, John 5
T(ownsend), Jr.
BURWELL, Lewis Carter, 10
Jr.
BURWELL, Lina 8
BURWELL, William H
Armisted
BURWELL, William 5
Russell
BURWELL, William 1
Turnbull
BURYAN, Edmund 9
Frederick
BUSA, Peter 9
BUSBEE, Charles Manly 1
BUSBEE, Charles Manly 5
BUSBEE, Fabius Haywood 1
BUSBEE, Jacques 5
BUSBEY, Fred E. 4
BUSBEY, Hamilton 1
BUSBEY, Katherine Graves 5
BUSBEY, L. White 1
BUSBY, George Henry H
BUSBY, Leonard Asbury 1

BUSBY, Orel 4
BUSCH, Adolf Georg 3
Wilhelm
BUSCH, Adolphus 1
BUSCH, Adolphus, III 2
BUSCH, Alfred H. 7
BUSCH, Alfred H. 8
BUSCH, August A., Jr. 10
BUSCH, Bonnie 7
BUSCH, Francis Xavier 6
BUSCH, Fritz 3
BUSCH, H.A. 4
BUSCH, Henry Miller 5
BUSCH, Joseph Francis 1
BUSCH, Joseph Peter 6
BUSCH, Niven 10
BUSCH, Noel 9
BUSCHEMEYER, John 1
Henry
BUSCHMAN, Leonard 7
Victor
BUSCHMAN, S.L. 2
BUSEY, Paul Graham 1
BUSEY, Samuel Clagett 1
BUSEY, Samuel Thompson 3
BUSH, Albert Peyton 1
BUSH, Alvin Ray 3
BUSH, Archibald Granville 4
BUSH, Asahel 1
BUSH, Benjamin Franklin 1
BUSH, Benjamin Jay 3
BUSH, Beverly 10
BUSH, Charles G. 1
BUSH, Earl J. 4
BUSH, Edith Linwood 7
BUSH, Florence Lilian 4
BUSH, Frederic Andrew 10
BUSH, George H
BUSH, Gordon Kenner 4
BUSH, Henry Tatnall 2
BUSH, Ira Benton 1
BUSH, Irving T. 2
BUSH, John A. 4
BUSH, Katherine Jeannette 1
BUSH, Leonard T. 3
BUSH, Lincoln 1
BUSH, Lucius Mason 8
BUSH, Prescott Sheldon 5
BUSH, Robert R(ay) 5
BUSH, Royal Robert 4
BUSH, Thomas Greene 1
BUSH, Vannevar 6
BUSH, Wendell T. 1
BUSH-BROWN, Harold 8
BUSH-BROWN, Henry 1
Kirke
BUSHBY, Wilkie 5
BUSHEE, Frederick 5
Alexander
BUSHER, George Dewey 6
BUSHER, John Joseph 7
BUSHFIELD, Harlan J. 2
BUSHMAN, Francis X 4
BUSHMILLER, Ernie 8
BUSHNELL, Asa Smith 1
BUSHNELL, Asa Smith 6
BUSHNELL, Asa Smith 7
BUSHNELL, Charles 3
Joseph
BUSHNELL, David H
BUSHNELL, David I., Jr. 1
BUSHNELL, Edward 2
BUSHNELL, George 4
Edward
BUSHNELL, George 1
Ensign
BUSHNELL, Henry Allen 4
BUSHNELL, Henry Davis 5
BUSHNELL, Herbert 1
Martin
BUSHNELL, Horace H
BUSHNELL, John Edward 4
BUSHNELL, Leland David 6
BUSHNELL, Madeline 5
Vaughan (Abbott)
BUSHNELL, Robert T. 2
BUSHNELL, Winthrop 1
Grant
BUSHONG, Robert Grey 3
BUSICK, Adrien Fowler 5
BUSIEL, Charles Albert 1
BUSIGNIES, Henri Gaston 2
BUSKIN, Martin 6
BUSKIN, Martin 7
BUSSER, Ralph Cox 3
BUSSEWITZ, Maxilliam 2
Alfred
BUSSEY, Cyrus 1
BUSSEY, Gertrude Carman 4
BUSSEY, Henson Estes 7
BUSSEY, William Henry 6
BUSSING, Wilfrid Charles 8
BUSSMANN, Harry T. 8
BUSSOM, Thomas 3
Wainwright
BUSTAMANTE, William 7
Alexander

BUSTARD, William Walter 1
BUSTEED, Robert Charles 10
BUSWELL, Arthur Moses 4
BUSWELL, Henry Clark 4
BUSWELL, Henry Foster 1
BUSWELL, James Oliver, 7
Jr.
BUTCHER, Devereux 10
BUTCHER, Edwin 6
BUTCHER, Harold 10
BUTCHER, Harry C. 8
BUTCHER, Howard 6
BUTCHER, Howard, III 10
BUTCHER, Thomas 4
Campbell
BUTCHER, Thomas Walter 10
BUTCHER, William Lewis 1
BUTCHER, William Lewis 7
BUTIN, Romain Francois 1
BUTLER, Alfred Augustus 1
BUTLER, Amos William 1
BUTLER, Andrew Pickens H
BUTLER, Arthur Pierce 3
BUTLER, Benjamin H
Franklin*
BUTLER, Bert S. 4
BUTLER, Burridge Davenal 2
BUTLER, Charles H
BUTLER, Charles 3
BUTLER, Charles C. 2
BUTLER, Charles Henry 1
BUTLER, Charles St. John 1
BUTLER, Charles 3
Thompson
BUTLER, Charles William 5
BUTLER, Chester Pierce H
BUTLER, Clement Moore H
BUTLER, Dan B. 3
BUTLER, Doris Lane 6
BUTLER, Edmond Borgia 3
BUTLER, Edward Burgess 1
BUTLER, Edward Francis 7
BUTLER, Edward H. 1
BUTLER, Mrs. Edward H. 6
BUTLER, Edward Hubert 1
BUTLER, Edward Hubert 3
BUTLER, Ellis Parker 1
BUTLER, Elmer Grimshaw 5
BUTLER, Ethan Flagg 1
BUTLER, Ezra H
BUTLER, Francis Peabody 8
BUTLER, Frank Osgood 5
BUTLER, Fred Mason 1
BUTLER, George Alfred 1
BUTLER, George Bernard 1
BUTLER, George Frank 1
BUTLER, George Harrison, 2
Jr.
BUTLER, G(eorge) Paul 7
BUTLER, Glentworth 1
Reeve
BUTLER, G(ordon) 6
Montague
BUTLER, Harold Lancaster 3
BUTLER, Harold Lancaster 5
BUTLER, Henry Varnum 3
BUTLER, Howard Crosby 1
BUTLER, Howard Russell 1
BUTLER, Hugh 1
BUTLER, Hugh Alfred 3
BUTLER, J. Glentworth 4
BUTLER, J. Vernon 4
BUTLER, James Davie 1
BUTLER, James Gay 1
BUTLER, James Joseph 2
BUTLER, James Orval 5
BUTLER, Jerome Ambrose 3
BUTLER, Joe Beaty 3
BUTLER, John 1
BUTLER, John Ammi 1
BUTLER, John Cornelius 3
BUTLER, John Gazzam 1
BUTLER, John George 1
BUTLER, John Jay 1
BUTLER, John Wesley 1
BUTLER, John Winchel 3
Spencer
BUTLER, Joseph Green, Jr. 1
BUTLER, Josiah H
BUTLER, Lee David 8
BUTLER, Louis Fatio 1
BUTLER, Marion 1
BUTLER, Mary 2
BUTLER, Matthew 1
Calbraith
BUTLER, Nathaniel 1
BUTLER, Nicholas Murray 2
BUTLER, Ovid 6
BUTLER, Paul 8
BUTLER, Paul M. 6
BUTLER, Paul Temple 7
BUTLER, Peter Walton 2
BUTLER, Pierce H
BUTLER, Pierce 1
BUTLER, Pierce* H
BUTLER, Pierce Mason H
BUTLER, Ralph 3

BUTLER, Richard H
BUTLER, Richard 1
BUTLER, Richard Austen 8
(Lord Butler)
BUTLER, Robert 3
BUTLER, Robert Gordon 1
BUTLER, Robert Paul 5
BUTLER, Robert Reyburn 1
BUTLER, Roy Francis 10
BUTLER, Rush Clark 3
BUTLER, Sampson Hale H
BUTLER, Samuel R. 4
BUTLER, Scot 1
BUTLER, Sheppard 7
BUTLER, Simeon H
BUTLER, Smedley 1
Darlington
BUTLER, T.J. 7
BUTLER, Tait 1
BUTLER, Thomas H
BUTLER, Thomas Baldwin 5
BUTLER, Thomas Belden H
BUTLER, Thomas Clifton 7
BUTLER, Thomas S. 1
BUTLER, Walter N. H
BUTLER, William* H
BUTLER, William 1
BUTLER, William Allen* 1
BUTLER, William 1
Frederick
BUTLER, William John 2
BUTLER, William Mill 2
BUTLER, William Morgan 1
BUTLER, William Morris 1
BUTLER, William Orlando 1
BUTLER, William Pitt 8
BUTLER, Willis Howard 1
BUTLER, Zebulon H
BUTMAN, Arthur 3
Benjamin
BUTMAN, Samuel H
BUTNER, Henry W. 1
BUTT, Archibald 1
Willingham
BUTT, Howard Edward 10
BUTT, John D. 4
BUTT, William 4
BUTTE, George Charles 1
BUTTELMAN, Clifford 7
Vincent
BUTTENHEIM, Edgar J. 4
BUTTENHIEM, Harold S. 4
BUTTENWIESER, 10
Benjamin Joseph
BUTTENWIESER, Moses 1
BUTTERFIELD, Consul 1
Willshire
BUTTERFIELD, Daniel H
BUTTERFIELD, Daniel 1
BUTTERFIELD, Ernest 5
Warren
BUTTERFIELD, John H
BUTTERFIELD, Kenyon 1
Leech
BUTTERFIELD, Lander 10
W(estgate)
BUTTERFIELD, Lyman 8
Henry
BUTTERFIELD, Martin 4
BUTTERFIELD, Ora 1
Elmer
BUTTERFIELD, Richard 7
Joseph
BUTTERFIELD, Victor 6
Lloyd
BUTTERFIELD, Victor 7
Lloyd
BUTTERICK, Ebenezer H
BUTTERWORTH, H
Benjamin
BUTTERWORTH, Charles 3
Fred
BUTTERWORTH, Frank 10
Willoughby, III
BUTTERWORTH, G. 3
Forrest
BUTTERWORTH, George 1
Forrest
BUTTERWORTH, 1
Hezekiah
BUTTERWORTH, Julian 4
Edward
BUTTERWORTH, Julian 7
Scott
BUTTERWORTH, Oliver 10
BUTTERWORTH, William 1
BUTTERWORTH, William 6
Walton
BUTTFIELD, W.J. 2
BUTTLE, Edgar Allyn 10
BUTTLES, John S. 2
BUTTON, Frank 1
Christopher
BUTTON, Robert Young 7
BUTTON, Stephen D. H
BUTTRAM, Frank 4
BUTTRE, John Chester H

BUTTRICK, George Arthur 7
BUTTRICK, James Tyler 4
BUTTRICK, Wallace 1
BUTTS, Alfred Benjamin 4
BUTTS, Allison 8
BUTTS, Annice Esther Bradford 1
BUTTS, Arthur Clarkson 4
BUTTS, Charles 3
BUTTS, Edmund Luther 3
BUTTS, Edward 4
BUTTS, Halleck Allison 8
BUTTS, Isaac H
BUTTZ, Henry Anson 1
BUTZ, Jesse Samuel Cooper 4
BUTZ, Reuben Jacob 3
BUTZEL, Fred M. 2
BUTZEL, Henry Magnus 4
BUTZEL, Leo Martin 4
BUTZLER, Albert George 5
BUWALDA, John Peter 3
BUXTON, Albert 1
BUXTON, Charles Lee 5
BUXTON, Edwin Orlando 4
BUXTON, Frank W. 6
BUXTON, G. Edward 2
BUXTON, John A. 4
BUXTON, L. Haynes 5
BUXTON, Robert William 5
BUYS, John L. 3
BUYSKE, Donald Albert 10
BUZBEE, Thomas Stephen 2
BUZBY, George Carroll 5
BUZZI, Alfred Antoni 4
BUZZNELL, Reginald W. 3
BYAM, Milton Sylvester 10
BYARS, Louis Thomas 5
BYARS, William Vincent 1
BYAS, Hugh 2
BYE, Carl R. 4
BYE, Frank Paxson 1
BYER, Herman Bailey 4
BYERLY, Perry 7
BYERLY, Theodore Carroll 10
BYERLY, William Elwood 1
BYERS, Clovis E. 6
BYERS, Gordon Leslie 6
BYERS, John Frederic 2
BYERS, Jonn Winford 5
BYERS, Joseph Perkins 4
BYERS, Maxwell Cunningham 1
BYERS, Mortimer W. 4
BYERS, Samuel Hawkins Marshall 1
BYERS, Vincent Gerard 4
BYERS, Walter Louis 5
BYERS, William Newton 1
BYFIELD, Ernest Lessing 4
BYFIELD, Joseph 1
BYFORD, Henry Turman 1
BYFORD, William Heath H
BYINGTON, Cyrus H
BYINGTON, Edwin Hallock 2
BYINGTON, Ezra Hoyt 1
BYINGTON, Homer Morrison 4
BYINGTON, Spring 5
BYINGTON, Steven Tracy 5
BYLES, Axtell J. 1
BYLES, Mather H
BYLLESBY, Henry Marison 1
BYNE, Arthur H
BYNNER, Edwin Lassetter H
BYNNER, Witter 5
BYNUM, Curtis 4
BYNUM, Jessee Atherton H
BYNUM, Marshall Francis 1
BYNUM, William Dallas 1
BYNUM, William Preston 1
BYOIR, Carl 3
BYRAM, George Logan 1
BYRAM, Harry E. 2
BYRD, Adam Monroe 1
BYRD, Anderson FLoyd 4
BYRD, Benjamin Franklin 7
BYRD, Elon Eugene 6
BYRD, Harry Clifton 5
BYRD, Harry Flood 4
BYRD, Richard Evelyn 1
BYRD, Richard Evelyn 1
BYRD, Samuel Craig 4
BYRD, William* H
BYRD, William Clifton 6
BYRER, Charles Emory 5
BYRER, Hrry Hopkins 5
BYRNE, Alice Hill 5
BYRNE, Amanda Austin 1
BYRNE, Austin Thomas 1
BYRNE, Barry 4
BYRNE, Bernard Albert 1
BYRNE, Charles Alfred 1
BYRNE, Charles Christopher 1

BYRNE, Christopher Edward 3
BYRNE, Cornelius James 6
BYRNE, Edwin Vincent 4
BYRNE, Emmet Francis 4
BYRNE, Eugene Hugh 7
BYRNE, Frank M. 6
BYRNE, Harry Vincent 6
BYRNE, James 2
BYRNE, James MacGregor 1
BYRNE, John 1
BYRNE, John Baird 1
BYRNE, Joseph 2
BYRNE, Joseph M., Jr. 1
BYRNE, Sister Marie Jose 3
BYRNE, Sister Marie Jose 5
BYRNE, Miriam 1
BYRNE, Thomas Sebastian 1
BYRNE, William 1
BYRNE, William Matthew 6
BYRNE, William Thomas 5
BYRNES, Allen William 1
BYRNES, Charles Metcalfe 1
BYRNES, Clifford Hamilton 6
BYRNES, Eugene Alexander 4
BYRNES, Hazel Webster 7
BYRNES, James Francis 5
BYRNES, John W. 8
BYRNES, Ralph Leonidas 5
BYRNES, Robert Dennison 5
BYRNES, Timothy Edward 1
BYRNES, William M. 4
BYRNS, Clarence Franklin 1
BYRNS, Joseph W. 1
BYRON, Arthur William 4
BYRON, Charles Loomis 4
BYRON, Goodloe Edgar 7
BYRON, Joseph Wilson 3
BYRON, Robert Burns, Jr. 5
BYRON, William Devereux 1
BYRUM, Enoch Edwin 4
BYWATERS, Jerry 10

C

CABANA, Oliver, Jr. 1
CABANISS, Edward Harman 1
CABANISS, Edward M. 4
CABANISS, Henry Harrison 1
CABANISS, Jelks Henry 8
CABANISS, Thomas Banks 4
CABEEN, Charles William 1
CABEEN, David Clark 4
CABELL, Benjamin Francis 1
CABELL, Charles Pearre 5
CABELL, De Rosey Carroll 1
CABELL, Earle 4
CABELL, Edward Carrington H
CABELL, George Craghead 1
CABELL, Isa Carrington 4
CABELL, James Alston 1
CABELL, James Branch 3
CABELL, James Lawrence H
CABELL, Joseph Carrington 1
CABELL, Nathaniel Francis H
CABELL, Robert Hervey 2
CABELL, Royal Eubank 3
CABELL, Samuel Jordan 1
CABELL, William H
CABELL, William H. H
CABELL, William Lewis 4
CABELL, Wymond 3
CABET, Etienne 1
CABLE, Benjamin Stickney 1
CABLE, Benjamin Taylor 1
CABLE, Emmett James 5
CABLE, Frank T. 2
CABLE, George Washington H
CABLE, John L. 5
CABLE, John Ray 3
CABLE, Joseph H
CABLE, Ranson R. 1
CABOT, Arthur Tracy 1
CABOT, Carolyn Sturgis 1
CABOT, Charles Codman 7
CABOT, Edward 1
CABOT, Edward Clarke H
CABOT, Ella Lyman 1
CABOT, Francis Higginson 3
CABOT, Frederick 1
CABOT, George H
CABOT, George E. 1
CABOT, Godfrey Lowell 4
CABOT, Henry B. 6
CABOT, Henry Bromfield 1
CABOT, Hugh 1
CABOT, John H
CABOT, John M. 7
CABOT, Philip 1

CABOT, Richard Clarke 1
CABOT, Samuel 7
CABOT, Sebastian H
CABOT, Stephen Perkins 3
CABOT, Ted 5
CABOT, William Brooks 2
CABRILLO, Juan Rodriguez H
CABRINI, Saint Frances Xavier H
CABRINI, Saint Frances Xavier 4
CACCIA, Harold Anthony (Caccia) 10
CADBURY, Henry Joel 6
CADBURY, Henry Joel 7
CADDELL, Albert D. 3
CADDICK, William Andrew 7
CADDOO, William Henry 4
CADDY, Edmund Harrington Homer 5
CADE, Cassuis Marcellus 3
CADE, C(laude) M(arshall) 7
CADE, George Newton 5
CADEK, Ottokar T. 3
CADELL, Victor 7
CADIEUX, Marcel 7
CADIGAN, Robert James 7
CADILLAC, Sieur de H
CADISH, Gordon Francis 1
CADLERHEAD, William Alexander 4
CADMAN, Charles Wakefield 2
CADMAN, Paul Fletcher 2
CADMAN, S. Parkes 1
CADOGAN, Alexander George Montagu 7
CADORIN, Ettore 6
CADWALADER, Charles Evert 1
CADWALADER, John* H
CADWALADER, John 1
CADWALADER, John Lambert 1
CADWALADER, Lambert H
CADWALADER, Richard McCall 1
CADWALADER, Thomas H
CADWALADER, Thomas Francis 5
CADWALLADER, Isaac Henry 1
CADWALLADER, Starr 1
CADWELL, Charles Stewart 5
CADY, Calvin Brainerd 4
CADY, Claude E. 6
CADY, Daniel H
CADY, Daniel Leavens 1
CADY, Edward Hammond 4
CADY, Everett Ware 4
CADY, George Luther 7
CADY, Gilbert Haven 4
CADY, Hamilton Perkins 2
CADY, Howard Stevenson 10
CADY, J. Cleveland 1
CADY, John Hutchins 5
CADY, John Watts H
CADY, Jonathan Rider 4
CADY, Philander Kinney 1
CADY, Putnam 1
CADY, Samuel Howard 2
CADY, Walter Guyton 5
CAEMMERER, H(ans) Paul 7
CAESAR, Doris 5
CAESAR, Kathleen 4
CAESAR, Orville Swan 4
CAETANI, Gelasio 1
CAFFEE, Robert Henderson 3
CAFFERT, James H. H
CAFFERY, Donelson 1
CAFFERY, Edward 8
CAFFERY, Eldon Lee 6
CAFFERY, Jefferson 6
CAFFEY, Eugene Mead 4
CAFFEY, Francis Gordon 3
CAFFIN, Charles Henry 1
CAFFREY, Donald John 7
CAFFREY, James Joseph 4
CAGE, Harry H
CAGE, John 10
CAGLE, Alvah Penn 4
CAGLE, Fred Ray 5
CAGLE, Fredric William, Jr. 9
CAGNEY, James 9
CAHALAN, (John) Donald 10
CAHAN, Abraham 3
CAHEN, Alfred 4
CAHILL, Arthur James 5
CAHILL, Bernard J.S. 2
CAHILL, Edward 1

CAHILL, Edward A. 4
CAHILL, Edward Cornelius 4
CAHILL, Fred Virgil 8
CAHILL, George Francis 3
CAHILL, Holger 4
CAHILL, Isaac Jasper 2
CAHILL, James Christopher 2
CAHILL, John Thomas 4
CAHILL, Marie 1
CAHILL, Michael Harrison 1
CAHILL, Michael Henry 1
CAHILL, Thaddeus 1
CAHN, Bertram Joseph 4
CAHN, Edmond 4
CAHN, Gladys D. Freeman 4
CAHNERS, Norman Lee 9
CAHOON, Edward Augustus 1
CAHOON, William H
CAILLE, Augustus 1
CAILLOUET, Adrian Joseph 2
CAIN, Arthur Leonard 7
CAIN, George R. 5
CAIN, James Clarence 10
CAIN, James Mallahan 7
CAIN, James William 1
CAIN, Joseph Alexander 7
CAIN, Joseph E. 4
CAIN, Richard Harvey H
CAIN, Rolly Morton 2
CAIN, Walter 1
CAIN, William 1
CAINE, John Thomas, III 3
CAINE, Lynn 9
CAINE, Milton A. 3
CAINE, Walter Eugene 8
CAINES, George H
CAIRNS, Alexander 3
CAIRNS, Anna Sneed 1
CAIRNS, Charles Andrew 1
CAIRNS, Frederick Irvan 2
CAIRNS, Huntington 9
CAIRNS, W.D. 3
CAIRNS, William B. 1
CAJORI, Florian 1
CAKE, Ralph Harlan 5
CAKE, Wallace Ellwood 4
CALABRESE, Giuseppe 4
CALDER, Alexander 3
CALDER, Alexander 7
CALDER, Alexander Milne 2
CALDER, Alexander Stirling 2
CALDER, Curtis Ernest 3
CALDER, Helen Barnetson 5
CALDER, Hugh Gordon 5
CALDER, Louis 4
CALDER, Louis, Jr. 4
CALDER, Robert (George) 8
CALDER, Robert Scott 5
CALDER, William M. 2
CALDERON, Ignacio 4
CALDERON, Luis 6
CALDERON, Manuel Alvarez 4
CALDERONE, Frank Anthony 9
CALDERON GUARDIA, Rafael Angel 5
CALDERWOOD, Alva John 2
CALDWELL, Alexander 1
CALDWELL, Ben Franklin 4
CALDWELL, Benjamin Palmer 3
CALDWELL, Bert Wilmer 3
CALDWELL, Capt Billy H
CALDWELL, Burns Durbin 1
CALDWELL, Charles H
CALDWELL, Charles Henry Bromedge H
CALDWELL, Charles Pope 4
CALDWELL, Clarence B. 4
CALDWELL, Clifford Douglas 1
CALDWELL, Daniel Templeton 3
CALDWELL, David H
CALDWELL, Edwin Valdivia 4
CALDWELL, Erskine 9
CALDWELL, Eugene Craighead H
CALDWELL, Eugene Wilson 1
CALDWELL, Francis Cary 3
CALDWELL, Frank Congleton 4
CALDWELL, Frank Merrill 1
CALDWELL, Fred T. 3
CALDWELL, George Alfred 1
CALDWELL, George Brinton 1

CALDWELL, George Chapman 1
CALDWELL, Greene Washington H
CALDWELL, Guy A. 9
CALDWELL, Harry Burkhead 7
CALDWELL, Henry Clay 1
CALDWELL, Howard Walter 1
CALDWELL, Hugh Milton 3
CALDWELL, Irene Catherine Smith 7
CALDWELL, J.G. 5
CALDWELL, James* H
CALDWELL, James E. 2
CALDWELL, James H. H
CALDWELL, James Henry 1
CALDWELL, James Russell 10
CALDWELL, Jessee Cobb 1
CALDWELL, John Curtis 1
CALDWELL, John Handly 1
CALDWELL, John Kenneth 6
CALDWELL, John Lawrence 1
CALDWELL, John Livy 5
CALDWELL, John Williamson 1
CALDWELL, Joseph Pearson H
CALDWELL, Joseph Pearson H
CALDWELL, Joseph Pearson 1
CALDWELL, Joshua William 1
CALDWELL, Josiah S. 4
CALDWELL, Lisle Bones 4
CALDWELL, Louis Goldsborough 3
CALDWELL, Mary Letitia 5
CALDWELL, Millard F., Jr. 7
CALDWELL, Morely Albert 1
CALDWELL, Oliver Johnson 10
CALDWELL, Orestes Hampton 4
CALDWELL, Orestes Hampton 5
CALDWELL, Otis William 2
CALDWELL, Patrick Calhoun H
CALDWELL, Ralph Merrill 7
CALDWELL, Robert Breckenridge 3
CALDWELL, Robert Granville 7
CALDWELL, Robert J. 3
CALDWELL, Robert Porter H
CALDWELL, Robert Tate 6
CALDWELL, Robert Tate 7
CALDWELL, Samuel Cushman 1
CALDWELL, Samuel Hawks 4
CALDWELL, Samuel Lunt H
CALDWELL, Sarah Campbell 7
CALDWELL, Stephen Aldophus 3
CALDWELL, Taylor (Janet Miriam) 9
CALDWELL, Thomas Jones 4
CALDWELL, Victor Bush 1
CALDWELL, Wallace Everett 8
CALDWELL, Waller Cochran 4
CALDWELL, Walter Bruce 8
CALDWELL, Walter Lindsay 4
CALDWELL, William Anthony 3
CALDWELL, William 9
CALDWELL, William Edgar 2
CALDWELL, William T., Jr. 7
CALE, Edgar Barclay 8
CALE, Thomas 4
CALEB, Frank 8
CALEF, Robert H
CALEY, Earle Radcliffe 8
CALEY, Glenn Hinton 8
CALEY, Llewellyn N. 1
CALFEE, John Edward 1
CALFEE, Robert Martin 6
CALHANE, Daniel Francis 3
CALHERN, Louis 3
CALHOON, John H

CALHOON, Richard Percival 8
CALHOON, Solomon Saladin 4
CALHOON, Thomas Bruce 7
CALHOUN, Abner Wellborn 1
CALHOUN, Alexander McConnell 1
CALHOUN, Arthur Wallace 7
CALHOUN, Byron E. 3
CALHOUN, David Randolph 1
CALHOUN, Fred Harvey Hall 3
CALHOUN, Galloway 4
CALHOUN, George Miller 2
CALHOUN, Hall Laurie 1
CALHOUN, John H
CALHOUN, John 1
CALHOUN, John Caldwell H
CALHOUN, John Calwell 1
CALHOUN, John Darr 4
CALHOUN, John William 2
CALHOUN, Joseph H
CALHOUN, Joseph Painter 4
CALHOUN, Newell Meeker 4
CALHOUN, Patrick 4
CALHOUN, Patrick, Jr. 8
CALHOUN, Philo Clarke 5
CALHOUN, Ralph Emerson
CALHOUN, Robert Lowry 10
CALHOUN, Wilbur Pere 8
CALHOUN, William Barron H
CALHOUN, William James 1
CALHOUN, William Lowndes 4
CALHOUN, William Lowndes 7
CALIFF, Joseph Mark 1
CALIFORNIA JOE H
CALIGA, Issac Henry
CALIGUIRI, Richard S. 9
CALISCH, Edward N. 1
CALIVER, Ambrose 4
CALKINS, Allard A. 4
CALKINS, Earnest Elmo 4
CALKINS, Francis Joseph 9
CALKINS, Franklin Welles
CALKINS, Gary Nathan 2
CALKINS, Harvey Reeves
CALKINS, Howard W. 6
CALKINS, James E. 5
CALKINS, John Uberto, Jr. 9
CALKINS, L.A. 4
CALKINS, Lyman Darrow 1
CALKINS, Mary Whiton 1
CALKINS, Norman Allison 4
CALKINS, Ransom M. 1
CALKINS, Raymond 5
CALKINS, Truesdel Peck 2
CALKINS, William Henry H
CALKINS, Wolcott
CALL, Arthur Deerin 2
CALL, Asa Vickrey 6
CALL, Charles Warren 6
CALL, Edward Payson 3
CALL, Jacob H
CALL, Leland Everett 1
CALL, Manfred 1
CALL, Margaret Flemming 6
CALL, Norman 1
CALL, Rhydon Mays 1
CALL, Richard Ellsworth 4
CALL, Richard Keith H
CALL, S. Leigh 1
CALL, Wilkinson 1
CALLAGHAN, Alfred 3
CALLAGHAN, Morley Edward 10
CALLAGHAN, Stephen 3
CALLAGHAN, William McCombe 10
CALLAHAN, Donald A. 3
CALLAHAN, Ethelbert
CALLAHAN, Frank Howard 8
CALLAHAN, George Harold 9
CALLAHAN, Henry White 4
CALLAHAN, James Yancy 4
CALLAHAN, Jeremiah Joseph 5
CALLAHAN, John 1
CALLAHAN, Kenneth 9
CALLAHAN, Patrick Henry 1
CALLAHAN, William Paul, Jr. 5
CALLAN, Albert Stevens 4
CALLAN, Charles Jerome 4
CALLAN, John Gurney 1
CALLAN, Peter A. 1
CALLAN, Robert Emmet 1

CALLAN, William Woody 9
CALLANAN, Carolyn Williams 4
CALLANAN, Edward A. 3
CALLANDER, Cyrus N. 1
CALLANDER, Cyrus N. 2
CALLANDER, William Forrest 5
CALLAWAY, Cason Jewell 4
CALLAWAY, Ely Reeves, Sr. 3
CALLAWAY, Enoch Howard 1
CALLAWAY, Fuller Earle 1
CALLAWAY, Fuller Earle, Jr. 10
CALLAWAY, Llewellyn Link 3
CALLAWAY, Merrel Price 3
CALLAWAY, Morgan, Jr. 1
CALLAWAY, Samuel Rodger 1
CALLAWAY, Trowbridge 4
CALLBREATH, James Finch 1
CALLCOTT, Wilfrid Hardy 5
CALLEN, Alfred Copeland 3
CALLEN, Irwin R. 9
CALLEN, J. Spencer 4
CALLENDER, Edward Belcher 1
CALLENDER, George Russell 5
CALLENDER, Guy Stevens 1
CALLENDER, Harold 3
CALLENDER, James Thomson H
CALLENDER, John H
CALLENDER, Romaine 1
CALLENDER, Sherman D. 3
CALLENDER, Walter Reid 4
CALLER, Mary ALice 5
CALLERY, Francis Anthony 5
CALLERY, James Dawson 1
CALLERY, Mary 7
CALLES, Plutarco Elias 2
CALLEY, Walter 1
CALLIERES BONNEVUE, Louis Hector de H
CALLIHAN, Harriet K. 10
CALLIMANOPULOS, Pericles Grigorios 7
CALLIS, Harold Baker 9
CALLISON, Tolliver Cleveland 4
CALLISTER, Edward Henry 1
CALLMANN, Rudolf 9
CALLOS, George John 4
CALLOW, John Michael 1
CALLOWAY, Alfred W. 1
CALLOWAY, Augustus James, Jr. 7
CALLOWAY, Thomas Clanton 6
CALLOWAY, Walter Bowles 5
CALLVERT, Ronald Glenn 3
CALMER, Ned 9
CALTHROP, Samuel Robert 1
CALVE, Emma 1
CALVE, Emma 2
CALVER, George Wehnes 5
CALVER, Homer Northup 5
CALVERLEY, Charles 1
CALVERLEY, Edwin Elliott 7
CALVERT, Cecil H
CALVERT, Charles H
CALVERT, Charles Benedict H
CALVERT, George 1
CALVERT, George Henry H
CALVERT, James Henry 10
CALVERT, John Betts 1
CALVERT, John F. 4
CALVERT, Leonard H
CALVERT, Philip Powell 5
CALVERT, Richard Creagh MacKubin 5
CALVERT, Robert 1
CALVERT, Robert S. 9
CALVERT, Thomas Elwood 1
CALVERT, William Jephtha 5
CALVERTON, Victor Francis 1
CALVERY, Herbert Orion 2
CALVIN, Edgar Eugene 1
CALVIN, Henrietta Willard (Mrs. John H. Calvin) 5
CALVIN, Samuel H
CALVIN, Samuel 1

CALVIN, William Austin 4
CALVO, Joaquin Bernardo 1
CALWELL, Charles Sheridan 1
CALYO, Nicolino H
CAM, Helen Maud 4
CAMAC, Charles Nicoll Bancker 1
CAMACHO, Carlos Garcia 7
CAMACHO, Manual Avila 3
CAMACHO FLORES, Felixberto 9
CAMAK, David English 6
CAMALIER, Renah F. 8
CAMBERE, Ara Angele 7
CAMBIAIRE, Célestin Pierre 7
CAMBIO, Frank Caesar 10
CAMBRELENG, Churchill Caldom H
CAMBRIDGE, Godfrey 7
CAMDEN, Aubrey Heyden 7
CAMDEN, Harry Poole 2
CAMDEN, Johnson Newlon 1
CAMDEN, Johnson Newlon 2
CAMERER, C(lyde) B(radley) 7
CAMERON, Adam Kirk 5
CAMERON, Albert Barnes 5
CAMERON, Alexander H
CAMERON, Andrew Carr H
CAMERON, Angus H
CAMERON, Archibald H
CAMERON, Arnold Guyot 2
CAMERON, Augustus Garfield 6
CAMERON, Barney 8
CAMERON, Basil 7
CAMERON, Benjamin Franklin 4
CAMERON, Charles Conrad 3
CAMERON, Charles Franklin 9
CAMERON, Charles Raymond 5
CAMERON, Colin Campbell 10
CAMERON, D(onald) Ewen 5
CAMERON, Donald Forrester 6
CAMERON, Edgar Spier 2
CAMERON, Edward Herbert 1
CAMERON, Edwin J. 3
CAMERON, Francis 6
CAMERON, Frank Kenneth 3
CAMERON, George Glenn 7
CAMERON, George Hamilton 2
CAMERON, George Toland 3
CAMERON, Gordon Wyatt 3
CAMERON, Harold William 5
CAMERON, Henry Clay 1
CAMERON, J. Walter 6
CAMERON, J. Walter 7
CAMERON, James Donald 1
CAMERON, John H
CAMERON, John Andrew 4
CAMERON, John M. 1
CAMERON, Norman W. 2
CAMERON, Ossian 1
CAMERON, Ralph Henry 3
CAMERON, Richard Ray 9
CAMERON, Robert Alexander H
CAMERON, Roderick William 1
CAMERON, Shelton Thomas 2
CAMERON, Simon H
CAMERON, Thomas Brown 6
CAMERON, Turner Christian, Jr. 5
CAMERON, William Donald 4
CAMERON, William Evelyn 1
CAMERON, William J. 4
CAMERON, William John 3
CAMERON, William Mcc 3
CAMILLO, Michael Francis 5
CAMINETTI, Anthony 1
CAMM, Frank 7
CAMM, John H
CAMMACK, Edmund Ernest 3
CAMMACK, Ira Insco 1

CAMMACK, James William 1
CAMMACK, James William 3
CAMMACK, John Walter 5
CAMMERHOFF, John Christopher Frederick H
CAMP, Albert Sidney 3
CAMP, Charles Lewis 6
CAMP, Charles Wadsworth 1
CAMP, David Nelson 1
CAMP, Edgar Whittlesey 1
CAMP, Ernest W. 8
CAMP, Frederic Edgar 4
CAMP, Hiram H
CAMP, Hugh Douglas 6
CAMP, Irving Luzerne 1
CAMP, James Leonidas, Jr. 8
CAMP, John Henry H
CAMP, John Lafayette H
CAMP, John M. 7
CAMP, John Spencer 2
CAMP, Lawrence Hicks 8
CAMP, Lawrence Sabyllia 2
CAMP, Mortimer Hart 4
CAMP, Thomas James 4
CAMP, Thomas Ringgold 5
CAMP, Walter 1
CAMP, Walter John Richard 4
CAMP, Wendell H. 4
CAMP, William Bacon 6
CAMP, William Bacon 7
CAMP, William McCutcheon 4
CAMP, Wofford Benjamin 9
CAMPAIGNE, Jameson Gilbert 8
CAMPANARI, Giuseppe 1
CAMPANINI, Cleofonte 1
CAMPANIUS, John H
CAMPAU, Daniel J. 1
CAMPAU, Francis Denis 3
CAMPAU, Joseph H
CAMPA Y CARAVEDA, Miguel Abgel 4
CAMPBELL, Albert Angus 9
CAMPBELL, Albert H. 1
CAMPBELL, Albert James 1
CAMPBELL, Alexander* 1
CAMPBELL, Alexander 7
CAMPBELL, Alexander Boyd 4
CAMPBELL, Alexander Morton 5
CAMPBELL, Alfred Hills 1
CAMPBELL, Allan H
CAMPBELL, Allan B. 4
CAMPBELL, Andrew 1
CAMPBELL, Anne (Mrs. George W. Stark) 8
CAMPBELL, Archibald Brush 4
CAMPBELL, Archibald Duncan 6
CAMPBELL, Archibald Murray 4
CAMPBELL, Archie James 7
CAMPBELL, Arthur Beri 7
CAMPBELL, Arthur Griffith 3
CAMPBELL, Arthur Russell 10
CAMPBELL, Bartley H
CAMPBELL, Benjamin H
CAMPBELL, Brookins H
CAMPBELL, Bruce Alexander 3
CAMPBELL, Bruce Jones 5
CAMPBELL, C. William 9
CAMPBELL, Cecil Raymond 7
CAMPBELL, Chandler 3
CAMPBELL, Charles Atwood H
CAMPBELL, Charles 1
CAMPBELL, Charles Diven 4
CAMPBELL, Charles E. 4
CAMPBELL, Charles King 1
CAMPBELL, Charles L. 3
CAMPBELL, Charles MacFie 2
CAMPBELL, Charles S. 3
CAMPBELL, Charles Sherman 3
CAMPBELL, Chesser M. 1
CAMPBELL, Chester I. 1
CAMPBELL, Clarence Sutherland 1
CAMPBELL, D. Scott 4
CAMPBELL, Daisy Rhodes 4
CAMPBELL, Dan Hampton 6
CAMPBELL, Daniel A. 4
CAMPBELL, Delwin Morton 3

CAMPBELL, Doak Sheridan 5
CAMPBELL, Donald Francis 5
CAMPBELL, Donald J. 2
CAMPBELL, Donald Malcolm 2
CAMPBELL, Douglas Houghton 3
CAMPBELL, Dwight 4
CAMPBELL, Ed Hoyt 7
CAMPBELL, Edmond Ernest 1
CAMPBELL, Edmund Schureman 3
CAMPBELL, Edward De Mille 1
CAMPBELL, Edward Hale 5
CAMPBELL, Edward Hastings 4
CAMPBELL, Edward K. 1
CAMPBELL, Eldridge 3
CAMPBELL, Elizabeth 4
CAMPBELL, Elmer Grant 5
CAMPBELL, E(rnest) Ray 5
CAMPBELL, Felix 1
CAMPBELL, Floyd D. 4
CAMPBELL, Frank 4
CAMPBELL, Frank L. 4
CAMPBELL, Frank Leslie 7
CAMPBELL, Gabriel 3
CAMPBELL, George Alexander 4
CAMPBELL, George Ashley 3
CAMPBELL, George Hollister 1
CAMPBELL, George Murray 7
CAMPBELL, George Washington* H
CAMPBELL, Gerald 4
CAMPBELL, Gilbert Whitney 1
CAMPBELL, Gordon Hensley 6
CAMPBELL, Gordon Peter 4
CAMPBELL, Gretna 9
CAMPBELL, H. Donald 5
CAMPBELL, H. Wood 1
CAMPBELL, Hardy Webster
CAMPBELL, Harold Denny 3
CAMPBELL, Harold George 2
CAMPBELL, Harry 7
CAMPBELL, H(arry) Brua 1
CAMPBELL, Harry Huse 1
CAMPBELL, Harvey J. 9
CAMPBELL, Hayward, Jr. 4
CAMPBELL, Helen Stuart 4
CAMPBELL, Henry Colin 1
CAMPBELL, Henry Donald 1
CAMPBELL, Henry Fraser H
CAMPBELL, Henry Munroe 1
CAMPBELL, Herbert Grant 1
CAMPBELL, Howard E. 8
CAMPBELL, Ian 7
CAMPBELL, Ira Alexander 4
CAMPBELL, J.W. 1
CAMPBELL, Jacob Miller H
CAMPBELL, James H
CAMPBELL, James A. 1
CAMPBELL, James Alexander 2
CAMPBELL, James Allan 8
CAMPBELL, James Archibald 1
CAMPBELL, James Arthur 10
CAMPBELL, James C. 4
CAMPBELL, James Daniels 1
CAMPBELL, James E. 1
CAMPBELL, James Hepburn H
CAMPBELL, James Hobart 5
CAMPBELL, James Leroy 2
CAMPBELL, James Mann 1
CAMPBELL, James Marshall 10
CAMPBELL, James Philander 2
CAMPBELL, James Romulus 1
CAMPBELL, James U. 1
CAMPBELL, James Valentine H
CAMPBELL, James Watson 5
CAMPBELL, John* H
CAMPBELL, John* H
CAMPBELL, John A. 1
CAMPBELL, John Allen H

CAMPBELL, John Archibald — H
CAMPBELL, John A(rthur) — 6
CAMPBELL, John Bradford — 4
CAMPBELL, John Bulow — 1
CAMPBELL, John Charles — 1
CAMPBELL, John Henry — 1
CAMPBELL, John Hull — 1
CAMPBELL, John Logan — 4
CAMPBELL, John Lorne — 4
CAMPBELL, John Lyle — 1
CAMPBELL, John Neal — 4
CAMPBELL, John Patrick — 7
CAMPBELL, John Pendleton — 4
CAMPBELL, John Pierce, Jr. — H
CAMPBELL, John Preston — 4
CAMPBELL, John Tenbrook — 1
CAMPBELL, John Thomas — 5
CAMPBELL, John Tucker — 10
CAMPBELL, John Wilson — H
CAMPBELL, Johnston B. — 3
CAMPBELL, Jon Bayard Taylor — 3
CAMPBELL, Joseph — 9
CAMPBELL, Josiah A. Patterson — 1
CAMPBELL, Kathleen Roseanne — 6
CAMPBELL, Killis — 1
CAMPBELL, L. Merle — 7
CAMPBELL, L.J. — 5
CAMPBELL, Leon — 3
CAMPBELL, Leory Walter — 4
CAMPBELL, Leroy Brotzman — 3
CAMPBELL, Leslie Hartwell — 9
CAMPBELL, Levin H., Jr. — 7
CAMPBELL, Lewis Davis — H
CAMPBELL, Lily Bess — 4
CAMPBELL, Prince Lucian — 1
CAMPBELL, Lucien Quitman — 2
CAMPBELL, Luther A. — 1
CAMPBELL, Macy — 1
CAMPBELL, Marcus B. — 2
CAMPBELL, Margaret Amelia — 10
CAMPBELL, Marguerite — 4
CAMPBELL, Marius Robison — 1
CAMPBELL, M(ary) Edith — 6
CAMPBELL, Murdoch A. — 8
CAMPBELL, Neil — 7
CAMPBELL, Nicholas Joseph, Jr. — 7
CAMPBELL, Oscar James, Jr. — 5
CAMPBELL, Mrs. Patrick — 1
CAMPBELL, Patrick Thomas — 1
CAMPBELL, Persia (Mrs. Edward Rice Jr.) — 6
CAMPBELL, Philip Pitt — 1
CAMPBELL, Price — 4
CAMPBELL, R. Granville — 1
CAMPBELL, Ralph Emerson — 1
CAMPBELL, Richard — 1
CAMPBELL, Richard Arthur — 10
CAMPBELL, Richard Kenna
CAMPBELL, Robert — H
CAMPBELL, Robert Argyll — 9
CAMPBELL, Robert Blair — H
CAMPBELL, Robert Donald — 4
CAMPBELL, Robert Erle — 7
CAMPBELL, Robert Fishburne — 2
CAMPBELL, Robert Kenneth — 10
CAMPBELL, Robert Morrell — 6
CAMPBELL, Robert Willis — 2
CAMPBELL, Rolla Dacres — 1
CAMPBELL, Ronald Ian — 8
CAMPBELL, Ronald Neil — 4
CAMPBELL, Ross Turner — 1
CAMPBELL, Rowland — 2
CAMPBELL, Roy Davies — 5
CAMPBELL, Roy E(lliott) — 9
CAMPBELL, Roy English — 7
CAMPBELL, Roy Hilton — 8
CAMPBELL, Roy Stuart — 8
CAMPBELL, Ruth Ramsdell (Mrs. James Francis Campbell)
CAMPBELL, Sam — 4
CAMPBELL, Samuel — H
CAMPBELL, Samuel Jones — 9

CAMPBELL, Stanley Howard — 7
CAMPBELL, Stewart — 7
CAMPBELL, Stuart Bland — 7
CAMPBELL, Stuart Bland, Jr. — 9
CAMPBELL, Theodorick Pryor
CAMPBELL, Thomas — H
CAMPBELL, Thomas A. — 5
CAMPBELL, Thomas Donald — 4
CAMPBELL, Thomas Edward — 2
CAMPBELL, Thomas Huffman — 2
CAMPBELL, Thomas Jefferson — H
CAMPBELL, Thomas Joseph — 1
CAMPBELL, Thomas Mitchell — 1
CAMPBELL, Thomas W. — 1
CAMPBELL, Thompson — H
CAMPBELL, Wallace — 3
CAMPBELL, Wallace Edwin — 5
CAMPBELL, Walter Gilbert — 5
CAMPBELL, Walter Stanley — 3
CAMPBELL, Wayne — 5
CAMPBELL, William* — H
CAMPBELL, William — 1
CAMPBELL, William A. — 8
CAMPBELL, William Alexander — 1
CAMPBELL, William Bowen — H
CAMPBELL, William Burnside — 7
CAMPBELL, William Carey — 4
CAMPBELL, William Francis — 1
CAMPBELL, William Henry — H
CAMPBELL, William J. — 9
CAMPBELL, William James — 2
CAMPBELL, William Lyman — 4
CAMPBELL, William Neal — 2
CAMPBELL, William Purnell — 5
CAMPBELL, William Rogers — 1
CAMPBELL, William Stuart — 9
CAMPBELL, William Taggart — 1
CAMPBELL, William W. — H
CAMPBELL, William W. — 4
CAMPBELL, William Wallace — 1
CAMPBELL, William Wilson — 5
CAMPBELL, William Wilson — 8
CAMPBELL, Willis Cohoon — 1
CAMPBELL, Willis L. — 10
CAMPBELL, Worthington — 4
CAMPELLO, Count Solone Di — 5
CAMPHOR, Alexander Priestly — 1
CAMPIOLI, Mario Ettore — 7
CAMPION, Donald Richard — 9
CAMPION, Frank Davis — 10
CAMPNEY, Ralph Osbiurne — 4
CAMPOS, Maria E. — 3
CAMROSE, 1st Viscount of Hackwood Park — 3
CAMSELL, Charles — 3
CAMUS, Albert — 3
CANADA, John Walter — 2
CANADA, John William — 3
CANADA, John William — 5
CANADA, Robert Owen, Jr. — 5
CANADA, William Wesley — 1
CANADAY, John Edwin — 8
CANADAY, John Edwin — 9
CANADAY, Paul O'Neal — 4
CANADAY, Ward Murphey — 7
CANARUTTO, Angelo — 2
CANARY, Martha Jane — H
CANARY, Martha Jane — 4
CANBY, Edward Richard Sprigg
CANBY, Henry Seidel — 4
CANBY, Richard Sprigg — H
CANBY, William Marriott — 1

CANDEE, Charles Lucius — 5
CANDEE, Helen Churchill — 2
CANDEE, Leverett — H
CANDEE, Lyman — 2
CANDLER, Allen Daniel — 1
CANDLER, Asa G. — 1
CANDLER, Asa Warren — 7
CANDLER, Charles Howard — 3
CANDLER, Charles Murphey — 1
CANDLER, Ezekiel Samuel, Jr. — 2
CANDLER, Henry E. — 5
CANDLER, John Slaughter — 2
CANDLER, Samuel Charles — 5
CANDLER, Thomas Slaughter — 5
CANDLER, Warren A. — 1
CANDLER, William — 1
CANDY, Albert Luther — 2
CANE, Melville Henry — 7
CANEVIN, J.F.Regis — 1
CANFIELD, Arthur Graves — 2
CANFIELD, Cass — 9
CANFIELD, Edward — 4
CANFIELD, Fayette Curtis — 9
CANFIELD, George Folger — 1
CANFIELD, Harry C. — 2
CANFIELD, James Hulme — 1
CANFIELD, Jane White — 9
CANFIELD, Leon H(ardy) — 7
CANFIELD, Roy Bishop — 1
CANFIELD, William Walker — 1
CANGELOSI, Vincent Emanuel — 10
CANHAM, Charles Draper William — 4
CANHAM, Erwin Dain — 8
CANHAM, Robert Allen — 9
CANIFF, Milton Arthur — 9
CANJAR, Lawrence Nicholas — 5
CANN, James Ferris — 2
CANN, Norman D. — 9
CANNAN, Robert Keith — 5
CANNIFF, William Henry — 1
CANNING, George — H
CANNON, A. Benson — 3
CANNON, Abram H. — 9
CANNON, Annie Jump — 1
CANNON, Austin Victor — 7
CANNON, Brown W. — 7
CANNON, Carl Leslie — 6
CANNON, Cavendish Welles — 4
CANNON, Charles A. — 5
CANNON, Charles James — H
CANNON, Clarence — 4
CANNON, Cornelia James (Mrs. Walter Bradford Cannon) — 5
CANNON, Frank Jenne — 4
CANNON, George Lyman, Jr.
CANNON, George Quayle — H
CANNON, George W. — 7
CANNON, Georgius Young — 9
CANNON, Grant Groesbeck
CANNON, Harriet Starr — H
CANNON, Henry White — 1
CANNON, Howard Henry — 7
CANNON, James, III — 3
CANNON, James, Jr. — 2
CANNON, James Graham — 1
CANNON, Jimmy — 6
CANNON, John — 1
CANNON, John Franklin — 1
CANNON, John Kenneth — 3
CANNON, Joseph Gurney — 1
CANNON, Le Grand Bouton
CANNON, Legrand, Jr. — 2
CANNON, Martin L. — 3
CANNON, Newton — H
CANNON, Paul Roberts — 9
CANNON, Raymond J. — 3
CANNON, Robert M. — 7
CANNON, Sylvester Quayle — 2
CANNON, Walter Bradford — 2
CANNON, William — 5
CANNON, William Cornelius — H
CANNY, Francis Charles — 8
CANOLES, M. Alice — 4
CANONCHET — H
CANONGE, Louis Placide — H
CANONICUS — H
CANOVA, Judy — 8
CANOVA, Leon Joseph — 2
CANRIGHT, Dudley Marvin — 1
CANSE, John Martin — 5
CANT, Gilbert — 8
CANT, William Alexander — 1

CANTACUZENE, Mme — 6
CANTAROW, Abraham — 7
CANTELLI, Guido — 4
CANTER, Howard Vernon — 5
CANTER, Joshua — H
CANTEY, James Willis — 9
CANTEY, Morgan Sabb — 4
CANTILLON, William David — 1
CANTILO, Jose Maria — 5
CANTIN, Marc — 10
CANTOR, Eddie — 4
CANTOR, Jacob Aaron — 1
CANTOR, Nathaniel — 3
CANTRALL, Arch Martin — 5
CANTRELL, Charles E. — 4
CANTRELL, Deaderick Harrell — 1
CANTRELL, James Randall — 8
CANTRELL, John Howard — 7
CANTRIL, Albert Hadley — 5
CANTRILL, James Campbell — 1
CANTRILL, James E. — 1
CANTWELL, Alfred W. — 7
CANTWELL, Conan — 4
CANTWELL, James William — 1
CANTWELL, John Joseph — 2
CANTWELL, Robert Emmett — 7
CANTWELL, Robert Murray — 3
CANTY, Thomas — 4
CAPA, Robert — 4
CAPAN, Edward Warren — 5
CAPARO, Jose Angel — 3
CAPE, Emily Palmer — 4
CAPEHART, Homer Earl — 7
CAPEK, Thomas — 3
CAPELLE, Henry Theodore — 7
CAPEN, Charles Laban — 1
CAPEN, Elmer Hewitt — 1
CAPEN, Nahum — H
CAPEN, Oliver Bronson — 3
CAPEN, Samuel Billings — 1
CAPEN, Samuel Paul — 3
CAPERS, Ellison — 1
CAPERS, John G. — 1
CAPERS, Walter Branham — 5
CAPERS, William Theodotus — H
CAPERS, William — 2
CAPERTO, William Banks — 1
CAPERTON, Allen Taylor — H
CAPERTON, Hugh — H
CAPES, William Parr — 2
CAPITMAN, William Gardiner — 7
CAPLAN, Harry — 10
CAPLAN, Harry — 7
CAPLAN, Louis — 7
CAPLENOR, Donald — 7
CAPLES, John — 10
CAPLES, Martin Joseph — 1
CAPLES, Russel B. — 5
CAPLES, William Goff — 10
CAPOGROSSI, Guiseppe — 6
CAPONIGRI, Aloysius Robert — 8
CAPOTE, Truman — 7
CAPOZZOLI, Louis Joseph — 8
CAPP, Al — 7
CAPPELLUCCI, Gabriel Orazio — 6
CAPPER, Arthur — 3
CAPPON, Lester Jesse — 8
CAPPS, Charles R. — 1
CAPPS, Edward — 3
CAPPS, Joseph Almarin — 4
CAPPS, Richard Brooks — 7
CAPPS, Stephen Reid — 2
CAPPS, Washington Lee — 1
CAPRA, Frank — 10
CAPRANO, Julius John — 7
CAPRON, Adin Ballou — 1
CAPRON, Charles Alexander — 3
CAPRON, Horace — H
CAPRON, Lawrence Rollin — 9
CAPSHAW, Hulon — 7
CAPSTAFF, Albert L. — 4
CAPSTAFF, John George — 3
CAPSTICK, John Henry — 2
CAPT, James Clyde — 2
CAPTAIN JACK — H
CARAWAY, Hattie Wyatt — 1
CARAWAY, Thaddeus H. — 1
CARBAJAL, Fernando — 6
CARBEE, Scott Clifton — 4
CARBO, Luis Felipe — 4
CARBONARA, E(mil) Vernon — 5
CARBONE, Agostino — 1
CARBONE, John Vito — 10

CARBONNIER, Claes Cecil — 4
CARD, Benjamin Cozzens — 1
CARD, Ernest Mason — 5
CARDELLI, Pietro — H
CARDEN, Cap R. — 1
CARDEN, Edward Walter — 3
CARDEN, George Alexander — 2
CARDEN, William Thomas — 1
CARDENAS, Garcia Lopez de — H
CARDENAS, Lazaro — 1
CARDER, Eugene Clayton — 6
CARDEW, Emily Craske — 6
CARDIFF, Ira D. — 1
CARDMAN, Cecilia — 10
CARDOFF, Thomas H. — 4
CARDON, Philip Vincent — 4
CARDOZO, Benjamin Nathan — 1
CARDOZO, Jacob Newton — H
CARDOZO, Manoel — 9
CARDWELL, James R. — 3
CARDY, Samuel — H
CARENS, Thomas Henry — 4
CAREW, Harold David — 2
CAREW, James — 1
CAREW, John F. — 3
CAREW, Sylvia — 8
CAREY, Archibald — 3
CAREY, Archibald J., Jr. — 7
CAREY, Archibald James — 1
CAREY, Arthur Astor — 1
CAREY, Asa Bacon — 1
CAREY, Charles Emerson — 3
CAREY, Charles Henry — 1
CAREY, Charles Irving — 5
CAREY, Charles Irving — 7
CAREY, Eben James — 2
CAREY, Eustace W. — 4
CAREY, Francis King — 2
CAREY, Hampson — 3
CAREY, Harvey Locke — 9
CAREY, Henry Charles — H
CAREY, Henry Westonrae — 1
CAREY, James Barron — 6
CAREY, James F. — 1
CAREY, James William — 5
CAREY, Jane Perry Clark — 8
CAREY, John Joseph — 1
CAREY, Joseph — 1
CAREY, Joseph Maull — 1
CAREY, Lawrence Bernard — 6
CAREY, Liguori John — 4
CAREY, Mathew — H
CAREY, Miriam Eliza — 1
CAREY, Peter Bernard — 1
CAREY, Robert — 4
CAREY, Robert Davis — 1
CAREY, Robert Lincoln — 4
CAREY, William Francis — 3
CAREY, William Gibson, Jr. — 2
CAREY, William Nelson — 7
CARGILL, Frank Valentine — 5
CARGILL, Frank Valentine — 5
CARGILL, Ian Peter M. — 8
CARGILL, James Nelson — 7
CARGILL, Oscar — 5
CARGILL, Otto Arthur — 7
CARGILL, Otto Arthur, Jr. — 10
CARHARDT, Raymond T. — 6
CARHART, Arthur Hawthorne — 9
CARHART, Daniel — 1
CARHART, Frank Milton — 4
CARHART, Henry Smith — 1
CARHART, Raymond T. — 7
CARHART, Winfield Scott — 4
CARHARTT, Hamilton — 1
CARHART, John Ernest — 2
CARHCART, James Leander — H
CARIANI, Anthony — 6
CARIAS ANDINO, Tiburcio — 5
CARIS, Albert Garfield — 6
CARKIN, Seth Ballou — 1
CARKNER, James W. — 4
CARL, Francis Augustus — 1
CARL, Katherine Augusta — 1
CARL, Melvin Latshaw — 3
CARL, William Crane — 1
CARLAND, John Emmett — 1
CARLE, E.E. — 6
CARLE, Frank Austin — 1
CARLE, Nathaniel Allen — 4
CARLE, Richard — 1
CARLEN, Raymond Nils — 10
CARLES, Arthur B. — 3
CARLETON, Bukk G. — 1
CARLETON, CLifford — 4
CARLETON, Edward Hercules — 6
CARLETON, Guy — 3
CARLETON, Henry — H

CARLETON, Henry Guy 1
CARLETON, John Walker 9
CARLETON, Mark Alfred 1
CARLETON, Murray H
CARLETON, Peter H
CARLETON, Philip 6
 Greenleaf
CARLETON, Robert 6
 Andrew Wood
CARLETON, Sprague 6
CARLETON, Will 1
CARLEY, Henry 4
 Thompson
CARLEY, Patrick J. 1
CARLEY, W.F. 3
CARLILE, John Snyder H
CARLILE, William Alonzo 8
CARLILE, William Buford 5
CARLIN, Andrew B. 1
CARLIN, Charles 1
 Creighton
CARLIN, Charles L. H
CARLIN, Edward 9
 Augustine
CARLIN, George Andrew 2
CARLIN, Henry A. 4
CARLIN, James Joseph 1
CARLIN, John H
CARLIN, Leo Joseph 9
CARLIN, Thomas H
CARLIN, Walter Jeffreys 3
CARLIN, William 1
 Passmore
CARLIN, William Worth H
CARLISLE, Charles Arthur 1
CARLISLE, Chester Lee 3
CARLISLE, Clifton Hugh 3
CARLISLE, Floyd Leslie 2
CARLISLE, G. Lister, Jr. 3
CARLISLE, Harold Walter 4
CARLISLE, Helen Grace 4
CARLISLE, Howard Bobo 5
CARLISLE, James Henry 1
CARLISLE, James H
 Mandeville
CARLISLE, James McCoy 4
CARLISLE, John Griffin 1
CARLISLE, John Nelson 1
CARLISLE, Marcus Lee 1
CARLISLE, Samuel 8
CARLL, John Franklin 4
CARLOCK, John Bruce 4
CARLOUGH, David 4
 Jacobus
CARLOUGH, Edward F. 8
CARLSEN, Carl Laurence 4
CARLSEN, Clarence J. 4
CARLSEN, Dines 1
CARLSEN, Emil 1
CARLSEN, Niels Christian 2
CARLSON, Albert Sigfrid 6
CARLSON, Albin Edmund 8
CARLSON, Anders Johan 10
CARLSON, Anders Johan 5
CARLSON, Anton Julius 5
CARLSON, Chester 5
CARLSON, Clarence Erick 9
CARLSON, Edgar Magnus 10
CARLSON, Edward Elmer 10
CARLSON, E(rnest) Leslie 5
CARLSON, Eskil 7
 Constantine
CARLSON, Evans Fordyce 2
CARLSON, Frank 9
CARLSON, George Alfred 1
CARLSON, Gunard Oscar 1
CARLSON, Harry Johan 5
CARLSON, Jack Wilson 10
CARLSON, James Alfred 1
CARLSON, John Fabian 2
CARLSON, Loren Daniel 5
CARLSON, T(horgny) 5
 C(edric)
CARLSON, Wally 4
CARLSON, Walter 9
CARLSON, William 10
 Donald
CARLSON, William Fitts 9
CARLSON, William Hugh 10
CARLSTON, Kenneth S. 5
CARLSTROM, Oscar E. 2
CARLTON, A.C. 3
CARLTON, Albert E. 1
CARLTON, Caleb Henry 1
CARLTON, Caleb Sidney 1
CARLTON, Clarence Clay 3
CARLTON, Doyle Elam 5
CARLTON, Ernest W. 4
CARLTON, Frank Tracy 5
CARLTON, Leslie Gilbert 3
CARLTON, Newcomb 3
CARLTON, Richard Paul 5
CARLTON, Romulus Lee 6
CARLTON, William 2
 Newnham Chattin
CARLYLE, Irving Edward 5
CARLYLE, William Levi 5

CARLYON, James Thomas 7
CARMACK, Edward Ward 1
CARMALT, James Walton 1
CARMALT, William Henry 1
CARMAN, Albert Pruden 3
CARMAN, Augustine 1
 Spencer
CARMAN, Bliss 1
CARMAN, Ezra Ayers 1
CARMAN, George Noble 2
CARMAN, Harry James 4
CARMELIA, Francis 2
 Albion
CARMER, Carl 7
CARMICHAEL, Archibald 3
 Hill
CARMICHAEL, Emmett 9
 Bryan
CARMICHAEL, Francis 6
 Abbott
CARMICHAEL, George 4
 Edgar
CARMICHAEL, George T. 4
CARMICHAEL, Harry 9
 John
CARMICHAEL, Henry 1
CARMICHAEL, Howard 8
 Hoagland (Hoagy
 Carmichael)
CARMICHAEL, Hugh 7
 Thompson
CARMICHAEL, James H 8
CARMICHAEL, James 6
 Vinson
CARMICHAEL, John 5
 Hugh
CARMICHAEL, John P. 9
CARMICHAEL, Katherine 8
 Kennedy
CARMICHAEL, Leonard 6
CARMICHAEL, Oliver 4
 Cromwell
CARMICHAEL, Oliver 7
 Cromwell, Jr.
CARMICHAEL, Omer 3
CARMICHAEL, Patrick 7
 Henry
CARMICHAEL, Richard H
 Bennett
CARMICHAEL, Robert 4
 Daniel
CARMICHAEL, Robert 6
 Daniel
CARMICHAEL, Thomas 2
 Harrison
CARMICHAEL, William H
CARMICHAEL, William 4
 Donald, Jr.
CARMICHAEL, William 2
 Perrin
CARMODY, John 3
CARMODY, John Michael 4
CARMODY, Martin Henry 3
CARMODY, Terence 2
 Francis
CARMODY, Thomas 1
CARMODY, Thomas 5
 Edward
CARMONA, Antonio 1
 Oscar de Fragoso
CARNAHAN, A.S.J. 5
CARNAHAN, David 5
 Hobart
CARNAHAN, George 1
 Holmes
CARNAHAN, Herschel L. 1
CARNAHAN, James H
CARNAHAN, James 1
 Richards
CARNAHAN, Paul Harvey 4
CARNAHAN, Wendell 4
CARNAP, Rudolf 5
CARNEGIE, Andrew 1
CARNEGIE, Dale 3
CARNEGIE, Hattie 3
CARNEGIE, Louise 2
 Whitfield
CARNEGIE, T(homas) 5
 Morris(on)
CARNEIRO LEAO, 8
 Antônio
CARNELL, Edward John 4
CARNELL, Laura Horner 1
CARNES, Cecil 3
CARNES, James Robert 10
CARNES, Thomas Petters H
CARNEY, Chesney M. 8
CARNEY, Francis Joseph 1
CARNEY, Frank 1
CARNEY, Harry Howell 6
CARNEY, James F. 10
CARNEY, James Lorring 4
CARNEY, Leonard T. 1
CARNEY, Mabel 7
CARNEY, Robert Bostwick 10
CARNEY, Robert Gibson 7
CARNEY, Thomas H

CARNEY, Thomas Joseph 2
CARNEY, William Roy 5
CARNOCHRAN, John H
 Murray
CARNOVSKY, Leon 7
CARNOVSKY, Morris 10
CARO, Marcus Rayner 4
CAROL, Kate H
CARONDELET, Baron 1
 Francisco Luis Hector de
CAROTHERS, Neil 7
CAROTHERS, Wallace H. 1
CARPENDER, Arthur S. 3
CARPENTER, Aaron 5
 Everly
CARPENTER, Alfred Saint 6
 Vrain
CARPENTER, Allen Fuller 2
CARPENTER, Allen 5
 Harmon
CARPENTER, Alva Edwin 1
CARPENTER, Arthur 3
 Devere
CARPENTER, Arthur 3
 Howe
CARPENTER, Arthur 8
 Whiting
CARPENTER, B. Platt 1
CARPENTER, Benjamin 1
CARPENTER, Carlos Clay 7
CARPENTER, Charles 1
 Carroll
CARPENTER, Charles 5
 Colcock Jones
CARPENTER, Charles E. 1
CARPENTER, Charles 2
 Ernest
CARPENTER, Charles 4
 Francis
CARPENTER, Charles 1
 Lincoln
CARPENTER, Clarence 5
CARPENTER, Clarence 6
 Ray
CARPENTER, Clark Bailey 8
CARPENTER, Clifford 8
 Earl
CARPENTER, CLinton E. 2
CARPENTER, Coy 5
 Cornelius
CARPENTER, Cyrus Clay H
CARPENTER, David 10
 Bailey
CARPENTER, Davis H
CARPENTER, Dean 8
CARPENTER, Decatur H
 Merritt Hammond
CARPENTER, Delph E. 3
CARPENTER, Edmund 1
 Janes
CARPENTER, Edward 5
 Childs
CARPENTER, Elbert 2
 Lawrence
CARPENTER, Ellen Maria 4
CARPENTER, Esther 8
CARPENTER, Eugene R. 1
CARPENTER, Fanny 5
 Hallock
CARPENTER, Farrington 7
 Reed
CARPENTER, Ford 2
 Ashman
CARPENTER, Francis 1
 Bicknell
CARPENTER, Frank 1
 George
CARPENTER, Frank 4
 Oliver
CARPENTER, Frank 1
 Pierce
CARPENTER, Frank 5
 Watson
CARPENTER, Franklin 4
 Reuben
CARPENTER, Fred Green 4
CARPENTER, Fred 5
 Warner
CARPENTER, Frederic 1
 Ives
CARPENTER, Frederic 1
 Walton
CARPENTER, George 2
 Albert
CARPENTER, George 1
 Oliver
CARPENTER, George Rice 1
CARPENTER, George 7
 Wayland
CARPENTER, Gilbert 1
 Saltonstall
CARPENTER, H. Beach 3
CARPENTER, Harry 8
 Gordon
CARPENTER, Homer 6
 Wilson

CARPENTER, Horace 1
 Francis
CARPENTER, Hubert 2
 Vinton
CARPENTER, J. Henry 3
CARPENTER, James D. 5
CARPENTER, James 10
 Morton
CARPENTER, James W .* 4
CARPENTER, Jay Arnold 7
CARPENTER, John Alden 3
CARPENTER, John 1
 Slaughter
CARPENTER, John 6
 William
CARPENTER, Julia 1
 Wiltberger
CARPENTER, Karen Anne 8
CARPENTER, Leroy 9
 Leonidas
CARPENTER, Leslie E. 6
CARPENTER, Levi D. H
CARPENTER, Louis 1
 George
CARPENTER, Louis 1
 Henry
CARPENTER, Matthew H
 Hale
CARPENTER, Miriam 6
 Feronia
CARPENTER, Monte 7
 Cutler
CARPENTER, Myron Jay 4
CARPENTER, Newton 1
 Henry
CARPENTER, Ralph 4
 Emerson
CARPENTER, Ray Wilford 4
CARPENTER, Reid 1
CARPENTER, Rhys 7
CARPENTER, Robert 2
 Ruliph Morgan
CARPENTER, Robert 5
 Wilfred
CARPENTER, Rolla 1
 Clinton
CARPENTER, Russell 8
 Phelps
CARPENTER, Samuel H. H
CARPENTER, Samuel 7
 Theodore
CARPENTER, Stanley 9
 Sherman
CARPENTER, Stephen H
 Cullen
CARPENTER, Stephen H
 Haskins
CARPENTER, W.T. 6
 Coleman
CARPENTER, Walter 6
 Samuel
CARPENTER, Walter 7
 Samuel, Jr.
CARPENTER, William E. 1
CARPENTER, William H. 4
CARPENTER, William 1
 Henry
CARPENTER, William 1
 Leland
CARPENTER, William 3
 Seal
CARPENTER, William 5
 Weston
CARPENTER, William 8
 Weston
CARR, Albert Zolotkoff 5
CARR, Alexander 2
CARR, Archie F. 9
CARR, Arthur Japheth 10
CARR, Arthur R. 3
CARR, Benjamin H
CARR, Camillo Casatti 1
 Cadmus
CARR, Ceylon Spencer 8
CARR, Chalmers Rankin 8
CARR, Charles Hardy 7
CARR, Charlotte 3
CARR, Clarence Alfred 1
CARR, Clark E. 1
CARR, Clyde Mitchell 1
CARR, Dabney H
CARR, Dabney Smith H
CARR, Earl Ingram 7
CARR, Edward Hallett 8
CARR, Elias 1
CARR, Emma Perry 5
CARR, Ernest James 10
CARR, Eugene Asa 1
CARR, Floyd Leverne 2
CARR, Francis H
CARR, Gene 3
CARR, George H. 1
CARR, George Wallace 3
CARR, Harold John 10
CARR, Harry 1
CARR, Harry C. 3
CARR, Harvey 3

CARR, Henry James 1
CARR, Herbert Wildon 1
CARR, Hobart Cecil 10
CARR, Irving J. 5
CARR, James H
CARR, James Kennedy 7
CARR, James O. 3
CARR, James Ozborn 2
CARR, Joe Cordell 8
CARR, John H
CARR, John Dickson 7
CARR, John Foster 1
CARR, John Wesley 3
CARR, Joseph Bradford H
CARR, Julian Shakespeare 1
CARR, Lawrence 5
CARR, Leland Walker 5
CARR, Lewis E. 1
CARR, Lucien 1
CARR, Nathan Tracy H
CARR, Ophelia Smith Todd 8
CARR, Oscar Clark, Jr. 7
CARR, Ossian Elmer 5
CARR, Ralph L. 3
CARR, Raymond Norman 8
CARR, Reid Langdon 2
CARR, Robert Franklin 2
CARR, Robert Kenneth 7
CARR, Samuel 1
CARR, Sarah Pratt 4
CARR, Sterling Douglas 5
CARR, Thomas Matthew H
CARR, Walter Lester 4
CARR, Walter Scott 4
CARR, Wilbert Lester 5
CARR, Wilbur John 2
CARR, William Henry 9
CARR, William Jarvis 6
CARR, William John 1
CARR, William Kearny 1
CARR, William Phillips 4
CARR, Wooda Nichols 1
CARRADINE, John 9
 Richmond
CARRE, Henry Beach 1
CARRE, Jean Marie 3
CARREIRO, Joseph 7
 Alvarez
CARREL, Alexis 2
CARRELL, George H
 Aloysius
CARRELL, Ora W. 7
CARRELL, William Beall 2
CARRERE, John Merven 1
CARRICK, Alice Van Leer 5
 (Mrs. Prescott Orde
 Skinner)
CARRICK, Lynn 4
CARRICK, Manton Marble 1
CARRICK, Samuel H
CARRICO, Joseph Leonard 2
CARRIER, Augustus Stiles 1
CARRIER, Wilbur Oscar 1
CARRIER, Willis Haviland 3
CARRIERE, Charles 9
 Montbrun
CARRIGAN, Clarence 1
CARRIGAN, Edward 2
CARRIGAN, John Willard 7
CARRIGAN, William L. 1
CARRINGTON, Alexander 6
 Berkeley
CARRINGTON, Edward H
CARRINGTON, Edward 1
 Codrington
CARRINGTON, Elaine 3
CARRINGTON, Fitzroy 1
CARRINGTON, Frances 1
 Courtney
CARRINGTON, Francis 6
 Louis
CARRINGTON, Gordon 2
 de L.
CARRINGTON, Henry 1
 Beebee
CARRINGTON, Hereward 6
 (Hubert Lavington)
CARRINGTON, James 1
 Beebee
CARRINGTON, John 7
 Claiborne
CARRINGTON, Paul H
CARRINGTON, Philip 9
CARRINGTON, Richard 1
 Adams, Jr.
CARRINGTON, William 2
 John
CARRINGTON, William 1
 Thomas
CARRIS, Lewis Herbert 3
CARRITHERS, Howard 4
CARRIUOLO, Christopher 9
 Wilfred
CARROLL, Anna Ella H
CARROLL, Augustus John 5
CARROLL, B. Harvey 1
CARROLL, Ben 2

CASEY, George J. 4
CASEY, Hugh John 8
CASEY, John Francis 2
CASEY, John J. 1
CASEY, John Schuyler 2
CASEY, Joseph H
CASEY, Lawrence B. 7
CASEY, Lee 3
CASEY, Levi H
CASEY, Lyman R. 1
CASEY, Ralph Droz 8
CASEY, Ralph Edward 8
CASEY, Lord Richard 7
  Gardiner
CASEY, Richard Gardiner 8
CASEY, Robert Joseph 4
CASEY, Robert Pierce 3
CASEY, Samuel Brown 4
CASEY, Silas H
CASEY, Silas 1
CASEY, Thomas Lincoln 1
CASEY, Warren Peter 10
CASEY, William Joseph 3
CASEY, William Joseph 9
CASEY, Zadoc H
CASH, Albert D. 3
CASH, James (Robert) 6
CASH, Wilbur Joseph 2
CASH, William Thomas 3
CASHEN, Thomas Cecil 3
CASHIN, John Martin 5
CASHMAN, Earl William 3
CASHMAN, Edwin James 5
CASHMAN, Joseph 1
  Thomas
CASHMAN, Robert 7
CASHMAN, Robert J. 10
CASHMORE, John 4
CASILEAR, John William H
CASKEY, John Fletcher 4
CASKEY, John Langdon 9
CASKIE, John Samuels H
CASKIE, Marion Maxwell 4
CASKODEN, Edwin 1
CASLER, Lester Alonzo 6
CASNER, Andrew James 10
CASON, Hulsey 3
CASPARI, Charles, Jr. 1
CASPARI, Charles Edward 2
CASPARY, Vera 4
CASPER, Henry Weber 8
CASPERSEN, O(laus) 10
  W(estby)
CASS, Alonzo Beecher 1
CASS, Charles Anderson 3
CASS, George Washington H
CASS, Joseph Kerr 4
CASS, Lewis H
CASS, Louis S. 4
CASSADY, John Howard 5
CASSADY, Morley 5
  Franklin
CASSADY, Ralph, Jr. 7
CASSADY, Thomas Gantz 5
CASSANDRA 4
CASSARD, Paul 8
CASSARETTO, Frank 9
CASSAT, David Berryhill 10
CASSAT, David Berryhill 8
CASSATT, Alexander 1
  Johnston
CASSATT, Mary 1
CASSAVETES, John 9
CASSEDY, George H
CASSEDY, John Irvin 1
CASSEL, Henry Burd 4
CASSEL, John H. 5
CASSELBERRY, William 1
  Evans
CASSELL, Wallace Lewis 4
CASSELMAN, Arthur Vale 3
CASSELS, Edwin Henry 2
CASSELS, Louis Welborn 6
CASSERLY, Eugene H
CASSIDY, George 4
  Livingston
CASSIDY, George 1
  Washington
CASSIDY, George Williams H
CASSIDY, Gerald 3
CASSIDY, Hélène Monod 7
CASSIDY, James E. 3
CASSIDY, James H. 5
CASSIDY, John Edward A. 8
CASSIDY, Leslie Martin 4
CASSIDY, Lewis Cochran 2
CASSIDY, M. Joseph 3
CASSIDY, Massilon 1
  Alexander
CASSIDY, William H
CASSIDY, William Joseph 6
CASSIL, Harold E. 3
CASSIL, Hurd Alexander 6
CASSILLY, Francis 4
CASSILLY, Philip 6
  Jacquemn
CASSIN, John H

CASSIN, Rene 6
CASSIN, William Bourke 10
CASSINGHAM, John W. 3
CASSINGHAM, Roy B. 4
CASSINGHAM, Roy B. 8
CASSINO, Samuel Edson 1
CASSIRER, Ernst 4
CASSODAY, John B. 1
CASSON, Herbert Newton 5
CASTAÑEDA, Hector-Neri 10
CASTANDEDA, Carlos 3
  Eduardo
CASTAÑEDA CASTRO, 8
  Salvador
CASTANO, Giovanni 7
CASTEGNIER, Georges 4
CASTELHUN, Dorothea 8
  (Mrs. W. K. Bassett)
CASTELLANI, Aldo 5
  (Count Of Chisimaio)
CASTELLANI, Maria 10
CASTELLANO, Richard S. 9
CASTELLANOS 7
  ARTEAGE, Daniel
CASTELLO, Eugene 1
CASTELLO BRANCO, 4
  Humberto de Alencar
CASTELLOW, Bryant 5
  Thomas
CASTEN, Daniel Francis 6
CASTER, George Brown 2
CASTIGLIONI, Arturo 3
CASTILLO, Ramon S. 2
CASTILLO NAJERA, 3
  Francisco
CASTLE, Alfred L. 6
CASTLE, Alfred Lowrey 7
CASTLE, Edward Sears 6
CASTLE, Eugene Winston 3
CASTLE, Frederick Albert 1
CASTLE, Gordon Benjamin 8
CASTLE, Harold Kainalu 4
  Long
CASTLE, Henry Anson 1
CASTLE, Homer Levi 4
CASTLE, John H., Jr. 5
CASTLE, Kendall Brooks 5
CASTLE, Lewis Gould 4
CASTLE, Nicholas 1
CASTLE, Ralph 7
CASTLE, Samuel Northrup 6
CASTLE, Vernon 4
CASTLE, William 3
CASTLE, William 5
CASTLE, William Bosworth 10
CASTLE, William Ernest 4
CASTLE, William Richards 1
CASTLE, William Richards 4
CASTLEBERRY, John 1
  Jackson
CASTLEBERRY, Winston 6
CASTLEMAN, Francis Lee, 3
  Jr.
CASTLEMAN, John 1
  Breckinridge
CASTLEMAN, Virginia 3
  Carter
CASTLEMON, Harry 1
CASTLENUOVO-TEDES- 1
  CO, Mario
CASTLES, Alfred Guldo 2
  Ruldolph
CASTNER, Joseph 2
  Compton
CASTO, C. Everett 3
CASTON, Saul 4
CASTRO, Albert 10
CASTRO, Americo 6
CASTRO, Frank Monroe 6
CASTRO, Hector David 4
CASTRO, Jose H
CASTRO, Matilde (Mrs. 6
  James H. Tufts)
CASTROVIEJO, Ramon 9
CASWELL, Albert Edward 3
CASWELL, Alexis H
CASWELL, Edward C. 6
CASWELL, Hollis L. 5
CASWELL, Irving A. 5
CASWELL, Lucien B. 4
CASWELL, Mary S. 1
CASWELL, Richard 1
CASWELL, Thomas 1
  Hubbard
CASWELL, Thomas 1
  Thompson
CASWELL, Wilbur 7
  Larremore
CATCHINGS, Thomas 4
  Clendinen
CATCHINGS, Waddill 4
CATE, Bert Clarence 8
CATE, Curtis Wolsey 7
CATE, Horace Nelson 2
CATE, Roscoe Simmons, Jr. 4
CATE, Wirt Armistead 10

CATES, Charles Theodore, 1
  Jr.
CATES, Clifton Bledsoe 5
CATES, Gordon Dell 5
CATES, Junius sidney 3
CATES, Louis Shattuck 3
CATES, Walter Thruston 5
CATESBY, Mark H
CATHARINE, Robert 8
  MacFarland
CATHCART, Arthur 2
  Martin
CATHCART, Charles 2
  Sanderson
CATHCART, Charles H
  William
CATHCART, Robert 2
  Spann
CATHCART, Stanley H. 3
CATHCART, Thomas 5
  Edward (Tom Cathcart)
CATHCART, Wallace 4
  Hugh
CATHCART, William 1
  Ledyard
CATHCART, William 1
CATHELL, Danid Webster 4
CATHELL, William T. 4
CATHER, David Clark 2
CATHER, Willa Sibert 2
CATHERWOOD, Cummins 10
CATHERWOOD, Mary 1
  Hartwell
CATHEY, Cornelius Oliver 9
CATHLES, Lawrence 5
  MacLagan
CATION, William Ritchie 7
CATLEDGE, Turner 8
CATLETT, Fred Wayne 7
CATLIN, Albertus Wright 1
CATLIN, Charles Albert 1
CATLIN, George H
CATLIN, George Edward 7
  Gordon
CATLIN, George Smith H
CATLIN, Henry Guy 4
CATLIN, Isaac Swartwood 1
CATLIN, Louise Ensign 4
CATLIN, Randolph 4
CATLIN, Robert Mayo 1
CATLIN, Roy George 1
CATLIN, Theron Ephron 3
CATLIN, Warren Benjamin 5
CATON, Arthur J. 1
CATON, Harry Anderson 6
CATON, John Dean 4
CATOR, George 1
CATRON, Charles 4
  Christopher
CATRON, John H
CATRON, Thomas Benton 1
CATT, Carrie Chapman 2
CATT, George William 1
CATTELL, Alexander H
  Gilmore
CATTELL, Edward James 1
CATTELL, Henry Ware 1
CATTELL, James McKeen 2
CATTELL, Jaques 4
CATTELL, Richard Bartley 4
  Channing
CATTELL, Roscoe Arnold 9
CATTELL, William 1
  Ashburn
CATTELL, William H
  Cassaday
CATTELLE, Wallis 1
  Richard
CATTERALL, Ralph 1
  Charles Henry
CATTO, Lord Thomas 6
  Sivewright
CATTON, Bruce 7
CATTON, Charles, Jr. H
CATTS, Sidney Johnston 1
CAUDILL, Harry Monroe 10
CAUDILL, Rebecca (Mrs. 9
  James Ayars)
CAUDILL, William Wayne 8
CAUFFMAN, Frank 4
  Guernsey
CAUGHRAN, B. Howard 8
CAULDWELL, Frederic 5
  Wadsworth
CAULDWELL, John 4
  Britton
CAULDWELL, Leslie 1
  Giffen
CAULDWELL, Oscar Ray 3
CAULEY, Frank William 8
CAULEY, John Rowan 7
CAULFIELD, Bernard H
  Gregory
CAULFIELD, Henry 4
  Stewart
CAULFIELD, Joan 10
CAULFIELD, John Francis 6

CAULFIELD, Leo Patrick 7
CAULK, John Roberts 1
CAULLERY, Maurice Jules 3
  Gaston Corneille
CAUSEY, James Campbell 6
CAUSEY, William Bowdoin 1
CAUSIN, John M.S. H
CAUTHEN, Baker James 8
CAUTHORN, Joseph 5
  Lurton
CAVADAS, Athenagoras 4
CAVAGNARO, James 5
  Francis
CAVAGNARO, Robert 5
  John
CAVALIERI, Lina (Mrs. 5
  Lucien Muratore)
CAVALLARO, Joseph B. 3
CAVALLITO, Albino 4
CAVALLON, Giorgio 10
CAVAN, Marie (Mary 5
  Cawein)
CAVANA, Martin 4
CAVANAGH, C.J. 1
CAVANAGH, Edward 9
  Francis, Jr.
CAVANAGH, Jerome 7
  Patrick
CAVANAGH, John Alexis 6
CAVANAGH, James H
  Michael
CAVANAUGH, John 1
  William
CAVANAUGH, John 5
  William
CAVANAUGH, Robert 4
  Joseph
CAVANAUGH, William 9
  Thomas
CAVE, Edward Powell 4
CAVE, H.W. 3
CAVE, Henry Wisdom 4
CAVE, Reuben Lindsay 4
CAVELIER, Robert H
CAVERLY, Raymond N. 8
CAVERNO, Charles 1
CAVERS, David Farquhar 9
CAVERT, Samuel McCrea 7
CAVERT, Walter Dudley 9
CAVICCHIA, Peter Angelo 4
CAVINS, Lorimer Victor 2
CAWEIN, Madison Julius 1
CAWL, Franklin Robert 4
CAWLEY, Edgar Moore 5
CAWLEY, Francis Riggs 8
CAWLEY, Robert Ralston 6
CAWTHORN, Joseph 2
  Bridger
CAYCE, Edgar 4
CAYLOR, John H
CAYTON, Horace Roscoe 5
CAYVAN, Georgia 1
CAYWOOD, Roland 3
  Blanchard
CAZAYOUX, Francis Earle 7
CAZAYOUX, Lawrence 10
  Marius
CAZEDESSUS, Eugene 1
  Romain
CAZENOVE, Theophile H
CAZIARC, Louis Vasmer 1
CECERE, Gaetano 10
CECIL, Arthur Bond 7
CECIL, Charles Purcell 3
CECIL, George W. 4
CECIL, James McCosh 3
CECIL, John Giles 5
CECIL, Lamar 3
CECIL, Russell 2
CECIL, Russell Lafayette 4
CECIL OF CHELWOOD, 3
  Viscount
CEDERGERG, William 5
  Emanuel
CEDERGREN, Hugo 5
CEDERSTROM, Albert 1
  Gustaf
CEFOLA, Michael 8
CEHANOVSKY, George 4
CEHRS, Charles Harold 5
CEKADA, Emil Bogomir 6
CELENTANO, William C. 5
CELERON DE 1
  BLAINVILLE, Pierre
  Joseph de
CELINE, Louis Ferdinand 4
CELIO, Enrico 8
CELL, George C. 1
CELL, John W(esley) 5
CELLA, John G. 6
CELLER, Emanuel 7
CELLINI, Renato 5
CENNAMO, Ralph 9
CERACCHI, Guiseppe H
CERF, Barry* 2
CERF, Benett Alfred 5
CERF, Edward Owen 3

CERF, Jay Henry 6
CERMAK, Anton Joseph 1
CERNY, Robert George 8
CERRACCHIO, Enrico 6
  Filiberto
CERRE, Jean Gabriel H
CERRONE, Jean Baptiste 10
CERVANTES, Alfonse J. 8
CESAR, Alejandro 7
CESARI, Lamberto 10
CESNOLA, Louis Palma Di 1
CESPEDES Y ORTIZ, 3
  Carlos Miguel
CESSNA, John H
CESSNA, Orange Howard 1
CESTARO, Michael Paul 6
CHABRAT, Guy Ignatius H
CHABRIER, Jacques Rene 9
CHACE, Arnold Buffum 1
CHACE, Arthur Freeborn 6
CHACE, Elizabeth Buffum H
CHACE, George Hart 3
CHACE, Jonathan 1
CHACE, Malacolmn 3
  Greene
CHACE, William N(iels) 6
CHADBOURN, Erlon R. 4
CHADBOURN, William 4
  Hobbs, Jr.
CHADBOURNE, George 1
  Storrs
CHADBOURNE, Paul H
  Ansel
CHADBOURNE, Thomas 1
  Lincoln
CHADBOURNE, William 4
  Merriam
CHADDOCK, Charles 1
  Gilbert
CHADDOCK, Robert 1
  Emmet
CHADSEY, Charles Ernest 1
CHADWICK, Charles 3
CHADWICK, Charles 1
  Wesley
CHADWICK, Clarence 1
  Wells
CHADWICK, E. Wallace 7
CHADWICK, E. Wallace 5
CHADWICK, French 1
  Ensor
CHADWICK, George 3
  Halcott
CHADWICK, George 1
  Whitefield
CHADWICK, Henry 5
  Dexter
CHADWICK, James 6
CHADWICK, James 6
  Carroll
CHADWICK, James Read 1
CHADWICK, John 4
  Raymond
CHADWICK, John White 1
CHADWICK, Lee Sherman 5
CHADWICK, Leigh 6
  E(dward)
CHADWICK, Stephen 6
  Fowler
CHADWICK, Stephen 1
  James
CHAFEE, Adna Romanza 1
CHAFEE, Francis 10
  H(asseltine)
CHAFEE, Henry Sharpe 4
CHAFEE, Zechariah, Jr. 3
CHAFER, Lewis Sperry 3
CHAFFEE, Adna Romanza 1
CHAFFEE, Arthur Billings 3
CHAFFEE, Calvin Clifford H
CHAFFEE, Emory Leon 6
CHAFFEE, Emory Leon 7
CHAFFEE, Eugene Bernard 10
CHAFFEE, Henry Hansell 5
CHAFFEE, Jerome Bunty H
CHAFFEE, Jerome Stuart 2
CHAFFEE, Paul Stanley 10
CHAFFEE, Robert Emory 6
CHAFFEY, Andrew M. 1
CHAFFEY, George 1
CHAFFIN, Lucien Gates 1
CHAFIN, Eugene Wilder 1
CHAGALL, Marc 8
CHAIKIN, Sol Chick 10
CHAILLE, Stanford 1
  Emerson
CHAILLE-LONG, Charles 1
CHAINEY, George 4
CHAISSON, John Robert 5
CHAIT, Frederick 9
CHALFANT, Alexander 4
  Steele
CHALFANT, Harry 1
  Malcolm
CHALIAPIN, Boris 7
CHALIAPIN, Feodor H

CHUBB, Thomas Caldecot 5
CHUBBUCK, Thomas H
CHUJOY, Anatole 5
CHUNDRIGAR, Ismail Ibrahim 4
CHUNN, Calvin Ellsworth 8
CHUPP, Charles David 5
CHURCH, Albert Thomas 7
CHURCH, Alonzo H
CHURCH, Alonzo 1
CHURCH, Aloysuis Stanislaus 6
CHURCH, Angelica Schuyler 3
CHURCH, Archibald 4
CHURCH, Arthur Latham 1
CHURCH, Augustus Byington 1
CHURCH, Benjamin* H
CHURCH, Benjamin Butler 3
CHURCH, Brooks Davis 10
CHURCH, Denver Samuel 3
CHURCH, Donald (Eisenbrey) 7
CHURCH, Earl D. 1
CHURCH, Earl Frank 8
CHURCH, Edward Bentley 1
CHURCH, Edwin Fayette, Jr. 6
CHURCH, Elihu 6
CHURCH, Ernest Elliott 10
CHURCH, Francis Pharcellus 1
CHURCH, Frank 8
CHURCH, Frank Henry 1
CHURCH, Frederick Edwin 1
CHURCH, Frederick Stuart 1
CHURCH, Gaylord 7
CHURCH, George Dudley 6
CHURCH, George Hervey 1
CHURCH, Henry Ward 1
CHURCH, I.W. 7
CHURCH, Irving Porter 1
CHURCH, James Edward 4
CHURCH, James Marion 7
CHURCH, John Adams 1
CHURCH, John Fertig 4
CHURCH, John Huston 3
CHURCH, Marguerite Stitt 9
CHURCH, Melville 1
CHURCH, Pharcellus H
CHURCH, Ralph Edwin 2
CHURCH, Randolph 5
CHURCH, Richard Cassius 6
CHURCH, Samuel Harden 2
CHURCH, William Conant 1
CHURCH, William E. 1
CHURCH, William Farr 7
CHURCH, William Howell 1
CHURCHILL, Alfred Vance 2
CHURCHILL, Charles Samuel 1
CHURCHILL, Edward Delos 5
CHURCHILL, Edward Perry 7
CHURCHILL, Everett Avery 3
CHURCHILL, Frank Edwin 2
CHURCHILL, Frank Spooner 4
CHURCHILL, George Bosworth 1
CHURCHILL, George Morton 5
CHURCHILL, Henry Stern 4
CHURCHILL, John Charles 1
CHURCHILL, John Wesley 1
CHURCHILL, Joseph Richmomd 1
CHURCHILL, Julius Alonzo 4
CHURCHILL, Lida A. 5
CHURCHILL, Marlborough 2
CHURCHILL, Ralph Loren 6
CHURCHILL, Lady Randolph Spencer 1
CHURCHILL, Thomas J. 1
CHURCHILL, Thomas William 1
CHURCHILL, William 1
CHURCHILL, Sir Winston 4
CHURCHILL, Winston 2
CHURCHMAN, John Woolman 1
CHURCHMAN, Philip Hudson 5
CHURCHMAN, William Henry H
CHURCHWELL, William Montgomery H
CHUTE, A(aron) Hamilton 5
CHUTE, Arthur Hunt 1
CHUTE, Arthur Lambert 1
CHUTE, (Beatrice) Joy 9
CHUTE, Charles Lionel 3
CHUTE, Horatio Nelson 1
CHU TEH, (GEN.) 7
CHWOROWSKY, Martin Philip 6
CHYNOWETH, Bradford G. 8
CIAMPAGLEA, Carlo 7
CIANCA, Bernard Joseph 6
CIARDI, John 9
CICOGNANI, Amleto Giovanni 6
CILLEY, Bradbury H
CILLEY, C.C. 5
CILLEY, Gordon Harper 1
CILLEY, Greenleaf 4
CILLEY, Jonathan Longfellow 1
CILLEY, Jonathan Prince 1
CILLEY, Joseph* H
CIMIOTTI, Gustave 5
CINELLI, Albert Arthur 6
CIOBANU, Ioan 6
CIOCCO, Antonio 5
CIPOLLARO, Anthony Caesar 6
CIRESI, Anthony David 10
CISLER, Walker Lee 10
CIST, Charles* H
CIST, Henry Martyn 1
CIST, Jacob H
CITRON, William Micheal 7
CLAAS, Gerhard 9
CLAASSEN, Peter Walter 1
CLABAUGH, Harry M. 1
CLABAUGH, Hinton Graves 2
CLABAUGH, Samuel Francis 8
CLACK, Robert Wood 7
CLAESSENS, Maria 6
CLAFLIN, Arthur Whitman 1
CLAFLIN, Avery 7
CLAFLIN, Horace Brigham H
CLAFLIN, John 1
CLAFLIN, W(alter) Harold 6
CLAFLIN, William 1
CLAFLIN, William Henry, III 7
CLAGETT, Clifton H
CLAGETT, Henry B. 7
CLAGETT, John Rozier 1
CLAGETT, Oscar Theron 10
CLAGETT, Robert Horatio 8
CLAGETT, Wyseman H
CLAGGETT, Strabo V(ivian) 9
CLAGHORN, George H
CLAGHORN, Kate Holladay 1
CLAGUE, Frank 3
CLAIBORNE, James Robert 7
CLAIBORNE, John H
CLAIBORNE, John Francis Hamtramck H
CLAIBORNE, John Herbert 1
CLAIBORNE, Nathaniel Herbert H
CLAIBORNE, Thomas* H
CLAIBORNE, William H
CLAIBORNE, William Charles Coles H
CLAIBORNE, William Stirling 1
CLAIR, Edward L . 3
CLAIR, Matthew W., Jr. 8
CLAIR, Matthew Wesley 2
CLAIR, Miles Nelson 7
CLAIR, Miles Nelson 8
CLAIR, Rene 7
CLAIRE, Richard Shaw 5
CLAMER, Guilliam Henry 4
CLAMPETT, Bob 8
CLANCY, Albert Worthington 4
CLANCY, Frank J. 3
CLANCY, Frank Willey 1
CLANCY, George Carpenter 4
CLANCY, John Richard 1
CLANCY, John Thomas 8
CLANCY, John W. 5
CLANCY, Maurice Lee 9
CLANCY, Robert H. 4
CLANCY, Robert H. 7
CLAP, Nathaniel H
CLAP, Thoms H
CLAPHAM, Thomas 4
CLAPP, Alfred Comstock 9
CLAPP, Alfred Lester 8
CLAPP, Asa H
CLAPP, Asa William Henry H
CLAPP, Augustus Wilson 2
CLAPP, Charles Horace 1
CLAPP, Clift Rogers 2
CLAPP, Clyde Alvin 3
CLAPP, Cornelia Maria 1
CLAPP, Earle Hart 5
CLAPP, Edward Bull 1
CLAPP, Edwin Jones 1
CLAPP, Elmer Frederick 1
CLAPP, Frank Leslie 1
CLAPP, Franklin Halsted 2
CLAPP, Frederick Gardner 2
CLAPP, Gordon Rufus 4
CLAPP, Harold L. 4
CLAPP, Henry Austin 1
CLAPP, Herbert Codman 1
CLAPP, Jacob Crawford 4
CLAPP, John Mantle 5
CLAPP, Leallyn Burr 9
CLAPP, Margaret 6
CLAPP, Moses Edwin 1
CLAPP, Paul Spencer 3
CLAPP, Philip Greeley 3
CLAPP, Verner Warren 5
CLAPP, William Jacob 8
CLAPP, William Warland H
CLAPPER, Raymond 2
CLAPPER, Samuel Mott Duryea 1
CLARAHAN, Leo E. 4
CLARDY, John D. 4
CLARDY, Kit 4
CLARE, Arthur James 1
CLARE, Israel Smith 1
CLARITY, Frank Edmund 1
CLARK, A. Howard 1
CLARK, Abraham H
CLARK, Addison 4
CLARK, Albert Montgomery 3
CLARK, Albert Warren 1
CLARK, Alden Hyde 4
CLARK, Alfred Edward 3
CLARK, Allan 3
CLARK, Allan Jay 3
CLARK, Allen Culling 2
CLARK, Alson Skinner 2
CLARK, Alva Benson 3
CLARK, Alvan H
CLARK, Alvan Graham H
CLARK, Ambrose Williams H
CLARK, Andrew Giles 7
CLARK, Andrew Hill 6
CLARK, Ann Nolan 10
CLARK, Anne Kinnier 5
CLARK, Annie Maria Lawrence 4
CLARK, Anson Luman 3
CLARK, Anthony Morris 7
CLARK, Arthur Bridgman 2
CLARK, Arthur Bryan 2
CLARK, Arthur Elwood 3
CLARK, Arthur Henry 3
CLARK, Augusta F(arnum) 7
CLARK, Austin Hobart 3
CLARK, B. Preston 1
CLARK, Badger 3
CLARK, Barrett H. 3
CLARK, Barzilla Worth 2
CLARK, Bennett Champ 3
CLARK, Bert Boone 5
CLARK, Berton S. 8
CLARK, Birge Malcolm 10
CLARK, Bobby 3
CLARK, Bonnell Wetmore 3
CLARK, Byron Bryant 9
CLARK, C.P. 4
CLARK, Calvin Montague 2
CLARK, Cameron 3
CLARK, Caroline Richards 5
CLARK, Carroll D. 7
CLARK, Champ 1
CLARK, Charles H
CLARK, Charles Benjamin H
CLARK, Charles Cleveland 5
CLARK, Charles Dickson 1
CLARK, Charles Edgar 1
CLARK, Charles Edward 4
CLARK, Charles Finney 1
CLARK, Charles Heber 1
CLARK, Charles Hopkins 1
CLARK, Charles Martin 1
CLARK, Charles Martin, Jr. 9
CLARK, Charles Spencer 8
CLARK, Charles Upson 4
CLARK, Charles Walker 1
CLARK, Charles William 1
CLARK, Chase Addison 4
CLARK, Chester Frederic 3
CLARK, Christopher Henderson H
CLARK, Clare Clyde 8
CLARK, Clarence C. 10
CLARK, Clarence Don 1
CLARK, Clarence Munroe 1
CLARK, Clarence Sewall 4
CLARK, Claude Lester 4
CLARK, Clifford Pease 3
CLARK, Cyrus J. 3
CLARK, D. Worth 3
CLARK, Dan Elbert 3
CLARK, Daniel* H
CLARK, David L. 1
CLARK, David Wasgate H
CLARK, Davis Wasgatt 1
CLARK, Dean Alexander 8
CLARK, Derral Leroy 5
CLARK, Donald Lemen 4
CLARK, Donald Sherman 7
CLARK, Duncan Campbell 4
CLARK, Dwight Edwin 3
CLARK, Earl Wesley 10
CLARK, Edgar Erastus 1
CLARK, Edith Kirkwood Ormsby 6
CLARK, Edson Lyman 1
CLARK, Edward 1
CLARK, Edward Brayton 5
CLARK, Edward Gay 2
CLARK, Edward Hardy 2
CLARK, Edward L. 3
CLARK, Edward Lee. 4
CLARK, Edward Lord 1
CLARK, Edward P. 1
CLARK, Edward W. 2
CLARK, Elijah H
CLARK, Eliot Candee 7
CLARK, Eliot Round 4
CLARK, Ellery Harding 2
CLARK, Elmer Talmage 4
CLARK, Elroy Newton 4
CLARK, Emily 3
CLARK, Emmons 1
CLARK, Emory T. 8
CLARK, Emory W. 3
CLARK, Ernest John 10
CLARK, Eugene Augustine 7
CLARK, Eugene Bradley 2
CLARK, Eugene Edwin 8
CLARK, Eugene Francis 1
CLARK, Evans 8
CLARK, Ezra Jr. H
CLARK, Ezra Westcote 2
CLARK, F. Lewis 1
CLARK, Felicia Buttz 4
CLARK, Felton Grandison 5
CLARK, Fontaine Riker 4
CLARK, Francis Edward 1
CLARK, Frank 4
CLARK, Frank Donald 7
CLARK, Frank Hodges 3
CLARK, Frank Sylvester 3
CLARK, Frank William 2
CLARK, Franklin H
CLARK, Franklin Jones 4
CLARK, Fred 5
CLARK, Fred Emerson 2
CLARK, Fred George 5
CLARK, Fred Pope 1
CLARK, Frederic Simmons 1
CLARK, Frederick Huntington 5
CLARK, Frederick John 1
CLARK, Frederick M. 5
CLARK, Frederick Pareis 5
CLARK, Frederick R. 10
CLARK, Frederick Timothy 1
CLARK, Friend Ebenezer 5
CLARK, Gaylord Parsons 1
CLARK, George 4
CLARK, George Archibald 1
CLARK, George Campbell 4
CLARK, George Crawford 1
CLARK, George Halford 3
CLARK, George Hardy 4
CLARK, George Harlow 5
CLARK, George J. 3
CLARK, George L. 9
CLARK, George Lindenberg 5
CLARK, George Luther 5
CLARK, George McMurry 7
CLARK, Sir George Norman 9
CLARK, George Ramsey 2
CLARK, George Rogers H
CLARK, George Thomas 1
CLARK, George Whitefield 1
CLARK, Geroge Larkin 4
CLARK, Gilbert Edward 8
CLARK, Glenn W(hitmire) 6
CLARK, Grady William 10
CLARK, Grenville 4
CLARK, Grenville 5
CLARK, Grenville 7
CLARK, Grover 1
CLARK, Hamilton Burdick 5
CLARK, Hannah Belle 4
CLARK, Harold Benjamin 3
CLARK, Harold Johnson 3
CLARK, Harold Terry 4
CLARK, Harry Camp 3
CLARK, Harry Granville 1
CLARK, Harry Henderson 3
CLARK, Harry Willard 4
CLARK, Harvey Cyrus 1
CLARK, Henry A. 3
CLARK, Henry Benjamin 5
CLARK, Henry Hunt 5
CLARK, Henry James H
CLARK, Henry Selby H
CLARK, Henry W. 2
CLARK, Henry Wadsworth 7
CLARK, Herbert Allen 8
CLARK, Herbert W. 4
CLARK, Herma N. 3
CLARK, Homer Pierce 6
CLARK, Horace Francis H
CLARK, Horace Spencer 1
CLARK, Horatio David 3
CLARK, Howard J. 1
CLARK, Howard V. 4
CLARK, Hubert Lyman 2
CLARK, Imogen 1
CLARK, Isaac 1
CLARK, Isaiah Raymond 1
CLARK, J. Reuben, Jr. 4
CLARK, J. Ross 1
CLARK, J. Scott 1
CLARK, Mrs. J.C. (Milam Ava Bertha) 7
CLARK, James H
CLARK, James Anthony 7
CLARK, James Edward 5
CLARK, James Edwin 2
CLARK, James G. 5
CLARK, James H. 7
CLARK, James Lippitt 7
CLARK, James Richard 8
CLARK, James Truman 1
CLARK, James Waddey 1
CLARK, James West H
CLARK, Janet Howell 5
CLARK, Jerome Bayard 7
CLARK, Jesse Redman 1
CLARK, John H
CLARK, John Alden 6
CLARK, John Arvine 3
CLARK, John Balfour 8
CLARK, John Bates 1
CLARK, John Brittan 2
CLARK, John Bullock H
CLARK, John Bullock 1
CLARK, John Bunyan 7
CLARK, John Chamberlain H
CLARK, John Cheesman 2
CLARK, John Clinton 9
CLARK, John Conrad 10
CLARK, John Davidson 7
CLARK, John Edward 1
CLARK, John Emory 1
CLARK, John Goodrich 1
CLARK, John Henry 9
CLARK, John Howe 1
CLARK, John Jesse 4
CLARK, John Lewis 5
CLARK, John Marshall 1
CLARK, John Maurice 4
CLARK, John Robert 3
CLARK, John Spencer 4
CLARK, Jonas H
CLARK, Jonas Gilman H
CLARK, Joseph Bourne 1
CLARK, Joseph James 5
CLARK, Joseph Leon 4
CLARK, Joseph S. 10
CLARK, Joseph Sylvester H
CLARK, Josephine Adelaide 4
CLARK, Julian Jerome 5
CLARK, Kate Upson 1
CLARK, Keith 3
CLARK, Kenneth Willis 7
CLARK, L. Pierce 1
CLARK, Lee Hinchman 4
CLARK, Leigh Mallet 10
CLARK, Leroy Walter 7
CLARK, Lester Williams 1
CLARK, Lewis Gaylord H
CLARK, Lewis Whitehouse 1
CLARK, Lincoln H
CLARK, Lindley Daniel 4
CLARK, Linwood L. 5
CLARK, Lloyd Montgomery 5
CLARK, Lord Kenneth McKenzie 8
CLARK, Lot H
CLARK, Lucius Charles 2
CLARK, Malcolm Emery 7
CLARK, Mallie Adkin 1
CLARK, Marguerite 1
CLARK, Marguerite Sheridan 8
CLARK, Mark Wayne 8
CLARK, Marsh 9
CLARK, Martin 9
CLARK, Melville 1
CLARK, Melville 3

CLARK, Melvin Green 1
CLARK, Meriweather Lewis H
CLARK, Myron H. 3
CLARK, Myron Holley H
CLARK, Nathaniel Walling 1
CLARK, Nelson Raymond 8
CLARK, Olynthus B. 1
CLARK, Paul Burroughes 4
CLARK, Paul Dennison 5
CLARK, Paul Foster 5
CLARK, Paul Franklin 7
CLARK, Pendleton Scott 10
CLARK, Percy Hamilton 4
CLARK, Ralph B. 8
CLARK, Randolph 4
CLARK, Ray Henry 3
CLARK, Reed Paige 3
CLARK, Rensselaer Weston 4
CLARK, Richard Elijah 7
CLARK, Richard Francis Maplestone 6
CLARK, Robert H
CLARK, Robert Bruce 5
CLARK, Robert Cariton 1
CLARK, Robert Fry 6
CLARK, Robert Lanier 4
CLARK, Robert Thomas, Jr. 3
CLARK, Roe Sidney 3
CLARK, Roland Eugene 3
CLARK, Rollin M. 3
CLARK, Roscoe W. 8
CLARK, Roy Wallace 2
CLARK, Rufus Wheelwright H
CLARK, Rufus Wheelwright 1
CLARK, Rush H
CLARK, Russell 9
CLARK, Sam L. 4
CLARK, Samuel H
CLARK, Samuel M. 1
CLARK, Samuel Orman 6
CLARK, Samuel Orman, Jr. 8
CLARK, Samuel Wesley 3
CLARK, Sheldon H
CLARK, Sheldon 3
CLARK, Sherman Edward 7
CLARK, Sherman Rockwell 8
CLARK, Solomon Henry 1
CLARK, Stephen Carlton 4
CLARK, Stephen Cutter 3
CLARK, Sydney Aylmer 8
CLARK, Taliaferro 2
CLARK, Theodore 3
CLARK, Theodore Minot 1
CLARK, Thomas Arkle 1
CLARK, Thomas Collier 1
CLARK, Thomas Curtis 3
CLARK, Thomas Frederic 4
CLARK, Thomas Harvey 1
CLARK, Thomas March 1
CLARK, Thomas Winder Young 7
CLARK, Tom C. 7
CLARK, Victor Selden 3
CLARK, Virginius E. 2
CLARK, W.A. Graham 3
CLARK, Wallace 2
CLARK, Walter* 1
CLARK, Walter Appleton 1
CLARK, Walter Eli 2
CLARK, Walter Ernest 3
CLARK, Walter Eugene 4
CLARK, Walter Loane 1
CLARK, Walter Vantilburg 5
CLARK, Walton 1
CLARK, Warren William Herman 8
CLARK, Washington A. 2
CLARK, Wesley Clarke 10
CLARK, Wesley Plummer 7
CLARK, Wilber Dale 9
CLARK, Wilbur 4
CLARK, Will L. 4
CLARK, William* H
CLARK, William 3
CLARK, William Andrews 1
CLARK, William Andrews, Jr. 1
CLARK, William Anthony 4
CLARK, William Arthur 1
CLARK, William Bell 8
CLARK, William Braddock 1
CLARK, William Bullock 1
CLARK, William Burt 7
CLARK, William Clifford 3
CLARK, William E. 4
CLARK, William Francis 4
CLARK, William Heermans 1
CLARK, William Henry 5
CLARK, William Irving 3
CLARK, William Mansfield 4
CLARK, William R. 5
CLARK, William Smith H
CLARK, William Smith, II 5
CLARK, William Thomas 4
CLARK, William Timothy 4
CLARK, William Van Alan 7
CLARK, William Walker 3
CLARK, Willis Gaylord H
CLARK, Willis Winfield 4
CLARK, Wilson D., Jr. 8
CLARK, Winfred Newcomb 3
CLARKE, Albert 1
CLARKE, Alfred 1
CLARKE, Andrew Stuart Currie 1
CLARKE, Archibald Smith H
CLARKE, Arthur Edward 2
CLARKE, Augustus Peck 1
CLARKE, Bascom B. 1
CLARKE, Bayard H
CLARKE, Benjamin Franklin 1
CLARKE, Beverly Leonidas H
CLARKE, Bruce Cooper 9
CLARKE, Caspar Purdon Kt 1
CLARKE, Caspar William 3
CLARKE, Charles Cameron 1
CLARKE, Charles Ezra H
CLARKE, Charles Galloway 8
CLARKE, Charles Lorenzo 1
CLARKE, Charles S. 3
CLARKE, Charles W.E. 4
CLARKE, Charles Walter 4
CLARKE, Clement George 1
CLARKE, Creston 1
CLARKE, David Andrew 6
CLARKE, David Roland 3
CLARKE, Donald Henderson 3
CLARKE, Dumont 1
CLARKE, Dwight L. 7
CLARKE, Edith Emily 1
CLARKE, Edmund Arthur Stanley 1
CLARKE, Edwin Leavitt 2
CLARKE, Elijah H
CLARKE, Eliot Channing 1
CLARKE, Elizabeth Crocker Lawrence 4
CLARKE, E(lwyn) L(orenzo) 6
CLARKE, Ernest Perley 1
CLARKE, Ernest Swope 2
CLARKE, Francis West 1
CLARKE, Frank G. 1
CLARKE, Frank Wigglesworth 1
CLARKE, Freeman H
CLARKE, George H
CLARKE, George Herbert 1
CLARKE, George W. 1
CLARKE, Gilmore David 8
CLARKE, Hans Thacher 5
CLARKE, Harley Lyman 3
CLARKE, Helen Archibald 1
CLARKE, Herbert Lincoln 2
CLARKE, Herman Frederick 2
CLARKE, Hopewell 1
CLARKE, Horace Donald 3
CLARKE, Hugh Archibald 4
CLARKE, Ida Clyde 3
CLARKE, J. Calvitt 5
CLARKE, James Augustine 5
CLARKE, James Everitt 4
CLARKE, James Franklin 1
CLARKE, James Frederic 2
CLARKE, James Freeman H
CLARKE, James I. 4
CLARKE, James P. 1
CLARKE, James Whyte 9
CLARKE, Joe Alexander 5
CLARKE, John H
CLARKE, John Davenport 1
CLARKE, John Hessin 2
CLARKE, John Hopkins H
CLARKE, John L. 10
CLARKE, John Mason 1
CLARKE, John Proctor 1
CLARKE, John Sleeper 1
CLARKE, John Vaughan 1
CLARKE, J(oseph) Henry 10
CLARKE, Jospeh Ignatius Constantine 1
CLARKE, Lorenzo Mason 2
CLARKE, Mary Bayard Devereux H
CLARKE, Mary Evelyn 8
CLARKE, Mary Francis H
CLARKE, McDonald H
CLARKE, Norris Jay 7
CLARKE, Philip Ream 4
CLARKE, R. Floyd 1
CLARKE, Reader Wright H
CLARKE, Rebecca Sophia 1
CLARKE, Richard H
CLARKE, Richard Henry 1
CLARKE, Richard Wilton 5
CLARKE, Robert 1
CLARKE, Robert Bradstreet 10
CLARKE, Robert Warner 10
CLARKE, Samuel Fessenden 1
CLARKE, Sarah J. 4
CLARKE, Staley Nichols H
CLARKE, Thomas Benedict 1
CLARKE, Thomas Howard 6
CLARKE, Thomas Shields 1
CLARKE, Thurmond 5
CLARKE, Walter H
CLARKE, Walter Irving 1
CLARKE, Walter James 2
CLARKE, William A. 4
CLARKE, William Fayal 1
CLARKE, William Francis 3
CLARKE, William Hawes Crichton 1
CLARKE, William Horatio 1
CLARKE, William Newton 1
CLARKIN, Franklin 5
CLARKSON, Coker Fiffield 1
CLARKSON, Coker Fifield H
CLARKSON, Edward Everett 3
CLARKSON, Edward Rycroft 3
CLARKSON, Grosvenor B. 1
CLARKSON, Henry Mazyck 4
CLARKSON, Heriot 2
CLARKSON, James A(ndrew) 5
CLARKSON, James C. 1
CLARKSON, James Willis, Jr. 3
CLARKSON, Jesse Dunsmore 6
CLARKSON, Louise 4
CLARKSON, Matthew* H
CLARKSON, Percy William 4
CLARKSON, Ralph 3
CLARKSON, Richard Perkinhon 1
CLARKSON, Robert Livingston 5
CLARKSON, Ross 8
CLARKSON, Thaddeus Stevens 4
CLARKSON, W. Palmer 1
CLARKSON, Wright 2
CLARY, Albert G. 1
CLARY, Harold Franklin 4
CLARY, Joseph Monroe 4
CLARY, William Webb 5
CLARY-SQUIRE, Mary Louise 4
CLAS, Angelo Robert 5
CLASON, Charles Russell 8
CLASSEN, Anton H. 1
CLASSON, David Guy 1
CLATWORTHY, Fred Payne 3
CLATWORTHY, Linda May 1
CLAUDE, Albert 8
CLAUDEL, Paul 3
CLAUDY, Carl Harry 6
CLAUGE, Ewan 9
CLAUS, Henry Turner 4
CLAUSE, Robert Lewis 8
CLAUSE, William Lewis 1
CLAUSEN, Claus Lauritz H
CLAUSEN, Donald Neath 10
CLAUSEN, Frederick Harold 2
CLAUSEN, Jens (Christian) 5
CLAUSEN, Leon R. 4
CLAUSEN, Robert Theodore 8
CLAUSEN, Roy Elwood 3
CLAUSEN, Samuel Wolcott 3
CLAUSER, Milton U. 7
CLAUSO, Gerard Leslie Makins 6
CLAUSO, J. Earl 3
CLAUSON, Andrew Gustav, Jr. 9
CLAUSON, Clinton Amos 3
CLAUSON, Ivy P. Stewart (Mrs. Edwin Clauson) 5
CLAUSSEN, George 2
CLAUSSEN, Julia 1
CLAVAN, Irwin 8
CLAWSON, Benjamin J. 6
CLAWSON, Clinton Dudley 3
CLAWSON, Isaih Dunn H
CLAWSON, Marion Don 3
CLAWSON, Rudger 2
CLAXTON, Allen Enes 4
CLAXTON, Brooke 4
CLAXTON, C. Porter 4
CLAXTON, John Wilbert 7
CLAXTON, Kate 1
CLAXTON, Mary Hannah Johnston 3
CLAXTON, Philander Priestley 3
CLAY, Albert Tobias 1
CLAY, Alexander Stephens 1
CLAY, Brutus Junius H
CLAY, Brutus Junius 1
CLAY, Cassius Marcellus 1
CLAY, Cecil 1
CLAY, Christopher Field 1
CLAY, Clement Claiborne H
CLAY, Clement Comer H
CLAY, Edward Williams H
CLAY, Green H
CLAY, Henry H
CLAY, Henry 7
CLAY, Henry Brevard 5
CLAY, James Brown H
CLAY, James Lloyd 6
CLAY, John 1
CLAY, John Cecil 5
CLAY, Joseph* H
CLAY, Laura 1
CLAY, Lucius Dub 7
CLAY, Matthew H
CLAY, Ryburn Glover 3
CLAY, William Rogers 1
CLAYBERG, John Bertrand 1
CLAYBERGER, Raymond Pierce 6
CLAYBORN, John Henry 3
CLAYBOURN, John G. 4
CLAYBOURN, John Geronold 5
CLAYBOURN, Leslie WIlliam 7
CLAY-CLOPTON, Virginia Carolina 4
CLAYPOLE, Edith Jane 5
CLAYPOLE, Edward Waller 1
CLAYPOLE, James Vernon 4
CLAYPOOL, Harold K. 3
CLAYPOOL, Horatio C. 4
CLAYPOOL, J(ohn) Gordon 5
CLAYTON, Augustin H
CLAYTON, Bertram Tracy 1
CLAYTON, Charles H
CLAYTON, Charles Curtis 9
CLAYTON, Christine B. 7
CLAYTON, Claude Feemster 6
CLAYTON, Ernest 3
CLAYTON, Everett McCord 6
CLAYTON, H.G. 4
CLAYTON, Henry De Lamar 1
CLAYTON, Henry Helm 2
CLAYTON, James Benjamin 4
CLAYTON, Jean Paul 8
CLAYTON, John H
CLAYTON, John Middleton H
CLAYTON, Joshua H
CLAYTON, Lawrence 2
CLAYTON, Philip Thomas Byard 5
CLAYTON, Powell 1
CLAYTON, Thomas H
CLAYTON, Victoria Virginia 1
CLAYTON, William Brasher 3
CLAYTON, William Lockhart 4
CLAYTON, Willis Sherman 1
CLAYTOR, Archer Adams 4
CLAYTOR, Arthur Adams 10
CLAYTOR, Graham 7
CLAYTOR, Thomas Ash 1
CLEARWATER, Alphonso Trumpbour 1
CLEARY, Alfred John 1
CLEARY, Daniel Francis 3
CLEARY, Edward John 8
CLEARY, George Edward 7
CLEARY, George J. 3
CLEARY, James M. 4
CLEARY, James Mansfield 5
CLEARY, John Joseph 9
CLEARY, John Vincent 10
CLEARY, Michael Joseph 2
CLEARY, Owen J. 4
CLEARY, Peter Joseph Augustine 1
CLEARY, Theresa Anne 10
CLEARY, Walter Henry 8
CLEARY, William E. 1
CLEASBY, Harold Loomis 5
CLEAVELAND, Agnes Morely 5
CLEAVELAND, Elizabeth Hannah Jocelyn 1
CLEAVELAND, Harry Hayes 2
CLEAVELAND, Harry Hayes, Jr. 3
CLEAVELAND, Livingston Warner 1
CLEAVELAND, Moses H
CLEAVELAND, Parker H
CLEAVER, J. Benjamin 7
CLEAVER, William Joseph 8
CLEAVES, Arthur Wordsworth 1
CLEAVES, Henry Bradstreet 1
CLEAVES, Herbert Martin 7
CLEAVES, Nelson C. 4
CLEAVES, Willis Everett 4
CLEAVINGER, John Simeon 3
CLEBORNE, Christopher James 1
CLEBORNE, Guy Miller 7
CLEBSCH, William Anthony 8
CLEBURN, Patrick Ronayne H
CLEE, Frederick Raymond 3
CLEE, Gilbert Harrison 5
CLEE, Lester Harrison 8
CLEEMANN, Richard Alsop 1
CLEETON, Glen Uriel 7
CLEGG, Cecil Hunter 5
CLEGG, Lee Milton 3
CLEGG, Moses Tran 1
CLEGHORN, Sarah Norcliffe 3
CLELAND, Alexander McIntosh 4
CLELAND, Charles S. 4
CLELAND, George L. 9
CLELAND, Hance H. 7
CLELAND, Henry Lloyd 8
CLELAND, Herdman Fitzgerald 1
CLELAND, James T. 7
CLELAND, John Scott 3
CLELAND, Joseph P. 6
CLELAND, McKenzie 1
CLELAND, Ralph Erskine 5
CLELAND, Robert Glass 3
CLELAND, Robert Wickliffe 4
CLELAND, Thomas Hann 1
CLELAND, Thomas Maitland 4
CLEM, John Lincoln 1
CLEMEN, Rudolf Alexander 5
CLEMENCE, Gerald Maurice 6
CLEMENCE, Richard Vernon 8
CLEMENS, Charles Edwin 1
CLEMENS, James Ross 3
CLEMENS, Jeremiah H
CLEMENS, Samuel Langhorne 1
CLEMENS, Sherrard H
CLEMENS, Wilbur T. 4
CLEMENS, William Marshall 1
CLEMENS, William Montgomery 1
CLEMENT, Allan Montgomery 3
CLEMENT, Charles Maxwell 1
CLEMENT, Clay 1
CLEMENT, Edmond 1
CLEMENT, Edward Henry 1
CLEMENT, Ernest Wilson 1
CLEMENT, Frank Goad 5
CLEMENT, George Clinton 1
CLEMENT, John Addison 2
CLEMENT, Kenneth Witcher 6
CLEMENT, Martin Withington 4
CLEMENT, Percival Wood 1
CLEMENT, Rugus Early H
CLEMENT, Samuel Averett 7
CLEMENT, Stephen Merrell 1
CLEMENT, William Tardy 3
CLEMENTE, Roberto Walker 5
CLEMENTS, Andrew Vernon 4
CLEMENTS, Berthold A. 2
CLEMENTS, C.R. 4
CLEMENTS, Charles L. 8

CLEMENTS, Colin Campbell 2
CLEMENTS, Courtland Cushing 1
CLEMENTS, Earle C. 8
CLEMENTS, Edith Schwartz
CLEMENTS, Edward Bates 1
CLEMENTS, Francis Washington 4
CLEMENTS, Frederic Edward 2
CLEMENTS, George L. 8
CLEMENTS, George P. 3
CLEMENTS, Sir John 9
CLEMENTS, Judson C. 1
CLEMENTS, Newton N. 1
CLEMENTS, Robert 1
CLEMENTS, William Lawrence 1
CLEMMER, Henry Austin 8
CLEMMER, Mary 1
CLEMMONS, Joe Rainey 2
CLEMMONS, Slaton 10
CLEMONS, Charles Frederic 1
CLEMONS, Harry 6
CLEMSON, Thomas Green H
CLEMSON, Walter John 4
CLENDENIN, David H
CLENDENIN, Frank Montrose 1
CLENDENIN, George Morey 7
CLENDENIN, Henry Wilson 1
CLENDENIN, William Ritchie 8
CLENDENIN, William Wallace 4
CLENDENING, Logan 2
CLENDINEN, James Augustus 10
CLEOPHAS, Mother Mary 1
CLEPHANE, James Ogilvie 1
CLEPHANE, Walter Collins 3
CLERC, Laurent H
CLERGUE, Francis Hector 4
CLERK, Ira 2
CLERKIN, James Joseph 6
CLERKIN, James Joseph, Jr. 7
CLEVA, Fausto 5
CLEVELAND, Aaron H
CLEVELAND, Abner Coburn 1
CLEVELAND, Alexander Sessums 4
CLEVELAND, Austin C(arl) 5
CLEVELAND, Benjamin H
CLEVELAND, Chauncey Fitch H
CLEVELAND, Chester Wilson 4
CLEVELAND, Clement 1
CLEVELAND, Cynthia Eloise 4
CLEVELAND, Forrest Fenton 8
CLEVELAND, Frank Ernest 3
CLEVELAND, Frederick Albert 2
CLEVELAND, George Gilbert 7
CLEVELAND, George Henry
CLEVELAND, Grover 1
CLEVELAND, Helen M. H
CLEVELAND, Horace William Shaler H
CLEVELAND, James 10
CLEVELAND, James Wray 4
CLEVELAND, Jesse Franklin
CLEVELAND, John Bomar 4
CLEVELAND, John Luther 8
CLEVELAND, Lemuel Roscoe 5
CLEVELAND, Orestes H
CLEVELAND, Paul W. 4
CLEVELAND, Reginald McIntosh 5
CLEVELAND, Richard Jeffry H
CLEVELAND, Rose Elizabeth 1
CLEVELAND, Treadwell, Jr.
CLEVELAND, William Davis 5
CLEVEN, Nels Andrew Nelson 5
CLEVENGER, Cliff 4

CLEVENGER, Galen Howell 6
CLEVENGER, Joseph R. 6
CLEVENGER, Shobal Vail H
CLEVENGER, Shobal Vail 4
CLEVER, Charles P. H
CLEVER, Conrad 1
CLEVERDON, Ernest Grove 8
CLEVERLEY, Frank T. 3
CLEW, William Joseph 8
CLEWELL, Edgar L. 6
CLEWELL, John Henry 1
CLEWIS, Alonzo Charles 2
CLEWS, Henry 1
CLEWS, James Blanchard 1
CLEXTON, Edward William 4
CLIFFE, Adam C. 1
CLIFFORD, Sr. Adele 9
CLIFFORD, Chandler R. 1
CLIFFORD, Charles P. 5
CLIFFORD, Charles Warren 1
CLIFFORD, Edward Laurence 4
CLIFFORD, Elmer 5
CLIFFORD, Harry 3
CLIFFORD, James Lowry 7
CLIFFORD, John David 3
CLIFFORD, John Fenn 7
CLIFFORD, John Henry 1
CLIFFORD, John McLean 7
CLIFFORD, Leslie Forbes 5
CLIFFORD, Nathan H
CLIFFORD, Philip Greely 7
CLIFFORD, Ralph Kibbe 8
CLIFFORD, Reese F(rancis) 5
CLIFFORD, Walter 4
CLIFFORD, William Schofield 6
CLIFFTON, William H
CLIFT, Albert Earl 1
CLIFT, David Horace 6
CLIFT, Denison Halley 7
CLIFT, Montgomery 4
CLIFTON, Albert Turner 2
CLIFTON, Chalmers Dancy 4
CLIFTON, Charles 1
CLIFTON, Chester Victor, Jr. 10
CLIFTON, Ernest Smith 7
CLIFTON, John Leroy 3
CLIFTON, Joseph Clinton 4
CLIFTON, Josephine H
CLIFTON, Leonard Leroy 7
CLIFTON, Louis 3
CLINCH, Charles Powell H
CLINCH, Duncan Lamont H
CLINCH, Edward Sears 1
CLINCH, R. Floyd 7
CLINCHY, Everett Ross 9
CLINE, Arthur Raymond 7
CLINE, Cyrus 4
CLINE, Earl 7
CLINE, Genevieve R. 6
CLINE, Howard Francis 5
CLINE, Howard Francis 5
CLINE, Isaac Monroe 3
CLINE, John Wesley 6
CLINE, Lewis Manning 5
CLINE, Lyle Stanley 5
CLINE, Pierce 2
CLINE, Robert Alexander 3
CLINE, Russell Walter 4
CLINE, Sheldon Scott 1
CLINE, Thomas Sparks 5
CLINE, Walter Branks 1
CLINEDINST, B. West 1
CLINGAN, William H
CLINGMAN, Charles 7
CLINGMAN, Thomas Lanier H
CLINKSCALES, John George 1
CLINNIN, John V. 3
CLINTON, Dewitt H
CLINTON, Fred S. 5
CLINTON, Garriet Pettibone (Mrs. Fred Davidson Clinton) 6
CLINTON, George* H
CLINTON, George 1
CLINTON, George Perkins 1
CLINTON, George Wylie 1
CLINTON, Sir Henry H
CLINTON, James H
CLINTON, Lawrence Martin 8
CLINTON, Louis Adelbert 1
CLINTON, Marshall 2
CLIPPINGER, Arthur Raymond 6
CLIPPINGER, Donald Roop 5

CLIPPINGER, Erle Elsworth 1
CLIPPINGER, Roy 7
CLIPPINGER, Walter Gillan 2
CLISE, James William 4
CLITHEROE, Lord (Sir Ralph Assheton) 8
CLIVE, John Leonard 10
CLOAK, Evelyn Kimmel Campbell (Mrs. F. Theodore Cloak) 6
CLOAK, Frank Valentine Centennial 3
CLOCK, Henry Harriman 7
CLOCK, John G. 7
CLOCK, Ralph H. 2
CLOETE, Stuart 7
CLOKE, Harvey Walton 6
CLOKE, Harvey Walton 7
CLOKE, John Benjamin 9
CLOKE, Paul 4
CLONNEY, James Goodwyn H
CLOONAN, John Joseph 6
CLOOS, Ernst 10
CLOOS, Ernst 10
CLOPPER, Edward Nicholas 3
CLOPTON, David H
CLOPTON, John H
CLOPTON, Malvern Bryan 2
CLORAN, Timothy 1
CLORVIERE, Joseph-pierre Picot ed Limoelan de
CLOSE, Charles Mollison 5
CLOSE, Charles William 1
CLOSE, Frederick Jacob 9
CLOSE, Hugh William 8
CLOSE, James William 5
CLOSE, Lewis Raymond 5
CLOSE, Lyman Withrow 5
CLOSE, Ralph William 2
CLOSE, Stuart 1
CLOSS, Gerhard Ludwig 10
CLOSSON, Henry Whitney 1
CLOSSON, William B. 1
CLOSTERMAN, Donald Franks 7
CLOTHIER, Isaac Hallowell 1
CLOTHIER, Morris Lewis 2
CLOTHIER, Robert Clarkson 5
CLOTHIER, William Jackson 6
CLOUCHEK, Emma Olds 1
CLOUD, Arthur David 4
CLOUD, Charles H. 2
CLOUD, Henry Roe 2
CLOUD, James Henry 1
CLOUD, John Hofer 1
CLOUD, Marshall Morgan 1
CLOUD, Noah Bartlett 1
CLOUD, Preston 10
CLOUD, William Woodward 3
CLOUES, William Jacob 4
CLOUGH, Charles A. 4
CLOUGH, Charles C. 3
CLOUGH, David Marston 1
CLOUGH, Francis Edgar 3
CLOUGH, Frank C. 3
CLOUGH, George Albert 1
CLOUGH, George Hatch 3
CLOUGH, George Obadiah 6
CLOUGH, John H. 6
CLOUGH, Merrill H. 5
CLOUGH, Paul Wiswall 5
CLOUGH, Raphael Floyd 3
CLOUGH, S. Dewitt 3
CLOUGH, Shepard 10
CLOUGH, W.P. 1
CLOUGH, William Plummer, Jr. 7
CLOUGH, Wilson Ober 10
CLOUGH-LEIGHTER, Henry 3
CLOUS, John Walter 1
CLOUSE, John Henry 8
CLOUSE, Wynne F. 1
CLOVER, George Frederick 1
CLOVER, Lewis P., Jr. 1
CLOVER, Richardson 1
CLOVER, Samuel Travers 1
CLOVIS, Paul Curtis 6
CLOW, Allan Bowman 5
CLOW, Harry Beach 1
CLOW, James Beach 3
CLOW, Kent Sarver 3
CLOW, William Ellsworth, Jr. 3
CLOWES, George Henry Alexander 3
CLOWNEY, William Kennedy H

CLOWRY, Robert Charles 1
CLUBB, Merrel Dare 5
CLUESMANN, Leo 4
CLUETT, E. Harold 3
CLUETT, Robert 1
CLUETT, Sanford Lockwood 5
CLUETT, W. Scott 5
CLUFF, Harvey H. 5
CLUGSTON, Herbert Andrews 7
CLURMAN, Harold Edgar 4
CLUTE, Walker Stillwell 4
CLUTE, Walter Marshall 1
CLUTE, Willard Nelson 3
CLUTTS, Oliver Perry 4
CLUTZ, Jacob Abraham 1
CLUVERIUS, Wat Tyler 3
CLUYTENS, Andre 4
CLYCE, Thomas Stone 2
CLYDE, George Dewey 5
CLYDE, John Cunningham 1
CLYDE, Norman Asa 5
CLYDE, Wilford Woodruff 8
CLYDE, William Gray 1
CLYDE, William Pancoast 1
CLYMAN, James H
CLYMER, George H
CLYMER, George E. H
CLYMER, Hiester 1
CLYMER, John Ford 10
CLYMER, Meredith 1
CLYMER, R(euben) 5
Swinburne
CLYNE, Charles F. 4
CLYNE, Charles F. 5
CLYNE, Charles Terence 8
CLYNE, James Francis, Jr. 5
CLYNE, John Valentine 10
COADY, Charles Pearce 1
COADY, John Martin 10
COAKLEY, Cornelius Godfrey 1
COAKLEY, Daniel Henry 4
COAKLEY, Joseph Charles 9
COALE, Griffith Baily 3
COALE, Isaac, Jr. 4
COALE, James Johnson 2
COALE, Robert Dorsey 1
COAN, Charles Florus 1
COAN, Frank Speer 8
COAN, Frederick Gaylord 4
COAN, Titus H
COAN, Titus Munson 1
COAPMAN, Eugene H. 1
COAR, John Firman 1
COASH, Louis E. 5
COATE, Alvin Teague 5
COATE, Roland Eli 3
COATES, Albert 9
COATES, Charles Edward 1
COATES, Charles F. 3
COATES, David C. 4
COATES, Edward Hornor 1
COATES, Edwin Morton 1
COATES, Eric 3
COATES, Florence Earle 1
COATES, Foster 1
COATES, Grace Stone 6
COATES, Henry Troth 1
COATES, James Otis 9
COATES, Joseph Hornor 1
COATES, Robert Harry 6
COATES, Robert Myron 10
COATES, Robert Myron 3
COATES, Samuel H
COATES, Thomas Jackson 1
COATS, Adelbert Sumpter 4
COATS, Albert B. 4
COATS, Marion (Mrs. Clifford L. Graves) 7
COATSWORTH, Elizabeth (Mrs. Henry Beston) 9
COBB, Albert Clifford 1
COBB, Amasa 1
COBB, Andrew Jackson 1
COBB, Beatrice 4
COBB, Bernard C. 3
COBB, Bertha Browning 3
COBB, Bruce Benson 5
COBB, Calvin 1
COBB, Candler 3
COBB, Carolus Melville 5
COBB, Charles Wellington 5
COBB, Clinton Levering H
COBB, Collier 1
COBB, Cully Alton 6
COBB, Cully Alton 7
COBB, Cyrus 1
COBB, Darius 1
COBB, David H
COBB, Dudley Manchester, Jr. 5
COBB, Ebenezer Baker 1
COBB, Elijah H
COBB, Ernest 4
COBB, Florence Etheridge 2

COBB, Frank Irving 1
COBB, George Thomas H
COBB, Henry Evertson 2
COBB, Henry Ives 1
COBB, Henry Nitchie 1
COBB, Herbert Edgar 1
COBB, Howell* H
COBB, Irvin Shrewsbury 2
COBB, James A. 3
COBB, James Blaine 7
COBB, James Harrel 6
COBB, James Shepard 3
COBB, John Blackwell 1
COBB, John Candler 1
COBB, John Nathan 1
COBB, John Robert 5
COBB, Jonathan Holmes H
COBB, Joseph Pettee 1
COBB, Lee J. 6
COBB, Lee J. 7
COBB, Levi Henry 1
COBB, Lloyd Joseph 5
COBB, Lyman H
COBB, Meta R. 7
COBB, Nathan Augustus 1
COBB, Randell Smith 2
COBB, Robert 4
COBB, Roger Burnham 7
COBB, Rufus Wills 4
COBB, Samuel Ernest 1
COBB, Sanford Hoadley 1
COBB, Seth Wallace 1
COBB, Stanley 4
COBB, Stanwood 7
COBB, Stephen Alonzo H
COBB, Sylvanus* H
COBB, Thomas Reed H
COBB, Thomas Reed Rootes H
COBB, Thomas Willis H
COBB, Tyrus Raymond H
COBB, Tyrus Raymond 4
COBB, W.R. 7
COBB, William Ballinger 8
COBB, William Henry 1
COBB, William J. 8
COBB, William Montague 10
COBB, William Titcomb 1
COBB, Williamson Robert Winfield H
COBBETT, William H
COBBEY, Charles Elliott 1
COBBEY, Joseph Elliott 1
COBBLEDICK, Gordon 10
COBBS, John Lewis 10
COBBS, Susan Parker 6
COBBS, Thomas Harper 6
COBE, Ira Maurice 1
COBERN, Camden McCormack 1
COBERO, Pedro Rodriguez H
COBLE, Arthur Byron 6
COBLEIGH, Nelson Simmons 1
COBLEIGH, William Merriam 5
COBLENTZ, Edmond David 3
COBLENTZ, Emory Lorenzo 1
COBLENTZ, Stanton Arthur 8
COBLENTZ, Virgil 1
COBLENTZ, William Weber 4
COBO, Albert E. 3
COBURN, Abner H
COBURN, Alvin F. 6
COBURN, Charles 4
COBURN, Donald Ellsworth 6
COBURN, Foster Dwight 1
COBURN, Frederick William 3
COBURN, John 1
COBURN, Nelson Francis 2
COBURN, Robert D. 6
COBURN, Stephen H
COBURN, William 4
COBURN, William Gibson 4
COCA, Arthur Fernandez 6
COCHEL, Wilber Andrew 3
COCHEMS, Henry Frederick 1
COCHEL, Frank Sherwood 2
COCHISE H
COCHRAN, Alexander G. 1
COCHRAN, Alexander Smith 10
COCHRAN, Andrew McConnell January 1
COCHRAN, Archelaus M. 3
COCHRAN, Archibald Prentice 5
COCHRAN, Burt 7
COCHRAN, Carlos Bingham 1

COLE, Frank L. 8
COLE, Frank Nelson 1
COLE, Franklin 5
COLE, Fred Carrington 9
COLE, George Douglas Howard 3
COLE, George E.* 1
COLE, George Lamont 1
COLE, George Lee 6
COLE, George W. 1
COLE, George Watson 1
COLE, Geroge Clarence 5
COLE, Glen Walker 3
COLE, Gordon Henry 9
COLE, Harold Harrison 7
COLE, Harold Mercer 5
COLE, Harold Newton 7
COLE, Harry Outen 1
COLE, Henry Tiffany 1
COLE, Howard Ellsworth 3
COLE, Howard I. 4
COLE, Howard Ware 5
COLE, Jack 6
COLE, James P. 8
COLE, Jean Dean 1
COLE, John Adams 4
COLE, John Nelson 1
COLE, John Tupper 6
COLE, Joseph Foxcroft H
COLE, Kenneth S(tewart) 8
COLE, Lawrence Thomas 5
COLE, Lawrence Wooster 2
COLE, Leon Jacob 2
COLE, Lewis Gregory 3
COLE, Louis Maurice 1
COLE, Louis William 8
COLE, Nat King 4
COLE, Nathan, Jr. 1
COLE, Nelson 1
COLE, Patience Bevier 7
COLE, Ralph Dayton 1
COLE, Ralph R. 3
COLE, Redmond Selecman 6
COLE, Richard Beverly 1
COLE, Robert Franklin 7
COLE, Robert Hugh 10
COLE, Robert Lee 9
COLE, Robert Taylor 10
COLE, Rossetter Gleason 3
COLE, Roy 6
COLE, Rufus 4
COLE, Rufus 5
COLE, Russell D. 4
COLE, Samuel Valentine 1
COLE, Samuel Winkley 1
COLE, Sandford Stoddard 9
COLE, Sylvan 8
COLE, Theodore Lee 1
COLE, Thomas H
COLE, Thomas (Raymond) 6
COLE, Thomas F. 4
COLE, Timothy 1
COLE, W. Storrs 10
COLE, Walton Adamson 4
COLE, Warren Henry 10
COLE, Whitfoord R. 1
COLE, Willard W. 6
COLE, William Carey 1
COLE, William H. 4
COLE, William Hinson H
COLE, William Isaac 1
COLE, William Morse 4
COLE, William Purrington, Jr. 3
COLE, Willim R. (Cozy Cole) 7
COLE, Wilson Giffin 3
COLEAN, Miles Lanier 7
COLEBAUGH, Charles Henry 2
COLEFAX, Peter 7
COLEGROVE, Chauncey Peter 7
COLEGROVE, Frederick Welton 4
COLEGROVE, Kenneth Wallace 6
COLEGROVE, Kenneth Wallace 7
COLEMAN, Algernon 1
COLEMAN, Alice Blanchard 1
COLEMAN, Arch 4
COLEMAN, Arch 5
COLEMAN, Arthur Prudden 6
COLEMAN, Beatrice 10
COLEMAN, Benjamin Wilson 1
COLEMAN, Bertram 7
COLEMAN, Chapman 1
COLEMAN, Charles Caryl 1
COLEMAN, Charles Elliott 4
COLEMAN, Charles Philip 1
COLEMAN, Charles Washington 4

COLEMAN, Christopher Bush 2
COLEMAN, Clarence J. 10
COLEMAN, Claude C. 3
COLEMAN, Cornelius Cunningham 5
COLEMAN, Cynthia Beverley Tucker 1
COLEMAN, Cyril 3
COLEMAN, D'Alton Corry 3
COLEMAN, Elliott 7
COLEMAN, Francis Carter 9
COLEMAN, Frank Joseph 1
COLEMAN, Frederick W.B. 2
COLEMAN, Frederick William 2
COLEMAN, George Anthony 9
COLEMAN, George Hopkins 9
COLEMAN, George Preston 2
COLEMAN, George Whitfield 1
COLEMAN, George William 3
COLEMAN, Gilbert Payson 4
COLEMAN, J.T. 7
COLEMAN, James Daniel Stetson 6
COLEMAN, James Melville 4
COLEMAN, James Plemon 10
COLEMAN, John 4
COLEMAN, John A. 7
COLEMAN, John Dawson 4
COLEMAN, John Francis 2
COLEMAN, John Hamline 4
COLEMAN, John Shields 5
COLEMAN, John Strider 3
COLEMAN, John Winston 10
COLEMAN, Kathleen Blake 4
COLEMAN, Leighton 1
COLEMAN, Lewis Minor 1
COLEMAN, Lyman H
COLEMAN, Nicholas Daniel H
COLEMAN, Philip Frantz 5
COLEMAN, Ralph Pallen 5
COLEMAN, Ralph Pallen, JR. 7
COLEMAN, Richard B. 4
COLEMAN, Robert 6
COLEMAN, Rowland Henry 7
COLEMAN, S. Waldo 6
COLEMAN, Satis Narrona 4
COLEMAN, Sheldon 9
COLEMAN, Sidney Andrew 6
COLEMAN, Stewart P. 5
COLEMAN, Sydney Haines 3
COLEMAN, Sylvan Clarence 1
COLEMAN, Thomas Davies 1
COLEMAN, THomas Emmet 4
COLEMAN, Thomas Wilkes 1
COLEMAN, Walter Moore 4
COLEMAN, Warren 2
COLEMAN, William H
COLEMAN, William Caldwell 4
COLEMAN, William Carlton 7
COLEMAN, William Coffin 3
COLEMAN, William Emmette 1
COLEMAN, William Harold 4
COLEMAN, William Henry 1
COLEMAN, William John 5
COLEMAN, William Magruder 1
COLEMAN, William Smith 7
COLEMAN, William Tell H
COLEMAN, William Wheeler 4
COLER, Bird Sim 1
COLES, Albert Leonard 7
COLES, Alfred Porter 2
COLES, David Smalley 4
COLES, Edward H
COLES, Isaac H
COLES, J. Ackerman 1
COLES, John William 9
COLES, Walter H
COLESTOCK, Henry Thomas 4
COLETTE 3
COLETTI, Joseph Arthur 6
COLEY, Bradley Lancaster 3
COLEY, Edward Huntington 2

COLEY, Francis Chase 1
COLEY, William Bradley 1
COLFAX, Schuyler H
COLFELT, Lawrence MacLay 4
COLFLESH, Robert William 4
COLFORD, William Edward 5
COLGATE, Gilbert 1
COLGATE, Henry A. 3
COLGATE, James Boorman 1
COLGATE, James Colby 2
COLGATE, Russell 1
COLGATE, S. Bayard 1
COLGATE, Sidney Morse 1
COLGATE, William H
COLGROVE, Philip Taylor 1
COLHOUN, John Ewing H
COLIE, Edward Martin 1
COLIE, Rosalie Littell 5
COLIN, Ralph Frederick 8
COLKADAY, Thomas 7
COLKET, Edward Burton 5
COLKET, Meredith Bright, Jr. 9
COLL, Raymond S. 4
COLLACOTT, Robert Hover 7
COLLADAY, Edgar Bergman 7
COLLADAY, Edward Francis 4
COLLADAY, Samuel Rakestraw 2
COLLAMER, Jacob H
COLLAMORE, Harry Bacon 6
COLLAR, William Coe 1
COLLBOHM, Franklin Rudolf 10
COLLBRAN, Henry 1
COLLEDGE, William A. 1
COLLENS, Arthur Morris 6
COLLENS, Charles 3
COLLENS, Clarence Lyman 5
COLLENS, Thomas Wharton H
COLLENS, William S. 10
COLLER, Frederick Amasa 4
COLLER, Julius A. 4
COLLERY, Arnold 10
COLLES, Alvin Robert 1
COLLES, Christopher H
COLLET, John Caskie 3
COLLETT, Armand René 6
COLLETT, C(harles T(aggart) 8
COLLETT, Frederick George 7
COLLETT, George Richard 2
COLLETT, Joan 10
COLLETT, John 1
COLLETT, Robert Arthur 6
COLLEY, Robert H. 7
COLLIE, George Lucius 3
COLLIE, Marvin Key 10
COLLIER, Alan Caswell 10
COLLIER, Barron 1
COLLIER, Charles Allen 8
COLLIER, Daniel Lewis H
COLLIER, David Charles 1
COLLIER, Edward Augustus 3
COLLIER, Everett Dolton 10
COLLIER, Frank Wilbur 2
COLLIER, George Haskell 1
COLLIER, Harry D. 3
COLLIER, Henry Watkins H
COLLIER, James William 1
COLLIER, John H
COLLIER, John Allen H
COLLIER, John Howard 3
COLLIER, Marie Elizabeth 5
COLLIER, Neil Rex 7
COLLIER, Paul Stanley 7
COLLIER, Peter H
COLLIER, Peter Fenelon 1
COLLIER, Price 1
COLLIER, Robert Arthur 9
COLLIER, Robert Joseph 1
COLLIER, Theodore 4
COLLIER, William 2
COLLIER, William Armistead 4
COLLIER, William Miller 1
COLLIGAN, Francis James 6
COLLIN, Alonzo 1
COLLIN, Charles Avery 1
COLLIN, Frederick 1
COLLIN, Harry E. 5
COLLIN, John Francis H
COLLINGE, Patricia 6
COLLINGE, Robert Joy 7
COLLINGS, Clyde Wilson 3

COLLINGS, Crittenden Taylor 1
COLLINGS, Ellsworth 8
COLLINGS, Gilbert Hooper 4
COLLINGS, Harry Thomas 1
COLLINGS, Howard Paxton 3
COLLINGS, John Ayres 5
COLLINGS, John Kempthorne, Jr. 8
COLLINGS, Kenneth Brown 1
COLLINGS, Samuel Posey 1
COLLINGWOOD, Charles (Cummings) 9
COLLINGWOOD, Francis Harris 1
COLLINGWOOD, G. Harris 3
COLLINGWOOD, Herbert Winslow 1
COLLINS, Alan Copeland 4
COLLINS, Albert Hamilton 2
COLLINS, Alfred Morris 1
COLLINS, Alfred Quinton 1
COLLINS, A(rchie) Frederick 5
COLLINS, Arden Leroy 7
COLLINS, Arthur Sylvester, Jr. 8
COLLINS, Atwood 1
COLLINS, Bertrand Robson Torsey 4
COLLINS, Carl Ingersoll 8
COLLINS, Carr P., Jr. 9
COLLINS, Carr Pritchett 5
COLLINS, Carter 6
COLLINS, Carvel 1
COLLINS, Charles Bertine 6
COLLINS, Charles E. 5
COLLINS, Charles Edwin 1
COLLINS, Charles Joseph 9
COLLINS, Charles Wallace 6
COLLINS, Charles William 4
COLLINS, Clem Weizell 7
COLLINS, Clifford Ulysses 2
COLLINS, Clinton Dewitt 1
COLLINS, Conrad Green 5
COLLINS, Cornelius Vallance 4
COLLINS, Cornelius Van Santvoord 1
COLLINS, Dennis Alphonsus 7
COLLINS, Edgar Thomas 1
COLLINS, Edward Day 1
COLLINS, Edward Knight H
COLLINS, Edwin R. 1
COLLINS, Ela 1
COLLINS, Everell Stanton 1
COLLINS, Forres McGraw 8
COLLINS, Foster K. 1
COLLINS, Francis Arnold 3
COLLINS, Francis Dolan 1
COLLINS, Frank Shipley 3
COLLINS, Franklin Wallace 2
COLLINS, Frederick Lewis 1
COLLINS, George Lewis 1
COLLINS, George Stuart 1
COLLINS, George W. 5
COLLINS, George William 4
COLLINS, Gilbert 1
COLLINS, Guy N. 1
COLLINS, Harold Moorman 3
COLLINS, Henry 1
COLLINS, Henry W. 5
COLLINS, Herman Leroy 1
COLLINS, Howard Dennis 1
COLLINS, Hubert Edwin 1
COLLINS, J. Franklin 1
COLLINS, James A., Jr. 9
COLLINS, James Daniel 1
COLLINS, James Francis 9
COLLINS, James Franklin 2
COLLINS, James H(iram) 1
COLLINS, James Lawton 4
COLLINS, James Mitchell 10
COLLINS, John H
COLLINS, John Anderson H
COLLINS, John Bartholomew 1
COLLINS, John Joseph 1
COLLINS, John Martin 3
COLLINS, John Mathewson 4
COLLINS, John Timothy 1
COLLINS, Joseph 5
COLLINS, Joseph Dorsey 4
COLLINS, Joseph Henry 1
COLLINS, Joseph Howland 1
COLLINS, Joseph Lawton 10
COLLINS, Joseph Martin 3
COLLINS, Joseph Victor 1
COLLINS, Joseph William 1
COLLINS, Joshua H

COLLINS, Laura G. 4
COLLINS, Leroy 10
COLLINS, Leroy Pierce 7
COLLINS, Loren Warren 1
COLLINS, Lorin Cone 1
COLLINS, Mark 5
COLLINS, Mary Love 7
COLLINS, Matthew Garrett 1
COLLINS, Mauney D. 4
COLLINS, Maurice 8
COLLINS, Michael Francis 1
COLLINS, Napoleon H
COLLINS, Orell Tex 8
COLLINS, Patrick A. 1
COLLINS, Paul Fisk 5
COLLINS, Paul Valorous 1
COLLINS, Philip Sheridan 2
COLLINS, Ralph L. 4
COLLINS, Richard Edward 8
COLLINS, Robert Alexander 6
COLLINS, Robert Moore 4
COLLINS, Ross Alexander 5
COLLINS, Ross Alexander 6
COLLINS, Rowland Lee 8
COLLINS, Roy Charles 5
COLLINS, Samuel Cornette 8
COLLINS, Stewart G. 2
COLLINS, Thomas Hightower 7
COLLINS, Truman Edward 10
COLLINS, Truman W. 4
COLLINS, Varnum Lansing 1
COLLINS, Virgil Dewey 4
COLLINS, Vivian 3
COLLINS, Walter Lansing 8
COLLINS, Whitley Charles 3
COLLINS, Wilbur M(ausly) 6
COLLINS, William H
COLLINS, William 3
COLLINS, William 4
COLLINS, William Dennis 6
COLLINS, William Henry 3
COLLINS, William Howes 9
COLLINS, Winifred 2
COLLINS, Yyvonne Deakins (Mrs. Carr P. Collins Jr.) 6
COLLINSON, Joseph Bruerd 7
COLLIP, James Bertram 4
COLLIS, Charles H.T. 1
COLLISON, Wilson 1
COLLISSON, Norman Harvey 4
COLLITZ, Hermann 1
COLLITZ, Klara Hechtenberg 2
COLLOFF, Roger David 10
COLLVER, Clinton 7
COLLYER, Robert 1
COLM, Benjamin H
COLMAN, George Tilden 8
COLMAN, Henry H
COLMAN, James Douglas 5
COLMAN, John H
COLMAN, Norman Jay 1
COLMAN, Ronald 3
COLMAN, Samuel 1
COLMER, William Meyers 7
COLMERY, Harry Walter, Jr. 7
COLMORE, Charles Blayney 3
COLNON, Aaron 3
COLNON, Stuart James 9
COLON, Doris E. 10
COLONNA, Paul Crenshaw 4
COLOWICK, Sidney Paul 8
COLPITTS, Edwin Henry 2
COLPITTS, Herbert Granger 8
COLPITTS, Walter William 3
COLQUHOUN, Walter Alexander 4
COLQUITT, Alfred Holt H
COLQUITT, Oscar Branch 1
COLQUITT, Walter T. 1
COLQUITT, Walter Terry H
COLSKY, Jacob 9
COLSON, Clyde Lemuel 4
COLSON, David Grant 1
COLSTON, Edward H
COLSTON, Edward 1
COLSTON, J. A. Campbell 9
COLSTON, James Allen 8
COLSTON, Raleigh H
COLSTON, William Ainslie 1
COLT, Harris Dunscomb 3
COLT, Le Baron Bradford 1
COLT, Samuel H
COLT, Samuel Pomeroy 1
COLT, Samuel Sloan 4
COLT, Thomas Clyde, Jr. 8
COLTER, Frederick Tuttle 1

COLTER, John — H
COLTMAN, Robert — 4
COLTMAN, William George — 4
COLTON, A.M.F. — H
COLTON, Arthur Willis — 2
COLTON, Calvin — H
COLTON, Charles Adams — 4
COLTON, Charles Henry — 1
COLTON, Don Byron — 5
COLTON, Elizabeth Avery — 1
COLTON, Elizabeth Sweetser — 3
COLTON, Ethan Theodore — 5
COLTON, Ferry Barrows — 3
COLTON, Gardner Quincy — H
COLTON, George Henry — 1
COLTON, George Radcliffe — 1
COLTON, Harold Sellers — 6
COLTON, James Hooper — 1
COLTON, Julia M. — 5
COLTON, Roger B. — 8
COLTON, Walter — 1
COLTON, Winfred Rufus — 6
COLTRANE, Eugene J. — 4
COLTRANE, John William — 4
COLUM, Mary M. — 3
COLUM, Padraic — 5
COLUM, Padraic — 7
COLUMBUS, Christopher — H
COLUMBUS, Diego — H
COLUMBUS, Fernando Colon — H
COLVER, Alice Ross (Mrs. Frederic B. Colver) — 9
COLVER, Benton Noble — 3
COLVER, Nathaniel — H
COLVER, William Byron — 1
COLVIN, Addison Beecher — 3
COLVIN, Allan Dewitt — 3
COLVIN, D. Leigh — 3
COLVIN, Fred Herbert — 4
COLVIN, George — 1
COLVIN, H. Milton — 3
COLVIN, James G. — 5
COLVIN, Mamie White — 3
COLVIN, Oliver Dyer — 4
COLVIN, Stephen Sheldon — 1
COLVIN, Verplanck — 1
COLVIN, W.H., Jr. — 5
COLVOCORESSES, George Musalas — H
COLVOCORESSES, George Partridge — 1
COLWELL, Alexander Hunter — 8
COLWELL, Archie Trescott — 7
COLWELL, Arthur Ralph, Sr. — 7
COLWELL, Ernest Cadman — 6
COLWELL, Felton — 6
COLWELL, Lula Pulliam (Mrs. Howard G. Colwell) — 8
COLWELL, Nathan Porter — 1
COLWELL, Robert Talcott — 4
COLWELL, Stephen — H
COLYER, Douglas — 3
COLYER, Vincent — H
COMAN, Charlotte Buell — 1
COMAN, Edwin Truman — 5
COMAN, Henry Benjamin — 1
COMAN, Katharine — 1
COMAN, Mary Meriam — 4
COMAN, Wilber Edmund — 1
COMAR, Cyril Lewis — 7
COMAR, Jerome Morton — 6
COMAY, Amos — 9
COMAY, Sholom David — 10
COMBA, Richard — 1
COMBES, W. Elmer — 9
COMBEST, Earl Edgar — 6
COMBS, Bert Thomas — 10
COMBS, Everett Randolph — 5
COMBS, George W. — 3
COMBS, Gilbert Raynolds — 5
COMBS, Hugh D(unlap) — 8
COMBS, J.M. — 3
COMBS, James Horton — 3
COMBS, Josiah Henry — 7
COMBS, Lee, Jr. — 7
COMBS, Leslie — H
COMBS, Leslie — 1
COMBS, Morgan Lafayette — 3
COMBS, Moses Newell — H
COMBS, Pat (William Malone) — 6
COMBS, Thomas Selby — 4
COMBS, William Hobart — 7
COMEAUX, C. Stewart — 1
COMEGYS, Joseph Parsons — H
COMER, Braxton Bragg — 1
COMER, Donald, Jr. — 9
COMER, Edward Trippe — 1
COMER, Geroge Legare — 4
COMER, Harry D. — 5
COMER, Hugh Moss — 4

COMER, James McDonald — 4
COMERFORD, Frank — 1
COMERFORD, Frank Dowd — 2
COMEY, Arthur Coleman — 3
COMEY, Arthur Messinger — 1
COMEY, David Dinsmore — 7
COMFORT, Anna Manning — 1
COMFORT, Charlotte Walrath — 5
COMFORT, Frank J. — 3
COMFORT, George Fisk — 1
COMFORT, Mandred Whitset — 3
COMFORT, Walter R. — 4
COMFORT, Will Levington — 1
COMFORT, William Wistar — 3
COMINGO, Abram — H
COMINS, Linus Bacon — H
COMINSKY, Jacob R(obert) — 5
COMISH, Newel Howland — 8
COMLEY, Arthur M. — 7
COMLY, Samuel Pancoast — 1
COMMAGER, Henry Steele — 8
COMMONS, John Rogers — 2
COMO, William Michael — 9
COMPARETTE, T. Louis — 1
COMPERE, Clinton Lee — 10
COMPERE, Ebenezer Lattimore — 1
COMPHER, Wilber G. — 4
COMPTON, Alfred Donaldson — 2
COMPTON, Alfred George — 1
COMPTON, Arthur H. — H
COMPTON, Arthur H. — 4
COMPTON, Charles Elmer — 1
COMPTON, Elias — 1
COMPTON, Fred A(rthur) — 9
COMPTON, George Brokaw — 1
COMPTON, James C. — 7
COMPTON, Karl Taylor — 2
COMPTON, Lewis — 1
COMPTON, Loulie — 1
COMPTON, Randolph Parker — 9
COMPTON, Ranulf — 6
COMPTON, Richard J. — 3
COMPTON, Walter — 3
COMPTON, William Randall — 6
COMPTON, William Randolph — 3
COMPTON, Wilson Martindale — 4
COMPTON-BURNETT, Ivy — 5
COMROE, Jerome Hiram, Jr. — 9
COMSTOCK, A. Barr — 3
COMSTOCK, Ada Louise — 6
COMSTOCK, Albert H. — 1
COMSTOCK, Alzada — 3
COMSTOCK, Anna Botsford — 1
COMSTOCK, Anthony — 1
COMSTOCK, Clarence Elmer — 2
COMSTOCK, Cyrus Ballou — 1
COMSTOCK, Daniel Frost — 5
COMSTOCK, Daniel Frost — 7
COMSTOCK, Elizabeth L. — H
COMSTOCK, Elting Houghtaling — 5
COMSTOCK, F. Ray — 2
COMSTOCK, Frank Mason — 1
COMSTOCK, George Cary — 1
COMSTOCK, George Franklin — H
COMSTOCK, Harriet Theresa — 5
COMSTOCK, Henry Tompkins Paige — H
COMSTOCK, John Henry — 1
COMSTOCK, Louis Kossuth — 4
COMSTOCK, Oliver Cromwell — H
COMSTOCK, Ralph J. — 4
COMSTOCK, Sarah — 3
COMSTOCK, Solomon Gilman — 1
COMSTOCK, Theodore Bryant — 1
COMSTOCK, William Alfred — 2
COMTOIS, Paul — 4
CONAGHAN, Brian Francis — 6
CONANT, Alban Jasper — 1
CONANT, C. Everett — 1
CONANT, Charles Arthur — 1
CONANT, Charlotte Howard — 1

CONANT, Ernest Bancroft — 5
CONANT, Frederic Warren — 7
CONANT, Frederick Odell — 1
CONANT, Gordon Daniel — 4
CONANT, Hannah O'Brien Chaplin — H
CONANT, Harold Wright — 4
CONANT, Harrison Josiah — 7
CONANT, Helen Peters Stevens — 1
CONANT, Henry Dunning — 4
CONANT, Hezekiah — H
CONANT, James Bryant — 7
CONANT, John Willis — 4
CONANT, Kenneth John — 10
CONANT, Levi Leonard — 1
CONANT, Roger — H
CONANT, Thomas Jefferson — H
CONANT, Thomas Oakes — 1
CONANT, W(illis) Garrett — 8
CONARD, Frederick Underwood — 3
CONARD, Henry Shoemaker — 5
CONARD, John — H
CONARRO, Harry Wiborg — 4
CONARRO, Harry Wiborg — 8
CONARROE, George W. — 4
CONATY, Thomas James — 1
CONAWAY, Charles Herman — 3
CONAWAY, Christine Yerges — 10
CONAWAY, Paul Brewer — 6
CONBOY, Martin — 2
CONBOY, Sara Agnes — 1
CONCANNON, Charles Cuthbert — 3
CONCHESO, Aurelio Fernandez — 3
CONCHON, Georges — 10
CONDE, Bertha — 5
CONDEE, Robert Asa — 1
CONDICT, George Herbert — 1
CONDICT, Lewis — H
CONDICT, Silas — H
CONDIT, Blackford — 1
CONDIT, John — H
CONDIT, Kenneth Hamilton — 6
CONDIT, Silas — H
CONDLIFFE, John B. — 8
CONDO, Gus S. — 3
CONDON, Eddie (Albert Edwin Condon) — 6
CONDON, Edward J. — 4
CONDON, Edward U. — 6
CONDON, Francis Bernard — 4
CONDON, Harry Ruth — 8
CONDON, Herbert Thomas — 3
CONDON, John Thomas — 1
CONDON, Martin J., III — 7
CONDON, Randall Judson — 1
CONDON, Richard William — 4
CONDON, Thomas Gerald — 4
CONDRA, George Evert — 6
CONDRON, Theodore Lincoln — 5
CONE, Burtis Octavius — 4
CONE, Fairfax Mastick — 7
CONE, Frederick Preston — 2
CONE, Helen Gray — 2
CONE, Herman — 3
CONE, Hutchinson Ingham — 1
CONE, John Carroll — 7
CONE, Martin — 4
CONE, Marvin Dorwart — 4
CONE, Orello — 1
CONE, Russell G. — 4
CONE, Spencer Houghton — H
CONEL, Jesse Leroy — 7
CONEY, Aims Chamberlain — 4
CONEY, Jabez — H
CONEY, John — H
CONFER, Ogden Palmer — 9
CONFREY, Edward Elzear (Zez) — 5
CONGDON, Charles Harris — 1
CONGDON, Charles Howard — 1
CONGDON, Charles Taber — 1
CONGDON, Chester Adgate — 1
CONGDON, Clement Hilman — 4
CONGDON, Edward Chester — 1
CONGDON, Ernest Arnold — 4
CONGDON, Gilbert Maurice — 4
CONGDON, Harriet Rice — 5
CONGDON, Joseph William — 1
CONGDON, Leon Abel — 7
CONGDON, Sidney Bishop — 9

CONGDON, Wray Hollowell — 9
CONGER, Abraham Benjamin — 3
CONGER, Albert C. — 5
CONGER, Allen C(lifton) — 8
CONGER, Edward A. — 4
CONGER, Edwin Hurd — 1
CONGER, Everett Lorentus — 1
CONGER, George Perrigo — 4
CONGER, Harmon Sweatland — H
CONGER, James Lockwood — H
CONGER, John Leonard — 5
CONGER, John William — 1
CONGER, John William — 1
CONGER, N. — 7
CONGER, Robert Alan — 4
CONGER, Seymour Beach — 1
CONGER, Seymour Beach, III — 5
CONGLETON, Jerome Taylor — 1
CONGLETON, Richard J. — 7
CONICK, Harold C. — 4
CONIGLIARO, Salvatore Alfred — 4
CONKEY, Elizabeth A. — 4
CONKEY, Henry Phillips — 3
CONKLIN, Abran — 4
CONKLIN, Arthur Stewart — 4
CONKLIN, Charles — 1
CONKLIN, Clarence Robert — 9
CONKLIN, Clifford Tremaine — 3
CONKLIN, Edmund Smith — 2
CONKLIN, Edwin Grant — 3
CONKLIN, Everett Lawson — 9
CONKLIN, Franklin, Jr. — 4
CONKLIN, Fredric L. — 8
CONKLIN, Jennie Maria Drinkwater — 1
CONKLIN, John F. — 5
CONKLIN, Roland Ray — 1
CONKLIN, Viola A. — 4
CONKLIN, William Augustus — 1
CONKLIN, William Judkins — 1
CONKLING, Alfred — H
CONKLING, Alfred Ronald — 4
CONKLING, Donald Herbert — 6
CONKLING, Frederick Augustus — H
CONKLING, Grace Hazard — 3
CONKLING, Mark Le Roy — 4
CONKLING, Roscoe — H
CONKLING, Roscoe Powers — 3
CONLAND, Henry H. — 2
CONLEN, William J. — 3
CONLEY, Alonzo Theodore — 4
CONLEY, Carey Herbert — 4
CONLEY, Clyde — 5
CONLEY, Clarence G. — 6
CONLEY, Dudley Steele — 6
CONLEY, Edgar Thomas — 3
CONLEY, Elmo Hansford — 2
CONLEY, Eugene — 8
CONLEY, George J. — 3
CONLEY, John Wesley — 1
CONLEY, Phebe Briggs — 9
CONLEY, William Gustavius — 3
CONLEY, William H. — 6
CONLEY, William Maxwell — 3
CONLIN, Earl Edgar — 4
CONLON, Mrs. William F. (Sara Frances Smith Conlon) — 6
CONN, Donald Deans — 3
CONN, George Chester — 4
CONN, Granville Priest — 1
CONN, Harold Joel — 7
CONN, Harry L. — 1
CONN, Herbert William — 1
CONN, Ulysses Sylvester — 1
CONNAH, Douglas John — 1
CONNALLY, Ben C. — 6
CONNALLY, Ben C. — 7
CONNALLY, Elijah L. — 4
CONNALLY, Tom — 4
CONNAR, Richard Grigsby — 10
CONNAWAY, Jay Hall — 10
CONNELL, Albert James — 2
CONNELL, Arthur J. — 4
CONNELL, Carl W. — 2
CONNELL, Charles R. — 1
CONNELL, Francis J. — 4
CONNELL, Frederick Martin — 7

CONNELL, George Boyce — 3
CONNELL, Horatio — 1
CONNELL, James Mark — 4
CONNELL, Karl — 1
CONNELL, Kenneth Hugh — 6
CONNELL, Louis Fred — 7
CONNELL, Richard — 2
CONNELL, Richard E. — 1
CONNELL, Wilfrid Thomas — 4
CONNELL, William — 1
CONNELL, William Henry — 2
CONNELL, William Lawrence — 1
CONNELL, William Phillips — 1
CONNELL, Wilson Edward — 1
CONNELLEY, Clifford Brown — 1
CONNELLEY, Earl John — 3
CONNELLEY, William Elsey — 1
CONNELLY, Bernard Chamberlin — 7
CONNELLY, Celia Logan — 1
CONNELLY, Cornelia — H
CONNELLY, Edward Michael — 2
CONNELLY, Emma Mary — 5
CONNELLY, Henry — H
CONNELLY, James H. — 1
CONNELLY, John Francis — 10
CONNELLY, John Peter — 9
CONNELLY, John R. — 5
CONNELLY, Marc (Marcus Cook) — 7
CONNELLY, Mathew J. — 7
CONNELLY, Pierce Francis — H
CONNELY, Emmett Francis — 3
CONNELLY, Willard — 4
CONNER, Albert Holmes — 6
CONNER, Benjamin Coulbourn — 1
CONNER, Benjamin F. — 7
CONNER, Benjamin Howe — 6
CONNER, Bruce — 5
CONNER, David — H
CONNER, Eli Taylor — 1
CONNER, Fox — 5
CONNER, James — H
CONNER, James Keys — 1
CONNER, James Moyer — 4
CONNER, James Perry — 4
CONNER, John Coggswell — H
CONNER, Lewis Atterbury — 3
CONNER, Martin Sennett — 2
CONNER, Norval White — 7
CONNER, Phineas Sanborn — 1
CONNER, Sabra — 7
CONNER, Samuel Shepard — H
CONNER, Walter Thomas — 5
CONNERAT, William Spencer — 8
CONNERS, William James — 1
CONNERS, William James, Jr. — 3
CONNERY, Lawrence J. — 1
CONNERY, Thomas Bernard Joseph — 4
CONNERY, William Patrick, Jr. — 1
CONNESS, John — 1
CONNESS, Leland Stanford — 2
CONNICK, Arthur Elswell — 4
CONNICK, Charles Jay — 2
CONNICK, Harris De Haven — 4
CONNIFF, Frank — 5
CONNIFF, Paul R. — 5
CONNING, John Stuart — 2
CONNOLLY, Brendan — 6
CONNOLLY, Christopher Powell — 1
CONNOLLY, Daniel Ward — H
CONNOLLY, Donald Hilary — 7
CONNOLLY, Francis X. — 4
CONNOLLY, James Austin — 1
CONNOLLY, James Brendan — 3
CONNOLLY, James J. — 3
CONNOLLY, James Louis — 10
CONNOLLY, John* — H
CONNOLLY, John L(awrence) — 9
CONNOLLY, Joseph Peter — 2
CONNOLLY, Joseph Vincent — 2
CONNOLLY, Louise — 4
CONNOLLY, Maurice — 1
CONNOLLY, Michael William — 1
CONNOLLY, Mike — 4
CONNOLLY, Paul Raymond — 7

CONNOLLY, Robert Emmet 3
CONNOLLY, Terence Leo 4
CONNOLLY, Thomas Arthur 10
CONNOLY, Theodore 4
CONNOR, Aloysius J. 4
CONNOR, Charles Ashley Richard 6
CONNOR, Charles Francis 6
CONNOR, Charles William 7
CONNOR, Edward 5
CONNOR, Fred (Wallace) 7
CONNOR, George L. 1
CONNOR, George Whitfield 1
CONNOR, Guy Leartus 2
CONNOR, Henry Groves 1
CONNOR, Henry William H
CONNOR, Jacob Elon 4
CONNOR, Leartus 1
CONNOR, Louis George 4
CONNOR, Patrick Edward H
CONNOR, Ray 1
CONNOR, Robert Digges Wimberly
CONNOR, Seldon 1
CONNOR, Washington Everett 1
CONNOR, William Durward 4
CONNOR, William Neil 4
CONNOR, William Ott 1
CONNORS, C(harles) H(enry) 7
CONNORS, Chuck Kevin Joseph 10
CONNORS, Edward Joseph 9
CONNORS, Gerald Anthony 9
CONNORS, James Joseph* 6
CONNORS, John P. 4
CONNORS, John Stanley 8
CONNORS, Joseph Mathew 4
CONNORS, Stephen Wilfred 10
CONOLLY, Richard L. 4
CONOVER, Adams Jewett 1
CONOVER, Charles H. 1
CONOVER, Elbert Moore 3
CONOVER, Frederic L(eroy) 9
CONOVER, Harvey 3
CONOVER, James Milton 5
CONOVER, Obediah Milton H
CONOVER, Samuel Seymour 4
CONQUEST, Ida 1
CONQUEST, Victor 8
CONRAD, Arcturus Z. 1
CONRAD, Carl Nicholas 1
CONRAD, Casper Hauzer, Jr. H
CONRAD, Charles 3
CONRAD, Charles Magill H
CONRAD, Charles Wearne 3
CONRAD, Cuthbert Powell 3
CONRAD, Frank 1
CONRAD, Frank L. 2
CONRAD, Frederick H
CONRAD, Frowenus 1
CONRAD, G. Miles 4
CONRAD, Henry Clay 1
CONRAD, James Lawson 6
CONRAD, Larry Allyn 10
CONRAD, Lowell Edwin 6
CONRAD, Marus Edward 4
CONRAD, Nicholas John 3
CONRAD, Paul C. 4
CONRAD, Robert Taylor H
CONRAD, Stephen 1
CONRAD, Timothy Abbot H
CONRAD, Victor Allen 4
CONRADI, Edward 2
CONRATH, Philip Allen 9
CONRIED, Hans (Frank Foster) 8
CONRIED, Heinrich 1
CONROW, Wilford Seymour 3
CONROY, Jack (John Wesley Conroy) 10
CONROY, John Joseph H
CONROY, Joseph H. 1
CONROY, Peter Joseph 3
CONROY, Thomas Francis 3
CONROY, Thomas Michael 5
CONRY, Michael Francis 1
CONRY, Thomas 2
CONS, Louis 2
CONSIDERANT, Victor Prosper H
CONSIDINE, James W(illiam) 5
CONSIDINE, John Joseph 8

CONSIDINE, Robert Bernard 6
CONSIDINE, Robert Bernard 7
CONSTABLE, Albert H
CONSTABLE, Stuart 7
CONSTABLE, William George 6
CONSTABLE, William George 7
CONSTANGY, Frank Alan 5
CONSTANT, Frank Henry 2
CONSTANT, George Zachary 9
CONSTANT, Samuel Victor 1
CONSTANTINE, Earl Gladstone 3
CONSTANTINOPLE, Panglotes S. 4
CONTA, Lewis Dalcin 10
CONTE, RIchard 6
CONTE, Silvio Otto 10
CONTEE, Benjamin H
CONTINI, Gianfranco 10
CONTOIS, David Ely 9
CONVERSE, Amasa R. H
CONVERSE, C. Crozat 1
CONVERSE, Costello C. 1
CONVERSE, Edmund Cogswell 1
CONVERSE, Florence 6
CONVERSE, Francis Bartlett 1
CONVERSE, Frederick Shepherd 1
CONVERSE, George Albert 1
CONVERSE, George Leroy H
CONVERSE, George Peabody 4
CONVERSE, Harriet Maxwell 1
CONVERSE, Harry E. 1
CONVERSE, Harry Pollard 3
CONVERSE, James Booth 1
CONVERSE, John Heman 1
CONVERSE, John Marquis 7
CONVERSE, Marquis Mills 1
CONVERSE, Miriam Sewall 6
CONVERSE, Myron Frederick 3
CONVERSE, Paul D. 8
CONVERY, Neil Joseph 4
CONVY, Bert 10
CONWAY, Albert 5
CONWAY, Barret 2
CONWAY, Carl Frederick 7
CONWAY, Carle Cotter 4
CONWAY, Edwin Stapleton 1
CONWAY, Elias Nelson H
CONWAY, Frederick Bartlett H
CONWAY, Henry Wharton H
CONWAY, Herbert 5
CONWAY, James Ignatius 4
CONWAY, James Sevier H
CONWAY, John Edward 2
CONWAY, John Sebastian 6
CONWAY, John Severinus 1
CONWAY, Joseph M. 4
CONWAY, Joseph W. 2
CONWAY, Katherine Eleanor 1
CONWAY, Marinus Willett 8
CONWAY, Martin Franklin H
CONWAY, Moncure Daniel 1
CONWAY, Patrick 1
CONWAY, Thomas 4
CONWAY, Thomas, Jr. 4
CONWAY, Timothy J. 9
CONWAY, Walter 3
CONWAY, William Ignatius 8
CONWELL, Hugh Earle 6
CONWELL, Russell Herman 1
CONWELL, Russell Herman 9
CONWELL, Walter Lewis 2
CONWILL, Allan Franklin 10
CONYNGHAM, Gustavus H
CONYNGHAM, William Hillard 2
COOGAN, Edward Francis 4
COOGAN, John Leslie 1
COOGAN, Peter Francis 9
COOGAN, Thomas James 6
COOGAN, Thomas Phillips 10
COOK, Albert John 1
COOK, Albert Samuel 3
COOK, Albert Stanburrough 1
COOK, Alfred A. 2
COOK, Alfred Newton 1
COOK, Alice Rice 5
COOK, Allan Nehrands 4

COOK, Alton 4
COOK, Andrew Bruce 5
COOK, Ansel Granville 1
COOK, Arthur Leroy 6
COOK, Burton Chauncey H
COOK, Carroll Blaine 1
COOK, Cary Wilson 4
COOK, Cecil Newton 7
COOK, Charles Alston 1
COOK, Charles Augustus 1
COOK, Charles Emerson 4
COOK, Charles R. 3
COOK, Charles Sumner 1
COOK, Charles T. 1
COOK, Chauncey William 2
COOK, Chester Aquila 3
COOK, Clarence Chatham H
COOK, Clinton Dana 5
COOK, Daniel Pope H
COOK, David C. 1
COOK, David Charles, III 10
COOK, David S. 10
COOK, Donald 4
COOK, Donald C. 8
COOK, Earl Ferguson 4
COOK, Ebenezer H
COOK, Edward Noble 4
COOK, Elmer Jay 4
COOK, Ermond Edson 4
COOK, Ernest Fullerton 4
COOK, Eugene 4
COOK, Everett Richard 6
COOK, Fannie 2
COOK, Fayette Lamartine 1
COOK, Francis Augustus 1
COOK, Frank Gaylord 2
COOK, Frederic White 3
COOK, Frederick Albert 1
COOK, George Andrus 8
COOK, George Brinton 1
COOK, George Cram 1
COOK, George Crouse 4
COOK, George Fox 4
COOK, George Frederick 1
COOK, George Hammell H
COOK, George Roy 5
COOK, George Thomas 9
COOK, George Washington 4
COOK, George Wythe 4
COOK, Gilbert Richard 4
COOK, Grant L. 3
COOK, H. Earl 5
COOK, Harold Huntting 8
COOK, Harold James 4
COOK, Henry Clay 1
COOK, Henry Mudd 4
COOK, Henry Webster 4
COOK, Howard 8
COOK, Howard Norton 7
COOK, Howard Willard 8
COOK, Irving Winthrop 1
COOK, Isaac H
COOK, J. Clinton, Jr. 4
COOK, James H
COOK, James Curtis 10
COOK, James Henry 2
COOK, James Merrill H
COOK, Joe 1
COOK, Joel 1
COOK, John 1
COOK, John 3
COOK, John Belmont 6
COOK, John Henry 5
COOK, John Parsons H
COOK, John Richard 8
COOK, John Williston 1
COOK, Joseph 1
COOK, Joseph Platt H
COOK, Marc H
COOK, Martha Elizabeth Duncan Walker 1
COOK, May Elizabeth 6
COOK, Melville Thurston 4
COOK, Orator Fuller, Jr. 3
COOK, Orchard 1
COOK, Orval R. 7
COOK, Otis Seabury 1
COOK, Paul 1
COOK, Peter, Jr. 5
COOK, Philip H
COOK, Philip 1
COOK, Raymond Mack 4
COOK, Richard Briscoe 1
COOK, Richard Yerkes 1
COOK, Robert Carter 10
COOK, Robert Cecil 7
COOK, Robert George 4
COOK, Robert Harvey 2
COOK, Roy Bird 1
COOK, Roy H. 4
COOK, Russell S. H
COOK, Samuel A. 1
COOK, Samuel C. 4
COOK, Samuel E. 4
COOK, Samuel Henry 7
COOK, Samuel Richard 1
COOK, Sidney Albert 2

COOK, Theodore Augustus 4
COOK, Thomas Ira 7
COOK, Vernon 3
COOK, Virgil Y. 1
COOK, Waldo Lincoln 3
COOK, Walter 1
COOK, Walter W. 4
COOK, Walter Wheeler 2
COOK, Walter William Spencer 4
COOK, William Cassius 3
COOK, William Henry* 1
COOK, William Locke 2
COOK, William Sutton 10
COOK, William Wallace 1
COOK, William Wilson 1
COOK, Willis Clifford 1
COOK, Willis Clifford 2
COOK, Zadock H
COOK, Zebedee H
COOKE, A. Wayland 1
COOKE, Alexander Bennett 2
COOKE, Arthur Bledsoe 5
COOKE, Bates 1
COOKE, Charles Maynard, Jr. 5
COOKE, Charles Montague, Jr. 2
COOKE, C(harles) Wythe 8
COOKE, Clarence Hyde 2
COOKE, Douglas H. 2
COOKE, Ebenezer H
COOKE, Edmund Francis 1
COOKE, Edmund Vance 1
COOKE, Edward Dean 4
COOKE, Elbridge Clinton 4
COOKE, Eleutheros H
COOKE, Elisha* H
COOKE, Flora Juliette 3
COOKE, George 1
COOKE, George Anderson 1
COOKE, George Henry 1
COOKE, George Willis 1
COOKE, Grace MacGowan 4
COOKE, Harold Groves 3
COOKE, Harrison Rice 5
COOKE, Helen Temple 3
COOKE, Henry D. 3
COOKE, Henry David H
COOKE, Hereward Lester 2
COOKE, James Francis 3
COOKE, James Negley, Jr. 7
COOKE, Jay 1
COOKE, Jay 4
COOKE, John Daniel 5
COOKE, John Esten* 1
COOKE, John Rogers H
COOKE, Joseph Brown 4
COOKE, Joseph Platt 3
COOKE, Josiah Parsons H
COOKE, Juan Isaac 3
COOKE, Leslie Edward 4
COOKE, Lorenzo Wesley 1
COOKE, Lorrin Alanson 1
COOKE, Lucy Finkel (Mrs. S. Jay Cooke) 6
COOKE, Marjorie Benton 1
COOKE, Morris Llewellyn 3
COOKE, Paul Denvir 10
COOKE, Philip Pendleton H
COOKE, Philip St. George H
COOKE, Richard Dickson 3
COOKE, Richard Joseph 1
COOKE, Robert Anderson 4
COOKE, Robert Locke 3
COOKE, Rose Terry H
COOKE, Roy Francis 8
COOKE, Samuel 4
COOKE, Strathmore Ridley Barnott 8
COOKE, Terence James 8
COOKE, Thomas Burrage 1
COOKE, Thomas Turner 4
COOKE, Thorton 1
COOKE, Walter Platt 1
COOKE, Willard Richardson 8
COOKE, William Parker 1
COOKENBOO, John B. 7
COOKINGHAM, L. Perry 10
COOKMAN, Alfred H
COOKSEY, George Robert 2
COOKSON, Frank Barton 7
COOKSON, Walter John 4
COOL, Rodney Lee 9
COOLBAUGH, Melville Fuller 3
COOLBRITH, Ina Donna 1
COOLE, Thomas Henry 1
COOLEDGE, Helen McGregor 8
COOLEY, Alford Warriner 1
COOLEY, Anna Maria 5
COOLEY, Arthur Edward 7
COOLEY, Arthur Henderson 5
COOLEY, Charles Horton 1

COOLEY, Charles Parsons 5
COOLEY, Charles Parsons 6
COOLEY, Edwin Gilbert 1
COOLEY, Ethel Halcrow (Mrs. John B. Cooley) 5
COOLEY, Frederick Boyden 2
COOLEY, George Ralph 9
COOLEY, Harold Dunbar 6
COOLEY, Hollis Eli 1
COOLEY, Leroy Clark 1
COOLEY, Lyman Edgar 1
COOLEY, McWhorter Stephens 6
COOLEY, Mortimer Elwyn 2
COOLEY, Robert Allen 5
COOLEY, Robert Lawrence 3
COOLEY, Robert Nelson 9
COOLEY, Roger William 1
COOLEY, Stoughton 1
COOLEY, Thomas Benton 2
COOLEY, Thomas MacIntyre H
COOLEY, Thomas McIntyre, II 10
COOLEY, Thomas Ross 3
COOLEY, Victor E. 8
COOLEY, William Forbes 4
COOLIDGE, Algernon 1
COOLIDGE, Amory 3
COOLIDGE, Archibald Cary 1
COOLIDGE, Arthur William 3
COOLIDGE, Calvin 1
COOLIDGE, Charles Allerton 1
COOLIDGE, Charles Austin 1
COOLIDGE, Cora Helen 1
COOLIDGE, Cornelius H
COOLIDGE, Dane 1
COOLIDGE, Edgar D. 6
COOLIDGE, Elizabeth Sprague 3
COOLIDGE, Emelyn Lincoln 2
COOLIDGE, Emma Downing 4
COOLIDGE, George Greer 3
COOLIDGE, Grace Goodhue 3
COOLIDGE, Harold Jefferson 1
COOLIDGE, Harold Jefferson 8
COOLIDGE, Herbert 5
COOLIDGE, J. Randolph 1
COOLIDGE, James Henry 4
COOLIDGE, John Gardner 1
COOLIDGE, John 8
COOLIDGE, John Templeman, Jr. 1
COOLIDGE, Joseph 4
COOLIDGE, Julian Lowell 3
COOLIDGE, Lawrence 3
COOLIDGE, Louis Arthur 1
COOLIDGE, Marcus ALlen 2
COOLIDGE, Mary Roberts 2
COOLIDGE, Richard Bradford 4
COOLIDGE, Sherman 1
COOLIDGE, Sidney 1
COOLIDGE, T. Jefferson 1
COOLIDGE, T. Jefferson 3
COOLIDGE, T. Jefferson, Jr. 1
COOLIDGE, William David 6
COOLIDGE, William Henry 1
COOLING, William Peter 8
COOM, Charles Sleeman 4
COOMARASWAMY, Ananda Kentish 2
COOMBE, Harry E. (James) 5
COOMBE, Reginald Gorton 7
COOMBE, Thomas H
COOMBES, Ethel Russell 6
COOMBS, C. Whitney 1
COOMBS, Charles Anthony 8
COOMBS, Edwin Seeger, Jr. 7
COOMBS, Frank L. 1
COOMBS, George Holden 2
COOMBS, Harrison S. 5
COOMBS, Ralph Roland 8
COOMBS, William Jerome 1
COOMBS, Zelotes Wood 2
COON, Byron S. 9
COON, Carleton Stevens 7
COON, Charles Lee 1
COON, Ernest D. 4
COON, J.R. 4
COON, Jesse Drake 3
COON, John Sayler 4
COON, Leland A(very) 9

COON, Owen L. 2
COON, Stephen Mortimer 1
COONAN, Frederick Leo 4
COONE, Henry Herbert 1
COONEY, Charles Edwin 3
COONEY, Frank H. 1
COONEY, James 4
COONEY, James D. 5
COONEY, Joseph Patrick 9
COONEY, Michael 1
COONEY, Percival John 1
COONEY, Russell Conwell 4
COONLEY, Howard 3
COONLEY, Lydia Avery 1
COONLEY, Prentiss 5
Loomis
COONRADT, Arthur C. 3
COONS, Albert 3
COONS, Albert Hewett 7
COONS, Arthur Gardiner 5
COONS, Clifford Vernon 10
COONS, Henry N. 4
COONS, James Ephraim 5
COONS, Leroy Wilson 2
COONS, Samuel Warwick 4
COONS, Sheldon R. 7
COONTZ, Robert Edward 1
COOPE, George Frederick 6
COOPER, Albert 6
Hudlburgh
COOPER, ALfred Duff 3
COOPER, Allen Foster 4
COOPER, Armwell 5
Lockwood
COOPER, Brainard 4
COOPER, Bryant Syms 3
COOPER, Charles 1
Champlin
COOPER, Charles 4
Hermance
COOPER, Charles 1
Lawrence
COOPER, Charles Phillips 3
COOPER, Charles Proctor 4
COOPER, Chauncey Ira 8
COOPER, Clayton 1
Sedgwick
COOPER, Colin Campbell 1
COOPER, Courtney Ryley 1
COOPER, Cyril Bernard 5
COOPER, David Acron 6
COOPER, Delmar Clair 10
COOPER, Douglas Harold 4
COOPER, Drury W. 3
COOPER, Edward 1
COOPER, Edward 3
COOPER, Edward Nathan 5
COOPER, Elias Samuel H
COOPER, Elisha Hillard 2
COOPER, Elizabeth (Mrs. 5
Clayton Sedgwick
Cooper)
COOPER, Ellwood 4
COOPER, Emma Lampert 1
COOPER, Ezekiel H
COOPER, Frank 2
COOPER, Frank B. 4
COOPER, Frank Edward 5
COOPER, Frank Irving 1
COOPER, Frederic Taber 1
COOPER, G. Wilhelmina 8
COOPER, Gary 4
COOPER, George 3
COOPER, George Bryan H
COOPER, George Franklin 3
COOPER, George Victor 3
COOPER, Gladys 5
COOPER, Grant Burr 10
COOPER, Harold 5
COOPER, Henry H
COOPER, Henry Allen 1
COOPER, Henry Elliot 3
COOPER, Henry Ernest 1
COOPER, Henry Noble 10
COOPER, Herman Charles 5
COOPER, Homer Eber 3
COOPER, Homer H. 4
COOPER, Hugh Lincoln 1
COOPER, Irving S. 9
COOPER, Irving Steiger 1
COOPER, Isabelle Mitchell 5
COOPER, Jacob 1
COOPER, James H
COOPER, James Fenimore H
COOPER, James Graham H
COOPER, James Wayne 10
COOPER, James Wesley 1
COOPER, Jere 3
COOPER, Job A. 1
COOPER, John H
COOPER, John Cobb 4
COOPER, John Crossan, Jr. 8
COOPER, John Gordon 5
COOPER, John 3
Montgomery
COOPER, John Sherman 10
COOPER, Joseph David 6

COOPER, Kenneth Ezelle 9
Phoebe
COOPER, Kent 4
COOPER, Lane 3
COOPER, Lester Irving 8
COOPER, Linton Leander 6
COOPER, Louise Field 10
COOPER, Mark Anthony H
COOPER, Merian C. 5
COOPER, Myers Y. 3
COOPER, Myles H
COOPER, Oscar Henry 1
COOPER, Peter H
COOPER, Philip 6
COOPER, Philip Henry 1
COOPER, Prentice 5
COOPER, Richard Matlack 1
COOPER, Richard Watson 3
COOPER, Robert Archer 3
COOPER, Robert Arthur, 10
Jr.
COOPER, Robert Franklin 4
COOPER, Robert Muldrow 4
COOPER, Russell Morgan 3
COOPER, Sam Bronson 1
COOPER, Samuel* H
COOPER, Samuel Inman 6
COOPER, Samuel Williams 1
COOPER, Sanson Milligan 4
COOPER, Sarah Brown H
Ingersoll
COOPER, Stuart 8
COOPER, Susan Fenimore H
COOPER, Theodore 1
COOPER, Thomas* H
COOPER, Thomas H
Abthorpe
COOPER, Thomas H
Buchecker
COOPER, Thomas Franklin 7
COOPER, Tom Richardson 4
COOPER, Wade Hampton 4
COOPER, Wade Hampton 5
COOPER, William* H
COOPER, William Albert 4
COOPER, William Alpha 1
COOPER, William 5
Goodwin
COOPER, William Irenaeus 1
COOPER, William John 1
COOPER, William Knowles 1
COOPER, William Lee 6
COOPER, William Raworth H
COOPER, William Skinner 7
COOPER, Wyllis 3
COOPERMAN, Philip 8
COOPER-POUCHER, H
Matilda S.
COOPERRIDER, George 1
T.
COORS, D. Stanley 4
COORS, Henry G(eorge) 7
(Coors)
COOTE, Colin Reith 10
COOTE, Richard H
COOTER, James Thomas 4
COOTNER, Paul Harold 7
COOVER, John Edgar 1
COOVER, Melanchthon 3
COOVER, Mervin Sylvester 8
COPASS, Benjamin Andrew 4
COPE, Alexis 4
COPE, Arthur Clay 4
COPE, Caleb H
COPE, Edward Drinker H
COPE, Gilbert 3
COPE, Henry Frederick 1
COPE, Millard 5
COPE, Quill Evan 5
COPE, Robert S. 3
COPE, Thomas Pym H
COPE, Walter H
COPELAN, Robert W. 4
COPELAND, Alfred Bryant 4
COPELAND, Arthur 1
H(erbert), Sr.
COPELAND, Charles 2
COPELAND, Charles 3
Townsend
COPELAND, Charles W. H
COPELAND, Clarence 9
Edmund
COPELAND, Edward 3
Rivers
COPELAND, Edwin 5
Bingham
COPELAND, Fayette 4
COPELAND, Foster 1
COPELAND, Frederick 1
Kent
COPELAND, Guild 1
Anderson
COPELAND, Jo 8
COPELAND, Kenneth 6
Wilford
COPELAND, Lammot du 8
Pont

COPELAND, Lennie 3
Phoebe
COPELAND, Manton 6
COPELAND, Melvin 6
Thomas
COPELAND, Melvin 7
Thomas
COPELAND, Morris Albert 10
COPELAND, Oren S. 3
COPELAND, Paul L. 4
COPELAND, Royal Samuel 1
COPELAND, Theodore 1
COPELAND, Walter Scott 1
COPELAND, William 4
Adams
COPELAND, William 3
Franklin
COPLAND, Aaron 10
COPLAND, Douglas Berry 5
COPLEY, Ira Clifton 2
COPLEY, James Strohn 6
COPLEY, John Singleton H
COPLEY, Lionel H
COPLIN, William Michael 1
Late
COPP, Arthur Woodward 1
COPP, Owen 1
COPPEDGE, Roy Flemister 8
COPPEE, Henry H
COPPEE, Henry St Leger 1
COPPENS, Charles 1
COPPER, Joseph Benjamin 5
COPPERNOLL, William D. 4
COPPERS, George Henry 4
COPPIN, Levi J. 3
COPPINGER, John Joseph 1
COPPINI, Pompeo 3
COPPOCK, Fred Douglass 6
COPPOCK, William Homer 6
COPPOLA, Carmine 10
COPPRIDGE, William 3
Maurice
COPWAY, George H
COQUARD, Leon 4
COQUELIN, Benoit H
Constant
COQUELIN, Benoit 4
Constant
COQUILLETT, Daniel 1
William
COQUILLETTE, St. Elmo 5
CORAM, Joseph A. 5
CORAM, Thomas* H
CORBALEY, Gordon Cook 4
CORBE, Zenan M. 5
CORBET, Darrah 7
CORBETT, Cletus John 10
CORBETT, Elizabeth 7
CORBETT, Gail Sherman 5
(Mrs. Harvey Wiley C.)
CORBETT, Gerald Robert 6
CORBETT, Harvey Wiley 3
CORBETT, Henry L. 3
CORBETT, Henry Winslow 1
CORBETT, Hiram Stevens 7
CORBETT, Hunter 1
CORBETT, J. Ralph 10
CORBETT, James John H
CORBETT, James John 4
CORBETT, Jim 3
CORBETT, Lamert 2
Seymour
CORBETT, Laurence Jay 3
CORBETT, Lee Cleveland 1
CORBETT, Robert James 5
CORBETT, Roger Bailey 8
CORBETT, Timothy 1
CORBETTA, Roger Henry 6
CORBIN, Alvin Leroy 5
CORBIN, Arthur Linton 4
CORBIN, Arthur Linton, 5
Jr.
CORBIN, Austin H
CORBIN, Caroline Fairfield 1
CORBIN, Charles Russell 2
CORBIN, Clement K. 6
CORBIN, Daniel C. 1
CORBIN, Henry Clark 1
CORBIN, Henry Pinkney 1
CORBIN, Horace Kellogg 3
CORBIN, John 3
CORBIN, Joseph Carter 4
CORBIN, Margaret H
CORBIN, Philip 1
CORBIN, William Herbert 2
CORBIN, William Lee 3
CORBIND, Jon 4
CORBIT, John Darlington 1
CORBIT, Ross 6
CORBITT, Charles 1
Linwood
CORBITT, James Howard 2
CORBLY, Lawrence 4
Jugurtha
CORBUS, Budd Clarke 3
CORBY, William H
CORCORAN, Brewer 5

CORCORAN, Charles 7
Robert
CORCORAN, Francis 1
Vincent
CORCORAN, George 4
Fancis
CORCORAN, Howard 10
Francis
CORCORAN, John William 1
CORCORAN, Katherine H
CORCORAN, Michael H
CORCORAN, Sanford 2
William
CORCORAN, Thomas 8
Gardiner
CORCORAN, Thomas J. 3
CORCORAN, William 8
Harrison
CORCORAN, William 4
Warwick
CORCORAN, William H
Wilson
CORCOS, Lucille 6
CORD, Errett Lobban 6
CORDELL, Harry William 7
CORDELL, Howard 9
William
CORDELL, Joe B. 10
CORDELL, Oscar L. 8
CORDELL, Wayne 4
Wellington
CORDES, Frank 3
CORDES, Frederick Carl 4
CORDIER, Andrew 6
Wellington
CORDINER, Ralph Jarron 6
CORDLEY, Arthur Burton 1
CORDON, Guy 5
CORDOVA, Gabriel 3
CORDOVA, Valdemar A. 9
CORDOVA-DAVILA, 1
Felix
COREA, George Claude 4
Stanley
COREA, Luis Felipe 1
CORENA, Fernando 9
CORETTE, John Earl 6
COREY, Albert B. 4
COREY, Alfred Adams, Jr. 1
COREY, Charles Henry 1
COREY, Fred Daniel 1
COREY, George Raymond 8
COREY, Herbert 3
COREY, Horace Harold 4
COREY, James William 1
COREY, Lester Spaulding 6
COREY, Marian Edith 8
COREY, Merton Leroy 9
COREY, Robert Brainard 5
COREY, Stephen Jared 1
COREY, Stephen Maxwell 8
COREY, Wendell Reid 5
COREY, William Ellis 1
CORFMAN, Elmer 5
Ellsworth
CORGAN, Joseph Aloysius 6
CORI, Carl Ferdinand 8
CORI, Gerty Theresa 3
CORIAT, Isador Henry 2
CORIELL, Louis Duncan 6
CORK, James M. 3
CORKER, Stephen Alfestus H
CORKERY, Francis E. 5
CORKEY, Alexander 1
CORKILL, James Frederick 4
CORLE, Edwin 3
CORLETT, Allen N. 7
CORLETT, Ben Callister 8
CORLETT, Charles 8
Harrison
CORLETT, George Milton 3
CORLETT, Webster David 5
CORLETT, William 4
Thomas
CORLETT, William H
Wellington
CORLETTE, Lyle H. 8
CORLEY, Francis Joseph 7
CORLEY, Frederick Dexter 4
CORLEY, James Henry 4
CORLEY, Jesse Lee 2
CORLISS, Augustus 1
Whittemore
CORLISS, Charles Albert 1
CORLISS, Frederick 4
William
CORLISS, George Henry H
CORLISS, Guy Carleton 3
Haynes
CORLISS, john Blaisdell 1
CORLISS, Leland Marchant 5
CORMENY, Alvin 5
E(ugene)
CORN, Herbert F. 4
CORN, Ira George, Jr. 8
CORN, N.S. 1
CORN, Samuel Thompson 1

CORNBROOKS, Thomas 2
Mullan
CORNBURY, Viscount H
CORNE, Michel Felice H
CORNEAU, Barton H
CORNELIUS, Adam E. 3
CORNELIUS, Charles Le 5
Sueur
CORNELIUS, Charles Over 1
CORNELIUS, David 7
William
CORNELIUS, Edward 10
Gordon
CORNELIUS, Martin 3
Phelps
CORNELIUS, Marty 7
CORNELIUS, Mary Ann 1
CORNELIUS, Olivia Smith 7
CORNELIUS, Ralph E. 5
CORNELIUS, Samuel 1
Anderson
CORNELIUS, Willard M. 3
CORNELL, Alonzo B. 1
CORNELL, Ezekiel H
CORNELL, Ezra H
CORNELL, Herbert 7
Watson
CORNELL, Irwin H. 4
CORNELL, Joseph 5
CORNELL, Katharine 6
CORNELL, Sarah Hughes 5
CORNELL, Thomas H
CORNELL, Walter Stewart 5
CORNELL, William Bouck 3
CORNELLIER, Philip 9
CORNELSON, George 1
Henry
CORNER, George 8
Washington
CORNER, George 1
Washington, Jr.
CORNER, Thomas 1
Cromwell
CORNETET, Noah E. 1
CORNETT, Olive Byram 9
CORNETTE, James P. 9
CORNFIELD, Jerome 7
CORNICK, Howard 2
CORNICK, Philip H. 5
CORNING, Charles Robert 1
CORNING, Edwin 4
CORNING, Erastus 3
CORNING, Erastus, 2d 8
CORNING, Frederick 1
Gleason
CORNING, Hobart M. 5
CORNING, J. Leonard 1
CORNISH, Albert Judson 4
CORNISH, Ed 1
CORNISH, Edward Joel 1
CORNISH, George 10
Anthony
CORNISH, Gertrude 6
Eleanor
CORNISH, Leslie Colby 1
CORNISH, Lorenzo Dana 1
CORNISH, Louis Craig 2
CORNISH, William D. 1
CORNMAN, Daniel 3
CORNMAN, James Welton 7
CORNMAN, Noel 6
CORNMAN, Oliver Perry 1
CORNOYER, Paul 1
CORNSTALK H
CORNWALL, Edward 1
Everett
CORNWALL, Henry 1
Bedinger
CORNWALL, Joseph 8
Spencer
CORNWALLIS, Charles H
CORNWALLIS, Kinahan 1
CORNWELL, Alfred L. 5
CORNWELL, Dean 4
CORNWELL, Forest 6
Augustus
CORNWELL, John J. 3
CORNWELL, William 4
Caryl
CORNYN, John Hubert 1
COROMILAS, Lambros A. 4
COROMINAS SEGURA, 9
Rodolfo
CORONADO, Francisco H
Vazquez de
CORP, Paul Metzger 6
CORPER, Harry John 6
CORRADI, Peter 9
CORRADO, Gaetano 1
CORRE, Joseph H
CORREA, Henry A. 10
CORREGAN, Charles 2
Hunter
CORREIA, Oscar 8
CORRELL, Charles J. 5
CORRIE, Walter Samuel 4
CORRIGAN, Emmett 3

CORRIGAN, Francis Patrick 4
CORRIGAN, James Joseph Patrick 9
CORRIGAN, John 3
CORRIGAN, Jones Irwin Joseph 2
CORRIGAN, Joseph Moran 2
CORRIGAN, Leo Francis 6
CORRIGAN, Michael Augustine 1
CORRIGAN, Owen Bernard 1
CORRIGAN, Severinus John 4
CORRIGAN, Walter Dickson, Sr. 3
CORRIGAN, William John 4
CORRIN, Brownlee Sands 9
CORRINGTON, John W. 7
CORRINGTON, Julian Dana 7
CORRINGTON, Louis Earle, Jr. 9
CORROON, Richard Aloysius 2
CORROON, Richard Francis 7
CORROTHERS, James David 5
CORRSIN, Stanley 9
CORRUCCINI, Roberto 4
CORRY, Edgar Clayton 5
CORSE, John Murray 4
CORSE, William Malcolm 2
CORSER, Harry Prosper 1
CORSI, Edward 4
CORSON, Caroline Rollins 1
CORSON, David Birdsall 1
CORSON, Dighton 1
CORSON, Eugene Rollin 4
CORSON, Fred Pierce 8
CORSON, Harry Herbert 5
CORSON, Hiram 1
CORSON, John Jay 10
CORSON, Juliet H
CORSON, Oscar Taylor 1
CORSON, Philip Langdon 10
CORSON, Robert William 8
CORSON, William Russell Cone 2
CORT, Stewart J. 3
CORT, Stewart Shaw 7
CORTAMBERT, Louis Richard H
CORTELYOU, George Bruce 1
CORTESI, Arnaldo 4
CORTÉS PÉREZ, Fidel 8
CORTEZ, Hernando H
CORTHALL, Arthur Bateman 1
CORTHALL, Nellis Eugene 1
CORTHELL, Elmer Lawrence 1
CORTILET, Michael P. 3
CORTISSOZ, Ellen MacKay Hutchinson 1
CORTISSOZ, Royal 2
CORTNEY, Philip 5
CORTRIGHT, Ernest Everett 5
CORUM, Martene Windsor 3
CORWIN, Arthur Frank 3
CORWIN, Arthur Mills 1
CORWIN, Charles Edward 3
CORWIN, Edward Samuel 4
CORWIN, Edward Tanjore 1
CORWIN, Franklin H
CORWIN, George B. 5
CORWIN, Margaret Trumbull 8
CORWIN, Moses Biedso H
CORWIN, Richard Warren 1
CORWIN, Robert Nelson 2
CORWIN, Thomas H
CORWINE, Aaron H. 1
CORWITH, Howard Post 4
CORWITH, James Carlton 4
CORY, Abram Edward 5
CORY, Charles Barney 1
CORY, Charles Edward 1
CORY, Clarence Linus 1
CORY, David 4
CORY, Ernest Neal 7
CORY, Harry Thomas 5
CORY, Herbert Ellsworth 4
CORY, Merton M(aine) 7
CORY, Thomas J. 4
CORY, Virgil 4
CORYELL, Charles Dubois 9
COSBY, Frank Carvill 1
COSBY, George Blake 1
COSBY, Spencer 4
COSBY, William H

COSDEN, Jeremiah H
COSDEN, Joshua S. 1
COSENZA, Mario Emilio 4
COSGRAVE, George 2
COSGRAVE, Jessica Garretson 2
COSGRAVE, John O'Hara 2
COSGRAVE, John O'Hara, II 5
COSGRAVE, William Thomas 4
COSGRIFF, James E. 1
COSGRIFF, Walter Everett 4
COSGROVE, Edward Bradley 4
COSGROVE, Emilie Dohrmann (Mrs. John Charles Cosgrove) 5
COSGROVE, Henry 1
COSGROVE, James J. 4
COSGROVE, John C. 7
COSGROVE, John Phillips 3
COSGROVE, Michael Frank 4
COSGROVE, Robert 7
COSGROVE, Terence Byrne 3
COSGROVE, William Hugh 9
COSHOW, Oliver Perry 1
COSS, John J. 2
COSSENTINE, Erwin Earl 10
COSSON, George 4
COSTA, Joseph 9
COSTAIN, Thomas Bertram 4
COSTANSO, Miguel H
COSTANTINO, Mark Americus 10
COSTE, Paul F. 4
COSTELLO, Frederick Hankerson 1
COSTELLO, Harry Todd 4
COSTELLO, J.F. 3
COSTELLO, John A(loysius) 6
COSTELLO, John Cornelius 6
COSTELLO, John Martin 7
COSTELLO, Joseph A. 7
COSTELLO, Lou 3
COSTELLO, Louis B. 3
COSTELLO, Peter E. 4
COSTELLO, William Aloysious 5
COSTELLO, William Francis 7
COSTER, Frank Donald 1
COSTIGAN, Edward Prentiss 1
COSTIGAN, Francis H
COSTIGAN, George Purcell, Jr. 1
COSTIGAN, Giovanni 10
COSTIGAN, John Edward 5
COSTIKYAN, S. Kent 2
COSTLEY, Elizabeth Christine 6
COSTOLOW, William Evert 4
COTE, Alcide 3
COTE, Raymond Henri 7
COTHERN, Leland 4
COTHRAN, Frank Harrison 2
COTHRAN, James Sproull H
COTHRAN, Perrin Chiles 3
COTHRAN, Thomas Perrin 1
COTLOW, Lewis Nathaniel 5
COTNAREANU, Leon 5
COTNER, F(rank) B(oyd) 3
COTNER, Thomas Ewing 7
COTT, Ted 6
COTTAM, Clarence 6
COTTAM, Gilbert Geoffrey 2
COTTAM, Howard Rex 8
COTTEN, Sallie Southall 1
COTTER, Carl Henry 4
COTTER, Charles F. 3
COTTER, James Edward 4
COTTER, John F. 3
COTTER, John M. 10
COTTER, John W. 4
COTTER, Joseph B. 1
COTTER, Michael Dennis 10
COTTER, William 4
COTTER, William Edward 3
COTTER, William Ross 8
COTTERAL, John Hazleton 1
COTTERILL, George Fletcher 5
COTTERILL, Robert Spencer 7
COTTERMAN, Charles Mason 4
COTTERMAN, Harold F. 8
COTTING, Charles Edward 8
COTTING, John Ruggles H

COTTINGHAM, Claybrook 2
COTTINGHAM, George W. 2
COTTINGHAM, Harold Fred 8
COTTINGHAM, Irven A. 1
COTTIS, George W. 4
COTTLE, Brooks 4
COTTMAN, James Hough 1
COTTMAN, Joseph Stewart H
COTTMAN, Vincendon Lazarus 1
COTTON, Alfred Cleveland 1
COTTON, Charles Stanhope 1
COTTON, Edward Howe 6
COTTON, Elizabeth Jane 4
COTTON, Emile Louis 7
COTTON, Fassett Allen 4
COTTON, Francis Ridgely 1
COTTON, Frederic Jay 1
COTTON, Henry Andrews 1
COTTON, Jesse Lee 3
COTTON, John H
COTTON, John 9
COTTON, Joseph Bell 1
COTTON, Joseph Potter 1
COTTON, Norris H
COTTON, William Davis 10
COTTON, William Edwin 3
COTTON, William H. 1
COTTON, William Joseph Henry 1
COTTON, William Wick 1
COTTRELL, Calvert Byron H
COTTRELL, Donald C. 3
COTTRELL, Edwin Angell 3
COTTRELL, Elias 1
COTTRELL, Frederick Gardner 2
COTTRELL, James La Fayette H
COTTRELL, Jesse Samuel 2
COTTRELL, Leonard 6
COTTRELL, Leonard S., Jr. 8
COTTRELL, Mary James 1
COTTRELL, Samuel 6
COTTRELL, Will Rea, Jr. 5
COTY, Rene 7
COTZIAS, George C. 7
COUCH, Albert Irving 2
COUCH, Benjamin Warren 2
COUCH, Charles Peter 4
COUCH, Darius Nash H
COUCH, George W. 6
COUCH, Harvey Crowley 1
COUCH, Harvey Crowley, Jr. 4
COUCH, Herbert Newell 3
COUCH, John Nathaniel 9
COUCH, Natalie Frances 4
COUCHMAN, Charles Bennington 4
COUCHMAN, Gaylord M. 7
COUDEN, Albert Reynolds 1
COUDEN, Henry Noble 1
COUDERT, Alexis Carrel 7
COUDERT, Amalia Kussner 5
COUDERT, Frederic Rene 1
COUDERT, Frederic Rene 3
COUDERT, Frederic Rene, Jr. 5
COUDREY, Harry Marcy 1
COUES, Elliott 1
COUES, Samuel Franklin 1
COUEY, James Henry, Jr. 5
COUGHLAN, Robert Edward, Jr. 5
COUGHLIN, Clarence Dennis 3
COUGHLIN, Edward Joseph 6
COUGHLIN, Howard 8
COUGHLIN, John William 1
COUGHLIN, Timothy J. 3
COUGHLIN, W.G. 4
COUGHLIN, Walter James 4
COUGHLIN, William Thomas 1
COULDOCK, Charles Walter H
COULETTE, Henri Anthony 9
COULL, James 10
COULSON, Charles Alfred 6
COULSON, Edwin Ray 5
COULSON, Robert E. 4
COULSTON, John Bishop 1
COULSTON, Melvin Herbert 4
COULTAS, Andrew Jackson 1
COULTER, Charles M. 3
COULTER, Charles Wellsley 7

COULTER, Ellis Merton 8
COULTER, Glenn Monroe 7
COULTER, John Lee 3
COULTER, John Merle 1
COULTER, John Stanley 4
COULTER, Kirkley Schley 7
COULTER, Mary Geigus 4
COULTER, Merle Crowe 3
COULTER, Richard H
COULTER, Sidney Beech 5
COULTER, Stanley 2
COULTER, Victor Aldine 9
COULTER, William S(ummey) 6
COULTHARD, George William 5
COULTON, George A. 1
COULTON, Thomas Evans 4
COUNCIL, Carl C. 4
COUNCIL, Walter Wooten 2
COUNCILL, William Hooper 1
COUNCILMAN, William Thomas 1
COUNCILOR, James Allan 2
COUNIHAN, Edward Augustine, Jr. 7
COUNSELMAN, Charles 1
COUNSELMAN, Theodore Benton 7
COUNTERMINE, John Donnan 4
COUNTRYMAN, Edwin 1
COUNTRYMAN, Gratia Alta 3
COUNTRYMAN, J.E. 5
COUNTRYMAN, Marcellus L. 4
COUNTRYMAN, Willis Arthur 4
COUNTS, George Sylvester 6
COUNTS, Gerald Alford 4
COUNTWAY, Francis A. 3
COUNTY, Albert John 2
COUPAL, James Francis 1
COUPER, Edgar Williams 9
COUPER, James Hamilton 4
COUPER, Louise Pettigrew 9
COUPER, William 2
COURANT, Richard 5
COURCHESNE, Georges 3
COURNAND, Andre F. 9
COURNAND, Edward L. 6
COURSAULT, Jesse Harliaman 1
COURSEY, Oscar William 3
COURT, Frank Willard 4
COURTENAY, William Ashmead 1
COURTENAY, William Howard 1
COURTER, Claude V. 4
COURTIS, Frank 1
COURTIS, Stuart Appleton 5
COURTIS, William Munroe 1
COURTLEIGH, William Louis 1
COURTNEY, Frederick 1
COURTNEY, Joseph William 1
COURTNEY, Luther Weeks 6
COURTNEY, Thomas J(ames) 5
COURTNEY, Walter 1
COURTNEY, Wirt 8
COURTRIGHT, Hernando 9
COURTS, Malon Clay 9
COURVILLE, Cyril Brian 1
COUSE, E. Irving 1
COUSENS, John Albert 1
COUSINS, C(larence) E(dwin) 7
COUSINS, Frank 4
COUSINS, Frank 9
COUSINS, Norman 10
COUSINS, Paul Mercer 8
COUSINS, Ralph P. 4
COUSINS, Robert Bartow 1
COUSINS, Robert Gordon 1
COUSINS, Solon Bolivar, Jr. 7
COUSINS, William E. 9
COUSIS, Arthur George 3
COUSLEY, Paul Sparks 9
COUSLEY, Stanley W. 3
COUTANT, Frank Raymond 6
COUTURIER, Hendrick H
COUZENS, Frank 3
COUZENS, James 1
COUZINS, Phoebe 1
COVALT, Donald A. 7
COVARRUBIAS, Miguel 3
COVAULT, Clarence Hartley 4
COVELL, David Ransom 8

COVELL, Louis Chapin 5
COVELL, William Edward Raab 9
COVENEY, Charles Carden 5
COVER, John Higson 9
COVER, Ralph 5
COVER, Rodney Addison 4
COVERDALE, John Walter 7
COVERDALE, William Hugh 2
COVERLEY, Robert 4
COVERT, Charles Edward 5
COVERT, Frank Manning 9
COVERT, John Cutler 1
COVERT, Lloyd W. 4
COVERT, William Chalmers 1
COVEY, Arthur Sinclair 3
COVILLE, Frederick V. 1
COVINGTON, Euclid M. 6
COVINGTON, Harry Stockdell 3
COVINGTON, J. Harry 1
COVINGTON, James Edward 9
COVINGTON, Leonard H
COVINGTON, William Slaughter 10
COVINO, Benjamin Gene 10
COVINTON, Harry Franklin 1
COVODE, John H
COWAN, Andrew 1
COWAN, Clyde Lorrain 6
COWAN, Edgar H
COWAN, Edward Payson 4
COWAN, Frank 1
COWAN, Frank Augustus 3
COWAN, Frank Irving 2
COWAN, Jacob Pitzer H
COWAN, James Raymo 3
COWAN, John Franklin 4
COWAN, Leslie 2
COWAN, Louis G. 7
COWAN, Robert Ernest 2
COWAN, Robert George 9
COWAN, Samuel Kinkade 5
COWAN, Wood Messick 8
COWAP, Charles Richardson 10
COWARD, Edward Fales 1
COWARD, Noel Peirce 5
COWARD, Thomas Ridgway 3
COWART, Harry Maciemore 6
COWART, Ralph W. 8
COWDEN, Howard Austin 6
COWDEN, John Brandon 5
COWDEN, Robert E., Jr. 5
COWDEN, Roy W(illiam) 7
COWDEN, Thomas Kyle 8
COWDERY, Edward Gilmore 1
COWDERY, Robert Holmes 6
COWDIN, J. Cheever 4
COWDRY, Edmund Vincent 6
COWELL, Alfred Lucius 5
COWELL, Henry Dixon 4
COWELL, Hervey Sumner 1
COWELL, Joseph Goss 7
COWELL, Joseph Leathley H
COWELL, Sylvester E. 5
COWEN, Benjamin Rush 1
COWEN, Benjamin Sprague H
COWEN, Benjamin Sprague 4
COWEN, John King 1
COWEN, Joshua Lionel 4
COWEN, Lawrence 5
COWEN, Myron Melvin 4
COWEN, William B. 4
COWEN, Wilson Walker 10
COWGER, William Owen 5
COWGILL, Clinton Harriman 9
COWGILL, Donald Olen 9
COWGILL, George Raymond 6
COWGILL, James Joseph 7
COWHERD, William Strother 1
COWIE, Alexander 7
COWIE, Charles Durno 8
COWIE, David Murray 1
COWIE, Jack Baron 4
COWIE, Thomas Jefferson 1
COWIN, John Clay 1
COWING, Hugh Alvin 2
COWL, Jane 3
COWLES, Alfred 1
COWLES, Alfred 1
COWLES, Alfred Hutchinson
COWLES, Augustus Woodruff 1

CRANNELL, Philip Wendell 1
CRANSTON, Claudia 2
CRANSTON, Earl 1
CRANSTON, Earl 5
CRANSTON, Henry Young H
CRANSTON, John H
CRANSTON, Mildred Welch 10
CRANSTON, Robert Bennie H
CRANSTON, Samuel H
CRANWELL, James Logan 4
CRANWELL, Thomas George 1
CRAPO, Philip M. 1
CRAPO, Stanford Tappan 1
CRAPO, William Wallace 1
CRAPSEY, Algernon Sidney 1
CRARY, Albert Paddock 9
CRARY, George Waldo 1
CRARY, Gordon B. 4
CRARY, Isaac Edwin H
CRASSWELLER, Frank 2
CRATER, Robert Winfield 8
CRATHORNE, Arthur Robert 2
CRATSLEY, Edward Kneeland 7
CRATTY, Mabel 1
CRATTY, Robert Irvin 4
CRAVATH, Erastus Milo 1
CRAVATH, Paul Drennan 1
CRAVEN, Alex 4
CRAVEN, Alfred 1
CRAVEN, Avery Odelle 7
CRAVEN, Braxton H
CRAVEN, Charles Edmiston 4
CRAVEN, Elijah Richardson 1
CRAVEN, Frank 2
CRAVEN, George Warren 1
CRAVEN, Hermon Wilson 4
CRAVEN, James Braxton 2
CRAVEN, James Braxton, Jr. 7
CRAVEN, John Joseph H
CRAVEN, Leslie 3
CRAVEN, Margaret 7
CRAVEN, Thomas 5
CRAVEN, Thomas Tingey H
CRAVEN, Thomas Tingey 3
CRAVEN, Tunis Augustus MacDonough 5
CRAVEN, Tunus Augustus MacDonough H
CRAVEN, Wesley Frank 7
CRAVEN, William Reno 4
CRAVENS, Ben 1
CRAVENS, Du Val Garland 5
CRAVENS, James Addison H
CRAVENS, James Harrison H
CRAVENS, John William 1
CRAVENS, Kenton Robinson 5
CRAVENS, Oscar Henry 5
CRAVER, Arthur William 7
CRAVER, Harrison Warwick 3
CRAVER, Samuel Porch 1
CRAWFORD, Andrew Murray 1
CRAWFORD, Andrew Wright 1
CRAWFORD, Angus 4
CRAWFORD, Angus 5
CRAWFORD, Arch 4
CRAWFORD, Arthur 1
CRAWFORD, Charles 3
CRAWFORD, Charles Wallace 3
CRAWFORD, Clarence K. 4
CRAWFORD, Coe Isaac 4
CRAWFORD, David A. 3
CRAWFORD, David McLean 4
CRAWFORD, Earl Stetson 5
CRAWFORD, Eben G. 2
CRAWFORD, Edward Grant 1
CRAWFORD, Edwin Robert 1
CRAWFORD, Eugene Lowther 1
CRAWFORD, F. Stuart 1
CRAWFORD, Finia Goff 5
CRAWFORD, Francis Marion 1
CRAWFORD, Fred Lewis 3
CRAWFORD, George Gordon 1
CRAWFORD, George Washington H
CRAWFORD, Harry Clement 6
CRAWFORD, Harry J. 3
CRAWFORD, Harry Jennings 3
CRAWFORD, Isabel 4
CRAWFORD, Ivan Charles 4
CRAWFORD, Jack Randall 5
CRAWFORD, J(ames) C(hamberlain) 6
CRAWFORD, James Pyle Wickersham 1
CRAWFORD, James Stoner 4
CRAWFORD, Jerry Tinder 1
CRAWFORD, Joan 7
CRAWFORD, Joel H
CRAWFORD, John H
CRAWFORD, John Calvin, Jr. 8
CRAWFORD, John Forsyth 5
CRAWFORD, John Jones 4
CRAWFORD, John M. 3
CRAWFORD, John Martin 1
CRAWFORD, John Raymond 1
CRAWFORD, John Wallace 1
CRAWFORD, Joseph E(manuel) 5
CRAWFORD, Kenneth Gale 8
CRAWFORD, Leonard Jacob 1
CRAWFORD, Leonidas Wakefield 3
CRAWFORD, Martin Jenkins H
CRAWFORD, Mary Caroline 1
CRAWFORD, Mary Sinclair 4
CRAWFORD, Medorem 1
CRAWFORD, Meriwether Lewis 4
CRAWFORD, Milo Hicks 6
CRAWFORD, Morris Barker 1
CRAWFORD, Morris Barker 2
CRAWFORD, Morris De Camp 7
CRAWFORD, Nelson Antrim 4
CRAWFORD, Porter James 2
CRAWFORD, Ralph Dixon 3
CRAWFORD, Ralston 7
CRAWFORD, Robert A. 1
CRAWFORD, Robert Platt 10
CRAWFORD, Russell Tracy 3
CRAWFORD, Samuel Johnson 1
CRAWFORD, Stanton Chapman 4
CRAWFORD, Thomas H
CRAWFORD, Thomas Dwight 1
CRAWFORD, Thomas Hartley H
CRAWFORD, Thomas Henry 4
CRAWFORD, Walter Joshua 1
CRAWFORD, William* H
CRAWFORD, William Alfred 1
CRAWFPRD, William Campbell 1
CRAWFORD, William Donham 8
CRAWFORD, William Harris H
CRAWFORD, William Henry 2
CRAWFORD, William Hopkins 4
CRAWFORD, William Hulfish 8
CRAWFORD, William L. 1
CRAWFORD, William T. 4
CRAWFORD, William Thomas 1
CRAWFORD, William Walt 6
CRAWFORD, William Webb 1
CRAWFORD-FROST, William Albert 1
CRAWFPRD, Cheryl 9
CRAWLEY, Clyde B. 3
CRAWLEY, David Ephraim 2
CRAWLEY, Edwin Schoffield 1
CRAWLEY, George E(dwin) 7
CRAWLEY, Thomas Edward 9
CRAWSHAW, Fred Duane 5
CRAWSHAW, William Henry 1
CRAYTON, Jenkins Street 6
CRAZY HORSE H
CREAGER, Charles E. 5
CREAGER, John Oscar 2
CREAGER, Marvin H. 3
CREAGER, Rentfro Banton 3
CREAGER, William Pitcher 3
CREAL, Edward Wester 2
CREAMER, David H
CREAMER, Thomas J. 4
CREAMER, Walter J(oseph) 7
CREAN, Robert 6
CREANZA, Joseph 9
CREASER, Charles W. 4
CREASEY, John 6
CREASY, William Neville 6
CREATH, Jacob* H
CREBS, John Montgomery H
CRECRAFT, Earl Willis 3
CREE, Albert Alexander 10
CREE, Archibald Cunningham 2
CREECH, Harris 2
CREECH, John W. 3
CREECH, Oscar, Jr. 4
CREECH, Oscar, Jr. 5
CREED, Thomas Percival 5
CREED, Wigginton Ellis 1
CREEDE, Frank J. 4
CREEDEN, Daniel W. 3
CREEDY, Frederick 7
CREEGAN, Charles Cole 1
CREEK, Herbert LeSourd 6
CREEKMORE, Edward Fitzgerald 7
CREEL, Cecil Willis 8
CREEL, Enrique C. 2
CREEL, George 3
CREEL, Robert Calhoun 5
CREELMAN, Harlan 3
CREELMAN, James 1
CREESE, James 4
CREESE, Wadsworth 5
CREESY, Josiah Perkins H
CREEVEY, Caroline Alathea Stickney 1
CREEVY, Charles Donald 7
CREHORE, Albert Cushing 4
CREHORE, William Williams 1
CREIGHTON, Albert Morton 4
CREIGHTON, Edward H
CREIGHTON, Elmer Ellsworth Farmer 1
CREIGHTON, Frank Whittington 2
CREIGHTON, Henry Jermain Maude 7
CREIGHTON, James Edwin 1
CREIGHTON, John Thrale 1
CREIGHTON, John Wallis 7
CREIGHTON, Martha Gladys 4
CREIGHTON, Thomas Hawk 8
CREIGHTON, William H
CREIGHTON, William Forman 9
CREIGHTON, William Henry 1
CREIGHTON, William J. 3
CREIM, Ben Wilton 3
CREITZ, Charles Erwin 1
CRELLIN, Edward Webster 2
CREMER, Jacob Theodoor 1
CREMIN, Lawrence Arthur 10
CRENIER, Henri 2
CRENNEN, Robert Earl 8
CRENSHAW, Bolling Hall 1
CRENSHAW, George Webster 8
CRENSHAW, H. F. 1
CRENSHAW, James Llewellyn 3
CRENSHAW, Ollinger 5
CRENSHAW, Thomas C. 4
CRERAR, Henry Duncan Graham 4
CRERAR, John H
CRESAP, Mark W., Jr. 4
CRESAP, Mark Winfield 2
CRESAP, Michael H
CRESAP, Thomas H
CRESKOFF, Jacob Joshua 7
CRESON, Larry Barkley 5
CRESPI, Juan H
CRESPO Y MARTINEZ, Gilberto 4
CRESS, George Clifford 3
CRESS, George Oscar 3
CRESSE, Wadsworth 7
CRESSEY, Donald Ray 9
CRESSEY, George Babcock 4
CRESSEY, George Croswell 1
CRESSLER, Alfred Miller 1
CRESSLER, Isabel Bonbrake 3
CRESSMAN, Paul Leroy 7
CRESSON, Elliott H
CRESSON, Ezra Townsend 4
CRESSON, Margaret French 6
CRESSON, W. Penn 1
CRESSWELL, Robert 2
CRESSY, Warren Francis 3
CRESSY, Wilfred Wesley 1
CRESSY, Will Martin 1
CRESTON, Paul 8
CRESWELL, Edward J. 3
CRESWELL, Harry I. T. 5
CRESWELL, John Angel James H
CRESWELL, Mary E. 6
CRET, Paul Philippe 2
CRÊTE, Marcel 9
CRETIN, Joseph H
CREVECOEUR, Michel-guillaume Jean De H
CREVISTON, Russell Good 8
CREW, Henry 3
CREW, William Binford 1
CREWS, Floyd Houston 4
CREWS, Leslie F. 5
CREWS, Ralph 1
CRICHTON, Alexander Fraser 1
CRICHTON, John Henderson 7
CRICHTON, Kyle S. 4
CRICKARD, Mason 8
CRIDER, Blake 6
CRIDER, John Henshaw 4
CRIDLAND, Charles 5
CRIDLER, Thomas Wilbur 4
CRIKELAIR, Robert John 7
CRILE, Austin Daniel 3
CRILE, Dennis Rider Wood 1
CRILE, George, Jr. 10
CRILE, George Washington 2
CRILLEY, A. Cyril 3
CRIM, John William Henry 1
CRIMI, James Ernest 6
CRIMMINS, Harry Benedict 4
CRIMMINS, John Daniel 1
CRIMONT, Joseph Raphael 2
CRINKLEY, Matthew S. 4
CRIPPA, Edward David 4
CRIPPEN, Henry Durrell 1
CRIPPEN, Lloyd Kenneth 5
CRIPPS, Sir Stafford 3
CRISCUOLO, Luigi 3
CRISFIELD, John Woodland H
CRISP, Arthur 6
CRISP, Charles Frederick H
CRISP, Charles R. 1
CRISP, Donald 6
CRISPIN, M. Jackson 3
CRISPO, Andrew J(ohn) 8
CRISS, Clair C. 3
CRISS, Mabel Leone 7
CRISS, Neil Louis 5
CRISS, Nell Louis 7
CRISSEY, Forrest 2
CRISSINGER, Daniel Richard 2
CRIST, Bainbridge 5
CRIST, Frederic Eugene 8
CRIST, Harris McCabe 2
CRIST, Henry H
CRIST, Raymond Fowler 2
CRISTY, Albert Barnes 4
CRISTY, Albert Moses 2
CRISWELL, George Stuart 1
CRITCHFIELD, Howard Emmett 4
CRITCHLOW, Francis B. 3
CRITES, Aure Brian 7
CRITES, Lowry Hyer 6
CRITTENBERGER, George Dale 4
CRITTENBERGER, Willis Dale 8
CRITTENDEN, Christopher 5
CRITTENDEN, Eugene Casson 3
CRITTENDEN, George Bibb H
CRITTENDEN, John Jordan H
CRITTENDEN, Thomas Leonidas H
CRITTENDEN, Thomas Theodore 1
CRITTENDEN, Walter Hayden 2
CRITZ, Harry Herndon 8
CRITZ, Hugh 5
CRITZ, Richard 5
CROASDALE, Jack Finch 4
CROASDALE, Stuart 1
CROCE, Benedette 3
CROCHERON, Henry H
CROCHERON, Jacob H
CROCKARD, Frank Hearne 3
CROCKER, Alvah H
CROCKER, Arthur W. 4
CROCKER, Augustus Luther 4
CROCKER, Bosworth 2
CROCKER, Charles H
CROCKER, Charles Henry 1
CROCKER, Edward Savage 5
CROCKER, Francis Bacon 1
CROCKER, Frank Longfellow 2
CROCKER, George 1
CROCKER, George Glover 1
CROCKER, Hannah Mather H
CROCKER, Henry E. 1
CROCKER, Lionel George 10
CROCKER, Michaux Henly 7
CROCKER, Samuel E. M. 7
CROCKER, Samuel Leonard H
CROCKER, Sarah G. H
CROCKER, Stuart Miller 3
CROCKER, Templeton 2
CROCKER, Templeton 7
CROCKER, Theodore D. 2
CROCKER, Uriel H
CROCKER, Uriel Haskell 1
CROCKER, Walter James 2
CROCKER, William 2
CROCKER, William Henry 1
CROCKER, William Willard 4
CROCKETT, Albert Stevens 5
CROCKETT, Arthur Jay 4
CROCKETT, Campbell 9
CROCKETT, Charles Winthrop 1
CROCKETT, David H
CROCKETT, Eugene Anthony 1
CROCKETT, Franklin Smith 6
CROCKETT, Horace Guy 4
CROCKETT, Ingram 4
CROCKETT, John Wesley H
CROCKETT, Montgomery Adams 4
CROCKETT, Walter Hill 1
CROCKETT, William Day 1
CROCKETT, William Goggin 1
CROES, John James Robertson 1
CROFFUT, William Augustus 1
CROFT, Albert Jefferson 1
CROFT, A(rthur) C. 7
CROFT, Delmer Eugene 1
CROFT, Edward 1
CROFT, George William 1
CROFT, Harry William 2
CROFT, Richard Graham 6
CROFTAN, Alfred Careno 1
CROFTS, Frederick Sharer 3
CROGHAN, George H
CROGHAN, Hubert McLeod 4
CROGMAN, William Henry, Sr. 1
CROHN, Burrill Bernard 7
CROISSANT, De Witt Clinton 2
CROIX, Teodoro de H
CROKER, Richard 1
CROLL, Morris William 2
CROLL, Philip C. 4
CROLL, William M. 1
CROLY, David Goodman H
CROLY, Herbert 1
CROLY, Jane Cunningham 1
CROMBIE, David Joseph 7
CROMELIN, Paul Bowen 3
CROMER, George Benedict 1
CROMER, George Washington 4
CROMER, S. S. 4

CULBERTSON, Henry Coe 1
CULBERTSON, Horace 9
Coe
CULBERTSON, Hugh 7
Emmett
CULBERTSON, James Coe 1
CULBERTSON, James 5
Gordon
CULBERTSON, John 7
Giffen
CULBERTSON, John 10
Harrison
CULBERTSON, John J. 1
CULBERTSON, Walter 7
Leroy
CULBERTSON, Walter 8
LeRoy
CULBERTSON, William 5
CULBERTSON, William 6
H(oward)
CULBERTSON, William 4
Smith
CULBRETH, David Marvel 4
Reynolds
CULBRETH, Thomas H
CULHANE, Frank James 7
CULIG, Ivan Conrad 4
CULIN, Alice Mumford 5
(Mrs. Stewart Culin)
CULIN, Frank Lewis 4
CULIN, Stewart 1
CULKIN, Francis D. 2
CULKINS, William 1
Clement
CULLEN, Bill (William 10
Lawrence Cullen)
CULLEN, Countee 2
CULLEN, Edgar 1
Montgomery
CULLEN, Elisha Dickerson H
CULLEN, Frederick John 5
CULLEN, Glenn E. 1
CULLEN, Hugh Roy 3
CULLEN, James Aloysius 6
CULLEN, Richard J. 2
CULLEN, Stuart Chester 7
CULLEN, Thomas Ernest 5
CULLEN, Thomas H. 2
CULLEN, Thomas Joseph 4
Vincent
CULLEN, Thomas Stephen 3
CULLEN, Vincent 4
CULLEN, William George 6
CULLER, Arthur Jerome 1
CULLER, Arthur Merl 4
CULLER, Elmer Augustin 8
Kurtz
CULLER, Joseph Albertus 1
CULLEY, Fenton Bayard 7
CULLIMORE, Allan 3
Reginald
CULLIMORE, Clarence 1
CULLINAN, Craig Francis 3
CULLINAN, Edith Phillips 3
CULLINAN, Joseph 1
Stephen
CULLIS, Charles H
CULLISON, James 1
Buchanan
CULLITON, Edward 10
Milton
CULLITY, Bernard Dennis 7
CULLMAN, Howard S(tix) 5
CULLOM, Alvan H
CULLOM, Marvin 4
McTyeire
CULLOM, Neil P. 8
CULLOM, Shelby Moore 1
CULLOM, William 8
CULLOM, Willis Richard 5
CULLOP, William Allen 1
CULLUM, George H
Washington
CULLUM, Robert Brooks 8
CULMER, Henry L. A. 1
CULP, Charles Cantrell 4
CULP, John M. 1
CULPEPER, John H
CULPEPER, Thomas H
CULPEPPER, James Henry 6
CULPEPPER, John 1
CULTER, Mary McCrae 4
CULVER, Bernard Mott 3
CULVER, Bertram Beach 3
CULVER, Charles Aaron 6
CULVER, Charles Beach 5
CULVER, Charles 1
Mortimer
CULVER, Erastus Dean 1
CULVER, Frank Pugh 2
CULVER, Harry Hazel 2
CULVER, Helen 1
CULVER, Henry S. 4
CULVER, John Yapp 5
CULVER, Montgomery 3
Morton
CULVER, Raymond B. 1

CULVER, Romulus Estep 4
CUMBERLAND, William 3
Wilson
CUMBERLEGE, Geoffrey 9
Fenmwick Jocelyn
CUMING, Sir Alexander 1
CUMING, Fortescue H
CUMINGS, Edgar Roscoe 5
CUMMER, Clyde Lottridge 3
CUMMIN, Gaylord Church 7
CUMMING, Alfred H
CUMMING, Charles 1
Atherton
CUMMING, Charles 7
Gordon
CUMMING, Hugh S. 2
CUMMING, Hugh Smith, 9
Jr.
CUMMING, Joseph Bryan 10
CUMMING, Thomas H
William
CUMMING, William H
CUMMING, William Albon 8
CUMMING, William 10
Patterson
CUMMINGHAM, William 2
Burgess
CUMMINGS, Amos 1
CUMMINGS, Mrs. 4
Bertrude Fields
CUMMINGS, Bob (Robert 10
Orville Cummings)
CUMMINGS, Charles 1
Amos
CUMMINGS, Clara Eaton 1
CUMMINGS, D. Mark 1
CUMMINGS, Edward 1
CUMMINGS, Edward 4
Estlin
CUMMINGS, George Bain 6
CUMMINGS, George 4
Donald
CUMMINGS, George W. 1
CUMMINGS, Gordon H
Parker
CUMMINGS, Harold Neff 4
CUMMINGS, Henry H
Johnson Brodhead
CUMMINGS, Henry 4
Johnson Brodhead
CUMMINGS, Homer Stille 3
CUMMINGS, James 1
Howell
CUMMINGS, Jeremiah H
Williams
CUMMINGS, Joe Brown 3
CUMMINGS, John H
CUMMINGS, John 1
CUMMINGS, Joseph H
CUMMINGS, L(eslie) 8
O(lin)
CUMMINGS, Marshall 5
Baxter
CUMMINGS, Marvin Earl 1
CUMMINGS, Nathan 8
CUMMINGS, O. Sam 4
CUMMINGS, Parke 9
CUMMINGS, Thomas Seir H
CUMMINGS, Tilden 9
CUMMINGS, Walter J. 4
CUMMINGS, Wilbur Love 1
CUMMINS, Albert Baird 1
CUMMINS, Albert Sheldon 9
CUMMINS, Albert Wilson 1
CUMMINS, Alexander H
CUMMINS, Alexander 2
Griswold
CUMMINS, Alfred Byron 10
CUMMINS, Claude 4
CUMMINS, Claude 5
CUMMINS, Clessie Lyle 5
CUMMINS, George David H
CUMMINS, George 9
Manning, Jr.
CUMMINS, James 8
Dirickson
CUMMINS, John 1
CUMMINS, John D. H
CUMMINS, Joseph Michael 3
CUMMINS, Maria Susanna 4
CUMMINS, Ralph 4
CUMMINS, Robert Rankin 3
CUMMINS, William 4
Fletcher
CUMMINS, William J. 1
CUMMINS, William Taylor 3
CUMMINS, William Taylor 6
CUMNOCK, Robert 1
McLean
CUNEO, Ernest L. 10
CUNEO, Gilbert Anthony 7
CUNEO, John F. 7
CUNHA, Felix 4
CUNINGGIM, Jesse Lee 3
CUNLIFFE, John William 2
CUNLIFFE-OWEN,
Frederick

CUNLIFFE-OWEN, Sir 2
Hugo
CUNNIFF, Michael Glen 1
CUNNINGHAM, Alan 8
Gordon
CUNNINGHAM, Albert 4
Benjamin
CUNNINGHAM, Andrew 1
Chase
CUNNINGHAM, Andrew 1
Oswald
CUNNINGHAM, Ann H
Pamela
CUNNINGHAM, 3
Augustine Joseph
CUNNINGHAM, Benjamin 1
B.
CUNNINGHAM, Benjamin 5
Frazier
CUNNINGHAM, Bert 2
CUNNINGHAM, Bess 7
Virginia
CUNNINGHAM, Burris 5
Bell
CUNNINGHAM, C. 5
Frederick
CUNNINGHAM, Charles 6
Barnard
CUNNINGHAM, Charles 7
Crehore
CUNNINGHAM, Charles 2
Henry
CUNNINGHAM, Cornelius 3
Carman
CUNNINGHAM, David F. 7
CUNNINGHAM, David 1
West
CUNNINGHAM, Donnell 1
Lafayette
CUNNINGHAM, Edward 1
Henry
CUNNINGHAM, Edwin 3
Sheddan
CUNNINGHAM, Edwin 4
W.
CUNNINGHAM, Elijah 1
William
CUNNINGHAM, Eugene 3
CUNNINGHAM, Firman 5
CUNNINGHAM, Floyd 8
Franklin
CUNNINGHAM, Francis H
Alanson
CUNNINGHAM, Frank 4
CUNNINGHAM, Frank 1
Harrison
CUNNINGHAM, Frank 1
Simpson
CUNNINGHAM, George 4
A.
CUNNINGHAM, George 3
William
CUNNINGHAM, Gustavus 6
Watts
CUNNINGHAM, Harrison 6
Edward
CUNNINGHAM, Harry A. 4
CUNNINGHAM, Harry 8
Francis
CUNNINGHAM, Henry 1
Vincent
CUNNINGHAM, Holly 3
Estil
CUNNINGHAM, Horace 5
Herndon
CUNNINGHAM, I. A. 1
CUNNINGHAM, James A. 4
CUNNINGHAM, James 4
Dalton
CUNNINGHAM, James 7
Hutchings
CUNNINGHAM, James 8
Vincent
CUNNINGHAM, Jesse 7
CUNNINGHAM, John 8
Bissell
CUNNINGHAM, John 5
Charles
CUNNINGHAM, John 3
Ferguson
CUNNINGHAM, John 5
Henry
CUNNINGHAM, John 4
Lovell
CUNNINGHAM, John 8
Phillip
CUNNINGHAM, Joseph 1
Oscar
CUNNINGHAM, Julian 1
W.
CUNNINGHAM, Louis 1
Wyborn
CUNNINGHAM, Maurice 7
Patrick
CUNNINGHAM, Milton 1
Joseph
CUNNINGHAM, Paul 4

CUNNINGHAM, Paul 1
Davis
CUNNINGHAM, Paul 8
Harvey
CUNNINGHAM, Paul 7
James
CUNNINGHAM, Paul 8
Millard
CUNNINGHAM, Richard 1
Hoope
CUNNINGHAM, Robert 4
Sydney
CUNNINGHAM, Ross 4
MacDuffee
CUNNINGHAM, Russell 1
McWhorter
CUNNINGHAM, Solomon 4
M.
CUNNINGHAM, Sumner 1
Archibald
CUNNINGHAM, Thomas 1
F.
CUNNINGHAM, Thomas 5
Mayhew
CUNNINGHAM, Wallace 6
McCook
CUNNINGHAM, Warren 3
W.
CUNNINGHAM, Wilfred 5
Harris
CUNNINGHAM, William 4
Alexander, III
CUNNINGHAM, William 4
Francis
CUNNINGHAM, William 5
James
CUNNINGHAM, William 7
Pilpel
CUNZ, Dieter 5
CUPP, Paul J. 9
CUPPIA, Jerome Chester 1
CUPPLES, Samuel 1
CUPPY, Hazlitt Alva 1
CUPPY, William Jacob 2
CURETON, Calvin Maples 2
CURIE, Robert James 6
CURL, Robert Floyd 7
CURLEE, Francis M. 3
CURLESS, Howard Marion 6
CURLEY, Daniel J. 1
CURLEY, Edward W. 1
CURLEY, Frank E. 1
CURLEY, James H
CURLEY, James Michael 3
CURLEY, Michael Joseph 2
CURLEY, Walter J. 5
CURLEY, William A. 3
CURME, George Oliver 2
CURME, George Oliver, Jr. 7
CUROE, Philip R(aphael) 2
V(incent)
CURRAN, Charles 2
Courtney
CURRAN, Edward 6
Lawrence
CURRAN, Edward 9
Matthew
CURRAN, Henry Hastings 1
CURRAN, Jean Alonzo 7
CURRAN, Kenneth James 5
CURRAN, Peter Ferguson 6
CURRAN, Thomas Jerome 3
CURRAN, William Reid 4
CURRELL, William 2
Spenser
CURRENS, Frederick 7
Hawley
CURREY, Brownlee Own 3
CURREY, J. Seymour 1
CURREY, John 1
CURRICK, Max Cohen 2
CURRIE, Barton Wood 4
CURRIE, Brainerd 4
CURRIE, Donald Herbert 4
CURRIE, Edward James 4
CURRIE, George Graham 1
CURRIE, George Selkirk 9
CURRIE, George 7
Washington
CURRIE, Gilbert Archibald 4
CURRIE, Gilbert Archibald 1
CURRIE, James Nimrod 7
CURRIE, John S. 3
CURRIE, Lauchlin 10
MacLaurin
CURRIE, Thomas White 4
CURRIE, William Mark 7
CURRIER, Albert Dean 1
CURRIER, Albert Henry 4
CURRIER, Amos Noyes 1
CURRIER, Charles Francis 1
Adams
CURRIER, Charles Warren 1
CURRIER, Frank Dunklee 1
CURRIER, George Harvey 5
CURRIER, J. Frank 1

CURRIER, John C. 4
CURRIER, Moody H
CURRIER, Nathaniel H
CURRIER, Raymond 5
Pillsbury
CURRIER, Richard Dudley 2
CURRIER, Thomas 2
Franklin
CURRY, Albert Bruce 1
CURRY, Allen 5
CURRY, Andrew Gibson 9
CURRY, Arthur Mansfield 4
CURRY, Arthur Ray 8
CURRY, Bryce Quention 9
CURRY, Charles Forrest 1
CURRY, Charles Madison 2
CURRY, Edward Rufus 1
CURRY, Edward Thomas 9
CURRY, George 2
CURRY, George Law H
CURRY, Haskell Brooks 8
CURRY, Jabez Lamar 1
Monroe
CURRY, James Bernard 1
CURRY, James J. 4
CURRY, James Rowland 5
CURRY, John F. 3
CURRY, John Francis 6
CURRY, John Steuart 2
CURRY, Michael John 3
CURRY, Neil James 4
CURRY, Peter H. 3
CURRY, R. Granville 4
CURRY, Samuel Silas 1
CURRY, William Melville 1
CURTICE, Harlow Herbert 4
CURTIN, Andrew Gregg H
CURTIN, Austin 4
CURTIN, D. Thomas 4
CURTIN, Frank Daniel 7
CURTIN, Jeremiah 1
CURTIN, Roland Gideon 1
CURTIS, A. J. R. 3
CURTIS, Alfred Allen 1
CURTIS, Arthur Melvin 2
CURTIS, Asahel 5
CURTIS, Augustus Darwin 1
CURTIS, Benjamin Robbins H
CURTIS, C. Densmore 1
CURTIS, Carlton Brandaga H
CURTIS, Carlton Clarence 1
CURTIS, Charles 1
CURTIS, Charles Albert 1
CURTIS, Charles Boyd 1
CURTIS, Charles Clarence 4
CURTIS, Charles Edgar 7
CURTIS, Charles Gordon 3
CURTIS, Charles Minot 2
CURTIS, Charles Pelham 2
CURTIS, Charles Pelham 3
CURTIS, Charlotte Murray 9
CURTIS, Claude Davis 8
CURTIS, Constance 3
CURTIS, Cyrus Hermann 1
Kotzschmar
CURTIS, David A. 1
CURTIS, Earl A. 6
CURTIS, Edward H
CURTIS, Edward 1
CURTIS, Edward Ely 8
CURTIS, Edward Gillman 3
CURTIS, Edward Gillman 1
CURTIS, Edward Glion, Jr. 5
CURTIS, Edward Harvey 4
CURTIS, Edward Lewis 1
CURTIS, Edward Peck 9
CURTIS, Edward S. 4
CURTIS, Edwin Upton 1
CURTIS, Eugene Judson 3
CURTIS, Eugene Newton 2
CURTIS, F. Kingsbury 1
CURTIS, Florence Rising 2
CURTIS, Francis 4
CURTIS, Francis Day 8
CURTIS, Francis Joseph 4
CURTIS, Frederic Colton 1
CURTIS, Frederick Smillie 1
CURTIS, George H
CURTIS, George Carroll 4
CURTIS, George Lenox 4
CURTIS, George Lewis 1
CURTIS, George Martin 4
CURTIS, George Martin, II 5
CURTIS, George Milton 4
CURTIS, George Morris 4
CURTIS, George Ticknor H
CURTIS, George William H
CURTIS, Georgina Pell 1
CURTIS, Gerald Beckwith 3
CURTIS, H. Holbrook 1
CURTIS, Harry Alfred 7
CURTIS, Harry Alfred 4
CURTIS, Harvey Lincoln 3
CURTIS, Heber Doust 1
CURTIS, Henry G. 1
CURTIS, Henry Stoddard 3

CURTIS, Howard James 5
CURTIS, Howard Junior 1
CURTIS, Hugh Everett, Jr. 7
CURTIS, Isabel Gordon 1
CURTIS, James Freeman 3
CURTIS, James Washington 8
CURTIS, Jesse William 5
CURTIS, John Green 1
CURTIS, John Jay 1
CURTIS, John Kimberly 8
CURTIS, John Talbot 3
CURTIS, John Thomas 4
CURTIS, Josiah 8
  Montgomery
CURTIS, Kent Krueger 9
CURTIS, Laurence 10
CURTIS, Lewis Perry 7
CURTIS, Louis 9
CURTIS, Mattoon Monroe 4
CURTIS, Melville Goss 3
CURTIS, Moses Ashley H
CURTIS, Nathaniel 6
  Cortlandt
CURTIS, Newton Martin 1
CURTIS, Oakley Chester 1
CURTIS, Olin Alfred 1
CURTIS, Otis Freeman 2
CURTIS, Paul Allan, Jr. 8
CURTIS, Richard Cary 3
CURTIS, Roger Ernest 9
CURTIS, Roy Emerson 4
CURTIS, Samuel Ryan H
CURTIS, Sumner 1
CURTIS, Vivian Critz 1
CURTIS, Walter Louis, Jr. 8
CURTIS, Wardon Allan 1
CURTIS, William 1
  Buckingham
CURTIS, William Edmond 1
CURTIS, William Eleroy 1
CURTIS, William Franklin 1
CURTIS, William Fuller 5
CURTIS, William Hall 10
CURTIS, William John 1
CURTIS, William Rodolph 6
CURTIS, William Samuel 1
CURTIS, Winterton 5
  Conway
CURTISS, Charles 1
  Chauncey
CURTISS, Charles Dwight 8
CURTISS, Charles Franklin 2
CURTISS, David Raymond 3
CURTISS, George 4
  Boughton
CURTISS, Glenn 1
  Hammond
CURTISS, John Hamilton 7
CURTISS, Julian Wheeler 2
CURTISS, Lawrence 5
  Meredith
CURTISS, Philip 4
CURTISS, Ralph Hamilton 4
CURTISS, Richard Sydney 4
CURTISS, Samuel Ives 1
CURTISS, Ursula Reilly 8
CURTISS, William Hanford 3
CURTISS, William John 3
CURTIZ, Michael 4
CURTS, Lewis 1
CURTS, Maurice Edwin 6
CURTS, Maurice Edwin 1
CURTS, Paul Holroyd 7
CURWEN, John 1
CURWEN, Samuel H
CURWEN, Samuel M. 1
CURWOOD, James Oliver 1
CURZON, Clifford 8
CURZON, Mary Victoria 1
CUSACK, John Francis 8
CUSACK, Thomas Francis 1
CUSHING, Caleb H
CUSHING, Charles C. S. 1
CUSHING, Charles Cook 8
CUSHING, Charles Phelps 6
CUSHING, Edward Harvey 1
CUSHING, Ernest Watson 1
CUSHING, Frank H
  Hamilton
CUSHING, George Holmes 5
CUSHING, Grafton Dulany 1
CUSHING, Harry Alonzo 3
CUSHING, Harry Cooke 4
CUSHING, Harvey 1
CUSHING, Henry Platt 1
CUSHING, Herbert 5
  Howard
CUSHING, Herbert Lewis 9
CUSHING, Howard 1
  Gardiner
CUSHING, John E. 3
CUSHING, John Pearsons 1
CUSHING, John Perkins H
CUSHING, John Thayer 1
CUSHING, Luther Stearns H
CUSHING, Oscar K. 2

CUSHING, Cardinal 5
  Richard
CUSHING, Samuel Tobey 1
CUSHING, Stephen S. 3
CUSHING, Thomas H
CUSHING, William H
CUSHING, William Barker 1
CUSHING, William Erastus 1
CUSHING, William Lee 1
CUSHMAN, Allerton 1
  Seward
CUSHMAN, Arlon 3
  Vannevar
CUSHMAN, Austin 1
  Sprague
CUSHMAN, Austin 7
  Thomas
CUSHMAN, Beulah 4
CUSHMAN, Charlotte H
  Saunders
CUSHMAN, Clarissa White 8
  Fairchild
CUSHMAN, Edward 1
  Everett
CUSHMAN, Edward L. 10
CUSHMAN, Francis W. 1
CUSHMAN, Frank 3
CUSHMAN, George Hewitt 1
CUSHMAN, Henry W. 4
CUSHMAN, Herbert Ernest 4
CUSHMAN, Horace O. 5
CUSHMAN, John Paine H
CUSHMAN, Joseph 2
  Augustine
CUSHMAN, Joshua H
CUSHMAN, Lewis Arthur 4
CUSHMAN, Martelle 9
  Loreen
CUSHMAN, Pauline H
CUSHMAN, Ralph 4
  Spaulding
CUSHMAN, Robert H
CUSHMAN, Robert 5
  Eugene
CUSHMAN, Robert 8
  Everton, Jr.
CUSHMAN, Samuel H
CUSHMAN, Susan Webb H
CUSHMAN, William 4
  Michael
CUSHWA, Charles B. 6
CUSICK, James Francis 6
CUSTER, Elizabeth Bacon 1
CUSTER, George H
  Armstrong
CUSTER, Omer Nixon 2
CUSTIS, George H
  Washington Parke
CUSTIS, John Trevor 2
CUSTIS, Marvin A. 3
CUSTIS, Vanderveer 4
CUSUMANO, Stefano 6
CUSUMANO, Stefano 7
CUTBUSH, James H
CUTCHEON, Byron M. 1
CUTCHEON, Franklin W. 1
  M.
CUTHBERT, Alfred H
CUTHBERT, Frederick 7
  Alexander
CUTHBERT, John Alfred H
CUTHBERT, Lucius 1
  Montrose
CUTHBERTSON, George 7
  Raymond
CUTHELL, Chester Welde 2
CUTHRELL, Hugh H. 3
CUTLER, Anna Alice 3
CUTLER, Arthur Hamilton 1
CUTLER, Augustus H
  William
CUTLER, Bertram 3
CUTLER, Carroll H
CUTLER, Charles Frederic 1
CUTLER, Condict Walker 1
CUTLER, Condict Walker, 3
  Jr.
CUTLER, Elbridge Gerry 1
CUTLER, Elliott Carr 2
CUTLER, Everett Alonzo 1
CUTLER, Frederick Morse 2
CUTLER, Garnet Homer 4
CUTLER, George Chalmers 1
CUTLER, Harry Morton 1
CUTLER, Henry Edwin 1
CUTLER, Henry Franklin 4
CUTLER, Ira Eugene 1
CUTLER, Ivan Burton 7
CUTLER, Ivan Burton 8
CUTLER, James Elbert 1
CUTLER, James Goold H
CUTLER, James Gould 4
CUTLER, James Gould 1
CUTLER, John Christopher 1
CUTLER, John W. 3
CUTLER, Joseph A. 7
CUTLER, Lawrence Mark 8

CUTLER, Leland Whitman 7
CUTLER, Lizzie Petit H
CUTLER, Manasseh 10
CUTLER, Max 10
CUTLER, Max H
CUTLER, Otis Henderson 1
CUTLER, Ralph William 1
CUTLER, Richard Schuyler 10
CUTLER, Robert 6
CUTLER, Samuel 8
CUTLER, Timothy H
CUTLER, William Frye 3
CUTLER, William Parker 1
CUTRIGHT, Harold Glen 4
CUTSHALL, Elmer Guy 8
CUTSHALL, H. Walton, 4
  Jr.
CUTTEN, Arthur W. 1
CUTTEN, George Barton 4
CUTTEN, Ruloff Edward 4
CUTTER, Benjamin 1
CUTTER, Charles Ammi 1
CUTTER, Ephraim 1
CUTTER, Mrs. George 5
  Albert (Florence Maxim
  Cutter)
CUTTER, George H
  Washington
CUTTER, Irving Samuel 2
CUTTER, John Ashburton 4
CUTTER, K. K. 4
CUTTER, Robert Kennedy 6
CUTTER, Victor 3
  MacOmber
CUTTER, Victor 4
  MacOmber, Jr.
CUTTER, William Dick 1
CUTTER, William Parker 1
CUTTING, Bronson 1
CUTTING, Charles Sidney 1
CUTTING, Charles Suydam 5
CUTTING, Charles Suydam 7
CUTTING, Churchill 1
  Hunter
CUTTING, Elisabeth 2
  Brown
CUTTING, Francis H
  Brockholst
CUTTING, Fulton 7
CUTTING, Hiram H
  Adolphus
CUTTING, James Ambrose H
CUTTING, John Clifton 8
CUTTING, Mary Stewart 1
CUTTING, R. Fulton 1
CUTTING, Starr Willard 1
CUTTING, W. Bayard 1
CUTTING, Windsor 5
  Cooper
CUTTLE, Francis 5
CUTTS, Charles 4
CUTTS, Elmer Henry 4
CUTTS, Marsena Edgar 1
CUTTS, Richard H
CUTTS, Richard Malcolm 6
CUYLER, Cornelius Cuyler 1
CUYLER, Lewis B(aker) 9
CUYLER, T. De Witt 1
CUYLER, Theodore H
CUYLER, Theodore 1
  Ledyard
CYBIS, Jan 6
CYBULSKI, Waclaw 1
  Boleslaw
CYR, Paul Narcisse 2
CZARNOMSKA, Marie 1
  Elizabeth Josephine
CZECH, Bruno C. 9
CZERNIK, Stanislaw 6
CZERWONKY, Richard 2
  Rudolph

D

DABLON, Claude H
DABNEY, Charles William 2
DABNEY, Edwin 1
DABNEY, Francis Lewis 6
DABNEY, Julia Parker 1
DABNEY, Lewis Stackpole 1
DABNEY, Richard 2
DABNEY, Richard Heath 2
DABNEY, Robert Lewis H
DABNEY, Samuel Gordon 1
DABNEY, Thomas Smith H
  Gregory
DABNEY, Virginius H
DABNEY, William C. 4
DABO, Leon 4
DABO, Theodore Scott 1
DABOLL, Nathan H
DABROWSKI, Joseph H
DACHÉ, Lilly 10
DACK, Gail Monroe 7
DACOSTA, Albert Lloyd 5
DA COSTA, Chalmers 1
DA COSTA, Jacob M. 1

DA COSTA, John C., Jr. 1
DACOSTA, Morton 9
DACSO, Michael Mihaly 6
DACSO, Michael Mihaly 7
DADANT, Camille Pierre 1
DADE, Alexander Lucien 1
DADMUN, Frances May 5
DADOURIAN, Haroutune 6
  Mugurdich
DADY, Sister Mary 8
  Rachael
DAEGER, Albert Thomas 1
DAFOE, Carmie R. 6
DAFOE, John Wesley 2
DAFT, Leo H
DAFT, Leo 4
DA GAMA, Vasco H
DAGER, Forrest Eugene 1
DAGG, John Leadley H
DAGGETT, Aaron Simon 1
DAGGETT, Albert H. 10
DAGGETT, Athern Park 5
DAGGETT, David 1
DAGGETT, Eleanor Nina 7
DAGGETT, Ellsworth 1
DAGGETT, Harriet Spiller 4
DAGGETT, Leonard 2
  Mayhew
DAGGETT, Mabel Potter 1
DAGGETT, Mary Stewart 1
DAGGETT, Napthali H
DAGGETT, Parker 4
  Hayward
DAGGETT, Robert Frost 3
DAGGETT, Stuart 1
DAGGETT, Windsor Pratt 7
DAGGY, Maynard Lee 5
DAGLEY, Stanley 9
DAGNESE, Joseph 9
  Martocci
DAGUE, Paul Bartram 6
DAGWELL, Benjamin 4
  Dunlap
DAHL, Francis W. 5
DAHL, George 4
DAHL, George Leighton 10
DAHL, Gerhard Melvin 3
DAHL, Myrtle Hooper 3
DAHL, Roald 10
DAHL, Roland J(ohn) 7
DAHL, Theodore H. 1
DAHL, Thomas Moore 9
DAHLBERG, Arthur 4
  Chester
DAHLBERG, Bror Gustave 3
DAHLBERG, Edward* 1
DAHLBERG, Edwin 9
  Lennart
DAHLBERG, Edwin 9
  Theodore
DAHLE, Herman B. 3
DAHLE, Herman Bjorn H
DAHLE, Herman Bjorn 1
DAHLERUP, Ioost Baron 2
DAHLGREEN, Charles W. 4
DAHLGREN, B. E. 4
DAHLGREN, John H
  Adolphus Bernard
DAHLGREN, John 10
  Onsgard
DAHLGREN, Lawrence 8
  Jungblom
DAHLGREN, Sarah H
  Madeleine Vinton
DAHLGREN, Ulric 2
DAHLING, Louis 9
  Ferdinand
DAHLMAN, James Charles 1
DAHLQUIST, John E. 6
DAHLQUIST, Thomas 4
  Wilford
DAICOVICIU, Constantin 6
DAIGNEAU, Ralph H. 1
DAILEY, James A. 7
DAILEY, Morris Elmer 1
DAILY, Francis L. 4
DAILY, Harry Parker 7
DAILY, James Wallace 10
DAILY, Joseph Earl 4
DAILY, Samuel Gordon H
DAINE, Robert 3
DAINES, Lyman Luther 2
DAINGERFIELD, Elliott 1
DAINGERFIELD, Foxhall 1
  Alexander
DAINS, Frank Burnett 2
DAISH, John Broughton 1
DAISLEY, Robert Henry 4
DAKAN, Everett LeRoy 8
DAKE, Charles 1
DAKE, Charles Laurence 1
DAKIN, Edwin Franden 5
DAKIN, Henry Drysdale 3
DAKIN, Roger 1
DAKINS, John Gordon 4
DALAND, Judson 1
DALAND, William Clifton 1

DALBEY, Josiah T. 4
DALBY, Zachary Lewis 5
DALE, Alan 1
DALE, Albert Ennis 3
DALE, Chester 4
DALE, Coudoashia Bernice 5
  Watts (Mrs. Luther W.
  Dale)
DALE, Edward Everett 5
DALE, Essie Rock 6
DALE, Frank 1
DALE, Harrison Clifford 7
DALE, Harry Howard 1
DALE, Sir Henry Hallett 5
DALE, James G. 8
DALE, James Wilkinson 1
DALE, Nelson Clark 4
DALE, Paul Newton 7
DALE, Porter Hinman 1
DALE, Richard H
DALE, Samuel H
DALE, Thomas H
DALE, Thomas Henry 1
DALE, Thomas Nelson 1
DALE, Warren Jefferson 4
D'ALELIO, Gaetano 7
  Francis
D'ALESANDRO, Thomas, 9
  Jr.
DALESIO, Carmine 1
DALEY, Arthur John 6
DALEY, Edmund Leo 7
DALEY, John F. 4
DALEY, John Joseph, Jr. 7
  (Bud)
DALEY, John Phillips 4
DALEY, Joseph T. 8
DALEY, Joseph T. 9
DALEY, Richard Joseph 7
DALEY, Robert Morris 3
DALEY, William Raymond 5
DALGETY, George S. 7
DALGLEISH, Oakley 4
  Hedley
DALI, Salvador 8
DALI, Salvador 9
DALL, Caroline Healey 4
DALL, William Healey 1
DALLAPICCOLA, Luigi 6
DALLAS, Alexander James H
DALLAS, Charles Donald 3
DALLAS, George Mifflin H
DALLAS, George Mifflin 4
DALLAS, Jacob A. H
DALLAS, John Thomson 4
DALLAS, Trevanion 4
  Barlow
DALLA VALLE, Joseph 3
  Maria
DALLDORF, Gilbert 7
DALLENBACH, Karl M. 5
DALLIN, Cyrus Edwin 2
DALLIN, David Julievich 4
DALLIS, Nicholas Peter 10
DALLMAN, Vincent Y. 4
DALLMANN, William 3
DALLSTREAM, Andrew 4
  John
DALMAU, Edward 10
  Martinez
DALMORES, Charles 1
DALRYMPLE, Louis 1
DALRYMPLE, Sherman 8
  Harrison
DALRYMPLE, William 1
  Haddock
DALSIMER, Philip T. 6
DALSIMER, Samuel 5
DALSTROM, Oscar 5
  Frederick
DALTON, Albert Clayton 5
DALTON, Carter 7
DALTON, Dorothy Upjohn 8
DALTON, Harry Lee 10
DALTON, Henry George 1
DALTON, James L. 2
DALTON, John Call H
DALTON, John Henry 6
DALTON, John 5
  M(ontgomery)
DALTON, John Nichols 9
DALTON, Joseph N. 4
DALTON, Marshall 7
  Bertrand
DALTON, Mary Louise 1
DALTON, Robert H
DALTON, Sidna Poage 4
DALTON, Ted 10
DALTON, Test 2
DALTON, Tristram H
DALTON, Van Broadus 7
DALTON, W. R. Inge 1
DALTON, William 1
DALY, Arnold 1
DALY, Augustin 1
DALY, Brenton L. 3
DALY, Caroll John 3

DALY, Sister Cecilia 5
DALY, Charles Frederick 1
DALY, Charles Patrick 1
DALY, David 6
DALY, E. A. 9
DALY, Edward C. 4
DALY, Edward James 3
DALY, Edward Joseph 8
DALY, Edwin King 3
DALY, George Joseph 7
DALY, Howard J., Sr. 4
DALY, Ivan de Burgh 6
DALY, J. Burrwood 1
DALY, J. J. 2
DALY, James 7
DALY, John Charles, Jr. 10
DALY, John Fidlar 5
DALY, John Francis 6
DALY, John J. 4
DALY, John Wallace 4
DALY, Joseph Francis 1
DALY, Kay Frances 6
DALY, Leo Anthony 8
DALY, Lloyd William 10
DALY, Marcus 1
DALY, Reginald Aldworth 3
DALY, Thomas Augustine 2
DALY, Thomas Francis 10
DALY, William Barry 2
DALY, William D. 1
DALY, William Jerome, Jr. 7
DALZELL, John 1
DALZELL, Lloyd Howland 4
DALZELL, Robert Duff 2
DALZELL, Robert M. H
DALZELL, William Sage 1
DAM, Carl Peter Henrik 2
DAM, Henry Jackson Wells 1
DAMBACH, Charles Arthur 5
DAME, Elizabeth L. 5
DAME, Frank Libby 1
DAME, Harriet Patience 1
DAME, J. Frank 5
DAME, Lawrence 8
DAMESHEK, William 5
DAMIANO, Celestine Joseph 4
DAMIANOV, Georgi 3
DAMM, Henry Christian Augustus 1
DAMM, Walter J. 4
DAMMANN, John Francis 4
DAMMANN, Milton 4
DAMMANN, Richard Weil 10
DAMMANN, Theodore 3
DAMMIN, Gustave John 10
DAMON, Alexander Martin 1
DAMON, Alonzo Willard 1
DAMON, Cathryn 9
DAMON, Frank Hardy 5
DAMON, George Alfred 1
DAMON, Howard Franklin H
DAMON, Lindsay Todd 1
DAMON, Mason Orne 8
DAMON, Norman Clare 5
DAMON, Ralph Shepard 3
DAMON, Richard Winslow 10
DAMON, Robert Hosken 3
DAMON, S(amuel) Foster 5
DAMON, Samuel Mills 1
DAMON, Terry Allen 9
DAMON, William Emerson 1
D'AMOURS, Ernest R. 4
DAMPIER, Joseph Henry 9
DAMRELL, William Shapleigh H
DAMROSCH, Frank Heino 1
DAMROSCH, Leopold H
DAMROSCH, Walter Johannes 3
DANA, Amasa H
DANA, Charles Anderson H
DANA, Charles Anderson 6
DANA, Charles Edmund 1
DANA, Charles Loomis 1
DANA, Edward 9
DANA, Edward Salisbury 1
DANA, Floyd G. 4
DANA, Francis H
DANA, Francis E. 1
DANA, Frank M. 5
DANA, Harvey Eugene 2
DANA, Henry Wadsworth Longfellow 3
DANA, Israel Thorndike 1
DANA, James H
DANA, James Dwight H
DANA, James Dwight 3
DANA, James Freeman H
DANA, John Cotton 1
DANA, John Fessenden 4
DANA, Judah H
DANA, Lynn Boardman 4
DANA, Marshall Newport 7
DANA, Marvin 4
DANA, Myron T. 4

DANA, Napoleon Jackson Tecumseh 1
DANA, Paul 1
DANA, Richard H
DANA, Richard Henry* H
DANA, Richard Henry 1
DANA, Richard Henry 8
DANA, Richard Turner 1
DANA, Samuel H
DANA, Samuel Luther 4
DANA, Samuel Trask 7
DANA, Samuel Whittelsey 1
DANA, Stephen Winchester 1
DANA, William Franklin 1
DANA, William Henry 1
DANA, William Parsons Winchester 1
DANAHER, John Anthony 10
DANBY, John Blench 8
DANCEL, Christian H
DANCER, H. M. 3
DANCKAERTS, Jasper 1
DANCY, Alexander Brown 1
D'ANDREA, Albert Philip 10
DANDRIDGE, Danske 4
DANDRIDGE, Dorothy 4
DANDRIDGE, N. Pendleton 1
DANDY, George Brown 1
DANDY, John Percy 6
DANDY, Walter Edward 2
DANE, Ernest Blaney 2
DANE, Joseph 1
DANE, Nathan H
DANE, Nathan, II 7
DANE, Walter Alden 5
DANE, Walter Alden 7
DANELY, Alfred Marion 4
DANENBERG, Emil Charles 8
DANENBERG, Leigh 7
DANENHOWER, John Wilson H
DANEY, Eugene 2
DANFORD, Lorenzo 1
DANFORD, Robert Melville 6
DANFORTH, Charles H
DANFORTH, Charles H. 5
DANFORTH, Charles Haskell 7
DANFORTH, David Newton 10
DANFORTH, Donald 6
DANFORTH, Elliott 1
DANFORTH, George Jonathan 3
DANFORTH, George Washington 4
DANFORTH, Henry Gold 1
DANFORTH, Isaac Newton 1
DANFORTH, Joseph D. 8
DANFORTH, Joshua Noble H
DANFORTH, Loomis Le Grand 4
DANFORTH, Moseley Isaac H
DANFORTH, Thomas H
DANFORTH, William H. 3
DANGAIX, William Joseph 2
D'ANGELO, Louis 8
DANGERFIELD, George 9
DANGERFIELD, Royden (James) 6
DANHOF, John James 6
DANHOF, Ralph John 5
DANIEL, Charles Ezra 4
DANIEL, Charles William 5
DANIEL, Cullen Coleman 4
DANIEL, David R. 4
DANIEL, Ferdinand 1
DANIEL, Hawthorne 8
DANIEL, Henry 1
DANIEL, J. McTyeire 5
DANIEL, James Martin, Jr. 7
DANIEL, Jaquelin James 10
DANIEL, John 2
DANIEL, John Franklin 2
DANIEL, John Laurence 7
DANIEL, John Moncure 1
DANIEL, John Reeves Jones H
DANIEL, John Warwick 1
DANIEL, Lewis C. 3
DANIEL, Peter Vivian H
DANIEL, Price, Sr. 9
DANIEL, Richard Potts 5
DANIEL, Robert Edwin 10
DANIEL, Robert Norman 3
DANIEL, Robert Prentiss 4
DANIEL, Rollin Augustus, Jr. 7
DANIEL, Ruby Kathryn 7
DANIEL, Walter Fletcher 6

DANIELIAN, Noobar Retheos 6
DANIELIAN, Noobar Rethesos 7
DANIELL, Francis Raymond 5
DANIELL, Moses Grant 1
DANIELLS, Arthur Grosvenor 2
DANIELLS, William Willard 1
DANIEL-ROPS, Henry 4
DANIELS, Arthur Hill 1
DANIELS, Arthur Simpson 4
DANIELS, Benjamin 3
DANIELS, Charles H
DANIELS, Charles Herbert 1
DANIELS, Charles Nelson 1
DANIELS, Clarence White 2
DANIELS, Cora Linn 4
DANIELS, Dominick Vincent 9
DANIELS, Draper 8
DANIELS, Elmer Harland 5
DANIELS, Farrington 5
DANIELS, Francis Cummings 3
DANIELS, Francis Potter 2
DANIELS, Frank 1
DANIELS, Frank Arthur 9
DANIELS, Fred Harold 8
DANIELS, Fred Harris 1
DANIELS, George Henry 1
DANIELS, Harold Kennan 4
DANIELS, Henry H. 3
DANIELS, John 3
DANIELS, John Karl 5
DANIELS, Jonathan Worth 8
DANIELS, Joseph 7
DANIELS, Joseph J. 5
DANIELS, Joseph Leonard 1
DANIELS, Josephus 2
DANIELS, Josephus, Jr. 4
DANIELS, Lilla Wood 4
DANIELS, Mark (Roy) 1
DANIELS, Milton J. 2
DANIELS, William S. 1
DANIELS, Winthrop More 2
DANIELS, Worth Bagley 7
DANIELSON, Clarence 3
DANIELSON, Gordon Charles 8
DANIELSON, Jacques 3
DANIELSON, John Oswald 8
DANIELSON, Reuben Gustaf 3
DANIELSON, Richard Ely 3
DANIELSON, Stig 7
DANIELSON, Wilmot Alfred 4
DANILEVICIUS, Zenonas 8
DANIS, Peter Godfrey 9
DANKMEYER, Theodore Rognald 7
DANLEY, William L. 4
DANN, Alexander William 4
DANN, Hollis Ellsworth 1
DANNAT, William T. 1
DANNAY, Frederic 8
DANNE, Gilbert Leonard 7
DANNELLY, Clarence Moore 8
DANNELLY, John Milton 1
DANNENBAUM, Walter 4
DANNER, Arthur Vincent 5
DANNER, Harris Leslie 1
DANNER, Joel Buchanan H
DANNER, Max Smith 9
DANNER, Peter C. 1
DANNREUTHER, Gustav H
DANNREUTHER, Gustav 4
DANNREUTHER, Walter T. 3
DANOWSKI, Thaddeus Stanley 9
DANSINGBERG, Paul 2
DANTON, George Henry 6
D'ANTONI, Joseph Steven 7
D'ANTONI, Salvador 3
DANTZIG, Henry Poincare 6
DANTZIG, Tobias 7
DANTZLER, Lehre L(ivingston) 6
DANZANSKY, Joseph Baer 7
DANZIGER, Frederick Simon 7
DANZIGER, Henry 1
DA PONTE, Lorenzo H
DA PONTE, Lorenzo Brooke 3
DAPPING, William Osborne 1
DARBAKER, James Mateer 10

D'ARBELOFF, Dimitri Vladimir 9
DARBY, Ada Claire 3
DARBY, Alfred Ellery 9
DARBY, Edwin Tyler 1
DARBY, Ezra H
DARBY, Harry 9
DARBY, John* H
DARBY, John Eaton 1
DARBY, John Fletcher H
DARBY, John Frederick 3
DARBY, William H
DARBY, William Johnson 1
DARBY, William Lambert 3
DARBYSHIRE, Leonard 4
DARCY, Donald 9
D'ARCY, Martin Cyril 7
DARCY, Thomas Francis, Jr. 10
D'ARCY, William Cheever 2
DARDEN, Colgate Whitehad, Jr. 7
DARDEN, Thomas Francis 2
DARE, Virginia H
D'AREZZO, Joseph Paul 7
DARGAN, Edmond Strother H
DARGAN, Edwin Charles 5
DARGAN, Edwin Preston 1
DARGAN, Henry McCune 5
DARGAN, Olive Tilford 5
DARGAVEL, John William 4
DARGEON, Harold William 5
DARGUE, Herbert Arthur 2
DARGUSCH, Carlton Spencer 6
DARGUSCH, Carlton Spencer 8
DARIN, Bobby 6
D'ARISTA, Robert 9
DARKE, William H
DARKEN, Lawrence Stamper 7
DARKENWALD, Gordon Gerald 4
DARLEY, Felix Octavius Carr H
DARLEY, Jane Cooper H
DARLEY, John Gordon 10
DARLEY, Ward 7
DARLING, Arthur Beebe 5
DARLING, Arthur Burr 5
DARLING, C. Coburn 4
DARLING, Charles Douglas 9
DARLING, Charles Ellett 6
DARLING, Charles Hial 2
DARLING, Charles Kimball 1
DARLING, Charles William 1
DARLING, Chester Arthur 6
DARLING, C(hester) Coburn 8
DARLING, Edward 6
DARLING, Flora Adams 1
DARLING, Henry H
DARLING, Herbert Franklin 5
DARLING, Jay Norwood 4
DARLING, John Augustus 5
DARLING, Joseph Robinson 5
DARLING, Louis, Jr. 4
DARLING, Mary Greenleaf 4
DARLING, Mason Cook H
DARLING, Philip Grenville 6
DARLING, Robert Ensign 5
DARLING, Samuel Taylor 1
DARLING, Sid L(ouis) 5
DARLING, Stephen Foster 10
DARLING, William Augustus H
DARLING, William Lafayette 1
DARLINGTON, Charles Francis 1
DARLINGTON, Charles Francis, Jr. 9
DARLINGTON, Charles Goodliffe 4
DARLINGTON, Charles Joseph 4
DARLINGTON, Edward H
DARLINGTON, Frederick 3
DARLINGTON, Henry 3
DARLINGTON, Isaac H
DARLINGTON, James Henry 1
DARLINGTON, Joseph James 1
DARLINGTON, Thomas 1
DARLINGTON, Thomas 2
DARLINGTON, Urban Valentine W. 3

DARLINGTON, William H
DARLOW, Arthur Edward 4
DARMS, John Martin George 2
DARNALL, Carl Rogers 1
DARNALL, Marcy Bradshaw 4
DARNALL, William Edgar 1
DARNELL, Henry Faulkner 1
DARNELL, Linda 4
DARNTON, Eleanor Choate 5
DARR, Earl A. 4
DARR, Edward A. 3
DARR, John Whittier 5
DARR, Leslie Rogers 7
DARR, Loren Robert 5
DARRACH, William 2
DARRAGH, Ann Sophia Towne H
DARRAGH, Archibald Bard 4
DARRAGH, Cornelius H
DARRAH, David Harley 7
DARRAH, Thomas W. 3
DARRAH, William Lee 6
DARRELL, Robert Donaldson 9
DARRIN, Erwin N. 4
DARROW, Chester William 5
DARROW, Clarence 1
DARROW, Daniel Cady 4
DARROW, George McMillan 8
DARROW, George Potter 2
DARROW, Karl Kelchner 9
DARROW, Richard William 7
DARSEY, Joseph Frederick 9
DARSIE, Darsie Lloyd 4
DARSIE, Marvin Lloyd 1
DARST, Joseph Miltenberger 3
DARST, Thomas Campbell 1
DART, Carlton Rollin 1
DART, Donald Edward 7
DART, Edward Dupaquier 4
DART, Henry P., Jr. 9
DART, Henry Plauche 1
DART, Justin 8
DART, Raymond Arthur 9
DART, Raymond Osborne 6
DARTON, Nelson Horatio 2
DARVAS, Lili 1
D'ARVILLE, Camille 1
DARWIN, Charles Carlyle 1
DARWIN, Charles Galton 4
DARWIN, Gertrude Bascom 1
DARWIN, Sir Robin (Robert Vere Darwin) 6
DAS, Rajani Kanta 6
DAS, Taraknath 3
D'ASCENZO, Nicola 3
DASCH, George 2
DASHER, Benjamin Joseph 5
DASHER, Charles Lanier, Jr. 5
DASHER, George Franklin 7
DASHIELL, Alfred Sheppard 5
DASHIELL, John Frederick 6
DASHIELL, Paul Joseph 3
DASHIELL, William Robert 1
DA SILVA, Howard 9
DASKAM, Walter Duryee 1
DASPIT, Lawrence Randall 7
DATER, Alfred Warner 1
DATES, Henry Baldwin 5
DATTNER, Bernhard 3
DAU, Frederick Jensen 7
DAU, William Herman Theodore 2
DAUB, Guido Herman 8
DAUBER, Clarence Andrew 7
DAUBIN, Fredland Allen 3
DAUERTY, James Shackelford 8
DAUGETTE, Clarence William 2
DAUGHERTY, Arthur Cornelius 5
DAUGHERTY, Carroll Roop 9
DAUGHERTY, Charles M. 1
DAUGHERTY, Duncan W(ilmer) 5
DAUGHERTY, Edgar Fay 3
DAUGHERTY, Harry Kerr 3
DAUGHERTY, Harry Micajah 1
DAUGHERTY, James Alexander 4

DAUGHERTY, James Henry 6
DAUGHERTY, Jerome 4
DAUGHERTY, Lewis Sylvester 1
DAUGHERTY, Robert Long 7
DAUGHTERS, Freeman 3
DAUGHTON, Ralph Hunter 7
D'AULAIRE, Ingri (Mrs. Edgar Parin D'Aulaire) 7
DAULTON, Agnes McClelland 2
DAULTON, George 1
DAUMONT, Simon Francois H
D'AUNOY, Rigney 1
DAUPHIN, Claude Le Grand Maria Eugene 7
DAUTEN, Carl Anton 7
DAUTERMAN, Carl Christian 10
DAUZVARDIS, Petras Paulius 5
DAVANT, Thomas S. 5
DAVEE, Henry A. 3
DAVEE, Thomas H
DAVEIS, Charles Stewart H
DAVEISS, Joseph Hamilton H
DAVELER, Erle Victor 3
DAVENPORT, Basil 4
DAVENPORT, Bennett Franklin 1
DAVENPORT, Charles Benedict 2
DAVENPORT, Edward Loomis H
DAVENPORT, Erwin R. 4
DAVENPORT, Eugene 1
DAVENPORT, Fanny Lily Gypsy H
DAVENPORT, Frances Gardiner 1
DAVENPORT, Franklin H
DAVENPORT, Fred Marshall 8
DAVENPORT, Frederick M. 3
DAVENPORT, Frederick Parker 1
DAVENPORT, George H
DAVENPORT, George Edward 1
DAVENPORT, George William 5
DAVENPORT, Gideon I. 4
DAVENPORT, Henry Joralemon 4
DAVENPORT, Herbert Joseph 1
DAVENPORT, Holton 4
DAVENPORT, Homer Calvin 1
DAVENPORT, Ira 1
DAVENPORT, Ira Erastus H
DAVENPORT, Ira Erastus 4
DAVENPORT, James* H
DAVENPORT, James Henry 1
DAVENPORT, James Leroy 1
DAVENPORT, James Sanford 1
DAVENPORT, John* H
DAVENPORT, John Gaylord 1
DAVENPORT, John Sidney, III 8
DAVENPORT, Leroy Benjamin 4
DAVENPORT, Louis M. 5
DAVENPORT, Louise Strong 9
DAVENPORT, R. Briggs 1
DAVENPORT, Raymond Ripley 7
DAVENPORT, Richard Graham 1
DAVENPORT, Roy Leonard 4
DAVENPORT, Russell 3
DAVENPORT, Samuel Arza 4
DAVENPORT, Stanley Woodward 4
DAVENPORT, Thomas* H
DAVENPORT, Walter H
DAVENPORT, Walter Rice 2
DAVENPORT, William Henry Harrison H
DAVES, Delmer Lawrence 7
DAVES, Jessica 6
DAVEY, James Charles 1
DAVEY, John 1
DAVEY, Martin L. 2
DAVEY, Randall 4

DAVEY, Robert C. 1
DAVEY, Wheeler P. 3
D'AVEZAC, Auguste Genevieve Valentin H
DAVID, Bert Alison 7
DAVID, Charles Wendell 7
DAVID, Donald Kirk 10
DAVID, Edward M. 9
DAVID, Edward Wandell 4
DAVID, Henry 8
DAVID, John Baptist Mary H
DAVID, Vernon Cyrenius 4
DAVID, William M(orris) 7
DAVIDGE, John Beale H
DAVIDGE, William Pleater H
DAVIDOFF, Leo Marx 6
DAVIDOW, H. M. 3
DAVIDS, James 8
DAVIDS, Mark 8
DAVIDS, Richard Carlyle 8
DAVIDSOHN, Israel 7
DAVIDSON, Alexander Caldwell H
DAVIDSON, Alfred James 1
DAVIDSON, Anstruther 1
DAVIDSON, Arnold 4
DAVIDSON, Arthur Ole 7
DAVIDSON, Augustus Cleveland 1
DAVIDSON, Benjamin 1
DAVIDSON, Carter 4
DAVIDSON, Charles 1
DAVIDSON, David J. 2
DAVIDSON, David W. 7
DAVIDSON, De Witt A. 6
DAVIDSON, Donald (Grady) 5
DAVIDSON, Donald Miner 4
DAVIDSON, Edwin Lee 1
DAVIDSON, George 4
DAVIDSON, George 4
DAVIDSON, George A. 1
DAVIDSON, Hannah Amelia 1
DAVIDSON, Harlan Page 1
DAVIDSON, Harold Prescott 7
DAVIDSON, Henry Alexander 6
DAVIDSON, Herbert Coolidge 7
DAVIDSON, Herbert Marc 9
DAVIDSON, Howard Calhoun 8
DAVIDSON, Ian Douglas 10
DAVIDSON, Irville Fay 1
DAVIDSON, Irwin Delmore 9
DAVIDSON, Israel 1
DAVIDSON, J. Brownlee 3
DAVIDSON, J. Edward 7
DAVIDSON, James Edward 2
DAVIDSON, James Edward 3
DAVIDSON, James Hamilton 3
DAVIDSON, James Henry 1
DAVIDSON, James Joseph, Jr. 10
DAVIDSON, James O. 1
DAVIDSON, James Wheeler 1
DAVIDSON, James Wood 1
DAVIDSON, Jo 3
DAVIDSON, John Frederick 9
DAVIDSON, John Wynn H
DAVIDSON, Joseph G. 5
DAVIDSON, J(oseph) LeRoy 8
DAVIDSON, Joseph Quentin 5
DAVIDSON, Laura Lee 5
DAVIDSON, Leroy 10
DAVIDSON, Levette Jay 3
DAVIDSON, Loucretia Isobel 5
DAVIDSON, Louis Rogers 1
DAVIDSON, Lucretia Maria H
DAVIDSON, Lyal Ament 3
DAVIDSON, Margaret Miller H
DAVIDSON, Marshall Bowman 10
DAVIDSON, Mary Blossom (Mrs. Charles S. Davidson) 5
DAVIDSON, Maurice P. 3
DAVIDSON, Rita Charmatz 8
DAVIDSON, Robert* H
DAVIDSON, Robert James 1
DAVIDSON, Roy Elton 4
DAVIDSON, Royal Page 2

DAVIDSON, Samuel Presley 1
DAVIDSON, Sidney Wetmore 7
DAVIDSON, Theodore Fulton 1
DAVIDSON, Thomas 1
DAVIDSON, Thomas Green H
DAVIDSON, Thomas Whitfield 6
DAVIDSON, Thomas William 4
DAVIDSON, Vanda Arthur, Jr. 9
DAVIDSON, Victor H. 3
DAVIDSON, Ward Follett 4
DAVIDSON, Wilbur Leroy 1
DAVIDSON, William 3
DAVIDSON, William Andrew 3
DAVIDSON, William Lee H
DAVIDSON, William Mehard 1
DAVID-WEILL, Pierre Sylvain Desire Gerard 6
DAVIE, Eugenie Mary (Mrs. Preston Davie) 7
DAVIE, Maurice R. 4
DAVIE, Preston 6
DAVIE, William Richardson H
DAVIES, Acton 1
DAVIES, Arthur B. 1
DAVIES, Arthur Ernest 4
DAVIES, Arthur Powell 3
DAVIES, Caroline Stodder 4
DAVIES, Charles 1
DAVIES, Charles Frederick H
DAVIES, Clarence Ebenezer 1
DAVIES, David Charles 1
DAVIES, David Lloyd 9
DAVIES, David William 8
DAVIES, Edward 4
DAVIES, Ernest Coulter 4
DAVIES, George Reginald 5
DAVIES, Harry William 3
DAVIES, Henry Eugene 1
DAVIES, Hester Rogers 8
DAVIES, Hywel 1
DAVIES, Isaiah 1
DAVIES, James 1
DAVIES, James William Frederick 4
DAVIES, John Newton 6
DAVIES, John Rumsey 1
DAVIES, John Sherrard 10
DAVIES, John Vipond 1
DAVIES, Joseph Edward 3
DAVIES, Julian Tappan 1
DAVIES, Julien Townsend 7
DAVIES, Marion 4
DAVIES, Martin 6
DAVIES, Paul Lewis 6
DAVIES, Paul Lewis 7
DAVIES, Percy Albert 4
DAVIES, Ralph Kenneth 10
DAVIES, Ray 7
DAVIES, Rhys 7
DAVIES, Robert Holborn 4
DAVIES, Rodger Paul 6
DAVIES, Samuel 1
DAVIES, Stanley Powell 9
DAVIES, Thomas Frederick* 1
DAVIES, Thomas Stephen 5
DAVIES, Thurston Jynkins 4
DAVIES, Valentine 4
DAVIES, Walter L. J. 8
DAVIES, William Gilbert 1
DAVIES, William Preston 2
DAVIES, William Rupert 4
DAVIES, William Walter 1
DAVIESS, Maria Thompson 1
D'AVIGDOR-GOLDSMI-D, Henry Joseph 7
DAVILA, Carlos 3
DAVILA, Céleo 6
DAVILA, Charles Alexander 4
DAVILA, Charles Alexander 7
DAVIN, John Wysor 2
DAVIS, A. M. 5
DAVIS, Abel 1
DAVIS, Achilles Edward 4
DAVIS, Addison D. 4
DAVIS, Adelle (Mrs. Frank V. Sieglinger) 6
DAVIS, Albert Gould 1
DAVIS, Alexander Jackson H
DAVIS, Alexander MacDonald 4
DAVIS, Alexander Mathews H
DAVIS, Alfred Cookman 2

DAVIS, Allison 8
DAVIS, Alton Frank 3
DAVIS, Alva Raymond 4
DAVIS, Amos H
DAVIS, Andrew Jay 3
DAVIS, Andrew McFarland 1
DAVIS, Arlene 4
DAVIS, Arlene (Mrs. Max T. Davies) 5
DAVIS, Arnold Lyman 1
DAVIS, Arthur Cayley 4
DAVIS, Arthur Kyle 3
DAVIS, Arthur Marshall 4
DAVIS, Arthur Newton 5
DAVIS, Arthur Powell 4
DAVIS, Arthur Vining 4
DAVIS, Arthur Vining 5
DAVIS, Arthur William 2
DAVIS, Asa Barnes 1
DAVIS, Beale 1
DAVIS, Benjamin Bernard 7
DAVIS, Benjamin Marshall 4
DAVIS, Benson Willis 3
DAVIS, Bergen 3
DAVIS, Bernard George 5
DAVIS, Bert Byron 2
DAVIS, Bette Ruth Elizabeth 10
DAVIS, Boothe Colwell 1
DAVIS, Brad 10
DAVIS, Bradley Moore 3
DAVIS, Brinton Beauregard 5
DAVIS, Bruce Gregory 6
DAVIS, Byron Bennett 1
DAVIS, Calvin Olin 3
DAVIS, Cameron Josiah 3
DAVIS, Carl Braden 3
DAVIS, Carlisle R. 4
DAVIS, Carroll Melvin 1
DAVIS, Cecil Clark 3
DAVIS, Charles Albert 1
DAVIS, Charles B. 2
DAVIS, Charles Belmont 1
DAVIS, Charles Edward 1
DAVIS, Charles Ernest, Jr. 5
DAVIS, Charles Gilbert 1
DAVIS, Charles Harold 1
DAVIS, Charles Henry H
DAVIS, Charles Henry 1
DAVIS, Charles Henry Stanley 1
DAVIS, Charles Hubbard 6
DAVIS, Charles Hubbard 7
DAVIS, Charles K. 4
DAVIS, Charles Lukens 1
DAVIS, Charles Malcolm 7
DAVIS, Charles Moler 5
DAVIS, Charles Palmer 1
DAVIS, Charles Russell 1
DAVIS, Charles Strout 3
DAVIS, Charles Thornton 4
DAVIS, Charles Wellington H
DAVIS, Chester Charles 6
DAVIS, Chester R. 4
DAVIS, Clarence Alba 6
DAVIS, Claude Jefferson 5
DAVIS, Clifford 5
DAVIS, Clinton Wildes 3
DAVIS, Clyde Brion 4
DAVIS, Curtis Wheeler 9
DAVIS, Curtis Woodward 8
DAVIS, Cushman Kellogg 1
DAVIS, D. Dwight 4
DAVIS, Daniel Franklin H
DAVIS, Darrell Haug 4
DAVIS, Darrey Adkins 9
DAVIS, David H
DAVIS, David Jackson 1
DAVIS, David John 3
DAVIS, David Lyle 7
DAVIS, David William 5
DAVIS, Deane Chandler 10
DAVIS, Don A(bner) 7
DAVIS, Donald Derby 4
DAVIS, Donald Goodwin, Jr. 7
DAVIS, Donald W. 3
DAVIS, Dwight Filley 2
DAVIS, E. Asbury 3
DAVIS, E. Asbury 5
DAVIS, E. Gorton 1
DAVIS, Earl Fred 4
DAVIS, Earl J. 1
DAVIS, Eddie 9
DAVIS, Edith Smith 1
DAVIS, Edmund Jackson H
DAVIS, Edward 1
DAVIS, Edward C. P. 3
DAVIS, Edward E. 5
DAVIS, Edward Everett 3
DAVIS, Edward Parker 4
DAVIS, Edward Wilson 8
DAVIS, Edwin 4
DAVIS, Edwin G. 5
DAVIS, Edwin Hamilton H

DAVIS, Edwin Weyerhaeuser 4
DAVIS, Effa Vetina 1
DAVIS, Ellery Williams 1
DAVIS, Elmer 3
DAVIS, Elmer Joseph 5
DAVIS, Emerson H
DAVIS, Eugene W. 8
DAVIS, Ewin Lamar 2
DAVIS, Fay 2
DAVIS, Floyd Arnold 8
DAVIS, Mrs. Foster Bowdle 7
DAVIS, Francis A. 10
DAVIS, Francis Breese, Jr. 4
DAVIS, Frank, Jr. 4
DAVIS, Frank De Montibirt 4
DAVIS, Frank Garfield 3
DAVIS, Frank Parker 3
DAVIS, Franklin Milton, Jr. 7
DAVIS, Fred Henry 1
DAVIS, Frederick Barton 6
DAVIS, Frederick Henry 1
DAVIS, Garret H
DAVIS, Gaylord 5
DAVIS, Gene Bernard 8
DAVIS, George H
DAVIS, George Arthur 6
DAVIS, George Breckenridge 1
DAVIS, George Burwell 4
DAVIS, George Gilman 1
DAVIS, George H. 3
DAVIS, George Harvey 3
DAVIS, George Philip 9
DAVIS, George Royal 1
DAVIS, George Russell 4
DAVIS, George Samler 1
DAVIS, George Thomas H
DAVIS, George Thompson Brown 5
DAVIS, George Washington 1
DAVIS, George Whitefield 1
DAVIS, George William 8
DAVIS, Gifford 4
DAVIS, Gladys Rockmore 4
DAVIS, Glenn B. 8
DAVIS, Glenn Robert 9
DAVIS, Graham Lee 3
DAVIS, Gwilym George 1
DAVIS, H. L. 4
DAVIS, Hal Charles 7
DAVIS, Hal Strange 3
DAVIS, Hale Virginius 9
DAVIS, Hallam Walker 7
DAVIS, Hallie Flanagan 5
DAVIS, Hamilton Seymour 9
DAVIS, Harold Eugene 4
DAVIS, Harold Thayer 6
DAVIS, Harry 10
DAVIS, Harry Douglas 9
DAVIS, Harry Ellerbe 5
DAVIS, Harry Lyman 3
DAVIS, H(arry) Norman 8
DAVIS, Harry Orville 4
DAVIS, Harry Phillips 1
DAVIS, Harvey Henry 5
DAVIS, Harvey Nathaniel 5
DAVIS, Harwell Goodwin 7
DAVIS, Hassoldt 5
DAVIS, Hayne 5
DAVIS, Helen Clarkson Miller (Mrs. Harvey Nathaniel Davis) 5
DAVIS, Henry H
DAVIS, Henry 4
DAVIS, Henry Edgar 1
DAVIS, Henry Gassaway 1
DAVIS, Henry Gassett 1
DAVIS, Henry Winter H
DAVIS, Herbert Burnham 1
DAVIS, Herbert John 4
DAVIS, Herbert Perry 8
DAVIS, Herbert Spencer 4
DAVIS, Herman S. 1
DAVIS, Horace 1
DAVIS, Howard 4
DAVIS, Howard 7
DAVIS, Howard Clarke 6
DAVIS, Howland Shippen 5
DAVIS, Hugh Orton 5
DAVIS, Ira Cleveland 4
DAVIS, Irving Gilman 1
DAVIS, J. Dewitt 4
DAVIS, J. F. 5
DAVIS, J. Frank 1
DAVIS, J. McCan 1
DAVIS, Jackson 2
DAVIS, Jacob Cunningham H
DAVIS, Jacqueline Marie Vincent (Mrs. Louis Reid Davis) 10
DAVIS, James 1
DAVIS, James Burnam 7
DAVIS, James Burnam 1
DAVIS, James Cox 1
DAVIS, James Curran 8

DENNISTON, Henry Martyn 1
DENNY, Charles Eugene 4
DENNY, Collins 2
DENNY, Collins, Jr. 4
DENNY, Ebenezer
DENNY, Emery Byrd 9
DENNY, Frank Lee 1
DENNY, George Hutcheson 3
DENNY, George Parkman 8
DENNY, George Vernon, Jr. 3
DENNY, Harmar H
DENNY, Harmar Denny 4
DENNY, Harold Norman 2
DENNY, Henry Wadhams 7
DENNY, James W. 5
DENNY, Ludwell 5
DENNY, Reginald Leigh 4
DENNY, Robert H. 3
DENNY-BROWN, Derek Ernest 7
DE NOGALES, Pedro Rafael (y Mendez) 6
DE NORMANDIE, James 1
DE NORMANDIE, Robert L. 3
DE NOYAN, Pierre-jacques Payen H
DENOYELLES, Peter H
DENOYER, L. Philip 4
DENSFORD, Katharine Jane (Mrs. Carl A. Dreves) 8
DENSLOW, Dorothea Henrietta 5
DENSLOW, Herbert McKenzie 2
DENSLOW, John Stedman 9
DENSLOW, Theodore North 7
DENSLOW, William Wallace 1
DENSMORE, Emmet 1
DENSMORE, Frances 3
DENSMORE, Harvey Bruce 6
DENSMORE, Hiram D.
DENSMORE, John B. 3
DENSMORE, John Hopkins 2
DENSON, Nimrod Davis 1
DENSON, Samuel Crawford 1
DENSTEDT, Orville Frederick 6
DENT, Albert Walter 8
DENT, Frederick Rodgers, Jr. 5
DENT, Frederick Tracy H
DENT, George H
DENT, Hawthorne K. 3
DENT, John H(erman) 9
DENT, John K. 8
DENT, John Marshall 6
DENT, L. Bruce 7
DENT, Louis Addison 4
DENT, Louis Linton
DENT, Marmaduke Herbert 1
DENT, Stanley Hubert 1
DENT, William Barton Wade H
DENTLER, Clara Louise (Mrs. William J. Dentler) 8
DENTON, Eugene Kenneth 9
DENTON, George Kirkpatrick
DENTON, J. Furman 5
DENTON, James Clarence 2
DENTON, James Edgar 5
DENTON, James G. 8
DENTON, Lyman Morse 5
DENTON, Minna Caroline 3
DENTON, Willard Kirkpatrick 8
DENTON, Winfield K. 5
DEN UYL, Simon Danker 10
DENVER, James William H
DENVER, Matthew Rombach 3
DENYES, John Russell 1
DE ONATE, Juan H
DE ONIS, Federico 4
DE OTERMEN, Antonio H
DE PADILLA, Juan H
DEPALMA, John T. 9
DE PAOLIS, Alessio 4
DE PARIS, Wilbur 5
DE PAUGHER, Adrien H
DE PAULA GUTIERREZ, Don Francisco 6
DEPAUW, Washington Charles H
DE PENA, Carlos Maria 1

DE PENALOSA BRICENO, Diego Dionsio H
DE PERALTA, Pedro H
DEPEW, Chauncey Mitchell 2
DEPEW, Claude Ira 3
DEPEW, Joseph William 5
DE PEYSTER, Abraham 1
DE PEYSTER, Frederic James 1
DE PEYSTER, John Watts 1
DEPINET, Ned E. 6
DEPONAI, John Martin 1
DE PORTOLA, Gaspar H
DE POUILLY, Jacques Nicholas Bussiere H
DE POURTALES, Louis Francois H
DEPPERMANN, William Herman 5
DE PRIEST, Oscar 3
DE PRIMA, Charles Raymond 10
DEPUE, David A. 1
DEPUTY, Manfred Wolfe 2
DE PUY, William Harrison H
DE QUILLE, Dan H
DERAMUS, William Neal 4
DERAMUS, William Neal, III 10
DERBIGNY, Irving A. 3
DERBIGNY, Pierre Auguste Charles Bourguignon H
DERBY, Ashton Philander 6
DERBY, Donald 5
DERBY, Elias Hasket* H
DERBY, Ethel Roosevelt 9
DERBY, George Horatio H
DERBY, George McClellan 3
DERBY, George Strong 1
DERBY, Jeanette Barr 4
DERBY, Orville Adelbert 4
DERBY, Palmer Portner 9
DERBY, Richard 2
DERBY, Richard 4
DERBY, Samuel Carroll 1
DERBY, Stephen Hasket 2
DERBY, Wilfrid Neville 8
DERCUM, Francis X. 1
DE REMER, John A. 1
DE RESZKE, Edouard 1
DE RESZKE, Jean 2
DERHAM, John P(ickens) 10
DERICK, Clarence George 7
DERICKSON, Donald 4
DERICKSON, Samuel Hoffman
DERIEUX, James Clarkson 7
DERIEUX, Samuel Arthur 1
DE RIVERA, Jose 8
DERLETH, August (William) 5
DERLETH, Charles, Jr. 5
DERN, Alfred L. 2
DERN, George Henry 1
DERN, John 1
DERN, John 8
DERNER, Gordon Frederick
DE ROALDES, Arthur Washington 1
DE ROBURT, Hammer 10
DE ROCHEMONT, Louis Charles 7
DE ROCHEMONT, Richard Guertis 8
DERONDE, Philip 7
DE ROSE, Peter 3
DE ROSSET, Frederick Ancrum
DE ROSSET, Moses John H
DE ROSSET, William Lord 3
DE ROTHSCHILD, Alain James Gustave Jules 8
DE ROUEN, Rene L. 2
DE ROUGEMONT, Denis
DEROULET, Vincent W. 6
DE ROUSSY DE SALES, Raoul 2
DERR, Cyrus George 1
DERR, Homer Munro 5
DERR, Louis 1
DERRICK, Leland Eugene 5
DERRICK, Samuel Melanchthon 5
DERRICK, Sidney Jacob 2
DERRICK, William Sheldon 9
DERRY, Duncan Ramsay 9
DERRY, George Hermann 5
DERSE, Alexander Anthony 4
DERSHEM, Franklin Lewis 1
DERTHICK, Frank A. 4
DERTHICK, Henry J. 5
DERTINGER, Georg 4

DERUJINSKY, Gleb W. 6
DE RUSSY, Isaac Denniston 1
DERWENT, Clarence 3
DERY, D. Geofge 3
DE SAINT EXUPERY, Antoine 2
DE SAINT-MEMIN, Charles Balthazar Jullen Fevret H
DE SALVIO, Alfonso 5
DESANCTIS, Adolph George 4
DE SANTILLANA, Glorgio Diaz 6
DE SAULLES, Charles August Heckscher 5
DE SAUSSURE, Henry William H
DESAUTELS, Pierre G. 7
DE SAUZE, Emile Blais 6
DE SAVITSCH, Eugene Constantine 4
DESBOROUGH, Alma Hinchman 8
DESCHAMPS, Paul 6
DESCHLER, Lewis 7
DE SCHWEINITZ, Edmond Alexander H
DE SCHWEINITZ, Karl 4
DE SCHWEINITZ, Paul 1
DESHA, Joseph H
DESHA, Lucius Junius 7
DESHA, Mary 1
DESHA, Robert H
DESHON, George 1
DE SICA, Vittorio 6
DESIDERIO, Anthony 5
DE SIEYES, Jean 7
DESIMONE, Salvatore Vincent 8
DESJARDINS, Arthur Ulderic 4
DESKEY, Donald 10
DESLOGE, Joseph 5
DE SMET, Pierre Jean H
DESMOND, Alice Curtis 10
DESMOND, Alton Harold 7
DESMOND, Charles S. 9
DESMOND, Daniel Francis 2
DESMOND, Humphrey Joseph 1
DESMOND, John J(oseph), Jr. 8
DESMOND, Johnny Alfred 9
DESMOND, Robert William 9
DESMOND, Thomas Charles 5
DESMOND, Thomas Henry 3
DE SOLLAR, Tenney Cook 4
DE SOTO, Hernando H
DE SOTO, Hernando 1
DESPARD, Clement L. 3
DES PLANCHES, Baron Ed Mayor 4
DES PORTES, Fay Allen 2
D'ESPOSITO, Joshua 3
DESPRADELLE, Constant Desire 1
DESPRES, Emile 5
DESPRES, Maurice Samuel 3
DESRUISSEAUX, Paul 8
DESSAR, Leo Charles 1
DESSAR, Louis Paul 3
DESSES, Jean 5
DESSEZ, Mrs. Elizabeth Richey 6
DESSION, George Hathaway 3
DESSUREAULT, Jean Marie 8
DE ST. AUBIN, Percival Ovide 1
DE ST. DENIS, Louis Juchereau H
DE STEIGUER, Louis Rodolph 2
DESTINN, Emmy 1
DESTLER, Chester McArthur 8
DESTREHAN, John Noel H
DE ST. VRAIN, Ceran De Hault Delassus H
DESVERNINE, Raoul Eugene 4
DE SYLVA, George Gard 3
DE TAKATS, Geza 9
DETCHON, Adelaide 5
DETELS, Martin Paul 5
DETGEN, Edward Joseph 7
DETHMERS, John R. 5
DETLEFSEN, John A. 7
DETMAR, Charles F., Jr. 9
DETMER, Julian Francis 4
DETMOLD, Christian Edward H

DE TOCQUEVILLE, Alexis Henri Maurice Clerel H
DE TONTY, Henry H
DE TORRENTE, Henry 4
DE TOUSARD, Anne Louis H
DETRE, Làszlò 6
DE TREVILLE, Yvonne 3
DETRICK, Jacob Stoll 4
DE TROBRIAND, Regis Denis de Kereden H
DETT, Robert Nathaniel 2
DETWEILER, A(lbert) Henry 5
DETWEILER, Charles Samuel 4
DETWEILER, Frederick German 3
DETWEILER, George H. 3
DETWEILER, Herbert K(nudsen) 7
DETWILER, Frederick Knecht 3
DETWILER, Samuel Randall 3
DETWILER, W. Frank 3
DETZER, Karl 9
DEUEL, Alanson Chase
DEUEL, Harry James, Jr. 3
DEUEL, Thorne
DEUEL, Wallace Rankin 6
DE ULLOA, Antonio H
DEUPREE, John Greer 4
DEUPREE, Richard Redwood 6
DE URSO, James Joseph 6
DE URZAIZ, Luis 10
DEUSING, Murl 8
DEUSSEN, Alexander 4
DEUTSCH, Adolph 6
DEUTSCH, Albert 4
DEUTSCH, Alcuin Henry 2
DEUTSCH, Babette 8
DEUTSCH, Bernard Seymour
DEUTSCH, Eberhard Paul 7
DEUTSCH, George Carl 10
DEUTSCH, Gotthard 1
DEUTSCH, Henry 3
DEUTSCH, Monroe Emanuel 3
DEUTSCHER, Isaac 5
DEVALERA, Eamon 6
DEVAN, Harriet Beecher Scoville 5
DEVANE, Dozier A(dolphus) 7
DE VANE, William Clyde 4
DEVANEY, John Patrick 1
DEVANEY, Michael R. 5
DE VARGAS ZAPATA Y LUJAN PONCE DE, Leon Diego H
DE VAULT, Samuel H. 6
DE VEGH, Imrie 6
D'EVELYN, Charlotte 8
DEVENDORF, George E. 1
DEVENDORF, Irving R. 1
DEVENDORF, James Franklin 2
DEVENS, Charles H
DEVER, Paul Andrew 4
DEVER, William Emmett 1
DEVEREAUX, Helena Trafford
DEVEREUX, F. Ramsey 4
DEVEREUX, Frederick Leonard 7
DEVEREUX, Helena Trafford (Mrs. James Fentress) 7
DEVEREUX, John C. H
DEVEREUX, John Henry H
DEVEREUX, Mary 1
DEVEREUX, Nicholas H
DEVERS, Jacob Loucks 5
DEVILBISS, Howard P. 5
DE VILBISS, Lydia Allen (Mrs. George Henry Bradford) 9
DE VILLAFRANCA, George Warren 7
DEVIN, Thomas Casimer H
DEVIN, William Augustus 3
DEVINE, C. Robert 10
DEVINE, David Francis 6
DEVINE, Edward Thomas 2
DEVINE, Gregory S. 7
DEVINE, James Gasper 5
DE VINE, James Herbert 3
DEVINE, John M. 5
DEVINE, Joseph McMurray 4
DEVINE, Thomas Hume
DE VINNE, Theodore Low 1
DEVINS, John Bancroft 1

DEVINY, John Joseph 3
DEVISSCHER, Charles 7
DEVITT, Edward James 10
DE VLIEG, Ray Albert 3
DEVLIN, Paul 10
DEVLIN, Robert Thomas 1
DEVLIN, Thomas Francis 3
DEVOE, Alan 3
DE VOE, Emma Smith
DEVOE, Frederick William 1
DEVOE, Jenner Higbee 9
DE VOE, John M. 2
DEVOE, Ralph Godwin 4
DEVOE, Robert W. 3
DE VOE, Walter 5
DEVOE, William Beck 3
DEVOL, Carroll Augustine 1
DE VOLL, F. Usher 1
DEVOORE, Ann (Mrs. Reginald Prescott Walden) 5
DEVOR, Donald Smith 3
DEVORE, Daniel Bradford 4
DEVORE, Harry S. 2
DE VORE, Nicholas 7
DE VORE, Rebecca Jane 5
DE VOS, Julius Emilius 4
DEVOSS, James Clarence 3
DE VOTO, Bernard Augustine 3
DEVOY, John H
DEVOY, John 4
DEVREE, Howard 4
DE VRIES, David Pieterson H
DE VRIES, Henry Peter 9
DEVRIES, Herman 2
DEVRIES, Louis 6
DEVRIES, Louis 7
DE VRIES, Marion 1
DE VRIES, Tiemen 4
DE VRIES, William 1
DEVYVER, Frank Traver 7
DEW, Louise E. 4
DEW, Thomas Roderick H
DEW, Thomas Roderick 4
DE WAHA, Baron Raymond 5
DEWALT, Arthur Granville 1
DEWAR, Henry Hamilton 6
DEWAR, Henry Hamilton Hal 7
DEWART, Frederick Wesley 5
DEWART, Lewis H
DEWART, Murray Wilder 4
D'EWART, Wesley Abner 6
DEWART, William Herbert 1
DEWART, William Lewis H
DEWART, William Thompson 2
DEWDNEY, Selwyn Hanington 7
DEWEERD, Harvey A. 7
DEWEERD, James A. 5
DEWEES, William Potts H
DEWEESE, David Downs 10
DE WEESE, Truman Armstrong 4
DEWELL, Wilbur 8
DEWESSE, Arville Ottis 5
DEWEY, Bradley 5
DEWEY, Byrd Spilman 5
DEWEY, Charles 1
DEWEY, Charles Almon 3
DEWEY, Charles Melville 1
DEWEY, Charles Schuveldt 6
DEWEY, Charles Schuveldt 7
DEWEY, Chester H
DEWEY, Chester Robert 6
DEWEY, Daniel H
DEWEY, Davis Rich 2
DEWEY, Edward Russell 7
DEWEY, Ernest Wayne 8
DEWEY, Evelyn 8
DEWEY, Francis Henshaw 1
DEWEY, Francis Henshaw, Jr. 9
DEWEY, Frederic Perkins 1
DEWEY, George 1
DEWEY, Godfrey 8
DEWEY, Harry Pinneo 1
DEWEY, Henry Bingham 1
DEWEY, Henry Sweetser 4
DEWEY, James F.* 3
DEWEY, John 3
DEWEY, Julian Hiland 4
DEWEY, Lloyd Ellis 4
DEWEY, Lyster Hoxie 2
DEWEY, Malcolm Howard 6
DEWEY, Mary Elizabeth 1
DEWEY, Melvil 1
DEWEY, Orville H
DEWEY, Richard 1
DEWEY, Stoddard 1
DEWEY, Thomas Edmund 5
DEWEY, W. A. 1

DIFFENDERFER, Lloyd Herr 4
DIFFENDERFFER, Frank Ried 4
DIFFENDORFER, Ralph Eugene 3
DIGBY, Bassett 8
DIGGES, Dudley 2
DIGGES, Isaac Watlington 3
DIGGES, J. Dudley 8
DIGGES, Sam Cook 10
DIGGES, Thomas Atwood H
DIGGES, Walter Mitchell 1
DIGGLE, Roland 3
DIGGS, Annie Leporte 1
DIGGS, James Robert Lincoln 4
DIGGS, Marshall Ramsey 5
DI GIORGIO, Joseph 3
DI GIORGIO, Robert 10
DIGNAN, Thomas G. 4
DIKE, Chester Thomas 5
DIKE, George Phillips 6
DIKE, Henry B. 4
DIKE, Kenneth Onwuka 8
DIKE, Norman Staunton 3
DIKE, Phil 10
DIKE, Samuel Warren 1
DILES, Dorothy Vernon 5
DILGER, Walter Linnell 5
DILKS, Walter Howard, Jr. 4
DILL, Clarence C. 7
DILL, David Bruce 9
DILL, Franklin Geselbracht 1
DILL, Homer Ray 4
DILL, James Brooks 1
DILL, Leonard Carter 6
DILL, Lewis 1
DILLARD, Allyn 5
DILLARD, Dudley 10
DILLARD, Frank Clifford 1
DILLARD, George Henderson Lee 6
DILLARD, Hardy Cross 8
DILLARD, James Edgar 3
DILLARD, James Hardy 1
DILLARD, Paul 1
DILLARD, William Elbert 10
DILLAYE, Blanche 1
DILLE, John Flint 3
DILLEHUNT, Richard Benjamin 3
DILLENBACK, Lemuel Cross 8
DILLER, George E. 5
DILLER, Joseph Silas 1
DILLER, Neal V. 3
DILLER, Theodore 2
DILLER, Theodore Craig 9
DILLEY, Arthur Urbane 5
DILLING, Albert Wallwick 9
DILLING, Mildred 8
DILLINGER, Joseph Rollen 7
DILLINGHAM, Albert Caldwell 1
DILLINGHAM, Charles Bancroft 1
DILLINGHAM, Frances Bent 5
DILLINGHAM, Frank 4
DILLINGHAM, Frank Ayer 1
DILLINGHAM, James Darius 4
DILLINGHAM, John Hoag 1
DILLINGHAM, Lowell Smith 9
DILLINGHAM, Paul, Jr. H
DILLINGHAM, W. O. 6
DILLINGHAM, Walter Francis 4
DILLINGHAM, William Paul 1
DILLMAN, Ray Eugene 8
DILLON, Charles 2
DILLON, Charles Hall 1
DILLON, Clarence 7
DILLON, Edmond Bothwell 1
DILLON, Edmond Bothwell 2
DILLON, Edward Saunders 8
DILLON, Fannie Charles 2
DILLON, George 5
DILLON, J. Clifford 3
DILLON, James 4
DILLON, Jesse William 5
DILLON, John Forest 1
DILLON, John Henry 8
DILLON, John Irving 1
DILLON, John J. 2
DILLON, John Jordan 2
DILLON, John Joseph 8
DILLON, John Richard 2
DILLON, John Thomas 3
DILLON, Mary 1
DILLON, Paul Washington 7
DILLON, Paul Washington 8
DILLON, Philip Robert 5
DILLON, Richard Charles 4
DILLON, Robert E. 3
DILLON, Robert E. 7
DILLON, Sidney H
DILLON, Theodore Harwood 7
DILLON, Thomas Church 9
DILLON, Thomas J. 2
DILLON, Thomas Joseph 4
DILLON, W. Martin 10
DILLON, William Thomas 4
DILNOT, Frank 5
DILUZIO, Nicholas Robert 9
DILWORTH, John Richard 8
DILWORTH, Richardson 6
DIMAN, Jeremiah Lewis H
DIMAN, John Hugh 2
DIMAND, Maurice Sven 9
DIMIT, Charles Parson 8
DIMITROFF, George Zakharieff 4
DIMITROV, Georgi 3
DIMITRY, Alexander H
DIMITRY, Charles Patton 1
DIMITRY, John Bull Smith 1
DIMMERLING, Harold J. 10
DIMMICK, Eugene Dumont 1
DIMMICK, Milo Melankthon H
DIMMICK, William Arthur 9
DIMMICK, William Harrison H
DIMMITT, Lillian English 4
DIMMOCK, George 1
DIMNENT, Edward D. 5
DIMOCK, Anthony Weston 1
DIMOCK, Davis, Jr. H
DIMOCK, Edward Jordan 9
DIMOCK, Hedley S. 3
DIMOCK, Marshall Edward 10
DIMOCK, William Wallace 3
DIMON, Raymond Clark 4
DIMOND, Anthony Joseph 3
DINAND, Joseph Nicholas 2
DINEHART, Alan 2
DINERMAN, Helen Schneider 6
DINES, Homer Duncan 3
DINES, Lloyd Lyne 7
DINES, Thomas A. 6
DINES, Tyson S. 1
DINGELL, John David 3
DINGEMAN, James Herbert 9
DINGER, Harold Eugene 6
DINGLE, John Holmes 6
DINGLEY, Edward Nelson 1
DINGLEY, Frank Lambert 1
DINGLEY, Nelson H
DINGMAN, Reed Othelbert 9
DINGS, Peter Conrad 1
DINKELOO, John Gerard 8
DINKELSPIEL, Lloyd W. 3
DINKELSPIEL, Martin J(errold) 10
DINKEY, Alva Clymer 1
DINKINS, James 1
DINKINS, Philip M. 5
DINKLAGE, Ralph Dietrich 7
DINKLER, Carling 4
DINKMEYER, Henry William 3
DIN MOHOMED 7
DINNEEN, Fitz-george 2
DINNICK, John Savery 8
DINNING, James Smith 10
DINNING, Robert John 7
DINSMOOR, Robert H
DINSMOOR, Samuel H
DINSMORE, Carlos Millson 2
DINSMORE, Charles Allen 1
DINSMORE, Frank F. 6
DINSMORE, Hugh Anderson 1
DINSMORE, John Walker 1
DINSMORE, John Wirt 4
DINSMORE, Joseph Campbell 5
DINSMORE, Ray Putnam 7
DINSMORE, Robert Scott 3
D'INVILLIERS, Edward Vincent 1
D'INVILLIERS, Edward Vincent 4
DINWIDDIE, Albert Bledsoe 1
DINWIDDIE, Courtenay 2
DINWIDDIE, Edwin Courtland 1
DINWIDDIE, George Summey 5
DINWIDDIE, John Ekin 4
DINWIDDIE, Robert H
DINWIDDIE, William 1
DION, Gerard 10
DIOR, Christian 3
DIPALMA, Joseph Alfred 6
DI PIETRO, Robert Joseph 10
DIPPEL, Andreas 1
DI PRIMA, Richard Clyde 8
DIRAC, Paul Adrien Maurice 8
DIRKS, Edward 7
DIRKS, John Edward 9
DIRKS, Louis Herman 4
DIRKSEN, Everett McKinley 5
DIRLAM, Arland Augustus 7
DIRR, Peter George 4
DIRSTINE, Pearl H. 7
DISALLE, Michael Vincent 8
DISCHER, Charles Dale 8
DISERENS, Paul 3
DISESA, Joseph Daniel 8
DISHER, John Howard 10
DISHMAN, John Wesley, Jr. 4
DISKIN, Carlton Fine 4
DISKIN, Michel Angelo 7
DISMUKES, Douglas Eugene 2
DISNEY, David Tiernan H
DISNEY, Doris Miles (Mrs. George J. Disney) 7
DISNEY, Richard Lester 8
DISNEY, Roy O. 5
DISNEY, Walter E. 4
DISNEY, Wesley Ernest 4
DISQUE, Brice P. 3
DISQUE, Robert Conrad 5
DISSTON, Harry 10
DISSTON, Henry H
DISTLER, Carl Martin 2
DISTLER, Theodore August 10
DISTURNELL, John H
DITCHY, Clair William 4
DITHMAR, Edward Augustus 1
DITISHEIM, Hanns 4
DITMARS, Raymond Lee 2
DITMARS, Walter Earl 4
DITRICHSTEIN, Leo 1
DITSON, Charles Healy 1
DITSON, George Leighton H
DITSON, Oliver H
DITTEMORE, John Valentine 1
DITTENHAVER, Sarah Louise 6
DITTENHOEFER, Abram Jesse 1
DITTER, J. William 2
DITTMAN, Marion Martha 7
DITTMAR, George Walter 2
DITTMER, Clarence Christian 10
DITTO, Rollo C. 2
DITTRICK, Howard 3
DITZ, George Armand 8
DITZLER, Charlotte Weber 5
DIVELY, George Samuel 9
DIVEN, Alexander Samuel H
DIVEN, George Miles 5
DIVEN, Robert Joseph 5
DIVERTY, Marshall Hand 8
DIVINE, Charles 8
DIVINE, Frank Henry 1
DIVINE, Thomas Francis 8
DIX, Charles Hewitt 8
DIX, Dorothea Lynde H
DIX, Edwin Asa 1
DIX, George Oscar 9
DIX, John Adams H
DIX, John Alden 1
DIX, John Homer H
DIX, Morgan 1
DIX, Otto 5
DIX, William Frederick 2
DIX, William Shepherd 7
DIXEY, Henry E. 2
DIXEY, John H
DIXON, Amzi Clarence 1
DIXON, Archibald H
DIXON, Arminius Gray 5
DIXON, Brandt Van Blarcom 1
DIXON, Dean 7
DIXON, Edgar H. 4
DIXON, Frank 1
DIXON, Frank Haigh 2
DIXON, Frank Joseph 4
DIXON, Frank Murray 4
DIXON, Frederick 1
DIXON, George Dallas 1
DIXON, George Hall 4
DIXON, George Peleg 3
DIXON, George W., Jr. 4
DIXON, George William 1
DIXON, Henry Aldous 4
DIXON, Ira Allen 8
DIXON, James H
DIXON, James M. 1
DIXON, James Main 1
DIXON, John 4
DIXON, John Aldous 10
DIXON, John Edward 4
DIXON, Joseph* H
DIXON, Joseph Andrew 6
DIXON, Joseph Moore 1
DIXON, L. A., Sr. 5
DIXON, Lincoln 1
DIXON, Luther Swift H
DIXON, Mary Quincy Allen 4
DIXON, Maynard 2
DIXON, Nathan Fellows* H
DIXON, Owen 7
DIXON, Pierson 4
DIXON, Robert Ellington 8
DIXON, Robert Galloway, Jr. 7
DIXON, Robert M. 1
DIXON, Rolland Burrage 1
DIXON, Royal 4
DIXON, Russell Alexander 6
DIXON, Sam Houston 4
DIXON, Samuel Gibson 1
DIXON, Sherwood 6
DIXON, Susan Bullitt 1
DIXON, Thomas 2
DIXON, Wesley Moon 5
DIXON, William H
DIXON, William 4
DIXON, William Palmer 1
DIXON, William Palmer 5
DIXON, William Wirt 4
DIXON, Willie James 10
DIXON, Zella Allen 1
DIXWELL, John H
DJUANDA KARTAWIDJAJA, Raden Hadji 4
DOAK, Samuel H
DOAK, William Nuckles 1
DOAN, Charles Austin 10
DOAN, Fletcher Morris 1
DOAN, Frank Carleton 1
DOAN, Gilbert Everett 5
DOAN, James Burton 5
DOAN, Leland Ira 6
DOAN, William H
DOANE, D(uane) Howard 7
DOANE, George Hobart 4
DOANE, George Washington H
DOANE, Gilbert H(arry) 10
DOANE, Ralph Harrington 2
DOANE, Richard Congdon 5
DOANE, Samuel Everett 5
DOANE, Thomas H
DOANE, William Croswell 1
DOANE, William Howard 4
DOBBIE, Elliott Van Kirk 5
DOBBIE, George Alexander 3
DOBBIN, Carroll Edward 5
DOBBIN, George W. 1
DOBBIN, James 4
DOBBIN, James Cochran H
DOBBINS, Charles Gordon 9
DOBBINS, Cris 7
DOBBINS, Donald Claude 2
DOBBINS, Gaines Stanley 7
DOBBINS, Harry Thompson 5
DOBBINS, James T(almage) 5
DOBBINS, James T(almage) 8
DOBBINS, Samuel Atkinson H
DOBBS, Arthur H
DOBBS, Hoyt McWhorter 3
DOBBS, John Francis 2
DOBBS, S. A. 9
DOBBS, Samuel Candler 5
DOBBS, Stuart Piper 4
DOBERSTEIN, John Walter 4
DOBI, Istvan 5
DOBIE, Armistead Mason 4
DOBIE, Charles Caldwell 2
DOBIE, James Frank 4
DOBLE, Kendall Dyer 4
DOBLIN, Jay 10
DOBRINER, Konrad 3
DOBSON, George Frederick 1
DOBSON, Herbert Gordon 9
DOBSON, Mason Henry 3
DOBSON, Sir Roy Hardy 5
DOBSON, William Arthur Charles Harvey 8
DOBYNS, Ashbel Webster 2
DOBYNS, Fletcher 2
DOBYNS, John Robert 1
DOBYNS, William Ray 1
DOBZHANSKY, Theodosius 6
DOBZHANSKY, Theodosius 7
DOCHEZ, Alphonse Raymond 4
DOCK, Christopher H
DOCK, George 3
DOCK, Lavinia L. 4
DOCKERAY, Floyd Carlton 6
DOCKERAY, James Carlton 8
DOCKERY, Alexander Monroe 1
DOCKERY, Alfred H
DOCKERY, Henry Clay 8
DOCKING, George 4
DOCKING, James Tippet 1
DOCKING, Robert Blackwell 8
DOCKWEILER, Isidore Bernard 2
DOCKWEILER, John Francis 2
DOCKWEILER, Thomas A. J. 4
DOCTOROFF, John 5
DOD, Albert Baldwin H
DOD, Daniel H
DOD, Thaddeus H
DODD, Alvin Earl 3
DODD, Amzl 1
DODD, Anna Bowman 2
DODD, Charles Harold 6
DODD, Charles Hastings 1
DODD, David Lefevre 9
DODD, Edward H
DODD, Ed(ward Benton) 10
DODD, Edward Howard 4
DODD, Edward Howard, Jr. 9
DODD, Edwin Merrick 3
DODD, Francis Joseph 4
DODD, Frank Courtenay 4
DODD, Frank Howard 1
DODD, George Allan 1
DODD, Harold 8
DODD, Henry Martyn 1
DODD, Ira Seymour 4
DODD, John Morris 3
DODD, Lee Wilson 1
DODD, Lester Paul 10
DODD, Monroe Elmon 3
DODD, Norris E. 5
DODD, Samuel C. T. 1
DODD, Thomas Joseph 5
DODD, Verne Adams 6
DODD, Walter Fairleigh 4
DODD, William Clifton 1
DODD, William Edward 1
DODD, William George 4
DODDRIDGE, Joseph H
DODDRIDGE, Philip H
DODDRIDGE, Philip 8
DODDRIDGE, William Brown 4
DODDS, Alexander 1
DODDS, B. L. 3
DODDS, Chauncey Y. 3
DODDS, Eugene Maxwell 4
DODDS, Francis Henry 4
DODDS, George William 2
DODDS, Harold Willis 7
DODDS, Harold Willis 8
DODDS, Jesse Truesdell 7
DODDS, John Richard 9
DODDS, John Wendell 10
DODDS, Nugent 8
DODDS, Ozro John H
DODDS, Robert J. 5
DODDS, Samuel 2
DODDS, Warren 4
DODGE, Augustus Ceasar H
DODGE, Barnett Fred 5
DODGE, Bayard 5
DODGE, Bernard Ogilvie 4
DODGE, Charles Richards 1
DODGE, Charles Wright 1
DODGE, Clarence Phelps 1
DODGE, Cleveland E. 8
DODGE, Cleveland Hoadley 1
DODGE, D. Stuart 1
DODGE, Daniel Kilham 1
DODGE, David Child 1
DODGE, David Low H
DODGE, Ebenezer H
DODGE, Ernest Stanley 7
DODGE, Francis Safford 1
DODGE, Frederic 1
DODGE, Grace Hoadley 1
DODGE, Grenville Mellen 1
DODGE, H. Percival 1

DODGE, Harris T. 4
DODGE, Henry H
DODGE, Henry Irving 1
DODGE, Henry Nehemiah 4
DODGE, Homer Levi 8
DODGE, Jacob Richards 1
DODGE, James Mapes 1
DODGE, Jeremiah H
DODGE, John Wood H
DODGE, Joseph Morrell 4
DODGE, Josephine Marshall Jewell 1
DODGE, Joshua Eric 1
DODGE, Kern 6
DODGE, Louis 5
DODGE, M. Hartley 4
DODGE, M(arcellus) Hartley 9
DODGE, Martin* 3
DODGE, Mary Abigail H
DODGE, Mary Mapes 1
DODGE, Melvin Gilbert 3
DODGE, Murray Witherbee 1
DODGE, Nathan Phillips 3
DODGE, Omenzo George 4
DODGE, Philip Tell 1
DODGE, R. E. Neil 1
DODGE, Raymond 2
DODGE, Raynal 4
DODGE, Richard Elwood 3
DODGE, Robert Gray 4
DODGE, Sherwood 5
DODGE, Theodore Ayrault 1
DODGE, Walter Phelps 5
DODGE, Washington 7
DODGE, Wendell Phillips 7
DODGE, William De Leftwich 1
DODGE, William Earl H
DODGE, William Earl 1
DODGE, Willis Edward 4
DODINGTON, Sven H. M. 10
DODS, John Bovee H
DODSHON, Joseph Henry 2
DODSON, Daniel Boone 10
DODSON, Edwin Stanton 8
DODSON, George Rowland 1
DODSON, Harry Lea 3
DODSON, John E. 1
DODSON, John Milton 1
DODSON, Loren Ralph 5
DODSON, Martha Ethel 5
DODSON, Owen Vincent 8
DOE, Charles H
DOE, Edward M. 1
DOE, Joseph Bodwell 4
DOE, Nicholas Bartlett H
DOE, Thomas Bartwell 4
DOEBLER, Errol W(eber) 9
DOERFLER, Christian 1
DOERFLINGER, Charles Hermann 1
DOERFLINGER, Jon Arno 6
DOERING, Carl Rupp 7
DOERING, Edmund Janes 2
DOERING, Grace Bernardina 8
DOERING, Otto Charles, Jr. 8
DOERMANN, Henry John 1
DOERR, John Edward 4
DOERSCHUK, Anna Beatrice 6
DOESCHER, Waldemar Oswald 4
DOETSCH, James F. 4
DOFT, Floyd Shelton 7
DOGAN, Matthew Winfred 2
DOGGETT, John L. 1
DOGGETT, Laurence Locke 3
DOGLIOTTI, Achille Mario 4
DOHAN, Edward G. 5
DOHENY, Edward Laurence 1
DOHENY, William Joseph 8
DOHERTY, Edward J. 6
DOHERTY, Henry Latham 1
DOHERTY, Philip Joseph 1
DOHERTY, Richard P. 8
DOHERTY, Robert Ernest 3
DOHERTY, Robert P(ace) 9
DOHERTY, Robert Remington 4
DOHME, Alfred Robert Louis 5
DOHNANYI, Erno (Ernest Von Dohnanyi) 5
DOIDGE, Frederick Widdowson 3
DOIG, Andrew Wheeler H
DOIG, James Rufus 5
DOIG, Thomas W. 3
DOING, Mahlon B. 4
DOISY, Edward Adelbert 9
DOKTOR, Paul Karl 10
DOLAK, Michael Charles 3
DOLAN, Arthur W. 2
DOLAN, Daniel Leo 4
DOLAN, Elizabeth Honor 3
DOLAN, Francis James 1
DOLAN, George W. 2
DOLAN, James Edward 4
DOLAN, Margaret Baggett (Mrs. Charles E. Dolan) 6
DOLAN, Patrick 9
DOLAN, Robert Emmett 5
DOLAN, Thomas 1
DOLAN, Tom 5
DOLAND, Jack Van Kirk 10
DOLAND, James Joseph 4
DOLBEAR, Amos Emerson 1
DOLBEAR, Samuel Hood 7
DOLCHO, Frederick H
DOLD, Jacob C. 1
DOLE, Arthur, Jr. 5
DOLE, Charles Fletcher 1
DOLE, Edmund Pearson 1
DOLE, Helen James Bennett 2
DOLE, Hollis Mathews 9
DOLE, James Drummond 3
DOLE, Malcolm 10
DOLE, Margaret Femald (Mrs. John S. Dole) 5
DOLE, Nathan Haskell 1
DOLE, Sanford Ballard 1
DOLE, William 8
DOLGE, Alfred 1
D'OLIER, Franklin 3
DOLIN, Anton 8
DOLKART, Leo 4
DOLL, Alfred W. 3
DOLL, August Phillip 8
DOLL, Charles George 10
DOLL, William Deberge 2
DOLLAHON, James Clifford 7
DOLLAR, R. Stanley 3
DOLLAR, Robert 1
DOLLARD, John 7
DOLLARD, Paul M. 4
DOLLARD, Stewart Edward 6
DOLLARD, Stewart Edward 7
DOLLARD, William H
DOLLENS, Burl Austin 3
DOLLEY, Charles Sumner 4
DOLLEY, David Hough 1
DOLLEY, James Clay 7
DOLLIVER, George Benton 6
DOLLIVER, Jonathan Prentiss 1
DOLLIVER, Margaret Gay 4
DOLMAN, John, Jr. 3
DOLOWITZ, Francis Marie Fleisher (Mrs. David A. Dolowitz) 5
DOLPH, John H. 1
DOLPH, Joseph Norton H
DOLPHY, Eric Allan 4
DOLSON, Charles Herbert 10
DOLVE, Robert M. 7
DOMAGK, Gerhard 4
DOMENEC, Michael H
DOMENICALI, Charles Angelo 8
DOMERATZKY, Louis 6
DOMERS, Henry Russell 5
DOMINIAN, Leon 1
DOMINICI, Santos Anibal 5
DOMINICK, Frank 1
DOMINICK, Fred H. 5
DOMINICK, Gayer Gardner 4
DOMINICK, James Robert 5
DOMINICK, Peter Hoyt 7
DOMM, Lincoln Valentine 10
DOMONKOS, Anthony Nicholas 7
DOMONOSKE, Arthur B(oquer) 6
DONAGAN, Alan Harry 10
DONAGHEY, Frederick 1
DONAGHEY, George W. 1
DONAGHY, William Andrew 6
DONAHEY, James Harrison 2
DONAHEY, John William 4
DONAHEY, Mary Dickerson 4
DONAHEY, Vic 2
DONAHEY, William 7
DONAHO, Glynn Robert 9
DONAHOE, Daniel Joseph 1
DONAHOE, Patrick H
DONAHUE, Charles 5
DONAHUE, Charles Henry 5
DONAHUE, Edward Joseph 8
DONAHUE, John Bartholomew 5
DONAHUE, Joseph Michael 4
DONAHUE, Joseph P. 3
DONAHUE, Lester 9
DONAHUE, Maurice H. 1
DONAHUE, Patrick James 1
DONAHUE, Peter H
DONAHUE, Russell B. 8
DONAHUE, Stephen J. 8
DONALD, George H. 5
DONALD, George Kenneth 8
DONALD, Joseph Marion 4
DONALD, Norman Henderson 4
DONALD, William Goodricke 3
DONALD, William John Alexander 4
DONALDSON, Albert Eeley 6
DONALDSON, Allyn Capron 6
DONALDSON, Charles M. 6
DONALDSON, Charles Russell 10
DONALDSON, Ethelbert Talbot 9
DONALDSON, Frank Arthur, Jr. 10
DONALDSON, Fred Kermit 4
DONALDSON, Henry Herbert 1
DONALDSON, J. A. 5
DONALDSON, James Rider 6
DONALDSON, Jesse Monroe 5
DONALDSON, John 3
DONALDSON, John M. 1
DONALDSON, Kenneth Hume 3
DONALDSON, Norman Vaux 4
DONALDSON, Robert Golden 1
DONALDSON, Thomas Quint 1
DONALDSON, Walter Foster 6
DONALDSON, William Raymond 4
DONALDSON, William V. 10
DONALSON, Erle Meldrim 6
DONALSON, John Ernest 1
DONAT, Robert 3
DONATELLI, August 10
DONATI, Pine 6
DONATO, Giuseppe 4
DONAVIN, Kirkwood Harry 7
DONDERO, George Anthony 5
DONDINEAU, Arthur 7
DONDLINGER, Peter Tracy 3
DONDO, Mathurin 5
DONDORE, Dorothy Anne 2
DONEGAN, Alfred William 7
DONEGAN, Edmund Joseph 3
DONEGAN, Harold Hand 4
DONEGAN, Maurice Francis 3
DO-NE-HO-GA-WA H
DONEHOO, George Patterson 1
DONEHUE, Francis McGarvey 6
DONEHUE, Vincent Julian 4
DONELSON, Andrew Jackson H
DONER, Dean Benton 10
DONER, Wilfred B. 10
DONEY, Carl Gregg 3
DONGAN, Thomas H
DONGES, Ralph Waldo Emerson 5
DONGES, Theophilus Ebenaezer 4
DONHAM, C. R. 3
DONHAM, Harold Gregory 2
DONHAM, Wallace Brett 3
DONHAUSER, J. Lewi 4
DONIGER, William 5
DONIPHAN, Alexander William H
DONKIN, McKay 5
DONLEVY, Alice Heighes 1
DONLEVY, Harriet Farley 1
DONLEY, Charles Sherman 4
DONLEY, William Henry 1
DONLON, Alphonsus John 1
DONN, Edward Wilton, Jr. 3
DONN, William L. 9
DONNAN, Elizabeth 3
DONNELL, Annie Hamilton 3
DONNELL, Ben Dobyns 3
DONNELL, Forrest C. 7
DONNELL, Harold Eugene 4
DONNELL, James J. 1
DONNELL, Otto Dewey 4
DONNELL, Philip Stone 4
DONNELL, Richard Spaight H
DONNELL, Robert H
DONNELLAN, Thomas A. 9
DONNELLEY, Dixon 9
DONNELLEY, Elliott 6
DONNELLEY, Gaylord 10
DONNELLEY, Thomas Elliott 3
DONNELLON, James Augustine 5
DONNELLY, Arthur Barrett 1
DONNELLY, Charles 1
DONNELLY, Charles Edward 8
DONNELLY, Dorothy Agnes 1
DONNELLY, Edward Terence 1
DONNELLY, Eleanor Cecilia 1
DONNELLY, Frederick William 1
DONNELLY, George J. 3
DONNELLY, Harold Irvin 1
DONNELLY, Henry Edmund 5
DONNELLY, Horace James 6
DONNELLY, Ignatius 1
DONNELLY, James L(eonard) 5
DONNELLY, John C. 1
DONNELLY, Joseph Gordon 1
DONNELLY, June Richardson 5
DONNELLY, Lucy Martin 2
DONNELLY, Percy John 9
DONNELLY, Phil M. 4
DONNELLY, Richard Carter 5
DONNELLY, Samuel Bratton 2
DONNELLY, Simon Peter 4
DONNELLY, Thomas Frederick 1
DONNELLY, Thomas James 4
DONNELLY, Walter Joseph 5
DONNER, Arvin Nehemiah 10
DONNER, Frederick G. 9
DONNER, George H
DONNER, Tamsen H
DONNER, William Henry 3
DONOGHUE, John Daniel 9
DONOGHUE, Thomas J. 5
DONOHO, Ruger 1
DONOHOE, Charles 1
DONOHOE, Denis 1
DONOHOE, Francis Michael 1
DONOHOE, James A. 3
DONOHOE, Michael 4
DONOHOE, Thomas Joseph 1
DONOHOE, William A. 4
DONOHUE, Harold Daniel 8
DONOHUE, Mark Neary 8
DONOHUGH, Thomas Smith 5
DONOVAN, Bernard Eugene 7
DONOVAN, Dennis Francis 8
DONOVAN, Edward Francis 2
DONOVAN, George Francis 5
DONOVAN, Gerald 9
DONOVAN, Hedley Williams 10
DONOVAN, Henry A(ugustus) 8
DONOVAN, Herman Lee 4
DONOVAN, James Alport, Jr. 7
DONOVAN, James Britt 5
DONOVAN, James J. 5
DONOVAN, James Norton 7
DONOVAN, Jeremiah 1
DONOVAN, Jerome Francis 2
DONOVAN, John Charles, Jr. 7
DONOVAN, John Chauncey 9
DONOVAN, John Joseph 1
DONOVAN, Richard 2
DONOVAN, Richard Joseph 6
DONOVAN, Thomas Leroy 6
DONOVAN, Timothy Paul 10
DONOVAN, William Joseph 3
DONOVAN, Winfred Nichols 4
DONWORTH, Charles Tenney 7
DONWORTH, George 2
DONWORTH, Grace 2
D'OOGE, Benjamin Leonard 3
D'OOGE, Martin Luther 1
DOOLAN, John Calvin 2
DOOLAN, Leonard Weakley 2
DOOLE, George Arntzen 8
DOOLEY, Channing Rice 3
DOOLEY, Dennis A. 8
DOOLEY, Edwin Benedict 8
DOOLEY, Henry Williamson 1
DOOLEY, James A. 7
DOOLEY, Joseph Brannon 4
DOOLEY, Lucy 3
DOOLEY, M. S. 3
DOOLEY, Michael F. 1
DOOLEY, Thomas Anthony, III 4
DOOLEY, Virginia Perrin Corttis 6
DOOLEY, William Francis 1
DOOLEY, William Henry 2
DOOLIN, John B. 1
DOOLING, Henry Cheesman 8
DOOLING, John Francis, Jr. 7
DOOLING, Maurice T. 1
DOOLING, Maurice T., Jr. 9
DOOLING, Peter J. 1
DOOLITTLE, Amos H
DOOLITTLE, Arthur K(ing) 10
DOOLITTLE, Charles Camp 1
DOOLITTLE, Charles Leander 1
DOOLITTLE, Dudley 3
DOOLITTLE, Eric 1
DOOLITTLE, Frederick William 3
DOOLITTLE, Gillum Hotchkiss 9
DOOLITTLE, Hilda 4
DOOLITTLE, Hooker Austin 4
DOOLITTLE, James Rood H
DOOLITTLE, Roscoe Edward 1
DOOLITTLE, Thomas Benjamin 1
DOOLY, Oscar Earle 5
DOOMAN, Eugene Hoffman 8
DOORLY, Henry 4
DOPP, Katherine Elizabeth 5
DORAN, Earl D. 7
DORAN, Edwin Beale 7
DORAN, James M. 2
DORAN, Joseph Ingersoll 1
DORAN, Thomas Francis 1
DORAN, William Thomas 3
DORATI, Antal 9
DORCHESTER, Daniel 1
DORCHESTER, Daniel 2
DORCHESTER, Liverus Hull 3
DORE, John F. 1
DOREMUS, Charles Avery 1
DOREMUS, Frank Ellsworth 2
DOREMUS, Henry M. 4
DOREMUS, Robert Barnard 8
DOREMUS, Robert Ogden 1
DOREMUS, Sarah Platt Haines H
DOREN, Electra Collins 1
DORESAM, Charles Henry 2
DORETY, Frederic Gerber 6
DOREY, Halstead 2
DORF, Erling 8
DORFMAN, Albert 8
DORFMAN, Joseph 10
DORFMAN, Ralph Isadore 9
DORFMAN, Saul 8

DORGAN, Thomas Aloysius — H
DORGAN, Thomas Aloysius — 4
DORIA, Clara — 1
DORIGAN, Harry William — 4
DORIGAN, Harry William — 5
DORION, Eustache Charles Edouard — 1
DORION, Marie — H
DORLAND, Ralph E., Sr. — 2
DORLAND, William Alexander Newman — 4
DORMAN, Edmund Lawrence — 4
DORMAN, William Edwin — 1
DORMER, Charles Joseph — 4
DORN, Francis Edwin — 9
DORN, Harold F. — 4
DORN, John Emil — 6
DORNE, Albert — 4
DORNIN, Bernard — H
DORNIN, Thomas Aloysius — H
DOROSHAW, Jennis Milford — 4
DORR, Carl E. — 6
DORR, Dudley Huntington — 4
DORR, Edward Monroe — 4
DORR, George Bucknam — 4
DORR, Goldthwaite Higginson — 7
DORR, Harold M. — 5
DORR, John A., Jr. — 9
DORR, John Van Nostrand — 1
DORR, Julia Caroline Ripley — 1
DORR, Rheta Childe — 2
DORR, Robert East Apthoep —
DORR, Robert John — 4
DORR, Thomas Wilson — H
DORRANCE, Arthur Calbraith — 2
DORRANCE, Charles — 7
DORRANCE, George Morris — 2
DORRANCE, Gordon — 3
DORRANCE, John Thompson — 1
DORRANCE, John Thompson, Jr. — 10
DORRANCE, Sturges Dick — 5
DORRELL, William — H
DORRITIE, John Francis — 10
DORROH, John Hazard — 6
D'ORSAY, Lawrance — 1
DORSCH, Eduard — 1
DORSCHEL, Querin Peter — 7
DORSET, Marion — 1
DORSETT, P. H. — 4
DORSETT, Walter Balckburn — 1
DORSEY, Cam Dawson — 4
DORSEY, Charles Howard — 6
DORSEY, Clarence Wilbur — 5
DORSEY, Clayton Chauncey — 2
DORSEY, Clement — H
DORSEY, Ella Loraine — 4
DORSEY, Francis Oswald — 1
DORSEY, Frank J. G. — 2
DORSEY, George Amos — 1
DORSEY, Harry Woodward — 5
DORSEY, Herbert Grove — 5
DORSEY, Hugh Manson — 2
DORSEY, Jack Sidney — 6
DORSEY, James Emmet — 4
DORSEY, James Owen — H
DORSEY, John Morris — 7
DORSEY, John Syng — H
DORSEY, Leo Patrick — 6
DORSEY, Leroy Howard — 3
DORSEY, Maxwell J. — 4
DORSEY, Montgomery — 4
DORSEY, Ray — 9
DORSEY, Sarah Ann Ellis — H
DORSEY, Stephen Michael — 9
DORSEY, Stephen Palmer — 4
DORSEY, Stephen W. — 1
DORSEY, Susan M. — 4
DORSEY, Thomas Brookshier — 9
DORSEY, Thomas Francis — 3
DORSEY, W. Roderick — 4
DORSHEIMER, William Edward —
DORSON, Richard M. — 8
DORST, Joseph Haddox — 1
DORST, Stanley Elwood — 10
DORT, J. Dallas — 1
DORTICOS, Torrado Osvaldo* — 8
DORWARD, William Thompson — 4
DORWIN, Oscar John — 6
DOSDALL, Chester Arthur — 3

DOSKER, Henry E. — 1
DOS PASSOS, John (Roderigo) — 5
DOS PASSOS, John Randolph — 1
DOSS, Clay — 3
DOSS, Roscoe James — 2
DOSTAL, Charles Antoine — 7
DOSTER, Frank — 1
DOSTER, James Jarvis — 2
DOSTERT, Leon Emile — 5
DOTEN, Carroll Warren — 2
DOTEN, Samuel Bradford — 3
DOTSON, Floyd D. — 5
DOTSON, George Edgar — 6
DOTT, Robert Henry, Sr. — 9
DOTTER, Charles Theodore —
DOTTERWEICH, June (Mrs. Frank Henry Dotterweich) — 5
DOTTS, Harold William — 10
DOTY, Alvah Hunt — 4
DOTY, Carl Babcock — 6
DOTY, Douglas Zabriskie — 1
DOTY, Elihu — H
DOTY, James Duane — H
DOTY, John Williams — 4
DOTY, Madeleine Zabriskie (Mrs. Roger N. Baldwin) — 6
DOTY, Paul — 1
DOTY, Robert Clark — 4
DOTY, Robert McIntyre — 10
DOTY, William Furman — 5
DOUB, George Cochran — 8
DOUB, Howard P. — 8
DOUBLEDAY, Abner — H
DOUBLEDAY, Frank Nelson — 1
DOUBLEDAY, George — 3
DOUBLEDAY, Nelson — 2
DOUBLEDAY, Netje De Graff — 1
DOUBLEDAY, Russell — 2
DOUBLEDAY, Ulysses Freeman — H
DOUDNA, Edgar George — 2
DOUDNA, Quincy Von Ogden — 9
DOUDOROFF, Michael — 6
DOUDS, Charles Tucker — 4
DOUGAL, William H. — H
DOUGHERTY, Blanford Barnard — 3
DOUGHERTY, Charles Frederick — 8
DOUGHERTY, Curtis — 1
DOUGHERTY, David Mitchell — 9
DOUGHERTY, Denis J. — 3
DOUGHERTY, Edward Archer —
DOUGHERTY, Edward E. — 2
DOUGHERTY, George A. — 1
DOUGHERTY, George S. — 1
DOUGHERTY, Gregg — 9
DOUGHERTY, Hugh — 1
DOUGHERTY, J. Hampden —
DOUGHERTY, James Henry — 7
DOUGHERTY, James L(awrence) — 7
DOUGHERTY, John — 1
DOUGHERTY, John L. — 7
DOUGHERTY, Joseph P(atrick) — 5
DOUGHERTY, Lee J. — 6
DOUGHERTY, Paul — 2
DOUGHERTY, Philip Hugh — 9
DOUGHERTY, Proctor Lambert — 5
DOUGHERTY, Raymond Philip — 1
DOUGHERTY, Richard — 9
DOUGHERTY, Richard Erwin — 4
DOUGHERTY, Thomas Francis — 6
DOUGHERTY, William Edgeworth — 1
DOUGHERTY, William H. — 6
DOUGHTIE, Venton Levy — 10
DOUGHTON, Robert L. — 3
DOUGHTY, Mrs. Alla Waters —
DOUGHTY, Howard — 2
DOUGHTY, Thomas — H
DOUGHTY, Walter Francis — 1
DOUGHTY, William Ellison — 5
DOUGHTY, William Henry — 1
DOUGHTY, William Henry, Jr. — 1
DOUGLAS, Albert — 4
DOUGLAS, Alexander — 4

DOUGLAS, Alexander Edgar — 8
DOUGLAS, Alice May — 2
DOUGLAS, Amanda Minnie — 1
DOUGLAS, Archibald — 2
DOUGLAS, Arthur F. — 3
DOUGLAS, Benjamin — H
DOUGLAS, Beverly Browne — H
DOUGLAS, Bruce Hutchinson — 2
DOUGLAS, Charles A. — 1
DOUGLAS, Charles Henry — 3
DOUGLAS, Charles Winfred — 2
DOUGLAS, Clarence Brown — 5
DOUGLAS, David Dwight — 3
DOUGLAS, Davison McDowell — 1
DOUGLAS, Donald B. — 6
DOUGLAS, Donald Wills, Jr. — 9
DOUGLAS, Ernest — 4
DOUGLAS, Fred James — 2
DOUGLAS, Frederic Huntington — 3
DOUGLAS, Frederick A. — 4
DOUGLAS, George Bruce — 1
DOUGLAS, George William — 1
DOUGLAS, George William — 2
DOUGLAS, Gilbert Franklin — 9
DOUGLAS, Grace Parsons — 6
DOUGLAS, Hamilton — 3
DOUGLAS, Helen Gahagan (Mrs. Melvyn Douglas) — 7
DOUGLAS, Henry Kyd — 1
DOUGLAS, Henry Trovert, Jr. — 4
DOUGLAS, James — 1
DOUGLAS, James H. — 1
DOUGLAS, James H., Jr. — 8
DOUGLAS, James Marsh — 6
DOUGLAS, James Stuart — 1
DOUGLAS, John — 1
DOUGLAS, John Francis — 3
DOUGLAS, John Frederick Howard —
DOUGLAS, John Gray — 6
DOUGLAS, John Jefferson — 8
DOUGLAS, Julia S. — 1
DOUGLAS, Kenneth Wallace — 6
DOUGLAS, Lee — 3
DOUGLAS, Lewis Williams — 10
DOUGLAS, Lewis Williams — 6
DOUGLAS, Lloyd C. — 3
DOUGLAS, Lloyd Virgil — 7
DOUGLAS, Marjory Stoneman —
DOUGLAS, Melvyn — 4
DOUGLAS, Lord Of Kirtleside (William Sholto Douglas) —
DOUGLAS, Orlando Benajah — 1
DOUGLAS, Oscar Berry — 4
DOUGLAS, Paul Howard — 7
DOUGLAS, Paul Howard — 9
DOUGLAS, Percy Liningston — 4
DOUGLAS, Richard — 4
DOUGLAS, Robert Martin — 1
DOUGLAS, Silas Hamilton — H
DOUGLAS, Stephen Arnold —
DOUGLAS, Stephen Arnold — 1
DOUGLAS, Thaddeus — 4
DOUGLAS, Theodore Wayland —
DOUGLAS, Thomas Clement — 9
DOUGLAS, Wallace Barton — 4
DOUGLAS, Walter — 2
DOUGLAS, Walter G. — 5
DOUGLAS, Walter John — 6
DOUGLAS, Walter Spalding — 8
DOUGLAS, William — 3
DOUGLAS, William Archer Sholte — 3
DOUGLAS, William Harris — 2
DOUGLAS, William Lewis — 1
DOUGLAS, William Orville — 7
DOUGLAS, William Wilberforce —
DOUGLASS, Alfred Eugene — 8
DOUGLASS, Andrew Elliott — 1
DOUGLASS, Andrew Ellicott — 4

DOUGLASS, Aubrey Augustus — 3
DOUGLASS, Benjamin Wallace — 1
DOUGLASS, Dana Carroll — 5
DOUGLASS, David Bates — H
DOUGLASS, Earl — 1
DOUGLASS, Earl Leroy — 5
DOUGLASS, Edwin Herbert — 4
DOUGLASS, Frank Harvey — 4
DOUGLASS, Frederick — H
DOUGLASS, Frederick Melvin — 3
DOUGLASS, Gaylord William — 5
DOUGLASS, George C. — 1
DOUGLASS, George Shearer — 3
DOUGLASS, H. Paul — 3
DOUGLASS, Harl Roy — 5
DOUGLASS, H(erbert) Ellwood — 5
DOUGLASS, John Joseph — 5
DOUGLASS, John Watkinson — 1
DOUGLASS, Joseph Henry — 6
DOUGLASS, Lathrop — 7
DOUGLASS, Lucille Sinclair — 4
DOUGLASS, Mabel Smith — 5
DOUGLASS, Matthew Hale — 2
DOUGLASS, Paul F. — 5
DOUGLASS, Ralph Benjamin — 9
DOUGLASS, Raymond Donald — 7
DOUGLASS, Robert M. J. — 1
DOUGLASS, Rufus Collins — 4
DOUGLASS, Thomas Vankirk — 4
DOUGLASS, Truman Bartlett — 5
DOUGLASS, Truman Orville — 1
DOUGLASS, William — H
DOULL, James Angus — 4
DOUNCE, Harry Esty — 3
DOUTHIRT, Walstein F. — 3
DOUTHIT, Claude — 3
DOUTHIT, Harold — 4
DOUTHIT, Jasper L. — 4
DOUTRICH, Isaac H. — 1
DOUTY, Nicholas — 5
DOVE, David James — H
DOVE, W(illiam) Franklin — 5
DOVELL, Ray C. — 5
DOVENER, Blackburn Barrett — 4
DOVENMUEHLE, George Henry — 8
DOVER, Elmer — 1
DOW, Alden Ball — 9
DOW, Alex — 2
DOW, Allan Wade — 3
DOW, Arthur Wesley — 1
DOW, Blanche Hinman — 6
DOW, Caroline Bell — 1
DOW, Charles Mason — 1
DOW, Earle Wilbur — 4
DOW, Edward Albert — 2
DOW, Fayette Brown — 4
DOW, Frank — 8
DOW, Frederick Neal — 1
DOW, George Francis — 1
DOW, Grove Samuel — 8
DOW, Henry — H
DOW, Herbert Henry — 1
DOW, Howard Malcolm — 1
DOW, James Wilson — 8
DOW, Jennings Bryan — 10
DOW, John Reneau — 6
DOW, Lorenzo — H
DOW, Neal — H
DOW, Peter Staub — 8
DOW, Robert C. — 8
DOW, Roger — 4
DOW, Wilbur Egerton, Jr. — 10
DOW, Willard Henry — 2
DOWD, Charles Ferdinand — 1
DOWD, Charles North — 1
DOWD, David L(loyd) — 5
DOWD, Fred A. — 6
DOWD, James Edward — 4
DOWD, Jerome — 4
DOWD, John Worthington — 1
DOWD, Laurence Phillips — 7
DOWD, Thomas Nathan — 9
DOWD, W. Carey, Jr. — 3
DOWD, Wallace Rutherford — 4
DOWD, William — 1
DOWDALL, Edward — 4
DOWDALL, Guy Grigsby — 5
DOWDELL, James Ferguson — H
DOWDELL, James Render — 3

DOWDEN, Raymond Baxter — 8
DOWDEY, Clifford Shirley, Jr. — 8
DOWDLE, Walter Reid — 8
DOWDNEY, Abraham — H
DOWDY, Andrew Hunter — 7
DOWDY, George Winston — 7
DOWE, Jennie Elizabeth Tupper — 1
DOWELL, Alvis Yates — 5
DOWELL, Austin Allyn — 9
DOWELL, Benjamin B. — 3
DOWELL, Carr Thomas — 6
DOWELL, Cassius C. — 1
DOWELL, Dudley — 7
DOWELL, Floyd Dee — 4
DOWELL, Greensville — H
DOWELL, Spright — 4
DOWER, Walter H. — 1
DOWLER, Francis Walton — 8
DOWLING, Alexander — 1
DOWLING, Austin — 1
DOWLING, Eddie — 6
DOWLING, Edward C. — 6
DOWLING, Emmett Patrick — 4
DOWLING, George Thomas — 4
DOWLING, John Joseph — 2
DOWLING, John William — 1
DOWLING, Judson Davie — 6
DOWLING, Michael John — 1
DOWLING, Noel Thomas — 5
DOWLING, Noel Thomas — 7
DOWLING, Oscar — 1
DOWLING, Robert Whittle — 6
DOWLING, Victor James — 1
DOWLING, Walter — 7
DOWLING, William E. — 4
DOWMAN, Charles Edward — 1
DOWNER, Alan Seymour — 5
DOWNER, Charles Alfred — 1
DOWNER, Eliphalet — H
DOWNER, James Walker — 1
DOWNER, Samuel — H
DOWNER, Samuel Forsythe — 7
DOWNES, Anne Miller — 4
DOWNES, Bruce — 4
DOWNES, Dennis Sawyer — 6
DOWNES, James R. — 3
DOWNES, John — H
DOWNES, John — 3
DOWNES, Olin — 3
DOWNES, William Augustus — 2
DOWNES, William Howe — 1
DOWNEY, David George — 1
DOWNEY, Fairfax Davis — 10
DOWNEY, Francis X. — 4
DOWNEY, Francis Xavier — 2
DOWNEY, George Eddy — 1
DOWNEY, George Faber — 1
DOWNEY, Hal — 3
DOWNEY, Hermon Horatio — 5
DOWNEY, John — H
DOWNEY, John Florin — 1
DOWNEY, John Irving — 9
DOWNEY, June E. — 1
DOWNEY, Mary Elizabeth — 3
DOWNEY, Morton — 9
DOWNEY, Sheridan — 4
DOWNEY, Stanley Wilson Crowell — 1
DOWNEY, Stephen Wheeler — 7
DOWNEY, Walter Francis — 4
DOWNEY, William H. — 3
DOWNIE, Robert C. — 4
DOWNING, Andrew Jackson — H
DOWNING, Augustus — 1
DOWNING, Charles* — H
DOWNING, Elliot Rowland — 2
DOWNING, Frances Murdaugh — H
DOWNING, George — H
DOWNING, H(arold) H(ardesty) — 7
DOWNING, Harold Kemp — 2
DOWNING, Maj Jack — 4
DOWNING, John Franklin — 1
DOWNING, John Robert — 1
DOWNING, King Lewis — 5
DOWNING, Paul M. — 2
DOWNING, Robert Everard —
DOWNING, Robert L. — 2
DOWNING, Russell Vincent — 5
DOWNING, Warwick Miller — 4
DOWNS, Charles Raymond — 8

DUNKLE, John Lee 7
DUNKLE, William Frederick, Jr. 9
DUNKLEY, Ferdinand Luis 3
DUNLAP, Andrew 1
DUNLAP, Arthur Ray 6
DUNLAP, Boutwell 1
DUNLAP, Charles Bates 1
DUNLAP, Charles Edward 4
DUNLAP, Charles Graham 1
DUNLAP, Charles Kephart 2
DUNLAP, David Richardson 5
DUNLAP, Elbert 5
DUNLAP, Frederick 6
DUNLAP, Frederick Levy 5
DUNLAP, George Washington H
DUNLAP, George Wesley 9
DUNLAP, Harry 4
DUNLAP, Hiram J. 1
DUNLAP, James Boliver H
DUNLAP, James Eugene 8
DUNLAP, John H
DUNLAP, John Bettes 4
DUNLAP, John Robertson 1
DUNLAP, John T. 6
DUNLAP, Knight 2
DUNLAP, Maurice P. 7
DUNLAP, Millard Fillmore 4
DUNLAP, Orrin Elmer, Jr. 5
DUNLAP, Renick William 2
DUNLAP, Robert 1
DUNLAP, Robert Finley 1
DUNLAP, Robert Henry 5
DUNLAP, Robert Pinckney H
DUNLAP, Roy J. 1
DUNLAP, Roy John, Jr. 5
DUNLAP, S(amuel) Benjamin 8
DUNLAP, William H
DUNLAP, William Claiborne H
DUNLAVY, Edwin Wesley 5
DUNLEVY, Robert Baldwin 3
DUNLOP, Edward Arunah 8
DUNLOP, James H
DUNLOP, Walter Scott 6
DUNMIRE, Glenn DeWitt 6
DUNMORE, 4th earl H
DUNMORE, Earl William 7
DUNMORE, Walter Thomas 2
DUNN, Alan 6
DUNN, Alexander Gordon H
DUNN, Arthur David 1
DUNN, Arthur Wallace 1
DUNN, Arthur William 1
DUNN, Ballard 5
DUNN, Beverly Charles 5
DUNN, Burton 8
DUNN, Byron Archibald 4
DUNN, Charles H
DUNN, Charles Alfred 7
DUNN, Charles Gwyllym 4
DUNN, Charles John 1
DUNN, Charles Putnam 4
DUNN, Charles Wesley 3
DUNN, Colon H. 7
DUNN, Daniel Francis 9
DUNN, Edward Gregory 2
DUNN, Edward K. 7
DUNN, Elias Bound 4
DUNN, Emmett Reid 3
DUNN, Esther Cloudman 9
DUNN, Fannie Wyche 2
DUNN, Fayette Smith 7
DUNN, Frank Harold 4
DUNN, Frank Kershner 4
DUNN, Frederick Julian 4
DUNN, Frederick Sherwood 4
DUNN, Gano 3
DUNN, George Grundy H
DUNN, George Hedford H
DUNN, George M. 4
DUNN, Harris Ashton 4
DUNN, Harry Lippincott 10
DUNN, Harry Thatcher 5
DUNN, Harvey 3
DUNN, Henry Wesley 5
DUNN, Herbert Omar 1
DUNN, Ignatius J. 3
DUNN, Jacob Piatt 1
DUNN, James Arthur 7
DUNN, James Clement 9
DUNN, Sir James Hamet 3
DUNN, James Phillip 1
DUNN, Jesse James 1
DUNN, John Joseph 1
DUNN, John Randall 2
DUNN, Joseph 3
DUNN, Joseph Allan 1
DUNN, Justin Stephen 9
DUNN, Kenneth 7
DUNN, Leslie Clarence 6
DUNN, Martha Baker 4
DUNN, Matthew A. 2
DUNN, Neil Harrison 8
DUNN, R. Roy 6
DUNN, Ray A. 6
DUNN, Richard J. 2
DUNN, Robert 3
DUNN, Robert A. 2
DUNN, Roger Elliott 8
DUNN, Ross Joseph 7
DUNN, Samuel O. 3
DUNN, Thomas B. 1
DUNN, Waldo Hilary 5
DUNN, William Carleton 8
DUNN, William Edward 4
DUNN, William Frank 5
DUNN, William Le Roy 1
DUNN, William Lewis 7
DUNN, William McKee H
DUNN, William Warren 4
DUNN, Williamson H
DUNNACK, Henry E. 1
DUNNE, Charles D. 4
DUNNE, Edmond M. 1
DUNNE, Edward Fitzsimons 1
DUNNE, Edward Joseph 1
DUNNE, Finley Porter 1
DUNNE, Irene 10
DUNNE, James Edward 2
DUNNE, James Edward Craven 4
DUNNE, Peter Francis 1
DUNNE, Philip 10
DUNNE, Robert Elmer 8
DUNNELL, Elbridge Gerry 1
DUNNELL, Mark Boothby 1
DUNNELL, Mark Hill 1
DUNNER, Joseph 7
DUNNETT, Alexander 1
DUNNIGAN, Frank Joseph 10
DUNNING, Albert Elijah 1
DUNNING, Alden W. 4
DUNNING, Charles A. 3
DUNNING, Edwin James 1
DUNNING, George Freeman 1
DUNNING, Harrison F. 6
DUNNING, Harry Westbrook 5
DUNNING, Henry Armitt Brown 4
DUNNING, Henry Sage 3
DUNNING, James Edmund 5
DUNNING, James Edwin 3
DUNNING, James Henry Fitzgerald 7
DUNNING, James Morse 10
DUNNING, John Ray 6
DUNNING, John Sullivan 5
DUNNING, John Wirt 3
DUNNING, Lehman H. 1
DUNNING, Morton Dexter 5
DUNNING, N. Max 2
DUNNING, Philip 5
DUNNING, Robert M(ackenzie) 5
DUNNING, Stewart N. 3
DUNNING, William Archibald 1
DUNNINGER, Joseph 6
DUNNINGTON, Francis Perry 4
DUNNINGTON, John Hughes 7
DUNNINGTON, Walter Grey 5
DUNNOCK, Mildred 10
DUNOYER DE SEGONZAC, Andre 6
DUNPHY, Charles 1
DUNPHY, John Englebert 9
DUNPHY, William Henry 1
DUNSCOMB, Charles Ellsworth 1
DUNSCOMB, Samuel Whitney, Jr. 1
DUNSHEE, Jay Dee 3
DUNSMORE, Andrew B. 1
DUNSMORE, John Ward 2
DUNSMORE, Philo Cordon 5
DUNSTAN, Arthur St. Charles 5
DUNSTAN, Edmund Fleetwood 5
DUNSTER, Henry H
DUNTLEY, John Wheeler 1
DUNTON, A. Davidson 9
DUNTON, Edith Kellogg 3
DUNTON, Frank Holt 4
DUNTON, Larkin 1
DUNTON, Lewis Marion 4
DUNTON, William Herbert 1
DUNWELL, Charles Tappan 1
DUNWELL, James Winslow 1
DUNWODY, Thomas Edgar 4
DUNWODY, William Elliott 3
DUNWOODY, Henry Harrison Chase 3
DUNWOODY, William Hood 1
DUPALAIS, Virginia Poullard H
DUPEE, Frederick Wilcox 7
DUPEE, John 5
DUPIUS, Charles W(illiam) 6
DUPLESSIS, Maurice L. 3
DUPONCEAU, Pierre Etinne H
DUPONG, Pierre 7
DU PONT, A. Felix 2
DU PONT, Alfred I. 1
DU PONT, Alfred Rhett 5
DU PONT, Eleuthere Irenee H
DUPONT, Emile Francis 6
DUPONT, Francis V. 4
DU PONT, Henry H
DU PONT, Henry Algernon 1
DUPONT, Henry B. 5
DUPONT, Henry Francis 5
DUPONT, Irenee 4
DUPONT, Irenee 5
DUPONT, Jesse Ball (Mrs. Alfred Ireneee Dupont) 5
DU PONT, Lammot 3
DU PONT, Pierre Samuel 3
DU PONT, Pierre Samuel, III 9
DU PONT, Samuel Francis H
DU PONT, T. Coleman 1
DU PONT, Victor Marie H
DU PONT, William, Jr. 4
DUPRATZ, Antoine Simon Le Page H
DU PRE, Arthur Mason 2
DU PRE, Daniel Allston 4
DUPRE, Henry Garland 1
DU PRÉ, Jacqueline 9
DUPRE, Marcel 5
DUPRE, Marcel 7
DUPREE, Louis Benjamin 10
DUPREY, John Paul 9
DUPUIS, Charles W(illiam) 9
DUPUIS, Raymond 5
DUPUIS, Rene 10
DUPUIS, Robert Newell 9
DUPUY, Eliza Ann H
DU PUY, Herbert 1
DUPUY, Pierre 5
DU PUY, Raymond 1
DUPUY, R(ichard) Ernest 6
DUPUY, Samuel Stuart 6
DU PUY, William Atherton 1
DUQUE, Ernest Eloy 9
DUQUE, Gabriel Carlos 8
DUQUE, Henry O'Melveny 5
DUQUE, Jose Luciano 9
DUQUESNE DE MENNEVILLE, Marquis H
DURAN, F. Mutis 4
DURAN, Narcisco H
DURAND, Asher Brown H
DURAND, Cyrus H
DURAND, David 5
DURAND, E(dward) Dana 5
DURAND, Elias Judah 1
DURAND, Elle Magioire H
DURAND, G(eorge) Harrison 5
DURAND, Sir Henry Mortimer 2
DURAND, James Harrison 6
DURAND, Loyal, Jr. 5
DURAND, William Frederick 3
DURANT, Ariel 8
DURANT, Charles Person H
DURANT, Frederick Clark, Jr. 4
DURANT, Henry H
DURANT, Henry Fowle H
DURANT, Thomas Clark H
DURANT, Thomas Jefferson H
DURANT, Thomas Morton 7
DURANT, William Crapo 2
DURANT, William James 7
DURANTE, Jimmy (James Francis) 7
DURANTE, Oscar 2
DURANTY, Walter 3
DURAS, Victor Hugo 6
DURBIN, Elisha John H
DURBIN, Fletcher McCullough 7
DURBIN, James Harold 10
DURBIN, John Price H
DURBIN, Winfield Taylor 1
DURBROW, Chandler Wolcott 6
DURDEN, Charles 7
DURELL, Daniel Meserve H
DURELL, Edward Henry H
DURELL, Edward Hovey 4
DURELL, George B. 4
DU RELLE, George 4
DURET, Miguel Lanz 3
DUREY, Cyrus 4
DUREY, John C. 5
DURFEE, Edgar Noble 3
DURFEE, Herbert Augustus 4
DURFEE, James Randall 7
DURFEE, Job H
DURFEE, Nathaniel Briggs H
DURFEE, Thomas 1
DURFEE, Walter Hetherington 6
DURFEE, William Franklin 1
DURFEE, William Pitt 1
DURFEE, William Pitt 2
DURFEE, Winthrop Carver 1
DURFEE, Zoheth Sherman H
DURFREY, John Cooper 4
DURGIN, Calvin Thornton 4
DURGIN, Cyrus W. 4
DURGIN, George Francis 4
DURGIN, Samuel Holmes 4
DURHAM, Caleb Wheeler H
DURHAM, Calen Wheeler 4
DURHAM, Carl Thomas 6
DURHAM, Charles Love 2
DURHAM, Donald B. 3
DURHAM, Edward 1
DURHAM, Edward Miall, Jr. 3
DURHAM, Fred Stranahan 3
DURHAM, George Homer 8
DURHAM, Harry Dixon 9
DURHAM, Henry Welles 5
DURHAM, Hobart Noble 5
DURHAM, Isreal W. 4
DURHAM, James Ware 5
DURHAM, John Stephens 1
DURHAM, Knowlton 4
DURHAM, Milton Jamison 1
DURHAM, Nelson Wayne 1
DURHAM, Philip Calvin 7
DURHAM, Plato Tracy 1
DURHAM, Robert Lee 2
DURIER, Antoine 1
DURIVAGE, Francis Alexander H
DURKEE, Arthur Bowman 10
DURKEE, Charles H
DURKEE, Frank Williams 1
DURKEE, John H
DURKEE, Rodney Stuart 8
DURKEE, William Porter 8
DURKIN, Martin 3
DURLAND, Kellogg 1
DURLAND, Lewis Hudson 8
DURLING, Edgar Vincent 3
DUROCHER, Leo (The Lip) 10
DURR, Clifford Judkins 6
DURR, Clifford Judkins 7
DURRANT, Stephen David 7
DURRELL, Joseph H. 4
DURRELL, Laurence Wood 8
DURRELL, Lawrence George 10
DURRENMATT, Friedrich 10
DURRETT, James J(ohnson) 8
DURRETT, Reuben Thomas 1
DURRETT, William Yancy 8
DURRIE, Daniel Steele H
DURRIE, George Henry H
DURST, William Arthur 1
DURSTINE, Roy Sarles 4
DURSTON, John Hurst 1
DURUFLE, Maurice 9
DURY, Charles 4
DURYEA, Charles Edgar H
DURYEA, Charles Edgar 4
DURYEA, Dan(iel) (Edwin) 5
DURYEA, Edwin 4
DURYEA, Hiram 1
DURYEA, Nina Larrey 3
DURYEA, Wright 4
DURYEE, Abram H
DURYEE, Samuel Sloan 7
DU SABLE, Jean Baptiste Point H
DU SACRE COEUR, Mother Marie 4
DUSCHAK, Lionel Herman 2
DUSE, Eleonora H
DUSE, Eleonora 4
DUSENBERRY, William Howard 7
DUSHAM, E(dward) H(enry) 6
DU SHANE, Donald 2
DUSHANE, Graham 4
DUSHMAN, Saul 3
DU SIMITIERE, Pierre Eugene H
DUSSER DE BARENNE, Joannes Gregorius 1
DUSTIN, Hannah H
DUSTMAN, Robert Barclay 9
DUTCHER, Charles Mason 1
DUTCHER, Clinton Harvey 9
DUTCHER, Francis Edward 6
DUTCHER, Francis Edward 7
DUTCHER, George Matthew 3
DUTCHER, Raymond Adams 7
DUTCHER, Silas Belden 1
DUTCHER, William 1
DUTRA, Eurico Gaspar 6
DUTREMBLAY, Pamphile-real 3
DUTROW, Howard Victor 6
DUTTON, Benjamin F. 1
DUTTON, Charles Judson 4
DUTTON, Clair C. 6
DUTTON, Clarence Edward 1
DUTTON, Edward A. 3
DUTTON, Edward Payson 1
DUTTON, Emily Helen 2
DUTTON, George Burwell 1
DUTTON, George Elliott 2
DUTTON, Henry H
DUTTON, Henry Post 7
DUTTON, Joseph 1
DUTTON, Leland Summers 10
DUTTON, Richard King 5
DUTTON, Samuel Train 1
DUTTON, Walter C. 4
DUTTON, William Jay 4
DUTY, Tony Edgar 10
DUVAL, Charles Warren 6
DU VAL, Frederic Beale 4
DUVAL, H. Rieman 1
DUVAL, Isaac Harding 1
DUVAL, Laurel 3
DUVAL, William Pope H
DUVALIER, Francois 5
DUVALL, Charles Raymond 1
DUVALL, Donald Chauncey 5
DUVALL, Gabriel H
DUVALL, James William 4
DUVALL, Trumbull Gillette 4
DUVALL, William Penn 1
DUVEL, Joseph William Tell 2
DUVENECK, Frank 1
DUVERNAY, Ludger H
DU VIGNEAUD, Vincent 7
DUVOISIN, Roger Antoine 9
DUWE, George E. 5
DUWEZ, Pol Edgard 8
DUWEZ, Pol Edgard 9
DUX, Claire 8
DUXBURY, George H. 3
DUYCKINCK, Evert Augustus H
DUYCKINCK, George Long H
DUYCKINCK, Gerrit H
DVORAK, Antonin H
DVORAK, August 7
DVORAK, Raymond Francis 8
DVORNIK, Francis 6
DVORNIK, Francis 7
D'VYS, George Whitefield 1
DWAN, Allan 8
DWAN, Ralph Hubert 5
DWENGER, Joseph H
DWIGGINS, Clare Victor 3
DWIGGINS, William Addison 3
DWIGHT, Arthur Smith 2
DWIGHT, Benjamin Franklin H
DWIGHT, Benjamin Woodbridge H
DWIGHT, Edmund H
DWIGHT, Edmund 1
DWIGHT, Edward Harold 8
DWIGHT, Edwin Welles 1
DWIGHT, Francis H
DWIGHT, Harrison Griswold 3

EBERLE, John H
EBERLEIN, Harold Donaldson 4
EBERLEIN, William Frederick 9
EBERLY, George Agler 5
EBERMAN, Paul Wilmot 7
EBERSOLE, Ezra Christian 1
EBERSOLE, J(acob) Scott 5
EBERSOLE, John Franklin 2
EBERSOLE, William Stahl 3
EBERSTADT, Ferdinand 5
EBERSTADT, Rudolph 4
EBERT, Edmund Francis 5
EBERT, Robert Edwin 5
EBERT, Rudolph Gustav 4
EBLE, Charles E. 9
EBLE, Frank Xavier A. 6
EBLEN, Amos Hall 8
EBRIGHT, Homer Kingsley 6
EBY, Frederick 4
EBY, Frederick 5
EBY, Ivan David 4
EBY, Kermit 4
EBY, Kerr 2
EBY, Margarette Fink 9
EBY, Robert Killian 4
ECCLES, George Stoddard 8
ECCLES, James A. 3
ECCLES, Marriner Stoddard 7
ECCLES, Robert G. 1
ECCLES, Willard L. 9
ECCLESTON, J(ames) Houston 8
ECCLESTON, Samuel H
ECHLIN, John Edward 10
ECHOLS, Angus B. 4
ECHOLS, Charles Patton 1
ECHOLS, John H
ECHOLS, John Minor 8
ECHOLS, John Warnock 1
ECHOLS, Leonard Sidney 5
ECHOLS, Oliver P. 3
ECHOLS, Robert 3
ECHOLS, William Graham 9
ECHOLS, William Holding, Jr. 1
ECHOLS, William Joseph 1
ECIJA, Juan de H
ECKARD, Elisabeth Ellen Gilliland 5
ECKARD, James Read H
ECKARD, Leighton Wilson 1
ECKARDT, Lisgar Russell 2
ECKART, Carl 6
ECKART, E. Albert 5
ECKEL, Clarence Lewis 5
ECKEL, Edwin Clarence 2
ECKELS, James Herron 1
ECKENRODE, Hamilton James 6
ECKENRODE, Robert Thomas 8
ECKER, Enrique E. 4
ECKER, Frederic W. 4
ECKER, Frederick H. 4
ECKERMAN, William Charles 8
ECKERSALL, Edwin Robert 4
ECKERSALL, Walter H. 1
ECKERT, Charles R. 4
ECKERT, George Nicholas H
ECKERT, Howard Haines 4
ECKERT, Otto E. 8
ECKERT, Ruth Elizabeth (Mrs. John H. McComb) 9
ECKERT, Samuel Baltz 7
ECKERT, Thomas Thompson 1
ECKERT, Wallace J. 5
ECKERT, William D(ole) 5
ECKFELDT, Howard 2
ECKFELDT, Thomas Hooper 1
ECKFORD, Henry H
ECKHARD, George Frederick 2
ECKHART, Bernard Albert 1
ECKHART, Harold 7
ECKHART, Percy Bernard 5
ECKHOUSE, Joseph L. 4
ECKLER, A. Ross 10
ECKLES, Clarence Henry 1
ECKLES, Isabel Lancaster 5
ECKLEY, Frederick Ralph, Jr. 8
ECKLEY, William Thomas 1
ECKMAN, Donald Preston 4
ECKMAN, George Peck 1
ECKMAN, James Russell 9
ECKMANN, Janos 6
ECKOFF, William Julius 1
ECKRICH, Richard P. 6
ECKSTEIN, Alexander 7
ECKSTEIN, Frederick H
ECKSTEIN, Gustav 8
ECKSTEIN, John H
ECKSTEIN, Louis 1
ECKSTEIN, Nathan 2
ECKSTEIN, Otto 8
ECKSTORM, Fannie Hardy 2
ECKSTROM, Lawrence Joel 4
ECTON, Zales Nelson 4
ED, Carl Frank Ludwig 3
EDBROOKE, Willoughby J. H
EDDINGER, Wallace 1
EDDINS, Daniel Stonewall 8
EDDINS, Henry A. 4
EDDIS, William H
EDDISON, William Barton 7
EDDLEMAN, Thomas Stricker 6
EDDY, Alfred Delavan 1
EDDY, Allen 3
EDDY, Arthur Jerome 1
EDDY, Brayton 3
EDDY, Charles Brown 3
EDDY, Clarence 1
EDDY, Clyde 8
EDDY, Condit Nelson 4
EDDY, Corbin Theodore 7
EDDY, Daniel Clarke H
EDDY, David Brewer 2
EDDY, Forrest Greenwood 1
EDDY, Francis Rollin 7
EDDY, Frank Woodman 1
EDDY, Gerald Ernest 7
EDDY, Harrison Prescott 1
EDDY, Henry Brevoort 5
EDDY, Henry Stephens 2
EDDY, Henry Turner 1
EDDY, Isaac H
EDDY, Lee Moin 6
EDDY, Manton S. 4
EDDY, Mary Baker Glover 1
EDDY, Milton Walker 4
EDDY, Nathan Browne 5
EDDY, Nelson 4
EDDY, Norman H
EDDY, Oliver Tarbell H
EDDY, Paul Dawson 6
EDDY, Richard 1
EDDY, Samuel H
EDDY, Sherwood 4
EDDY, Spencer 1
EDDY, Thomas H
EDDY, Thomas Mears H
EDDY, Walter Hollis 3
EDDY, Walter Lewis 8
EDDY, William Abner 1
EDDY, William Alfred 4
EDDY, William Crawford 10
EDDY, Zachary H
EDEBOHLS, George Michael 1
EDELHERTZ, Bernard 1
EDELMAN, John W. 5
EDELMAN, Maurice 6
EDELMAN, Nathan 5
EDELSTEIN, Ludwig 4
EDELSTEIN, M. Michael 2
EDEN, Charles H
EDEN, Charles Henry 10
EDEN, Frank Ernest 7
EDEN, Robert H
EDENBORN, William 1
EDENS, Arthur Hollis 5
EDENS, James Benjamin 5
EDENS, James Drake, Jr. 8
EDENS, William Grant 3
EDER, Phanor James 5
EDES, Benjamin H
EDES, Henry Herbert 1
EDES, Robert Thaxter 1
EDES, William Cushing 1
EDESON, Robert 1
EDEY, Maitland Armstrong 10
EDGAR, Alvin Randall 6
EDGAR, Alvin Randall 7
EDGAR, Campbell Dallas 8
EDGAR, Charles Bloomfield 1
EDGAR, Charles Leavitt 1
EDGAR, Earl Eugene 7
EDGAR, Graham 3
EDGAR, J. Clifton 1
EDGAR, Randolph 1
EDGAR, Randolph 2
EDGAR, Robert Franklin 4
EDGAR, Thomas Delbert 1
EDGAR, William Crowell 1
EDGCOMB, Ernest Isaac 4
EDGCOMB, Leslie 7
EDGE, Joseph H(enry) 7
EDGE, Rosalie (Mrs. Charles Noel) 6
EDGE, Walter Evans 3
EDGECOMBE, Samuel 3
EDGELL, George Harold 3
EDGELL, Robert Louis 10
EDGERLY, Beatrice (Mrs. J. Havard MacPherson) 6
EDGERLY, Winfield Scot 1
EDGERTON, Alanson Harrison 8
EDGERTON, Alfred Peck H
EDGERTON, Alice Craig 2
EDGERTON, Alonzo Jay H
EDGERTON, Charles Eugene 1
EDGERTON, Edward Keith 6
EDGERTON, Franklin 4
EDGERTON, Glen Edgar 7
EDGERTON, Halsey Charles 4
EDGERTON, Harold Eugene 10
EDGERTON, Henry White 5
EDGERTON, Herbert Oliver 5
EDGERTON, Hiram H. 1
EDGERTON, James Arthur 1
EDGERTON, John Emmett 1
EDGERTON, John Warren 1
EDGERTON, Justin Lincoln 5
EDGERTON, William Franklin 5
EDGETT, Edwin Francis 2
EDGINGTON, Ralph 7
EDGINGTON, Thomas Benton 1
EDGREN, John Alexis 1
EDHOLM-SIBLEY, Mary G. Charlton 4
EDIE, Guy Lewis 1
EDIE, John Rufus H
EDIE, Lionel Danforth 4
EDINGS, William Seabrook 4
EDINGTON, Arlo Channing 3
EDINGTON, William Edmund 7
EDISON, Charles 5
EDISON, Charles B. 5
EDISON, Harry 4
EDISON, Mark Aaron 3
EDISON, Oskar E. 4
EDISON, Samuel Bernard 5
EDISON, Thomas A. 1
EDLUND, Roscoe Claudius 9
EDLUND, Sidney Wendell 7
EDMAN, Irwin 3
EDMAN, V. Raymond 4
EDMANDS, John 1
EDMANDS, John Wiley H
EDMANDS, Samuel Sumner 1
EDMINSTER, Talcott W. 8
EDMISTER, Floyd (Harris) 6
EDMISTON, Andrew 4
EDMISTON, R. W. 4
EDMISTON, William Sherman 5
EDMOND, William H
EDMONDS, Dean Stockett 5
EDMONDS, Douglas Lyman 4
EDMONDS, Francis William H
EDMONDS, Frank Norman, Jr. 9
EDMONDS, Franklin Spencer 2
EDMONDS, George Washington 1
EDMONDS, Harry Marcus Weston 2
EDMONDS, Henry Morris 4
EDMONDS, Ira Clement 6
EDMONDS, James E. 6
EDMONDS, John Worth H
EDMONDS, Richard Hathaway 1
EDMONDS, Thomas Sechler 6
EDMONDS, Thomas Sechler 7
EDMONDSON, Cathrine Elizabeth 5
EDMONDSON, Clarence Edmund 2
EDMONDSON, Hugh Allen 9
EDMONDSON, James Howard 5
EDMONDSON, John Preston 7
EDMONDSON, Thomas William 1
EDMONDSON, William John 5
EDMONSON, James Bartlett 7
EDMUNDS, Albert Joseph 1
EDMUNDS, Albert Joseph 2
EDMUNDS, Charles Carroll 4
EDMUNDS, Charles Keyser 2
EDMUNDS, Charles Wallis 1
EDMUNDS, George Franklin 1
EDMUNDS, Harry Nicholas 1
EDMUNDS, James Richard, Jr. 3
EDMUNDS, John Ollie 8
EDMUNDS, Palmer Daniel 9
EDMUNDS, Samuel Henry 1
EDMUNDS, Sterling Edwin 2
EDMUNDS-HEMINGWAY, Mme 3
EDMUNDSON, Henry Alonzo H
EDMUNDSON, James Depew 1
EDOUART, Alexander H
EDOUART, Auguste H
EDQUIST, Erhart David 10
EDRINGTON, William Reynolds 1
EDROP, Percy T. 5
EDSALL, David Linn 2
EDSALL, Geoffrey 7
EDSALL, Joseph E. H
EDSALL, Preston William 5
EDSALL, Samuel Cook 1
EDSFORTH, Charles Dugdale 4
EDSON, Andrew Wheatley 1
EDSON, Carroll Everett 1
EDSON, Cyrus 1
EDSON, Franklin 1
EDSON, Gus 4
EDSON, Howard Austin 5
EDSON, Job Adolphus 1
EDSON, John Joy 1
EDSON, Katherine Philips 1
EDSON, Merritt Austin 3
EDSON, Peter 7
EDSON, Robert Clay 4
EDSON, Stephen Reuben 5
EDSON, Tracy R. H
EDSON, Winfield 3
EDSTROM, David 1
EDWARD, Harvey 2
EDWARDS, Alanson W. 1
EDWARDS, Alba M. 5
EDWARDS, Alfred Shenstone 4
EDWARDS, Arthur Robin 1
EDWARDS, Austin Southwick 7
EDWARDS, Bela Bates H
EDWARDS, Benjamin H
EDWARDS, Benjamin D. 1
EDWARDS, Benjamin Franklin 4
EDWARDS, Billy Matt 9
EDWARDS, Bryan C. 9
EDWARDS, Byron Malet 8
EDWARDS, Carleton Bailey 9
EDWARDS, Charles H
EDWARDS, Charles Gordon 1
EDWARDS, Charles Lincoln 1
EDWARDS, Charles Mundy, Jr. 9
EDWARDS, Charles Peter 7
EDWARDS, Charles Reid 8
EDWARDS, Charles Vernon 5
EDWARDS, Charles William 3
EDWARDS, Chauncey Theodore 5
EDWARDS, Clarence Ransom 1
EDWARDS, Clement Stanislaus 5
EDWARDS, Corwin D. 7
EDWARDS, Daniel James 10
EDWARDS, Daniel Richmond 8
EDWARDS, David Frank 4
EDWARDS, David George 4
EDWARDS, David Morton 1
EDWARDS, Dayton J(ames) 7
EDWARDS, Deltus Malin 5
EDWARDS, Don Calvin 1
EDWARDS, Douglas 10
EDWARDS, Edward B. 2
EDWARDS, Edward Everett 9
EDWARDS, Edward Irving 1
EDWARDS, Edward William 3
EDWARDS, Elisha Jay 4
EDWARDS, Everett Eugene 3
EDWARDS, F. Boyd 2
EDWARDS, Francis Henry 10
EDWARDS, Frank 4
EDWARDS, Frank William 7
EDWARDS, Frederick 5
EDWARDS, George Herbert 2
EDWARDS, George Lane 5
EDWARDS, George Porter 1
EDWARDS, George Thornton 1
EDWARDS, George Wharton 2
EDWARDS, George William 3
EDWARDS, Gordon L. 3
EDWARDS, Granville Dennis 3
EDWARDS, Gurney 3
EDWARDS, Harrison Griffith 5
EDWARDS, Harry Stillwell 1
EDWARDS, Heber L. 4
EDWARDS, Henry Waggaman H
EDWARDS, Hiram W(heeler) 7
EDWARDS, Howard 1
EDWARDS, Howard Wesley 4
EDWARDS, Ira 2
EDWARDS, James D. 8
EDWARDS, James Ellis 9
EDWARDS, James Thomas 1
EDWARDS, John* H
EDWARDS, John Cummins H
EDWARDS, John Harrington 4
EDWARDS, John Homer 2
EDWARDS, John Palmer 4
EDWARDS, John Richard 1
EDWARDS, John Rogers 2
EDWARDS, John S. 9
EDWARDS, Jonathan* H
EDWARDS, Joseph Lee 4
EDWARDS, Joseph Lee 5
EDWARDS, Julian 1
EDWARDS, Justin H
EDWARDS, Kate Flournoy 7
EDWARDS, Landon Brame 1
EDWARDS, Le Roy Mallory 4
EDWARDS, Lena Frances 9
EDWARDS, Leroy D. 3
EDWARDS, Lester Richard 8
EDWARDS, Leverett 10
EDWARDS, Linden Forest 5
EDWARDS, Loren McClain 2
EDWARDS, Louise Betts 1
EDWARDS, Lyford Paterson 8
EDWARDS, Marcia 8
EDWARDS, Margaret Messenger 4
EDWARDS, Morgan H
EDWARDS, Murray French 4
EDWARDS, Myrtle Sassman (Mrs. Harlan H. Edwards) 5
EDWARDS, Nathaniel Marsh 1
EDWARDS, Ninian H
EDWARDS, Ninian Wirt H
EDWARDS, Ogden Matthias 1
EDWARDS, Paul Carroll 7
EDWARDS, Paul Kenneth 3
EDWARDS, Percy Noyes 5
EDWARDS, Philip R. 4
EDWARDS, Pierpont H
EDWARDS, Prentice Dearing 10
EDWARDS, Ray Gwyther 5
EDWARDS, Ray Lee 7
EDWARDS, Richard 1
EDWARDS, Richard Ambrose 10
EDWARDS, Richard Henry 3
EDWARDS, Richard Stanislaus 3
EDWARDS, Robert Ernest 5
EDWARDS, Robert Wilkinson 5
EDWARDS, Ronald Stanley 6
EDWARDS, Russell 10
EDWARDS, Samuel H
EDWARDS, Samuel 1
EDWARDS, Sherman 7
EDWARDS, Stephen Ostrom 1
EDWARDS, Talmadge H

ELLINGSON, Harold Victor 7
ELLINGSON, Steve 10
ELLINGTON, Buford 5
ELLINGTON, Edward Kennedy (Duke) 6
ELLINGTON, Elmer Verne 8
ELLINGTON, Harold S(laight) 9
ELLINGTON, Jesse Thompson 5
ELLINGWOOD, Albert Russell 1
ELLINGWOOD, Finley 1
ELLINWOOD, Everett E. 2
ELLINWOOD, Frank Field 1
ELLINWOOD, Ralph Everett 1
ELLINWOOD, Truman Jeremiah 1
ELLIOT, Charles H
ELLIOT, Daniel Giraud 1
ELLIOT, George Thomson 1
ELLIOT, Henry M. 8
ELLIOT, Henry Rutherford 1
ELLIOT, James H
ELLIOT, John Wheelock 1
ELLIOT, Jonathan H
ELLIOTT, A. Marshall 1
ELLIOTT, Albert Randle 10
ELLIOTT, Alfred J. 5
ELLIOTT, Arthur Richard 4
ELLIOTT, Ben G. 8
ELLIOTT, Benjamin H
ELLIOTT, Byron Kosciusko 1
ELLIOTT, Charles Addison 1
ELLIOTT, Charles Burke 1
ELLIOTT, Charles Gleason 1
ELLIOTT, Charles Herbert 6
ELLIOTT, Charles Loring H
ELLIOTT, Claude 3
ELLIOTT, Colin Fraser 8
ELLIOTT, Curtis Miller 5
ELLIOTT, Dabney Otey 7
ELLIOTT, Daniel Stanley 2
ELLIOTT, Denholm Mitchell 10
ELLIOTT, Edward 2
ELLIOTT, Edward Charles 4
ELLIOTT, Edward Loomis 3
ELLIOTT, Ernest Eugene 1
ELLIOTT, Errol Thomas 10
ELLIOTT, Francis Perry 1
ELLIOTT, Frank Rumsey 4
ELLIOTT, George 1
ELLIOTT, George Blow 2
ELLIOTT, George Frank 1
ELLIOTT, George Frederick 4
ELLIOTT, George Paul 7
ELLIOTT, G(eorge) R(oy) 7
ELLIOTT, Gertrude 3
ELLIOTT, Grace Loucks 7
ELLIOTT, Harold Hirsch 6
ELLIOTT, Harold Hirsch 7
ELLIOTT, Harriet Wiesman 2
ELLIOTT, Harrison Sacket 3
ELLIOTT, Henry Wood 4
ELLIOTT, Homer 3
ELLIOTT, Howard 1
ELLIOTT, Huger 2
ELLIOTT, Ivan A. 8
ELLIOTT, J. M. 2
ELLIOTT, Jackson S. 2
ELLIOTT, James H
ELLIOTT, James Douglas 1
ELLIOTT, James Lewis 5
ELLIOTT, James Robert 4
ELLIOTT, James Thomas H
ELLIOTT, Jesse Duncan H
ELLIOTT, John H
ELLIOTT, John 1
ELLIOTT, John Asbury 1
ELLIOTT, John B. 4
ELLIOTT, John Barnwell 5
ELLIOTT, John Henry* 4
ELLIOTT, John Lovejoy 2
ELLIOTT, John M. 4
ELLIOTT, John MacKay 1
ELLIOTT, John Milton H
ELLIOTT, John Stuart 4
ELLIOTT, John Wesley 4
ELLIOTT, John Wesley 5
ELLIOTT, Joseph Alexander 4
ELLIOTT, Lewis Grimes 2
ELLIOTT, Louis D. 8
ELLIOTT, Mabel Agnes 10
ELLIOTT, Martha Virginia Beggs 9
ELLIOTT, Martin Anderson 9
ELLIOTT, Martin Kelso 4
ELLIOTT, Maud Howe 2
ELLIOTT, Maxine 1
ELLIOTT, Middleton Stuart 3
ELLIOTT, Milton Courtright 1
ELLIOTT, Oliver Morton 1
ELLIOTT, Orrin Leslie 1
ELLIOTT, Owen N. 7
ELLIOTT, Philip Lovin 4
ELLIOTT, Phillips Packer 4
ELLIOTT, Richard Hammond 5
ELLIOTT, Richard Maurice 8
ELLIOTT, Richard Nash 2
ELLIOTT, Robert Brown H
ELLIOTT, Robert Carl 7
ELLIOTT, Robert Hare Egerton 7
ELLIOTT, Robert Irving 2
ELLIOTT, Robert Michael 4
ELLIOTT, Roy Gordon 3
ELLIOTT, Sarah Barnwell 1
ELLIOTT, Shelden Douglass 5
ELLIOTT, Simon Bolivar 4
ELLIOTT, Stephen H
ELLIOTT, Stuart Rhett 5
ELLIOTT, Thompson Coit 2
ELLIOTT, Walter 1
ELLIOTT, Washington Lafayette H
ELLIOTT, Willard Buford 7
ELLIOTT, William H
ELLIOTT, William 1
ELLIOTT, William 2
ELLIOTT, William Arthur 1
ELLIOTT, William Henry 1
ELLIOTT, William John 6
ELLIOTT, William Sanders 3
ELLIOTT, William Swan 1
ELLIOTT, William Yandell 7
ELLIS, Aileen Virginia 7
ELLIS, Alexander Caswell 2
ELLIS, Alston 1
ELLIS, Anderson Nelson 2
ELLIS, Anna M. B. 1
ELLIS, Arthur McDonald 1
ELLIS, Brooks Fleming 7
ELLIS, Caleb H
ELLIS, Calvin H
ELLIS, Carleton 1
ELLIS, Carlyle 6
ELLIS, Challen Blackburn 2
ELLIS, Charles Alton 2
ELLIS, Charles Calvert 10
ELLIS, Charles Calvert 3
ELLIS, Charles S. 4
ELLIS, Chesselden H
ELLIS, Clyde Taylor 7
ELLIS, Crawford Hatcher 4
ELLIS, David Abram 1
ELLIS, Don Carlos 3
ELLIS, Donald Johnson 7
ELLIS, Edgar Clarence 2
ELLIS, Edward Sylvester 1
ELLIS, Edwin Erastus 1
ELLIS, Ezekiel John H
ELLIS, Frank Burton 5
ELLIS, G. Corson 4
ELLIS, George Adams 3
ELLIS, George C(arrington) 7
ELLIS, George David 4
ELLIS, George Edward H
ELLIS, George Edwin 4
ELLIS, George Price, Sr. 3
ELLIS, George Washington 1
ELLIS, George William 5
ELLIS, Gilbert R. 8
ELLIS, Gordon 6
ELLIS, Griffith Ogden 2
ELLIS, H. Bert 1
ELLIS, Harold Milton 2
ELLIS, Harvey 1
ELLIS, Hayne 5
ELLIS, Henry H
ELLIS, Horace 1
ELLIS, Howard 4
ELLIS, Howard 5
ELLIS, Howard Sylvester 10
ELLIS, Hubert Summers 8
ELLIS, Ira Howell 4
ELLIS, J. Breckenridge 3
ELLIS, James 6
ELLIS, James Tandy 4
ELLIS, Job Bicknell 1
ELLIS, John Dayhuff 3
ELLIS, John Henry 6
ELLIS, John Tracy 10
ELLIS, John Washington H
ELLIS, John Washington 4
ELLIS, John William 1
ELLIS, John Willis H
ELLIS, Katharine Ruth 6
ELLIS, Leighton Arthur 4
ELLIS, Lewis Ethan 7
ELLIS, Marvin Earl 10
ELLIS, Mary 1
ELLIS, Max Mapes 3
ELLIS, Milton Andrew 4
ELLIS, Overton Gentry 1
ELLIS, Perry Canby 1
ELLIS, Perry Edwin 9
ELLIS, Powhatan H
ELLIS, Ralph 3
ELLIS, Richard Hastings 10
ELLIS, Robert H. 8
ELLIS, Robert Walpole 1
ELLIS, Roy 8
ELLIS, Rudolph 1
ELLIS, Samuel Mervyl 2
ELLIS, Seth H. 1
ELLIS, Tharon J. 4
ELLIS, Theodore Thaddeus 1
ELLIS, Thomas Cargill Warner 4
ELLIS, Thomas David 3
ELLIS, W. R. 3
ELLIS, Wade H. 2
ELLIS, Willard Drake 2
ELLIS, William Cox H
ELLIS, William D. 4
ELLIS, William Edward 8
ELLIS, William Hull 2
ELLIS, William John 2
ELLIS, William Leigh 10
ELLIS, William Russell 1
ELLIS, William Thomas 3
ELLISON, Andrew H
ELLISON, Daniel 7
ELLISON, Everett Monroe 1
ELLISON, George Robb 3
ELLISON, Jerome 8
ELLISON, J(ohn) Malcus 8
ELLISON, Joseph Roy 5
ELLISON, Robert S(purrier) 5
ELLISON, Thomas Emmet 1
ELLISON, William Bruce 1
ELLISTON, George 2
ELLISTON, Grace 3
ELLISTON, Herbert Berridge 3
ELLITHORP, John Stafford, Jr. 4
ELLMAKER, Amos H
ELLMAKER, Lee 3
ELLMANN, Richard 9
ELLS, Arthur Fairbanks 4
ELLSBERG, Edward 8
ELLSBERRY, William Wallace H
ELLSLER, Effie 1
ELLSLER, Effie 2
ELLSWORTH, Albert Leroy 3
ELLSWORTH, Donald William 7
ELLSWORTH, Elmer Ephriam H
ELLSWORTH, Franklin Fowler 3
ELLSWORTH, Fred Winthrop 3
ELLSWORTH, Harris 9
ELLSWORTH, Henry Leavitt H
ELLSWORTH, James Drummond 1
ELLSWORTH, James William 1
ELLSWORTH, John Jay 5
ELLSWORTH, John Orval 6
ELLSWORTH, Lincoln 3
ELLSWORTH, Oliver H
ELLSWORTH, Oliver B. 5
ELLSWORTH, Samuel Stewart H
ELLSWORTH, Sidney Ernest 4
ELLSWORTH, William Webster 1
ELLSWORTH, William Wolcott H
ELLWANGER, George Herman 1
ELLWANGER, William De Lancey 1
ELLWOOD, Charles Abram 2
ELLWOOD, Isaac Leonard 1
ELLWOOD, John Kelley 4
ELLWOOD, Reuben H
ELLYSON, J. Taylor 1
ELMAN, Mischa 4
ELMAN, Robert 3
ELMEN, Gustaf Waldemar 3
ELMENDORF, Dwight Lathrop 1
ELMENDORF, Francis Littleton 5
ELMENDORF, Henry Livingston 1
ELMENDORF, Joachim 1
ELMENDORF, John E., Jr. 4
ELMENDORF, John Van Gaasbeek 7
ELMENDORF, Lucas Conrad H
ELMENDORF, Theresa Hubbell 1
ELMER, Ebenezer H
ELMER, Henry Whiteley 1
ELMER, Herbert Charles 4
ELMER, Jonathan H
ELMER, Lucius Quintius Cincinnatus H
ELMER, Manuel Conrad 7
ELMER, S. Lewis 4
ELMER, S(amuel) Lewis 5
ELMER, William 1
ELMER, William 3
ELMER, William Price 3
ELMHIRST, Leonard Knight 6
ELMLARK, Harry Eugene 8
ELMORE, Franklin Harper H
ELMORE, George Sutherland 3
ELMORE, Jefferson 1
ELMORE, Samuel Edward 1
ELMORE, Wilber Theodore 1
ELMQUIST, Axel Louis 2
ELMSLIE, George Grant 3
ELOESSER, Leo 6
ELOFSON, Carl L. 3
ELONEN, Anna Sivia 9
ELROD, Morton John 4
ELROD, Ralph 3
ELROD, Samuel Harrison 1
ELSASSER, Theodore Herman 9
ELSASSER, Walter Maurice 10
ELSBERG, Charles Albert 2
ELSBERG, Louis H
ELSBREE, Wayland Hoyt 10
ELSE, Gerald Frank 8
ELSENBAST, Arthur S. 6
ELSER, Frank B. 1
ELSER, Maximilian, Jr. 4
ELSER, William James 5
ELSEY, Charles 6
ELSING, William Taddes 8
ELSNER, Henry Leopold 1
ELSOM, James Claude 4
ELSON, Alfred Walter 2
ELSON, Arthur 1
ELSON, Henry William 3
ELSON, Louis Charles 1
ELSON, Robert T. 9
ELSON, Sam 7
ELSON, Sam 8
ELSON, William Harris 1
ELSSFELDT, Otto Hermann Wilheim Leonhard 6
ELSTAD, Leonard M. 10
ELSTAD, Rudolph T. 3
ELSTON, Dorothy Andrews (Mrs. Walter L. Kabis) 5
ELSTON, Isaac Compton 1
ELSTON, Isaac Compton, Jr. 4
ELSTON, John Arthur 1
ELSWORTH, Edward 1
ELTHON, Leo 4
ELTING, Arthur Wells 2
ELTING, Howard 3
ELTING, Victor 3
ELTING, Victor, Jr. 7
ELTING, Winston 5
ELTINGE, Julian 1
ELTINGE, Leroy 1
ELTON, Frederic Garfield 6
ELTON, J. O. 3
ELTON, James Samuel 1
ELTON, John Prince 2
ELTON, Reuel William 8
ELTON, Wallace Wesley 10
ELTSE, Ralph R. 7
ELTZHOLTZ, Carl Frederick 1
ELVEHJEM, Conrad Arnold 4
ELVERSON, James 1
ELVEY, Christian Thomas 5
ELVIDGE, Ford Quint 9
ELVING, Philip Juliber 8
ELVINS, Politte 2
ELWELL, Charles Clement 1
ELWELL, Clarence Edward 6
ELWELL, Francis Edwin 1
ELWELL, Herbert 6
ELWELL, John Johnson H
ELWELL, Levi Henry 1
ELWELL, Richard E. 6
ELWOOD, Everett Sprague 6
ELWOOD, John Worden 4
ELWOOD, Philip Homer, Jr. 4
ELWOOD, Robert Arthur 3
ELWYN, Alfred Langdon H
ELY, Albert Heman 1
ELY, Alfred H
ELY, Charles Russell 1
ELY, Charles Wright 1
ELY, Elizabeth L. 5
ELY, Frederick David 1
ELY, Grosvenor 4
ELY, Hanson Edward 3
ELY, John H
ELY, John Hugh 1
ELY, John Slade 1
ELY, Joseph Buell 3
ELY, Lafayette G. 4
ELY, Leonard Wheeler 4
ELY, Richard R(oyal) 5
ELY, Richard Theodore 2
ELY, Robert Erskine 2
ELY, Roy J. W. 4
ELY, Sims 3
ELY, Smith 1
ELY, Sterling 4
ELY, Sumner Boyer 5
ELY, Theodore Newel 1
ELY, Thomas Southgate 6
ELY, Walter Raleigh, Jr. 8
ELY, Wayne 3
ELY, William H
ELY, Wilson C. 3
ELZAS, Barnett Abraham 1
ELZEY, Arnold H
ELZNER, Alfred Oscar 1
EMANUEL, Victor 4
EMBER, Aaron 1
EMBLETON, Harry 3
EMBODY, George Charles 1
EMBREE, Charles Fleming 1
EMBREE, Edwin Rogers 2
EMBREE, Elihu H
EMBREE, Elisha H
EMBREE, William Dean 9
EMBRIE, Jonas Reece H
EMBRY, John 4
EMBRY, Lloyd Bowers 7
EMBRY, Norris Wulkop 8
EMBRY, Thomas Eric 10
EMBRY, Thomas Eric 8
EMBURY, Aymar, II 4
EMBURY, David A. 4
EMBURY, Philip H
EMCH, Arnold 5
EMCH, Arnold Frederick 10
EMENY, Brooks 7
EMERICH, Ira 6
EMERICH, Ira 7
EMERICH, Martin 4
EMERICK, Charles Franklin 1
EMERICK, Edson James 3
EMERMAN, David 6
EMERSON, Alfred Edwards 7
EMERSON, Benjamin Kendall 1
EMERSON, Charles Franklin 1
EMERSON, Charles Phillips 1
EMERSON, Charles Wesley 1
EMERSON, Cherry Logan 4
EMERSON, Chester Burge 6
EMERSON, Chester Burge 7
EMERSON, Earl Arthur 9
EMERSON, Edward Randolph 1
EMERSON, Edward Waldo 1
EMERSON, Edwin 4
EMERSON, Edwin, Jr. 5
EMERSON, Ellen Russell 1
EMERSON, Evalyn (Stage Name, Evalyn Earle) 5
EMERSON, Faye Margaret 8
EMERSON, Frank Collins 1
EMERSON, Frank Nelson 5
EMERSON, George Barrell H
EMERSON, George H. 5
EMERSON, Gladys Anderson 8
EMERSON, Gouverneur H
EMERSON, Gouverneur Vincent 8
EMERSON, Guy 5
EMERSON, Harold Logan 4
EMERSON, Harrington 1
EMERSON, Haven 3
EMERSON, Henry Pendexter 1
EMERSON, Jabez Oscar 5
EMERSON, James Ezekiel 1
EMERSON, James Gordon 8
EMERSON, Jay Noble 2
EMERSON, John 3
EMERSON, Joseph H
EMERSON, Justin Edwards 4
EMERSON, Kendall 5
EMERSON, Linn 5
EMERSON, Lousis W. 4
EMERSON, Luther Orlando 1

EMERSON, Lynn Arthur 8
EMERSON, Merton Leslie 2
EMERSON, Nathaniel Bright
EMERSON, Nathaniel Waldo 1
EMERSON, Oliver Farrar 1
EMERSON, Paul 1
EMERSON, Philip 4
EMERSON, Ralph H
EMERSON, Ralph 1
EMERSON, Ralph Waldo H
EMERSON, Robert 3
EMERSON, Robert Alton 1
EMERSON, Robert Greenough 10
EMERSON, Robert Stephen 1
EMERSON, Rollins Adams 2
EMERSON, Rupert 7
EMERSON, Sam W. 6
EMERSON, Samuel Franklin
EMERSON, Summer Brooks 5
EMERSON, Susan Mabel 4
EMERSON, Thomas Irwin 10
EMERSON, Willard I. 4
EMERSON, William
EMERSON, William 3
EMERSON, Willis George
EMERTON, Ephraim 1
EMERTON, James H. 1
EMERY, Albert Hamilton 1
EMERY, Albert Waldron, Jr. 9
EMERY, Alden H(ayes) 6
EMERY, Ambrose R. 2
EMERY, Charles Edward H
EMERY, Dewitt McKinley 3
EMERY, Earnest Wesley 8
EMERY, Edward Kellogg 1
EMERY, Fred Azro 4
EMERY, Fred Parker 1
EMERY, Grenville C. 1
EMERY, Harlan Julien 7
EMERY, Henry Crosby 1
EMERY, Ina Capitola 1
EMERY, James Augustan 3
EMERY, John Garfield 6
EMERY, John Runkle 1
EMERY, Lewis, Jr. 1
EMERY, Lucilius Alonzo 1
EMERY, Matthew Gault 1
EMERY, Natt Morrill 1
EMERY, Richard Runkel 1
EMERY, Roe 3
EMERY, Sarah Anna 1
EMERY, Stephen Albert H
EMERY, Susan L. 1
EMERY, William Marshall* 1
EMERY, William Morrell 4
EMERY, William Orrin 3
EMERY, Z. Taylor 1
EMGE, Ludwig Augustus 7
EMHARDT, William Chauncey 3
EMIG, Arthur S. 1
EMIG, Elmer Jacob 3
EMIL, Allan D. 6
EMIL, Allan D. 7
EMILE, Anders 9
EMISON, John C. 4
EMISON, John C. 5
EMKEN, Cecil Wheeler 5
EMLAW, Harlan Stigand 1
EMME, Earle E(dward) 9
EMMERICH, F. J. 5
EMMERICH, Herbert 5
EMMERSON, Henry Read 3
EMMERSON, Louis Lincoln 1
EMMERT, Arthur Philip 7
EMMERT, John Harley 2
EMMET, Grenville Temple 1
EMMET, Herman LeRoy 8
EMMET, John Patten H
EMMET, Lydia Field 3
EMMET, Robert R(utherford) M(orris) 8
EMMET, Thomas Addis H
EMMET, Thomas Addis 1
EMMET, William Leroy 1
EMMET, William Temple 1
EMMETT, Daniel Decatur H
EMMETT, Daniel Decatur 2
EMMONS, Arthur Brewster, III 4
EMMONS, Charles Demoss 1
EMMONS, Delos Carleton 4
EMMONS, Ebenezer H
EMMONS, George Foster H
EMMONS, George Thorton 2
EMMONS, Glenn Leonidas 7
EMMONS, Grover Carlton 1
EMMONS, Harold Hunter 4
EMMONS, Lloyd C. 3

EMMONS, Nathanael H
EMMONS, Peter Kenneth 9
EMMONS, Ralph Lewis 8
EMMONS, Samuel Franklin 1
EMMONS, William Harvey 1
EMORY, Frederic 1
EMORY, Frederick Lincoln 1
EMORY, John H
EMORY, Samuel T. 3
EMORY, William Hemsley 1
EMORY, William Hermsley 1
EMOTT, James* 1
EMPEY, Arthur Guy 4
EMPEY, Arthur Guy 7
EMPIE, Paul Chauncey 7
EMPRINGHAM, James 5
EMPSON, William 8
EMRICH, Duncan Black 7
EMRICH, Frederick Ernest 1
EMRICH, Jeannette Wallace 2
EMSHWILLER, Ed 10
EMSWELLER, Samuel Leonar 5
ENANDER, John Alfred 1
ENCKELL, Carl J. A. 3
ENDALKACHEW, Makonnen 6
ENDALKATCHOU, Bitwoded Makonnen 4
ENDECOTT, John H
ENDELMAN, Julio 2
ENDERS, George Christian 4
ENDERS, Howard Edwin 1
ENDERS, John Franklin 9
ENDERS, John Ostrom 3
ENDICOTT, Charles Moses 1
ENDICOTT, Frank 10
ENDICOTT, Frank Simpson
ENDICOTT, George H
ENDICOTT, H. Wendell 1
ENDICOTT, Henry 1
ENDICOTT, James Lawrence 7
ENDICOTT, Mordecal Thomas 1
ENDICOTT, Robert Rantoul 7
ENDICOTT, William H
ENDICOTT, William 1
ENDICOTT, William Crowninshield* 1
ENDLICH, Gustav Adolf 1
ENDORE, Samuel Guy 5
ENDRESS, Henry 8
ENELOW, Heman Gerson 1
ENERSEN, Lawrence Albert 9
ENESCO, Georges 3
ENFIELD, Gertrude Dixon (Mrs. John Enfield)
ENGBERG, Carl Christian 1
ENGBERG, Edward John 8
ENGBLOM, Alexander Natanael 7
ENGDAHL, John Louis 7
ENGEBRETSON, Oscar Edwin
ENGEL, Albert Joseph 3
ENGEL, Antonie Jacobus 10
ENGEL, Carl 7
ENGEL, Carl Henry 5
ENGEL, Edward J. 2
ENGEL, Irving M. 7
ENGEL, K. August 4
ENGEL, Katharine Asher 8
ENGEL, Lehman 8
ENGEL, Lewis Libman 7
ENGEL, Lyle Kenyon 9
ENGEL, Marian Ruth 8
ENGEL, Michael Martin 5
ENGEL, Peter 1
ENGEL, Samuel Gamilel 7
ENGEL, William 8
ENGELBART, Roger William 9
ENGELHARD, Joseph A. 2
ENGELHARDT, Francis Ernest 4
ENGELHARDT, Fred 2
ENGELHARDT, Nickolaus Louis 3
ENGELHARDT, Nickolaus Louis, Jr. 8
ENGELHARDT, William R. 6
ENGELHARDT, Zephyrin 1
ENGELKEMEIR, Donald William 5
ENGELMANN, George H
ENGELMANN, George Julius 1
ENGELMORE, Irwin B. 6
ENGEN, Hans Kristian 3
ENGER, Melvin Lorenius 3
ENGERRAND, George C. 4

ENGERT, Cornelius Van H.* 8
ENGERUD, Edward 1
ENGGAS, Carl E. 9
ENGH, Harold V. 7
ENGLAND, Bayard L(anning) 7
ENGLAND, Edward Theodore 5
ENGLAND, George Allan 1
ENGLAND, John H
ENGLAND, William Henry 5
ENGLAR, D. Roger 3
ENGLE, Clair 4
ENGLE, Earl T. 3
ENGLE, Jesse A. 4
ENGLE, John Raymond 7
ENGLE, John Summerfield 5
ENGLE, Paul Hamilton 10
ENGLE, Robert H. 10
ENGLE, Wilbur Dwight 5
ENGLEBRIGHT, Harry Lane 2
ENGLEBRIGHT, William F. 4
ENGLEHARD, Charles William
ENGLEHART, Francis Augustus 8
ENGLEHART, O(tto) T(heodore) 9
ENGLEHART, Robert William 4
ENGLEMAN, James Ozro 2
ENGLER, Edmund Arthur 1
ENGLER, Kyle 7
ENGLIS, Charles Mortimer 1
ENGLIS, John H
ENGLISH, Ada Jeannette 8
ENGLISH, Charles Henry 2
ENGLISH, Conover 4
ENGLISH, David Combs 1
ENGLISH, Earl Forman 7
ENGLISH, Earle Walter 4
ENGLISH, Elbert Hartwell H
ENGLISH, E(ugene) Schuyler 7
ENGLISH, E(ugene) Schuyler 8
ENGLISH, Frank A. 3
ENGLISH, Frank Clare 5
ENGLISH, George Bethune H
ENGLISH, George Letchworth 2
ENGLISH, George Washington 4
ENGLISH, Harold Medvin 9
ENGLISH, Harry David Williams 1
ENGLISH, Horace Bidwell 4
ENGLISH, James Edward H
ENGLISH, James Henry 7
ENGLISH, John Francis 5
ENGLISH, John Mahan 8
ENGLISH, Maurice 8
ENGLISH, Merle Neville 2
ENGLISH, Paul X. 8
ENGLISH, Robert Byrns 3
ENGLISH, Robert Henry 2
ENGLISH, Sara Ann (Mrs. Henry W. English) 5
ENGLISH, Spofford Grady 7
ENGLISH, Spofford Grady 8
ENGLISH, Thomas Dunn 1
ENGLISH, Virgil P. 4
ENGLISH, William Eastin 1
ENGLISH, William Hayden H
ENGMAN, Martin Feeney 2
ENGRAM, William Carl 8
ENGSTROM, Adolph (Hjaimar) 6
ENGSTROM, Elmer William 8
ENGSTROM, Howard Theodore 4
ENGSTROM, Sigfrid Emanuel 3
ENGSTROM, William Weborg 6
ENLOE, Benjamin Augustine 1
ENLOW, Robert Cooke 4
ENMAN, Horace Luttrell 4
ENNALS, Martin Francis Antony 10
ENNEKING, John Joseph 1
ENNEN, Robert Campion 8
ENNIS, Alfred 1
ENNIS, George Pearse 1
ENNIS, H. Robert 3
ENNIS, Joseph 3
ENNIS, Luna May 1
ENNIS, Thomas Elmer, Jr. 9
ENNIS, Thomas Leland 2
ENNIS, William Duane 2
ENO, William Phelps 1

ENOCHS, Herbert Alexander 5
ENOCHS, William Henry H
ENOS, George M. 3
ENRIETTO, John 6
ENRIGHT, Earl F. 4
ENRIGHT, Elizabeth 3
ENRIGHT, Richard Edward
ENRIGHT, Walter J(oseph) 5
ENRIGHT, William Fairleigh 7
ENRIQUEZ, René 10
ENSEY, Lot
ENSIGN, Forest Chester 5
ENSIGN, Josiah Davis
ENSIGN, Mary Jane (Mrs. Dwight Chester Ensign) 6
ENSIGN, Orville Hiram 1
ENSIGN, Raymond Powell 7
ENSIGN, Willis Lee 1
ENSLEN, Eugene F. 2
ENSLEY, Enoch H
ENSLEY, Francis Gerald 4
ENSLIN, Morton Scott 9
ENSLOW, Linn Harrison 3
ENSOR, James 9
ENSOR, Lowell Skinner 6
ENSTROM, William N. 3
ENT, Uzal Girard 2
ENTENZA, John Dymock 8
ENTERS, Angna 10
ENTIZMINGER, Louis 8
ENTRATTER, Jack 5
ENTREKIN, Paul Brinton 3
ENTRIKIN, John Bennett 4
ENTWISTLE, James 1
ENTZ, John A. 6
ENWALL, Hasse Octavius 2
ENYART, Arthur Delano 7
EPES, Louis Spencer 1
EPES, Sydney P. 1
EPLER, Percy H(arold) 5
EPLEY, Dean George 7
EPLEY, Lloyd L. 5
EPLEY, Malcolm 7
EPP, George Edward 5
EPPELSHEIMER, Daniel Snell 9
EPPENBERGER, Fred Arnold 9
EPPERLY, James Melvin 6
EPPERT, Ray R. 9
EPPES, John Wayles H
EPPINGER, Eugene 7
EPPINGER, Josua, Jr. 7
EPPINK, Norman Roland 8
EPPLER, William Burgess 5
EPPLEY, Eugene C. 3
EPPLEY, Geary Francis 7
EPSTEIN, Abraham 5
EPSTEIN, Benjamin Robert 8
EPSTEIN, Eleni Sakes (Sidney Epstein) 10
EPSTEIN, Henry 4
EPSTEIN, Henry David 7
EPSTEIN, Jacob 3
EPSTEIN, Joseph Hugo 4
EPSTEIN, Louis M. 1
EPSTEIN, Max 3
EPSTEIN, Paul Sophus 8
EPSTEIN, Ralph C. 3
EPSTEIN, Richard Lewis 9
EPSTEIN, Saul Leon 4
EPSTEIN, Stephan 6
EPSTINE, Harry M. 1
EPTING, Lawrence 9
EPTON, Bernard Edward 4
EQUEN, Murdock 4
ERB, Allen H. 6
ERB, Carl Lee, Jr. 5
ERB, Donald Milton 2
ERB, Frank Otis 2
ERB, John Lawrence 2
ERB, John Warren 7
ERB, Newman 2
ERB, Paul 10
ERBEN, Henry Vander Bogert 7
ERBES, Philip Henry 5
ERDLAND, Bernard August 5
ERDMAN, Charles Rosenbury 4
ERDMAN, Frederick Seward 5
ERDMAN, Helga Mae 6
ERDMAN, Jacob H
ERDMAN, John Frederic 1
ERDMAN, William James, II 10
ERDMANN, Charles Albert 4
ERDMANN, William Lawrence 4
ERHARDT, Joel Benedict 5

ERHARDT, John George 3
ERICHSEN, Hugo 2
ERICKSEN, Ephraim Edward 7
ERICKSON, Alfred William 1
ERICKSON, Arvel Benjamin 6
ERICKSON, Charles Watt 6
ERICKSON, Clifford E. 4
ERICKSON, Cyrus 3
ERICKSON, E(dwin) R. 6
ERICKSON, Ernest I. 8
ERICKSON, Frank Morton 3
ERICKSON, Franklin Carl 7
ERICKSON, George Abraham 9
ERICKSON, John E. 2
ERICKSON, J(ulius) L(yman) E(dward) 5
ERICKSON, Knut Eric 4
ERICKSON, Peter W. 6
ERICKSON, Reinhart H
ERICKSON, Rolf Herbert 10
ERICKSON, Sidney 7
ERICKSON, Statie Estelle 9
ERICSON, Charles John Alfred 1
ERICSON, John Ernst 1
ERICSSON, Frans August 3
ERICSSON, John H
ERICSSON, Leif H
ERIC THE RED H
ERIKSON, Carl Anthony 3
ERIKSON, David Junkin 4
ERIKSON, Henry Anton 3
ERIKSSON, Erik McKinley 1
ERIKSSON, Herman 2
ERIM, Kenan Tevfik 10
ERK, Edmund Frederick 3
ERLAGDER, Abraham Lincoln 1
ERLAGDER, Joseph 4
ERLAGDER, Milton S. 5
ERLAGDER, Mitchell Louis 1
ERLANDER, Tage 8
ERLICH, Alvin Lewis 7
ERMATINGER, Francis H
ERMENTROUT, Daniel 1
ERMINGER, Howell B., Jr. 3
ERN, Henri 4
ERNEST, Albert 4
ERNEST, John Henry 6
ERNSBERGER, Millard Clayton 1
ERNST, Alwin Charles 2
ERNST, August Frederic 3
ERNST, Bernard Morris Lee 1
ERNST, Carl Clark 4
ERNST, Carl Wilhelm 4
ERNST, Clayton Holt 2
ERNST, Edward Cranch 2
ERNST, Edwin Charles 5
ERNST, Frederic 7
ERNST, Fritz B. 3
ERNST, George Alexander Otis 1
ERNST, Hans 2
ERNST, Harold Clarence 1
ERNST, Henry 1
ERNST, Jimmy 9
ERNST, John Louis 8
ERNST, Max 9
ERNST, Morris Leopold 7
ERNST, Oswald Herbert 1
ERNST, Richard Pretlow 1
ERNSTENE, Arthur Carlton 5
ERNY, Charles G. 4
ERPF, Armand Grover 5
ERPF, Carl K. 9
ERRETT, Edwin Reader 2
ERRETT, Isaac H
ERRETT, Russell H
ERSKINE, Albert Russel 1
ERSKINE, Ebenezer 1
ERSKINE, Emma Payne 1
ERSKINE, George Chester 6
ERSKINE, Graves Blanchard 6
ERSKINE, Howard Major 1
ERSKINE, John H
ERSKINE, John 3
ERSKINE, Laurie York 10
ERSKINE, Robert H
ERTE, Romain de Tirtoff 10
ERTEGUN, Mehmet Munir 2
ERTZ, R. B. A. Edward 2
ERVIN, Charles Edwin 2
ERVIN, James H
ERVIN, James S. 2
ERVIN, Jee W. 2
ERVIN, John Wesley 8
ERVIN, Morris Donaldson 3

FEDIN, Konstantin Alexandrovich 9
FEE, Charles S. 1
FEE, Chester Anders 3
FEE, George Edward 7
FEE, James Alger 3
FEE, Jerome John 5
FEE, John Gregg H
FEE, William Thomas 1
FEEHAN, Daniel F. 1
FEEHAN, Patrick A. 1
FEELEY, James Patrick 4
FEELEY, William P. 1
FEELY, Edward Francis 4
FEELY, John Joseph 1
FEEMAN, Harlan Luther 3
FEEMSTER, Robert M. 4
FEENBERG, Eugene 7
FEENEY, Daniel J. 5
FEENEY, Joseph Gerald 5
FEENEY, Leonard 7
FEERICK, Robert J. 1
FEEZOR, Forrest Chalmers 9
FEGAN, Hugh J. 3
FEGAN, Joseph Charles 2
FEGTLY, Samuel Marks 2
FEHLANDT, August Frederick 1
FEHN, Ed J. 7
FEHR, Arthur 5
FEHR, Harrison Robert 1
FEHR, Herman 5
FEHRENBACH, John 4
FEHSENFELD, John Diedrich 9
FEIBELMAN, Herbert U. 5
FEIBELMAN, Julian Beck 7
FEIBUS, Arthur 6
FEIDELSON, Charles N. 4
FEIDLER, Ernest Reynold 7
FEIERABEND, Raymond H. 5
FEIGL, Hugo 4
FEIKER, Frederick Morris 4
FEIL, Harold 8
FEILCHENFELD, Ernst H. 3
FEIN, A. Edwin 9
FEIN, Marvin Michael 10
FEINBERG, Gerald 10
FEINBERG, Louis 6
FEINBERG, Samuel Maurice 6
FEINGOLD, Benjamin Franklin 8
FEININGER, Lyonel Charles Adrian 3
FEINSINGER, Nathan Paul 8
FEIR, James 7
FEIRER, William Anthony 7
FEISALII
FEISE, Ernst (Karl Richard Wilhelm) 7
FEISS, Paul Louis 3
FEIST, Irving J. 7
FEITEL, Donald Gottschalk 7
FEJOS, Paul 4
FEKE, Robert H
FELAND, Faris Robison, II 3
FELAND, John J. 7
FELAND, Logan 1
FELCH, Alpheus H
FELD, Irvin 9
FELD, Jacob 6
FELDBERG, Morris 5
FELDBUSH, Harry A. 4
FELDER, C. S. 3
FELDER, John Myers H
FELDMAN, A. Harry 6
FELDMAN, Alvin Lindbergh 9
FELDMAN, Arbraham Jehiel 10
FELDMAN, Charles K. 5
FELDMAN, Herman 2
FELDMAN, Marty 8
FELDMAN, Maurice 7
FELDMAN, William H(ugh) 6
FELDMANN, Charles Russell 6
FELDMANN, Henry 10
FELDMANN, Leonard G. 5
FELDMANN, Markus 3
FELDMANN, Robert Lincoln 6
FELDMANS, Jules 3
FELDMEIR, Daryle Matthew 9
FELDSTEIN, David 6
FELGAR, James Huston 2
FELITTO, Raymond Nicholas 6

FELIX, Anthony G. 3
FELIX, Elizabeth Rachel H
FELKEL, Herbert 1
FELKER, Samuel Demeritt 1
FELL, Alpheus Gilbert 1
FELL, Charles Albert 5
FELL, D. Newlin 1
FELL, Frank J., Jr. 4
FELL, George Edward 1
FELL, Harold Bertels 3
FELL, John H
FELL, John R. 4
FELL, Thomas 2
FELLAND, Ole Gunderson 1
FELLER, Abraham Howard 3
FELLER, Alto Edmund 4
FELLER, William 5
FELLERS, Bonner Frank 6
FELLERS, Carl Raymond 3
FELLHEIMER, Alfred 1
FELLINGHAM, John Henry 5
FELLNER, William John 8
FELLOWS, C. Gurnee 1
FELLOWS, Dorkas 1
FELLOWS, Eugene Hilpert 6
FELLOWS, Frank 3
FELLOWS, George Emory 1
FELLOWS, Grant 5
FELLOWS, Harold E. 3
FELLOWS, John Ernest 4
FELLOWS, John R. 5
FELLOWS, Oscar F. 1
FELLOWS, William Bainbridge 1
FELLOWS, William Kinne 2
FELMLEY, David 1
FELS, Joseph 1
FELS, Mary 3
FELS, Samuel S. 3
FELS, William Carl 4
FELSING, William August 3
FELSKE, Benjamin 9
FELT, Charles Frederick Wilson 1
FELT, Dorr Eugene 1
FELT, Edward Webster 1
FELT, Ephraim Porter 2
FELT, Joseph Barlow H
FELT, Truman Thomas 4
FELTER, Harvey Wickes 1
FELTES, Nicholas Rudolph 3
FELTIN, Maurice 6
FELTON, Charles 1
FELTON, Cornelius Conway H
FELTON, Edgar Conway 1
FELTON, George Hurlburt 4
FELTON, Lloyd Derr 3
FELTON, Ralph A. 1
FELTON, Rebecca Latimer 1
FELTON, Samuel Morse H
FELTON, Samuel Morse 1
FELTON, Samuel Morse 5
FELTON, William Hamilton 1
FELTS, Sam Lee 8
FELTS, Wayne Moore 9
FENDALL, Josias H
FENDER, Clarence Leo 10
FENETRY, Clare Gerald 3
FENGER, Christian 1
FENGER, Frederic(k) Abildgaard 7
FENHAGEN, George Corner 3
FENHAGEN, James Corner 3
FENKELL, George Harrison 3
FENLEY, Oscar 1
FENLON, John F. 2
FENN, E. Hart 4
FENN, George Karl 4
FENN, Harry 10
FENN, Henry Courtesy 10
FENN, Stephen Southmyd H
FENN, Wallace Osgood 1
FENN, William Wallace 1
FENNELL, Earle James 1
FENNELL, Edward O'Brien 7
FENNELL, James H
FENNELL, William George 1
FENNELLY, John Fauntleroy 6
FENNELLY, Leo C. 7
FENNEMAN, Nevin M. 2
FENNER, Arthur 1
FENNER, Burt L. 1
FENNER, Charles E. 4
FENNER, Charles Erasmus 1
FENNER, Charles Payne 1
FENNER, Clarence Norman 3
FENNER, Darwin Schriever 7

FENNER, Edward Blaine 2
FENNER, Erasmus Darwin 2
FENNER, Goodrich Robert 9
FENNER, Harlan K. 4
FENNER, Hiram Walter 1
FENNER, James H
FENNER, Mildred Sandison (Mrs. Ernest G. Reid) 9
FENNER, Robert Coyner 5
FENNING, Frederick Alexander 2
FENNINGER, Carl W(iker) 7
FENNO, John H
FENOLLOSA, Ernest Francisco 1
FENOLLOSA, Mary McNeill 3
FENSHAM, Florence 1
FENSKE, Merrell Robert 5
FENSKE, Theodore H. 4
FENSTERBUSCH, Jack Alvin 9
FENSTERMACHER, R. 4
FENSTERSTOCK, Howard Warren 7
FENSTERWALD, Bernard 3
FENSTON, Earl J. 3
FENTON, Beatrice 9
FENTON, Frederick Charles 9
FENTON, Hector Tyndale 1
FENTON, Howard Withrow 3
FENTON, Jerome D. 4
FENTON, John E. 10
FENTON, Joseph Clifford 5
FENTON, Lucien Jerome 1
FENTON, Martin 8
FENTON, Ralph Albert 4
FENTON, Reuben Eaton H
FENTON, William David 1
FENTRESS, Calvin 3
FENTRESS, Calvin, Jr. 8
FENWICK, Benedict Joseph H
FENWICK, Charles G. 5
FENWICK, Charles Ghequiere 6
FENWICK, Charles Philip 3
FENWICK, Edward Dominic H
FENWICK, Edward Taylor 2
FENWICK, George H
FENWICK, John H
FENWICK, Millicent Hammond 10
FERBER, Edna 5
FERBER, Herbert 10
FERBER, Robert 9
FERBERT, Adolph Henry 2
FERDON, John William 4
FEREBEE, Enoch Emory 4
FERENBAUGH, Claude Birkett 6
FERGER, Roger H(enry) 8
FERGUS, E(rnest) N(ewton) 8
FERGUSON, Alexander Hugh 1
FERGUSON, Alfred Lynn 7
FERGUSON, Ardale Wesley 10
FERGUSON, Charles 4
FERGUSON, Charles 4
FERGUSON, Charles Eugene 4
FERGUSON, Charles W. 9
FERGUSON, Chester Howell 8
FERGUSON, Clarence Clyde, Jr. 8
FERGUSON, Clarence Meadd 7
FERGUSON, Delancey 4
FERGUSON, Donald Nivison 7
FERGUSON, Edmund Sheppard 5
FERGUSON, Edward 5
FERGUSON, Elsie 4
FERGUSON, Emma Henry 1
FERGUSON, Everard D. 1
FERGUSON, Farquhar H
FERGUSON, Fenner H
FERGUSON, Finlay Forbes 1
FERGUSON, Frank Cardwell 4
FERGUSON, Frank William 1
FERGUSON, Franklin La Du 4
FERGUSON, Fred Swearengin 3
FERGUSON, Garland Sevier, Jr. 4

FERGUSON, George Albert 1
FERGUSON, George Victor 7
FERGUSON, Georgia Ransom 4
FERGUSON, Harley B(ascom) 5
FERGUSON, Harriet R. 4
FERGUSON, Harry George 1
FERGUSON, Henry 1
FERGUSON, Henry A. 1
FERGUSON, Henry Gardiner 4
FERGUSON, Hill 5
FERGUSON, Homer 8
FERGUSON, Homer Lenoir 9
FERGUSON, Ira Alfred 5
FERGUSON, James Edward 2
FERGUSON, James Sharbrough 8
FERGUSON, John A(lexander) 9
FERGUSON, John Calvin 2
FERGUSON, John Donald 4
FERGUSON, John Howard 7
FERGUSON, John Lambuth 5
FERGUSON, John William 1
FERGUSON, Kenneth Reinhard 3
FERGUSON, Leonard Wilton 9
FERGUSON, Louis Aloysius 1
FERGUSON, Lucia (Caroline) Loomis (Mrs Walter Ferguson) 8
FERGUSON, Malcolm P. 10
FERGUSON, Margaret Clay 3
FERGUSON, Melville Foster 5
FERGUSON, Milton James 3
FERGUSON, Miriam A. 4
FERGUSON, Olin Jerome 1
FERGUSON, Phil Moss 9
FERGUSON, R. J. 3
FERGUSON, Robert Gracey 1
FERGUSON, Robert Gracey 5
FERGUSON, Roy King 6
FERGUSON, Samuel 2
FERGUSON, Samuel David 1
FERGUSON, Smith Farley 3
FERGUSON, Thomas Ewing 4
FERGUSON, Thompson B. 1
FERGUSON, Walter 1
FERGUSON, Whitworth 8
FERGUSON, William Blair Morton (William Morton) 6
FERGUSON, William H. 1
FERGUSON, William J. 1
FERGUSON, William Law 4
FERGUSON, William Porter Frisbee 1
FERGUSON, William Scott 3
FERGUSON, Arthur Walsh 1
FERGUSSON, E. Morris 2
FERGUSSON, Erna 8
FERGUSSON, Francis 9
FERGUSSON, Frank Kerby 1
FERGUSSON, Harvey 8
FERGUSSON, Harvey Butler 8
FERLAINO, Frank Ralph 3
FERM, Vergilius Ture Anselm 6
FERMAN, Joseph Wolfe 6
FERMI, Enrico 3
FERMI, Laura 7
FERN, Fanny H
FERNALD, Bert M. 1
FERNALD, Charles Edward 10
FERNALD, Charles Henry 1
FERNALD, Chester Bailey 1
FERNALD, David Gordon 10
FERNALD, Frank Lysander 1
FERNALD, Gustavus Stockman 1
FERNALD, Henry Barker 4
FERNALD, Henry Torsey 3
FERNALD, James Champlin 1
FERNALD, Merritt Caldwell 1
FERNALD, Merritt Lyndon 1
FERNALD, Robert Foss 4

FERNALD, Robert Heywood 1
FERNALD, Walter Elmore 1
FERNANDEL, Ferdinand Joseph Desire (Contandin) 5
FERNANDEZ, Antonio M. 3
FERNANDEZ, John D. 4
FERNANDEZ, Royes 7
FERNBACH, R(obert) Livingston 5
FERNBERGER, Samuel Weiller 3
FERNLEY, George Anderson 5
FERNOS-ISERN, Antonio 10
FERNOW, Bernhard Eduard 1
FERNOW, Berthold 1
FERNSTROM, Henning 1
FERNSTROM, Karl D(ickson) 8
FERON, Madame H
FERRARA, Orestes 5
FERRARA, Ruth Reiordan 9
FERRARI, Louis 3
FERRARI-FONTANA, Edoardo 1
FERRATA, Giuseppe 1
FERRE, Nels Fredrik Solomon 5
FERREE, Barr 1
FERREE, Clarence Errol 2
FERREE, John Willard 6
FERREE, John Willard 7
FERREL, William 1
FERRELL, Chiles Clifton 1
FERRELL, Harrison Herbert 7
FERRELL, John Appley 2
FERRELL, John Atkinson 4
FERREN, John (Millard) 5
FERRER, José Vicente 10
FERRERO, Edward 1
FERREY, Edgar Eugene 10
FERREYROS, Alfredo 8
FERRI, Antonio 6
FERRIER, Kathleen H
FERRIER, Kathleen 4
FERRIER, William Warren 2
FERRIL, Thomas Hornsby 10
FERRIN, Augustin William 5
FERRIN, Dana Holman 4
FERRIN, Evan F(isher) 3
FERRIN, William Nelson 4
FERRIS, Albert Warren 4
FERRIS, Charles Edward 5
FERRIS, Charles Goadsby H
FERRIS, Cornelius 4
FERRIS, David 1
FERRIS, David Lincoln 2
FERRIS, Deward Olmsted 7
FERRIS, Elmer Ellsworth 3
FERRIS, Eugene B., Jr. 3
FERRIS, Frank Halliday 7
FERRIS, George Floyd 4
FERRIS, George Hooper 1
FERRIS, George Mallette 10
FERRIS, George Washington Gale H
FERRIS, Harry Burr 1
FERRIS, Helen (Josephine) 5
FERRIS, Isaac H
FERRIS, Jean Leon Gerome 1
FERRIS, Joel Edward 6
FERRIS, John Mason 1
FERRIS, John Orland 8
FERRIS, John Wallace de Beque 6
FERRIS, Mary Lanman Douw 1
FERRIS, Melton 10
FERRIS, Morris Patterson 1
FERRIS, Ralph Hall 3
FERRIS, Scott 5
FERRIS, Theodore Parker 5
FERRIS, Walter 7
FERRIS, Walter Rockwood 5
FERRIS, Walton C. 3
FERRIS, Woodbridge Nathan 5
FERRISS, Franklin 1
FERRISS, Hugh 4
FERRISS, James Henry 1
FERRISS, Orange 1
FERROGGIARO, F. A. 8
FERRY, David William 3
FERRY, Dexter Mason 1
FERRY, Dexter Mason, Jr. 1
FERRY, E. Hayward 1
FERRY, Elisha Peyre H
FERRY, Ervin Sidney 5
FERRY, Frederick Carlos 5
FERRY, George Bowman 1
FERRY, George Francis 3
FERRY, Hugh J. 5
FERRY, Orris Sanford H

FORGAN, David Robertson 1
FORGAN, James Berwick 1
FORGAN, James Berwick 8
FORGAN, James Russell 6
FORGASH, Morris 4
FORIO, Edgar Joseph 5
FORKER, John Norman 3
FORKNER, Hamden Landon 6
FORMAN, Allan 1
FORMAN, David H
FORMAN, Harrison 7
FORMAN, H(enry) Chandlee 10
FORMAN, Henry James 4
FORMAN, Jonathan 9
FORMAN, Joshua H
FORMAN, Justus Miles 1
FORMAN, Phillip 7
FORMAN, Samuel Eagle 4
FORMAN, William St. John 1
FORMENTO, Felix 1
FORMES, Karl Johann H
FORNANCE, Joseph H
FORNELL, Earl Wesley 5
FORNES, Charles Vincent 1
FORNEY, Daniel Munroe H
FORNEY, James 1
FORNEY, John H. 1
FORNEY, John Wien H
FORNEY, Peter H
FORNEY, William H
FORNEY, William R(ufus) 5
FORNIA, Rita 1
FORNOF, John Renchin 7
FORNOFF, Charles Wright 8
FORREST, Aubrey Leland 3
FORREST, Earle Robert 7
FORREST, Edwin H
FORREST, French H
FORREST, Jacob Dorsey 1
FORREST, Leonard Joseph 7
FORREST, Matthew Galbraith 8
FORREST, Nathan Bedford H
FORREST, Nathan Bedford 2
FORREST, Thomas H
FORREST, Uriah H
FORREST, Wilbur Studley 8
FORREST, William Mentzel 4
FORREST, William Sylvester 4
FORRESTAL, Frank Vincent 3
FORRESTAL, James 2
FORRESTAL, James 4
FORRESTAL, Michael Vincent 9
FORRESTER, Alvin Theodore 9
FORRESTER, D. Bruce 3
FORRESTER, Elijah Lewis 5
FORRESTER, Graham 2
FORRESTER, Henry 4
FORRESTER, James Joseph 1
FORREY, George C., Jr. 3
FORRY, John Harold 4
FORSANDER, Nils 1
FORSBERG, Edward Carl Albin, Sr. 9
FORSBERG, Robert Lee 7
FORSBERG, Robert Lee 8
FORSCH, Albert 6
FORSE, Charles Thomas 1
FORSEE, Aylesa 9
FORSGREN, John H., Jr. 10
FORSTALL, Armand William 2
FORSTALL, Walton 9
FORSTER, Alexius Mador 4
FORSTER, Donald Frederick 8
FORSTER, E(dward) M(organ) 5
FORSTER, Frank Joseph 2
FORSTER, Henry 8
FORSTER, James Franklin 5
FORSTER, Rudolph 5
FORSTER, Walter Leslie 8
FORSTER, Weidman Wallace 5
FORSTER, William Blair 6
FORSTER, William Blair 7
FORSTMANN, Curt Erwin 3
FORSTMANN, Julius G. 4
FORSYTH, David Dryden 1
FORSYTH, George Alexander 1
FORSYTH, George Howard, Jr. 10
FORSYTH, Henry Hazlett 1
FORSYTH, James McQueen 1
FORSYTH, James W. 1
FORSYTH, Jessie 4
FORSYTH, John* H
FORSYTH, Robert 1
FORSYTH, Thomas H
FORSYTH, Volney King 9
FORSYTH, William 1
FORSYTHE, Donald Taylor 9
FORSYTHE, Edwin B. 8
FORSYTHE, George Elmer 5
FORSYTHE, John Evans 7
FORSYTHE, Newton Melville 4
FORSYTHE, Robert Stanley 1
FORSYTHE, W. B. 3
FORSYTHE, Warren Ellsworth 7
FORT, Carl Allen 6
FORT, Franklin William 1
FORT, George Franklin H
FORT, George Hudson 6
FORT, Gerrit 3
FORT, Greenbury Lafayette H
FORT, J. Franklin 1
FORT, Jardine Carter 3
FORT, Joel B., Jr. 3
FORT, John Porter 8
FORT, Marion Kirkland, Jr. 4
FORT, Rufus Elijah 2
FORT, Tomlinson H
FORTAS, Abe 8
FORTE, Felix 7
FORTEN, James H
FORTENBAUGH, Abraham 4
FORTENBAUGH, Robert 3
FORTENBAUGH, Samuel Byrod, Jr. 9
FORTESCUE, Granville 3
FORTH, Edward Walter 4
FORTIER, Alcee 1
FORTIER, Donald Robert 9
FORTIER, Louis J. 6
FORTIER, Michel J. 3
FORTIER, Samuel 1
FORTIN, Jacques 8
FORTMILLER, Hubert Clare 6
FORTSON, Benjamin Wynn, Jr. 7
FORTUNE, Alonzo Willard 3
FORTUNE, J(ohn) Robert 5
FORTUNE, Porter Lee, Jr. 10
FORTUNE, William 1
FORWARD, Charles Hamilton 7
FORWARD, Chauncey H
FORWARD, DeWitt Arthur 10
FORWARD, John F., Jr. 5
FORWARD, Walter H
FORWOOD, William Henry 1
FOSBROKE, Gerald Elton 4
FOSBROKE, Hughell Edgar Woodall 3
FOSBURGH, James Whitney 7
FOSCO, Peter 6
FOSCO, Peter 7
FOSCUE, Edwin Jay 5
FOSCUE, Henry Armfield 8
FOSDICK, Charles Austin 1
FOSDICK, James William 1
FOSDICK, Lucian John 4
FOSDICK, Nicoll H
FOSDICK, Raymond Blaine 5
FOSDICK, William Whiteman H
FOSHAG, William Frederick 3
FOSHAY, James A. 1
FOSKETT, James Hicks 4
FOSS, Carl Ludvigsen 7
FOSS, Claude William 1
FOSS, Cyrus David 1
FOSS, Eugene Noble 1
FOSS, Feodore Feodorovich 5
FOSS, Florence Winslow 7
FOSS, George Edmund 1
FOSS, George Ernest 3
FOSS, Harold Leighton 7
FOSS, Martin Moore 6
FOSS, Noble 5
FOSS, Sam Walter 1
FOSS, Thomas E. 10
FOSS, Wilson, Jr. 3
FOSSE, Bob 9
FOSSEEN, Carrie S. (Mrs. Manley L. Fosseen) 5
FOSSLER, Laurence 1
FOSTER, A. Lawrence H
FOSTER, Abiel H
FOSTER, Abigail Kelley H
FOSTER, Addison Gardner 1
FOSTER, Adriance S. 6
FOSTER, Agnes Greene 1
FOSTER, Albert Douglas 5
FOSTER, Alexis Caldwell 2
FOSTER, Alfred Dwight 1
FOSTER, Allen Evarts 7
FOSTER, Allyn King 1
FOSTER, Ardeen 4
FOSTER, Arthur Borders 4
FOSTER, Austin Theophilus 4
FOSTER, Ben 1
FOSTER, Bernard Augustus, Jr. 5
FOSTER, Blair 8
FOSTER, Major Bronson 3
FOSTER, Cassius G. 1
FOSTER, Cedric 6
FOSTER, Charles 1
FOSTER, Charles Elwood 1
FOSTER, Charles Henry Wheelwright 3
FOSTER, Charles James H
FOSTER, Charles Kendall 2
FOSTER, Charles Richard 1
FOSTER, Clyde Tanner 6
FOSTER, David Johnson 1
FOSTER, David Nathaniel 1
FOSTER, David Skaats 1
FOSTER, Dorothy 7
FOSTER, Dwight H
FOSTER, Edna Abigail 2
FOSTER, Edward K. 4
FOSTER, Elizabeth Andros 7
FOSTER, Ellsworth D. 1
FOSTER, Enoch 1
FOSTER, Ephraim Hubbard H
FOSTER, Ernest Le Neve 4
FOSTER, Eugene Clifford 1
FOSTER, Eugene Martin 8
FOSTER, Fay 4
FOSTER, Fern Allen (Fern Allen Meroney)* 10
FOSTER, Finley M. K. 3
FOSTER, Frances Allen 8
FOSTER, Francis Apthorp 5
FOSTER, Frank Hugh 1
FOSTER, Frank Keyes 1
FOSTER, Frank Pierce 1
FOSTER, George Buchanan 9
FOSTER, George Burgess, Jr. 3
FOSTER, George Burman 1
FOSTER, George Nimmons 3
FOSTER, George P. 4
FOSTER, George Sanford 2
FOSTER, Glen Edward 4
FOSTER, Hannah Webster H
FOSTER, Harold Rudolf 8
FOSTER, Harry Ellsworth 4
FOSTER, Harry Latourette 1
FOSTER, Harvey Goodson 9
FOSTER, Henry Allen H
FOSTER, Henry Bacon 3
FOSTER, Henry Donnel H
FOSTER, Henry Hubbard 2
FOSTER, Herbert Darling 1
FOSTER, Herbert Hamilton 2
FOSTER, Horatio Alvah 1
FOSTER, Irving Lysander 1
FOSTER, Israel Moore 3
FOSTER, J. J. 8
FOSTER, J. T. 7
FOSTER, James Peers 4
FOSTER, James William 4
FOSTER, Jeanne Robert (Mrs. Matlack Foster) 5
FOSTER, Jeanne Robert (Mrs. Matlack Foster) 7
FOSTER, John H
FOSTER, John Early 1
FOSTER, John Gilman 1
FOSTER, John Gray H
FOSTER, John Hopkins 1
FOSTER, John McGaw 1
FOSTER, John Merrill 10
FOSTER, John Morrell 3
FOSTER, John Morton 5
FOSTER, John Pierrepont Codrington 1
FOSTER, John Shaw 2
FOSTER, John Strickland 8
FOSTER, John Watson 1
FOSTER, John Wells H
FOSTER, John Winthrop 6
FOSTER, Joseph 1
FOSTER, Joseph C. 6
FOSTER, Joseph Franklin 6
FOSTER, Joshua Hill 5
FOSTER, Judith Ellen Horton 1
FOSTER, Julian Barringer 2
FOSTER, Lafayette Sabine H
FOSTER, Laurence 5
FOSTER, Lee Byron 7
FOSTER, Luther 4
FOSTER, Mable Grace 5
FOSTER, Marcellus Elliott 2
FOSTER, Martin D. 1
FOSTER, Matthias Lanckton 4
FOSTER, Maximilian 5
FOSTER, Milton Hugh 5
FOSTER, Minard Irwin 7
FOSTER, Murphy James 1
FOSTER, Nathaniel Greene H
FOSTER, Nellis Barnes 1
FOSTER, Norman 7
FOSTER, Paul F. 5
FOSTER, Paul Hadley 4
FOSTER, Paul Pinkerton 5
FOSTER, Percy Semple 1
FOSTER, Randolph Sinks 1
FOSTER, Reginald 2
FOSTER, Richard Clarke 2
FOSTER, Robert Arnold 5
FOSTER, Robert Frederick 2
FOSTER, Robert Sandford 1
FOSTER, Robert Verrell 1
FOSTER, Roger 1
FOSTER, Rufus Edward 2
FOSTER, Rufus James 4
FOSTER, Samuel Monell 1
FOSTER, Scott 4
FOSTER, Sheppard Walter 2
FOSTER, Stanhope 8
FOSTER, Stephen Clark H
FOSTER, Stephen Collins H
FOSTER, Stephen Symonds H
FOSTER, T. Stewart 4
FOSTER, Ted 6
FOSTER, Theodore H
FOSTER, Theodosia Toll 3
FOSTER, Theodosia Toll 4
FOSTER, Thomas Arnold 5
FOSTER, Thomas Flournoy H
FOSTER, Thomas Henry 3
FOSTER, Thomas Jefferson H
FOSTER, Thomas Jefferson 4
FOSTER, Vernon Whit 6
FOSTER, Virgll Elwood 5
FOSTER, Volney William 1
FOSTER, W(alter) Bert(ram) 5
FOSTER, Walter Herbert 6
FOSTER, Warren Dunham 7
FOSTER, Warren William 2
FOSTER, Wilder De Ayr H
FOSTER, William 1
FOSTER, William Chapman 8
FOSTER, William Davis 1
FOSTER, William Eaton 1
FOSTER, William Edward* 1
FOSTER, William Frederick 3
FOSTER, William Garnett 2
FOSTER, William Heber Thompson 2
FOSTER, William Henry 3
FOSTER, William James 3
FOSTER, William Trufant 3
FOSTER, William Wallace 3
FOSTER, William Wilson, Jr. 1
FOSTER, William Z. 4
FOTH, Joseph Henry 8
FOTH, Joseph H(enry) 8
FOTHERGILL, John Vincent 3
FOTITCH, A. Constantin 3
FOUGNER, Ernest Hjalmar 5
FOUGNER, G. Selmer 1
FOUILHOUX, Jacques Andre 2
FOUKE, Philip Bond H
FOUKE, William Hargrave 1
FOULDS, Henry W. 3
FOULET, Alfred Lucien 9
FOULK, Charles William 3
FOULK, Claude Claude 5
FOULK, George Clayton H
FOULK, William Henry 4
FOULKE, Elizabeth E. 5
FOULKE, William Dudley 1
FOULKES, Howard Tallmadge 9
FOULKROD, Harry Ellsworth 5
FOULKROD, Raymond 9
FOULKROD, William W. 1
FOULOIS, Benjamin Delahauf 4
FOUNTAIN, Claude Russell 2
FOUNTAIN, Percy Coleman 3
FOUNTAIN, Reginald Morton 5
FOUNTAIN, Richard Tillman 2
FOUNTAIN, Samuel Warren 1
FOUNTAIN, William Alfred, Sr. 3
FOURNET, John Baptiste 8
FOURNIER, Alexis Jean 2
FOURNIER, Alphonse 4
FOURNIER, Leslie Thomas 4
FOUSE, Levi Garner 1
FOUSE, Winfred Eugene 3
FOUSEK, Peter 9
FOUST, Alan Shivers 9
FOUST, Julius Isaac 2
FOUT, Henry H. 2
FOWKE, Gerard 1
FOWKES, Frederick Mayhew 10
FOWLE, Daniel H
FOWLE, Frank Fuller 2
FOWLE, James Luther 7
FOWLE, Luther Richardson 5
FOWLE, Luther Richardson 7
FOWLE, William Bentley H
FOWLER, Alfred 3
FOWLER, Arthur Thomas 5
FOWLER, Ben B. 10
FOWLER, Benjamin Austin 1
FOWLER, Burton Philander 4
FOWLER, C. Lewis 5
FOWLER, Carl Hitchcock 2
FOWLER, Charles A(rman) 9
FOWLER, Charles Evan 2
FOWLER, Charles Henry 1
FOWLER, Charles Newell 1
FOWLER, Charles Rollin 3
FOWLER, Charles Wesley 4
FOWLER, Chester Almeron 2
FOWLER, Clifton Lefevre 4
FOWLER, Cody 7
FOWLER, David 1
FOWLER, Edmund P., Jr. 4
FOWLER, Edmund Prince 4
FOWLER, Elbert Hazelton 1
FOWLER, Elbert Hazelton 2
FOWLER, Elting Alexander 1
FOWLER, Francis E., Jr. 9
FOWLER, Frank 1
FOWLER, Frederick Curtis, II 5
FOWLER, Frederick Hall 2
FOWLER, Gene 4
FOWLER, George Albert 8
FOWLER, George Little 1
FOWLER, George Ryerson 1
FOWLER, George S. 4
FOWLER, George Starkweather 7
FOWLER, H. Robert 1
FOWLER, Harold Lees 7
FOWLER, Harold North 3
FOWLER, Harry Atwood 5
FOWLER, Helen Frances Wose (Mrs. Albert Vann Fowler) 5
FOWLER, Henry Thatcher 2
FOWLER, James Alexander 3
FOWLER, James Alexander, Jr. 9
FOWLER, James Randlett 7
FOWLER, Jessie Allen 1
FOWLER, John H
FOWLER, John 1
FOWLER, Joseph Smith 1
FOWLER, Joseph William 10
FOWLER, Laura 6
FOWLER, Laurence Hall 5
FOWLER, Leonard Burke 2
FOWLER, Ludlow Sebring 4
FOWLER, Mel 9
FOWLER, Nathaniel Clark, Jr. 1
FOWLER, Orin H
FOWLER, Orson Squire H
FOWLER, Raymond Foster 2
FOWLER, Rex H. 5
FOWLER, Richard Brosing 7
FOWLER, Richard Labbitt 5
FOWLER, Robert Lambert 3
FOWLER, Robert Ludlow 1
FOWLER, Russell Story 3
FOWLER, Samuel H
FOWLER, Thomas Powell 1
FOWLER, Trevor Thomas H
FOWLER, Walter William 3
FOWLER, William Charles 1
FOWLER, William Edward 5
FOWLER, William Eric 6
FOWLKES, John Guy 10
FOX, Abijah Upson 7
FOX, Abraham Manuel 2
FOX, Albert Charles 1
FOX, Alex P. 4
FOX, Andrew Fuller 3
FOX, Augustus Henry 6
FOX, Austen George 1
FOX, Carl 3
FOX, Carol 8
FOX, Charles Eben 1

FULTON, Albert Cooley 5
FULTON, Andrew Steele H
FULTON, Charles Darby 9
FULTON, Charles Herman 5
FULTON, Charles William 1
FULTON, Chester Alan 3
FULTON, Elmer Lincoln 4
FULTON, Frank Taylor 4
FULTON, Fraser Fowler 7
FULTON, Hugh 4
FULTON, James A. 3
FULTON, James Grove 5
FULTON, James Murdock 10
FULTON, John 1
FULTON, John Allen 1
FULTON, John Farquhar 4
FULTON, John Hall H
FULTON, John Hamilton 1
FULTON, John Samuel 1
FULTON, Joseph Samuel 4
FULTON, Justin Dewey 1
FULTON, Kerwin Holmes 3
FULTON, Marshall Nairne 7
FULTON, Maurice Garland 5
FULTON, Robert H
FULTON, Robert Burwell 1
FULTON, Robert Irving 1
FULTON, Samuel Alexander 3
FULTON, Wallace H. 6
FULTON, Walter Scott 3
FULTON, Weston Miller, Sr. H
FULTON, Weston Miller, Sr. 4
FULTON, Will Huston 8
FULTON, William H
FULTON, William John 4
FULTON, William John, Jr. 7
FULTON, William Pomeroy 1
FULTON, William Savin H
FULTON, William Shirley 4
FULTON, William Stewart 1
FULTON, William Yost 7
FULTZ, Francis Marion 4
FULWOOD, Charles Allen 4
FUMASONI-BIONDI, Peter 4
FUNCHESS, Marion Jacob 3
FUNDERBURK, James Ernest 6
FUNK, Casimir 4
FUNK, Charles Earle 3
FUNK, Clarence Sidney 1
FUNK, Erwin Charles 5
FUNK, Eugene Duncan 2
FUNK, Frank Hamilton 1
FUNK, Henry Daniel 1
FUNK, Isaac Kaufman 1
FUNK, John Clarence 3
FUNK, Miles Conrad 5
FUNK, Wilfred 4
FUNK, Wilhelm Heinrich 4
FUNK, William R. 1
FUNKE, Erich (Alfred) 6
FUNKE, Erich (Alfred) 7
FUNKHOUSER, Abram Paul 4
FUNKHOUSER, George A. 1
FUNKHOUSER, John William 6
FUNKHOUSER, William Delbert 2
FUNSTEN, Benjamin Reed 5
FUNSTEN, Benjamin Reed 8
FUNSTEN, James Bowen 1
FUNSTON, Edward Hogue 1
FUNSTON, Frederick 1
FUOSS, Raymond Matthew 9
FUOSS, Robert 7
FUQUA, Henry 1
FUQUA, Isham W. 6
FUQUA, James Henry 4
FUQUA, Stephen Ogden 2
FURAY, James Henry 3
FURAY, John Baptist 5
FURBER, Edward Parker 10
FURBER, Fred Nason 3
FURBER, Henry Jewett 3
FURBER, Percival Elverton 7
FURBER, Pierce T. H
FURBERSHAW, Virginia Lawton 6
FURBRINGER, Max Henry 3
FURBUSH, Charles Lincoln 1
FURCHES, David Moffatt 1
FURER, Julius Augustus 4
FURER, Samuel Henry 9
FURER, William Charles 4
FUREY, Francis James 9
FUREY, Francis Thomas 4
FUREY, John Vincent 1
FURGUSON, Elizabeth Graeme H

FURLONG, Atherton Bernard, Sr. 4
FURLONG, Charles Wellington 4
FURLONG, Clair Willits 7
FURLONG, Nadine Mary 10
FURLONG, Philip Joseph 9
FURLONG, Thomas J. H
FURLONG, Thomas Raphael 7
FURLONG, William Rea 6
FURLONG, William Rea 7
FURLOW, Floyd Charles 1
FURMAN, Bess (Mrs. Robert B. Armstrong, Jr.) 5
FURMAN, Franklin De Ronde 2
FURMAN, James Cement H
FURMAN, John Myers 1
FURMAN, Lucy 3
FURMAN, N. Howell 4
FURMAN, Richard H
FURNALD, Henry Natsch 2
FURNAS, Clifford Cook 5
FURNAS, Elwood 1
FURNAS, Robert Wilkinson 1
FURNESS, Caroline Ellen 1
FURNESS, Clifton Joseph 3
FURNESS, Horace Howard 1
FURNESS, Horace Howard, Jr. 1
FURNESS, James Wilson 5
FURNESS, William Henry H
FURNESS, William Henry, III 1
FURNISS, Edgar Stephenson 5
FURNISS, Edgar Stephenson, Jr. 4
FURNISS, Henry Dawson 1
FURNISS, John Neilson, M.D. 7
FURR, Roy 6
FURRER, Rudolph 4
FURROW, Clarence Lee 3
FURRY, Wendell Hinkle 8
FURRY, William Davis 5
FURST, Clyde 1
FURST, Joseph 4
FURST, Milton 9
FURST, Moritz H
FURST, Sidney Dale 5
FURSTENBERG, Albert Carl 5
FURTH, Albert Lavenson 4
FURTH, Jacob 7
FURTSEVA, Yekaterina Alekseevna 6
FURTWANGLER, Wilhelm 3
FURUSETH, Andrew 1
FUSFELD, Irving Sidney 10
FUSON, Samuel Dillard 3
FUSSELL, Bartholomew H
FUSSELL, Joseph Hall 2
FUSSELL, Lewis 1
FUSSELL, M. Howard 1
FUSSELL, Paul 10
FUSTING, Frederick Erwin 3
FUTCHER, Thomas Barnes 1
FUTHEY, Bruce 4
FUTHEY, John Smith H
FUTRALL, John Clinton 1
FUTRELL, Junius Marion 3
FUTRELLE, Jacques 1
FUTRELLE, May 5
FYAN, Robert Washington H
FYE, Paul McDonald 10
FYFE, John William 4
FYLES, Franklin 1

G

GAARDE, Fred William 2
GABA, Meyer Grupp 4
GABALDON, Isauro 5
GABB, William More H
GABBARD, Elmer Everett 4
GABBERT, Mont Robertson 3
GABBERT, William Henry 1
GABEL, Arthur Bertram 9
GABEL, Carl W. 4
GABIN, Jean (Alexis Jean Montcorgel) 7
GABLE, Clark 4
GABLE, George Daniel 1
GABLE, Morgan Edwards 1
GABLE, William Russell 6
GABLEMAN, Edwin Wilson 3
GABO, Naum 7
GABRIEL, Charles L. 3
GABRIEL, Gilbert Wolf 3
GABRIEL, John Huston 4

GABRIEL, Mgrditch Simbad 4
GABRIEL, Ralph Henry 8
GABRIEL, Ralph Henry 9
GABRIELS, Henry 1
GABRIELSON, Guy George 7
GABRIELSON, Ira Noel 7
GABRILOWITSCH, Ossip 1
GABRO, Jaroslav 7
GABUZDA, George Joseph 6
GACCIONE, Anthony Salvatore 10
GADDIS, Cyrus Jacob 4
GADDUM, Leonard W(illiam) 8
GADE, John Allyne 3
GADLOW, David Berman 4
GADSBY, Edward Northup 6
GADSBY, George M. 3
GADSBY, Robert Charles 4
GADSDEN, Henry White 7
GADSDEN, Philip Henry 2
GADSEN, Christopher H
GADSEN, James H
GADSKI, Madame Johanna 1
GAEBELEIN, Arno Clemens 2
GAEBELEIN, Frank Ely 8
GAEDE, William R. 4
GAEHR, Paul Frederick 3
GAENSLEN, Frederick Julius 1
GAERTNER, Carl Frederick 3
GAERTNER, Fred, Jr. 4
GAERTNER, Herman Julius 3
GAERTNER, William 2
GAERTNER, Wolfgang Wilhelm 10
GAERTTNER, Erwin Rudolf 6
GAFFEY, Hugh J. 2
GAFFNEY, Dale V. 3
GAFFNEY, Emmett Lawrence 4
GAFFNEY, Hugh H. 4
GAFFNEY, John Jerome 2
GAFFNEY, John Marshall 5
GAFFNEY, Leo Vincent 5
GAFFNEY, Matthew Page 4
GAFFNEY, Thomas St John 2
GAFFORD, Burns Newman 7
GAG, Wanda 2
GAGARIN, Yuri (Alekseyevich) 5
GAGE, Alfred Payson 1
GAGE, Brownell 2
GAGE, Charles Amon 5
GAGE, Charles Ellsworth 7
GAGE, Elbert Mauney 5
GAGE, Frances Dana Barker H
GAGE, George Williams 1
GAGE, Harry Morehouse 4
GAGE, H(enry) Phelps 7
GAGE, Henry Tifft 1
GAGE, Homer 1
GAGE, John Bailey 5
GAGE, John Balley 6
GAGE, John H. 4
GAGE, Joshua H
GAGE, Lyman Judson 1
GAGE, Matilda Joslyn H
GAGE, Philip Steams 8
GAGE, Robert 10
GAGE, Simon Henry 2
GAGE, Susanna Phelps 1
GAGE, Thomas H
GAGE, Thomas Hovey 1
GAGE, Walter Boutwell 5
GAGE, Walter Henry 7
GAGE-DAY, Mary M. D. 1
GAGEL, Edward 1
GAGER, Charles Stuart 2
GAGER, Curtis H. 4
GAGER, Edwin Baker 1
GAGER, Leslie Tracy 8
GAGGIN, Edwin Hall 3
GAGLIARDI, Tommaso H
GAGNON, J-romeo 5
GAGNON, Onesime 4
GAGNON, Wilfrid 4
GAHMAN, Floyd 7
GAHN, Harry C. 4
GAIGE, Crosby 2
GAIL, William Wallace 3
GAILLARD, David Du Bose 1
GAILLARD, Edwin Samuel H
GAILLARD, Edwin White 1
GAILLARD, Felix 5
GAILLARD, John H

GAILLARD, William Dawson 6
GAILLARDET, Theodore Frederick H
GAILOR, Frank Hoyt 3
GAILOR, Thomas Frank 1
GAINE, Hugh H
GAINER, Denzil Lee 6
GAINER, Joseph Henry 2
GAINES, Alexander Pendleton 10
GAINES, Charles Kelsey 2
GAINES, Clement Carrington 4
GAINES, Edmund Pendleton H
GAINES, Edward Franklin 2
GAINES, Francis Pendleton 4
GAINES, Francis Pendleton, Jr. 9
GAINES, Frank Henry 1
GAINES, George Strother H
GAINES, James Marshall 6
GAINES, John Pollard H
GAINES, John Wesley 1
GAINES, John William 5
GAINES, Joseph Holt 4
GAINES, L. Ebersole 3
GAINES, Lewis McFarland 1
GAINES, Paschal Clay 4
GAINES, Reuben Reid 1
GAINES, Robert Edwin 4
GAINES, Ruth 6
GAINES, Tilford Craig 7
GAINES, Wesley John 1
GAINES, William Maxwell 10
GAINEY, Daniel Charles 7
GAINEY, Percy Leigh 5
GAINSBOURG, Serge (Lucien Ginsburg)* 10
GAINSBRUGH, Martin Reuben 7
GAIR, George West 1
GAISMAN, Henry Jacques 6
GAITHER, Frances 3
GAITHER, H. Rowan, Jr. 4
GAITHER, Nathan H
GAITHER, P(erry) Stokes 5
GAITHER, William Cotter, Jr. 4
GAITSKELL, Hugh Todd Naylor 4
GAITSKILL, Bennett S. 1
GALAMIAN, Ivan Alexander 7
GALAMIAN, Ivan Alexander 8
GALANTIERE, Lewis 7
GALARNEAULT, John Toan 5
GALATTI, Stephen 4
GALBERRY, Thomas H
GALBRAITH, Anna Mary 1
GALBRAITH, Archibald Victor 5
GALBRAITH, Clinton Alexander 1
GALBRAITH, Francis Joseph 9
GALBRAITH, John H
GALBRAITH, Nettie May 2
GALBRAITH, Virginia Lee 8
GALBRAITH, William James, Jr. 7
GALBREATH, John Morrison 1
GALBREATH, John Wilmer 9
GALBREATH, Robert Ferguson 4
GALE, Arthur Sullivan 5
GALE, Benjamin H
GALE, Clement Rowland 4
GALE, Edward Chenery 2
GALE, Edward Justus 5
GALE, Esson McDowell 4
GALE, George H
GALE, George Gordon 7
GALE, George Washington H
GALE, Henry Gordon 2
GALE, Hoyt Stoddard 3
GALE, Joseph Wasson 5
GALE, Laurence Edward 4
GALE, Levin H
GALE, Minna K. 5
GALE, Noel 4
GALE, Oliver Marble 5
GALE, Philip Bartlett 2
GALE, Richard Nelson 8
GALE, Richard Pillsbury 6
GALE, Samuel Chester 4
GALE, Stephen Henry 1
GALE, Walter John 7
GALE, William Holt 1
GALE, Willis Donald 4
GALE, Zona 1
GALEN, Albert John 1

GALER, Roger Sherman 3
GALES, George M. 3
GALES, Joseph* H
GALITZEN, Elizabeth H
GALITZINE, Nicholas 8
GALKIN, Elliott Washington 10
GALL H
GALL, Edward Alfred 7
GALL, Edward B. 8
GALL, John Christian 3
GALLAGHER, Bernard Patrick 10
GALLAGHER, Buell Gordon 7
GALLAGHER, Charles Eugene 3
GALLAGHER, Charles Theodore 1
GALLAGHER, Charles Wesley 1
GALLAGHER, Daniel J. 3
GALLAGHER, Edward George 6
GALLAGHER, Francis Edward 3
GALLAGHER, Harold John 8
GALLAGHER, Henry M. 4
GALLAGHER, Howard William 5
GALLAGHER, Hugh 5
GALLAGHER, Hugh Clifford 1
GALLAGHER, Hugh Patrick H
GALLAGHER, James Joseph, Jr. 7
GALLAGHER, John Bentley 10
GALLAGHER, John James 5
GALLAGHER, Louis Joseph 5
GALLAGHER, Louis Joseph 7
GALLAGHER, Michael 3
GALLAGHER, Michael James 1
GALLAGHER, Nicholas Aloysius 1
GALLAGHER, Ralph Aloysius 4
GALLAGHER, Ralph W. 3
GALLAGHER, Raymond Joseph 10
GALLAGHER, Sears 3
GALLAGHER, Thomas 1
GALLAGHER, William 1
GALLAGHER, William Davis H
GALLAGHER, William Henry 7
GALLAGHER, William J. 2
GALLAHER, Ernest Yale 5
GALLAHUE, Dudley Richard 5
GALLAHUE, Edward Francis 5
GALLALEE, John Morin 4
GALLAND, Joseph Stanislaus 2
GALLANT, Albert Ernest 1
GALLANT, Wade Miller, Jr. 10
GALLATIN, Albert H
GALLATIN, Albert Eugene 3
GALLATIN, Francis Dawson 1
GALLAUDET, Bern Budd 1
GALLAUDET, Edward Miner 1
GALLAUDET, Thomas 1
GALLAUDET, Thomas Hopkins H
GALLAWAY, Robert Macy 1
GALLEGOS, Jose Manuel H
GALLEGOS FREIRE, Rómulo 7
GALLEN, Hugh J. 8
GALLEN, John James 6
GALLICO, Paul William 7
GALLICO, Poole 3
GALLI-CURCI, Amelita 4
GALLIE, William Edward 3
GALLIER, James H
GALLIGAN, Matthew James 4
GALLIHER, William Thompson 1
GALLINGER, Jacob H. 1
GALLISON, Henry Hammond 1
GALLITZIN, Demetrius Augustine H
GALLIVAN, James Ambrose 1

GARNER, Harry Hyman 6
GARNER, James Bert 5
GARNER, James Wilford 1
GARNER, John Nance 4
GARNER, Richard Lynch 4
GARNER, Robert 6
Livingston
GARNER, Wightman Wells 5
GARNET, Henry Highland H
GARNETT, Alexander H
Yelverton Peyton
GARNETT, David 9
GARNETT, Edward 7
Bernard
GARNETT, George 4
Harrison
GARNETT, James Mercer 1
GARNETT, James Mercur H
GARNETT, Judith
Livingston Cox
GARNETT, Louise Ayres 1
GARNETT, Muscoe Russel H
Hunter
GARNETT, Porter 3
GARNETT, Robert Selden* H
GARNETT, Theodore
Stanford
GARNSEY, Daniel Greene H
GARNSEY, Elmer 2
Ellsworth
GARNSEY, Leon Leslie 7
GARRABRANT, Arthur 3
Anderson
GARRAN, Frank W. 2
GARRARD, James H
GARRARD, Jeanne 6
GARRARD, Jeptha 1
GARRARD, Kenner H
GARRATT, George Alfred 8
GARREAU, Armand 4
GARRECHT, Francis 2
Arthur
GARRELS, Arthur 2
GARRELS, Robert Minard 9
GARRETSON, Abram 1
Quick
GARRETSON, Arthur 4
Samuel
GARRETSON, Austin 1
Bruce
GARRETSON, Cornelius 5
David
GARRETSON, Garret 1
James
GARRETSON, George 1
Armstrong
GARRETSON, James H
Edmund
GARRETSON, Joseph 1
GARRETSON, Oliver 6
Kelleam
GARRETT, Alexander 1
Charles
GARRETT, Alfred Cope 2
Deane
GARRETT, Campbell 4
Deane
GARRETT, Clyde D. 6
GARRETT, Clyde L. 7
GARRETT, Daniel Edward 1
GARRETT, David 1
Claiborne
GARRETT, Donald 5
Wallace
GARRETT, Edmund Henry 1
GARRETT, Edward Isaiah 6
GARRETT, Eileen Jeanette 5
GARRETT, Erwin 3
Clarkson
GARRETT, Ethel Shields 9
GARRETT, Finis James 3
GARRETT, Garet 3
GARRETT, George Angus 5
GARRETT, Guy Thomas 10
GARRETT, Harry Freeland 8
GARRETT, Homer
L(ycurgus)
GARRETT, J. Tracy 1
GARRETT, James Harold, 9
Jr.
GARRETT, James 5
Madison, Jr.
GARRETT, James William 5
GARRETT, John Biddle 1
GARRETT, John Clifford 4
GARRETT, John Work H
GARRETT, John Work 2
GARRETT, Johnson 7
GARRETT, Leroy Allin 1
GARRETT, Paul 9
GARRETT, Paul Loos 3
GARRETT, Pearson 10
Beverly
GARRETT, Philip C. 1
GARRETT, Ray 5
GARRETT, Ray 8
GARRETT, Ray, Jr. 7
GARRETT, Robert H

GARRETT, Robert 4
GARRETT, Robert Edwin 6
GARRETT, Robert Young, 9
Jr.
GARRETT, Ruby Dwight 7
GARRETT, Rufus 2
Napoleon
GARRETT, Thomas H
GARRETT, William Abner 1
GARRETT, William Adelor 5
GARRETT, William 1
Robertson
GARRETTSON, Freeborn 1
GARREY, George Henry 3
GARREY, Walter Eugene 3
GARRICK, James P. 2
GARRIGA, Mariano Simon 5
GARRIGAN, Philip Joseph 1
GARRIGUE, Jean 5
GARRIGUES, Henry 1
Jacques
GARRIGUES, James 4
Edward
GARRIOTT, Edward 1
Bennett
GARRIS, Edward Walter 9
GARRISON, Carl Louise 5
GARRISON, Charles Grant 1
GARRISON, Cornelius H
Kingsland
GARRISON, Daniel H
GARRISON, Daniel 1
Mershon
GARRISON, Edwin 10
Ronald
GARRISON, Fielding 1
Hudson
GARRISON, Francis 1
Jackson
GARRISON, F(rank) 5
Lynwood
GARRISON, George 7
Nelvin
GARRISON, George Pierce 1
GARRISON, George H
Tankard
GARRISON, Harrell 5
Edmond
GARRISON, Homer, Jr. 5
GARRISON, James Carr 1
GARRISON, James Harvey 4
GARRISON, John Boggs 3
GARRISON, John Dorsey 7
GARRISON, John R. 1
GARRISON, Lemuel 5
Addison
GARRISON, Lemuel 9
Alonzo
GARRISON, Lindley Miller 1
GARRISON, Lloyd Amos 6
GARRISON, Lloyd 10
Kirkham
GARRISON, Mabel 4
Clarence
GARRISON, Sidney 2
Clarence
GARRISON, Walter 4
Raymond
GARRISON, Wendell 1
Phillips
GARRISON, William Hart 5
GARRISON, William H
Lloyd
GARRISON, William 1
Lloyd
GARRISON, William Re H
Tallack
GARRISON, Winfred 5
Ernest
GARRITY, Devin Adair 7
GARROU, Albert Francis 7
GARROW, Nathaniel H
GARROWAY, Dave 8
GARRY, Charles R. 10
GARRY, Harold Bernard 5
GARRY, Spokane H
GARSIDE, Charles 4
GARST, Perry 1
GARST, Warren 1
GARSTANG, John 4
GARTH, Schuyler Edward 2
GARTH, Thomas Russell 1
GARTHE, Louis 1
GARTIN, Carroll 4
GARTLAND, Joseph 3
Francis
GARTLEY, Harold 5
McKinley
GARTNER, Arthur 7
Edward
GARTON, Will Melville 2
GARTRELL, Lucius H
Jeremiah
GARVAN, Francis Patrick 1
GARVER, Austin Samuel 1
GARVER, Chauncey 5
Brewster
GARVER, Earl S. 5

GARVER, Francis Marion 5
GARVER, Frank Harmon 3
GARVER, Frederic 2
Benjamin
GARVER, John Anson 5
GARVER, John Newton, 3
Jr.
GARVER, William Henry 4
Harrison
GARVER, William Lincoln 4
GARVEY, Dan E. 7
GARVEY, Eugene A. 1
GARVEY, Helen Marie 5
GARVEY, James Allen 5
GARVEY, John L. 4
GARVEY, Marcus Moziah H
GARVEY, Marcus Moziah 4
GARVEY, Sister Mary 3
Patricia
GARVIN, Edwin Louis 4
GARVIN, George Kinne* 5
GARVIN, Jay Earle 3
GARVIN, Joseph F. 4
GARVIN, Lucius 7
GARVIN, Lucius Fayette 1
Clark
GARVIN, Margaret Root 2
GARVIN, William Swan H
GARVY, George 9
GARWOOD, Harry 7
Crawford
GARWOOD, Hiram 1
Morgan
GARWOOD, Irving 3
GARWOOD, Sterling
Marion
GARWOOD, Wilmer St. 9
John
GARY, E. Stanley 4
GARY, Elbert Henry 1
GARY, Eugene Blackburn 1
GARY, Frank Boyd 1
GARY, Hampson 3
GARY, Howland R. 7
GARY, Hunter Larrabee 2
GARY, J. Vaughan 6
GARY, James Albert 1
GARY, Joseph Easton 1
GARY, Martin H
Witherspoon
GARY, Romain 7
GARY, Theodore 1
GARY, Theodore Sauvinet 8
GARY, Wyndham Lewis 10
GASAWAY, Howard 4
Hamilton
GASCON, Jean 9
GASCOYNE, John J. 5
GASIOROWSKA, Xenia 10
GASKILL, Alfred 3
GASKILL, David Abram 10
GASKILL, Francis Almon 1
GASKILL, Harold Vincent 6
GASKILL, Harvey Freeman H
GASKINS, Lossie Leonard 6
GASPARD, Leon 7
GASQUE, Allard Henry 1
GASS, Howard Allan 1
GASS, Patrick H
GASS, Sherlock Bronson 2
GASSAWAY, Franklin 7
Drennan
GASSAWAY, Percy Lee 1
GASSER, Henry Martin 9
GASSER, Herbert Spencer 1
GASSER, Lorenzo Dow 3
GASSER, Roy Cullen 3
GASSER, William Daniel 7
GASSNER, John Waldhorn 1
GASSON, Thomas Ignatius 1
GAST, Charles E. 1
GAST, Frederick Augustus 1
GAST, Gustav Carl 8
GAST, Paul Frederick 1
GAST, Robert Shaeffer 2
GASTON, Arthur Lee 4
GASTON, Athelston 4
GASTON, Charles Robert 2
GASTON, Edward F. 9
GASTON, Edward Page 4
GASTON, Ernest B. 1
GASTON, Everett Thayer 5
GASTON, George Albert 1
GASTON, James 1
McFadden
GASTON, John 5
Montgomery
GASTON, Joseph Alfred 1
GASTON, Lloyd H. 4
GASTON, Lucy Page 1
GASTON, William* H
Alexander
GASTON, William 1
Alexander
GATCH, Lee 5
GATCH, Thomas Leigh 5
GATCH, Thomas Milton 1
GATCH, Willis Dew 4

GATCHELL, Charles 4
GATCHELL, George 1
Washington
GATELY, H. Prescott 1
GATELY, James Hayes 5
GATELY, James Hayes 7
GATENBY, John William 6
GATES, Albert R. 5
GATES, Artemus L. 7
GATES, Arthur Irving 5
GATES, Caleb Frank 1
GATES, Caleb Frank 3
GATES, Cassius Emerson 5
GATES, Charles Cassius 5
GATES, Charles Gilbert 1
GATES, Charles Winslow 5
GATES, Clarence Ray 2
GATES, Clifford Elwood 5
GATES, Earle Winslow 4
GATES, Edmund O. 5
GATES, Edward Dwight 8
GATES, Edward Percy 7
GATES, Eleanor 3
GATES, Ellen M. 1
Huntington
GATES, Elmer 1
GATES, Errett 5
GATES, Fanny Cook 1
GATES, Frederick Taylor 1
GATES, George Augustus 1
GATES, Herbert Wright 2
GATES, Horatio H
GATES, Isaac Edgar 1
GATES, James Edward 7
GATES, Jasper Calvin 4
GATES, Jay Raymond 7
GATES, John Howard 1
GATES, John Warne 1
GATES, Joseph Wilson 4
GATES, Josephine Scribner 1
GATES, Kermit Hoyt 4
GATES, Lewis Edwards 4
GATES, Merrill Edwards 1
GATES, Milo Hudson 5
GATES, Moody Bliss 6
GATES, Owen Hamilton 1
GATES, Paul Hayden 3
GATES, Philetus Warren 1
GATES, Robert McFarland 4
GATES, Robert Moores 5
GATES, Robert S. 4
GATES, Seth Merrill H
GATES, Susa Young 1
GATES, Sylvester Govett 6
GATES, Sir Thomas H
GATES, Thomas Sovereign 2
GATES, Thomas 8
S(overeign), Jr.
GATES, W. Francis 4
GATES, William Benjamin 1
GATES, William Byram 6
GATES, William Fred, Jr. 9
GATES, William Frederick 1
GATESON, Daniel Wilmot 4
GATESON, Daniel Wilmot 7
GATESON, Marjorie 7
GATEWOOD, Arthur 5
Randolph
GATEWOOD, James 1
Duncan
GATEWOOD, James 4
Edwin
GATHERCOAL, Edmund 3
Norris
GATHINGS, Ezekiel 7
Candler
GATHINGS, James 7
Anderson
GATHMANN, Louis 4
GATLEY, George Grant 4
GATLIN, Alfred Moore H
GATLIN, John C(hristian) 10
GATLING, Richard Jordan 1
GATSCHET, Albert Samuel 1
GATTI-CASAZZA, Giulio 7
GATTON, Roy Harper 4
GATTS, Robert Roswell 6
GATY, Lewis Rumsey 4
GATZKE, Hans Wilhelm 9
GAUCH, Donald Eugene 4
GAUCHAT, Robert David 6
GAUD, William Steen 7
GAUDIN, Antoine Marc 6
GAUGENGIGL, Ignaz 1
Marcel
GAUGLER, Ray C. 3
GAUL, Gilbert William 1
GAUL, Harvey B. 2
GAULEY, Robert David 3
GAULIN, Alphonse, Jr. 5
GAULT, Arthur Eugene 1
GAULT, Franklin Benjamin 1
GAULT, Harry G. 9
GAULT, James Sherman 1
GAULT, Mark R. 5
GAULT, Norman Cox 3

GAUMNITZ, Walter 7
Herbert
GAUNT, Alfred Calvin 3
GAUS, Charles H. 1
GAUSE, Frank Ales 5
GAUSE, Fred C. 2
GAUSE, Lucien Coatsworth H
GAUSEWITZ, Alfred Leroy 4
GAUSS, Christian 3
GAUSS, Clarence Edward 3
GAUT, John McReynolds 1
GAUTHIER, Eva 3
GAUVREAU, Emile Henry 3
GAVAGAN, Joseph 5
Andrew
GAVAN, Paul A. 7
GAVEGAN, Edward James 4
GAVER, Harry Hamilton 3
GAVER, Jack 6
GAVIN, Frank Stanton 1
Burns
GAVIN, James M. 10
GAVIN, John Anthony 9
GAVIN, Leon Harry 4
GAVISK, Francis Henry 1
GAVIT, Bernard Campbell 3
GAVIT, John E. H
GAVIT, John Palmer 3
GAVIT, Joseph 5
GAVRILOVIC, Stoyan 4
GAW, Allison 3
GAW, Cooper 3
GAW, Esther Allen 6
GAW, William A. 9
GAWTRY, Harrison E. 1
GAY, Carl Warren 5
GAY, Charles Richard 2
GAY, Ebenezer H
GAY, Edward 1
GAY, Edward James H
GAY, Edward Randolph 4
GAY, Edwin Francis 2
GAY, Eustace, Sr. 9
GAY, Frank Butler 1
GAY, Frederick Lewis 1
GAY, Frederick Parker 1
GAY, Frederick Parker 3
GAY, George Washington 1
GAY, H. Nelson 1
GAY, John Longdon 4
GAY, Leslie Newton 7
GAY, Maria 3
GAY, Maude Clark 3
GAY, Norman Russell 4
GAY, Robert Malcolm 4
GAY, Sydney Howard H
GAY, Taylor Scott 4
GAY, Thomas Benjamin 7
GAY, W. Allan 1
GAY, Walter 1
GAYARRE, Charles H
Etienne Arthur
GAYE, Marvin 8
GAYER, Arthur David 3
GAYLE, Addison 10
GAYLE, John H
GAYLE, R. Finley, Jr. 3
GAYLER, Charles H
GAYLEY, Charles Mills 1
GAYLEY, Henry Clifford 6
GAYLEY, James 1
GAYLORD, Bradley 7
GAYLORD, Charles Seeley H
GAYLORD, Clifford 3
Willard
GAYLORD, Edward King 6
GAYLORD, Fay Claude 8
GAYLORD, Franklin 2
Augustus
GAYLORD, Harvey 1
Russell
GAYLORD, James H
Madison
GAYLORD, Joseph Searle 4
GAYLORD, Robert March 7
GAYLORD, Truman
Penfield
GAYLORD, Willis H
GAYMAN, Harvey Ellison 8
GAYNOR, Frank R. 1
GAYNOR, Janet 8
GAYNOR, Jessie Smith 1
GAYNOR, Paul 6
GAYNOR, William Jay 1
GAYOSO DE LEMOS, H
Manuel
GAZIANO, Joseph 8
Salvatore
GAZLAY, P.M. 4
GAZLEY, James William H
GAZZAM, Joseph M. 1
GEALY, Fred Daniel 10
GEAR, Harry Barnes 3
GEAR, Hiram Lewis 4
GEAR, John Henry 1
GEAR, Joseph H
GEARE, Randolph Iltyd 1

GEARHART, Bertrand Wesley 3
GEARHART, Ephraim Maclay 6
GEARHART, Harry A(lonzo) 8
GEARIN, John M. 1
GEARY, George Reginald 5
GEARY, John White H
GEARY, Joseph James 4
GEBELEIN, George Christian 2
GEBERT, Herbert George 4
GEBHARD, Bruno Frederic 9
GEBHARD, Heinrich 6
GEBHARD, John H
GEBHARD, Willrich 4
GEBHARDT, Ernest A. 4
GEBHARDT, George Frederic
GEBHARDT, Raymond L. 3
GEDDES, Alice Spencer 5
GEDDES, Sir Auckland Campbell 3
GEDDES, Frederick Lyman 1
GEDDES, George Washington H
GEDDES, James H
GEDDES, James, Jr. 2
GEDDES, James Loraine H
GEDDES, John Joseph 2
GEDDES, Norman Bel 3
GEDDES, Ross Campbell 6
GEDDES, William Findlay 4
GEDDES, Williamson Nevin
GEDDY, Vernon Meredith 3
GEDYE, George Eric Rowe 5
GEE, A.M. 6
GEE, Clarence Stafford 7
GEE, Edward 3
GEE, James Gilliam 10
GEE, Nathaniel Gist 1
GEE, Wilson 4
GEEHAN, Robert William 10
GEELAN, Peter Brian Kenneth 10
GEER, Bennette, Eugen 4
GEER, Curtis Manning 1
GEER, Danforth 4
GEER, E. Harold 3
GEER, Everett Kinne 3
GEER, George Jarvis H
GEER, Theodore Thurston 4
GEER, Walter 1
GEER, Will 7
GEER, William Chauncey 4
GEER, William Clarke 2
GEER, William Drennan 7
GEER, William Henry 1
GEER, William Montague 1
GEERY, William Beckwith 7
GEFFEN, Maxwell Myles 7
GEHAN, John Francis 4
GEHL, Edward J. 3
GEHLBACH, Herman Hunter 4
GEHLE, Frederick W. 4
GEHLE, Frederick W. 7
GEHLKE, Charles Elmer 5
GEHMAN, Henry Snyder 8
GEHRES, Leslie E. 7
GEHRES, Leslie Edward 6
GEHRIG, Lou 4
GEHRING, Albert 1
GEHRING, Benjamin Robert 9
GEHRING, John George 3
GEHRKENS, Karl Wilson 7
GEHRMANN, Adolph 1
GEHRMANN, Bernard John 3
GEHRMANN, George Howard
GEHRON, William 3
GEHRS, John Henry 1
GEIBEL, Adam 1
GEIBEL, Victor B. 4
GEIER, Ernest Conrad 7
GEIER, Frederick August 1
GEIER, Philip Otto 3
GEIER, Philip Otto 4
GEIFFERT, Alfred, Jr. 3
GEIGER, Alfred B. 3
GEIGER, C. Harve 6
GEIGER, Ferdinand A. 1
GEIGER, Jacob 1
GEIGER, Jacob Casson 7
GEIGER, Joseph Roy 8
GEIGER, Marlin George 4
GEIGER, Roy Stanley 2
GEIGER, William Frederick 5
GEIGER-TOREL, Herman Berthold 7
GEIGLE, Francis R. 6
GEIJSBEEK, John Bart 5

GEIL, William Edgar 1
GEILING, Eugene Maximilian Karl 9
GEIRINGER, Karl 9
GEIS, George (Sherman) 5
GEISEKING, Walter Wilhelm 3
GEISEL, Carolyn 1
GEISEL, Theodor Seuss (Seuss)* 10
GEISER, Karl Frederick 3
GEISER, Karl Frederick 8
GEISER, Samuel Wood 8
GEISINGER, William Robert 9
GEISLER, John George 1
GEISLER, Richard Marcus 8
GEISLER, Richard Marcus 9
GEISMAR, Maxwell David 1
GEISSINGER, James Allen 1
GEISSINGER, John Blank 10
GEISSLER, Arthur H. 2
GEISSLER, Ludwig Reinhold 1
GEISSMAN, Theodore Albert 7
GEIST, Clarence Henry 1
GEIST, Emil Sebastian 1
GEIST, Jacob Myer 10
GEIST, Samuel Herbert 2
GEIST, Walter 3
GELB, Ignace Jay 9
GELBACH, Loring Lusk 4
GELDARD, Frank Arthur 8
GELEERD, Elisabeth Rozetta (Mrs. Rudolph M. Loewenstein) 5
GELERT, Johannes Sophus 1
GELLATLY, John Arthur 5
GELLER, Bruce 7
GELLER, David 4
GELLERMANN, William 4
GELLERT, N. Henry 4
GELLES, Paul P. 4
GELLHORN, Ernst 5
GELLHORN, George 1
GELMAN, Frank Herman 9
GELMAN, Samuel Joseph 5
GELSINGER, Michael George Howard 4
GELSTON, David H
GELTZ, Charles Gottlieb 10
GEMMELL, George Albert 7
GEMMELL, Robert Campbell 1
GEMMELL, William Henry 4
GEMMILL, Benjamin McKee 1
GEMMILL, Chalmers Laughlin 9
GEMMILL, Paul Fleming 8
GEMMILL, Robert Andrew 10
GEMMILL, Willard Beharrell 1
GEMMILL, William Headrick 3
GEMMILL, William Nelson 1
GEMUNDER, August Martin Ludwig H
GENDRON, John Wilbrod 8
GENET, Arthur Samuel 3
GENET, Edmond Charles H
GENET, Jean 9
GENGEMBRE, Charles Antoine Colombo 1
GENGLER, Leonard 6
GENGRAS, E. Clayton 8
GENIN, John Nicholas H
GENIN, Sylvester H
GENNET, Charles Westcott, Jr. 2
GENNETT, Nathaniel Chapman Weems 6
GENRY, William Richard 4
GENSMAN, Lorrain M. 6
GENT, Mrs. Sophia S. Daniell H
GENTELE, C. Goran H.A. 5
GENTH, Frederick Augustus H
GENTH, Frederick Augustus, Jr. 1
GENTH, Lillian 3
GENTHE, Arnold 2
GENTHE, Karl Wilhelm 5
GENTILE, Edward 5
GENTILE, Felix Michael 4
GENTLE, Alice True 3
GENTRY, Charles Burt 4
GENTRY, Cyrus S. 4
GENTRY, Martin Butler 5
GENTRY, Meredith Poindexter H
GENTRY, North Todd 2
GENTRY, Thomas George 4
GENTRY, William Lee 4

GENTZKOW, Cleon Joseph 9
GENUNG, George Frederick 1
GENUNG, John Franklin 1
GEOBEL, Herman Philip 1
GEOFFROY, W.J. 3
GEOGHAN, William F.X. 3
GEOGHEGAN, Anthony Vincent Barrett 4
GEOHEGAN, William Anthony 4
GEORG, Walter Ferdinand 5
GEORGE I H
GEORGE II H
GEORGE III H
GEORGE, Albert Eugene 4
GEORGE, Albert Joseph 4
GEORGE, Andrew Jackson 1
GEORGE, Andrew Jackson 1
GEORGE, Charles Albert 3
GEORGE, Charles Carlton 1
GEORGE, Charles P. 2
GEORGE, Collins Crusor 8
GEORGE, Chief Dan 8
GEORGE, Edgar Jesse 1
GEORGE, Edwin Black 4
GEORGE, Harold Coulter 1
GEORGE, Harold Lee 10
GEORGE, Henry 1
GEORGE, Henry 1
GEORGE, James Zachariah H
GEORGE, Jennings Burton 5
GEORGE, John J. 4
GEORGE, Joseph Henry 1
GEORGE, Joseph Johnson 6
GEORGE, Joseph Warren 4
GEORGE, Manfred 4
GEORGE, Newell A. 8
GEORGE, Nicholas Apostolos 8
GEORGE, Robert Hudson 8
GEORGE, Robert James 1
GEORGE, Robert Mabry 4
GEORGE, Rufus Lambert 4
GEORGE, Russell D. 4
GEORGE, Vesper Lincoln 1
GEORGE, Vi 3
GEORGE, W. Kyle 6
GEORGE, W. Perry 4
GEORGE, Walter Franklin 3
GEORGE, W(esley) C(ritz) 8
GEORGE, William 2
GEORGE, William Reuben 1
GEORGEN, W. Donald 9
GEORGESON, Charles Christian 1
GEORGI, Carl Eduard 9
GEOTHALS, George Washington 1
GEPPERT, Otto Emil 5
GEPPERT, Otto Emil 8
GEPPERT, William L. 7
GEPSON, John Morgan 2
GERAGHTY, Helen Tieken 9
GERAGHTY, James 8
GERAGHTY, James M. 1
GERAGHTY, John James 8
GERAGHTY, Martin John 1
GERALD, Mother Mary 4
GERAN, Elmer Hendrickson 3
GERARD, Felix Roy 2
GERARD, James Watson H
GERARD, James Watson 1
GERARD, James Watson 3
GERARD, Ralph Waldo 6
GERARDI, Joseph A. 4
GERASIMOV, Mikhail Mikhaylovich 5
GERBER, Daniel F. 6
GERBER, Frank 3
GERBER, John Jay 10
GERBER, Thomas William 10
GERBERDING, George Henry 1
GERBERDING, Richard Henry 5
GERBODE, Frank Leven Albert 9
GERBRANDY, P.S. 4
GERCKE, Daniel James 4
GERDEMANN, Herbert Edmund 5
GERDES, John 3
GERDES, Robert H. 9
GERDINE, Thomas Golding 1
GERE, Brewster Huntington 6
GERE, Charles Henry 1
GERE, George Grant 3
GERE, George Washington 4
GEREN, Paul Francis 9
GERETY, Pierce Joseph 8
GERGEN, John Jay 4
GERHARD, Dietrich 9

GERHARD, Gerhard Russell 5
GERHARD, William Paul 1
GERHARD, William Wood H
GERHARDT, August Edward 2
GERHARDT, Charles H. 4
GERHARDT, Harrison Alan 7
GERHARDT, Karl 4
GERHARDT, Paul, Jr. 4
GERHART, Emanuel Vogel 1
GERHART, John K. 7
GERHAUSER, William Henry 3
GERHOLZ, Robert Paul 9
GERICKE, Wilhelm 1
GERIG, Benjamin 7
GERIG, John Lawrence 1
GERIG, William 2
GERITY, James, Jr. 6
GERKEN, Rudolph A. 5
GERKEN, Walter Diedrick 5
GERLACH, Arch C. 2
GERLACH, Charles L. 2
GERLACH, George W. 8
GERLACH, John Joseph 1
GERLAUGH, Paul 3
GERLING, Henry Joseph 5
GERLOUGH, Daniel Lauder 7
GERMAIN, Edward Bennett 8
GERMAIN, George H
GERMAN, Donald Robert 9
GERMAN, John S. 2
GERMAN, Obadiah H
GERMAN, William J. 4
GERMANE, Charles E. 2
GERMANI, Gino 7
GERMANN, Frank E(rhart) E(mmanuel) 6
GERMANOS 3
GERMANY, Eugene Benjamin 5
GERMER, Lester Halbert 5
GERMESHAUSEN, Kenneth Joseph 10
GERMUTH, Frederick George 4
GERNERD, Fred Benjamin 2
GERNERT, Robert Eugene 7
GERNON, Frank E. 2
GERNREICH, Rudi 8
GERNSBACK, Hugo 4
GEROLD, Nicholas John 2
GERONIMO 9
GERONIMO H
GEROULD, Gordon Hall 4
GEROULD, James Thayer 3
GEROULD, John Hiram 3
GEROULD, Katharine Fullerton 2
GEROULD, Winifred Gregory 3
GEROW, Leonard Townsend 5
GEROW, Richard Oliver 7
GERRER, Gregory 3
GERRISH, Frederic Henry 1
GERRISH, Theodore 4
GERRISH, Thorton 4
GERRISH, Willard Peabody 5
GERRITY, Joe Warren 9
GERRITY, Thomas Patrick 4
GERRY, Elbridge* H
GERRY, Elbridge Thomas 1
GERRY, James 4
GERRY, Louis Cardell 4
GERRY, Margarita Spalding 5
GERRY, Martin Hughes, Jr.
GERRY, Peter Goelet 3
GERSBACHER, Eva Nina Oxford (Mrs. W.M. Gersbacher)
GERSCHENKRON, Alexander 7
GERSHAW, Frederick William
GERSHENFELD, Louis 7
GERSHON, Richard Keve 8
GERSHON-COHEN, Jacob 5
GERSHOVITZ, Samuel D. 4
GERSHOY, Leo 6
GERSHWIN, George 4
GERSHWIN, Ira 8
GERSON, Feliz Napoleon 7
GERSON, Noel Bertram 9
GERSON, Oscar 5
GERSON, Theodore Perceval 8
GERST, Francis Joseph 5

GERSTELL, Robert Sinclair 5
GERSTEN, E. Chester 5
GERSTENBERG, Charles William 2
GERSTENBERGER, Henry John 3
GERSTENFELD NORMAN 5
GERSTENMAIER, John Herbert 10
GERSTER, Arpad Geyza 1
GERSTER, Jack Alan 5
GERSTLE, Lewis H
GERSTLE, Mark Lewis 5
GERTH, Hans Heinrich 7
GERTKEN, Severin (James) 6
GERVAIS, John Lewis H
GERVASI, Frank 10
GERWIG, George William 3
GESCHICKTER, Charles Freeborn 9
GESCHWIND, Irving I. 7
GESCHWIND, Norman 8
GESELL, Arnold 4
GESELL, Robert 3
GESELL, William H. 8
GESNER, Anthon Temple 1
GESNER, Bertram Melvin 5
GESSLER, A(lbert) E(dward)
GESSLER, A(lbert) E(dward) 7
GESSLER, Theodore A.K. 1
GESSNER, Hermann Bertram 2
GESSNER, James Walter 8
GESSNER, Robert 5
GEST, John Marshall 1
GEST, Joseph Henry 1
GEST, Morris 2
GEST, William Purves 1
GESTEFELD, Ursula Newell 1
GESTER, George Clark 7
GESTIDO, General Oscar 4
GETCHELL, Charles Munro 4
GETCHELL, J. Stirling 1
GETCHELL, Noble Hamilton 5
GETHOEFER, Louis Henry 2
GETHRO, Fred William 5
GETLER, Charles 4
GETMAN, Arthur Kendall 8
GETMAN, Frederick Hutton 2
GETSCHOW, Roy Martin 5
GETSINGER, Edward Christopher 4
GETTE, Warren Andrews 9
GETTELL, Raymond Garfield 3
GETTEMY, Charles Ferris 1
GETTS, Clark H. 8
GETTY, George Franklin 6
GETTY, George Washington H
GETTY, Jean Paul 6
GETTY, Jean Paul 7
GETTY, Robert 5
GETTY, Robert N. 4
GETTYS, Warner Ensign 9
GETZ, Donald Andrew 7
GETZ, Forry Rohrer 4
GETZ, George Fulmer 1
GETZ, George Fulmer, Jr. 10
GETZ, Hiram Landis 4
GETZ, James Lawrence H
GETZ, Oscar 8
GETZ, Stan 10
GEWEHR, Wesley Marsh 7
GEWIN, Walter Pettus 7
GEYELIN, Philip Laussat 7
GEYER, Benjamin Franklin 7
GEYER, Bertram Birch 4
GEYER, Ellen M. 3
GEYER, Henry Sheffie H
GEYER, Lee Edward 1
GEYL, Pieter 4
GEZORK, Herbert 8
GHALI, Paul 5
GHEEN, Edward Hickman 1
GHENT, William James 2
GHEORGHIU-DEJ, Gheorghe 4
GHERARDI, Bancroft* 1
GHERARDI, Walter Rockwell 1
GHOLSON, James Herbert H
GHOLSON, Samuel Jameson H
GHOLSON, Thomas, Jr. H
GHOLSON, Thomas Saunders H
GHOLSON, William Yates H

GHORMLEY, Alfred M. 4
GHORMLEY, John Wallace 5
GHORMLEY, Ralph K. 3
GHORMLEY, Robert Lee 3
GHULAM, Mohammed 3
GIACCONE, John S. 6
GIACOMETTI, Alberto 4
GIAMATTI, A. Bartlett 10
GIANERA, W(illiam) C(harles) 7
GIANILLONI, Vivian Joseph 3
GIANNINI, Armadeo Peter 2
GIANNINI, Attillo H. 2
GIANNINI, Gabriel Maria 10
GIANNINI, Lawrence Mario 3
GIANNINI, Vittorio 4
GIAUQUE, Florien 1
GIAUQUE, William Francis 8
GIAVER, Joachim G. 1
GIBAULT, Pierre H
GIBB, Arthur Norman 3
GIBB, Frederick William 5
GIBB, Hamilton Alexander Rosskeen 5
GIBB, John McGregor, Jr. 7
GIBBES, Heneage 1
GIBBES, Robert Wilson H
GIBBINS, Henry 2
GIBBON, John H
GIBBON, John Heysham 3
GIBBON, John Heysham, Jr. 5
GIBBON, Thomas Edward 1
GIBBONEY, Stuart Gatewood 2
GIBBONS, Abigail Hopper H
GIBBONS, Cedric 3
GIBBONS, Charles David 5
GIBBONS, Douglas 4
GIBBONS, Edmund F. 4
GIBBONS, Edmund F. 5
GIBBONS, Edward F. 8
GIBBONS, Floyd 1
GIBBONS, George Rison 3
GIBBONS, Helen Davenport (Mrs. Herbert Adams Gibbons) 7
GIBBONS, Henry H
GIBBONS, Henry 1
GIBBONS, Henry, Jr. 1
GIBBONS, Herbert Adams 1
GIBBONS, James Cardinal 1
GIBBONS, James Edmund 3
GIBBONS, James Sloan H
GIBBONS, John 1
GIBBONS, Myles F. 7
GIBBONS, Stephen B. 3
GIBBONS, Thomas H
GIBBONS, Walter Bernard 5
GIBBONS, William* H
GIBBONS, William Cephus 4
GIBBONS, William Futhey 4
GIBBONS, Willis Alexander 8
GIBBS, A. Hamilton 4
GIBBS, Alfred Wolcott 1
GIBBS, Carey A. 5
GIBBS, Delbridge Lindley 10
GIBBS, Edwin C. 1
GIBBS, Federic A. 10
GIBBS, Frederick Seymour 1
GIBBS, George* H
GIBBS, George 1
GIBBS, George 2
GIBBS, George Couper 2
GIBBS, George Sabin 2
GIBBS, Harry Drake 1
GIBBS, James Ethan Allen H
GIBBS, Jeannette Phillips 5
GIBBS, John Sears, Jr. 3
GIBBS, Josiah Willard H
GIBBS, Josiah Willard 1
GIBBS, Julian Howard 8
GIBBS, Lincoln Robinson 2
GIBBS, Sir Philip 4
GIBBS, Ralph A. 4
GIBBS, Robert Adams 3
GIBBS, Roswell Clifton 6
GIBBS, William Francis 4
GIBBS, William Hasell H
GIBBS, Willis Benjamin 1
GIBBS, Winifred Stuart 1
GIBBS, Wolcott 1
GIBBS, Wolcott 3
GIBIER, Paul 1
GIBLIN, Walter M. 4
GIBNEY, Virgil Pendleton 1
GIBSON, Anna Lemira 4
GIBSON, Arrell Morgan 9
GIBSON, Axel Emil 1
GIBSON, Ben J. 2
GIBSON, Cable Morgan 5
GIBSON, Carleton Bartlett 1
GIBSON, Charles 9
GIBSON, Charles Brockway 4
GIBSON, Charles Dana 2
GIBSON, Charles Donnel 4
GIBSON, Charles Hammond 3
GIBSON, Charles Hopper 1
GIBSON, Charles Langdon 2
GIBSON, Colin William George 9
GIBSON, Daniel Parke 7
GIBSON, Daniel Zachary 8
GIBSON, Edgar J. 1
GIBSON, Edwin T. 3
GIBSON, Ernest Willard 1
GIBSON, Ernest William 5
GIBSON, Eva Katherine Clapp 1
GIBSON, Finley F. 5
GIBSON, Foye Goodner 8
GIBSON, Frank Markey 1
GIBSON, Frederic Everett 9
GIBSON, George H
GIBSON, George Miles 1
GIBSON, Hamilton (William) 7
GIBSON, Harvey Dow 3
GIBSON, Henry Richard 1
GIBSON, Horatio Gates 1
GIBSON, Hugh 3
GIBSON, Isaac Howard 7
GIBSON, James 10
GIBSON, James Alexander 1
GIBSON, James Edgar 3
GIBSON, James J. 7
GIBSON, James King H
GIBSON, James Lambert 2
GIBSON, James Robert 9
GIBSON, John H
GIBSON, John Bannister H
GIBSON, J(ohn) J(oseph) 5
GIBSON, John W. 7
GIBSON, Joseph Edward 10
GIBSON, Joseph Thompson 1
GIBSON, Joseph Vincent 7
GIBSON, Kasson Stanford 7
GIBSON, Lorenzo P. 1
GIBSON, Louis Henry 1
GIBSON, Norman Rothwell 6
GIBSON, Paris 1
GIBSON, Paul Emil 4
GIBSON, Phil Sheridan 8
GIBSON, Preston 1
GIBSON, Ralph Edward 8
GIBSON, Ralph Milton 8
GIBSON, Randall Lee H
GIBSON, Robert Atkinson 1
GIBSON, Robert Edward Lee 4
GIBSON, Robert Fisher 10
GIBSON, Robert McKenzie 7
GIBSON, Robert Murray 2
GIBSON, Robert Newcomb 4
GIBSON, Robert Williams 1
GIBSON, Russell 8
GIBSON, Samuel Carrol 4
GIBSON, Stanley 3
GIBSON, Thomas L. 6
GIBSON, Truman Kella 5
GIBSON, Truman Kella 7
GIBSON, Walter Murray H
GIBSON, William H
GIBSON, William Campbell 1
GIBSON, William Hamilton H
GIBSON, William Meredith 1
GIBSON, William Merriam 9
GIBSON, William Richie 1
GIBSON, William Wesley 4
GIBSON, William Willard 10
GIDDINGS, Franklin Henry 1
GIDDINGS, Howard Andrus 2
GIDDINGS, Joshua Reed H
GIDDINGS, Napoleon Bonaparte H
GIDE, Andre Paul Guillaume 3
GIDEON, Abram 4
GIDEON, Dave 2
GIDEON, Peter Miller H
GIDEON, Valentine 3
GIDEONSE, Harry David 8
GIDLEY, James Williams 1
GIDLEY, William Francis 7
GIDNEY, Dean Robert 8
GIDNEY, Herbert Alfred 4
GIE, Stefanus Francois Naude 2
GIEDION, Siegfried 5
GIEG, L. Frederick 8
GIEGENGACK, Augustus E. 6
GIEGERICH, Leonard Anthony 1
GIELNIAK, Jozef 5
GIELOW, Martha Sawyer 1
GIERING, Eugene Thomas 1
GIERSBACH, Walter C. 10
GIERULA, Jerzy Kazimierz 6
GIES, Thomas George 8
GIES, William John 3
GIESE, Augustus Albert 4
GIESE, Henry 9
GIESE, Herman Robert 5
GIESE, Oscar W. 3
GIESE, William Frederic 4
GIESECKE, Albert Anthony 7
GIESECKE, Frederick Ernest 5
GIESECKE, Friederich Ernst 5
GIESEL, Frederick W. 4
GIESLER, Jerry 4
GIESLER-ANNEKE, Mathilde Franzisha H
GIESY, John Ulrich 2
GIFFEN, Ernest Clyde 8
GIFFEN, James Kelly 1
GIFFEN, John Kelly 1
GIFFEN, Robert Carlisle 7
GIFFIN, William M. 4
GIFFORD, Augusta Hale 1
GIFFORD, Charles L. 2
GIFFORD, Fannie Stearns Davis (Mrs. Augustus McKinstry Gifford) 7
GIFFORD, Frances Eliot 4
GIFFORD, Franklin Kent 4
GIFFORD, George 1
GIFFORD, George 3
GIFFORD, George Hussey 9
GIFFORD, Glen J. 3
GIFFORD, Harold 1
GIFFORD, James Meacham 1
GIFFORD, John Clayton 2
GIFFORD, Kenneth C. 4
GIFFORD, L.C. 5
GIFFORD, Livingston 1
GIFFORD, Miram Wentworth 4
GIFFORD, Orrin Philip 1
GIFFORD, Ralph Clayton 3
GIFFORD, Ralph Waldo 1
GIFFORD, Robert Ladd 4
GIFFORD, Robert Swain 1
GIFFORD, Roy Wellington 3
GIFFORD, Sanford Robinson H
GIFFORD, Sanford Robinson 2
GIFFORD, Seth Kelley 1
GIFFORD, Sidney Brooks 4
GIFFORD, Walter John 3
GIFFORD, Walter Sherman 4
GIFFORD, William Logan Rodman 5
GIGLI, Benjimino 3
GIGLIOTTI, Frank Bruno 10
GIGNILLIAT, Leigh Robinson 5
GIGNILLIAT, Leigh R(obinson), Jr. 5
GIGNOUX, Edward Thaxter 9
GIGNOUX, Regis Francois H
GIGOT, Francis Ernest 1
GIGRICH, Curvin Henry 3
GIGUÈRE, Paul Antoine 9
GIHON, Albert Dakin 5
GIHON, Albert Leary 1
GIKOW, Ruth 8
GILBANE, Thomas Freeman 8
GILBER, James Henry 5
GILBERT, Abijah H
GILBERT, Albert Clark 3
GILBERT, Alexander 4
GILBERT, Alfred Carlton 4
GILBERT, Alfred Carlton, Jr. 4
GILBERT, Arthur Hill 5
GILBERT, Arthur Witter 1
GILBERT, Benjamin Davis 4
GILBERT, Carl Joyce* 8
GILBERT, Carol Jeanne 6
GILBERT, Cass 1
GILBERT, Charles Allan 1
GILBERT, Charles Benajah 1
GILBERT, Charles Calvin, Sr. 3
GILBERT, Charles Henry 1
GILBERT, Charles Kendall 3
GILBERT, Charles Pierrepont H. 3
GILBERT, Clinton Wallace 1
GILBERT, Dale Winston 8
GILBERT, Donald Wood 3
GILBERT, Douglas 8
GILBERT, Earl C. 4
GILBERT, Edward H
GILBERT, Edward Martinius 5
GILBERT, Eliphalet Wheeler H
GILBERT, Elizabeth Ann Dinwiddie 7
GILBERT, Ezekiel H
GILBERT, Frank Bixby 1
GILBERT, Frederick Augustus 6
GILBERT, Frederick Spofford 5
GILBERT, George Blodgett 2
GILBERT, George Burton 3
GILBERT, George Gilmore 1
GILBERT, Mrs. George Henry 1
GILBERT, George Holley 1
GILBERT, Grove Karl 1
GILBERT, Gustave Mark 7
GILBERT, Harvey Wilbarger 3
GILBERT, Helen Homans 10
GILBERT, Henderson 4
GILBERT, Henry Boas 7
GILBERT, Henry Franklin Belknap 1
GILBERT, Hiram Thornton 1
GILBERT, Horace Mark 1
GILBERT, Sir Humphrey H
GILBERT, Jacob H. 7
GILBERT, James Eleazer 1
GILBERT, James Henry 6
GILBERT, John 1
GILBERT, John 4
GILBERT, John Gibbs H
GILBERT, John Ingersoll 1
GILBERT, Joseph Oscar 5
GILBERT, Joseph Walter 2
GILBERT, Katharine 3
GILBERT, Kenneth 8
GILBERT, Levi 1
GILBERT, Linda H
GILBERT, Lou 7
GILBERT, L(ouis) Wolfe 5
GILBERT, Lyman D. 1
GILBERT, Mahlon Norris 1
GILBERT, Marie Dolores Eliza Rosanna H
GILBERT, Marion L. 4
GILBERT, Matthew William 1
GILBERT, Nathan 7
GILBERT, Nelson Rust 4
GILBERT, Newell Clark 3
GILBERT, Newton Whiting 1
GILBERT, Osceola Pinckney 2
GILBERT, Prentiss Bailey 1
GILBERT, Ralph 1
GILBERT, Robert Randle 5
GILBERT, Rufus Henry H
GILBERT, S. Price 3
GILBERT, Samuel T. 2
GILBERT, Seymour Parker 1
GILBERT, Sylvester H
GILBERT, Vedder Morris 5
GILBERT, Virgil O. 4
GILBERT, Walter Bond 4
GILBERT, William Augustus H
GILBERT, William Ball 1
GILBERT, William Edward 2
GILBERT, William Lewis H
GILBERT, William Marshall 6
GILBERT, William Paul 7
GIL-BORGES, Esteban 6
GILBOY, Glennon 3
GILBREATH, Frederick 8
GILBREATH, James Richard 4
GILBREATH, Sidney Gordon 5
GILBREATH, W(illiam) Sydnor, Jr. 5
GILBRETH, Frank Bunker 1
GILBRETH, Lillian Moller 5
GILBRETH, Lillian Moller 6
GILCHRIST, Albert Waller 1
GILCHRIST, Alexander 1
GILCHRIST, Beth Bradford 3
GILCHRIST, Clarence Thomas 6
GILCHRIST, Donald Bean 1
GILCHRIST, Fred C. 3
GILCHRIST, Gibb 8
GILCHRIST, Harry Lorenzo 2
GILCHRIST, Huntington 6
GILCHRIST, Jack Cecil 5
GILCHRIST, John Foster 4
GILCHRIST, John Raymond 5
GILCHRIST, Ralph Towns 7
GILCHRIST, Robert H
GILCHRIST, T. Caspar 1
GILCHRIST, Thomas Byron 4
GILCHRIST, William Wallace 1
GILCREASE, Thomas 4
GILCREEST, Edgar Lorrington 7
GILDER, Jeannette Leonard 1
GILDER, John Francis 1
GILDER, Joseph B. 1
GILDER, Richard Watson 1
GILDER, Robert Fletcher 1
GILDER, Rodman 3
GILDER, Rosamond 9
GILDER, William Henry H
GILDERSLEEVE, Basil Lanneau 1
GILDERSLEEVE, Ferdinand 1
GILDERSLEEVE, Henry Alger 1
GILDERSLEEVE, Oliver 1
GILDERSLEEVE, Thomas Arthur 8
GILDERSLEEVE, Virginia Crocheron 4
GILE, John Fowler 3
GILE, John Martin 1
GILE, M. Clement 1
GILELS, Emil 9
GILES, Barney McKinney 8
GILES, Chauncey H
GILES, Dorothy 4
GILES, Howard Everett 3
GILES, J. Edward 4
GILES, Malcolm R. 3
GILES, Warren Crandall 7
GILES, William Alexander 1
GILES, William Branch H
GILES, William Fell H
GILFILLAN, S(eabury) Colum 8
GILFORD, Jack (Jacob Gellman)* 10
GILHAMS, Clarence C. 3
GILKEY, Charles Whitney 5
GILKEY, Charles Whitney 7
GILKEY, Geraldine Gunsaulus Brown 3
GILKEY, Herbert James 7
GILKEY, James Gordon 8
GILKINSON, Howard 4
GILKISON, Frank E. 3
GILKYSON, Thomas Walter 5
GILL, Adam Capen 1
GILL, Atticus James 7
GILL, Augustus Herman 1
GILL, Benjamin 1
GILL, Bennett Lloyd 1
GILL, Charles A. 7
GILL, Charles Clifford 2
GILL, Corrington 2
GILL, Elbyrne Grady 4
GILL, Ernest Clark 10
GILL, Everett 3
GILL, George Carleton 4
GILL, Henry Z. 1
GILL, James Presley 4
GILL, Joe Henry 2
GILL, John H
GILL, John, Jr. 1
GILL, John Edward 1
GILL, John Goodner 4
GILL, John Kermode, Jr. 7
GILL, John Paul 7
GILL, Joseph A. 1
GILL, Joseph J. 4
GILL, Joseph Kaye 1
GILL, Kermode Frederic 5
GILL, Laura Drake 1
GILL, Louis John (Gil) 7
GILL, McCune (Mc-cune Gill) 7
GILL, Murray Francis 8
GILL, Patrick Francis 1
GILL, Paul Ludwig 1
GILL, Richard C. 3
GILL, Robert Sutherland 9
GILL, Stanley Jensen 10
GILL, Theodore Nicholas 1
GILL, Thomas Augustus 1
GILL, Thomas Harvey 5
GILL, Waltus Hughes 1
GILL, William Andrew 1
GILL, William Fearing 1
GILL, William Francis 1
GILL, William Hanson 6
GILL, William Hugh 1
GILL, Wilson Lindsley 1
GILLAM, Bernhard H
GILLAM, Clifford Riggs 10
GILLAM, Manly Marcus 4
GILLAN, Silas Lee 4
GILLANDERS, John Gordon 2

GLEASON, Lafayette B. 1
GLEASON, Ralph Joseph 6
GLEASON, Sarell Everett 1
GLEASON, William Palmer 1
GLEASON, William 6
  Thomas
GLEAVES, Albert 1
GLEDHILL, Franklin 6
GLEED, Charles Sumner 1
GLEED, James Willis 1
GLEED, Thomas F. 7
GLEESON, Francis Doyle 1
GLEESON, Joseph Michael 1
GLEESON, William F. 7
GLEIS, Paul G. 3
GLEISS, Henry Crete 1
GLEISSNER, John M. 1
GLEN, Henry H
GLEN, Irving MacKey 1
GLEN, James Allison 3
GLENDINNING, Malcolm 5
GLENDINNING, Robert 1
GLENN, Benjamin Duke, 8
  Jr.
GLENN, Charles Bowles 5
GLENN, Charles Leslie 7
GLENN, Edgar Eugene 3
GLENN, Edwin Forbes 5
GLENN, Frank 8
GLENN, Garrard 2
GLENN, Gustavus Richard 1
GLENN, J. Lyles 1
GLENN, James Dryden 1
GLENN, James W. 4
GLENN, John Brodnax 4
GLENN, John Mark 3
GLENN, John McGaw 6
GLENN, Leonidas 3
  Chalmers
GLENN, Mary Wilcox 1
GLENN, Milton Willits 4
GLENN, Oliver Edmunds 4
GLENN, Otis Ferguson 3
GLENN, Robert Brodnax 1
GLENN, Thomas Kearney 2
GLENN, Thomas L. 4
GLENN, William Schaeffer 1
GLENNAN, Arthur Henry 4
GLENNON, James Henry 1
GLENNON, John Joseph 2
GLESMANN, Louis 7
  George
GLESSING, Thomas B. H
GLESSNER, John Jacob 1
GLICK, Carl 5
GLICK, George 1
  Washington
GLICK, Walter R. 9
GLICKMAN, Irving 5
GLICKMAN, Mendel 4
GLICKSMAN, Frank 8
  Leonard
GLICKSMAN, Harry 6
GLIDDEN, Charles Jasper 1
GLIDDEN, Joseph Farwell H
GLIDDEN, Joseph Farwell 4
GLIDDEN, Minnie Maud 1
GLIDDEN, William Roy 8
GLINES, Earle Stanley 4
GLINES, Victor Leroy 10
GLINSKY, Vincent 6
GLINTENKAMP, Hendrik 2
GLOCK, Carl 4
GLOCKLER, George 8
GLOGAUER, Fritz 1
GLONINGER, John H
GLORE, Charles Foster 3
GLORIEUX, Alphonsus 1
  Joseph
GLOSE, Adolf 4
GLOSSBRENNER, Adam H
  John
GLOTZBACH, William 1
  Edward
GLOVER, Arthur James 2
GLOVER, Charles 1
GLOVER, Charles Carroll 1
GLOVER, Charles Carroll, 7
  Jr.
GLOVER, Conrad Nathan 10
GLOVER, David D. 3
GLOVER, Frederick Samuel 3
GLOVER, George Henry 1
GLOVER, James Waterman 1
GLOVER, John Desmond 1
GLOVER, John Desmond 8
GLOVER, John George 5
GLOVER, John H
  Montgomery
GLOVER, Lyman Beecher 1
GLOVER, Robert Hall 2
GLOVER, Roy Henry 4
GLOVER, Sheldon Latta 9
GLOVER, Townend 1
GLOVER, W(arren) Irving 6
GLOVER, William Howard H
GLUCK, Alma 1

GLUECK, Bernard 5
GLUECK, Bernard 7
GLUECK, Eleanor Touroff 5
  (Mrs. Sheldon Glueck)
GLUECK, Nelson 5
GLUECK, Sheldon 7
GLUECKSMAN, J(oe) 7
  D(ave)
GLUHAREFF, Michael E. 4
GLYNDON, Howard 4
GLYNN, James H
GLYNN, James P. 1
GLYNN, Martin H. 1
GLYNN, William Edward 8
GMEINER, Hermann 9
GMEINER, John 1
GOAD, Louis Clifford 7
GOAN, Orrin S. 4
GOAR, Everett L. 7
GOBBI, Tito 8
GOBBLE, Aaron Ezra 4
GOBEIL, Samuel 4
GOBEILLE, Harold Le 3
  Fevre
GOBEL, George Leslie 10
GOBER, William Mathis 5
GOBETZ, Wallace 6
GOBIN, Hillary Asbury 1
GOBIN, John Peter Shindel 1
GOBLE, George 4
  Washington
GOBRECHT, Christian H
GOCK, A.J. 4
GODARD, George 1
  Seymour
GODBE, William Samuel H
GODBEER, George H. 4
GODBER, Frederick 8
GODBER, Frederick (Lord 9
  1st Baron Godber of
  Mayfield)
GODBEY, Allen Howard 2
GODBEY, Earle 2
GODBEY, John Campbell 5
GODBEY, John Emory 1
GODBOLD, Albert 10
GODBOLD, Edgar 3
GODBOLD, Norman 1
  Dosier
GODBOUT, Joseph 3
  Adelard
GODCHARLES, Frederick 2
  Antes
GODCHAUX, Charles 1
GODCHAUX, Frank A. 4
GODCHAUX, Jules 3
GODDARD, Calvin H
GODDARD, Calvin 1
  Hooker
GODDARD, Calvin Luther H
GODDARD, Charles 3
  William
GODDARD, Christopher 4
  Marsh
GODDARD, David 8
  Rockwell
GODDARD, Edwin C. 2
GODDARD, George 8
  W(illiam)
GODDARD, Harold Clarke 2
GODDARD, Harry 1
  Williams
GODDARD, Henry 4
  Herbert
GODDARD, Henry Newell 4
GODDARD, Henry Warren 4
GODDARD, James (H.) 7
GODDARD, John H
GODDARD, John Calvin 2
GODDARD, Karl B. 3
GODDARD, Leroy Albert 1
GODDARD, Loring 3
  Hapgood
GODDARD, Luther M. 1
GODDARD, Morrill 1
GODDARD, O. Fletcher 4
GODDARD, Oscar Elmo 3
GODDARD, Paul Beck H
GODDARD, Paulette 10
GODDARD, Pliny Earle 1
GODDARD, Ralph Bartlett 1
GODDARD, Ralph Willis 1
GODDARD, Robert Hale 2
  Ives
GODDARD, Robert Hales 1
  Ives
GODDARD, Robert 2
  Hutchings
GODDARD, Roy William 8
GODDARD, William H
GODDARD, William 1
GODDING, Adelaide M. 4
  Smith
GODDING, John Granville 1
GODDING, William 1
  Whitney
GODEFROY, Maximilian H

GODEHN, Paul M. 3
GÖDEL, Kurt 7
GODEY, Louis Antoine 4
GODFREY, Alfred 5
  Laurance
GODFREY, Alfred 8
  Laurance
GODFREY, Arthur 8
GODFREY, Benjamin 1
GODFREY, Darwin Foote 10
GODFREY, Edward Settle 1
GODFREY, Fletcher 1
GODFREY, Hollis 1
GODFREY, Lincoln 1
GODFREY, Stuart C. 2
GODFREY, Thomas* H
GODIN, Edgar 9
GODING, Frederick 1
  Webster
GODKIN, Edwin Lawrence 1
GODLEY, Frederick 4
  Augustus
GODLOVE, Isaac Hahn 3
GODMAN, John Davidson H
GODOLPHIN, Francis 6
  Richard Borroum
GODOWSKY, Leopold 1
GODOY, Jose Francisco 4
GODSHALK, William H
GODSHALL, Lincoln 5
  Derstine
GODSHALL, Wilson Leon 3
GODSOE, Joseph Gerald 7
GODSON, Joseph 9
GODWIN, Blake More 10
GODWIN, Earl 3
GODWIN, Edward Allison 1
GODWIN, Hannibal La 1
  Fayette
GODWIN, Harold 1
GODWIN, Herbert 5
GODWIN, Parke 1
GOEBEL, Frank J. 4
GOEBEL, Julius 1
GOEBEL, Julius 6
GOEBEL, Louis William 6
GOEBEL, Max Theodore 7
GOEBEL, Peter W. 1
GOEBEL, William H
GOEKE, John Henry 1
GOELET, Augustin Hardin 1
GOELET, Robert 4
GOELET, Robert Walton 1
GOEPP, Philip Henry 1
GOERKE, Lenor Stephen 6
GOERTNER, Francis B. 4
GOERTZ, Raymond C. 5
GOESS, Frederick V. 10
GOESSMANN, Charles 1
  Anthony
GOESSMANN, Helena 3
  Theresa
GOETCHIUS, Henry 1
  Richard
GOETHALS, George 7
  Rodman
GOETHALS, Robert 8
  Joseph
GOETHE, Charles Matthias 4
GOETSCHIUS, John Henry H
GOETSCHIUS, Percy 4
GOETTE, John 6
GOETTELMANN, Paul 7
  Auguste
GOETZ, Albert Gillies 4
GOETZ, George H
  Washington
GOETZ, Norman S. 5
GOETZ, Philip Becker 1
GOETZ, William 5
GOETZE, Albrecht 5
GOETZE, Arthur Burton 3
GOETZE, Frederick Arthur 3
GOETZENBERGER, 9
  Ralph L(eon)
GOETZMANN, Jule 3
  Lawrence
GOFF, Bruce 8
GOFF, Charles Ray 8
GOFF, Charles Weer 6
GOFF, Emmet Stull H
GOFF, Ernest Lucius 4
GOFF, Frederick Harris 1
GOFF, Guy Despard 1
GOFF, Harold 1
GOFF, James Matthew 9
GOFF, John W. 1
GOFF, Nathan 1
GOFF, Thomas Theodore 2
GOFFE, J. Riddle 1
GOFFE, William H
GOFFMAN, Erving 8
GOFORTH, William 1
GOGARTY, Oliver St John 1
GOGGIN, Catharine 5
GOGGIN, William Leftwich H
GOH, Choo San 9

GOHDES, Conrad Bruno 3
GOHEEN, Harry Earl 10
GOHEN, Charles Marsh 5
GOIN, Sanford Williams 3
GOING, Charles Buxton 5
GOING, Jonathan H
GOING, Maud 1
GOING, Richard Fuller 10
GOINS, John Clement 10
GOLATKA, Walter Francis 4
GOLAY, John Ford 5
GOLD, Aaron Michael 8
GOLD, Arthur 10
GOLD, Harry 5
GOLD, Howard R. 3
GOLD, Nathan Jules 5
GOLD, Pleasant Daniel, Jr. 5
GOLD, Thomas Ruggles H
GOLD, William Henry 4
GOLD, William Jason 1
GOLDBECK, Albert 4
  Theodore
GOLDBECK, Edward 1
GOLDBECK, Robert 1
GOLDBERG, Abraham 6
  Isaac
GOLDBERG, Albert Levi 10
GOLDBERG, Arthur 10
  Joseph
GOLDBERG, Isaac 1
GOLDBERG, Leo 5
GOLDBERG, Leo 9
GOLDBERG, Leon Isadore 10
GOLDBERG, Morrell 7
GOLDBERG, Reuben 1
  Lucius (Rube)
GOLDBERG, Reuben 7
  Lucius (Rube)
GOLDBERG, Samuel 6
  Auron
GOLDBERGER, Isidore 5
  Harry
GOLDBERGER, Joseph 1
GOLDBLATT, Joel 8
GOLDBLATT, Maurice 8
GOLDBLATT, Maurice 4
  Henry
GOLDBLATT, Nathan 5
GOLDBLOOM, Alton 8
GOLDEN, Ben Hale 5
GOLDEN, Clinton Strong 4
GOLDEN, Grace 5
GOLDEN, Harry 8
GOLDEN, Hawkins 9
GOLDEN, James S. 5
GOLDEN, John 3
GOLDEN, John Matthew 10
GOLDEN, Michael Joseph 4
GOLDEN, Richard 1
GOLDEN, Ross 6
GOLDEN, S. Herbert 1
GOLDEN, S.M. 5
GOLDENBERG, Louis 9
GOLDENBERG, Morris 5
GOLDENHERSH, Joseph 10
  Herman
GOLDENWEISER, 1
  Alexander
GOLDENWEISER, 3
  Emanuel Alexander
GOLDER, Benjamin M. 2
GOLDER, Boyd E. 1
GOLDER, Frank Alfred 1
GOLDESBERRY, John 5
  Milford
GOLDET, Antoine Gustave 4
GOLDFARB, Jacob A. 7
GOLDFINE, William 7
GOLDFINGER, Nathaniel 7
GOLDFOGLE, Henry M. 1
GOLDFORB, Abraham 6
  Jules
GOLDING, Frank Henry 1
GOLDING, Jerrold R. 4
GOLDING, Louis 4
GOLDING, Louis Thorn 4
GOLDING, Samuel H. 5
GOLDING, Stuart Samuel 10
GOLDMAN, Albert 4
GOLDMAN, Alfred 6
GOLDMAN, Alvin 6
  D(amascus)
GOLDMAN, Edward 2
  Alphonse
GOLDMAN, Edwin Franko 3
GOLDMAN, Emma H
GOLDMAN, Emma 4
GOLDMAN, Eric Frederick 9
GOLDMAN, Frank 4
GOLDMAN, Henry 10
  Maurice
GOLDMAN, Hetty 5
GOLDMAN, Leon 6
GOLDMAN, Maurice 4
  Harry
GOLDMAN, Mayer C. 1
GOLDMAN, Morris H. 6

GOLDMAN, Ralph 10
GOLDMAN, Richard 7
  Franko
GOLDMAN, Robert Philip 7
GOLDMAN, Samuel P. 5
GOLDMAN, Solomon 3
GOLDMANN, Franz 5
GOLDMANN, Nahum 8
GOLDMANN, Sidney 8
GOLDMARK, Pauline 4
  Dorothea
GOLDMARK, Pauline 5
  Dorothea
GOLDMARK, Peter Carl 7
GOLDMARK, Rubin 1
GOLDNER, Jacob Henry 5
GOLDRING, William 7
GOLDSBERRY, Louise 5
  Dunham
GOLDSBOROUGH, H
  Charles
GOLDSBOROUGH, Laird 3
  S.
GOLDSBOROUGH, Laird 2
  Shields
GOLDSBOROUGH, Louis H
  Malesherbes
GOLDSBOROUGH, 2
  Phillips Lee
GOLDSBOROUGH, 1
  Richard Francis
GOLDSBOROUGH, H
  Robert
GOLDSBOROUGH, H
  Robert Henry
GOLDSBOROUGH, T. 3
  Alan
GOLDSBOROUGH, W. 3
  Elwell
GOLDSBOROUGH, 5
  Washington Laird
GOLDSBOROUGH, 1
  Worthington
GOLDSCHMIDT, Jakob 3
GOLDSCHMIDT, Richard 3
  Benedict
GOLDSCHMIDT, Samuel 1
  Anthony
GOLDSMITH, Alan 4
  Gustavus
GOLDSMITH, Brooks P. 5
GOLDSMITH, Clarence 9
  Earl
GOLDSMITH, Clifford 5
GOLDSMITH, Deborah H
GOLDSMITH, Edward Ira 9
GOLDSMITH, Goldwin 5
GOLDSMITH, Grace 6
  Arabell
GOLDSMITH, Jonathan H
GOLDSMITH, Middleton H
GOLDSMITH, Milton 3
GOLDSMITH, Philip H. 3
GOLDSMITH, Raymond 9
  William
GOLDSMITH, Robert 1
GOLDSMITH, Robert 10
  Hillis
GOLDSMITH, William 10
  Wallace
GOLDSPOHN, Albert 1
GOLDSTEIN, Benjamin 6
  Franklin
GOLDSTEIN, David Henry 7
GOLDSTEIN, Harold 9
GOLDSTEIN, Irving 9
GOLDSTEIN, Israel 9
GOLDSTEIN, Jerome 9
GOLDSTEIN, Louis 4
GOLDSTEIN, Mark E. 7
GOLDSTEIN, Max Aaron 1
GOLDSTEIN, Max 7
  Fullmore
GOLDSTEIN, Moise 7
  Herbert
GOLDSTEIN, Molse 5
  Herbert
GOLDSTEIN, Nathaniel 7
  Lawrence
GOLDSTEIN, Robert 9
  V(ernon)
GOLDSTEIN, Sidney 9
GOLDSTEIN, Sidney 3
  Emanuel
GOLDSTINE, Harry 3
GOLDSTON, Eli 6
GOLDSTON, Robert 1
  Conroy
GOLDSWORTHY, William 6
  Arthur
GOLDTHWAIT, James 2
  Walter
GOLDTHWAIT, Joel 5
  Ernest
GOLDTHWAIT, Nathan 3
  Edward

Name	
GOLDTHWAIT, Sheldon Forrest	4
GOLDTHWAITE, Anne	2
GOLDTHWAITE, du Val R.	3
GOLDTHWAITE, George	H
GOLDTHWAITE, George Edgar	4
GOLDTHWAITE, Henry Barnes	H
GOLDTHWAITE, Nellie Esther	2
GOLDTHWAITE, Ralph Harvard	7
GOLDTHWAITE, Vere	5
GOLDWATER, Leonard John	10
GOLDWATER, Richard M.	5
GOLDWATER, Robert	5
GOLDWATER, Robert	7
GOLDWATER, Sigismund Schultz	2
GOLDWYN, Samuel	6
GOLDWYN, Samuel (Surname Adopted)	7
GOLEMON, Albert Sidney	10
GOLENBOCK, Justin Merton	9
GOLER, George W.	1
GOLER, William Harvey	4
GOLIGHTLY, Trueman Harlan	10
GOLINKIN, Joseph Webster	7
GOLINO, Carlo Luigi	10
GOLLADAY, Edward Isaac	H
GOLLADAY, Jacob Shall	H
GOLLOMB, Joseph	3
GOLLONG, Paul Bernhard Werner	10
GOLOVIN, Nicholas Erasmus	5
GOLSCHMANN, Vladimir	5
GOLTMAN, Maximilian	1
GOLTRA, Edward Field	1
GOLUB, Jacob Joshua	3
GOLUB, William	10
GOMBERG, Morris	6
GOMBERG, Moses	2
GOMBERG, William	9
GOMBROWICZ, Witold	5
GOMEZ, Fortino	9
GOMEZ, Laureano	4
GOMEZ-MORENO MARTINEZ, Manuel	5
GOMORL, Pal	6
GOMORY, Andrew Louis	7
GOMPERS, Samuel	1
GOMPERT, William Henry	2
GOMULKA, Wladyslaw	9
GONCE, John Eugene, Jr.	3
GONDA, Thomas Andrew	9
GONDELMAN, Sidney	5
GONGWER, Lillian May	5
GONNERMAN, Harrison Frederick	7
GONS, James Walker	H
GONZALES, Ambrose Elliott	1
GONZALES, Bienvenido M.	3
GONZALES, Mario Flores	6
GONZALES, Rosa Mangual	4
GONZALES, William Elliott	1
GONZALEZ, Xavier	10
GOOCH, D. Linn	4
GOOCH, Daniel Wheelwright	H
GOOCH, Frank Austin	1
GOOCH, James Thomas	8
GOOCH, Robert Kent	8
GOOCH, Tom Carbry	3
GOOCH, Wilby T.	7
GOOCH, Sir William	H
GOOD, Adolphus Clemens	H
GOOD, Albert Irwin	7
GOOD, Alice Campbell	3
GOOD, Carter Victor	10
GOOD, Charles Winfred	3
GOOD, Clarence Allen	9
GOOD, Edward Ellsworth	1
GOOD, Edwin Stanton	5
GOOD, Frederick Hopkins	5
GOOD, Grover Charles	5
GOOD, Howard Harrison	4
GOOD, Irby J.	2
GOOD, James Isaac	1
GOOD, James William	1
GOOD, Jeremiah Haak	H
GOOD, John Walter	6
GOOD, Paul Francis	5
GOOD, Robert Crocker	9
GOODALE, Charles Warren	1
GOODALE, Dora Read	4
GOODALE, Francis Greenleaf	7
GOODALE, George Lincoln	1
GOODALE, George Pomeroy	1
GOODALE, Greenleaf Austin	1
GOODALE, Hubert Dana	6
GOODALE, Joseph Lincoln	4
GOODALE, Joseph Lincoln	5
GOODALE, Stephen Lincoln	H
GOODALE, Stephen Lincoln	3
GOODALL, Albert Gallatin	H
GOODALL, Charles Edward	5
GOODALL, Harvey L.	H
GOODALL, Herbert Whittaker	7
GOODALL, Louis Bertrand	1
GOODALL, Newman	10
GOODBAR, Joseph Ernest	3
GOODBODY, Harold P.	9
GOODBODY, John Collett	10
GOODBODY, Marcus	7
GOODCHILD, Chauncey George	7
GOODCHILD, Frank Marsden	1
GOODDING, T(homas) H(omer)	8
GOODE, Clement Tyson	2
GOODE, Delmer Morrison	8
GOODE, George Brown	H
GOODE, George William	5
GOODE, J. Paul	1
GOODE, John	1
GOODE, John Chambers, Jr.	8
GOODE, Patrick Gaines	1
GOODE, Richard Livingston	1
GOODE, Richard Urquhart	1
GOODE, Samuel	H
GOODE, William Athelstane Meredith	5
GOODE, William Osborne	H
GOODELL, Charles Ellsworth	9
GOODELL, Charles Elmer	1
GOODELL, Charles Le Roy	1
GOODELL, David Harvey	1
GOODELL, Henry Hill	1
GOODELL, Raymond Batchelder	3
GOODELL, Reginald Rusden	2
GOODELL, Roswell Eaton	1
GOODELL, Thomas Dwight	1
GOODELL, William*	H
GOODEN, Robert Burton	6
GOODEN, Robert Burton	7
GOODENOUGH, Erwin Ramsdell	4
GOODENOUGH, George Alfred	1
GOODENOUGH, Luman W.	3
GOODENOW, John Milton	H
GOODENOW, Robert	H
GOODENOW, Rufus King	H
GOODERHAM, Melvill Ross	3
GOODFELLOW, Edward	1
GOODFELLOW, Millard Preston	6
GOODFRIEND, James Herman	9
GOODHART, Arthur Lehman	7
GOODHARTZ, Abraham Samuel	6
GOODHEART, William Raymond, Jr.	4
GOODHUE, Benjamin	H
GOODHUE, Bertram Grosvenor	1
GOODHUE, Edward Solon	4
GOODHUE, Everett Walton	6
GOODHUE, Francis Abbot	4
GOODHUE, James Madison	1
GOODHUE, William Joseph	5
GOODIER, James Norman	5
GOODIN, John Randolph	1
GOODING, Frank R.	1
GOODKIND, Gilbert E.	3
GOODKIND, Maurice Louis	1
GOODKNIGHT, James Lincoln	1
GOODLAND, Walter Samuel	2
GOODLING, George A.	8
GOODLOE, Daniel Reaves	H
GOODLOE, Don Speed Smith	6
GOODLOE, William Cassius	H
GOODMAN, Benedict Kay	4
GOODMAN, Benny	9
GOODMAN, Charles	H
GOODMAN, Charles	2
GOODMAN, Clark Drouillard	8
GOODMAN, Daniel Carson	3
GOODMAN, David	5
GOODMAN, DeWitt Stetten	10
GOODMAN, E(dward) Urner	7
GOODMAN, Frank Bartlett	3
GOODMAN, Frank Croly	3
GOODMAN, George Hill	5
GOODMAN, Herman Edward	9
GOODMAN, Howard	3
GOODMAN, Jack Arthur	3
GOODMAN, James E.	4
GOODMAN, Mrs. Jean R.	1
GOODMAN, Jess Dee	5
GOODMAN, John	4
GOODMAN, John Forest	2
GOODMAN, Jules Eckert	4
GOODMAN, Leo Magill	9
GOODMAN, Louis Earl	4
GOODMAN, Martin Wise	8
GOODMAN, Mary Ellen	5
GOODMAN, Michael A.	10
GOODMAN, Nathan Gerson	3
GOODMAN, Oscar R.	9
GOODMAN, Paul	5
GOODMAN, Percival	10
GOODMAN, Steven Benjamin	8
GOODMAN, William Edward	4
GOODMAN, William M.	3
GOODMAN, William Owen	1
GOODNIGHT, Charles	H
GOODNIGHT, Charles	4
GOODNIGHT, Clarence James	9
GOODNIGHT, Cloyd Herschel	1
GOODNIGHT, Isaac Herschel	1
GOODNIGHT, Scott Holland	5
GOODNO, William Colby	5
GOODNOW, Charles Allen	1
GOODNOW, Frank Johnson	1
GOODNOW, Isaac Tichenor	H
GOODNOW, John	1
GOODNOW, Minnie	5
GOODPASTURE, Ernest William	4
GOODPASTURE, Wendell Williamson	5
GOODRELL, Mancil Clay	1
GOODRICH, Alfred John	4
GOODRICH, Alva Curtis	6
GOODRICH, Annie Warburton	3
GOODRICH, Arthur	1
GOODRICH, Ben	4
GOODRICH, Benjamin Franklin	H
GOODRICH, Carter	6
GOODRICH, Caspar Frederick	1
GOODRICH, Charles Augustus	H
GOODRICH, Chauncey*	H
GOODRICH, Chauncey	1
GOODRICH, Chauncey Allen	H
GOODRICH, Chauncey William	3
GOODRICH, David Marvin	3
GOODRICH, Donald Reuben	2
GOODRICH, Donald Wells	10
GOODRICH, Edgar Jennings	5
GOODRICH, Edward Thayer	7
GOODRICH, Elizur	H
GOODRICH, Elizus	H
GOODRICH, Ernest Payson	3
GOODRICH, Forest Jackson	8
GOODRICH, Foster Edward	5
GOODRICH, Frances	8
GOODRICH, Francis Lee Dewey	5
GOODRICH, Frank	1
GOODRICH, Frank Boott	H
GOODRICH, Frederick William	4
GOODRICH, Hale Caldwell	5
GOODRICH, Herbert F.	4
GOODRICH, Hubert Baker	4
GOODRICH, James Clarence	3
GOODRICH, James Edward	3
GOODRICH, James Putnam	1
GOODRICH, John Ellsworth	1
GOODRICH, John Zacheus	H
GOODRICH, Joseph King	1
GOODRICH, L(awrence) Keith	5
GOODRICH, Leland Matthew	10
GOODRICH, Levi	H
GOODRICH, Lowell Pierce	2
GOODRICH, Milo	H
GOODRICH, Nathaniel Lewis	3
GOODRICH, Paul W.	8
GOODRICH, Pierre Frist	6
GOODRICH, Ralph Dickinson	6
GOODRICH, Ralph Leland	4
GOODRICH, Robert Eugene	5
GOODRICH, Samuel Griswold	H
GOODRICH, Wallace	3
GOODRICH, William Marcellus	H
GOODRICH, William W.	1
GOODRIDGE, John	4
GOODRIDGE, Malcolm	3
GOODRIDGE, Sarah	H
GOODSELL, Charles True	1
GOODSELL, Charles True	2
GOODSELL, Daniel Ayres	H
GOODSELL, Fred Field	6
GOODSELL, Henry Guy	6
GOODSELL, Willystine	6
GOODSON, Edward Fletcher	4
GOODSON, Louis Hoffman	8
GOODSON, Max Reed	8
GOODSPEED, Arthur Willis	H
GOODSPEED, Charles Barnett	2
GOODSPEED, Charles Ten Broeke	2
GOODSPEED, Edgar Johnson	4
GOODSPEED, Frank Lincoln	1
GOODSPEED, George Edward	8
GOODSPEED, George Stephen	1
GOODSPEED, Thomas Harper	4
GOODSPEED, Thomas Wakefield	1
GOODSPEED, Walter Stuart	5
GOODWILLIE, David Herrick	3
GOODWILLIE, David Lincoln	1
GOODWIN, Angier Louis	6
GOODWIN, Arthur C.	2
GOODWIN, Cardinal Leonidas	2
GOODWIN, Charles Archibald	3
GOODWIN, Charles Jaques	1
GOODWIN, Clarence Norton	3
GOODWIN, Daniel	H
GOODWIN, Daniel Raynes	H
GOODWIN, E. McKee	5
GOODWIN, Edward C.	1
GOODWIN, Edward Jasper	1
GOODWIN, Edward Jewett	1
GOODWIN, Elijah	H
GOODWIN, Elliot H.	1
GOODWIN, Ernest Vance	4
GOODWIN, Francis M.	6
GOODWIN, Frank Judson	3
GOODWIN, Frederick C.	2
GOODWIN, Frederick Deane	8
GOODWIN, Godfrey G.	1
GOODWIN, Grace Duffield (Mrs. Frank J. Goodwin)	5
GOODWIN, Guy Spencer	8
GOODWIN, Hannibal Williston	H
GOODWIN, Harold	1
GOODWIN, Harry Manley	3
GOODWIN, Henry Charles	H
GOODWIN, Howard	7
GOODWIN, Ichabod	H
GOODWIN, J. Cheever	1
GOODWIN, James Junius	1
GOODWIN, John Benjamin	1
GOODWIN, John Edward	2
GOODWIN, John Noble	1
GOODWIN, Kathryn Dickinson	5
GOODWIN, Lavinia Stella	1
GOODWIN, Leo, Sr.	1
GOODWIN, Leo, Sr.	8
GOODWIN, Mark London	5
GOODWIN, Maud Wilder	1
GOODWIN, Nat C.	1
GOODWIN, Philip Arnold	1
GOODWIN, Philip Lippincott	3
GOODWIN, Richard Vanderburgh	3
GOODWIN, Robert Cabaniss	10
GOODWIN, Robert Eliot	6
GOODWIN, Russell Parker	1
GOODWIN, Wilder	3
GOODWIN, Willard T.	3
GOODWIN, William Archer Rutherfoord	1
GOODWIN, William Hall	1
GOODWIN, William N.	6
GOODWIN, William N.	7
GOODWIN, William Watson	1
GOODWYN, Kendall Wirt	10
GOODWYN, Peterson	H
GOODY, Marvin Edward	7
GOODYEAR, Anson Conger	4
GOODYEAR, Bradley	7
GOODYEAR, Charles*	H
GOODYEAR, Charles Waterhouse	1
GOODYEAR, John	4
GOODYEAR, William Henry	1
GOODYKOONTZ, Bess	10
GOODYKOONTZ, Colin Brummitt	3
GOODYKOONTZ, Wells	2
GOOKIN, Daniel	H
GOOLD, Herbert Stewart	7
GOOLD, Marshall Newton	1
GOOLRICK, C. O'Conor	4
GOOLSBY, Robert Edwin Moorman	4
GOONETILLEKE, Oliver Ernest	9
GOOSSENS, Eugene Sir	4
GORALSKI, Robert	10
GORAN, Morris	9
GORBACH, Alfons	5
GORBY, Paul Ford	5
GORDIN, Harry Mann	1
GORDINIER, Charles H.	4
GORDINIER, Hermon Camp	4
GORDIS, Robert	10
GORDON, Adoniram Judson	H
GORDON, Alfred	5
GORDON, Ambrose	9
GORDON, Andrew	H
GORDON, Anna Adams	1
GORDON, Archibald D.	H
GORDON, Armistead Churchill	1
GORDON, Armistead Churchill, Jr.	3
GORDON, Arthur Ernest	10
GORDON, Arthur Horace	1
GORDON, Burgess Lee	9
GORDON, Caroline (Mrs. Gordon Tate)	7
GORDON, Charles	2
GORDON, Charles A.	6
GORDON, Charles Henry	1
GORDON, Clarence	4
GORDON, Clarence McCheyne	5
GORDON, Colln Stuart	6
GORDON, David Stuart	1
GORDON, Dexter Keith	10
GORDON, Donald	5
GORDON, Donald Edward	8
GORDON, Dorothy	5

GORDON, Douglas 2
GORDON, Edgar Stillwell 7
GORDON, Edward Clifford 1
GORDON, Edward S. 7
GORDON, Edwin Seamer 1
GORDON, Eleanor Elizabeth 4
GORDON, Eleanor Kinzie 1
GORDON, Elizabeth 1
GORDON, Elliott Morton 7
GORDON, Ernest (Barron) 5
GORDON, Francis 1
GORDON, Frank Malcolm 2
GORDON, Fred George Russ 4
GORDON, Frederic Sutterle 3
GORDON, Frederick Charles 1
GORDON, George Anderson 3
GORDON, George Angier 1
GORDON, George Breed 1
GORDON, George Byron 1
GORDON, George C. 4
GORDON, George Henry H
GORDON, George Longan, Jr. 7
GORDON, George Phineas H
GORDON, George Washington 1
GORDON, Glen E. 10
GORDON, Gurdon Wright 3
GORDON, Harold John 10
GORDON, Harry Haskin 9
GORDON, Herbert Ford 7
GORDON, Hirsch Loeb 5
GORDON, Irwin Leslie 3
GORDON, Jack Murphy 8
GORDON, Jacques 2
GORDON, James H
GORDON, James 1
GORDON, James Fleming 10
GORDON, James Herndon 1
GORDON, James Logan 1
GORDON, James Marcus 3
GORDON, James Roycroft 10
GORDON, John 1
GORDON, John 3
GORDON, John 8
GORDON, John Boyle 9
GORDON, John Brown 1
GORDON, John Everett 9
GORDON, Joseph Claybaugh 1
GORDON, Julien 1
GORDON, Kermit 7
GORDON, Laura De Force H
GORDON, Laura De Force 4
GORDON, Leon 4
GORDON, Louis 4
GORDON, M. Lafayette 1
GORDON, Margaret 4
GORDON, Max 10
GORDON, Max 7
GORDON, Merritt J. 4
GORDON, Milton A. 10
GORDON, Mortimor S. 8
GORDON, Neil Elbridge 4
GORDON, Ney Kingsley 4
GORDON, Peter Benjamin 6
GORDON, Peyton 2
GORDON, Ray P(ercival) 5
GORDON, Richard Sammons 5
GORDON, Robert 3
GORDON, Robert Aaron 7
GORDON, Robert Charles 1
GORDON, Robert Donaldson 8
GORDON, Robert Lashbrook 7
GORDON, Robert Loudon 2
GORDON, Robert S. 5
GORDON, Robert S. 7
GORDON, Robert Sirkosky, Jr. 9
GORDON, Robert Winslow 8
GORDON, Ruth 3
GORDON, S.D. 1
GORDON, Samuel 8
GORDON, Seth 8
GORDON, Seth Chase 1
GORDON, Thomas Sylvy 4
GORDON, Thurlow Marshall 6
GORDON, Thurlow Marshall 7
GORDON, Walter Arthur 7
GORDON, Walter Henry 1
GORDON, Walter Lockhart 9
GORDON, William* H
GORDON, William 1
GORDON, William 2
GORDON, William Duncan 4

GORDON, William Fitzhugh H
GORDON, William Knox 2
GORDON, William Lawrence Sanford 5
GORDON, William Robert H
GORDON, William St. Clair 1
GORDON, William W. 1
GORDON, William Washington H
GORDON-DAVIS, Alfred Burwell (Davis Brinton) 5
GORDY, J.P. 1
GORDY, Walter 9
GORDY, Wilbur Fisk 1
GORE, Christopher H
GORE, Claude 3
GORE, Elbert Brutus 4
GORE, George William, Jr. 8
GORE, Herbert Charles 5
GORE, Howard Mason 2
GORE, Jack Worter 8
GORE, James Howard 4
GORE, John Kinsey 2
GORE, Joshua Walker 1
GORE, Quentin Pryor 4
GORE, Robert Hayes 6
GORE, Thomas Pryor 2
GORE, W.A. 1
GORE, Wilbert Lee 10
GOREN, Charles Henry 10
GORES, Landis 10
GORGAS, Ferdinand James Samuel 4
GORGAS, Josiah H
GORGAS, William Crawford 1
GORGES, Sir Ferdinando H
GORHAM, Benjamin H
GORHAM, Frederic Poole 1
GORHAM, George Congdon 1
GORHAM, Jabez H
GORHAM, John H
GORHAM, Nathaniel H
GORHAM, Sidney Smith, Jr. 7
GORHAM, Willis Arnold H
GORIN, Orville B. 1
GORINI, Luigi 7
GORKIN, Jess 8
GORKY, Arshile 4
GORMAN, Arthur Pue 1
GORMAN, Arthur Pue, Jr. 1
GORMAN, Charles Edmund 1
GORMAN, Daniel M. 1
GORMAN, George Edmond 1
GORMAN, Herbert Sherman 3
GORMAN, James Edward 2
GORMAN, John Jerome 7
GORMAN, John Leonard 9
GORMAN, Lawrence Clifton 1
GORMAN, Michael Arthur 3
GORMAN, Patrick Emmet 7
GORMAN, Robert Nestor 4
GORMAN, Thomas Francis (Mike Gorman) 10
GORMAN, Thomas J. 5
GORMAN, William Joseph 7
GORMLEY, Robert Emmett 8
GORNITZKA, Odd 8
GORNOWSKI, Edward John 8
GORNTO, Albert Brooks, Jr. 10
GORODNITZKI, Sascha 9
GOROSTIZA, Jose 5
GORRELL, Edgar Staley 2
GORRELL, Faith Lanman 1
GORRIE, John H
GORRINGE, Henry Honeychurch H
GORSKI, Martin 2
GORSLINE, George William 9
GORSUCH, John Elliott 9
GORTATOWSKY, Jacob Dewey 4
GORTHY, Willis Charles 4
GORTNER, Ross Aiken 1
GORTNER, Ross Aiken, Jr. 9
GORTON, David Allyn 4
GORTON, Eliot 1
GORTON, Samuel H
GOSA, Robert Earl 6
GOSE, Mack F. 3
GOSE, Thomas Phelps 5
GOSHEN, Elmer Isaac 9
GOSHEY, Frank Joseph 8
GOSHORN, Alfred Traber 1

GOSHORN, Clarence Baker 3
GOSHORN, Lenore Rhyno 3
GOSHORN, R. C. 8
GOSHORN, R.C. 3
GOSLEE, Hart John 2
GOSLINE, William A., Jr. 2
GOSLING, Glen Donald 6
GOSLING, Thomas Warrington 1
GOSNELL, Harold Foote 10
GOSNELL, John Ansley 5
GOSNEY, Ezra Seymour 2
GOSNOLD, Bartholomew H
GOSS, Albert S. 3
GOSS, Arthur 8
GOSS, Bert Crawford 5
GOSS, Charles A. 1
GOSS, Charles Frederic 1
GOSS, Chauncey P. 1
GOSS, Chauncey Porter 1
GOSS, Edward Otis 1
GOSS, Elbridge Henry 1
GOSS, Evan Benson 1
GOSS, Francis Webster 1
GOSS, Harold Isaac 7
GOSS, Harvey Theo 3
GOSS, Howard Archibald 7
GOSS, James Hassell 9
GOSS, John Henry 2
GOSS, Nathaniel Stickney 1
GOSS, Robert Whitmore 5
GOSS, Warren Lee 1
GOSS, Wesley Perry 9
GOSS, William Freeman Myrick 1
GOSS, William Middlebrook 4
GOSSARD, George Daniel 1
GOSSARD, Harry Clinton 3
GOSSELIN, Edward N. 9
GOSSETT, Alfred Newton 2
GOSSETT, Benjamin Brown 1
GOSSETT, Charles C. 8
GOSSETT, Earl J. 4
GOSSETT, John Taylor 1
GOSSETT, Robert Kenneth 5
GOSSICK, Ben Roger 7
GOSSLER, Philip Green 2
GOSTELOWE, Jonathan H
GOTAAS, Harold Benedict 7
GOTCH, Arthur Edward 5
GOTFRYD, Alexander 10
GOTHAL, Sylvan 5
GOTSHALK, Dilman Water 6
GOTSHALL, William Charles 1
GOTT, Charles 1
GOTT, Daniel H
GOTT, Edgar Nathaniel 2
GOTT, Edwin Hays 9
GOTT, Philip Porter 8
GOTT, William Thomas 1
GOTTESMAN, D. Samuel 3
GOTTFRIED, Louis Elio 5
GOTTHEIL, Gustave 1
GOTTHEIL, Richard James Horatio 1
GOTTHEIL, William Samuel 4
GOTTLIEB, Aldolph 6
GOTTLIEB, Bertram 9
GOTTLIEB, James E. 6
GOTTLIEB, Lewis 1
GOTTLIEB, Polly Rose (Mrs. Alex Gottlieb) 6
GOTTSCHALK, Alfred 6
GOTTSCHALK, Alfred L. Moreau 1
GOTTSCHALK, Hans W. 7
GOTTSCHALK, Louis 6
GOTTSCHALK, Louis Ferdinand 4
GOTTSCHALK, Louis Moreau H
GOTTSCHALL, Morton 5
GOTTSCHALL, Oscar M. 4
GOTTSHALL, Ralph K(err) 8
GOTTWALD, Floyd Dewey 8
GOTTWALD, Floyd Dewey, Jr. 8
GOTTWALD, Klement 3
GOTWALD, Luther Alexander 4
GOTWALS, John C. 5
GOUBEAU, Vincent de Paul 10
GOUCHER, John Franklin 1
GOUDSMIT, Samuel 7
GOUDY, Frank Burris 2
GOUDY, Franklin Curtis 1
GOUDY, Frederic William 2
GOUDY, William Charles H
GOUGAR, Helen M. 1

GOUGE, Sir Arthur 8
GOUGE, William M. H
GOUGH, Emile Jefferson 2
GOUGH, Harold Robert 8
GOUGH, John Bartholomew H
GOUGH, Lewis Ketcham 4
GOUGH, Robert E. 5
GOUIN, Leon Mercier 9
GOULART, Joao Belchlor Marques 7
GOULD, Albert J. 7
GOULD, Anna Laura 5
GOULD, Arthur Robinson 2
GOULD, Ashley Mulgrave 1
GOULD, Augustus Addison H
GOULD, Benjamin Apthorp H
GOULD, Benjamin Z. 9
GOULD, Bernard Albert 10
GOULD, Carl Frelinghuysen 1
GOULD, Charles Lessington 9
GOULD, Charles Newton 1
GOULD, Charles Winthrop 1
GOULD, Chester 8
GOULD, Clarence Pembroke 5
GOULD, Clarence Pembroke 7
GOULD, Edward Sherman 1
GOULD, Edward Shuman H
GOULD, Edwin 1
GOULD, Edwin Miner Lawrence 3
GOULD, Edwin Sprague 1
GOULD, Elgin Ralston Lovell 1
GOULD, Elizabeth Lincoln 1
GOULD, Ezra Palmer 1
GOULD, Frank 4
GOULD, Frank Horace 1
GOULD, Frank Jay 3
GOULD, Frank Miller 2
GOULD, Fredrick G. 8
GOULD, George Jay 1
GOULD, George Milbry 1
GOULD, Glenn Herbert 8
GOULD, Gordon Thomas, Jr. 7
GOULD, Hannah Flagg H
GOULD, Harley Nathan 8
GOULD, Harris Perley 2
GOULD, Harry 2
GOULD, Harry Edward 5
GOULD, Herman Day H
GOULD, Howard 1
GOULD, James H
GOULD, Jay H
GOULD, Kenneth Miller 5
GOULD, Kingdon 2
GOULD, Laura Stedman 1
GOULD, Lawrence McKinley 10
GOULD, Leslie 7
GOULD, Lyman Jay 7
GOULD, Moses Joseph 4
GOULD, Nathaniel Duren 4
GOULD, Norman Judd 4
GOULD, Norman Judd 5
GOULD, Samuel Wadsworth 1
GOULD, Theodore Pennock 4
GOULD, Thomas Ridgeway H
GOULD, William Drum 10
GOULD, William Edward 3
GOULDEN, Joseph Augustus 1
GOULDER, Harvey 1
GOULDER, Harvey Danforth 4
GOULDING, Edmund 3
GOULDING, Francis Robert H
GOULDING, Raymond Walter 10
GOULDNER, Alvin Ward 7
GOULETT, Paul R. 4
GOULEY, John William Severin 4
GOUPIL, St. Rene H
GOURDIN, Theodore H
GOURLEY, James Edwin 8
GOURLEY, Joseph Harvey 2
GOURLEY, Louis Hill 3
GOURLEY, Robert John 6
GOURLEY, Wallace S. 7
GOURLEY, William B. 1
GOUVERNEUR, Marian 1
GOUWENS, Teunis Earl 7
GOVAN, Andrew Robison H
GOVAN, Gilbert Eaton 9
GOVAN, Mary Christine Noble 9
GOVE, Aaron 1

GOVE, Charles Augustus 1
GOVE, Frank Edward 4
GOVE, George 3
GOVE, George 6
GOVE, Philip Babcock 5
GOVIN, Rafael R. 1
GOW, Arthur Sidney 6
GOW, Charles R(ice) 5
GOW, George Coleman 4
GOW, James Steele 5
GOW, John Russell 1
GOW, Paul A. 7
GOW, Robert MacGregor 4
GOWAN, Sister M. Olivia 8
GOWANS, Ephraim Gowan 4
GOWANS, William H
GOWDY, John Kennedy 1
GOWDY, Robert Clyde 3
GOWDY, Roy Cotsworth 1
GOWEN, Francis Innes 1
GOWEN, Franklin Benjamin H
GOWEN, Herbert Henry 5
GOWEN, Isaac William 1
GOWEN, James Bartholomew 3
GOWEN, James Emmet 5
GOWEN, John Knowles, Jr. 4
GOWEN, John Wittemore 4
GOWEN, Robert Fellows 4
GOWEN, Samuel Emmett 6
GOWENLOCK, Thomas Russell 4
GOWER, John Henry 4
GOWETZ, Irene 10
GOWIN, Enoch Burton 7
GOWMAN, T. Harry 4
GOYEN, Charles William 8
GRABACH, John Robert 8
GRABAU, Amadeus William 5
GRABAU, Johannes Andreas August H
GRABAU, Martin 4
GRABAU, Richard Fred 8
GRABB, William Clarence 8
GRABER, Edward Darwin 1
GRABER, Laurence Frederick 8
GRABFELDER, Samuel 1
GRABILL, Ethelbert Vincent 5
GRABLE, Betty (Elizabeth Ruth) 5
GRABLE, E.F. 4
GRABLE, Errett Marion 8
GRACE, Princess of Monaco 8
GRACE, Atonzo G. 5
GRACE, Carl Guy 5
GRACE, Edward Raymond 4
GRACE, Eugene Gifford 4
GRACE, Francis Mitchell 1
GRACE, Frank W. 2
GRACE, Harry Holder 4
GRACE, James Thomas, Jr. 4
GRACE, John Joseph 5
GRACE, John Joseph 7
GRACE, Joseph Peter 3
GRACE, Louise Carol 4
GRACE, Oliver Russell 10
GRACE, Thomas 1
GRACE, Thomas L. 5
GRACE, Thomas Langdon H
GRACE, William 1
GRACE, William Joseph 3
GRACE, William Russell 1
GRACE, William Russell 2
GRACEY, Samuel Levis 1
GRACEY, Wilbur Tirrell 5
GRACEY, William Adolphe 2
GRACIE, Archibald H
GRAD, Harold 9
GRADLE, Harry Searls 5
GRADLE, Henry 1
GRADWOHL, Bernard Sam 9
GRADY, Daniel Henry 3
GRADY, Eleanor Hundson 5
GRADY, Henry Francis 3
GRADY, Henry W. 4
GRADY, Henry Woodfin H
GRADY, John Henry 9
GRADY, Paul Davis 9
GRADY, Roy Israel 9
GRAEBNER, August Lawrence 1
GRAEBNER, Martin Adolph Henry 3
GRAEBNER, Theodore 3
GRAEBNER, Walter 7
GRAEFE, James Arthur 9
GRAEFFE, Edwin O(tto) 5
GRAESSER, Roy French 5
GRAESSL, Lawrence H
GRAF, Herbert 5
GRAF, Homer William 5

GRAF, John E(nos) 8
GRAF, Julius Eicher 9
GRAF, Oskar Maria 5
GRAF, Paul Luther 9
GRAF, Robert Joseph 2
GRAF, Samuel Herman 8
GRAFE, Paul 7
GRAFF, Ellis U. 5
GRAFF, Everett D. 4
GRAFF, Frederic H
GRAFF, Frederick H
GRAFF, Fritz William 3
GRAFF, George E. 1
GRAFF, Joseph Verdi 1
GRAFFENRIED, H
  Christopher
GRAFFLI, Douglas 3
  Gordon
GRAFLY, Charles 1
GRAFLY, Dorothy 7
GRAFTON, Charles 1
  Chapman
GRAFTON, Robert 1
  Wadsworth
GRAH, Rudolf Ferdinand 7
GRAHAM, Albert D. 3
GRAHAM, Alexander 2
  William
GRAHAM, Allen Jordan 1
GRAHAM, Arthur Butler 6
GRAHAM, B.A. 3
GRAHAM, Balus Joseph 5
  Windsor
GRAHAM, Ben George 2
GRAHAM, Benjamin 7
GRAHAM, Bill 10
GRAHAM, Chalmers 10
  George
GRAHAM, Charles H
  Kinnaird
GRAHAM, Charles 4
  Vanderveer
GRAHAM, Christopher 3
GRAHAM, Clarence Henry 5
GRAHAM, Dale 3
GRAHAM, David H
GRAHAM, David 7
GRAHAM, David Wilson 1
GRAHAM, Donald 7
GRAHAM, Donald Earl 4
GRAHAM, Donald 5
  Goodnow
GRAHAM, Dorothy 3
GRAHAM, Edward Kidder 1
GRAHAM, Edwin Charles 3
GRAHAM, Edwin Eldon 3
GRAHAM, Edwin R. 1
GRAHAM, Ernest Robert 1
GRAHAM, Evarts 3
  Ambrose
GRAHAM, Frank 4
GRAHAM, Frank 2
  Dunstone
GRAHAM, Frank Porter 1
GRAHAM, Frederick J. 6
GRAHAM, George Edward 4
GRAHAM, George Scott 1
GRAHAM, Geroge Rex H
GRAHAM, Gwethalyn 4
GRAHAM, Henry Tucker 3
GRAHAM, Horace French 1
GRAHAM, Horace French 2
GRAHAM, Horace 3
  Reynolds
GRAHAM, Hoyt Conlin 1
GRAHAM, Hugh 3
GRAHAM, Inez 4
GRAHAM, Isabella H
  Marshall
GRAHAM, James* H
GRAHAM, James Arthur 4
GRAHAM, James B. 5
GRAHAM, James Duncan 1
GRAHAM, James Francis 4
GRAHAM, James Harper 1
GRAHAM, James Hiram 4
GRAHAM, James M. 2
GRAHAM, John* 1
GRAHAM, John Andrew H
GRAHAM, John Howard 3
GRAHAM, John Hugh H
GRAHAM, John Joseph 6
GRAHAM, John Meredith 5
GRAHAM, John Stephens 7
GRAHAM, John William 6
GRAHAM, Jonathan 1
  Thomas
GRAHAM, Joseph H
GRAHAM, Joseph 4
  Alexander
GRAHAM, Kelley H
GRAHAM, Lawrence Pike 1
GRAHAM, Lena Forney 5
  Reinhardt (Mrs. Joseph
  Graham)
GRAHAM, Louis Edward 4

GRAHAM, Malbone 4
  Watson
GRAHAM, Margaret 1
  Collier
GRAHAM, Martha 10
GRAHAM, Mary Owen 5
GRAHAM, Neil F. 4
GRAHAM, Palmer 8
  Hampton
GRAHAM, Philip L. 4
GRAHAM, Ray Austin 9
GRAHAM, Robert 9
GRAHAM, Robert Cabel 4
GRAHAM, Robert Henry 5
GRAHAM, Robert 10
  Montrose
GRAHAM, Robert Orlando 1
GRAHAM, Robert X. 3
GRAHAM, Samuel Jordan 3
GRAHAM, Shirley Lola 7
  (Mrs. W.E.B. Dubois)
GRAHAM, Stephen A. 4
GRAHAM, Stephen Victor 5
GRAHAM, Sterling 5
  Edward
GRAHAM, Sylvester H
GRAHAM, Thomas Wesley 5
GRAHAM, Thomas Wesley 7
GRAHAM, Walter James 2
GRAHAM, Walter Waverly 6
GRAHAM, Wilard J. 4
GRAHAM, William H
  Alexander
GRAHAM, William 3
  Alexander
GRAHAM, William Donald 7
GRAHAM, William 4
  Harrison
GRAHAM, William Hugh 8
GRAHAM, William 1
  Johnson
GRAHAM, William Joseph 4
GRAHAM, William 1
  Montrose
GRAHAM, William Pratt 4
GRAHAM, William Roger 9
GRAHAM, William Tate 5
GRAHAME, Gloria 8
GRAHAME, Laurance Hill 4
GRAHL, Charles Harry 7
  Hans
GRAIG, Frank Andrew 6
GRAINGER, Percy 4
GRALTON, Richard T. 9
GRAM, Moltke Stefanus 4
GRAMATKY, Hardie 7
GRAMBLING, Allen 5
  Rowell
GRAMBSCH, Paul Victor 9
GRAMLICH, Francis 6
  W(illiam)
GRAMLICH, Howard John 8
GRAMM, Donald 8
GRAMMER, Allen 5
  L(uther)
GRAMMER, Carl 2
  Eckhardt
GRAMMER, Elijah 1
  Sherman
GRAMMER, Jacob 1
GRAMSTORFF, Emil 9
  Anton
GRANAHAN, Kathryn E. 7
GRANAHAN, William 3
  Thomas
GRANBERRY, C. Read 4
GRANBERRY, John Cowper 1
GRANBERY, John Cowper 3
GRAND, Gordon, Jr. 4
GRANDFIELD, Charles 4
  Paxton
GRANDGENT, Charles 1
  Hall
GRANDIN, Egbert Henry 4
GRANDIN, Thomas B. 7
GRANDJANY, Marcel 6
GRANDY, Cyrus Wiley 7
GRANFIDLE, William 3
  Joseph
GRANGE, Red (Harold) 10
  Edward (The Galloping
  Ghost)
GRANGER, Alfred Hoyt 1
GRANGER, Amédée 6
GRANGER, Amos Phelps H
GRANGER, Armour 5
  Townsend
GRANGER, Arthur Otis 1
GRANGER, Barlow 1
GRANGER, Bradley H
  Francis
GRANGER, Charles 1
  Trumbull
GRANGER, Christopher 7
  Mabley

GRANGER, Daniel Larned 1
  Davis
GRANGER, Francis H
GRANGER, Frank Butler 1
GRANGER, Gideon H
GRANGER, Gordon H
GRANGER, Jeffrey Solon 8
GRANGER, Lester B. 6
GRANGER, Miles Tobey H
GRANGER, Moses 1
  Moorhead
GRANGER, Sherman 5
  Moorhead
GRANGER, Walter 1
GRANGER, William 1
  Alexander
GRANICK, David 10
GRANIK, Theodore 5
GRANIT, Ragnar Arthur 10
GRANJON, Henry Regis 4
GRANNAN, Charles P. 5
GRANNIS, Elizabeth 4
  Bartlett
GRANNIS, Robert 5
  Maitland
GRANNISS, Anna Jane 4
GRANNISS, Robert 1
  Andrews
GRANOVSKY, Alexander 8
  A.
GRANRUD, Carl Frithjof 10
GRANT, Abraham 1
GRANT, Abraham Phineas 1
GRANT, Albert Weston 1
GRANT, Alsie Raymond 4
GRANT, Amy (Allison) 6
GRANT, Archie C. 10
GRANT, Arthur Rogers 2
GRANT, Asahel H
GRANT, Ben Joseph 8
GRANT, Benjamin William 9
GRANT, Bishop F(ranklin) 5
GRANT, Carroll Walter 5
GRANT, Cary 10
GRANT, Chapman 8
GRANT, Charles Henry 1
GRANT, Charles Leon 6
GRANT, Claudius 1
  Buchanan
GRANT, David Alexander 7
GRANT, David Elias 5
GRANT, David Norvell 4
  Walker
GRANT, Deforest 5
GRANT, Duncan Campbell 6
GRANT, Edward Donald 9
GRANT, Elihu 2
GRANT, Elliott Mansfield 5
GRANT, Eugene Lodewick 10
GRANT, Evva H. 7
GRANT, Frederick Clifton 6
GRANT, Frederick Dent 1
GRANT, George Barnard 1
GRANT, George Barnard 4
GRANT, George Camron 3
GRANT, George Ernest 3
GRANT, George McInvale 8
GRANT, Gordon 2
GRANT, Harry Johnston 4
GRANT, Heber J. 2
GRANT, Henry Horace 1
GRANT, Henry William 1
GRANT, Hugh Gladney 8
GRANT, Hugh John 1
GRANT, James Benton 1
GRANT, James Benton 2
GRANT, James Richard 3
GRANT, Jesse R. 4
GRANT, John Benjamin 9
GRANT, John Black 1
GRANT, John Cowles 1
GRANT, John Francis 8
GRANT, John Gaston 4
GRANT, John Henry 1
GRANT, John MacGregor 1
GRANT, John Prescott 1
GRANT, John Thomas H
GRANT, Joseph Donohoe 2
GRANT, Joseph Henry 1
GRANT, Julia Dent 1
GRANT, Lester Strickland 5
GRANT, Lewis Addison 1
GRANT, M. Earl 9
GRANT, Madison 1
GRANT, Margaret 4
GRANT, Percy Stickney 1
GRANT, Richard Frank 3
GRANT, Richard Ralph 3
  Hallam
GRANT, Robert 1
GRANT, Robert John 2
GRANT, Roderick 4
  McLellan
GRANT, Rollin P. 1
GRANT, Thirza Eunice 1
GRANT, Thomas McMillan 3
GRANT, Ulysses S., III 5

GRANT, Ulysses S, Jr. 1
GRANT, Ulysses Sherman 1
GRANT, Ulysses Simpson H
GRANT, Walter Bruce 1
GRANT, Walter Schuyler 6
GRANT, Whit McDonough 1
GRANT, William Daniel 6
GRANT, William Thomas 3
GRANT, William Thomas 5
GRANT, William West 1
GRANT, William West 3
GRANTGES, William 8
  Fidelas
GRANTHAM, Edwin 1
  Lincoln
GRANTLAND, Seaton H
GRANT-SMITH, U. 4
GRANVILLE, 4th Earl 3
GRANVILLE, Keith 10
GRANVILLE, William 5
  Anthony
GRANVILLE-SMITH, W. 1
GRANVILLE-SMITH, 6
  Walter, Jr.
GRAPER, Elmer Diedrich 7
GRAS, Norman Scott Brien 7
GRASON, C. Gus 3
GRASS, John H
GRASS, John 4
GRASSE, Edwin 3
GRASSE, Francois Joseph H
  Paul de
GRASSELLI, Caesar 1
  Augustin
GRASSELLI, Thomas Fries 5
GRASSELLI, Thomas 2
  Saxton
GRASSHAM, Charles C. 2
GRASSHOFF, Frank O. 3
GRASSIE, Herbert J. 6
GRASSO, Ella T. (Mrs. 7
  Thomas A. Grasso)
GRASTY, Charles Henry 1
GRASTY, John Sharshall 1
GRATACAP, Louis Pope 1
GRATIOT, Charles H
GRATKE, Charles Edward 2
GRATON, L(ouis) (C(aryl) 6
GRATTAN, Clinton 7
  Hartley
GRATZ, Bernard H
GRATZ, Michael H
GRATZ, Rebecca H
GRATZ, W. Edward J. 3
GRAU, Frederick 10
  Vahlcamp
GRAU, Maurice 1
GRAUDAN, Nikolai 5
GRAUEL, George Edward 4
GRAUER, A.E. 4
GRAUER, Ben 7
GRAUER, Natalie Eynon 3
GRAUER, Theophil Paul 4
GRAUL, Donald Philip 7
GRAUPNER, Adolphus 2
  Earhart
GRAUPNER, Johann H
  Christian Gottlieb
GRAU SAN MARTIN, 5
  Ramon
GRAUSTEIN, Archibald 5
  R(obertson)
GRAUSTEIN, William 1
  Caspar
GRAVATT, John James 6
GRAVATT, William Loyall 2
GRAVE, Caswell 1
GRAVE, Frederick David 4
GRAVELY, Joseph Jackson H
GRAVELY, William S. 8
GRAVEN, Bruce 6
GRAVEN, Henry Norman 4
GRAVES, Abbott Fuller 1
GRAVES, Alvin C. 4
GRAVES, Anson Rogers 1
GRAVES, Austin Taylor 10
GRAVES, Benjamin 7
  Clifford
GRAVES, Bibb 2
GRAVES, Charles 2
GRAVES, Charles Alfred 4
GRAVES, Charles Burleigh 1
GRAVES, C(harles) 7
  Edward
GRAVES, Charles Hinman 1
GRAVES, Charles Mrashall 3
GRAVES, Dixie Bibb 7
GRAVES, Eli Edwin 4
GRAVES, Eugene Silas 1
GRAVES, Frank Pierrepont 3
GRAVES, Frank Xavier, Jr. 10
GRAVES, Frederick Rogers 1
GRAVES, George Keene 2
GRAVES, Grant Ostrander 1
GRAVES, Harold Nathan 4
GRAVES, Henry Solon 3

GRAVES, Herbert 1
  Cornelius
GRAVES, Ireland 5
GRAVES, Jackson Alpheus 1
GRAVES, James Robinson H
GRAVES, James Wesley 3
GRAVES, Jay P. 2
GRAVES, John 3
GRAVES, John Temple 1
GRAVES, John Temple 4
GRAVES, Lawrence 10
  Murray
GRAVES, Lester Herbert 8
GRAVES, Louis 4
GRAVES, Louis 7
GRAVES, Lulu Grace 2
GRAVES, Mark 4
GRAVES, Marvin Lee 4
GRAVES, Mary Wheat 5
  (Mrs. Billy Z. Graves)
GRAVES, Nelson Zuingle 1
GRAVES, Ralph A. 1
GRAVES, Ralph H. 1
GRAVES, Robert (Von 9
  Ranke)
GRAVES, Robert John 3
GRAVES, Roger Colgate 8
GRAVES, Schuyler Colfax 1
GRAVES, Waller W. 1
GRAVES, William Blair 1
GRAVES, William H(orace) 10
GRAVES, William Jordan H
GRAVES, William Lucius 2
GRAVES, William Phillips 1
GRAVES, William Sidney 1
GRAVES, William 3
  Washington
GRAVES, Zuinglius Calvin H
GRAVETT, Joshua 5
GRAVIER, Charles H
GRAVIER, Jacques H
GRAWE, Oliver Rudolph 4
GRAWN, Charles Theodore 4
GRAY, Albert F(rederick) 5
GRAY, Alexander 1
GRAY, Alfred Leftwich 1
GRAY, Alfred Walter 1
GRAY, Andrew Caldwell 1
GRAY, Arthur 7
GRAY, Arthur Irving 4
GRAY, Arthur Romeyn 1
GRAY, Asa H
GRAY, Augustine Heard 8
GRAY, Baron De Kalb 1
GRAY, Bowman 1
GRAY, Bowman 5
GRAY, Bowman, III 9
GRAY, Campbell 1
GRAY, Carl Raymond 1
GRAY, Carl Raymond, Jr. 3
GRAY, Charles Harold 4
GRAY, Charles Oliver 4
GRAY, Charlotte Elvira 1
GRAY, Chester Earl 2
GRAY, Chester H. 4
GRAY, Clarence Truman 5
GRAY, Clifton Daggett 2
GRAY, Clifton Merritt 1
GRAY, Cyrus S. 1
GRAY, Daniel Thomas 6
GRAY, David H
GRAY, David 1
GRAY, David L. 1
GRAY, Donald Joseph 1
GRAY, Dudley Guy 1
GRAY, Duncan 4
  Montgomery
GRAY, E. McQueen 4
GRAY, Earl Quincy 9
GRAY, Earle* 5
GRAY, Edward 9
GRAY, Edward C. 10
GRAY, Edward Winthrop 2
GRAY, Edwin H
GRAY, Elisha 1
GRAY, Ernest Weston 6
GRAY, Finly H. 3
GRAY, Francis Calley H
GRAY, Francis Calley 7
GRAY, Frank, Jr. 7
GRAY, Franklin Dingwall 10
GRAY, G. Charles 8
GRAY, George 1
GRAY, George Edward 4
GRAY, George Herbert 2
GRAY, George William 4
GRAY, George Zabriskie H
GRAY, Giles Wilkeson 7
GRAY, Giles Wilkeson 8
GRAY, Gordon 8
GRAY, Gordon 8
GRAY, Hamilton 8
GRAY, Harold (Lincoln) 5
GRAY, Harold Edwin 5
GRAY, Harold Parker 4
GRAY, Henry 9
GRAY, Henry David 5

GRAY, Henry G. 3
GRAY, Henry Peteers H
GRAY, Hiram H
GRAY, Hob 5
GRAY, Horace 1
GRAY, Horace 10
Montgomery
GRAY, Howard Adams 3
GRAY, Howard Kramer 3
GRAY, Isaac Pusey H
GRAY, J.P. 4
GRAY, J.S. 5
GRAY, James 1
GRAY, James Alexander 3
GRAY, James Burdis 4
GRAY, James M. 1
GRAY, James Richard 1
GRAY, Jessie 2
GRAY, John Chipman 1
GRAY, John Clinton 1
GRAY, John Cowper H
GRAY, John Henry 2
GRAY, John Pinkham 1
GRAY, John Purdue 1
GRAY, John Stephens 10
GRAY, Joseph M.M. 3
GRAY, Joseph Phelps 4
GRAY, Joseph Preston 1
GRAY, Joseph W. H
GRAY, Joslyn 5
GRAY, Leon Fowler 5
GRAY, Lewis Cecil 6
GRAY, Louis Herbert 3
GRAY, Maria Freeman 4
GRAY, Mat 5
GRAY, Morris 1
GRAY, Norman Briggs 7
GRAY, Oscar Lee 4
GRAY, Philip F. 8
GRAY, Prentiss Nathaniel 1
GRAY, Ralph Weld 6
GRAY, Richard George 8
GRAY, Richard J. 4
GRAY, Robert H
GRAY, R(obert) A. 7
GRAY, Robert Davis 7
GRAY, Roland 5
GRAY, Thomas 1
GRAY, Truman Stretcher 10
GRAY, Walter H. 6
GRAY, Wellington Burbank 7
GRAY, Willard Franklin 4
GRAY, William H
GRAY, William C. 4
GRAY, William H. H
GRAY, William John 4
GRAY, William Lafayette, 7
Jr.
GRAY, William Price, Jr. 4
GRAY, William Rensselaer 1
GRAY, William Scott 4
GRAY, William Steele 4
GRAY, William Steele, Jr. 8
GRAYDON, Alexander H
GRAYDON, Allan 10
GRAYDON, James Weir 4
GRAYDON, Joseph 5
Spencer
GRAYDON, William H
GRAYSON, Cary Travers 1
GRAYSON, Charles 4
Prevost
GRAYSON, Clifford 4
Prevost
GRAYSON, Theodore J. 1
GRAYSON, Thomas 4
Jackson
GRAYSON, Thomas Wray 1
GRAYSON, William H
GRAYSON, William Bandy 4
GRAYSON, William John H
GREACEN, Edmund 2
GREATHOUSE, Charles 1
A.
GREATHOUSE, Clarence 1
R.
GREATHOUSE, Clarence H
Ridgeby
GREATON, John H
GREATON, Joseph H
GREATOREX, Eliza Pratt H
GREATOREX, Kathleen 3
Honora
GREAVES, Donald 8
Critchfield
GREAVES, Frederick 6
Clarence
GREAVES, Joseph Eames 3
GREBANIER, Bernard 7
GREBE, John Josef 8
GREBE, Marguerite 5
Luckett
GREBENSTCHIKOFF, 4
George
GREBLE, Edwin St John 1
GREBLE, John T. H
GRECH, Anthony Paul 10

GREDE, William J. 10
GREEAR, Fred Bonham 4
GREEF, Robert Julius 4
GREEFF, Theodore 7
GREELEY, Dana McLean 9
GREELEY, Edwin Seneca 4
GREELEY, Horace H
GREELEY, Louis May 1
GREELEY, Mellen Clark 6
GREELEY, Paul Webb 9
GREELEY, Samuel Arnold 5
GREELEY, William B. 3
GREELEY, William Roger 4
Washington
GREELY, Antoinette 6
GREELY, Edward H
GREELY, John Nesmith 4
GREEN, Abel 6
GREEN, Addison Loomis 2
GREEN, Adolphus 1
Williamson
GREEN, Adwin Wigfall 4
GREEN, Adwin Wigfall 5
GREEN, Alexander Little H
Page
GREEN, Allen Percival 3
GREEN, Andrew Haswell 1
GREEN, Arthur Laurence 4
GREEN, Asa H
GREEN, Ashbel H
GREEN, Bartholomew H
GREEN, Ben Charles 8
GREEN, Beriah H
GREEN, Bernard 1
Richardson
GREEN, Berryman 1
GREEN, Bert 2
GREEN, Byram H
GREEN, Charles 7
GREEN, Charles Boden 5
GREEN, Charles Carrol 4
GREEN, Charles Edward 4
GREEN, Charles Edward 7
GREEN, Charles Henry 1
GREEN, Charles Henry 3
GREEN, Charles 1
Montraville
GREEN, Conant Lewis 3
GREEN, Constance 6
McLaughlin
GREEN, Crawford 6
Richmond
GREEN, Daniel Crandall 7
GREEN, Darrell Bennet 3
GREEN, David Edward 1
GREEN, David Ezra 8
GREEN, David I. 1
GREEN, Duff H
GREEN, Dwight H. 3
GREEN, Dwight Phelps 6
GREEN, Edith 9
GREEN, Edward Averill 4
GREEN, Edward Brodhead 3
GREEN, Edward Henry 7
GREEN, Edward Howland 1
Robinson
GREEN, Edward Melvin 1
GREEN, Edward Melvin 7
GREEN, Edwin George 7
GREEN, Edwin Luther 3
GREEN, Estill J. 6
GREEN, Fitzhugh 10
GREEN, Fitzhugh 2
GREEN, Fletcher Melvin 7
GREEN, Francis H
GREEN, Francis Harriet H
Whipple
GREEN, Francis Harvey 3
GREEN, Francis Mathews 1
GREEN, Frank Russell 3
GREEN, Fred Warren 1
GREEN, Frederick 3
GREEN, Frederick Robin 4
GREEN, Frederick William H
GREEN, Garner Leland 6
GREEN, George Rex 2
GREEN, George Walter 4
GREEN, Grafton 2
GREEN, H.T.S. 2
GREEN, Harold L. 3
GREEN, Harold Roy 6
GREEN, Harry E. 6
GREEN, Harry Edward 9
GREEN, Harry Joseph 5
GREEN, Henry 1
GREEN, Henry Irvin 3
GREEN, Henry Woodhull H
GREEN, Henry Woodhull 1
GREEN, Hetty Howland 1
Robinson
GREEN, Horace H
GREEN, Horace 2
GREEN, Howard Whipple 3
GREEN, Innis 3
GREEN, Isiah Lewis 4
GREEN, Jacob* H

GREEN, James 1
GREEN, James Benjamin 5
GREEN, James F. 4
GREEN, James Gilchrist 1
GREEN, James Monroe 1
GREEN, James Stephen H
GREEN, James Woods 1
GREEN, Jerome Joseph 4
GREEN, Jesse Cope 1
GREEN, John* 1
GREEN, John 2
GREEN, John 1
GREEN, John Cleve H
GREEN, John Edgar, Jr. 2
GREEN, John F. 1
GREEN, John Garside 4
GREEN, John M. 6
GREEN, John Orne 1
GREEN, John Pugh 1
GREEN, John Raeburn 10
GREEN, John Webb 3
GREEN, Jonas H
GREEN, Joseph H
GREEN, Joseph Andrew 4
GREEN, Joseph Coy 7
GREEN, Joshua 6
GREEN, Julia M. 4
GREEN, Leon 7
GREEN, Leslle H. 6
GREEN, Lewis Warner H
GREEN, Lot 4
GREEN, Marcellus 2
GREEN, Marcus Herbert 7
GREEN, Melville Saul 5
GREEN, Nathan H
GREEN, Nathan 1
GREEN, Nathan Williams 3
GREEN, Norvin 4
GREEN, Norvin Hewitt 3
GREEN, Paul Eliot 7
GREEN, Paul Martin 6
GREEN, Percy Warren 3
GREEN, Perry Luther 3
GREEN, Richard Calvin 8
GREEN, Robert Gladding 2
GREEN, Robert Holt 9
GREEN, Robert McCay 5
GREEN, Robert Morris 9
GREEN, Robert N. 4
GREEN, Robert Stockton 4
GREEN, Rolland Lester 5
GREEN, Roy Melvin 9
GREEN, Roy Monroe 2
GREEN, Rufus Lot 1
GREEN, Samuel H
GREEN, Samuel Abbott 1
GREEN, Samuel Bowdlear 1
GREEN, Samuel Swett 2
GREEN, Seth 1
GREEN, Theodore Francis 4
GREEN, Theodore Meyer 5
GREEN, Thomas H
GREEN, Thomas Dunbar 3
GREEN, Thomas Edward 1
GREEN, Thomas Henry 8
GREEN, Thomas Samuel 7
GREEN, Walter Lawrence 4
GREEN, Walton Atwater 3
GREEN, Warren Everett 2
GREEN, Wharton Jackson 1
GREEN, William 1
GREEN, William 1
GREEN, William Charles 3
GREEN, William Elza 1
GREEN, William Henry 1
GREEN, William John 3
GREEN, William Joseph, 4
Jr.
GREEN, William Marvin 2
GREEN, William Mercer H
GREEN, William Mercer 1
GREEN, William Paul 8
GREEN, William Raymond 2
GREEN, Willis 1
GREEN, Wyman Reed H
GREENAWALD, Paul 3
Benjamin
GREENAWAY, Donald 10
GREENAWAY, Emerson 10
GREENBAUM, David 6
GREENBAUM, Dorothea 9
Schwarcz
GREENBAUM, Edward S. 5
GREENBAUM, Edward S. 8
GREENBAUM, Leo 1
GREENBAUM, Max 1
GREENBAUM, Samuel 1
GREENBAUM, Sigmund 2
Samuel
GREENBERG, Ben Norton 10
GREENBERG, Bernard 4
Samuel
GREENBERG, Carl 8
GREENBERG, Charles 9
GREENBERG, Frank 8
GREENBERG, Noah 4

GREENBERG, Sam U. 7
GREENBERG, Sarah K. 6
GREENBERRY, Nicholas 4
Barstow
GREENBIE, Marjorie 4
Barstow
GREENBIE, Marjorie 6
Barstow
GREENBLATT, Jacob 6
GREENBLATT, Louis 5
GREENBLATT, Robert 9
Benjamin
GREENBLATT, Samuel 7
GREENDLINGER, Leo 1
GREENE, A. Crawford 1
GREENE, Aella 1
GREENE, Albert Collins H
GREENE, Albert Gorton H
GREENE, Anne Bosworth 6
GREENE, Arthur Dale H
GREENE, Arthur Maurice, 5
Jr.
GREENE, Balcomb 10
GREENE, Benjamin Allen 1
GREENE, Charles Arthur 5
GREENE, Charles Emmett 7
GREENE, Charles Ezra 1
GREENE, Charles Jerome 2
GREENE, Charles Jerome 8
GREENE, Charles Lyman 1
GREENE, Charles Samuel 1
GREENE, Charles Warren 4
GREENE, Charles Wilson 4
GREENE, Chester W. 4
GREENE, Christopher H
GREENE, Clay Meredith 1
GREENE, Condon Lorntz 6
GREENE, D. Crosby 1
GREENE, Daniel Crosby 1
GREENE, David Gorham 10
GREENE, David Maxson 1
GREENE, Edward Belden 3
GREENE, Edward Lee 1
GREENE, Edward Martin 3
GREENE, Edwin Farnham 3
GREENE, Ernest 7
W(oodruff)
GREENE, Esther 7
GREENE, Evarts Boutell 2
GREENE, Flora Hartley 4
GREENE, Floyd L. 3
GREENE, Francis Vinton 1
GREENE, Frank Lester 1
GREENE, Fred T. 4
GREENE, Frederick Stuart 1
GREENE, Gardiner 1
GREENE, George C. 1
GREENE, George Francis 1
GREENE, George Louis 5
GREENE, George Sears H
GREENE, George Sears, Jr. 1
GREENE, George 1
Washington
GREENE, George 1
Wellington
GREENE, George H
Woodward
GREENE, Graham 10
GREENE, Harry Irving 4
GREENE, Harry Sylvestre 5
Nutting
GREENE, Henry Alexander 1
GREENE, Henry Copley 1
GREENE, Henry Fay 1
GREENE, Henry Vincent 1
GREENE, Herbert Eveleth 2
GREENE, Herbert Wilber 1
GREENE, Homer 1
GREENE, Howard 3
GREENE, Sir Hugh 9
Carleton
GREENE, Isabel Catherine 1
GREENE, Jacob L. 1
GREENE, James E(dward) 5
GREENE, James Etheridge 1
GREENE, James H. 4
GREENE, James Leon 5
GREENE, James Nicholas 5
GREENE, James Sonnett 3
GREENE, Jerome Davis 3
GREENE, John 4
GREENE, John Ernest 1
GREENE, John Holden H
GREENE, John James 7
GREENE, John Morton 4
GREENE, John Priest 5
GREENE, Joseph Ingham 3
GREENE, Joseph Nathaniel 5
GREENE, Katherine Glass 2
GREENE, Laurence Francis 9
GREENE, Laurence 6
Whitridge
GREENE, Laurenz 7
GREENE, Lee Seifert 9
GREENE, Lionel Y. 4
GREENE, Lorne 9
GREENE, Marc Tiffany 4
GREENE, M(aria) Louise 5

GREENE, Mary Anne 4
GREENE, Myron Wesley 1
GREENE, Nathanael H
GREENE, Nathaniel H
GREENE, Oliver D. 1
GREENE, Patterson 5
GREENE, Peyton W(illiam) 7
GREENE, Raleigh W. 3
GREENE, Ray H
GREENE, Richard Gleason 1
GREENE, Richard 8
Leighton
GREENE, Richard 3
Thurston
GREENE, Robert Holmes 1
GREENE, Roger Sherman 1
GREENE, Roger Sherman 2
GREENE, S. Harold 1
GREENE, Sam 4
GREENE, Samuel Dana H
GREENE, Samuel Harrison 4
GREENE, Samuel Stillman H
GREENE, Samuel Webb 5
GREENE, Sarah Pratt 1
GREENE, Sherman 9
Lawrence
GREENE, Stephen 7
GREENE, Theodore 3
Ainsworth
GREENE, Thomas L. 1
GREENE, Thomas Marston H
GREENE, Ward 3
GREENE, Warwick 1
GREENE, William* H
GREENE, William Bertram 7
GREENE, William Brenton 4
GREENE, William Chase 8
GREENE, William Cornell 1
GREENE, William Houston 1
GREENE, William L. 1
GREENE, William Milbury 4
GREENE, William Stedman 1
GREENE, Winfield 1
Wardwell
GREENEBAUM, Henry 1
Everett
GREENEBAUM, Leon 5
Charles
GREENEBAUM, Moses 1
Ernest
GREENEBAUM, Samuel 6
Lewis
GREENEFIELD, Nathan 1
R.
GREENER, John Hunter 5
GREENER, Richard 4
Theodore
GREENFIELD, Albert 4
Monroe
GREENFIELD, Alfred M. 8
GREENFIELD, Eric Viele 1
GREENFIELD, Joseph A. 6
GREENFIELD, Kent 4
Roberts
GREENFIELD, Taylor 10
Hatton
GREENHALGE, Frederick H
Thomas
GREENHILL, J.P. 6
GREENHILL, J.P. 7
GREENHILL, Maurice H. 7
GREENHOW, Robert H
GREENING, Harry Cornell 5
GREENLAW, Edwin 1
GREENLAW, Lowell M. 5
GREENLEAF, Benjamin H
GREENLEAF, Carl 3
Dimond
GREENLEAF, Charles 1
Ravenscroft
GREENLEAF, Edmund H
GREENLEAF, Elizabeth 7
Adele
GREENLEAF, Georgie H. 1
Franck
GREENLEAF, James Leal 1
GREENLEAF, Johathan H
GREENLEAF, Moses* H
GREENLEAF, Robert 10
Kiefner
GREENLEAF, Simon H
GREENLEAF, Thomas H
GREENLEE, John Reece 6
GREENLEE, Karl B. 4
GREENLEY, Howard 4
GREENMAN, A.V. 8
GREENMAN, Frances 8
Cranmer
GREENMAN, Frederick 4
Francis
GREENMAN, Jesse More 3
GREENMAN, Judd 7
GREENMAN, Milton J. 1
GREENMAN, Walter 2
Folger
GREENMAN, William 8
Garrett

GREENOUGH, Allen 6
Jackson
GREENOUGH, Allen 7
Jackson
GREENOUGH, Chester 1
Noyes
GREENOUGH, George 1
Gordon
GREENOUGH, Henry H
GREENOUGH, Horatio H
GREENOUGH, James 1
Bradstreet
GREENOUGH, James 1
Carruthers
GREENOUGH, Jeanie 4
Ashley Bates
GREENOUGH, John 1
Lloyd
GREENOUGH, Robert 1
Battey
GREENOUGH, William 2
GREENOUGH, William 10
Croan
GREENQUIST, Kenneth 5
Lloyd
GREENSFELDER, Albert 3
Preston
GREENSHIELDS, Donn 4
D.
GREENSLADE, John Wills 2
GREENSLADE, Rush 7
Molland
GREENSLET, Ferris 3
GREENSON, Ralph 7
Romeo
GREENSON, Ralph 8
Romeo
GREENSPUN, H. M. 10
Hank
GREENSTEIN, Jesse P. 3
GREENSTOE, Julius Hillel 3
GREENSTONE, J(ohn) 10
David
GREENUP, Christopher H
GREENWALD, Emanuel 1
GREENWALD, Herbert S. 3
GREENWALL, Frank 10
Koehler
GREENWALT, Elmer 1
Ellsworth
GREENWAY, Charles 1
Moore
GREENWAY, Isabella 3
Selmes
GREENWAY, James 5
Cowan
GREENWAY, John 1
Campbell
GREENWAY, Walter H
Burton
GREENWELL, Darrell J. 4
GREENWELL, Hiliary 4
Johnson
GREENWOOD, Alfred H
Burton
GREENWOOD, Allen 2
GREENWOOD, Arthur H. 4
GREENWOOD, Elizabeth 4
Ward
GREENWOOD, Ernest 3
GREENWOOD, Ethan H
Allen
GREENWOOD, Frederick 8
GREENWOOD, George 7
Herbert
GREENWOOD, Grace 1
GREENWOOD, Isaac 1
GREENWOOD, James A. 8
GREENWOOD, James M. 4
GREENWOOD, John H
GREENWOOD, John 5
Joseph
GREENWOOD, Marion 5
GREENWOOD, Miles H
GREENWOOD, Thomas 2
Benton
GREER, Benjamin Brinton 1
GREER, David Hummell 1
GREER, Everett 8
GREER, Frank U. 2
GREER, Herbert Chester 2
GREER, Hilton Ross 3
GREER, Isaac Garfield 6
GREER, James Agustin 1
GREER, Lawrence 1
GREER, Margaret R. 3
GREER, Marshall 8
Raymond
GREER, Robert Evans 7
GREER, Samuel Miller 2
GREET, William Cabell 5
GREEVER, Garland 4
GREEVER, Walton 4
Harlowe
GREGERSEN, Magnus 5
Ingstrup
GREGG, Alan 3
GREGG, Alexander H

GREGG, Alexander White 1
GREGG, Alexander White 3
Jr.
GREGG, Andrew H
GREGG, Curtis Hussey 1
GREGG, David 1
GREGG, David McMurtrie 1
GREGG, Donald Crowther 8
GREGG, Earl Lamont 6
GREGG, Florence Clara 1
GREGG, Francis Whitlock 5
GREGG, Frank Moody 4
GREGG, Fred Marion 4
GREGG, Godfrey Robert 6
GREGG, J.A. 3
GREGG, James Bartlett 1
GREGG, James Edgar 2
GREGG, James Madison H
GREGG, John 1
GREGG, John Andrew 3
GREGG, John B. 3
GREGG, John Price 3
GREGG, John Robert 2
GREGG, John William 6
GREGG, Josiah H
GREGG, Maxcy 1
GREGG, Paul L.* 3
GREGG, Robert 1
GREGG, Russell Taaffe 6
GREGG, Russell Taaffe 7
GREGG, William H
GREGG, William C. 2
GREGG, William Henry 4
GREGG, William Lee 7
GREGG, Willis Ray 1
GREGOR, Elmer Russell 3
GREGORY, Carl C. 1
GREGORY, Caspar Rene 1
GREGORY, Charles Noble 1
GREGORY, Chester 1
Arthur
GREGORY, Christopher 8
GREGORY, Clifford V. 2
GREGORY, Daniel Seelye 1
GREGORY, David 8
Albertus
GREGORY, David Thomas 3
GREGORY, Dudley H
Sanford
GREGORY, Edmund 4
Bristol
GREGORY, Edward 7
Wadsworth, Jr.
GREGORY, Eliot 1
GREGORY, Elisha Hall 1
GREGORY, Eufemia 7
Giannini
GREGORY, H. W. 8
GREGORY, Herbert Bailey 1
GREGORY, Herbert E. 3
GREGORY, Hollingsworth 7
Franklin
GREGORY, Horace Victor 8
GREGORY, Jackson 2
GREGORY, John 3
GREGORY, John Goadby 3
GREGORY, John Henry 1
GREGORY, John Herbert 1
GREGORY, John Milton H
GREGORY, L.H. 2
GREGORY, Laurence 2
Wilcoxson
GREGORY, Leslie Roscoe 3
GREGORY, Louis Hoyt 3
GREGORY, Luther 1
Elwood
GREGORY, Martin Leroy 6
GREGORY, Maurice 3
Clinton
GREGORY, Menas Sarkis 1
GREGORY, Noble Jones 5
GREGORY, Oliver Fuller 1
GREGORY, Raymond 3
William
GREGORY, Robert Todd 9
GREGORY, Samuel H
GREGORY, Stephen 1
Strong
GREGORY, Thomas B. 4
GREGORY, Thomas T.C. 1
GREGORY, Thomas Watt 1
GREGORY, Thorne 8
GREGORY, Virginia 1
Whitney
GREGORY, Warren 1
GREGORY, Warren Fenno 1
GREGORY, William 1
GREGORY, William 2
Benjamin
GREGORY, William 3
Edward
GREGORY, William 4
Hamilton, Jr.
GREGORY, William 1
K(ing)
GREGORY, William Logan 3

GREGORY, William 5
Mumford
GREGORY, William Voris 1
GREGORY, Willis George 1
GREHAN, Bernard H. 3
GREIG, Alexander Simpson 4
GREIG, John H
GREINER, John E. 2
GREINER, Tuisco 4
GREIS, Henry Nauert 2
GRELL, Louis 4
GRELLET, Stephen H
GREMSE, Albert Rudolph 7
GRENDON, Felix 7
GRENELL, Zelotes 1
GRENFELL, Elton Watters 7
GRENFELL, Helen Loring 1
GRENFELL, Nicholas 6
Pirie, Jr.
GRENFELL, Sir Wilfred 1
Thomason
GRENIER, Arthur 1
Sylvester
GRENIER, Pierre 8
GRENNELL, George, Jr. H
GRESHAM, James Wilmer 1
GRESHAM, Leroy 3
GRESHAM, Rupert N. 4
GRESHAM, Thomas Dew 6
GRESHAM, Walter Quintin H
GRESS, Ernest Milton 5
GRESSENS, O. 10
GRESSETTE, Lawrence 8
Marion
GRETSCH, Fred, Jr. 7
GREUSEL, John Hubert 1
GREVE, Charles Theodore 1
GREVE, William Marcus 7
GREVILLE, Mr. H
GREVSTAD, Nicolay 1
Andrew
GREW, Henry S. 3
GREW, Joseph Clark 4
GREW, Theophilus H
GREWEN, Robert Francis 7
GREY, Benjamin Edwards 4
GREY, Elmer 4
GREY, Frank Herbert 7
GREY, James David 9
GREY, Samuel Howell 4
GREY, Zane 1
GRIBBEL, John 1
GRIBBIN, George Homer 8
GRIBBIN, Robert Emmet 8
GRIBBLE, Stephen Charles 9
GRIBBLE, William Charles, 7
Jr.
GRICE, David Stephen 4
GRICE, Homer Lamar 7
GRICE, Warren 2
GRIDER, George William 10
GRIDER, Henry 4
GRIDLEY, Charles O. 4
GRIDLEY, Charles Vernon H
GRIDLEY, Jeremiah H
GRIDLEY, Marion Eleanor 6
(Mrs. Robinson Johnson)
GRIDLEY, Richard H
GRIER, Albert Oliver 3
Herman
GRIER, Alvan Ruckman 1
GRIER, Boyce McLaughlin 6
GRIER, Francis Ebenezer 3
GRIER, Harry Dobson 6
Miller
GRIER, James Alexander* 4
GRIER, James Harper 4
GRIER, Maurice Edward 10
GRIER, Norman 3
MacDowell
GRIER, Robert Calvin 8
GRIER, Robert Cooper 1
GRIER, Robert Maxwell 6
GRIER, William 1
GRIER, William Moffatt 4
GRIERSON, Benjamin H. 4
GRIERSON, Benjamin 1
Henry
GRIERSON, Elmer Presley 4
GRIERSON, John 5
GRIES, John Matthew 3
GRIESEDIECK, Alvin 4
GRIEST, Theodore Reed 6
GRIEST, William Walton 1
GRIEVE, Miller H
GRIFFENHAGEN, Edwin 8
O.
GRIFFES, Charles H
Tomlinson
GRIFFES, Charles 4
Tomlinson
GRIFFETH, Ross John 10
GRIFFIN, Angus MacIvor 5
GRIFFIN, Anthony Jerome 1
GRIFFIN, Appleton 1
Prentiss Clark

GRIFFIN, Bulkley 5
Southworth
GRIFFIN, Cardinal 3
Bernard
GRIFFIN, Carroll Wardlaw 3
GRIFFIN, Charles H
GRIFFIN, Charles Carroll 7
GRIFFIN, Clare Elmer 6
GRIFFIN, Cyrus H
GRIFFIN, Daniel J. 1
GRIFFIN, David Burton 7
GRIFFIN, Delia Isabel 4
GRIFFIN, Edward Dorr H
GRIFFIN, Edward Herrick 1
GRIFFIN, Emmet D. 6
GRIFFIN, Eugene 1
GRIFFIN, Eugene Leonard 6
GRIFFIN, Frank H. 7
GRIFFIN, Frank Loxley 5
GRIFFIN, Frederick 5
Robertson
GRIFFIN, Henry Lyman 1
GRIFFIN, Isaac H
GRIFFIN, James Aloysius 2
GRIFFIN, James Arthur 3
GRIFFIN, James H. 3
GRIFFIN, James Owen 4
GRIFFIN, John 1
GRIFFIN, John Howard 3
GRIFFIN, John Howard 7
GRIFFIN, John Joseph 1
GRIFFIN, John King H
GRIFFIN, John W. 4
GRIFFIN, Lawrence 5
Edmonds
GRIFFIN, Lee Henry 5
GRIFFIN, Levi Thomas 1
GRIFFIN, Mark Alexander 5
GRIFFIN, Martin Eugene 4
GRIFFIN, Martin Ignatius 1
GRIFFIN, Martin 9
I(gnatius) J(oseph), Jr.
GRIFFIN, Martin Luther 2
GRIFFIN, Michael 1
GRIFFIN, Nathaniel 1
Edward
GRIFFIN, Norval Burris 8
GRIFFIN, Robert Melville 6
GRIFFIN, Robert Melville 8
GRIFFIN, Robert 1
Stanislaus
GRIFFIN, S. Marvin 8
GRIFFIN, Samuel H
GRIFFIN, Simon Goddell 1
GRIFFIN, Solomon Bulkley 1
GRIFFIN, Thomas 1
GRIFFIN, Walter 1
GRIFFIN, William 2
Aloysius
GRIFFIN, William Richard 2
GRIFFIN, William Thomas 10
GRIFFIN, William Vincent 3
GRIFFING, Josephine H
Sophie White
GRIFFING, Robert 7
Perkins, Jr.
GRIFFIS, Elliot 4
GRIFFIS, Lawrence W. 4
GRIFFIS, Stanton 6
GRIFFIS, William Elliot 1
GRIFFITH, Armond 4
Harrold
GRIFFITH, Benjamin H
GRIFFITH, Benjamin 1
Whitfield
GRIFFITH, C.J. 4
GRIFFITH, Chauncey H. 3
GRIFFITH, Clark 3
GRIFFITH, Coleman 4
Roberts
GRIFFITH, David Lewelyn 2
Wark
GRIFFITH, David Wark H
GRIFFITH, David Wark 4
GRIFFITH, Dudley David 7
GRIFFITH, Earl L. 4
GRIFFITH, Elmer 1
Cummings
GRIFFITH, Francis Marion 4
GRIFFITH, Frank Carlos 1
GRIFFITH, Frank Leslie 1
GRIFFITH, Franklin 3
Thomas
GRIFFITH, F(ranklin) 7
Webb
GRIFFITH, Frederic 5
Richardson
GRIFFITH, George 1
GRIFFITH, George Cupp 6
GRIFFITH, Griffith Jenkins 1
GRIFFITH, Griffith 4
Pritchard
GRIFFITH, Hall McAlister 3
GRIFFITH, Harry Elmer 4
GRIFFITH, Harry Melvin 5
GRIFFITH, Heber Emlyn 5
GRIFFITH, Helen Sherman 4

GRIFFITH, Herbert 1
Eugene
GRIFFITH, Hugh 7
GRIFFITH, Ivor 4
GRIFFITH, J.P. Crozer 1
GRIFFITH, Jefferson Davis 1
GRIFFITH, John 5
GRIFFITH, John Edwin, 9
Jr.
GRIFFITH, John Keller 7
GRIFFITH, John L. 2
GRIFFITH, Louis Eugene 8
GRIFFITH, Lynn B. 7
GRIFFITH, M. Dison 6
GRIFFITH, P. Merrill 1
GRIFFITH, Paul Howard 6
GRIFFITH, Reginald 3
Harvey
GRIFFITH, Richard 5
GRIFFITH, Robert H
Eglesfield
GRIFFITH, Samuel H
GRIFFITH, Samuel 5
Henderson
GRIFFITH, Theodore 8
Barton
GRIFFITH, Thomas Stuart 4
GRIFFITH, Virgil A. 5
GRIFFITH, W.M. 3
GRIFFITH, Wendell 5
Horace
GRIFFITH, William H
GRIFFITH, William 1
GRIFFITH, William G. 4
GRIFFITHS, Arthur Floyd 1
GRIFFITHS, David 1
GRIFFITHS, Edwin 6
Patterson
GRIFFITHS, Edwin 1
Stephen
GRIFFITHS, Farnham 3
Pond
GRIFFITHS, Frederick J. 2
GRIFFITHS, George 7
Findley
GRIFFITHS, James Henry 4
GRIFFITHS, John Lewis 1
GRIFFITHS, John Willis 1
GRIFFITHS, William John, 4
Jr.
GRIFFITTS, Charles 8
Hurlbut
GRIGEBY, Hugh Blair H
GRIGGS, Chauncey Wright 1
GRIGGS, David Cullen 3
GRIGGS, David Tressel 6
GRIGGS, David Tressel 7
GRIGGS, Edward Howard 1
GRIGGS, Everett Gallup 1
GRIGGS, Frederick 2
GRIGGS, Herbert Lebau 2
GRIGGS, James Henry 10
GRIGGS, James M. 1
GRIGGS, John William 1
GRIGGS, Milton Wright 9
GRIGGS, Nathan Kirk 1
GRIGGS, Richard Leslie 1
GRIGGS, Richard Leslie 9
GRIGGS, Thomas Newell 4
GRIGGS, William 4
Cornelius
GRIGSBY, Bertram James 3
GRIGSBY, William Fred 3
GRIM, Allan K. 4
GRIM, David H
GRIM, Paul Ridgeway 3
GRIMBALL, Elizabeth 3
Berkeley
GRIME, Sarah Lois 4
GRIMES, Charles 4
Pennebaker
GRIMES, Donald Robert 5
GRIMES, Fern Edith 4
Munroe (Mrs. William
Schuyler Grimes)
GRIMES, Frances 4
GRIMES, Frank 4
GRIMES, George 4
GRIMES, George Simon 1
GRIMES, J. Bryan 1
GRIMES, J. Frank 6
GRIMES, James Stanley H
GRIMES, James Wilson H
GRIMES, John 1
GRIMES, John Wesley 7
GRIMES, Samuel 7
GRIMES, Waldo Ernest 4
GRIMES, William 7
Alexander
GRIMES, William Henry 5
GRIMES, William 3
Middleton
GRIMKE, Angelina Emily H
GRIMKE, Angelina Weld 4
GRIMKE, Archibald Henry 1
GRIMKE, Francis James 4
GRIMKE, Frederick H

HABOUSH, Edward Joseph 6
HACK, Elizabeth Jane 4
  Miller
HACK, George H
HACK, Gwendolyn 5
  Dunlevy Kelly
HACK, John Tilton 10
HACK, Roy Kenneth 2
HACKEMANN, Louis 4
  Frederick
HACKENBURG, William 4
  Bower
HACKER, Fred A. 3
HACKER, Louis Morton 9
HACKER, Newton 3
HACKER, Victor N. 7
HACKETT, Arthur 5
HACKETT, Bobby 1
HACKETT, Charles 5
HACKETT, Charles 5
  Megginson
HACKETT, Charles Wilson 3
HACKETT, Chauncey 1
HACKETT, E. Byrne 3
HACKETT, Francis 4
HACKETT, Frank D. 3
HACKETT, Frank S. 3
HACKETT, Frank Warren 1
HACKETT, Horatio Balch 1
HACKETT, James 5
  Dominick
HACKETT, James Henry 1
HACKETT, James J. 6
HACKETT, James Keteltas 8
HACKETT, Joan 8
HACKETT, Karleton 1
  Spalding
HACKETT, Lewis Wendell 4
HACKETT, Raymond E. 8
HACKETT, Richard 3
  Nathaniel
HACKETT, Robert Phillip 4
HACKETT, Samuel Everett 5
HACKETT, Thomas C. 6
HACKETT, Thomas Paul 9
HACKETT, Wallace 4
HACKETT, William 1
  Stormont
HACKH, Ingo W.D. 1
HACKL, George F. 6
HACKLER, Victor 6
HACKLEY, Aaron Jr. H
HACKLEY, Charles Elihu 4
HACKLEY, Charles H. 1
HACKMAN, Abe 3
HACKMAN, Pearl E(stella) 6
HACKNEY, Ed T. 3
HACKNEY, Leonard J. 4
HACKNEY, Thomas 2
HACKNEY, Walter S. 1
HACKWORTH, Werter 10
  Shipp
HADAMARD, Jacques 5
  Salomon
HADAS, Moses 4
HADDAD, Eugene 9
HADDEN, Alexander 1
HADDEN, Archibald 1
HADDEN, Charles 3
HADDEN, Crowell 1
HADDEN, John Alexander 10
HADDEN, John Alexander 1
HADDEN, Maude Miner 4
HADDOCK, Charles H
  Brickett
HADDOCK, Frank 1
  Channing
HADDOCK, John 4
  Courtney
HADDON, William, Jr. 8
HADDOW, Alexander 3
HADEN, Annie Bates (Mrs. 5
  Charles J. Haden)
HADEN, Charles Jones 5
HADEN, Russell Landram 3
HADER, Berta Hoerner 6
HADER, Berta Hoerner 7
  (Mrs. Elmer Stanley
  Hader)
HADER, Elmer Stanley 7
HADFIELD, Barnabas 4
  Burrows
HADFIELD, George H
HADING, Hane 4
HADJIMARKOS, 6
  Demetrios Markos
HADLAY, Carleton 2
  Sturtevant
HADLAY, Chalmers 1
HADLEY, Arthur Twining 1
HADLEY, Cassius Clay 1
HADLEY, Charles William 3
HADLEY, Edwin Marshall 3
HADLEY, Egbert Charles 8
HADLEY, Ernest Elvin 1
HADLEY, Everett Addison 1
HADLEY, Hamilton 6

HADLEY, Hamilton 7
HADLEY, Henry Harrison* 1
HADLEY, Henry K. 1
HADLEY, Herbert Spencer 1
HADLEY, Hiram 1
HADLEY, Hiram Elwood 1
HADLEY, James H
HADLEY, John Vestal 1
HADLEY, Lindley Hoag 2
HADLEY, Morris 7
HADLEY, Philip Bardwell 6
HADLEY, Rollin Van 10
  Nostrand
HADLOCK, Wendell 7
  Stanwood
HADSALL, Harry Hugh 1
HADSELL, Irving W. 4
HADZSITS, George Depue 3
HAEBERLE, Arminius T. 1
HAEBERLE, Frederick 6
  Edward
HAEBERLIN, John 9
  Benjamin, Jr.
HAECKER, Theophilus 2
  Levi
HAEHNEL, William Otto, 10
  Jr.
HAENSEL, Fitzhugh 2
  William
HAENSEL, Paul 2
HAERING, George John 4
HAERTLEIN, Albert 4
HAESCHE, William Edwin 1
HAESHMAN, Walter Scott 1
HAESSLER, Carl 4
HAESSLER, F. Herbert 8
HAEUSSLER, Armin 4
HAFEN, Ann Woodbury 1
  (Mrs. Leroy R. Hafen)
HAFEN, LeRoy R. 10
HAFEY, William Joseph 3
HAFF, Delbert James 2
HAFFENREFFER, Rudolf 3
  Frederick
HAFFNER, Charles 7
  Christian, Jr.
HAFNER, Charles Andrew 8
HAFNER, john A. 3
HAFNER, Theodore 10
HAGA, Oliver Owen 2
HAGAN, Clarence 1
  W(estervelt)
HAGAN, Edward James 3
HAGAN, Horace Henry 1
HAGAN, John Campbell, 1
  Jr.
HAGAN, William Arthur 4
HAGAR, Edward McKim 1
HAGAR, George Jotham 1
HAGAR, Gerald Hanna 4
HAGAR, Stansbury 5
HAGEBOECK, Alfons 1
  Ludwig
HAGEDORN, Hermann 4
HAGEL, William 8
HAGEMAN, Harry 1
  Andrew
HAGEMAN, Richard 4
HAGEMANN, Harry H. 5
HAGEMEYER, Jesse 4
  Kalper
HAGEN, Harold C. 3
HAGEN, Hermann August H
HAGEN, Jere 5
HAGEN, John George 1
HAGEN, John P. 10
HAGEN, Oscar Carl 7
HAGEN, Oskar Frank 3
  Leonard
HAGEN, Sam 3
HAGEN, William John 6
HAGENBARTH, Francis 1
  Joseph
HAGER, Albert Davis H
HAGER, Albert Ralph 5
HAGER, Alice Rogers 5
HAGER, Clint Wood 2
HAGER, Dorsey 8
HAGER, Eric Hill 2
HAGER, George Caldwell 1
HAGER, John Sharpenstein H
HAGER, Joseph Arthur 9
HAGER, Lawrence White, 1
  Sr.
HAGER, Luther George 2
HAGERMAN, Edward 1
  Thomson
HAGERMAN, Frank 1
HAGERMAN, Herbert 1
  James
HAGERMAN, James 1
HAGERTY, Christian Dane 1
HAGERTY, Edward Daniel 1
HAGERTY, George James 1
HAGERTY, Harry C. 9
HAGERTY, James C. 8
HAGERTY, James Edward 2

HAGERTY, William Walsh 9
HAGGARD, Alfred Martin 1
HAGGARD, Fred Porter 4
HAGGARD, Sir Godfrey 5
  Digsby Napier
HAGGARD, Howard 3
  Wilcox
HAGGARD, Sewell 1
HAGGARD, William 1
  David
HAGGARD, William Wade 9
HAGGE, Hans Jergen 1
HAGGERSON, Fred H. 3
HAGGERTY, Cornelius J. 5
HAGGERTY, James E. 5
HAGGERTY, John James 6
HAGGERTY, Melvin 5
  Everett
HAGGERTY, Patrick 7
  Eugene
HAGGERTY, William J. 6
HAGGETT, Arthur Sewall 1
HAGGIN, Ben Ali 3
HAGGIN, James B. 1
HAGGIN, Louis Terah 1
HAGGOTT, Warren 4
  Armstrong
HAGIN, Fred Eugene 1
HAGNER, Alexander 1
  Burton
HAGNER, Francis Randall 1
HAGNER, Peter H
HAGOOD, Johnson 1
HAGOOD, Johnson 2
HAGOPIAN, Peter B. 4
HAGSPIEL, Bruno Martin 4
HAGSTROM, G. Arvid 3
HAGUE, Arnold 1
HAGUE, Eliott Baldwin 4
HAGUE, Frank 3
HAGUE, James Duncan 1
HAGUE, Louis Marchand 1
HAGUE, Maurice Stewart 2
HAGUE, Parthenia 4
  Antionette Vardaman
HAGUE, William H
HAGY, Harry B. 3
HAHN, Adolf 1
HAHN, Albert George 5
HAHN, Benjamn Daviese 1
HAHN, Calvin 1
HAHN, Conrad Velder 1
HAHN, Edgar A. 7
HAHN, Frederic Halsted 5
HAHN, Frederick E. 2
HAHN, George Philip 1
HAHN, Herman F. 3
HAHN, J. Jerome 1
HAHN, John H
HAHN, Lew 3
HAHN, Michael Georg H
  Decker
HAHN, Nancy Coonsman 6
HAHN, Otto 5
HAHN, Paul M. 4
HAHN, Willard E. 4
HAHNE, Ernest Herman 3
HAID, Leo 1
HAID, Paul L. 2
HAIDER, Michael 9
  Lawrence
HAIDT, John Valentine H
HAIEN, John 7
HAIG, John T. 4
HAIG, Robert Murray 3
HAIG, Vernon Lester 5
HAIG-BROWN, Roderick 7
  Langmere
HAIGH, Frank Coyal 7
HAIGHT, Albert 1
HAIGHT, Cameron 5
HAIGHT, Charles H
HAIGHT, Charles Coolidge 1
HAIGHT, Charles S. 5
HAIGHT, Edward H
HAIGHT, Elizabeth 4
  Hazelton
HAIGHT, George Ives 3
HAIGHT, Gordon Sherman 3
HAIGHT, H.W. 5
HAIGHT, Henry Huntly 1
HAIGHT, Raymond Leroy 2
HAIGHT, Thomas Griffith 1
HAIGIS, John William 1
HAILE, Colombus 1
HAILE, William H
HAILER, Florin J. 8
HAILES, Patrick Buchan- 6
  Hepburn
HAILE SELLASSIE 6
HAILEY, Orren Luico 1
HAILEY, Thomas Griffin 4
HAILMANN, William 4
  Nicholas
HAILPERIN, Herman 5
HAILS, Raymond Richard 4

HAIN, Edward Wiles 6
HAIN, Jacob L. 5
HAINDS, John Robert 6
HAINER, Bayard Taylor 1
HAINES, Charles Glidden H
HAINES, Charles Grove 2
HAINES, Charles Grove 7
HAINES, Charles Henry 4
HAINES, Charles James 1
HAINES, Daniel H
HAINES, Edmund Thomas 6
HAINES, Elwood Lindsay 2
HAINES, Frank David 3
HAINES, Harry B. 5
HAINES, Harry L. 2
HAINES, Helen 5
HAINES, Helen Elizabeth 5
HAINES, Henry Cargill 1
HAINES, Jennie Day 4
HAINES, John Allen 1
HAINES, John Michener 1
HAINES, John Peter 1
HAINES, Lewis Francis 10
HAINES, Matthias Loring 4
HAINES, Ralph Edward 7
HAINES, Richard 8
HAINES, Richard Carleton 7
HAINES, Robert Terrel 5
HAINES, Samuel Faitoute 9
HAINES, Thomas Harvey 5
HAINES, Walter Stanley 1
HAINES, William T. 1
HAINES, William Wister 10
HAINS, Peter Conover 1
HAINS, Thornton Jenkins 4
HAIRE, Andrew J. 3
HAISH, Jacob H
HAISH, Jacob 4
HAISLIP, Wade Hampton 5
HAISS, Catherine Nugent 6
  (Mrs. John D Haiss)
HAJI ALI H
HAKANSSON, Erik Gosta 3
HAKE, Don Franklin 8
HAKE, Harry 3
HAKLUYT, Richard H
HALAGS, George Stanley, 7
  Jr.
HALAS, George Stanley 8
HALAS, George Stanley, Jr. 8
HALASI-KUN, Tibor 10
HALBERSTADT, Baird 1
HALBERSTRM, Michael 7
  Joseph
HALBERT, Henry Sale 1
HALBERT, Homer 1
  Valmore
HALD, Henry Martin 4
HALDANE, William 6
  George
HALDEMAN, Bruce 2
HALDEMAN, Frederick 4
  Dwight
HALDEMAN, Harry 1
  Marston
HALDEMAN, Isaac 1
  Massey
HALDEMAN, Jack Carroll 9
HALDEMAN, Richard H
  Jacobs
HALDEMAN, Samuel H
  Steman
HALDEMAN, Walter 1
  Newman
HALDEMAN, William 1
  Birch
HALDEMAN, William 7
  S(trubhar)
HALDEMAN-JULIUS, E. 3
HALDEN, Alfred A. 3
HALDEN, Leon Gilbert 3
HALDERMAN, John A. 1
HALDIMAND, Lois 8
  DeForrest
HALE, Albert 1
HALE, Albert Cable 1
HALE, Anne Gardner 1
HALE, Annie Riley 2
HALE, Artemas H
HALE, Beatrice Forbes- 7
  robertson
HALE, Benjamin H
HALE, Chandler 3
HALE, Charles H
HALE, Charles Reuben 1
HALE, Clarence H
HALE, David H
HALE, David C. H
HALE, Earl Melvin 4
HALE, Edward Everett* H
HALE, Edward Joseph 1
HALE, Edward Russell 4
HALE, Edwin Moses H
HALE, Edwin Moses 1
HALE, Ellen Day 2
HALE, Enoch H
HALE, Eugene H

HALE, Fletcher 1
HALE, Florence 3
HALE, Floyd Orlin 1
HALE, Frank Connell 7
HALE, Frank J. 6
HALE, Frank Judson 5
HALE, Franklin Darius 1
HALE, Fred Douglas 4
HALE, Frederick 4
HALE, Gardner 1
HALE, George Ellery 1
HALE, Harris Grafton 4
HALE, Harrison 6
HALE, Harry Clay 2
HALE, Horatio Emmons H
HALE, Hugh Ellmaker 3
HALE, Irving 4
HALE, J. A. 8
HALE, James Tracy H
HALE, John Howard 1
HALE, John Parker H
HALE, John Philetus 4
HALE, Ledyard Park 1
HALE, Lillian Westcott 4
HALE, Lincoln Bell 3
HALE, Louise Closser 1
HALE, Lucretia Peabody 1
HALE, Marice Rutledge 7
  (Mrs. Gardner Hale)
HALE, Mark Pendleton 7
HALE, Marshal 2
HALE, Matthew 1
HALE, Morris Smith 1
HALE, Nancy 9
HALE, Nathan* H
HALE, Nathan Wesley 4
HALE, Newton Johnston 9
HALE, Oron James 10
HALE, Oscar 3
HALE, Philip 1
HALE, Philip Leslie 1
HALE, Philip Thomas 1
HALE, Prentis Cobb 1
HALE, Ralph Tracy 3
HALE, Reuben Brooks 3
HALE, Richard Walden 2
HALE, Richard Walden, Jr. 7
HALE, Robert 7
HALE, Robert Beverly 9
HALE, Robert Lee 5
HALE, Robert Safford H
HALE, Salma H
HALE, Sarah Josepha Buell H
HALE, Susan 1
HALE, Walter 1
HALE, Will T. 4
HALE, William* H
HALE, William Barton 1
HALE, William Bayard 1
HALE, William Benjamin 1
HALE, William Browne 2
HALE, William Gardner 1
HALE, William Green 1
HALE, William Harlan 6
HALE, William Henry 1
HALE, William J. 3
HALE, William Thomas 1
HALE, William Wetherla 8
HALE, Willis H. 4
HALE, Wyatt Walker 2
HALECKI, Oscar 6
HALEY, Alex Palmer 10
HALEY, Andrew Gallagher 4
HALEY, Dennis C. 4
HALEY, Elisha H
HALEY, George Franklin 1
HALEY, Jack 7
HALEY, James Andrew 8
HALEY, James Frederick 5
HALEY, Jesse James 1
HALEY, John Leslie 4
HALEY, Mrs. Lovick Pierce 6
HALEY, Molly Anderson 8
  (Mrs. Frank LeRoy
  Haley)
HALEY, Ora 1
HALEY, William J. 3
HALFHILL, James Wood 1
HALFORD, Albert James 1
HALFORD, Elijah Walker 1
HALFORD, John Henry 5
HALFORD, Ralph Stanley 7
HALIFAX, Earl of 3
HALL, A. Cleveland 1
HALL, A. Neely 1
HALL, Abraham Oakey H
HALL, Alaistair Cameron 5
HALL, Albert Richardson 1
HALL, Alexander Wilford 1
HALL, Allen Garland 1
HALL, Alonzo Cleveland 7
HALL, Alton Parker 1
HALL, Alvin Percy 6
  McDonald
HALL, Alvin William 5
HALL, Ansel Franklin 4
HALL, Arethusa H

HAMILBURG, Ira M. 4
HAMILBURG, Joseph M. 5
HAMILL, Alfred Ernest 3
HAMILL, Charles 1
  Humphrey
HAMILL, Ernest Alfred 1
HAMILL, Howard M. 1
HAMILL, James A. 1
HAMILL, Patrick 1
HAMILL, Robert Lyon 6
HAMILL, Samuel 2
  McClintock
HAMILTON, A.J. 5
HAMILTON, Albert Hine H
HAMILTON, Alexander* H
HAMILTON, Alexander* 4
HAMILTON, Alexander 5
HAMILTON, Alice 1
HAMILTON, Allan 1
  McLane
HAMILTON, Alston 1
HAMILTON, Andrew* H
HAMILTON, Andrew H
  Holman
HAMILTON, Andrew H
  Jackson
HAMILTON, Ann Ruth 7
  Frances
HAMILTON, Anthony 10
  Robert
HAMILTON, Arthur 2
  Stephen
HAMILTON, Aymer Jay 4
HAMILTON, Bertis Frank 3
HAMILTON, Charles 7
  Edgar
HAMILTON, Charles 1
  Elbert
HAMILTON, Charles 7
  Horace
HAMILTON, Charles H
  Memorial
HAMILTON, Charles 3
  Robert
HAMILTON, Charles H
  Smith
HAMILTON, Charles 1
  Sumner
HAMILTON, Charles 8
  Walter
HAMILTON, Charles 5
  Whiteley
HAMILTON, Clarence 1
  Grant
HAMILTON, Clarence 7
  Herbert
HAMILTON, Clarence Otis 8
HAMILTON, Clayton 2
  Meeker
HAMILTON, Cliff 9
  Struthers
HAMILTON, Cornelius H
  Springer
HAMILTON, Daniel 4
  Webster
HAMILTON, David 1
  Gilbert
HAMILTON, David Wiley 6
HAMILTON, Dexter 5
HAMILTON, Donald Ross 5
HAMILTON, Duncan 8
  Alexander
HAMILTON, Earl Jefferson 10
HAMILTON, Edith 2
HAMILTON, Edward John 1
HAMILTON, Edward 8
  Joseph
HAMILTON, Edward La 1
  Rue
HAMILTON, Edward 7
  Parmelee
HAMILTON, Edward 10
  Pierpont
HAMILTON, Edward 2
  Wilbur Dean
HAMILTON, Edwin S. 8
HAMILTON, Elwood 2
HAMILTON, F.F. H
HAMILTON, Fay W. 9
HAMILTON, Finley 1
HAMILTON, Fowler 8
HAMILTON, Francis 4
  Frazee
HAMILTON, Frank H
  Hastings
HAMILTON, Frank 1
  Hastings
HAMILTON, Franklin 1
  Elmer Ellsworth
HAMILTON, Frederic 3
  Rutherford
HAMILTON, Frederick 1
  William
HAMILTON, Gail H
HAMILTON, Garrison W. 4
HAMILTON, George 1
  Anson

HAMILTON, George E. 2
HAMILTON, George E., 10
  Jr.
HAMILTON, George Hall 1
HAMILTON, George 2
  Henry
HAMILTON, George 1
  Livingstone
HAMILTON, Gilbert Van 2
  Tassel
HAMILTON, Grant E. 4
HAMILTON, Hamilton 1
HAMILTON, Harold Lee 5
HAMILTON, Harry Heber 6
HAMILTON, Henry H
HAMILTON, H(enry) 10
  G(lenn)
HAMILTON, Hollister 1
  Adelbert
HAMILTON, Holman 7
HAMILTON, Hugh 4
  Ralston
HAMILTON, Isaac Miller 3
HAMILTON, J. Kent 1
HAMILTON, J. Taylor 3
HAMILTON, James* H
HAMILTON, James, Jr. H
HAMILTON, James 5
  Alexander
HAMILTON, James E. 3
HAMILTON, James 1
  Edward
HAMILTON, James Henry 4
HAMILTON, James 4
  Lemmon, Jr.
HAMILTON, James 1
  McLellan
HAMILTON, James 5
  Wallace
HAMILTON, Jamin 4
  Hannibal
HAMILTON, Jay Benson 1
HAMILTON, John* H
HAMILTON, John 1
HAMILTON, John Alan 1
HAMILTON, John C. 5
HAMILTON, John Carroll 3
HAMILTON, John Daniel 6
  Miller
HAMILTON, John L. 1
HAMILTON, John Leonard 3
HAMILTON, John 1
  Marshall
HAMILTON, John McLure 1
HAMILTON, John 5
  Sherman
HAMILTON, John Taylor 1
HAMILTON, John William 1
HAMILTON, J(oseph) 6
  G(régoire) de Roulbac
HAMILTON, Kate 5
  Waterman
HAMILTON, Kenneth 6
  Gardiner
HAMILTON, Leicester 10
  Forsyth
HAMILTON, Louis 6
  Franklin
HAMILTON, Maxwell M. 3
HAMILTON, Morgan H
  Calvin
HAMILTON, Norman 4
  Rond
HAMILTON, Paul H
HAMILTON, Peter H
HAMILTON, Peter Joseph 1
HAMILTON, Peter Myers H
  Adam
HAMILTON, Pierpont 10
  Morgan
HAMILTON, Ralph Scott 1
HAMILTON, Raphael 9
  Noteware
HAMILTON, Robert H
HAMILTON, Robert 5
  Patrick
HAMILTON, Roger 7
  Stanton
HAMILTON, Rolland 4
  Jerome
HAMILTON, Roy William 1
HAMILTON, Samuel King 1
HAMILTON, Samuel L. 3
HAMILTON, Schuyler 1
HAMILTON, Stanislaus 1
  Murray
HAMILTON, Thomas 1
  Benton
HAMILTON, Thomas Hale 7
HAMILTON, Thomas 1
  Jefferson
HAMILTON, Thomas 9
  Jefferson
HAMILTON, Thompson A. 5
HAMILTON, Walter 6
  Raleigh

HAMILTON, Walton Hale 3
HAMILTON, Wesley D. 7
HAMILTON, Willard I. 3
HAMILTON, William 4
HAMILTON, William 4
  Benjamin
HAMILTON, William F. 3
HAMILTON, William 5
  Henry
HAMILTON, William Peter 1
HAMILTON, William 3
  Pierson
HAMILTON, William 1
  Reeve
HAMILTON, William H
  Thomas*
HAMILTON, William 4
  Thomas
HAMILTON, William 4
  Wistar
HAMILTON, Wilson H. 3
HAMLEN, James C. 1
HAMLEN, Joseph 3
  Rochemont
HAMLET, Harry Gabriel 3
HAMLETT, Barksdale 1
HAMLETT, Barksdale 7
HAMLEY, Frederick 6
  George
HAMLIN, Alfred Dwight 1
HAMLIN, Augustus Choate 1
HAMLIN, Charles 1
HAMLIN, Charles Sumner 1
HAMLIN, Chauncey J. 4
HAMLIN, Clarence Clark 4
HAMLIN, Conde 4
HAMLIN, Conde 6
HAMLIN, Courtney Walker 1
HAMLIN, Cyrus 1
HAMLIN, Edward 6
HAMLIN, Edward Stowe H
HAMLIN, Elbert Bacon 1
HAMLIN, Emmons H
HAMLIN, Frank 7
  Thompson
HAMLIN, Fred 3
HAMLIN, George John 1
HAMLIN, Hannibal H
HAMLIN, Hannibal Emery 1
HAMLIN, Huybertie 6
  Lansing Pruyn (Mrs.
  Charles S. Hamlin)
HAMLIN, John 3
HAMLIN, John N(ellis) 5
HAMLIN, Oliver Deveta, 9
  Jr.
HAMLIN, Simon Moulton 1
HAMLIN, Talbot Faulkner 3
HAMLIN, Teunis 1
  Slingerland
HAMLIN, Walter Bergen 8
HAMLIN, William H
HAMLINE, John Henry 1
HAMLINE, Leonidas Lent H
HAMM, Beth Creevey 3
HAMM, Edward Frederick, 9
  Jr.
HAMM, Margherita Arlina 1
HAMM, William 1
HAMM, William, Jr. 5
HAMMAKER, Wilbur 5
  Emery
HAMMAN, Louis 2
HAMMARSKJOLD, Dag 4
  Hjalmar Agne Carl
HAMMEL, Wilbert C. 4
HAMMEL, William Charles 3
  Adam
HAMMELL, Alfred 4
  Lawson
HAMMELL, George M. 1
HAMMER, Armand 10
HAMMER, Edwin Wesley 3
HAMMER, John 1
  Shackelford
HAMMER, Kenneth S. 5
HAMMER, Sanford S. 10
HAMMER, Thorvald 10
  Frederick
HAMMER, Trygve 2
HAMMER, William C. 1
HAMMER, William Joseph 1
HAMMERLING, Louis 1
  Nicholas
HAMMERSTEIN, Oscar 1
HAMMERSTEIN, Oscar, 4
  2d
HAMMETT, Edward 5
HAMMETT, Frederick 7
  Simonds
HAMMETT, Henry 3
  Pinckney
HAMMETT, Louis Plack 9
HAMMETT, Samuel H
  Adams

HAMMETT, Samuel 4
  Dashiell
HAMMETT, William H. H
HAMMILL, Fred H. 1
HAMMILL, John H
HAMMITT, Frederick 10
  Gnichtel
HAMMITT, Jackson Lewis 1
HAMMITT, Joseph Otis 7
HAMMON, Jupiter H
HAMMON, William 10
  McDowell
HAMMOND, Alonzo John 2
HAMMOND, Andrew B. 1
HAMMOND, Bray 5
HAMMOND, Charles H
HAMMOND, Charles 5
  Herrick
HAMMOND, Charles 7
  Herrick
HAMMOND, Charles 3
  Parker
HAMMOND, Creed 1
  Cheshire
HAMMOND, Datus Miller 1
HAMMOND, Dean B(urt) 6
HAMMOND, Edward H
HAMMOND, Edward 9
  Cuyler
HAMMOND, Edward 1
  Payson
HAMMOND, Edward 5
  Sanford
HAMMOND, Edwin H
HAMMOND, Edwin 1
  Pollock
HAMMOND, Eleanor 1
  Prescott
HAMMOND, Eli Shelby 1
HAMMOND, Frank Clinch 5
HAMMOND, George 4
  Francis
HAMMOND, George 1
  Henry
HAMMOND, George 1
  Young
HAMMOND, Godfrey 1
HAMMOND, Graeme 2
  Monroe
HAMMOND, Harold 1
HAMMOND, Harold Earl 9
HAMMOND, Harry Parker 3
HAMMOND, Jabez Dean 1
HAMMOND, Jabez Delano 1
HAMMOND, Jack 5
HAMMOND, James, Jr. 3
HAMMOND, James H
  Bartlett
HAMMOND, James 4
  Bartlett
HAMMOND, James Henry H
HAMMOND, James Wright 9
HAMMOND, Jason E. 1
HAMMOND, John H
HAMMOND, John 9
HAMMOND, John Dennis 1
HAMMOND, John Hays 1
HAMMOND, John Hays, 1
  Jr.
HAMMOND, John Henry 2
HAMMOND, John Wikes 1
HAMMOND, John, 1
  Winthrop
HAMMOND, Laurens 6
HAMMOND, Lily Hardy 1
HAMMOND, Lyman Pierce 3
HAMMOND, Matthew 1
  Brown
HAMMOND, Monroe 1
  Percy
HAMMOND, Nathaniel H
  Job
HAMMOND, Norma Mae 1
HAMMOND, Ogden 3
  Haggerty
HAMMOND, Paul Lyman 7
HAMMOND, Percy 1
  Hanna
HAMMOND, Robert H
HAMMOND, Roland 4
HAMMOND, Samuel 1
HAMMOND, Stevens Hill 1
HAMMOND, Theodore 1
  Augustus
HAMMOND, Thomas Guy 7
HAMMOND, Thomas 3
  Stevens
HAMMOND, Walter Willis 8
HAMMOND, William 6
HAMMOND, William 1
  Alexander
HAMMOND, William 4
  Alexander
HAMMOND, William 2
  Churchill
HAMMOND, William H
  Gardiner

HAMMOND, William Phin 8
HAMMOND, William 10
  Rogers
HAMMOND, Winfield 1
  Scott
HAMMONS, David H
HAMMONS, Earle 4
  Wooldridge
HAMMONS, Earle 1
  Woolridge
HAMMONS, Joseph H
HAMMONS, Paul Edward 6
HAMMONS, Walter Scott 7
HAMP, Sidford Frederick 1
HAMPDEN, Walter 3
HAMPSON, Alfred Aubert 2
HAMPSON, Philip F. 6
HAMPTON, Ambrose 7
  Gonzales
HAMPTON, Aubrey Otis 3
HAMPTON, Benjamin 1
  Bowles
HAMPTON, Edgar Lloyd 1
HAMPTON, George 4
HAMPTON, Harry Horton 8
HAMPTON, Ireland 2
HAMPTON, James Giles H
HAMPTON, John Peyton 7
HAMPTON, Moses H
HAMPTON, Wade H
HAMPTON, Wade 1
HAMPTON, Wiley Bishop 8
HAMRICK, Kenneth 10
  Edison
HAMRIN, SHirley Austin 3
HAMSUN, Knut 3
HAMSUN, Knut 4
HAMTRAMCK, John 1
  Francis
HAMUDA PASHA H
HAN, Yu-Shan 9
HANAN, John H. 1
HANAU, Kenneth John 3
HANAUER, Jerome J. 1
HANAW, Henry 1
HANBACK, Lewis H
HANBURY, Una 10
HANBY, Albert Thatcher 6
HANBY, Benjamin Russell H
HANCEY, Carlos 4
HANCH, Charles Connard 2
HANCHER, John William 4
HANCHER, Virgil Melvin 4
HANCHETT, Benton 1
HANCHETT, Edwin Lani 6
HANCHETT, George 5
  Tilden
HANCHETT, Henry 1
  Granger
HANCHETT, Lafayette 3
HANCHETT, Luther H
HANCOCK, Albert Elmer 1
HANCOCK, Arthur Boyd 5
HANCOCK, Clarence 2
  Eugene
HANCOCK, Elizabeth 1
  Hazlewood
HANCOCK, G. Allan 4
HANCOCK, George H
HANCOCK, Glover Dunn 1
HANCOCK, H. Irving 1
HANCOCK, Harris 4
HANCOCK, Harry D(avid) 8
HANCOCK, James Cole 1
HANCOCK, James Ralph 9
HANCOCK, John 10
HANCOCK, John* H
HANCOCK, John M. 3
HANCOCK, La Toucha 1
HANCOCK, Ralph Lowell 9
HANCOCK, Stewart 7
  Freeman
HANCOCK, Theodore E. 1
HANCOCK, Thomas 2
  Hightower
HANCOCK, W(alter) Scott 5
HANCOCK, William 4
  Wayne
HANCOCK, Winfield Scott H
HAND, Alfred 1
HAND, Augustus H
  Cincinnatus
HAND, Augustus Noble 3
HAND, Charles Connor 9
HAND, Chauncey Harris 1
HAND, Clifford Jay 8
HAND, Daniel H
HAND, Edward H
HAND, George Trowbridge 1
HAND, Harold Curtis 5
HAND, John Pryor 1
HAND, Learned 4
HAND, Richard Lockhart 1
HAND, Thomas Millet 3
HAND, Wayland Debs 9
HAND, William Flowers 2

HARDWICK, Katharine Davis 6
HARDWICK, Thomas William 2
HARDWICKE, Sir Cedric Webster 4
HARDY, Alexander George 6
HARDY, Allster Clavering 8
HARDY, Arthur C. 7
HARDY, Arthur Sherburne 1
HARDY, Ashley Kingsley 1
HARDY, Caldwell 1
HARDY, Charles J. 3
HARDY, Charles J. 1
HARDY, Charles Oscar 2
HARDY, David Keith 6
HARDY, David Phillip 3
HARDY, David Ross 5
HARDY, Edward Lawyer 5
HARDY, Edward Rochie 9
HARDY, Edwin Noah 3
HARDY, Ewing Lloyd 5
HARDY, George 10
HARDY, George Erastus 4
HARDY, George Fiske 3
HARDY, Guy U. 2
HARDY, H(arrison) Claude 6
HARDY, Irene 4
HARDY, James Daniel 9
HARDY, James Graham 3
HARDY, John Crumpton 1
HARDY, John Forster 9
HARDY, John Henry 1
HARDY, Joseph Johnston 1
HARDY, Josiah H
HARDY, Kenneth Burnham 5
HARDY, Lamar 3
HARDY, Le Grand Haven 4
HARDY, Marjorie 2
HARDY, Martha Eugenia Sidebottom (Mrs. Donald Hardy) 5
HARDY, Mary Earle 1
HARDY, Oscar J. 3
HARDY, Osgood 8
HARDY, Ralph W. 3
HARDY, Robert Marion 4
HARDY, Rufus 4
HARDY, Samuel H
HARDY, Summers 3
HARDY, Thomas Walter 4
HARDY, Warren Follansbee 1
HARDY, William Edwin 1
HARE, Arley Munson (Mrs. James A.) 5
HARE, Clifford Leroy 2
HARE, Darius Dodge H
HARE, Emlen Spencer 4
HARE, Francis Hutcheson 9
HARE, George Andrew 1
HARE, George Emien H
HARE, Hobart Amory 1
HARE, Hugh F. 4
HARE, James H. 2
HARE, James Madison 4
HARE, John Innes Clark 4
HARE, Marmaduke 3
HARE, Robert H
HARE, S. Herbert 4
HARE, T(homas) Truxtun 4
HARE, William Hobart 1
HARER, William Benson 5
HARGADON, I. Leo 3
HARGER, Charles Moreau 3
HARGER, Rolla Neil 8
HARGEST, William Milton 2
HARGETT, Ira Mason 6
HARGIS, Andrew Broadus 8
HARGIS, Thomas Frazier 1
HARGITT, Charles Wesley 1
HARGITT, George Thomas 6
HARGRAVE, Frank Flavius
HARGRAVE, Helen Pearson 10
HARGRAVE, Homer 4
HARGRAVE, Thomas Jean 4
HARGRAVE, William Loftin 6
HARGRAVE, William Walter 8
HARGREAVES, John Morris 3
HARGREAVES, Richard T(heodore) 5
HARGROVE, Reginald Henry 3
HARGROVE, Robert Kennon 1
HARINELL, Timothy V. 8
HARING, Alexander 3
HARING, Clarence Henry 4
HARING, Clarence Melvin 1
HARING, Douglas Gilbert 5
HARING, John H

HARING, Nikolaus Martin 9
HARING, Philip Erwin 5
HARISON, Beverly Drake 1
HARK, J. Max 1
HARKAVY, Minna 9
HARKER, Catherine 1
HARKER, Joseph Ralph 1
HARKER, Oliver Albert 1
HARKER, Ray Clarkson 5
HARKEY, Simeon Walcher H
HARKINS, Edward Francis 5
HARKINS, George Frederick 10
HARKINS, Henry Nelson 4
HARKINS, Matthew 1
HARKINS, Thomas J. 6
HARKINS, William Draper 3
HARKNESS, Albert 1
HARKNESS, Albert 7
HARKNESS, Albert Granger 1
HARKNESS, Charles William 1
HARKNESS, Earl 10
HARKNESS, Edward Stephen 1
HARKNESS, Georgia Elma 6
HARKNESS, Gordon Follette 1
HARKNESS, Harvey W. 1
HARKNESS, Hope Knight Hodgman (Mrs. Albert Harkness) 9
HARKNESS, James Stewart 4
HARKNESS, Rebekah West 8
HARKNESS, Richard Long 7
HARKNESS, Robert 9
HARKNESS, William 1
HARKNESS, William Hale 3
HARKRADER, Charles Johnston 7
HARL, Maple Talbot 3
HARLAN, Aaron H
HARLAN, Byron Berry 2
HARLAN, Campbell Allen 1
HARLAN, Edgar Rubey 1
HARLAN, George Cuvier 1
HARLAN, Henry David 2
HARLAN, James* 1
HARLAN, James 1
HARLAN, James Elliott 1
HARLAN, James S. 1
HARLAN, John Graydon, Jr. 10
HARLAN, John Marshall 1
HARLAN, John Marshall 5
HARLAN, John Maynard 1
HARLAN, Josiah 1
HARLAN, Mabel Margaret 9
HARLAN, Otis 1
HARLAN, Richard H
HARLAN, Richard Davenport 1
HARLAN, Rolvix 4
HARLAN, W. Glen 10
HARLAND, Edward 1
HARLAND, Henry 1
HARLAND, James Penrose 5
HARLAND, Lewis E. 6
HARLAND, Thomas 4
HARLEY, Alvin E. 7
HARLEY, Charles Richard 1
HARLEY, Lewis Reifsneider 1
HARLING, W. Franke 3
HARLLEE, William Curry 5
HARLOR, John Clayton 10
HARLOW, Agnes Virginia 8
HARLOW, Alvin Fay 4
HARLOW, Bryce Nathaniel 9
HARLOW, Harry F. 8
HARLOW, James Gindling, Sr. 7
HARLOW, Jean H
HARLOW, Jean 4
HARLOW, John Brayton 4
HARLOW, Louis Kinney 4
HARLOW, Ralph Volney 3
HARLOW, Rex Francis 9
HARLOW, Richard Cresson 4
HARLOW, S. Ralph 7
HARLOW, S. Ralph 5
HARLOW, Victor Emmanuel 3
HARLOW, Virginia 8
HARLOW, William Burt 4
HARLOW, William Elam 3
HARLOW, William Page 1
HARMAN, Arthur Fort 2
HARMAN, Avraham 10
HARMAN, Harvey John 5
HARMAN, Henry Elliott 1
HARMAN, Jacob Anthony 5

HARMAN, James Lewie 5
HARMAN, John 7
HARMAN, Pinckney Jones 1
HARMAN, Pinckney Jones 4
HARMANSON, John Henry H
HARMAR, Josiah H
HARMATI, Sandor 1
HARMELING, Henry 4
HARMELING, Stephen John 3
HARMER, Alfred C. 1
HARMON, Andrew Davidson 3
HARMON, Arthur Loomis 3
HARMON, Austin Morris 3
HARMON, Benjamin Smith 1
HARMON, Cameron 3
HARMON, Claude Moore 3
HARMON, Daniel L(ewis) 10
HARMON, Daniel Williams H
HARMON, Darrell Victor 6
HARMON, Ernest N. 7
HARMON, Francis Stuart 3
HARMON, Frank Wilson 4
HARMON, Harold Elliott 4
HARMON, Henry Gadd 4
HARMON, Hubert Reilly 3
HARMON, John Francis 3
HARMON, John Millard 6
HARMON, Judson 1
HARMON, Leo Clinton 5
HARMON, Miliard Fillmore 2
HARMON, Nolan Bailey 9
HARMON, Paul M. 4
HARMON, William Elmer 1
HARMONY, David Buttz 1
HARMS, Herm 8
HARMS, John Henry 2
HARMSWORTH, Harry Clayton 7
HARN, Orlando Clinton 3
HARNDEN, William Frederick H
HARNED, Herbert 8
HARNED, Malcolm Stuart 7
HARNED, Perry L. 4
HARNED, Robert Ellsworth 5
HARNED, Robey Wentworth 7
HARNED, Thomas Biggs 4
HARNED, Virginia 2
HARNER, Nevin Cowger 3
HARNESS, Edward Granville 8
HARNETT, Cornelius H
HARNEY, George Edward 1
HARNEY, John Milton 1
HARNEY, William Selby H
HARNISH, Jay Dewey 10
HARNISH, William Max 7
HARNLY, Andrew Hoerner 4
HARNO, Albert James 1
HARNSBERGER, Harry Scott 8
HARNWELL, Gaylord P. 8
HAROLD, Raymond Paget 5
HARPER, Alexander H
HARPER, Carrie Anna 1
HARPER, Claude 9
HARPER, Cornelius Allen 3
HARPER, Donald 3
HARPER, Earl Enyeart 4
HARPER, Edward Thomson 1
HARPER, Fletcher H
HARPER, Floyd Arthur H
HARPER, Fowler Vincent 4
HARPER, Francis Jacob H
HARPER, George Andrew 1
HARPER, George McLean 2
HARPER, George Washington Finley 3
HARPER, H. Mitchell 4
HARPER, Harold 5
HARPER, Harry F. 2
HARPER, Harvey W. 3
HARPER, Heber (Reece) 7
HARPER, Henry Winston 2
HARPER, Herbert E. 6
HARPER, Horace William 9
HARPER, Howard Vincent 3
HARPER, Ida Husted 1
HARPER, Jacob Chandler 1
HARPER, James* H
HARPER, James Clarence H
HARPER, James Patterson, Jr. 1
HARPER, James R. 5
HARPER, James Wright 8
HARPER, Jene 10
HARPER, John 8
HARPER, John Adams H

HARPER, John Dickson 8
HARPER, John Erasmus 1
HARPER, John Lyell 1
HARPER, Joseph Morrill H
HARPER, Marion, Jr. 10
HARPER, Mary McKibbin 5
HARPER, Merritt Wesley 3
HARPER, Paul Tompkins 1
HARPER, Paul Vincent 2
HARPER, Robert Almer 1
HARPER, Robert Francis 1
HARPER, Robert Goodloe H
HARPER, Robert Henry 7
HARPER, Robert N. 1
HARPER, Robert S. 4
HARPER, Roland M. 4
HARPER, Samuel Northrup 2
HARPER, Samuel Williams 3
HARPER, Sinclair Ollason 7
HARPER, Theodore Acland 2
HARPER, Thomas 10
HARPER, Thomas Henry 4
HARPER, Wilhelmina 6
HARPER, William H
HARPER, William Allen 2
HARPER, William Rainey 1
HARPER, William St John 1
HARPER, William Taylor 10
HARPER, William Wade 1
HARPHAM, Gertrude Tressel Rider 5
HARPSTER, Charles Melvin 1
HARPSTER, John Henry 1
HARPUR, Robert H
HARR, Luther 3
HARR, William R. 3
HARRAH, Charles Jefferson H
HARRAH, Charles Jefferson 4
HARRAH, William 3
HARRAH, William Fisk 7
HARRAL, Jared Alphonso 4
HARRAL, Stewart 4
HARRAR, Ellwood Scott 6
HARRAR, J. George 8
HARRE, T. Everett 2
HARRELD, John William 5
HARRELL, Alfred 2
HARRELL, Charles Adair 10
HARRELL, Eugene Flowers 8
HARRELL, Joel Ellis 5
HARRELL, John 1
HARRELL, Linwood Parker 5
HARRELL, Luther Alonzo 8
HARRELL, Mack 4
HARRELSON, John William 3
HARRELSON, William Louis 7
HARRER, Gustave Adolphus 2
HARRIES, George Herbert 1
HARRIGAN, Edward 1
HARRIGAN, Nolan 4
HARRILL, Paul Eugene 8
HARRIMAN, Alice 1
HARRIMAN, ALonzo Jesse 5
HARRIMAN, Charles Conant 2
HARRIMAN, E. Roland 7
HARRIMAN, Edward Avery 5
HARRIMAN, Edward Henry 1
HARRIMAN, Florence Jaffray 4
HARRIMAN, Frank Black 1
HARRIMAN, Frederick William 1
HARRIMAN, Henry Ingraham 3
HARRIMAN, Job 1
HARRIMAN, John Walter 5
HARRIMAN, Joseph Wright 2
HARRIMAN, Karl Edwin 1
HARRIMAN, Lewis Gildersleeve 5
HARRIMAN, Mary W. 1
HARRIMAN, Oliver 1
HARRIMAN, Raymond Davis 5
HARRIMAN, Walter H
HARRIMAN, William Averell 9
HARRINGTON, Arthur William 4

HARRINGTON, Bob (Robert William Harrington) 10
HARRINGTON, Charles 1
HARRINGTON, Charles A. 5
HARRINGTON, Charles Kendall 1
HARRINGTON, Charles Medbury 1
HARRINGTON, Daniel 6
HARRINGTON, David L. 4
HARRINGTON, Emerson Columbus 4
HARRINGTON, Francis Bishop 1
HARRINGTON, Francis Clark 1
HARRINGTON, Frank Annibal 3
HARRINGTON, George Bates 4
HARRINGTON, Harry Franklin 1
HARRINGTON, Henry Hill 4
HARRINGTON, Henry William H
HARRINGTON, Howard DeWitt 6
HARRINGTON, John Lyle 2
HARRINGTON, John T. 1
HARRINGTON, John Thomas 2
HARRINGTON, John Walker 3
HARRINGTON, Joseph 5
HARRINGTON, Karl Pomeroy 4
HARRINGTON, Leon W. 1
HARRINGTON, Louis Clare 3
HARRINGTON, Marion Thomas 10
HARRINGTON, Mark Raymond 5
HARRINGTON, Mark Walrid 4
HARRINGTON, Mark Walrod H
HARRINGTON, Michael 10
HARRINGTON, Mildred P(riscilla) 7
HARRINGTON, Philip 2
HARRINGTON, Purnell Frederick 1
HARRINGTON, Robert Stuckey 8
HARRINGTON, Russell Chase 5
HARRINGTON, Samuel Maxwell H
HARRINGTON, Samuel Milby 2
HARRINGTON, Stuart William 5
HARRINGTON, Thomas F. 3
HARRINGTON, Thomas Francis 1
HARRINGTON, Vincent Francis 2
HARRINGTON, William Watson 5
HARRINGTON, Willis F. 4
HARRIOTT, Frank 4
HARRIS, Abram Lincoln 4
HARRIS, Abram Winegardner 1
HARRIS, Addison C. 1
HARRIS, Agnes Ellen 3
HARRIS, Albert Hall 4
HARRIS, Albert Mason 4
HARRIS, Albert Wadsworth 5
HARRIS, Alexander 5
HARRIS, Alexandrina Robertson 7
HARRIS, Alfred F. 2
HARRIS, Alfred S. 2
HARRIS, Amanda Bartlett 1
HARRIS, Andrew Lintner 1
HARRIS, Arthur Emerson 4
HARRIS, Arthur I. 4
HARRIS, Arthur M. 1
HARRIS, Arthur Ringland 8
HARRIS, Arvil Ernest 4
HARRIS, Basil 2
HARRIS, Benjamin H
HARRIS, Benjamin Bee 1
HARRIS, Benjamin Franklin 1
HARRIS, Benjamin Gwinn H
HARRIS, Beverly Dabney 2
HARRIS, Bravid Washington 4
HARRIS, C. Addison, Jr. 7

HART, William Lee 3
HART, William Leroy 9
HART, William Lincoln 5
HART, William Michael 4
HART, William Octave 1
HART, William Richard 4
HART, William S. 2
HARTE, Bret 1
HARTE, Emmett Forrest 5
HARTE, Houston 5
HARTE, Richard 5
HARTE, Richard Hickman 1
HARTE, Robert Adolph 7
HARTE, Thomas John 4
HARTECK, Paul 8
HARTENSTEIN, Robert Franklin 4
HARTER, Donald Robert 7
HARTER, Dow W(atters) 5
HARTER, Dow W(atters) 7
HARTER, George Abram 2
HARTER, Isaac 3
HARTER, J. Francis 2
HARTER, Michael Daniel H
HARTER, Robert Lawrence 10
HARTFIELD, David, Jr. 9
HARTFIELD, John McCallum 4
HARTFIELD, Joseph Manuel 4
HARTFORD, Ellis Ford 7
HARTFORD, Fernando Wood 1
HARTFORD, George Huntington H
HARTFORD, George Huntington 4
HARTFORD, George L. 3
HARTFORD, John A. 3
HARTHORN, Drew Thompson 5
HARTIG, Henry Edward 9
HARTIG, Robert Lee 7
HARTIGAN, Charles Conway 2
HARTIGAN, John Patrick 8
HARTIGAN, Joseph John 7
HARTIGAN, Raymond Harvey 5
HARTINGER, William Calvert 5
HARTKE, Gilbert Vincent 9
HARTLEY, Charles Pinckney 5
HARTLEY, Ellis Taylor 1
HARTLEY, Eugene Fuller 4
HARTLEY, Frank 1
HARTLEY, Fred Allan, Jr. 5
HARTLEY, Fred Lloyd 10
HARTLEY, Harold H. 4
HARTLEY, Henry Alexander Saturnin 4
HARTLEY, Isaac Smithson 1
HARTLEY, James Joseph 2
HARTLEY, Jonathan Scott 1
HARTLEY, Leslie Poles 5
HARTLEY, Lowrie C. 5
HARTLEY, Robert Willard 5
HARTLEY, Roland H. 3
HARTLEY, Thomas H
HARTLINE, Haldan Keffer 8
HARTLINE, Haldan Keffer 9
HARTMAN, Carl G. 4
HARTMAN, Carl Henry 8
HARTMAN, Charles Dudley 7
HARTMAN, Charles S. 1
HARTMAN, Charles William 5
HARTMAN, Douglas William 4
HARTMAN, Dwight Dryden 9
HARTMAN, Edwin Mitman 2
HARTMAN, Elizabeth 9
HARTMAN, Ernest Herman 5
HARTMAN, Frank Alexander 5
HARTMAN, George Edward 10
HARTMAN, Gertrude 3
HARTMAN, Glen Walter 10
HARTMAN, Harold Hoover 4
HARTMAN, Harvey Clarence 4
HARTMAN, Henry 4
HARTMAN, Howard Russell 3
HARTMAN, Irvin H. 8
HARTMAN, Jesse L. 4
HARTMAN, John A. 5
HARTMAN, John Adams, Jr. 8
HARTMAN, John Clark 1
HARTMAN, John Daniel 6
HARTMAN, John Jacob 8
HARTMAN, John Maurice 8
HARTMAN, John Peter 2
HARTMAN, Lee Foster 1
HARTMAN, Leon Wilson 2
HARTMAN, Lewis Oliver 3
HARTMAN, Louis Francis 5
HARTMAN, Louis H. 4
HARTMAN, Paul William 6
HARTMAN, Ralph Maxwell 9
HARTMAN, Robert S. 6
HARTMAN, Sara 5
HARTMAN, Siegfried Frisch 3
HARTMANN, Alexis Frank 4
HARTMANN, Arthur (Martinus) 7
HARTMANN, Carl Sadakichi 5
HARTMANN, F. Norman 6
HARTMANN, F.M. 1
HARTMANN, George W. 3
HARTMANN, Jacob Wittmer 2
HARTMANN, Reina Kate Goldstein 6
HARTMANN, William V. 5
HARTNESS, James 1
HARTNETT, Robert Clinton 9
HARTNETT, Timothy V. 6
HARTNEY, Harold Evans 2
HARTRANFT, Chester David 1
HARTRANFT, John Frederick H
HARTRATH, Lucie 4
HARTREE, Douglas Rayner 3
HARTRIDGE, Clifford Wayne 4
HARTRIDGE, Emelyn Battersby 2
HARTRIDGE, John Earle 1
HARTRIDGE, Julian H
HARTS, William Wright 4
HARTSFIELD, William Berry 5
HARTSFIELD, William Berry 8
HARTSHORN, Edwin Simpson 6
HARTSHORN, William Henry 1
HARTSHORN, William Newton 1
HARTSHORNE, Charles 1
HARTSHORNE, Charles Hopkins 1
HARTSHORNE, Henry H
HARTSHORNE, Hugh 4
HARTSHORNE, Marion Holmes 9
HARTSHORNE, Richard 9
HARTSING, Ralph H., Sr. 10
HARTSON, Louis D(unton) 7
HARTSON, Nelson Thomas 7
HARTSOOK, Arthur J. 9
HARTSTEIN, Jacob I. 10
HARTSUCH, Paul Jackson 8
HARTSUFF, Albert 1
HARTSUFF, George Lucas H
HARTT, Charles Frederick H
HARTT, Frederick 10
HARTT, George Montgomery 3
HARTT, Mary Bronson 5
HARTT, Rollin Lynde 2
HARTUNG, Albert Michael 3
HARTUNG, Hans Heinrich Ernst 10
HARTWELL, Alfred Stedman 1
HARTWELL, Burt Laws 4
HARTWELL, Edward Mussey 1
HARTWELL, Ernest Clark 4
HARTWELL, Henry Walker 3
HARTWELL, John Augustus 1
HARTWELL, Oliver Whitcomb 7
HARTWELL, Shattuck Osgood 3
HARTWICH, Herman 2
HARTWICK, Elbert Stuart 10
HARTWIG, Cleo 9
HARTWIG, Johann Christopher H
HARTY, Jeremiah J. 1
HARTZ, Louis 9
HARTZ, William Homer 5
HARTZELL, Charles 1
HARTZELL, J. Culver 1
HARTZELL, Joseph Crane 1
HARTZELL, Milton Bixler 4
HARTZELL, Thomas B. 5
HARTZLER, Henry Burns 1
HARTZLER, John Ellsworth 4
HARTZOG, Henry Simms 4
HARTZOG, Justin R. 4
HARVARD, John H
HARVEY, Alexander 2
HARVEY, Andrew Magee 2
HARVEY, Basil Coleman Hyatt 3
HARVEY, Byron 4
HARVEY, Byron Schermerhorn 3
HARVEY, Charles Daggett 7
HARVEY, Charles Henry 1
HARVEY, Charles Milton 3
HARVEY, Charles Mitchell 1
HARVEY, Daniel Robert 4
HARVEY, Edmund Newton 3
HARVEY, Eli 3
HARVEY, Ethel Browne 4
HARVEY, Ford 1
HARVEY, Frederick Loviad 1
HARVEY, George H
HARVEY, George 1
HARVEY, George Cockburn 1
HARVEY, George U. 2
HARVEY, Harold Brown 2
HARVEY, Haywood Augustus H
HARVEY, Holman 5
HARVEY, Horace 3
HARVEY, I.J., Jr. 4
HARVEY, James Madison H
HARVEY, Jasper Elliott 7
HARVEY, Jean Charles 5
HARVEY, Johathan H
HARVEY, John (Lacey) 5
HARVEY, Sir John H
HARVEY, Kenneth G. 5
HARVEY, Laurence 6
HARVEY, Lawson Moreau 1
HARVEY, Leo M. 6
HARVEY, Leroy 1
HARVEY, Lester Schley 10
HARVEY, Lillian A. (Mrs. Raymond F. Harvey) 5
HARVEY, Lorenzo Dow 1
HARVEY, Louis Powell H
HARVEY, M.J. 7
HARVEY, Matthew H
HARVEY, Mose Lofley 8
HARVEY, Paul 2
HARVEY, P(aul) Casper 6
HARVEY, Philip Francis 1
HARVEY, Ralph Hicks 3
HARVEY, Ray Forrest 5
HARVEY, Robert Otto 8
HARVEY, Rodney Beecher 2
HARVEY, Roger Allen 6
HARVEY, Roland Bridendall 1
HARVEY, Rowland Hill 2
HARVEY, Samuel Clark 3
HARVEY, Theodore H. 9
HARVEY, William Edwin 1
HARVEY, William Hope 1
HARVEY, William Lemuel 1
HARVEY, William Patrick 4
HARVEY, William Riggs 3
HARVEY, W(illiam) W(est) 5
HARVIE, Eric Lafferty 6
HARVIE, John H
HARVIE, John Bruce 2
HARVIE, Peter Lyons 2
HARVILL, Halbert 9
HARVILL, Richard Anderson 9
HARVIN, Edwin Lawrence 10
HARVIN, Lucius Herman, Jr. 9
HARWI, Frank Edwin 7
HARWICK, Harry John 8
HARWOOD, Albert Leslie, Jr. 7
HARWOOD, Andrew Allen H
HARWOOD, Charles 3
HARWOOD, Charles McHenry 4
HARWOOD, Cole Leslie 4
HARWOOD, Edwin 1
HARWOOD, Frank James 1
HARWOOD, George Alexander 1
HARWOOD, John H
HARWOOD, John E. H
HARWOOD, Thomas A. 4
HARWOOD, William Sumner 1
HARZA, Leroy Francis 3
HASBROOK, Charles Phillips 7
HASBROUCK, Abraham Bruyn H
HASBROUCK, Abraham Joseph H
HASBROUCK, Alfred 1
HASBROUCK, Charles Alfred 4
HASBROUCK, Gilbert D.B. 2
HASBROUCK, Henry Cornelius 1
HASBROUCK, Josiah H
HASBROUCK, Louise Seymour 7
HASBROUCK, Lydia Sayer H
HASBROUCK, Lydia Sayer 4
HASCALL, Augustus Porter H
HASCALL, Milo Smith 1
HASCALL, Wilbur 1
HASCHE, Rudolph Leonard 3
HASE, William Frederick 1
HASELDEN, Kyle Emerson 5
HASELHORST, Donald Duane 9
HASELTINE, Burton 2
HASELTINE, George 1
HASELTINE, Herbert 4
HASELTINE, Nathan Stone 5
HASELTON, Norris Swift 7
HASELTON, Page Smith 5
HASELTON, Seneca 1
HASEMAN, Charles 1
HASENCLEVER, Peter H
HASKELL, Charles Nathaniel 1
HASKELL, Clinton Howard 3
HASKELL, Douglas 7
HASKELL, Duane Hedrick 6
HASKELL, Dudley Chase H
HASKELL, Earl Stanley 4
HASKELL, Edward Howard 1
HASKELL, Edwin Bradbury 1
HASKELL, Ella Louise Knowles H
HASKELL, Ella Louise Knowles 4
HASKELL, Eugene Elwin 1
HASKELL, Freda Rew (Mrs. George S. Haskell) 5
HASKELL, Frederick Tudor 1
HASKELL, Glenn Leach 5
HASKELL, Harold Clifford 3
HASKELL, Harriet Newell 1
HASKELL, Harry Garner 3
HASKELL, Harry Leland 1
HASKELL, Helen Eggleston 5
HASKELL, Henry Joseph 3
HASKELL, Horace Bray 5
HASKELL, J. Amory 1
HASKELL, John Henry Farrell 9
HASKELL, Lewis Wardlaw 4
HASKELL, Llewellyn Frost 4
HASKELL, Mellen Woodman 2
HASKELL, Reuben L. 6
HASKELL, Thomas Hawes 1
HASKELL, William Edwin 1
HASKELL, William Edwin, Jr. 3
HASKELL, William Nafew 3
HASKELL, William T. H
HASKET, Elias H
HASKIN, Frederic J. 2
HASKIN, John Bussing h
HASKIN, William Lawrence 1
HASKINS, Caryl Davis 1
HASKINS, Charles Homer 1
HASKINS, Charles Nelson 2
HASKINS, Charles Waldo 1
HASKINS, George Lee 10
HASKINS, John Christopher 7
HASKINS, Kittredge 1
HASKINS, Samuel Moody 3
HASKINS, Sylvia Shaw Judson 10
HASLAM, Charles Raymond 4
HASLAM, Robert Thomas 4
HASLER, Frederick Edward 5
HASLER, Frederick Edward 7
HASLER, Henry 4
HASLUP, Lemuel A. 3
HASPEL, Joseph 4
HASS, Anthony 10
HASS, Henry Bohn 9
HASSAM, Childe 1
HASSAM, John Tyler 1
HASSARD, John Greene H
HASSAUREK, Friedrich H
HASSE, Adelaide 3
HASSEL, Karl Elmer 6
HASSELBRING, Heinrich 5
HASSELMANS, Louis 3
HASSELQUIST, Tuve Nilsson H
HASSELTINE, Hermon Erwin 5
HASSENFELD, Merrill Lloyd 8
HASSENFELD, Stephen David 10
HASSETT, William D. 6
HASSKARL, Joseph F. 1
HASSLER, Elizabeth Emily 4
HASSLER, Ferdinand Augustus 1
HASSLER, Fredinand Rudolph H
HASSLER, Russell Herman 5
HASSLER, Simon 1
HASSOLD, Ernest Christopher 10
HASSRICK, Romain Calvin 7
HASTIE, Reid William 9
HASTIE, William Henry 7
HASTINGS, Albert Baird 9
HASTINGS, Charles Douglas 1
HASTINGS, Charles Harris 5
HASTINGS, Charles Sheldon 1
HASTINGS, Daniel Hartman 1
HASTINGS, Daniel O. 4
HASTINGS, Earl Freeman 4
HASTINGS, Edgar Morton 3
HASTINGS, Edwin George 5
HASTINGS, Edwin Kilpatrick 7
HASTINGS, Elizabeth Thomson 9
HASTINGS, Francis William 4
HASTINGS, Frank Seymour 1
HASTINGS, Frank Warren 1
HASTINGS, George H
HASTINGS, George Aubrey 3
HASTINGS, George Buckland 4
HASTINGS, George Everett 2
HASTINGS, George Henry 1
HASTINGS, Harry George 4
HASTINGS, Hugh 4
HASTINGS, John H
HASTINGS, John Russell 2
HASTINGS, John Simpson 7
HASTINGS, Lansford W. H
HASTINGS, Paul Pardee 2
HASTINGS, Reuben C.M. 4
HASTINGS, Samuel Dexter 1
HASTINGS, Samuel Miles 2
HASTINGS, Serramus Clinton H
HASTINGS, Seth h
HASTINGS, Thomas H
HASTINGS, Thomas 1
HASTINGS, Thomas Samuel 1
HASTINGS, Thomas Wood 5
HASTINGS, Walter Scott 8
HASTINGS, Wells Southworth 1
HASTINGS, William Granger 1
HASTINGS, William Soden H
HASTINGS, William Walter 4
HASTINGS, William Wirt 1
HASTY, Frederick Emerson 8
HASWELL, Alanson Mason 4
HASWELL, Anthony H
HASWELL, Charles Haynes 1
HASWELL, Ernest Bruce 9
HASWELL, Kanah Elizabeth Marcum (Mrs. Harold Alanson) 5
HATATHLI, Ned 6
HATCH, Abram 4
HATCH, Albert Sydney 4
HATCH, Alden 6
HATCH, Carl A. 4

Name		Name		Name		Name		Name	
HATCH, Chester Elbert	7	HATHAWAY, King	2	HAUSERMAN, Fredric Martin	5	HAWGOOD, Harry	1	HAWLEY, Albert Henry	1
HATCH, Edward	H	HATHAWAY, Lester Gordon	6	HAUSKENS, Peter Bert	5	HAWK, Carl Curtis	10	HAWLEY, Bostwick	1
HATCH, Edward, Jr.	4	HATHAWAY, Robert Joseph	3	HAUSMAN, Leon Augustus	4	HAWK, Eugene Blake	6	HAWLEY, Cameron	5
HATCH, Edward Wingate	1	HATHAWAY, Samuel Gilbert	H	HAUSMAN, Louis	5	HAWK, Philip Bovier	4	HAWLEY, Charles Anthony	4
HATCH, Edwin Glentworth	1	HATHAWAY, Starke R(osecrans)	8	HAUSMAN, Samuel	10	HAWK, Robert Moffett Allison	H	HAWLEY, Charles Arthur	8
HATCH, Emily Nichols	3	HATHAWAY, Stewart Southworth	4	HAUSMAN, William A., Jr.	2	HAWK, Wilbur C.	1	HAWLEY, Charles B.	4
HATCH, Everard E.	1	HATHAWAY, Warren	3	HAUSMANN, Emil John	9	HAWKE, James Albert	1	HAWLEY, Donly Curtis	4
HATCH, Francis March	1	HATHAWAY, William Lee	4	HAUSMANN, Erich	4	HAWKES, Albert Wahl	6	HAWLEY, Edmund Summers	9
HATCH, Frederick Thomas	1	HATHORN, Henry Harrison	H	HAUSNER, Gideon Maks	10	HAWKES, Anna L. Rose	8	HAWLEY, Edwin	1
HATCH, Harry C.	2	HATHORN, John	4	HAUSSERMANN, John William	4	HAWKES, Benjamin Carleton	1	HAWLEY, Fred Vermillia	1
HATCH, Henry James	1	HATHORN, Richmond Yancey	10	HAUSSERMANN, Oscar William	6	HAWKES, Clarence	3	HAWLEY, Frederick William	3
HATCH, Israel Thompson	h	HATHORNE, George	H	HAUSSLER, Arthur Glenn	6	HAWKES, Elden Earl	5	HAWLEY, Gideon*	H
HATCH, James Noble	4	HATHORNE, William	H	HAUSSMANN, Alfred Carl	4	HAWKES, Forbes	1	HAWLEY, Graham	7
HATCH, John Fletcher	6	HATHWAY, Calvin Sutliff	6	HAUT, Irvin Charles	5	HAWKES, Herbert Edwin	2	HAWLEY, Harry Franklin	5
HATCH, John Porter	1	HATHWAY, George W.	5	HAUTECOEUR, Louis	6	HAWKES, James	H	HAWLEY, James H.	1
HATCH, John Wood	4	HATHWAY, Marion	3	HAUXHURST, Henry Austin	6	HAWKES, Lester Litchfield	9	HAWLEY, Jean H.	2
HATCH, L. Boyd	3	HATLO, Jimmy	H	HAVARD, Valery	1	HAWKES, McDougall	1	HAWLEY, Jess Bradford	7
HATCH, Leonard Williams	3	HATOYAMA, Ichiro	3	HAVAS, George	4	HAWKES, Nathan William	7	HAWLEY, John Baldwin	H
HATCH, Lloyd A.	4	HATT, Paul Kitchener	3	HAVELL, Robert	H	HAWKES, Thomas Frederick	9	HAWLEY, John Blackstock	7
HATCH, Louis Clinton	5	HATT, William Kendrick	5	HAVEMEYER, Henry Osborne	1	HAWKES, William F.	1	HAWLEY, John Blackstock, Jr.	1
HATCH, Pascal Enos	3	HATTERSLEY, J(ohn) F(rank)	8	HAVEMEYER, Henry Osborne	H	HAWKESWORTH, Alan Spencer	2	HAWLEY, John Mitchell	1
HATCH, Philander Ellsworth	4	HATTON, Augustus Rutan	2	HAVEMEYER, Horace	3	HAWKINS, Prince Albert	1	HAWLEY, Joseph	H
HATCH, Richard Allen	8	HATTON, Charles Harold	1	HAVEMEYER, Horace, Jr.	10	HAWKINS, Alvin	1	HAWLEY, Joseph Boswell	1
HATCH, Robert Seymour	5	HATTON, E. Roy	4	HAVEMEYER, John Craig	1	HAWKINS, Arthur Hanson	3	HAWLEY, Julius Sargent	1
HATCH, Roy Winthrop	4	HATTON, Frank	H	HAVEMEYER, Loomis	5	HAWKINS, Benjamin	1	HAWLEY, Margaret Foote	1
HATCH, Rufus	H	HATTON, Moses Wesley	4	HAVEMEYER, Theodore Augustus	H	HAWKINS, Benjamin Waterhouse	H	HAWLEY, Newton Fremont	1
HATCH, Samuel Grantham	1	HATTON, Robert Hopkins	H	HAVEMEYER, William Frederick	H	HAWKINS, Bertram Spence	8	HAWLEY, Paul Ramsey	4
HATCH, Sinclair	10	HATTON, T. Chalkley	1	HAVEMEYER, William Frederick	1	HAWKINS, Charles Martyr	4	HAWLEY, Ralph Chipman	5
HATCH, Stephen D.	H	HATTSTAEDT, John James	1	HAVEN, Emily Bradley Neal	H	HAWKINS, Chauncey Jeddie	1	HAWLEY, Ransom Smith	6
HATCH, Theodore Frederick	9	HATTSTAEDT, John Robert	8	HAVEN, Erastus Otis	H	HAWKINS, Coleman	5	HAWLEY, Thomas Porter	1
HATCH, Vermont	3	HATZFELD, Helmut Anthony	7	HAVEN, Franklin	1	HAWKINS, David Robert	9	HAWLEY, Willis Chatman	1
HATCH, William Henry	H	HAUBER, Ulrich Albert	7	HAVEN, George Griswold	1	HAWKINS, Dexter Arnold	H	HAWN, Henry Gaines	1
HATCH, William Henry Paine	7	HAUBERG, John Henry	3	HAVEN, Gilbert	H	HAWKINS, Dexter Clarkson	1	HAWORTH, Erasmus	1
HATCH, Winslow Roper	7	HAUBIEL, Charles	7	HAVEN, Henry Philemon	H	HAWKINS, Earle T(aylor)	5	HAWORTH, Joseph	1
HATCHER, Eldridge Burwell	2	HAUBOLD, Herman A.	1	HAVEN, Joseph	H	HAWKINS, Edler Garnett	7	HAWORTH, Leland John	7
HATCHER, Harlan Henthorne	10	HAUCK, Fred	4	HAVEN, Joseph Emerson	1	HAWKINS, Edward Russell	4	HAWORTH, Paul Leland	1
HATCHER, James Donald	10	HAUCK, Herman John	7	HAVEN, Nathaniel Appleton	H	HAWKINS, Frank Lee	7	HAWORTH, Sir Walter Norman	2
HATCHER, James Fulton	3	HAUCK, Louise Platt	2	HAVEN, Solomon George	1	HAWKINS, George Andrew	7	HAWS, John Henry Hobart	H
HATCHER, John Bell	1	HAUCK, Minnie	2	HAVEN, Willi꞉ i Ingraham	1	HAWKINS, George K.	1	HAWTHORN, Horace Boies	8
HATCHER, John Henry	5	HAUGAN, Henry Alexander	1	HAVENHILL, L.D.	3	HAWKINS, George Sydney	H	HAWTHORNE, Charles Webster	1
HATCHER, Julian Sommerville	4	HAUGAN, Randolph Edgar	8	HAVENNER, Franck Roberts	4	HAWKINS, Hamilton Smith	1	HAWTHORNE, Edward William	9
HATCHER, Orle Latham	2	HAUGE, Gabriel	9	HAVENNER, George Clement	5	HAWKINS, Hamilton Smith	3	HAWTHORNE, Hildegarde	3
HATCHER, Robert Anthony	H	HAUGE, Hjalmar Christian	4	HAVENS, Donald	3	HAWKINS, Henry Gabriel	4	HAWTHORNE, Hugh Robert	4
HATCHER, Robert Anthony	2	HAUGE, Phillip Enoch	10	HAVENS, Frank Colton	1	HAWKINS, Horace Norman	2	HAWTHORNE, Julian	1
HATCHER, Samuel Claiborne	3	HAUGEN, Bernhart	7	HAVENS, George Remington	7	HAWKINS, Ira	1	HAWTHORNE, Nathaniel	H
HATCHER, William Bass	2	HAUGEN, Gilbert N.	1	HAVENS, James Dexter	4	HAWKINS, Isaac Roberts	1	HAWTHORNE, Rose	H
HATCHER, William E.	1	HAUGEN, Nils Penderson	1	HAVENS, James Smith	1	HAWKINS, J. Dawson	4	HAWTHORNE, Rose	4
HATCHER, Wirt Hargrove	6	HAUGH, Jesse Lee	4	HAVENS, Johathan Nicoll	4	HAWKINS, J.E.	4	HAWTREY, Charles Henry	1
HATCHETT, Stephen Pinckney	7	HAUGHEY, Thomas	H	HAVENS, Paul Egbert	1	HAWKINS, Jack	5	HAWTREY, Sir Ralph George	6
HATFIELD, Charles Albert Phelps	4	HAUGHT, Benjamin Franklin	4	HAVENS, Raymond Dexter	3	HAWKINS, J(esse) Mills	10	HAWXHURST, Robert, Jr.	5
HATFIELD, Charles Folsom	1	HAUGHT, David L.	7	HAVENS, Valentine Britton	2	HAWKINS, John Harold	9	HAXO, Henry Emile	6
HATFIELD, Charles James	3	HAUGHT, Thomas William	3	HAVENS, Walter Paul, Jr.	10	HAWKINS, John J.	1	HAY, Alexandre	10
HATFIELD, Charles Sherrod	2	HAUGHTON, Daniel Jeremiah	9	HAVERLY, Christopher	4	HAWKINS, John Parker	1	HAY, Andrew Kessler	H
HATFIELD, Edwin Francis	1	HAUHART, William Frederic	5	HAVERS, Lord Michael (Robert Olfield)*	10	HAWKINS, Joseph	H	HAY, Arthur Douglas	3
HATFIELD, George	3	HAUK, Minnie	H	HAVERSTICK, Edward Everett	3	HAWKINS, Joseph Elmer	7	HAY, Charles Augustus	H
HATFIELD, George Juan	4	HAUK, Minnie	4	HAVERSTICK, Edward Everett, Jr.	8	HAWKINS, Joseph H.	H	HAY, Charles Martin	2
HATFIELD, Henry Drury	4	HAUKE, Robert Charles	6	HAVERTY, Clarence	4	HAWKINS, Laurence Ashley	3	HAY, Clarence Leonard	5
HATFIELD, Henry Rand	2	HAULENBEEK, P. Raymond	4	HAVIGHURST, Alfred Freeman	10	HAWKINS, Layton S.	4	HAY, Earl Downing	1
HATFIELD, James Taft	2	HAUN, Burton Oliver	5	HAVIGHURST, Freeman Alfred	5	HAWKINS, Micajah Thomas	H	HAY, Eugene Gano	1
HATFIELD, James Tobias	1	HAUN, Henry Peter	H	HAVIGHURST, Harold Canfield	10	HAWKINS, Morris Seymour	2	HAY, George	1
HATFIELD, John Nye	10	HAUPERT, Raymond Samuel	5	HAVIGHURST, Robert J.	10	HAWKINS, Orwill Van Wickle	9	HAY, Henry Clinton	1
HATFIELD, Joseph Clayton	3	HAUPT, Alexander James Derbyshire	1	HAVILAND, Clarence Floyd	1	HAWKINS, Robert Bruce	7	HAY, Isaac Kline	7
HATFIELD, Joshua Alexander	1	HAUPT, Charles Elvin	1	HAVILAND, James Thomas	3	HAWKINS, Robert Bruce	8	HAY, James	1
HATFIELD, Lansing	3	HAUPT, Herman	1	HAVILAND, John	1	HAWKINS, Robert Dawson	9	HAY, James, Jr.	1
HATFIELD, Marcus Pattern	1	HAUPT, Ira	1	HAVILAND, Virginia	9	HAWKINS, Robert Martyr	8	HAY, John	1
HATFIELD, Oliver Perry	H	HAUPT, Lewis Muhlenberg	1	HAVNER, Horace Moore	3	HAWKINS, Rush Christopher	1	HAY, John W.	3
HATFIELD, R.G.	H	HAUPT, Paul	1	HAWES, Albert Gallatin	6	HAWKINS, Sion Boone	8	HAY, Logan	2
HATFIELD, Richard Bennett	10	HAUPT, Sarah Minerva	5	HAWES, Austin Foster	6	HAWKINS, Thomas Francis	7	HAY, Malcolm	5
HATFIELD, W. Wilbur	7	HAUPTMANN, Gerhart	2	HAWES, Aylett	H	HAWKINS, Thomas Hayden	1	HAY, Marion E.	1
HATFIELD, William Durell	9	HAUROWITZ, Felix	9	HAWES, Charles Henry	2	HAWKINS, Walter Lincoln	10	HAY, Mary Garrett	1
HATHAWAY, Alton Hastings	7	HAURY, Emil Walter	10	HAWES, Elizabeth	5	HAWKINS, William Bruce	6	HAY, Oliver Perry	1
HATHAWAY, Arthur Stafford	1	HAUSDORFER, Walter	5	HAWES, George Edward	4	HAWKINS, William Edward	1	HAY, Samuel Ross	2
HATHAWAY, Charles Montgomery, Jr.	3	HAUSEMAN, David Nathaniel	10	HAWES, Harriet Boyd	4	HAWKINS, William George	1	HAY, Stephen John	1
HATHAWAY, Edward Sturtevant	7	HAUSER, Charles R(oy)	2	HAWES, Harry Bartow	2	HAWKINS, William John	4	HAY, Thomas Abraham Horn	1
HATHAWAY, Evangeline	1	HAUSER, Conrad Augustine	2	HAWES, Henry Quinby	8	HAWKINS, William Waller	3	HAY, William Henry	2
HATHAWAY, Fons A.	5	HAUSER, Emil Daniel William	8	HAWES, James William	1	HAWKINSON, James R.	9	HAY, William Perry	2
HATHAWAY, Forrest Henry	1	HAUSER, Ernst A.	3	HAWES, Joel	H	HAWKS, Charles, Jr.	3	HAYAKAWA, Samuel Ichiye	10
HATHAWAY, Gail Abner	7	HAUSER, Gayelord (Helmut Eugene Benjamin Gellert Hauser)	9	HAWES, John Bromham, II	1	HAWKS, Francis Lister	H	HAYAKAWA, Sessue (Kintaro Hayakawa)	6
HATHAWAY, George Henry	1	HAUSER, Harry	5	HAWES, Richard	H	HAWKS, Frank Monroe	1	HAYCOX, Ernest	3
HATHAWAY, Harle Wallace	2	HAUSER, Nancy McKnight	10	HAWES, Richard S.	4	HAWKS, Howard Winchester	1	HAYCRAFT, Howard	10
HATHAWAY, Joseph Henry	5	HAUSER, Samuel Thomas	1	HAWES, Stewart S.	4	HAWKS, James Dudley	4	HAYCRAFT, Julius Everette	5
		HAUSER, Walter	4	HAWES, Stewart S(tarks)	5	HAWKS, John	1	HAYDEN, Amos Sutton	H
				HAWES, William Post	H	HAWLEY, Alan Ramsay	H	HAYDEN, Arthur Gunderson	4
								HAYDEN, Austin Albert	1
								HAYDEN, Carl (Trumbull)	5
								HAYDEN, Carl (Trumbull)	6
								HAYDEN, Charles	1
								HAYDEN, Charles H.	1
								HAYDEN, Charles Sidney	1
								HAYDEN, Edward Everett	1

HAYDEN, Ferdinand Vandiveer — H
HAYDEN, Frank — 1
HAYDEN, Frederick Smith — 4
HAYDEN, Horace Edwin — 1
HAYDEN, Horace H. — H
HAYDEN, Jay G. — 5
HAYDEN, Joel Babcock — 2
HAYDEN, John Louis — 1
HAYDEN, Joseph — H
HAYDEN, Joseph Ralston — 2
HAYDEN, Josiah Willard — 3
HAYDEN, Martin Scholl — 10
HAYDEN, Merrill A. — 6
HAYDEN, Moses — H
HAYDEN, Paul Vincent — 7
HAYDEN, Philip Cady — 4
HAYDEN, Robert Earl — 7
HAYDEN, Sterling — 1
HAYDEN, Velma Denison — 4
HAYDEN, Warren Sherman — 1
HAYDEN, William — H
HAYDN, Hiram — 6
HAYDN, Hiram Collins — 1
HAYDOCK, George Sewell — 5
HAYDON, Albert Eustace — 6
HAYDON, Glen — 10
HAYDON, Glen — 4
HAYEK, Friedrich August (von) — 10
HAYES, Albert J(ohn) — 8
HAYES, Alfred — 10
HAYES, Alfred — 1
HAYES, Anson — 4
HAYES, Arthur Badley — 2
HAYES, Arthur Hull — H
HAYES, Augustus Allen — 4
HAYES, C. Willard — 1
HAYES, Carlton Joseph Huntley — 1
HAYES, Charles Harris — 1
HAYES, Charles Willard, Jr. — 7
HAYES, Clara Edna — 7
HAYES, Clifford Barron — 4
HAYES, Daniel Webster — 3
HAYES, David J.A. — 3
HAYES, Doremus Almy — 1
HAYES, Edward Arthur — 3
HAYES, Edward Cary — 1
HAYES, Edward Francis — 6
HAYES, Edward Mortimer — 1
HAYES, Edward William — 1
HAYES, Ellen — 1
HAYES, Everis Anson — 1
HAYES, Francis Little — 1
HAYES, Frank J. — 7
HAYES, Frederick Albert — 4
HAYES, George Miller — 3
HAYES, Hammond Vinton — 4
HAYES, Harold M. — 4
HAYES, Harold Thomas Pace — 10
HAYES, Harvey Cornelius — 5
HAYES, Helen Hayden — 6
HAYES, Henry — 4
HAYES, Henry Reed — 3
HAYES, Hoyt E. — 8
HAYES, Isaac Israel — H
HAYES, James Edward — 2
HAYES, James Juvenal — 8
HAYES, James Leo — 5
HAYES, James Martin — 9
HAYES, Jay Orley — 2
HAYES, John Cornelius — 7
HAYES, John Herman — 4
HAYES, John Lord — H
HAYES, John Russell — 3
HAYES, John S. — 9
HAYES, John W. — 8
HAYES, John William — 2
HAYES, Johnson Jay — 5
HAYES, Joseph — 4
HAYES, Joseph P. — 5
HAYES, Lucy Webb — H
HAYES, L(uther) Newton — 9
HAYES, Mary Sanders (Mrs. William Henry Hays) — 5
HAYES, Max S. — 2
HAYES, Montrose W. — 1
HAYES, Myron J. — 3
HAYES, Nevin William — 9
HAYES, Patrick Joseph — H
HAYES, Philip — 2
HAYES, Philip Cornelius — 1
HAYES, R.S. — 5
HAYES, Ralph Leo — 7
HAYES, Ralph Wesley — 3
HAYES, Reginald Carroll — 8
HAYES, Roland — 7
HAYES, Rutherford Birchard — H
HAYES, Samuel Perkins — 3
HAYES, Samuel Walter — 1
HAYES, Simeon Mills — 4

HAYES, Stephen Quentin — 1
HAYES, Thomas Gordon — 1
HAYES, Thomas Jay — 8
HAYES, Thomas Michael — 8
HAYES, Thomas Sumner — 3
HAYES, Wade Hampton — 3
HAYES, Warren Howard — 1
HAYES, Watson McMillan — 2
HAYES, Wayland J(ackson) — 5
HAYES, Webb Cook — 1
HAYES, Webb Cook, II — 3
HAYES, William Patrick — 8
HAYFORD, John Fillmore — 1
HAYGOOD, Atticus Green — H
HAYGOOD, Laura Askew — H
HAYHOW, Edgar Charles — 3
HAYHURST, Emery Roe — 4
HAYKIN, David Judson — 3
HAYLER, Guy Wilfrid — 5
HAYLES, Alvin Beasley — 9
HAYLEY, John William — 1
HAYMAKER, Jesse N. — 1
HAYMAN, Al — 1
HAYMOND, Frank Cruise — 5
HAYMOND, Thomas S. — 5
HAYMOND, Thomas Sherwood — H
HAYMOND, William Summerville — 1
HAYNE, Arthur Peronneau — H
HAYNE, Coe — 5
HAYNE, Isaac — H
HAYNE, James Adams — 5
HAYNE, Paul Hamilton — H
HAYNE, Robert Young — H
HAYNE, William Hamilton — 1
HAYNER, J(ohn) Clifford — 10
HAYNER, Rutherford — 1
HAYNES, Arthur Edwin — 1
HAYNES, Benjamin Rudolph — 4
HAYNES, Carlyle Boynton — 3
HAYNES, Charles Eaton — 1
HAYNES, Charles H(enry) — 6
HAYNES, Daniel H. — 3
HAYNES, David Oliphant — 1
HAYNES, Donald — 10
HAYNES, Eli Stuart — 3
HAYNES, Elizabeth A. Ross — 3
HAYNES, Elwood — 1
HAYNES, Emerson Paul — 9
HAYNES, Emory James — 1
HAYNES, Evan — 3
HAYNES, Fred Emory — 4
HAYNES, George Edmund — 3
HAYNES, George Henry — 2
HAYNES, Harley A(rmand) — 3
HAYNES, Henry Williamson — 1
HAYNES, Hilda Mocile Lashley — 9
HAYNES, Ira Allen — 3
HAYNES, Irving Samuel — 4
HAYNES, John — H
HAYNES, John Randolph — 1
HAYNES, Joseph Walton — 5
HAYNES, Justin O'Brien — 2
HAYNES, Myron Wilbur — 1
HAYNES, Nathaniel Smith — 1
HAYNES, Robert Blair — 4
HAYNES, Rowland — 4
HAYNES, Roy Asa — 1
HAYNES, Sherwood Kimball — 10
HAYNES, Thornwell — 3
HAYNES, Williams (Nathan Gallup) — 7
HAYNIE, Henry — 1
HAYNSWORTH, Clement Furman, Jr. — 10
HAYS, Albert Theodore — 6
HAYS, Alexander — H
HAYS, Arthur Alexander — 3
HAYS, Arthur Garfield — 3
HAYS, Brooks — 8
HAYS, Calvin Cornwell — 1
HAYS, Charles — H
HAYS, Charles Melville — 1
HAYS, Charles Thomas — 2
HAYS, Daniel Peixotto — 1
HAYS, Donald C. — 8
HAYS, Edde K. — 4
HAYS, Edward D. — 1
HAYS, Edward Retilla — H
HAYS, Elmer D. — 1
HAYS, Frank Lazmer — 3
HAYS, Frank W. — 1
HAYS, George Omar — 8
HAYS, George Washington — 1
HAYS, Harry Thompson — H
HAYS, Howard H. — 5
HAYS, I. Minis — 1
HAYS, Isaac — H
HAYS, Jack Newton — H
HAYS, J(ames) Byers — 9
HAYS, John — 1

HAYS, John Coffee — H
HAYS, Margaret Gebbie — 1
HAYS, Mortimer — 4
HAYS, Mrs. Glenn G. — 10
HAYS, Paul R. — 7
HAYS, Paul R. — 8
HAYS, Samuel — H
HAYS, Samuel Lewis — H
HAYS, Silas B. — 4
HAYS, Walter Lee — 4
HAYS, Wayne Levere — 9
HAYS, Will H. — 3
HAYS, Willet Martin — 4
HAYS, William Charles — 4
HAYS, William Jacob — H
HAYS, William Jacob — 1
HAYS, William Shakespeare — 1
HAYT, Charles D. — 1
HAYWARD, Benjamin Dover — 1
HAYWARD, Edward Beardsley — 8
HAYWARD, Edward Farwell — 1
HAYWARD, Florence — 1
HAYWARD, Fred Preston — 5
HAYWARD, George — 1
HAYWARD, Harry — 1
HAYWARD, Harry Taft — 1
HAYWARD, Joseph Warren — 1
HAYWARD, Monroe Leland — 1
HAYWARD, Nathan — 2
HAYWARD, Nathaniel Manley — H
HAYWARD, Ralph A. — 3
HAYWARD, Susan — 6
HAYWARD, Walter Brownell — 1
HAYWARD, William — 2
HAYWARD, William, Jr. — H
HAYWARD, William Leete — 4
HAYWARD, Wilmer — 7
HAYWOOD, Allen S. — 3
HAYWOOD, Harry Leroy — 3
HAYWOOD, John — H
HAYWOOD, John Kerfoot — 1
HAYWOOD, John Wilfred — 5
HAYWOOD, John Wilfred — 7
HAYWOOD, Marshall, Jr. — 5
HAYWOOD, Marshall De Lancey — 1
HAYWOOD, Richard Mansfield — 7
HAYWOOD, Thomas Holt — 8
HAYWOOD, William Dudley — 1
HAYWOOD, William Dudley — 4
HAYWOOD, William Henry, Jr. — H
HAYWORTH, Don — 8
HAYWORTH, Rita (Margarita Carman Cansino) — 9
HAZAM, Louis Joseph — 8
HAZARD, Augustus George — H
HAZARD, Caroline — 2
HAZARD, Clifton T. — 4
HAZARD, Daniel Lyman — 3
HAZARD, Ebenezer — H
HAZARD, Elmer Clarke — 6
HAZARD, Frederick Rowland — 1
HAZARD, Henry Bernard — 3
HAZARD, Jonathan J. — H
HAZARD, Lauriston Hartwell — 1
HAZARD, Leland — 7
HAZARD, Marshall Curtiss Gibson — 1
HAZARD, Rowland Gibson — H
HAZARD, Rowland Gibson — 1
HAZARD, Samuel — H
HAZARD, Spencer Peabody — 3
HAZARD, Thomas — H
HAZARD, Thomas Pierrepont — 5
HAZARD, Thomas Robinson — H
HAZARD, Willis Hatfield — 3
HAZEL, John Raymond — 4
HAZELBAKER, Norval Denver — 1
HAZELET, Craig Potter — 9
HAZELIUS, Ernest Lewis — H
HAZELRIGG, James Hervey — 4
HAZELTINE, Abner — H
HAZELTINE, Alan — 4
HAZELTINE, George Cochran, Jr. — 1

HAZELTINE, Harold Dexter — 5
HAZELTINE, Horace — 4
HAZELTINE, Louis ALan — 7
HAZELTINE, Mary Emogene — 2
HAZELTINE, Mayo Williamson — 1
HAZELTON, John H. — 3
HAZELTON, John Wright — H
HAZELWOOD, John — H
HAZEN, Allen — 1
HAZEN, Allen Tracy — 7
HAZEN, Arlon Giberson — 7
HAZEN, Azel Washburn — 1
HAZEN, Ben H. — 8
HAZEN, Charles Downer — 1
HAZEN, Edward Gates — 9
HAZEN, Harold Locke — 7
HAZEN, Harold Locke — 8
HAZEN, Henry Allen* — 1
HAZEN, Henry Honeyman — 3
HAZEN, John Vose — 1
HAZEN, Joseph Chalmers — 4
HAZEN, Marshman Williams — 1
HAZEN, Maynard Thompson — 4
HAZEN, Moses — H
HAZEN, Richard — 10
HAZEN, William Babcock — H
HAZEN, William Livingston — 2
HAZLET, Stewart E(merson) — 6
HAZLETT, Harry Fouts — 4
HAZLETT, Robert — 2
HAZLETT, Samuel M. — 3
HAZLETT, Theodore Lyle — 7
HAZLEWOOD, Craig Beebe — 3
HAZZARD, Charles — 1
HAZZARD, Jesse Charles — 5
HAZZARD, John Edward — 1
H'DOUBLER, Francis Todd — 4
HEACOCK, Frank Ahern — 4
HEACOCK, Roger Lee — 4
HEACOX, Arthur Edward — 5
HEAD, Albert Joseph — 7
HEAD, Edith — 8
HEAD, Franklin Harvey — 1
HEAD, Hayden Wilson — 9
HEAD, Henry Oswald — 1
HEAD, Howard — 10
HEAD, James Butler — 1
HEAD, James Marshall — 1
HEAD, James Milne — 5
HEAD, Jerome Reed — 6
HEAD, John Benedict — 1
HEAD, John Frazier — 1
HEAD, Leon Oswald — 4
HEAD, Mabel — 5
HEAD, T. Grady — 4
HEAD, Walter Dutton — 4
HEAD, Walter William — 3
HEAD, Walton O. — 1
HEADDEN, William Parker — 1
HEADE, Martin Johnson — H
HEADLAND, Isaac Taylor — 2
HEADLEE, Thomas J. — 2
HEADLEY, Cleon — 3
HEADLEY, Joel Tyler — H
HEADLEY, John William — 3
HEADLEY, Leal Aubrey — 4
HEADLEY, Louis Sherman — 7
HEADLEY, Phineas Camp — 1
HEADLEY, Roy — 3
HEADLEY, Sherman Knight — 10
HEAFFORD, George Henry — 4
HEAL, Gilbert B. — 3
HEALD, Daniel Addison — 1
HEALD, Frederick De Forest — 3
HEALD, Henry Townley — 6
HEALD, Henry Townley — 7
HEALD, Kenneth Conrad — 5
HEALD, Kenneth Conrad — 8
HEALD, William Henry — 1
HEALE, Charles J. — 2
HEALEY, Arthur Daniel — 1
HEALEY, Charles C. — 1
HEALEY, George — 7
HEALEY, Michael J. — 5
HEALY, A. Augustus — 1
HEALY, Arthur Kelly David — 7
HEALY, Daniel Joseph — 1
HEALY, Daniel Joseph — H
HEALY, Daniel Ward, Jr. — 5
HEALY, Ezra Anthony — 1
HEALY, Fred Albert — 2
HEALY, George Peter Alexander — H

HEALY, George William, Jr. — 7
HEALY, James Augustine — 1
HEALY, Joseph — H
HEALY, Kent Tenney — 8
HEALY, Patrick Joseph — 1
HEALY, Paul Francis — 8
HEALY, Robert E. — 2
HEALY, Robert Wallace — 1
HEALY, Thomas Henry — 4
HEALY, Thomas Jefferson — 8
HEALY, William — 4
HEANEY, John William — 3
HEANEY, Noble Sproat — 3
HEANEY, Robert Cecil Curtis — 7
HEAP, David Porter — 1
HEAP, Samuel Davies — H
HEAPS, Alvin Eugene — 9
HEAPS, William James — 5
HEAPS, Wilson A. — 10
HEARD, Arthur Marston — 1
HEARD, Augustine — H
HEARD, Benjamin — 1
HEARD, Bill James — 5
HEARD, Dwight Bancroft — 1
HEARD, Franklin Fiske — H
HEARD, Gerald — 5
HEARD, Jack Whitehead — 7
HEARD, James Delavan — 5
HEARD, John J. — 9
HEARD, Manning Wright — 10
HEARD, Marstron — 10
HEARD, Oscar Edwin — 1
HEARD, William H. — 1
HEARD, William Wright — 1
HEARE, Clayton — 5
HEARN, Clint Calvin — 1
HEARN, David William — 1
HEARN, Hardie B. — 4
HEARN, Lafcadio — 1
HEARN, Thomas G — 8
HEARNE, Edward Dingle — 4
HEARNE, John J(oseph) — 5
HEARON, Charles Oscar — 5
HEARST, Austine McDonnell — 10
HEARST, Charles Ernest — 1
HEARST, David Whitmore — 9
HEARST, George — H
HEARST, George Randolph, Sr. — 5
HEARST, John Randolph — 3
HEARST, Phoebe Apperson — 1
HEARST, William Randolph — 3
HEATH, Clyde J(ames) — 5
HEATH, Daniel Collamore — 1
HEATH, Donald R. — 9
HEATH, Edward Charles — 8
HEATH, Edwin Joseph — 3
HEATH, Ferry Kimball — 1
HEATH, Fred H. — 2
HEATH, Frederick Carroll — 1
HEATH, Harold — 3
HEATH, Hubert A. — 4
HEATH, Hugh Austin — 2
HEATH, James Ewell — H
HEATH, James P. — H
HEATH, Janet Field (Mrs. S. Roy Heath) — 7
HEATH, John — 1
HEATH, Perry Sanford — 1
HEATH, Richard Nathan — 9
HEATH, S. Burton — 2
HEATH, William — H
HEATH, William Ames — 4
HEATH, William Womack — 5
HEATHCOTE, Caleb — H
HEATHCOTE, Charles William — 4
HEATLEY, Stuart Alden Goodyear — 4
HEATON, Augustus — 1
HEATON, Aurhur B . — 3
HEATON, Claude Edwin — 10
HEATON, David — 1
HEATON, Harry Clifton — 3
HEATON, Herbert — 5
HEATON, John Langdon — 1
HEATON, Leonard D(udley) — 8
HEATON, Lucia Elizabeth — 3
HEATON, Percy — 1
HEATON, Robert Douglas — 3
HEATTER, Gabriel — 8
HEATWOLE, Cornelius Jacob — 1
HEATWOLE, Joel Prescott — 1
HEATWOLE, Lewis James — 1
HEATWOLE, Timothy Oliver — 4
HEAVEY, John William — 2
HEAZEL, Francis — 9
HEBARD, Arthur Foster — 2
HEBARD, Grace Raymond — 1
HEBARD, William — H

HEBB, Donald Olding 9
HEBBARD, William Lawrence 7
HEBBEL, Robert 7
HEBBERD, John Bailey 6
HEBBLE, William Joseph 10
HEBDEN, John Calder 1
HEBEL, John William 1
HEBERT, F. Edward 7
HEBERT, Felix 5
HEBERT, Paul MacArius 7
HEBERT, Paul Octave H
HEBRARD, Jean 3
HECHT, Ben 4
HECHT, David Stanford 3
HECHT, Frank Abner 7
HECHT, George Joseph 7
HECHT, Hans H. 5
HECHT, Harold 8
HECHT, Julius Lawrence 3
HECHT, Moses S. 3
HECHT, Rudolph S. 3
HECHT, Samuel M. 7
HECHT, Selig 2
HECHT, Wilbur Hudson 6
HECHTMAN, Robert Aaron 8
HECK, Arch Oliver 7
HECK, Barbara Ruckle H
HECK, Charles Voisin* 8
HECK, Frank Hopkins 8
HECK, Nicholas Hunter 3
HECK, Robert Culbertson Hays 3
HECK, William Harry 1
HECKE, G. H. 4
HECKEL, Albert Kerr 6
HECKEL, Charles Willard 9
HECKEL, Edward Balthasar 1
HECKEL, George Baugh 1
HECKEL, Norris Julius 4
HECKER, Arthur Orr 8
HECKER, Frank Joseph 1
HECKER, Friedrich Karl Franz H
HECKER, Isaac Thomas H
HECKER, John Valentine 4
HECKER, William Frantz 7
HECKERLING, Philip Ephraim 8
HECKERT, Charles Girven 1
HECKERT, John Walter 3
HECKERT, Josiah Brooks 10
HECKETT, Eric Harlow 4
HECKEWELDER, John Gottlieb Ernestus H
HECKLER, Edwin Little 4
HECKMAN, James Robert 2
HECKMAN, Samuel B. 3
HECKMAN, Wallace 1
HECKMAN, William Robert 9
HECKSCHER, August 1
HECKSCHER, August 2
HECKSCHER, Celeste Delongpre 1
HECKSCHER, Robert Valentine 7
HEDBACK, Axel Emanuel 3
HEDBERG, Hollis Dow 9
HEDBLOM, Carl Arthur 1
HEDBROOKE, Andrew H
HEDDENS, Barret Spencer, Jr. 7
HEDENSTROM, Paul Henry 5
HEDERMAN, T.M. 2
HEDERMAN, Thomas Martin, Jr. 8
HEDGCOCK, George Grant 4
HEDGE, Charles Gorham 1
HEDGE, Frederic Henry H
HEDGE, Frederic Henry 4
HEDGE, Henry Rogers 5
HEDGE, Levi H
HEDGE, Thomas 4
HEDGE, William Russell 2
HEDGES, Benjamin Van Doren 5
HEDGES, Frank Hinckley 1
HEDGES, J. Edward 4
HEDGES, James Blaine 4
HEDGES, Job Elmer 1
HEDGES, Joseph Harold 3
HEDGES, Marion Hawthorne 3
HEDGES, Samuel Hamilton 2
HEDLESTON, Winn David 1
HEDLEY, Frank 3
HEDLUND, Floyd Frederick 8
HEDLUND, Glenn Wilber 7
HEDLY, Arthur Howard 4
HEDMAN, Martha 8
HEDMEG, Andrew 10
HEDRICH, Arthur William 8
HEDRICH, Kenneth 5
HEDRICK, Bayard Murphy 4
HEDRICK, Charles Baker 2
HEDRICK, Charles Embury 3
HEDRICK, E.H. 3
HEDRICK, Earle Raymond 2
HEDRICK, Ira Grant 1
HEDRICK, Lawrence E. 6
HEDRICK, Lawrence Hyskell 8
HEDRICK, Tubman Keene 5
HEDRICK, Ulysses Prentiss 3
HEDRICK, Wyat Cephas 4
HEDSTROM, Carl Oscar 5
HEDTOFT, Hans 3
HEEBNER, Charles 1
HEED, Thomas D. 3
HEEKIN, Albert Edward, Jr. 5
HEELAN, Edmond 2
HEELY, Allan Vanderhoef 3
HEENAN, John Carmel H
HEENEHAN, James T. 3
HEENEY, Arnold Danford Patrick 5
HEERMAN, Ritz Edwin 4
HEERMANCE, Edgar Laing 5
HEERMANCE, Radcliffe 7
HEERMANN, Adolphus L. H
HEERMANS, Augustyn H
HEERMANS, Charles Abram 4
HEERMANS, Forbes 1
HEERMANS, Josephine Woodbury 4
HEES, William Rathbun 2
HEETER, Silvanus Laurabee 5
HEEZEN, Bruce Charles 7
HEFELBOWER, Samuel Gring 3
HEFFELFINGER, Frank Peavey 10
HEFFELFINGER, Frank Totton 3
HEFFELFINGER, George W.P. 5
HEFFELFINGER, William Stewart 9
HEFFERAN, Thomas Hume 5
HEFFERAN, W.S., Jr. 4
HEFFERLINE, Ralph Franklin 6
HEFFERLINE, Ralph Franklin 7
HEFFERN, Andrew Duff 1
HEFFERNAN, James Joseph 4
HEFFERNAN, John Baptist 10
HEFFERNAN, Joseph Lawrence 8
HEFFERNAN, Joseph Victor 9
HEFFERNAN, Paul Malcolm 9
HEFFNER, Edward Hoch 7
HEFFNER, Hubert Crouse 8
HEFFNER, R(oe)-M(errill) S(ecrist) 9
HEFFRON, John Lorenzo 1
HEFFRON, Patrick Richard 1
HEFFRON, Robert James 8
HEFLEBOWER, Richard Brooks 8
HEFLEBOWER, Roy Cleveland 7
HEFLIN, Aubrey Newbill 6
HEFLIN, J. Thomas 3
HEFLIN, Van 5
HEFLING, Arthur William 6
HEFNER, Frank Karl 8
HEFNER, Ralph A(ubrie) 5
HEFNER, Robert Arthur 9
HEFTY, Thomas R. 4
HEG, Elmer Ellsworth 4
HEGEMAN, John Rogers 1
HEGER, Anthony 1
HEGGEN, Thomas Orlo 2
HEGLAND, Martin 5
HEGNER, Mrs. Bertha Hofer 4
HEGNER, Robert William 2
HEGRE, Theodore A. 8
HEHER, Harry 5
HEHIR, Martin A. 1
HEHRE, Frederick William 7
HEIDBREDER, Edna Frances 8
HEIDEGGER, Martin 6
HEIDEL, William Arthur 1
HEIDELBERGER, Charles 8
HEIDELBERGER, Michael 10
HEIDEN, Konrad 6
HEIDER, Raphael 5
HEIDINGER, James Vandaveer 2
HEIDINGSFIELD, Myron S(amuel) 5
HEIDT, Lawrence Joseph 9
HEIFETZ, Benar 6
HEIFETZ, Jascha 9
HEIGES, Donald Russel 10
HEIGES, Jesse Gibson 10
HEIKES, Victor Conrad 2
HEIL, Charles Emile 3
HEIL, Julius Peter 2
HEIL, Walter 8
HEIL, William Franklin 1
HEILAND, Carl August 3
HEILBRONNER, Louis 5
HEILBRUNN, Lewis Victor 3
HEILEMAN, Frank A. 4
HEILIG, Sterling 4
HEILMAN, Charles George 9
HEILMAN, Ernest A. 8
HEILMAN, Fordyce R. 4
HEILMAN, Ralph Emerson 1
HEILMAN, Russell Howard 4
HEILMAN, William H
HEILMAN, William Clifford 2
HEILNER, Samuel 1
HEILNER, Van Campen 5
HEILPRIN, Angelo 1
HEILPRIN, Louis 1
HEILPRIN, Michael H
HEIM, Herbert E. 5
HEIM, Jacques 4
HEIM, Leo Edward 10
HEIM, Raymond Walter 7
HEIM, Schuyler F(ranklin) 7
HEIMANN, Henry Herman 3
HEIMANN, Robert Karl 10
HEIMBACH, Arthur E. 3
HEIMBACH, Howard Anders 5
HEIMBERGER, William Wengerd 10
HEIMERICH, John James 5
HEIMKE, William 1
HEIMROD, George 4
HEIN, Carl 2
HEIN, Carl Christian 1
HEIN, Otto Louis 4
HEIN, Walter Jacob 4
HEINBERG, John Gilbert 3
HEINDEL, Augusta Foss 2
HEINDEL, Richard Heathcote 7
HEINE, Peter Bernard William H
HEINEICKE, Arthur John 5
HEINEMAN, Walter Ben 1
HEINEMANN, E. 1
HEINEMANN, Edward H. 10
HEINEMANN, Gustav W. 7
HEINEMANN, Mitchell 9
HEINER, Gordon Graham 2
HEINER, Moroni 5
HEINER, Robert Graham 7
HEINFELDEN, Curt H. G. 9
HEINGARTNER, Robert Wayne 2
HEINICKE, Arthur John 9
HEINISCH, Don 6
HEINISCH, Don 7
HEINITSH, George W. 6
HEINL, Robert D. 3
HEINL, Robert Debs, Jr. 7
HEINLEIN, Mary Virginia 4
HEINLEIN, Robert Anson 9
HEINMILLER, Louis Edward 1
HEINMULLER, John P.V. 4
HEINO, Albert Frederic 3
HEINRICH, Antony Philip H
HEINRICH, Edward Oscar 3
HEINRICH, Helmut Gustav 7
HEINRICH, Rudolf 7
HEINRICH, Wilhelm 1
HEINRICHS, Charles E. 4
HEINRICHS, Jacob 2
HEINROTH, Charles 5
HEINS, Albert Edward 10
HEINS, George Lewis 1
HEINSHEIMER, Edward Lewis 1
HEINSOHN, Alvin 5
HEINTZ, Philip Benjamin 2
HEINTZELMAN, Arthur William 4
HEINTZELMAN, Samual Peter H
HEINTZELMAN, Stuart 1
HEINTZLEMAN, B. Frank 9
HEINTZLEMAN, Percival Stewart 2
HEINZ, Fred C. 4
HEINZ, Henry John 1
HEINZ, Henry John, II 10
HEINZ, Henry John, III 10
HEINZ, Howard 1
HEINZ, John Bernard 4
HEINZE, F. Augustus 1
HEINZE, Otto Charles 5
HEINZE, Robert Harold 8
HEINZE, Walter O. 9
HEINZEN, Karl Peter H
HEINZERLING, Lynn Louis 8
HEIRES, John Hopkins 9
HEISCHMANN, John J. 1
HEISE, Fred H. 2
HEISE, Herman Alfred 9
HEISEL, Thoms Bayard 1
HEISEN, Aaron Jonah 5
HEISENBERG, Werner 6
HEISER, Victor George 5
HEISERMAN, Arthur Ray 6
HEISERMAN, Clarence Benjamin 3
HEISING, Raymond Alphonsus 4
HEISKELL, Augustus Longstreet 8
HEISKELL, Frederick Hugh 1
HEISKELL, Henry Lee 1
HEISKELL, John Netherland 5
HEISKELL, Samuel G. 1
HEISLER, Charles Harrington 8
HEISLER, John Clement 1
HEISS, Austin Elmer 4
HEISS, Gerson Kirkland 5
HEISS, Marion Welch 4
HEISS, Michael H
HEISSENBUTTEL, John Diedrich 4
HEISTAND, Henry Olcot Sheldon 1
HEITFELD, Henry 1
HEITMAN, Charles Easton 3
HEITMAN, Francis Bernard 4
HEITSCHMIDT, Earl T. 5
HEIZER, Oscar Stuart 4
HEIZER, Robert Fleming 7
HEIZMANN, Charles Lawrence 4
HEKKING, William Mathews 5
HEKMA, Jacob 2
HEKMAN, Edward John 7
HEKMAN, John 3
HEKTOEN, Ludvig 3
HELANDER, Linn 9
HELBRON, Peter H
HELBURN, Theresa 3
HELCK, (Clarence) Peter 10
HELD, Adolph 7
HELD, Anna 1
HELD, John, Jr. 3
HELDER, H.A. 4
HELEN MADELEINE, Sister 8
HELFEN, Mathias 3
HELFENSTEIN, Edward Trail 2
HELFENSTEIN, Ernest H
HELFENSTEIN, John Albert Conrad H
HELFFERICH, Donald Lawrence 9
HELGESEN, Henry T. 1
HELLAND, Andreas 5
HELLBAUM, Arthur Alfred 4
HELLEGERS, Andre E. 8
HELLEMS, Fred Burton Renney 1
HELLENTHAL, John Albertus 2
HELLER, A. Arthur 4
HELLER, Ann Williams 10
HELLER, Edmund 1
HELLER, Edward Hellman 4
HELLER, Elinor Raas 9
HELLER, Erich 10
HELLER, Florence Grunsfeld 5
HELLER, Frank Henry 5
HELLER, Frank Morley 5
HELLER, George 3
HELLER, Helen West 3
HELLER, James Gutheim 5
HELLER, John Roderick, Jr. 10
HELLER, Joseph Milton 2
HELLER, Maximiliam 1
HELLER, Otto 1
HELLER, Philip Alter 7
HELLER, Philip Henri 10
HELLER, Robert 6
HELLER, Robert G. 8
HELLER, Victor H. 4
HELLER, Walter E. 5
HELLER, Walter Wolfgang 9
HELLER, William 4
HELLERSON, Charles Benedict 9
HELLIER, Charles Edward 1
HELLINGER, Ernst David 2
HELLINGER, Mark 2
HELLIWELL, Paul Lionel Edward 7
HELLMAN, C(larisse) Doris (Mrs. Morton Pepper) 6
HELLMAN, F.J. 4
HELLMAN, Geoffrey Theodore 7
HELLMAN, George Sidney 3
HELLMAN, Hugo Edward 6
HELLMAN, Isias William 1
HELLMAN, Isias William, Jr. 1
HELLMAN, Lillian 8
HELLMAN, Louis M. 10
HELLMAN, Marco H. 6
HELLMAN, Maurice S. 4
HELLMAN, Milo 2
HELLMAN, Morton J. 7
HELLMAN, Morton J. 8
HELLMAN, Sam 7
HELLMAN, Yehuda 9
HELLMUND, Rudolph Emil 2
HELLMUTH, Paul Francis 9
HELLRING, Bernard 10
HELLSTROM, Carl Reinhold 4
HELLWEG, J.F. 6
HELLYER, George Maclean 9
HELM, Charles Alton 8
HELM, Ebe Walter, Jr. 8
HELM, Harold Holmes 9
HELM, Harry Sherman 2
HELM, Harvey 1
HELM, James Meredith 1
HELM, (John) Blakey 9
HELM, John Charles H
HELM, John Larue H
HELM, Joseph Church 1
HELM, Margie May 10
HELM, Nathan Wilbur 6
HELM, Nelson 4
HELM, Roy 3
HELM, Thaddeus Geary 4
HELM, Thomas Kennedy 1
HELM, Wilbur 5
HELM, William P. 3
HELMBOLD, F. Wilbur 10
HELMER, B. Bradwell 1
HELMER, Frank Ambrose 1
HELMER, Hugh Joslin 8
HELMHOLZ, Henry Frederic 3
HELMICK, Eli Alva 2
HELMICK, Milton John 3
HELMICK, William H
HELMING, Oscar Clemens 1
HELMKE, Walter Edward 7
HELMLE, Frank J. 1
HELMPRAECHT, Joseph H
HELMS, Charles Brumm, Jr. 9
HELMS, E. Allen 7
HELMS, Edgar James 4
HELMS, Elmer Ellsworth 3
HELMS, Paul Hoy 3
HELMS, William H
HELMSLEY, William H
HELMUTH, Justus Henry Christian H
HELMUTH, William Tod* 1
HELPER, Hinton Rowan 1
HELPERN, Milton 7
HELPMAN, Dell A. 1
HELSER, Albert D. 5
HELSER, Maurice David 3
HELSON, Harry 7
HELSTEIN, Ralph L. 8
HELTMAN, Harry Joseph 4
HELTON, Roy Addison 7
HELVERING, Guy Tresillian 2
HELYAR, Frank G. 4
HEMANS, Lawton Thomas 1
HEMBDT, Phil Harold 1
HEMBORG, Carl August 4
HEMENWAY, Alfred 1
HEMENWAY, Augustus 1
HEMENWAY, Charles Clifton 5

HEMENWAY, Charles Francis 7
HEMENWAY, Charles Reed 2
HEMENWAY, Henry Bixby 1
HEMENWAY, Herbert Daniel 2
HEMENWAY, James Alexander 1
HEMENWAY, Mary Porter Tileston H
HEMEON, Wesley C. L. 9
HEMING, Arthur 1
HEMINGTON, Francis 2
HEMINGWAY, Allan 5
HEMINGWAY, Ernest 4
HEMINGWAY, Harold Edgar 2
HEMINGWAY, Harry J. 4
HEMINGWAY, James S. 4
HEMINGWAY, Louis Lee 7
HEMINGWAY, Samuel Burdett 3
HEMINGWAY, Walter Clarke 3
HEMINGWAY, Wilson Edwin 1
HEMINGWAY, Wilson Linn 3
HEMKE, Paul Emil 8
HEMLEY, Cecil 4
HEMLEY, Cecil 4
HEMLEY, Samuel 5
HEMMETER, Henry Bernard 2
HEMMETER, John Conrad 1
HEMPEL, Charles Julius H
HEMPEL, Frieda 3
HEMPHILL, Alexander Julian 1
HEMPHILL, Charles Robert 1
HEMPHILL, Clifford 4
HEMPHILL, James C. 7
HEMPHILL, James Calvin 1
HEMPHILL, John H
HEMPHILL, John James 1
HEMPHILL, Joseph 1
HEMPHILL, Joseph Newton 1
HEMPHILL, Robert Witherspoon 8
HEMPHILL, Victor Herman 3
HEMPHILL, William Arnold 1
HEMPHILL, William P. 4
HEMPL, George 1
HEMPSTEAD, Clark 3
HEMPSTEAD, Edward H
HEMPSTEAD, Fay 1
HEMRY, Charles W. 4
HEMSTREET, Charles 4
HENCH, Atcheson Laughlin 6
HENCH, Jay Lyman 4
HENCH, Philip Showalter 4
HENCHMAN, Daniel H
HENCK, John Benjamin 4
HENCKEN, Hugh O'Neill 8
HENDEE, George Ellsworth 1
HENDEE, Searle 8
HENDEL, Charles William 8
HENDEL, John William H
HENDEL, Samuel 9
HENDELSON, William H. 6
HENDERLITE, James Henry 3
HENDERSHOT, Clarence 7
HENDERSON, Alexander Iselin 4
HENDERSON, Alfred Edwin 5
HENDERSON, Algo Donmyer 9
HENDERSON, Archibald H
HENDERSON, Archibald 1
HENDERSON, Bennett H. H
HENDERSON, Bruce Doolin 10
HENDERSON, Byrd Everett 4
HENDERSON, C. Hanford 1
HENDERSON, Charles 1
HENDERSON, Charles Belknap 3
HENDERSON, Charles English 1
HENDERSON, Charles J. 4
HENDERSON, Charles Richmond 1
HENDERSON, Charles William 2
HENDERSON, Daniel 3
HENDERSON, David 1

HENDERSON, David Bremner 1
HENDERSON, David E. 6
HENDERSON, David English H
HENDERSON, Earl C. 3
HENDERSON, Edward 5
HENDERSON, Eldon Hazelton 5
HENDERSON, Elmer Lee 3
HENDERSON, Ernest 4
HENDERSON, Ernest Flagg 1
HENDERSON, Ernest Norton 1
HENDERSON, Everette L(on) 10
HENDERSON, George Bunsen 5
HENDERSON, George Logan 4
HENDERSON, Gerard C. 1
HENDERSON, Grace Mildred 5
HENDERSON, Harold Gould 6
HENDERSON, Harry Oram 8
HENDERSON, Harry Peters 6
HENDERSON, Helen Weston 5
HENDERSON, Herschel Bradford 10
HENDERSON, Howard Andrew Millet 1
HENDERSON, Isaac 1
HENDERSON, James Fletcher 4
HENDERSON, James Henry Dickey H
HENDERSON, James Michael 9
HENDERSON, James Monroe 4
HENDERSON, James Pinckney H
HENDERSON, John H
HENDERSON, John Armstrong 1
HENDERSON, John Brooks* 1
HENDERSON, John H. 4
HENDERSON, John Joseph 1
HENDERSON, John Moreland 1
HENDERSON, John O. 6
HENDERSON, John Steele 1
HENDERSON, John Thompson 3
HENDERSON, John William, Jr. 7
HENDERSON, Joseph H
HENDERSON, Joseph Lindsey 4
HENDERSON, Joseph W. 3
HENDERSON, Junius H
HENDERSON, Kenneth Manning 5
HENDERSON, Lawrence Joseph 1
HENDERSON, Leland John 5
HENDERSON, Leon 9
HENDERSON, Leon N. 4
HENDERSON, Leonard H
HENDERSON, Lester Dale 7
HENDERSON, Lizzie George 4
HENDERSON, Loy Wesley 9
HENDERSON, Lucile Kelling 10
HENDERSON, Mary N. Foote 4
HENDERSON, Melvin Starkey 3
HENDERSON, Paul 7
HENDERSON, Peronneau Finley 5
HENDERSON, Peter H
HENDERSON, Philip Eldon 3
HENDERSON, Ralph 10
HENDERSON, Richard Ernest H
HENDERSON, Robert 2
HENDERSON, Robert 3
HENDERSON, Robert Burns 1
HENDERSON, Robert Miller 1
HENDERSON, Samuel H
HENDERSON, Theodore Sommers 1
HENDERSON, Thomas H

HENDERSON, Thomas Howard 5
HENDERSON, Thomas Jefferson 1
HENDERSON, Thomas Stalworth 1
HENDERSON, Vivian Wilson 6
HENDERSON, Walter Brooks Drayton 2
HENDERSON, Walter C. 3
HENDERSON, William D. 2
HENDERSON, William James 1
HENDERSON, William Olin 1
HENDERSON, William Penallow 2
HENDERSON, William Price 2
HENDERSON, William Thomas 5
HENDERSON, William Williams 2
HENDERSON, Yandell 2
HENDERSON, Zach Suddath 8
HENDLER, L. Manuel 4
HENDON, Robert Randall 10
HENDREN, Linville Laurentine 6
HENDREN, Paul 3
HENDREN, William Mayhew 1
HENDRICK H
HENDRICK, Archer Wilmot 1
HENDRICK, Burton Jesse 2
HENDRICK, Calvin Wheeler 4
HENDRICK, Ellwood 1
HENDRICK, Frank 5
HENDRICK, Ives 5
HENDRICK, James Pomeroy 10
HENDRICK, John Thilman 2
HENDRICK, Michael J. 1
HENDRICK, Peter Aloysius 1
HENDRICK, Thomas Augustine 1
HENDRICK, William Jackson 4
HENDRICKS, ALlan Barringer, Jr. 5
HENDRICKS, Calvin 10
HENDRICKS, Eldo Lewis 1
HENDRICKS, Francis 4
HENDRICKS, Ira King 5
HENDRICKS, Thomas Andrews H
HENDRICKS, Thomas Armstrong 2
HENDRICKS, Walter 7
HENDRICKS, William H
HENDRICKSON, Charles Elvin 1
HENDRICKSON, George Lincoln 4
HENDRICKSON, Homer O. 3
HENDRICKSON, Robert C. 4
HENDRICKSON, William Woodbury 1
HENDRIX, Byron M. 7
HENDRIX, Eugene Russell 1
HENDRIX, Jimi 5
HENDRIX, Jospeh CLifford 1
HENDRIX, William Samuel 2
HENDRIXSON, Walter Scott 1
HENDRYSON, Irvin Edward 7
HENDRYX, James Beardsley 4
HENDY, Philip 9
HENEMANM, Harlow James 9
HENEY, Francis Joseph 1
HENGSBACH, Franz Cardinal 10
HENGST, James McCleery 4
HENGST, Raymond Guthrie 8
HENICAN, Joseph Padrick, Jr. 4
HENIE, Sonja 5
HENIGAN, George Francis 6
HENING, Benjamin Cabell 2
HENING, William Waller H
HENION, John Quint 8
HENIUS, Max 1
HENKE, Frederic Goodrich 4
HENKE, Robert Henry 7
HENKEL, Paul H

HENKIN, Daniel Zwie 9
HENKIND, Paul 9
HENKLE, Charles Zane 3
HENKLE, Eli Jones H
HENKLE, Rae Delancey 1
HENKLE, Roger Black 10
HENLE, Guy 10
HENLE, James 5
HENLEY, Robert H
HENLEY, Robert E. 4
HENLEY, Thomas Jefferson H
HENLEY, Walter Ervin 6
HENLINE, Henry Harrison 8
HENMON, Vivian Allen Charles 3
HENN, Albert William 3
HENN, Bernhart H
HENN, Mary J. 7
HENNE, Frances Elizabeth 9
HENNELLY, Mark M. 9
HENNEMAN, John Bell 1
HENNEMUTH, Robert George 6
HENNEPIN, Louis H
HENNEQUIN, Alfred 1
HENNESSEY, Thomas Michael 6
HENNESSY, Frank J. 6
HENNESSY, John 1
HENNESSY, John Francis 10
HENNESSY, John Francis 1
HENNESSY, John James 8
HENNESSY, John Joseph 1
HENNESSY, John Lawrence 3
HENNESSY, Michael Edmund 3
HENNESSY, Roland Burke 5
HENNESSY, Wesley Joseph 10
HENNESSY, William John 1
HENNESSY, William Thomas 4
HENNEY, Charles William F. 7
HENNEY, Richard Bernard 1
HENNEY, Richard Bernard 8
HENNEY, William Franklin 1
HENNI, John Martin H
HENNING, Arthur Sears 1
HENNING, Edward J. 1
HENNING, George Neeley 3
HENNING, O(scar) A(dam) 8
HENNINGER, G(eorge) Ross 10
HENNINGS, E. Martin 3
HENNINGS, Josephine Silva 9
HENNINGS, Thomas Carey 6
HENNINGS, Thomas Carey, Jr. 4
HENNINGSEN, Charles Frederick H
HENNISEE, Argalus Garey 1
HENNOCK, Frieda B. 4
HENNRICH, Kilian Joseph 2
HENNY, David Christian 1
HENREID, Paul (Paul Georg Julius von Hernried Ritter von Wasel-Waldingau)* 10
HENRETTA, James Edward 5
HENRI, Robert 1
HENRICH, John B. 7
HENRICH, V. C. 4
HENRICHS, Henry Frederick 6
HENRICI, Arthur Trautwein 2
HENRICI, Max 7
HENRICKS, Coleman Bresee 5
HENRICKS, Harold H. 3
HENRICKS, Namée (Mrs. Walter A Henricks) 8
HENRIQUES, Robert David Quixano 4
HENRIQUEZ-URENA, Max 5
HENRIQUEZ-URENA, Pedro 2
HENROTIN, Charles Martin H
HENROTIN, Ellen M. 1
HENROTIN, Fernand 1
HENRY, Albert P. H
HENRY, Alexander H
HENRY, Alexander 1
HENRY, Alfred Hylas 4
HENRY, Alfred Judson 1
HENRY, Andrew H
HENRY, Arnold Kahle 5
HENRY, Arthur 4

HENRY, Barklie McKee 4
HENRY, Bayard 1
HENRY, Caleb Sprague H
HENRY, Carl French 1
HENRY, Charles Daniel, II 8
HENRY, Charles Lewis 1
HENRY, Charles William 1
HENRY, Claude Morrison 1
HENRY, David W. 3
HENRY, Donald Lee 9
HENRY, Douglas Selph 5
HENRY, E. Stevens 1
HENRY, Edward Atwood 6
HENRY, Edward Lamson 1
HENRY, Eugene John 4
HENRY, Frank Anderson 7
HENRY, Frederick Augustus 2
HENRY, Frederick Porteous 4
HENRY, George Francis 4
HENRY, George Frederick 2
HENRY, George McClellan 5
HENRY, George William 4
HENRY, Guy Vernor 1
HENRY, Guy Vernor 4
HENRY, Harry DeWitte 8
HENRY, Heth H
HENRY, Horace Chapin 1
HENRY, Howard James 5
HENRY, Howell Meadors 3
HENRY, Hugh Carter 2
HENRY, Hugh Thomas 4
HENRY, J. Norman 1
HENRY, James H
HENRY, James Addison 1
HENRY, James Buchanan 8
HENRY, James McClure 3
HENRY, Jerry Maurice 6
HENRY, John* H
HENRY, John A. 10
HENRY, John Flournoy H
HENRY, John Martin 8
HENRY, J(ohn) Porter 5
HENRY, J(ohn) Porter 7
HENRY, John Robert 6
HENRY, John Robertson 4
HENRY, Joseph H
HENRY, Joseph Ward 7
HENRY, Jules 5
HENRY, Kate Kearney 1
HENRY, Langdon C. 4
HENRY, Lemuel H. 1
HENRY, Matthew George 6
HENRY, Morris Henry H
HENRY, Myron Ormell 3
HENRY, Nelson B(ollinger) 9
HENRY, Nelson Herrick 1
HENRY, O. 1
HENRY, Patrick H
HENRY, Patrick 3
HENRY, Philip Solomon 1
HENRY, Philip Walter 2
HENRY, Phineas McCray 8
HENRY, Ralph Coolidge 5
HENRY, Robert H
HENRY, Robert K. 2
HENRY, Robert Lee 1
HENRY, Robert Llewellyn, Jr. 7
HENRY, Robert Llewellyn, Jr. 5
HENRY, Robert Patterson 6
HENRY, Robert Pryor H
HENRY, Robert Selph 5
HENRY, Samuel Clements 5
HENRY, Sidney Morgan 3
HENRY, Stuart 3
HENRY, Thomas H
HENRY, Thomas P. 2
HENRY, Waights Gibbs 4
HENRY, Waights Gibbs, Jr. 10
HENRY, William* H
HENRY, William Arnon 1
HENRY, William Elmer 5
HENRY, William M. (Bill) 5
HENRY, William M. 8
HENRY, William Thomas 4
HENRY, William Wirt 1
HENRY-HAYE, Gaston 8
HENSCHEL, George 2
HENSCHEL, Lillian June Bailey H
HENSEL, H. Struve 10
HENSEL, William Uhler 1
HENSHALL, James Alexander 1
HENSHAW, Albert Melville 3
HENSHAW, Clement Long 10
HENSHAW, David H
HENSHAW, Francis Harold 7
HENSHAW, Frederic Rich 1
HENSHAW, Frederick William 1

HENSHAW, Harry Preston 7
HENSHAW, Henry Wetherbee 1
HENSHAW, Marshall B. 8
HENSHAW, Samuel 2
HENSHEL, Harry Davis 4
HENSKE, John M. 10
HENSKE, Joseph Aloysius 7
HENSLEY, Adelia Gates 1
HENSLEY, Richard Gibson 4
HENSLEY, Samuel J. H
HENSLEY, Sophia Almon 1
HENSLEY, Walter Lewis 2
HENSLEY, William Nicholas, Jr. 1
HENSON, Albert Lee 10
HENSON, Aubrey Eugene 5
HENSON, Clarence Cherrington 5
HENSON, Elmer D. 6
HENSON, James Maury 10
HENSON, John O'Neal 3
HENSON, Josiah 1
HENSON, Poindexter Smith 1
HENTHORNE, Norris Gifford 4
HENTZ, Caroline Lee Whiting H
HENTZ, Nicholas Marcellus H
HENWOOD, Berryman 3
HENYEY, Louis G(eorge) 1
HENZE, Henry Rudolf 6
HEPBRON, James M(erritt) 9
HEPBURN, A. Barton 1
HEPBURN, Andrew Dousa 1
HEPBURN, Andrew Hopewell 4
HEPBURN, Arthur Japy 4
HEPBURN, Charles Keith 5
HEPBURN, Charles McGuffey 1
HEPBURN, Frederick Taylor 3
HEPBURN, James Curtis 1
HEPBURN, Joseph Samuel 7
HEPBURN, Neil Jamieson 4
HEPBURN, Samuel 6
HEPBURN, William McGuffey 3
HEPBURN, William Murray 4
HEPBURN, William Peters 1
HEPLER, Alexander Brenner 8
HEPNER, Harry Walker 10
HEPNER, Walter Ray 6
HEPP, Maylon Harold 9
HEPPENHEIMER, Ernest J. 3
HEPPENHEIMER, William Christian
HEPPENSTALL, Robert B. 4
HEPPENSTALL, Thomas Earl 3
HEPTING, George Henry 9
HEPWORTH, Barbara 6
HEPWORTH, George Hughes 1
HERBEIN, B. William 5
HERBEN, Stephen Joseph 4
HERBER, Elmer Charles 8
HERBERG, Will 7
HERBERICK, Bernard Felix 7
HERBERMANN, Charles George 1
HERBERT, Addie Hibler 6
HERBERT, Sir A(lan) Patrick 5
HERBERT, Albert 1
HERBERT, Charles Jerome 9
HERBERT, Donald Roy 10
HERBERT, Edward 9
HERBERT, F. Hugh 3
HERBERT, F. M., Jr. 5
HERBERT, Frank Marion 8
HERBERT, Frank Patrick 9
HERBERT, Frederick Davis
HERBERT, Harold Harvey 8
HERBERT, Hilary Abner 1
HERBERT, Hugh 7
HERBERT, J. Joseph 3
HERBERT, James Cassidy 5
HERBERT, James M. 1
HERBERT, John Carlyle H
HERBERT, John F. J. 1
HERBERT, John I. H. 4
HERBERT, John Kingston 5
HERBERT, John Warne 1
HERBERT, Louis H
HERBERT, Paul M. 8
HERBERT, Philemon Thomas H
HERBERT, Thomas J(ohn) 6
HERBERT, Victor 1

HERBERT, Walter 6
HERBERT, William Henry H
HERBST, Josephine Frey 5
HERBST, Stanislaw 6
HERBST, William Parker 7
HERBSTER, Ben Mohr 9
HERBUT, Peter Andrew 7
HERD, John Victor 9
HERDER, Ralph Barnes 3
HERDIC, Peter 9
HERDMAN, Margaret M. 8
HERDMAN, William James 1
HEREFORD, Frank 1
HEREFORD, William Richard 1
HERFORD, Beatrice 5
HERFORD, Oliver 1
HERGESHEIMER, Joseph 3
HERGET, Paul 8
HERHOLZ, Alfred 4
HERHOLZ, Ottilie 4
HERING, Carl 1
HERING, Constantine H
HERING, Daniel Webster 1
HERING, Frank Earl 1
HERING, Henry 2
HERING, Hermann S. 1
HERING, Hollis Webster 2
HERING, Oswald Constantin 1
HERING, Rudolph 1
HERIOT, George H
HERKIMER, John H
HERKIMER, Nicholas H
HERLANDS, William Bernard* 5
HERLIHY, Charles Michael 2
HERLIHY, David Joseph 10
HERLIHY, Ernest Herbert 10
HERLIHY, John Albert 4
HERLY, Louis 2
HERMAN, Abraham 2
HERMAN, Alexander C. 6
HERMAN, Henry Edson Todd 3
HERMAN, James R. 3
HERMAN, Lebrecht Frederick H
HERMAN, Leon Emerson 3
HERMAN, Raphael 2
HERMAN, Robert Dixon 10
HERMAN, Stewart Winfield 6
HERMAN, Theodore Frederick 2
HERMAN, Woodrow Charles (Woody Herman) 9
HERMANCE, William Ellsworth 1
HERMANN, Binger 1
HERMANN, Edward Adolph 4
HERMANN, Grover Martin 8
HERMANNSSON, Halldor 3
HERMANOVSKI, Egils P. 10
HERMLE, Leo David 8
HERMS, William Brodbeck 3
HERMSEN, Edward Herman 5
HERNANDEZ, Benigno Cardenas 4
HERNANDEZ, Jose Conrado 1
HERNANDEZ, Joseph Marion 1
HERNANDEZ, Roberto 4
HERNDON, Charles Traverse 3
HERNDON, Fred E. 8
HERNDON, James B., Jr. 3
HERNDON, John Goodwin 3
HERNDON, Thomas Hord H
HERNDON, William Henry H
HERNDON, William Lewis H
HERNE, James A. 1
HERNE, Katherine Corcoran
HERNON, William Seton 3
HERO, Andrew, Jr. 1
HEROD, William 1
HEROD, William Pirtle 1
HEROD, William Pirtle
HEROD, William Rogers 6
HEROD, William Rogers 7
HEROLD, Amos Lee 7
HEROLD, Don 1
HEROLD, Don 8
HEROLD, Donald George 9
HEROLD, Jean Christopher 4
HERON, Alexander Richard 9
HERON, James Henry (Jamie Heron) 5
HERON, Matilda Agnes H

HERON, S. D. 4
HERON, William H
HEROY, James Harold 3
HEROY, William Bayard 5
HERR, Dan 10
HERR, Edwin Musser 1
HERR, Herbert Thacker 1
HERR, Hiero Benjamin 1
HERR, John H
HERR, John Knowles 6
HERR, Vincent V. 5
HERRE, Albert W. C. T. 4
HERREID, Charles N. 1
HERREID, Myron Tillman 4
HERRESHOFF, Charles Frederick 3
HERRESHOFF, J. B. Francis 1
HERRESHOFF, James Brown 1
HERRESHOFF, John Brown 1
HERRESHOFF, Nathaniel Greene 1
HERRICK, Alan Adair 10
HERRICK, Albert Bledsoe 4
HERRICK, Anson H
HERRICK, Charles Judson 3
HERRICK, Cheesman Abiah 3
HERRICK, Christine Terhune 2
HERRICK, Clarence Luther 1
HERRICK, Clinton B. 4
HERRICK, Curtis James 5
HERRICK, D-cady 1
HERRICK, Ebenezer H
HERRICK, Edward Claudius H
HERRICK, Elinore Morehouse 4
HERRICK, Elizabeth 5
HERRICK, Everett Carleton 3
HERRICK, Francis Hobart 1
HERRICK, Frederick Cowles 2
HERRICK, Genevieve Forbes (Mrs. John Origen Herrick) 5
HERRICK, George Frederick 1
HERRICK, George Marsh 4
HERRICK, George Q. 7
HERRICK, Glenn Washington 5
HERRICK, H. T. 7
HERRICK, H.T. 8
HERRICK, Harold 1
HERRICK, Harold Edward 8
HERRICK, Henry W. 1
HERRICK, Howard U. 7
HERRICK, Huldah 4
HERRICK, James Bryan 3
HERRICK, John Origen 5
HERRICK, Joshua H
HERRICK, Lott Russell 1
HERRICK, Lucius Carroll 1
HERRICK, Manuel 5
HERRICK, Mrs. Margaret Buck 7
HERRICK, Marvin Theodore 4
HERRICK, Myron T. 1
HERRICK, Parmely Webb 1
HERRICK, Paul Murray 5
HERRICK, Ray W. 5
HERRICK, Richard Platt H
HERRICK, Robert 1
HERRICK, Robert Frederick 2
HERRICK, Samuel H
HERRICK, Samuel H
HERRICK, Samuel Edward 1
HERRICK, Sophia M'Ilvaine Bledsoe 1
HERRICK, Stephen Solon 1
HERRICK, Walter R. 5
HERRIDGE, William Duncan 4
HERRIDGE, William Duncan 8
HERRIN, William Franklin 1
HERRING, Clyde Edsel 7
HERRING, Clyde Laverne 2
HERRING, Herbert James 5
HERRING, Hubert Clinton 3
HERRING, Hubert Clinton 5
HERRING, James H
HERRING, John Woodbridge 9
HERRING, Robert Ray 8
HERRING, Silas Clark H
HERRING, William 4

HERRINGTON, Arthur William Sidney 5
HERRINGTON, Cass E. 1
HERRINGTON, Hunley W(hatley) 7
HERRINGTON, Lewis Butler 6
HERRIOT, Edouard Marie 3
HERRIOTT, Frank Irving 2
HERRIOTT, Frank Wilbur 10
HERRIOTT, Irving 3
HERRIOTT, James Homer 5
HERRIOTT, Maxwell Haines 6
HERRLE, Colin 3
HERRMAN, Augustine H
HERRMAN, Esther 1
HERRMANN, Alexander H
HERRMANN, Bernard 6
HERRMANN, Carl Strauss 8
HERRMANN, Ernest Edward 3
HERRMANN, Henry Francis 4
HERRMANN, Richard 2
HERROLD, Lloyd Dallas William 9
HERRON, Charles 2
HERRON, Charles Douglas 5
HERRON, Clark Lincoln 1
HERRON, George Davis 1
HERRON, James Hervey 2
HERRON, John S. 2
HERRON, Rufus Hills 4
HERSCHDORFER, Manuel 3
HERSCHEL, Clemens 1
HERSCHELL, William 1
HERSCHER, Irenaeus Joseph 8
HERSCHLER, Edgar J. 10
HERSEY, George Dallas 1
HERSEY, Heloise Edwina 1
HERSEY, Henry Blanchard 2
HERSEY, Henry Johnson 1
HERSEY, Ira Greenlief 2
HERSEY, Jacob Daniel Temple 1
HERSEY, Mark Leslie 1
HERSEY, Mayo Dyer 7
HERSEY, Samuel Freeman H
HERSH, A. H. 3
HERSHEY, Amos Shartle 1
HERSHEY, Burnet 3
HERSHEY, Charlie Brown 3
HERSHEY, Harry Bryant 4
HERSHEY, John Willard 1
HERSHEY, Lewis Blaine 7
HERSHEY, Milton Snavely 1
HERSHEY, Omer F. 4
HERSHEY, Oscar H. 1
HERSHEY, Paris N. 3
HERSHEY, Robert Landis 6
HERSHEY, Scott F. 1
HERSHMAN, Mendes 10
HERSHMAN, Oliver Sylvester 1
HERSHOLT, Jean 3
HERSKOVITS, Melville Jean 4
HERSMAN, Charles Campbell 4
HERSMAN, Christopher C. 4
HERSMAN, Hugh Steel 3
HERSTEIN, Israel Nathan 9
HERT, Alvin Tobias 1
HERT, Sally Aley 2
HERTEL, Robert Russell 4
HERTER, Albert 3
HERTER, Christian H
HERTER, Christian Archibald 1
HERTER, Christian Archibald 4
HERTER, Christian Archibald 8
HERTERICK, Vincent Richard 5
HERTIG, Arthur Tremain 10
HERTS, B. Russell 3
HERTWIG, Charles Christian 9
HERTY, Charles Holmes 1
HERTY, Charles Holmes, Jr. 3
HERTZ, Alfred 2
HERTZ, Emanuel 1
HERTZ, Gustav Crane 5
HERTZ, John, Jr. 5
HERTZ, John Daniel 1
HERTZ, Richard Otto 4
HERTZBERG, Halfdan Fenton Harbo 7
HERTZBERG, Hans Rudolph Reinhart 1

HERTZBERG, Hazel Whitman 9
HERTZKA, Wayne Solomon 6
HERTZLER, Arthur Emanuel 2
HERTZLER, Charles William 4
HERTZLER, John Rowe 7
HERTZOG, Charles D(emetrius) 5
HERTZOG, Donald Paul 8
HERTZOG, Walter Scott 5
HERTZOG, Walter Sylvester 6
HERVAS Y PANDURO, Lorenzo H
HERVEY, Alpheus Baker 1
HERVEY, Daniel E. 4
HERVEY, Donald Franklin 6
HERVEY, Harcourt 5
HERVEY, Harcourt, Jr. 5
HERVEY, Harry Clay 3
HERVEY, James Madison 5
HERVEY, John Gaines 5
HERVEY, Walter Lowrie 3
HERVEY, William Addison 1
HERVEY, William Rhodes 3
HERZ, Martin Florian 8
HERZBERG, Donald Gabriel 7
HERZBERG, Joseph Gabriel 7
HERZBERG, Max J. 3
HERZBERGER, Maximillan Jakob 8
HERZBRUN, Helene McKInsey 9
HERZFELD, Karl Ferdinand 7
HERZIG, Charles Simon 1
HERZOG, Anna Edes 3
HERZOG, Felix Benedict 1
HERZOG, Maximilian Joseph 1
HERZOG, Paul M. 9
HERZSTEIN, Joseph 5
HESCHEL, Abraham Joshua 5
HESKETT, R(olland) M(cCartney) 9
HESKIN, Oscar E. 7
HESLER, Lexemuel Ray 7
HESLIN, Thomas 1
HESS, Alfred Fabian 1
HESS, Eckhard Heinrich 9
HESS, Elmer 4
HESS, Finley B. 5
HESS, Frank L. 3
HESS, Franklin 1
HESS, George (J.) 7
HESS, Harry Hammond 4
HESS, Henry 1
HESS, Herbert William 2
HESS, Jerome Sayles 5
HESS, Jerome Sayles 7
HESS, John Ambrose 7
HESS, Julius Hays 3
HESS, Leslie Elsworth 3
HESS, Max 5
HESS, Myra 4
HESS, Richard Cletus 10
HESS, Robert Lee 10
HESS, Seymour Lester 8
HESS, Thomas B. 7
HESS, Victor Francis 4
HESS, Walter J. 6
HESS, Walter Norton 8
HESS, Walter Rudolf 4
HESS, Wendell Frederick 3
HESSBERG, Albert 1
HESSBERG, Irving Kapp 2
HESSE, Bernard Conrad 1
HESSE, Frank McNeil 3
HESSE, Herman Carl 6
HESSE, Hermann 4
HESSE, Richard 6
HESSE, Seymour David 4
HESSELBERG, Edouard Gregory 1
HESSELIUS, Gustavus H
HESSELIUS, John H
HESSELLUND-JENSEN, Aage 6
HESSELTINE, William Best 4
HESSER, Ernest George 7
HESSER, Frederic William 3
HESSEY, John Hamilton 8
HESSLER, John Charles 2
HESSLER, William Henry 4
HESSON, Samuel Moodie 1
HESTER, Clinton Monroe 10
HESTER, Clinton Monroe 5
HESTER, E. Elizabeth 7
HESTER, Hugh Bryan 8
HESTER, John Hutchison 6

HILDRETH, Horace A. 9
HILDRETH, John Lewis 1
HILDRETH, Joseph S. 4
HILDRETH, Melvin Andrew 2
HILDRETH, Melvin Davis 3
HILDRETH, Richard H
HILDRETH, Samuel Prescott H
HILDRETH, William Sobieski 4
HILDT, John Coffey 1
HILDUM, Clayton Edward 3
HILEMAN, Donald Goodman 8
HILGARD, Eugene Woldemar 1
HILGARD, Ferdinand Heinrich Gustav H
HILGARD, Julius Erasmus H
HILGARTNER, Henry Louis 1
HILKEY, Charles Joseph 4
HILL, Adams Sherman 1
HILL, Agnes Leonard 1
HILL, Albert Hudgins 1
HILL, Albert Ross 2
HILL, Alferd J. 3
HILL, Alfred Gibson 5
HILL, Ambrose Powell H
HILL, Arthur B. 6
HILL, Arthur Dehon 2
HILL, Arthur Edward 1
HILL, Arthur Joseph 4
HILL, Arthur Middleton 5
HILL, Arthur Turnbull 1
HILL, Sir Austin Bradford 10
HILL, Bancroft 3
HILL, Benjamin Harvey H
HILL, Bert Hodge 3
HILL, Carlton 5
HILL, Mrs. Caroline Miles 3
HILL, Carolyn Bailey 4
HILL, Charles 4
HILL, Charles Edward 1
HILL, Charles Leander 3
HILL, Charles Lewis 3
HILL, Charles Shattuck 4
HILL, Chester James, Jr. 5
HILL, Claiborne Milton 3
HILL, Clarence Edwin 8
HILL, Claude Eugene 3
HILL, Clyde Milton 4
HILL, Crawford 1
HILL, Daniel A. 10
HILL, Daniel Grafton, Jr. 7
HILL, Daniel Harvey H
HILL, Daniel Harvey 1
HILL, David Bennett 1
HILL, David Garrett 5
HILL, David Jayne 1
HILL, David Spende 3
HILL, Derek Leonard 10
HILL, Donald MacKay 6
HILL, Douglas Green 9
HILL, Dudley Toll 7
HILL, Dumont Peck 1
HILL, Eben Clayton, M. D. 1
HILL, Ebenezer J. 1
HILL, Edgar Preston 1
HILL, Edmund Walton 6
HILL, Edward Burlingame 4
HILL, Edward Curtis 4
HILL, Edward Gurney 1
HILL, Edward Lee 6
HILL, Edward Llewellyn 3
HILL, Edward W. 8
HILL, Edward Yates 1
HILL, Edwin Conger 3
HILL, Emory 1
HILL, Ernest Rowland 2
HILL, Ernest W. 4
HILL, Ernie 3
HILL, Eugene DuBose 8
HILL, Eugene Lott 6
HILL, Everett Wentworth 7
HILL, Felix Robertson, Jr. 5
HILL, Francis (Charles) 5
HILL, Frank Alpine 1
HILL, Frank Davis 1
HILL, Frank Ernest 5
HILL, Frank Pierce 4
HILL, Fred Burnett 1
HILL, Frederic Stanhope H
HILL, Frederic Stanhope 4
HILL, Frederick Sinclair 3
HILL, Frederick Thayer 5
HILL, Frederick Trevor 3
HILL, G. Albert 4
HILL, George Alfred, Jr. 2
HILL, George Andrews 1
HILL, George Anthony 1
HILL, George Griswold 1
HILL, George Handel H
HILL, George Robert 6
HILL, George Washington 2
HILL, George William* 1

HILL, Gershom Hyde 1
HILL, Grace Livingston 2
HILL, Grover Bennett 4
HILL, Harold O. 4
HILL, Harry Granison 3
HILL, Harry Harrison 4
HILL, Harry W. 5
HILL, Henry Albert 3
HILL, Henry Alexander 4
HILL, Henry Clarke 3
HILL, Henry Wayland 4
HILL, Herbert Wynford 2
HILL, Hiram Warner 1
HILL, Horace Greeley 2
HILL, Howard Copeland 1
HILL, Hugh Lawson White H
HILL, Hyacinthe (Virginia Anderson Kain)* 10
HILL, Irving 5
HILL, Isaac H
HILL, Isaac William 4
HILL, J. B. P. Clayton 1
HILL, J. Gilbert 4
HILL, J. Murray 4
HILL, J. Stacy 1
HILL, James H
HILL, James 4
HILL, James, Jr. 3
HILL, James Brents 2
HILL, James Daniel 8
HILL, James Ewing 1
HILL, James J. 1
HILL, James Julian 9
HILL, James Langdon 1
HILL, James Levan 7
HILL, James Michael 4
HILL, James Norman 1
HILL, James Perminter 3
HILL, James Tomilson, Jr. 7
HILL, James W. 3
HILL, Janet McKenzie 1
HILL, Jim Dan 10
HILL, Joe H
HILL, Joe 4
HILL, John* H
HILL, John A. 3
HILL, John Alexander 1
HILL, John Calvin 6
HILL, John D(owning) 8
HILL, John Edward 1
HILL, John Ethan 4
HILL, John Fremont 1
HILL, John Godfrey 5
HILL, John Henry H
HILL, John Hub 9
HILL, John Leonard 6
HILL, John Lindsay 1
HILL, John M(cMurry) 8
HILL, John Sprunt 1
HILL, John Warren 8
HILL, John Wesley 1
HILL, John Wiley 8
HILL, John William H
HILL, Joseph Adna 1
HILL, Joseph Henry 1
HILL, Joseph Knoerle 1
HILL, Joseph Morrison 5
HILL, Joseph St Clair 4
HILL, Joshua 1
HILL, Judson Sudborough 1
HILL, Julien Harrison 2
HILL, Karl Allen 8
HILL, Knute 5
HILL, Lamar 1
HILL, Laurance Landreth 1
HILL, Lawrence 6
HILL, Lee H. 6
HILL, Leslie Pinckney 5
HILL, Lister 8
HILL, Lon Carrington 8
HILL, Louis A. 4
HILL, Louis Clarence 1
HILL, Louis Warren 2
HILL, Luther Lyons 10
HILL, Lysander 1
HILL, Mabel Jones 3
HILL, Marion 1
HILL, Mark Langdon H
HILL, Max 2
HILL, Merton Earle 1
HILL, Mozell Clarence 5
HILL, Nathaniel Peter 1
HILL, Nathaniel Peter 1
HILL, Noble H
HILL, Norman Llewellyn 7
HILL, Norman Stewart 5
HILL, Owen Aloysius 1
HILL, Owen Duffy 4
HILL, Patty Smith 2
HILL, Percival Smith 1
HILL, Pierre Bernard 3
HILL, Ralph Waldo Snowden 3
HILL, Randolph William 3
HILL, Reese Franklin 5
HILL, Reuben L.* 3

HILL, Reuben Lorenzo, Jr. 9
HILL, Rey Marshall 9
HILL, Richard H
HILL, Richard Johnson 10
HILL, Robert Andrews H
HILL, Robert Burns 8
HILL, Robert C. 7
HILL, Robert Carmer 2
HILL, Robert E. Lee 3
HILL, Robert Leland 9
HILL, Robert Madden 9
HILL, Robert Potter 1
HILL, Robert Thomas 1
HILL, Robert White 8
HILL, Robert William 4
HILL, Rolla Bennett 4
HILL, Roscoe R. 4
HILL, Ross D. 7
HILL, Samuel 1
HILL, Samuel S. 8
HILL, Sherwin A. 4
HILL, Theodore Albert 8
HILL, Theophilus Hunter 1
HILL, Thomas H
HILL, Thomas Bowen, Jr. 8
HILL, Thomas Edie 1
HILL, Thomas Foster 4
HILL, Thomas Guthrie Franklin 1
HILL, Thomas Russell 6
HILL, Thomas Russell 7
HILL, Tom Burbridge 4
HILL, Ureli Corelli H
HILL, Vassie James 3
HILL, Walker 1
HILL, Walter Barnard 1
HILL, Walter Clay 4
HILL, Walter Henry 1
HILL, Walter Newell 3
HILL, Warren E. 4
HILL, Whitmel H
HILL, William H
HILL, William A. 1
HILL, William Austin 3
HILL, William Bancroft 2
HILL, William Calvin 7
HILL, William Edwin 1
HILL, William Free 1
HILL, William H. 5
HILL, William Henry H
HILL, William Henry 1
HILL, William S. 1
HILL, William Silas 5
HILL, Wilson Shedric 1
HILLAIRE, Marcel 9
HILLARD, Charles W. 1
HILLARD, George Stillman H
HILLARD, Mary Robbins 1
HILLAS, Robert M. 3
HILLBRAND, Earl K. 4
HILLE, Einar (Carl) 7
HILLE, Gustav 4
HILLE, Hermann 4
HILLEARY, Edgar D. 5
HILLEBOE, Gertrude Miranda 8
HILLEBOE, Herman Ertresvaag 6
HILLEBRAND, Harold Newcomb 3
HILLEBRAND, William Francis 1
HILLEGAS, Howard Clemens 1
HILLEGAS, Michael H
HILLEN, Solomon, Jr. H
HILLENBRAND, Harold 9
HILLENKOETTER, Roscoe Henry 8
HILLENMEYER, Louis Edward 4
HILLER, Alfred 3
HILLER, Ernest Theodore 7
HILLER, Hiram Miliken 1
HILLES, Charles Dewey 2
HILLES, Frederick Vantyne Holbrook 5
HILLES, Frederick Whiley 4
HILLES, Frederick Whiley 7
HILLES, William Samuel 1
HILLHOUSE, James H
HILLHOUSE, James Abraham H
HILLHOUSE, James T(heodore) 8
HILLHOUSE, William 1
HILLIARD, Benjamin Clark 3
HILLIARD, Benjamin Clark, Jr. 5
HILLIARD, Curtis Morrison 1
HILLIARD, Edmund Bayfield 6
HILLIARD, Francis H

HILLIARD, Henry Washington H
HILLIARD, Isaac 5
HILLIARD, John Northern 1
HILLIARD, Raymond Marcellus 4
HILLIARD, Robert Cochran 1
HILLIARD, Thomas C. 4
HILLIER, William Herbert 9
HILLINGER, Raymond Peter 5
HILLIS, David H
HILLIS, Mrs. Newell Dwight 1
HILLIS, Newell Dwight 1
HILLIS, William H. 7
HILLMAN, Alex L. 5
HILLMAN, Arthur 8
HILLMAN, Bill (Clarence William Hillman) 10
HILLMAN, Charles Clark 8
HILLMAN, Christine Huff (Mrs. Howard S. Hillman) 6
HILLMAN, Herman David 7
HILLMAN, James Frazer 8
HILLMAN, James Noah 7
HILLMAN, John Hartwell, Jr. 3
HILLMAN, John William 5
HILLMAN, Lucy Rosaltha 4
HILLMAN, Sidney 2
HILLMAN, William 4
HILLQUIT, Morris 1
HILLS, Ada A. 1
HILLS, Elijah Clarence 1
HILLS, Elmer Walker 8
HILLS, Franklin Grant 4
HILLS, George Burkhart 8
HILLS, George Strough 7
HILLS, Joseph Lawrence 5
HILLS, Laura Coombs 3
HILLS, Laurence 1
HILLS, Lewis Samuel 1
HILLS, Oscar Armstrong 3
HILLS, Ralph Gorman 7
HILLS, Richard Charles 1
HILLS, Thomas McDougall 6
HILLS, Victor Gardiner 1
HILLS, William Henry 1
HILLYER, H. Stanley 3
HILLYER, Junius H
HILLYER, Robert Silliman 4
HILLYER, Thomas Arthur 4
HILLYER, Virgil Mores 1
HILLYER, William Hurd 4
HILMER, William Charles 5
HILPERT, Elmer Ernest 6
HILPRECHT, Herman Volrath 1
HILSBERG, Alexander 4
HILSON, Edwin I. 3
HILTABIDLE, William Orme, Jr. 10
HILTMAN, John Wolfe 1
HILTNER, Seward 9
HILTNER, William Albert 10
HILTON, Alexander 1
HILTON, Clifford L. 2
HILTON, Conrad N. 7
HILTON, David Clark 4
HILTON, Henry Hoyt 2
HILTON, Hugh Gerald 5
HILTON, James 7
HILTON, James Carroll 7
HILTON, James H. 8
HILTON, Warren 1
HILTON, William Atwood 6
HIMEBAUGH, Keith 1
HIMELICK, Alan Edward 10
HIMES, Charles Francis H
HIMES, Charles Francis 3
HIMES, Chester Bomar 8
HIMES, John Andrew 1
HIMES, Joseph Hendrix 4
HIMES, Joshua Vaughan H
HIMES, Norman Edwin 2
HIMLER, Leonard E. 5
HIMMEL, Joseph 1
HIMMELBLAU, David 4
HIMMELWRIGHT, Abraham Lincoln Artman H
HIMSTEAD, Ralph E. 3
HIMSWORTH, Winston E. 5
HINCHEE, Fred Lee 6
HINCHMAN, Walter Swain 6
HINCKLE, William H
HINCKLEY, Allen Carter 3
HINCKLEY, Edwin Smith 2
HINCKLEY, Frank Erastus 4
HINCKLEY, Frank L. 3
HINCKLEY, Frederic Allen 1

HINCKLEY, Frederick Wheeler 1
HINCKLEY, George Lyman 1
HINCKLEY, George W. 4
HINCKLEY, Julian 7
HINCKLEY, Robert 1
HINCKLEY, Robert Henry 9
HINCKS, Carroll Clark 4
HINCKS, Clarence Meredith 4
HINCKS, Edward Winslow 8
HINCKS, Edward Young 1
HINDEMITH, Paul 4
HINDERLIDER, Michael Creed 5
HINDLE, Norman Frederick 4
HINDLEY, George 4
HINDLEY, Howard Lister 2
HINDMAN, Albert Clare 1
HINDMAN, Baker Michael 5
HINDMAN, James Edward 4
HINDMAN, Thomas Carmichael H
HINDMAN, William H
HINDMARSH, Harry Comfort 3
HINDS, Anthony Keith 3
HINDS, Asher Crosby 1
HINDS, Ernest 2
HINDS, Frederick Wesley 1
HINDS, Henry 4
HINDS, James H
HINDS, John Iredelle Dillard 1
HINDS, Julian 6
HINDS, Thomas H
HINDS, Warren Elmer 1
HINDS, William Alfred 1
HINDS, William Lawyer 5
HINDUS, Maurice Gerschon 5
HINE, Charles Daniel 1
HINE, Charles De Lane 1
HINE, Clint C. 1
HINE, Francis Lyman 1
HINE, Jack 9
HINEBAUGH, William Henry 4
HINER, Louis Chase 9
HINER, Robert L. 6
HINERFELD, Benjamin 3
HINES, Charles 4
HINES, Charles Anderson 7
HINES, Duncan 3
HINES, Earl Kenneth 8
HINES, Earle Garfield 4
HINES, Edgar Alphonso 2
HINES, Edward 1
HINES, Edward Norris 1
HINES, Edward Warren 1
HINES, Frank Thomas 3
HINES, Harold H., Jr. 4
HINES, Harry Matlock 4
HINES, Herbert Waldo 7
HINES, Hugh Tim 7
HINES, J. F. 8
HINES, James Kollock 1
HINES, John Fore 5
HINES, John Leonard 3
HINES, Laurence Edward 3
HINES, Linnaeus Neal 1
HINES, Marion 8
HINES, Murray Arnold 5
HINES, Ralph J. 3
HINES, Richard H
HINES, Vincent Joseph 10
HINES, Walker Downer 1
HINGELEY, Joseph Beaumont 1
HINITT, Frederick William 1
HINKE, Frederick William 4
HINKE, Karl 10
HINKE, William John 2
HINKLE, Beatrice M. 3
HINKLE, Elmer Forry 3
HINKLE, Frederick Wallis 3
HINKLE, James Fielding 4
HINKLE, Ross Oel 3
HINKLE, Samuel Forry 8
HINKLE, Thomas Clark 2
HINKLE, Thornton Mills 1
HINKLEY, Alonzo Gibbs 4
HINKLEY, H. Lawrence 4
HINKLEY, J. William, III 3
HINKLEY, John 1
HINKS, Kennett Webb 10
HINKS, Kennett Webb 8
HINMAN, Alice Hamlin 1
HINMAN, Charlton Joseph Kadio 7
HINMAN, Dale Durkee 1
HINMAN, E(dgar) Harold 5
HINMAN, Elisha H
HINMAN, George Elijah 5

HINMAN, George Warren 1
HINMAN, George Wheeler 1
HINMAN, Harold J. 3
HINMAN, Harvey Deforest 3
HINMAN, Joel 1
HINMAN, John Holmes 7
HINMAN, Russell 1
HINMAN, Thomas Philip 1
HINRICHS, Carl Gustav 6
HINRICHS, Gustavus Detlef
HINRICHS, Gustavus Detlef 4
HINRICHSEN, Walter 5
HINRICHSEN, William H. 4
HINSCH, Charles Arthur 1
HINSDALE, Burke Aaron 1
HINSDALE, Ellen Clarinda 4
HINSDALE, Grace Webster
HINSDALE, Guy 2
HINSDALE, John Wetmore 1
HINSDALE, Wilbert B. 2
HINSEY, Joseph Clarence 7
HINSHAW, Carl 3
HINSHAW, Clifford Reginald 8
HINSHAW, David 1
HINSHAW, Edmund Howard 4
HINSHAW, Joseph Howard 5
HINSHAW, Melvin Taliaferro 6
HINSHAW, Virgil Goodman 3
HINSHAW, William Russell 8
HINSHAW, William Wade 2
HINSHELWOOD, Sir Cyril 4
HINSHELWOOD, Sir Cyril (Norman) 5
HINSMAN, Carl B. 5
HINSON, M. R. 4
HINSON, Noel Bertram 3
HINSON, Walter Benwell 1
HINTON, Charles Louis 3
HINTON, Edward Wilcox 1
HINTON, Fanny Darling 8
HINTON, H. D. 3
HINTON, Harold B. 3
HINTON, James William 5
HINTON, L. W. 6
HINTON, Ralph C. 7
HINTON, Raymond J. 3
HINTON, Walter 8
HINTON, William Miller 7
HINTZ, Alfred Edward 4
HINTZ, August McCurdy 7
HINTZ, Howard William 4
HINTZE, William Robert 7
HIPCHEN, Donald Eugene 10
HIPP, Herman Neel 8
HIPPLE, Alpheus Hugh 4
HIPPLE, Frank K. 1
HIPSHER, Edward Ellsworth 2
HIPSLEY, Elmer R. 5
HIRAMOTO, Masaji 8
HIRE, Chas
HIRES, Charles Elmer H
HIRES, Charles Elmer 4
HIRES, Harrison Streeter 1
HIROHITO, His Majesty 9
HIRONS, Frederic C. 1
HIRONS, Frederic Charles 4
HIRSCH, Alcan 1
HIRSCH, Arthur Henry 1
HIRSCH, Edwin Frederick 5
HIRSCH, Edwin Frederick 7
HIRSCH, Emil Gustav 8
HIRSCH, Felix Edward 8
HIRSCH, Frank E. 7
HIRSCH, Gustav 3
HIRSCH, Harold 1
HIRSCH, Harold Seller 10
HIRSCH, Howard Carlyle 10
HIRSCH, Irene Dorothea 5
HIRSCH, Isaac E. 2
HIRSCH, I(saac) Seth 6
HIRSCH, James Gerald 9
HIRSCH, John Frederick 4
HIRSCH, John Stephen 10
HIRSCH, Joseph 8
HIRSCH, Julius 7
HIRSCH, Leo Henry, Jr. 7
HIRSCH, Maurice 5
HIRSCH, Max 5
HIRSCH, Monroe Jerome 6
HIRSCH, Nathaniel David M'ttron 10
HIRSCHBERG, Michael Henry 1
HIRSCHBERG, Sanford Leon 4
HIRSCHFELD, Hans M. 4
HIRSCHFELD, Tomas Beno 9

HIRSCHFELDER, Arthur Douglass 2
HIRSCHFELDER, Joseph Oakland 10
HIRSCHFELDER, Joseph Oakland 1
HIRSCHHORN, Fred 2
HIRSCHLER, Frederic Salz 5
HIRSCHMAN, Louis Jacob 6
HIRSH, Herbert William 5
HIRSH, Hugo 1
HIRSHBERG, Albert Simon 6
HIRSHBERG, Herbert Simon 3
HIRSHBERG, Leonard Keene 5
HIRSHFELD, Clarence Floyd 1
HIRST, Barton Cooke 1
HIRST, Claude Marvin 8
HIRST, Henry Beck 1
HIRST, Robert Lincoln 4
HIRTH, Emma P. 3
HIRTH, Friedrich 1
HISAW, Frederick Lee 1
HISCOCK, Frank 1
HISCOCK, Frank Harris 2
HISCOCK, Ira Vaughan 9
HISE, Elijah H
HISE, Harley 8
HISGEN, Thomas Louis 1
HISLOP, Joseph 8
HISSONG, Clyde 9
HITCH, Arthur Martin 3
HITCH, Calvin Milton 5
HITCH, Robert Mark 1
HITCHCOCK, Abner Edward 4
HITCHCOCK, Albert Spear 1
HITCHCOCK, Alfred H
HITCHCOCK, Alfred Joseph 7
HITCHCOCK, Alfred Marshall 3
HITCHCOCK, Alvirus Nelson 4
HITCHCOCK, Caroline Hanks 4
HITCHCOCK, Charles A. 1
HITCHCOCK, Charles Baker 5
HITCHCOCK, Charles Henry 1
HITCHCOCK, Curtice 2
HITCHCOCK, Edward H
HITCHCOCK, Edward Asbury 1
HITCHCOCK, Embury 2
HITCHCOCK, Enos H
HITCHCOCK, Ethan Allen 1
HITCHCOCK, Frank Harris 1
HITCHCOCK, Frank Lauren 3
HITCHCOCK, Fred A(ndrews) 1
HITCHCOCK, Frederick Collamore 1
HITCHCOCK, Frederick Hills 1
HITCHCOCK, George 1
HITCHCOCK, George Collier 5
HITCHCOCK, Gilbert Monell 1
HITCHCOCK, Henry 1
HITCHCOCK, Henry Booth 1
HITCHCOCK, Henry-Russell 9
HITCHCOCK, Herbert E. 4
HITCHCOCK, Lauren Blakely 5
HITCHCOCK, Lucius Wolcott 2
HITCHCOCK, Peter 1
HITCHCOCK, Philip Stanley 7
HITCHCOCK, Phineas Warrener H
HITCHCOCK, Ripley 1
HITCHCOCK, Romyn 4
HITCHCOCK, Roswell Dwight H
HITCHENS, Arthur Parker 2
HITCHENS, William Frank 7
HITCHLER, Theresa 3
HITCHLER, Walter Harrison 3
HITCHMAN, Robert Bruce 8
HITCHNER, Elmer Reeve 9
HITE, Bert Holmes 1
HITE, George E., Jr. 3
HITE, Jost H

HITE, Lewis Field 2
HITE, Omar 8
HITER, Frank Ambrose 3
HITESMAN, Walter Wood 9
HITLER, Adolf 4
HITREC, Joseph George 5
HITSCHFELD, Walter Francis 9
HITT, Francis Guy 8
HITT, R. S. Reynolds 1
HITT, Robert Melvin, Jr. 5
HITT, Robert Roberts 1
HITTEL, Charles J. 4
HITTELL, John Sherzer 1
HITTI, Philip Khurl 7
HITZ, John 1
HITZ, Ralph 1
HITZ, William 1
HITZIG, William Maxwell 8
HIX, Asa Witt 4
HIX, Charles H. 1
HIXON, Ernest Howard 5
HIXON, A(rthur) Norman 7
HIXSON, Arthur Warren 6
HIXSON, Fred White 1
HIXSON, William Aase 6
HJELLE, John Orlo 8
HLAVATY, Vaclav 5
HNIZDO, Jaroslav 8
HO, Chi-minh 9
HO, Chinn 9
HOAD, William Christian 4
HOADLEY, David H
HOADLEY, Franklin Rogers 8
HOADLEY, George Arthur 1
HOADLEY, John Chipman H
HOADLEY, Leigh 6
HOADLY, George 1
HOAG, Arthur Edmund 7
HOAG, Clarence Gilbert 6
HOAG, David Doughty 1
HOAG, Ernest Bryant 1
HOAG, Frank Stephen 4
HOAG, George Grant 5
HOAG, Gilbert Thomas 4
HOAG, Joseph H
HOAG, Junius Clarkson 1
HOAG, Truman Harrison 4
HOAG, William Ricketson 4
HOAGE, Robert J. 5
HOAGLAND, Denis Robert 3
HOAGLAND, Henry E. 6
HOAGLAND, Hudson 9
HOAGLAND, John Hurle 4
HOAGLAND, Moses H
HOAGLAND, Warren Eugene 5
HOAGLUND, James B. 9
HOAN, Daniel Webster 4
HOAR, Ebenezer Rockwood H
HOAR, George Frisbie 1
HOAR, Leonard 4
HOAR, Rockwood 1
HOAR, Samuel H
HOARD, Charles Brooks H
HOARD, William Dempster H
HOARE, Elmer Joseph 5
HOBAN, Edward Francis 4
HOBAN, James 1
HOBAN, Michael John 1
HOBART, Aaron 1
HOBART, Alice Tisdale 4
HOBART, Alvah Sabin 1
HOBART, Douglas Roseberry 7
HOBART, Edward A. 8
HOBART, Franklin Gatfield 4
HOBART, Garret Augustus 1
HOBART, George Vere 1
HOBART, Harold Peckham 8
HOBART, Harrison Clayton 1
HOBART, Henry Metcalf 2
HOBART, Horace Reynolds 1
HOBART, John Henry H
HOBART, John Sloss H
HOBART, Lewis Parsons 3
HOBART, Mrs. Lowell Fletcher (Edith Liela) 5
HOBART, Marie Elizabeth Jefferys 1
HOBBES, Alan Buxton 5
HOBBIE, Henry Martin 3
HOBBIE, Selah Reeve H
HOBBINS, James R. 4
HOBBLE, Deborah Sharp 5
HOBBS, Alfred Charles H
HOBBS, Allan Wilson 4
HOBBS, Charles Seright 5
HOBBS, Charles Wood 4
HOBBS, Clark Simpson 8
HOBBS, Edward H. 1

HOBBS, Franklin Warren 3
HOBBS, George Sayward 4
HOBBS, Gustavus Warfield, Jr. 3
HOBBS, Ichabod Goodwin 1
HOBBS, James Randolph 2
HOBBS, John Edward 1
HOBBS, John Weston 4
HOBBS, Leland Stanford 4
HOBBS, Lewis Lyndon 4
HOBBS, Morris Henry 4
HOBBS, Nicholas 8
HOBBS, Perry L. 4
HOBBS, Ralph Waller 1
HOBBS, Roe Raymond 1
HOBBS, Roscoe Conklin 6
HOBBS, Sam Francis 3
HOBBS, William Herbert 3
HOBBS, William J. 4
HOBBY, William Pettus 4
HOBDY, John Buford 5
HOBEN, Allan 1
HOBEN, Lindsay 4
HOBGOOD, Charles Goyne 6
HOBGOOD, Frank P. 5
HOBLER, Atherton W. 6
HOBLER, Atherton W. 8
HOBLIT, Harris Keys 7
HOBLITZELL, John Dempsey, Jr. 4
HOBLITZELLE, Harrison 2
HOBLITZELLE, Karl 4
HOBSON, Alfred Norman 5
HOBSON, A(lphonso) Augustus
HOBSON, Asher 8
HOBSON, Benjamin Lewis 1
HOBSON, Edward Henry 1
HOBSON, Henry Wise 9
HOBSON, James Richard 10
HOBSON, Jesse Edward 5
HOBSON, John Peyton 1
HOBSON, Joseph Reid Anderson
HOBSON, Katherine Thayer 8
HOBSON, Laura Zametkin 5
HOBSON, Richmond Pearson 1
HOBSON, Robert Louis 5
HOBSON, Robert P. 4
HOBSON, Sarah Matilda 4
HOBSON, Stanley H. 4
HOBSON, T. Francis 4
HOBSON, Thayer 4
HOBSON, Wilder 4
HOBSON, William Andrew 5
HOBSON, William Horace 4
HOCA, Myron Myroslaw 5
HOCH, August 1
HOCH, Daniel K. 4
HOCH, Edward Wallis 1
HOCH, Homer 2
HOCH, Paul H. 4
HOCHBAUM, Hans Weller 3
HOCHDOERFER, Richard 4
HOCHE, Herman Emanuel 4
HOCHMUTH, Bruno Arthur 4
HOCHSCHILD, Harold K. 7
HOCHSTETTER, Robert William 5
HOCHWALD, Fritz G(abriel) 5
HOCHWALD, Werner 10
HOCHWALT, Albert Frederick 1
HOCHWALT, Carroll Alonzo 9
HOCHWALT, Frederick G. 4
HOCKADAY, Ela 5
HOCKEMA, Frank C. 3
HOCKENBEAMER, August Frederick 1
HOCKENSMITH, Wilbur Darwin 3
HOCKER, Lon O. 2
HOCKER, William Adam 4
HOCKETT, Homer Carey 5
HOCKING, Brian 6
HOCKING, William Ernest 4
HOCKLEY, Chester Fox 4
HOCKSTADER, Leonard Albert 4
HODDER, Alfred 1
HODDER, Frank Heywood 1
HODDINOTT, Ira Seymour 10
HODDINOTT, Mary Loretta 5
HODELL, Charles Wesley 1
HODES, Barnet 7
HODES, Henry Irving 4
HODES, Horace Louis 10
HODGDON, Albion Reed 4
HODGDON, Charles 3
HODGDON, Daniel Russell 7

HODGDON, Frank 1
Wellington
HODGDON, Frank Wilbert 4
HODGE, Archibald H
Alexander
HODGE, Bachman 4
Gladstone
HODGE, Caspar Wistar 1
HODGE, Charles H
HODGE, Clifton Fremont 4
HODGE, Edward B. 1
HODGE, Edward Blanchard 2
HODGE, Edwin, Jr. 9
HODGE, Edwin Rose, Jr. 4
HODGE, Elbert J. 9
HODGE, Frederick Webb 3
HODGE, Henry Wilson 1
HODGE, Hugh Lenox H
HODGE, Hugh Lenox 1
HODGE, James Campbell 8
HODGE, John Aspinwall 1
HODGE, John R. 4
HODGE, Kenneth Lavern 4
HODGE, Oliver 4
HODGE, Raymond Joseph 10
HODGE, Richard Morse 4
HODGE, Tobe 1
HODGE, Walter Hartman 6
HODGE, Walter Roberts 1
HODGE, Willard Wellington 4
HODGE, William 1
HODGE, William Irvine 5
HODGE, William Vallance Douglas 6
HODGEN, John Thompson H
HODGES, Arthur 4
HODGES, Brandon Patton 3
HODGES, Campbell Blackshear 2
HODGES, Charles 4
HODGES, Charles Drury H
HODGES, Charles H. 1
HODGES, Charles Libbens 1
HODGES, Courtney H. 4
HODGES, Elmer Burkett 9
HODGES, Frank 5
HODGES, Fred Murchison 9
HODGES, George 1
HODGES, George Hartshorn 2
HODGES, George Tisdale H
HODGES, Gilbert 5
HODGES, Gilbert Tennent 3
HODGES, Harry Foote 4
HODGES, Harry Marsh 4
HODGES, Henry Clay 1
HODGES, J(ames) Allison 7
HODGES, James Leonard H
HODGES, John Cunyus 4
HODGES, John Cunyus 5
HODGES, John Irel Hall 7
HODGES, John Sebastian Bach 1
HODGES, Johnny 5
HODGES, Joseph Gilluly 5
HODGES, Joseph Howard 8
HODGES, Leigh Mitchell 3
HODGES, Leroy 2
HODGES, Louise Threete 5
HODGES, Luther Hartwell 5
HODGES, Nathaniel Dana Carlile 1
HODGES, Richard Edward 4
HODGES, Richard Gilbert 6
HODGES, Thomas Edward 4
HODGES, Walter Edward 2
HODGES, William Franklin 3
HODGES, William Thomas 2
HODGES, William V. 4
HODGHEAD, Beverly Lacy 1
HODGIN, Charles Elkanah 4
HODGIN, Cyrus Wilburn 1
HODGINS, Eric 5
HODGKIN, Henry Theodore 1
HODGKIN, Wilfred Reginald Haughton 6
HODGKIN, William Newton 4
HODGKINS, Alton Ross 3
HODGKINS, Henry Follett 9
HODGKINS, Howard Lincoln 1
HODGKINS, Louise Manning 1
HODGKINS, William Candler 1
HODGKINSON, Francis 2
HODGKINSON, Harold Daniel 8
HODGKINSON, John H
HODGKINSON, Robert 9
HODGMAN, Burns P. 1
HODGMAN, T. Morey 4

HOWARD, Hubert Elmer 7
HOWARD, Jacob Merritt H
HOWARD, James E. 1
HOWARD, James J. 9
HOWARD, James Leland 6
HOWARD, James Quay 1
HOWARD, James Raley 3
HOWARD, John Don 6
HOWARD, John Eager H
HOWARD, John Eager 8
HOWARD, John Galen 1
HOWARD, John Raymond 1
HOWARD, John Tasker 4
HOWARD, John Zollie 10
HOWARD, Joseph, Jr. 1
HOWARD, Joseph Henry 3
HOWARD, Joseph Whitney 5
HOWARD, Julia Palmer 5
HOWARD, Karl S. 8
HOWARD, Kathleen 3
HOWARD, Lawrence 6
Augustus
HOWARD, Leland Ossian 3
HOWARD, Leon 8
HOWARD, Leslie 2
HOWARD, Louis Orrin 2
HOWARD, Lowry Samuel 2
HOWARD, Margaret 6
Douglas
HOWARD, Marion Edith 3
HOWARD, Mildred 6
Langford
HOWARD, Milford W. 4
HOWARD, Nathaniel 2
Lamson
HOWARD, Nathaniel 7
Richardson
HOWARD, Oliver Otis 1
HOWARD, Perry W. 4
HOWARD, Perry Wilbon 1
HOWARD, Philip Eugene 2
HOWARD, Ralph Hills 1
HOWARD, Rhea 7
HOWARD, Robert 8
Boardman
HOWARD, Robert Lorenzo 9
HOWARD, Robert 4
Mayburn
HOWARD, Rossiter 2
HOWARD, Roy Wilson 4
HOWARD, Seth Edwin 1
HOWARD, Sidney Coe 1
HOWARD, Stanley Edwin 8
HOWARD, Thomas Benton 1
HOWARD, Tilgham H
Ashurst
HOWARD, Timothy 1
Edward
HOWARD, Trevor Wallace 9
HOWARD, Velma 1
Swanston
HOWARD, Volney Erskine H
HOWARD, Walter 1
HOWARD, Walter Eugene 1
HOWARD, Walter 2
Lafayette
HOWARD, Wendell 4
Stanton
HOWARD, Wesley O. 1
HOWARD, Wilbert 4
Harvard
HOWARD, William H
HOWARD, William H
Alanson
HOWARD, William Clyde 3
HOWARD, William Eager, 5
Jr.
HOWARD, William 7
Edwards
HOWARD, William Gibbs 2
HOWARD, William 1
Lauriston
HOWARD, William Lee 1
HOWARD, William 1
Marcellus
HOWARD, William Schley 5
HOWARD, William Travis 5
HOWARD, Willie 3
HOWARTH, Ellen 1
Clementine
HOWAT, William Frederick 1
HOWBERT, Irving 1
HOWDEN, Frederick 1
Bingham
HOWE, Albert Richards H
HOWE, Albion Parris H
HOWE, Andrew Jackson H
HOWE, Anna Belknap 1
HOWE, Archibald Murray 1
HOWE, Arthur 3
HOWE, Arthur Millidge 2
HOWE, Burton Alonzo 3
HOWE, Carl 2
HOWE, Carl Ellis 4
HOWE, Charles Sumner 1
HOWE, Church 1
HOWE, Clarence Decatur 4

HOWE, Daniel Wait 1
HOWE, David Willard 9
HOWE, Edgar F. 5
HOWE, Edgar Watson 3
HOWE, Edmund Grant 3
HOWE, Edward Gardner 4
HOWE, Edward Leavitt 1
HOWE, Elias H
HOWE, Ernest 1
HOWE, Ernest Joseph 9
HOWE, Frank William 1
HOWE, Frederic Clemson 1
HOWE, Frederic William 3
HOWE, Frederic William, 5
Jr.
HOWE, Frederick Stanley 1
HOWE, Frederick Webster H
HOWE, Gene Alexander 1
HOWE, George H
HOWE, George 1
HOWE, George 3
HOWE, George 5
HOWE, George Augustus 1
HOWE, George Maxwell 5
HOWE, Harland Bradley 1
HOWE, Harley Earl 4
HOWE, Harold* 1
HOWE, Harold 7
HOWE, Harrison Estell 2
HOWE, Helen 6
HOWE, Henry H
HOWE, Henry Marion 1
HOWE, Henry Saltonstall 1
HOWE, Henry V(an 6
Wagsten)
HOWE, Herbert Alonzo 1
HOWE, Herbert Crombie 1
HOWE, Herbert Marshall 1
HOWE, J. Olin 1
HOWE, James Blake 1
HOWE, James Lewis 3
HOWE, James Wong 7
HOWE, Jerome Willard 7
HOWE, John Benedict 2
HOWE, John H. H
HOWE, John Ireland H
HOWE, John Lynn 6
HOWE, John W. H
HOWE, Jonas Holland H
HOWE, Julia Ward 1
HOWE, Lois Lilley 1
HOWE, Louis McHenry 1
HOWE, Lucien 1
HOWE, Malverd Abijah 4
HOWE, Mark Anthony De 1
Wolfe
HOWE, Mark Anthony De H
Wolfe
HOWE, Mark De Wolfe 4
HOWE, Marshall Avery 1
HOWE, Mary 4
HOWE, Oscar 9
HOWE, Percival S., Jr. 4
HOWE, Percival Spurr 1
HOWE, Percy Rogers 2
HOWE, Quincy 7
HOWE, Ralph S. 4
HOWE, Reginald Heber* 1
HOWE, Richard Flint 1
HOWE, Robert 2
HOWE, Samuel H
HOWE, Samuel Burnett 1
HOWE, Samuel Gridley H
HOWE, Stanley H. 3
HOWE, Stewart Samuel 5
HOWE, Thomas Carr 1
HOWE, Thomas Marshall H
HOWE, Thomas Y., Jr. H
HOWE, Timothy Otis H
HOWE, Wallis Eastburn 4
HOWE, Walter 1
HOWE, Walter 4
HOWE, Walter Bruce 3
HOWE, Will David 2
HOWE, Willard B. 1
HOWE, William* H
HOWE, William Augustus 1
HOWE, William Francis 1
HOWE, William Henry 1
HOWE, William Wirt 1
HOWE, Wirt 1
HOWELL, Clayton James 6
HOWELL, A. Brazier 4
HOWELL, Albert Charles 7
HOWELL, Alfred Corey H
HOWELL, Almonte Charles 9
HOWELL, Arthur Holmes 1
HOWELL, Benjamin 1
Franklin
HOWELL, Benjamin 7
Franklin
HOWELL, Benjamin 7
Randolph
HOWELL, Charles Cook 4
HOWELL, Charles Fish 2
HOWELL, Charles Robert 6
HOWELL, Clark 1

HOWELL, Clark 4
HOWELL, Corwin 6
HOWELL, Daniel Lane 4
HOWELL, Daniel William 2
HOWELL, David 1
HOWELL, David J. 9
HOWELL, Edward H
HOWELL, Edward Vernon 2
HOWELL, Edwin Eugene 1
HOWELL, Edwin Hite 1
HOWELL, Elias H
HOWELL, Elsworth 9
Seaman
HOWELL, Evan (George) 7
HOWELL, Evan P. 1
HOWELL, Francis 1
Singleton
HOWELL, George 4
HOWELL, George Blaine 1
HOWELL, Hannah Johnson 9
HOWELL, Herbert P. 2
HOWELL, Hilton Emory 5
HOWELL, J. Morton 1
HOWELL, James Albert 6
HOWELL, James Bruen H
HOWELL, James Edward 1
HOWELL, Jeremiah Brown 1
HOWELL, John Adams 1
HOWELL, John Adams 4
HOWELL, John Carnett 4
HOWELL, John White 1
HOWELL, Joseph 1
HOWELL, Joseph A. 3
HOWELL, Julius Franklin 2
HOWELL, Marion 8
Gertrude
HOWELL, Mary Seymour 1
HOWELL, Max Don 4
HOWELL, Meta Pauline 5
HOWELL, Nathaniel 1
Woodhull
HOWELL, R. Beecher 1
HOWELL, Reese M. 4
HOWELL, Richard H
HOWELL, Robert Boyte H
Crawford
HOWELL, Roger, Jr. 10
HOWELL, Roger William 5
HOWELL, Walter Rufus 2
HOWELL, Wilbur Samuel 10
HOWELL, William Barberle 1
HOWELL, William Henry 2
HOWELL, Williamson S., 1
Jr.
HOWELLS, John Mead 3
HOWELLS, Mildred 1
HOWELLS, William Dean 1
HOWER, Harry Sloan 2
HOWER, Milton Otis 1
HOWER, Paul Allen 4
HOWER, Ralph M. 6
HOWERTH, Ira Woods 1
HOWERTON, James 1
Robert
HOWERY, Bill Nelson 8
HOWES, Benjamin Alfred 3
HOWES, Ernest Grant 3
HOWES, Ethel Dench 4
Puffer
HOWES, Frank Stewart 1
HOWES, George Edwin 4
HOWES, Herbert Harold 1
HOWES, Royce B. 5
HOWES, William 4
Washington
HOWEY, Benjamin H
Franklin
HOWEY, Walter Crawford 3
HOWEY, William John 2
HOWIE, David Heath 7
HOWIE, Robert George 3
HOWISON, George Holmes 1
HOWISON, Henry 1
Lycurgus
HOWISON, Robert Reid 1
HOWKINS, Elizabeth 5
Penrose
HOWLAND, Alfred 1
Cornelius
HOWLAND, Alice 7
Gulielma
HOWLAND, Arthur 3
Charles
HOWLAND, Benjamin H
HOWLAND, Charles P. 1
HOWLAND, Charles 2
Roscoe
HOWLAND, Emily 1
HOWLAND, Frances 4
Louise
HOWLAND, Fred Arthur 4
HOWLAND, Frederick 1
Hoppin
HOWLAND, Gardiner 1
Greene
HOWLAND, Gardiner 1
Greene

HOWLAND, Garth A. 3
HOWLAND, Harold 4
HOWLAND, Harold 9
(Jacobs)
HOWLAND, Henry Elias 1
HOWLAND, Henry 1
Raymond
HOWLAND, Hewitt 2
Hanson
HOWLAND, John 1
HOWLAND, Joseph Briggs 5
HOWLAND, Leroy Albert 6
HOWLAND, Louis 1
HOWLAND, Marguerite 6
Elizabeth Smith (Mrs.
Cecil M. Howland)
HOWLAND, Murray 3
Shipley
HOWLAND, Paul 2
HOWLAND, Richard 10
Henry
HOWLAND, Richard 4
Smith
HOWLAND, Silas Wilder 1
HOWLAND, Thomas 1
Smith
HOWLAND, William 1
HOWLAND, William 1
Bailey
HOWLETT, Freeman 5
S(mith)
HOWLETT, James David 5
HOWLETT, Robert 10
Glasgow
HOWLETT, Walter Main 5
HOWLEY, Lee Christopher 8
HOWLEY, Richard 1
HOWORTH, M. Beckett 9
HOWRY, Charles Bowen 1
HOWSE, Hilary Ewing 1
HOWSE, W. L., Jr. 2
HOWSE, William Massy 6
Godwin
HOWSER, Richard Alton 9
HOWSON, Carl R(obert) 7
HOWSON, Elmer Thomas 4
HOWSON, Louis Richard 9
HOWSON, Roger 4
HOWZE, Henry Russell 5
HOWZE, Robert Lee 1
HOXIE, George Luke 5
HOXIE, Harold Jennings 5
HOXIE, Richard Leverige 1
HOXIE, Robert Franklin 1
HOXIE, Solomon 1
HOXIE, Vinnie Ream 1
HOXTON, Archibald 5
Robinson
HOXTON, Llewellyn 4
Griffith
HOXTON, William 1
Winslow
HOXWORTH, Stephen A. 4
HOY, Albert Harris 5
HOY, Carson 1
HOY, Patrick Henry 6
HOY, William Edwin 8
HOYER, Theodore 4
HOYLE, Eli Dubose 1
HOYLE, Rene Edward 7
Derussy
HOYME, Gjermund H
HOYNE, Archibald 4
Lawrence
HOYNE, Thomas MacLay 1
HOYNE, Thomas Temple 2
HOYNES, William 1
HOYOS, Henry 2
HOYO, John Charles 3
HOYT, Albert Ellis 4
HOYT, Albert Harrison 4
HOYT, Alex Crawford 6
HOYT, Allen Grey 1
HOYT, Arthur Stephen 1
HOYT, Austin 7
HOYT, Burnham 3
HOYT, Charles Albert 1
HOYT, Charles Hale 4
HOYT, Charles Kimball 1
HOYT, Charles Oliver 1
HOYT, Colgate 1
HOYT, Colgate 3
HOYT, Creig Simmons 3
HOYT, David Webster 1
HOYT, Deristhe Lavinta 5
HOYT, Edward C. 1
HOYT, Elizabeth Stone 3
HOYT, Elton, II 3
HOYT, Francis Southack 1
HOYT, Franklin Chase 1
HOYT, Gile Calvert 8
HOYT, Harold Wardwell 7
HOYT, Harrison Val 7
HOYT, Helen Brown 4
HOYT, Henry Augustus 4
HOYT, Henry Hamilton 10
HOYT, Henry Martyn H

HOYT, Henry Martyn 1
HOYT, Homer 8
HOYT, James Alfred 3
HOYT, James Humphrey 1
HOYT, James Phillips 4
HOYT, John Clayton 2
HOYT, John Philo 4
HOYT, John Sherman 3
HOYT, John Wesley 1
HOYT, Lucius Warner 1
HOYT, Minerva Hamilton 2
HOYT, Phillis Lucille 5
HOYT, Ralph H
HOYT, Ralph Melvin 9
HOYT, Ralph Wilson 1
HOYT, Richard Farnsworth 1
HOYT, Robert Joseph 10
HOYT, Robert Stuart 5
HOYT, Samuel Leslie 9
HOYT, Vance Joseph 8
HOYT, W. Henry 3
HOYT, Wayland 1
HOYT, Wilbur Franklin 1
HOYT, William Dana 2
HOYT, William Greeley 1
HRDLICKA, Ales 2
HROMADKA, Josef Luki 5
HSIA, David Yi-yung 5
HSU, Mo 3
HSU, Shuhsi 9
HUARD, Frances Wilson 7
(Baroness Huard)
HUARD, Leo A(lbert) 5
HUBACHEK, Frank 9
Brookes
HUBARD, Edmund Wilcox H
HUBARD, Robert 1
Thruston
HUBARD, William James H
HUBAY, Charles Alfred 10
HUBBARD, Adolphus 1
Skinner
HUBBARD, Alice 1
HUBBARD, Allen Skinner 9
HUBBARD, Anita Day 4
HUBBARD, Asahel H
Wheeler
HUBBARD, Bernard 4
Rosecrans
HUBBARD, Carlisle Le 6
Compte
HUBBARD, Charles J. 3
HUBBARD, Charles Wells 3
HUBBARD, Chester H
Dorman
HUBBARD, David H
HUBBARD, Demas, Jr. H
HUBBARD, Elbert 1
HUBBARD, Elbert 1
Hamilton
HUBBARD, Elijah Kent 1
HUBBARD, Elizabeth 10
Wright
HUBBARD, Frances 5
Virginia
HUBBARD, Frank Gaylord 4
HUBBARD, Frank 1
McKinney
HUBBARD, Frank W. 2
HUBBARD, Frank William 7
HUBBARD, Frederick A. 3
HUBBARD, Gardiner 1
Greene
HUBBARD, George David 3
HUBBARD, George Henry 4
HUBBARD, George 4
Whipple
HUBBARD, Giles Munro 3
HUBBARD, Gurdon H
Saltonstall
HUBBARD, Harry 1
HUBBARD, Havrah 5
William Lines
HUBBARD, Henry H
HUBBARD, Henry H
Griswold
HUBBARD, Henry 1
Guernsey
HUBBARD, Henry Vincent 2
HUBBARD, Henry Wright 1
HUBBARD, Howard S. 4
HUBBARD, John* H
HUBBARD, John 1
HUBBARD, John Charles 3
HUBBARD, John Henry H
HUBBARD, John Perry 10
HUBBARD, John W. 2
HUBBARD, Jonathan H
Hatch
HUBBARD, Joseph H
Stillman
HUBBARD, Kin 1
HUBBARD, L. Ron 9
HUBBARD, Leslie Elmer 4
HUBBARD, Lester 1
A(ndrews)

HUNTINGTON, Emily 1
HUNTINGTON, Faye 4
HUNTINGTON, Ford 2
HUNTINGTON, Frances Carpenter (Mrs. William Chapin) 5
HUNTINGTON, Frank 1
HUNTINGTON, Frederic Dan 1
HUNTINGTON, George 1
HUNTINGTON, George Herbert 3
HUNTINGTON, George Sumner 1
HUNTINGTON, Harwood 1
HUNTINGTON, Henry Alonzo 1
HUNTINGTON, Henry Barrett 4
HUNTINGTON, Henry Edwards 1
HUNTINGTON, Jabez H
HUNTINGTON, Jabez Williams H
HUNTINGTON, James Otis Sargent 1
HUNTINGTON, Jedediah H
HUNTINGTON, John Willard 7
HUNTINGTON, Lloyd Lee 4
HUNTINGTON, Margaret Evans 1
HUNTINGTON, Oliver Whipple 1
HUNTINGTON, Richard Lee 5
HUNTINGTON, Robert Watkinson 2
HUNTINGTON, Samuel* H
HUNTINGTON, Samuel 9
HUNTINGTON, Theodore Sollace 1
HUNTINGTON, Thomas Waterman 1
HUNTINGTON, Thomas Waterman 6
HUNTINGTON, Tuley Francis 1
HUNTINGTON, Warner Dare 1
HUNTINGTON, Whitney Clark 4
HUNTINGTON, William Chapin 3
HUNTINGTON, William Edwards 1
HUNTINGTON, William Reed 1
HUNTLEY, Charles R. 1
HUNTLEY, Chester Robert (Chet) 6
HUNTLEY, Elias Dewitt 1
HUNTLEY, Florence 1
HUNTLEY, Michel Carter 7
HUNTLEY, Samantha Littlefield 2
HUNTLEY, Victoria Hutson 5
HUNTLEY, William Russell 6
HUNTLY, Philip Conrad 7
HUNTON, Deane (Edward) 7
HUNTON, Eppa 1
HUNTON, Eppa, IV 7
HUNTON, Eppa, Jr. 1
HUNTON, William Lee 1
HUNTOON, Benjamin Bussey 1
HUNTOON, Gardner A. 5
HUNTOON, Louis Doremus 2
HUNTRESS, Carroll Benton 3
HUNTRESS, Frank G. 3
HUNTSMAN, Adam H
HUNTSMAN, Owen Benjamin 1
HUNTSMAN, Robert F. R. 2
HUNTZICKER, Harry Noble 8
HUNZIKER, Otto Frederick 3
HUNZIKER, Richard Overton 6
HUPP, James Lloyd 7
HUPP, John Cox 4
HUPPELER, Lambert Mathias 7
HUPPER, Roscoe Henderson 4
HUPPERTZ, John William 6
HUPPUCH, Winfield A. 4
HURBAN, Vladimir S. 2
HURD, Albert Arthur 1
HURD, Archer Willis 3
HURD, Arthur William 1
HURD, Carl Bently 10
HURD, Charles DeWitt 10
HURD, Charles Edwin 1
HURD, Charles W. B. 5
HURD, Edward Melville 1
HURD, Edward Payson* 1
HURD, Eugene 1
HURD, Frank Hunt H
HURD, Frederick William 8
HURD, George Arthur 1
HURD, George Edward 5
HURD, Guilford Lansing 5
HURD, Harry Boyd 2
HURD, Harvey Bostwick 1
HURD, Henry Mills 1
HURD, John Codman H
HURD, Lee Maidment 2
HURD, Louis Guthrie 1
HURD, Nathaniel H
HURD, Peter 9
HURD, Richard Melancthon 1
HURD, William Daniel 1
HURDLE, James Ernest 5
HURDON, Elizabeth 4
HURFF, Lindley Scarlett 5
HURIE, Wiley Lin 3
HURLBERT, William Henry H
HURLBURT, William Blair 7
HURLBUT, Byron Satterlee 1
HURLBUT, Edwin Wilcox 1
HURLBUT, Jesse Lyman 1
HURLBUT, Stephen Augustus H
HURLBUT, William N. 3
HURLEIGH, Robert Francis 7
HURLEY, Charles Francis 2
HURLEY, Donald Joseph 7
HURLEY, Edward Nash 1
HURLEY, Edward Timothy 3
HURLEY, George 3
HURLEY, James E. 1
HURLEY, James Franklin 1
HURLEY, John Patrick 2
HURLEY, John Richard 3
HURLEY, Joseph Patrick 4
HURLEY, Julien A. 7
HURLEY, Lawrence Francis 3
HURLEY, Leonard B. 4
HURLEY, Margaret Helene 4
HURLEY, Neil C. 2
HURLEY, Neil C., Jr. 4
HURLEY, Patrick Jay 4
HURLEY, Pearley B(liss) 6
HURLEY, Robert Augustine 5
HURLEY, Roy T. 5
HURLEY, Ruby 7
HURLEY, Stephen Edward 3
HURLEY, Thomas Dreux 8
HURLEY, William E. 3
HURLIN, Ralph Gibney 8
HURLL, Estelle May 1
HUROK, Sol 6
HURRELL, Alfred 1
HURREY, Clarence Barzillai 5
HURSH, Ralph Kent 4
HURST, Albert S. 2
HURST, Carlton Bailey 2
HURST, Charles Warner 2
HURST, Clarence Thomas 2
HURST, Fannie 4
HURST, Harold Emerson 5
HURST, John 1
HURST, John Fletcher 1
HURST, M. L. 7
HURST, Peter F(rederick) 5
HURST, William Henry 4
HURSTON, Zora Neale 3
HURT, Huber William 4
HURT, John Jeter 5
HURT, John Smith 4
HURT, John Tom 7
HURT, Rollin 4
HURTH, Peter Joseph 1
HURTY, John N. 1
HURTZ, Leonard E. 6
HURWITZ, Abraham 8
HURWITZ, Henry 4
HURWITZ, Henry, Jr. 10
HURWITZ, Leo 10
HURWITZ, Wallie Abraham 3
HUSAIN, Zaklr 5
HUSAK, Gustav 10
HUSBAND, Alexander Chapman 7
HUSBAND, George Rosewall 3
HUSBAND, Joseph 1
HUSBAND, Richard Wellington 1
HUSBAND, William Walter 2
HUSBANDS, Hermon H
HUSBANDS, Sam Henry 3
HUSE, Charles Phillips 3
HUSE, Charles Wells 6
HUSE, Harry Pinckney 2
HUSE, Howard Russell 8
HUSE, Raymond Howard 3
HUSE, William 3
HU-SHIH 4
HUSIK, Isaac 1
HUSING, Edward B. 4
HUSKINS, C. Leonard 3
HUSKINS, James Preston 2
HUSKINS, William Everett, Jr. 9
HUSS, George Morehouse 2
HUSS, Henry Holden 3
HUSSAKOF, Louis 6
HUSSEIN, Taha 6
HUSSERL, Edmond H
HUSSERL, Edmond 4
HUSSEY, Allen Sanborn 7
HUSSEY, Charles Lincoln 1
HUSSEY, Curtis Grubb H
HUSSEY, George Frederick, Jr. 8
HUSSEY, Hugh Hudson 8
HUSSEY, John Brennan 4
HUSSEY, Obed H
HUSSEY, Raymond 3
HUSSEY, Roland Dennis 4
HUSSEY, Russell Claudius 8
HUSSEY, Tacitus 4
HUSSEY, William Joseph 1
HUSSLEIN, Joseph 3
HUSSMAN, George H
HUSSON, Chesley Hayward 5
HUSTED, Elbert Ervin 9
HUSTED, James Delno 1
HUSTED, James William 1
HUSTED, James William 6
HUSTED, Ladley* 5
HUSTING, Berthold Juneau 2
HUSTING, Paul Oscar 1
HUSTIS, James H. 2
HUSTON, Abraham Francis 1
HUSTON, Charles H
HUSTON, Charles Andrews 1
HUSTON, Charles Lukens 3
HUSTON, Claudius Hart 3
HUSTON, Henry Augustus 5
HUSTON, Howard Riggins 3
HUSTON, John 9
HUSTON, Joseph Waldo 1
HUSTON, Luther Allison 6
HUSTON, Luther Allison 7
HUSTON, McCready 9
HUSTON, Ralph Chase 3
HUSTON, Ralph Ernest 5
HUSTON, S(imeon) Arthur 5
HUSTON, Stewart 5
HUSTON, Thad 1
HUSTON, Walter 4
HUSTVEDT, Sigurd Bernhard 7
HUTAFF, G. Harry 7
HUTCHENS, Francis Case 8
HUTCHENS, Frank Townsend 1
HUTCHENS, Raymond Paul 8
HUTCHEON, Robert James 1
HUTCHERSON, Dudley Robert 4
HUTCHESON, Allen Carrington, Jr. 4
HUTCHESON, David 4
HUTCHESON, Grote 2
HUTCHESON, John Bell 1
HUTCHESON, John Redd 4
HUTCHESON, Joseph C., Jr. 5
HUTCHESON, Joseph Chappell 4
HUTCHESON, Martha Brookes 5
HUTCHESON, Thomas Barksdale, Jr. 9
HUTCHESON, William Anderson 2
HUTCHESON, William L. 3
HUTCHIN, Clair Elwood, Jr. 7
HUTCHINGS, Frank Day 1
HUTCHINGS, George Ernest 6
HUTCHINGS, John Richard, Jr. 3
HUTCHINGS, Leslie Morton 3
HUTCHINGS, Leslie Morton 4
HUTCHINGS, Lester 3
HUTCHINGS, Paul Raymond 7
HUTCHINGS, Richard Henry 2
HUTCHINGS, William Lawrence 7
HUTCHINS, Augustus Schell 2
HUTCHINS, Charles Clifford 4
HUTCHINS, Charles Henry 1
HUTCHINS, Charles Lewis 4
HUTCHINS, Charles Pelton 1
HUTCHINS, Charles Thomas 1
HUTCHINS, Curtis Marshall 9
HUTCHINS, Edward Webster 1
HUTCHINS, Frank Avery 3
HUTCHINS, Frank Frazier 2
HUTCHINS, Harry Burns 1
HUTCHINS, James Calhoun 1
HUTCHINS, Jere Chamberlain 3
HUTCHINS, John H
HUTCHINS, John Corbin 1
HUTCHINS, John Sellers 8
HUTCHINS, Lee Milo 7
HUTCHINS, Lee Wilson 3
HUTCHINS, Robert Maynard 7
HUTCHINS, Robert Maynard 8
HUTCHINS, Robert Senger 10
HUTCHINS, Ross Elliott 8
HUTCHINS, Stilson 1
HUTCHINS, Thomas H
HUTCHINS, Waldo H
HUTCHINS, Wells Andrews H
HUTCHINS, Will 2
HUTCHINS, William J. 3
HUTCHINSON, Adoniram Judson Joseph H
HUTCHINSON, Anne H
HUTCHINSON, Aubry Vaughan 4
HUTCHINSON, B. Edwin 4
HUTCHINSON, Benjamin Peters H
HUTCHINSON, Cary Talcott 1
HUTCHINSON, Charles Lawrence 1
HUTCHINSON, Edith Stotesbury 5
HUTCHINSON, Edward 8
HUTCHINSON, Edward Prince 10
HUTCHINSON, Elijah Cubberley 1
HUTCHINSON, E(lizabeth) B(artol) Dewing 7
HUTCHINSON, Ely Champion 3
HUTCHINSON, Emlen 4
HUTCHINSON, Forney 5
HUTCHINSON, Frederick Lane 1
HUTCHINSON, George Alexander 3
HUTCHINSON, Howard 7
HUTCHINSON, J. Edward 9
HUTCHINSON, J. Raymond B. 4
HUTCHINSON, James H
HUTCHINSON, James Herbert 8
HUTCHINSON, John 1
HUTCHINSON, John Corrin 4
HUTCHINSON, John Harrison 9
HUTCHINSON, John Irwin 1
HUTCHINSON, John Wallace 1
HUTCHINSON, Joseph Baldwin 1
HUTCHINSON, Knox Thomas 3
HUTCHINSON, Mark Eastwood 5
HUTCHINSON, Maynard 9
HUTCHINSON, Melvin Tyler 6
HUTCHINSON, Myron Wells, Jr. 3
HUTCHINSON, Norman 1
HUTCHINSON, Paul 3
HUTCHINSON, Ray Coryton 6
HUTCHINSON, Robert Orland 3
HUTCHINSON, S. Pemberton 1
HUTCHINSON, Thomas H
HUTCHINSON, William K. 3
HUTCHINSON, William Spencer 2
HUTCHINSON, William Thomas 7
HUTCHINSON, Woods 1
HUTCHISON, Benjamin Franklin 1
HUTCHISON, Claude Burton 7
HUTCHISON, Frances Kinsley 4
HUTCHISON, Frederick William 3
HUTCHISON, George Wayland 2
HUTCHISON, Harvey Macleary 6
HUTCHISON, James Brewster 3
HUTCHISON, James Edgar 4
HUTCHISON, Joseph Carson 9
HUTCHISON, Martin Bell 1
HUTCHISON, Miller Reese 2
HUTCHISON, Ralph Cooper 4
HUTCHISON, Robert Alden 1
HUTCHISON, Stuart Nye 3
HUTCHISON, Stuart Nye 5
HUTCHISON, Stuart Nye, Jr. 9
HUTCHISON, Thomas L. 4
HUTCHISON, William Easton 3
HUTCHMAN, J(ohnston) Harper 5
HUTH, Donald Earl 9
HUTHMACHER, Jacob Joseph 10
HUTSON, Charles Woodward 1
HUTSON, Frederick Leroy 3
HUTSON, John B. 4
HUTSON, Joshua Brown 4
HUTSON, Leander C. 5
HUTSON, Richard H
HUTT, Henry 2
HUTT, Robert Bines Woodward 7
HUTTER, Donald Stephen 10
HUTTER, Francis 4
HUTTIG, Charles Henry 1
HUTTON, Barbara 7
HUTTON, Colin Osborne 5
HUTTON, Edward F. 4
HUTTON, Edward Hyatt 1
HUTTON, Frederick Remsen 1
HUTTON, Hugh McMillen 6
HUTTON, Hugh McMillen 7
HUTTON, James 7
HUTTON, James Buchanan 1
HUTTON, James Franklin 9
HUTTON, James Morgan 1
HUTTON, John Edward H
HUTTON, Josiah Lawson 5
HUTTON, Laurence 1
HUTTON, Leon 4
HUTTON, Levi W. 1
HUTTON, Mancius Holmes 1
HUTTON, Norman 1
HUTTON, Samuel Reed 4
HUTTON, Sidney Buchanan 7
HUTTON, William Edward 3
HUTTY, Alfred 3
HUTZLER, Albert David 4
HUTZLER, Albert David, Jr. 9
HUTZLER, Joel Gutman David 7
HUXFORD, Walter Scott 3
HUXLEY, Aldous Leonard 4
HUXLEY, Henry Minor 3
HUXLEY, Sir Julian Sorell 6
HUXMAN, Walter A. 5
HUXTABLE, Richard Scott 7
HUYCK, Edmund Niles 1
HUYKE, Juan Bernardo 6
HUYLER, John H
HUYSMANS, Camille 4
HYAM, Leslie Abraham 4
HYAMSON, Moses 2
HYATT, Alpheus 1
HYATT, Carl Britt 5
HYATT, Charles Eliot 1
HYATT, Edward 1
HYATT, Francis Marion 6
HYATT, Frank Kelso 3
HYATT, Gerhardt Wilfred 9
HYATT, Harry Middleton 8
HYATT, James Philip 6
HYATT, John Wesley 1
HYDE, Albert Alexander 1

IRVINE, Ralstone Robert 10
IRVINE, Robert Tate 1
IRVINE, William* H
IRVINE, William 1
IRVINE, William 4
IRVINE, William Bay 4
IRVINE, William Burriss 1
IRVINE, William Mann 1
IRVINE, Wilson Henry 4
IRVING, Frederick Carpenter 3
IRVING, George Henry, Jr. 1
IRVING, George Milton 4
IRVING, Sir Henry Brodribb 1
IRVING, Isabel 2
IRVING, John Beaufain H
IRVING, John Duer 1
IRVING, John Treat 1
IRVING, Jules 7
IRVING, Laurence 7
IRVING, Minna 4
IRVING, Paulus A. 4
IRVING, Peter 1
IRVING, Pierre Munro H
IRVING, Robert Augustine 10
IRVING, Robert Shippen 7
IRVING, Roland Duer H
IRVING, Thomas Patrick 4
IRVING, Washington H
IRVING, William H
IRWIN, Agnes 1
IRWIN, Bernard John Dowling 1
IRWIN, Charles Walter 1
IRWIN, Clinton Fillmore 5
IRWIN, David D. 8
IRWIN, Edith Alice 6
IRWIN, Edward M. 1
IRWIN, Elisabeth Antoinette 2
IRWIN, Forrest Atlee 7
IRWIN, Frederick Charles 5
IRWIN, George Le Roy 1
IRWIN, Graham Wilkie 10
IRWIN, Harry H(arrison) 8
IRWIN, Harry N. 3
IRWIN, Harvey S. 4
IRWIN, Herbert Milton 8
IRWIN, Inez Haynes 1
IRWIN, James Benson 10
IRWIN, James Ellis 6
IRWIN, James William 1
IRWIN, Jared H
IRWIN, John 1
IRWIN, John Arthur 4
IRWIN, John Nichol 1
IRWIN, John Scull 1
IRWIN, Kilshaw McHenry 1
IRWIN, Leon 10
IRWIN, May 1
IRWIN, Noble Edward 1
IRWIN, Richard Dorsey 10
IRWIN, Richard William 1
IRWIN, Robert Benjamin 1
IRWIN, Robert Forsythe, Jr. 4
IRWIN, Robert Winfred 5
IRWIN, Solden 1
IRWIN, Staford Leroy 3
IRWIN, Thomas H
IRWIN, W. Francis 1
IRWIN, Wallace 3
IRWIN, Walter McMaster 1
IRWIN, Warren W. 4
IRWIN, William Andrew 4
IRWIN, William Glanton 2
IRWIN, William Henry 2
IRWIN, William Wallace H
ISAAC, Charles Martin 7
ISAAC, Joseph Elias 6
ISAAC, Walter 10
ISAACS, Abram Samuel 1
ISAACS, Asher 4
ISAACS, Charles Applewhite 1
ISAACS, Edith J. R. 3
ISAACS, Harold Robert 9
ISAACS, Hart 4
ISAACS, Hart 1
ISAACS, Henry G. H
ISAACS, John Dove 4
ISAACS, John Dove, III 1
ISAACS, Kenneth L. 10
ISAACS, Lewis Montefiore 2
ISAACS, Moses Legis 5
ISAACS, Myer Samuel 1
ISAACS, Nathan 1
ISAACS, Raphael 4
ISAACS, Reginald Roderic 9
ISAACS, Rufus Philip 7
ISAACS, Samuel Myer 1
ISAACS, Stanley Myer 4
ISAACS, Walter F. 1
ISAACSON, Charles David 1
ISAACSON, Thorpe Beal 10

ISAACSON, William Joseph 8
ISAAK, Nicholas 6
ISACKS, Jacob C. H
ISBELL, Egbert Raymond 5
ISBELL, Horace Smith 10
ISBELL, Marion William 9
ISBRANDTSEN, Hans J. 3
ISE, John 7
ISELIN, Adrian 1
ISELIN, Charles Oliver 1
ISELIN, Columbus O'Donnell 5
ISELIN, Columbus O'Donnell 1
ISELIN, Ernest 3
ISELIN, Oliver 4
ISELIN, Philip H. 7
ISELY, Frederick B. 2
ISENSTEAD, Joseph Herman 6
ISERMAN, Maurice 7
ISERMAN, Michael 2
ISGRIG, Frederick Arthur 7
ISHAM, Asa Brainerd 4
ISHAM, Frederic Stewart 1
ISHAM, Henry Porter 5
ISHAM, Howard Edwin 4
ISHAM, Mary Keyt 2
ISHAM, Norman Morrison 2
ISHAM, Ralph Heyward 3
ISHAM, Samuel 1
ISHERWOOD, Benjamin Franklin 1
ISHERWOOD, Christopher 9
ISHIBASHI, Shojiro 8
ISHIDA, Reisuke 8
ISHIDA, Taizo 8
ISLE, John Stanley 10
ISLE, Walter Whitfield 3
ISMAY, Lord 4
ISOM, Edward Whitten 4
ISOM, Mary Frances 1
ISRAEL, Adrian Cremieux 10
ISRAEL, Arthur, Jr. 1
ISRAEL, Edward L. 1
ISRAEL, Harold Edward 4
ISRAEL, Rogers 1
ISRAEL, Sam, Jr. 4
ISRAELS, Carlos Lindner 5
ISRAELS, Sydney 7
ISSEKS, Samuel Shepp 3
ISSERMAN, Ferdinand Myron 5
ISTEL, Andre 4
ITTEL, George Alfred 4
ITTLESON, Henry 2
ITTLESON, Henry 6
ITTNER, Martin Hill 2
ITTNER, William Butts 1
ITURBI, José 7
IVAN, Franklin Baker 8
IVANISSEVICH, Oscar 1
IVANOWSKI, Sigismond De 5
IVEAGH, The Earl of 4
IVERSEN, Lorenz 4
IVERSEN, Lorenz 6
IVERSEN, Robert William 9
IVERSON, Alfred H
IVERSON, Marvin Alvin 7
IVERSON, Samuel Gilbert 1
IVES, Autustus Wright 4
IVES, Brayton 1
IVES, Charles E. 3
IVES, Charles John 4
IVES, Charles Taylor 4
IVES, Chauncey Bradley H
IVES, Clarence Albert 5
IVES, Eli H
IVES, Ernest Linwood 8
IVES, Frederic Eugene 1
IVES, Frederick Manley 1
IVES, George Burnham 1
IVES, Halsey Cooley 1
IVES, Herbert Eugene 3
IVES, Howard Chapin 2
IVES, Irving McNeil 4
IVES, James Edmund 2
IVES, James Merritt 1
IVES, Joel Stone 1
IVES, John Hiett 5
IVES, John Winsor 3
IVES, Joseph Christmas H
IVES, Joseph Moss 1
IVES, Levi Silliman H
IVES, Percy 1
IVES, Philip 9
IVES, Ralph Burkett 4
IVES, Sarah Noble 5
IVES, Sumner Albert 2
IVES, Willard H
IVEY, Alphonso Lynn 2
IVEY, Charles Herbert 4
IVEY, George Melvin 5
IVEY, Herbert Dee 4
IVEY, Joseph Benjamin 3

IVEY, Thomas Neal 1
IVEY, Zida Caswell 7
IVIE, John Mark 6
IVIE, Joseph Henry 2
IVIE, William Noah 5
IVINS, Anthony W. 1
IVINS, Antoine Ridgway 5
IVINS, Benjamin Franklin Price 4
IVINS, James S. Y. 4
IVINS, Lester Sylvan 4
IVINS, William Mills 5
IVINSON, Edward 1
IVISON, David Brinkerhoff 1
IVISON, Maynard C. 7
IVY, Andrew Conway 7
IVY, Hardy H
IVY, Horace MacAulay 7
IVY, Robert Henry 6
IVY, Robert Henry 7
IYENAGA, Toyokichi 3
IZARD, George H
IZARD, Ralph H
IZARD, Thomas C. 4

J

JABLONSKI, Wanda Mary 10
JABLONSKY, Harvey Julius 10
JACCARD, Walter M. 5
JACCHIA, Agide 1
JACK, Frederick Lafayette 3
JACK, George Whitfield 1
JACK, Glen Robert 10
JACK, James Robertson 3
JACK, John George 3
JACK, Summers Melville 4
JACK, Theodore Henley 4
JACK, William H
JACK, William Blake 2
JACK, William Harry 8
JACKLIN, Edward G. 5
JACKLING, Daniel Cowan 3
JACKMAN, Charles Lyman 4
JACKMAN, Howard Hill 4
JACKMAN, Wilbur Samuel 1
JACKS, Allen 6
JACKS, Horace Leonard 6
JACKS, Leo Vincent 5
JACKSON, A. V. Williams 1
JACKSON, Abraham Reeves H
JACKSON, Abraham Willard 1
JACKSON, Al 6
JACKSON, Albert Atlee 1
JACKSON, Albert Mathews 1
JACKSON, Allan 4
JACKSON, Amos Henry 3
JACKSON, Amos Wade 5
JACKSON, Andrew H
JACKSON, Andrew 4
JACKSON, Archer L. 7
JACKSON, Arnold S. 4
JACKSON, Arthur C. 3
JACKSON, Arthur Conard 6
JACKSON, Bennett Barron 4
JACKSON, Burris C. 4
JACKSON, Carl Newell 2
JACKSON, Carlton 6
JACKSON, Charles H
JACKSON, Charles (Reginald) 5
JACKSON, Charles Akerman 4
JACKSON, Charles Cabot 1
JACKSON, Charles Douglas 4
JACKSON, Charles H. Spurgeon 4
JACKSON, Charles Loring 1
JACKSON, Charles Samuel 1
JACKSON, Charles Shattuck 8
JACKSON, Charles Tenney 5
JACKSON, Charles Thomas H
JACKSON, Charles Warren 1
JACKSON, Chevalier 3
JACKSON, Chevalier L. 4
JACKSON, C(icero) Floyd 7
JACKSON, Claiborne Fox H
JACKSON, Clarence A. 7
JACKSON, Clarence Evert 9
JACKSON, Clarence Martin 2
JACKSON, Clifford Linden 1
JACKSON, Daniel Dana 1
JACKSON, David 1
JACKSON, David E. H
JACKSON, David H
JACKSON, David Sherwood 1
JACKSON, Dorothy Branch 1
JACKSON, Dugald Caleb 3
JACKSON, Dunham 2

JACKSON, E. Hilton 3
JACKSON, Ebenezer, Jr. H
JACKSON, Ed 3
JACKSON, Edith Banfield 7
JACKSON, Edward 1
JACKSON, Edward Brake H
JACKSON, E(dward) Franklin 6
JACKSON, Edward Payson 1
JACKSON, Elihu Emory 1
JACKSON, Elizabeth Noland 6
JACKSON, Elmore 9
JACKSON, Ernest Bryan 4
JACKSON, Francis H
JACKSON, Frank Dar 1
JACKSON, Frank Lee 5
JACKSON, Fred 7
JACKSON, Fred Schuyler 1
JACKSON, Frederic Ellis 2
JACKSON, Frederick John Foakes 1
JACKSON, Frederick Mitchell 3
JACKSON, Gabrielle Snow 4
JACKSON, George H
JACKSON, George Anson 1
JACKSON, George B. 2
JACKSON, George Edwards 1
JACKSON, George K. H
JACKSON, George Leroy 5
JACKSON, George Pullen 1
JACKSON, George Somerville 1
JACKSON, George Thomas 1
JACKSON, George Washington 1
JACKSON, Glenn Edward 8
JACKSON, Hall 4
JACKSON, Harold Pineo 8
JACKSON, Hazel Brill 10
JACKSON, Helen Maria Fiske Hunt 1
JACKSON, Henry 1
JACKSON, Henry Ezekiel 1
JACKSON, Henry Hollister 3
JACKSON, Henry Martin 8
JACKSON, Henry Melville 1
JACKSON, Henry Rootes 1
JACKSON, Henry S. 1
JACKSON, Herbert Spencer 3
JACKSON, Herbert W., Jr. 4
JACKSON, Herbert Worth 1
JACKSON, Hezekiah 7
JACKSON, Hezekiah 8
JACKSON, Holland Taylor Condict 1
JACKSON, Holmes 1
JACKSON, Howard Campbell, Sr. 4
JACKSON, Howell Edmunds H
JACKSON, J. Hugh 4
JACKSON, Jabez North 1
JACKSON, Jabez Young 1
JACKSON, James* H
JACKSON, James A. H
JACKSON, James Arthur 3
JACKSON, James Caleb 1
JACKSON, James F. 1
JACKSON, James Frederick 1
JACKSON, James Hathaway 1
JACKSON, James Kirkman 4
JACKSON, James Streshly H
JACKSON, Jesse Benjamin 2
JACKSON, John Adams 1
JACKSON, John Brinckerhoff 1
JACKSON, John Davies H
JACKSON, John Day 4
JACKSON, John Edward* 5
JACKSON, John Edwin 7
JACKSON, John Ellett 10
JACKSON, John George 3
JACKSON, John Gillespie 3
JACKSON, John Gillespie 6
JACKSON, John Henry 1
JACKSON, John J. 5
JACKSON, John Jay 1
JACKSON, John Long 2
JACKSON, John Nelson 9
JACKSON, Jonathan H
JACKSON, Joseph Cooke 1
JACKSON, Joseph Henry 2
JACKSON, Joseph Henry 5
JACKSON, Joseph Raymond 5
JACKSON, Joseph Webber H
JACKSON, Josephine Agnes 2
JACKSON, Katharine Johnson 3

JACKSON, Katherine Gauss 6
JACKSON, Lambert Lincoln 3
JACKSON, Laura (Laura Riding)* 10
JACKSON, Lee R. 9
JACKSON, Leonara (Mrs. William Duncan McKim) 6
JACKSON, Leroy Freeman 6
JACKSON, Lyman E. 6
JACKSON, Mahalia 6
JACKSON, Margaret Doyle 4
JACKSON, Margaret Weymouth 6
JACKSON, Martha 5
JACKSON, Mary Anna 1
JACKSON, McStay 4
JACKSON, Mercy Ruggles Bisbe H
JACKSON, Mortimer Melville H
JACKSON, N. Baxter 6
JACKSON, Patrick Tracy H
JACKSON, Paul Rainey 5
JACKSON, Percival E. 5
JACKSON, Percy 1
JACKSON, Philip Ludwell 3
JACKSON, Rachel Donelson H
JACKSON, Ralph Leroy 3
JACKSON, Raymond Thomas* 5
JACKSON, Reginald Henry 1
JACKSON, Richard 7
JACKSON, Richard, Jr. H
JACKSON, Richard Arbuthnot 1
JACKSON, Richard Harrison 5
JACKSON, Richard Seymour 6
JACKSON, Richard Seymour 7
JACKSON, Richard Webber 3
JACKSON, Robert 6
JACKSON, Robert Arnold 7
JACKSON, Robert Charles, Jr. 7
JACKSON, Robert Henry 10
JACKSON, Robert Houghwout 3
JACKSON, Robert Manson 6
JACKSON, Robert Tilden 8
JACKSON, Robert Tracy 2
JACKSON, Roscoe Bradbury 1
JACKSON, Russell 1
JACKSON, Samuel H
JACKSON, Samuel Charles 8
JACKSON, Samuel Dillon 3
JACKSON, Samuel MacAuley 1
JACKSON, Samuel Morley 2
JACKSON, Samuel P. H
JACKSON, Schuyler Wood 4
JACKSON, Seymour Scott 10
JACKSON, Sheldon 1
JACKSON, Shirley 4
JACKSON, Theodore Fredlinghuysen 4
JACKSON, Thomas Birdsall H
JACKSON, Thomas Broun 5
JACKSON, Thomas Herbert 1
JACKSON, Thomas Jonathan H
JACKSON, Thomas Woodrow 8
JACKSON, Thomas Wright 5
JACKSON, V. T. 3
JACKSON, Virgil Thomas, Sr. 4
JACKSON, Wilfred J. 3
JACKSON, Will Woodward 8
JACKSON, William* H
JACKSON, William 1
JACKSON, William Alexander 4
JACKSON, William Benjamin 1
JACKSON, William H(arding) 5
JACKSON, William Henry 2
JACKSON, William Hicks 1
JACKSON, William Humphreys 1
JACKSON, William J. 1
JACKSON, William Kenneth 2
JACKSON, William Neil 6
JACKSON, William Nichols 5
JACKSON, William Payne 2
JACKSON, William Purnell 1
JACKSON, William Terry H

JACKSON, William Thomas Hobdell 8
JACKSON, William Trayton 1
JACKSON, Willis Carl 8
JACKVONY, Louis V. 3
JACOB, Cary Franklin 7
JACOB, Charles Waldemar 10
JACOB, Frederick Murray 9
JACOB, Leonard 10
JACOB, Peyton 7
JACOB, Philip Ernest 9
JACOB, Richard Taylor 1
JACOB, Robert Byron 5
JACOBBERGER, Francis Benedict 4
JACOBI, Abraham 1
JACOBI, Frederick 3
JACOBI, Herbert J. 8
JACOBI, Herbert P. 5
JACOBI, Mary Putnam 1
JACOBS, Arthur P. 6
JACOBS, Benjamin Franklin 1
JACOBS, Bernard 6
JACOBS, Carl Marlon 4
JACOBS, Carl Nicholas 10
JACOBS, Charles M. 1
JACOBS, Charles Michael 1
JACOBS, Edwin Elmore 3
JACOBS, Elbridge Churchill 5
JACOBS, Fenton Stratton 4
JACOBS, Ferris, Jr. H
JACOBS, Fred Clinton 4
JACOBS, Harold 8
JACOBS, Harold Duane 3
JACOBS, Henry Barton 1
JACOBS, Henry Eyster 1
JACOBS, Henry L. 4
JACOBS, Israel H
JACOBS, J. Arthur 1
JACOBS, James Albert 7
JACOBS, James Najeeb 9
JACOBS, Jay Wesley 5
JACOBS, John Hall 4
JACOBS, John Marshall 4
JACOBS, Joseph 1
JACOBS, Joseph Benjamin 8
JACOBS, Joseph Earle 5
JACOBS, Joshua W. 1
JACOBS, Lawrence Pierce 7
JACOBS, Melville 5
JACOBS, Michael H
JACOBS, Michael William 4
JACOBS, Michel 3
JACOBS, Morris Elias 9
JACOBS, Myrl Lamont 3
JACOBS, Nathan Bernd 3
JACOBS, Nathan Ellis 9
JACOBS, Nathan L. 9
JACOBS, Nehemiah Pitman Mann 4
JACOBS, Norman Ernest 8
JACOBS, Pattie Ruffner 1
JACOBS, Paul 7
JACOBS, Randall 4
JACOBS, Tevis 6
JACOBS, Thornwell 3
JACOBS, Walter Abraham 4
JACOBS, Walter Ballou 1
JACOBS, Walter William 8
JACOBS, Whipple 3
JACOBS, William Plummer 2
JACOBS, William States 3
JACOBS, Woodrow Cooper 10
JACOBSEN, A. P. 6
JACOBSEN, Alfred 4
JACOBSEN, Bernhard Martin 1
JACOBSEN, Carlyle 6
JACOBSEN, Christian F. 7
JACOBSEN, Einar A. 5
JACOBSEN, Elnar A. 5
JACOBSEN, Ernest A. 8
JACOBSEN, Jerome Vincent 5
JACOBSEN, Lydik Slegumfeldt 7
JACOBSEN, Norman 6
JACOBSEN, Oscar Thorklid 10
JACOBSOHN, Simon Eberhard 1
JACOBSON, Alma Frank 10
JACOBSON, Arthur Clarence 3
JACOBSON, Avrohm 8
JACOBSON, Belle Elizabeth 5
JACOBSON, Carl Alfred 5
JACOBSON, Carl Frederick 2
JACOBSON, Edmund 8
JACOBSON, Fritz 1
JACOBSON, Gabe 2
JACOBSON, Irving 7
JACOBSON, Joel Ross 10
JACOBSON, John Christian H
JACOBSON, Leon Orris 10
JACOBSON, Morris Lazarev 4
JACOBSON, Moses Abraham 5
JACOBSON, Robert 9
JACOBSON, Samuel 6
JACOBSON, Samuel David 7
JACOBSSON, Per 4
JACOBSTEIN, Meyer 4
JACOBUS, David Schenck 3
JACOBUS, Donald Lines 8
JACOBUS, Melancthon Williams 1
JACOBY, George Alonzo 10
JACOBY, George W. 1
JACOBY, Harold 1
JACOBY, Henry Sylvester 3
JACOBY, J(ames) Ralph 6
JACOBY, Ludwig Sigmund H
JACOBY, Neil Herman 7
JACOBY, Oswald 8
JACOBY, Raymond W. 4
JACOBY, Robert Bird 9
JACOBY, Sidney Bernhard 10
JACOBY, William Lawall 1
JACOWAY, Henderson Madison 5
JACQUES, Sidney Bennett 4
JACQUES, William White 1
JACUZZI, Aldo Joseph 9
JADWIN, Edgar 1
JAECKEL, Theodore 1
JAECKLE, Edwin F. 10
JAEGER, Alphons Otto 3
JAEGER, Edmund Carroll 8
JAEGER, Gebhard 4
JAEGER, Richard L. 10
JAEGER, Werner Wilhelm 4
JAEGERS, Albert 1
JAEGERS, Augustine 6
JAEKEL, Frederic Blair 2
JAFFA, Myer Edward 1
JAFFÉ, Bernard Frederick Victor 8
JAFFE, David 10
JAFFE, David Lawrence 6
JAFFE, Hans H. 10
JAFFE, Louis Isaac 2
JAFFE, Sam 8
JAFFRAY, Clive Palmer 9
JAFFRAY, Clive Talbot 3
JAGEMANN, Hans Carl Gunther von 1
JAGENDORF, Moritz Adolph 9
JAGGAR, Thomas Augustus 1
JAGGAR, Thomas Augustus 3
JAGGARD, Edwin Ames 1
JAGGER, Dean 10
JAHN, Gunnar 5
JAHN, Theodore Louis 7
JAHN, Walter J. 5
JAHNCKE, Ernest Lee 4
JAHNCKE, P. F., Sr. 5
JAHNS, Richard Henry 8
JAHR, Torstein (Knutsson Torstensen) 5
JAINSEN, Wilson Carl 6
JAKOBSON, Roman 8
JAKOSKY, John Jay 4
JALBERT, Eugene Louis 9
JALLADE, Louis Eugene 3
JALONICK, George Washington, III 8
JALVING, Clarence Louis 10
JAMERSON, G(eorge) H. 5
JAMES, Marquis 3
JAMES, Addison Davis 4
JAMES, Albert Calder 4
JAMES, Albert William 6
JAMES, Alexander 2
JAMES, Alfred Farragut 3
JAMES, Alice Archer Sewall 3
JAMES, Amaziah Bailey H
JAMES, Aphie 5
JAMES, Arthur Curtiss 1
JAMES, Arthur Horace 5
JAMES, Arthur Horace 7
JAMES, Bartlett Burleigh 3
JAMES, Ben 4
JAMES, Benjamin F. 4
JAMES, Bushrod Washington 1
JAMES, Charles 1
JAMES, Charles Fenton 1
JAMES, Charles Franklin 9
JAMES, Charles P. 1
JAMES, Charles Tillinghast H
JAMES, Clifford Cyril 8
JAMES, D. Bushrod 1
JAMES, D. Willis 1
JAMES, Daniel, Jr. 7
JAMES, Darwin Rush* 1
JAMES, Donald Denny 5
JAMES, Edmund James 1
JAMES, Edward Christopher H
JAMES, Edward David 5
JAMES, Edward Holton 3
JAMES, Edward Washington 5
JAMES, Edwin H
JAMES, Edwin Leland 3
JAMES, Edwin Warley 5
JAMES, Eldon Revare 2
JAMES, Elias Olan 6
JAMES, Eric G. 9
JAMES, Ernest Kelly 7
JAMES, Fleming 3
JAMES, Fleming, Jr. 9
JAMES, Francis H
JAMES, Francis Bacon 1
JAMES, Frank Cyril 5
JAMES, Frank Lowber 1
JAMES, George 5
JAMES, George Francis 1
JAMES, George Oscar 1
JAMES, George Roosa 1
JAMES, George Wharton 1
JAMES, Harlean 6
JAMES, Harry Haag 8
JAMES, Henry* H
JAMES, Henry 1
JAMES, Henry 2
JAMES, Henry 4
JAMES, Herman Brooks 5
JAMES, James Alton 4
JAMES, James Charles 5
JAMES, James Charles 7
JAMES, Jesse Woodson H
JAMES, John 8
JAMES, John Edwin 4
JAMES, John V. 10
JAMES, Joseph B. 9
JAMES, Joseph Hidy 2
JAMES, Jules 7
JAMES, Louis 1
JAMES, Mary E. 1
JAMES, May Hall (May Winsor Hall) 6
JAMES, M(azey) Stephen 8
JAMES, Minnie Kennedy (Mrs. Wm. Carey James) 5
JAMES, Newton 8
JAMES, Ollie M. 1
JAMES, Ollie Murray 5
JAMES, Philip (Frederick Wright) 6
JAMES, Phillip 6
JAMES, Phillip 7
JAMES, Reese D. 4
JAMES, Richard Vernon 9
JAMES, Samuel Catlett 4
JAMES, Samuel Humphreys 4
JAMES, Thomas H
JAMES, Thomas Chalkley H
JAMES, Thomas Lemuel 1
JAMES, Thomas Potts H
JAMES, W. Frank 2
JAMES, Walter Belknap 1
JAMES, Walter Gilbert 2
JAMES, Warren William 2
JAMES, William 1
JAMES, William 4
JAMES, William Carey 3
JAMES, William Fleming 10
JAMES, William Hartford 1
JAMES, William John 1
JAMES, William Knowles 1
JAMES, William M. 3
JAMES, William P. 1
JAMES, William Roderick 2
JAMES, William Stubbs 4
JAMES, Wright Elwood 8
JAMESON, Edwin Cornell 4
JAMESON, Henry 1
JAMESON, Horatio Gates H
JAMESON, Jay Paul 7
JAMESON, John H
JAMESON, John Alexander H
JAMESON, John Butler 5
JAMESON, John Franklin 1
JAMESON, P. Henry 4
JAMESON, Patrick Henry 4
JAMESON, Robert Willis 3
JAMESON, Russell Parsons 3
JAMIESON, Charles Clark 1
JAMIESON, Donald Campbell 9
JAMIESON, Douglas James 6
JAMIESON, Edmund Scudder 1
JAMIESON, Francis Anthony 3
JAMIESON, Guy Arthur 4
JAMIESON, John Calhoun 8
JAMIESON, Robert Arthur 8
JAMIESON, Robert Cary 2
JAMIESON, Robert Gordon 8
JAMIESON, Thomas N. 4
JAMIESON, William D. 2
JAMIESON, William Edward 4
JAMISON, Alpha Pierce 5
JAMISON, Atha Thomas 2
JAMISON, Cecilia Viets 4
JAMISON, Charles Laselle 4
JAMISON, David H
JAMISON, David Lee 2
JAMISON, Joseph Warren 1
JAMISON, Minnie Lou 4
JAMISON, Monroe Franklin 1
JAMISON, Paul Bailey 5
JAMISON, Robert H. 4
JAMISON, Thomas Worth, Jr. 4
JAMISON, William Arbuckle 1
JANE, Robert Stephen 3
JANES, George Milton 1
JANES, Henry Fisk H
JANES, John Valle 5
JANES, Lewis George H
JANES, Lewis George 1
JANEWAY, Charles Alderson 7
JANEWAY, Edward Gamaliel 1
JANEWAY, Frank Latimer 4
JANEWAY, Phineas Allen 4
JANEWAY, Theodore Caldwell 1
JANIS, Elsie 3
JANIS, Irving Lester 10
JANIS, Jay 10
JANIS, Sidney 10
JANISSE, Denis R. 4
JANNEY, O. Edward 1
JANNEY, Russell 4
JANNEY, Samuel McPherson H
JANNEY, Thomas B. 1
JANNOTTA, Alfred Vernon 5
JANOWITZ, Morris 9
JANSEN, Ernest George 3
JANSEN, Marie 1
JANSEN, Peter 4
JANSEN, Reinier H
JANSEN, William 4
JANSON, Horst Woldemar 8
JANSS, Peter W(illiam) 5
JANSSEN, David 7
JANSSEN, E. C. 2
JANSSEN, Henry 2
JANSSEN, John 1
JANSSEN, Werner 10
JANSSENS, Francis H
JANSSON, Edward Fritiof 4
JANTZEN, Alice Catherine 8
JANUARY, William Louis 4
JANUASHEK, Francesca 1
JANVIER, Caesar A. Rodney 1
JANVIER, Catharine Ann 1
JANVIER, Charles 1
JANVIER, Margaret Thomson 1
JANVIER, Thomas Allibone 1
JANVRIN, Joseph Edward 1
JANZEN, Assar Gotrik 5
JANZEN, Cornelius Cicero 8
JANZEN, Danile H(ugo) 5
JAQUA, Albert Roscoe 3
JAQUA, Ernest James 5
JAQUA, Ernest James 7
JAQUES, Alfred 1
JAQUES, Bertha E. 2
JAQUES, Charles Everett 3
JAQUES, Florence Page 8
JAQUES, Francis Lee 5
JAQUES, Herbert 1
JAQUES, Willard W. 1
JAQUES, William Henry 1
JAQUESS, James Frazier H
JAQUESS, William Thomas 4
JAQUITH, Harold Clarence 2
JARBOE, Henry Lee 4
JARCHOW, Charles Christian 10
JARCHOW, Christian E. 9
JARDINE, David H
JARDINE, James Tertius 3
JARDINE, John Earle 3
JARDINE, John Earle, Jr. 5
JARDINE, William M. 3
JARECKY, Herman 4
JARMAN, John 8
JARMAN, Joseph Leonard 2
JARMAN, Lewis Wilson 3
JARMAN, Pete 3
JARMAN, Sanderford 3
JARMAN, Walton Maxey 7
JARMAN, Walton Maxey 8
JARMAN, William Jackson 7
JARNAGIN, Milton Preston 6
JARNAGIN, Spencer H
JARNEFELT, Eero 8
JARRATT, Devereaux H
JARRATT, Hill 5
JARRELL, Albert Polk 4
JARRELL, Albert Polk 5
JARRELL, Charles Crawford 5
JARRELL, James Hoyt 7
JARRELL, John Williams 7
JARRELL, Randall 4
JARRETT, Benjamin 2
JARRETT, Cora Hardy 5
JARRETT, Edwin Seton 1
JARRETT, Harry B. 6
JARRETT, William Ambrose 3
JARRETT, William Paul 1
JARRETT, William Paul 2
JARROLD, Ernest 4
JARVES, James Jackson H
JARVIE, James Newbegin 1
JARVIS, Charles H. H
JARVIS, Chester Deacon 2
JARVIS, David Henry 4
JARVIS, De Forest Clinton 4
JARVIS, Deming H
JARVIS, Edward H
JARVIS, George Tibbals 5
JARVIS, Harry Aydelotte 5
JARVIS, Howard Arnold 9
JARVIS, John Wesley H
JARVIS, Leonard H
JARVIS, Porter M. 10
JARVIS, Robert Edward Lee 5
JARVIS, Samuel M. 1
JARVIS, Thomas Jordan 1
JARVIS, Thomas Neilson 2
JARVIS, William H
JARVIS, William Chapman H
JASLOW, Robert Irwin 10
JASPER, Martin Theophilus 9
JASPER, William H
JASPERS, Karl 9
JASSPON, William Henry 3
JASTRAM, Edward Perkins 3
JASTROW, Joseph 2
JASTROW, Marcus 1
JASTROW, Morris, Jr. 1
JASZI, Oscar 3
JAUNCEY, George Eric MacDonnell 2
JAUREGUI, Guillermo Patterson y 1
JAVIS, Abraham H
JAVITS, Benjamin Abraham 6
JAVITS, Benjamin Abraham 7
JAVITS, Jacob Koppel 9
JAWORSKI, Leon 8
JAY, Clarence Hollingsworth 3
JAY, Eric George 10
JAY, Sir James H
JAY, John* H
JAY, John Clarkson 1
JAY, John Edwin 4
JAY, Lawrence Merton 1
JAY, Mary Rutherford 3
JAY, Milton 1
JAY, Nelson Dean 5
JAY, Peter Augustus H
JAY, Peter Augustus 1
JAY, Pierre 2
JAY, William* H
JAY, William 1
JAYCOX, Walter Husted 1
JAYNE, Anselm Helm 4
JAYNE, Benaiah Gustin 4
JAYNE, Caroline Furness 1
JAYNE, Henry Labarre 1
JAYNE, Horace 1
JAYNE, Horace Howard Furness 6
JAYNE, Joseph Lee 1
JAYNE, Walter Addison 1
JAYNES, Allan Brown 1
JAYNES, Lawrence C. 7
JEAN, Sister Anne 5
JEAN, Joseph 8
JEAN, Sally Lucas 5
JEANMARD, Jules Benjamin 3
JEANNERET, Marsh 10
JEANS, Philip Charles 3
JECK, George G. 5
JEFFE, Ephraim F. 9
JEFFEE, Saul 10
JEFFERDS, Vincent Harris 10
JEFFERIES, Emily Brown 6
JEFFERIS, Albert Webb 4
JEFFERIS, William W. 1
JEFFERS, Clyde G. 6

JEFFERS, Dwight Smithson 7
JEFFERS, Eliakim Tupper 1
JEFFERS, Henry William 3
JEFFERS, John Leroy 7
JEFFERS, Katharine R. 3
JEFFERS, Leroy 1
JEFFERS, Lewis Francis 8
JEFFERS, Robinson 4
JEFFERS, William 1
Hamilton
JEFFERS, William Martin 3
JEFFERS, William H
Nicholson
JEFFERSON, Benjamin 5
Lafayette
JEFFERSON, Bradley 4
Carter
JEFFERSON, Charles 1
Edward
JEFFERSON, Clarence 4
Ernest
JEFFERSON, Cornelia H
Burke
JEFFERSON, Elmer L. 9
JEFFERSON, Floyd 5
Wellman
JEFFERSON, Floyd 6
Wellman
JEFFERSON, Floyd 4
Wellman, Jr.
JEFFERSON, Howard B. 8
JEFFERSON, John Percival 1
JEFFERSON, Joseph H
JEFFERSON, Joseph* 1
JEFFERSON, Mark 4
JEFFERSON, Martha H
Wayles
JEFFERSON, Robert 4
JEFFERSON, Samuel 1
Mitchell
JEFFERSON, Thomas H
JEFFERY, Alexander Haley 9
JEFFERY, Edward Turner 1
JEFFERY, Edwin T. 7
JEFFERY, Elmore Berry 1
JEFFERY, Robert Emmett 1
JEFFERY, Rosa Griffith H
Vertner Johnson
JEFFERY, Warren Craig 7
JEFFERY, William Prentiss 3
JEFFERYS, Charles 3
William
JEFFERYS, Edward Miller 2
JEFFERYS, William 2
Hamilton
JEFFORDS, Elza H
JEFFORDS, Joe Sam 6
JEFFORDS, Lawrence 6
Suggs
JEFFORDS, Olin Merrill 4
JEFFORDS, Walter M., Jr. 10
JEFFRESS, Edwin Bedford 8
JEFFREY, A(rthur) A(llan) 7
JEFFREY, Edward Charles 4
JEFFREY, Frank Rumer 2
JEFFREY, Robert Hutchins 6
JEFFREY, Walter Roland 5
JEFFREYS, Charles
JEFFRIES, Benjamin Joy 1
JEFFRIES, Edward J. 3
JEFFRIES, John H
JEFFRIES, Louis Eugene 1
JEFFRIES, Millard Dudley 1
JEFFRIES, Walter Sooy 3
JEFFRIES, William 10
Worthington
JEFFRIS, Zay 4
JEFFRIS, Malcolm George 3
JEFFS, Charles Richardson 3
JEIDELS, Otto 2
JELINEK, Hans 10
JELKE, Ferdinand Frazier 3
JELKE, John Faris 4
JELKS, James Thomas 4
JELKS, John Lemuel 1
JELKS, William Dorsey 1
JELLEMA, William Harry 6
JELLIFF, Horatio F. H
JELLIFFE, Russell Wesley 9
JELLIFFE, Smith Ely 2
JELLIFFE, Walter Scribner 7
JELLINEK, Elvin M. 6
JELLINGHAUS, C. L. 3
JELLISON, Walter Fremont 1
JEMISON, David Vivian 3
JEMISON, Mary H
JEMISON, Robert 6
JEMISON, Robert, Sr. 1
JENCKES, Joseph* H
JENCKES, Joseph 5
Sherburne, Jr.
JENCKES, Marcien 5
JENCKES, Thomas Allen H
JENCKES, Virginia Ellis 6
JENCKES, Virginia Ellis 7
JENCKS, Millard Henry 1
JENIFER, Daniel* H
JENKINS, Ab 7

JENKINS, Albert Gallatin H
JENKINS, Alfred 3
Alexander, Jr.
JENKINS, Arthur 1
JENKINS, Burris, Jr. 4
JENKINS, Burris Atkins 2
JENKINS, C. Bissell 1
JENKINS, Charles Francis 1
JENKINS, Charles Francis 3
JENKINS, Charles Jones H
JENKINS, Charles Rush 5
JENKINS, Daniel Edwards 1
JENKINS, David Rhys 3
JENKINS, Douglas 6
JENKINS, E. Fellows 1
JENKINS, Edward Corbin 5
JENKINS, Edward Elmer 5
JENKINS, Edward Hopkins 1
JENKINS, Florence Foster 4
JENKINS, Frances 5
JENKINS, Francis A. 4
JENKINS, Frank Edwin 4
JENKINS, Frederick 1
Warren
JENKINS, George Franklin 1
JENKINS, Glenn Llewellyn 7
JENKINS, Harold Richard 10
JENKINS, Harry Earle 8
JENKINS, Harry Hibbs 6
JENKINS, Herbert 5
F(ranklin)
JENKINS, Herbert 5
Theodore
JENKINS, Hermon Dutilh 1
JENKINS, Herschel V. 4
JENKINS, Hilger Perry 5
JENKINS, Howard 1
Malcolm
JENKINS, J. Caldwell 3
JENKINS, James Alexander 4
JENKINS, James Alexander 5
JENKINS, James Graham 1
JENKINS, John H
JENKINS, John Henry 10
JENKINS, John J. 1
JENKINS, John Murray 3
JENKINS, John S., Jr. 5
JENKINS, John Stilwell H
JENKINS, Joseph Alton 7
JENKINS, Joseph Harley 6
JENKINS, Joseph J. 4
JENKINS, Lemuel H
JENKINS, MacGregor 1
JENKINS, Martin David 7
JENKINS, Micah H
JENKINS, Michael 1
JENKINS, Nathaniel H
JENKINS, Olaf Pitt 8
JENKINS, Oliver Peebles 1
JENKINS, Paul Burrill 1
JENKINS, Perry Wilson 3
JENKINS, Ralph Carlton 2
JENKINS, Ray Howard 7
JENKINS, Robert H
JENKINS, Robert Edwin 1
JENKINS, Robert Spurgeon 10
JENKINS, Romily James 5
Heald
JENKINS, Stephen 1
JENKINS, Thomas 5
JENKINS, Thomas Albert 4
JENKINS, Thomas 1
Atkinson
JENKINS, Thornton H
Alexander
JENKINS, Timothy H
JENKINS, Vernon Henry 3
JENKINS, William Adrian 6
JENKINS, William Dunbar 1
JENKINS, Will(iam) 6
F(itzgerald)
JENKINS, William J. 3
JENKINS, William Leroy 3
JENKINS, William M. 1
JENKINS, William Oscar 4
JENKINS, William Robert 10
JENKINS, William Robert 5
JENKINSON, Edward 9
Lealand
JENKINSON, Isaac 1
JENKINSON, Richard C. 1
JENKS, Albert Ernest 3
JENKS, Almet 4
JENKS, Almet Francis 1
JENKS, Arthur Byron 2
JENKS, Arthur Whipple 1
JENKS, Benjamin L. 4
JENKS, Clarence Wilfred 6
JENKS, Edward Watrous 1
JENKS, Edwin Hart 1
JENKS, Frank William 1
JENKS, George Augustus 1
JENKS, George Charles 1
JENKS, Henry Fitch 1
JENKS, James Lawrence 1
JENKS, Jeremiah Whipple 1
JENKS, John Edward 1

JENKS, John Story 2
JENKS, John Whipple H
Potter
JENKS, Joseph H
JENKS, Michael H
Hutchinson
JENKS, Orrin Roe 3
JENKS, Phoebe A. 1
Pickering
JENKS, Stephen Moore 6
JENKS, Thomas Elijah 9
JENKS, Tudor 1
JENKS, William H
JENKS, William Jackson 3
JENNE, James Nathaniel 1
JENNER, Albert Ernest, Jr. 9
JENNER, William Ezra 8
JENNESS, Benning H
Wentworth
JENNESS, Leslie George 5
JENNESS, Lyndon Yates 1
JENNESS, Theodora 4
Robinson
JENNETT, William Armin 8
JENNEWEIN, Carl Paul 7
JENNEY, Charles Albert 3
JENNEY, Charles Francis 1
JENNEY, Chester Ezekiel 6
JENNEY, Melvin Richard 7
JENNEY, Ralph E. 2
JENNEY, William Le 1
Baron
JENNEY, William Sherman 5
JENNINGS, Alvin R. 10
JENNINGS, Andrew 1
Jackson
JENNINGS, B. Brewster 5
JENNINGS, Charles 1
Godwin
JENNINGS, David H
JENNINGS, David 3
JENNINGS, Dean Southern 5
JENNINGS, Duncan 8
Tallmadge
JENNINGS, Edward Henry 1
JENNINGS, Edwin B. 4
JENNINGS, Elmer 1
Hayward
JENNINGS, Elzy Dee 1
JENNINGS, Frank 8
JENNINGS, Frank E. 5
JENNINGS, Frank Lamont 8
JENNINGS, Frederic Beach 4
JENNINGS, Hennen 1
JENNINGS, Henry Burritt 5
JENNINGS, Henry C. 1
JENNINGS, Herbert 2
Spencer
JENNINGS, Isaac, Jr. 5
JENNINGS, Joe Leslie 4
JENNINGS, John H
JENNINGS, John, Jr. 3
JENNINGS, John Edward 6
JENNINGS, John Joseph 1
JENNINGS, Jonathan 1
JENNINGS, Judson Toll 2
JENNINGS, Leslie Nelson 5
JENNINGS, Lewellyn A. 8
JENNINGS, Louis John 1
JENNINGS, Maria Croft 4
JENNINGS, Martin Luther 1
JENNINGS, Newell 1
JENNINGS, O. E. 4
JENNINGS, Oliver Gould 1
JENNINGS, Paul 9
JENNINGS, Percy Hall 6
JENNINGS, Richard 1
William
JENNINGS, Robert 4
William
JENNINGS, Roscoe G. 4
JENNINGS, Rudolph D. 3
JENNINGS, Samuel 3
Clemens
JENNINGS, Sidney 1
Johnston
JENNINGS, Stephen 5
Richard
JENNINGS, T. Albert 1
JENNINGS, W. Beatty 1
JENNINGS, Walter 1
JENNINGS, Walter Louis 2
JENNINGS, Wesley 5
William
JENNINGS, William 8
Howard
JENNINGS, William 9
Mitchell
JENNINGS, William 1
Sherman
JENNISON, Marshall 7
Walker
JENNISON, Ralph Drury 7
JENSEN, Alfred Julius 7
JENSEN, Alfred Julius 8
JENSEN, Ben Franklin 5
JENSEN, Cecil Leon 7

JENSEN, Christen 6
JENSEN, Christian Nephi 6
JENSEN, Elmer C. 3
JENSEN, Frank A. 2
JENSEN, George Albert 10
JENSEN, Howard C. 5
JENSEN, Jens 3
JENSEN, Jens 7
JENSEN, Johannes V. 3
JENSEN, John Christian 3
JENSEN, Leslie 1
JENSEN, Merrill Monroe 7
JENSEN, Merrill Monroe 8
JENSEN, Moroni Lundby 7
JENSEN, Moroni Lundby 8
JENSEN, Ralph Adelbert 2
JENSON, Sherman Milton 10
JENSON, Theodore Joel 8
JENT, John William 1
JENTE, Richard 3
JENTZSCH, Richard Alvin 1
JEPPSON, George 4
Nathaniel
JEPSEN, Glenn Lowell 6
JEPSON, Harry B. 3
JEPSON, Ivar Per 5
JEPSON, Samuel L. 1
JEPSON, William 2
JERGENS, Andrew 4
JERGER, Edward 7
Remington
JERITZA, Maria 8
JERMAIN, Louis Francis 1
JERMAN, Mrs. Cornelia 5
Petty
JERMAN, Thomas Palmer 6
JERMANE, William 4
Wallace
JERNBERG, Reinert 1
August
JERNEGAN, Marcus 2
Wilson
JERNEGAN, Prescott Ford 4
JERNIGAN, Charlton C. 3
JEROLOMAN, John 4
JEROME, Brother 3
JEROME, Chauncey H
JEROME, F(rank) J(ay) 7
JEROME, Harry 1
JEROME, William Travers 1
JERRARD, Jerry 4
JERSILD, Marvin A(mble) 5
JERTBERG, Gilbert H. 6
JERVEY, Harold Edward 6
JERVEY, Henry 2
JERVEY, Huger Wilkinson 2
JERVEY, James Postell 2
JERVEY, James Wilkinson 2
JERVIS, John Bloomfield H
JESNESS, Oscar Bernard 4
JESSE, Richard Henry 2
JESSE, Richard Henry 1
JESSE, William H(erman) 5
JESSEL, George 7
JESSEN, Carl Arthur 4
JESSEN, Herman Fredrick 8
JESSEN, Karl Detlev 1
JESSEPH, John Ervin 8
JESSOPP, Dudley Frederick 4
JESSUP, Andrew Simes 7
JESSUP, Charles Augustus 4
JESSUP, Edgar B. 4
JESSUP, Elon 7
JESSUP, Everett Colgate 1
JESSUP, Henry Harris 1
JESSUP, Henry Wynans 1
JESSUP, John Knox 7
JESSUP, Joseph John 3
JESSUP, Philip C. 9
JESSUP, Samuel 1
JESSUP, Walter Albert 2
JESTER, Beauford Halbert 2
JESTER, John Roberts 5
JESUP, Henry Griswold 1
JESUP, Morris Ketchum 1
JESUP, Thomas Sidney H
JETER, Frank Hamilton 3
JETER, Jeremiah Bell H
JETT, Daniel Boone 7
JETT, Ewell Kirk 4
JETT, Robert Carter 5
JETT, Thomas M. 4
JETTON, Clyde Thomas 10
JEWELL, Bert Mark 6
JEWELL, Edmund Francis 10
JEWELL, Edward Alden 2
JEWELL, Edward Oswell 9
JEWELL, Frederick Swartz 1
JEWELL, Harvey H
JEWELL, James Ralph 6
JEWELL, Jesse Dale 6
JEWELL, John Franklin 1
JEWELL, Louise Pond 2
JEWELL, Marshall H
JEWELL, Mary Frances 8
JEWELL, Theodore 1
Frelinghuysen

JEWELL, William Henry 3
JEWETT, Arthur Crawford 3
JEWETT, Charles 1
JEWETT, Charles Coffin H
JEWETT, Charles Webster 7
JEWETT, David H
JEWETT, Edward Hurtt 1
JEWETT, Frances Gulick 4
JEWETT, Frank Baldwin 2
JEWETT, Frank Baldwin, 9
Jr.
JEWETT, Frank Fanning 3
JEWETT, Frederick Stiles H
JEWETT, Freeborn H
Garretson
JEWETT, George Anson 1
JEWETT, George Franklin 1
JEWETT, George Frederick 3
JEWETT, Harry Mulford 1
JEWETT, Harvey C. 1
JEWETT, Harvey Chase, Jr. 3
JEWETT, Hugh 6
JEWETT, Hugh Judge 10
JEWETT, Hugh Judge H
JEWETT, James Richard 2
JEWETT, John Howard 1
JEWETT, John Howard 4
JEWETT, John Punchard H
JEWETT, Joshua Husband H
JEWETT, Luther H
JEWETT, Milo Parker H
JEWETT, Nelson J. 3
JEWETT, Rutger Bleecker 1
JEWETT, Sarah Orne 1
JEWETT, Sophie 1
JEWETT, Stephen Perham 5
JEWETT, Stephen Shannon 1
JEWETT, William H
JEWETT, William Cornell H
JEWETT, William Samuel H
Lyon
JEWETT, William Smith H
JIGGITTS, Louis Meredith 4
JILLSON, Willard Rouse 8
JIMENEZ, Enrique A. 8
JIMENEZ, Juan Ramon 3
JIMENEZ OREAMUNO, 2
Ricardo
JIMERSON, James 10
Compere, Sr.
JINNAH, Mahomed Ali 2
JLLEK, Lubor 6
JOANIS, John Weston 9
JOANNES, Francis Y. 3
JOAREZ, Benito H
JOB, Frederick William 4
JOB, Herbert Keightley 1
JOB, Robert 4
JOB, Thomas 2
JOBE, Morris Butler 8
JOBES, Harry C. 5
JOBIN, Raoul 6
JOBLING, James Wesley 4
JOBST, Norbert Raymond 6
JOBUSCH, Frederick Henry 9
JOCELYN, Nathaniel H
JOCELYN, Simeon Smith H
JOCELYN, Stephen Perry 1
JOCHEM, Anita M. 6
JOCHEMS, William Dennis 4
JOCHER, Katharine 8
JOCHER, Ernst 9
JOCKERS, Leslie Harter 9
JOECKEL, Carleton Bruns 7
JOEHR, Adolf 6
JOEKEL, Samuel Levinson 3
JOEL, George William 1
Freeman
JOERG, W. L. G. 3
JOESTING, Henry 4
Rochambeau
JOFFE, J(acob) S(amuel) 7
JOFFREY, Robert 9
(Abdullah Jaffa Bey
Khan)
JOHANN, Albert Eugene 8
JOHANN, Carl 1
JOHANNES, Francis 1
JOHANNSEN, Oskar 4
Augustus
JOHANSEN, Frederick 8
Andrew
JOHANSEN, George P. 4
JOHANSEN, John C. 4
JOHANSON, Perry Bertil 8
JOHL, Edwin Phillips 4
JOHN, Augustus E. 2
JOHN, Dewitt 9
JOHN, Sister Mary Francis 5
JOHN, John Price Durbin 1
JOHN, Otto Marion 7
JOHN, Samuel Will 4
JOHN, Waldemar Alfred 4
Paul
JOHN, William Mestrezat 4
JOHN, William Scott 3
JOHNES, Edward Rodolph 1

JOHNS, Carl Oscar 2
JOHNS, Charles A. 1
JOHNS, Choate Webster 4
JOHNS, Clarence D. 3
JOHNS, Clayton 1
JOHNS, Cyrus N. 10
JOHNS, Cyrus N. 5
JOHNS, Dale Martin 7
JOHNS, Frank Stoddert 5
JOHNS, George Sibley 1
JOHNS, Jay Winston 7
JOHNS, Jay Winston 8
JOHNS, John H
JOHNS, Joshua Leroy 2
JOHNS, Kensey H
JOHNS, Kensey, Jr. H
JOHNS, Ralph Stanley 7
JOHNS, Roy William 4
JOHNS, William Franklin 8
JOHNS, William Hingston 2
JOHNSEN, Erik Kristian 1
JOHNSEN, Harvey M. 10
JOHNSON, A. Dexter 9
JOHNSON, A. Theodore 4
JOHNSON, Aben 4
JOHNSON, Adam Rankin 4
JOHNSON, Adelaide 4
McFadyen
JOHNSON, Adna Romulus 4
JOHNSON, Alba Boardman 1
JOHNSON, Albert 3
JOHNSON, Albert Garfield 8
JOHNSON, Albert Henry 5
JOHNSON, Albert Mussey 2
JOHNSON, Albert Richard 4
JOHNSON, Albert 3
Rittenhouse
JOHNSON, Albert Williams 3
JOHNSON, Albin Iver 7
JOHNSON, Albinus Alonzo 4
JOHNSON, Alden Porter 5
JOHNSON, Alex Carlton 1
JOHNSON, Alexander 1
JOHNSON, Alexander H
Bryan
JOHNSON, Alexander H
Smith
JOHNSON, Alfred Le Roy 4
JOHNSON, Alfred Sidney 1
JOHNSON, Alice Frein 6
JOHNSON, Allan Chester 3
JOHNSON, Allen 1
JOHNSON, Alvin Saunders 5
JOHNSON, Amos Neill 6
JOHNSON, Andrew H
JOHNSON, Andrew 1
Gustavus
JOHNSON, Andrew N. 9
JOHNSON, Andrew W. 4
JOHNSON, Anna 2
JOHNSON, Anton J. 6
JOHNSON, Arlien 10
JOHNSON, Arnold Milton 3
JOHNSON, Arthur B. 7
JOHNSON, Arthur Charles 3
JOHNSON, Arthur E. 9
JOHNSON, Arthur Monrad 2
JOHNSON, Arthur Newhall 1
JOHNSON, Ashley Sidney 1
JOHNSON, Axel A. 4
JOHNSON, Axel Petrus 3
JOHNSON, B. Eleanor 7
JOHNSON, Bascom 3
JOHNSON, Ben* 2
JOHNSON, Benjamin Alvin 3
JOHNSON, Benjamin 1
Franklin
JOHNSON, Benjamin 1
Newhall
JOHNSON, Benjamin H
Pierce
JOHNSON, Bernard Lyman 2
JOHNSON, Bob 10
JOHNSON, Bolling Arthur 1
JOHNSON, Bradley Tyler 1
JOHNSON, Briard Poland 1
JOHNSON, Buford Jeanette 6
JOHNSON, Burt W. 1
JOHNSON, Bushrod Rust H
JOHNSON, Byron 3
JOHNSON, Byron 1
JOHNSON, Byron Arthur 4
JOHNSON, Byron Bancroft 4
JOHNSON, Campbell 5
Carrington
JOHNSON, Carl Edward 5
JOHNSON, Carl Gunnard 5
JOHNSON, Carl W. 3
JOHNSON, Carl Wright 10
JOHNSON, Carlton Myles 7
JOHNSON, Cave H
JOHNSON, Chapman H
JOHNSON, Charles H
JOHNSON, Charles D. 9
JOHNSON, Charles Ellicott 5
JOHNSON, Charles Eugene 1
JOHNSON, Charles F., Jr. 3

JOHNSON, Charles F. H. 3
JOHNSON, Charles 1
Fletcher
JOHNSON, Charles 1
Frederick
JOHNSON, Charles Henry 2
JOHNSON, Charles Nelson 1
JOHNSON, Charles Oscar 4
JOHNSON, Charles Philip 1
JOHNSON, Charles Price 5
JOHNSON, Charles 3
Spurgeon
JOHNSON, Charles Sumner 4
JOHNSON, Charles 4
Williamson
JOHNSON, Charles Willis 2
JOHNSON, Charles 1
Willison
JOHNSON, Charles 2
Willison
JOHNSON, Charlotte Buel 8
JOHNSON, Clarence 6
Hazelton
JOHNSON, Clarence 10
Leonard
JOHNSON, Clarence S. 3
JOHNSON, Clarke Howard 1
JOHNSON, Claude M. 4
JOHNSON, Clayton Errold 10
JOHNSON, Clifton 1
JOHNSON, Clinton Charles 6
JOHNSON, Cone 4
JOHNSON, Constance 6
Fuller Wheeler (Mrs.
Burges Johnson)
JOHNSON, Crawford Toy 2
JOHNSON, Crawford Toy 5
JOHNSON, Crockett 6
(David Johnson Leisk)
JOHNSON, Curtis Boyd 3
JOHNSON, Davenport 8
JOHNSON, David 1
JOHNSON, David Bancroft 1
JOHNSON, David Clayton 2
JOHNSON, David 9
Livingstone
JOHNSON, Donald Milton 9
JOHNSON, Douglas 7
Valentine
JOHNSON, Douglas Wilson 2
JOHNSON, Duncan Starr 1
JOHNSON, E. Fred 5
JOHNSON, Earl A. 5
JOHNSON, Earl Mortimer 9
JOHNSON, Earl Shepard 9
JOHNSON, Earle Frederick 3
JOHNSON, Earle George 4
JOHNSON, Eastman 1
JOHNSON, Eben Samuel 1
JOHNSON, Edgar 5
Augustus Jerome
JOHNSON, Edgar 10
Frederick
JOHNSON, Edgar 2
Hutchinson
JOHNSON, Edgar 5
N(athaniel)
JOHNSON, Edith Christina 3
JOHNSON, Edward* H
JOHNSON, Edward Bryant 1
JOHNSON, Edward 10
Crosby, II
JOHNSON, Edward Gilpin 5
JOHNSON, Edward Payson 1
JOHNSON, Edward 4
Roberts
JOHNSON, Edwin Carl 5
JOHNSON, Edwin Clifford 1
JOHNSON, Edwin Ferry H
JOHNSON, Edwin S. 1
JOHNSON, Effie 1
JOHNSON, Elbert Leland 2
JOHNSON, Eldon V. 8
JOHNSON, Eldridge 2
Reeves
JOHNSON, Elias Finley 1
JOHNSON, Elias Henry 1
JOHNSON, Elijah H
JOHNSON, Elizabeth H
JOHNSON, Elizabeth 6
Forrest
JOHNSON, Elizabeth 4
Winthrop
JOHNSON, Ellen H
JOHNSON, Ellen Cheney H
JOHNSON, Ellis Adolph 6
JOHNSON, Elvera Crosby 6
(Mrs. John Alex Johnson)
JOHNSON, Emil Fritiof 4
JOHNSON, Emory Richard 2
JOHNSON, Emsley Wright 3
JOHNSON, Ernest Amos 3
JOHNSON, Evan Malbone 1
JOHNSON, Francis H
JOHNSON, Francis Ellis 5
JOHNSON, Francis Howe 4
JOHNSON, Francis Kirk 4

JOHNSON, Francis Rarick 4
JOHNSON, Francis 4
Raymond
JOHNSON, Frank Asbury 4
JOHNSON, Frank Fisk 1
JOHNSON, Frank Harris 10
JOHNSON, Frank Ludwig 8
JOHNSON, Frank Pearson 1
JOHNSON, Frank Seward 1
JOHNSON, Frank Tenney 1
JOHNSON, Franklin 1
JOHNSON, Franklin 2
Paradise
JOHNSON, Franklin 3
Winslow
JOHNSON, Fred G. 5
JOHNSON, Fred Page 1
JOHNSON, Frederick 5
JOHNSON, Frederick H
Avery
JOHNSON, Frederick 5
Ernest
JOHNSON, Frederick Foote 2
JOHNSON, Frederick 3
Green
JOHNSON, Frederick 3
William
JOHNSON, Fridolf Lester 10
JOHNSON, George 2
JOHNSON, George 4
JOHNSON, George C. 4
JOHNSON, George D. 7
JOHNSON, George E. Q. 4
JOHNSON, George 1
Ellsworth
JOHNSON, George Francis 2
JOHNSON, George H. 4
JOHNSON, George K. 1
JOHNSON, George Marion 9
JOHNSON, George 7
Tewksbury
JOHNSON, George W. 1
JOHNSON, George William 2
JOHNSON, Gerald White 7
JOHNSON, Glover 6
JOHNSON, Gove Griffith 2
JOHNSON, Grace Allen 3
JOHNSON, Gustavus 4
JOHNSON, Guy H
JOHNSON, Guy Benton 10
JOHNSON, Guy Dibble 7
JOHNSON, Hale 1
JOHNSON, Hall 8
JOHNSON, Hallet 8
JOHNSON, Hallett 5
JOHNSON, Hansford 4
Duncan
JOHNSON, Harold Bowtell 2
JOHNSON, Harold Keith 8
JOHNSON, Harold Lester 7
JOHNSON, Harold T. 9
JOHNSON, Harry Gordon 7
JOHNSON, Harry 1
McCrindell
JOHNSON, Harry Miles 3
JOHNSON, Harvey Hull H
JOHNSON, Hayden 1
JOHNSON, Hayden Briggs 7
JOHNSON, Helen Kendrick 1
JOHNSON, Helgi 6
JOHNSON, Henry H
JOHNSON, Henry 1
JOHNSON, Henry Clark 1
JOHNSON, Henry Herbert 1
JOHNSON, Henry Lincoln 1
JOHNSON, Henry Lowry 1
Emilius
JOHNSON, Henry 3
Mortimer
JOHNSON, Henry U. 4
JOHNSON, Henry Viley 1
JOHNSON, Herbert 2
JOHNSON, Herbert Conrad 10
JOHNSON, Herbert Fisk 5
JOHNSON, Herbert Fisk 7
JOHNSON, Herbert Martin 1
JOHNSON, Herbert Morris 1
JOHNSON, Herbert 2
Spencer
JOHNSON, Herman E. 5
JOHNSON, Herrick 1
JOHNSON, Herschel V. 4
JOHNSON, Herschel H
Vespasian
JOHNSON, Hewlett 1
JOHNSON, Hiram Warren 2
JOHNSON, Hollis Eugene 10
JOHNSON, Homer Hosea 4
JOHNSON, Horace 4
JOHNSON, Howard 1
JOHNSON, Howard Albert 6
JOHNSON, Howard 3
Cooper
JOHNSON, Howard J. 4
JOHNSON, Hugh 9
JOHNSON, Hugh Albert 7
JOHNSON, Hugh Bailey 10

JOHNSON, Hugh McCain 2
JOHNSON, Hugh S. 2
JOHNSON, Irving Harding 8
(Mrs. Curtis B. Johnson)
JOHNSON, Irving Peska 2
JOHNSON, Isaac Cureton 3
JOHNSON, Iver Magni 7
JOHNSON, J. Ford 4
JOHNSON, J. Lovell 1
JOHNSON, J. Sidney 5
JOHNSON, Jack Vernon 7
JOHNSON, Jackson 1
JOHNSON, Jacob 3
JOHNSON, James* H
JOHNSON, James 7
JOHNSON, James H
Augustus
JOHNSON, James Buford 4
JOHNSON, James Clarence 4
JOHNSON, James Gibson 1
JOHNSON, James Granville 1
JOHNSON, James H. 8
JOHNSON, James Hutchins H
JOHNSON, James Leeper H
JOHNSON, James 3
McIntosh
JOHNSON, James Weldon 8
JOHNSON, Jed Joseph 4
JOHNSON, Jefferson 4
Deems, Jr.
JOHNSON, Jeremiah 1
Augustus
JOHNSON, Jeromus H
JOHNSON, Jesse 3
JOHNSON, Jesse Charles 10
JOHNSON, Jesse Lee, Jr. 9
JOHNSON, John H
JOHNSON, John 1
JOHNSON, Sir John H
JOHNSON, John A. 1
JOHNSON, John Albert 1
JOHNSON, John Arthur 9
JOHNSON, John B. 1
JOHNSON, John 6
Beauregard
JOHNSON, John Bockover, 5
Jr.
JOHNSON, John Burlin 8
JOHNSON, John Butler 1
JOHNSON, John Charles 8
JOHNSON, John David 6
JOHNSON, John Davis 4
JOHNSON, John Edward 1
JOHNSON, John Edward 5
JOHNSON, John Gilmore 1
JOHNSON, John Graver 1
JOHNSON, John Harold 9
JOHNSON, John Lipscomb 2
JOHNSON, John Mitchell 4
JOHNSON, John Monroe 7
JOHNSON, John Samuel 1
Adolphus
JOHNSON, John Seward 8
JOHNSON, John T. 4
JOHNSON, John H
Telemachus
JOHNSON, John Theodore 4
JOHNSON, John William 1
JOHNSON, Jonathan H
Eastman
JOHNSON, Jonathan 4
Eastman
JOHNSON, Joseph* H
JOHNSON, Joseph Esrey 10
JOHNSON, Joseph French 1
JOHNSON, Joseph H. 10
JOHNSON, Joseph Horsfall 1
JOHNSON, Joseph Kelly 10
JOHNSON, Joseph Lowery 5
JOHNSON, Joseph Taber 1
JOHNSON, Joseph Travis 4
JOHNSON, Joseph Travis 4
JOHNSON, Josephine 10
Winslow (Grant G.
Cannon)*
JOHNSON, Jotham 4
JOHNSON, Julia 1
MacFarlane
JOHNSON, Justin H
JOHNSON, Justin 4
JOHNSON, Karl Richard 10
JOHNSON, Kate Burr 6
(Mrs. Clarence A.
Johnson)
JOHNSON, Keen 1
JOHNSON, Kenneth D. 3
JOHNSON, Kenneth Leroy 7
JOHNSON, Kermit Alonzo 9
JOHNSON, Lambert 3
Dunning
JOHNSON, Lee Payne 4
JOHNSON, Lee Saltonstall 1
JOHNSON, Leighton Foster 3
JOHNSON, Leland Parrish 9
JOHNSON, Leon H. 5
JOHNSON, Lester 6
JOHNSON, Lester Bicknell 5

JOHNSON, Levi H
JOHNSON, Lewis Edgar 3
JOHNSON, Lewis Jerome 3
JOHNSON, Ligon 3
JOHNSON, Lilian Wyckoff 3
JOHNSON, Lincoln 3
JOHNSON, Lindsay 6
Franklin
JOHNSON, Livingston 1
JOHNSON, Loren Bascom 2
Tabor
JOHNSON, Lorenzo M. 1
JOHNSON, Louis Arthur 4
JOHNSON, Lowell Rexford 10
JOHNSON, Lucius E. 1
JOHNSON, Lucius Henry 1
JOHNSON, Luther 4
Alexander
JOHNSON, Luther Appeles 1
JOHNSON, Lyndon Baines 5
JOHNSON, Magnus 1
JOHNSON, Malcolm 3
JOHNSON, Margaret 4
JOHNSON, Margaret 1
Louise
JOHNSON, Marian Willard 9
(Mrs. Dan R. Johnson)
JOHNSON, Marietta Louise 1
JOHNSON, Marion Alvin 4
JOHNSON, Marmaduke H
JOHNSON, Martin 1
JOHNSON, Martin Nelson 1
JOHNSON, Martin Wigge 10
JOHNSON, Maurice O. 7
JOHNSON, Max Sherred 4
JOHNSON, Melvin 3
Maynard
JOHNSON, Melvin 4
Maynard, Jr.
JOHNSON, Merle Devore 1
JOHNSON, Milbank 2
JOHNSON, Mordecai 7
Wyatt
JOHNSON, Mortimer 1
Lawrence
JOHNSON, Napoleon 9
B(onaparte)
JOHNSON, Nathan 4
Robinson
JOHNSON, Nathaniel H
JOHNSON, Nels G. 3
JOHNSON, Nelson Trusler 3
JOHNSON, Noadiah H
JOHNSON, Noye Monroe 9
JOHNSON, Nunnally 7
JOHNSON, Ogden Carl 10
JOHNSON, Oliver H
JOHNSON, Oliver Francis 1
JOHNSON, Osa Helen 3
JOHNSON, Oscar John 2
JOHNSON, Otis Coe 1
JOHNSON, Otis R. 3
JOHNSON, Owen 3
JOHNSON, Palmer O. 3
JOHNSON, Pamela 8
Hansford (The Lady
Snow)
JOHNSON, Paul Burney 2
JOHNSON, Paul Emanuel 6
JOHNSON, Paul Luther 6
JOHNSON, Paul Rodgers 2
JOHNSON, Paul Sheldon 9
JOHNSON, Perley Brown 6
JOHNSON, Philander 1
Chase
JOHNSON, Philip H
JOHNSON, Philip Gustav 2
JOHNSON, Pyke 8
JOHNSON, Ralph Blake 4
JOHNSON, Randall 6
Edward
JOHNSON, Ray Prescott 4
JOHNSON, Redford 9
K(ohlsaat)
JOHNSON, Reginald Davis 3
JOHNSON, Reverdy H
JOHNSON, Richard Ellis 3
JOHNSON, Richard H. 3
JOHNSON, Richard Harvey 1
JOHNSON, Richard 5
Mentor
JOHNSON, Richard 5
Newhall
JOHNSON, Richard W. H
JOHNSON, Richard Zina 1
JOHNSON, Robert 5
JOHNSON, Robert Davis 7
JOHNSON, Robert Edward 7
JOHNSON, Robert Elliott 10
JOHNSON, Robert 7
Emerson Lamb
JOHNSON, Robert Kellogg 10
JOHNSON, Robert 4
Livingston
JOHNSON, Robert 5
Livingston, Jr.

JOHNSON, Robert Underwood 1
JOHNSON, Robert V. 6
JOHNSON, Robert W. 4
JOHNSON, Robert Ward H
JOHNSON, Robert Wilkinson 1
JOHNSON, Robert Wood 5
JOHNSON, Robert Wood, Jr. 5
JOHNSON, Roger Bruce Cash 3
JOHNSON, Rosamond 3
JOHNSON, Rossiter 1
JOHNSON, Roy 8
JOHNSON, Roy Everard 7
JOHNSON, Roy Ivan 8
JOHNSON, Roy Melisander 6
JOHNSON, Roy William 4
JOHNSON, Royal Cleaves 1
JOHNSON, Royal Kenneth 8
JOHNSON, S. Arthur 4
JOHNSON, Samuel* H
JOHNSON, Samuel William 1
JOHNSON, Searcy Lee 10
JOHNSON, Sherman Ellsworth 7
JOHNSON, Silas 3
JOHNSON, Simeon Moses 3
JOHNSON, Stanley 2
JOHNSON, Stanley Bryce 9
JOHNSON, Stanley H. 1
JOHNSON, Sveinbjorn 1
JOHNSON, Sylvanus Elihu 1
JOHNSON, Talmage Casey 4
JOHNSON, Theodore 3
JOHNSON, Thomas 1
JOHNSON, Thomas Cary 1
JOHNSON, Thomas E. 7
JOHNSON, Thomas Humrickhouse 1
JOHNSON, Thomas Joseph Allan 1
JOHNSON, Thomas Moore 1
JOHNSON, Tillman Davis 3
JOHNSON, Tom Loftin 1
JOHNSON, Treat Baldwin 2
JOHNSON, Victor Long 7
JOHNSON, Virgil Lamont 4
JOHNSON, Virginia Wales 1
JOHNSON, Vivian Wells 10
JOHNSON, W. Ogden 4
JOHNSON, Waldo Porter H
JOHNSON, Wallace 4
JOHNSON, Wallace Clyde 1
JOHNSON, Wallace Edwards 9
JOHNSON, Walter H. 4
JOHNSON, Walter Lathrop 4
JOHNSON, Walter Nathan 3
JOHNSON, Walter Perry 1
JOHNSON, Walter Perry 4
JOHNSON, Walter Richard 6
JOHNSON, Walter Samuel 7
JOHNSON, Wanda Mae 5
JOHNSON, Warren C. 8
JOHNSON, Wayne 2
JOHNSON, Wendell A. L. 4
JOHNSON, Wendell Eugene 9
JOHNSON, Wentworth Paul 10
JOHNSON, Wilfrid Estill 8
JOHNSON, Willard Lyon 9
JOHNSON, Sir William H
JOHNSON, William* H
JOHNSON, William Allen 1
JOHNSON, William Arthur 3
JOHNSON, William Bullein H
JOHNSON, William Burdett 3
JOHNSON, William C. 3
JOHNSON, William Christie 1
JOHNSON, William Cost H
JOHNSON, William Driscoll 5
JOHNSON, William Eugene 2
JOHNSON, William F. 4
JOHNSON, William Franklin 4
JOHNSON, William Geary 4
JOHNSON, William Hallock 4
JOHNSON, William Hannibal 1
JOHNSON, William Harold 5
JOHNSON, William Henry 1
JOHNSON, William Houston 4
JOHNSON, William Howard 1
JOHNSON, William Martin 4
JOHNSON, William Mindred 1
JOHNSON, William Ransom H

JOHNSON, William Samuel H
JOHNSON, William Samuel 1
JOHNSON, William Templeton 3
JOHNSON, William Woolsey 1
JOHNSON, Willis Ernest 3
JOHNSON, Willis Fletcher 1
JOHNSON, Willis Grant 1
JOHNSON, Wingate M. 4
JOHNSTON, Adelia Antoinette Field 1
JOHNSTON, Albert Sidney H
JOHNSTON, Alexander H
JOHNSTON, Alva 3
JOHNSTON, Alvanley 3
JOHNSTON, Annie Fellows 1
JOHNSTON, Archibald 4
JOHNSTON, Archibald Anderson 7
JOHNSTON, Augustus 1
JOHNSTON, Bruce Gilbert 10
JOHNSTON, Charles H
JOHNSTON, Charles 1
JOHNSTON, Charles Clement H
JOHNSTON, Charles Eugene 3
JOHNSTON, Charles G. 4
JOHNSTON, Charles Haven Ladd 2
JOHNSTON, Charles Hughes 1
JOHNSTON, Charles Worth 1
JOHNSTON, Christopher 1
JOHNSTON, Clarence Howard 1
JOHNSTON, Clarence Thomas 5
JOHNSTON, Clement Dixon 7
JOHNSTON, David Claypoole H
JOHNSTON, David E. 4
JOHNSTON, David Ira 3
JOHNSTON, Don P(orter) 7
JOHNSTON, Douglas T. 4
JOHNSTON, Edward R. 7
JOHNSTON, Elizabeth Bryant 1
JOHNSTON, Ella Bond 1
JOHNSTON, Ellis Murray 7
JOHNSTON, Eric A. 4
JOHNSTON, Forney 4
JOHNSTON, Frances Benjamin 3
JOHNSTON, Francis Wayland 4
JOHNSTON, Frank Evington 8
JOHNSTON, Franklins Davis 5
JOHNSTON, Gabriel H
JOHNSTON, Garvin Howell 7
JOHNSTON, George Ben 1
JOHNSTON, George Doherty 1
JOHNSTON, George Sim 10
JOHNSTON, Gordon 1
JOHNSTON, Gordon 3
JOHNSTON, Harold Whetstone 1
JOHNSTON, Harry Lang 2
JOHNSTON, Harry Raymond 6
JOHNSTON, Harvey Pollard 5
JOHNSTON, Henrietta H
JOHNSTON, Henry Alan 3
JOHNSTON, Henry Donaldson 4
JOHNSTON, Henry Phelps 1
JOHNSTON, Henry Rust 8
JOHNSTON, Herrick Lee 4
JOHNSTON, Howard Agnew 1
JOHNSTON, Howard Andrews 10
JOHNSTON, Hugh 1
JOHNSTON, Ivan Murray 4
JOHNSTON, J. Stoddard 1
JOHNSTON, James 3
JOHNSTON, James A. 3
JOHNSTON, James Ambler 4
JOHNSTON, James Hugo, Jr. 9
JOHNSTON, James Martin 4
JOHNSTON, James Steptoe 1
JOHNSTON, John H
JOHNSTON, John 1
JOHNSTON, John 3
JOHNSTON, John Alexander 1
JOHNSTON, John Black 2

JOHNSTON, John Robert 3
JOHNSTON, John Maclin 10
JOHNSTON, John T. M. 1
JOHNSTON, John Taylor 1
JOHNSTON, John Warfield H
JOHNSTON, Joseph Eggleston H
JOHNSTON, Joseph Forney 1
JOHNSTON, Josiah Stoddard 1
JOHNSTON, Julia Harriette 1
JOHNSTON, Kilbourne 5
JOHNSTON, L. S. 3
JOHNSTON, Lawrence Albert 1
JOHNSTON, Leon H. 4
JOHNSTON, Leslie Morgan 5
JOHNSTON, Lucy Browne 1
JOHNSTON, Marbury 1
JOHNSTON, Maria Isabella 5
JOHNSTON, Mary 1
JOHNSTON, Means, Jr. 10
JOHNSTON, Myrtle Alice Dean (Mrs. Carl Edward Johnston) 6
JOHNSTON, Olin Dewitt 4
JOHNSTON, Oliver Martin 4
JOHNSTON, Oscar Goodbar 3
JOHNSTON, Paul Alexander 9
JOHNSTON, Paul William 9
JOHNSTON, Percy Hampton 1
JOHNSTON, Peter H
JOHNSTON, Richard Hall 5
JOHNSTON, Richard Holland 3
JOHNSTON, Richard Malcolm H
JOHNSTON, Richard Wyckoff 8
JOHNSTON, Rienzi Melville 1
JOHNSTON, Robert Born 5
JOHNSTON, Robert Daniel 4
JOHNSTON, Robert Matteson 1
JOHNSTON, Robert Story 2
JOHNSTON, Rowland L. 1
JOHNSTON, Rufus Perry 1
JOHNSTON, Russell M. 4
JOHNSTON, Samuel H
JOHNSTON, Samuel 4
JOHNSTON, Samuel M. 5
JOHNSTON, S(amuel) Paul 9
JOHNSTON, Stanley 4
JOHNSTON, Stewart 1
JOHNSTON, Thomas 1
JOHNSTON, Thomas Alexander 10
JOHNSTON, Thomas McElree 10
JOHNSTON, Thomas Murphy H
JOHNSTON, Thomas William 1
JOHNSTON, Victor A. 4
JOHNSTON, W. Dawson* 1
JOHNSTON, W. Fenton 4
JOHNSTON, Walter Vail 4
JOHNSTON, Wayne Andrew 4
JOHNSTON, William H
JOHNSTON, William Agnew 1
JOHNSTON, William Atkinson 1
JOHNSTON, William Drumm, Jr. 5
JOHNSTON, William Greer 3
JOHNSTON, William Hugh 1
JOHNSTON, William Milton 1
JOHNSTON, William Norville 10
JOHNSTON, William Pollock 1
JOHNSTON, William Preston 1
JOHNSTON, William Waring 1
JOHNSTON, Wirt 1
JOHNSTON, Zachariah H
JOHNSTONE, Alan 8
JOHNSTONE, Arthur Edward 5
JOHNSTONE, Bruce 5
JOHNSTONE, Burton Kenneth 7
JOHNSTONE, Edward Ransom 2

JOHNSTONE, Edward Robert 1
JOHNSTONE, Ernest Kinloch 2
JOHNSTONE, Henry Fraser 4
JOHNSTONE, Henry Webb 5
JOHNSTONE, Job H
JOHNSTONE, John Humphreys 4
JOHNSTONE, William Jackson 1
JOHN XXIII, His Holiness H
JOHONNOTT, Edwin Sheldon 1
JOINER, Otis William 6
JOLIET, Louis H
JOLINE, Adrian Hoffman 1
JOLIOT-CURIE, Frederic 3
JOLIOT-CURIE, Irene 3
JOLIVET, Andre 6
JOLLES, Otto Jolle Matthijs 5
JOLLEY, Harold Dean 9
JOLLIFFE, Charles Byron 5
JOLLIFFE, Norman H. 4
JOLLY, Austin Howell 4
JOLLY, Robert Garland 3
JOLSON, Al 3
JOME, Hiram L. 3
JONAH, David Alonzo 8
JONAH, Frank Gilbert 2
JONAS, August Frederick 1
JONAS, Benjamin Franklin 1
JONAS, Charles Andrew 5
JONAS, Charles Raper 9
JONAS, Edgar A. 4
JONAS, Franz 6
JONAS, H(arry) A(lfred) 7
JONAS, Jack Henry 5
JONAS, Maryla 3
JONAS, Nathan S. 4
JONAS, Ralph 3
JONAS, Russell E. 5
JONES, Aaron 4
JONES, Aaron Edward 8
JONES, Abner H
JONES, Ada 4
JONES, Adam Leroy 1
JONES, Albert Marshall 2
JONES, Albert Monmouth 4
JONES, Albert Pearson 10
JONES, Albert R. 5
JONES, Alexander H
JONES, Alexander Francis 4
JONES, Alfred 1
JONES, Alfred 2
JONES, Alfred B. 4
JONES, Alfred Miles 1
JONES, Alfred William 8
JONES, Alice Hanson 9
JONES, Allen H
JONES, Allen Northey 1
JONES, Amanda Theodosia 1
JONES, Andrieus Aristieus 1
JONES, Anson H
JONES, Archibald A. 4
JONES, Archie Neff 7
JONES, Arnold Roosevelt 7
JONES, Arthur Carhart 10
JONES, Arthur Gray 1
JONES, Arthur Julius 5
JONES, Arthur Woodruff 6
JONES, Augustine 1
JONES, Barton Mills 3
JONES, Bassett 3
JONES, Belling, Jr. 10
JONES, Benjamin H
JONES, Benjamin Franklin* 1
JONES, Benjamin Franklin, Jr. 1
JONES, Benjamin Rowlands 7
JONES, Bob 4
JONES, Breckinridge 1
JONES, Brian 5
JONES, Bruce Carr 3
JONES, Buell Fay 2
JONES, Burnie Edward 8
JONES, Burr W. 1
JONES, Burton Rensselaer 1
JONES, C. Edward 1
JONES, C. Hampson 1
JONES, Calvin H
JONES, Carl H. 3
JONES, Carl Waring 3
JONES, Carlton Allen 1
JONES, Carolyn 8
JONES, Carter Helm 2
JONES, Catesby Ap Roger H
JONES, Charles Alfred 2
JONES, Charles Alvin 3
JONES, Charles Andrews 3
JONES, Charles Aubrey 7
JONES, Charles Colcock H
JONES, Charles Colcock, III 5

JONES, Charles Davies 1
JONES, Charles F. 5
JONES, Charles Franklin 10
JONES, Charles Fremont 1
JONES, Charles Henry 1
JONES, Charles Hodge 6
JONES, Charles Paul 6
JONES, Charles Reading 2
JONES, Charles S. 5
JONES, Charles Sherman 7
JONES, Charles Sumner 1
JONES, Charles Williams 10
JONES, Cheney Church 3
JONES, Chester Lloyd 1
JONES, Chester Morse 5
JONES, Claud Ashton 2
JONES, Clement Ross 1
JONES, Cliff C. 4
JONES, Clifford Bartlett 7
JONES, Clyde E. 3
JONES, Cranston Edward 10
JONES, Cyril Hamlen 5
JONES, Daniel Fiske 1
JONES, Daniel Jonathan 4
JONES, Daniel Terryll H
JONES, Daniel Webster 1
JONES, David H
JONES, David 6
JONES, David Dallas 3
JONES, David Hugh 4
JONES, David John 7
JONES, David Percy 1
JONES, David Rumph H
JONES, Donald Forsha 4
JONES, Dorothy Cameron 10
JONES, Dwight Bangs 3
JONES, E. Lester 1
JONES, Earl Gardner 9
JONES, Earl J. 3
JONES, Edgar Dewitt 3
JONES, Edgar Laroy 1
JONES, Edith Kathleen 4
JONES, Edmund Adams 1
JONES, Edmund Lyddane 7
JONES, Edward Brant 7
JONES, Edward Campbell 1
JONES, Edward Cole 8
JONES, Edward David 3
JONES, Edward E. 3
JONES, Edward Franc 1
JONES, Edward Groves 1
JONES, Edward Perry 5
JONES, Edward Vason 1
JONES, Edwin Donatus, Jr. 8
JONES, Edwin Frank 1
JONES, Edwin Howard, Jr. 9
JONES, Edwin Lee 5
JONES, Edwin Leslie 6
JONES, Edwin Whiting 4
JONES, Eleanor Louise 1
JONES, Eli Sherman (Jack) 8
JONES, Eli Stanley 5
JONES, E(li) Stanley 7
JONES, Eliot 5
JONES, Elizabeth 10
JONES, Elizabeth Dickson 4
JONES, Ella Virginia 4
JONES, Elmer Ellsworth 5
JONES, Elmer Ray 4
JONES, Elmer Rutledge 9
JONES, Elton B. 4
JONES, E(mmett) Milton 5
JONES, Ernest Carl 9
JONES, Ernest Victor 7
JONES, Eugene Kinckle 7
JONES, Evan J. 7
JONES, Evelyn Tubb 5
JONES, Everett Starr 4
JONES, Evert Leon 7
JONES, F. Robertson 1
JONES, Fernando 1
JONES, Floyd William 5
JONES, Forrest Robert 4
JONES, Francis H
JONES, Francis Coates 1
JONES, Francis Ilah 3
JONES, Frank 1
JONES, Frank Cazenove 2
JONES, Frank Johnston 1
JONES, Frank Leonard 3
JONES, Frank Pierce 6
JONES, Frank Pierce 7
JONES, Franklin D. 1
JONES, Franklin Elmore 1
JONES, Fred 9
JONES, Frederic Marshall 1
JONES, Frederic Randolph 6
JONES, Frederick E. 6
JONES, Frederick Robertson 2
JONES, Gabriel H
JONES, Gaius J. 4
JONES, Galen 1
JONES, Gardner Maynard 1
JONES, George* H
JONES, George E. 10
JONES, George H. 1

KENDIG, Bess Horton 6
(Mrs. Andrew LeRoy Kendig)
KENDIG, Calvin Miles 3
KENDIG, H. Evert 3
KENDRICK, Asahel Clark H
KENDRICK, Baynard 7
Hardwick
KENDRICK, Benjamin 2
Burks
KENDRICK, Charles 5
KENDRICK, E. S. 4
KENDRICK, Eliza Hall 1
KENDRICK, Georgia 1
KENDRICK, Herbert 10
Spencer, Jr.
KENDRICK, James Blair, 10
Jr.
KENDRICK, John H
KENDRICK, John 1
Benjamin
KENDRICK, John Mills 1
KENDRICK, John William 1
KENDRICK, Nathaniel 5
Cooper
KENDRICK, Pearl L. 8
KENDRICK, Philip Eugene 6
KENDRICK, W. Freeland 3
KENDRICKS, Edward 3
James
KENE, Joseph Alphonse 4
KENEALY, Ahmed John 4
KENEALY, Alexander C. 4
KENEALY, William James 6
KENEFICK, Daniel Joseph 2
KENERSON, Edward 6
Hibbard
KENERSON, William 6
Herbert
KENGLA, Hannah M. 3
Egan
KENIN, Herman David 5
KENISON, Frank Rowe 7
KENISTON, Hayward 7
(Ralph)
KENISTON, Hayward 5
(Ralph)
KENISTON, James 1
Mortimer
KENKEL, Frederick P. 3
KENLON, John 1
KENLY, John Reese 1
KENLY, Julie Woodbridge 2
Terry
KENLY, Ritchie Graham 1
KENLY, William Lacy 1
KENNA, Edward Dudley 4
KENNA, F. Regis 9
KENNA, Frank 2
KENNA, Howard James 6
KENNA, John Edward H
KENNA, Joseph Norris 3
KENNA, Roger 4
KENNALLY, Vincent 7
Ignatius
KENNAMER, Charles 3
Brents
KENNAMER, Franklin 6
Elmore
KENNAN, George 1
KENNARD, Earle Hesse 7
KENNARD, Frederic 1
Hedge
KENNARD, Joseph 2
Spencer
KENNARD, Samuel M. 1
KENNARD, William 6
Jeffers
KENNEBECK, George 5
Robert
KENNEDY, Albert Joseph 6
KENNEDY, Ambrose J. 3
KENNEDY, Andrew H
KENNEDY, Annie 3
Richardson
KENNEDY, Anthony H
KENNEDY, Archibald H
KENNEDY, Arthur 3
Garfield
KENNEDY, Bernard R. 10
KENNEDY, Charles A. 5
KENNEDY, Charles Rann 2
KENNEDY, Charles 5
William
KENNEDY, Charles 7
William
KENNEDY, Chase Wilmot 1
KENNEDY, Clarence 5
KENNEDY, Clarence 3
Hamilton
KENNEDY, Clement 7
KENNEDY, Clyde 5
Raymond
KENNEDY, Crammond 1
KENNEDY, Daniel Joseph 1
KENNEDY, David Scott 1

KENNEDY, Edward 10
Eugene
KENNEDY, Elijah 1
Robinson
KENNEDY, Elizabeth 6
Smith
KENNEDY, Emma Baker 1
KENNEDY, F. Lowell 1
KENNEDY, Foster 3
KENNEDY, Frances 9
Midlam (Mrs. Joseph Conrad Kennedy)
KENNEDY, Francis 1
Willard
KENNEDY, Frank Brittain 8
KENNEDY, Frank J. 6
KENNEDY, Fred 5
J(ohnston)
KENNEDY, Fredrick C. 8
KENNEDY, G. Donald 9
KENNEDY, Gall 5
KENNEDY, George A. 4
KENNEDY, George 7
Clayton
KENNEDY, Gerald 7
Hamilton
KENNEDY, Gerald 8
Hamilton
KENNEDY, Gerald S. 7
KENNEDY, Gilbert 5
Falconer
KENNEDY, Harry 9
Sherbourne
KENNEDY, Hayes 5
KENNEDY, Henry L. 3
KENNEDY, Howard 7
Ernest
KENNEDY, Howard 1
Samuel
KENNEDY, Howard 4
Samuel
KENNEDY, J. Lawson 9
KENNEDY, James 1
Aloysius Charles
KENNEDY, James 6
Edwin
KENNEDY, James Arthur 4
KENNEDY, James Francis 6
KENNEDY, James Henry 1
KENNEDY, James 1
Madison
KENNEDY, James Melvin 4
KENNEDY, James Walter 7
KENNEDY, John A. 10
KENNEDY, John Bright 4
KENNEDY, John Bright 5
KENNEDY, John Doby H
KENNEDY, John Fisher 10
KENNEDY, John 1
Fitzgerald
KENNEDY, John J. 7
KENNEDY, John 4
Lauderdale
KENNEDY, John Louis 4
KENNEDY, John Lyon 9
KENNEDY, John H
Pendleton
KENNEDY, John 3
Pendleton
KENNEDY, John Stewart 1
KENNEDY, John Thomas 3
KENNEDY, Joseph 1
KENNEDY, Joseph Camp H
Griffith
KENNEDY, Joseph Patrick 5
KENNEDY, Joseph 3
William
KENNEDY, Josiah Forrest 4
KENNEDY, Julian 1
KENNEDY, Keith Furnival 10
KENNEDY, Lloyd Ellison 4
KENNEDY, Lorne Edward 4
KENNEDY, Margaret 4
KENNEDY, Margaret 4
KENNEDY, Martin J. 3
KENNEDY, Merton Grant 4
KENNEDY, Michael 2
Joseph
KENNEDY, Miles 4
Coverdale
KENNEDY, Moorhead 1
Cowell
KENNEDY, Olin Wood 5
KENNEDY, Paca 1
KENNEDY, Paul A(lfred) 8
KENNEDY, Philip 4
Benjamin
KENNEDY, Ralph Dale 1
KENNEDY, Raymond 3
KENNEDY, Richard 3
Oakley
KENNEDY, Ridgway, Jr. 8
KENNEDY, Robert 5
Francis
KENNEDY, Robert 9
Hayward
KENNEDY, Robert 5
MacMillan

KENNEDY, Robert Morris 2
KENNEDY, Robert 1
Patterson
KENNEDY, Roger L. J. 4
KENNEDY, Ruby Jo 5
Reeves
KENNEDY, Ruth Lee 9
KENNEDY, Samuel 1
Macaw
KENNEDY, Sara 1
Beaumont
KENNEDY, Selden Brown 7
KENNEDY, Sidney 5
Robinson
KENNEDY, Stanley 5
Carmichael
KENNEDY, Sylvester 5
Michael
KENNEDY, T. Blake 3
KENNEDY, Thomas 4
KENNEDY, Thomas F. 1
KENNEDY, W. McNeil 5
KENNEDY, Walker 1
KENNEDY, Walter 7
Wallace
KENNEDY, Willard John 2
KENNEDY, William 10
KENNEDY, William H
KENNEDY, William 1
Dempsey
KENNEDY, William 7
KENNEDY, William Henry 2
Joseph
KENNEDY, William Jesse, 8
III
KENNEDY, William 5
Parker
KENNEDY, William Pierce 5
KENNEDY, William Sloane 1
KENNEDY, William 7
Thomson
KENNEDY, Wray David 5
KENNELLY, Arthur 1
Edwin
KENNELLY, Edward F. 4
KENNELLY, Martin H. 4
KENNER, Albert Walton 3
KENNER, Duncan Farrar H
KENNER, Frank Terry 4
KENNERLEY, Mitchell 6
KENNERLY, John Hanger 1
KENNERLY, Thomas 4
Martin
KENNERLY, Wesley 2
Travis
KENNESON, Taddeus 1
Davis
KENNETT, Luther Martin H
KENNEY, Edward A. 1
KENNEY, George 8
Churchill
KENNEY, James Francis 6
KENNEY, John Andrew 2
KENNEY, Richard Rolland 1
KENNEY, W. John 10
KENNEY, William Francis 1
KENNEY, William P. 1
KENNEY, William 9
Richardson
KENNGOTT, George 4
Frederick
KENNICOTT, Cass 5
(Langdon)
KENNICOTT, Donald 4
KENNICOTT, Robert H
KENNISH, John 4
KENNON, Jack Eccleston 4
KENNON, Lyman Walter 1
Vere
KENNON, William, Sr. H
KENNON, William, Jr. H
KENNON, William Lee 3
KENNY, Albert Sewall 1
KENNY, Dumont Francis 8
KENNY, Elizabeth 3
KENNY, James Donald 8
KENNY, John Edward 6
KENNY, John V. 6
KENNY, Michael 2
KENNY, Nicholas 6
Napoleon
KENNY, Nicholas 7
Napoleon (Nick Kenny)
KENNY, Robert Walker 5
KENNY, Thomas James 5
KENNY, William John 1
KENOYER, Leslie Alva 7
KENRICK, Francis Patrick H
KENRICK, Peter Richard H
KENRICK, William H
KENSETT, John Frederick H
KENT, Alexander 1
KENT, Amos Eugene 7
KENT, Arthur Atwater 2
KENT, Carleton Velney, Jr. 8
KENT, Charles Artemas 1
KENT, Charles Foster 1

KENT, Charles Stanton 5
KENT, Charles William 1
KENT, Corita 9
KENT, Donald Peterson 5
KENT, Edward H
KENT, Edward 1
KENT, Edward Mather 5
KENT, Elizabeth Thacher 4
KENT, Everett 8
KENT, Everett Leonard 9
KENT, Frank Richardson 3
KENT, Fred I. 5
KENT, Harry Christison 10
KENT, Harry Llewellyn 2
KENT, Harry Watson 2
KENT, Henry Oakes 1
KENT, Herbert A. 4
KENT, Hollister 6
KENT, Ira Rich 2
KENT, Jacob Ford 1
KENT, James H
KENT, James Tyler 1
KENT, John Harvey 4
KENT, Joseph H
KENT, Louise Andrews 5
KENT, Moss H
KENT, Norman 5
KENT, Norton Adams 2
KENT, R. H. 4
KENT, Raymond Asa 5
KENT, Richard T. 5
KENT, Robert Homer 3
KENT, Robert Thurston 2
KENT, Rockwell 5
KENT, Roland Grubb 3
KENT, Russell 1
KENT, Russell Alger 4
KENT, Sherman 9
KENT, Stephen G(irard) 5
KENT, Walter Henry 1
KENT, William* 1
KENT, William J., Jr. 5
KENT, W(illiam) Wallace 6
KENTON, Edna 3
KENTON, Simon H
KENTON, Stanley 7
Newcomb
KENWAY, Herbert 6
Winthrop
KENYON, Alfred Monroe 1
KENYON, Allan Titsworth 7
KENYON, Alpheus 1
Burdick
KENYON, Charles (Arthur) 6
KENYON, Dorothy 5
KENYON, Douglas 4
Houston
KENYON, Frederick 4
Courtland
KENYON, George Henry 4
KENYON, Helen 7
KENYON, James Benjamin 1
KENYON, John Samuel 4
KENYON, Otis Allen 2
KENYON, Theodore 1
Stanwood
KENYON, William 1
Houston
KENYON, William H
Scheuneman
KENYON, William Squire 1
KEOGH, Andrew 3
KEOGH, Eugene James 10
KEOGH, Martin Jerome 1
KEOGH, Thomas Bernard 4
KEOKUK H
KEOSIAN, John 8
KEOUGH, Austin 3
Campbell
KEOUGH, Francis Patrick 4
KEOWN, William Hamilton 8
KEPHART, Calvin Ira 5
KEPHART, Cyrus Jeffries 1
KEPHART, Ezekial Boring 1
KEPHART, Horace 1
Lafayette
KEPHART, John Wiliam 2
KEPLER, Charles Ober 1
KEPLER, Thomas Samuel 4
KEPLINGER, John Carper 7
KEPNER, Harold R. 4
KEPNER, Harry V. 4
KEPNER, William E. 10
KEPPEL, Charles John 4
KEPPEL, Francis 10
KEPPEL, Frederick 1
KEPPEL, Frederick Paul 2
KEPPLER, Joseph H
KEPPLER, Joseph 5
KER, Charles H. 7
KER, Severn Parker 2
KERBEY, Eric A. 3
KERBY, William Frederick 10
KERBY, William Joseph 1
KERCHER, John Wesley, 7
Jr.

KERCHEVAL, Royal 8
Dickson
KERCHEVILLE, F(rancis) 5
M(onroe)
KEREKES, Frank 4
KEREKES, Tibor 5
KERENS, Richard C. 1
KERENSKY, Alexander 5
Fedorovitch
KERESEY, Henry Donnelly 4
KERFOOT, John Barrett 1
KERFOOT, Samuel 1
Fletcher
KERFOTT, John Barrett H
KERKAM, William Barron 4
KERKER, Gustave Adolph 1
KERLEY, Charles Gilmore 2
KERLIN, Isaac Newton H
KERLIN, Robert Thomas 3
KERMATH, James Edward 6
KERN, Alfred Allan 6
KERN, Edith Kingman 5
KERN, Edward Meyer H
KERN, Frank Dunn 6
KERN, Frederick John 1
KERN, Harold G. 6
KERN, Herbert Arthur 4
KERN, Howard Lewis 2
KERN, Jerome David 2
KERN, John Adam 1
KERN, John Dwight 2
KERN, John Worth 1
KERN, John Worth 5
KERN, Josiah Quincy 1
KERN, Maximilan 4
KERN, Olly J. 4
KERN, Paul Bentley 3
KERN, Richard Arminius 8
KERN, Richard Hovenden 4
KERN, Robert H. 4
KERN, Walter McCollough 2
KERN, William Albert 4
KERNAHAN, Arthur Earl 1
KERNAN, Francis H
KERNAN, Francis Joseph 2
KERNAN, John Devereux 4
KERNAN, Thomas Jones 4
KERNAN, Walter Avery 6
KERNAN, Walter Avery 7
KERNAN, Warnick J. 6
KERNAN, Warnick J. 7
KERNAN, Will Hubbard 4
KERNE, Leo J. 4
KERNER, Otto 3
KERNER, Otto 6
KERNER, Otto 7
KERNER, Robert Joseph 3
KERNEY, James 1
KERNEY, Sarah M. 4
KERNO, Ivan 4
KERNOCHAN, Joseph 5
Frederick
KERNS, Shirley Kendrick 3
KEROUAC, Jack (Jean-
louis Kerouac) 5
KERPER, Hazel Bowman 6
KERR, Abram Tucker 1
KERR, Albert Boardman 2
KERR, Alexander 1
KERR, Alexander Taylor 5
KERR, Alexander Thomas 1
Warwick
KERR, Alvah Milton 1
KERR, Andrew 6
KERR, A(rthur) Stewart 10
KERR, Charles 2
KERR, Charles Volney 1
KERR, Charles William 3
KERR, Clarence D. 3
KERR, David Ramsey 1
KERR, Duncan J. 1
KERR, E. S. Wells 7
KERR, Edgar Davis 6
KERR, Edmund Hugh 10
KERR, Elmore Coe, Jr. 7
KERR, Eugene Wycliff 5
KERR, Ewing Thomas 10
KERR, Florence Stewart 8
KERR, Frank Marion 1
KERR, George Howard 6
KERR, Harold Dabney 6
KERR, Harrison 7
KERR, Harry Hyland 6
KERR, H(enry) 1
Farquharson
KERR, Henry H. 3
KERR, Henry Hampton 6
KERR, Howard Ickis 3
KERR, Hugh T. 3
KERR, Hugh Thomson 10
KERR, James H
KERR, James Bremer 1
KERR, James Taggart 1
KERR, John H
KERR, John, Jr. H
KERR, John Bozman 1
KERR, John Brown* 1

KIOKEMEISTER, Fred Ludwig 5
KIP, Abraham Lincoln 4
KIP, Frederic Ellsworth 4
KIP, Leonard 1
KIP, William Ingraham H
KIPLINGER, Ralph Ernest 9
KIPLINGER, Willard Monroe 5
KIPNIS, Alexander 7
KIPNIS, Claude 9
KIPP, Charles John 1
KIPP, George Washington 1
KIPP, Orin Lansing 3
KIPPAX, John R. 1
KIRBY, Absalom 1
KIRBY, Allan Price 9
KIRBY, Amos 8
KIRBY, C. Valentine 2
KIRBY, Daniel Bartholomew 3
KIRBY, Daniel Noyes 2
KIRBY, Edmund Burgis 1
KIRBY, Ephraim H
KIRBY, Frank E. 1
KIRBY, Fred Morgan 3
KIRBY, George Francis 8
KIRBY, George Hughes 1
KIRBY, Harold 3
KIRBY, J. Hudson H
KIRBY, James Cordell, Jr. 10
KIRBY, John, Jr. 1
KIRBY, John Henry 1
KIRBY, Laverne Howe 6
KIRBY, R. Harper 1
KIRBY, Robert J. 2
KIRBY, Rollin 3
KIRBY, William Fosgate 1
KIRBY, William Gerard 5
KIRBY, William Maurice 1
KIRBY, William Thomas 10
KIRBYE, J. Edward 1
KIRBY-SMITH, Edmund H
KIRCHHOFER, Alfred Henry 9
KIRCHHOFF, Charles 1
KIRCHHOFFER, Richard Ainslie 8
KIRCHMAYER, Leon Kenneth 8
KIRCHNER, Arthur Adolph 4
KIRCHNER, George H. 1
KIRCHNER, Henry Paul 3
KIRCHNER, Otto 1
KIRCHWEY, Freda 6
KIRCHWEY, George Washington 2
KIRCK, Charles Townsend 1
KIRK, Alan Goodrich 4
KIRK, Albert E. 6
KIRK, Alexander Comstock 8
KIRK, Arthur Dale 2
KIRK, Arthur Sherman 9
KIRK, Charles Albert 2
KIRK, Dolly Williams 5
KIRK, Edward Cameron 1
KIRK, Edward Norris H
KIRK, Ellen Olney 4
KIRK, Frank C. 4
KIRK, Haddon S(purgeon) 9
KIRK, Harris C. 4
KIRK, Harris Elliott 4
KIRK, James 8
KIRK, John Esben 6
KIRK, John Foster 1
KIRK, John Franklin 1
KIRK, John R. 1
KIRK, Lester King 5
KIRK, May 4
KIRK, Norman Thomas 4
KIRK, Ralph G. 6
KIRK, Raymond Eller 3
KIRK, Raymond V. 2
KIRK, Ronald T. (Rahsaan Roland Kirk) 7
KIRK, Rudolf 10
KIRK, Thomas Jefferson 4
KIRK, Waldorf Tilton 3
KIRK, Wilfred Bernard 4
KIRK, William 4
KIRK, William Frederick 1
KIRK, William Talbot 6
KIRKBRIDE, Franklin Butler 3
KIRKBRIDE, Thomas Story H
KIRKBRIDE, Walter George 6
KIRKCONNELL, Watson 10
KIRKEBY, Arnold S. 4
KIRKHAM, Harold Laurens Dundas 2
KIRKHAM, John Henry 1
KIRKHAM, Stanton Davis 2
KIRKHAM, William Barri 5

KIRKLAND, Archie Howard 1
KIRKLAND, Caroline Matilda Stansbury H
KIRKLAND, Edward Chase 6
KIRKLAND, James Hampton 1
KIRKLAND, James Robert 3
KIRKLAND, John Thornton H
KIRKLAND, Joseph* H
KIRKLAND, Samuel 1
KIRKLAND, Weymouth 4
KIRKLAND, William Lennox H
KIRKLAND, Winifred Margaretta 2
KIRKLIN, Byrl Raymond 3
KIRKMAN, Marshall Monroe 1
KIRKPATRICK, Andrew H
KIRKPATRICK, Andrew 1
KIRKPATRICK, Blaine Evron 3
KIRKPATRICK, Carlos Stevens 3
KIRKPATRICK, Charles Cochran 9
KIRKPATRICK, Clifford 5
KIRKPATRICK, Donald 7
KIRKPATRICK, Edwin Asbury 1
KIRKPATRICK, Elbert W. 1
KIRKPATRICK, George Holland 5
KIRKPATRICK, Ivone 4
KIRKPATRICK, Leonard Henry 4
KIRKPATRICK, Martin Glen 8
KIRKPATRICK, Milo Orton 8
KIRKPATRICK, Ralph 8
KIRKPATRICK, Richard Bogue 9
KIRKPATRICK, Sanford 4
KIRKPATRICK, Sidney Dale 5
KIRKPATRICK, Thomas Le Roy 2
KIRKPATRICK, William H
KIRKPATRICK, William Dawson 4
KIRKPATRICK, William Huntington 5
KIRKPATRICK, William Huntington 7
KIRKPATRICK, William James 1
KIRKPATRICK, William Sebring 1
KIRKS, Rowland Falconer 7
KIRKUS, William 1
KIRKWOOD, Arthur Carter 5
KIRKWOOD, Daniel H
KIRKWOOD, Irwin 1
KIRKWOOD, James 10
KIRKWOOD, John Gamble 5
KIRKWOOD, Joseph Edward 1
KIRKWOOD, Marion Rice 8
KIRKWOOD, Samuel Jordan H
KIRKWOOD, William Reeside 4
KIRN, George John 4
KIROACK, Howard 3
KIRSCH, John N. 4
KIRSCH, Robert 7
KIRSCHBAUM, Arthur 3
KIRSHMAN, John Emmett 2
KIRSHNER, Charles Henry 2
KIRST, Hans Hellmut 9
KIRSTEIN, Arthur 4
KIRSTEIN, George Garland 9
KIRSTEIN, Louis Edward 2
KIRSTEIN, Max 1
KIRSTEN, Dorothy 10
KIRSTEN, Frederick K. 7
KIRTLAND, Dorrance 1
KIRTLAND, Fred Durrell 5
KIRTLAND, Jared Potter 1
KIRTLAND, John Copeland 3
KIRTLAND, Lucian Swift 4
KIRTLEY, James Samuel 3
KIRWAN, Albert Dennis 5
KIRWAN, Michael Joseph 5
KIRWAN, Michael Joseph 7
KIRWAN, Thomas M. 10
KIRWIN, Thomas Joseph 3

KISELEV, Evgeny Dmitrievich 4
KISELEWSKI, Joseph 10
KISER, Samuel Ellsworth 1
KISER, Samuel Ellsworth 2
KISH, George 10
KISKADDON, Andrew Henry 7
KISSAM, Henry Snyder 1
KISSANE, Ray William 10
KISSEL, John 1
KISSELL, Harry Seaman 4
KISSNER, Franklin H. 9
KISSOCK, Alan 8
KISTER, George Raphael 4
KISTIAKOWSKY, George Bogdan 8
KISTLER, John Clinton 1
KISTLER, Joy William 10
KISTLER, Raymon M. 4
KISTLER, Samuel Stephens 6
KITAGAWA, Joseph Mitsuo 10
KITCH, Paul Richard 9
KITCHEL, Allan F. 7
KITCHEL, Lloyd 3
KITCHEL, William Lloyd 2
KITCHELL, Aaron 1
KITCHELL, Joseph Gray 2
KITCHEN, Bethuel 8
KITCHEN, Delmas Kendall 8
KITCHEN, Hyram 10
KITCHEN, Joseph Ambrose 6
KITCHENS, Wade Hampton 4
KITCHIN, Claude 1
KITCHIN, Thurman Delna 3
KITCHIN, William Copeman 1
KITCHIN, William Walton 1
KITSON, Geoffrey Herbert 6
KITSON, Harry Dexter 3
KITSON, Henry Hudson 4
KITSON, Samuel James 1
KITSON, Theo Alice Ruggles 1
KITTAY, Sol 8
KITTELL, Albert George 2
KITTELL, James Shepard 1
KITTELLE, Sumner Ely Wetmore 3
KITTERA, John Wilkes H
KITTERA, Thomas H
KITTINGER, Harold D. 2
KITTLE, Charles Morgan 1
KITTREDGE, Abbott Eliot 1
KITTREDGE, Alfred Beard 1
KITTREDGE, Frank Alvah 3
KITTREDGE, George 1
KITTREDGE, George Washington H
KITTREDGE, George Watson 2
KITTREDGE, Henry Crocker 8
KITTREDGE, Henry Grattan 1
KITTREDGE, Josiah Edwards 1
KITTREDGE, Mabel Hyde 3
KITTREDGE, Walter 1
KITTREDGE, Wheaton 1
KITTRELL, Flemmie Pansy 7
KITTRELL, Norman Goree 1
KITTS, Joseph Arthur 2
KITTS, Willard Augustus, 3rd 4
KITTSON, Norman Wolfred H
KIVEL, John 1
KIVETTE, Frederick Norman 6
KIVLIN, Vincent Earl 5
KIXMILLER, Edgar Byron 6
KIXMILLER, William 2
KIZER, Benjamin Hamilton 6
KIZER, Benjamin Hamilton 7
KIZER, Edwin Dicken 7
KJELLGREN, Bengt R. F. 5
KJERSTAD, Conrad Lund 4
KLABER, Eugene Henry 5
KLABUNDE, Earl Horace 4
KLAEBER, Frederick 4
KLAERNER, Richard Albert 4
KLAESTAD, Helge 4
KLAFFENBACH, Arthur O. 4
KLAIN, Zora 5
KLAMMER, Aloysius A. 3
KLAPP, William Henry 1
KLAPPER, Joseph Thomas 6
KLAPPER, Paul 3
KLARAGARD, Sever 7

KLARE, Robert Edward 4
KLARMANN, Adolf D. 6
KLASSEN, Elmer Theodore 10
KLASSEN, Karl Peter 7
KLASSEN, Peter Pierre 7
KLATH, Thormod Oscar 2
KLATSKIN, Gerald 9
KLAUBER, Adolph 1
KLAUBER, Edward 3
KLAUBER, Laurence Monroe 5
KLAUDER, Charles Zeller 1
KLAUS, Irving Goncer 5
KLAUS, Kenneth Blanchard 8
KLAUSER, Karl 1
KLAUSLER, Alfred Paul 10
KLAUSMEYER, David Michael 5
KLAVAN, Israel 7
KLAW, Marc 1
KLAWANS, Arthur Herman 6
KLEBAN, Edward Lawrence 10
KLEBANOFF, Philip Samuel 10
KLEBERG, Edward Robert 3
KLEBERG, Richard Miffin 3
KLEBERG, Robert Justus 6
KLEBERG, Rudolph 1
KLEBS, Arnold Carl 2
KLECKI, Paul 6
KLECKNER, Martin Seler 3
KLECZKA, John C. 7
KLEEGMAN, Sophia Josephine* 5
KLEEMAN, Arthur S. 4
KLEEMAN, Rita Halle 8
KLEENE, Gustav Adolph 2
KLEIN, Alfred 8
KLEIN, Arthur George 4
KLEIN, Arthur Jay 7
KLEIN, Arthur Warner 6
KLEIN, Bruno Oscar 1
KLEIN, Charles 1
KLEIN, Edward Elkan 9
KLEIN, Eugene S. 2
KLEIN, Francis Joseph 5
KLEIN, Frederick B. 3
KLEIN, Frederick Charles 1
KLEIN, George H. 6
KLEIN, Gerald Brown 5
KLEIN, Harry Martin John 5
KLEIN, Harry Thomas 4
KLEIN, Henry Weber 5
KLEIN, Herman William 3
KLEIN, Hermann 4
KLEIN, Horace C. 4
KLEIN, Jacob 1
KLEIN, John Warren 3
KLEIN, Joseph Frederic 1
KLEIN, Joseph J(erome) 6
KLEIN, Julius 1
KLEIN, Julius 8
KLEIN, Manuel 1
KLEIN, Melanie 1
KLEIN, Norma 10
KLEIN, Otto G(eorge) 9
KLEIN, Sandor Sidney 5
KLEIN, Seymour Miller 5
KLEIN, Simon Robert 4
KLEIN, Walter Conrad 4
KLEIN, William, Jr. 5
KLEIN, William Henry 7
KLEIN, William M. 1
KLEINER, Hugo Gustav 5
KLEINER, Israel S. 4
KLEINMAN, Abraham Morris 7
KLEINPELL, Robert Minssen 9
KLEINPELL, William Darwin 3
KLEINSCHMIDT, Edward Ernst 6
KLEINSCHMIDT, Rudolph August 2
KLEINSMID, Rufus Bernard von 4
KLEINWAECHTER, Ludwig Paul Viktor 7
KLEISER, George William 3
KLEISER, Grenville 4
KLEISER, Lorentz 4
KLEISNER, George Harry 10
KLEIST, James Aloysius 4
KLEITZ, William L. 3
KLEMIN, Alexander 3
KLEMM, Louis Richard 1
KLEMME, Edward Julius 5
KLEMME, Randall Telford 6
KLEMME, Roland M. 5
KLEMPERER, Otto 5
KLENDSHOJ, Niels Christian 7
KLENKE, William Walter 4

KLEPETKO, Frank 4
KLEPPER, Frank B. 3
KLEPPER, Max Francis 1
KLERMAN, Gerald Lawrence 10
KLETZER, Virginia Mernes 8
KLETZKI, Paul 5
KLEVENOV, Louis H. 6
KLEYLE, Helen Murray 7
KLIBAN, B(ernard) 10
KLIBANOW, William J. 5
KLIEFORTH, Alfred Will 8
KLIEFORTH, Ralph George 4
KLIEN, Arthur Jay 3
KLIEWER, John Walter 1
KLIKA, Ervin Robert 4
KLIMAS, John Edward 6
KLIMAS, John Edward 7
KLINCK, Arthur William 3
KLINCK, Leonard Silvanus 5
KLINE, Allan Blair 5
KLINE, Allen Marshall 4
KLINE, Ardolph L. 1
KLINE, Barton Leeorie 6
KLINE, C. Mahlon 4
KLINE, Charles H. 1
KLINE, Charles Talcott 8
KLINE, Franz Josef 4
KLINE, George 2
KLINE, George Milton 1
KLINE, George Washington 1
KLINE, I. Clinton 3
KLINE, Ira M. 6
KLINE, Jacob 1
KLINE, John Robert 1
KLINE, Marcus C. L. 1
KLINE, Marion Justus 1
KLINE, Morris 10
KLINE, Nathan Schellenberg 8
KLINE, Paul Robert 5
KLINE, Quentin McKay 1
KLINE, Reamer 8
KLINE, Virgil Philip 1
KLINE, Walter Winter 6
KLINE, Whorten Albert 2
KLINE, William Fair 1
KLINE, William Jay 1
KLINEFELTER, Howard Emanuel 5
KLING, Charles Fergus 6
KLING, Samuel Grover 7
KLINGAMAN, Orie Erb 1
KLINGBERG, Frank Joseph 7
KLINGBIEL, Ray I. 5
KLINGE, Ernest F. 3
KLINGENSMITH, John, Jr. H
KLINGENSTEIN, Joseph 7
KLINGLER, Harry J. 4
KLINGMAN, Darwin Dee 10
KLINGMAN, William (Washington) 1
KLIPPART, John Hancock H
KLIPSTEIN, Ernest Carl 1
KLIPSTEIN, Louis Frederick H
KLITGAARD, Georgina 1
KLOAP, John Melnick 8
KLOCK, Mabie Crouse 3
KLOEB, Frank Le Blond 1
KLOEBER, Charles Edward 1
KLOEFFLER, Royce Gerald 6
KLOEFFLER, Royce Gerald 7
KLONIS, Stewart 10
KLONOWER, Henry 8
KLOPFER, Donald Simon 4
KLOPMAN, William 6
KLOPP, Edward Jonathan 1
KLOPP, Henry Irwin 2
KLOPPENBURG, Ralph Haase 10
KLOPSCH, Louis 1
KLOPSTEG, Paul Ernest 9
KLOSS, Charles Luther 1
KLOSS, John Anthony 10
KLOSSNER, Howard Jacob 4
KLOTS, Allen Trafford 4
KLOTS, Allen Trafford 9
KLOTZ, Oskar 1
KLOTZ, Robert H
KLOTZBURGER, Edwin Carl 4
KLUBERTANZ, George Peter 5
KLUCKHOHN, Clyde Kay Maben 4
KLUCKHOLN, Frank Louis 5
KLUCKMAN, Revone W. 8

KLUCZYNSKI, John C. 6
KLUG, Norman R. 4
KLUGER, Samuel B. 8
KLUGESCHEID, Richard 5
Charles
KLUGHERZ, John 3
Anthony
KLUSS, Charles Laverne 4
KLUSS, Wilfred Martin 9
KLUSZEWSKI, Theodore 10
Bernard
KLUTTS, Jerry 7
KLUTTZ, Theodore 4
Franklin
KLUTTZ, Whitehead 6
KLUVER, Heinrich 7
KLUYVER, Albert Jan 3
KLYCE, Scudder 1
KLYVER, Henry Peter 4
KNABE, Valentine Wilhelm H
Ludwig
KNABENSHUE, Paul 1
KNABENSHUE, Roy 3
KNABENSHUE, Samuel S. 1
KNAEBEL, Ernest 2
KNAGGS, Nelson Stuart 10
KNAPLUND, Paul 4
Alexander
KNAPP, Adeline 1
KNAPP, Andrew Stephen 4
KNAPP, Anthony Lausett 6
KNAPP, Arnold Herman 3
KNAPP, A(rthur) Blair 2
KNAPP, Arthur May 4
KNAPP, Bliss 3
KNAPP, Bradford 1
KNAPP, Charles H
KNAPP, Charles 1
KNAPP, Charles Luman 1
KNAPP, Charles Welbourne 1
KNAPP, Chauncey H
Langdon
KNAPP, Cleon Talboys 3
KNAPP, Daniel C. 10
KNAPP, David William 9
KNAPP, Francis Atherton 5
KNAPP, Frank Averill 4
KNAPP, Fred Church 2
KNAPP, George H
KNAPP, George C. 7
KNAPP, George Leonard 5
KNAPP, Grace Higley 5
KNAPP, Halsey B. 8
KNAPP, Harold Everard 4
KNAPP, Harry Shepard 1
KNAPP, Henry Alonzo 1
KNAPP, Herman* 1
KNAPP, John Joseph 1
KNAPP, Joseph Grant 8
KNAPP, Joseph Palmer 3
KNAPP, Kemper K. 2
KNAPP, Lyman Enos 1
KNAPP, Martin Augustine 1
KNAPP, Peter Hobart 10
KNAPP, Philip Coombs 1
KNAPP, Robert Hampden 4
KNAPP, Robert Talbot 3
KNAPP, Samuel Lorenzo H
KNAPP, Seaman Asahel 1
KNAPP, Shepherd 2
KNAPP, Sherman 9
Richmond
KNAPP, Stanley Merrill 4
KNAPP, Thad Johnson 1
KNAPP, Thomas McCartan 4
KNAPP, Walter I(rving) 5
KNAPP, Wilfrid McNaught 7
KNAPP, Willard A. 1
KNAPP, William Ireland 1
KNAPPEN, Loyal Edwin 1
KNAPPEN, Theodore 1
MacFarlane
KNAPPENBERGER, J. 4
William
KNAPPERTSBUSCH, 4
Hans
KNATCHBULL- 9
HUGESSEN, Adrian
KNATHS, Karl (Otto) 5
KNAUFFT, Edwin 4
KNAUSS, Francis J(acob) 7
KNAUSS, Harold Paul 4
KNAUTH, Arnold 4
Whitman
KNAUTH, Oswald 4
Whitman
KNEASS, George Bryan 5
KNEASS, Samuel H
Honeyman
KNEASS, Strickland H
KNEASS, Strickland Landis 1
KNEASS, William H
KNECHT, Andrew Wilson 4
KNECHT, Karl Kae 5
KNEEDLER, William L. 4
KNEELAND, Abner H

KNEELAND, George 5
Jackson
KNEELAND, Robert 5
Shepherd
KNEELAND, Robert 7
Shepherd
KNEELAND, Samuel* H
KNEELAND, Stillman 1
Foster
KNEELAND, Yale, Jr. 5
KNEIL, Robert Chipman 4
KNEIP, Frederick Evoy 10
KNEIP, Herbert Joseph 3
KNEIP, Richard Francis 9
KNEISEL, Franz 1
KNEISLY, Nathaniel 8
McKay
KNEISS, Gilbert Harold 4
KNEPPER, Edwin Garfield 4
KNERR, Hugh Johnston 8
KNEUBUHL, Emily 7
KNEVELS, Gertrude 4
KNIBBS, Harry Herbert 2
KNICKERBOCKER, Fred 3
Hugh
KNICKERBOCKER, H
Harmen Jansen
KNICKERBOCKER, H
Herman
KNICKERBOCKER, 2
Hubert Renfro
KNICKERBOCKER, 4
William E.
KNICKERBOCKER, 5
William Skinkle
KNIFFIN, William Henry 3
KNIGHT, Adele Ferguson 4
KNIGHT, Albion 1
Williamson
KNIGHT, Alfred 6
KNIGHT, Arthur Merrill 6
KNIGHT, Augustus Smith 2
KNIGHT, Austin Melvin 1
KNIGHT, Bruce Winton 9
KNIGHT, Charles 1
KNIGHT, Charles Landon 1
KNIGHT, Charles Mellen 2
KNIGHT, Charles Robert 3
KNIGHT, Charles 7
Strongman
KNIGHT, Clarence A. 1
KNIGHT, Claude Arthur 9
(Reynolds)
KNIGHT, Clifford 9
KNIGHT, Edgar Wallace 3
KNIGHT, Edward Collings H
KNIGHT, Edward Henry 4
KNIGHT, Edward Hooker 2
KNIGHT, Edward Wallace 2
KNIGHT, Erastus Cole 2
KNIGHT, Eric 4
KNIGHT, Eugene Herbert 5
KNIGHT, Eugene Herbert 7
KNIGHT, Felix Harrison 6
KNIGHT, Frances Gladys 8
KNIGHT, Francis 3
McMaster
KNIGHT, Frank A. 3
KNIGHT, Frank Burke 8
KNIGHT, Frank Hyneman 5
KNIGHT, Frederic 7
Butterfield
KNIGHT, Frederic 1
Harrison
KNIGHT, Frederick Irving 1
KNIGHT, George 1
Alexander
KNIGHT, George Laurence 2
KNIGHT, George Thomson 1
KNIGHT, George Wells 1
KNIGHT, Goodwin (Jess) 4
KNIGHT, Grant Cochran 1
KNIGHT, Harold Audas 3
KNIGHT, Harry Clifford 2
KNIGHT, Harry Edward 5
KNIGHT, Harry Hazelton 8
KNIGHT, Harry S. 1
KNIGHT, Harry Wallace 8
KNIGHT, Henry Cogswell H
KNIGHT, Henry Granger 2
KNIGHT, Howard Lawton 6
KNIGHT, Howard Roscoe 2
KNIGHT, James Ernest 1
KNIGHT, James L. 10
KNIGHT, Jesse 1
KNIGHT, Jesse William 4
KNIGHT, John 3
KNIGHT, John George 1
David
KNIGHT, John James 8
KNIGHT, John Shively 2
KNIGHT, John Thornton 1
KNIGHT, Jonathan* H
KNIGHT, Leona Kaiser 4
KNIGHT, Lester Benjamin 10
KNIGHT, Lester Lloyd 9
KNIGHT, Louis Aston 2

KNIGHT, Lucian Lamar 1
KNIGHT, Milton 5
KNIGHT, Montgomery 2
KNIGHT, Nehemiah H
KNIGHT, Nehemiah Rice H
KNIGHT, Nicholas 4
KNIGHT, Ora Willis 7
KNIGHT, Otis D. 4
KNIGHT, Peter Oliphant 2
KNIGHT, Ralph T(homas) 7
KNIGHT, Richard Bennett 8
KNIGHT, Ridgway 1
KNIGHT, Robert 1
KNIGHT, Robert Palmer 4
KNIGHT, Robert Patrick 10
KNIGHT, Ryland 3
KNIGHT, Samuel 1
KNIGHT, Samuel Bradley 9
KNIGHT, Samuel Howell 9
KNIGHT, Sarah Kemble H
KNIGHT, Stephen Albert 1
KNIGHT, Ted (Tadeus 9
Wladyslaw Konopka)
KNIGHT, Telfair 8
KNIGHT, Thomas A. 9
KNIGHT, Thomas Edmund 2
KNIGHT, Thomas 1
Edmund, Jr.
KNIGHT, Thomas J. 7
KNIGHT, Walter David 3
KNIGHT, Webster 1
KNIGHT, Wilbur Clinton 1
KNIGHT, William Allen 3
KNIGHT, William D. 4
KNIGHT, William Henry 1
KNIGHT, William Windus 9
KNIPE, Alden Arthur 4
KNIPE, Emilie Benson 3
KNIPE, James Launcelot 8
KNIPP, Charles Tobias 2
KNISKERN, Leslie Albert 4
KNISKERN, Philip 4
Wheeler
KNISKERN, Warren B. 1
KNOBLAUCH, Arthur 9
Lewis
KNOBLOCH, Henry 5
F(rederick) J(acob)
KNOCH, Win G. 8
KNODE, Oliver M. 4
KNODE, Ralph Howard 4
KNOLENBERG, Bernhard 6
KNOLES, Tully Cleon 3
KNOLL, Hans G. 4
KNOLLYS, Edward George 4
William Tyrwhitt
KNOOP, Frederick Barnes 5
KNOPF, Adolph 4
KNOPF, Alfred A. 9
KNOPF, Blanche 4
KNOPF, Blanche (Wolf) 5
KNOPF, Carl Sumner 2
KNOPF, Philip 4
KNOPF, S. Adolphus 1
KNOPF, William Cleveland, 7
Jr.
KNOPF, William Cleveland, 5
Jr.
KNOPP, Herbert William, 4
Sr.
KNORPP, Walter Wesley 7
KNORR, Fred August 4
KNORR, Klaus Eugene 10
KNORR, Nathan Homer 7
KNORR, Walter Hebert 6
KNORTZ, Karl 4
KNOTT, A. Leo 1
KNOTT, David H. 3
KNOTT, Emmet Kennard 4
KNOTT, J. Proctor 8
KNOTT, James E. 4
KNOTT, James Proctor 1
KNOTT, John Francis 4
KNOTT, J(oseph) C(arlton) 8
KNOTT, J(oseph) C(arlton) 8
KNOTT, Laura A. 4
KNOTT, Lester R. 4
KNOTT, Richard Gillmore 9
KNOTT, Richard Wilson 1
KNOTT, Stuart R. 4
KNOTT, Thomas Albert 4
KNOTT, Van Buren 5
KNOTTS, Armanis F. 1
KNOTTS, Edward C. 1
KNOTTS, Howard Clayton 4
KNOTTS, Raymond 5
KNOUFF, Ralph Albert 4
KNOUS, William Lee 3
KNOWER, Henry 1
McElderry
KNOWLAND, Joseph 4
Russell
KNOWLAND, William Fife 6
KNOWLES, Archibald 5
Campbell
KNOWLES, Asa Smallidge 10
KNOWLES, Daniel Clark 1

KNOWLES, Edward Gillett 5
KNOWLES, Edward 4
Randall
KNOWLES, Edwin 5
Blackwell
KNOWLES, Ellin J. 1
KNOWLES, Frederic 1
Lawrence
KNOWLES, Frederick 5
Milton
KNOWLES, Gladys 9
Ellsworth Heinrich (Mrs.
Aubrey Knowles)
KNOWLES, Harvey Coles 9
KNOWLES, Hiram 1
KNOWLES, Horace 1
Greeley
KNOWLES, Hugh Shaler 9
KNOWLES, John Hilton 7
KNOWLES, Lucius James H
KNOWLES, Melita 5
KNOWLES, Morris 1
KNOWLES, Nathaniel 5
KNOWLES, Richard 8
KNOWLES, Robert Bell 3
KNOWLSON, James S. 3
KNOWLTON, Ansel 3
Alphonse
KNOWLTON, Charles H
KNOWLTON, Charles 4
Osmond
KNOWLTON, Charles 5
Osmond
KNOWLTON, Daniel 5
Chauncey
KNOWLTON, Ebenezer H
KNOWLTON, Eliot A. 1
KNOWLTON, Frank Hall 1
KNOWLTON, Frank 5
P(attengill)
KNOWLTON, George 1
Willard
KNOWLTON, Helen Mary 1
KNOWLTON, Hosea 1
Morrill
KNOWLTON, Marcus 1
Perrin
KNOWLTON, P. Clarke 1
KNOWLTON, Philip 3
Arnold
KNOWLTON, Robert 4
Henry
KNOWLTON, Thomas H
KNOX, Adeline Trafton 4
KNOX, Mrs. Charles B. 3
KNOX, Clinton Everett 7
KNOX, Dudley Wright 4
KNOX, Mrs. Frank 5
KNOX, George William 1
KNOX, Harry 1
KNOX, Henry H
KNOX, James H
KNOX, James E. 3
KNOX, Jessie Juliet (Daily) 5
KNOX, John Barnett 1
KNOX, John Clark 4
KNOX, John Jay H
KNOX, John Marshall 10
KNOX, Louis 2
KNOX, Martin Van Buren 1
KNOX, Mary Alice 4
KNOX, Philander Chase 1
KNOX, Raymond Collyer 5
KNOX, Robert White 3
KNOX, Rush Hightower 4
KNOX, Samuel H
KNOX, Samuel Lippincott 2
Griswold
KNOX, Seymour H. 10
KNOX, Seymour Horace, 4
III
KNOX, Thomas Wallace H
KNOX, Walter Eugene, III 8
KNOX, William Carroll, Jr. 8
KNOX, William Edward 4
KNOX, William Elliott 1
KNOX, William Francis 7
KNOX, William Franklin 2
KNOX, William Russell 5
KNOX, William Shadrach 4
KNOX, William Wallace 8
KNOX, William White 1
KNUBEL, Frederick 2
Hermann
KNUBEL, Frederick 3
Ritscher
KNUDSEN, Arthur Miller 8
KNUDSEN, Charles 3
William
KNUDSEN, Thorkild R. 4
KNUDSEN, Vern O. 6
KNUDSEN, William S. 2
KNUDSON, Albert 1
Cornelius
KNUDSON, Bennett Olin 4
KNUDSON, Charles 7
Anthony

KNUDSON, James K. 4
KNUDSON, John 3
Immanuel
KNUDSON, Lewis 7
KNUTSON, Harold 3
KNUTSON, Herbert Claus 9
KNUTSON, Kent Siguart 5
KOBAK, Alfred Julian 6
KOBAK, Edgar 4
KOBBE, Gustav 1
KOBBE, William August 1
KOBELT, Karl 4
KOBER, Arthur 6
KOBER, George Martin 1
KOCH, Alfred 3
KOCH, Arnold Theodor 7
KOCH, Carl Galland 10
KOCH, Charles Rudolph 1
Edward
KOCH, Edward William 2
KOCH, Elers 3
KOCH, Felix John 1
KOCH, Fred Chase 5
KOCH, Fred Conrad 2
KOCH, Frederick Henry 2
KOCH, George Price 5
KOCH, Harlan Clifford 9
KOCH, Henry G. H
KOCH, John 7
KOCH, Julius Arnold 3
KOCH, Otto 3
KOCH, Raymond Joseph 7
KOCH, Richard 3
KOCH, Sumner Leibnitz 7
KOCH, Theodore Wesley 1
KOCHAN, Edward John 5
KOCHENDORFER, Fred 9
Daniel
KOCHER, A. Lawrence 5
KOCHERSPERGER, 4
Hiram Miller
KOCHERTHAL, Josua von H
KOCHIN, Louis Mordecai 5
KOCHS, August 4
KOCIALKOWSKI, Leo 3
KOCK, Winston Edward 8
KOCKRITZ, Ewald 1
KOCOUREK, Albert 5
KOCSIS, Ann 6
KOCUREK, Louis Joe 9
KODALY, Zoltan 4
KOEBEL, Ralph Francis 4
KOEGEL, Otto Erwin 6
KOEGEL, Otto Erwin 6
KOEHLER, John Theodore 10
KOEHLER, Otto A. 5
KOEHLER, Robert 1
KOEHLER, Sylvester Rosa 1
KOEHLER, Walter Allos 7
KOEHLER, Wilhelm 3
Reinhold Walter
KOEHRING, William J. 5
KOENIG, Adolph 1
KOENIG, Egmont Francis 6
KOENIG, Frederick 7
Gilman, Jr.
KOENIG, George Augustus 1
KOENIG, Joseph Pierre 4
KOENIG, Louis F. 5
KOENIG, M(arshall) Glenn 6
KOENIG, Myron L(aw) 5
KOENIG, Robert P. 8
KOENIG, Virgil 10
KOENIGSBERG, Moses 2
KOENKER, Robert Henry 3
KOEPEL, Norbert Francis 4
KOEPPEL, Donald Allen 9
KOERBLE, Charles 6
Edward
KOERNER, Andrew 4
KOERNER, Gustave H
KOERNER, Henry 10
KOERNER, Theodor 3
KOERNER, Theodor 3
KOERNER, William 3
KOERNER, William Henry 1
Dethlep
KOESTER, Frank 1
KOESTER, George Arthur 6
KOESTLER, Arthur 8
KOFFKA, Kurt 1
KOGAN, Herman 10
KOGAN, Leonld 8
KOGEL, Marcus David 10
KOGLER, James Foley 10
KOGSTAD, Arthur 7
Woodrow
KOHL, Edwin Phillips 4
KOHLBECK, Valentine 1
KOHLBERG, Lawrence 9
KOHLER, Arthur W. 8
KOHLER, Elmer Peter 1
KOHLER, Eric Louis 6
KOHLER, Foy David 10
KOHLER, Fred 1
KOHLER, G. A. Edward 1
KOHLER, Herbert Calvin 3

LAFFERTY, Abraham Walter 5
LAFFERTY, Alma V. 4
LAFFERTY, John James 1
LAFFERTY, William Thornton 1
LAFFITE, Jean H
LAFFOON, Ruby 1
LAFLECHE, Leo Richer 3
LA FLESCHE, Francis 1
LA FLESCHE, Susette H
LAFLIN, Addison Henry H
LA FOLLETTE, Belle Case 1
LA FOLLETTE, Fola 5
LA FOLLETTE, Harvey Marion 1
LA FOLLETTE, Philip Fox 4
LA FOLLETTE, Robert Marion 1
LA FOLLETTE, Robert Marion, Jr. 3
LA FOLLETTE, Robert Russell 4
LA FOLLETTE, Suzanne 8
LA FOLLETTE, William L. 1
LAFON, Thomy H
LAFONTAINE, Jean-Marie 9
LA FONTAINE, Rachel Adelaide 1
LAFORE, Laurence Davis 9
LA FORGE, Laurence 3
LAFOUNT, Harold Arundel 3
LAFRENTZ, Ferdinand William 3
LA GARDE, Louis Anatole 1
LAGEN, Mary Huneker (Mrs.) 5
LAGER, Eric W. 6
LAGERCRANTZ, Herman Ludvig Fabian de 4
LAGERGREN, Carl Gustaf 1
LAGERKVIST, Par (Fabian) 6
LAGERQUIST, Walter Edwards 2
LAGERSTROM, Paco Axel 10
LAGINESTRA, Rocco Michael 8
LA GORCE, John Oliver 3
LAGRANGE, Frank Crawford 4
LAGRONE, Cyrus Wilson, Jr. 9
LA GUARDIA, Fiorello H. 2
LAGUNA, Theodore de Leo de 1
LAHEE, Frederic Henry 9
LAHEE, Henry Charles 4
LAHEY, Edwin A. 5
LAHEY, Frank Howard 3
LAHEY, Richard Francis 7
LAHM, Frank Purdy 4
LAHM, Frank Purdy 5
LAHM, Samuel H
LAHONTAN, baron de H
LAHR, Bert 4
LAHR, Raymond Merrill 6
LAI, Chia-chiu 5
LAIDLAW, Alexander Hamilton 1
LAIDLAW, Alexander Hamilton, Jr. 1
LAIDLAW, Harriet Barton 2
LAIDLAW, John Blake 6
LAIDLAW, Robert Alexander 7
LAIDLAW, Robert W. 7
LAIDLAW, Walter 1
LAIDLER, Harry Wellington 5
LAIDLER, Harry Wellington 7
LAIDLEY, Roy Russell 5
LAING, Alexander Kinnan 7
LAING, Arthur 7
LAING, Chester William 4
LAING, Gordon Jennings 2
LAING, James Tamplin 7
LAING, John 2
LAING, John Albert 3
LAING, Peter Marshall 9
LAING, Samuel McPherson 2
LAIPPLY, Thomas Charles 5
LAIRD, Allison White 1
LAIRD, Donald Anderson 10
LAIRD, Edmund Cody 4
LAIRD, Helen Connor 8
LAIRD, James H
LAIRD, John Baker 5
LAIRD, John Kenneth, Jr. 6
LAIRD, John King 7
LAIRD, John Wesley 7
LAIRD, Linnie 8
LAIRD, Samuel 1
LAIRD, Warren Powers 2
LAIRD, William J. 7
LAIRD, William Ramsey 6
LAIRY, Moses Barnett 1
LAIST, Theodore Frederick 1
LAISTNER, Max Ludwig Wolfram 3
LAIT, Jacquin L. 3
LAKANAL, Joseph H
LAKE, Charles H. 4
LAKE, Devereux 5
LAKE, Everett John 2
LAKE, Forrest U(nna) 8
LAKE, Fred Wrightman 3
LAKE, George Burt 2
LAKE, Harry Beaston 5
LAKE, Harry Beaston 7
LAKE, John 3
LAKE, Kirsopp 2
LAKE, Leonora Marie 4
LAKE, Mack Clayton 3
LAKE, Marshall E. 3
LAKE, Richard Harrington 9
LAKE, Simon 2
LAKE, William Augustus H
LAKES, Arthur 4
LAKEY, Alice 1
LAKIN, Herbert Conrad 5
LAKIN, James Sansome 1
LAL, Gobind Beharl 8
LALANDE, Gilles 10
LA LANNE, Frank Dale 1
LALLEY, Joseph M(ichael) 7
LALLEY, William H. 7
LALLY, Francis Joseph 9
LALLY, John Peter 9
LALONE, Emerson Hugh 4
LALOR, Alice H
LALUMIER, Edward Louis 6
LAMADE, Dietrick 1
LAMADE, George R. 4
LAMADE, Howard John 3
LAMAR, Andrew Jackson 1
LAMAR, Clarinda Pendleton 2
LAMAR, Gazaway Bugg H
LAMAR, Henry Graybill H
LAMAR, James Sanford 4
LAMAR, John Basil H
LAMAR, Joseph Rucker 1
LAMAR, Lucius Quintus Cincinnatus H
LAMAR, Mirabeau Bounaparte H
LAMAR, William Harmong 1
LA MARR, Esther Bernice Randall 5
LAMARSH, John Raymond 8
LAMARSH, Judy (Julia Verlyn) 7
LAMAS, Fernando 8
LAMASTER, Slater 8
LAMB, Albert Richard 3
LAMB, Alfred William H
LAMB, Arthur Becket 3
LAMB, B(urley) F(rank) 7
LAMB, Charles Rollinson 2
LAMB, Daniel Smith 1
LAMB, Edward 9
LAMB, Edwin Travis 1
LAMB, Ella Condie 3
LAMB, Franklin 7
LAMB, Frederick Stymetz 1
LAMB, Harold Albert 4
LAMB, Henry Whitney 1
LAMB, Horace Rand 7
LAMB, Hugh Louis 3
LAMB, Isaac Wixom 1
LAMB, James Gibson 5
LAMB, John H
LAMB, John 4
LAMB, John Edward 1
LAMB, John Wallace 7
LAMB, Joseph F. 4
LAMB, Martha Joanna Reade Nash H
LAMB, Peter Oswald 1
LAMB, Richard Hubbert 4
LAMB, Robert Scott 3
LAMB, Roland O. 1
LAMB, William 1
LAMB, William Frederick 3
LAMB, William Hollinshead 7
LAMBDIN, Alfred Cochran 1
LAMBDIN, James Reid H
LAMBDIN, Jerry Elmer 4
LAMBDIN, Milton Bennett 1
LAMBDIN, William Wallace 1
LAMBE, Sir Charles Edward 4
LAMBERSON, Ray Guernsey 6
LAMBERT, Adrian Van Sinderen 5
LAMBERT, Albert Bond 2
LAMBERT, Alexander 1
LAMBERT, Avery Eldorus 5
LAMBERT, Byron James 3
LAMBERT, Charles H
LAMBERT, Charles Frederic 10
LAMBERT, Charles Irwin 3
LAMBERT, Fred Dayton 1
LAMBERT, Gerard Barnes 4
LAMBERT, Henry Lewis 8
LAMBERT, Hubert Cottrell 6
LAMBERT, Jack Lincoln 4
LAMBERT, Joe Calvin 7
LAMBERT, John H
LAMBERT, John 1
LAMBERT, John S. 3
LAMBERT, Louis A. 1
LAMBERT, Oscar Doane 4
LAMBERT, Robert Archibald 4
LAMBERT, Robert Eugene 5
LAMBERT, Robert Joe 10
LAMBERT, Samuel Waldron 2
LAMBERT, T. Arthur 4
LAMBERT, Tallmadge Augustine 4
LAMBERT, Walter Davis 6
LAMBERT, William Harrison 1
LAMBERT, W(illiam) V(incent) 6
LAMBERT, Wilton John 1
LAMBERTON, Benjamin Peffer 1
LAMBERTON, Chess 5
LAMBERTON, James McCormick 1
LAMBERTON, James Wilson 9
LAMBERTON, John A. 2
LAMBERTON, John Porter 1
LAMBERTON, Robert Eneas 1
LAMBERTON, William Alexander 1
LAMBERTSON, Genio Madison 1
LAMBERTSON, William Purnell 3
LAMBETH, William Alexander 2
LAMBETH, William Arnold 3
LAMBIE, Morris Bryan 8
LAMBIE, William S. 7
LAMBLE, John W. 5
LAMBRIGHT, Edwin Dart 3
LAMBRIX, Joseph H. 5
LAMBUTH, James William H
LAMBUTH, Walter Russell 1
LA MER, Victor Kuhn 4
LAMEY, Arthur Francis 4
LAMEY, Carl Arthur 9
LAMM, Henry 4
LAMM, Lynne M. 3
LAMME, Benjamin G. 1
LAMON, Ward Hill H
LAMONT, Daniel Scott 1
LAMONT, Forrest 1
LAMONT, Hammond 1
LAMONT, Peter T. 5
LAMONT, Robert Patterson 2
LAMONT, Thomas Stilwell 4
LAMONT, Thomas William 2
LA MONTE, John Life 3
LAMORISSE, Albert 5
LA MOTHE, John Dominique 1
LA MOTTE, Ellen Newbold 4
LAMOUNTAIN, John H
L'AMOUR, Louis Dearborn 9
LA MOURE, Howard Alexander 5
LAMOUREUX, Silas Wright 1
LAMPE, John Harold 9
LAMPE, Joseph Joachim 1
LAMPE, M(atthew) Willard 7
LAMPE, William Blakeman 7
LAMPE, William Edmund 3
LAMPEN, Albert Eugene 4
LAMPERT, Floran 1
LAMPERT, James Benjamin 7
LAMPERTI, A. Charles 7
LAMPLAND, Carl Otto 3
LAMPMAN, Ben Hur 3
LAMPMAN, Lewis 4
LAMPORT, Harold 6
LAMPORT, Harold 7
LAMPORT, William Henry H
LAMPRECHT, Sterling Power 6
LAMPREY, Louise 3
LAMPRON, Edward John 8
LAMPSON, Sir Curtis Miranda H
LAMPTON, Dinwiddie 7
LAMPTON, Robert Benjamin 7
LAMPTON, Thaddeus Booth 1
LAMPTON, Walter M. 4
LAMPTON, William James 1
LAMSA, George Mamishisho 9
LAMSON, Charles Henry 1
LAMSON, Charles Marion 1
LAMSON, Fred Mason 1
LAMSON, George Herbert, Jr. 1
LAMSON, Guy Caleb 5
LAMSON, Julius Gustavus 2
LAMSON, Paul Dudley 4
LAMSON-SCRIBNER, Frank 1
LAMY, John Baptist H
LANAHAN, Francis H. 6
LANAHAN, Henry 4
LANAHAN, William Wallace 2
LANCASTER, Billy Jack 7
LANCASTER, Bruce 4
LANCASTER, Chester L. 3
LANCASTER, Columbia H
LANCASTER, Dabney Stewart 6
LANCASTER, Ellsworth Gage 3
LANCASTER, Henry Carrington 3
LANCASTER, Hewes 1
LANCASTER, John Herrold 5
LANCASTER, John Lynch 4
LANCASTER, Lane W. 9
LANCASTER, Richard Venable 4
LANCASTER, Walter B. 3
LANCE, Thomas Jackson 7
LANCEFIELD, Rebecca Craighill 7
LANCHESTER, Elsa 9
LAND, Aldred Dillingham 1
LAND, Charles Henry 1
LAND, Edwin Herbert 10
LAND, Emory Scott 5
LAND, Fort Elmo 1
LAND, Francis LaVerne 8
LAND, Frank Sherman 3
LAND, Frank Sherman 4
LAND, William Jesse Goad 2
LANDA, Louis A. 10
LANDACRE, Francis Leroy 1
LANDACRE, Paul Hambleton 4
LANDAHL, Carl William 5
LANDAIS, Pierre H
LANDAU, Jacob 5
LANDAU, Lev Davidovich 5
LANDAUER, Jerry Gerd 7
LANDAUER, Jerry Gerd 8
LANDEEN, William Martin 9
LANDEGGER, Karl Francis 6
LANDER, Edward 1
LANDER, Frederick West H
LANDER, Jean Margaret 1
LANDER, Louisa 4
LANDER, Mamie Stubbs 8
LANDER, Toni (Toni Pihl Petersen) 8
LANDERHOLM, Edwin Francis 4
LANDERS, George Foreman 1
LANDERS, George Marcellus H
LANDERS, Howe Stone 2
LANDERS, Joseph Samuel 4
LANDERS, Mary Kenny 10
LANDERS, Warren Prince 2
LANDERS, Wilbur Nelson 4
LANDES, Bertha Knight 2
LANDES, Henry 1
LANDES, Herbert Ellis 3
LANDES, Ruth 10
LANDES, William Grant 5
LANDFIELD, Jerome 3
LANDGREBE, Earl Frederick 9
LANDIS, Benson Young 4
LANDIS, Carney 4
LANDIS, Cary D. 1
LANDIS, Charles Beary 1
LANDIS, Charles Israel 1
LANDIS, Charles William 5
LANDIS, Frederick 10
LANDIS, Frederick 1
LANDIS, Gerald Wayne 5
LANDIS, Harry Dewitt 3
LANDIS, Henry Robert Murray 1
LANDIS, James McCauley 4
LANDIS, Jessie Royce 5
LANDIS, John Howard 1
LANDIS, Josiah Pennabecker 1
LANDIS, Kenesaw Mountain 2
LANDIS, Kenesaw Mountain, II 2
LANDIS, Mark Homer 7
LANDIS, Mary Green (Mrs. Judson Taylor Landis) 6
LANDIS, Paul Nissley 5
LANDIS, Robert Kumler 4
LANDIS, William Weldman 2
LANDMAN, Isaac 2
LANDMAN, Jacob Henry 4
LANDMAN, Louis W. 3
LANDON, Alfred Mossman 9
LANDON, Charles Raeburne 5
LANDON, Chauncey Louis 9
LANDON, Edward August 9
LANDON, Hal D. 4
LANDON, Hugh McKennan 2
LANDON, Judson Stuart 1
LANDON, Melville De Lancey 1
LANDON, Michael (Eugene Maurice Orowitz)* 10
LANDON, Thomas Durland 1
LANDON, Thompson Hoadley 1
LANDON, Warren Hall 1
LANDONE, Leon Elbert 4
LANDOWSKA, Wanda 3
LANDRES, Morris M. 10
LANDRETH, Burnet 1
LANDRETH, David H
LANDRETH, Earl 5
LANDRETH, Olin Henry 1
LANDRETH, Symington Phillips 6
LANDRETH, William Barker 4
LANDRIGAN, Charles Raymond 4
LANDRITH, Harold Fochone 9
LANDRITH, Ira 1
LANDRUM, John Morgan H
LANDRUM, Philip Mitchell 10
LANDRUM, Robert Dallas 2
LANDRUM, William Warren 1
LANDRY, Aubrey Edward 5
LANDRY, George A. 4
LANDRY, Joseph Aristide H
LANDSBERG, Helmut E(rich) 9
LANDSBERG, Max 1
LANDSBERG, Mortimer 7
LANDSHOFF, Fritz Helmut 9
LANDSIEDEL, Harry 4
LANDSMAN, Herbert Samuel 7
LANDSTEINER, Karl 2
LANDSTREET, Fairfax Stuart 1
LANDY, James H
LANE, Albert Grannis 1
LANE, Alfred Church 2
LANE, Sir Allen 5
LANE, Amos H
LANE, Anna Eichberg King 4
LANE, Arthur Bliss 3
LANE, Arthur Willis 7
LANE, Charles Elmaar 5
LANE, Charles Homer 1
LANE, Charles Homer 2
LANE, Charles Stoddard 1
LANE, Chester T. 3
LANE, Clarence Guy 3
LANE, Clement Quirk 3
LANE, Donald Edward 7
LANE, Edward Binney 1
LANE, Edward Hudson 6
LANE, Edward Wood 2
LANE, Elbert Clarence 3
LANE, Elinor MacArtney 1
LANE, Ernest Preston 7
LANE, Everett Hale 6
LANE, Francis Ransom 4
LANE, Frank Hardy 5
LANE, Franklin Knight 1
LANE, Frederic Chapin 8

LA SALLE, Joseph Pierre 8
LA SALLE, sieur de H
LASATER, Ed 1
  Cunningham
LASBY, William Frederick 5
LASCARI, Salvatore 4
LASDON, William Stanley 8
LASELLE, Mary Augusta 4
LASER, Marvin 9
LA SERE, Emile H
LASH, Israel George H
LASH, James Hamilton 3
LASH, Joseph P. 9
LASHAR, Walter B. 1
LA SHELLE, Kirke 1
LASHER, George Starr 4
LASHER, George William 1
LASHINSKY, Herbert 7
LASHLEY, K. S. 3
LASHLY, Arthur Valentine 3
LASHLY, Jacob Mark 4
LASHLY, John Henderson 9
LASKE, Arthur Charles 9
LASKER, Albert Davis 3
LASKER, Bruno 4
LASKER, Edward 7
LASKER, Loula Davis 4
LASKEY, John Ellsworth 2
LASKI, Harold Joseph 1
LASKIN, Bora 8
LASKOSKE, Aloysius 5
  William
LASKY, Jesse L. 3
LASKY, Victor 10
LASKY, Wayne Edward 5
LA SPISA, Jake Anthony 5
LASS, Ernest William 7
LASSEN, Peter H
LASSER, Jacob Kay 3
LASSETER, Dillard Brown 10
LASSETTER, William 8
  Casper
LASSETTRE, Edwin 10
  Nichols
LASSINGER, Larry Wayne 6
LASSITER, Francis Rives 1
LASSITER, Herbert Carlyle 3
LASSITER, Newton Hance 5
LASSITER, Robert 5
LASSITER, William 3
LASSWELL, Harold 7
  Dwight
LASTER, Howard Joseph 9
LASTFOGEL, Abe 8
LASTINGER, John 5
  Williams
LASZLO, Ernest 8
LATANE, James Allen 1
LATANE, James Wilson 9
LATANE, John Holladay 1
LATCH, Edward Biddle 1
LATCHAW, David Austin 2
LATCHAW, John Roland 3
  Harris
LATHAM, Carl Ray 1
LATHAM, Charles Louis 5
LATHAM, Dana 6
LATHAM, Earl 2
LATHAM, Harold Strong 5
LATHAM, Louis Charles H
LATHAM, Milton Slocum 1
LATHAM, Orval Ray 1
LATHAM, Rex Knight 3
LATHAM, Vida A. 4
LATHAN, Robert 1
LATHBURY, Albert 4
  Augustus
LATHBURY, Clarence 1
LATHBURY, Mary 1
  Artemisia
LATHE, Herbert William 1
LATHEM, Abraham Lance 1
LATHERS, Richard 3
LATHROP, Alanson P. 3
LATHROP, Austin Eugene 1
LATHROP, Bryan 1
LATHROP, Charles 1
  Newton
LATHROP, Dorothy Pulis 9
LATHROP, Francis 1
LATHROP, Gardiner 1
LATHROP, George Parsons H
LATHROP, Gertrude 10
  Katherine
LATHROP, Henry 1
  Burrowes
LATHROP, John H
LATHROP, John 1
LATHROP, John Carroll 1
LATHROP, John Hiram H
LATHROP, John Howland 1
LATHROP, Julia Clifford 1
LATHROP, Palmer Jadwin 1
LATHROP, Rose 1
  Hawthorne
LATHROP, Samuel H
LATHROP, Walter W. 6

LATHROP, William 1
  Langson
LATHROPE, George 7
  Haines
LATIL, Alexandre H
LATIMER, Asbury 1
  Churchwell
LATIMER, Claiborne 4
  Green
LATIMER, Clyde Burney 3
LATIMER, Elizabeth 1
  Wormeley
LATIMER, Henry H
LATIMER, John Austin 6
LATIMER, John Francis 10
LATIMER, John Leslie 10
LATIMER, Jonathan Wyatt 8
LATIMER, Julian Lane 1
LATIMER, Margery 1
LATIMER, Samuel Lowry 6
LATIMER, Thomas Erwin 1
LATIMER, Thomas 1
  Sargent
LATIMER, Wendell 3
  Mitchell
LA TOUR, Le Blonde de H
LATOURETTE, Earl C. 3
LATOURETTE, Howard 3
  Fenton
LA TOZA, Charles Anton 9
LATROBE, Benjamin H
  Henry*
LATROBE, Charles H
  Hazelhurst
LATROBE, Fredinand 1
  Claiborne
LATROBE, John H
  Hazelhurst Boneval
LATSHAW, David Gardner 5
LATT, Samuel Arch 10
LATTA, Alexander Bonner H
LATTA, James P. 1
LATTA, Robert Edward 3
LATTA, Samuel Whitehill 4
LATTA, Thomas Albert 1
LATTIG, Herbert Elmer 1
LATTIMER, George W. 1
LATTIMORE, John Aaron 1
  Cicero
LATTIMORE, John 1
  Compere
LATTIMORE, Offa Shivers 1
LATTIMORE, Owen 10
LATTIMORE, Richmond 8
LATTIMORE, Samuel 1
  Allan
LATTIMORE, William H
LATTIN, Leroy Emory 6
LATTMAN, Walter 4
LATTRE DE TASSIGNY, 3
  Jean Joseph Marie
  Gabriel de
LATTY, Elvin Remus 9
LATZER, John A. 3
LATZER, Robert Louis 8
LAU, Robert Frederick 2
LAUB, Desmond Kenneth 8
LAUBACH, Charles 1
LAUBACH, Frank Charles 5
LAUBACH, Howard L. 5
LAUBENGAYER, Richard 4
  August
LAUBENGAYER, Robert 3
  J.
LAUBER, Joseph 2
LAUCHHEIMER, Charles 1
  Henry
LAUCK, Gerold McKee 9
LAUCK, William Jett 2
LAUCKS, Irving Fink 7
LAUD, Sam 4
LAUDEMAN, Randolph 1
  Douglass
LAUDER, Andrew B. 8
LAUDER, Harry 4
LAUER, Conrad Newton 2
LAUER, Edward Henry 7
LAUER, Stewart Ellwood 4
LAUER, Walter Ernest 4
LAUFER, Berthold 1
LAUFER, Calvin Weiss 1
LAUFMAN, Sidney 9
LAUGEL, Raymond 6
  William
LAUGHINGHOUSE, 1
  Charles O'Hagan
LAUGHLIN, Clara 1
  Elizabeth
LAUGHLIN, Frank C. 2
LAUGHLIN, Gail 3
LAUGHLIN, George 1
  Ashton
LAUGHLIN, George Mark 2
LAUGHLIN, George 2
  McCully, Jr.

LAUGHLIN, Harry 2
  Hamilton
LAUGHLIN, Henry 9
  Alexander
LAUGHLIN, Hugh C. 6
LAUGHLIN, Irwin 1
LAUGHLIN, James 1
  Laurence
LAUGHLIN, John Edward, 5
  Jr.
LAUGHLIN, Julian 1
LAUGHLIN, Napoleon 4
  Bonaparte
LAUGHLIN, Reginald S. 10
LAUGHLIN, Samuel Ott, 3
  Jr.
LAUGHLIN, Sceva Bright 5
LAUGHTON, Charles 4
LAUGHTON, George 1
LAUGHTON, Sarah 4
  Elizabeth
LAUGIER, Henri 8
LAUHOFF, Howard Joseph 4
LAUNT, Francis Albemarle 1
  Delbretons
LAUPP, Hugo E. 9
LAURANCE, John H
LAURENCE, Margaret 9
LAURENCE, William 7
  Leonard
LAURENS, Henry H
LAURENS, John H
LAURENT, Robert 5
LAURENTI, Mario 1
LAURGAARD, Olaf 2
LAURIAT, Charles Emelius 1
LAURIE, James 1
LAURIE, James Woodin 5
LAURIE, Wilfrid Rhodes 6
LAURIE, William 1
LAURITIS, Joseph 7
  Aloysius
LAURITSEN, Charles 5
  Christian
LAURITZEN, Ivar 6
LAURSON, Phillip Gustave 7
LAURVIK, J(ohn) Nilsen 5
LAURYSSEN, Gaston 4
LAUSCHE, Frank John 10
LAUSE, Charles Joseph 9
LAUT, Agnes C. 1
LAUTERBACH, Edward 1
LAUTERBACH, Jacob 2
  Zallel
LAUTERBACH, Richard 3
  E.
LAUTERBACH, Robert 10
  Alan
LAUTERPACHT, Hersch 4
LAUTMANN, Herbert 5
  Moses
LAUTZ, Henry B(itzel) 1
LAUX, August 1
LAVAKE, Rae Thornton 6
LAVAL, Jean M. 1
LAVALLE, John 5
LAVALLEE, Calixa H
LAVAN, Peter Ichabod 9
  Baer
LA VARRE, William 10
LAVEILLE, Joseph H
LAVELL, Cecil Fairfield 4
LAVELLE, John Daniel 7
LAVELLE, Michael J. 1
LAVELY, Henry Alexander 4
LAVELY, Horace Thomas 8
LAVENDER, Harrison 1
  Morton
LAVENTURE, William 8
  Burrows
LA VERENDRYE, Pierre H
  Gaultier de Varennes
LAVERTY, Roger 8
  Montgomery
LAVERY, Charles Joseph 1
LAVERY, Emmet Godfrey 9
LAVERY, Urban A. 3
LAVES, Kurt 2
LAVES, Walter Herman 8
  Carl
LAVIALLE, Peter Joseph H
LAVIDGE, A. W. 4
LAVINDER, Claude 1
  Hervey
LAVINE, Harold 9
LAVINO, Edwin M. 7
LAVIS, Fred 5
LAW, Andrew H
LAW, Arthur Ayer 1
LAW, Charles Blakeslee 1
LAW, Evander McIver 1
LAW, Francis Marion 5
LAW, Fred Hayes 2
LAW, Frederick Houk 1
LAW, George H
LAW, Herbert Edward 5

LAW, James 1
LAW, James Richard 3
LAW, John H
LAW, John Adger 2
LAW, Jonathan H
LAW, Lyman 1
LAW, Mrs. Marc A. 9
LAW, Marie Hamilton 7
LAW, Richard H
LAW, Robert 1
LAW, Robert Adger 4
LAW, Russell 2
LAW, Sallie Chapman H
  Gordon
LAW, Thomas Hart 1
LAW, William Adger 1
LAWALL, Charles Elmer 5
LA WALL, Charles Herbert 1
LAWDER, Henry Miller 4
LAWES, Lewis E. 2
LAWFORD, Peter 8
LAWLAH, John Wesley 7
LAWLER, Frank H
LAWLER, Joab H
LAWLER, John J. 2
LAWLER, Joseph 8
  Christopher
LAWLER, Richard 8
  H(arold)
LAWLER, Thomas 2
  Bonaventure
LAWLER, Thomas G. 1
LAWLER, Thomas 8
  Newman
LAWLESS, John T. 4
LAWLESS, Theodore 5
  Kenneth
LAWLOR, Daniel J. 3
LAWLOR, William F. 3
LAWLOR, William Patrick 1
LAWRANCE, Charles 3
  Lanier
LAWRANCE, Marion 1
LAWRANCE, William 1
  Irvin
LAWRENCE, Abbott H
LAWRENCE, Abraham 7
  Riker
LAWRENCE, Albert 4
  Lathrop
LAWRENCE, Alexander 7
  Atkinson
LAWRENCE, Amory 1
  Appleton
LAWRENCE, Amos H
LAWRENCE, Amos H
  Adams
LAWRENCE, Andrew 2
  Middleton
LAWRENCE, Armon Jay 4
LAWRENCE, Arthur 7
  Brewster
LAWRENCE, Benjamin 4
  Franklin
LAWRENCE, Carl 3
  Gustavus
LAWRENCE, Charles 6
  Drummond
LAWRENCE, Charles 2
  Kennedy
LAWRENCE, Charles 9
  Radford, II
LAWRENCE, Charles 1
  Solomon
LAWRENCE, Cornelius H
  Van Wyck
LAWRENCE, David 5
LAWRENCE, David Leo 4
LAWRENCE, E. George 6
LAWRENCE, Edwin 3
  Gordon
LAWRENCE, Edwin 6
  Winship
LAWRENCE, Effingham H
LAWRENCE, Egbert 1
  Charles
LAWRENCE, Ellis Fuller 2
LAWRENCE, Ernest 3
  Orlando
LAWRENCE, Florus 4
  Fremont
LAWRENCE, Frank 9
  Dudley
LAWRENCE, Frank Pell 3
LAWRENCE, Frederic 10
  Cunningham
LAWRENCE, George 6
  Andrew
LAWRENCE, George Hill 7
  Mathewson
LAWRENCE, George H
  Newbold
LAWRENCE, George 1
  Pelton
LAWRENCE, George 1
  Warren
LAWRENCE, Gertrude 3

LAWRENCE, Henry F. 4
LAWRENCE, Henry Wells 1
LAWRENCE, Howard C. 4
LAWRENCE, Isaac 1
LAWRENCE, James H
LAWRENCE, James 1
  Cooper
LAWRENCE, James 3
  Earnest
LAWRENCE, James 4
  Peyton Stuart
LAWRENCE, John 6
  Benjamin
LAWRENCE, John Henry 7
LAWRENCE, John 10
  Hundale
LAWRENCE, John 6
  Marshall
LAWRENCE, John Silsbee 6
LAWRENCE, John 1
  Strachan
LAWRENCE, John Watson H
LAWRENCE, John William 5
LAWRENCE, Joseph H
LAWRENCE, Joseph Stagg 3
LAWRENCE, Josephine 7
LAWRENCE, Justus 10
  Baldwin
LAWRENCE, Margaret 1
LAWRENCE, Nathaniel 9
  Morris
LAWRENCE, Newbold 5
  Trotter
LAWRENCE, Ralph 5
  Restieaux
LAWRENCE, Ray 6
  Ellsworth
LAWRENCE, Richard 9
  Elmer
LAWRENCE, Richard H
  Smith
LAWRENCE, Richard 2
  Wesley
LAWRENCE, Robert 1
LAWRENCE, Robert H., 5
  Jr.
LAWRENCE, Robert H., 4
  Jr.
LAWRENCE, Robert 1
  Means
LAWRENCE, Samuel H
LAWRENCE, Samuel 1
  Crocker
LAWRENCE, Samuel 9
  Eugene
LAWRENCE, Sidney H
LAWRENCE, Thomas 4
LAWRENCE, Victor H. 3
LAWRENCE, W. Vernon 10
LAWRENCE, William* H
LAWRENCE, William* 1
LAWRENCE, William 5
  Appleton
LAWRENCE, William H
  Beach
LAWRENCE, William 3
  Henry
LAWRENCE, William 5
  Hereford
LAWRENCE, William 1
  Howard
LAWRENCE, William 1
  Mangam
LAWRENCE, William H
  Thomas
LAWRENCE, William Van 1
  Duzer
LAWRENCE, William 3
  Witherle
LAWRIE, Harold Newbold 7
LAWRIE, Lee 4
LAWRIE, Ritchie, Jr. 4
LAWS, Annie 1
LAWS, Bolitha James 3
LAWS, Curtis Lee 2
LAWS, Elijah 1
LAWS, Frank Arthur 1
LAWS, George William 2
LAWS, Robert Franklin 10
LAWS, Robert Harry 9
LAWS, Samuel Spahr 1
LAWSHE, Abraham 1
  Lincoln
LAWSON, Albert Gallatin 1
LAWSON, Albert Thomas 4
LAWSON, Alexander H
LAWSON, Alfred Henry 9
LAWSON, Alfred William 3
LAWSON, Andrew Cowper 3
LAWSON, Andrew Werner, 7
  Jr.
LAWSON, Claude Sims 4
LAWSON, David A. 6
LAWSON, Donald Elmer 10
LAWSON, Douglas E. 4
LAWSON, Edward Burnett 4

LAWSON, Ernest 1
LAWSON, Evald Benjamin 4
LAWSON, Fred Alexander 7
LAWSON, George 3
LAWSON, George Benedict 3
LAWSON, Huron Willis 5
LAWSON, James H
LAWSON, James Gilchrist 2
LAWSON, James Joseph 4
LAWSON, John H
LAWSON, John Daniel H
LAWSON, John Davison 1
LAWSON, Joseph Albert 4
LAWSON, Joseph Warren 6
LAWSON, Laurin Leonard 3
LAWSON, Leonidas Merion H
LAWSON, Martin Emert 3
LAWSON, Paul Bowen 3
LAWSON, Publius Virgilius 1
LAWSON, Robert 3
LAWSON, Roberta Campbell 1
LAWSON, Thomas H
LAWSON, Thomas Goodwin 1
LAWSON, Thomas R. 3
LAWSON, Thomas William 1
LAWSON, Victor Fremont 1
LAWSON, W. Elsworth 4
LAWSON, Walter Carson 6
LAWSON, Warner 5
LAWSON, William C. 3
LAWTHER, Harry Preston 2
LAWTON, Alexander Robert H
LAWTON, Alexander Robert 5
LAWTON, Alexander Rudolf 1
LAWTON, Ben Redmond 9
LAWTON, Ezra Mills 1
LAWTON, Frederick 3
LAWTON, Frederick Joseph 6
LAWTON, Henry W. 1
LAWTON, Louis Bowen 5
LAWTON, Robert Oswald 7
LAWTON, Robert Oswald 8
LAWTON, Samuel Tilden 4
LAWTON, Shailer Upton 10
LAWTON, Shailer Upton 4
LAWTON, William Cranston 4
LAWTON, William Henry 4
LAWWILL, Stewart 5
LAWYER, George 1
LAWYER, Jay 4
LAWYER, Thomas H
LAX, Stephen Girard 7
LAY, Alfred Morrison H
LAY, Benjamin H
LAY, Charles Downing 3
LAY, Chester Frederic 6
LAY, Frank Morrill 3
LAY, George Washington H
LAY, George William 4
LAY, Henry Champlin H
LAY, Herman Warden 8
LAY, James Selden, Jr. 9
LAY, John Louis H
LAY, Julius Gareche 1
LAY, Robert Dwight 1
LAY, Tracy Hollingsworth 7
LAY, Walter E. 7
LAY, Wilfrid 5
LAYBOURNE, Lawrence Eugene 6
LAYBOURNE, Lawrence Eugene 7
LAYCOCK, Charles Wilbur 1
LAYCOCK, Craven 4
LAYDEN, Elmer Francis 6
LAYLIN, John Gallup 7
LAYLIN, Lewis Cass 1
LAYMAN, Waldo Arnold 3
LAYNE, J. Gregg 3
LAYNG, James D. 1
LAYTE, Ralph R. 4
LAYTHE, Leo L. 9
LAYTON, Caleb Rodney 1
LAYTON, Caleb S. 7
LAYTON, Frank Davis 3
LAYTON, Frederick 1
LAYTON, Joseph E. 4
LAYTON, Olivia Higgins 6
LAYTON, Walter Thomas 4
LAYTON, Warren K(enneth) 8
LAZAN, Benjamin J. 4
LAZAR, Benedict Joseph 3
LAZARO, Hipolito 6
LAZARO, Ladislas 1
LAZARON, Morris Samuel 8
LAZAROVICH-HREBELIANOVICH, Princess 3
LAZAROW, Arnold 6
LAZARSFELD, Paul Felix 7
LAZARUS, A(rnold) L(eslie) 10
LAZARUS, Emma H
LAZARUS, Fred 6
LAZARUS, Herman 9
LAZARUS, Jeffrey L. 7
LAZARUS, Marvin Paul 8
LAZARUS, Ralph 9
LAZARUS, Reuben Avis 5
LAZARUS, Robert 5
LAZARUS, Simon 2
LAZEAR, Jesse H
LAZEAR, Jesse William H
LAZELLE, Henry Martyn 1
LAZENBY, Albert 4
LAZENBY, Marion Elias 7
LAZENBY, William Rane 1
LAZO, Hector 4
LAZRUS, Benjamin 10
LAZRUS, Oscar M. 7
LAZRUS, S. Ralph 3
LAZZARI, Carolina Antoinette 2
LAZZARI, Pietro 7
LÉGER, Paul-Emile Cardinal 10
LEA, Clarence Frederick 4
LEA, Fanny Heaslip 3
LEA, Henry Charles 1
LEA, Homer 1
LEA, Isaac H
LEA, John McCormick 1
LEA, Luke H
LEA, Luke 2
LEA, Mathew Carey H
LEA, Mathew Carey 4
LEA, Preston 1
LEA, Pryor H
LEA, Robert Wentworth 3
LEA, William Sentelle 9
LEACH, Abby 1
LEACH, Agnes Brown (Mrs. Henry Goddard Leach) 7
LEACH, Albert Ernest 1
LEACH, Arthur Burtis 1
LEACH, Charles Nelson 5
LEACH, Daniel Dyer H
LEACH, Dewitt Clinton 4
LEACH, Edmund C. 4
LEACH, Edward Giles 1
LEACH, Ellis 5
LEACH, Eugene Walter 1
LEACH, Frank Aleamon 4
LEACH, Frank Aleamon, Jr. 5
LEACH, George E. 3
LEACH, Henry Goddard 5
LEACH, Howard Seavoy 3
LEACH, Hugh 5
LEACH, J. Granville 1
LEACH, James Madison H
LEACH, John Enfield 6
LEACH, John Sayles 4
LEACH, Julian Gilbert 10
LEACH, MacEdward 4
LEACH, Margaret Kernochan (Mrs. Ralph Pulitzer) 6
LEACH, Ralph Waldo Emerson 5
LEACH, Raymond Hotchkiss 2
LEACH, Shepherd H
LEACH, W(alter) Barton 5
LEACH, Wilford 9
LEACH, William Fillmore 5
LEACH, William Herman 4
LEACOCK, Arthur Gordner 2
LEACOCK, Stephen Butler 2
LEADBETTER, Caroline Pittock 5
LEADBETTER, Daniel Parkhurst H
LEADBETTER, Frederick William 2
LEADBETTER, Wyland F. 6
LEAF, Erle Mervin 7
LEAF, Munro 7
LEAHY, Edward L. 3
LEAHY, Frank 5
LEAHY, Lamar Richard 3
LEAHY, Osmund A. 10
LEAHY, Paul 4
LEAHY, Timothy John 1
LEAHY, William Augustine 1
LEAHY, William D. 3
LEAHY, William Edward 3
LEAK, Clarence Elmer 7
LEAKE, Arthur Cyrus 8
LEAKE, Chauncey D. 7
LEAKE, Eugene W. 3
LEAKE, Frank 4
LEAKE, Gerald 7
LEAKE, James Miller 6
LEAKE, James Payton 5
LEAKE, Joseph Bloomfield 1
LEAKE, Shelton Farrar H
LEAKE, Walter H
LEAKEY, Louis Seymour Bazett 5
LEALE, Charles Augustus 1
LEALE, Medwin 1
LEAMAN, William Gilmore 6
LEAMING, Edmund Bennett 1
LEAMING, Jacob Spicer H
LEAMING, Jeremiah H
LEAMING, Thomas H
LEAMY, Frank Ashton 4
LEAMY, Frederick Walter 3
LEAMY, Hugh 1
LEAMY, James Patrick 2
LEAN, Sir David 10
LEANDER, Hugo Austin 5
LEAR, Ben 4
LEAR, Floyd Seyward 10
LEAR, Fred Roy 3
LEAR, Harry Bonnell 4
LEAR, Tobias H
LEAR, Willian Powell 7
LEARNARD, George Edward 5
LEARNARD, Henry Grant 1
LEARNED, Amasa H
LEARNED, Arthur Garfield 3
LEARNED, Dwight Whitney 4
LEARNED, Ebenezer H
LEARNED, Ellin Craven 1
LEARNED, Henry Barrett 1
LEARNED, Henry Dexter 10
LEARNED, Marion Dexter 1
LEARNED, Walter 1
LEARNED, William Law 1
LEARNED, William Setchel 2
LEARSI, Rufus 4
LEARY, Cornelius Lawrence Ludlow H
LEARY, Daniel Bell 2
LEARY, Francis Thomas 5
LEARY, Frederick 3
LEARY, Herbert Fairfax 3
LEARY, John Digney 6
LEARY, John Joseph, Jr. 2
LEARY, Leo H. 4
LEARY, Lewis 10
LEARY, Lewis Gaston 3
LEARY, Montgomery Elihu 5
LEARY, Peter, Jr. 1
LEARY, Richard Phillips 1
LEARY, Robert Michael 9
LEARY, Timothy 3
LEARY, William Henry 3
LEASE, Emory Bair 1
LEASE, Mrs. Mary Elizabeth 1
LEATH, Edward Magruder, Jr. 7
LEATHAM, Charles H(enry) 8
LEATHERS, Waller Smith 2
LEATHERS OF PURFLEET, Baron 4
LEATHERWOOD, Elmer O. 1
LEAVELL, Byrd Stuart 8
LEAVELL, Frank Hartwell 2
LEAVELL, Hugh Rodman 7
LEAVELL, James Berry 1
LEAVELL, James Reader 6
LEAVELL, Landrum Pinson 1
LEAVELL, Richard Marion 3
LEAVELL, Ullin Whitney 4
LEAVELL, William Hayne 1
LEAVELLE, Arnaud Bruce 3
LEAVELLE, Robert Bryan 5
LEAVENS, Robert French 6
LEAVENWORTH, Elias Warner H
LEAVENWORTH, Francis Preserved 1
LEAVENWORTH, Henry H
LEAVITT, Ashley Day 3
LEAVITT, Burke Fay 4
LEAVITT, Charles Welford 1
LEAVITT, Dudley H
LEAVITT, Erasmus Darwin 1
LEAVITT, Frank McDowell 1
LEAVITT, Halsey B. 4
LEAVITT, Humphrey Howe H
LEAVITT, John McDowell H
LEAVITT, Joseph 10
LEAVITT, Joshua H
LEAVITT, Julius Adelbert 1
LEAVITT, Mary Greenleaf Clement 1
LEAVITT, Milo David, Jr. 8
LEAVITT, Roger 3
LEAVITT, Scott 4
LEAVITT, Sheldon 1
LEAVITT, Sturgis Elleno 8
LEAVY, Charles Henry 3
LEAYCRAFT, J. Edgar 1
LE BARON, John Francis 1
LE BARON, John Kittredge 4
LEBARON, Robert 9
LE BARON, William 3
LEBER, Charles Tudor 4
LEBHAR, Godfrey Montague 4
LEBLANC, Camille (Andre) 10
LE BLANC, Moreland Paul, Jr. 9
LE BLANC, Thomas John 2
LE BLOND, Charles Hubert 3
LE BLOND, Harold R. 5
LEBO, Thomas Coverley 1
LE BOEUF, Randall James 1
LE BOEUF, Randall James 6
LEBOLD, Foreman M. 3
LEBOUTILLIER, George 3
LEBOUTILLIER, Philip 8
LEBRA, William Philip 9
LE BRETON, Tomas Alberto 5
LE BRUN, Napoleon Eugene Henry Charles H
LEBRUN, Rico 4
LECHE, Paul 4
LECHE, Richard Webster 4
LECHER, Louis Arthur 2
LECHFORD, Thomas H
LECHNER, Carl Bernard 5
LECKIE, Adam Edward Lloyd 1
LECKIE, Katherine 1
LECKRONE, Walter 4
LECKWIJCK, William Peter Edward van 6
LECLAIR, Edward E(mile), Jr. 5
LECLAIR, Titus G. 5
LE CLAIRE, Harry Walter 10
LE CLEAR, Thomas H
LE CLERC, J. Arthur 3
LECLERG, Erwin Louis 8
LECOMPTE, Irville Charles 5
LECOMPTE, Joseph H
LECOMPTE, Karl Miles 5
LECONTE, John H
LECONTE, John Lawrence H
LE CONTE, Joseph 1
LE CONTE, Joseph Nisbet 2
LE CONTE, Robert Grier 1
LE CORBEILLER, Philippe 9
LE CORBUSIER, Charles-edouard 4
LECOUNT, Edwin Raymond 1
LECUONA, Ernesto 4
LEDBETTER, Allison Woodville 4
LEDBETTER, G. Edward 8
LEDBETTER, Huddie 4
LEDBETTER, Walter A. 1
LEDDEN, Walter Earl 8
LEDDY, Bernard Joseph 5
LEDDY, Raymond G(regory) 7
LEDERER, Albrecht Misa 8
LEDERER, Charles 1
LEDERER, Charles 3
LEDERER, Erwin Reginald 2
LEDERER, Francis Loeffler 10
LEDERER, Francis Loeffler 5
LEDERER, George W. 1
LEDERER, John H
LEDERER, Ludwig George 7
LEDERER, Norbert Lewis 3
LEDERER, Richard M. 3
LEDERLE, Arthur F. 8
LEDERLE, Ernst Joseph 1
LEDLIE, George 1
LEDNICKI, Waclaw 4
LEDNICKI, Waclaw 5
LEDOUX, Albert Reid 1
LEDOUX, John Walter 1
LEDOUX, Louis Vernon 2
LE DUC, William Gates 1
LEDVINA, Emmanuel B. 5
LEDWITH, William Laurence 1
LEDYARD, Erwin 1
LEDYARD, Henry 1
LEDYARD, Henry Brockholst 1
LEDYARD, John H
LEDYARD, Joshua Heard 5
LEDYARD, Lewis Cass 1
LEDYARD, Lewis Cass, Jr. 1
LEDYARD, William H
LEE, Agnes 1
LEE, Albert 2
LEE, Albert Lindley 1
LEE, Alexander Edmund 6
LEE, Alfred H
LEE, Alfred Emory 4
LEE, Alfred McClung 10
LEE, Algernon 3
LEE, Alice Louise 4
LEE, Alonzo Hester 6
LEE, Andrew Ericson 1
LEE, Ann H
LEE, Archie Laney 3
LEE, Arthur H
LEE, Arthur 4
LEE, Bee Virginia 4
LEE, Benjamin 1
LEE, Benjamin Fisler 1
LEE, Benjamin Franklin 1
LEE, Blair 2
LEE, Blewett 4
LEE, Bradner Wells 1
LEE, Burton James 1
LEE, Calvin Bow Tong 8
LEE, Canada 3
LEE, Charles* H
LEE, Charles Alfred H
LEE, Charles Hamilton 4
LEE, Charles Henry 8
LEE, C(harles) O(ren) 7
LEE, David Aaron 6
LEE, David B. 5
LEE, David Russell 1
LEE, Delia Foreacre (Mrs. Blewett Lee) 5
LEE, Dwight Erwin 10
LEE, E. Trumbull 1
LEE, Edgar Desmond 6
LEE, Edward Edson 2
LEE, Edward Hervey 1
LEE, Edward Thomas 2
LEE, Edwin Augustus 4
LEE, Edwin F. 2
LEE, Elisha 1
LEE, Eliza Buckminster H
LEE, Elmer 4
LEE, Elmo Pearce 2
LEE, Fitzhugh 1
LEE, Francis Bazley 1
LEE, Francis D. H
LEE, Francis Lightfoot H
LEE, Frank 1
LEE, Frank Augustus 4
LEE, Frank Herbert 8
LEE, Frank Hood 3
LEE, Frank Theodosius 2
LEE, Fredeick Crosby 6
LEE, Frederic Edward 3
LEE, Frederic Girard 1
LEE, Frederic Paddock 5
LEE, Frederic Schiller 1
LEE, Gentry 4
LEE, George Bolling 2
LEE, George Cabot 3
LEE, George Hamor 8
LEE, George Joseph 7
LEE, George Washington Curtis 1
LEE, George Winthrop 2
LEE, Gerald Stanley 2
LEE, Gertrude Adams 3
LEE, Gordon 1
LEE, Gordon Canfield 5
LEE, Graham 3
LEE, Guy Carleton 1
LEE, Gypsy Rose (Rose Louise Hovick) 5
LEE, Halfdan 6
LEE, Hannah Sawyer H
LEE, Harold 8
LEE, Harold B. 6
LEE, Harry 1
LEE, Harry Winfield 4
LEE, Henry* H
LEE, Henry 4
LEE, Henry Haworth 1
LEE, Henry Thomas 4
LEE, Hildegarde L. 1
LEE, Homer 1
LEE, Howard Burton 7
LEE, Hugh Johnson 2
LEE, Ivy Ledbetter 1
LEE, James Beveridge 2
LEE, James Grafton Carleton 1
LEE, James J. 5
LEE, James Melvin 1
LEE, James P. 3
LEE, James Paris 1
LEE, James T. 4
LEE, James Wideman 1
LEE, Jason H
LEE, Jennette 3
LEE, Jennette 4
LEE, Jesse H

LEWIS, Clarke — H
LEWIS, Claude Isaac — 1
LEWIS, Cleona — 7
LEWIS, Clive Staples — 4
LEWIS, Dale Morgan — 7
LEWIS, Daniel — 1
LEWIS, Daniel Curtis, Jr. — 9
LEWIS, Daniel F. — 4
LEWIS, Dave — 5
LEWIS, David John — 3
LEWIS, David Thomas — 8
LEWIS, Dean — 1
LEWIS, Diocesian — H
LEWIS, Dixon Hall — 1
LEWIS, D(ominic) B(evan) Wyndham — 5
LEWIS, Dorothy Moore — 7
LEWIS, Dudley Cushman — 9
LEWIS, Earl Ramage — 8
LEWIS, Ebenezer Ellesville — 1
LEWIS, Edmund Harris — 5
LEWIS, Edward Gardner — 1
LEWIS, Edward Mann — 2
LEWIS, Edward McElhiney — 3
LEWIS, Edward Morgan — 1
LEWIS, Edward Samuel — 1
LEWIS, Edward Shakespear — 9
LEWIS, Edward Van Vliet — 10
LEWIS, Edwin Herbert — 1
LEWIS, Edwin James, Jr. — 1
LEWIS, Edwin Owen — 6
LEWIS, Edwin Seelye — 1
LEWIS, Elijah Banks — 3
LEWIS, Elizabeth Foreman — 3
LEWIS, Ellis — H
LEWIS, Emanuel P. — 9
LEWIS, Enoch — H
LEWIS, Ernest Irvin — 2
LEWIS, Ernest Sidney — 1
LEWIS, Ernest William — 1
LEWIS, Ervin Eugene — 7
LEWIS, Essington — 4
LEWIS, Estelle Anna Blanche Robinson — H
LEWIS, Eugene Howard — 1
LEWIS, Eugene W. — 3
LEWIS, Exum Percival — 1
LEWIS, F. Park — 1
LEWIS, Fielding — H
LEWIS, Fletcher — 3
LEWIS, Francis — H
LEWIS, Francis Albert — 1
LEWIS, Frank Grant — 2
LEWIS, Frank J. — 4
LEWIS, Frank M(endell) — 7
LEWIS, Franklin Allan — 3
LEWIS, Franklin Crocker — 1
LEWIS, Franklin Fillmore — 3
LEWIS, Fred — 7
LEWIS, Fred B(radley) — 6
LEWIS, Fred Ewing — 2
LEWIS, Fred Justin — 3
LEWIS, Frederic Thomas — 3
LEWIS, Frederick Wheeler — 5
LEWIS, Freeman — 7
LEWIS, Fulton, Jr. — 4
LEWIS, G. Griffin — 4
LEWIS, Gayle F. — 10
LEWIS, George Albert — 1
LEWIS, George Francis — 3
LEWIS, George (Mathews) — 8
LEWIS, George Morris — 4
LEWIS, George William — 1
LEWIS, Gilbert Newton — 2
LEWIS, Grant Kirkland — 7
LEWIS, H. Edgar — 2
LEWIS, Harold C. — 2
LEWIS, Harold Gregg — 10
LEWIS, Harold M(acLean) — 6
LEWIS, Harry Herbert — 3
LEWIS, Harry Reynolds — 7
LEWIS, Henry — H
LEWIS, Henry — 1
LEWIS, Henry Carleton — 5
LEWIS, Henry Harrison — 4
LEWIS, Henry Steele — 3
LEWIS, Henry Thomas — 1
LEWIS, Herbert Lefkovitz — 5
LEWIS, Herbert Wesley — 4
LEWIS, Homer Pierce — 4
LEWIS, Howard — 3
LEWIS, Howard Augustus — 4
LEWIS, Howard Bishop — 3
LEWIS, Howard Corwin — 1
LEWIS, Howard Phelps — 9
LEWIS, Hugh Alban — 4
LEWIS, Ida — 1
LEWIS, Irving Jefferson — 1
LEWIS, Irving Stanton — 5
LEWIS, Isaac Newton — 1
LEWIS, Ivy Foreman — 4
LEWIS, J. Wilbur — 1
LEWIS, James — H
LEWIS, James Hamilton — 1
LEWIS, James M. — 1
LEWIS, James Malcolm — 3
LEWIS, James Ogier — 3

LEWIS, James Otto — H
LEWIS, Jesse Willard — 3
LEWIS, John — 7
LEWIS, John Beavens — 1
LEWIS, John E. — 8
LEWIS, John F., Jr. — 4
LEWIS, John Francis — H
LEWIS, John Frederick — 1
LEWIS, John Henry — 3
LEWIS, John Kent — 4
LEWIS, John L. — 1
LEWIS, John Milligan — 6
LEWIS, John Neher — 5
LEWIS, John Philip — 4
LEWIS, John Reece — 9
LEWIS, Joseph — 5
LEWIS, Joseph — 8
LEWIS, Joseph, Jr. — H
LEWIS, Joseph H. — 1
LEWIS, Joseph Hilliard — 10
LEWIS, J(oseph) Volney — 5
LEWIS, Joseph William — 1
LEWIS, Judd Mortimer — 2
LEWIS, Kathryn — 4
LEWIS, Kemp Plummer — 3
LEWIS, L. Logan — 4
LEWIS, Lafayette Arthur — 4
LEWIS, Lawrence — H
LEWIS, Lawrence — 2
LEWIS, Lee Rich — 2
LEWIS, Leicester Crosby — 2
LEWIS, L(eo) Rhodes — 10
LEWIS, Leon Patteson — 1
LEWIS, Lillian — 2
LEWIS, Lloyd Downs — 2
LEWIS, Lloyd Griffith — 3
LEWIS, Loran Ludowick — 1
LEWIS, Lowery Lamon — 1
LEWIS, Lucy May — 1
LEWIS, Lunsford Lomax — 4
LEWIS, Mahlon Everett — 1
LEWIS, Marion L. — 3
LEWIS, Marvin Harrison — 5
LEWIS, Mary Sybil — 1
LEWIS, Mary Sybil — 2
LEWIS, Mason Avery — 4
LEWIS, Mead A(llyn) — 9
LEWIS, Mel (Melvin Sokoloff)* — 10
LEWIS, Melvin S(owles) — 5
LEWIS, Meriwether — H
LEWIS, Merton Elmer — 1
LEWIS, Merton Harry — 5
LEWIS, Morgan — H
LEWIS, Morris James — 3
LEWIS, Nancy Duke — 4
LEWIS, Nelson Peter — 1
LEWIS, Nolan Don Carpenter, M.D. — 7
LEWIS, Norman — 8
LEWIS, Olin Bailey — 4
LEWIS, Oren Ritter — 9
LEWIS, Orlando Faulkland — 1
LEWIS, Orme — 10
LEWIS, Oscar — 5
LEWIS, Otto O. — 8
LEWIS, Paul A. — 1
LEWIS, Preston W(ilhelm) — 10
LEWIS, Ralph Ferguson — 7
LEWIS, Read — 8
LEWIS, Reuben Alexander, Jr. — 2
LEWIS, Richard Henry — 1
LEWIS, Richard Welborne — 1
LEWIS, Richmond — 7
LEWIS, Robert — 1
LEWIS, R(obert) Donald — 10
LEWIS, Robert E. — 1
LEWIS, Robert James — 9
LEWIS, Roger — 9
LEWIS, Roger Labaree — 7
LEWIS, Samuel — H
LEWIS, Samuel J. — 8
LEWIS, Sinclair — 3
LEWIS, Spearman — 3
LEWIS, Spencer Steen — 3
LEWIS, Ted (Theodore Friedman) — 5
LEWIS, Theodore Leonard — 3
LEWIS, Thomas — H
LEWIS, Thomas E. — 8
LEWIS, Thomas Hamilton — 3
LEWIS, Tracy Hammond — 8
LEWIS, Virgil Anson — 1
LEWIS, Vivian M. — 2
LEWIS, Walker — 1
LEWIS, Walter Oliver — 4
LEWIS, Warren Harmon — 4
LEWIS, Warren Kendall — 6
LEWIS, Wilfred — 1
LEWIS, Willard Potter — 8
LEWIS, William Alexander — 1
LEWIS, Sir William Arthur — 10
LEWIS, William Bennett — 6
LEWIS, William Berkeley — H
LEWIS, William David — H

LEWIS, William Dodge — 4
LEWIS, William Draper — 2
LEWIS, William Eugene — 1
LEWIS, William Fisher — 4
LEWIS, William Henry — 4
LEWIS, William J. — H
LEWIS, William Luther — 3
LEWIS, William Mather — 3
LEWIS, William Stanley — 2
LEWIS, Sir Willmett Harsant — 5
LEWIS, Wilmarth Sheldon — 7
LEWIS, Wilmarth Sheldon — 8
LEWIS, Wilson Seeley — 1
LEWIS, Winford Lee — 2
LEWIS, Winslow — H
LEWIS, Yancey — 1
LEWISOHN, Adolph — 1
LEWISOHN, Ludwig — 3
LEWISOHN, Margaret S. — 3
LEWISOHN, Sam A. — 3
LEWMAN, Frank C. — 4
LEWTON, Frederick Lewis — 3
LEWY, Hans — 9
LEX, Charles E. — H
LEXOW, Clarence — 1
LEY, Frederick Theodore — 3
LEY, Harold Alexander — 3
LEY, Katherine Louise — 8
LEY, Willy — 5
LEYDON, John Koebig — 1
LEYENDECKER, Frank X. — 1
LEYENDECKER, Joseph Christian — 3
LEYMAN, Harry Stoll — 5
LEYPOLDT, Frederick — H
LEYS, James Farquharson — 1
LEYS, Wayne Albert Risser — 5
LEYSEN, Ralph J. — 3
LEYSHON, Hal Irwin — 4
L'HALLE, Constantin de — 4
L'HEUREUX, Camille — 4
L'HEUREUX, Herve Joseph — 3
LHEVINNE, Josef — 2
LHEVINNE, Rosina — 2
L'HOMMEDIEU, Ezra — H
LHOTE, Andre — 9
LI, Choh Hao — 9
LI, Kuo-ching — H
LIAUTAUD, Andre — 3
LIBBEY, Edward Drummond — 1
LIBBEY, Fay Wllmott — 7
LIBBEY, Jonas Marsh — 1
LIBBEY, Laura Jean — 1
LIBBEY, William — 2
LIBBY, Arthur Stephen — 2
LIBBY, Arthur Stephen — 5
LIBBY, Charles Freeman — 1
LIBBY, Edward Norton — 1
LIBBY, Frederick Joseph — 5
LIBBY, Melanchthon Fennessy — 1
LIBBY, Orin Grant — 3
LIBBY, Raymond Loring — 7
LIBBY, Samuel Hammonds — 3
LIBBY, Warren Edgar — 3
LIBBY, Willard Frank — 8
LIBBY, William Charles — 8
LIBERACE (Wladziu Valentino Liberace) — 9
LIBERMAN, Samuel Halpern — 5
LIBERTE, Jean — 10
LIBERTE, Jean — 1
LIBMAN, Emanuel — 2
LICHTER, McLlyar Hamilton — 4
LICHTENSTEIN, Jacob — 10
LICHT, Frank — 1
LICHTEN, Robert Lyon — 6
LICHTENBERG, Bernard — 2
LICHTENBERG, Leopold — 1
LICHTENBERGER, Arthur Carl — 5
LICHTENBERGER, James Pendleton — 3
LICHTENSTEIN, Joy — 1
LICHTENSTEIN, Manuel E. — 7
LICHTENSTEIN, Walter — 4
LICHTENTAG, Alexander — 1
LICHTENWALNER, Norton Lewis — 8
LICHTENWALTER, Franklin H. — 1
LICHTMANN, Samuel Arthur — 10
LICHTNER, William Otto — 7
LICHTY, George M. — 8
LICHTY, John Alden — 1
LICHTY, L(ester) (Clyde) — 5
LICK, Charles Jacob — 7
LICK, James — H
LICK, Maxwell John — 2

LIDBURY, Frank Austin — 6
LIDDEL, Urner — 7
LIDDELL, Donald Macy — 3
LIDDELL, Eva Louise — 1
LIDDELL, Frank Austin — 4
LIDDELL, Henry — 4
LIDDELL, Howard Scott — 4
LIDDELL, Mark Harvey — 1
LIDDLE, Charles Allen — 4
LIDDON, Benjamin Sullivan — 1
LIDSTONE, Herrick Kenley — 9
LIE, Jonas — 1
LIEB, Charles — 3
LIEB, Charles Christian — 3
LIEB, Irwin Chester — 10
LIEB, John William — 1
LIEB, Joseph Patrick — 6
LIEBEL, Michael, Jr. — 5
LIEBEL, Willard Koehler — 1
LIEBER, B. Franklin — 1
LIEBER, Eugene — 4
LIEBER, Francis — H
LIEBER, G. Norman — 1
LIEBER, Hugh Gray — 4
LIEBER, Lillian R(osanoff) — 7
LIEBER, Richard — 2
LIEBERMAN, Elias — 5
LIEBERMAN, Saul — 8
LIEBERS, Otto Hugo — 4
LIEBERSON, Goddard — 7
LIEBES, Mrs. Dorothy Wright — 5
LIEBHAFSKY, Herman Alfred — 8
LIEBLING, Abbott Joseph — 4
LIEBLING, Emil — 1
LIEBLING, George — 4
LIEBLING, Leonard — 2
LIEBMAN, Joshua Loth — 2
LIEBMAN, Julius — 1
LIEBMAN, Max — 8
LIEBMAN, William Lewis — 9
LIEBMANN, Philip — 5
LIEBOW, Averill Abraham — 7
LIECTY, Austin N. — 5
LIEDER, Frederick William Charles — 3
LIEDER, Paul Robert — 3
LIEFELD, Albert — 1
LIEFERANT, Henry — 8
LIEN, Arnold Johnson — 4
LIEN, Elias Johnson — 4
LIEN, Robert Cowles — 6
LIENAU, Detlef — H
LIERLE, Dean McAllister — 5
LIES, Eugene Theodore — 5
LIEURANCE, Thurlow — 4
LIFE, Andrew Creamor — 1
LIFE, Frank Mann — 1
LIFSCHEY, Samuel — 4
LIFSON, Nathan — 10
LIGGETT, Hunter — H
LIGGETT, Louis Kroh — 2
LIGGETT, Walter William — 1
LIGGINS, John — 1
LIGGIT, Clarence Reed — 1
LIGGITT, Earle O. — 8
LIGHT, Charles Porterfield — 3
LIGHT, Charles Porterfield, Jr. — 7
LIGHT, Enoch Henry — 9
LIGHT, Evelyn — 3
LIGHT, George Augustus — 6
LIGHT, Israel — 6
LIGHT, Rudolph Alvin — 5
LIGHT, Sidney — 4
LIGHTBURN, George William — 4
LIGHTBURN, Joseph A. J. — 1
LIGHTNER, Clarence Ashley — 1
LIGHTNER, Edwin Allan, Jr. — 10
LIGHTNER, Ezra Wilberforce — 5
LIGHTNER, Milton C. — 5
LIGHTON, William Rheem — 4
LIGON, Elvin Seth* — 6
LIGON, Thomas Watkins — H
LIGUTTI, Luigi Gino — 9
LIHME, C. Bai — 2
LIKERT, Rensis — 9
LIKLY, William F. — 4
LIKOFF, William — 9
LILE, William Minor — 1
LILES, Luther Brooks — 2
LILIENFELD, Abraham Morris — 8
LILIENFELD, Abraham Morris — 9
LILIENFIELD, Henry Jacob — 7
LILIENTHAL, David Eli — 7
LILIENTHAL, Howard — 2

LILIENTHAL, Jesse Warren — 1
LILIENTHAL, Joseph Leo, Jr. — 3
LILIENTHAL, Max — H
LILIENTHAL, Samuel — 3
LILIUOKALANI — H
LILIUOKALANI — 4
LILJE, Johannes Ernst Richard — 7
LILJENCRANTZ, Ottilie Adaline — 1
LILJESTRAND, Goran — 5
LILLARD, Benjamin — 4
LILLARD, Walter Huston — 4
LILLARD, Walter Huston — 5
LILLARD, William Parlin — 7
LILLEHEI, Richard Carlton — 7
LILLEHEI, Richard Carlton — 8
LILLEY, Alexander Neil — 7
LILLEY, Charles Sumner — 1
LILLEY, George — 1
LILLEY, George Leavens — 1
LILLEY, Mial E. — 4
LILLEY, Robert — 4
LILLEY, Robert Dodd — 9
LILLEY, Tom — 8
LILLIBRIDGE, William Otis — 1
LILLICK, Ira S. — 4
LILLIE, Abraham Bruyn Hasbrouck — 1
LILLIE, Beatrice (Lady Peel) — 9
LILLIE, Charles A. — 4
LILLIE, Frank Rattray — 2
LILLIE, Gordon William — 1
LILLIE, Gordon William — 2
LILLIE, Harold Irving — 3
LILLIE, Howard Russell — 4
LILLIE, Lucy Cecil — 1
LILLIE, Ralph Dougall — 7
LILLIE, Ralph Stayner — 3
LILLIE, Samuel Morris — 4
LILLIS, Donald Chace — 5
LILLIS, James F. — 4
LILLIS, Thomas F. — 1
LILLY, D. Clay — 10
LILLY, Doris — 10
LILLY, Eli — 7
LILLY, John Francis — 8
LILLY, Josiah Kirby — 2
LILLY, Josiah Kirby — 4
LILLY, Linus Augustine — 2
LILLY, Richard C. — 3
LILLY, Samuel — H
LILLY, Thomas Jefferson — 3
LILLY, William — H
LIM, Pilar Hidalgo (Mrs. Vicente Lim) — 6
LIM, Robert Kho-Seng — 10
LIMA, Manoel de Oliveira — 1
LIMB, Ben C. — 7
LIMBACH, Rusell Theodore — 5
LIMBERT, Lee Middleton — 4
LIMERICK, 2nd earl — H
LIMING, Melville Darst — 7
LIMOGES, Joseph Eugene — 6
LIMON, Jose Arcadio — 5
LIN, Piao — 5
LINCECUM, Gideon — H
LINCOLN, Abraham — H
LINCOLN, Allen B. — 1
LINCOLN, Arleigh Leon — 4
LINCOLN, Asa Liggett — 6
LINCOLN, Azariah Thomas — 3
LINCOLN, Benjamin — H
LINCOLN, Charles Clark — 1
LINCOLN, Charles Monroe — 3
LINCOLN, Charles Perez — 1
LINCOLN, Charles Sherman
LINCOLN, Charles Zebina — 4
LINCOLN, Daniel Waldo — 5
LINCOLN, Daniel Waldo — 7
LINCOLN, David Francis — 1
LINCOLN, Edmond E. — 3
LINCOLN, Enoch — H
LINCOLN, Francis Church — 5
LINCOLN, Gatewood — 3
LINCOLN, George Arthur — 6
LINCOLN, George Gould — 6
LINCOLN, J. Freeman — 4
LINCOLN, James Claiborne — 1
LINCOLN, James Finney — 4
LINCOLN, James Rush — 4
LINCOLN, James Sullivan — H
LINCOLN, Jeanie Gould — 1
LINCOLN, John Cromwell — 3
LINCOLN, John Larkin — H

LORING, Augustus Peabody 1
LORING, Augustus Peabody 9
LORING, Augustus Peabody, Jr. 3
LORING, Charles 4
LORING, Charles Greely 1
LORING, Charles Harding 1
LORING, Edward Greely H
LORING, Ellis Gray H
LORING, Emilie 3
LORING, Frederick Wadsworth H
LORING, George Bailey H
LORING, Homer 5
LORING, John Alden 1
LORING, Joshua* H
LORING, Paule Stetson 2
LORING, Ralph Alden 3
LORING, Richard Tuttle 1
LORING, Victor Joseph 2
LORING, William Caleb 1
LORING, William Wing 10
LORMAN, William Rudolph
LORNE, Marion 5
LORRE, Peter 4
LORTON, Eugene 2
LORWIN, Lewis L. 5
LORY, Charles Alfred 5
LOSE, George William 4
LOSER, Joseph Carlton 1
LOSEY, Frederick Douglas 1
LOSEY, Joseph 8
LOSKIEL, George Henry H
LOSSING, Benson John H
LOSSING, Helen S. 4
LOTHIAN, Marquess of 1
LOTHROP, Amy 1
LOTHROP, Daniel H
LOTHROP, Fannie Mack 5
LOTHROP, George Van Ness H
LOTHROP, Harriett Mulford 1
LOTHROP, Howard Augustus 1
LOTHROP, Marcus Thompson 1
LOTHROP, Samuel Kirkland 4
LOTHROP, Thornton Kirkland 1
LOTHROPP, John H
LOTKA, Alfred James 2
LOTSPEICH, Ethel Moore 1
LOTSPEICH, Roy Nicholas 3
LOTSPEICH, William Douglas 5
LOTT, Abraham Grant 5
LOTT, Charles H. 3
LOTT, Edson Schuyler 2
LOTTE, Edward F. L. 1
LOTTRIDGE, Silas A. 1
LOTZ, John 6
LOTZ, John R. 4
LOTZ, Oscar 3
LOUBAT, Joseph Florimund Duc de
LOUCHHEIM, Walter Clinton, Jr. 5
LOUCKS, Charles Ernest 9
LOUCKS, Charles Olney 4
LOUCKS, Daniel K(yle) 8
LOUCKS, Elton Crocker 9
LOUCKS, Philip G. 4
LOUCKS, Vernon Reece 7
LOUCKS, William Dewey 5
LOUD, Annie Frances 4
LOUD, Eugene Francis 1
LOUD, Frank Herbert 1
LOUD, George Alvin 4
LOUD, Henry Martin 1
LOUD, John Hermann 5
LOUDEN, Frederic Alic 4
LOUDEN, William 1
LOUDENSLAGER, Henry Clay 1
LOUDERBACK, George Davis 3
LOUDERBACK, Harold 1
LOUDERBACK, William Johnson 1
LOUDON, A. 3
LOUDON, Johkheer John A. 4
LOUDON, Samuel H
LOUDOUN, 4th earl H
LOUGEE, Francis Eaton 4
LOUGEE, Norman Arthur 8
LOUGEE, Willis Eugene 1
LOUGH, James Edwin 3
LOUGH, Samuel Alexander 4
LOUGH, William Henry 6
LOUGHAN, Mrs. Katherine O'Neil 6

LOUGHBOROUGH, James Fairfax 2
LOUGHEAD, Flora Haines 4
LOUGHEED, William Foster 4
LOUGHIN, Charles A. 4
LOUGHLIN, Gerald Francis 2
LOUGHLIN, John H
LOUGHRAN, John T. 3
LOUGHRIDGE, Robert Hills 4
LOUGHRIDGE, Robert McGill H
LOUGHRIDGE, William H
LOUGHRY, Howard K. 7
LOUHI, Kullervo 7
LOUIS, Andrew 7
LOUIS, Jean Francois 9
LOUIS, Joe 7
LOUIS, John Jeffry 3
LOUIS, Max C. 4
LOUISELL, David William 7
LOUNSBERRY, Frank Burton
LOUNSBURY, Charles Edwin 3
LOUNSBURY, George Edward 1
LOUNSBURY, George Fenner 3
LOUNSBURY, James Breckinridge 6
LOUNSBURY, Phineas Chapman 1
LOUNSBURY, Ralph Reed 1
LOUNSBURY, Thomas Raynesford 1
LOURIE, Arthur 4
LOURIE, David A. 1
LOURIE, Donald Bradford 10
LOURIE, Reginald Spencer 9
LOUTFI, Omar 4
LOUTHAN, Hattie Horner Thompson 5
LOUTHAN, Henry Thompson 3
LOUTHERBOURG, Annibale Christian Henry de H
LOUTTIT, Chauncey McKinley 3
LOUTTIT, George William 4
LOUTTIT, Thomas Robley 7
LOUTTIT, Thomas Robley 8
LOUTTIT, William Easton, Jr. 5
LOUTZENHEISER, Joe L. 2
LOUW, Eric Hendrik 2
LOUW, Eric Hendrick 8
LOVATT, George Ignatius 5
LOVE, Albert Gallatin 5
LOVE, Albert Irving 5
LOVE, Alfred Henry 1
LOVE, Andrew Leo 4
LOVE, Charles Everts 3
LOVE, Charles Marion, Jr. 9
LOVE, Cornelius Ruxton, Jr. 5
LOVE, Don Lathrop 5
LOVE, Edgar Amos 6
LOVE, Edward Bainbridge 5
LOVE, Emanuel King H
LOVE, Frank Samuel 1
LOVE, George Hutchinson 10
LOVE, Harold Oren 9
LOVE, Harry Houser 4
LOVE, J. Mack 4
LOVE, James H
LOVE, James Jay 4
LOVE, James Lee 3
LOVE, James Lowrey 5
LOVE, James Sanford, Jr. 5
LOVE, James Spencer 4
LOVE, John H
LOVE, John, Jr. 10
LOVE, John W. 3
LOVE, Julian Price 5
LOVE, Malcolm A. 10
LOVE, Peter Early H
LOVE, Robertus 1
LOVE, Smoloff Palace 1
LOVE, Stephen 9
LOVE, Stephen Hunter 1
LOVE, Thomas Bell 2
LOVE, Thomas Cutting H
LOVE, Thomas J. 3
LOVE, William Carter 4
LOVE, William De Loss 1
LOVEJOY, Arthur Oncken 4
LOVEJOY, Asa Lawrence 4
LOVEJOY, Clarence Earle 6
LOVEJOY, Donald Meston 10
LOVEJOY, Elijah Parish H
LOVEJOY, Esther Pohl 4
LOVEJOY, Francis Thomas Fletcher 1
LOVEJOY, Frank William 2

LOVEJOY, George Edwards 1
LOVEJOY, George Newell 4
LOVEJOY, Hatton 6
LOVEJOY, Jesse Robert 2
LOVEJOY, John Meston 5
LOVEJOY, Owen H
LOVEJOY, Owen Reed 4
LOVEJOY, Philip 4
LOVEJOY, Robert Carr 9
LOVEJOY, Thomas E. 1
LOVEJOY, Thomas Eugene, Jr. 7
LOVELACE, Curtis M. 4
LOVELACE, Delos Wheeler 4
LOVELACE, Francis H
LOVELACE, William Randolph, II 4
LOVELAND, Albert J. 4
LOVELAND, Chester H. 7
LOVELAND, Edward Rutherford 4
LOVELAND, Francis William 1
LOVELAND, Gilbert 3
LOVELAND, Hansell William 4
LOVELAND, Seymour 4
LOVELAND, William Austin Hamilton 4
LOVELESS, Herschel Cellel 10
LOVELL, Alfred Henry 4
LOVELL, Earl B. 2
LOVELL, Endicott Remington 9
LOVELL, Ernest James 6
LOVELL, George Blakeman 6
LOVELL, James H
LOVELL, John H
LOVELL, John Epy H
LOVELL, John Harvey 1
LOVELL, Joseph H
LOVELL, Malcolm R. 6
LOVELL, Mansfield 4
LOVELL, Moses 2
LOVELL, Richardson H
LOVELL, Ralph L. 2
LOVELL, Ralph Marston 9
LOVELL, Stanley Platt 7
LOVELL, Walter Raleigh 5
LOVELY, John A. 1
LOVEMAN, Amy 3
LOVEMAN, Robert 1
LOVERIDGE, Blanche Grosbec 5
LOVERIDGE, Earl W. 3
LOVERING, Charles T. 4
LOVERING, Henry Bacon 1
LOVERING, Joseph H
LOVERING, William C. 1
LOVESTONE, Jay 10
LOVET-LORSKI, Boris 5
LOVETT, Archibald Battle 4
LOVETT, Edgar Odell 3
LOVETT, Israel Herrick 8
LOVETT, John H
LOVETT, Ralph Brundidge 8
LOVETT, Robert Abercrombie 9
LOVETT, Robert H. 1
LOVETT, Robert Morss 3
LOVETT, Robert Scott 1
LOVETT, Robert Williamson 1
LOVETT, William Cuyler 1
LOVETTE, Joyce Metz 4
LOVETTE, Leland Pearson 1
LOVETTE, Leland Pearson 5
LOVETTE, Oscar Byrd 1
LOVEWELL, John H
LOVEWELL, Joseph Taplin 1
LOVEWELL, Samuel Harrison 4
LOVING, Starling 1
LOVINS, William Thomas 4
LOVITT, William Vernon 6
LOVRE, Harold O. 5
LOW, A. Augustus 4
LOW, Sir A. Maurice 1
LOW, Abiel Abbot H
LOW, Abraham Adolph 3
LOW, Albert Howard 4
LOW, Benjamin Robbins Curtis 1
LOW, Berthe Julienne 1
LOW, Clarence Harry 7
LOW, David 4
LOW, Edmon 4
LOW, Ethelbert Herrick 10
LOW, Ethelbert Ide 2
LOW, Francis Stuart H
LOW, Frederick Ferdinand H
LOW, Frederick Rollins 1
LOW, George Michael H
LOW, Isaac H
LOW, Juliette Gordon H

LOW, Juliette Gordon 4
LOW, Lawrence David 7
LOW, Marcus A. 1
LOW, Mrs. Marie Dickson 3
LOW, Mary Fairchild 4
LOW, Nicholas H
LOW, Seth 1
LOW, V. Theodore 8
LOW, Will Hicok 1
LOW, William Gilman 1
LOWBER, James William 1
LOWDEN, Frank Orren 4
LOWDEN, Isabel 3
LOWDERMILK, Patricia Cannales 1
LOWDERMILK, Walter Clay 6
LOWE, Arthur Houghton 1
LOWE, Boutelle Ellsworth 8
LOWE, Charles H
LOWE, Clarence George 4
LOWE, Clement Belton 4
LOWE, Clowney Oswald 6
LOWE, David Perley H
LOWE, Donald Vaughn 5
LOWE, Elias Avery 5
LOWE, Emily Lynch 4
LOWE, Ephraim Noble 4
LOWE, Frank E. 5
LOWE, Frank Melville, Jr. 7
LOWE, George Hale 4
LOWE, Herman A. 5
LOWE, Joe 5
LOWE, John 1
LOWE, John Smith 3
LOWE, John William 2
LOWE, John Zollikoffer 7
LOWE, Louis Robert 5
LOWE, Louise 1
LOWE, Malcolm Branson 5
LOWE, Martha Perry 4
LOWE, Mildred 9
LOWE, Ralph Phillips H
LOWE, Richard Barrett 5
LOWE, Stanley 5
LOWE, Thaddeus S. C. 1
LOWE, Thomas Merritt 4
LOWE, Titus 1
LOWE, Victor (Augustus) 9
LOWE, Walter Irenaeus 1
LOWE, William Baird 1
LOWE, William Henry, Sr. 9
LOWE, William Herman 6
LOWE, William Webb 1
LOWELL, Abbott Lawrence
LOWELL, Amy 1
LOWELL, Daniel Ozro Smith 1
LOWELL, Delmar Rial 1
LOWELL, Edward Jackson H
LOWELL, Francis Cabot 1
LOWELL, Francis Cabot 1
LOWELL, Guy 1
LOWELL, James Arnold 1
LOWELL, James Harrison 2
LOWELL, James Russell H
LOWELL, Joan 4
LOWELL, John* 1
LOWELL, John 1
LOWELL, Josephine Shaw 1
LOWELL, Joshua Adams H
LOWELL, Orson 3
LOWELL, Percival 1
LOWELL, Ralph 7
LOWELL, Robert (Traill Spence, Jr.) 7
LOWELL, Robert Traill Spence H
LOWELL, Sherman James 1
LOWEN, Charles Jules, Jr. 3
LOWENBERG, Bettie 4
LOWENBERG, Miriam Elizabeth 10
LOWENFELS, Walter 7
LOWENS, Irving 8
LOWENSTEI, Melvyn Gordon 5
LOWENSTEIN, Allard Kenneth 7
LOWENSTEIN, Henry Polk 4
LOWENSTEIN, Leah Miriam Hiller 8
LOWENSTEIN, Leon 7
LOWENSTEIN, Lloyd L. 4
LOWENSTEIN, Solomon 1
LOWENSTINE, Mandel 3
LOWENTHAL, Esther 7
LOWER, Christian H
LOWER, William Edgar 2
LOWEREE, F. Harold 4
LOWERY, Doane McKendry 8
LOWERY, Martin Joseph 8
LOWERY, Percival C. 7
LOWES, John Livingston 2

LOWETH, Charles Frederick 1
LOWIE, Robert Harry 3
LOWINSKY, Edward Elias 5
LOWMAN, Arthur Ames 6
LOWMAN, Charles Le Roy 6
LOWMAN, Harmon 5
LOWMAN, Seymour 1
LOWMAN, Webster B. 1
LOWMASTER, A. T. 7
LOWNDES, Arthur 1
LOWNDES, Charles Henry Tilghman 5
LOWNDES, Charles Lucien Baker 4
LOWNDES, Lloyd 1
LOWNDES, Mary Elizabeth 2
LOWNDES, Rawlins H
LOWNDES, Thomas H
LOWNDES, William H
LOWNEY, Walter M. 1
LOWNSBERY, Charles Hatch 5
LOWRANCE, John Witherspoon 8
LOWREY, Bill G. 2
LOWREY, Frederick Dwight 7
LOWREY, Frederick Jewett 4
LOWREY, Harvey H. 4
LOWREY, Lawrence Tyndate 8
LOWREY, Lawson Gentry 3
LOWREY, Mark Perrin H
LOWRIA, Rebecca Lawrence 6
LOWRIE, James Walter 4
LOWRIE, John Cameron 1
LOWRIE, Samuel Thompson 1
LOWRIE, Selden Gale 7
LOWRIE, Walter H
LOWRIE, Walter 5
LOWRIE, Will Leonard 2
LOWRY, D. R. 3
LOWRY, Edith Belle 2
LOWRY, Edith C. 5
LOWRY, Edward George 2
LOWRY, Fesington Carlyle 4
LOWRY, Frank Clifford 5
LOWRY, Frank J. 3
LOWRY, George Maus 8
LOWRY, Hiram Harrison 4
LOWRY, H(omer) H(iram) 1
LOWRY, Horace 1
LOWRY, Howard Foster 4
LOWRY, Howard James 5
LOWRY, John 4
LOWRY, Joseph E. 4
LOWRY, Malcolm 4
LOWRY, Ralph 8
LOWRY, Robert* 1
LOWRY, Thomas 1
LOWRY, Thomas Claude 2
LOWSLEY, Oswald Swinney 3
LOWSTUTER, William Jackson* 3
LOWTH, Frank James 5
LOWTHER, Florence De Loiselle 1
LOWTHER, Granville 1
LOWTHER, Hugh Sears 3
LOWY, Alexander 1
LOWY, Louis 10
LOY, Matthias 1
LOY, Sylvester K. 3
LOYALL, George H
LOYALL, George Robert 1
LOZIER, Clemence Sophia Harned H
LOZIER, Ralph Fulton 2
LOZNER, Joseph 6
LOZOWICK, Louis 6
LOZZIO, Bismarck Berto 7
LUBALIN, Herbert Frederick 7
LUBALIN, Herbert Frederick 9
LUBBOCK, Francis Richard 1
LUBECK, Henry 1
LUBELL, Samuel 9
LUBERG, Leroy Edward 8
LUBEROFF, George 6
LUBIN, Charles W. 9
LUBIN, David 1
LUBIN, Isador 7
LUBIN, Simon Julius 1
LUBITSCH, Ernst 2
LUBKE, Carl Heinrich 5
LUBOFF, Norman 9
LUBOMIRSKI, Prince Casimir
LUBSCHEZ, Ben Judah 6
LUBY, James 1

LYNCH, James Mathew 1
LYNCH, James William 4
LYNCH, Jeremiah 1
LYNCH, Jerome Morley 3
LYNCH, John H
LYNCH, John A. 1
LYNCH, John David 2
LYNCH, John Fairfield 1
LYNCH, John Joseph H
LYNCH, John Roy 1
LYNCH, Joseph Bertram 4
LYNCH, Joseph Patrick 3
LYNCH, Kenneth Merrill 6
LYNCH, Kevin 8
LYNCH, Matthew 1
Christopher
LYNCH, Patrick Neeson H
LYNCH, Raymond A. 5
LYNCH, Robert Joseph 10
LYNCH, Robert Newton 1
LYNCH, Russell George 7
LYNCH, Thomas* H
LYNCH, Thomas Connor 9
LYNCH, Thomas Francis 5
LYNCH, Vincent de Paul 8
LYNCH, Walter A. 3
LYNCH, Walton D. 4
LYNCH, Warren 7
LYNCH, Warren J. 3
LYNCH, Willard A. 3
LYNCH, William Francis H
LYNCH, William Joseph 7
LYNCH, William Orlando 3
LYNCH-STAUNTON, 10
Frank C.
LYND, Robert Staughton 5
LYNDE, Benjamin H
LYNDE, Carleton John 5
LYNDE, Francis 1
LYNDE, Paul Edward 9
LYNDE, Samuel Adams 1
LYNDE, William Pitt H
LYNDON, Lamar 5
LYNDS, Elam H
LYNE, James Garnett 4
LYNE, Wickliffe Campbell 1
LYNEN, Feodor 7
LYNES, (Joseph) Russell, 10
Jr.
LYNETT, Edward James 2
LYNETT, Edward James 4
LYNETT, Elizabeth Ruddy 3
LYNHAM, John 9
Marmaduke
LYNN, Charles J. 3
LYNN, Chester Bernard 8
LYNN, David 4
LYNN, Harry Hudson 5
LYNN, Henry Sharpe 10
LYNN, Klonda 10
LYNN, Robert Henry 3
LYNN, Robert Marshall 7
LYNN, Robert T. 10
LYNN, Thomas Edward 6
LYNN, Wilbert 5
LYNN, William Harcourt 10
LYON, A. Maynard 7
LYON, Adrian 5
LYON, Alfred E. 4
LYON, Andrew Hutchinson 4
LYON, Anne Bozeman 4
LYON, Arlon Everett 7
LYON, Asa H
LYON, B. B. Vincent 6
LYON, Bertrand 6
LYON, Caleb H
LYON, Cecil Andrew 1
LYON, Charles Gershom 6
LYON, Charles Stuart 10
LYON, Clyde Laten 6
LYON, David Gordon 2
LYON, Dorsey Alfred 2
LYON, Edmund 1
LYON, Edmund Daniel 2
LYON, Edwin Bowman 5
LYON, Eldridge Merick 1
LYON, Elias Potter 3
LYON, Elijah Wilson 10
LYON, Ernest 2
LYON, Ernest Neal 1
LYON, Francis Strother H
LYON, Frank 3
LYON, Frank Emory 6
LYON, Frederick Saxton 2
LYON, George Armstrong 1
LYON, George F. 1
LYON, George Harry 5
LYON, George Robert 10
LYON, Gideon Allen 7
LYON, Harley Wesley 7
LYON, Harris Merton 7
LYON, Harvey William 3
LYON, Hastings 3
LYON, Henry Ware 3
LYON, Herb 5
LYON, Homer LeGrand 6
LYON, James H

LYON, J(ames) Adair 5
LYON, James Alexander 3
LYON, John Denniston 1
LYON, John Stanley 4
LYON, Leonard Saxton 4
LYON, Leroy Springs 1
LYON, Leverett Samuel 3
LYON, Lucius H
LYON, Marcus Ward, Jr. 1
LYON, Mary H
LYON, Matthew H
LYON, Milford Hall 5
LYON, Nathaniel H
LYON, Nelson Reed 5
LYON, Pritchett Alfred 4
LYON, Quinter M(arcellus) 10
LYON, Roger Adrian 8
LYON, Scott Cary 2
LYON, T. Lyttleton 1
LYON, Tom 8
LYON, Walter Jefferson 1
LYON, William Alexander 6
LYON, William Henry 1
LYON, William Penn 1
LYONS, Albert Brown 4
LYONS, Chalmers J. 1
LYONS, Champ 4
LYONS, Charles William 1
LYONS, Charlton Havard 6
LYONS, Clifford Pierson 10
LYONS, Coleburke 5
LYONS, Dennis Francis 1
LYONS, Eugene 5
LYONS, Gerald Edward 2
LYONS, Harold Aloysius 9
LYONS, James J. 4
LYONS, John Frederick 6
LYONS, John H. 9
LYONS, John Sprole 2
LYONS, Joseph Henry 6
LYONS, Judson Whitlocke 1
LYONS, Julius J. 1
LYONS, Katharine 1
LYONS, Leonard 7
LYONS, Louis Martin 8
LYONS, Lucile Manning 3
LYONS, M. Arnold 9
LYONS, Peter H
LYONS, Richard Joseph 10
LYONS, Richard Thomas 7
LYONS, Robert Edward 2
LYONS, Samuel Ross 4
LYONS, Thomas Daniel 7
LYONS, Thomas Richard 1
LYONS, Thomas William 9
LYONS, Timothy Augustine 1
LYONS, William Aloysius 8
LYSENKO, Trofim 7
Denisovich
LYSTER, Henry Francis Le H
Hunte
LYSTER, Theodore Charles 1
LYTE, E. Oram 1
LYTELL, Bert 3
LYTER, Jean Curtis 1
LYTLE, Almon Wheeler 4
LYTLE, Clyde Francis 8
LYTLE, J. Horace 4
LYTLE, Robert Todd H
LYTLE, W(ilbert) Vernon 8
LYTLE, William Haines H
LYTTELTON, Oliver 5
LYTTLE, Charles Harold 7
LYTTLETON, William H
Henry
LYTTON, Bart 5

M

MAAG, William Frederick, 5
Jr.
MAAS, Anthony J. 1
MAAS, Carlos J. 5
MAAS, Melvin Joseph 4
MAASKE, Roben J. 3
MAASS, Herbert Halsey 3
MAASS, Otto 4
MABBOTT, Thomas Ollive 5
MABEE, George W. 2
MABERY, Charles Frederic 1
MABEY, Charles R. 5
MABIE, Edward Charles 3
MABIE, Hamilton Wright 1
MABIE, Henry Clay 1
MABIE, Louise Kennedy 3
MABLEY, Jackie Moms 6
MABON, John Scott 7
MABON, Thomas McCance 3
MABRY, Edward L. 9
MABRY, George Lafayette, 10
Jr.
MABRY, Giddings Eldon 9
MABRY, Harry Cooper 9
MABRY, Milton Harvey 4
MABRY, Thomas Jewett 7
MABURY, Margaret Ellis 1

MAC ADAM, George 4
Hartley
MAC AFEE, John Blair 1
MACAGY, Douglas 6
Guernsey
MACALARNEY, Robert 2
Emmet
MACALESTER, Charles* H
MACALISTER, Sir Ian 3
MAC ALISTER, James 1
MACALLISTER, 4
Archibald Thomas, Jr.
MAC ALPINE, Robert 1
John
MACANALLY, James R. 5
MACARTHUR, Alfred 4
MAC ARTHUR, Archibald 1
MAC ARTHUR, Arthur* 1
MAC ARTHUR, Arthur 1
Frederic
MACARTHUR, Charles 3
MACARTHUR, Donald 10
MAC ARTHUR, Donald 10
Malcolm
MACARTHUR, Douglas 4
MACARTHUR, Harry 6
MAC ARTHUR, James 1
MACARTHUR, John D. 1
MACARTHUR, John R. 3
MACARTHUR, Robert 5
Helmer
MAC ARTHUR, Robert 1
Stuart
MACARTHUR, Ruth 6
Alberta Brown
MAC ARTHUR, Walter 4
MACARTNEY, Clarence 3
Edward Noble
MACARTNEY, John W. 5
MACARTNEY, Thomas 1
Benton, Jr.
MACAULAY, Fannie 2
Caldwell
MACAULAY, Fannie 4
Caldwell
MACAULAY, Frederick 5
Robertson
MACAULAY, Malcolm 6
George
MACAULAY, Peter 4
Stewart
MACAULEY, Alvan 3
MACAULEY, Charles 1
Raymond
MACAULEY, Charles 5
Raymond
MACAULEY, Edward 4
MACAULEY, Irving P. 4
MACAUSLAND, Earle 7
Rutherford
MACBAIN, Gavin Keith 5
MACBAIN, Richard 10
Norman
MACBETH, Alexander 2
Barksdale
MACBETH, Florence 4
MACBETH, George 1
Alexander
MACBETH, George Duff 5
MACBETH, Henry 4
MACBETH, Norman 4
MACBRAYNE, Lewis E. 3
MACBRIDE, D. S. 3
MACBRIDE, Philip 4
Douglas
MACBRIDE, Thomas 1
Huston
MACCAFFREY, Isabel 7
Gamble
MACCALLA, Clifford 1
Sheron
MACCALLUM, John 2
Archibald
MAC CALLUM, John 5
Bruce
MACCALLUM, William 2
George
MAC CAMERON, Robert 1
MACCARTHY, Gerald 6
R(aleigh)
MACCARTY, William 4
Carpenter
MACCAUD, Francis 5
William
MACCAUGHEY, Vaughan 3
MAC CAULEY, Clay 1
MACCHENSNEY, Chester 4
M.
MACCHESNEY, Brunson, 7
III (Alfred)
MACCHESNEY, Clara 5
Taggart
MACCHESNEY, Nathan 3
William
MACCKEY, William 4
Fleming

MACCLINTOCK, Paul 5
MACCLINTOCK, Samuel 5
MAC CLINTOCK, William 1
Darnall
MACCLOSKEY, James 5
Edward, Jr.
MACCOLL, Alexander 5
MAC COLL, James 1
Roberton
MAC COLL, William Bogle 1
MACCOLL, William 1
Hamilton
MAC CONNELL, Charles 1
Jenkins
MACCONNELL, John 3
Wilson
MACCONOCHIE, Arthur 9
F(rancis)
MAC CORD, Charles 1
William
MACCORKLE, Emmett 1
Wallace
MAC CORKLE, Stuart 8
Alexander
MAC CORKLE, William 1
Alexander
MACCORMACK, Daniel 1
William
MACCORMICK, Austin 7
Harbutt
MACCORMNACK, Walter 4
Roy
MACCORRY, P. J. 4
MAC COUN, Townsend 4
MACCOY, William Logan 2
MAC CRACKEN, Henry 1
Mitchell
MACCRACKEN, Henry 5
Noble
MACCRACKEN, John 2
Henry
MACCRACKEN, William 5
Patterson, Jr.
MACCRATE, John 7
MACCREA, John 9
Livingstone
MACCREAGH, Gordon 7
MACCULLOUGH, 3
Gleason Harvey
MACCURDY, George 2
Grant
MACCUTCHEON, Aleck 3
MAC DANIEL, Frank 1
MACDANIEL, Robert D. 4
MACDIARMID, Hugh 9
(Christopher Murray
Grieve)
MAC DILL, David 1
MACDONALD, Alexander 1
Black
MACDONALD, Alexander 2
Lewis
MACDONALD, Angus 3
Addams
MACDONALD, Anna 5
Addams
MACDONALD, Archibald 1
Arnott
MAC DONALD, Arthur 1
Jay
MACDONALD, Arthur 4
MACDONALD, Augustin 5
Sylvester
MACDONALD, Bernard 4
Callaghan
MACDONALD, Betty 5
MACDONALD, Byrnes 3
MACDONALD, Carlos 1
Frederick
MACDONALD, Charles 1
MAC DONALD, Daniel 7
Joseph
MACDONALD, D(eloss) 7
K(ent)
MACDONALD, Duncan 2
Black
MACDONALD, Dwight 8
MACDONALD, Edwina 6
LeVin
MACDONALD, George 1
Alexander
MACDONALD, George 3
Everett
MACDONALD, George 2
Saxe
MACDONALD, Godfrey 4
MACDONALD, Gordon 1
MACDONALD, Gordon 7
Andrew
MACDONALD, H. E. 7
MACDONALD, Henry 3
MACDONALD, Ian 5
(Gibbs)
MACDONALD, James 1
Allan
MACDONALD, James R. 4

MACDONALD, James H
Wilson Alexander
MACDONALD, James 4
Wilson Alexander
MACDONALD, Jeanette 4
MACDONALD, Jesse Juan 5
MACDONALD, John 2
Alexander
MACDONALD, John 9
Dann
MACDONALD, John H. 4
MAC DONALD, John 10
(Haskell)
MACDONALD, John 1
William
MACDONALD, John 7
Winchester
MACDONALD, Katherine 6
Cunningham (Mrs.
George Field MacDonald)
MACDONALD, Lillias 7
Margaret
MACDONALD, Malcolm 7
John
MACDONALD, Mary 10
Elizabeth
MACDONALD, Milton 4
Tenney
MACDONALD, Milton 6
Theodore
MACDONALD, Moses H
MACDONALD, Neil 1
Carnot
MACDONALD, Nestor 10
Joseph
MACDONALD, Pirie 2
MACDONALD, Ranald H
MACDONALD, Robert 4
MACDONALD, Thomas 3
Harris
MACDONALD, Torbert 7
Hart
MAC DONALD, William 4
MACDONALD, William 4
Alexander
MACDONALD, William 1
H.
MAC DONALD, William J. 5
MACDONALD, William 7
Ross
MACDONALD, Willis 1
Goss
MACDONALD-WRIGHT, 6
Stanton
MACDONELL, Angus 1
MACDONELL, James 7
Donald
MACDONELL, James 8
Johnson
MACDONNELL, James 6
Francis Carlin
MACDONNELL, James 9
Mackerras
MACDONNELL, Robert 8
George
MACDONNELL, Ronald 6
Macalister
MACDONOUGH, Thomas H
MACDOUGAL, Daniel 3
Trembly
MACDOUGALD, Dan 3
MACDOUGALL, Mrs. 4
Alice Foote
MAC DOUGALL, Clinton 1
Dugald
MACDOUGALL, Curtis 9
Daniel
MACDOUGALL, Edward 3
Archibald
MACDOUGALL, Frank 6
Henry
MACDOUGALL, Hamilton 2
Crawford
MACDOUGALL, Mary 7
Stuart
MACDOUGALL, Ranald 6
MAC DOUGALL, Robert 1
MACDOUGALL, Roderick 8
Martin
MACDOUGALL, Roderick 9
Martin
MACDOUGALL, William 1
Dugald
MACDOWELL, Charles 3
Henry
MACDOWELL, Mrs. 3
Edward
MACDOWELL, Edward 1
Alexander
MACDOWELL, Elmer 9
George
MACDOWELL, Katherine H
Sherwood Bonner
MACDOWELL, Noah 7
MACDOWELL, Thain 4
Wendell

Name	
MACDUFFEE, Cyrus Colton	4
MACDUFFIE, John	1
MACE, Daniel	H
MACE, David Robert	10
MACE, Frances Laughton	1
MACE, Frank William	4
MACE, Harold Loring	2
MACE, William Harrison	1
MACEACHERN, Malcolm T.	3
MACEACHRAN, Clinton Edson	8
MACEDO SOARES, Jose Carlos	5
MAC ELREE, Wilmer W.	4
MAC ELROY, Andrew Jackson	4
MACELROY, Andrew Jackson	5
MACELWANE, Geraldine Frances	6
MACELWANE, James B.	3
MACELWANE, John Patrick	5
MACELWEE, Roy Samuel	2
MACENULTY, John Forrest	6
MACEWEN, Ewen Murchison	2
MACEWEN, Walter	2
MACFADDEN, Bernarr	3
MACFADDEN, William Semple	10
MACFADYEN, Alexander	1
MACFARLAN, William Charles	2
MACFARLAND, Charles Stedman	3
MACFARLAND, Finlay Leroy	
MACFARLAND, Frank Mace	3
MACFARLAND, Hays	6
MACFARLAND, Henry Brown Floyd	1
MACFARLAND, Lanning	5
MACFARLAND, Robert Alfred	3
MACFARLANE, Alexander	4
MACFARLANE, Catharine	5
MACFARLANE, Charles William	5
MACFARLANE, David Laing	3
MACFARLANE, Howard Pettingill	5
MACFARLANE, James	6
MACFARLANE, John C.	3
MACFARLANE, John Muirhead	4
MACFARLANE, Joseph Arthur	4
MACFARLANE, Peter	3
MACFARLANE, Peter Clark	1
MACFARLANE, Robert	H
MACFARLANE, W. E.	2
MACFARLANE, William	6
MACFEE, William Frank	9
MACFEELY, Robert	1
MAC GAHAN, Barbara	1
MACGAHAN, Januarius Aloysius	H
MACGILL, Charles Frederick	7
MAC GILLIVRAY, Alexander Dyer	1
MACGILLIVRAY, William	H
MACGILVARY, Norwood	2
MAC GILVARY, Paton	1
MACGINLEY, John Bernard	5
MAC GINNISS, John	1
MACGLASHAN, David Pollock	6
MAC GOVERN, Stan(ley) Raymond Eugene)	7
MAC GOWAN, Alice	4
MACGOWAN, David Bell	5
MAC GOWAN, Gault	5
MAC GOWAN, Granville	1
MAC GOWAN, John Encil	5
MACGOWAN, John Koe	2
MACGOWAN, Kenneth	4
MAC GRATH, Harold	1
MACGREGOR, Charles Peter	5
MACGREGOR, Clarence	3
MACGREGOR, David Hutchison	3
MACGREGOR, David Hutchison	5
MACGREGOR, Frank Silver	5
MAC GREGOR, Henry Frederick	1
MACGREGOR, John Murdoch	10
MACGREGOR, Lawrence John	9
MACGREGOR, Theodore Douglas	6
MACHADO, Alfredo C.	10
MACHADO, Luis	7
MACHARG, John Brainerd	3
MACHARG, William	3
MACHEBEUF, Joseph Projectus	H
MACHEN, Arthur Webster	3
MACHEN, J. Gresham	1
MACHEN, Willis Benson	H
MACHIR, James	H
MACHLETT, Raymond R.	3
MACHLIS, Leonard	7
MACHLUP, Fritz	4
MACHMER, William Lawson	3
MACHOLD, Earle John	6
MACHOLD, Henry Edmund	4
MACHROWICZ, Thaddeus M(ichael)	5
MACHT, Stuart Martin	10
MACHUM, Waldo Carson	7
MACIEJEWSKI, Anton Frank	4
MACINNES, Duncan	4
MAC INNES, Helen (Mrs. Gilbert Highet)	9
MAC INNIS, John Murdoch	1
MACINTOSH, Douglas Clyde	2
MACINTOSH, Frank Campbell	10
MAC INTOSH, John Alexander	1
MACINTOSH, William James	10
MACINTYRE, Archibald James	5
MACINTYRE, Christine Melba	9
MACINTYRE, Malcolm Ames	10
MACINTYRE, W(illiam) Ralph	10
MACIOCE, Thomas Matthew	10
MACISAAC, Fred	1
MACIVER, Robert Morrison	5
MACIVER, Robert Morrison	7
MACIVOR, John William	6
MACK, A. B.	3
MACK, Andrew	1
MACK, Augustus Frederick, Jr.	4
MACK, Carl Theodore	5
MACK, Clifton Eugene	7
MACK, Connie	3
MACK, Edgar M.	2
MACK, Edward	3
MACK, Edwin S.	2
MACK, George Herbert	5
MACK, Henry Whitcomb	4
MACK, Howard	3
MACK, Isaac Foster	1
MACK, J(ames) S(tephen)	5
MACK, John E.	3
MACK, John Givan Davis	1
MACK, John M.	1
MACK, John Sephus	5
MACK, Julian Ellis	4
MACK, Julian William	2
MACK, Marion	10
MACK, Norman Edward	1
MACK, Pauline Beery	6
MACK, Peter Francis, Jr.	9
MACK, Richard Alfred	4
MACK, Russell Herbert	10
MACK, Russell Vernon	3
MACK, Ted	7
MACK, Walter Staunton	10
MACK, Warren Bryan	5
MACK, William	2
MACKALL, Alexander Lawton	5
MACKALL, Colin MacKenzie	7
MACKALL, Henry Clinton	7
MACKALL, Leonard Leopold	1
MACKALL, Louis	1
MACKALL, Paul	3
MACKAY, Albert Calder	9
MACKAY, Albert George	7
MACKAY, Clarence Hungerford	1
MACKAY, Constance D'Arcy	4
MACKAY, Donald Dundas	4
MACKAY, Donald Sage	1
MACKAY, Helen	4
MACKAY, Helen (Mrs. Archibald MacKay)	5
MACKAY, Henry Squarebriggs, Jr.	3
MACKAY, James	H
MACKAY, John Alexander	8
MACKAY, John Alexander	9
MACKAY, John Keiller	5
MACKAY, John Keiller	8
MACKAY, John William	1
MACKAY, Louis	8
MACKAY, Louis Alexander	3
MACKAY, Margaret	5
MACKAY, Robert	5
MACKAY, Roland Parks	4
MACKAY, William Andrew	1
MACKAY, William Eshorne	1
MACKAYE, Arthur Loring	4
MACKAYE, Benton	6
MACKAYE, Harold Steele	1
MACKAYE, James	1
MACKAYE, James Morrison Steele	H
MACKAYE, Percy	3
MACKAY-SMITH, Alexander	1
MACKEACHIE, Douglas Cornell	2
MACKECHNIE, Hugh Neil	4
MACKEE, George Miller	3
MACKEEN, Henry Poole	9
MACKEEVER, John C.	3
MACKELLAR, Patrick	H
MACKELLAR, Thomas	H
MAC KELLAR, Thomas	4
MACKELLAR, William Henry Howard	2
MACKELVIE, Jay Ward	8
MACKEN, Walter	4
MACKENDRICK, Lilian	9
MACKENZIE, A. Cameron	1
MACKENZIE, Alastair St. Clair	5
MACKENZIE, Alexander	1
MACKENZIE, Alexander	H
MACKENZIE, Alexander Slidell	1
MACKENZIE, Arthur	5
MACKENZIE, Arthur Stanley	4
MACKENZIE, Cameron	1
MACKENZIE, Chalmers Jack	9
MACKENZIE, Compton	7
MACKENZIE, Donald	H
MACKENZIE, Donald	2
MACKENZIE, Donald Hector	3
MACKENZIE, Eric Francis	10
MACKENZIE, Frederick William	1
MACKENZIE, George Henry	H
MACKENZIE, Harold Orville	7
MACKENZIE, Ian Alistair	8
MACKENZIE, J. Gazzam	5
MACKENZIE, James Cameron	1
MACKENZIE, Jean Kenyon	1
MACKENZIE, John Douglas	6
MACKENZIE, John Noland	1
MACKENZIE, Kenneth	H
MACKENZIE, Kenneth Alexander J.	1
MACKENZIE, Kenneth Gerard	1
MACKENZIE, Morris Robinson Slidell	1
MACKENZIE, Murdo	1
MACKENZIE, Norman Archibald Macrae	9
MAC KENZIE, Ossian	7
MACKENZIE, Ossian	8
MACKENZIE, Philip Edward	2
MACKENZIE, Ranald Slidell	H
MACKENZIE, Robert	1
MACKENZIE, Robert Shelton	H
MACKENZIE, Roderick Dempster	1
MACKENZIE, Tandy	4
MACKENZIE, Thomas Hanna	2
MACKENZIE, William	H
MACKENZIE, William Adams	2
MACKENZIE, William Douglas	1
MACKENZIE, William Ross	3
MACKENZIE, William Roy	3
MACKEOWN, Samuel Stuart	3
MACKERSKY, L(indsay) Stuart	9
MACKEY, Albert Gallatin	H
MACKEY, Charles Osborn	4
MACKEY, Charles William	1
MACKEY, David Ray	6
MACKEY, Edmund William McGregor	1
MACKEY, Harry A.	1
MACKEY, Joseph T.	4
MACKEY, Levi Augustus	1
MACKICHAN, Keith B.	7
MACKIE, Alexander	4
MACKIE, David Ives	4
MACKIE, Ernest Lloyd	5
MACKIE, Joseph Bolton Cooper	2
MACKIE, Pauline Bradford (Mrs. Herbert M. Hopkins)	5
MACKIE, Thomas Turlay	3
MACKILLOP, Malcolm Andrew	9
MACKIN, Catherine	8
MACKIN, Joseph Hoover	4
MACKINNEY, Loren Carey	4
MACKINNEY, Paul R.	7
MACKINNON, Alexander Donald	10
MACKINNON, Allan P.	1
MACKINNON, Eugene	4
MACKINNON, George V.	1
MACKINNON, Harold Alexander	5
MACKINNON, James Angus	3
MACKINNON, John C.	6
MACKINNON, Lee Warner	5
MACKINTOSH, Alexander	2
MACKINTOSH, George Lewis	1
MACKINTOSH, Harold Vincent	4
MACKINTOSH, Hugh	6
MACKINTOSH, Kenneth	5
MACKINTOSH, William Archibald	5
MACKLIN, James Edgar	1
MACKLIN, John Farrell	7
MACKLIN, Justin Wilford	4
MACKLIN, W. A. Stewart	1
MACKNIGHT, Dodge	3
MACKRELL, Franklin Cunningham	10
MACKUBIN, Florence	1
MACKY, Eric Spencer	3
MACLACHAN, David Cathcart	1
MACLACHLAN, Daniel A.	1
MACLACHLAN, James A.	4
MACLACHLAN, James Morrill	10
MACLACHLAN, John Miller	3
MAC LACHLAN, Lachlan	1
MACLACHLAN, Margery Jean	4
MACLAFFERTY, James Henry	1
MACLANE, Gerald Robinson	5
MACLANE, M. Jean	4
MAC LANE, Mary	1
MACLANE, Mary	2
MAC LAREN, Archibald	1
MACLAREN, Gay	7
MACLAREN, Malcolm	2
MACLAURIN, Richard Cockburn	1
MACLAURIN, William Rupert	3
MACLAY, Edgar Stanton	4
MACLAY, Isaac Walker	1
MACLAY, James	1
MACLAY, Otis Hardy	1
MACLAY, Robert Samuel	1
MACLAY, Samuel	H
MACLAY, William*	H
MACLAY, William Brown	1
MACLAY, William	H
MACLAY, William Plunkett	1
MACLAY, William Walter	3
MACLEAN, Alexander Tweedie	3
MACLEAN, Alistair	9
MACLEAN, Angus Dhu	1
MACLEAN, Angus Hector	9
MACLEAN, Annie Marion	1
MACLEAN, Arthur Winfield	2
MACLEAN, Basil Clarendon	4
MACLEAN, Charles Fraser	1
MACLEAN, Charles Thomas Agnew	1
MACLEAN, Charles Waldo	10
MACLEAN, Clara Dargan	1
MACLEAN, Daniel	4
MAC LEAN, Donald Drew	8
MACLEAN, Donald Isidore	4
MACLEAN, George Edwin	1
MAC LEAN, Grace Edith	7
MACLEAN, Henry Coit	4
MACLEAN, James Alexander	2
MACLEAN, John*	H
MACLEAN, John Allan	8
MACLEAN, John Norman	2
MACLEAN, Joseph Brotherton	8
MACLEAN, Malcolm Shaw	6
MACLEAN, Munroe Deacon	5
MACLEAN, Norman Fitzroy	10
MACLEAN, Paul Robert	5
MACLEAN, Ray Butts	2
MACLEAN, Samuel Richter	4
MACLEAN, Stuart	5
MACLEAN, William	10
MACLEAR, Anne Bush	1
MACLEARY, Bonnie	6
MACLEISH, Andrew	1
MAC LEISH, Archibald	8
MACLEISH, Bruce	6
MACLEISH, Bruce	7
MACLEISH, John E.	5
MACLELLAN, Kenneth F.	5
MACLELLAN, Robert J.	3
MACLELLAN, Robert Llewellyn	5
MACLENNAN, Francis	1
MACLENNAN, Francis William	2
MACLENNAN, Frank Pitts	1
MACLENNAN, Hugh	10
MACLENNAN, Simon Fraser	5
MACLEOD, Annie Louise Hamilton	7
MACLEOD, Bruce	4
MACLEOD, Colln Munro	5
MACLEOD, Donald Campbell	2
MACLEOD, Frederick Joseph	1
MACLEOD, Iain Norman	5
MACLEOD, John Holmes	8
MACLEOD, John James Rickard	1
MACLEOD, Malcolm James	1
MACLEOD, Robert Brodie	5
MAC LEOD-THORP, L. E. G.	2
MACLIN, Edward Silver	7
MACLOSKIE, George	1
MACLURE, William	H
MACMAHON, Arthur W.	2
MACMAHON, Lloyd Francis	10
MACMANUS, Seumas	4
MACMANUS, Seumas	5
MACMILLAN, Cargill	2
MACMILLAN, Conway	3
MACMILLAN, Cyrus	3
MACMILLAN, Donald Baxter	6
MACMILLAN, Dougald, III (William)	6
MACMILLAN, Sir Ernest Campbell	5
MACMILLAN, George Whitfield	5
MACMILLAN, Harold (Earl of Stockton)	10
MACMILLAN, Harvey Reginald	6
MACMILLAN, Hugh Alexander	9
MACMILLAN, Hugh R.	3
MACMILLAN, Jason Leon	4
MACMILLAN, John Alwyn	3
MACMILLAN, John Hugh, Jr.	4
MACMILLAN, Sir Kenneth	10

MACMILLAN, Kerr Duncan 1
MACMILLAN, Lucy Hayes 4
MACMILLAN, Norman John 7
MACMILLAN, Richard F. 6
MAC MILLAN, Thomas C. 1
MACMILLAN, William Duncan 2
MACMILLEN, Francis 7
MACMONNIES, Frederick 1
MAC MULLAN, Ralph A. 5
MACMULLEN, Wallace 4
MACMURRAY, Frederick Martin 10
MACMURRAY, James E. 2
MACMURRAY, John Van Antwerp 4
MACNAIR, Florence Wheelock Ayscough 2
MACNAIR, Harley Farnsworth 2
MACNAIR, James Duncan 2
MACNAMARA, Arthur James 4
MACNAMARA, G. Allan 4
MACNAUGHT, J. Watson 8
MACNAUGHTON, Boyd 7
MACNAUGHTON, Edgar 5
MACNAUGHTON, Ernest Boyd 4
MACNAUGHTON, James 2
MACNAUGHTON, Lewis Winslow 5
MACNAUGHTON, Moray Fraser 4
MACNEAL, Robert E. 4
MACNEAL, Ward J. 2
MACNEICE, Louis 4
MACNEIL, Carol Brooks 5
MACNEIL, Hermon Atkins 4
MACNEIL, Neil 5
MACNEIL, Sayre 4
MACNEIL, Virginia Allen Bagby 6
MAC NEILL, Charles Mather 1
MACNEILL, Earl S(chworm) 10
MACNEILLE, Holbrook Mann 6
MACNEILLE, Stephen Mann 4
MACNEISH, Noel Stones 4
MACNEVEN, William James H
MACNICOL, Roy Vincent 5
MACNICOL, Roy Vincent 8
MACNIDER, Hanford 4
MACNIDER, Hanford 5
MACNIDER, William de Berniere 3
MACNULTY, William K. 4
MACNUTT, Glenn Gordon 10
MACNUTT, J(oseph) Scott 7
MACOBER, William Butts, Jr. 7
MACOMB, Alexander H
MACOMB, Augustus Canfield 4
MACOMB, David Betton 1
MACOMB, Montgomery Meigs 1
MACOMBER, Alexander 3
MACOMBER, Allison Rufus 8
MACOMBER, John R. 5
MACOMBER, William 1
MACON, Nathaniel H
MACON, Robert Bruce 1
MACPHAIL, Leland Stanford (Larry) 6
MACPHAIL, William 4
MACPHERSON, Crawford Brough 9
MACPHERSON, Daniel Allan 7
MAC PHERSON, Earle Steele 3
MACPHERSON, Leslie Coombs 6
MACPHERSON, Thomas George 7
MACPHERSON, Walter Henry 3
MACPHIE, Elmore I. 3
MAC PHIE, John Peter 4
MAC QUEARY, Thomas Howard 1
MACQUEARY, Thomas Howard 2
MACQUEEN, Donald Bruce 5
MAC QUEEN, Lawrence Inglis 8
MAC QUEEN, Peter 1

MACQUIDDY, Ernest Lynn 9
MACQUIGG, Charles Ellison 3
MACRAE, Durant Loomis 7
MACRAE, Elliott Beach 4
MACRAE, Elmer Livingston 3
MACRAE, Emma Fordyce (Mrs. Homer Swift) 7
MAC RAE, Floyd Willcox 4
MAC RAE, George Winsor 9
MACRAE, George Wythe 4
MACRAE, Gordon 9
MACRAE, Harry B. 4
MACRAE, Hugh 5
MAC RAE, James Cameron 1
MACRAE, John 2
MACRAE, John, Jr. 8
MACRAE, William Alexander 1
MACRIDIS, Roy Constantine 10
MACRUM, George Herbert 8
MACSHERRY, Charles Whitman 6
MACSPARRAN, James H
MACTAVISH, William Caruth 5
MACVANE, Edith 4
MACVANE, John Franklin 8
MACVANE, Silas Marcus 3
MACVEAGH, Charles 1
MACVEAGH, Ewen Cameron 5
MACVEAGH, Franklin 1
MACVEAGH, Lincoln 5
MAC VEAGH, Wayne 4
MAC VEY, William Pitt 5
MAC VICAR, John 4
MACVICAR, John George 2
MAC VICAR, Margaret Love Agnes 10
MACVITTY, Karl de G. 5
MACWHITE, Michael 7
MACWHORTER, Alexander H
MACY, Anne Mansfield Sullivan 4
MACY, Arthur 1
MACY, C. Ward 3
MACY, Carleton 3
MACY, Clarence Edward 7
MACY, Edith Dewing 4
MACY, Edward Warren 3
MACY, George 1
MACY, Jesse 1
MACY, John 3
MACY, John B. H
MACY, John Williams, Jr. 9
MACY, Josiah H
MACY, Josiah, Jr. 7
MACY, Josiah, Jr. 3
MACY, Josiah Noel 7
MACY, Nelson 3
MACY, Paul Griswold 4
MACY, V. Everit 4
MACY, Valentine E(verit), Jr. 4
MACY, W. Kingsland 4
MACY-HOOBLER, Icie G(ertrude) 9
MADDEN, Carl Halford 7
MADDEN, Clifford John 8
MADDEN, Edwin Charles 4
MADDEN, Eva Anne 4
MADDEN, Henry Miller 8
MADDEN, James Loomis 5
MADDEN, John 4
MADDEN, John Beckwith 9
MADDEN, John Fitz 2
MADDEN, John Griffith 4
MADDEN, John Joseph 4
MADDEN, John T. 10
MADDEN, John Thomas 2
MADDEN, Joseph Warren 6
MADDEN, Lillian Gertrude 6
MADDEN, M. Lester 4
MADDEN, Martin Barnaby 1
MADDEN, Mrs. Maude Whitmore
MADDEN, Ray J(ohn) 9
MADDIN, Percy Downs 2
MADDOCK, Catharine Young Glen 5
MADDOCK, Sydney Dean 8
MADDOCK, Walter Grierson 4
MADDOCK, William Eli 5
MADDON, John W. 3
MADDOX, Dwayne Depew 4
MADDOX, Fletcher 1
MADDOX, James Gray 6
MADDOX, John J. 2
MADDOX, Louis Wilson 3
MADDOX, Robert Charles 6

MADDOX, Robert Foster 5
MADDOX, Samuel T. 1
MADDOX, William Arthur 1
MADDOX, William Percy 5
MADDRY, Charles Edward 4
MADDUX, Jared 5
MADDUX, Parker Simmons 3
MADDY, Joseph Edgar 4
MADEIRA, Crawford Clark 10
MADEIRA, Jean Browning 5
MADEIRA, Louis Childs 1
MADEIRA, Percy Childs, Jr. 9
MADELEVA, Sister Mary 4
MADERNA, Bruno 6
MADIERA, Percy Child 2
MADIGAN, Laverne 2
MADIGAN, Michael J. 9
MADILL, Grant Charles 2
MADISON, Charles A(llan) 9
MADISON, Charles C. H
MADISON, Dorothea Payne Todd H
MADISON, Edmond H. 1
MADISON, Frank Dellno 2
MADISON, Harold Lester 3
MADISON, James* H
MADISON, James Buford 7
MADISON, Lucy Foster 1
MADISON, Norman Arthur 4
MADSEN, Charles Clifford 10
MADSEN, Mattias 8
MADSON, Ben A(dolph) 8
MAEDER, LeRoy M. A. 6
MAEGLI, Hallo 6
MAENNER, Theodore Henry 3
MAERZ, Joseph 7
MAES, Camillus Paul 1
MAES, Robert Adamson 10
MAES, Urban 6
MAESTRE, Sidney 4
MAESTRI, Robert S(idney) 6
MAETERLINCK, Maurice 2
MAFFETT, Minnie Lee 7
MAFFITT, David H
MAFFITTZ, John Newland 4
MAFFRY, August 8
MAFOR, Ralph Hermon 7
MAFOR, William Warner H
MAG, Arthur 8
MAG, Edward Arnold 7
MAGAN, Percy Tilson 2
MAGARY, Alvin Edwin 4
MAGAW, Charles Albert 5
MAGDSICK, Henry Herbert 8
MAGEE, Carlton Cole 2
MAGEE, Charles Lohr 5
MAGEE, Christopher Lyman 1
MAGEE, Clare 5
MAGEE, Elizabeth Stewart 5
MAGEE, Frank Lynn 10
MAGEE, James Carre 6
MAGEE, James Carre 7
MAGEE, James Dysart 2
MAGEE, James M. 2
MAGEE, John H
MAGEE, John 4
MAGEE, John Benjamin 2
MAGEE, John Fackenthal 4
MAGEE, J(unius) Ralph 5
MAGEE, Rena Tucker 5
MAGEE, Walter Warren 1
MAGEE, Wayland Wells 6
MAGEE, William Addison 1
MAGEE, William Michael 4
MAGELLAN, Ferdinand 1
MAGELSSEN, William Christian 1
MAGER, Charles Augustus 3
MAGEVNEY, Eugene A. 4
MAGGARD, Edward Harris 4
MAGGS, Douglas Blount 4
MAGIE, David 5
MAGIE, William Francis 2
MAGIE, William Jay 1
MAGIL, Mary Ellen Ryan (Mrs. Elias Magil) 5
MAGILL, Edmund Charles 1
MAGILL, Edward Hicks 1
MAGILL, Frank Stockton 3
MAGILL, George Paull 3
MAGILL, Hugh Stewart 3
MAGILL, James Marion 10
MAGILL, James Phineas 6
MAGILL, Robert Edward 1
MAGILL, Robert Nathaniel 4
MAGILL, Roswell 4
MAGILL, Samuel Edward 1
MAGILL, William Seagrove 5

MAGILLIGAN, Donald James 5
MAGIN, Francis W. 4
MAGINN, Edward Joseph 8
MAGINNES, Albert Bristol 4
MAGINNIS, Charles Donagh 3
MAGINNIS, Martin 1
MAGINNIS, Samuel Abbot 1
MAGISTAD, Oscar Conrad 3
MAGLIN, William Henry 3
MAGNA, Edith Scott (Mrs. Russell William Magna) 7
MAGNANI, Anna 6
MAGNER, F. J. 2
MAGNER, James Edmund 7
MAGNER, James Joseph 5
MAGNER, John F. 4
MAGNER, Thomas Francis 2
MAGNES, Judah Leon 2
MAGNEY, Clarence Reinbold 7
MAGNIER, Anthony Aloysius 3
MAGNIN, Cyril 9
MAGNUS, Finn Haakon 7
MAGNUS, Joseph Emil 4
MAGNUS, Percy Cecil 3
MAGNUS, Wilhelm 10
MAGNUSON, Donald 7
MAGNUSON, Paul Budd 7
MAGNUSON, Warren Grant 10
MAGNUSSON, Carl Edward 1
MAGNUSSON, Leifur 7
MAGNUSSON, Magnus Vignir 5
MAGNUSSON, Peter Magnus 4
MAGOFFIN, Beriah H
MAGOFFIN, James Wiley H
MAGOFFIN, Ralph Van Deman 2
MAGONE, Daniel 1
MAGONIGLE, Edith Marion 5
MAGONIGLE, H. Van Buren 5
MAGOON, Charles E. 1
MAGOON, Henry Sterling H
MAGOON, Wallace Herbert 9
MAGOR, S. F. 3
MAGOUN, Francis Peabody, Jr. 7
MAGOUN, George Frederic H
MAGOUN, Henry A. 1
MAGOUN, Herbert William 3
MAGOUN, Jeanne Bartholow (Mrs. Francis P.) 5
MAGOVERN, John J., Jr. 4
MAGOWAN, Sir John Hall 9
MAGOWEN, Robert Anderson 9
MAGRADY, Frederick W. 3
MAGRATH, Andrew Gordon H
MAGRATH, George Burgess 1
MAGRATH, William 3
MAGRAW, Lester Andrew 2
MAGRISH, Alfred E. 7
MAGRITTE, Rene 4
MAGRUDDER, Benjamin Drake 1
MAGRUDDER, David Lynn H
MAGRUDER, Allan Bowie H
MAGRUDER, Bruce 3
MAGRUDER, Calvert 5
MAGRUDER, Cary Walthall 7
MAGRUDER, Frank Abbott 3
MAGRUDER, George Lloyd 1
MAGRUDER, John 3
MAGRUDER, John Bankhead H
MAGRUDER, John H., Jr. 4
MAGRUDER, Julia 1
MAGRUDER, Marshall 7
MAGRUDER, Patrick H
MAGRUDER, Thomas Pickett 1
MAGRUDER, William Thomas 1
MAGSAYSAY, Ramon 3
MAGUIRE, Bassett 10
MAGUIRE, Hamilton Ewing 5
MAGUIRE, James G. 4

MAGUIRE, Jeremiah De Smet 4
MAGUIRE, John Arthur 5
MAGUIRE, John MacArthur 7
MAGUIRE, Matthew 4
MAGUIRE, Philip Francis 6
MAGUIRE, Raymer Francis 4
MAGUIRE, Russell 4
MAGUIRE, Walter N. 4
MAGUIRE, William G. 4
MAHAFFEY, Jesse Lynn 2
MAHAFFEY, John Quincy 4
MAHAFFIE, Chrales Delahunt 5
MAHAN, Alfred Thayer 1
MAHAN, Archie Irvin 9
MAHAN, Asa H
MAHAN, Bruce Ellis 8
MAHAN, Bruce Herbert 3
MAHAN, Bryan Francis 1
MAHAN, Dennis Hart H
MAHAN, Dennis Hart 1
MAHAN, Edgar Clyde 2
MAHAN, George Addison 1
MAHAN, Lawrence Elmer 2
MAHAN, Milo H
MAHAN, Patrick Joseph 1
MAHANA, C. R. 5
MAHANEY, C.R. 6
MAHANY, Rowland Blennerhassett 1
MAHAR, Edward Albert 5
MAHENDRA, Bir Bikram Shah Deva 5
MAHER, Aldea 3
MAHER, Aly Pacha 4
MAHER, Chauncey Carter 5
MAHER, Dale Wilford 4
MAHER, Frank Barry 7
MAHER, George Washington 1
MAHER, James Denis 4
MAHER, James P. 4
MAHER, Leo Thomas 10
MAHER, Philip Brooks 10
MAHER, Stephen John 1
MAHESHWARI, Panchanan 4
MAHEU, Rene Gabriel Eugene 6
MAHIN, Edward Garfield 3
MAHIN, Frank Cadle 2
MAHIN, Frank Webster 1
MAHIN, John Lee 1
MAHL, William 1
MAHLE, Arthur Edwin 4
MAHLER, Ernst 4
MAHLER, Fritz 6
MAHLER, Gustav H
MAHLER, Gustav 4
MAHLER, Henry Ralph 8
MAHLSTEDT, Walter 8
MAHON, George Herman 9
MAHON, J. D. 4
MAHON, James Samuel 8
MAHON, Margaret Mary 10
MAHON, Paul Thomas 9
MAHON, Russell C. 3
MAHON, Stephen Keith 5
MAHON, Thaddeus MacLay 4
MAHON, Wilfred John 1
MAHON, William D. 2
MAHONE, William H
MAHONEY, Bernard Joseph 4
MAHONEY, Caroline Smith 1
MAHONEY, Charles H. 4
MAHONEY, Daniel Joseph 4
MAHONEY, Edward R. 1
MAHONEY, George William 8
MAHONEY, James Bonaparte 8
MAHONEY, James Owen 9
MAHONEY, Jeremiah T. 5
MAHONEY, John C. 2
MAHONEY, John Dennis 5
MAHONEY, John Friend 3
MAHONEY, John Joseph 2
MAHONEY, Joseph Nathaniel
MAHONEY, Louis A. 8
MAHONEY, Peter Paul 8
MAHONEY, Tom 8
MAHONEY, Walter Butler 3
MAHONEY, William Frank 1
MAHONEY, William J. 2
MAHONY, Emon Ossian 1
MAHONY, Michael Joseph 1
MAHONY, Thomas Harrison 5
MAHOOD, J. W. 4
MAHOOL, John Barry 1

MANNING, Richard 10
MANNING, Richard Irvine H
MANNING, Richard Irvine 1
MANNING, Robert H
MANNING, Thomas Courtland H
MANNING, Timothy Cardinal 10
MANNING, Van H. 1
MANNING, Vannoy Hartrog H
MANNING, Walter Webster 1
MANNING, Warren Henry 1
MANNING, William Albert 5
MANNING, William Ray 2
MANNING, William T. 1
MANNING, William Thomas 2
MANNIX, Henry 7
MANNON, Floyd Ralph 4
MANNY, Frank Addison 5
MANSELL, Irving Lawson 9
MANSELL, O. S. 4
MANSER, Harry 4
MANSERGH, Robert 5
MANSFIELD, Archibald Romaine 1
MANSFIELD, Beatrice Cameron 4
MANSFIELD, Burton 1
MANSFIELD, Donald Bruce 9
MANSFIELD, Edward Deering H
MANSFIELD, Frederick William 3
MANSFIELD, George Rogers 5
MANSFIELD, Harvey Claflin, Sr. 9
MANSFIELD, Henry Buckingham 1
MANSFIELD, Howard 1
MANSFIELD, Ira Franklin 4
MANSFIELD, Jared H
MANSFIELD, Jayne 4
MANSFIELD, Joseph Jefferson 2
MANSFIELD, Joseph King Fenno H
MANSFIELD, Luther Stearns 7
MANSFIELD, Orlando Augustine 4
MANSFIELD, Richard H
MANSFIELD, Richard 1
MANSFIELD, Robert E. 1
MANSFIELD, Samuel Mather 1
MANSFIELD, Thomas Robert 9
MANSFIELD, Walter Roe 9
MANSFIELD, William Douglass 3
MANSHEL, Warren Demian 10
MANSHIP, Charles Phelps 2
MANSHIP, Paul 4
MANSKE, Walter Earl 6
MANSON, Alexander Malcolm 7
MANSON, Daniel Edgar 2
MANSON, Frederic E. 4
MANSON, John Thomas 2
MANSON, Mahlon Dickerson H
MANSON, Marsden 1
MANSON, Otis Frederick H
MANSON, Ray H. 4
MANSON, Richard 3
MANSS, Harvey McKnight 3
MANSUR, Charles Harley H
MANSUR, Zophar M. 1
MANSURE, Edmund F. 10
MANTELL, Charles L. 10
MANTELL, John J. 7
MANTELL, Robert Bruce 1
MANTER, Harold W(infred) 5
MANTEUFFEL, Tadeusz 6
MANTEY, Julius Robert 8
MANTHORNE, Mary Elizabeth Arnold 7
MANTLE, Burns 2
MANTLE, Gladys Ann Doyle (Mrs. Arthur Claud-mantle) 5
MANTLE, Lee 1
MANTON, Martin Thomas 2
MANTON, Walter Porter 1
MANTOVANI, Annunzio Paolo 7
MANTYNBAND, Louis M(artin) 5
MANTZ, H. J. 5
MANUCY, Dominic H
MANUEL, Herschel Thurman 7
MANUEL, Wiley William 7
MANUEL, W(illiam) A(sbury) 5
MANUILSKY, Dmitry Zakharavish 3
MANVILLE, Alfred R. 10
MANVILLE, Edward Britton 2
MANVILLE, Hiram Edward 2
MANVILLE, (Hiram) Edward, Jr. 8
MANWARING, A. Homer, II 3
MANWARING, Elizabeth Wheeler 2
MANWARING, Wilfred Hamilton 5
MANWELL, Reginald Dickinson 10
MANZANARES, Francisco Antonio 1
MAO, Tse-tung 7
MAO TSE-TUNG 6
MAPEL, William 8
MAPES, Carl Edgar 1
MAPES, Carl Herbert 4
MAPES, Charles Victor 1
MAPES, Clarel Bowman 5
MAPES, James Jay H
MAPES, Russell Wesley 9
MAPES, Victor 5
MAPHIS, Charles Gilmore 1
MAPLE, Clair George 9
MAPLES, Harold E. 2
MAPOTHER, Wible Lawrence 1
MAPOW, Abraham B. 6
MAPPA, Adam Gerard H
MAPPLETHORPE, Robert 10
MARABLE, Fate 4
MARABLE, John Hartwell H
MARAIS, Josef 7
MARAVICH, Pete (Peter Press) 9
MARAZITI, Joseph J. 10
MARBLE, Annie Russell 1
MARBLE, Arthur H. 2
MARBLE, Charles Baldwin 1
MARBLE, Danforth H
MARBLE, Edgar M. 1
MARBLE, Fred Elmer 1
MARBLE, George Watson 1
MARBLE, Henry Chase 7
MARBLE, John Hobart 1
MARBLE, John Putnam 3
MARBLE, Manton 1
MARBLE, Mitchell Stewart 4
MARBLE, Samuel Davey 10
MARBLE, Thomas Littlefield 3
MARBLE, William Allen 1
MARBURG, Edgar 1
MARBURG, Otto 2
MARBURG, Theodore 2
MARBURGER, Ralph E. 3
MARBURY, Elisabeth 1
MARBURY, Ogle 7
MARBURY, William G. 5
MARBURY, William L. 1
MARBURY, William Luke 9
MARBUT, Curtis Fletcher 1
MARBY, Giddings Edlon 6
MARC, Henri M. 4
MARCANTONIO, Vito 3
MARCEAU, Henri 5
MARCEL, Gabriel Honore 6
MARCH, Abraham W. 5
MARCH, Alden H
MARCH, Alden 2
MARCH, Anthony 6
MARCH, Cecil Clifford 7
MARCH, Charles Hoyt 2
MARCH, Daniel 1
MARCH, Francis Andrew 1
MARCH, Francis Andrew, Jr. 1
MARCH, Fredric 6
MARCH, Hal 5
MARCH, H(erman) W(illiam) 6
MARCH, John Lewis 5
MARCH, Peyton Conway 3
MARCH, Thomas Stone 1
MARCH, William A. 7
MARCHAND, Albert Gallatin H
MARCHAND, David H
MARCHAND, Jean 9
MARCHAND, John Bonnett H
MARCHANT, Edward Dalton H
MARCHANT, Henry H
MARCHANT, Trelawney E. 3
MARCHBANKS, Tom Earl 6
MARCHER, Royal 8
MARCHETTI, Andrew A. 5
MARCHEV, Alfred 2
MARCIAL-DORADO, Carolina 1
MARCIN, Max 6
MARCKWARDT, Albert Henry 6
MARCO, Herbert Francis 5
MARCO, Salvatore Michael 6
MARCONI, William 1
MARCOS, Ferdinand E. 10
MARCOSSON, Isaac Frederick 4
MARCOSSON, Sol 1
MARCOTTE, Henry 3
MARCOU, John Belknap 4
MARCOU, Jules H
MARCOUX, Vanni (Vanni-Marcoux) 6
MARCUM, Thomas 4
MARCUS, Joseph Anthony 4
MARCUS, Louis 1
MARCUS, Louis William 1
MARCUS, Miah 9
MARCUS, Ralph 3
MARCUS, Sumner 7
MARCUS, William Arthur 8
MARCUSE, Herbert 7
MARCUSE, Milton E. 2
MARCUSSEN, William Henry 8
MARCY, Carl Milton 10
MARCY, Daniel H
MARCY, Erastus Edgerton 1
MARCY, George Edward 1
MARCY, Henry Orlando 1
MARCY, Milton Asa 8
MARCY, Oliver 1
MARCY, Randolph Barnes H
MARCY, William Learned H
MARDAGA, Thomas Joseph 8
MARDEN, Charles Carroll 1
MARDEN, George Augustus 1
MARDEN, Jesse Krekore 5
MARDEN, Orison Swett 1
MARDEN, Orison Swett 6
MARDEN, Oscar Avery 1
MARDEN, Philip Sanford 4
MARDEN, Robert Fiske 1
MARDEN, Virginia McAvoy (Mrs. Orison Swett Marden) 9
MARDER, Arthur Jacob 7
MARDIS, Samuel Wright H
MAREAN, Emma Endicott 1
MAREAN, Josiah Taylor 1
MAREAN, Willis Adams 1
MARECHAL, Ambrose H
MAREK, George Richard 9
MAREK, Kurt W. (C. W. Ceram) 5
MAREMONT, Arnold Harold 7
MARENO, Francisco Ildefonse H
MARES, Joseph R. 7
MARES, Lumir Martin 5
MARESCA, Virginia Keller 6
MAREST, Pierre Gabriel H
MARETZEK, Max H
MARGARET, Sister Patricia 8
MARGET, Arthur William 4
MARGETTS, Walter Thomas, Jr. 8
MARGIL, Antonio H
MARGIOTTI, Charles Joseph 3
MARGOLD, Nathan Ross 2
MARGOLIES, Joseph Aaron 8
MARGOLIS, Max Leopold 1
MARGOLIUS, Sidney Senier 7
MARGOULIES, Vladimir de 4
MARGRAF, Gustav Bernhard 5
MARGULIES, Joseph 10
MARGULIES, Walter Pierre 9
MARIE, Jean Henri Theophile 9
MARIENTHAL, George Edward 5
MARIETTA, Shelley Uriah 6
MARIGNY, Bernard H
MARIL, Herman 9
MARIN, John 3
MARIN, Joseph 4
MARIN, William Peyton 7
MARINDIN, Henri Louis Francois 1
MARINE, David 7
MARINO, Anthony Wayne Martin 7
MARINO, Pasquale Augustine 8
MARINONI, Antonio 2
MARIO, Queena 3
MARION, Frances 6
MARION, Francis H
MARION, Jerry Baskerville 8
MARION, John Hardin 2
MARION, Robert H
MARIS, Albert Branson 9
MARIS, Paul Vestal 7
MARITAIN, Jacques 5
MARITAIN, Jacques 7
MARIX, Adolph 1
MARJERISON, Howard Mitchell 3
MARK, Clarence 3
MARK, Clayton 1
MARK, Edgar H. 4
MARK, Edward Laurens 2
MARK, Herman Francis 10
MARK, Julius 10
MARK, Kenneth Lamartine 3
MARK, Mary Louise 6
MARK, Peter Herman 7
MARKBREIT, Leopold 1
MARKEE, Joseph Eldridge 5
MARKEL, Lester 7
MARKEL, Samuel A. 3
MARKELEY, Philip Swenk H
MARKELIUS, Sven Gottfrid 9
MARKELL, Charles 3
MARKELL, Charles Frederick 1
MARKELL, Henry H
MARKELL, Isabella Banks 9
MARKELL, Jacob H
MARKENS, Isaac 1
MARKERT, Frederic Schaefer 3
MARKEVITCH, Igor 8
MARKEY, Daniel Peter 4
MARKEY, D(avid) John 9
MARKEY, Gene 7
MARKEY, John Clifton 5
MARKEY, Lawrence Morris 3
MARKEY, Lucille Parker 8
MARKHAM, Charles Henry 1
MARKHAM, Edgar 7
MARKHAM, Edward M. 3
MARKHAM, Edwin 1
MARKHAM, Edwin C. 4
MARKHAM, George C. 5
MARKHAM, George Dickson 2
MARKHAM, Henry Harrison 1
MARKHAM, Herbert Ira 4
MARKHAM, James Morris 10
MARKHAM, James Walter 5
MARKHAM, Jared Clark 4
MARKHAM, John Raymond 5
MARKHAM, Joseph Leo 8
MARKHAM, Osmon Grant 2
MARKHAM, R. H. 3
MARKHAM, Reuel Finney 3
MARKHAM, Thomas F. 3
MARKHAM, Walter Tipton 2
MARKHAM, William H
MARKHAM, William Guy 1
MARKHAM, William Hugh 3
MARKIN, Morris 5
MARKINO, Yoshio 5
MARKLE, Alvan 1
MARKLE, Donald 9
MARKLE, John 1
MARKLEY, Alfred Collins 1
MARKLEY, Edward Anthony 3
MARKLEY, Frank Ranck 9
MARKLEY, Herbert Emerson 8
MARKLEY, Joseph Lybrand 1
MARKLEY, Klare S(tephen) 10
MARKLEY, Klare S(tephen) 6
MARKLEY, Rodney Weir 9
MARKOE, Abraham H
MARKOE, Peter H
MARKOE, Thomas Masters 1
MARKS, Avery C., Jr. 1
MARKS, Barry Alan 8
MARKS, Bernard 1
MARKS, Carl 4
MARKS, Edward Bennett 2
MARKS, Edwin Hall 8
MARKS, Edwin I. 5
MARKS, Elias H
MARKS, Henry Kingdon 2
MARKS, Henry Thomas 10
MARKS, Herbert S. 4
MARKS, J(ames) Christopher 5
MARKS, James Harmon 7
MARKS, Jeanette 4
MARKS, Johnny (John D.) 9
MARKS, Mrs. L. S. 1
MARKS, Laurence Mandeville 3
MARKS, Lawrence 9
MARKS, Lawrence Irwin 10
MARKS, Leon John 5
MARKS, Lewis Hart 7
MARKS, Lionel Simeon 3
MARKS, Marcus M. 1
MARKS, Mary E(lla) 7
MARKS, Mary Helen 7
MARKS, Meyer Benjamin 10
MARKS, Percy 3
MARKS, Sam Reynolds 7
MARKS, Sidney Jerome 5
MARKS, Solon 1
MARKS, Willard Leighton 2
MARKS, William H
MARKS, William Dennis 1
MARKS, Wirt Peebles, Jr. 4
MARKUS, Frank H. 10
MARKWARD, John Oliver 7
MARKWARD, Joseph Bradley 1
MARKWARDT, L(orraine) J(oseph) 10
MARKWART, Arthur Hermann 1
MARKWOOD, Michael Edward 3
MARLAND, Ernest Whitworth 2
MARLAND, Sidney Percy, Jr. 10
MARLAND, William C. 4
MARLATT, Abby Lillian 5
MARLATT, Charles Lester 3
MARLATT, Earl Bowman 7
MARLENS, Al 7
MARLER, Herbert Meredith 1
MARLEY, Francis Matthias 9
MARLEY, James Preston 3
MARLEY, John 8
MARLIN, Harry Halpine 1
MARLING, Alfred Erskine 1
MARLING, James H. H
MARLING, John Leake H
MARLIO, Louis 6
MARLOR, Henry S. 4
MARLOW, Frank William 2
MARLOW, Thomas A. 1
MARLOWE, Julia 3
MARLOWE, Sylvia 8
MARMADUKE, John Sappington H
MARMER, Harry Aaron 3
MARMER, Milton Jacob 5
MARMIER, Pierre Edouard 6
MARMION, Keith Robert 5
MARMION, Robert Augustine 1
MARMON, Howard C. 2
MARMON, Jeff Berry 1
MARMORSTON, Jessie 7
MARMUR, Jacland 5
MARNELL, Robert Overton 1
MARNEY, Leonard Carlyle 7
MARON, Samuel Herbert 6
MARONEY, Frederick William 3
MAROT, Helen 1
MAROT, Mary Louise 5
MAROTTA, Nicholas G(ene) 10
MARQUAND, Allan 1
MARQUAND, Henry Gurdon 1
MARQUAND, John Phillips 4
MARQUARDT, Carl Eugene 5
MARQUARDT, Walter William 6
MARQUART, Edward John 3
MARQUAT, William Frederic 4
MARQUESS, William Hoge 1
MARQUETT, Turner Mastin H

MARTIN, Joseph I. 3
MARTIN, Joseph J. 8
MARTIN, Joseph William, Jr. 4
MARTIN, Joshua Lanier H
MARTIN, Josiah H
MARTIN, Julius Corpening 2
MARTIN, Kiel 10
MARTIN, Kingsley Leverich 2
MARTIN, Larkin Morris 1
MARTIN, Laurence Janney 8
MARTIN, Lawrence 6
MARTIN, Lawrence Crawford 5
MARTIN, Leroy Albert 5
MARTIN, Lester 3
MARTIN, Lillien Jane 2
MARTIN, Louis Adolphe, Jr. 1
MARTIN, Luther H
MARTIN, Luther, III 4
MARTIN, Mabel Wood 3
MARTIN, Marion Elizabeth 9
MARTIN, Martha Evans 1
MARTIN, Mary 10
MARTIN, Melissa Margaret 9
MARTIN, Mellen Chamberlain 3
MARTIN, Melvin Albert 1
MARTIN, Miles Macon 4
MARTIN, Milward Wyatt 6
MARTIN, Morgan Lewis H
MARTIN, Motte 3
MARTIN, Otis Orval 9
MARTIN, Park Hussey 9
MARTIN, Patrick Minor 5
MARTIN, Paul Alexander 4
MARTIN, Paul Curtis 1
MARTIN, Paul Elliott 10
MARTIN, Paul Leo 4
MARTIN, Paul Logan 7
MARTIN, Paul Sidney 6
MARTIN, Percy Alvin 2
MARTIN, Quinn 9
MARTIN, Ralph Andrew 5
MARTIN, Raymond George 6
MARTIN, Reginald Wesley 4
MARTIN, Renwick Harper 5
MARTIN, Riccardo 3
MARTIN, Richard Milton 9
MARTIN, Robert Grant 1
MARTIN, Robert Hugh 1
MARTIN, Robert Nicols H
MARTIN, Robert William 5
MARTIN, Roscoe Coleman 5
MARTIN, Royce George 3
MARTIN, Samuel Albert 1
MARTIN, Santford 3
MARTIN, Selden Osgood 2
MARTIN, Stanley Hubert 8
MARTIN, Strother 7
MARTIN, Sydney Errington 7
MARTIN, Sylvester Mitchell 1
MARTIN, T. T. 3
MARTIN, Thomas Baldwin 10
MARTIN, Thomas Commerford 1
MARTIN, Thomas Ellsworth 5
MARTIN, Thomas Joseph 5
MARTIN, Thomas Paul 3
MARTIN, Thomas Powderly 4
MARTIN, Thomas Staples 1
MARTIN, Thomas Wesley 5
MARTIN, Townsend Bradley 8
MARTIN, V. G. 3
MARTIN, Victoria Claflin Woodhull 1
MARTIN, Wallace Harold 5
MARTIN, Walter Bramblette 7
MARTIN, W(alter) Reid 9
MARTIN, Walton 3
MARTIN, Warren Frederic 6
MARTIN, Whitmell Pugh 1
MARTIN, William 4
MARTIN, William Alexander Parsons 1
MARTIN, William C. 10
MARTIN, William Dobbin H
MARTIN, William Elejius 5
MARTIN, William Franklin 1
MARTIN, William Harris 9
MARTIN, William H(ennick) 6
MARTIN, William Hope 1
MARTIN, William Joseph 2
MARTIN, William Joseph 5
MARTIN, William Leslie 4

MARTIN, William Logan 3
MARTIN, William Logan 4
MARTIN, William McChesney 3
MARTIN, William Oliver 6
MARTIN, William Thomas 4
MARTIN, William Thompson 3
MARTIN, William Thornton (Pete Martin)
MARTIN, Winfred Robert 7
MARTINDALE, Don Albert 8
MARTINDALE, Earl Henry
MARTINDALE, F. Carew 4
MARTINDALE, Henry Clinton
MARTINDALE, James Vaughan 8
MARTINDALE, John Henry H
MARTINDALE, Thomas 1
MARTIN DU GARD, Roger
MARTINE, James Edgar 4
MARTINEAU, Harriet H
MARTINEAU, John Ellis 1
MARTINEAU, Roland Guy
MARTINEK, Frank V(ictor) 5
MARTINELLI, Giovanni 5
MARTINET, Marjorie Dorsey 7
MARTINEZ, Felix 1
MARTINEZ, Maria Antonita 7
MARTINEZ, Maximiliano H. 7
MARTINEZ, Xavier 2
MARTINEZ-VARGAS, Ricardo 7
MARTINEZ ZUVIRIA, Gustavo (Hugo Wast, Nom De Plume)
MARTING, Walter Adelbert 7
MARTINI, Roland 4
MARTINO, Antonio P. 10
MARTINO, Gaetano 4
MARTINON, Jean 6
MARTINOT, Sadie 4
MARTINS, Jorge Dodsworth 7
MARTINS, Maria Alves 5
MARTINSON, Henry R. 7
MARTINU, Bohuslav 3
MARTINY, Philip 1
MARTS, Arnaud Cartwright 5
MARTS, Carroll Hartman 4
MARTWICK, William Lorimer 5
MARTY, Martin H
MARTYN, Carlos 1
MARTYN, Chauncey White 1
MARTYN, Sarah Towne Smith
MARTZ, Charles E. 8
MARTZ, Hyman Scher 5
MARTZ, Velorus 6
MARTZ, William Edward 8
MARTZLOFF, Karl H(enry) 7
MARUSZEWSKI, Mariusz 6
MARVEL, Carl Shipp 9
MARVEL, Josiah 3
MARVEL, Ik
MARVEL, Richard Douglas 9
MARVEL, Robert Wiley 6
MARVEL, Robert Wiley 4
MARVEL, William 10
MARVEL, William Worthington 7
MARVELL, George Ralph 2
MARVIN, Burton Wright 7
MARVIN, Charles Frederick 2
MARVIN, Cloyd Heck 5
MARVIN, Dudley H
MARVIN, Dwight 5
MARVIN, Dwight Edwards 1
MARVIN, Enoch Mather H
MARVIN, Frank Olin 1
MARVIN, Fred Richard 1
MARVIN, Frederic Rowland
MARVIN, George 3
MARVIN, Harold Myers 10
MARVIN, Henry Howard 3
MARVIN, James Arthur 4
MARVIN, Joseph Benson 1
MARVIN, Langdon Parker 3
MARVIN, Lee 9
MARVIN, Richard Pratt H

MARVIN, Thomas O. 3
MARVIN, Walter S(ands) 5
MARVIN, Walter Taylor 2
MARVIN, William Glenn 1
MARVIN, Winthrop Lippitt 1
MARWEDEL, Emma Jacobina Christiana H
MARX, Alexander 3
MARX, Charles David 1
MARX, Groucho (Julius Marx) 10
MARX, Guido Hugo 3
MARX, Harry S. 2
MARX, Henry Mosler 8
MARX, Karl H
MARX, Oscar B. 1
MARX, Otto 4
MARX, Otto, Jr. 10
MARX, Robert S. 4
MARX, Rudolf 9
MARX, Samuel Abraham 4
MARYE, George Thomas 1
MARZALL, John Adams 3
MARZO, Eduardo 1
MASARYK, Jan 3
MASCHKE, Maurice 1
MASCUCH, John Thomas 3
MASE, Stanley Wilson 4
MASEFIELD, John 4
MASENG, Sigurd 3
MASER, Edward Andrew 4
MASHBURN, Arthur Gray 5
MASHBURN, Lloyd A. 4
MASIKO, Peter, Jr. 8
MASLACH, George 7
MASLAND, John Wesley, Jr. 5
MASLOW, Abraham Harold 5
MASON, A. Lawrence 4
MASON, Abraham John H
MASON, Alfred Bishop 1
MASON, Alfred De Witt 1
MASON, Alpheus Thomas 10
MASON, Alvin Hughlett 6
MASON, Amelia Gere 1
MASON, Armistead Thomson H
MASON, Arthur Ellery 4
MASON, August H(oward) 7
MASON, Augustus Lynch 1
MASON, Bernard Sterling 5
MASON, C. Avery 5
MASON, Caroline Atwater 1
MASON, Cassity E. 1
MASON, Charles H
MASON, Charles Ellis 7
MASON, Charles Frederick 4
MASON, Charles Harrison 4
MASON, Charles Noble 5
MASON, Charles Walter 8
MASON, Claibourne Rice 4
MASON, Clyde Walter 8
MASON, Daniel Gregory 3
MASON, David Hastings 1
MASON, David Malcolm 9
MASON, Edith (Barnes) 6
MASON, Edward Campbell 1
MASON, Edward Sagendorph 10
MASON, Edward Tuckerman
MASON, Edward Wilson 2
MASON, Emily Virginia 1
MASON, Francis H
MASON, Francis Van Wyck 7
MASON, Frank Earl 10
MASON, Frank Holcomb 1
MASON, Frank Stuart 1
MASON, George* H
MASON, George Allen 3
MASON, George Champlin H
MASON, George Dewitt 5
MASON, George Grant 5
MASON, G(eorge) Grant, Jr. 5
MASON, George Jefferson 4
MASON, George W. 3
MASON, Guy 3
MASON, Harold Carlton 8
MASON, Harold Jesse 10
MASON, Harold Whitney 2
MASON, Harriet L. 4
MASON, Harry Howland 2
MASON, Henry H
MASON, Henry Freeman 1
MASON, Herbert Delavan 2
MASON, J. Alden 5
MASON, James 9
MASON, James Brown 4
MASON, James Monroe 5
MASON, James Murray H
MASON, James Orley 3
MASON, James Tate 1
MASON, James Weir 1

MASON, Jeremiah H
MASON, Jerry 10
MASON, Jesse Henry 2
MASON, John H
MASON, John 1
MASON, J(ohn) Alden 10
MASON, John Calvin H
MASON, John Henry 1
MASON, John Mitchell H
MASON, John Russell 7
MASON, John Thomson H
MASON, John William 1
MASON, John Young H
MASON, Jonathan H
MASON, Joseph Warren Teets 1
MASON, Julian Starkweather 3
MASON, Karl Ernest 7
MASON, L. Walter 1
MASON, Leslie Fenton 5
MASON, Lewis Duncan 1
MASON, Lowell H
MASON, Lowell Blake 8
MASON, Lucius Randolph 7
MASON, Luther Whiting 1
MASON, Madison Charles Butler 1
MASON, Martin Alexander 8
MASON, Mary Augusta 5
MASON, Mary Knight Wood 4
MASON, Mary Stuard Townsend 7
MASON, Maud M. 3
MASON, Max 4
MASON, Michael L. 4
MASON, Miriam Evangeline (Mrs. Miriam Mason Swain) 6
MASON, Mortimer Phillips 5
MASON, Moses, Jr. H
MASON, Newton Eliphalet 2
MASON, Noah Morgan 4
MASON, Norman Pierce 10
MASON, Otis Tufton 1
MASON, Ralph Schweizer 10
MASON, Richard Barnes H
MASON, Roy Martell 5
MASON, Rufus Osgood 1
MASON, Samson 4
MASON, Samuel H
MASON, Silas Boxley 1
MASON, Silas Cheever 1
MASON, Stanley George 10
MASON, Stevens Thomson* H
MASON, Thomson H
MASON, Victor Louis 1
MASON, Wallace Edward 2
MASON, Walt 5
MASON, Wilbur Nesbitt 5
MASON, William* H
MASON, William 1
MASON, William Clarke 9
MASON, William D(aniel) 7
MASON, William Ernest 1
MASON, William Madison 5
MASON, William Pitt 1
MASON, William Sanford H
MASON, William Smith 4
MASON, William Woodman 1
MASQUERAY, Emmanuel Louis 1
MASQUERIER, Lewis H
MASSAGLIA, Joseph, Jr. 5
MASSASSOIT H
MASSECK, Clinton Joseph 1
MASSEE, Edward Kingsley 3
MASSEE, Jasper Cortenus 5
MASSEE, May 4
MASSEE, William Wellington 2
MASSELL, Benjamin Joseph 7
MASSENGALE, John Edward, III 10
MASSER, Harry L. 8
MASSET, Wilbur Fisk 1
MASSEY, George Betton 1
MASSEY, George Valentine 1
MASSEY, Harris Benton 9
MASSEY, John 4
MASSEY, Louis Melville 8
MASSEY, Lucius Saunders 1
MASSEY, Luther M. 6
MASSEY, Mary Elizabeth 6
MASSEY, Raymond 8
MASSEY, Richard W. 1
MASSEY, Vincent 4
MASSEY, William Alexander 1
MASSIE, David Meade 1
MASSIE, Eugene Carter 1
MASSIE, Robert Kinloch 1

MASSIE, Robert Kinloch, Jr. 1
MASSINE, Leonide 7
MASSINGALE, Sam Chapman 1
MASSLICH, Chester Bentley 1
MASSMANN, Frederick H. 5
MASSON, Andre 9
MASSON, Henry Jan ? 6
MASSON, Robert Lou ? 5
MASSON, Thomas L. 1
MAST, Burdette Pond 4
MAST, Casper Leo, Jr. 7
MAST, Gerald 9
MAST, Phineas Price H
MAST, Samuel Ottmar 2
MASTEN, Samuel William 7
MASTER, Arthur Matthew 6
MASTER, Henry Buck 3
MASTERS, Dexter Wright 9
MASTERS, Edgar Lee 2
MASTERS, Frank Meriro 3
MASTERS, Frank Milton 7
MASTERS, Harris Kennedy 5
MASTERS, Howard Russell 3
MASTERS, John 8
MASTERS, John Volney 5
MASTERS, Josiah H
MASTERS, Keith 5
MASTERS, Victor Irvine 3
MASTERSON, John Joseph 4
MASTERSON, Kate 5
MASTERSON, Patrick J. 3
MASTERSON, Robert Ernest 7
MASTERSON, William Barclay H
MASTERSON, William Barclay 4
MASTERSON, William Edward 5
MASTERSON, William Henry 8
MASTERSON, William Wesley 1
MASTICK, Seabury Cone 5
MASTIN, Claudius Henry H
MASTIN, William McDowell 1
MASTON, Robert H. 3
MASTON, Thomas Bufford 10
MASUR, Ernest Frank 9
MASUR, Gerhard Strassman 7
MASUR, Jack 5
MASURSKY, Harold 10
MASURY, John Wesley H
MATAS, Rudolph 3
MATCHETT, Charles Horatio 1
MATCHETT, David Fleming 2
MATCHETT, Gerald James 7
MATE, Hubert Emery 8
MATECHECK, Richard Vincent 7
MATEER, Calvin Wilson 1
MATEER, John Gaston 8
MATELIGER, Jan Ernst H
MATHENY, Ezra Stacy 5
MATHER, Alonzo Clark 1
MATHER, Arthur 2
MATHER, Cotton H
MATHER, Elmer James 3
MATHER, Frank Jewett, Jr. 3
MATHER, Fred 1
MATHER, Frederic Gregory 1
MATHER, Gordon MacDonald 3
MATHER, Increase H
MATHER, John Waterhouse
MATHER, Katharine 10
MATHER, Kirtley Fletcher 7
MATHER, Margaret Morgan Herbert 1
MATHER, Norman Wells 3
MATHER, Philip R. 10
MATHER, Richard H
MATHER, Robert H
MATHER, Rufus Graves 3
MATHER, S. Livingston 4
MATHER, Samuel H
MATHER, Samuel 1
MATHER, Samuel Holmes H
MATHER, Samuel Livingston 8
MATHER, Stephen Tyng 1
MATHER, Thomas Ray 2
MATHER, William Allan 4
MATHER, William Gwinn 3
MATHER, William Tyler 1
MATHER, William Williams H

MAXWELL, William Henry 1
MAXWELL, William John 4
MAY, A. Wilfred 5
MAY, Alonzo Beryl 5
MAY, Andrew Jackson 3
MAY, Arthur James 5
MAY, Charles Henry 2
MAY, Clarence E(arl) 7
MAY, Dan 8
MAY, David 4
MAY, David William 1
MAY, Earl Chapin 4
MAY, Edna 1
MAY, Edward 1
MAY, Edward Harrison H
MAY, Edwin H
MAY, Ernest H. 1
MAY, Geoffrey 4
MAY, George Oliver 4
MAY, George Storr 4
MAY, H(arold) Cameron 7
MAY, Henry 1
MAY, Herbert Arthur 4
MAY, Herbert Gordon 7
MAY, Herbert Louis 4
MAY, Irving 4
MAY, J. T. 9
MAY, Jacques Meyer 6
MAY, James Vance 2
MAY, Julia Harris 1
MAY, Kenneth Ownsworth 7
MAY, Luke S. 4
MAY, Mark Arthur 9
MAY, Max 1
MAY, Max Benjamin 1
MAY, Mortimer 6
MAY, Morton J. 5
MAY, Orville Edward 7
MAY, Philip Reginald Aldridge 9
MAY, Samuel Chester 3
MAY, Samuel Joseph H
MAY, Stella Burke 4
MAY, Thomas 1
MAY, Thomas 5
MAY, William Andrew 1
MAY, William Henry 5
MAY, William L. H
MAYALL, Samuel H
MAYBANK, Burnet Rhett 3
MAYBECK, Bernard Ralph 5
MAYBELL, Claude 5
MAYBURY, William Cotter 1
MAYER, Albert 8
MAYER, Albert J., Jr. 4
MAYER, Alfred Marshall 5
MAYER, Andre 3
MAYER, Arthur L. 7
MAYER, Augustus Kiefer 9
MAYER, Brantz H
MAYER, Carl G. 8
MAYER, Charles Herbert 4
MAYER, Charles Holt 5
MAYER, Charles Raphael 4
MAYER, Constant 1
MAYER, Edgar 6
MAYER, Edward Everett 5
MAYER, Elias 4
MAYER, Emil 1
MAYER, Ernest De W(ael) 5
MAYER, Ferdinand Lathrop 8
MAYER, Francis Blackwell H
MAYER, Frederick 8
MAYER, George B(aker) 7
MAYER, Gottfried Oscar 5
MAYER, Harry Hubert 5
MAYER, Henrik Martin 5
MAYER, Herbert Carleton 7
MAYER, Hy 3
MAYER, Isaac Henry 4
MAYER, John Anton 9
MAYER, John Ignatius 6
MAYER, Joseph 6
MAYER, Joseph Bell 3
MAYER, Julius M. 1
MAYER, Levy 1
MAYER, Lewis H
MAYER, Louis Burt 5
MAYER, Lucius W. 2
MAYER, Manfred Martin 8
MAYER, Maria Goeppert 4
MAYER, Oscar F. 4
MAYER, Oscar Gottried 4
MAYER, Philip Frederick 8
MAYER, Rene 5
MAYER, Richard 4
MAYER, Robert B. 6
MAYERS, Lawrence Seymour 3
MAYES, Lewis 6
MAYES, Edward 4
MAYES, Joel Bryan H
MAYES, Robert Burns 1
MAYES, William Harding 1

MAYFIELD, Charles Herbert 8
MAYFIELD, Earle Bradford 4
MAYFIELD, Frank Henderson 10
MAYFIELD, FRANK MCCONNELL 8
MAYFIELD, Irving Hall 4
MAYFIELD, Samuel Martin 8
MAYFIRLD, James Jefferson 1
MAYHAM, Ray Edwin 3
MAYHER, Laurence Thompson 9
MAYHEW, Experience H
MAYHEW, George Noel 4
MAYHEW, Jonathan H
MAYHEW, Joseph Howard 8
MAYHEW, Thomas* H
MAYLATH, Heinrich 4
MAYNADIER, Gustavus Howard 4
MAYNARD, A. Rogers 7
MAYNARD, Allegra 10
MAYNARD, Charles Johnson 4
MAYNARD, Edward H
MAYNARD, Edwin Post 2
MAYNARD, Fred Augustus 4
MAYNARD, George Colton 1
MAYNARD, George William 1
MAYNARD, George Willoughby 1
MAYNARD, Gilbert P. 7
MAYNARD, Harold Howard 3
MAYNARD, Harry Lee 4
MAYNARD, Horace H
MAYNARD, James 1
MAYNARD, John 4
MAYNARD, John Albert 4
MAYNARD, John Blackwell 2
MAYNARD, John Walter 4
MAYNARD, John William 3
MAYNARD, La Salle Almeron 1
MAYNARD, Laurens Amby 4
MAYNARD, Leonard 5
MAYNARD, Lester 5
MAYNARD, Mila Tupper 4
MAYNARD, Poole H
MAYNARD, Reuben Leslie 4
MAYNARD, Rezin Augustus 4
MAYNARD, Richard Field 4
MAYNARD, Robert Washburn 5
MAYNARD, Roger 5
MAYNARD, Samuel Taylor 1
MAYNARD, Theodore 3
MAYNARD, Walter 5
MAYNARD, Walter Effingham 1
MAYNARD, Washburn 1
MAYNARD, William Hale 4
MAYNE, Arthur Ferdinand 5
MAYNE, Dexter Dwight 1
MAYNE, Walter R. 7
MAYNOR, Hal Wharton, Jr. 8
MAYO, Amory Dwight 1
MAYO, Arthur H. 7
MAYO, Bernard 7
MAYO, Braxton Davis 7
MAYO, Charles George 9
MAYO, Charles Horace 1
MAYO, Chester Garst 9
MAYO, Earl Edmund 7
MAYO, Earl Williams 4
MAYO, Edmund Cooper 5
MAYO, Frank H
MAYO, Frank Rea 10
MAYO, Frederick Joseph 5
MAYO, George Elton 8
MAYO, Henry Thomas 1
MAYO, Katherine 1
MAYO, Nelson Slater 3
MAYO, Robert H
MAYO, Robert Murphy H
MAYO, Robert William Bainbridge 1
MAYO, Sarah Carter Edgarton H
MAYO, Selz Cabot 8
MAYO, Thomas Tabb, IV 8
MAYO, William H
MAYO, William Benson 2
MAYO, William James 1
MAYO, William Kennon H

MAYO, William Kennon 1
MAYO, William Starbuck H
MAYOR, A. Hyatt 7
MAYOR, Alfred 1
MAYO-SMITH, Richmond 1
MAYRANT, William H
MAYROSE, Herman Everett 10
MAYROSE, Herman Everett 7
MAYS, Benjamin Elijah 8
MAYS, Calhoun Allen 5
MAYS, Dannitte Hill 1
MAYS, David John 5
MAYS, Floyd Rosenbaum 3
MAYS, James H. 4
MAYS, Paul Kirtland 4
MAYS, Paul Kirtland 8
MAYS, Percy Joseph 6
MAYTAG, Fred, II 4
MAYTAG, Frederick L. 1
MAYTAG, Lewis B. 4
MAYTHAM, Thomas Northrup 1
MAZA, Jose 4
MAZAN, Walter Lawrence 10
MAZE, Matthew T. 1
MAZER, Jacob 5
MAZET, Robert 2
MAZUR, Paul Myer 7
MAZUREAU, Etienne H
MAZYCK, William Gaillard 2
MAZZANOVICH, Lawrence 4
MAZZEI, Philip H
MAZZILLI, Ranieri 6
MAZZOLA, Vincent Pontorno 9
MAZZONELLI, Rudy William 9
MAZZUCHELLI, Samuel Charles H
M'BA, Leon 4
MCADAM, Charles Vincent, Sr. 10
MCADAM, David 1
MCADAM, Dunlap Jamison 1
MCADAM, Edward Lippincott, Jr. 5
MCADAM, George Harrison 1
MCADAMS, Clark 1
MCADAMS, John Pope 4
MCADAMS, Joseph Edward 6
MCADAMS, Thomas Branch 3
MCADIE, Alexander George 2
MC ADOO, Donald Eldridge 10
MCADOO, Henry Molseed 3
MCADOO, Mary Faith Floyd 1
MCADOO, William 1
MCADOO, William Gibbs 1
MCAFEE, Almer McDuffie 2
MCAFEE, Cleland Boyd 2
MCAFEE, Helen 7
MCAFEE, John Armstrong 4
MCAFEE, Joseph Ernest 2
MC AFEE, Kenneth Emberry 9
MCAFEE, Larry Benjamin 1
MCAFEE, Lowell Mason 1
MCAFEE, Ralph Canfield 1
MCAFEE, Robert Breckinridge H
MCAFEE, Robert William 6
MCAFEE, William A(rchibald) 5
MCALEER, William 4
MCALESTER, Andrew Walker 1
MCALESTER, Andrew Walker, Jr. 3
MCALEXANDER, Ulysses Grant 1
MCALISTER, Alexander Worth 3
MCALISTER, Heber Lowrey 3
MCALISTER, Hill 3
MCALISTER, John Barr 2
MCALISTER, Samuel Bertran 4
MCALISTER, William King 1
MCALL, Reginald Ley 4
MCALLESTER, Samuel Jackson 3
MCALLISTER, Addams Stratton 2
MCALLISTER, Alan H. 5

MCALLISTER, Archibald H
MCALLISTER, Charles Albert 1
MCALLISTER, Charles Eldridge 3
MCALLISTER, David 1
MC ALLISTER, Decker Gordon 8
MCALLISTER, Elliott 5
MCALLISTER, Frank Winton 2
MCALLISTER, George Franklin 5
MCALLISTER, Hall 1
MCALLISTER, Harry Lee 6
MCALLISTER, Henry 3
MCALLISTER, J(ames) Gray 5
MCALLISTER, Joseph Thompson 1
MCALLISTER, Matthew Hall H
MCALLISTER, Samuel Ward H
MCALLISTER, Samuel Wilson 8
MCALLISTER, Sydney G. 2
MCALLISTER, Walter Williams* 8
MC ALLISTER, Walter Williams 8
MCALLISTER, Ward 1
MCALONEY, Thomas Simpson 1
MCALPIN, Benjamin Brandreth 1
MCALPIN, David H(unter) 10
MCALPIN, Edwin Augustus 1
MCALPINE, Charles Alonzo 2
MCALPINE, Kenneth 4
MCALPINE, William H. 3
MCALPINE, William Jarvis H
MCALVAY, Aaron Vance 1
MCANALLY, Arthur Monroe 5
MCANALLY, David Rice H
MCANANY, Edwin Sebast 5
MCANDLESS, Alva John 3
MCANDREW, Gordon Leslie 10
MCANDREW, James William 1
MCANDREW, William 1
MCANDREW, William Robert 5
MCANDREWS, James Joseph 2
MCANEENY, William Joseph 1
MCANENY, George 3
MCANNEY, B. O. 4
MCARDLE, Joseph A. 4
MCARDLE, Montrose Pallen 4
MCARDLE, Thomas Eugene 4
MCARTHUR, Charles Mortimer 6
MCARTHUR, Clifton Nesmith 1
MCARTHUR, Duncan H
MCARTHUR, Edwin 9
MCARTHUR, James Neville 9
MCARTHUR, John H
MCARTHUR, John 1
MCARTHUR, Lewis Linn 4
MCARTHUR, Lewis Linn, Jr. 4
MCARTHUR, William Pope H
MCARTHUR, William Taylor 1
MCATEE, John Lind 1
MCATEE, Waldo Lee 7
MCAULEY, Thomas H
MCAULIFF, Cornelius 1
MCAULIFFE, Anthony C. 6
MCAULIFFE, Daniel J. 3
MCAULIFFE, Eugene 3
MCAULIFFE, John 1
MCAULIFFE, Joseph John 2
MCAULIFFE, Maurice Francis 1
MCAUSLAND, Robert Donald 7
MCAVITY, Malcolm 2
MCAVOY, Charles D. 1
MCAVOY, John Vincent 1
MC AVOY, Thomas D. 4
MCAVOY, Thomas Timothy 5
MCBAIN, Howard Lee 1
MCBAIN, James William 3
MCBAINE, James Patterson 4

MC BATH, James Harvey 10
MCBEAN, Atholl 6
MCBEAN, Thomas H
MCBEATH, James Mark 4
MCBEE, Earl Thurston 5
MCBEE, Mary Vardrine 4
MCBEE, Silas 1
MCBRAYER, Louis Burgin 1
MCBRIDE, Allan Clay 2
MCBRIDE, Andrew Jay 4
MCBRIDE, Earl Duwain 9
MCBRIDE, F. Scott 3
MCBRIDE, George McCutchen 5
MCBRIDE, George Wickliffe 1
MCBRIDE, Harold Herkimer 4
MCBRIDE, Harry Alexander 4
MCBRIDE, Henry 1
MCBRIDE, James Harvey 1
MCBRIDE, Karl R., Sr. 3
MCBRIDE, Katharine Elizabeth 7
MC BRIDE, Lloyd 8
MCBRIDE, Lloyd Merrill 8
MCBRIDE, Malcolm Lee 2
MCBRIDE, Mary Margaret 7
MCBRIDE, Robert Edwin 1
MCBRIDE, Robert H. 8
MCBRIDE, Robert W. 1
MCBRIDE, Thomas Allen 1
MCBRIDE, Wilbert George 6
MCBRIDE, William Manley 3
MCBRIEN, Dean Depew 4
MCBRIEN, Jasper Leonidas 1
MCBROOM, Charles Emmett 4
MCBRYDE, Archibald H
MCBRYDE, Charles Neil 5
MCBRYDE, James Bolton 1
MCBRYDE, John McLaren 1
MCBRYDE, Warren Horton 5
MC BURNEY, Andrew Marvell 10
MCBURNEY, Charles 1
MCBURNEY, John White 4
MCBURNEY, Ralph 4
MCBURNEY, Robert Ross H
MCCABE, Charles B. 5
MCCABE, Charles Cardwell 1
MCCABE, Charles Martin 8
MCCABE, Charles Raymond 8
MC CABE, Cynthia Jaffee 9
MCCABE, David Aloysius 6
MCCABE, Edward Raynsford Warner 5
MCCABE, Francis Xavier 1
MCCABE, Frank Wells 9
MCCABE, Harriet Calista 1
MCCABE, James Dabney H
MCCABE, James Harvey 8
MCCABE, John Collins H
MCCABE, Lida Rose 1
MC CABE, Thomas Bayard 8
MCCABE, Thomas Bayard, Jr. 7
MCCABE, W. Gordon 1
MCCABE, William Gordon, Jr. 7
MCCABE, William Hugh 4
MCCADDEN, John Edward 4
MCCAFFERTY, Don 6
MCCAFFERTY, Thomas Bowles 3
MCCAFFERY, Richard Stanislaus 2
MCCAFFREY, John H
MCCAFFREY, John Lawrence 9
MCCAGG, Ezra Butler 1
MCCAHAN, David 3
MCCAHEY, James B. 8
MCCAHEY, James B. 8
MCCAHILL, David Ignatius Bartholomew 7
MCCAI, William Ross 6
MCCAIG, William Dougal 2
MCCAIN, Charles Curtice 2
MCCAIN, Charles Simonton 3
MCCAIN, Dewey Marven 2
MCCAIN, Donald Rockefeller 7
MCCAIN, George Nox 1
MCCAIN, Henry Pinckney 1
MCCAIN, James Ross 4
MCCAIN, John Sidney 2
MCCAIN, John Sidney, Jr. 1
MCCAIN, Paul Pressly 2
MCCAIN, Samuel Adams 4

MCCLUNG, George Harlan 3
MCCLUNG, Hugh Lawson 1
MCCLUNG, Lee 1
MCCLUNG, Reid Lage 4
MCCLUNG, Will Clinton 3
MCCLUNG, William H. 3
MCCLURE, Abbot 6
MCCLURE, Alexander Kelly 1
MCCLURE, Alexander Wilson H
MCCLURE, Alfred James Pollock 4
MCCLURE, Charles H
MCCLURE, Charles Freeman Williams 3
MCCLURE, Charles Wylie 4
MCCLURE, Daniel E. 4
MCCLURE, Donald C. 1
MCCLURE, Frank James 7
MCCLURE, George H
MCCLURE, George Henry 4
MCCLURE, Grace Latimer Jones 6
MCCLURE, Harry A. 7
MCCLURE, Harry Bell 6
MCCLURE, Howard (Orton) 5
MCCLURE, James Gore King 1
MCCLURE, James Gore King 3
MCCLURE, John Clarence 4
MCCLURE, John Elmer 10
MCCLURE, John Elmer 7
MCCLURE, John Quayle 10
MCCLURE, Marjorie Barkley
MCCLURE, Martha 2
MCCLURE, Matthew Thompson, Jr. 4
MCCLURE, Meade Lowrie 1
MCCLURE, Nathaniel Fish 2
MCCLURE, Norman Egbert 4
MCCLURE, Robert A. 7
MCCLURE, Robert Owen 3
MCCLURE, Roy Donaldson 3
MCCLURE, Russell Everett 6
MCCLURE, Russell Schee 3
MCCLURE, Samuel Grant 2
MCCLURE, Samuel Sidney 2
MCCLURE, W. Frank 3
MCCLURE, Wallace 8
MCCLURE, Walter Tennant 4
MCCLURE, William L. 3
MCCLURE, Worth 4
MCCLURG, Alexander Caldwell 1
MCCLURG, James H
MCCLURG, Joseph Washington H
MCCLURG, Walter Audubon 1
MCCLURKIN, John Knox 1
MCCLURKIN, Robert 3
MCCLURKIN, Robert J. G. 3
MCCLUSKEY, Edmund Roberts 4
MC CLUSKEY, Ellen L. 8
MCCLUSKEY, Thomas Joseph
MCCLUSKY, Howard Yale 8
MCCOACH, David, Jr. 3
MCCOARD, Albert Babcock 8
MCCOBB, Paul (Winthrop) 5
MCCOLE, Cornelius (Con) J. 8
MCCOLL, Clarke Munro 7
MCCOLL, Jay Robert 1
MCCOLL, Robert Boyd 5
MCCOLL, Robert Boyd 8
MCCOLLESTER, Lee Sullivan 2
MCCOLLESTER, Parker 3
MCCOLLESTER, Sullivan Holman 1
MCCOLLOCH, Claude 8
MCCOLLOCH, Frank Cleveland 5
MCCOLLOM, John Hildreth 1
MCCOLLOM, Vivian C. 4
MCCOLLOUGH, Walter 10
MCCOLLUM, Earl 2
MCCOLLUM, Elmer Verner
MCCOLLUM, John Isaac, Jr. 9
MC COLLUM, Robert Stuart 9
MCCOMAS, Francis John 1

MCCOMAS, Henry Clay 5
MCCOMAS, Louis Emory 1
MCCOMAS, O. Parker 3
MCCOMAS, William H
MCCOMB, Arthur James 3
MCCOMB, Edgar 3
MCCOMB, Eleazer H
MCCOMB, John* H
MCCOMB, John Hess 10
MCCOMB, Marshall Francis 9
MCCOMB, Samuel 4
MCCOMB, William 4
MCCOMB, William Andrew 1
MCCOMB, William Randolph 3
MCCOMBS, Carl Esselstyn 2
MCCOMBS, Nelson Wilbor 8
MCCOMBS, Vernon Monroe 3
MCCOMBS, William Frank 1
MCCONACHIE, Harry Steele 4
MCCONACHIE, Lauros Grant 5
MCCONAGHA, William Albert 8
MCCONATHY, Osbourne 2
MCCONAUGHY, James 1
MCCONAUGHY, James Lukens 2
MCCONAUGHY, Robert 1
MCCONE, Alan 7
MCCONE, John A. 10
MCCONIHE, Malcolm Stuart 5
MCCONKEY, Frederick Paul 8
MCCONKEY, George McDonald 7
MCCONLEY, George E(lmer) 8
MCCONN, Charles Maxwell 3
MCCONN, William Finney 8
MCCONNAUGHEY, George Carlton 4
MCCONNAUGHEY, Robert Kendall 4
MCCONNEL, John Ludlum H
MCCONNEL, Mervin Gilbert 3
MCCONNEL, Murray 4
MCCONNEL, Roger Harmon 5
MCCONNELL, Andrew M. 5
MCCONNELL, Burt 8
MCCONNELL, Charles Melvin 3
MCCONNELL, Felix Grundy H
MCCONNELL, Fernando Coello 1
MCCONNELL, Fowler Beery 4
MCCONNELL, Francis John 3
MCCONNELL, Frank Charles 8
MCCONNELL, Franz Marshall 5
MCCONNELL, H. Hugh 3
MCCONNELL, H. S. 3
MCCONNELL, Henry 6
MCCONNELL, Herbert S(tevenson) 5
MCCONNELL, Ira Welch 1
MCCONNELL, James Eli 1
MCCONNELL, James Hoge Tyler 10
MCCONNELL, James Moore 1
MC CONNELL, James Vernon 10
MCCONNELL, John Griffith 6
MCCONNELL, John Paul 9
MCCONNELL, John Preston 4
MCCONNELL, Joseph Moore 1
MCCONNELL, Lincoln 1
MCCONNELL, Luther Graham 4
MCCONNELL, Philip I. 9
MCCONNELL, Raymond Arnott, Jr. 7
MCCONNELL, Robert Darll 5
MCCONNELL, Robert Perche 5
MCCONNELL, Roy F. 4
MCCONNELL, Samuel David 1

MCCONNELL, Samuel Parsons 1
MC CONNELL, Thomas Raymond 9
MCCONNELL, W. Joseph 3
MCCONNELL, Wallace Robert 4
MCCONNELL, William J. 1
MCCONNICO, Andrew Jackson 5
MCCONOCHIE, William Robert 7
MCCONWAY, William 1
MCCOOK, Alexander McDowell 1
MCCOOK, Anson George 1
MCCOOK, Edward Moody 1
MCCOOK, Henry Christopher 1
MCCOOK, John James* 1
MCCOOK, Willis Fisher 1
MCCORD, Alvin Carr 3
MCCORD, Andrew H
MCCORD, Andrew King 6
MCCORD, Carey Pratt 7
MCCORD, David James H
MCCORD, George Herbert 1
MC CORD, James Iley 10
MCCORD, James Nance 5
MCCORD, Joseph 2
MCCORD, Joseph Alexander 4
MCCORD, Leon 3
MCCORD, Louisa Susanna Cheves H
MCCORD, May Kennedy 6
MCCORD, Myron Hawley 1
MCCORD, Robert D. 4
MCCORD, William Clay 4
MCCORD, William H. 4
MCCORKLE, Donald MacOmber 7
MCCORKLE, Graham K. 4
MCCORKLE, Joseph Walker H
MCCORKLE, Thomas Smith 3
MCCORMAC, Eugene Irving 2
MCCORMACK, Alfred 3
MCCORMACK, Arthur Thomas 2
MCCORMACK, Buren H. 1
MCCORMACK, Emmet J. 4
MCCORMACK, George Bryant 1
MCCORMACK, James 6
MCCORMACK, John 2
MCCORMACK, John W. 7
MCCORMACK, Joseph Nathaniel 1
MCCORMACK, M. Harriet Joyce (Mrs. John W. McCormack) 5
MCCORMACK, Thomas Joseph 1
MCCORMICK, Albert Edward 4
MCCORMICK, Albert M. D. 1
MCCORMICK, Alexander Agnew 1
MCCORMICK, Alexander Hugh 1
MCCORMICK, Andrew Phelps 1
MCCORMICK, Anne O'Hare 3
MCCORMICK, Bradley Thomas 3
MCCORMICK, Charles O(wen) 7
MCCORMICK, Charles Perry 5
MCCORMICK, Charles Tilford 4
MCCORMICK, Charles Wesley 1
MCCORMICK, Chauncey 3
MCCORMICK, Cyrus 5
MCCORMICK, Cyrus Hall H
MCCORMICK, Cyrus Hall 1
MCCORMICK, David 4
MCCORMICK, Donald 4
MCCORMICK, Edith Rockefeller 1
MCCORMICK, Edmund Burke 1
MCCORMICK, Edward James 6
MCCORMICK, Ernest O. 5
MCCORMICK, Fowler 5
MCCORMICK, Frederick 5
MCCORMICK, George Chalmers 5
MCCORMICK, George Wellesley 3

MCCORMICK, George Winford 6
MCCORMICK, Gertrude Howard 3
MCCORMICK, Gertrude Howard (Mrs. Vance C. McCormick) 5
MCCORMICK, Harold Fowler 1
MCCORMICK, Harriet Hammond 1
MCCORMICK, Harry Benton 7
MCCORMICK, Henry Buehler 1
MCCORMICK, Henry J. 9
MCCORMICK, Howard 2
MCCORMICK, James Byron 10
MCCORMICK, James Robinson H
MCCORMICK, James Thomas 3
MCCORMICK, John Dale 4
MCCORMICK, John Francis 2
MCCORMICK, John Henry 5
MCCORMICK, John Newton 1
MCCORMICK, John Vincent 5
MCCORMICK, Langdon 1
MCCORMICK, Leander Hamilton 1
MCCORMICK, Leander J. 1
MCCORMICK, Lynde Dupuy 3
MCCORMICK, Marshall 1
MCCORMICK, Medill 1
MCCORMICK, Myron 4
MCCORMICK, Patrick Joseph 3
MCCORMICK, Paul 1
MCCORMICK, Paul John 4
MCCORMICK, R. Hall 1
MCCORMICK, Richard Cunningham 1
MCCORMICK, Robert H
MCCORMICK, Robert Elliott 5
MCCORMICK, Robert Hall 4
MCCORMICK, Robert Laird 1
MCCORMICK, Robert Louis Laing 6
MCCORMICK, Robert Rutherford 3
MCCORMICK, Robert Sanderson 1
MCCORMICK, Samuel Black 1
MCCORMICK, Stephen H
MCCORMICK, Thomas Carson 3
MCCORMICK, Thomas Gerard 4
MCCORMICK, Vance Criswell 2
MCCORMICK, Washington Jay 7
MC CORMICK, Wilfred 10
MCCORMICK, Willard F. 10
MCCORMICK, William 1
MCCORMICK, William Bernard 5
MCCORMICK, William Laird 3
MC CORMICK, William Morgan 8
MCCORMICK, William Thomas 7
MCCORMICK, William Wallace 9
MCCORMICK, Willoughby M. 1
MCCORNACK, John Knox 1
MCCORT, John J. 1
MCCORVEY, Gessner Tutwiler 4
MCCORVEY, Thomas Chalmers 1
MCCOSH, Andrew J. 1
MCCOSH, James H
MCCOSKER, Alfred Justin 3
MCCOTTER, Cyrus Rawson 4
MCCOURT, Walter Edward 2
MCCOWEN, Edward Oscar 3
MCCOWN, Albert 3
MCCOWN, Chester Charlton 5
MCCOWN, Edward C. 2

MCCOWN, Theodore Doney 5
MCCOY, Bernice 5
MCCOY, Cornelius Joseph 8
MCCOY, Daniel 1
MCCOY, Elijah H
MCCOY, Elijah 4
MCCOY, Ernest B. 7
MCCOY, Frank Ross 3
MCCOY, George Walter 5
MCCOY, Henry Bayard 1
MCCOY, Henry Kent H
MCCOY, Herbert Newby 2
MCCOY, Horace Lyman 2
MCCOY, Isaac H
MCCOY, James Henry 1
MCCOY, John Hall 3
MCCOY, John Willard 4
MCCOY, Lester 8
MCCOY, Oliver Rufus 8
MCCOY, Philbrick 6
MCCOY, Ralph Richard 10
MCCOY, Robert H
MCCOY, Samuel Duff 4
MCCOY, Samuel Duff 7
MCCOY, Tim 7
MCCOY, Walter Irving 1
MCCOY, Whitley Peterson 10
MCCOY, Whitley Peterson 5
MCCOY, William H
MCCOY, William Daniel 5
MCCRACKEN, Charles Chester 3
MCCRACKEN, Harlan Linneus 4
MC CRACKEN, Harold 8
MC CRACKEN, James 9
MCCRACKEN, Robert James 5
MCCRACKEN, Robert McDowell 5
MCCRACKEN, Robert Thompson 9
MCCRACKEN, Samuel Cooke 3
MCCRACKEN, Thomas 4
MCCRACKEN, William Denison 1
MCCRACKIN, Josephine Clifford 1
MCCRADY, Edward 1
MCCRADY, John 5
MCCRAE, Thomas 1
MC CRAKEN, Robert Stanton 10
MCCRAKEN, Tracy Stephenson 4
MCCRARY, Alvin Jasper 4
MCCRARY, George Washington H
MCCRARY, John Alva 5
MCCRARY, John Raymond 3
MCCRATE, John Dennis H
MCCRAW, William 3
MCCRAY, Warren T. 1
MCCREA, Allan 7
MCCREA, Annette E. 1
MCCREA, Archie Elbert 3
MCCREA, Charles Harold 2
MCCREA, James 1
MCCREA, James Alexander 1
MCCREA, Nelson Glenn 2
MCCREA, Roswell Cheney 3
MCCREA, Tully 1
MCCREADY, J(ames) Homer 7
MCCREADY, Robert Thompson Miller 2
MCCREARY, George Boone 5
MCCREARY, George Deardorff 1
MCCREARY, James Bennett 1
MCCREARY, John H
MCCREARY, John Ferguson 7
MCCREATH, Andrew S. 4
MCCREDIE, Marion MacMaster 4
MC CREE, Wade Hampton, Jr. 9
MCCREEDY, Jo Ann 6
MCCREEDY, John 7
MCCREERY, Charles H
MCCREERY, Donald Chalmers 4
MCCREERY, Elbert L. 3
MCCREERY, Fenton Reuben 1
MCCREERY, Hugh Pete 6
MCCREERY, James W. 1
MCCREERY, Thomas Clay H
MCCREERY, William* H

MCKINSTRY, Addis Emmett 1
MCKINSTRY, Alexander H
MCKINSTRY, Charles Hedges 4
MCKINSTRY, Elisha Williams H
MCKINSTRY, Grace E. 1
MCKINSTRY, Helen May 2
MCKISICK, Lewis 2
MCKISSICK, Anthony Foster 1
MCKISSICK, Floyd Bixler 10
MCKISSICK, James Rion 2
MCKISSOCK, Thomas H
MCKISSON, Robert Erastus 4
MCKITTRICK, Roy 4
MCKITTRICK, Thomas Harrington 5
MCKITTRICK, William James 1
MCKNEW, Thomas Willson 10
MCKNIGHT, Alexander G. 3
MCKNIGHT, Alexander Hearne 1
MCKNIGHT, Anna Caulfield 2
MCKNIGHT, Charles 1
MCKNIGHT, Douglas 6
MCKNIGHT, George Harley 5
MCKNIGHT, Harvey Washington 1
MCKNIGHT, Henry Turney 5
MCKNIGHT, James Rankin 3
MCKNIGHT, Lynn B(oyd) 9
MCKNIGHT, Robert* H
MCKNIGHT, Robert James George 6
MC KNIGHT, Robert Kellogg 10
MCKNIGHT, Roy Jerome 4
MCKNIGHT, Sumner Thomas 7
MCKNIGHT, Timothy Irle 9
MCKNIGHT, William Hodges 6
MCKNIGHT, William Lester 8
MCKONE, Don Townsend 4
MCKOWEN, John Clay 4
MCKOWN, Edgar M. 6
MCKOWN, Harry Charles 4
MCKOWN, Roberta Ellen 8
MCKOWNE, Frank A. 2
MCKUSICK, Marshall Noah 3
MCLACHLAN, Archibald C. 4
MCLACHLAN, James 4
MCLACHLEN, Archibald Malcolm 4
MCLAGAN, Thomas Rodgle 10
MCLAGLEN, Victor 3
MCLAIN, Bobby Maurice 6
MCLAIN, Chester Alden 4
MCLAIN, Frank Alexander 4
MC LAIN, John David, Jr. 8
MCLAIN, John Scudder 1
MCLAIN, John Speed 1
MC LAIN, Joseph Howard 8
MCLAIN, Raymond S. 3
MCLALLEN, Walter Field 4
MCLANAHAN, Austin 2
MCLANAHAN, James Xavier H
MCLANE, A. V. 5
MCLANE, Allan H
MCLANE, Charles Keith 6
MCLANE, Charles Lourie 4
MCLANE, James Woods 1
MCLANE, John 1
MCLANE, John Roy 5
MCLANE, Louis H
MCLANE, Patrick 5
MCLANE, Robert Milligan H
MCLANE, Ruby Roach 6
MCLANE, William Ward 1
MCLAREN, Arthur Douglas 7
MCLAREN, Donald 1
MCLAREN, Norman 9
MCLAREN, Norman Loyall 7
MCLAREN, Richard Wellington 6
MCLAREN, Richard Wellington 7
MCLAREN, Walter Wallace
MCLAREN, William Edward

MCLAREN, William Gardner 5
MCLARIN, W(illiam) S(anford), Jr. 8
MCLARNAN, Charles Walter 7
MCLARTY, Norman Alexander 2
MCLAUGHLIN, Allan Joseph 5
MCLAUGHLIN, Andrew Cunningham 2
MCLAUGHLIN, Charles Borromeo 7
MCLAUGHLIN, Charles F. 6
MCLAUGHLIN, Charles Hemphill 8
MCLAUGHLIN, Charles V(incent) 5
MCLAUGHLIN, Chester Bentline 1
MCLAUGHLIN, Chester Bond 3
MCLAUGHLIN, Dean Benjamin 4
MC LAUGHLIN, Donald Hamilton 8
MCLAUGHLIN, Dorsey Elmer 2
MCLAUGHLIN, Edward Aloysius 6
MCLAUGHLIN, Edward H. 4
MCLAUGHLIN, Emma Moffat (Mrs. Alfred McLaughlin) 5
MCLAUGHLIN, Francis 9
MCLAUGHLIN, Frank 10
MCLAUGHLIN, George Asbury 1
MCLAUGHLIN, George Dunlap 2
MCLAUGHLIN, George Vincent 8
MCLAUGHLIN, Harold Newell 5
MCLAUGHLIN, Henry Woods 3
MCLAUGHLIN, Hugh 1
MCLAUGHLIN, J. Frank 4
MCLAUGHLIN, James Campbell 1
MCLAUGHLIN, James Matthew 4
MCLAUGHLIN, James W. H
MCLAUGHLIN, John 7
MCLAUGHLIN, Joseph 1
MCLAUGHLIN, Mary Louise 1
MCLAUGHLIN, Melvin Orlando 1
MCLAUGHLIN, Paul 5
MCLAUGHLIN, Robert Samuel 5
MCLAUGHLIN, Robert William 10
MCLAUGHLIN, Robert William 1
MCLAUGHLIN, Roland Rusk 5
MCLAUGHLIN, Stuart Watts 5
MCLAUGHLIN, Thomas H. 2
MCLAUGHLIN, Walter Wylie 8
MC LAUGHLIN, William Earle 10
MCLAURIN, Anselm Joseph 1
MCLAURIN, John Lowndes 1
MCLAUTHLIN, Herbert Weston 1
MCLAWS, Lafayette H
MCLEAISH, Robert Burns H
MCLEAN, A. Neil 4
MCLEAN, Alney 1
MCLEAN, Andrew 1
MCLEAN, Angus 1
MCLEAN, Angus Wilton 1
MCLEAN, Archibald 1
MCLEAN, Arthur Edward 4
MCLEAN, David J. 6
MCLEAN, Donald 1
MCLEAN, Edward Beale 1
MCLEAN, Edward Cochrane 5
MCLEAN, Emily Nelson Ritchie 1
MCLEAN, Finis Ewing H
MCLEAN, Franklin Chambers 5
MCLEAN, Fred 6
MCLEAN, George Payne 1

MCLEAN, Heber Hampton 5
MCLEAN, Helen Vincent 10
MCLEAN, James Henry H
MCLEAN, James Stanley 3
MCLEAN, John* H
MCLEAN, John Emery 4
MCLEAN, John Godfrey 6
MCLEAN, John Knox 1
MCLEAN, John M(ilton) 5
MCLEAN, John Roll 1
MCLEAN, Leslie Alexander 8
MCLEAN, Milton Robbins 3
MCLEAN, Noel B. 8
MCLEAN, Ridley 1
MCLEAN, Robert 7
MCLEAN, Robert Norris 4
MCLEAN, Samuel H
MCLEAN, Simon James 3
MCLEAN, Thomas Chalmers 5
MCLEAN, Wallace Donald 6
MCLEAN, Walter 1
MCLEAN, William H
MC LEAN, William Burdette 7
MCLEAN, William L. 1
MCLEAN, William L., Jr. 3
MCLEAN, William Swan, Jr. 1
MCLEARN, Frank Cecil 6
MCLEARY, James Harvey 1
MCLEES, Archibald H
MCLEISTER, Ira Ford 6
MC LELLAN, Adrian Oswald 7
MCLELLAN, Archibald 1
MCLELLAN, Asahel Walker 2
MCLELLAN, Hugh Dean 5
MCLELLAN, Isaac 1
MCLELLAN, Thomas George 5
MCLEMORE, Albert Sydney 5
MCLEMORE, Jeff 1
MCLEMORE, Richard Aubrey 7
MCLENDON, Gordon Barton 9
MCLENDON, Lennox Polk 5
MCLENDON, Robert Burns 6
MCLENDON, Sol Brown 4
MCLENE, Jeremiah H
MCLENEGAN, Charles Edward 1
MCLENNAN, Charles Evart 9
MCLENNAN, Donald Roderick 2
MCLENNAN, Grace Tytus 1
MCLENNAN, Peter Baillie 1
MCLEOD, Alexander H
MCLEOD, Clarence John 3
MC LEOD, Daniel Rogers 9
MCLEOD, Duncan Allen 4
MCLEOD, Frank Hilton 2
MCLEOD, Hugh H
MC LEOD, James Currie 7
MC LEOD, James Currie 8
MCLEOD, James Currie 9
MCLEOD, Malcolm 4
MCLEOD, Martin H
MCLEOD, Mary Louise Demarco 5
MCLEOD, Murdoch 3
MCLEOD, N. H. F. 5
MCLEOD, Nelson Wesley 4
MCLEOD, Scott 4
MCLEOD, Thomas Gordon 1
MCLEOD, Walter Herbert 4
MCLEOD, William Norman 4
MCLESKEY, Waymon B. 4
MCLESTER, James Somerville 3
MCLESTER, Judson Cole, Jr. 4
MCLEVY, Jasper 1
MCLIN, Anna Eva 5
MCLINTOCK, (George) Gordon 10
M'CLINTOCK, John H
MC LOUGHLIN, Ellen Veronica 10
MCLOUGHLIN, John H
MCLOUTH, Donald B. 3
MCLOUTH, Lawrence Amos 1
MCLUCAS, Walter Scott 3
MC LUHAN, Herbert Marshall 7
MCLURE, Charles Derickson 4
MCLURE, John Rankin 8
MCLYMAN, Benjamin Murray 7

MCMAHAN, Anna Benneson 1
MCMAHAN, George Thomas 5
MCMAHON, Alphonse 5
MCMAHON, Amos Philip 2
MCMAHON, Arthur Laurence 5
MCMAHON, Bernard H
MCMAHON, Bernard John 9
MCMAHON, Brien 3
MCMAHON, Ernest Edward 10
MCMAHON, Francis Elmer 9
MCMAHON, Frank Murray Patrick 9
MCMAHON, Gerald J. 9
MCMAHON, Henry George 5
MCMAHON, Howard Oldford 10
MCMAHON, James 1
MCMAHON, John A. 1
MCMAHON, John E., Jr. 8
MCMAHON, John Joseph 1
MCMAHON, John Lasalle 1
MCMAHON, John Robert 3
MCMAHON, John Van Lear H
MCMAHON, Joseph H. 1
MCMAHON, Joseph Henry 9
MCMAHON, Lawrence Stephen H
MCMAHON, Martin Thomas 1
MCMAHON, Stephen John 3
MCMAHON, Thomas F. 2
MCMAHON, Thomas J. 3
MCMAIN, Eleanor Laura 2
MCMANAMAN, Edward Peter 4
MCMANAMON, James Emmett 3
MCMANAMY, Frank 2
MCMANES, James H
MCMANES, Kenmore Mathew 5
MCMANIS, John Thomas 5
MCMANUS, Charles Edward 2
MCMANUS, George 2
MCMANUS, George Henry 5
MCMANUS, Howard 6
MC MANUS, James Norbert 7
MCMANUS, John B., Jr. 7
MCMANUS, John Joseph 2
MCMANUS, William H
MCMARTIN, Charles 3
MCMARTIN, William Joseph 5
MCMASTER, Fitz Hugh 1
MCMASTER, Florence R. 6
MCMASTER, Guy Humphreys H
MCMASTER, James Alphonsus H
MCMASTER, John Bach 1
MCMASTER, John Stevenson 1
MCMASTER, Leroy 2
MCMASTER, Philip Duryee 2
MCMASTER, Robert Charles 9
MCMASTER, Ross Huntington 4
MCMASTER, William Henry 4
MCMASTER, William Henry* 5
MCMATH, Francis Charles 1
MCMATH, Robert Edwin 5
MCMATH, Robert Emmett 4
MCMATH, Robert R. 4
MCMEANS, George Beale 4
MCMECHAN, Francis Hoeffer 1
MCMEEN, Samuel Groenendyke 1
MCMEIN, Neysa 2
MCMENAMIN, Hugh L. 2
MCMENAMY, Francis Xavier H
MCMENIMEN, Walter L. 7
MCMENIMEN, William V. 4
MCMICHAEL, Clayton 1
MCMICHAEL, Morton H
MCMICHAEL, Thomas Hanna 1
MCMILLAN, Alexander H
MCMILLAN, Alexander 1
MCMILLAN, Alfred E. 5
MCMILLAN, Charles 1

MCMILLAN, Claude Richelieu 4
MCMILLAN, Daniel Hugh 4
MCMILLAN, Donald 8
MCMILLAN, Duncan J. 1
MCMILLAN, Edward John 4
MCMILLAN, Edwin Mattison 10
MCMILLAN, Franklin R. 7
MCMILLAN, Fred Orville 3
MCMILLAN, George Scholefield 5
MCMILLAN, Homer 3
MCMILLAN, James 1
MCMILLAN, James Thayer 2
MCMILLAN, James Winning 1
MCMILLAN, John Lanneau 7
MC MILLAN, Kenneth 9
MCMILLAN, Malcolm Cook 10
MCMILLAN, Neil Alexander 1
MCMILLAN, Philip Hamilton 1
MCMILLAN, Putnam Dana 4
MCMILLAN, Robert Johnston 2
MCMILLAN, Samuel 4
MCMILLAN, Samuel James Renwick H
MCMILLAN, Thomas M. 7
MCMILLAN, Thomas Sanders 1
MCMILLAN, William H
MCMILLAN, William Benton 7
MCMILLAN, William Charles 1
MCMILLAN, William H.
MCMILLAN, William Joshua 5
MCMILLAN, William Linn 1
MCMILLEN, Alonzo Bertram 1
MCMILLEN, Dale Wilmore 5
MCMILLEN, Fred Ewing 3
MCMILLEN, James Adelbert 3
MC MILLEN, Wheeler 10
MCMILLIN, Alvin Nugent 3
MCMILLIN, Benton 1
MCMILLIN, Emerson 1
MCMILLIN, Francis Briggs Nelson 1
MCMILLIN, Frederick 1
MCMILLIN, George Johnson 8
MCMILLIN, John Milton 3
MCMILLIN, Lucille Foster 2
MC MILLIN, Miles James 8
MCMILLIN, Stewart Earl 3
MCMINN, Bryan Towne 7
MCMINN, Joseph H
MCMORAN, George Andrew 6
MCMORRAN, Henry 3
MCMORRIS, Charles H. 4
MCMORROW, Francis Joseph 4
MCMORROW, Thomas 3
MCMULLAN, Harry 3
MCMULLAN, Oscar 4
MCMULLEN, Adam 5
MCMULLEN, Charles Bell 5
MCMULLEN, Chester Bartow 3
MCMULLEN, Clements 3
MCMULLEN, Fayette H
MCMULLEN, Hugh Aloysius 1
MCMULLEN, John H
MCMULLEN, John Joseph 5
MCMULLEN, Lynn Banks 4
MCMULLEN, Richard Cann 2
MCMULLIN, Joseph J(ohn) A(nthony) 7
MCMULLIN, Thomas Edison 9
MCMURDY, Robert 2
MCMURRAY, Charles Backman 1
MCMURRAY, Dewitt 4
MCMURRAY, Howard Johnstone 4
MCMURRAY, James Donald 5
MCMURRAY, James Henry 1
MCMURRAY, John 5
MCMURRAY, Orrin Kip 2
MC MURRAY, Paul Ray 9

MCMURRAY, William Josiah 1
MCMURRICH, J. Playfair 3
MCMURRICH, James Playfair H
MCMURRICH, James Playfair 4
MCMURRY, Charles Alexander 1
MCMURRY, Frank Morton 1
MCMURRY, Lida Brown 2
MC MURRY, Robert Noleman 8
MC MURRY, Robert Noleman 9
MCMURRY, William Fletcher 1
MCMURTREY, James Edward, Jr. 10
MCMURTRIE, Douglas Crawford 2
MCMURTRIE, Uz 4
MCMURTRIE, William 1
MCMURTRY, James Gilmer 3
MCMURTRY, John H
MCMURTRY, Lewis S. 1
MCMURTRY, Robert Gerald 9
MCMURTRY, William John 4
MCNAB, Alexander J. 3
MCNAB, Allan 8
MCNAB, Archibald Peter 2
MCNAB, John 8
MCNABB, Joe Hector 2
MCNABB, Samuel W. 1
MCNAGNY, Phil McClellan 5
MC NAGNY, Phil McClellan, Jr. 7
MCNAIR, Alexander H
MC NAIR, Andrew Hamilton 7
MCNAIR, Frank 6
MCNAIR, Fred Walter 1
MCNAIR, Fredeick Vallette 1
MCNAIR, James Birtley 5
MCNAIR, John H
MCNAIR, John Babbitt 5
MCNAIR, Laurance North 7
MCNAIR, Lesley James 1
MCNAIR, Malcom Perrine 9
MCNAIR, Ronald Erwin 9
MCNAIR, William Sharp 1
MCNALLY, Andrew 3
MCNALLY, Frederick George 1
MCNALLY, George Frederick 6
MCNALLY, Harold Joseph 7
MCNALLY, James Clifford 1
MCNALLY, Joseph Thomas 5
MCNALLY, Paul Aloysius 3
MCNALLY, William Duncan 4
MCNALLY, William J. 1
MCNAMARA, Francis Joseph 7
MCNAMARA, Harley Vincent 4
MCNAMARA, John 8
MCNAMARA, John Arthur 8
MCNAMARA, John M. 1
MCNAMARA, Joseph Augustine 5
MCNAMARA, Martin D. 4
MCNAMARA, Patrick Vincent 4
MC NAMARA, Paul James 9
MCNAMARA, Robert Charles 4
MCNAMARA, Robert Charles 5
MCNAMEE, C. Declan 4
MCNAMEE, Charles Joseph 4
MCNAMEE, Daniel V., Jr. 7
MCNAMEE, Frank A. 9
MCNAMEE, Graham 2
MCNAMEE, Luke 2
MCNAMEE, William John, Jr. 2
MCNARNEY, Josehh T. 5
MCNARY, Charles Linza 2
MCNARY, Henrietta Williamson 4
MCNARY, James Graham 4
MCNARY, William S. 4
MCNARY, William Selwyn 8
MCNAUGHER, John 2
MCNAUGHT, Francis Hector 1
MCNAUGHT, James 4
MCNAUGHT, James B. 3

MCNAUGHTON, Andrew George Latta 4
MCNAUGHTON, John Hugh 1
MCNAUGHTON, John Theodore 4
MCNAUGHTON, William Francis 4
MCNAUGHTON, William Francis 5
MCNEAL, Alice 4
MCNEAL, Donald Hamlin 4
MCNEAL, Edgar Holmes 3
MCNEAL, Joshua Vansant 1
MCNEAL, Thomas Allen 2
MCNEAL, William Horton 6
MCNEALY, Raymond William 3
MCNEAR, George Plummer, Jr. 2
MC NEE, Robert Bruce 10
MC NEELY, E. L. 10
MCNEELY, Eugene J(ohnson) 6
MCNEELY, Harry G(regory) 5
MCNEELY, Robert Whitehead 5
MCNEES, Sterling G. 3
MC NEESE, Aylmer Green, Jr. 10
MCNEIL, Archibald 7
MCNEIL, Edwin Colyer 4
MCNEIL, Elton Burbank 6
MCNEIL, Everett 1
MC NEIL, Gomer Thomas 8
MC NEIL, Henry Slack 8
MCNEIL, Hiram Colver 1
MCNEIL, John Eugene 1
MCNEIL, Kenneth Gordon 5
MCNEIL, Sister Mary Donald 5
MC NEIL, Neil Venable 8
MC NEIL, Robert Lincoln 5
MCNEIL, Robert Lincoln 7
MC NEIL, Wilfred James 7
MCNEILL, Archibald H
MCNEILL, Daniel 1
MCNEILL, Edwin Ruthven 5
MCNEILL, George Edwin 1
MCNEILL, George Rockwell 1
MCNEILL, Hector H
MCNEILL, I. C. 4
MCNEILL, John Charles 1
MCNEILL, John Hanson H
MCNEILL, John Thomas 6
MCNEILL, Neal Edward 3
MCNEILL, Robert Hayes 6
MCNEILL, Thomas W. 3
MCNEILL, William Gibbs H
MCNEILL, Winfield Irving 8
MCNEIR, George 1
MCNEIR, William 4
MCNEIRNY, Francis H
MCNELLY, Walter C. 10
MCNEW, John Thomas Lamar 2
MCNICHOL, Paul John 5
MCNICHOLAS, John T. 3
MC NICHOLAS, Joseph Alphonsus 8
MCNICHOLS, John Patrick 1
MC NICHOLS, Ray 9
MCNIECE, Harold Francis 5
MCNIECE, Renwick Sloane 7
MCNIECE, Robert Gibson 3
MCNINCH, Frank R. 3
MCNULTA, John 1
MCNULTA, John 4
MCNULTY, C. H. 3
MCNULTY, Frank J. 5
MC NULTY, Frederick Charles 9
MCNULTY, George Albert 4
MCNULTY, James 5
MCNULTY, John Laurence 3
MC NULTY, Kneeland 10
MCNULTY, Robert Wilkinson 4
MCNULTY, William Charles 7
MCNUTT, Alexander H
MCNUTT, Anna Mary 5
MCNUTT, Paul Vories 5
MCNUTT, William Fletcher 4
MCNUTT, William Roy 6
MCORMOND, Raymond Richards 7
MCPEAK, William Wallace 4
MCPHAIL, Harvey Franklin 9
MCPHEE, Eugene Roderick 6
MCPHEE, Julian A. 4
MCPHEETERS, Chester Amos 4
MCPHEETERS, Julian C. 8

MC PHEETERS, Thomas S., Jr. 9
MCPHEETERS, William Emmett 4
MCPHEETERS, William Marcellus 1
MCPHERREN, Charles Elmo 5
MCPHERRIN, John Weitz 6
MCPHERSON, Aimee Semple H
MCPHERSON, Aimee Semple 2
MCPHERSON, Aimee Semple 4
MCPHERSON, Charles 2
MCPHERSON, Edward H
MCPHERSON, Harry Wright 3
MCPHERSON, Hobart M. 3
MCPHERSON, Isaac V. 4
MCPHERSON, Isaac V. 4
MCPHERSON, James Birdseye H
MCPHERSON, John Bayard 1
MCPHERSON, John Dallas 9
MCPHERSON, John Edward 1
MCPHERSON, John Hanson Thomas 3
MCPHERSON, John Rhoderic H
MCPHERSON, Logan Grant 1
MCPHERSON, Ross 1
MCPHERSON, Samuel Dace 3
MCPHERSON, Sherman Tecumseh 4
MCPHERSON, Simon John 1
MCPHERSON, Smith 1
MCPHERSON, William Lenhart 3
MCPHERSON, William Doddridge 1
MCPIKE, Henry H. 1
MCQUADE, Vincent Augustine 5
MCQUAID, Bernard John 1
MCQUAID, William Ravenel 4
MCQUARRIE, Irvine 4
MCQUEEN, Elizabeth Lippincott 6
MCQUEEN, Frederick Emil 4
MCQUEEN, Henry Clay 1
MCQUEEN, John H
MCQUEEN, L(oren) A(ngus) 5
MCQUEEN, Steve 7
MCQUEEN, Stewart 1
MCQUIGG, John Rea 1
MCQUILKIN, Robert Crawford 1
MC QUILKIN, William Winter 10
MCQUILLEN, John Hugh H
MCQUILLIN, Eugene 1
MCQUILLIN, Raymond E(ugene) 8
MCQUISTON, Irving Matthew 8
MC QUOWN, O. Ruth 8
MCRAE, Austin Lee 1
MCRAE, Bruce 1
MCRAE, Duncan Kirkland 8
MCRAE, Floyd Willcox 8
MCRAE, George W. 3
MCRAE, Hamilton Eugene, Jr. 10
MCRAE, James Henry 1
MCRAE, James Wilson 3
MCRAE, John Finley 10
MCRAE, John Jones H
MCRAE, Milton A. 1
MCRAE, Roderick 1
MCRAE, Thomas Chipman 1
MCRAE, William Allan 6
MCRCLOSKEY, George V. A. 1
MCREYNOLDS, Frederick Wilson 5
MCREYNOLDS, George Edgar 3
MCREYNOLDS, James Clark 2
MCREYNOLDS, John Oliver 2
MCREYNOLDS, Peter Wesley 1
MCREYNOLDS, Samuel Davis 1
MCREYNOLDS, William Henry 3
MCRILL, Albert Leroy 3
MCROBERTS, Harriet Pearl Skinner 2

MCROBERTS, Robert M. 10
MCROBERTS, Samuel H
MCROY, Paul Furgeson 10
MCRUER, James Chalmers 8
MCSHAIN, John 10
MCSHANE, Andrew James 1
MCSHANE, Edward James 10
MCSHANE, Ralph E(dward) 8
MCSHEA, Joseph 10
MCSHERRY, Frank David 7
MCSHERRY, James 3
MCSHERRY, Richard H
MCSKIMMON, William Bingham 5
MCSOLEY, Raymond Joseph 3
MCSORLEY, Edward 4
MCSORLEY, Joseph 4
MCSPADDEN, Joseph Walker 4
MCSPARRAN, John Aldus 5
MCSURELY, William Harvey 2
MCSWAIN, Eldridge Tracy 10
MCSWAIN, John Jackson 1
MC SWAIN, William Adney 10
MCSWEENEY, Henry 2
MCSWEENEY, John Morgan 5
MCSWEENEY, Miles Benjamin 1
MCTAGUE, Charles Patrick 4
MCTAMMANY, John H
MCTAMMANY, John 4
MCTARNAHAN, William Chamberlin 3
MCTYEIRE, Holland Nimmons H
MCULLOCH, Philip 4
MCVAY, Charles Butler, Jr.* 2
MCVEA, Emilie Watts 1
MCVEAN, Charles 4
MCVEIGH, John Newburn 3
MCVEY, Frank Lerond 3
MCVEY, William E. 1
MCVEY, William Estus 3
MCVICAR, Nelson 4
MCVICKAR, John H
MCVICKAR, William Neilson 1
MCVICKER, James Hubert H
MCVINNEY, Russell J. 5
MCVITTIE, George Cunliffe 10
MCWADE, Robert Malachi 1
MCWANE, James Ransom 1
MCWHINNEY, Thomas Martin 1
MCWHIRTER, Felix Marcus 7
MCWHIRTER, Felix T. 1
MCWHIRTER, Luella Frances Smith 3
MCWHIRTER, William Allan 4
MCWHORTER, Ashton Waugh 1
MCWHORTER, Ernest D. 2
MCWHORTER, Henry Clay 1
MCWHORTER, Roger Barton 8
MCWILLIAM, John R. 4
MC WILLIAMS, Carey 7
MC WILLIAMS, Carey 7
MCWILLIAMS, Clarence A. 1
MCWILLIAMS, John Probasco 5
MC WILLIAMS, John Wesley 7
MCWILLIAMS, Roland Fairbairn 3
MCWILLIAMS, Thomas Samuel 4
MCWILLIE, Thomas Anderson 1
MCWILLIE, William H
MEACHAM, Harry Monroe 7
MEACHAM, James H
MEACHAM, Malcolm 1
MEACHAM, W(illiam) Banks 5
MEACHAM, William Shands 7
MEAD, Albert Davis 2
MEAD, Albert Edward 1
MEAD, Arthur Emett 4
MEAD, Arthur Raymond 6

MEAD, Charles Larew 1
MEAD, Charles Marsh 1
MEAD, Cowles H
MEAD, D. Irving 3
MEAD, Daniel Webster 2
MEAD, Edward Campbell 1
MEAD, Edward Sherwood 5
MEAD, Edwin Doak 1
MEAD, Elizabeth Storrs 1
MEAD, Elwood 1
MEAD, Frank Spencer 8
MEAD, Frederick Sumner 1
MEAD, George Herbert 1
MEAD, George Houk 4
MEAD, George Jackson 2
MEAD, George Whitefield 2
MEAD, George Wilson 4
MEAD, Gilbert Wilcox 2
MEAD, Harry L. 4
MEAD, James M. 4
MEAD, John Abner 1
MEAD, Kate Campbell Hurd 1
MEAD, Larkin Goldsmith 1
MEAD, Leon 4
MEAD, Leonard Charles 1
MEAD, Lucia True Ames 1
MEAD, Margaret 7
MEAD, Nelson Prentiss 4
MEAD, Robert Gillespie, 2d 7
MEAD, Solomon Cristy 5
MEAD, Stanton Witter 10
MEAD, Sterling V. 5
MEAD, Theodore Hoe 4
MEAD, Warren Judson 4
MEAD, William Edward 5
MEAD, William Henry 6
MEAD, William Rutherford 1
MEAD, William Whitman 1
MEADE, Edwin Ruthwen H
MEADE, Eleanore Hussey H
MEADE, Eleanore Hussey 7
MEADE, Francis Louis 3
MEADE, Frank B. 2
MEADE, George 1
MEADE, George Edward 5
MEADE, George Gordon 8
MEADE, George Peterkin 6
MEADE, George Peterkin 7
MEADE, James J. 4
MEADE, Janifer Dewitt 4
MEADE, Richard Andrew 4
MEADE, Richard Hardaway 10
MEADE, Richard Kidder* H
MEADE, Richard Kidder 1
MEADE, Richard Worsam* H
MEADE, Richard Worsam 1
MEADE, Robert Douthat 6
MEADE, Robert Heber 7
MEADE, Robert Leamy 1
MEADE, William H
MEADER, Clarence Linton 7
MEADER, George Farnham 8
MEADER, Stephen Warren 7
MEADOR, Chastain Clark 1
MEADOR, Clifton Kirkpatrick 7
MEADOW, H(enry) Grady 9
MEADOW, William King 1
MEADOWCROFT, William Henry 1
MEADOWS, Algur Hurtle 7
MEADOWS, Clarence Watson 4
MEADOWS, James Allen 5
MEADOWS, John Cassius 7
MEADOWS, Leon Renfroe 7
MEADOWS, Paul 9
MEADOWS, Robert Merle 9
MEAGHER, James Francis 1
MEAGHER, James Luke 1
MEAGHER, Raymond H
MEAGHER, Thomas Francis H
MEAKER, Samuel Raynor 8
MEAKIN, L. H. 1
MEALEY, Carroll Edward 4
MEANEY, Sir Patrick Michael 10
MEANEY, Thomas Francis 5
MEANS, Cyril Chesnut, Jr. 10
MEANS, David MacGregor 1
MEANS, Earl A. 3
MEANS, Eldred Kurtz 3
MEANS, Emily Adams 1
MEANS, Florence Crannell 7
MEANS, Frank Wilson 3
MEANS, Gardiner Coit 9
MEANS, Gaston Bullock 4
MEANS, George Hamilton 2
MEANS, Haston Bullock 1
MEANS, Hugh J(ackson) 7
MEANS, James Howard 4
MEANS, Lewis M. 8

MEANS, Paul Banwell 10
MEANS, Philip Ainsworth 2
MEANS, Rice William 2
MEANS, Stewart 2
MEANS, Thomas Herbert 5
MEANWELL, Walter E. 3
MEANY, Edmond Stephen 1
MEANY, Edward P. 1
MEANY, George 1
MEARA, Frank S. 1
MEARNS, David Chambers 7
MEARNS, Edgar A. H
MEARNS, Edgar Alexander 1
MEARNS, Hughes 4
MEARS, Brainerd 6
MEARS, David Otis 1
MEARS, Eliot Grinnell 2
MEARS, Frederick 1
MEARS, Helen Farnsworth 1
MEARS, J. Ewing 1
MEARS, John William H
MEARS, Leverett 1
MEARS, Louise Wilhelmina 5
MEARS, Mary 5
MEARSON, Lyon 8
MEASE, James H
MEASON, Isaac H
MEBANE, Alexander H
MEBANE, B. Frank 4
MEBANE, Daniel 1
MEBANE, Harry Bartlett, Jr. 5
MEBANE, Robert Sloan 1
MECH, Stephen John 5
MECHAU, Frank, Jr. 2
MECHEM, Floyd Russell 1
MECHEM, Merritt Cramer 5
MECHEM, Philip 5
MECHERLE, George Jacob 3
MECHERLE, Raymond Perry 8
MECHLIN, Leila 2
MECK, John Foster 8
MECKLENBURGER, Albert F. 8
MECKLIN, John Martin 5
MECKLIN, John Moffatt 3
MECKSTROTH, Jacob Adolf 8
MECLEARY, Howard Blaine 7
MECOM, Benjamin H
MECOM, John Whitfield 8
MECOM, Philip Henry 8
MEDALIE, Carrie Kaplan (Mrs. George Z. Medalie) 7
MEDALIE, George Zerdin 2
MEDARY, Milton Bennett 1
MEDARY, Samuel H
MEDAWAR, Peter Brian 9
MEDBURY, Charles Sanderson 1
MEDEARIS, T(homas) W(hittier) 5
MEDEIROS, Humberto Sousa 8
MEDFORD, William 5
MEDHURST, Sir Charles E. H. 3
MEDILL, Joseph H
MEDILL, William H
MEDINA, Harold R. 10
MEDINA, William A. 8
MEDLEY, Mat H
MEDLRUM, Herbert Alexander 5
MEDSGER, Oliver Perry 5
MEDSKER, Leland L. 7
MEDUNA, Ladislas Joseph 10
MEE, John F. 9
MEE, William 1
MEECH, Charles Braddock 7
MEECH, Ezra H
MEEHAN, M. Joseph 4
MEEHAN, Thomas 1
MEEHAN, Thomas A. 4
MEEK, Alexander Beaufort 1
MEEK, Benjamin Franklin 1
MEEK, Charles Simpson 3
MEEK, Devon Walter 9
MEEK, Edward Roscoe 5
MEEK, Fielding Bradford 1
MEEK, Frederick Mayer 7
MEEK, Harry E. 8
MEEK, Howard Bagnall 5
MEEK, John Henry 1
MEEK, Joseph A(icinus) 8
MEEK, Joseph Henry 8
MEEK, Joseph L. H
MEEK, Peter Gray 10
MEEK, Robert Abner 3
MEEK, Samuel Williams 8
MEEK, Seth Eugene 1
MEEK, Sterner St Paul 5
MEEK, Theophile James 6
MEEK, Thomas Bradfield 7
MEEK, Tom Jones 7

MEEK, Walter Joseph 6
MEEKER, Arthur 2
MEEKER, Arthur 5
MEEKER, Claude 1
MEEKER, Ezra 1
MEEKER, Frank Leroy 2
MEEKER, George Herbert 2
MEEKER, Jacob Edwin 1
MEEKER, James Rusling H
MEEKER, Jonathan Magie 1
MEEKER, Jotham H
MEEKER, Moses H
MEEKER, Nathan Cook H
MEEKER, Ralph Inman 5
MEEKER, Royal 3
MEEKINS, Isaac Melson 2
MEEKINS, Lynn Roby 1
MEEKISON, David 4
MEEKS, Benjamin Wiltshire 6
MEEKS, Carroll Louis Vanderslice 4
MEEKS, Clarence Gardner 3
MEEKS, Everett Victor 3
MEEKS, James A. 3
MEEM, Harry Grant 2
MEEM, John Gaw 8
MEEMAN, Edward John 4
MEENES, Max 6
MEERSCHAERT, Theophile 1
MEES, Arthur 1
MEES, Carl Leo 3
MEES, Charles Edward Kenneth 4
MEES, Otto 3
MEES, Theophilus 1
MEESE, Alfred Hall 4
MEESE, William Giles 8
MEESE, William Henry 4
MEESER, Spenser Byron 1
MEESKE, Fritz 9
MEESSEN, Hubert Joseph 4
MEFTAH, Davood Khan 5
MEGAN, Charles P. 2
MEGAN, Graydon 4
MEGAPOLENSIS, Johannes H
MEGARGEE, Edwin 3
MEGARO, Gaudens 3
MEGEE, Vernon Edgar 10
MEGGERS, William Frederick 4
MEGGINSON, William 5
MEGOWEN, Carl Robert 4
MEGOWN, John William 10
MEGRAN, Herbert Brown 3
MEGRAW, Herbert Ashton 3
MEGRUE, Roi Cooper 1
MEHAFFY, Pat 7
MEHAFFY, Tom Miller 4
MEHAN, John Dennis 4
MEHAN, Mona Catharine 4
MEHEGAN, John Francis 8
MEHL, Joseph Martin 7
MEHL, Robert Franklin 6
MEHL, Robert Franklin 7
MEHLBERG, Josephine Janina Bednarski Spinner (Mrs. Henry) 7
MEHLER, John Sauter 4
MEHLIN, Theodore Grefe 4
MEHLING, Theodore John 4
MEHORNAY, Robert Lee 5
MEHOS, Charles Arthur 4
MEHR, Robert Irwin 9
MEHRBACH, Albert, Jr. 7
MEHREN, Edward J. 4
MEHREN, George Louis 10
MEHRING, Howard William 7
MEHRTENS, William Osborne 7
MEHRTENS, William Osborne 8
MEHTA, Gaganvihari L. 6
MEHUS, Oscar Myking 9
MEI, Alexis Itale 10
MEID, George Donald 7
MEIDELL, Harold M. 5
MEIER, Fabian Allan 4
MEIER, Fred Campbell 1
MEIER, Julius L. 1
MEIER, Norman Charles 4
MEIER, Walter Frederick 4
MEIERE, M. Hildreth 4
MEIERS, Ruth Lenore 9
MEIGGS, Henry H
MEIGHAN, Thomas 1
MEIGHEN, Arthur 3
MEIGHEN, John Felix 3
Dryden
MEIGS, Arthur Ingersoll 3
MEIGS, Arthur Vincent 1
MEIGS, Charles Delucena H
MEIGS, Cornelia Lynde 6
MEIGS, Cornelia Lynde 7

MEIGS, Grance Lynde 6
MEIGS, Henry H
MEIGS, James Aitken 1
MEIGS, Joe Vincent 9
MEIGS, John 1
MEIGS, John Forsyth H
MEIGS, Josiah H
MEIGS, Merrill Church 4
MEIGS, Montgomery 1
MEIGS, Montgomery Cunningham H
MEIGS, Return Jonathan H
MEIGS, Return Jonathan, Jr.* H
MEIGS, Robert Van 5
MEIGS, William Montgomery 1
MEIKLE, George Stanley 5
MEIKLEJOHN, Alexander 4
MEIKLEJOHN, David Shirra 10
MEIKLEJOHN, George De Rue 1
MEIKS, Lyman Thompson 5
MEILING, Richard Lewis 5
MEILINK, John Girard 3
MEIN, John Gordon 5
MEIN, William Wallace 4
MEINBERG, Carl Herman 8
MEINE, Franklin Julius 5
MEINECKE, Emilio Pepe Michael 3
MEINECKE, Willard Henry 7
MEINEL, William John 4
MEINERS, (Henrich) William W. 7
MEINHOLD, H. E. 6
MEINHOLD, H. E. 6
MEINHOLTZ, Frederick E. 4
MEINRATH, Joseph 1
MEINS, Carroll Leach 3
MEINZER, Oscar Edward 2
MEIR, Golda (Changed Name From Golda Myerson 1956) 7
MEISEL, Emanuel George 8
MEISENHELDER, Edmund W. 3
MEISENHELTER, L. R. 6
MEISLE, Kathryn (Mrs. Calvin M. Franklin) 5
MEISS, Millard 6
MEISSNER, Edwin Benjamin 3
MEISSNER, K. W. 3
MEISTEN, John Nicholas 5
MEISTER, John William 4
MEITNER, Lise 5
MEJIA, Federico 4
MEKEEL, Haviland Scudder 2
MELANDER, A. L. 4
MELANDER, George Harold 6
MELAUGH, Edward Gerard 7
MELBA, Mme Nellie 1
MELBY, Ernest Oscar 9
MELCHER, Carl A. 3
MELCHER, Columbus Rudolph 2
MELCHER, Daniel 9
MELCHER, Frank Otis 5
MELCHER, Frederic Gershom 4
MELCHER, George 4
MELCHER, George B. 4
MELCHER, Joseph H
MELCHER, Leroy, Jr. 8
MELCHERS, Gari 1
MELCHERS, Leo Edward 6
MELCHETT, Julian Edward Alfred 8
MELCHIOR, Lauritz 2
MELCHIOR, Lebrecth Hommel 1
MELCHOR, Oliver Hoffman 1
MELDEN, Charles Manly 4
MELDRIM, Peter W. 1
MELDRUM, Andrew Barclay 1
MELDRUM, A(ndrew) MacKenzie 5
MELDRUM, William Buell 3
MELEAR, James Melville 3
MELENCIO, Jose P. 3
MELENDY, Mary Ries 4
MELENEY, Clarence Edmund 1
MELENEY, Frank Lamont 4
MELHORN, Donald Franklin 7
MELHORN, Kent C. 1
MELHORN, Nathan R. 5
MELHUS, Irving E. 6
MELICK, Dermont Wilson 9

MELICK, John Vliet 9
MELICK, William Frank 9
MELINE, Frank L. 2
MELINE, James Florant 1
MELIODON, Jules Andre 5
MELISH, John H
MELISH, John Howard 5
MELISH, William Bromwell 4
MELIUS, L. Malcolm 4
MELL, Patrick H. H
MELL, Patrick Hues 1
MELLE, Rosine 1
MELLEN, Charles Sanger 1
MELLEN, Chase 1
MELLEN, George Frederick 1
MELLEN, Grenville H
MELLEN, Ida M. 6
MELLEN, J. Grenville 8
MELLEN, Prentiss 1
MELLER, Harry Bertine 2
MELLETT, John Calvin 8
MELLETT, Lowell 1
MELLETTE, Arthur Calvin H
MELLIN, Carl Johan 1
MELLIN, Oscar Alvin 10
MELLINGER, Aubrey Hugo 4
MELLINGER, Samuel 4
MELLISH, David Batcheller H
MELLISH, Mary 3
MELLISS, David Ernest 1
MELLITZ, Samuel 1
MELLMAN, William Jules 7
MELLON, Andrew William 1
MELLON, Eleanor Mary 10
MELLON, James R. 1
MELLON, Richard Beatty 1
MELLON, Richard King 5
MELLON, Thomas 1
MELLON, Thomas Alexander 2
MELLON, William Larimer 2
MELLOR, Charles Chauncey 1
MELLOR, Walter 1
MELLOTT, Arthur J. 3
MELLUISH, James George 5
MELNITZ, William Wolf 9
MELONEY, Marie Mattingly 2
MELONEY, William Brown 1
MELONEY, William Brown 5
MELOY, Francis Edward, Jr. 7
MELOY, Harry 9
MELROSE, Alice Gunhild 7
MELS, Edgar 4
MELSHEIMER, Friedrich Valentin 1
MELSON, Charles Leroy H
MELTON, Charles Lewis 3
MELTON, James 4
MELTON, Leroy 1
MELTON, Oliver Quimby 8
MELTON, Wightman Fletcher 1
MELTON, William D. 1
MELTON, William Walter 6
MELTZER, Abraham 1
MELTZER, Charles Henry 1
MELTZER, Doris 7
MELTZER, Leon 1
MELTZER, Samuel James 1
MELVILLE, David H
MELVILLE, Frank, Jr. 1
MELVILLE, George Wallace 1
MELVILLE, Henry 1
MELVILLE, Herman H
MELVILLE, K(enneth) I(van) 6
MELVILLE, Rose 2
MELVILLE, Ward 1
MELVIN, Alonzo Dorus 1
MELVIN, Bradford Morse 4
MELVIN, Crandall 1
MELVIN, Frank Worthington 5
MELVIN, Harold Wesley 9
MELVIN, Henry Alexander 1
MELVIN, Marion Edmund 8
MELVIN, Myron S. 4
MELVIN, Ridgely Prentiss 1
MELZAR, Frederic Preston 10
MEMBRE, Zenobius 1
MEMBRENO, Alberto 4
MEMINGER, James Wilbert 1
MEMMINGER, Allard 1
MEMMINGER, Christopher Gustavus H
MEMMINGER, Christopher Gustavus 1
MEMMINGER, Lucien 6

MEMORY, Jasper Livingston 10
MEMPHIS SLIM (Peter Chatman)* 10
MENAGH, Louis Randolph 6
MENARD, Henry William 9
MENARD, Michel Branamour H
MENARD, Pierre H
MENARD, Rene H
MENCHER, Ely 7
MENCKEN, August 4
MENCKEN, Henry Louis 3
MENCKEN, Sara Powell Haardt 1
MENCONI, Ralph Joseph 6
MENDEL, Arthur 7
MENDEL, Lafayette Benedict 1
MENDEL, Warner H(umphrey) 5
MENDEL, Werner Max 10
MENDELL, Clarence Whittlesey 5
MENDELL, M(ordecai) Lester 9
MENDELL, Seth 1
MENDELL, Wayne 7
MENDELS, Walter Bass 7
MENDELSOHN, Albert 8
MENDELSOHN, Charles Jastrow 1
MENDELSOHN, Erich H
MENDELSOHN, Erich 4
MENDELSOHN, Robert Saul 9
MENDELSOHN, Samuel 1
MENDELSSOHN, Louis 1
MENDENHALL, Charles Elwood 1
MENDENHALL, George Newton 6
MENDENHALL, Harlan George 1
MENDENHALL, Thomas Corwin 1
MENDENHALL, Walter Curran 3
MENDENHALL, William Orville 6
MENDERES, Adnan 4
MENDES, Frederick de Sola 1
MENDES, Henry Pereira 1
MENDES, Murilo Monteiro 6
MENDES FRANCE, Pierre 8
MENDEZ, Joaquin 1
MENDEZ, Pereira Octavio 8
MENDLESON, Alan N. 3
MENEELY, A. Howard 4
MENEELY, Andrew H
MENEELY, George Rodney 9
MENEES, Thomas 1
MENEFEE, F(erdinand) N(orthrup) 5
MENEFEE, F(erdinand) N(orthrup) 7
MENEFEE, Richard Hickman H
MENEFFE, Guy Clifton 7
MENEN, Aubrey (Salvator Aubrey Clarence Menon) 9
MENENDEZ, Pedro de Aviles H
MENETREY, Joseph 1
MENEWA H
MENG, John Joseph 9
MENGARINI, Gregory H
MENGE, Edward John Von Komorowski 7
MENGE, Frederick 3
MENGEL, Levi Walter 1
MENGEL, Robert Morrow 10
MENGER, Carl S. 8
MENGERT, William Felix 7
MENGES, Franklin 3
MENGLE, Glenn A. 4
MENIHAN, John Conway 10
MENJOU, Adolphe Jean 2
MENK, Louis 9
MENKEN, Adah Isaacs H
MENKEN, Helen 4
MENKEN, S. Stanwood 3
MENKES, Sigmund Josef 10
MENN, Joe Karl 7
MENN, Thorpe 7
MENNAN, William Gerhard 4
MENNER, Robert James 3
MENNIN, Peter 8
MENNINGER, Charles August 1
MENNINGER, Karl Augustus* 10

MENNINGER, William Claire 4
MENOCAL, Aniceto G. 1
MENOHER, Charles Thomas 1
MENOHER, Pearson 3
MENON, Maniketh Gopala 4
MENSEL, Ernst Edmund 4
MENSEL, Ernst Heinrich 2
MENSHIKOV, Mikhail Alekseevich 7
MENTON, A(ndrew) Paul 5
MENTSCHIKOFF, Soia 8
MENTZ, George Francis Millen 3
MENTZER, William Cyrus 5
MENVILLE, Leon 3
MENVILLE, Raoul Louis 2
MENZEL, Donald Howard 1
MENZEL, Margaret Young 9
MENZIES, Alan Wilfrid Cranbrook 4
MENZIES, Alan Wilfrid Cranbrook 5
MENZIES, Duncan Cameron 8
MENZIES, John Thomson 4
MENZIES, John William H
MENZIES, Percival Keith 6
MENZIES, Robert James 7
MERAS, Albert Amedee 1
MERCADANTE, Joseph 7
MERCER, Alfred Clifford 1
MERCER, Archibald 4
MERCER, Beverly Howard 6
MERCER, Charles 9
MERCER, Charles Fenton H
MERCER, David Henry 1
MERCER, Elwyn Jarvis 10
MERCER, Eugene Leroy 3
MERCER, Frederick Olin 4
MERCER, Henry Chapman 1
MERCER, Henry Dickson 10
MERCER, Hugh H
MERCER, Hugh Victor 5
MERCER, James H
MERCER, Jesse H
MERCER, John Francis H
MERCER, Johnny (John H.) 7
MERCER, Johnny (John H.) 8
MERCER, Lauron W. 4
MERCER, Margaret 1
MERCER, Marion Everett (Mrs. Charles D. Mercer) 8
MERCER, Samuel Alfred Browne 6
MERCER, Saul Erastus 4
MERCER, William Fairfield 1
MERCHANT, Frank Ivan 3
MERCHANT, Livingston Tallmadge 7
MERCIER, Armand Theodore 3
MERCIER, Charles Alfred H
MERCK, George Wilhelm 3
MERCUR, Rodney Augustus 1
MERCUR, Ulysses H
MEREDITH, Albert Barrett 2
MEREDITH, Edna Elliott 6
MEREDITH, Edwin Thomas 1
MEREDITH, Edwin Thomas, Jr. 4
MEREDITH, Ernest Sidney 6
MEREDITH, James Alva 2
MEREDITH, James Hargrove 9
MEREDITH, Joseph Carroll 1
MEREDITH, Samuel H
MEREDITH, Virginia Claypool 1
MEREDITH, William Henry 1
MEREDITH, William Morris H
MEREDITH, William Morton 4
MERGEN, Francois 10
MERGENTHALER, Ottmar H
MERGLER, Marie Josepha H
MERIAM, Lewis 7
MERICA, Charles Oliver 1
MERICA, Paul Dyer 3
MERICKA, William John 5
MERIGOLD, Benjamin Shores 5
MERILH, Edmond L. 4
MERILLAT, Louis Adolph 6
MERINGTON, Marguerite 3
MERITT, Edgar Briant 5
MERIVALE, Philip 2

MERIWETHER, Colyer 1
MERIWETHER, David* H
MERIWETHER, Elizabeth Avery 1
MERIWETHER, James H
MERIWETHER, James A. H
MERIWETHER, Lee 4
MERK, Frederick 7
MERKER, Harvey Milton 5
MERKLE, Edward Arrol 8
MERLE, Lawrence J. 9
MERLEAU-PONTY, Maurice
MERLE-SMITH, Van Santvoord 2
MERLE-SMITH, Wilton 1
MERMAN, Ethel 8
MERMEY, Maurice 6
MERMOD, Camille 7
MERNER, Garfield David 5
MÉRO, Yolanda (Mrs. Hermann Irion) 8
MEROLA, Gaetano 6
MEROLA, Mario 9
MERONEY, William Penn 1
MERORY, Joseph 5
MERRELL, Edgar Sanford Keen 2
MERRELL, George R. 4
MERRELL, Herman Stroup 4
MERRELL, Irvin Seward 3
MERRELL, John Hastings 3
MERRELL, John Porter 1
MERRELL, William Dayton 4
MERRIAM, Alan (Parkhurst) 7
MERRIAM, Alexander Ross 1
MERRIAM, Augustus Chapman H
MERRIAM, Carroll Burnham 1
MERRIAM, Charles H
MERRIAM, Charles Edward 3
MERRIAM, Charles J. 7
MERRIAM, Clinton Hart 2
MERRIAM, Edmund Franklin 1
MERRIAM, Eve 10
MERRIAM, Frank Finley 3
MERRIAM, George Spring 1
MERRIAM, Harold Guy 7
MERRIAM, Henry Clay 1
MERRIAM, Henry M. 3
MERRIAM, John Campbell 2
MERRIAM, John Everett 4
MERRIAM, John Francis 9
MERRIAM, Kenneth Gerald 7
MERRIAM, Robert Edward 9
MERRIAM, (Syms) Allen 7
MERRIAM, William Rush 1
MERRIAMN, Myra Hunt Kingman 1
MERRICK, Edward Steele 5
MERRICK, Edwin Thomas Anderson 1
MERRICK, Frank 2
MERRICK, Frederick H
MERRICK, George Edgar 2
MERRICK, George Peck 1
MERRICK, Harry Hopkins 5
MERRICK, Harry L. 1
MERRICK, J. Hartley 3
MERRICK, John Vaughan H
MERRICK, Pliny H
MERRICK, Samuel Vaughan H
MERRICK, Walter Chapman 4
MERRICK, William Duhurst H
MERRICK, William Matthew
MERRIFIELD, Fred 1
MERRIFIELD, Webster 1
MERRILL, Aaron Stanton 1
MERRILL, Abner Hopkins 1
MERRILL, Albert B. 3
MERRILL, Allyne Litchfield 4
MERRILL, Alma Lowell 4
MERRILL, Almos Newlove 5
MERRILL, Ambrose Pond, Jr. 10
MERRILL, Barzille Winfred 3
MERRILL, Beardslee Bliss 4
MERRILL, Cassius Exum 4
MERRILL, Charles Boughton 9
MERRILL, Charles Clarkson 4
MERRILL, Charles Edward 3

MERRILL, Charles Washington 3
MERRILL, Charles White 1
MERRILL, Charles White 5
MERRILL, Cyrus Strong 1
MERRILL, Dana True 3
MERRILL, Daniel 1
MERRILL, Daniel Roy 8
MERRILL, Edward Bagley 1
MERRILL, Edward D. 7
MERRILL, Edward Folsom 4
MERRILL, Edwin Godfrey 2
MERRILL, Edwin Katte 4
MERRILL, Elmer Drew 1
MERRILL, Elmer Truesdell 1
MERRILL, Ezra 9
MERRILL, Francis Ellsworth 5
MERRILL, Frank D. 1
MERRILL, Frank Thayer 4
MERRILL, Frederick Augustus 5
MERRILL, Frederick James Hamilton 1
MERRILL, George Arthur 4
MERRILL, George Earnest 1
MERRILL, George Edmands 1
MERRILL, George Perkins 1
MERRILL, Hamilton 8
MERRILL, Harwood Ferry 8
MERRILL, Henry Ferdinand 1
MERRILL, Hugh Davis 3
MERRILL, James Andrew 1
MERRILL, James Cushing 1
MERRILL, James Griswold 1
MERRILL, James Milford 4
MERRILL, John Buxton 3
MERRILL, John Fuller 2
MERRILL, John Lenord Appleton 2
MERRILL, John Lisgar 5
MERRILL, John Ogden 1
MERRILL, John Putnam 8
MERRILL, Joseph Francis 3
MERRILL, Joseph L. 5
MERRILL, Joseph L. 8
MERRILL, Julia Wright 6
MERRILL, Leon Stephen 1
MERRILL, Louis Taylor 4
MERRILL, Lucius Herbert 1
MERRILL, Maruice Hitchcock 10
MERRILL, Maud Amanda Clarence 8
MERRILL, Melvin 7
MERRILL, Oliver Boutwell 9
MERRILL, Orsamus Cook 1
MERRILL, Oscar Charles 3
MERRILL, Paul Willard 4
MERRILL, Payson 1
MERRILL, Reed Miller 9
MERRILL, Richard Nye 6
MERRILL, Robert Taylor 1
MERRILL, Robert V. 3
MERRILL, Samuel H
MERRILL, Samuel* 1
MERRILL, Selah 1
MERRILL, Stephen Mason 1
MERRILL, Thais A. 4
MERRILL, Thomas Emery 1
MERRILL, William Augustus 4
MERRILL, William Bradford 1
MERRILL, William Emery H
MERRILL, William Fessenden* 1
MERRILL, William Henry 1
MERRILL, William J. 4
MERRILL, William Pierson 3
MERRIMAN, Daniel 1
MERRIMAN, Daniel 8
MERRIMAN, Harry Morton 3
MERRIMAN, Helen Bigelow 4
MERRIMAN, Heminway 9
MERRIMAN, Mansfield 1
MERRIMAN, Myra Hunt Kingman (Mrs. Josiah C.) 1
MERRIMAN, Roger Bigelow 2
MERRIMAN, San Lorenzo 3
MERRIMAN, Thaddeus 1
MERRIMAN, Truman Adams H
MERRIMON, Augustus Summerfield H
MERRING, Harry Lloyd 8
MERRITT, Abraham 2
MERRITT, Anna Lea 4
MERRITT, Arthur Donald 9
MERRITT, Arthur Hastings 4
MERRITT, Dixon Lanier 5

MERRITT, Edwin Atkins 1
MERRITT, Emma Laura Sutro (Mrs. George Washington Merritt) 5
MERRITT, Ernest George 2
MERRITT, Frank 1
MERRITT, Hiram Houston 7
MERRITT, Hiram Houston 8
MERRITT, Hulett Clinton 3
MERRITT, James White 6
MERRITT, Leonidas 1
MERRITT, LeRoy Charles 6
MERRITT, Matthew J. 2
MERRITT, Percival 1
MERRITT, Ralph Palmer 7
MERRITT, Robert Clarence 1
MERRITT, Schuyler 3
MERRITT, Walter Gordon 5
MERRITT, Wesley 1
MERROW, Chester Earl 6
MERRY, Ann Brunton H
MERRY, John Fairfield 1
MERRY, Joseph James 5
MERRY, Robert Watson 4
MERRY, William Lawrence 1
MERRYFIELD, Mary Ainsworth 6
MERRYMAN, Andrew Curtis 1
MERRYWEATHER, George Edmund 1
MERSELES, Theodore Frelinghuysen 1
MERSEREAU, George Jefferson 2
MERSETH, Sidney Ingmar 5
MERSHEIMER, Walter Lyon 8
MERSHON, Martin Luther 1
MERSHON, Ralph Davenport 3
MERSHON, William Butts 2
MERSKEY, Clarence 8
MERSON, Alexander J(ames) 5
MERTENS, George William 6
MERTINS, Gustave Frederick 5
MERTINS, Marshall Louis 5
MERTINS, (Marshall) Louis 6
MERTON, Holmes Whittier 2
MERTON, Thomas 5
MERTZ, Albert 1
MERTZ, Henry Oliver 7
MERTZKE, Arthur John 8
MERVINE, William H
MERVIS, Meyer Bernard 3
MERWIN, Bruce Welch 8
MERWIN, Frederic Eaton 2
MERWIN, Frederic Eaton 7
MERWIN, Henry Childs 1
MERWIN, Herbert Eugene 4
MERWIN, Loring Chase 5
MERWIN, Milton Hervey 1
MERWIN, Orange H
MERWIN, Samuel 1
MERWIN, Samuel Edwin 1
MERWIN, Timothy Dwight 4
MERYMAN, Richard Sumner 4
MERYMAN, Richard Sumner 7
MESCON, Herbert 9
MESEROLE, Clinton V. 6
MESEROLE, Clinton Vanderbilt 1
MESERVE, Charles Francis 4
MESERVE, Frederic Hill 4
MESERVE, Harry Chamberlain 1
MESERVE, John Bartlett 2
MESERVE, Nathaniel H
MESERVE, Shirley Edwin 8
MESICK, Jane Louise 4
MESICK, William S. 4
MESS, Otto 1
MESSENGER, J. Franklin 3
MESSENGER, North Overton 1
MESSENGER, Robert Pocock 4
MESSER, Alpha 1
MESSER, Asa 1
MESSER, Edmund Clarence 1
MESSER, L. Wilbur 1
MESSER, Samuel 1
MESSER, William Stuart 4
MESSERSMITH, George S. 3
MESSERSMITH, George S. 4
MESSIAEN, Olivier 10
MESSICK, John Decatur 10
MESSINA, Angelina Rose 5
MESSING, Abraham Joseph 1

MESSINGER, Charles Raymond 1
MESSINGER, Edwin John 4
MESSINGER, William Henry 9
MESSITER, Arthur Henry 1
MESSLER, Eugene Lawrence 5
MESSLER, Thomas Doremus H
MESSMER, Sebastian Gebhard 1
MESSMORE, Fred W(ilber) 9
MESSNER, Julian 2
MESSNER, Kathryn G. 2
MESTA, Frank Albert 4
MESTA, L. W. 3
MESTA, Perle 6
MESTERN, H. Edward 5
MESTRES, Ricardo Angelo 8
MESTREZAT, Stephen Leslie 1
MESTROVIC, Ivan 4
METCALF, Arunah H
METCALF, Clarence Sheridan 6
METCALF, Clell Lee 2
METCALF, Edward Potter 4
METCALF, Frank Albert 7
METCALF, Frank Arthur 1
METCALF, George P. 3
METCALF, George Wallace 4
METCALF, Haven 2
METCALF, Henry Brewer 1
METCALF, Henry Harrison 1
METCALF, Irving Wight 1
METCALF, Jesse Houghton 2
METCALF, Joel Hastings 1
METCALF, John Calvin 2
METCALF, John Milton Putnam 4
METCALF, John Thomas 8
METCALF, Keyes DeWitt 8
METCALF, Lee 7
METCALF, Leonard 1
METCALF, Lorettus Sutton 1
METCALF, Martin Kellogg 6
METCALF, Maynard Mayo 1
METCALF, Michael Pierce 9
METCALF, Ralph 1
METCALF, Stephen Olney 3
METCALF, Theron H
METCALF, Thomas Nelson 8
METCALF, Victor Howard 1
METCALF, Wilder Stevens 1
METCALF, Willard Leroy 1
METCALF, William 1
METCALF, Zeno Payne 4
METCALFE, George Richmond 1
METCALFE, Henry 4
METCALFE, Henry Bleecker H
METCALFE, James Stetson 1
METCALFE, Ralph H. 2
METCALFE, Richard Lee 3
METCALFE, Samuel Lytler H
METCALFE, Thomas H
METCALFE, Tristram Walker 3
METEYARD, Thomas Buford 1
METHOD, Harold Lambert 9
METTAUER, John Peter H
METTEN, John Farrell 5
METTEN, William F. 5
METTLER, John Wyckoff 3
METTLER, L. Harrison 4
METTS, John Van Bokkelen 5
METZ, Abraham Louis 4
METZ, Albert Frederick 4
METZ, Arthur Ray 4
METZ, Carl Altgeld 9
METZ, Charles William 6
METZ, Christian H
METZ, Herman A. 1
METZDORF, Robert Frederick 6
METZENBAUM, Myron Firth 2
METZGAR, Charles Watson 4
METZGER, Delbert Everner 4
METZGER, Earl H. 8
METZGER, Fraser 3
METZGER, Frederick Elder 3
METZGER, Herman Arthur 6
METZGER, Hutzel 3
METZGER, Irvin Dilling 3
METZGER, Leon Daniel 9
METZGER, Ralph Alfred 5

MILLER, Charles Addison 2
MILLER, Charles Armand 1
MILLER, Charles C. 1
MILLER, Charles Ervine 1
MILLER, Charles Franklin 5
MILLER, Charles Henry 1
MILLER, Charles Lewis 4
MILLER, Charles Mosher 6
MILLER, C(harles) Phillip, 9
Jr.
MILLER, Charles R. 1
MILLER, Charles R. D. 4
MILLER, Charles Ransom 1
MILLER, Charles Russel 1
MILLER, Charles Wesley 1
MILLER, Charles Wilbur 3
MILLER, Charles William 1
Emil
MILLER, Christian Otto 3
Gerberding
MILLER, Cincinnatus 1
Heine
MILLER, Clarence A. 3
MILLER, Clarence B. 1
MILLER, Clarence Ross 8
MILLER, Claude Rue 9
MILLER, Clement 4
Woodnutt
MILLER, Clemmy Olin 7
MILLER, Clifton 9
McPherson
MILLER, Clyde Raymond 8
MILLER, Clyde Winwood 5
MILLER, Crosby Parke 1
MILLER, Daniel Fry H
MILLER, Daniel H. H
MILLER, Daniel Long 1
MILLER, Darius 1
MILLER, David Aaron 3
MILLER, David Franklin 9
MILLER, David Lewis 5
MILLER, David Louis 9
MILLER, David P. 7
MILLER, David Philip 10
MILLER, Dayton Clarence 1
MILLER, Dean Edgar 8
MILLER, Delmas Ferguson 9
MILLER, Dewitt 1
MILLER, Dick 5
MILLER, Dickinson 4
Sergeant
MILLER, Don Clark 5
MILLER, Don Hugo 5
MILLER, Donald Richard 10
MILLER, Donald Sidney 10
MILLER, Donald William 8
MILLER, Dudley 5
Livingston
MILLER, E. P. Smith 1
MILLER, Edgar Calvin 5
Leroy
MILLER, Edgar Grim, Jr. 3
MILLER, Edmund Howd 1
MILLER, Edmund 3
Thornton
MILLER, Edmund W. 4
MILLER, Edward Alanson 4
MILLER, Edward August 9
MILLER, Edward Furber 4
MILLER, Edward Godfrey 7
MILLER, Edward Godfrey, 5
Jr.
MILLER, Edward Terhune 1
MILLER, Edward Tylor 4
MILLER, Edward Waite 1
MILLER, Edward Whitney 6
MILLER, Edward William 10
MILLER, Edwin Lang 8
MILLER, Edwin Lee 2
MILLER, Edwin Lillie 1
MILLER, Edwin Morton 6
MILLER, Elihu Spencer H
MILLER, Elizabeth Cavert 9
MILLER, Elizabeth Smith 1
MILLER, Emerson R. 1
MILLER, Emily 5
Huntington
MILLER, Emily Van Dorn 8
MILLER, Emma Guffey 5
MILLER, Ephraim 1
MILLER, Ernest B. 3
MILLER, Ernest Henry 1
MILLER, Ernest Ivan 5
MILLER, Ethel Hull 4
MILLER, Eugene Harper 1
MILLER, E(ugene) 5
K(earfott)
MILLER, Eugene Walter 3
MILLER, Ezra H
MILLER, Fern V. 9
MILLER, Flora Whitney 9
MILLER, Florence Lowden 9
(Mrs. C. Phillip Miller)
MILLER, Francis Garner 1
MILLER, Francis Pickens 7
MILLER, Francis Trevelyn 2
MILLER, Frank 9

MILLER, Frank A. 4
MILLER, Frank Augustus 1
MILLER, Frank Ebenezer 1
MILLER, Frank Harvey 1
MILLER, Frank Justus 1
MILLER, Frank William 4
MILLER, Franklin Thomas 1
MILLER, Fred J. 1
MILLER, Fred W. 2
MILLER, Frederic Howell 4
MILLER, Frederic K(elper) 6
MILLER, Frederic Magoun 3
MILLER, Frederick A.* 3
MILLER, Freeman Edwin 4
MILLER, Frieda Segelke 6
MILLER, G. F. 5
MILLER, Galen 5
MILLER, George 3
MILLER, George 4
MILLER, George Abram 5
MILLER, George Carter 1
MILLER, George E. 1
MILLER, George Frederick 4
MILLER, George Funston H
MILLER, George Henry 5
MILLER, George Henry 6
MILLER, George Lee 1
MILLER, George M. H
MILLER, George 1
MacCulloch
MILLER, George McAnelly 4
MILLER, George Morey 1
MILLER, George Noyes 1
MILLER, George Paul 9
MILLER, George Roland 10
MILLER, George Stewart 5
MILLER, George Tyler 9
MILLER, Gerrit Smith 1
MILLER, Gerrit Smith, Jr. 3
MILLER, Gilbert Heron 5
MILLER, Gladys 10
MILLER, Glenn 2
MILLER, Grace Moncrieff 1
MILLER, Gray 2
MILLER, Gustavus 1
Hindman
MILLER, Harlan 5
MILLER, Harold C. 3
MILLER, Harold F. 5
MILLER, Harold William 7
MILLER, Harriet Mann 1
MILLER, Harry (Mckinley) 4
MILLER, Harry Edward 1
MILLER, Harry Irving 9
MILLER, Harry William 7
MILLER, Harvey H. 3
MILLER, Hazel Belle 6
MILLER, Helen Richards 2
Guthrie
MILLER, Helen Topping 3
MILLER, Helen Topping 1
MILLER, Henry* 1
MILLER, Henry 4
MILLER, Henry (Valentine) 7
MILLER, Henry B. 1
MILLER, Henry Russell 3
MILLER, Henry Watkins 1
MILLER, Henry Willard 7
MILLER, Herbert 5
Adolphus
MILLER, Herbert John 10
MILLER, Hilliard Eve 2
MILLER, Homer Virgil H
Milton
MILLER, Horace Alden 1
MILLER, Howard Shultz 6
MILLER, Hugh 6
MILLER, Hugo Eugene 6
MILLER, Humphreys 1
Henry Clay
MILLER, Irving Elgar 5
MILLER, Isaac Eugene 3
MILLER, J. Jay 1
MILLER, J. M. C. 4
MILLER, J. Martin 4
MILLER, J. Maxwell 1
MILLER, Jacob F. 1
MILLER, Jacob Welsh H
MILLER, Jacob William 1
MILLER, James 1
MILLER, James Alexander 2
MILLER, James Collins 1
MILLER, James Conelese 3
MILLER, James Decatur, 5
Jr.
MILLER, James Kenneth 5
MILLER, James Monroe 4
MILLER, James Roscoe 7
MILLER, James Russell 1
MILLER, Jesse H
MILLER, Jesse Isidor 2
MILLER, Joaquin 6
MILLER, John* H
MILLER, John 1
MILLER, John Anthony 1
MILLER, John Barnes 1
MILLER, John Bleecker 4

MILLER, John Briggs 4
MILLER, John Calvin 1
MILLER, John D. 2
MILLER, John Elvis 9
MILLER, John Eschelman 1
MILLER, John Ford 4
MILLER, John Franklin 1
MILLER, John Franklin* 1
MILLER, John Gaines H
MILLER, John Henderson 1
MILLER, John Henry 1
MILLER, John Jose 8
MILLER, John King 6
MILLER, John L. 7
MILLER, John Maffit, Jr. 1
MILLER, John Richardson 4
MILLER, John Robinson, 8
Jr.
MILLER, John Rulon, Jr. 1
MILLER, John S. 4
MILLER, John Stocker 1
MILLER, J(ohn) Wesley 7
MILLER, Jonathan H
Peckham
MILLER, Joseph H
MILLER, Joseph Dana 1
MILLER, Joseph Henry 3
MILLER, Joseph Hillis 3
MILLER, Joseph Leggett 1
MILLER, Joseph Nelson 1
MILLER, Joseph Torrence 1
MILLER, Josiah H
MILLER, Julian Creighton 10
MILLER, Julian Creighton 5
MILLER, Julian Howell 4
MILLER, Julian Malcolm 7
MILLER, Julian Sidney 2
MILLER, Julius Sumner 9
MILLER, Justin 5
MILLER, Kelly 2
MILLER, Kempster 1
Blanchard
MILLER, Kenneth Dexter 8
MILLER, Kenneth S. 6
MILLER, Kennth Hayes 5
MILLER, Knox Emerson 5
MILLER, Lawrence 4
William
MILLER, Lee Graham 4
MILLER, Leo P. 4
MILLER, Leo Edward 3
MILLER, Leo L. 5
MILLER, Leslie Andrew 5
MILLER, Leslie Andrew 7
MILLER, Leslie Freeland 3
MILLER, Leslie Haynes 10
MILLER, Leslie William 1
MILLER, Leverett 1
Saltonstall
MILLER, Lewis H
MILLER, Lewis Bennett 4
MILLER, Lloyd Ivan 10
MILLER, Logan C. 3
MILLER, Loren 4
MILLER, Loren Barker 3
MILLER, Louise Klein 2
MILLER, Loye Holmes 5
MILLER, Loye Wheat 9
MILLER, Lucius Hopkins 2
MILLER, Luther Deck 5
MILLER, Lyle Leslie 9
MILLER, M. Clare 7
MILLER, M. Hughes 10
MILLER, M. V. 3
MILLER, Malcolm E. 4
MILLER, Marcus P. 1
MILLER, Marie Tastevin 8
MILLER, Marion Mills 4
MILLER, Mary Britton 6
MILLER, Mary Rogers 4
MILLER, Maude Murray 1
MILLER, Max 4
MILLER, Max 5
MILLER, Max 7
MILLER, Max Arnold 10
MILLER, Melville Winans 4
MILLER, Merle 9
MILLER, Merrill 1
MILLER, Merritt Finley 5
MILLER, Michael A. 4
MILLER, Milton 5
MILLER, Milton A. 1
MILLER, Morris Smith H
MILLER, Nathan H
MILLER, Nathan L. 3
MILLER, Nellie Burget 3
MILLER, Neville 7
MILLER, Newton 4
MILLER, Ogden Dayton 5
MILLER, Olive Thorne 1
MILLER, Oliver Chester 6
MILLER, Orie Otis 7
MILLER, O(rris) J(oseph) 1
MILLER, Oscar Phineas 1
MILLER, Otto 3
MILLER, Park Hays 6

MILLER, Park Hays, Jr. 9
MILLER, Paul 10
MILLER, Paul Duryea 1
MILLER, Paul E. 3
MILLER, Paul Gerard 3
MILLER, Perry 4
MILLER, Perry B. 1
MILLER, Peter Paul 10
MILLER, Pleasant H
Moorman
MILLER, Pleasant Thomas 5
MILLER, R. Paul 4
MILLER, R. T., Jr. 3
MILLER, Ralph English 3
MILLER, Ralph James 8
MILLER, Ransford Stevens 1
MILLER, Ray Haggard 6
MILLER, Ray T. 4
MILLER, Raymond Wiley 10
MILLER, Reed 1
MILLER, Richard Arthur 10
MILLER, Richard E. 1
MILLER, Richard E. 2
MILLER, Richard Henry 3
MILLER, Richard 4
Thompson
MILLER, Robert Frederick 5
MILLER, Robert Johnson 1
MILLER, Robert Justin 9
MILLER, Robert Lee 7
MILLER, Robert 1
Netherland
MILLER, Robert Rowland 5
MILLER, Robert Talbott 1
MILLER, Robert Talbott, 4
Jr.
MILLER, Robert Walter 4
MILLER, Robert Warren 6
MILLER, Robert Watt 5
MILLER, Roger 2
MILLER, Roger Dean 10
MILLER, Roscoe Earl 1
MILLER, Roswell 1
MILLER, Rufus Wilder 1
MILLER, Russell 1
MILLER, Russell Benjamin 4
MILLER, Russell Cooper 6
MILLER, Russell King 1
MILLER, Rutger Bleecker H
MILLER, Samuel Charles 3
MILLER, Samuel Duncan 1
MILLER, Samuel Franklin H
MILLER, Samuel Freeman H
MILLER, Samuel Haas 3
MILLER, Samuel Howard 5
MILLER, Samuel Martin 8
MILLER, Samuel Warren 1
MILLER, Samuel William 1
MILLER, Seton Ingersoll 6
MILLER, Shackelford 1
MILLER, Sidney Lincoln 3
MILLER, Sidney 1
Trowbridge
MILLER, Smith H
MILLER, Spencer, Sr. 3
MILLER, Stephen Decatur H
MILLER, Stephen Ivan 5
MILLER, Stewart Edward 10
MILLER, Sydney 2
Robotham
MILLER, Theodore Joseph 3
MILLER, Thomas Condit 4
MILLER, Thomas Marshall 1
MILLER, Thomas Root 4
MILLER, Thomas 7
Woodnutt
MILLER, Thurman (Dusty 7
Miller)
MILLER, Troup 1
MILLER, Vaughn 4
MILLER, Vernon Xavier 9
MILLER, Victor Charles 4
MILLER, Victor Joseph 8
MILLER, W. Earl 4
MILLER, W. Leslie 2
MILLER, Walter 3
MILLER, Walter H. 9
MILLER, Walter John 1
MILLER, Walter McNab 4
MILLER, Walter Richard 1
MILLER, Walther Martin 10
MILLER, Ward (Amos) 8
MILLER, Warner 1
MILLER, Warren Drake 8
MILLER, Warren Hastings 1
MILLER, Watson B. 4
MILLER, Webb 1
MILLER, Wilbur K. 6
MILLER, Wilbur K. 1
MILLER, Wilhelm 5
MILLER, William H
MILLER, William 1
MILLER, William Christian 8
MILLER, William Davis 4
MILLER, William E. 3
MILLER, William Ernest 7

MILLER, William Henry H
MILLER, William Henry 1
Harrison
MILLER, William Jasper 4
MILLER, William Jennings 3
MILLER, William 10
McKinley
MILLER, William Morrison 4
MILLER, William 1
Niswonger
MILLER, William Rickarby H
MILLER, William Snow 1
MILLER, William Starr H
MILLER, William Todd 1
MILLER, William Whipple 7
MILLER, William Wilson 1
MILLER, Willis Dance 4
MILLES, Carl Wilhelm 3
Emil
MILLET, Clarence 3
MILLET, Francis Davis 1
MILLET, John Alfred 6
Parsons
MILLET, John Alfred 7
Parsons
MILLETT, Fred Benjamin 6
MILLETT, George Van 5
MILLETTE, John W. 2
MILLHAUSER, Dewitt 2
MILLICAN, George 10
Everett
MILLIGAN, Alexander 1
Reed
MILLIGAN, Burton 8
Aliviere
MILLIGAN, Edward 1
MILLIGAN, Ezra McLeod 1
MILLIGAN, Harold V. 3
MILLIGAN, Jacob L. 3
MILLIGAN, John Jones H
MILLIGAN, Lucy 8
Richardson (Mrs. Harold
V. Milligan)
MILLIGAN, Melvin Lee 4
MILLIGAN, Orlando 3
Howard
MILLIGAN, Robert Wiley 1
MILLIGAN, Samuel 4
MILLIGAN, William 1
Edwin
MILLIGAN, W(infred) 8
O(liver)
MILLIKAN, Clark 4
Blanchard
MILLIKAN, George Lee 2
MILLIKAN, Max Franklin 5
MILLIKAN, Robert 3
Andrews
MILLIKEN, Arnold White 4
MILLIKEN, Carl Elias 4
MILLIKEN, Charles M. 8
MILLIKEN, Edwin C. 4
MILLIKEN, Frank Roscoe 10
MILLIKEN, Gerrish H. 2
MILLIKEN, John Barnes 4
MILLIKEN, John David 4
MILLIKEN, Joseph K. 4
MILLIKEN, Joseph 1
Knowles
MILLIKEN, Mahlon 8
G(eorge)
MILLIKEN, Seth Llewellyn H
MILLIKEN, Seth Mellen 1
MILLIKEN, William 8
Mathewson
MILLIKEN, William 6
Thomas
MILLIKIN, Benjamin L. 1
MILLIKIN, Eugene Donald 3
MILLIKIN, Severance 10
Allen
MILLIMAN, Elmer 2
Edward
MILLIN, Lucinda Alfreda 9
MILLIN, Sarah Gertrude 5
MILLING, Robert Edward 2
MILLING, Robert Edward, 4
Jr.
MILLING, Roberts Clay 7
MILLINGTON, Charles 1
Stephen
MILLINGTON, Ernest 3
John Oldknow
MILLION, Elmer Mayse 10
MILLION, John Wilson 1
MILLIS, Harry Alvin 2
MILLIS, Harry Lee 2
MILLIS, John 3
MILLIS, Wade 1
MILLIS, Walter 5
MILLIS, William Alfred 2
MILLMAN, Edward 4
MILLMAN, Jacob 10
MILLMAN, Peter 10
MacKenzie
MILLMAN, Ronald Burton 10
MILLNER, Walker Leroy 4

MONTEZUMA, Carlos 1
MONTGOMERIE, John H
MONTGOMERY, A. E. 5
MONTGOMERY, Alfred 4
E.
MONTGOMERY, 5
Benjamin F.
MONTGOMERY, Charles 2
Carroll
MONTGOMERY, Daniel, H
Jr.
MONTGOMERY, Deane 10
MONTGOMERY, 4
Douglass William
MONTGOMERY, Edmund 1
Duncan
MONTGOMERY, Edna 5
Morley
MONTGOMERY, Edward 8
MONTGOMERY, Edward 1
Emmet
MONTGOMERY, Edward 6
Gerrard
MONTGOMERY, Edward 1
Louis
MONTGOMERY, Emery 7
W(atkins)
MONTGOMERY, Emily P. 5
(Mrs. E. Geoffrey
Montgomery)
MONTGOMERY, Fletcher 2
H.
MONTGOMERY, Francis 9
Rhodes
MONTGOMERY, Frank 1
Hugh
MONTGOMERY, George 1
MONTGOMERY, George 8
MONTGOMERY, George 6
Granville
MONTGOMERY, George 3
Hugh Alexander
MONTGOMERY, George 2
Redington
MONTGOMERY, George H
Washington
MONTGOMERY, Guy 3
MONTGOMERY, Harry 7
MONTGOMERY, Harry 10
Thomas
MONTGOMERY, Helen 1
Barrett
MONTGOMERY, Henry 3
Arthur
MONTGOMERY, Henry 7
Close, Jr.
MONTGOMERY, J. Knox 5
MONTGOMERY, Jack 5
Percival
MONTGOMERY, James H
MONTGOMERY, James 5
Alan
MONTGOMERY, James 7
Alan, Jr.
MONTGOMERY, James 1
Eglinton
MONTGOMERY, James 5
Llewellyn
MONTGOMERY, James 3
Shera
MONTGOMERY, Jeff 8
MONTGOMERY, John H
MONTGOMERY, John H
Berrien
MONTGOMERY, John 3
Flournoy
MONTGOMERY, John H
Gallagher
MONTGOMERY, John 1
Harold
MONTGOMERY, John 6
Rhea
MONTGOMERY, John 1
Rogerson
MONTGOMERY, Joseph H
MONTGOMERY, Joseph 8
Webster, Jr.
MONTGOMERY, Joseph 8
West
MONTGOMERY, Mack 4
Allen
MONTGOMERY, Mary 5
Williams
MONTGOMERY, Morris
Carpenter
MONTGOMERY, Oscar
Hilton
MONTGOMERY, Paul 7
Vaughn
MONTGOMERY, R. Ames 3
MONTGOMERY, Richard H
MONTGOMERY, Richard 3
D.
MONTGOMERY, Richard
Mattern
MONTGOMERY, Robert 1
MONTGOMERY, Robert 8

MONTGOMERY, Robert 3
Hiester
MONTGOMERY, Robert 8
Humphrey
MONTGOMERY, Robert 1
M.
MONTGOMERY, Robert 4
Nathaniel
MONTGOMERY, Roselle 1
Mercier
MONTGOMERY, Royal 10
Ewert
MONTGOMERY, 10
Rutherford George
MONTGOMERY, S. A. 4
MONTGOMERY, Samuel 1
Thomas
MONTGOMERY, Spencer 9
Bishop
MONTGOMERY, T. T. 7
MONTGOMERY, Thomas H
MONTGOMERY, Thomas 1
Harrison, Jr.
MONTGOMERY, Thomas 1
Lynch
MONTGOMERY, Valda 3
Stewart
MONTGOMERY, Victor 4
MONTGOMERY, Whitney 4
Maxwell
MONTGOMERY, William* H
MONTGOMERY, William 3
MONTGOMERY, William 1
Coons
MONTGOMERY, William 3
Woodrow, Jr.
MONTGOMERY OF 6
ALAMEIN, 1St Viscount
of Hindhead
MONTGOMERY OF 8
ALAMEIN, 1st Viscount
of Hindhead (Field
Marshal Bernard Law
Montgomery)
MONTHERLANT, Henry 5
De
MONTONNA, Ralph E. 3
MONTOYA, Atanasio 1
MONTOYA, Joseph M. 7
MONTOYA, Nestor 1
MONTRESOR, James H
Gabriel
MONTRESOR, John H
MONTROLL, Elliott 8
Waters
MONTROSS, Lynn 4
MONTZHEIMER, Arthur 5
MOOAR, Sherman 5
MOOD, Francis Asbury H
MOOD, Orlando Clarendon 3
MOODIE, Campbell 5
MOODIE, Roy Lee 1
MOODY, Blair 3
MOODY, Clarence 8
L(emuel)
MOODY, Dan 4
MOODY, Dwight Lyman 3
MOODY, Ernest Addison 6
MOODY, Frank Sims 1
MOODY, Gideon Curtis 1
MOODY, H. W. 3
MOODY, Herbert 2
Raymond
MOODY, James H
MOODY, Joseph Burnley 1
MOODY, Lewis Ferry 3
MOODY, Malcolm 4
Adelbert
MOODY, Nelson Kingsland 1
MOODY, Paul H
MOODY, Paul Dwight 2
MOODY, Robert Earle 8
MOODY, Sidney Clarke 6
MOODY, Virginia Green 1
MOODY, Walter Dwight 1
MOODY, Walter Sherman 1
MOODY, William Henry 1
MOODY, William Lewis, 3
Jr.
MOODY, William Revell 1
MOODY, William Vaughn 1
MOODY, Winfield Scott 4
MOODY, Zenas Ferry 1
MOOG, Wilson Townsend 3
MOON, Carl 2
MOON, Don P. 2
MOON, Edwin G. 1
MOON, Franklin 1
MOON, Grace 2
MOON, Henry Dukso 6
MOON, John Austin 1
MOON, Marjorie Ruth 10
MOON, Parker Thomas 1
MOON, Reuben Osborne 4
MOON, Truman Jesse 1
MOON, Virgil Holland 6
MOON, Warren G. 10

MOON, William Deaderick 8
MOONEY, Charles A. 1
MOONEY, Charles Patrick 1
Joseph
MOONEY, Daniel Francis 1
MOONEY, Edmund L. 1
MOONEY, Edward 3
Cardinal
MOONEY, Eugene Francis 5
MOONEY, Franklin D. 4
MOONEY, George Austin 7
MOONEY, Guy 4
MOONEY, Henry Keppler 7
MOONEY, James 1
MOONEY, James David 3
MOONEY, James Elliott 5
MOONEY, James Garth 5
MOONEY, Joseph F. 1
MOONEY, Joseph W. 4
MOONEY, Robert 1
Johnstone
MOONEY, Robert Lee 4
MOONEY, Urban Drening 1
MOONEY, William H
MOONEY, William C. 4
MOONEY, William M. 3
MOONEYHAM, Walter 10
Stanley
MOONLIGHT, Thomas 1
MOOR, Elizabeth I. 4
MOOR, Wyman Bradbury H
Seavy
MOORA, Robert L(orenzo) 5
MOORE, Addison Webster 1
MOORE, Albert Burton 4
MOORE, Albert Voorhis 3
MOORE, Albert Weston 4
MOORE, Alexander Pollock 1
MOORE, Alfred H
MOORE, Alfred Stibbs 1
MOORE, Alice Medora 1
Rogers
MOORE, Allen, II 5
MOORE, Allen Francis 5
MOORE, Andrew H
MOORE, Andrew Charles 1
MOORE, Anne Carroll 4
MOORE, Ansley 1
Cunningham
MOORE, Arthur Harry 3
MOORE, Arthur James 6
MOORE, Aubertine 1
Woodward
MOORE, Aubrey Shannon 3
MOORE, Austin Talley 4
MOORE, Barrington 7
MOORE, Bartholomew H
Figures
MOORE, Ben Wheeler 3
MOORE, Benjamin H
MOORE, Benson B(ond) 7
MOORE, Bertha Pearl 1
MOORE, Blaine Free 1
MOORE, Bob 3
MOORE, Bruce 7
MOORE, Bruce 8
MOORE, Bryant Edward 3
MOORE, Burton Evans 1
MOORE, C. Ellis 1
MOORE, C. Ulysses 1
MOORE, Carl Allphin 6
MOORE, Carl Richard 3
MOORE, Carl Vernon 5
MOORE, Charles 2
MOORE, Charles Albert 4
MOORE, Charles Alexander 4
MOORE, Charles Arthur 1
MOORE, Charles Arthur 3
MOORE, Charles Brainard 1
Taylor
MOORE, Charles Cadwell 1
MOORE, Charles Calvin 3
MOORE, Charles Forrest 1
MOORE, Charles Henkel 8
MOORE, Charles Herbert 1
MOORE, Charles James 2
MOORE, Charles Leonard 1
MOORE, Charles Lothrop 1
MOORE, Charles Napoleon 7
MOORE, Clarence 1
Bloomfield
MOORE, Clarence King 5
MOORE, Clarence Lemuel 1
Elisha
MOORE, Clement Clarke H
MOORE, Clifford Herschel 1
MOORE, Clyde B. 6
MOORE, D. McFarlan 1
MOORE, Dale Grant 8
MOORE, Dan Killian 9
MOORE, Daniel Decatur 1
MOORE, David Channing 7
MOORE, David Hastings 1
MOORE, David Richard 3
MOORE, Dewitt Van 5
Deusen
MOORE, Douglas Ross 9

MOORE, Douglas Stuart 5
MOORE, Dunlop 1
MOORE, Dwight Munson 9
MOORE, E. E. 4
MOORE, Earl Vincent 9
MOORE, Edmond H. 1
MOORE, Edmund Joseph 4
MOORE, Edward, Jr. 3
MOORE, Edward Bruce 1
MOORE, Edward Caldwell 2
MOORE, Edward Colman 1
MOORE, Edward Frederick 10
MOORE, Edward H. 3
MOORE, Edward James 2
MOORE, Edward Jay 1
MOORE, Edward Mott 1
MOORE, Edward Roberts 3
MOORE, Edward Small 2
MOORE, Edward W. 1
MOORE, Edwin King 1
MOORE, Edwin Ward 1
MOORE, Elbert Edmund 4
MOORE, Eliakim Hastings 1
MOORE, Ella Maude 3
MOORE, Elon Howard 3
MOORE, Ely H
MOORE, Emmett Burris 9
MOORE, Ernest Carroll 3
MOORE, Ernest Carroll, Jr. 5
MOORE, Escum Lionel 6
MOORE, Ethelbert Allen 3
MOORE, Eva Perry 1
MOORE, Filmore 1
MOORE, Forris Jewett 1
MOORE, Francis 1
MOORE, Francis Cruger 4
MOORE, Frank A. 1
MOORE, Frank Charles 10
MOORE, Frank Gardner 3
MOORE, Frank Horace 1
MOORE, Frank Lincoln 1
MOORE, Frank R. 4
MOORE, Frank Stanley 9
MOORE, Franklin 1
Benjamin
MOORE, Franklin 8
Harkness
MOORE, Fred Atkins 3
MOORE, Fred Holmsley 9
MOORE, Frederick 5
MOORE, Frederick 1
Ferdinand
MOORE, Frederick 1
Wightman
MOORE, Frontis H. 10
MOORE, G. Bedell 1
MOORE, Gabriel H
MOORE, George Andrew 2
MOORE, George Curtis 9
MOORE, George Edward 4
MOORE, George F. 2
MOORE, George Fleming 3
MOORE, George Foot 1
MOORE, George Gail 5
MOORE, George Godfrey 1
MOORE, George Gordon 6
MOORE, George Henry H
MOORE, George Herbert 1
MOORE, George Thomas 3
MOORE, George Thomas 2
MOORE, Grace 2
MOORE, H. Humphrey 1
MOORE, Harold Emerson 6
MOORE, Harold Emery, Jr. 7
MOORE, Harrie G. 5
MOORE, Harrison Bray 5
MOORE, Harry H. 3
MOORE, Harry Hascall 2
MOORE, Harry Lee 7
MOORE, Harry T. 7
MOORE, Harry T. 8
MOORE, Harry Tunis 1
MOORE, Harry William 6
MOORE, Harvey Wilson 7
MOORE, Helen 4
MOORE, Heman Allen 1
MOORE, Henrietta Greer 1
MOORE, Sir Henry H
MOORE, Henry 9
MOORE, H(enry) Coleman, 10
Jr.
MOORE, Henry Dunning H
MOORE, Henry Frank 1
MOORE, Henry Hoyt 4
MOORE, Henry Lynn 1
MOORE, Henry Thomas 7
MOORE, Henry Trumbull 6
MOORE, Herbert McComb 2
MOORE, Hight C. 3
MOORE, Hollis Andrew, 7
Jr.
MOORE, Houston Burger 4
MOORE, Howard Earle 7
MOORE, Hoyt Augustus 3
MOORE, Hudson, Jr. 1
MOORE, Hugh 5
MOORE, Hugh Benton 5

MOORE, Hugh Kelsea 1
MOORE, Hugh Ramsay 7
MOORE, Ira Allen 7
MOORE, Irwin L. 5
MOORE, Isaac Sadler 5
MOORE, J. Howard 1
MOORE, J. Percey 4
MOORE, J. W. E. 5
MOORE, Jacob Bailey H
MOORE, James* H
MOORE, James Edward 1
MOORE, James Gregory 5
MOORE, James Hobart 1
MOORE, James Miles 1
MOORE, James Patrick, Jr. 7
MOORE, James W. 1
MOORE, Jared Sparks 3
MOORE, Jean Oliver 10
MOORE, Jere 2
MOORE, Jesse Hale H
MOORE, John* H
MOORE, John* 1
MOORE, John Bassett 2
MOORE, John Cecil 5
MOORE, John Chandler 2
MOORE, John Cunningham 4
MOORE, John D. 1
MOORE, John Denis 10
Joseph
MOORE, John Ferguson 5
MOORE, John G. 4
MOORE, John Leverett 4
MOORE, John M. 1
MOORE, John Merrick 3
MOORE, John Milton 2
MOORE, John Monroe 2
MOORE, John Peabody 6
MOORE, John Small 5
MOORE, John Trotwood 1
MOORE, Mrs. John 3
Trotwood
MOORE, John W. 1
MOORE, John Walker 3
MOORE, John Weeks H
MOORE, John White 1
MOORE, John William 2
MOORE, Joseph 1
MOORE, Joseph Arthur 1
MOORE, Joseph B. 1
MOORE, Joseph Earle 3
MOORE, Joseph Haines 2
MOORE, J(oseph) 5
Hampton
MOORE, Joseph Marion 7
MOORE, Joseph Waldron 6
MOORE, Josiah John 4
MOORE, Josiah Staunton 4
MOORE, Julian H. 1
MOORE, Kenneth W. 5
MOORE, Laban Theodore H
MOORE, Laurence 10
MOORE, Leonard Page 8
MOORE, Lewis Baxter 4
MOORE, Lillian 4
MOORE, Lillian Russell 1
MOORE, Louis Herbert 1
MOORE, Lyle Stickley 3
MOORE, Lyman Sweet 3
MOORE, Marianne Craig 5
MOORE, Mark Egbert 5
MOORE, Mary 3
MOORE, Mary Norman 5
MOORE, Maurice H
MOORE, Maurice Edwin 9
MOORE, Maurice Malcolm 4
MOORE, Maurice 9
Thompson
MOORE, Merrill 3
MOORE, Miles Conway 1
MOORE, Miller 8
MOORE, Milton Harvey 5
MOORE, Mrs. N. Hudson 1
MOORE, Nathan Grier 2
MOORE, Nathaniel 1
Drummond
MOORE, Nathaniel Fish H
MOORE, O. Otto 10
MOORE, Olin Harris 7
MOORE, Orren Cheney H
MOORE, Orval Floyd 3
MOORE, Oscar Fitzallen H
MOORE, Paul 3
MOORE, Paul H. 4
MOORE, Paul J. 4
MOORE, Philip North 1
MOORE, Philip Wyatt 6
MOORE, Randle T. 5
MOORE, Ransom Asa 1
MOORE, Raymond Cecil 6
MOORE, Richard Albert 10
MOORE, Richard Bishop 1
MOORE, Richard Channing H
MOORE, Richard Curtis 4
MOORE, Robert H
MOORE, Robert 1
MOORE, Robert Allan 5
MOORE, Robert B(ryson) 9

MOORE, Robert Foster 4
MOORE, Robert H(arris) 5
MOORE, Robert Lee 4
MOORE, Robert Lee 5
MOORE, Robert Lee 6
MOORE, Robert Lee 7
MOORE, Robert Martin 3
MOORE, Robert McDonald 4
MOORE, Robert Murray 4
MOORE, Robert S. 1
MOORE, Robert Thomas 3
MOORE, Robert Walton 1
MOORE, Robert Webber 4
MOORE, Roberts Cosby 5
MOORE, Roderick Dunn 8
MOORE, Roger Allan 10
MOORE, Roy 3
MOORE, Roy W. 5
MOORE, Royal Archibald 7
MOORE, Rupert Eastmer 5
MOORE, Ruth 9
MOORE, Samuel H
MOORE, Samuel 1
MOORE, Samuel McDowell H
MOORE, Samuel Preston H
MOORE, Samuel Wallace 1
MOORE, Sherwood 4
MOORE, Stanford 8
MOORE, Stephen 1
MOORE, Sydenham H
MOORE, Thomas H
MOORE, Thomas Joseph 4
MOORE, Thomas Justin 3
MOORE, Thomas Love H
MOORE, Thomas Morrell 4
MOORE, Thomas Overton H
MOORE, Thomas Verner 1
MOORE, Thomas Verner 5
MOORE, Thomas Waterman 5
MOORE, Veranus Alva 1
MOORE, Victor 4
MOORE, Victor F. 5
MOORE, Vida Frank 1
MOORE, Walter Bedford 2
MOORE, Walter William 1
MOORE, Walton Norwood 4
MOORE, Ward Frederick 10
MOORE, Warren G., Sr. 4
MOORE, Wilbert Ellis 9
MOORE, William* H
MOORE, William Charles 4
MOORE, William Emmet 1
MOORE, William Emmet 2
MOORE, William Eves 1
MOORE, William F. 6
MOORE, William Garrett 2
MOORE, William George 5
MOORE, William Henry 1
MOORE, William J. 7
MOORE, William Sturtevant 1
MOORE, William Sutton H
MOORE, William Talman 7
MOORE, William Taylor 7
MOORE, William Thomas 4
MOORE, William Underhill 2
MOORE, Willis Luther 1
MOORE, Wilmer Lee 4
MOORE, Zephaniah Swift H
MOOREHEAD, Agnes Robertson 6
MOOREHEAD, Alan 8
MOOREHEAD, Frederick Brown 2
MOOREHEAD, Singleton Peabody 4
MOOREHEAD, Warren King 1
MOOREHEAD, William Gallogly 1
MOORES, Charles Bruce 1
MOORES, Charles Washington 1
MOORES, J. Henry 1
MOORES, Merrill 1
MOORHEAD, Dudley Thomas 5
MOORHEAD, Frank Graham 3
MOORHEAD, Harley G. 2
MOORHEAD, James Kennedy H
MOORHEAD, Louis David 1
MOORHEAD, Louis David 3
MOORHEAD, Maxwell K. 5
MOORHEAD, Paul Grady 9
MOORHEAD, Robert Lowry 5
MOORHEAD, William Singer 3
MOORHEAD, William Singer 9
MOORHOUSE, Harold Roy 4
MOORMAN, Charles Harwood 1
MOORMAN, Henry DeHaven 6
MOORMAN, Robert Burrus Buckner 6
MOORMAN, Robert Wardlaw 6
MOOS, Charles J. 6
MOOS, Malcolm Charles 8
MOOSBRUGGER, Frederick 6
MOOSER, William H
MOOSMULLER, Oswald William H
MOOT, Adelbert 1
MOOT, Welles Van Ness 7
MOOTS, Elmer Earl 7
MOQUE, Alice Lee 1
MORA, F. Luis 1
MORA, Jose Antonio 6
MORA, Joseph Jacinto 2
MORAIS, Sabato H
MORALES, Cecilio Jose 7
MORALES, Franklin E. 7
MORALES, Miquel Marcos 7
MORALES, Sanchez 1
MORA MIRANDA, Marcial 5
MORAN, Alfred E. 6
MORAN, Annette 1
MORAN, Benjamin H
MORAN, Daniel Edward 1
MORAN, Daniel James 2
MORAN, Douglas Edward 9
MORAN, Edward H
MORAN, Edward Carleton, Jr. 4
MORAN, Edwin Bryan 9
MORAN, Eugene Francis 4
MORAN, Francis Thomas 1
MORAN, Frank Goding 7
MORAN, Fred T. 4
MORAN, Hugh Anderson 7
MORAN, James D. 8
MORAN, James Thomas 1
MORAN, John Henry 3
MORAN, John Joseph 5
MORAN, Julia Porcelli 6
MORAN, Leon 1
MORAN, Percy 1
MORAN, Peter 1
MORAN, Richard Bartholomew 5
MORAN, Robert 4
MORAN, Thomas H
MORAN, Thomas 1
MORAN, Thomas 4
MORAN, Thomas A. 1
MORAN, Thomas Francis 1
MORAN, W(alter) H(arrison) 6
MORAN, William Edward, Jr. 5
MORAN, William Joseph 4
MORANDI, Giorgio 4
MORANTI, Paul Joseph 7
MORANZONI, Roberto 7
MORAUD, Marcel Jean 7
MORAVIA, Alberto (Pincherle) 10
MORAWETZ, Albert Richard 4
MORAWETZ, Victor 1
MORBY, Edwin Seth 8
MORCOM, Clifford Bawden 3
MORDE, Theodore A. 3
MORDECAI, Alfred H
MORDECAI, Alfred 1
MORDECAI, Moses Cohen H
MORDECAI, Samuel Fox 1
MORDECAI, T. Moultrie 4
MORDEN, William J. 3
MORDVINOFF, Nicolas 2
MORE, Brookes 2
MORE, Charles Church 3
MORE, E. Anson 1
MORE, Herman 5
MORE, John Herron 5
MORE, Lena Gay 8
MORE, Louis Trenchard 2
MORE, Nicholas H
MORE, Paul Elmer 1
MORE, Robert E(lmer) 9
MORE, William Gibb 8
MOREAU, Arthur Edmond 3
MOREAU, Arthur Stanley, Jr. 9
MOREAU DE SAINT MERY, Mederic-louis-elie H
MOREAU-LISLET, Louis Casimir Elisabeth H
MOREAUX, Amable Oli 2
MORECOCK, Earle Monroe 10
MOREELL, Ben 9
MOREHEAD, Albert Hodges 4
MOREHEAD, Charles Allen 3
MOREHEAD, Charles Slaughter H
MOREHEAD, French Hugh 3
MOREHEAD, James Turner* H
MOREHEAD, John Alfred 1
MOREHEAD, John Henry 2
MOREHEAD, John Lindsay 4
MOREHEAD, John Motley H
MOREHEAD, John Motley 1
MOREHEAD, John Motley 4
MOREHOUSE, Albert Kellogg 3
MOREHOUSE, Clifford Phelps 7
MOREHOUSE, Daniel Walter 1
MOREHOUSE, Edward Ward 7
MOREHOUSE, Frances Milton 2
MOREHOUSE, Frederic Cook 1
MOREHOUSE, George Pierson 4
MOREHOUSE, George Read 1
MOREHOUSE, Henry Lyman 1
MOREHOUSE, Juluis Stanley 4
MOREHOUSE, Linden Husted 1
MOREHOUSE, Linden Husted 4
MOREHOUSE, Lyman Foote 5
MOREHOUSE, Nye F. 8
MOREHOUSE, P. Gad Bryan 5
MOREHOUSE, Ward 4
MOREHOUSE, William Russell 1
MOREL, Jean 6
MORELAND, Charles F(red) 8
MORELAND, Edward Leyburn 3
MORELAND, Jesse Earl 10
MORELAND, John Richard 2
MORELAND, William Hall 2
MORELAND, William Haywood 2
MORELL, George Fowler 7
MORELL, George Webb H
MORELL, Parker 2
MORELL, Rosa Blanca Ortiz (Mrs. Ramon B. Morell) 6
MORELL, William Nelson 5
MORELOCK, George Leslie 6
MORELOCK, Horace Wilson 5
MORENCY, Paul Wilfrid 6
MORENO, Arthur Alphonse 3
MORENO, Jacob L. 6
MORENO-LACALLE, Julian 6
MORESCHI, Joseph V. 5
MORESI, Harry James 6
MORETZ, Owen Leonard 7
MORETZ, William Henry 10
MOREY, Albert Anderson 10
MOREY, Arthur Thornton 1
MOREY, Charles Rufus 3
MOREY, Charles William 4
MOREY, Chester S. 1
MOREY, Frank H
MOREY, George W(ashington) 8
MOREY, Henry Martyn 3
MOREY, John William 3
MOREY, Lee B. 6
MOREY, Lloyd 4
MOREY, Samuel H
MOREY, Sylvester Marvin 6
MOREY, Sylvester Marvin 7
MOREY, Victor Pinkerton 3
MOREY, Walter Nelson 10
MOREY, William Carey 1
MORFA, Raymond J. 3
MORFIT, Campbell H
MORFORD, Henry H
MORFORD, James Richard 4
MORGAN, Abel H
MORGAN, Alfred Powell 5
MORGAN, Alfred Y. 9
MORGAN, Angela 3
MORGAN, Ann Haven 4
MORGAN, Anna 1
MORGAN, Anne 3
MORGAN, Anne Eugenia Felicia 1
MORGAN, Appleton 1
MORGAN, Arthur Ernest 6
MORGAN, Barton 7
MORGAN, Bayard Quincy 4
MORGAN, Bayard Quincy 7
MORGAN, Brooks Sanderson 5
MORGAN, Byron 8
MORGAN, Carey E. 1
MORGAN, Caroline Starr 5
MORGAN, Casey Bruce 1
MORGAN, Charles H
MORGAN, Charles 3
MORGAN, Charles Carroll 1
MORGAN, Charles Eldridge 2
MORGAN, Charles Henry 1
MORGAN, Charles Herbert 1
MORGAN, Charles Hill 1
MORGAN, Charles Hill 8
MORGAN, Charles Stillman 9
MORGAN, Christopher H
MORGAN, Clifford Thomas 6
MORGAN, Clifford Thomas 7
MORGAN, Clifford Veryl 3
MORGAN, Clinton Emory 3
MORGAN, Clinton Gerard, Jr. 10
MORGAN, Clyde B. 9
MORGAN, Daniel H
MORGAN, Daniel Edgar 2
MORGAN, Daniel Nash 1
MORGAN, David E. 1
MORGAN, David Percy 6
MORGAN, D(avid) W(illiam) R(owsen) 9
MORGAN, Dewitt Schuyler 2
MORGAN, Dick Thompson 1
MORGAN, Donald Marvin 7
MORGAN, Edmund Morris, Jr. 4
MORGAN, Edward Broadbent 1
MORGAN, Edward M. 1
MORGAN, Edwin Barber H
MORGAN, Edwin Denison H
MORGAN, Edwin Franklin Abell 4
MORGAN, Edwin Lee 4
MORGAN, Edwin Vernon 1
MORGAN, Elford C(hapman) 5
MORGAN, Eliot S. N. H
MORGAN, Ephraim Franklin 2
MORGAN, Ezra Leonidas 1
MORGAN, F. Coelies 1
MORGAN, Forrest 1
MORGAN, Francis Patterson 4
MORGAN, Frank 3
MORGAN, Frank Millett 4
MORGAN, Fred Bogardus 3
MORGAN, Fred Bruce 6
MORGAN, Frederic Lindley 5
MORGAN, G. Campbell 4
MORGAN, Geoffrey Francis 3
MORGAN, George H
MORGAN, George 1
MORGAN, George Allen 5
MORGAN, George Hagar 1
MORGAN, George Horace 4
MORGAN, George O. 3
MORGAN, George Wagner 3
MORGAN, George Washbourne H
MORGAN, George Washington H
MORGAN, George Wilson 1
MORGAN, George Wilson 5
MORGAN, Gerald Demuth 7
MORGAN, Harcourt Alexander 3
MORGAN, Harry Dale 3
MORGAN, Harry Hays 1
MORGAN, Henry A. 4
MORGAN, Henry Sturgis 8
MORGAN, Henry William 1
MORGAN, Henry Williams 6
MORGAN, Herbert Rollo 3
MORGAN, Hugh Jackson 4
MORGAN, Ike 5
MORGAN, Ina Lucas 7
MORGAN, Isaac B. 3
MORGAN, J. D. 7
MORGAN, Jacob L. 5
MORGAN, James H
MORGAN, James 3
MORGAN, James Bright H
MORGAN, James Dada H
MORGAN, James Dudley 1
MORGAN, James Henry 1
MORGAN, James Norris 1
MORGAN, James W. 3
MORGAN, Jerome J. 4
MORGAN, Jesse Robert 6
MORGAN, John H
MORGAN, John Heath 5
MORGAN, John Hill 2
MORGAN, John Hunt H
MORGAN, John Jacob Brooke 2
MORGAN, John Jordan H
MORGAN, John Livingston Rutgers 1
MORGAN, John Paul H
MORGAN, John Pierpont 1
MORGAN, John Pierpont 2
MORGAN, John Thoburn 5
MORGAN, John Tyler 1
MORGAN, Joseph H. 7
MORGAN, Junius Spencer H
MORGAN, Junius Spencer 4
MORGAN, Justin H
MORGAN, Justin Colfax 3
MORGAN, Lewis Henry H
MORGAN, Lewis Lovering 5
MORGAN, Lloyd 9
MORGAN, Louis M. H
MORGAN, Sister M. Sylvia 4
MORGAN, Marshall Shapleigh 6
MORGAN, Matthew Somerville H
MORGAN, Maud 1
MORGAN, Michael Ryan 1
MORGAN, Minot Canfield 5
MORGAN, Monta B., Sr. 3
MORGAN, Morris Hicky 1
MORGAN, Octavius 1
MORGAN, Ora Sherman 4
MORGAN, Paul Beagary 3
MORGAN, Paul Winthrop 10
MORGAN, Percy Tredegar 4
MORGAN, Peto Whittaker 4
MORGAN, Philip Hicky H
MORGAN, Philip M. 4
MORGAN, Ralph 4
MORGAN, Raymond A. 4
MORGAN, Robert Kenneth 4
MORGAN, Robert M. 3
MORGAN, Roy Leonard 9
MORGAN, Russell Hedley 9
MORGAN, Russell Van Dyke 3
MORGAN, Samuel St. John 7
MORGAN, Samuel Tate 1
MORGAN, Shepard (Ashman) 7
MORGAN, Sherley Warner 7
MORGAN, Sidney 8
MORGAN, Stephen 4
MORGAN, Stokeley Williams 4
MORGAN, Tali Esen 1
MORGAN, Theodore Harding 9
MORGAN, Theophilous John 5
MORGAN, Thomas H
MORGAN, Thomas Alfred 4
MORGAN, Thomas Francis, Jr. 5
MORGAN, Thomas Hunt 2
MORGAN, Thomas J. 1
MORGAN, Thomas John 1
MORGAN, Thomas W. 1
MORGAN, Tom P. 1
MORGAN, Wallace 2
MORGAN, Walter Piety 3
MORGAN, Walter Sydney 3
MORGAN, William H
MORGAN, William 1
MORGAN, William Berry 4
MORGAN, William Conger 5
MORGAN, William Edgar, 2d 4
MORGAN, William Fellowes 2
MORGAN, William Forbes 1
MORGAN, William Gerry 2
MORGAN, William Henry* 1
MORGAN, William John 7
MORGAN, William M. 1
MORGAN, William McKendree 2
MORGAN, William Sacheus 5
MORGAN, William Stephen H
MORGAN, William Thomas 2

MORSE, Philip McCord 9
MORSE, Richard Cary 1
MORSE, Richard Cary 4
MORSE, Richard Stetson 9
MORSE, Robert Hosmer 4
MORSE, Robert Hosmer 6
MORSE, Robert McNeil 1
MORSE, Roy Francis 7
MORSE, Roy L. 1
MORSE, Samuel Finley Breese H
MORSE, Samuel Finley Brown 5
MORSE, Sidney 1
MORSE, Sidney Edwards H
MORSE, Waldo Grant 1
MORSE, Warner Jackson 1
MORSE, Wayne Lyman 6
MORSE, Wilbur, Jr. 3
MORSE, Withrow 3
MORSELL, Everett Graham 7
MORSELL, H(erndon) Tudor 8
MORSELL, John Albert 6
MORSMAN, Robert Porter 7
MORSS, Charles Anthony 1
MORSS, Everett 1
MORSS, Samuel E. 1
MORSTEIN MARX, Fritz 5
MORT, Paul R. 4
MORTENSEN, Martin 5
MORTENSEN, Otto Axel 7
MORTENSEN, Soren Hansen 6
MORTENSEN, William Henry 10
MORTENSON, Ernest Dawson 5
MORTENSON, Peter Alvin 1
MORTEZA 4
MORTHLAND, David Vernon 6
MORTIMER, Alfred Garnett 4
MORTIMER, Charles G. 7
MORTIMER, Frank Cogswell 3
MORTIMER, James Daniel 3
MORTIMER, Lee 4
MORTIMER, Mary H
MORTON, Alfred Hammond 6
MORTON, Asa Henry 4
MORTON, Ben L. 9
MORTON, Charles H
MORTON, Charles 1
MORTON, Charles Adams 4
MORTON, Charles Bruce, II 9
MORTON, Charles Gould 1
MORTON, Charles W. 4
MORTON, Conrad Vernon 5
MORTON, David 3
MORTON, Eliza Happy 1
MORTON, Ferdinand Joseph La Menthe H
MORTON, Ferdinand Joseph La Menthe 4
MORTON, Frank Roy 1
MORTON, Frederick William 4
MORTON, George* H
MORTON, George Carpenter 1
MORTON, George Edwin 1
MORTON, Harold Coleman 10
MORTON, Henry 1
MORTON, Henry H. 1
MORTON, Howard McIlvain 2
MORTON, Ira Abbott 3
MORTON, Jack A. 5
MORTON, Jackson H
MORTON, James Ferdinand 1
MORTON, James Geary 5
MORTON, James Madison, Jr. 1
MORTON, James Proctor 5
MORTON, James St Clair H
MORTON, Jay Robert 10
MORTON, Jennie Chinn 1
MORTON, Jeremiah H
MORTON, Jeremiah Rogers 1
MORTON, John H
MORTON, John 4
MORTON, John Jamieson, Jr. 7
MORTON, Joseph 2
MORTON, Joy 1
MORTON, Julius Sterling 1
MORTON, Lawrence 9
MORTON, Leon Lincoln 7
MORTON, Levi Parsons 1
MORTON, Louis 6
MORTON, Marcus* H
MORTON, Nathaniel H
MORTON, Oliver Hazard Perry H
MORTON, Oren Frederic 1
MORTON, Paul 1
MORTON, Perry William 4
MORTON, Richard Albert Dunlap 3
MORTON, Richard Lee 6
MORTON, Robert Lee 7
MORTON, Rogers Clark Ballard 7
MORTON, Rosalie Slaughter 5
MORTON, Roy Jay 10
MORTON, Samuel George H
MORTON, Samuel Walker 1
MORTON, Sarah Wentworth Apthorpe H
MORTON, Sterling 4
MORTON, Thomas H
MORTON, Thomas George 4
MORTON, Thruston Ballard 8
MORTON, W. Brown 4
MORTON, Walter Albert 8
MORTON, William Hanson 9
MORTON, William Henry Stephenson 4
MORTON, William Thomas Green H
MORTON, William W(ilson) 8
MORTON, W(oolridge) Brown 9
MORWITZ, Edward H
MORWITZ, Samuel Mordecai 6
MORY, E. Lawrence 6
MOSBY, Charles Virgil 2
MOSBY, Henry Sackett 8
MOSBY, John Singleton 1
MOSCHCOWITZ, Alexis Victor 1
MOSCHCOWITZ, Paul 2
MOSCONA, Nicola 6
MOSCONE, George Richard 7
MOSCOSO DE ALVARADO, Luis de H
MOSCOW, Warren 10
MOSCOWITZ, Grover M. 2
MOSCRIP, William Smith 6
MOSELEY, Ben Perley Poore 4
MOSELEY, Charles West 3
MOSELEY, Edward Augustus 1
MOSELEY, Edward Buckland 1
MOSELEY, Edwin M. 7
MOSELEY, Frederick S., Jr. 5
MOSELEY, George Van Horn 4
MOSELEY, Hal Walters 2
MOSELEY, John Ohleyer 3
MOSELEY, Jonathan Ogden H
MOSELEY, Lonzo B. 4
MOSELEY, Mercer Pamplin 1
MOSELEY, Ray Benjamin Franklin 7
MOSELEY, Robert David, Jr. 9
MOSELEY, William Abbott H
MOSELY, Philip Edward 5
MOSENTHAL, Herman 3
MOSENTHAL, Joseph H
MOSER, Alfred A. 5
MOSER, Arthur Hurst 7
MOSER, Charles Kroth 5
MOSER, Christopher Otto 1
MOSER, Clarence Patten 5
MOSER, Ellsworth 4
MOSER, Guy L. 4
MOSER, Henry S. 5
MOSER, Jefferson Franklin 1
MOSER, Paul 10
MOSER, William 4
MOSES, Alfred Geiger 6
MOSES, Alfred Joseph 1
MOSES, Andrew 2
MOSES, Anna Mary Robertson 4
MOSES, Bernard 1
MOSES, C. A. 4
MOSES, Colter Hamilton 4
MOSES, Elbert Raymond 6
MOSES, Emile Phillips 6
MOSES, Frederick Taft 3
MOSES, George Higgins 2
MOSES, Harry Morgan 3
MOSES, Henry L. 4
MOSES, Horace Augustus 2
MOSES, John 2
MOSES, Montrose Jonas 1
MOSES, Robert 8
MOSES, Siegfried 6
MOSES, Thomas 3
MOSES, Thomas Freeman 1
MOSES, Walter 10
MOSES, Walter H. 6
MOSESSOHN, David N. 1
MOSESSOHN, Moses Dayyan 1
MOSESSOHN, Nehemiah 1
MOSHER, Aaron Alexander Roland 3
MOSHER, Charles Adams 8
MOSHER, Clelia Duel 1
MOSHER, Eliza Maria 1
MOSHER, Esek Ray 2
MOSHER, Frederick Camp 10
MOSHER, George Clark 1
MOSHER, George Frank 1
MOSHER, Gouverneur Frank 1
MOSHER, Harris Payton 3
MOSHER, Howard Townsend 1
MOSHER, Ira 4
MOSHER, Raymond Mylar 3
MOSHER, Robert Brent 1
MOSHER, Samuel Barlow 5
MOSHER, Thomas Bird 1
MOSHER, William Allison 5
MOSHER, William Eugene 2
MOSIER, Harold Gerard 5
MOSIER, Jeremiah George 1
MOSIER, Maurice Lee 8
MOSIER, Orval McKinley 4
MOSIMAN, Samuel K. 1
MOSKOWITZ, Belle Israels 1
MOSKOWITZ, Charles C. 9
MOSLER, Edwin H. 3
MOSLER, Henry 1
MOSLEY, Earl Louis 7
MOSLEY, J(ohn) Brooke, Jr. 9
MOSS, Albert Bartlett 1
MOSS, Arnold 10
MOSS, Charles Malcolm 8
MOSS, Charles McCord 5
MOSS, Charles Melville 4
MOSS, Chase 6
MOSS, Emma Sadler 5
MOSS, Frank 1
MOSS, Frank J. 5
MOSS, Fred August 4
MOSS, Herbert James 3
MOSS, Howard 9
MOSS, Hunter Holmes, Jr. 1
MOSS, James Alfred 1
MOSS, James Mercer 9
MOSS, John Calvin H
MOSS, John Hall 7
MOSS, Joseph 3
MOSS, Joseph S., Jr. 10
MOSS, Lemuel 1
MOSS, Leonard Wallace 9
MOSS, Leslie Bates 2
MOSS, Louis John 2
MOSS, Mary 1
MOSS, Maxmilian 4
MOSS, Ralph W. 4
MOSS, Robert Verelle, Jr. 7
MOSS, Washington Irving 8
MOSS, William Lorenzo 3
MOSS, William Washburn 2
MOSS, Woodson 1
MOSSADEGH, Mohammed 4
MOSSE, Baskett Pershing 8
MOSSER, Charles Marcel 5
MOSSER, Sawyer McArthur 7
MOSSMAN, B. Paul 5
MOSSMAN, Frank E. 2
MOSSNER, Ernest Campbell 9
MOSSTELLER, Frank 7
MOST, Johann Joseph H
MOST, Johann Joseph 4
MOSTEL, Zero (Sam Mostel) 7
MOSTELLER, L. Karlton 5
MOSTOFI, Khosrow 10
MOSZYNSKI, Jerzy Robert 9
MOTCHAN, Louis A. 6
MOTE, Carl Henry 2
MOTE, Don Carlos 8
MOTE, Donald Roosevelt 5
MOTEN, Bennie 4
MOTEN, Roger Henwood 3
MOTHERSHEAD, John Leland, Jr. 10
MOTHERWELL, Robert 10
MOTHERWELL, Robert Burns, II 2
MOTLEY, Arthur Harrison 8
MOTLEY, Emery Tyler 3
MOTLEY, John Lothrop H
MOTLEY, Warren 5
MOTLEY, Warren 7
MOTLEY, Willard Francis 4
MOTON, Robert Russa 1
MOTRY, Hubert Louis 3
MOTT, Charles Stewart 5
MOTT, Charles Stewart Harding 10
MOTT, Francis Edward 6
MOTT, Frank Luther 4
MOTT, George Scudder 1
MOTT, Gershom H
MOTT, Gordon Newell H
MOTT, James* H
MOTT, James Wheaton 2
MOTT, John Griffin 2
MOTT, John R. 3
MOTT, Jordan Lawrence 1
MOTT, Lewis Freeman 1
MOTT, Lucretia Coffin H
MOTT, Luther Wright 1
MOTT, Omer Hillman 2
MOTT, Richard H
MOTT, Rodney Loomer 5
MOTT, T. Bentley 3
MOTT, Thomas Hezekiah, Jr. 9
MOTT, Valentine H
MOTT, Valentine 1
MOTT, William Elton 2
MOTTE, Isaac H
MOTTER, Orton B. 3
MOTTET, Henry 1
MOTTET, Jeanie Gallup (Mrs. Henry Mottet) 5
MOTTIER, David Myers 1
MOTZKIN, Theodore S. 5
MOUAT, Malcolm Palmer 7
MOUDY, Alfred L. 6
MOUDY, Walter Frank 5
MOUHTAR BEY, Ahmed 5
MOULD, Elmer Wallace King 3
MOULD, Jacob Wray H
MOULDER, Morgan M. 7
MOULDS, George Henry 6
MOULTON, Arthur Wheelock 4
MOULTON, Charles Robert 2
MOULTON, Charles Wells 1
MOULTON, Charles William 1
MOULTON, Dudley 6
MOULTON, Earl L. 3
MOULTON, Edwin F. 1
MOULTON, Elton James 8
MOULTON, Forest Ray 3
MOULTON, Frank Prescott 4
MOULTON, George Mayhew 1
MOULTON, Gertrude Evelyn 6
MOULTON, Harold Glen 4
MOULTON, Horace Platt 10
MOULTON, Louise Chandler 1
MOULTON, Mace H
MOULTON, Mary Kennington 6
MOULTON, Richard Green 1
MOULTON, Robert Hurt 6
MOULTON, Sherman Roberts 2
MOULTON, Vern 3
MOULTON, Warren Joseph 2
MOULTON, William Horace 4
MOULTON, Willis Bryant 1
MOULTRIE, John H
MOULTRIE, William H
MOULTROP, Irving Edwin 4
MOUNGER, W. M. 3
MOUNT, Arnold John 2
MOUNT, Finley Pogue 1
MOUNT, George Haines 6
MOUNT, James Atwell 1
MOUNT, Oliver Erskine 4
MOUNT, Russell Theodore 6
MOUNT, Wallace 1
MOUNT, William Sidney H
MOUNTAIN, Harry Montgomery 6
MOUNTAIN, Worrall Frederick 10
MOUNTCASTLE, George Williams 5
MOUNTCASTLE, Robert Edward Lee 1
MOUNTIN, Joseph W. 3
MOUNTREY, Robert Walther 7
MOURSUND, Andrew Fleming, Jr. 5
MOURSUND, Walter Henrik 3
MOUSEL, Lloyd Harvey 5
MOUSER, Grant Earl, Jr. 2
MOUTON, Alexander H
MOUZON, Edwin Dubose 1
MOUZON, James Carlisle 6
MOWAT, Magnus 5
MOWATT, Anna Cora Ogden H
MOWBRAY, Albert Henry 2
MOWBRAY, George Mordey H
MOWBRAY, H. Siddons 1
MOWBRAY-CLARKE, John 3
MOWER, Charles Drown 1
MOWER, Charles Drown 2
MOWER, Joseph Anthony H
MOWERY, William Byron 3
MOWITZ, Robert James 8
MOWRER, Edgar Ansel 7
MOWRER, Frank Roger 5
MOWRER, Orval Hobart 8
MOWRER, Paul Scott 5
MOWRY, Daniel, Jr. H
MOWRY, George Edwin 8
MOWRY, Harold 3
MOWRY, Ross Rutledge 3
MOWRY, William Augustus 1
MOXLEY, William J. 4
MOXOM, Philip Stafford 1
MOYER, Andrew Jackson 3
MOYER, Benton Leslie 4
MOYER, Burton James 5
MOYER, Charles Edward 7
MOYER, Charles H. 4
MOYER, David Gurstelle 5
MOYER, Gabriel Hocker 1
MOYER, Harold Nicholas 1
MOYER, Harvey Vernon 3
MOYER, James Ambrose 2
MOYER, Joseph Kearney 5
MOYER, Sheldon 7
MOYER, William Henry 1
MOYLAN, Stephen H
MOYLE, Henry Dinwoodey 4
MOYLE, James Henry 2
MOYLE, Walter Gladstone 5
MOYNE, Ernest John 7
MOYNIHAN, Charles Joseph 7
MOYNIHAN, James Humphrey 4
MOYNIHAN, P. H. 2
MOZDZER, Henry Anthony 10
MOZEE, Phoebe Anne Oakley H
MOZEE, Phoebe Anne Oakley 4
MOZIER, Joseph H
MRAK, Ignatius 1
MRAZEK, Robert Vernon 10
MUAN, Arnulf 10
MUCCIO, John Joseph 10
MUCKENFUSS, Anthony Moultrie 1
MUCKEY, Floyd Summer 1
MUCKLE, John Selser 1
MUCKLE, M. Richards 1
MUDD, Eugene J. 6
MUDD, Harvey Gilmer 1
MUDD, Harvey Seeley 3
MUDD, Mildred Esterbrook 3
MUDD, Seeley G. 4
MUDD, Seeley Wintersmith 1
MUDD, Stuart 6
MUDD, Sydney E. 1
MUDD, Sydney Emanuel 1
MUDD, William Swearingen 2
MUDGE, Alfred Eugene 2
MUDGE, Claire R. 4
MUDGE, Courtland Sawin 4
MUDGE, Edmund Webster 2
MUDGE, Enoch H
MUDGE, Henry U. 1
MUDGE, Isadore Gilbert 3
MUDGE, James 1
MUDGE, Lewis Seymour 2
MUDGE, Verne Donald 3
MUDGE, William Leroy 3
MUDGETT, Bruce D. 7
MUDRICK, Marvin 9
MUEHLBERGER, Clarence Weinert 4
MUEHLEISEN, Eugene Frederick 6
MUEHLENTHAL, Clarice Kelman 10
MUEHLING, John Adam 2
MUELLER, Adolph 2
MUELLER, Alfred H
MUELLER, Arthur E. A. 4
MUELLER, Edward 3
MUELLER, Erwin Wilhelm 7
MUELLER, Fred William 5

MUELLER, Frederick Henry 7
MUELLER, Gilbert John 7
MUELLER, Hans 4
MUELLER, Hans Alexander 4
MUELLER, Hermann 4
MUELLER, John Henry 4
MUELLER, John Howard 3
MUELLER, John Theodore 7
MUELLER, John Victor 4
MUELLER, Joseph M. 10
MUELLER, Karl Anton 5
MUELLER, Karl William 7
MUELLER, Kate Hevner 8
MUELLER, Merrill (Red) 7
MUELLER, Paul 4
MUELLER, Paul Albert 3
MUELLER, Paul Ferdinand 1
MUELLER, Paul John 5
MUELLER, Theodore Edward 3
MUELLER, Theodore Frederick 3
MUELLER, Theophil Herbert 4
MUELLER, Werner 4
MUENCH, Aloisius Joseph 4
MUENCH, George Arthur 8
MUENCH, Hugo 6
MUENCH, Hugo, Jr. 5
MUENNICH, Ferenc 4
MUENSCHER, Walter C. 4
MUENZINGER, Karl Friedrich 7
MUETTERTIES, Earl Leonard 8
MUGAVERO, Francis J. 10
MUGGERIDGE, Malcolm 10
MUGGLETON, Gerald Dean 7
MUHAMMED, Elijah (Elijah Poole) 6
MUHLBERG, William 9
MUHLEMAN, George Washington 5
MUHLEMAN, Maurice Louis 1
MUHLENBERG, Francis Swaine H
MUHLENBERG, Frederick A(ugustus) 8
MUHLENBERG, Frederick Augustus Conrad H
MUHLENBERG, Gotthilf Henry Ernest H
MUHLENBERG, Henry Augustus H
MUHLENBERG, Henry Augustus Philip H
MUHLENBERG, Henry Melchior H
MUHLENBERG, Henry Peter Gabriel H
MUHLENBERG, William Augustus H
MUHLFELD, George O. 2
MUHLMANN, Adolf 4
MUHSE, Albert Charles 4
MUILENBURG, James 6
MUIR, Andrew Forest 1
MUIR, Charles Henry 1
MUIR, Downie Davidson, Jr.
MUIR, E. Stanton 4
MUIR, James 3
MUIR, James 4
MUIR, James Irvin 4
MUIR, Jere T. 5
MUIR, John* 1
MUIR, Joseph Johnstone 1
MUIR, Malcolm 7
MUIR, Roy Cummings 6
MUIR, William 4
MUIRHEAD, David 4
MUIRHEAD, James Fullarton 1
MUKERJI, Dhan Gopal
MULATIER, Léon Frédéric 8
MULCAHY, Francis Patrick 6
MULDER, Arnold 7
MULDER, Bernard J. 10
MULDER, John 4
MULDER, Hugh Cornelius 3
MULDOON, Peter J. 1
MULDOON, Robert David 10
MULDOON, William H
MULDOON, William H
MULEY SOLIMAN H
MULFINGER, George Abraham 1
MULFORD, Clarence Edward 3
MULFORD, Donald Lewis 10
MULFORD, Elisha H

MULFORD, John Willett 4
MULFORD, Prentice H
MULFORD, Raymon Howard 5
MULFORD, Roland Jessup 5
MULFORD, Walter 5
MULHAUPT, Frederick J. 1
MULHAUSER, Frederick Ludwig 6
MULHAUSER, Ruth 7
MULHEARN, John Robert 7
MULHEARN, John Robert 8
MULHERIN, William Anthony 2
MULHERON, Anne Morton 2
MULHOLLAND, Edward J. 9
MULHOLLAND, Frank L. 2
MULHOLLAND, Henry Bearden 4
MULHOLLAND, John 5
MULHOLLAND, John Hugh 6
MULHOLLAND, William 1
MULKEY, Frederick William 1
MULL, George Fulmer 1
MULL, J. Harry 1
MULL, John Wesley 5
MULLAHY, John Henry 7
MULLALLY, Thornwell 2
MULLALY, Charles J. 2
MULLALY, John 1
MULLAN, Eugene Hagan 6
MULLAN, George Vincent 1
MULLAN, James McElwane 1
MULLAN, W. G. Read 1
MULLANEY, Eugene L(iguri) 6
MULLANEY, James Vincent 4
MULLANEY, John Barry 1
MULLANEY, Patrick J. 9
MULLANEY, Paul Lynch 8
MULLANPHY, John H
MULLANY, James Robert Madison H
MULLANY, John Francis 1
MULLANY, Patrick Francis H
MULLEN, Arthur Francis 1
MULLEN, Buell (Mrs. J. Bernard Mullen) 9
MULLEN, James 4
MULLEN, James Hanna 10
MULLEN, James William 1
MULLEN, John Francis 8
MULLEN, John Wilfred 10
MULLEN, Joseph 5
MULLEN, Robert Rodolf 9
MULLEN, Ruth Ackerman (Mrs. Frank A. Mullen) 5
MULLEN, Thomas Francis 1
MULLEN, Thomas Richard 3
MULLEN, Tobias 1
MULLEN, William E. 5
MULLENBACH, James 1
MULLENBACH, Philip 10
MULLENDORE, James Myers 10
MULLENIX, Charles A. 3
MULLENIX, Rollin Clarke 2
MULLER, Adolf Lancken 5
MULLER, Amelia A. 3
MULLER, Carl 4
MULLER, Carl Christian 1
MULLER, Edouard 2
MULLER, George P. 2
MULLER, Henry Nicholas 2
MULLER, Herbert Joseph 7
MULLER, Herman Edwin 4
MULLER, Hermann Joseph 4
MULLER, Hilgard 9
MULLER, James Arthur 2
MULLER, John H. 7
MULLER, Jonas Norman 4
MULLER, Margarethe 3
MULLER, Nichols 4
MULLER, Siegfried Hermann 4
MULLER, Siemon William 5
MULLER, W. Max 1
MULLER, Walter J. 4
MULLERGREN, Arthur L. 8
MULLER-URY, Adolfo 2
MULLETT, Mary B. 1
MULLGARDT, Louis Christian 4
MULLGARDT, William Oscar 6
MULLIGAN, Catharine A(rcher) 5
MULLIGAN, Charles J. 1
MULLIGAN, Charles Wise 5

MULLIGAN, David B. 3
MULLIGAN, Henry A. 8
MULLIGAN, James Hilary 1
MULLIGAN, Richard Thomas 1
MULLIGAN, William G(eorge) 10
MULLIGAN, William Joseph 6
MULLIKEN, Alfred Henry 1
MULLIKEN, Otis E. 5
MULLIKEN, Robert Sanderson 9
MULLIKEN, Samuel Parsons 1
MULLIKIN, Sidney Albert 1
MULLIN, Francis Anthony 2
MULLIN, Joseph H
MULLIN, Mark Joseph 2
MULLIN, Sam S. 5
MULLIN, Willard (Harlan) 7
MULLIN, William Valentine 1
MULLINNIX, Henry Maston 2
MULLINS, Charles Love, Jr. 7
MULLINS, D. Frank 4
MULLINS, David Wiley 9
MULLINS, Edgar Young 1
MULLINS, George Walker 3
MULLINS, Isla May 1
MULLINS, James H
MULLINS, Michael Gordon 10
MULLINS, Royal Leeman 10
MULLINS, Thomas C. 5
MULLINS, William Harvey Lowe 10
MULLOWNEY, John James 3
MULLOY, William Theodore 3
MULRONEY, John E. 7
MULROONEY, Edward Pierce 1
MULROY, Thomas Robert, Sr. 10
MULRY, Joseph Aloysius 1
MULTER, Abraham J. 9
MULTER, Smith Lewis 3
MULVANE, David Winfield 1
MULVANIA, Maurice 6
MULVIHILL, Michael Joseph 1
MUMAW, Lloyd Gerber 9
MUMFORD, Charles 4
MUMFORD, Charles Carney 1
MUMFORD, Emily Hamilton 10
MUMFORD, Ethel Watts 1
MUMFORD, Frederick Blackmar 3
MUMFORD, George H
MUMFORD, George Saltonstall 2
MUMFORD, Gurdon Saltonstall H
MUMFORD, Herbert Windsor 1
MUMFORD, James Gregory 1
MUMFORD, John Kimberly 1
MUMFORD, L. Quincy 8
MUMFORD, Lewis 10
MUMFORD, Mary Eno 4
MUMFORD, Philip G. 3
MUMFORD, Samuel Cranage 1
MUMFORD, William Walden, Sr. 9
MUMMA, Harlan L. 5
MUMMA, James Hebron 5
MUMMA, Morton Claire, Jr. 5
MUMMA, Walter Mann 4
MUMMART, Clarence Allen 3
MUMMERT, Arden John 8
MUMPER, Norris McAllister 2
MUMPER, William Norris 4
MUNCE, Robert J(ohn) 6
MUNCH, Edvard 4
MUNCIE, Curtis Hamilton 4
MUNCIE, J. H. 5
MUNDE, Paul Fortunatus 1
MUNDELEIN, George William 1
MUNDEN, Kenneth White 6
MUNDHEIM, Samuel 1
MUNDIE, William Bryce 6
MUNDT, G. Henry 4
MUNDT, Karl Earl 6

MUNDT, Walter J. 5
MUNDY, Ethel Frances 4
MUNDY, Ezekiel Wilson 1
MUNDY, Johnson Marchant H
MUNDY, Talbot 1
MUNDY, William Nelson 2
MUNFORD, Mary Cooke Branch 1
MUNFORD, Robert H
MUNFORD, Walter F. 3
MUNFORD, William H
MUNGEN, William H
MUNGER, Claude Worrell 3
MUNGER, Dell H. 4
MUNGER, Frank James 5
MUNGER, Harold Henry 5
MUNGER, Paul Francis 9
MUNGER, Royal Freeman 2
MUNGER, Theodore Thornton 1
MUNGER, Thomas Charles 4
MUNGER, William Henry 1
MUNHALL, Leander Whitcomb 1
MUNIZ, Joao Carlos 4
MUNK, Joseph Amasa 1
MUNKITTRICK, Richard Kendall 1
MUNN, Charles Allen 1
MUNN, Charles Clark 1
MUNN, Hiram H. 4
MUNN, James Buell 4
MUNN, John Calvin 9
MUNN, John Pixley 1
MUNN, John Randall 7
MUNN, Orson Desaix 1
MUNN, Orson Desaix 3
MUNN, Ralph 6
MUNN, Robert Ferguson 9
MUNN, William Phipps 1
MUNNIKHUYSEN, Henry D. F. 7
MUNNIKHUYSEN, Walter Farnandis 4
MUNNS, Mrs. Margaret Cairns 3
MUNOZ, Jorge 1
MUNOZ GRANDES, Agustin 5
MUNOZ-MARIN, Luis 1
MUNRO, Annette Gardner 3
MUNRO, Dana Carleton 1
MUNRO, Dana Gardner 10
MUNRO, David Alexander 1
MUNRO, Donald 5
MUNRO, Emily Gardner 1
MUNRO, George H
MUNRO, H. G. 3
MUNRO, Harry Clyde 8
MUNRO, Henry 1
MUNRO, James Alan 5
MUNRO, John Cummings 1
MUNRO, Leslie Knox 6
MUNRO, Robert Frater 5
MUNRO, Thomas 6
MUNRO, Walter J. 3
MUNRO, Walter Lee 1
MUNRO, Wilfred Harold 1
MUNRO, William Bennett 5
MUNROE, Charles Andrews 3
MUNROE, Charles Edward 1
MUNROE, Henry Smith 1
MUNROE, Hersey 1
MUNROE, James Phinney 1
MUNROE, John Alexander 5
MUNROE, Kirk 1
MUNROE, Robert Clifford 4
MUNROE, William Adams 1
MUNROE, William Robert 4
MUNSELL, Albert Henry 1
MUNSELL, Charles Edward 1
MUNSELL, Frank 4
MUNSELL, Harry B. 4
MUNSELL, Joel 1
MUNSELL, William Oliver 6
MUNSEY, Frank Andrew 1
MUNSN, John Maurice 3
MUNSON, C. La Rue 1
MUNSON, Charles Sherwood 7
MUNSON, Edward Lyman 2
MUNSON, Edwin Sterling 1
MUNSON, Frank C. 1
MUNSON, George S(harp) 7
MUNSON, Gorham B. 5
MUNSON, James Decker 1
MUNSON, James Eugene 1
MUNSON, John B. 4
MUNSON, John G. 3
MUNSON, John P. 1
MUNSON, Joseph Jones 8
MUNSON, Lewis S., Jr. 1
MUNSON, Loveland 1
MUNSON, Myron Andrews 1

MUNSON, Samuel Edgar 5
MUNSON, Samuel Lyman 1
MUNSON, Thomas Lewis 9
MUNSON, Thomas Volney 1
MUNSON, Townsend 7
MUNSON, Welton Marks 1
MUNSON, William Benjamin 1
MUNSTER, August W. 3
MUNSTER, Joe Henry, Jr. 8
MUNSTERBERG, Hugo 1
MUNTER, Evelyn LaVon (Mrs. Robert Duane Munter) 6
MUNTER, Godfrey L(eon) 10
MUNTER, Richard Strobach 6
MUNTZ, Earl Edward 4
MUNVES, William 9
MUNZ, Friedrich 1
MUNZ, Philip Alexander 6
MUNZIG, George Chickering 1
MURALT, Carl Leonard De 5
MURANE, Cornelius Daniel 4
MURANE, Edward E. 7
MURAT, Achille Napoleon H
MURATORE, Lucien 3
MURCH, Boynton Daggett 7
MURCH, Chauncey 1
MURCH, James DeForest 6
MURCH, Maynard Hale 4
MURCH, Thompson Henry H
MURCH, Walter Tandy 4
MURCHIE, Alexander 3
MURCHIE, Harold Hale 4
MURCHIE, Robert Charles 4
MURCHISON, Carl 4
MURCHISON, Charles Holton 9
MURCHISON, Claudius Temple 5
MURCHISON, Clinton W., Jr. 9
MURCHISON, Clinton Williams 5
MURCHISON, John D. 7
MURCHISON, Kenneth MacKenzie 1
MURDEN, Forrest Dozier 7
MURDOCH, Donald R. 9
MURDOCH, Frank Hitchcock H
MURDOCH, James Edward H
MURDOCH, James Vesey 6
MURDOCH, James Y. 4
MURDOCH, John 1
MURDOCH, John Gormley 1
MURDOCH, Thomas Chase 1
MURDOCK, Carleton 7
MURDOCK, Charles Albert 1
MURDOCK, George John 2
MURDOCK, George Peter 8
MURDOCK, Harold 1
MURDOCK, Harris H. 3
MURDOCK, Henry Taylor 5
MURDOCK, James H
MURDOCK, James Oliver 8
MURDOCK, John Robert 5
MURDOCK, John Robert 7
MURDOCK, John Samuel 2
MURDOCK, Joseph Ballard 1
MURDOCK, Kenneth Ballard 6
MURDOCK, Marcellus Marion 5
MURDOCK, Thomas Patrick 3
MURDOCK, Victor 2
MURFEE, Hopson Owen 3
MURFEE, James Thomas 1
MURFEE, Latimer 8
MURFIN, James Orin 1
MURFIN, Orin Gould 3
MURFREE, Mary Noailles 1
MURFREE, Walter Lee 3
MURFREE, William Hardy H
MURIE, Olaus Johan 4
MURKLAND, Charles Sumner 1
MURLIN, John Raymond 5
MURLIN, Lemuel Herbert 4
MURNAGHAN, Francis D. 10
MURNANE, George 5
MURPH, Daniel Shuford 5
MURPHEY, Archibald De Bow H
MURPHEY, Bradford 8
MURPHEY, Charles H
MURPHEY, Robert Joseph 5

NEWTON, Cosette Faust 6
(Mrs. Frank Hawley
Newton)
NEWTON, Eben H
NEWTON, Edith 6
NEWTON, Elbridge Ward 4
NEWTON, Glenn D. 5
NEWTON, Henry Jotham H
NEWTON, Homer Curtis 3
NEWTON, Howard 4
Chamberlian
NEWTON, Hubert Anson H
NEWTON, Isaac* H
NEWTON, Isaac Burkett 1
NEWTON, James 1
Thornwell
NEWTON, John H
NEWTON, John Henry 2
NEWTON, John Orville 4
NEWTON, John Wharton 5
NEWTON, Joseph Fort 2
NEWTON, Louie De Votie 9
NEWTON, Maurice 5
NEWTON, Maxwell 10
NEWTON, McGuire 1
NEWTON, Michael 9
NEWTON, Norman 10
Thomas (King)
NEWTON, Oscar 1
NEWTON, R. Heber 1
NEWTON, Richard H
NEWTON, Robert 8
NEWTON, Robert Park, Jr. 10
NEWTON, Robert Safford H
NEWTON, Thomas* H
NEWTON, Thomas H
Willoughby
NEWTON, Virgil Miller, Jr. 7
NEWTON, Walter Hughes 1
NEWTON, Walter Russell 4
NEWTON, Warren Childs 7
NEWTON, Watson J. 1
NEWTON, William H
Wilberforce
NEWTON, Willoughby H
NEXON, Hubert Henry 10
NEY, Jerome M. 9
NEY, Robert Leo 9
NEYER, Joseph 10
NEYLAN, John Francis 4
NEYLAND, Harry 3
NEYLAND, Robert Reese, 4
Jr.
NEYMAN, Jerzy 8
NEYMANN, Clarence 3
Adolph
NEZ COUPE H
NGO DINH DIEM 4
NIAS, Henry 3
NIBECKER, A(lfred) 8
S(anford), Jr.
NIBLACK, Albert Parker 1
NIBLACK, Silas Leslie H
NIBLACK, William Ellis H
NIBLEY, Charles Wilson 1
NIBLO, Urban 3
NIBLO, William H
NICCOLLS, Samuel Jack 1
NICE, Harry 1
NICE, Margaret Morse 6
(Mrs. Leonard Blaine
Nice)
NICELY, Harold Elliott 3
NICELY, James Mount 4
NICHOL, Edward Sterling 5
NICHOL, Francis David 10
NICHOL, Francis David 4
NICHOL, Frederick 3
William
NICHOLAS, Anna 1
NICHOLAS, Edwin August 3
NICHOLAS, George H
NICHOLAS, John 1
NICHOLAS, John Spangler 4
NICHOLAS, Lindsley 6
Vincent
NICHOLAS, Philip H
Norborne
NICHOLAS, Richard 3
Ulysses
NICHOLAS, Robert H
Carter*
NICHOLAS, William 1
Gardiner
NICHOLAS, William Oliver 5
NICHOLAS, Wilson Cary H
NICHOLL, Don 8
NICHOLL, Horace 1
Wadham
NICHOLL, William Evan 7
NICHOLLS, C. W. delyon 1
NICHOLLS, Francis Tillon 1
NICHOLLS, George 5
Heaton
NICHOLLS, John Calhoun H
NICHOLLS, Merrill Edgar 9

NICHOLLS, Rhoada 1
Holmes
NICHOLLS, Richard H
NICHOLLS, Samuel Jones 1
NICHOLLS, Thomas David 5
NICHOLLS, William 3
Durrett
NICHOLLS, William Hord 7
Lowber
NICHOLLS, Alexander 9
NICHOLS, Anne 4
NICHOLS, Arthur Burr 5
NICHOLS, Barbara 7
NICHOLS, Beverley 8
NICHOLS, Bill 9
NICHOLS, Bruce W. 10
NICHOLS, Charles A. 1
NICHOLS, Charles Gerry 4
NICHOLS, Charles Henry 1
NICHOLS, Charles Henry 1
NICHOLS, Charles Lemuel 1
NICHOLS, Charles Walter 4
NICHOLS, Charles Walter, 9
Jr.
NICHOLS, Clarina Irene H
Howard
NICHOLS, Clark Asahel 5
NICHOLS, Edward Hall 1
NICHOLS, Edward 1
Leamington
NICHOLS, Edward Tattnall 1
NICHOLS, Edward West 1
NICHOLS, Egbert Ray 3
NICHOLS, Ernest Fox 1
NICHOLS, Floyd Bruce 9
NICHOLS, Francis Henry 1
NICHOLS, Frank R. 4
NICHOLS, Frederick 8
Adams
NICHOLS, Frederick Day 5
NICHOLS, Frederick 3
George
NICHOLS, George Elwood 1
NICHOLS, George Ward H
NICHOLS, Harry Peirce 1
NICHOLS, Henry Drew 4
NICHOLS, Henry Joseph 6
NICHOLS, Henry Sargent 1
Prentiss
NICHOLS, Henry Windsor 4
NICHOLS, Herbert 1
NICHOLS, Herbert L. 4
NICHOLS, Hobart, Jr. 4
NICHOLS, Ichabod H
NICHOLS, Isabel 2
McIlhenny
NICHOLS, Jack John 2
Conover
NICHOLS, James 1
NICHOLS, James Robinson H
NICHOLS, James Walter 6
NICHOLS, Jeannette 8
Paddock
NICHOLS, J(esse) Brooks 7
NICHOLS, Jesse Clyde 5
NICHOLS, John Benjamin 3
NICHOLS, John Francis 5
NICHOLS, John Grayson 2
NICHOLS, John Richard 1
NICHOLS, John Treadwell 7
NICHOLS, John Wesley 6
NICHOLS, Joseph Clifford 7
NICHOLS, Leslie 9
NICHOLS, Malcolm E. 3
NICHOLS, Marie 7
Hochmuth
NICHOLS, Mark Lovel 5
NICHOLS, Marvin Curtis 6
NICHOLS, Mary Sargeant H
Neal Gove
NICHOLS, Matthias H. H
NICHOLS, Nathan 10
Lankford
NICHOLS, Neil Ernest 3
NICHOLS, Othniel Foster 1
NICHOLS, Philip, Jr. 10
NICHOLS, Pierrepont 3
Herrick
NICHOLS, Robert Hastings 3
NICHOLS, Roy Franklin 10
NICHOLS, Roy Franklin 5
NICHOLS, Ruth Rowland 4
NICHOLS, Shuford 10
Reinhardt
NICHOLS, Spencer Baird 3
NICHOLS, Spencer Van 2
Bokkelen
NICHOLS, Summer Ely 9
NICHOLS, Thomas Flint 5
NICHOLS, Walter Edmond 5
NICHOLS, Walter Franklin 2
NICHOLS, Walter 1
Hammond
NICHOLS, William Ford 1
NICHOLS, William Henry 1
NICHOLS, William Leroy 3
NICHOLS, William Robert 7

NICHOLS, William 1
Theophilus
NICHOLS, William Wallace 2
NICHOLSON, Alfred H
Osborn Pope
NICHOLSON, Ben 8
NICHOLSON, Donald W. 8
NICHOLSON, Dwight Roy 10
NICHOLSON, Edward 5
Everett
NICHOLSON, Eliza Jane H
Poitevent Holbrook
NICHOLSON, Francis H
NICHOLSON, Frank Lee 3
NICHOLSON, Frank 4
Walter
NICHOLSON, George 1
Edward
NICHOLSON, George 5
Mansel
NICHOLSON, George 2
Robert Henderson
NICHOLSON, George T. 1
NICHOLSON, Gunnar 9
Walfrid Enander
NICHOLSON, Hammond 4
Burke
NICHOLSON, Harold 5
George
NICHOLSON, Henry 1
Hudson
NICHOLSON, Isaac Lea 1
NICHOLSON, J. Lee 4
NICHOLSON, James H
Bartram
NICHOLSON, James H
Bartram
NICHOLSON, James 4
Thomas
NICHOLSON, James 5
William
NICHOLSON, James 1
William
NICHOLSON, James H
William Augustus
NICHOLSON, Jesse 9
Thompson
NICHOLSON, John* H
NICHOLSON, John 9
Burton, Jr.
NICHOLSON, John 6
Frederick
NICHOLSON, John Page 1
NICHOLSON, John Reed 1
NICHOLSON, John 4
Rutherford
NICHOLSON, Joseph H
Hopper
NICHOLSON, Leonard 3
Kimball
NICHOLSON, Meredith 2
Hayward
NICHOLSON, Nollie Davis 6
NICHOLSON, Norman 5
Edwin
NICHOLSON, P. J. 8
NICHOLSON, Paul Coe 3
NICHOLSON, Ralph 5
NICHOLSON, Reginald 1
Fairfax
NICHOLSON, Rex Lee 6
NICHOLSON, Rex Lee 7
NICHOLSON, Robert 5
Harvey
NICHOLSON, Robert 9
Lawrence
NICHOLSON, Samuel H
NICHOLSON, Samuel D. 1
NICHOLSON, Samuel 1
Edgar
NICHOLSON, Samuel M. 1
NICHOLSON, Samuel 1
Thorne
NICHOLSON, Seth Barnes 4
NICHOLSON, Somerville 1
NICHOLSON, Soterios 2
NICHOLSON, Thomas 2
NICHOLSON, Thomas 10
Dominic
NICHOLSON, Timothy 4
NICHOLSON, Vincent 2
Dewitt
NICHOLSON, Walter 4
Wicks
NICHOLSON, Watson 3
NICHOLSON, William 1
Jones
NICHOLSON, William 6
McNeal
NICHOLSON, William 6
Ramsey
NICHOLSON, William 1
Rufus
NICHOLSON, William H
Thomas
NICHT, Frank Joseph 9
NICKELL, Vernon Lewis 9
NICKELS, John Augustine 1
Heard

NICKELS, Mervyn Millard 5
NICKERSON, Frank 4
Stillman
NICKERSON, Hiram 1
Robert
NICKERSON, Hoffman 4
NICKERSON, John 3
NICKERSON, John 8
Winslow
NICKERSON, Kingsbury 4
S.
NICKERSON, Walter John 7
NICKEUS, Johnson 1
NICKLAS, Charles Aubrey 2
NICKLESS, Alfred Samuel 7
NICKS, F. William 5
NICKSON, James Joseph 9
NICODEMUS, Frank 3
Courtney, Jr.
NICOL, Alexander R. 4
NICOL, Charles Edgar 1
NICOL, Jacob 5
NICOLA, Lewis H
NICOLAI, Harry T. 3
NICOLASSEN, George 5
Frederick
NICOLAY, Helen 3
NICOLAY, John George 1
NICOLET, Jean H
NICOLL, Alfred Harris 8
NICOLL, De Lancey 1
NICOLL, Henry H
NICOLL, James Craig 1
NICOLL, Matthias, Jr. 1
NICOLLET, Joseph Nicolas H
NICOLLS, Matthias 1
NICOLLS, Richard H
NICOLLS, William H
NICOLLS, William Jasper 1
NICOLSON, Harold 7
(George)
NICOLSON, J(ohn) 7
U(rban)
NICOLSON, Marjorie 7
Hope
NICUM, John 1
NIDECKER, John E. 9
NIDEN, George 9
NIEBUHR, H. Richard 4
NIEBUHR, Reinhold 5
NIEDERLEHNER, 10
Leonard
NIEDERMAIR, John 8
Charles
NIEDERMEYER, 3
Frederick David
NIEDRINGHAUS, 1
Frederick G.
NIEDRINGHAUS, George 2
Hayward
NIEDRINGHAUS, George 1
W.
NIEDRINGHAUS, Henry 1
Frederick
NIEDRINGHAUS, J. P. 4
Erwin
NIEDRINGHAUS, 1
Thomas Key
NIEHAUS, Charles Henry 1
NIEHAUS, Fredrich 5
Wilhelm
NIELDS, John P. 2
NIELSEN, Alice 2
NIELSEN, Arthur Charles 5
NIELSEN, Fred Kenelm 4
NIELSEN, Harald Herborg 5
NIELSEN, Jens Rud 10
NIELSEN, Johannes 5
Maagaard
NIELSEN, Lawrence Ernie 10
NIELSEN, Otto R. 10
NIEMAN, Lucius W. 1
NIEMANN, Carl 4
NIEMEYER, John Henry 1
NIEMI, Taisto John 8
NIEMOELLER, Martin 9
NIEPORTE, Victor B. 7
NIERENSEE, John R. H
NIERMAN, John L. 3
NIES, James Buchanan 1
NIESET, Robert Thomas 6
NIESS, Robert Judson 9
NIESZ, Homer E. 1
NIETO DEL RIO, Felix 3
NIEUWLAND, Julius 1
Arthur
NIEZER, Charles M. 1
NIEZER, Louis Fox 8
NIFONG, Frank Gosney 4
NIGGEMAN, Louis 6
William
NIGHTINGALE, Augustus 1
Frederick
NIGHTINGALE, Earl 10
Clifford
NIGHTINGALE, William 4
Thomas

NIGRELLI, Ross Franco 10
NIHART, Benjamin 3
Franklin
NIJINSKY, Vaslav 4
NIKANDER, John Kustaa 1
NIKOLSKY, Alexander A. 4
NILAN, John Joseph 1
NILES, Alfred Salem 1
NILES, Alva Joseph 2
NILES, Blair 3
NILES, Edward Hulbert 3
NILES, Emory Hamilton 7
NILES, Frederick Adolph 8
NILES, George McCallum 1
NILES, Henry Carpenter 3
NILES, Henry Clay 1
NILES, Henry Clay 6
NILES, Hezekiah H
NILES, Jason H
NILES, John Jacob 7
NILES, John Jacob 8
NILES, John Milton H
NILES, Kossuth 1
NILES, Nathan Erie 1
NILES, Nathaniel* H
NILES, Nathaniel 1
NILES, Philip Bradford 3
NILES, Samuel H
NILES, Walter Lindsay 2
NILES, William Harmon 1
NILES, William Henry 4
NILES, William White 1
NILES, William Woodruff 1
NILLES, Herbert George 4
NILSEN, Arthur 7
NILSSON, Fritiof 6
NILSSON, Hjalmar 1
NILSSON, Victor 2
NIMITZ, Chester William 4
NIMKOFF, Meyer F. 4
NIMMONS, George Croll 2
NIMS, Eugene Dutton 3
NIMS, Harry Dwight 4
NIMS, Marshall Grant 9
NIN, Anais 7
NINDE, Edward 1
Summerfield
NINDE, William Xavier 1
NININGER, Harvey 9
Harlow
NINNIS, Frederick Charles 6
NIPHER, Francis Eugene 1
NISBET, Charles H
NISBET, Charles Richard 2
NISBET, Eugenius Aristides H
NISBET, James Douglas 1
NISBET, Robert Hogg 4
NISBET, Walter Olin, Jr. 5
NISKA, Maralin 10
NISLEY, Harold A. 4
NISONGER, Herschel 5
Ward
NISSEN, Harry 8
NISSEN, Harry Archibald 3
NISSEN, Hartvig 4
NISSEN, Henry W. 3
NISSEN, Ludwig 1
NISWONGER, C. Rollin 7
NISWONGER, C. Rollin 8
NITSCHMANN, David H
NITZE, William Albert 3
NITZSCHE, Elsa Koenig 3
NITZSCHE, George E. 4
NIVEN, Archibald H
Campbell
NIVEN, David 8
NIVEN, John Ballantine 3
NIVEN, William 1
NIVISON, Robert 6
NIVOLA, Costantino 9
NIX, Abit 8
NIX, James Thomas 2
NIX, Robert N. C. 9
NIXON, Brevard 1
NIXON, Charles Elston 4
NIXON, Elliott B. 4
NIXON, Elliott Bodley 10
NIXON, Eugene White 5
NIXON, George Felton 3
NIXON, George Stuart 1
NIXON, Howard Kenneth 4
NIXON, John* H
NIXON, John Thompson H
NIXON, Justin Wroe 3
NIXON, Lewis 1
NIXON, Louise Aldrich 10
NIXON, Oliver Woodson 1
NIXON, Pat Irland 4
NIXON, Paul 3
NIXON, Samuel F. 4
NIXON, Thomas Carlyle 5
NIXON, William C. 1
NIXON, William Penn 1
NIZA, Marcos de H
NKRUMAH, Kwame 5
NOA, Ernestine 5
NOA, Thomas Lawrence 7

NOSS, John Boyer 7
NOSS, Theodore Bland 1
NOSSITER, Bernard Daniel 10
NOSTRAND, Peter Elbert 4
NOSWORTHY, Thomas Arthur 4
NOTESTEIN, Frank Wallace 8
NOTESTEIN, Jonas O. 1
NOTESTEIN, Wallace 5
NOTESTEIN, William Lee 4
NOTHSTEIN, Ira Oliver 5
NOTMAN, Arthur H
NOTMAN, James Geoffrey 6
NOTMAN, John H
NOTNAGEL, Leland Hascall 3
NOTOPOULOS, James A. H
NOTT, Abraham H
NOTT, Charles Cooper 1
NOTT, Eliphalet H
NOTT, Henry Junius H
NOTT, Josiah Clark H
NOTT, Otis Fessenden H
NOTT, Samuel H
NOTT, Stanley Charles 3
NOTTE, John Anthony, Jr. 8
NOTTER, Harley A. 3
NOTTINGHAM, Wayne B. 4
NOTTINGHAM, William 1
NOTZ, Frederick William Augustus
NOTZ, William Frederick 1
NOURSE, Amos H
NOURSE, Charles Joseph 6
NOURSE, Edward Everett 1
NOURSE, Edwin Griswold 6
NOURSE, Elizabeth 1
NOURSE, Henry Stedman 1
NOURSE, John Thomas, Jr. 3
NOURSE, Joseph Pomeroy 3
NOVACK, Ben 8
NOVAES, Guiomar 7
NOVAK, Arthur Francis 8
NOVAK, Emil 7
NOVAK, Frank John, Jr. 2
NOVAK, Milan Vaclav 10
NOVAK, Ralph B(ernard) 5
NOVAK, Sonia 4
NOVARRO, Ramon (Real Name Ramon Gil Samaniego)
NOVELLO, Ivor 4
NOVER, Barnet 5
NOVIK, Ylda Farkas (Mrs. David Novik) 7
NOVIKOFF, Alex Benjamin 9
NOVILLE, George Ottilie 8
NOVINS, Louis A. 9
NOVOTNY, Antonin 6
NOVOTNY, Charles K. 4
NOVY, Frederick George 5
NOVY, Robert Lev 5
NOWACZYNSKI, Wojciech Jerzy 9
NOWELS, Trellyen Ernest 2
NOWLAN, Alden 8
NOWLAN, George Clyde 4
NOWLIN, William Dudley 4
NOXON, Frank Wright 2
NOXON, Herbert Richards 5
NOYAN, Pierre-jacques Payende H
NOYCE, Robert Norton 10
NOYER, Ralph 7
NOYES, Alexander Dana 3
NOYES, Alfred 3
NOYES, Arthur Amos 4
NOYES, Arthur P. 4
NOYES, Blancke 7
NOYES, C. Reinold 3
NOYES, Carleton 3
NOYES, Charles Floyd 1
NOYES, Charles Lothrop 1
NOYES, Charles Phelps 1
NOYES, Charles Rutherford 4
NOYES, Clara D. 1
NOYES, Crosby Stuart 1
NOYES, Daniel Rogers 1
NOYES, E. Louise 1
NOYES, Edward Allen 4
NOYES, Edward Follansbee H
NOYES, Edward MacArthur 1
NOYES, Eliot Fette 7
NOYES, Frank Brett 2
NOYES, Frank Eugene 1
NOYES, George Henry 1
NOYES, George Loftus 4
NOYES, George Rapall 5
NOYES, George Rapall 1
NOYES, Guy Lincoln 1
NOYES, Harry Alfred 5
NOYES, Henry Drury 1
NOYES, Henry Erastus 1
NOYES, Irving George

NOYES, James Atkins 3
NOYES, Jansen 6
NOYES, John H
NOYES, John Humphrey H
NOYES, John Rutherford 3
NOYES, Joseph Cobham
NOYES, La Verne W. 1
NOYES, Leigh 7
NOYES, Linwood Irving 4
NOYES, Marion Ingalls 4
NOYES, Morgan Phelps 5
NOYES, Newbold 2
NOYES, Nicholas Hartman 7
NOYES, Pierrepont Burt 1
NOYES, Pierrepont T. 10
NOYES, Robert Gale 4
NOYES, Theodore Richards 1
NOYES, Theodore Williams 2
NOYES, Walter Chadwick 1
NOYES, William Albert 3
NOYES, William Albert, Jr. 7
NOYES, William Curtis H
NSUBUGA, Emmanuel Cardinal 10
NUCKOLLS, Claiborne George 6
NUCKOLLS, Stephen Friel 1
NUEL, Percy (Edmond) 7
NUELLE, Joseph Henry 4
NUELSEN, John Louis 2
NUESSLE, Francis E. 5
NUESSLE, William L. 4
NUFER, Albert F. 3
NUFFER, Joseph Henry 5
NUFFIELD, Viscount 4
NUGEN, Robert Hunter 4
NUGENT, Daniel Cline 2
NUGENT, Elliott 7
NUGENT, Frank Stanley 4
NUGENT, Brother Gregory 10
NUGENT, James Alexander 2
NUGENT, John F. 1
NUGENT, Joseph C. 9
NUGENT, Paul Cook 4
NUGENT, Robert Logan 4
NUGENT, Thomas Joseph 5
NUGENT, Walter Henry 5
NUGENT, William A. 8
NUHN, Clifford Jeremiah 5
NUHN, John Alfred 4
NULSEN, Charles Kilbourne 3
NULTON, Louis McCoy 3
NUNEMAKER, John Horace 3
NUNES, Gordon Maxwell 10
NUNEZ, Alvar Cabeza de Vaca H
NUNEZ, Solón 7
NUNGESTER, Walter James 9
NUNLIST, Frank Joseph 4
NUNN, Clement Singleton 5
NUNN, Harold Francis 5
NUNN, Marshall 3
NUNN, Paul N. 1
NUNNEMACHER, Rudolph Fink 9
NUNO, Jaime H
NUNO, Jaime 4
NUQUIST, Andrew Edgerton 6
NUREYEV, Rudolf Hametovich 10
NURI AS-SAID 3
NURKSE, Ragnar 4
NURSE, Rebecca H
NUSBAUM, Jesse Logan 4
NUSE, Roy Cleveland 6
NUSSBAUM, Arthur 4
NUSSBAUM, Max 6
NUSSBAUM, Murray 8
NUSSBAUM, Paul Joseph 1
NUTE, Alonzo H
NUTE, Grace Lee 10
NUTHEAD, William H
NUTLY, William B. 8
NUTT, Clifford Cameron 4
NUTT, Hubert Wilbur 5
NUTT, Joseph Randolph 2
NUTT, Robert Lee 2
NUTTALL, George Henry Falkiner 1
NUTTALL, Leonard John, Jr. 2
NUTTALL, Thomas H
NUTTALL, Zelia 1
NUTTER, Donald Grant 4
NUTTER, Edmondson John Masters 3
NUTTER, Edward Hoit 1
NUTTER, Fred Jewett 7
NUTTER, George Read 1
NUTTER, G(ilbert) Warren 7
NUTTING, Charles Cleveland 1
NUTTING, George Edward 4

NUTTING, Harold Judd 4
NUTTING, Herbert Chester 1
NUTTING, John Danforth 3
NUTTING, Margaret Ogden
NUTTING, Mary Adelaide 2
NUTTING, Mary Olivia 1
NUTTING, Newton Wright H
NUTTING, Perley Gilman 2
NUTTING, Wallace 1
NUTTLE, Harry (Hopkins) 5
NUTTLE, Harry (Hopkins) 7
NUTTMAN, Louis Meredith 5
NUVEEN, John 2
NUVEEN, John 5
NUYTTENS, Pierre 3
NYBURG, Sidney Lauer 3
NYCE, Benjamin Markley 3
NYDAHL, Malvin John 7
NYDEGGER, James Archibald 1
NYDEN, John Augustus 1
NYE, Archibald 4
NYE, Arthur Wickes 7
NYE, Edgar Hewitt 2
NYE, Edgar Wilson H
NYE, Ernest Lewis 9
NYE, Frank E. 1
NYE, Frank Mellen 2
NYE, Frank Wilson 8
NYE, George Dewey 10
NYE, Gerald P. 5
NYE, Irene 5
NYE, James Gordon 9
NYE, James Warren H
NYE, John Hooper 4
NYE, Reuben Lovell 4
NYE, Wallace George 4
NYE, Ward Higley 5
NYGAARD, Harlan Kenneth 4
NYGAARD, Hjalmar C. 4
NYHOLM, Jens 8
NYLANDER, Lennart 4
NYQUIST, Carl 3
NYQUIST, Edna Elvera 4
NYQUIST, Ewald B(erger) 9
NYSTROM, Paul Henry 5
NYSTROM, Wendell Clarence 5
NYSWANDER, Reuben Edson, Jr. 1

O

OAKES, Clarence Perry 6
OAKES, Frederick Warren 4
OAKES, George Washington Ochs 1
OAKES, Herbert Walter 7
OAKES, James 1
OAKES, Robert A. 6
OAKES, Thomas Fletcher* 4
OAKES, Urian H
OAKEY, P. Davis 4
OAKLAND, Ralph Edward 9
OAKLAND, Simon Benjamin 8
OAKLEAF, Joseph 1
OAKLEY, Amy 4
OAKLEY, Annie H
OAKLEY, Annie 4
OAKLEY, Francis Clark 4
OAKLEY, Henry Augustus 4
OAKLEY, Horace Sweeney 4
OAKLEY, Imogen Brashear 1
OAKLEY, Seymour Adams 1
OAKLEY, Thomas Jackson H
OAKLEY, Thornton 3
OAKLEY, Violet 4
OAKMAN, Walter G. 1
OAKSEY, Geoffrey Lawrence 5
OAKSEY, Geoffrey Lawrence 6
OARE, Robert Lenn 4
OATES, Gordon Cedric 9
OATES, James Franklin 3
OATES, James Franklin, Jr. 8
OATES, Warren 8
OATES, Whitney J. 6
OATES, William Calvin 1
OBALDIA, Jose Doming de 4
OBEAR, Hugh Harris 5
OBEAR, Hugh Harris 7
OBEE, Charles Walter 6
OBENAUER, Marie Louise 2
OBENCHAIN, William Alexander 1
OBENSHAIN, Richard Dudley 7
OBENSHAIN, Wiley S(hackford) 5
OBER, Frank Benedict 9
OBER, Frank Roberts 4
OBER, Henry Kulp 1

OBER, Sarah Endicott 4
OBERBECK, Arthur William 10
OBERF, Frederick Albion 1
OBERFELL, George Grover
OBERG, Erik 3
OBERG, Kalervo 6
OBERHANSLEY, Henry Ernest 2
OBERHARDT, William 3
OBERHELMAN, Harry Alvin 9
OBERHOFFER, Emil 4
OBERHOLSER, Harry Church 4
OBERHOLTZER, Edison Ellsworth 7
OBERHOLTZER, Ellis Paxson 1
OBERHOLTZER, Sara Louisa 4
OBERHOLTZER, Sara Louisa Vickers H
OBERLAENDER, Gustav 1
OBERLINK, Boyd Stevenson 1
OBERLY, Henry Sherman 4
OBERMANN, Julian J. 3
OBERMAYER, Leon Jacob 7
OBERMEYER, Ernest David 9
OBERNAUER, Harold 8
OBERNDORF, Clarence Paul 3
OBERNDORFER, Anne Shaw Faulkner (Mrs. Marx E. Oberndorfer) 5
OBERON, Merle 7
O'BERRY, John E. 4
OBERTEUFFER, Delbert 7
OBERTEUFFER, George 3
OBERWINDER, John Ferdinand 8
OBERWORTMANN, Nugent Robert 4
OBICI, Amedeo 2
OBOLER, Eli Martin 9
O'BOYLE, Francis Joseph 4
O'BOYLE, Patrick Aloysius Cardinal 9
O'BRIAN, John Lord 5
O'BRIAN, John Lord 6
O'BRIAN, Robert Enlow 10
O'BRIEN, Charles F. 1
O'BRIEN, Dale 10
O'BRIEN, Daniel J. 8
O'BRIEN, David Vincent 10
O'BRIEN, Denis 1
O'BRIEN, Denis Augustine 1
O'BRIEN, Dennis Francis 2
O'BRIEN, Edgar David 5
O'BRIEN, Edmond 8
O'BRIEN, Edward Charles 1
O'BRIEN, Edward Francis 2
O'BRIEN, Edward James 3
O'BRIEN, Edward Joseph Harrington 1
O'BRIEN, Ernest Aloysius 7
O'BRIEN, Eugene 7
O'BRIEN, Eugene Louis 9
O'BRIEN, Fitz-james 4
O'BRIEN, Francis Patrick 4
O'BRIEN, Frank A. 1
O'BRIEN, Frank Cornelius 5
O'BRIEN, Frank James 4
O'BRIEN, Frank Michael 2
O'BRIEN, Frederick 1
O'BRIEN, Frederick William
O'BRIEN, George D. 3
O'BRIEN, George Miller 9
O'BRIEN, Henry Rust 5
O'BRIEN, Henry Xavier 10
O'BRIEN, Howard Vincent 2
O'BRIEN, James Edward 10
O'BRIEN, James H. 4
O'BRIEN, James Patrick 4
O'BRIEN, James Putnam 1
O'BRIEN, Jeremiah* H
O'BRIEN, John H
O'BRIEN, John 1
O'BRIEN, John A. 4
O'BRIEN, John A. 7
O'BRIEN, John Cornelius 4
O'BRIEN, John F. 1
O'BRIEN, John Joseph 1
O'BRIEN, John P. 2
O'BRIEN, Joseph John 3
O'BRIEN, Justin McCortney 5
O'BRIEN, Kenneth 3
O'BRIEN, Lawrence Francis 10
O'BRIEN, Leo Frederick 5
O'BRIEN, Leo William 8

O'BRIEN, Sister M. Raphael 3
O'BRIEN, Matthew Anthony H
O'BRIEN, Maxwell A. 8
O'BRIEN, Miles 4
O'BRIEN, Morgan Joseph 1
O'BRIEN, Patrick Henry 3
O'BRIEN, Patrick M. 7
O'BRIEN, Ray J. 8
O'BRIEN, Richard H
O'BRIEN, Richard Frank 10
O'BRIEN, Robert Lincoln 3
O'BRIEN, S. Weldon 4
O'BRIEN, Sara Redempta 5
O'BRIEN, Seumas 6
O'BRIEN, Thomas Charles 3
O'BRIEN, Thomas Dillon 1
O'BRIEN, Thomas George 5
O'BRIEN, Thomas Henry 2
O'BRIEN, Thomas J. 4
O'BRIEN, Thomas James 1
O'BRIEN, Thomas Stanley, III 8
O'BRIEN, Vincent 3
O'BRIEN, William Augustine 6
O'BRIEN, William Austin 2
O'BRIEN, William Claire 5
O'BRIEN, William David 4
O'BRIEN, William James 4
O'BRIEN, William L. 9
O'BRIEN, William Shoney H
O'BRIEN, William Smith 2
O'BRIEN, William V. O. 3
O'BRIEN, William W. 7
O'BRINE, David Edward, Jr. 4
O'BRYNE, Michael 5
O'BYRNE, Eleanor Mary 10
O'BYRNE, John Coates 10
O'BYRNE, John J. 5
O'CALLAGHAN, Edmund Balley H
O'CALLAGHAN, Jeremiah H
O'CALLAGHAN, Peter 1
OCAMPOS, Bernardo 3
O'CASEY, Sean 3
OCCOM, Samson H
OCHELTREE, John Burdon 7
OCHLEWSKI, Tadeusz 6
OCHS, Adolph S. 1
OCHS, Arthur, Jr. 5
OCHS, Clarence L. 5
OCHS, Julius H
OCHS, Milton Barlow 3
OCHS, Phil 7
OCHSNER, Albert John 1
OCHSNER, Alton 8
OCHSNER, Edward H. 3
OCHSNER, Erwin Charles 7
OCHTMAN, Dorothy 5
OCHTMAN, Leonard 1
OCKENDEN, Ina Marie Porter 4
OCKENGA, Harold John 9
OCKERBLAD, Nelse Frederick 3
OCKERSON, John Augustus H
OCKERSON, John Augustus 2
OCKERSON, John Augustus
O'CONNELL, Ambrose 4
O'CONNELL, Arthur 7
O'CONNELL, C. Leonard 3
O'CONNELL, Daniel Theodore 4
O'CONNELL, David Joseph 1
O'CONNELL, Dennis Joseph 1
O'CONNELL, Desmond Henry 5
O'CONNELL, Eugene H
O'CONNELL, Harold J. 4
O'CONNELL, Harold P. 9
O'CONNELL, James 1
O'CONNELL, James Timothy 4
O'CONNELL, John Henry 5
O'CONNELL, John James, III 8
O'CONNELL, John Joseph 1
O'CONNELL, John Joseph 2
O'CONNELL, John Matthew, Jr. 1
O'CONNELL, John Michael, Jr. 3
O'CONNELL, Joseph E. 4
O'CONNELL, Joseph Francis 2
O'CONNELL, Joseph Francis, Jr. 4

OLIFF, Charles 9
OLIN, Abram Baldwin H
OLIN, Arvin Solomon 1
OLIN, Franklin W. 3
OLIN, Gideon H
OLIN, Henry H
OLIN, Hubert Leonard 4
OLIN, John Merrill 8
OLIN, John Myers 1
OLIN, Richard M. 1
OLIN, Stephen H
OLIN, Stephen Henry 1
OLIN, Walter Herbert 1
OLIN, William Milo 1
OLINGER, Henri Cesar 4
OLINSKY, Ivan Gregorewitch 4
OLIPHANT, A. Dayton 4
OLIPHANT, Charles Lawrence 5
OLIPHANT, Ernest Henry Clark 4
OLIPHANT, Harold Duncan 5
OLIPHANT, Herman 1
OLITSKY, Peter Kosciusko 4
OLIVARES, Jose De 5
OLIVE, Edgar William 5
OLIVE, George Scott 4
OLIVE, John Ritter 6
OLIVE, John Ritter 7
OLIVE, Lindsay Shepherd 10
OLIVER, Allen Laws 5
OLIVER, Andrew* H
OLIVER, Andrew 8
OLIVER, Arthur L. 1
OLIVER, Augustus Kountze 3
OLIVER, Charles Augustus 1
OLIVER, Clarence Paul 10
OLIVER, Daniel Charles 1
OLIVER, Edna May 2
OLIVER, Edward Allen 3
OLIVER, Edwin Austin 1
OLIVER, Edwin Letts 3
OLIVER, Edwin Letts 4
OLIVER, Fitch Edward H
OLIVER, Frank 7
OLIVER, Fred Nash 9
OLIVER, George Jeffries 6
OLIVER, George Sturges 4
OLIVER, George Tener 1
OLIVER, Grace Atkinson 1
OLIVER, Grayden 10
OLIVER, Henry Kemble H
OLIVER, Henry Madison, Jr. 5
OLIVER, Henry W. 1
OLIVER, James 1
OLIVER, James Arthur 8
OLIVER, James Harrison 1
OLIVER, James Henry 7
OLIVER, Jean Redman 7
OLIVER, John Chadwick 4
OLIVER, John Rathbone 2
OLIVER, John Watkins 10
OLIVER, John William 8
OLIVER, Joseph H
OLIVER, Joseph 4
OLIVER, Joseph Doty 1
OLIVER, Joseph Hayden 7
OLIVER, L. Stauffer 4
OLIVER, Lunsford Errett 8
OLIVER, Martha Capps 1
OLIVER, Paul Ambrose 1
OLIVER, Peter H
OLIVER, Ralph Addison 9
OLIVER, Robert Shaw 1
OLIVER, Thomas Edward 2
OLIVER, Webster J. 5
OLIVER, William Bacon 4
OLIVER, William Burns 6
OLIVER, William F(rederick) 5
OLIVER, William Morrison H
OLIVETTI, Adriano 4
OLIVIER, Charles Pollard 6
OLIVIER, Charles Pollard 7
OLIVIER, Sir Laurence Kerr 10
OLIVIER, Stuart 6
OLLENHAUER, Erich 4
OLLESHEIMER, Henry 1
OLLMANN, Loyal Frank 4
OLMSTEAD, Albert Ten Eyck 2
OLMSTEAD, Dawson 7
OLMSTEAD, Frank Robert 3
OLMSTEAD, Ralph W. 9
OLMSTED, Charles Edward 7
OLMSTED, Charles Sanford 1
OLMSTED, Charles Tyler 1
OLMSTED, Clarence Edward 8
OLMSTED, Denison H
OLMSTED, E. Stanley 5
OLMSTED, Everett Ward 2
OLMSTED, Frederick Law 1
OLMSTED, Frederick Law 3
OLMSTED, George Welch 1
OLMSTED, Gideon H
OLMSTED, James Frederic 1
OLMSTED, James Greeley 1
OLMSTED, James Montrose Duncan 3
OLMSTED, John Bartow 4
OLMSTED, John Charles 1
OLMSTED, Marlin Edgar 1
OLMSTED, Mildred Scott (Allen Seymour Olmsted) 10
OLMSTED, Millicent 1
OLMSTED, Victor Hugo 4
OLMSTED, William Beach 1
OLNEY, Albert J. 3
OLNEY, George W. 1
OLNEY, Jesse H
OLNEY, Louis Atwell 2
OLNEY, Peter Butler 1
OLNEY, Richard* 1
OLNEY, Warren 1
OLNEY, Warren, Jr. 1
O'LOUGHLIN, John M(artin) 5
O'LOUGHLIN, Joseph Martin 9
OLP, Ernest Everett 1
OLPIN, A(lbert) Ray 10
OLPP, Archibald Ernest 7
OLRICH, Ernest Louis 4
OLSCHKI, Leonardo 7
OLSEN, Arden Beal 8
OLSEN, C. Arild 10
OLSEN, Clarence Edward 5
OLSEN, Einar Arthur 10
OLSEN, Eugene Field 10
OLSEN, Francis Richard 10
OLSEN, Herb 6
OLSEN, Herluf Vagn 4
OLSEN, Ingerval M. 4
OLSEN, John Charles 2
OLSEN, Julius 2
OLSEN, Leif Ericson 4
OLSEN, Marvin Elliott 10
OLSEN, Nils Andreas 1
OLSEN, Thomas Siegfried 3
OLSEN, William Anderson 6
OLSON, Arthur Andrew 9
OLSON, Axel Ragnar 1
OLSON, Bruce F. 7
OLSON, Carl Augustus 9
OLSON, Carl Walter 3
OLSON, Charles 5
OLSON, Conrad Patrick 7
OLSON, Culbert 4
OLSON, Edwin August 2
OLSON, Elder James 10
OLSON, Ernst William 3
OLSON, Floyd Bjerstjerne 1
OLSON, George Edgar 2
OLSON, George Leonard 7
OLSON, Gideon Carl Emil 8
OLSON, Grant Franklin 3
OLSON, Gus 8
OLSON, H. Edwin 4
OLSON, Harry 1
OLSON, Harry Edwin 7
OLSON, Harvey S. 9
OLSON, Henry 4
OLSON, James Chester 10
OLSON, James Edward 5
OLSON, John Frederick 5
OLSON, Julius Emil 4
OLSON, Julius Johann 5
OLSON, Karl John 7
OLSON, Kenneth Eugene 4
OLSON, Lawrence 10
OLSON, Norman O. 6
OLSON, Oscar Ludvig 3
OLSON, Oscar Thomas 4
OLSON, Oscar William 3
OLSON, Ralph J. 5
OLSON, Ralph O. 3
OLSON, Raymond 6
OLSON, Raymond Ferdinand 4
OLSON, Raymond Verlin 9
OLSON, Richard Hall 10
OLSON, Robert August 9
OLSON, Robert S. 8
OLSON, Roy Howard 6
OLSON, Sigurd Ferdinand 8
OLSON, Willard Clifford 7
OLSSEN, William Whittingham 4
OLSSON, Alexander 3
OLSSON, Elis 3
OLSSON, George Carl Phillip 10
OLSSON, Olof 1
OLSTEN, William 10
OLSTERLING, Anders Johan 7
OLSTON, Albert B. 4
OLT, George Russell 3
OLYPHANT, David Washington Cincinnatus H
OLYPHANT, John Kensett 6
OLYPHANT, Robert 1
OLYPHANT, Robert Morrison 1
O'MAHONEY, Joseph Christopher 4
O'MAHONEY, Joseph Michael 4
O'MAHONY, John H
O'MALLEY, Austin 1
O'MALLEY, Charles Acheson 10
O'MALLEY, Charles P. 5
O'MALLEY, Comerford J. 10
O'MALLEY, Edward Valentine 8
O'MALLEY, Francis Joseph 6
O'MALLEY, Frank Ward 1
O'MALLEY, Henry 1
O'MALLEY, John Francis 5
O'MALLEY, Joseph Edward 6
O'MALLEY, Mart J. 8
O'MALLEY, Thomas F. 5
O'MALLEY, Walter F. 7
OMAN, Carl R. 9
OMAN, Charles Malden 2
OMAN, Joseph Wallace 1
OMAR H
O'MEALIA, E. Leo 4
O'MEARA, Edward Thomas 10
O'MEARA, Joseph 10
O'MEARA, Mark 1
O'MEARA, Stephen 1
O'MEARA, Walter Andrew 10
O'MELVENY, Henry William 1
O'MELVENY, John 8
O'MELVENY, Stuart 8
OMMERLE, Harry Garner 7
OMWAKE, George L. 1
OMWAKE, Howard Rufus 2
OMWAKE, John 1
ONAHAN, William James 1
ONAN, David Warren 3
ONASSIS, Aristotle Socrates 6
ONATE, Juan de H
ONDERDONK, Adrian Holmes 5
ONDERDONK, Benjamin Tredwell H
ONDERDONK, Frank Scovill 1
ONDERDONK, Gilbert 4
ONDERDONK, Henry H
ONDERDONK, Henry Ustick H
ONDRAK, Ambrose Leo 4
O'NEAL, Charles Thomas 3
O'NEAL, Claude E(dgar) 5
O'NEAL, Claude E(dgar) 7
O'NEAL, Edward Asbury, III 3
O'NEAL, Edward Ashbury H
O'NEAL, Emmet 1
O'NEAL, Emmet 4
O'NEAL, Forest Hodge 10
O'NEAL, Frederick 10
O'NEAL, James 5
O'NEAL, Perry Ernest 10
O'NEAL, Samuel Amos 3
O'NEAL, William Russell 2
O'NEALE, Margaret H
O'NEALL, John Belton H
O'NEIL, Charles 1
O'NEIL, Frank R. 1
O'NEIL, George F. 5
O'NEIL, Hugh Roe 5
O'NEIL, James 1
O'NEIL, James Francis 8
O'NEIL, James Julian 6
O'NEIL, John Francis 1
O'NEIL, Joseph Henry 1
O'NEIL, Lew Drew 6
O'NEIL, Patrick Henry 4
O'NEIL, Ralph Thomas 1
O'NEIL, William Francis 4
O'NEIL, William J. 8
O'NEILL, Albert T. 3
O'NEILL, Burke 4
O'NEILL, C. William 7
O'NEILL, Charles H
O'NEILL, Charles 2
O'NEILL, Charles Austin 3
O'NEILL, Edmond 1
O'NEILL, Edward Emerson 3
O'NEILL, Edward J(oseph) 7
O'NEILL, Edward L. 2
O'NEILL, Eugene Gladstone 3
O'NEILL, Eugene M. 1
O'NEILL, Florence 4
O'NEILL, Frank J. 5
O'NEILL, Gerard Kitchen 10
O'NEILL, Harry P. 3
O'NEILL, Hugh 1
O'NEILL, J. Henry 4
O'NEILL, J. Vincent 4
O'NEILL, James Albert 6
O'NEILL, James Lewis 2
O'NEILL, James Milton 5
O'NEILL, John H
O'NEILL, John Edward 4
O'NEILL, John J. 3
O'NEILL, John William 7
O'NEILL, Lewis Patrick 5
O'NEILL, Merlin 7
O'NEILL, Michael C(ornelius) 10
O'NEILL, Michael Joyce 10
O'NEILL, Richard Winslow 8
O'NEILL, William James 8
ONG, David Graham 8
ONKEN, William Henry, Jr. 5
ONSAGER, Lars 7
ONTHANK, Pierce 7
OOMS, Casper W. 4
OOST, Stewart Irvin 8
OOSTERMEYER, Jan 4
OOSTING, Henry J. 5
OPDYCKE, John Baker 3
OPDYCKE, Leonard Eckstein 1
OPDYKE, George H
OPDYKE, William Stryker 1
OPERTI, Albert 1
OPHEIM, Leonard Bertinius 5
OPHULS, William 1
OPIE, Eugene Lindsay 5
OPIE, Thomas 4
OPLER, Marvin Kaufmann 7
OPP, Julie 1
OPPELT, Wolfgang Walter 6
OPPEN, George 8
OPPENHEIM, Adolf Leo 6
OPPENHEIM, Alfred 10
OPPENHEIM, Amy Schwartz 3
OPPENHEIM, Ansel 1
OPPENHEIM, Edward Phillips 2
OPPENHEIM, James 1
OPPENHEIM, Nathan 1
OPPENHEIM, Samuel 1
OPPENHEIM, Saul Chesterfield 10
OPPENHEIMER, Sir Ernest* 3
OPPENHEIMER, Francis J. (Francis Opp) 6
OPPENHEIMER, Frank Friedman 8
OPPENHEIMER, Fritz Ernest 10
OPPENHEIMER, Fritz Ernest 5
OPPENHEIMER, Jess 9
OPPENHEIMER, Julius John 8
OPPENHEIMER, Monroe 10
OPPENHEIMER, Reuben 8
OPPENHEIMER, Robert 4
OPPENHEIMER, Russell Henry 8
OPPER, Clarence Victor 4
OPPER, Frederick Burr 1
OPPERMANN, Paul 7
OPPICE, Harold Whinery 6
OPTIC, Oliver H
OPTON, Frank G. 10
O'QUIN, Leon 9
ORAHOOD, Harper M. 1
ORBISON, Roy 9
ORBISON, Thomas James 1
ORCHARD, Claude R. 7
ORCHARD, John Ewing 4
ORCUTT, Calvin B. 1
ORCUTT, Frederic Scott 7
ORCUTT, Hiram H
ORCUTT, William Dana 3
ORCUTT, William Warren 2
ORD, Edward Otho Cresap H
ORD, George H
ORD, James Garesché 7
ORDAL, Ola Johannessen 1
ORDAL, Zakarias J. 3
ORDEAN, Albert Le Grand 1
ORDONEZ, Castor 1
ORDOVER, Sondra T. 9
ORDRONAUX, John 1
ORDWAY, A(lonzo) B(enton) 8
ORDWAY, Edward Warren 4
ORDWAY, J. G. 4
ORDWAY, John H
ORDWAY, John Morse 1
ORDWAY, Samuel Hanson 1
ORDWAY, Samuel Hanson 5
ORDWAY, Thomas 3
ORE, Oystein 5
O'REAR, Edward Clay 5
O'REAR, James Bigstaff 9
O'REAR, John Davis 1
O'REGAN, Anthony H
O'REILLY, Alexander H
O'REILLY, Andrew John Goldsmith 2
O'REILLY, Bernard H
O'REILLY, Bernard Patrick 1
O'REILLY, Charles J. 1
O'REILLY, Edward Synnott 6
O'REILLY, Gabriel Ambrose 5
O'REILLY, Henry H
O'REILLY, James 1
O'REILLY, James Thomas 4
O'REILLY, John Boyle H
O'REILLY, Mary Boyle 1
O'REILLY, Peter J. 4
O'REILLY, Richard Thomas 9
O'REILLY, Robert Maitland 1
O'REILLY, Thomas Charles 1
ORELL, Bernard Leo 8
ORENDORFF, Alfred 1
ORFF, Carl 8
ORGAIN, William Edmund 7
ORIANS, George Harrison 10
ORKIN, Saul 8
ORLADY, George Boal 1
ORLOFF, Jack 10
ORMAN, James Bradley 4
ORMANDY, Eugene 8
ORME, James Booth Lockwood 6
ORME, John Pinckney 1
ORMES, Robert Verner 9
ORMOND, Alexander Thomas 1
ORMOND, Jesse Marvin 6
ORMOND, John Kelso 7
ORMONDROYD, Jesse 10
ORMSBEE, Ebenezer Jolls 1
ORMSBEE, Thomas Hamilton 5
ORMSBY, Oliver Samuel 3
ORMSBY, Ross R. 7
ORMSBY, Stephen H
ORMSBY, Waterman Lilly H
ORMSTON, Mark D. 4
ORNBURN, Ira M. 8
ORNDOFF, Benjamin Harry 5
ORNDORFF, William Ridgely 1
ORNDUFF, William Wilmer 5
ORNE, Caroline Frances 1
ORNE, John 1
ORNER, Irvin Melvin 4
ORNITZ, Samuel 3
ORNSTEIN, Leo 9
O'RORKE, Edward Arthur 8
O'ROURKE, Charles Edward 2
O'ROURKE, Fidelis (Arthur J.) 5
O'ROURKE, George Martin 8
O'ROURKE, John Thomas 2
O'ROURKE, John Thomas 8
O'ROURKE, Lawrence James 4
O'ROURKE, Patrick Ira 2
O'ROURKE, William Thomas 3
OROVITZ, Max 7
OROWAN, Egon 10
OROZCO, Jose Clemente 2
ORR, Alexander Dalrymple H
ORR, Alexander Ector 1
ORR, Benjamin H
ORR, Carey 4
ORR, Charles 4
ORR, Charles Prentiss 1
ORR, Douglas William 5
ORR, Douglass Winnett 10
ORR, Flora Gracia 3
ORR, George 1
ORR, Gustavus John H
ORR, H. Winnett 3
ORR, Hugh H
ORR, Isaac Henry 3
ORR, James Lawrence H
ORR, James Lawrence 1
ORR, James Washington 1
ORR, John 7
ORR, John Alvin 3

PALMER, Henry E. 1
PALMER, Henry L. 1
PALMER, Henry Robinson 4
PALMER, Henry Wilber 1
PALMER, Horatio Richmond 1
PALMER, Howard 2
PALMER, Howard Shirley 7
PALMER, Innis Newton H
PALMER, Irving Allston 1
PALMER, James Croxall 1
PALMER, James Lindley 7
PALMER, James Shedden H
PALMER, Joel H
PALMER, John 4
PALMER, John Alfred 8
PALMER, John McAuley 1
PALMER, John McAuley 3
PALMER, John Roy 8
PALMER, John William 3
PALMER, John Williamson 1
PALMER, Joseph H
PALMER, Julius Auboineau 1
PALMER, Kyle Dulaney 9
PALMER, Leigh Carlyle 3
PALMER, Leroy Sheldon 1
PALMER, Leslie Richard 1
PALMER, Lester Joerg 8
PALMER, Lilli 9
PALMER, Loren 1
PALMER, Lynde 1
PALMER, Martin Franklin 4
PALMER, Mary Bell 1
PALMER, Nathaniel Brown H
PALMER, Orville Henry 7
PALMER, Pauline 1
PALMER, Philip Mason 3
PALMER, Philip Motley 7
PALMER, Mrs. Potter 1
PALMER, Potter 1
PALMER, Potter 2
PALMER, Ray H
PALMER, Ray 2
PALMER, Richard Emery 9
PALMER, Robert 3
PALMER, Samuel Sterling 1
PALMER, Silas H. 4
PALMER, Stanley Gustavus 6
PALMER, Stephen Eugene 10
PALMER, Stephen S. 1
PALMER, Stuart 4
PALMER, Theodore Sherman 3
PALMER, Thomas Waverly 1
PALMER, Thomas Waverly 5
PALMER, Thomas Witherell 1
PALMER, Truman Garrett 1
PALMER, Walter Launt 1
PALMER, Walter Lincoln 10
PALMER, Walter Thomas 8
PALMER, Walter Walker 3
PALMER, Warren Sherman 4
PALMER, William Adams H
PALMER, William Beach 4
PALMER, William Charles 9
PALMER, William Henry 1
PALMER, William Jackson 1
PALMER, William Pendleton 1
PALMER, William Spencer 5
PALMER, Williston Birkhimer 6
PALMERSTON, 3d viscount H
PALMIERI, Edmund Louis 10
PALMISANO, Vincent L. 7
PALMORE, William Beverly 1
PALMQUIST, Elim Arthur Eugene 5
PALOU, Francisco H
PALTSITS, Victor Hugo 3
PALUMBO, Leonard 6
PAM, Max 1
PAMMEL, Louis Hermann 1
PAN, Hermes 10
PANARETOFF, Stephen 4
PANASSIE, Hughes Louis Marle Henri 6
PANBOURNE, Oliver 1
PANCOAST, Henry Khunrath 1
PANCOAST, Henry Spackman 1
PANCOAST, Joseph H
PANCOAST, Russell Thorn 1
PANCOAST, Seth H
PANCOAST, Thomas Jessup 1
PANCOST, E. Ellsworth 3
PANDOLFI, Frank Louis 6
PANE-GASSER, John 4
PANETH, F. A. 3
PANGBORN, Earl Leroy 4

PANGBORN, Frederic Werden 4
PANGBORN, Georgia Wood 5
PANGBORN, Thomas Wesley 4
PANICO, Giovanni 4
PANITZ, Murray Wolfe 10
PANNELL, Faye H
PANNELL, Henry Clifton 2
PANNILL, Charles Jackson 3
PANNKOKE, Otto Herman 1
PANOFF, Robert 9
PANOFSKY, Erwin 4
PANOFSKY, Hans Arnold 4
PANSY 1
PANTON, William H
PANTSIOS, Athan Anastason 6
PANTZER, Kurt Friedrich 7
PANUFNIK, Sir Andrzej 10
PANUNZIO, Constantine Maria 4
PANYUSHKIN, Alexander S(emyenovich) 6
PAOLINO, Thomas Joseph 9
PAPADOPOULOS, Dimitrios (Ecumenical Patriarch Dimitrios I)* 10
PAPAGOS, Alexander 3
PAPANEK, Ernst 6
PAPANEK, Jan 10
PAPANICOLAOU, George Nicholas 4
PAPE, Delbert Hill 7
PAPE, Eric 1
PAPE, William J. 4
PAPEN, George William 10
PAPESH, Alexander Anthony 6
PAPEZ, James Wenceslas 3
PAPI, Gennaro 1
PAPISH, Jacob 8
PAPP, Joseph 10
PAPPENHEIMER, Alwin M. 3
PAPPER, Solomon 9
PAPSDORF, Herman L. 8
PAQUET, Anthony C. H
PAQUETTE, Charles Alfred 5
PAQUIN, Albert Joseph, Jr. 4
PAQUIN, Lawrence G. 4
PAQUIN, Paul 1
PAQUIN, Samuel Savil 2
PARADISE, Frank Ilsley 1
PARAMANANDA, Swami 1
PARAY, Paul 7
PARCEL, John Ira 6
PARDEE, Ario H
PARDEE, Arthur McCay 7
PARDEE, Don Albert 1
PARDEE, George Cooper 1
PARDEE, Harold Ensign Bennett 5
PARDEE, Harold Ensign Bennett 7
PARDEE, Israel Platt 1
PARDEE, James Thomas 2
PARDO, Felipe 4
PARDO DE ZELA, Francisco 7
PARDOE, T(homas) Earl 7
PARDOE, William Edward 7
PARDOW, William O'Brien 1
PARDRIDGE, William Deweese 6
PARDUE, Austin 8
PARDUE, Louis A. 4
PAREDES, Quintin 7
PARENT, Alphonse Marie 5
PARENTE, Pascal Prosper 5
PARET, J(ahial) Parmly 5
PARET, Thomas Dunkin 1
PARET, William 1
PARFREY, Sydney Woodrow 7
PARGELLIS, Stanley 4
PARGNY, Eugene W(illiam) 7
PARHAM, Frederick William 1
PARHAM, James A. 6
PARHAM, William Eugene 7
PARIS, Auguste Jean, Jr. 3
PARIS, Charles Wesley 6
PARIS, Gordon Daniel 9
PARIS, W. Francklyn 5
PARIS, William Edward 3
PARISH, Elijah H
PARISH, Howard Wells 9
PARISH, John Carl H
PARISH, Margaret Cecile (Peggy) 9
PARISH, Walter Alvis 3
PARISH, William Jackson 4
PARK, Charles Abraham 7

PARK, Charles Caldwell 1
PARK, Charles Edwards 4
PARK, Charles Francis 2
PARK, Colin 7
PARK, Edward Amasa 1
PARK, Edward Cahill 5
PARK, Edwards Albert* 4
PARK, Frank 4
PARK, Franklin Atwood 1
PARK, Guy Brasfield 2
PARK, Isabelle Springer 6
PARK, J. A. 3
PARK, J. Edgar 3
PARK, James H
PARK, John Alsey 3
PARK, John Callaway 8
PARK, Julian 4
PARK, Lawrence 1
PARK, Lee I. 7
PARK, Linton H
PARK, Marion Edwards 4
PARK, Maud Wood 3
PARK, Milton 1
PARK, Orville Augustus 2
PARK, Philip Mulvena 8
PARK, Richard Leonard 7
PARK, Robert Emory 2
PARK, Robert Ezra 2
PARK, Roswell H
PARK, Roswell 1
PARK, Royal Wheeler 1
PARK, Sam 1
PARK, Samuel Culver 1
PARK, Samuel Culver, Jr. 1
PARK, Thomas 10
PARK, Trenor William H
PARK, William 4
PARK, William Hallock 1
PARK, William Lee 4
PARKE, Benjamin H
PARKE, Francis Neal 3
PARKE, Henry Walter 5
PARKE, John H
PARKE, John Grubb 1
PARKE, John Shepard 3
PARKE, William More 4
PARKER, A. Warner 1
PARKER, Addison Bennett 4
PARKER, Albert 8
PARKER, Albert George, Jr. 3
PARKER, Alexander Wilson 5
PARKER, Alexis du Pont 1
PARKER, Alfred Charles 9
PARKER, Alton Brooks 1
PARKER, Amasa Junius H
PARKER, Amasa Junius 1
PARKER, Amory 4
PARKER, Andrew H
PARKER, Arthur Caswell 3
PARKER, Ben Hutchinson 1
PARKER, Benjamin Franklin 1
PARKER, Bertha Morris 7
PARKER, Charles A. 3
PARKER, Charles Barnsdall 4
PARKER, Charles Christopher H
PARKER, Charles Christopher 1
PARKER, Charles Edward* 7
PARKER, Charles Morton 1
PARKER, Charles Wolcott 5
PARKER, Chauncey David 5
PARKER, Chauncey Goodrich 2
PARKER, Chauncey Goodrich, Jr. 3
PARKER, Clarence P(rentice) 7
PARKER, Clifford Stetson 9
PARKER, Cola Godden 4
PARKER, Cortlandt 1
PARKER, Cortlandt 1
PARKER, Daingerfield 1
PARKER, Daniel 10
PARKER, Daniel Francis 4
PARKER, David Bennett 7
PARKER, David Stuart 10
PARKER, Davis Raff 10
PARKER, Dewitt Henry 2
PARKER, Dorothy 4
PARKER, Edith Putnam 1
PARKER, Edmund Southard 1
PARKER, Edward Burns 3
PARKER, Edward Cary 1
PARKER, Edward Foster 7
PARKER, Edward Frost 1
PARKER, Edward J. 4
PARKER, Edward Melville 4
PARKER, Edward Pickering 6

PARKER, Edward Sanders, Jr. 1
PARKER, Edward Wheeler 4
PARKER, Edwin B. 1
PARKER, Edwin P., Jr. 8
PARKER, Edwin Pond 1
PARKER, Edwin Wallace H
PARKER, Eila Moore Johnson (Mrs. Barton Wise Parker) 6
PARKER, Ely Samuel H
PARKER, Emmett Newton 1
PARKER, Evan James 4
PARKER, Fitzgerald Sale 1
PARKER, Fletcher Douglas 4
PARKER, Foster 7
PARKER, Foxhall Alexander H
PARKER, Frances 5
PARKER, Francis Hubert 1
PARKER, Francis Lejau 1
PARKER, Francis Warner 1
PARKER, Francis Wayland 1
PARKER, Frank 2
PARKER, Frank Wilson 1
PARKER, Franklin Eddy 1
PARKER, Franklin Eddy, Jr. 1
PARKER, Franklin Nutting 5
PARKER, Frederic, Jr. 1
PARKER, Frederic Charles Wesby 2
PARKER, Gabe Edward 6
PARKER, George Albert 1
PARKER, George Amos 1
PARKER, George B. 2
PARKER, George Frederick 1
PARKER, George Howard 3
PARKER, George M., Jr. 8
PARKER, George Proctor 1
PARKER, George Swinnerton 3
PARKER, Glenn 10
PARKER, Glenn Lane 2
PARKER, Grady P. 5
PARKER, H. E. 3
PARKER, H. Wayne 5
PARKER, Harry D. 9
PARKER, Harry Lee 3
PARKER, Harry M. 9
PARKER, Henry Griffith 1
PARKER, Henry Taylor 1
PARKER, Herbert 1
PARKER, Herschel Clifford 4
PARKER, Hilon Adelbert 1
PARKER, Homer Cling 2
PARKER, Horatio Newton 2
PARKER, Horatio William 1
PARKER, Hosea 1
PARKER, Isaac Washington H
PARKER, Isaac Charles H
PARKER, J. Heber 3
PARKER, J. Roy 3
PARKER, James* H
PARKER, James 1
PARKER, James Cutler Dunn 1
PARKER, James Edmund 2
PARKER, James Henry 1
PARKER, James I. 4
PARKER, James Southworth 1
PARKER, James W. 3
PARKER, Jameson 5
PARKER, Jane Marsh 1
PARKER, Jo A. 5
PARKER, Joel* H
PARKER, John 3
PARKER, John Adams 4
PARKER, John Bernard 1
PARKER, John Castieregah 6
PARKER, John D. 4
PARKER, John Gowans 3
PARKER, John Henry 2
PARKER, John Johnston 3
PARKER, John Mason H
PARKER, John Milliken 1
PARKER, Joseph Benson 1
PARKER, Joseph E. 5
PARKER, Joseph Orville 10
PARKER, Josiah H
PARKER, Julia Evelina Smith H
PARKER, Julius Frederick 4
PARKER, Junius 1
PARKER, Karr 9
PARKER, Kenneth Colburn 1
PARKER, Laigh C. 3
PARKER, Lawton S. 1
PARKER, Leonard Fletcher 1
PARKER, Lewis Wardlwa 1
PARKER, Lottie Blair 1
PARKER, Louis Alexander 8

PARKER, Lovell Hallet 4
PARKER, Lovell Hallet 7
PARKER, Marion W. 4
PARKER, Maude 3
PARKER, Maurice 6
PARKER, Millard Mayhew 4
PARKER, Morgan 7
PARKER, Moses Greeley 1
PARKER, Myron Melvin 4
PARKER, Nahum H
PARKER, Norman Sallee 8
PARKER, Peter H
PARKER, R. Wayne 4
PARKER, Ralph Douglas 10
PARKER, Ralph Halstead 10
PARKER, Ralph Robinson 2
PARKER, Raymond 10
PARKER, Richard H
PARKER, Richard Alexander 10
PARKER, Richard Elliot H
PARKER, Richard Green H
PARKER, Robert 3
PARKER, Robert Hunt 5
PARKER, Robert L. 7
PARKER, Robert Plewes 9
PARKER, Robert Shumate Jr. 6
PARKER, Ross Isaac 6
PARKER, Roy Hartford 3
PARKER, Sam Diehl 7
PARKER, Samuel H
PARKER, Samuel Chester 1
PARKER, Samuel Wilson 1
PARKER, Severn Eyre H
PARKER, Stanley V. 5
PARKER, Theodore H
PARKER, Theodore Bissell 2
PARKER, Thomas H
PARKER, Thomas Cleveland 1
PARKER, Torrance 2
PARKER, Valeria Hopkins 3
PARKER, Walter Huntington 5
PARKER, Walter Huntington 7
PARKER, Walter Robert 3
PARKER, Walter Winfield 3
PARKER, Wesby Reed 4
PARKER, Willard H
PARKER, Willard 4
PARKER, William Amory 9
PARKER, William Belmont 1
PARKER, William Edward 2
PARKER, William Gordon 5
PARKER, William H. 1
PARKER, William Harwar 5
PARKER, William Henry 5
PARKER, William M. 2
PARKER, William Riley 5
PARKER, William Stanley 5
PARKERSON, Jesse Jones 5
PARKES, Charles Herbert 5
PARKES, Henry Bamford 5
PARKES, William Ross 5
PARKHILL, Charles Breckinridge 1
PARKHILL, James William 4
PARKHURST, C. Francis 1
PARKHURST, Charles Chandler 1
PARKHURST, Charles Chandler 8
PARKHURST, Charles Henry 1
PARKHURST, Frederic Augustus 5
PARKHURST, Frederic Hale 1
PARKHURST, George Leigh 10
PARKHURST, Helen 6
PARKHURST, Helen Huss 3
PARKHURST, Howard Elmore 1
PARKHURST, John Adelbert 1
PARKHURST, John Foster 1
PARKHURST, John Gibson 1
PARKHURST, Lewis 2
PARKIN, George Raleigh 7
PARKIN, John Hamilton 9
PARKIN, Walter H. 9
PARKINS, Almon Ernest 1
PARKINSON, Belvidera Ashleigh Dry 8
PARKINSON, Burney Lynch 5
PARKINSON, Daniel Baldwin 1
PARKINSON, Donald Berthold 2
PARKINSON, George Ambrose 8
PARKINSON, John Barber 1

PARKINSON, Robert Henry 1
PARKINSON, Roy Harvey 8
PARKINSON, Thomas Francis 10
PARKINSON, Thomas I. 3
PARKINSON, William Lynn 4
PARKINSON, William Nimon 5
PARKMAN, Francis H
PARKMAN, Henry 1
PARKMAN, Henry 3
PARKS, Addison Karrick 2
PARKS, Bert 10
PARKS, Charles Wellman 1
PARKS, Clifford C. 1
PARKS, E. Taylor 4
PARKS, Ed Horace, III 10
PARKS, Edd Winfield 5
PARKS, Edward Lamay 1
PARKS, Ethel R. 4
PARKS, Floyd Lavinius 3
PARKS, Frank Thomas 4
PARKS, George Sutton 8
PARKS, Gordon Roger, Jr. 7
PARKS, Gorham 8
PARKS, Henry Green 10
PARKS, Henry Martin 3
PARKS, James Lewis* 1
PARKS, John Louis 5
PARKS, John Shields 5
PARKS, Leighton 8
PARKS, Lewis Smith 8
PARKS, Marvin McTyeire 1
PARKS, Robert Lee McAllister 3
PARKS, Rufus 1
PARKS, Samuel Conant 2
PARKS, Tilman Bacon 8
PARKS, Wilbur George 6
PARKS, William 1
PARKS, Wythe Marchant 1
PARKYNS, George Isham H
PARLANGE, Charles 9
PARLEE, Norman Allen Devine 9
PARLETTE, Ralph 1
PARLEY, Peter H
PARLIN, Charles Coolidge 8
PARLIN, Frank Edson 1
PARLIN, H. T. 3
PARLIN, William Henry 1
PARLOA, Maria H
PARLOW, Kathleen 8
PARMELE, Harris Barnum 1
PARMELE, Mary Platt 1
PARMELEE, Amy Olgen 7
PARMELEE, Cullen Warner
PARMELEE, Henry Francis 1
PARMELEE, Howard Coon 3
PARMELEE, Julius Hall 4
PARMELEE, Lewis Dwight 3
PARMELEE, Maurice 7
PARMENTER, Bertice Marvin
PARMENTER, Charles Sylvester 1
PARMENTER, Charles Winfield 4
PARMENTER, Christine Whiting 3
PARMENTER, Clarence Edward 8
PARMENTER, Frederick James 6
PARMENTER, George Freeman 3
PARMENTER, Roswell A. 4
PARMENTER, William H
PARMENTIER, Andrew H
PARMLEY, Joseph William 1
PARMLEY, Walter Camp 1
PARMLY, Eleazar H
PARNALL, Christopher 4
PARNELL, Harvey 1
PARPART, Arthur Kemble 4
PARR, Albert Eide 10
PARR, Charles McKew 6
PARR, Charles McKew 7
PARR, Harry L. 4
PARR, Jerome Henry 3
PARR, Joseph Greer 3
PARR, Samuel Wilbur 9
PARR, Samuel Wilson 1
PARR, William David 5
PARRA, Francisco José 9
PARRAN, Thomas* 4
PARRA PEREZ, Caracciolo 8
PARRAVANO, Giuseppe 7
PARRETT, Arthur N. 3
PARRETT, William Fletcher H

PARRINGTON, Vernon Louis 1
PARRIOTT, F. B. 3
PARRIOTT, James Deforis 2
PARRIS, Albion Keith H
PARRIS, Alexander H
PARRIS, Samuel H
PARRIS, Virgil Delphini H
PARRISH, Albert Garrett 3
PARRISH, Anne 4
PARRISH, Anne 3
PARRISH, Carl 4
PARRISH, Celestia Susannah 1
PARRISH, Charles H
PARRISH, Clara Weaver 1
PARRISH, Edward H
PARRISH, Isaac* 1
PARRISH, John Bertrand 5
PARRISH, Joseph H
PARRISH, June Austin 7
PARRISH, Karl Calvin 1
PARRISH, Lucian Walton 1
PARRISH, Maxfield 4
PARRISH, Philip Hammon 3
PARRISH, Randall 1
PARRISH, Robert Lewis 5
PARRISH, Robert Milton 7
PARRISH, Stephen 1
PARROTT, Alonzo Leslie 6
PARROTT, Claude Byron 4
PARROTT, Enoch Greenleafe H
PARROTT, James Marion 1
PARROTT, John Fabyan H
PARROTT, Marcus Junius H
PARROTT, Percival John 3
PARROTT, Robert Belgrove 9
PARROTT, Robert Parker H
PARROTT, Thomas Marc 3
PARRY, Albert 10
PARRY, Carl Eugene 7
PARRY, Charles Christopher H
PARRY, Charles Thomas H
PARRY, David MacLean 1
PARRY, Emma Louise 3
PARRY, Florence Fisher 8
PARRY, John Horace 8
PARRY, John Jay 3
PARRY, John Stubbs H
PARRY, Sidney Loren 5
PARRY, Will H. 1
PARSELL, Charles Victor 1
PARSHALL, De Witt 3
PARSHALL, Douglass Ewell 10
PARSHLEY, Howard Madison 3
PARSON, Hubert Templeton 1
PARSONS, Albert Richard H
PARSONS, Albert Ross 1
PARSONS, Albert Stevens 1
PARSONS, Alice Beal 4
PARSONS, Alice Knight 4
PARSONS, Andrew Clarkson 6
PARSONS, Archibald Livingstone 3
PARSONS, Arthur Barrette 4
PARSONS, Arthur Hudson, Jr. 3
PARSONS, Azariah Worthington
PARSONS, Betty Pierson 8
PARSONS, Charles H
PARSONS, Charles* 1
PARSONS, Charles 4
PARSONS, Charles B. 4
PARSONS, Charles Baldwin 1
PARSONS, Charles Cutler 7
PARSONS, Charles Francis 2
PARSONS, Charles Lathrop 4
PARSONS, C(hauncey) Leland 6
PARSONS, Claude Van 1
PARSONS, Donald Johnson 5
PARSONS, Douglas Eugene 7
PARSONS, Eben Burt 1
PARSONS, Edmund Byrd 5
PARSONS, Edward Alexander 4
PARSONS, Edward Erskine, Jr. 9
PARSONS, Edward Lambe 1
PARSONS, Edward Smith 2
PARSONS, Edward Young 1
PARSONS, Elsie Clews 2
PARSONS, Emma Follin (Mrs. Clifford W. Parsons) 5
PARSONS, Ernest William 1
PARSONS, Eugene 1
PARSONS, Fannie Griscom 1
PARSONS, Floyd William 1

PARSONS, Frances Theodora 4
PARSONS, Francis 1
PARSONS, Frank 1
PARSONS, Frank Alvah 1
PARSONS, Frank Nesmith 1
PARSONS, Frederick Williams 3
PARSONS, Geoffrey 3
PARSONS, Geoffrey, Jr. 8
PARSONS, Harriet Oettinger 8
PARSONS, Harry deberkeley 1
PARSONS, Hayward Treat 10
PARSONS, Mrs. Henry 1
PARSONS, Herbert 1
PARSONS, J. Lester 3
PARSONS, James Graham 10
PARSONS, James Kelly 5
PARSONS, J(ames) Russell 5
PARSONS, James Russell, Jr. 1
PARSONS, John B. 4
PARSONS, John Calvin 5
PARSONS, John Edward 1
PARSONS, John Frederick 5
PARSONS, Lester Shields 4
PARSONS, Lewis Baldwin 1
PARSONS, Lewis Eliphalet H
PARSONS, Lewis Morgan 5
PARSONS, Llewellyn B. 4
PARSONS, Llewellyn B(radley) 5
PARSONS, Louella O. 5
PARSONS, Marion Randall 6
PARSONS, Payn Bigelow 1
PARSONS, Philip Archibald 2
PARSONS, Ralph Monroe 6
PARSONS, Reginald Hascall 1
PARSONS, Richard 1
PARSONS, Richard Torrence 8
PARSONS, Robert Stevens 1
PARSONS, Robert Wade 9
PARSONS, Rose Peabody (Mrs. William Barclay Parsons) 9
PARSONS, Samuel 1
PARSONS, Samuel Holden H
PARSONS, Starr 2
PARSONS, Talcott 7
PARSONS, Theophilus* 1
PARSONS, Thomas Smith 1
PARSONS, Thomas William H
PARSONS, Usher 3
PARSONS, Wallace Emery 3
PARSONS, Wilfrid 3
PARSONS, Willard H. 2
PARSONS, William 2
PARSONS, William Barclay 1
PARSONS, William Barclay 5
PARSONS, William Edward 1
PARSONS, William Lewis 5
PARSONS, William Sterling 5
PARSONS, William Walter 10
PARSONS, William Wood 1
PARSONS, Willis Edwards 4
PARTCH, Clarence Elmar 7
PARTCH, Harry 6
PARTCH, Virgil Franklin, II 1
PARTHEMOS, George Steven 8
PARTINGTON, Frederick Eugene 1
PARTIPILO, Anthony Victor 5
PARTLOW, Ira Judson 1
PARTLOW, William Dempsey 5
PARTNER, Winnie Leroy 4
PARTON, Arthur 1
PARTON, Ernest 1
PARTON, Henry Woodbridge 1
PARTON, James H
PARTON, Lemuel Frederick 2
PARTON, Sara Payson Willis H
PARTRIDGE, Albert Gerry 3
PARTRIDGE, Alden H
PARTRIDGE, Bellamy 4
PARTRIDGE, Charles Patrick 4
PARTRIDGE, Donald Barrows 10
PARTRIDGE, Donald Barrows 2
PARTRIDGE, Edward Lasell 1

PARTRIDGE, (Ernest) John 8
PARTRIDGE, Everett P(ercy) 5
PARTRIDGE, Frank Charles 2
PARTRIDGE, George H
PARTRIDGE, George Everett 3
PARTRIDGE, James Rudolph H
PARTRIDGE, John Francis 7
PARTRIDGE, John Francis 8
PARTRIDGE, John Slater 1
PARTRIDGE, Richard 1
PARTRIDGE, Richard Clare 7
PARTRIDGE, Roi 8
PARTRIDGE, Sidney Catlin 1
PARTRIDGE, William Ordway 1
PARVIN, Theodore Sutton 1
PARVIN, Theophilus H
PAS, Ion 6
PASANT, Athanase J. 10
PASCALIS-OUVRIERE, Felix H
PASCALL, Thomas M. 6
PASCHAL, Franklin Cressey 2
PASCHAL, George Washington H
PASCHALL, John 3
PASCHALL, J(oshue) E(rnest) 6
PASCHALL, Nathaniel 7
PASCHALL, Nathaniel 8
PASCO, Samuel 1
PASHKOVSKY, Theophilus Nicholas 3
PASKO, Wesly Washington H
PASLEY, Virginia Schmitz (Mrs. Fred Pasley) 9
PASMA, Henry Kay 2
PASMORE, Henry Bickford 2
PASOLINI, Pier Paolo 6
PASQUIN, Anthony H
PASSANNATE, Charles 3
PASSANO, Edward B. 2
PASSARELLI, Luigi Alfonso 3
PASSAVANT, William Alfred H
PASSMAN, Otto Ernest 9
PASSMORE, Ellis Pusey 1
PASSMORE, Eric William 8
PASSMORE, Lincoln K. 1
PASTA, John Robert 8
PASTERNAK, Boris Leonidovitch 4
PASTERNAK, Joseph 10
PASTORE, Peter Nicholas 10
PASTORIUS, Francis Daniel H
PASTORIUS, Jaco 9
PASTORIZA, Andrés 8
PASVOLSKY, Leo 3
PATCH, Alexander McCarrell, Jr. 2
PATCH, Edith Marion 3
PATCH, Frank Wallace 1
PATCH, Helen Elizabeth 3
PATCH, Howard Rollin 4
PATCH, Joseph D. 7
PATCH, Kate Whiting 1
PATCH, Nathaniel Jordan Knight 1
PATCH, Ralph Reginald 3
PATCH, Sam H
PATCHEN, Kenneth 5
PATCHIN, Frank Glines 1
PATCHIN, Philip Halsey 3
PATCHIN, Robert Halsey 3
PATE, John Ralston 8
PATE, John Ralston 9
PATE, Martha B. Lucas 8
PATE, Maurice 4
PATE, Randolph Mcc 4
PATE, Walter Romny 5
PATEK, Doris S. 10
PATEK, Stanislaw 4
PATENAUDE, Esioff Leon 5
PATENOTRE, Eleanor Elverson 5
PATERSON, Albert Barnett 3
PATERSON, Donald Gildersleeve 4
PATERSON, Isabel 4
PATERSON, James Venn 2
PATERSON, John H
PATERSON, Norman McLeod 7
PATERSON, Robert 7
PATERSON, Robert Gildersleeve 4

PATERSON, Van Rensselaer 1
PATERSON, William H
PATERSON, William Tait 5
PATES, Gordon 10
PATIGIAN, Haig 3
PATILLO, Henry H
PATINO, Antenor R. 8
PATINO, Simon I. 2
PATMAN, Wright 6
PATMOS, Martin 6
PATON, James Morton 2
PATON, Lewis Bayles 1
PATON, Stewart 2
PATON, Thomas Bugard 1
PATON, William Agnew 1
PATON, William Andrew 8
PATON, William Kennell 3
PATRI, Angelo 4
PATRICELLI, Leonard Joseph 8
PATRICK, David Lyall 5
PATRICK, Edwin Daviess 2
PATRICK, Fred Albert 1
PATRICK, George Edward 1
PATRICK, George Neill 6
PATRICK, George Thomas White 2
PATRICK, Hugh Talbot 1
PATRICK, John Hayward 5
PATRICK, Joseph Cecil 4
PATRICK, Luther 3
PATRICK, Marsena Rudolph H
PATRICK, Mary Mills 1
PATRICK, Mason Mathews 1
PATRICK, Ransom Rathbone 5
PATRICK, Rembert Wallace 6
PATRICK, Robert F. 5
PATRICK, Robert Goodlett 1
PATRICK, Robert John, Jr. 10
PATRICK, Roy Leonard 3
PATRICK, Ted 4
PATRICK, Walter Albert 8
PATT, John Francis 5
PATTANGALL, William Robinson 2
PATTBERG, Emil Joseph, Jr. 8
PATTEE, Ernest Noble 2
PATTEE, Fred Lewis 3
PATTEE, William Sullivan 1
PATTEN, Amos Williams 1
PATTEN, Bradley Merrill 5
PATTEN, Charles Harreld 5
PATTEN, David 6
PATTEN, David L(ongfellow) 10
PATTEN, Everett Frank 4
PATTEN, George Yager 3
PATTEN, Gilbert 2
PATTEN, Helen Philbrook 4
PATTEN, Henry 3
PATTEN, James A. 1
PATTEN, James Horace 1
PATTEN, John H
PATTEN, John A. 1
PATTEN, Lewis Byford 7
PATTEN, Simon Nelson 1
PATTEN, Thomas Gedney 1
PATTEN, William 1
PATTEN, Zeboim Charles 2
PATTERSON, A. L. 4
PATTERSON, Adoniram Judson 1
PATTERSON, Alexander Evans 2
PATTERSON, Alicia 4
PATTERSON, Alvah Worrell 1
PATTERSON, Andrew Henry 1
PATTERSON, Antoinette De Courcey 1
PATTERSON, Archibald Williams 4
PATTERSON, Austin McDowell 3
PATTERSON, Boyd Crumrine 9
PATTERSON, Bryan 7
PATTERSON, Burd Shippen 1
PATTERSON, C. Stuart 1
PATTERSON, Caleb Perry 6
PATTERSON, Catherine Norris 2
PATTERSON, Charles Brodie 1
PATTERSON, Charles Edward 1
PATTERSON, Charles H. 7

PHELPS, Edward Bunnell	1	PHILLIPS, Aris	9	...

PHELPS, Edward Bunnell 1
PHELPS, Edward John 1
PHELPS, Edward Shethar 1
PHELPS, Edwin Philbrook 7
PHELPS, Elisha H
PHELPS, Erskine Mason 1
PHELPS, Esmond 3
PHELPS, George Harrison 2
PHELPS, George Turner 1
PHELPS, Guy Fitch 1
PHELPS, Guy Merritt 2
PHELPS, Guy Rowland H
PHELPS, Harry 1
PHELPS, Helen Watson 2
PHELPS, Henry Willis 2
PHELPS, Isaac King 5
PHELPS, James H
PHELPS, James Ivey 2
PHELPS, J(ames) Manley 5
PHELPS, John Jay 2
PHELPS, John Noble 5
PHELPS, John Smith H
PHELPS, Joseph Barnwell 8
PHELPS, Lancelot H
PHELPS, Lawrence 4
PHELPS, Malcom Elza 10
PHELPS, Marian 4
PHELPS, M(arlin) 7
T(heophelus)
PHELPS, Oliver H
PHELPS, Phelps 9
PHELPS, Richard K. 8
PHELPS, Richardson 8
PHELPS, Ruth Shepard 5
PHELPS, Samuel Shethar H
PHELPS, Shelton Joseph 2
PHELPS, Stephen 1
PHELPS, Thomas Stowell 1
PHELPS, Thomas Stowell, 1
Jr.
PHELPS, Timothy Guy 1
PHELPS, William Franklin 4
PHELPS, William Henry 1
PHELPS, William Lyon 2
PHELPS, William Richard 7
PHELPS, William Wallace H
PHELPS, William Walter H
PHELPS, William 1
Woodward
PHELPS-RIDER, Alice 6
PHEMISTER, Dallas B. 3
PHENIX, George Perley 1
PHIFER, Fred Wood 1
PHIFER, Robert Smith 7
PHILARET, George 9
Voznesensky
PHILBIN, Eugene A. 1
PHILBIN, Philip J. 5
PHILBRICK, Donald Ward 9
PHILBRICK, Herbert Shaw 4
PHILBROOK, Warren 1
Coffin
PHILE, Philip H
PHILENIA H
PHILIP H
PHILIP, Andre 5
PHILIP, George 2
PHILIP, Hoffman 3
PHILIP, John Jay 6
PHILIP, John W. 1
PHILIPP, Cyrus L. 10
PHILIPP, Emanuel Lorenz 1
PHILIPP, Richard 3
PHILIPPE, Robert Rene 5
PHILIPPI, E. Martin 2
PHILIPPI, Julius Edward 7
PHILIPS, Allen Griffith 7
PHILIPS, Aurelius Edwin 8
PHILIPS, Carlin 5
PHILIPS, Edith 9
PHILIPS, Frederick Stanley 8
PHILIPS, George Morris 1
PHILIPS, Irving 10
PHILIPS, Jesse Evans 4
PHILIPS, John F. 1
PHILIPS, Joseph Leon 8
PHILIPS, Martin Wilson 1
PHILIPS, William Pyle 3
PHILIPSE, Frederick H
PHILIPSON, David 2
PHILLER, George 1
PHILLIP, Hardie H
PHILLIPPE, Gerald Lloyd 5
PHILLIPPI, Joseph Martin 1
PHILLIPPI, Stanley Isaac 1
PHILLIPPI, Albanus 2
PHILLIPS, Albanus, Jr. 5
PHILLIPS, Alexander 1
Hamilton
PHILLIPS, Alexander Lacy 1
PHILLIPS, Alexander Roy 2
PHILLIPS, Alexander Van 1
Cleve
PHILLIPS, Alfred Edward 1
PHILLIPS, Alfred Noroton 5
PHILLIPS, Andrew 1
Wheeler

PHILLIPS, Aris 9
PHILLIPS, Arthur 9
PHILLIPS, Arthur L. 1
PHILLIPS, Asa Emory 1
PHILLIPS, Barnet 1
PHILLIPS, Benjamin 5
Dwight
PHILLIPS, Benjamin 7
Dwight
PHILLIPS, Bernard 6
PHILLIPS, Bert Geer 5
PHILLIPS, Burr Wendell 9
PHILLIPS, Burrill 9
PHILLIPS, Cabell Beverly 6
Hatchett
PHILLIPS, Cabell Beverly 7
Hatchett
PHILLIPS, Carl Chrisler 3
PHILLIPS, Carl L. 4
PHILLIPS, Catherine Coffin 2
PHILLIPS, Channing 1
Emery
PHILLIPS, Charles 1
PHILLIPS, Charles Gordon 5
PHILLIPS, Charles Henry 3
PHILLIPS, Charles L. 1
PHILLIPS, Charles Leonard 4
PHILLIPS, Chauncey Hatch 1
PHILLIPS, Chester Arthur 7
PHILLIPS, Coles 1
PHILLIPS, David Atlee 9
PHILLIPS, David Graham 7
PHILLIPS, Dorothy 7
Williams
PHILLIPS, Duane Seneca 1
PHILLIPS, Duncan 2
PHILLIPS, Edgar John 7
PHILLIPS, Edna M. 5
PHILLIPS, Edward Charles 3
PHILLIPS, Elliot Schuyler 1
PHILLIPS, Ellis Laurimore 3
PHILLIPS, Ethel Calvert 2
PHILLIPS, Everett Franklin 5
PHILLIPS, Francis Clifford 1
PHILLIPS, Frank 3
PHILLIPS, Frank McGinley 1
PHILLIPS, Frank Reith 2
PHILLIPS, George H
PHILLIPS, George Felter 1
PHILLIPS, George Wallace 6
PHILLIPS, Glenn Randall 1
PHILLIPS, Guy Berryman 9
PHILLIPS, Harmon 6
PHILLIPS, Harold Cooke 1
PHILLIPS, Harry 9
PHILLIPS, Harry Clinton 1
PHILLIPS, Harry 1
Hungerford Spooner, Jr.
PHILLIPS, Harry Irving 4
PHILLIPS, Henry H
PHILLIPS, Henry A. 3
PHILLIPS, Henry Albert 3
PHILLIPS, Henry Bayard 1
PHILLIPS, Henry Disbrow 3
PHILLIPS, Henry Lee 6
PHILLIPS, Henry Myer H
PHILLIPS, Henry Wallace 4
PHILLIPS, Herbert S. 4
PHILLIPS, Irna 6
PHILLIPS, James Andrew 1
PHILLIPS, James David 5
PHILLIPS, James Emerson, 7
Jr.
PHILLIPS, James Frederick 5
PHILLIPS, James Frederick 6
PHILLIPS, James Paul, II 3
PHILLIPS, Jay 10
PHILLIPS, Jay A. 9
PHILLIPS, Jay Campbell 1
PHILLIPS, Jesse J. 1
PHILLIPS, Jesse Snyder 3
PHILLIPS, John* H
PHILLIPS, John 1
PHILLIPS, John Bakewell 1
PHILLIPS, John Burton 1
PHILLIPS, John C. 2
PHILLIPS, John Charles 1
PHILLIPS, John Charles 4
PHILLIPS, John George 4
PHILLIPS, John Goldsmith 10
PHILLIPS, John Herbert 1
PHILLIPS, John Marshall 3
PHILLIPS, John McFarlane 1
PHILLIPS, John Milton 8
PHILLIPS, John Nicholson 5
PHILLIPS, John Sanburn 2
PHILLIPS, John Spinning 9
PHILLIPS, Kathryn Sisson 1
(Mrs. Ellis L. Phillips)
PHILLIPS, Lee Allen 1
PHILLIPS, Lee Eldas 2
PHILLIPS, Lena Madesin 5
PHILLIPS, Leon C. 3
PHILLIPS, Leroy 5
PHILLIPS, Levi Benjamin 1
PHILLIPS, Llewellyn 1
PHILLIPS, Louis 3

PHILLIPS, Lyle Winston 7
PHILLIPS, Marie Tello 5
(Mrs. Charles J. Yaegle)
PHILLIPS, Marjorie 8
PHILLIPS, Maude Gillette 4
PHILLIPS, Merton Ogden 3
PHILLIPS, Michael James 5
PHILLIPS, Milton Eves 1
PHILLIPS, Morris 1
PHILLIPS, Nathaniel 7
PHILLIPS, Nathaniel Pope 10
PHILLIPS, Nelson 1
PHILLIPS, Norman 4
Ethelbert
PHILLIPS, Orie Leon 1
PHILLIPS, Paul Chrisler 3
PHILLIPS, Percival 1
PHILLIPS, Percy Toumine 7
PHILLIPS, Percy Wilson 5
PHILLIPS, Philip* H
PHILLIPS, Philip Lee 1
PHILLIPS, Ralph Wilbur 10
PHILLIPS, Ray Edmund 4
PHILLIPS, Richard Harvey 4
PHILLIPS, Richard Idler 9
PHILLIPS, Richard Jones 1
PHILLIPS, Robert 2
PHILLIPS, Robert Allan 7
PHILLIPS, Roger Sherman 5
PHILLIPS, Rowley Wilhelm 6
PHILLIPS, Samuel H
PHILLIPS, Samuel Cochran 10
PHILLIPS, Samuel Edgar 3
PHILLIPS, Samuel J. 9
PHILLIPS, Seymour 9
PHILLIPS, Stephen H
Clarendon
PHILLIPS, T. D. 4
PHILLIPS, T. Redfield 1
PHILLIPS, Thomas Ashley 3
PHILLIPS, Thomas Guthrie 8
PHILLIPS, Thomas I. 1
PHILLIPS, Thomas 4
Raphael
PHILLIPS, Thomas W. 1
PHILLIPS, Thomas, 1
Wharton, Jr.
PHILLIPS, Ulrich Bonnell 1
PHILLIPS, Velma 10
PHILLIPS, Waite 4
PHILLIPS, Wallace Banta 3
PHILLIPS, Wallace 8
Benjamin
PHILLIPS, Walter Sargeant 6
PHILLIPS, Watson Lyman 2
PHILLIPS, Wayne 9
PHILLIPS, Wendell H
PHILLIPS, Wendell 6
PHILLIPS, Wendell 1
Christopher
PHILLIPS, Willard H
PHILLIPS, William* H
PHILLIPS, William 4
Addison
PHILLIPS, William Battle 1
PHILLIPS, William Eric 4
PHILLIPS, William Fowke 1
Ravenel
PHILLIPS, William Irving 4
PHILLIPS, Ze Barney 2
Thorne
PHILLIPSON, Irving 3
Joseph
PHILLIPY, Lester Newton 7
PHILLPOTTS, Eden 4
PHILOON, Wallace 7
Copeland
PHILP, John W. 2
PHILPOTT, Albert Lee 10
PHILPOTT, Charles 8
Hughes
PHILPOTT, Gordon M. 4
PHILPOTT, Harvey Cloyd, 4
Sr.
PHILPOTT, Peter Willey 4
PHILPUTT, Allan Bearden 1
PHILPUTT, James M. 1
PHILSON, Robert H
PHIN, John 1
PHINIZY, Bowdre 1
PHINIZY, Ferdinand H
PHINIZY, Hamilton 1
PHIPPS, Don Holcomb 5
PHIPPS, Frank Huntington 1
PHIPPS, Henry 1
PHIPPS, John H. 8
PHIPPS, John Shaffer 3
PHIPPS, Lawrence Clinton, 7
Jr.
PHIPPS, Lawrence Cowle 1
PHIPPS, Michael Grace 5
PHIPPS, Oval Alexander 7
PHIPS, Sir William H
PHISTER, Elijah Conner 1
PHISTER, Montgomery 4
PHLEGAR, Archer A. 1

PHLEGER, Atherton 10
Macondray
PHLEGER, Herman 9
PHOENIX, Charles E. 5
PHOENIX, Jonas Phillips 1
PHOENIX, Lloyd 4
PHOLIEN, Joseph 4
PHRANER, Wilson 4
PHYFE, Duncan 1
PHYFE, William Henry 1
Pinkney
PHYSICK, Philip Syng H
PHYTHIAN, Robert Lees 1
PIAAT, Sarah Morgan 1
Bryan
PIAF, Edith 4
PIAGET, Jean 7
PIASECKI, Peter F. 1
PIASTRO, Mishel 5
PIATIGORSKY, Gregor 7
PIATT, Donn 1
PIATT, John James 1
PIAZZA, Ferdinand 5
PIAZZONI, Gottardo 5
PIBUL SONGGRAM, 4
Luang
PICARD, Frank A. 4
PICARD, George Henry 1
PICARD, Ralph Alan 3
PICARD, Robert (George) 1
PICASSO, Pablo Ruiz 5
PICCARD, Jean Felix 5
PICCARD, Jeannette 7
Ridlon
PICCIONI, Attilio 9
PICCIRILLI, Attilio 2
PICCIRILLI, Furio 6
PICHEL, Irving 3
PICK, Albert, Jr. 7
PICK, Bernhard 1
PICK, Lewis Andrew 3
PICKARD, Andrew Ezra 6
PICKARD, Florence 1
Willingham
PICKARD, Frederick 3
William
PICKARD, Greenleaf 3
Whittier
PICKARD, John 1
PICKARD, Josiah Little 1
PICKARD, Samuel Nelson 5
PICKARD, Samuel Thomas 1
PICKARD, Ward Wilson 2
PICKARD, William 1
Lowndes
PICKEL, Frank Welborn 1
PICKEL, Margaret Barnard 3
PICKELL, Frank Gerald 1
PICKELLS, Charles 5
William
PICKEN, Lillian Hoxie 4
PICKENS, Andrew H
PICKENS, Andrew 2
Calhoun
PICKENS, Francis H
Wilkinson
PICKENS, Israel H
PICKENS, James Madison 5
PICKENS, Samuel O. 1
PICKENS, Slim 8
PICKENS, William 3
PICKENS, William 1
Augustus
PICKER, Arnold Melville 10
PICKERELL, George 4
Henry
PICKERING, Abner 4
PICKERING, Charles 1
PICKERING, Edward 1
Charles
PICKERING, Ernest 6
PICKERING, Harold 8
Gregg
PICKERING, John* H
PICKERING, Loring 1
PICKERING, Nelson 8
Winslow
PICKERING, Timothy H
PICKERING, William 1
Alfred
PICKERING, William 1
Henry

PICKETT, Tom 7
PICKETT, Warren Wheeler 3
PICKETT, William 1
Clendenin
PICKETT, William Francis 10
PICKHARDT, William 1
Paul
PICKING, Henry F. 4
PICKLE, George Wesley 4
PICKLESIMER, Hayes 5
PICKMAN, Benjamin, Jr. H
PICKNELL, William Lamb H
PICKRAL, George Monroe 8
PICKREL, William 4
Gillespie
PICKRELL, Homer P. 5
PICKRELL, Kenneth Leroy 9
PICOFF, Ronald Chester 6
PICOT, Louis Julien 1
PICQUET, Francois H
PICTON, Thomas H
PIDCOCK, Brian Morris 6
Henzell
PIDDOCK, Charles Albert 1
PIDGE, John Bartholomew 4
Gough
PIDGEON, Walter 8
PIDGIN, Charles Felton 1
PIECK, Wilhelm 4
PIECZENTKOWSKI, 9
Herman Arnold
PIEPER, Charles John 8
PIEPER, Emil G. 1
PIEPER, Ezra H. 3
PIEPER, Franz August 1
Otto
PIEPER, John Jacob 1
PIEPER, William Charles 3
PIER, Arthur Stanwood 4
PIER, Garrett Chatfield 2
PIER, William Lauren 4
PIERCE, Alfred Mann 5
PIERCE, Allin Hugh 7
PIERCE, Anna Eloise 3
PIERCE, Anne E(lise) 9
PIERCE, Arthur Henry 1
PIERCE, Arthur Sylvanus 4
PIERCE, Benjamin H
PIERCE, Bessie Louise 6
PIERCE, Byron Root 1
PIERCE, Carleton Custer 5
PIERCE, Charles Curry 8
PIERCE, Charles Franklin 1
PIERCE, Charles Milton 6
PIERCE, Charles Sumner 1
PIERCE, Claude Connor 2
PIERCE, Clay Arthur 5
PIERCE, Clayton Baxter 9
PIERCE, Clifford Davis 6
PIERCE, Daniel Thompson 3
PIERCE, Dante Melville 1
PIERCE, Daren Laine 9
PIERCE, Earle Vaydor 5
PIERCE, Edward Allen 6
PIERCE, Edward J. 6
PIERCE, Edward Lillie H
PIERCE, Edward Lillie 3
PIERCE, Edward Peter 1
PIERCE, Francis Marshal 2
PIERCE, Frank 4
PIERCE, Frank Reynolds 4
PIERCE, Frank W. 4
PIERCE, Franklin 1
PIERCE, Frederick Clifton 1
PIERCE, Frederick Ernest 4
PIERCE, Frederick Louis 1
PIERCE, George Edwin 3
PIERCE, George Foster H
PIERCE, George Warren 4
PIERCE, George 3
Washington
PIERCE, George William 6
PIERCE, Gilbert Ashville 1
PIERCE, Grace Adele 1
PIERCE, H. Clay 1
PIERCE, Henry Hill 1
PIERCE, Henry Lillie H
PIERCE, Henry Niles 1
PIERCE, James Harvey 8
PIERCE, Jason Noble 2
PIERCE, John Davis H
PIERCE, Joseph Hart 1
PIERCE, Josiah, Jr. 1
PIERCE, Katharine Curtis 7
(Mrs. Henry Hill Pierce)
PIERCE, Lawrence Blunt 1
PIERCE, Lawrence Michael 7
PIERCE, Leonard A. 4
PIERCE, Lorne 1
PIERCE, Louis 10
PIERCE, Lyman L. 1
PIERCE, Marvin 5
PIERCE, Maurice Campbell 8
PIERCE, Newton Barris 1
PIERCE, Norval Harvey 2
PIERCE, Oliver Willard 5
PIERCE, Palmer Eddy 1

PIERCE, Ray Vaughn 4
PIERCE, Rice A. 4
PIERCE, Richard Donald 6
PIERCE, Robert Fletcher Young 4
PIERCE, Robert L. 4
PIERCE, Robert Willard (Bob) 7
PIERCE, Roger 4
PIERCE, Shelly 3
PIERCE, Truman Mitchell 9
PIERCE, Ulysses Grant Baker 2
PIERCE, Wallace Lincoln 1
PIERCE, Walter Marcus 3
PIERCE, Walworth 4
PIERCE, William H
PIERCE, William Heflin 7
PIERCE, William Kasson 4
PIERCE, William Leigh H
PIERCE, W(illis) Conway 6
PIERCE, Winslow Shelby 1
PIERI, Louis Arthur Raymond 4
PIERIOT, Lucille Georgette 6
PIERON, Henri 4
PIEROTTI, John 9
PIERPONT, Francis Harrison H
PIERPONT, Harlan Trimble 7
PIERPONT, Henry Edwards 5
PIERPONT, James H
PIERPONT, James 1
PIERPONT, John H
PIERRE, Edward Dienhart 8
PIERRE, William Henry 10
PIERREPONT, Edwards H
PIERREPONT, Robert Low 2
PIERROT, George Francis 7
PIERSEL, Alba Chambers 1
PIERSOL, George Arthur 1
PIERSOL, George Morris 4
PIERSON, Abraham* H
PIERSON, Arthur Tappan 1
PIERSON, Charles Ernest 4
PIERSON, Charles Wheeler 1
PIERSON, Coen Gallatin 5
PIERSON, Delavan Leonard 1
PIERSON, Earl Wendell 10
PIERSON, Elmer F. 10
PIERSON, Hamilton Wilcox H
PIERSON, Isaac H
PIERSON, Isaac 1
PIERSON, Israel Coriell 1
PIERSON, J. Fred 1
PIERSON, Jeremiah Halsey H
PIERSON, Job H
PIERSON, Joseph Brelsford 7
PIERSON, Lewis Eugene 3
PIERSON, Louise Randall 8
PIERSON, Richard Norris 7
PIERSON, Romaine 1
PIERSON, Silas Gilbert 2
PIERSON, Warren Lee 7
PIERSON, William* 1
PIERSON, William Whatley, Jr. 8
PIERZ, Franz H
PIETENPOL, Clarence John 7
PIETENPOL, William Brasser 7
PIETERS, Adrian John 1
PIETERS, Aleida Johanna 1
PIETRO, Cartaino di Sciarrine 1
PIETSCH, Karl 1
PIETSCH, Theodore Wells 1
PIEZ, Charles 1
PIFER, Drury Augustus 5
PIFFARD, Henry Granger 1
PIGA, Franco 10
PIGEON, Louis Phillipe 9
PIGEON, Richard 5
PIGFORD, Clarece E. 2
PIGFORD, Robert Lamar 10
PIGGOT, Charles Snowden 6
PIGGOT, James H
PIGGOT, Robert H
PIGMAN, George Wood 1
PIGMAN, W. Ward 7
PIGOTT, James M. 10
PIGOTT, James M. 5
PIGOTT, John Thomas 4
PIGOTT, Paul 4
PIGOTT, Reginald James Seymour 7
PIGOTT, William Trigg 2
PIGUET, Leon A. 4
PIHLBLAD, C. Terence 7
PIHLBLAD, Ernst Frederick 2
PIIP, Antonius 7
PIKARSKY, Milton 10
PIKE, Albert H
PIKE, Austin Franklin H
PIKE, Charles Burrall 2
PIKE, Clayton Warren 1
PIKE, Douglas Henry 6
PIKE, F. H. 3
PIKE, Frederick Augustus H
PIKE, Granville Ross 4
PIKE, H. Harvey 6
PIKE, Harry Hale 5
PIKE, James H
PIKE, James Albert 5
PIKE, James Shepherd H
PIKE, John D. 8
PIKE, Joseph Brown 4
PIKE, Nicolas H
PIKE, Percy M. 4
PIKE, Robert H
PIKE, Robert Gordon 1
PIKE, Sumner Tucker 6
PIKE, William John 1
PIKE, Zebulon Montgomery H
PILAT, Carl Francis 5
PILAT, Ignaz Anton H
PILAT, Oliver 9
PILCH, Judah 9
PILCHER, James Evelyn 1
PILCHER, James Taft 2
PILCHER, Joshua H
PILCHER, Lewis Frederick 1
PILCHER, Lewis Stephen 1
PILE, William Anderson H
PILES, Samuel Henry 1
PILGRIM, Charles Winfield 4
PILIÉ, Louis M. 10
PILLAI, K. C. Sreedharan 9
PILLARS, Charles Adrian 1
PILLEMER, Louis 3
PILLING, James Constantine H
PILLOW, Gideon Johnson H
PILLSBURY, Albert Enoch 1
PILLSBURY, Alfred Fiske 3
PILLSBURY, Arthur Judson 1
PILLSBURY, Charles Alfred H
PILLSBURY, Charles Alfred 1
PILLSBURY, Charles Stinson 1
PILLSBURY, Donald Marion 8
PILLSBURY, Edwin S. 4
PILLSBURY, Eleanor Bellows (Mrs. Philip Winston Pillsbury) 5
PILLSBURY, Evans Searle 4
PILLSBURY, George Bigelow 5
PILLSBURY, Harriette Brown 3
PILLSBURY, Harry N. 1
PILLSBURY, Henry Church 3
PILLSBURY, Horace Davis 1
PILLSBURY, John Elliott 1
PILLSBURY, John Henry 1
PILLSBURY, John Sargent 1
PILLSBURY, John Sargent 5
PILLSBURY, Parker H
PILLSBURY, Philip Winston 8
PILLSBURY, Rosecrans W. 1
PILLSBURY, Walter Bowers 4
PILLSBURY, Walter Bowers 5
PILLSBURY, William Howard 3
PILMORE, Joseph H
PILPEL, Harriet Fleischl 10
PILPEL, Robert 9
PILSBRY, Henry Augustus 3
PILSBURY, Amos H
PILSBURY, Timothy H
PILSWORTH, Malcolm Nevil 4
PILZER, Maximilian 3
PIM, W. Paul 3
PIMEN, Patriarch (Sergey Mikhailovich Isvekov) 10
PIMENTEL, George Claude 10
PINANSKI, Abraham Edward 2
PINANSKI, Samuel 5
PINAY, Antoine 9
PINCHBACK, Pinckney Benton Stewart 1
PINCHBECK, Raymond Bennett 3
PINCHOT, Amos Richard Eno 2
PINCHOT, Cornelia Bryce 4
PINCHOT, Gifford 2
PINCHOT, James W. 1
PINCKARD, Harold Recenus 5
PINCKNEY, Charles H
PINCKNEY, Charles Cotesworth H
PINCKNEY, Charles Cotesworth 1
PINCKNEY, Elizabeth Lucas H
PINCKNEY, Francis Douglas 6
PINCKNEY, Henry Laurens H
PINCKNEY, John Adams 5
PINCKNEY, Josephine Lyons Scott 3
PINCKNEY, Merritt Willis 1
PINCKNEY, Thomas H
PINCOFFS, Maurice Charles 7
PINCUS, Gregory 4
PINDALL, James H
PINDALL, Xenophon Overton 1
PINDELL, Henry Means 1
PINE, David Andrew 5
PINE, Frank Woodworth 1
PINE, James 3
PINE, John B. 1
PINE, Robert Edge H
PINE, William Bliss 2
PINERO, Jesus T. 3
PINES, Ned Lewis 10
PINESS, George 5
PINGER, Henry Ambrose 10
PINGREE, George Elmer 6
PINGREE, Hazen S. 1
PINGREE, Samuel Everett 1
PINK, Charlotte (Mrs. John M. Pink) 6
PINK, Louis Heaton 3
PINKERT, Joseph S. 10
PINKERTON, Allan H
PINKERTON, Henry 10
PINKERTON, Kathrene 4
PINKERTON, Lewis Letig H
PINKERTON, Lowell Call 3
PINKERTON, Roy David 6
PINKERTON, William Allan 1
PINKHAM, Lucile Deen 4
PINKHAM, Lucius Eugene 1
PINKHAM, Lydia Estes H
PINKLEY, Roy H(enry) 6
PINKNEY, Edward Coote H
PINKNEY, Ninian H
PINKNEY, William H
PINNELL, Emmett Louis 5
PINNELL, George Lewis 10
PINNELL, Leroy Kenneth 5
PINNELL, William George 10
PINNEO, Dotha Stone 1
PINNER, Max H
PINNER, Max 2
PINNEY, E. Jay 4
PINNEY, Edward Lee 7
PINNEY, Edward Stevenson 7
PINNEY, George Miller, Jr. 4
PINNEY, Harry Bowman 5
PINNEY, Jean Burrows 7
PINNEY, Norman H
PINO, Ralph Harrison 8
PINSKI, David 5
PINSON, William Washington 1
PINTARD, John H
PINTARD, Lewis H
PINTEN, Joseph Gabriel 2
PINTNER, Rudolf 2
PINTO, Alva Sherman 2
PINTO, Isaac H
PINTO, Salvator 4
PINZA, Ezio 3
PIOTROVSKY, Boris Borisovich 10
PIPER, Alexander Ross 3
PIPER, Arthur 4
PIPER, Charles Vancouver 1
PIPER, Sir David Towry 10
PIPER, Edgar Bramwell 1
PIPER, Edwin Ford 1
PIPER, Fred Leroy 3
PIPER, Harry Cushing 10
PIPER, Horace L. 4
PIPER, Howard 8
PIPER, James 4
PIPER, Margaret Rebecca 6
PIPER, Martha Kime 9
PIPER, Otto Alfred 9
PIPER, Raymond F. 4
PIPER, William H
PIPER, William Thomas 5
PIPES, Louis A(lbert) 5
PIPES, Martin Luther 1
PIPES, Samuel Wesley, III 9
PIPKIN, Charles Wooten 1
PIPKIN, Francis Marion 10
PIPKIN, George H. 7
PIPPEN, Rodger Hamill 8
PIPPENGER, Wayne Grise 6
PIPPETT, Roger 4
PIPPIN, Raymond Russell 7
PIPPING, Hugo Edvard 6
PIPPY, Chesley Alwyn 10
PIQUENARD, Alfred H. H
PIRANI, Eugenio di 4
PIRAZZINI, Agide 1
PIRCE, William Almy H
PIRE, Dominique Georges 5
PIRELLI, Alberto 5
PIRELLI, Alberto 7
PIRET, Edgar Lambert 9
PIRIE, Emma Elizabeth 3
PIRIE, Frederick W. 3
PIRIE, John Charles 9
PIRIE, John T., Jr. 7
PIRIE, John Taylor 1
PIRIE, Samuel Carson 1
PIRKEY, Everett Leighton 4
PIRKEY, Henry Warren 6
PIRLOT, Paul Leon 10
PIRNIE, Alexander 8
PIRNIE, Malcolm 9
PIRQUET, Clemens Freiherr Von 5
PIRRUNG, Gilbert Robinson 9
PIRSSON, James W. H
PIRSSON, Louis Valentine 1
PIRTLE, James Speed 1
PISACANO, Nicholas Joseph 10
PISAR, Charles Juneau 3
PISCATOR, Erwin 4
PISE, Charles Constantine H
PISER, Alfred Lionel 6
PISHTEY, Joseph Josephson 5
PISK, Paul Amadeus 10
PISTON, Walter 7
PISTOR, William Jacob 7
PITAMIC, Leonidas 7
PITAVAL, John Baptist 1
PITCAIRN, Harold Frederick 4
PITCAIRN, John H
PITCAIRN, Norman Bruce 2
PITCAIRN, Raymond 4
PITCAIRN, Robert 1
PITCHER, Arnold Ellis 7
PITCHER, Charles Sidney 5
PITCHER, Molly H
PITCHER, Nathaniel H
PITCHER, Zina H
PITCHFORD, John H. 1
PITCHLYNN, Peter Perkins H
PITFIELD, Robert Lucas 5
PITKIN, Francis Alexander 5
PITKIN, Frederick Walker H
PITKIN, Timothy H
PITKIN, Walter Boughton 3
PITKIN, William* H
PITKIN, Wolcott H. 3
PITMAN, Benn 1
PITMAN, Frank Wesley 2
PITMAN, J. Asbury 3
PITMAN, James Hall 4
PITMAN, John 1
PITMAN, Norman Hinsdale 1
PITNER, Thomas Jefferson 1
PITNEY, John Oliver Halsted 1
PITNEY, Mahlon 1
PITNEY, Shelton 2
PITOU, Augustus 1
PITT, Arthur Stuart 7
PITT, Carl Allen 8
PITT, David Alexander 3
PITT, Louis Wetherbee 3
PITT, Robert Healy 1
PITT, William H
PITTENGER, Benjamin Floyd 7
PITTENGER, Lemuel Arthur 3
PITTENGER, Paul Stewart 7
PITTENGER, William 1
PITTENGER, William Alvin 3
PITTERMAN, Brune 8
PITTMAN, Alfred 4
PITTMAN, Chalmers Van Anglen 7
PITTMAN, Charles Wesley H
PITTMAN, Ernest Wetmore 5
PITTMAN, Hannah Daviess 4
PITTMAN, Hobson 5
PITTMAN, Key 1
PITTMAN, Marvin Summers 3
PITTMAN, Nathan Rowland 1
PITTMAN, Vail Montgomery 4
PITTMAN, William Buckner 1
PITTOCK, Henry Lewis 1
PITTS, Alexander Davidson 1
PITTS, Alice Fox 7
PITTS, Hiram Avery H
PITTS, Llewellyn William 4
PITTS, Llewellyn William 5
PITTS, Mary Helen McCrea Weaver 5
PITTS, Robert Franklin 7
PITTS, Thomas Jefferson 10
PITZ, Henry Clarence 7
PITZER, Alexander White 1
PIUS XII 3
PIVER, Sara Elizabeth Early (Mrs. Sara Early Piver) 5
PIXLEY, Frank 1
PIXLEY, Henry David 4
PIZA, Samuel Emilio 8
PIZARRO, Francisco H
PIZER, Irwin Howard 10
PIZITZ, Louis 3
PIZZETTI, Iidebrando 4
PLACE, Edwin Bray 7
PLACE, Edwin Bray 8
PLACE, Ira Adelbert 1
PLACE, Perley Oakland 2
PLACE, Roland Percy 4
PLACE, Wilard Fiske 4
PLACHY, Fred Joseph 5
PLACHY, Fred Joseph 7
PLACIDE, Alexander H
PLACIDE, Henry H
PLACK, William L. 2
PLAEHN, Erma Belle 6
PLAFKER, Nathan Victor 6
PLAGENS, Joseph Casimir 2
PLAISTED, Frederick William 2
PLAISTED, Harris Merrill H
PLAMENATZ, John Petrov 6
PLAMONDON, Alfred Daniel, Jr. 4
PLANCK, Max Karl Ernst Ludwig 4
PLANJE, Christian William 6
PLANK, Harvey H. 9
PLANK, Kenneth Robert 6
PLANK, William Bertolette 3
PLANT, David H
PLANT, Henry Bradley 1
PLANT, Marcus Leo 8
PLANT, Marion Borchers 5
PLANT, Morton F. 1
PLANT, Oscar Henry 1
PLANTS, Tobias Avery H
PLANTZ, Myra Goodwin 1
PLANTZ, Samuel 1
PLASCHKE, Paul Albert 4
PLASS, Everett Dudley 7
PLASSMANN, Ernst H
PLASSMANN, Thomas 3
PLASTER, Jerry Glen 5
PLASTIRAS, Nicholas 3
PLATE, Walter 5
PLATER, George H
PLATER, Thomas H
PLATH, Sylvia 4
PLATNER, John Winthrop 1
PLATNER, Samuel Ball 1
PLATOU, Ralph Victor 5
PLATT, Casper 4
PLATT, Charles 1
PLATT, Charles Adams 1
PLATT, Charles Alexander 4
PLATT, Edmund 1
PLATT, Eleanor 6
PLATT, Franklin 1
PLATT, Frederick Joseph 3
PLATT, Geoffrey 9
PLATT, Harrison Gray 10
PLATT, Harvey P. 4
PLATT, Henry Clay 1
PLATT, Henry Russell 1
PLATT, Howard V. 4
PLATT, Isaac Hull 1
PLATT, James Henry, Jr. H
PLATT, James Perry 1
PLATT, James Westlake 10
PLATT, John 2
PLATT, John Henry 7
PLATT, John Osgood 2
PLATT, Jonas H
PLATT, Joseph Brereton 4
PLATT, Joseph Swan 8
PLATT, Kenneth Allan 10
PLATT, Livingston 5
PLATT, Orville Hitchcock 1

PLATT, Robert Swanton 4
PLATT, Rutherford 6
PLATT, Samuel 5
PLATT, Thomas Collier 1
PLATT, William 8
PLATT, William Popham 1
PLATT, Zephaniah H
PLATTEN, Donald Campbell 10
PLATTEN, John Wesley 3
PLATTS, Ralph H. 8
PLATZEK, M. Warley 1
PLATZMAN, Robert Leroy 6
PLAUT, Edward 5
PLAUT, Walter Sigmund 10
PLAXTON, Charles Percy 8
PLAYER, William Oscar, Jr. 3
PLAYTER, Harold 5
PLAZA, Galo 9
PLEADWELL, Frank Lester 3
PLEASANT, Earle Birtrum 7
PLEASANT, Ruffin Golson 1
PLEASANTS, Henry, Jr. 4
PLEASANTS, J. Hall 3
PLEASANTS, James H
PLEASANTS, James Jay, Jr. 3
PLEASANTS, John Hampden H
PLEASONTON, Alfred H
PLEASONTON, Augustus James H
PLEHN, Carl Copping 2
PLENZKE, Oswald H(enry) 8
PLESSET, Milton Spinoza 10
PLESSNER, Theodore 2
PLETSCH, George Burgess 8
PLIMPTON, Francis T. P. 8
PLIMPTON, George Arthur 1
PLIMPTON, George Lincoln 3
PLIMPTON, Russell Arthur 6
PLIMPTON, Russell Arthur 7
PLITT, Edwin August 9
PLOCK, Richard Henry 3
PLONK, Emma Laura 4
PLOUGH, Abe 8
PLOWDEN, Eldridge Rodgers 6
PLOWHEAD, Ruth Gipson 6
PLOWMAN, George Taylor 1
PLOWMAN, Laurence Carrington 8
PLUEMER, Adolph 4
PLUM, David Banks 2
PLUM, Harry Clarke 1
PLUM, Harry Grant 3
PLUMB, Albert Hale 1
PLUMB, Charles Sumner 1
PLUMB, Fayette Rumsey 4
PLUMB, Glenn Edward 1
PLUMB, John Jay 9
PLUMB, Preston B. H
PLUMBE, George Edward 1
PLUMBE, John H
PLUME, Joseph Williams 1
PLUME, Stephen Kellogg 3
PLUMER, Arnold H
PLUMER, George H
PLUMER, Paul Southworth 8
PLUMER, William H
PLUMER, William, Jr. H
PLUMER, William Swan H
PLUMLEY, Charles Albert 4
PLUMLEY, Frank 1
PLUMMER, Charles Griffin 1
PLUMMER, Daniel Clarence 3
PLUMMER, Edward Clarence 1
PLUMMER, Edward Hinkley 1
PLUMMER, Frank Arthur 9
PLUMMER, Frank Everett 4
PLUMMER, Franklin E. H
PLUMMER, Gladys Emily Serena 10
PLUMMER, Henry H
PLUMMER, James Kemp 3
PLUMMER, John Watrous 5
PLUMMER, Jonathan H
PLUMMER, Mary Wright 1
PLUMMER, Ralph Walter 5
PLUMMER, Samuel C. 5
PLUMMER, Walter Percy 1
PLUMMER, Wilbur Clayton 9
PLUMMER, William Alberto 1
PLUNKERT, William Joseph 6
PLUNKETT, Charles Peshall 1
PLUNKETT, Charles T. 1
PLUNKETT, Edward Milton 2
PLUNKETT, Robert Edward 9
PLUNKETT, William Brown 1
PLYLER, Alva Washington 5
PLYLER, Earle Keith 7
PLYLER, John Laney 4
PLYLER, Marion Timothy 5
PLYM, Francis John 1
PLYMIRE, Reginald Floyd 5
PLYMPTON, Eben 1
PLYMPTON, George Washington 1
POAG, Thomas E. 6
POAGE, William Robert 9
POBOISK, Donald Paul 10
POCAHONTAS H
PO-CHEDLEY, Donald Stephen 5
POCKMAN, Philetus Theodore 1
POCOCK, Philip F. 8
PODELL, David Louis 2
PODELL, Jacob Joseph 9
POE, Clarence 4
POE, Edgar Allan H
POE, Edgar Allan 4
POE, Elisabeth Ellicott 2
POE, Elizabeth Arnold H
POE, Floyd 5
POE, James 7
POE, John Prentiss 1
POE, John William 1
POE, Orlando Metcalfe H
POE, Pascal Eugene, Jr. 4
POEBEL, Arno 3
POEHLER, W(illiam) A(ugust) 5
POELKER, John Henry 10
POELS, Henry Andrew 4
POETKER, Albert H. 4
POFFENBARGER, George 4
POFFENBARGER, Livia Simpson 1
POFFENBERGER, Albert Theodore 7
POGANY, Willi 3
POGUE, Joseph Ezekiel 8
POHL, Herbert Ackland 9
POHL, John Florian 8
POHLERS, Richard Camillo 3
POHLMAN, Augustus Grote 3
POHLMANN, Julius 1
POILLON, Howard Andrews 3
POILLON, William Clark 5
POINDEXTER, Claude Hendricks 6
POINDEXTER, George H
POINDEXTER, Joseph Boyd 3
POINDEXTER, Miles 2
POINSETT, Joel Roberts H
POINT, Nicholas H
POINT DU SABLE, Jean Baptiste H
POINTS, Arthur Jones 5
POISTER, Arthur (William) 7
POISTER, R(alph) S(eymour) 10
POITRAS, Herman Arthur 7
POL, Sarah Childress H
POLACCO, Giorgi 4
POLACHEK, Victor Henry 1
POLACK, William Gustave 3
POLAK, John Osborn 1
POLAKOV, Walter Nicholas 6
POLAND, Luke Potter H
POLAND, Reginald 10
POLAND, William Carey 1
POLANYI, Karl 4
POLASEK, Albin 4
POLDERVAART, Arie 5
POLE, Elizabeth H
POLE, John William 3
POLEMAN, Horace Irvin 4
POLERI, David Samuel 4
POLEVITZKY, Igor Boris 7
POLHAMUS, Jose Nelson 5
POLHEMUS, James H. 4
POLIER, Justine Wise 9
POLIER, Shad 7
POLING, Daniel Alfred 5
POLING, Daniel V. 4
POLITELLA, Joseph 6
POLITZ, Alfred 8
POLIVKA, Jaroslav Joseph 3
POLK, Albert Fawcett 5
POLK, Charles Peale H
POLK, Forrest Raymond 4
POLK, Frank Lyon 2
POLK, James G. 3
POLK, James Hilliard 10
POLK, James Knox H
POLK, Leonidas H
POLK, Leonidas Lafayette H
POLK, Lucius Eugene H
POLK, Ralph Lane 1
POLK, Rufus King 1
POLK, Thomas H
POLK, Trusten H
POLK, William H
POLK, William Hawkins H
POLK, William Mecklenburg 1
POLLACK, Abou David 6
POLLACK, Ervin Harold 5
POLLACK, Herbert 10
POLLACK, Jack Harrison 8
POLLACK, Louis 5
POLLAK, Egon 6
POLLAK, Gustav 1
POLLAK, Harry Hamilton 7
POLLAK, Robert 5
POLLAK, Virginia Morris 4
POLLAK, Walter Hellprin 1
POLLAN, Arthur Adair 3
POLLARD, Arthur Gayton 1
POLLARD, Braxton 10
POLLARD, Cash Blair 3
POLLARD, Charles Louis 2
POLLARD, Claude 5
POLLARD, Edward Alfred H
POLLARD, Edward Bagby 1
POLLARD, Ernest Mark 5
POLLARD, Harold Stanley 3
POLLARD, Harry 9
POLLARD, Harry Strange 5
POLLARD, Henry Douglas 2
POLLARD, Herman Marvin 8
POLLARD, Isaac 1
POLLARD, John Garland 1
POLLARD, John William Hobbs 5
POLLARD, Percival 1
POLLARD, Robert Nelson 6
POLLARD, Violet McDougall (Mrs. John Garland Pollard) 8
POLLARD, Warren Randolph 10
POLLARD, Warren Randolph 4
POLLARD, William B., Sr. 3
POLLARD, William Jefferson 1
POLLEY, Joseph Crawford 10
POLLEY, Samuel Cleland 2
POLLIA, Joseph P. 3
POLLITT, Levin Irving 5
POLLITZER, Anita 6
POLLITZER, Sigmund 1
POLLMAN, William 1
POLLOCK, Benjamin Reathe 4
POLLOCK, Carl Arthur 8
POLLOCK, Channing 2
POLLOCK, Charles Andrew 1
POLLOCK, Clement Perry 6
POLLOCK, Davis Allen 10
POLLOCK, Edwin A. 8
POLLOCK, Edwin Taylor 2
POLLOCK, Frank Scott 7
POLLOCK, Horatio Milo 3
POLLOCK, Jackson H
POLLOCK, Jackson 4
POLLOCK, James H
POLLOCK, John C. 1
POLLOCK, Lawrence S. 9
POLLOCK, Lewis John 4
POLLOCK, Oliver H
POLLOCK, Pinckney Daniel 1
POLLOCK, Simon Oscar 4
POLLOCK, Thomas Cithcart 2
POLLOCK, Thomas Clark 9
POLLOCK, Walter Briesler 1
POLLOCK, Wayne 4
POLLOCK, William 8
POLMANTIER, Paul Churchill 7
POLSKY, Bert Alfred 6
POLSLEY, Daniel Haymond H
POLTORATZKY, Marianna A. 5
POLYA, George 9
POLYAK, Stephen 3
POLYZOIDES, Adamantios Theophilus 5
POMAREDE, Leon H
POMERANTZ, Abraham L(ouis) 8
POMERANTZ, Louis 9
POMERAT, Charles Marc 4
POMERENE, Atlee 1
POMEROY, Allan 4
POMEROY, Charles H
POMEROY, Cleve H. 8
POMEROY, Daniel Eleazer 4
POMEROY, Elizabeth Ella 4
POMEROY, Eltweed 1
POMEROY, Howard Edwin 6
POMEROY, John Larrabee 1
POMEROY, John Norton H
POMEROY, John Norton 1
POMEROY, Joseph George (Gilbert) 8
POMEROY, Marcus Mills H
POMEROY, Ralph Brouwer 1
POMEROY, Samuel Clarke H
POMEROY, Seth H
POMEROY, Theodore Medad 1
POMPA, Gilbert Gutierrez 9
POMPIDOU, Georges Jean Raymond 6
POMUS, Doc (Jerome Solon Felder)* 10
PONCE DE LEON, Juan H
PONCE ENRIQUEZ, Camilo 7
PONCHER, Henry George 3
POND, Allen Bartlit 1
POND, Alonzo Smith 3
POND, Alonzo William 9
POND, Anson Phelps 4
POND, Ashley 1
POND, Bremer Whidden 3
POND, Calvin Parker 8
POND, Charles Fremont 1
POND, Dana 4
POND, Enoch H
POND, Francis Jones 5
POND, Frederick Eugene 1
POND, George Augustus 8
POND, George Edward 1
POND, George Gilbert 1
POND, Horace B. 7
POND, Irving Kane 1
POND, James B. 4
POND, James Burton 1
POND, John Allan 5
POND, Peter H
POND, Philip 2
POND, Robert Andrew 5
POND, Samuel William H
POND, Silvanus Billings H
POND, Theodore Hanford 1
POND, Wilf Pocklington 1
PONDER, Amos Lee 8
PONIATOFF, Alexander Matthew 7
PONS, Lilly 6
PONSELLE, Rosa Melba 8
PONT-AU-SABLE, Jean Baptiste H
PONTI, Gio 7
PONTIAC H
PONTIUS, Albert William 1
PONTIUS, Clarence Isaiah 9
POOK, Samuel Hartt 1
POOL, David De Sola 5
POOL, Eugene Hillhouse 2
POOL, George Franklin 6
POOL, Ithiel Desola 9
POOL, Joe 5
POOL, John H
POOL, Judith Graham 6
POOL, Leonard Parker 7
POOL, Leonidas Moore 1
POOL, Maria Louise H
POOL, Raymond John 7
POOL, Tamar De Sola 7
POOL, Walter Freshwater H
POOLE, Abram 4
POOLE, Cecil Percy 1
POOLE, Charles Augustus 4
POOLE, Charles Hubbard 1
POOLE, Dewitt Clinton 3
POOLE, Ernest 2
POOLE, Eugene Alonzo 1
POOLE, Fanny Huntington Runnells 2
POOLE, Fenn E. 3
POOLE, Fitch H
POOLE, Franklin Osborne 2
POOLE, Frederic 1
POOLE, Herman 4
POOLE, James Plummer 8
POOLE, John 5
POOLE, John Bayard 10
POOLE, Lynn D. 5
POOLE, Murray Edward 1
POOLE, Robert Franklin 3
POOLE, Rufus Gilbert 5
POOLE, Sidman Parmelee 3
POOLE, William Frederick H
POOLER, Charles Alfred 5
POOLEY, Charles A. 1
POOLEY, Edward Murray 5
POOLEY, Robert C(ecil) 10
POOR, Agnes Blake 1
POOR, Alfred Easton 9
POOR, Charles Henry H
POOR, Charles Lane 3
POOR, Charles Marshall 5
POOR, Daniel H
POOR, Enoch H
POOR, Frank A. 3
POOR, Fred Arthur 3
POOR, Henry Varnum, III 5
POOR, Henry William 1
POOR, John H
POOR, John Alfred H
POOR, John Merrill 1
POOR, Ruel Whitcomb 1
POOR, Russell Spurgeon 5
POOR, Samuel Smith 7
POOR, Walter Everett 3
POOR, Wharton 6
POOR, William Bunker 6
POORE, Benjamin Andrew 1
POORE, Benjamin Perley H
POORE, Charles Graydon 5
POORE, Henry Rankin 1
POORMAN, Alfred Peter 3
POOS, Omer 7
POPE, Abner S. 7
POPE, Albert Augustus 1
POPE, Alexander 1
POPE, Alfred Atmore 1
POPE, Allan Melvill 4
POPE, Amy Elizabeth 5
POPE, Arthur 6
POPE, Arthur Edward 7
POPE, Arthur Upham 5
POPE, Bayard Foster 5
POPE, Carey Joseph 1
POPE, Clifford Hillhouse 6
POPE, Curran 1
POPE, Edward Waldron 4
POPE, Francis Horton 5
POPE, Franklin Leonard H
POPE, Frederick 5
POPE, Generoso Paul, Jr. 9
POPE, George 1
POPE, Gustavus Debrille 3
POPE, Harold Linder 6
POPE, Henry Francis 3
POPE, Herbert 3
POPE, James Pinckney 7
POPE, James Worden 1
POPE, John* H
POPE, John Alexander 8
POPE, John Dudley 4
POPE, John Russell 1
POPE, Larry Jacob 6
POPE, Liston 6
POPE, Maurice Arthur 8
POPE, Nathaniel H
POPE, Patrick Hamilton H
POPE, Percival Clarence 1
POPE, Ralph Elton 3
POPE, Ralph Wainwright 1
POPE, Roy L(eon) 6
POPE, Walter Lyndon 5
POPE, William Hayes 1
POPE, Young John 1
POPEJOY, Thomas Lafayette 6
POPEJOY, Thomas Lafayette 7
POPENOE, Frederick Wilson 9
POPHAM, Arthur C. 8
POPHAM, George H
POPHAM, Richard Allen 9
POPMA, Gerritt Jacob 4
POPOFF, Stephen 1
POPOVIC, Vladimir 5
POPOV-VENIAMINOV, Joann H
POPP, Henry William 9
POPPELE, Jacob R. 9
POPPEN, Emmanuel Frederick 4
POPPEN, Henry Albert 8
POPPEN, James L. 7
POPPENHEIM, Mary Barnett 1
POPPENHUSEN, Conrad Herman 2
POPPER, Hans 9
POPPER, William 4
PORCAYO URIBE, Juvenal 8
PORCHER, Francis Peyre H
PORMORT, Philemon H
PORRAS, Belisario 4
PORRITT, Edward 1
PORRO, Thomas J. 4
PORT, Edmund 9
PORT, Frederick James 7

PORTAL, Baron Wyndham Raymond 2
PORTELA, Epifanio 4
PORTER, A. Kingsley 1
PORTER, A. W. Noel 4
PORTER, Albert 1
PORTER, Albert Gallatin H
PORTER, Alexander H
PORTER, Andrew H
PORTER, Arthur Le Moyne 5
PORTER, Augustus Seymour H
PORTER, Benjamin Curtis 1
PORTER, Bruce 5
PORTER, Charles Allen 1
PORTER, Charles Burnham 1
PORTER, Charles Howell 5
PORTER, Charles Scott 4
PORTER, Charles Vernon 4
PORTER, Charley Lyman 4
PORTER, Charlotte Williams 4
PORTER, Claude R. 2
PORTER, Clifford Lewis 7
PORTER, Cole 4
PORTER, Dana 4
PORTER, David H
PORTER, David Dixon H
PORTER, David Dixon 2
PORTER, David Richard 6
PORTER, David Rittenhouse H
PORTER, David Stewart 10
PORTER, Delia Lyman 1
PORTER, Dwight 1
PORTER, Earle S. 3
PORTER, Ebenezer H
PORTER, Edward Arthur Gribbon 6
PORTER, Eleanor Hodgman 1
PORTER, Eliot Furness 10
PORTER, Ernest Warren 5
PORTER, Eugene Hoffman 1
PORTER, F. Addison 1
PORTER, Fairfield 6
PORTER, Fitz-john 1
PORTER, Florence Collins 1
PORTER, Frank Chamberlin 2
PORTER, Frank M. 4
PORTER, Frank Monroe 1
PORTER, Fred Thomas 5
PORTER, Frederic Hutchinson 7
PORTER, Gene Stratton 1
PORTER, George French 1
PORTER, Gilbert Edwin 2
PORTER, Gilchrist H
PORTER, H. M. 1
PORTER, Harold Everett 1
PORTER, Henry Alford 2
PORTER, Henry Dwight 1
PORTER, Henry H. 1
PORTER, Henry (Harry) Alanson 5
PORTER, Henry Hobart 2
PORTER, Henry Kirke 1
PORTER, Holbrook Fitz-john 1
PORTER, Horace 1
PORTER, Hugh 4
PORTER, Hugh Omega 4
PORTER, Irvin Lourie 6
PORTER, James H
PORTER, James A. 5
PORTER, James Davis 1
PORTER, James Dunlop 5
PORTER, James Hyde 4
PORTER, James Madison H
PORTER, James Madison, III 4
PORTER, James Pertice 3
PORTER, J(ames) Sherman 1
PORTER, James Temple 1
PORTER, James W. 3
PORTER, Jermain Gildersleeve 1
PORTER, Joe Frank 3
PORTER, John H
PORTER, John Addison H
PORTER, John Addison 1
PORTER, John Byron 10
PORTER, John Clinton 3
PORTER, John Henry 1
PORTER, John Jermain 6
PORTER, John Lincoln 1
PORTER, John Luke 5
PORTER, John Lupher 1
PORTER, John Roger 7
PORTER, John Wesley, Jr. 9
PORTER, John Willard 9
PORTER, John William 1
PORTER, Joseph Franklin 2
PORTER, Joseph Yates 1
PORTER, Katherine Anne 7

PORTER, Katherine Harriet 8
PORTER, Kirk Harold 5
PORTER, Lawrence Charles 7
PORTER, L(ester) G(ilbert) 5
PORTER, Lewis Cass 9
PORTER, Linn Boyd 1
PORTER, Louis Hopkins 2
PORTER, Lucius Chapin 3
PORTER, Miles Fuller 1
PORTER, Newton Hazelton 2
PORTER, Noah H
PORTER, Paul Aldermandt 6
PORTER, Paul Aldermandt 7
PORTER, Peter Buell H
PORTER, Phil 4
PORTER, Quincy 4
PORTER, Ralph E. 8
PORTER, Raymond Averill 1
PORTER, Robert Langley 4
PORTER, Robert Percival 1
PORTER, Robert William 10
PORTER, Rodney Robert 9
PORTER, Roland Guyer 3
PORTER, Rose 1
PORTER, Royal A(rthur) 5
PORTER, Rufus 1
PORTER, Russell Williams 2
PORTER, Samuel 1
PORTER, Sarah H
PORTER, Seton 3
PORTER, Silas Wright 1
PORTER, Stephen Geyer 1
PORTER, Sydney 1
PORTER, Sylvia 10
PORTER, Theodoric 1
PORTER, Thomas Conrad 1
PORTER, Timothy H. H
PORTER, Valentine Mott 1
PORTER, Verne Hardin 1
PORTER, Vernon Carroll 10
PORTER, Washington Tullis 1
PORTER, Whitney Clair 5
PORTER, William Arnold 6
PORTER, William Arnold 1
PORTER, William Curren 4
PORTER, William David 1
PORTER, William Gove 1
PORTER, William Henry* 1
PORTER, William J. 9
PORTER, William Luther 6
PORTER, William N(ichols) 5
PORTER, William Townsend 2
PORTER, William Trotter H
PORTER, William Wagener 1
PORTER, William Wallace Hawks 5
PORTERFIELD, Allen Wilson 3
PORTERFIELD, James H. 10
PORTERFIELD, Lewis Broughton 2
PORTERFIELD, Robert Huffard 5
PORTERIE, Gaston Louis 3
PORTEUS, Stanley David 7
PORTEVIN, Albert Marcel Germain Rene 4
PORTIER, Michael H
PORTINARI, Candido 4
PORTMAN, Eric 5
PORTMANN, Ursus Victor 4
PORTNOFF, Alexander 2
PORTOLA, Gaspar de H
PORTOR, Laura Spencer 3
PORY, John H
POSADAS, Juan 7
POSEGATE, Mabel 3
POSES, Jack I. 8
POSEY, Addison Cecil 8
POSEY, Chester Alfred 1
POSEY, Leroy R. 6
POSEY, Thomas 1
POSEY, William Campbell 1
POSNER, Edwin 5
POSNER, Ernst Maximilan 7
POSNER, Harry 4
POSNER, Louis Samuel 1
POSNER, Stanley I. 4
POSSE, Rose (Baroness) 1
POSSEL, René de 5
POSSUM, Peter Ever 10
POST, Alice Thacher 2
POST, Allen 9
POST, Chandler Rathfon 1
POST, Charles Addison 6
POST, Charles Johnson 3
POST, Charles William 1
POST, Chester Leroy 3
POST, Christian Frederick H
POST, Curtis Walter 9
POST, Edwin 1
POST, Elwyn Donald 4
POST, Emily 4

POST, Frank Truman 1
POST, Gaines 9
POST, George Adams 1
POST, George Browne 1
POST, George Edward 1
POST, Herbert Wilson 4
POST, Hoyt Garrod 3
POST, Isaac H
POST, James D. 1
POST, James Howell 1
POST, James Otis 1
POST, Josephine Fowler 2
POST, Jotham, Jr. H
POST, Kenneth 3
POST, Kirby Marion 7
POST, Lawrence T. 3
POST, L(eon) Abbett 10
POST, Levi Arnold 5
POST, Louis Freeland 1
POST, Marjorie Merriweather 6
POST, Martin Hayward 1
POST, Melville Davisson 1
POST, Philip Sidney H
POST, Regis Henri 2
POST, Roswell Olcott 4
POST, Truman Marcellus 1
POST, W. Merritt 1
POST, Waldron Kintzing 3
POST, Wilber E. 4
POST, Wiley 1
POST, William Stone 1
POST, Wright H
POSTL, Karl Anton H
POSTLE, Wilbur Everett 1
POSTLETHWAITE, Keith Thomson 9
POSTLETHWAITE, Robert Hodgshon 4
POSTLETHWAITE, William Wallace 5
POSTNIKOV, Fedor Alexis (F. A. Post) 5
POSTON, Charles Pebrille H
POSTON, Elias McClellan 1
POSTON, Gretchen 10
POSTON, Lawrence Sanford 6
POTEAT, Edwin McNeill 1
POTEAT, Edwin McNeill 3
POTEAT, Hubert McNeill 1
POTEAT, James Douglass 2
POTEAT, Wlilliam Louis 1
POTHIER, Aram J. 1
POTOCKI, Jerzy 1
POTOFSKY, Jacob S. 7
POTOK, Anna Maximillian 9
POTRATZ, Herbert August 6
POTT, Francis Lister Hawks 2
POTT, John H
POTT, William Sumner Appleton 1
POTTENGER, Francis Marion 4
POTTER, Albert Franklin 1
POTTER, Albert Knight 4
POTTER, Alfred Claghorn 1
POTTER, Alfred Knight 1
POTTER, Allen H
POTTER, Alonzo H
POTTER, Andrey Abraham 7
POTTER, Burton Willis 1
POTTER, Charles 5
POTTER, Charles Edward 7
POTTER, Charles Francis 4
POTTER, Charles Jackson 10
POTTER, Charles Lewis 1
POTTER, Charles Nelson 1
POTTER, Chester Magee 1
POTTER, Clarkson 6
POTTER, Clarkson Nott H
POTTER, Cora Urquhart 5
POTTER, David 5
POTTER, David Magle 5
POTTER, David Morris 5
POTTER, Delbert Maxwell 5
POTTER, Edward Clark 1
POTTER, Edward Eels 1
POTTER, Edwin Augustus 1
POTTER, Eliphalet Nott 1
POTTER, Elisha Reynolds* 1
POTTER, Ellen Culver 3
POTTER, Emery Davis H
POTTER, Ernest W. 8
POTTER, Frank B(ell) 5
POTTER, Frank Maxson 2
POTTER, George Frederick 9
POTTER, George Milton 5
POTTER, George W. 3
POTTER, Harry S. 1
POTTER, Henry Codman 1
POTTER, Henry Noel 5
POTTER, Henry Staples 1
POTTER, Homer Dexter 1
POTTER, Horatio H
POTTER, James H

POTTER, Mrs. James Brown 1
POTTER, James Harry 7
POTTER, John Fox 1
POTTER, John Milton 2
POTTER, John Wesley 4
POTTER, Justin 4
POTTER, Lars Sellstedt 8
POTTER, Louis 1
POTTER, Margaret Horton 4
POTTER, Marion E. 3
POTTER, Mark Winslow 2
POTTER, Mary Knight 1
POTTER, Mary Ross 1
POTTER, Nathaniel H
POTTER, Nathaniel Bowditch 5
POTTER, Orlando Brunson H
POTTER, Orrin W. 1
POTTER, Paul Meredith 1
POTTER, Pitman Benjamin 7
POTTER, Platt 1
POTTER, Robert H
POTTER, Robert Brown 1
POTTER, Robert Sturgis 9
POTTER, Rockwell Harmon 4
POTTER, Roderick 4
POTTER, Russell Sherwood 10
POTTER, Samuel John H
POTTER, Samuel Otway Lewis 4
POTTER, Stephen 5
POTTER, Thomas Albert 2
POTTER, Thomas Paine 5
POTTER, Waldo C. 7
POTTER, Wilfrid Carne 2
POTTER, William 1
POTTER, William Bancroft 1
POTTER, William Bleecker 1
POTTER, William Chapman 3
POTTER, William Everett 9
POTTER, William Henry 1
POTTER, William J. 4
POTTER, William James H
POTTER, William Parker 1
POTTER, William Plumer 1
POTTER, William W. 5
POTTER, William Warren 1
POTTER, William Wilson H
POTTERTON, Thomas Edward 1
POTTHAST, Edward Henry 1
POTTHOFF, Carl John 9
POTTLE, Emory Bemsley H
POTTLE, Frederick Albert 9
POTTS, Alfred Fremont 1
POTTS, Benjamin Franklin H
POTTS, Charles Edwin 3
POTTS, Charles Sower 1
POTTS, David, Jr. H
POTTS, David M. 7
POTTS, James Henry 1
POTTS, James Henry 2
POTTS, James Manning 10
POTTS, Jonathan 1
POTTS, Joseph McKean, II 7
POTTS, Joseph McKean, II 8
POTTS, Louis Moses 1
POTTS, Richard H
POTTS, Robert 1
POTTS, Robert Joseph 4
POTTS, Roy C. 6
POTTS, Templin Morris 1
POTTS, William 1
POTTS, Willis John 5
POTTS, Wylodine Gabbert (Mrs. Thomas C. Potts) 5
POTZGER, John E. 3
POU, Edward William 1
POU, James Hinton 1
POUCH, William Henry 3
POUDER, George Harry 10
POUILLY, Jacques Nicholas Bussiere de H
POUILLY, Joseph de H
POULENC, Francis* 4
POULOS, Raleigh Anest 6
POULSON, Donald Frederick 10
POULSON, Norris 8
POULSON, Zachariah H
POULSSON, Anne Emilie 1
POULTER, Thomas Charles 7
POULTERER, Henry E. 8
POUND, Arthur 4
POUND, Cuthbert Winfred 1
POUND, Earl Clifford 2
POUND, Ezra 5
POUND, Ezra Loomis 7
POUND, G(rellet) C. 5
POUND, Jere M. 1
POUND, Jere M. 1
POUND, Louise 3
POUND, Roscoe 4

POUND, Thomas H
POURTALES, Louis Francois de H
POUSETTE-DART, Nathaniel 4
POUSETTE-DART, Richard 10
POWDERLY, Terence Vincent 1
POWDERMAKER, Hortense 5
POWE, Thomas Erasmus 2
POWEL, Charles Alfred 7
POWEL, Harford 3
POWEL, John Hare H
POWELL H
POWELL, Aaron Macy 1
POWELL, Adam Clayton, Jr. 5
POWELL, Alden L. 3
POWELL, Alfred H. H
POWELL, Annie Marion 8
POWELL, Arthur Gray 3
POWELL, Arthur James Emery 3
POWELL, Benjamin Edward 7
POWELL, Benjamin Harrison 4
POWELL, Benjamin Harrison, IV 10
POWELL, Caroline Amelia 2
POWELL, Caroline Amelia 5
POWELL, Carroll A. 2
POWELL, Cecil Frank 1
POWELL, Charles Francis 1
POWELL, Charles L. 1
POWELL, Charles Stuart H
POWELL, Charles Underhill 3
POWELL, Clilan Bethany 10
POWELL, Cuthbert 1
POWELL, David 1
POWELL, Dawn 4
POWELL, Desmond Stevens 4
POWELL, Dick 4
POWELL, Doane 3
POWELL, Donald Adams 3
POWELL, E. Alexander 3
POWELL, E. Harrison 4
POWELL, Earl Alexander 1
POWELL, Edward 1
POWELL, Edward Angus 7
POWELL, Edward Henry 4
POWELL, Edward Lindsay 1
POWELL, Edward Payson 1
POWELL, Edward Thomson 5
POWELL, Eleanor Torrey 8
POWELL, Elmer Ellsworth 2
POWELL, Elmer Nathaniel 1
POWELL, Frank Marion, Sr. 7
POWELL, Fred Wilbur 2
POWELL, Frederick 4
POWELL, G. Harold 1
POWELL, G. Thomas 4
POWELL, G. Thomas 5
POWELL, George May 1
POWELL, Hunter Holmes 1
POWELL, John 4
POWELL, John Benjamin 2
POWELL, John H. 1
POWELL, John Lee 4
POWELL, John Wesley 1
POWELL, Joseph Wright 3
POWELL, Joseph Yancey 4
POWELL, Julius Cherry 10
POWELL, Junius L. 4
POWELL, Lazarus Whitehead H
POWELL, Legh Richmond, Jr. 7
POWELL, Levin H
POWELL, Lucien Whiting 1
POWELL, Lula E. 2
POWELL, Lyman Pierson 2
POWELL, Lyman Theodore 6
POWELL, Maud 1
POWELL, Nathan 5
POWELL, Noble Cilley 5
POWELL, Paul 5
POWELL, Paulus H
POWELL, Paulus Prince 4
POWELL, Philip Wayne 4
POWELL, Rachel Hopper 4
POWELL, Ralph Lorin 6
POWELL, Ray E. 6
POWELL, Raymond P. 7
POWELL, Richard Holmes 2
POWELL, Richard Roy Belden 8
POWELL, Richard Sterling 5
POWELL, Robert 1
POWELL, Robert Lee 9

RAGEN, Joseph Edward 5
RAGIR, Benjamin A. 3
RAGLAND, George 3
RAGLAND, James Black 10
RAGLAND, Joseph Pemberton 7
RAGLAND, Samuel Evan 3
RAGLAND, William T. 5
RAGO, Henry Anthony 5
RAGON, Heartsill 1
RAGONE, Stanley 7
RAGOZIN, Zenaide Alexeievna 5
RAGSDALE, A(rthur) C(hester) 8
RAGSDALE, Bartow Davis 2
RAGSDALE, Edward Tillottson 5
RAGSDALE, J. Willard 1
RAGSDALE, James W. 4
RAGSDALE, Jesse G(rant) 9
RAGSDALE, Tallulah 3
RAGSDALE, Van Hubert 3
RAGSDALE, Warner Bernice 9
RAGUET, Condy H
RAHI, Michel 6
RAHILLY, Thomas Francis 9
RAHMAN, Abdul 4
RAHMAN, Aneesur 9
RAHMAN, Fazlur 10
RAHMAN, Tunku Abdul 3
RAHMN, Elza Lothner 5
RAHN, Hermann 10
RAHN, Otto 3
RAHV, Philip 6
RAIBLE, John R. 2
RAICHLE, Frank G. 9
RAIFORD, Lemuel Charles 2
RAIGUEL, George Earle 6
RAILEY, Fleming G. 4
RAILEY, Thomas Tarlton 3
RAIMONDI, Luigi 6
RAINE, James Watt 2
RAINE, William MacLeod 3
RAINER, Joseph 4
RAINES, George Neely 3
RAINES, John 1
RAINES, John Marlin 5
RAINEY, Anson 1
RAINEY, Floyd Dean 7
RAINEY, Henry Thomas 1
RAINEY, Homer Price 9
RAINEY, John W. 1
RAINEY, Joseph Hayne H
RAINEY, Lilius Bratton 5
RAINEY, Ma H
RAINEY, Ma 4
RAINEY, Robert M. 7
RAINIE, Harrison McKinley 7
RAINS, Albert 10
RAINS, Claude 4
RAINS, Gabriel James H
RAINS, George Washington H
RAINS, Leon 3
RAINSFORD, William Stephen 1
RAINWATER, Clarence Elmer 1
RAINWATER, James 9
RAIRDEN, Bradstreet Stinson 2
RAISA, Rosa 4
RAITT, Effie Isabel 2
RAIZEN, Charles Sanford 4
RAJAGOPALACHARYA, Chakravarti 5
RAJAMAITRI, Phya Abhibal 7
RAJCHMAN, Jan Aleksander 10
RAK, Mary Kidder 3
RAKE, Geoffrey William 3
RAKE, John Frederick 6
RAKEMAN, Carl 6
RAKER, John Edward 1
RAKER, John Peter 9
RAKOTOMALALA, Louis 5
RALE, Sebastien H
RALEIGH, Henry Patrick 6
RALEIGH, Sir Walter H
RALEY, John Wesley 5
RALL, Edward Everett 5
RALL, Harris Franklin 4
RALL, Owen 9
RALLI, Elaine Pandia 5
RALLS, Arthur Williams 6
RALLS, Charles C. 7
RALPH, James H
RALPH, Lester 2
RALPH, Stuart Harrison 3
RALSTON, Anderson Wheeler 2
RALSTON, Burrell Otto 5
RALSTON, Byron Brown 5
RALSTON, Hon James Layton K. C. 2
RALSTON, Jackson Harvey 2
RALSTON, John Chester 1
RALSTON, Oliver Caldwell 4
RALSTON, Mrs. Samuel M. 3
RALSTON, Samuel Moffett 1
RALSTON, William Chapman H
RALSTON, William Chapman 5
RAMADIER, Paul 4
RAMAGE, Carroll Johnson 1
RAMAGE, James Savage 3
RAMAGE, John H
RAMAGE, Lawson Paterson 10
RAMAKER, Albert John 2
RAMALEY, Francis 2
RAMAN, Chandrasekhara 6
RAMANI, Radhakrishna 5
RAMBAUD, George Gibier 5
RAMBAUT, Mary Lucinda Bonney 1
RAMBEAU, Morjorie 5
RAMBO, Victor Clough 9
RAMEE, Joseph Jacques H
RAMEY, Frank Marion 3
RAMEY, Homer Alonzo 3
RAMIREZ, Pedro Pablo 4
RAMM, Charles Adolph 4
RAMMELKAMP, Charles Henry 1
RAMMELKAMP, Charles Henry, Jr. 8
RAMMER, August J. 4
RAMPY, Edgar Franklin 7
RAMPY, Thomas Randall 7
RAMSAY, Alexander H
RAMSAY, David H
RAMSAY, David Marshall 3
RAMSAY, Erskine 3
RAMSAY, Francis Munroe 1
RAMSAY, George Douglas H
RAMSAY, Grace Kirkpatrick 7
RAMSAY, Marion Livingston 10
RAMSAY, Nathaniel H
RAMSAY, Robert Lee 6
RAMSAY, Robert Lincoln 3
RAMSAY, Thomas Henry 1
RAMSAYE, Terry 3
RAMSBURG, C. J. 3
RAMSDELL, Charles William 2
RAMSDELL, Edwin George 3
RAMSDELL, Lewis Stephen 6
RAMSDELL, Washington Irving 4
RAMSDELL, Willett Forrest 8
RAMSEN, Halsey Edmund 3
RAMSER, Charles Ernest 4
RAMSEUR, Stephen Dodson H
RAMSEY, Alexander 1
RAMSEY, Alfred 4
RAMSEY, Arthur Michael (Lord Ramsey of Canterbury) 9
RAMSEY, D. Hiden 4
RAMSEY, Dewitt Clinton 4
RAMSEY, George 2
RAMSEY, George Junkin 1
RAMSEY, George Samuel 2
RAMSEY, Hobart C. 9
RAMSEY, Horace Marion 2
RAMSEY, James B. 4
RAMSEY, James Basil 5
RAMSEY, James Gettys McGready H
RAMSEY, John Patterson 4
RAMSEY, John Rathbone 1
RAMSEY, Joseph, Jr. 1
RAMSEY, Joseph Robert 9
RAMSEY, Leonidas Willing 2
RAMSEY, Marathon Montrose 4
RAMSEY, Norman Carnegie 7
RAMSEY, Norman Foster 4
RAMSEY, Paul Hubert 8
RAMSEY, Robert H
RAMSEY, Robert Paul 9
RAMSEY, Rolla Roy 3
RAMSEY, William H
RAMSEY, William F. 1
RAMSEY, William Sterrett H
RAMSEY, Willis Hinksman 1
RAMSEYER, Christian William 2
RAMSEYER, John Alvin 5
RAMSEYER, Lloyd Louis 7
RAMSOWER, Harry C(lifford) 6
RAMSPECK, Robert 5
RAMSTAD, N(iles) Oliver 5
RAMUS, Carl 5
RANARD, Donald Louis 10
RANCANS, Joseph 9
RANCE, Sir Hubert Elvin 6
RANCK, Clayton Haverstick 5
RANCK, Edward Carty 6
RANCK, George Washington 1
RANCK, Henry Haverstick 2
RANCK, John Allan 7
RANCK, Samuel H. 3
RANCK, Than Vanneman 2
RAND, Addison Crittenden H
RAND, Arthur Henry, Jr. 5
RAND, Austin Loomer 8
RAND, Ayn 8
RAND, Benjamin 1
RAND, Charles Frederic 1
RAND, Christopher 5
RAND, Clayton Thomas 5
RAND, Edgar Eugene 3
RAND, Edward Augustus 1
RAND, Edward Kennard 2
RAND, Edward Lothrop 1
RAND, Edward Sprague H
RAND, Elbridge Dexter 8
RAND, Ellen Emmet 2
RAND, Frank Chambless 2
RAND, Frank Prentice 5
RAND, Frederick Henry 2
RAND, George Franklin 2
RAND, Gertrude 5
RAND, Gertrude 7
RAND, Henry Hale 4
RAND, Herbert Wilbur 4
RAND, James Henry 5
RAND, John Goffe H
RAND, John Langdon 2
RAND, John Prentice 1
RAND, Mary Frances Abbott 4
RAND, Norfleet Hale 9
RAND, Stephen 1
RAND, Theodore Dehon 1
RAND, William, Jr. 1
RAND, William Blanchard 6
RAND, William McNear 9
RAND, William Wilberforce 1
RANDALL, Albert Borland 2
RANDALL, Alexander H
RANDALL, Alexander 3
RANDALL, Alexander Williams H
RANDALL, Benjamin* H
RANDALL, Blanchard 2
RANDALL, Burton Alexander 1
RANDALL, Charles Hiram 4
RANDALL, Clarence Belden 4
RANDALL, Clyde Nathaniel 5
RANDALL, Daniel Richard 1
RANDALL, David Anton 6
RANDALL, David Austin H
RANDALL, David Lindsey 7
RANDALL, Edward 2
RANDALL, Edward, Jr. 9
RANDALL, Edward Caleb 1
RANDALL, Edwin Jarvis 4
RANDALL, Edwin Mortimer 1
RANDALL, Emilius Oviatt 1
RANDALL, Eugene Wilson 1
RANDALL, Frank Alfred 3
RANDALL, Frank Hall 4
RANDALL, Frank Lange 1
RANDALL, George Archibald 1
RANDALL, George Morton 1
RANDALL, George William 6
RANDALL, Henry Stephens H
RANDALL, J. G. 3
RANDALL, James Ryder 1
RANDALL, Jesse W. 7
RANDALL, John Arthur 6
RANDALL, John Hammond 4
RANDALL, John Herman 2
RANDALL, John Herman, Jr. 7
RANDALL, Lawrence Merrill 5
RANDALL, Merle 2
RANDALL, Otis Everett 2
RANDALL, Paul King, Jr. 5
RANDALL, R. C. 3
RANDALL, Robert Henry 4
RANDALL, Robert Richard H
RANDALL, Ruth Painter 5
RANDALL, Samuel H
RANDALL, Samuel Bond 1
RANDALL, Samuel Jackson H
RANDALL, Samuel Sidwell H
RANDALL, William Harrison H
RANDALL, William Trafton 4
RANDALL, Wyatt William 1
RANDAU, Clem J. 3
RANDEGGER, Giuseppe Aldo 5
RANDEL, James Buford, Jr. 9
RANDELL, Choice Boswell 4
RANDLE, C. Wilson 4
RANDLE, Thurman 3
RANDLES, Andrew J. 5
RANDOLPH, Alfred Magill 1
RANDOLPH, Asa Philip 7
RANDOLPH, Bessie Carter 4
RANDOLPH, Bessie Carter 7
RANDOLPH, Beverley H
RANDOLPH, Carman Fitz 1
RANDOLPH, Edgar Eugene 6
RANDOLPH, Edmund H
RANDOLPH, Edmund Jennings H
RANDOLPH, Edward H
RANDOLPH, Edward Hughes 1
RANDOLPH, Epes 1
RANDOLPH, Francis Fitz 6
RANDOLPH, George F. 1
RANDOLPH, George Wythe H
RANDOLPH, Harold 1
RANDOLPH, Harrison 3
RANDOLPH, Hollins Nicholas 1
RANDOLPH, Isham 1
RANDOLPH, Jacob H
RANDOLPH, James Fitz H
RANDOLPH, John* H
RANDOLPH, Sir John H
RANDOLPH, John Cooper Fitz 1
RANDOLPH, Joseph Fitz H
RANDOLPH, Joseph Fitz 1
RANDOLPH, Lee F. 6
RANDOLPH, Lewis Van Syckle Fitz 1
RANDOLPH, Lingan Strother 1
RANDOLPH, Oscar Dewolf 7
RANDOLPH, Peyton H
RANDOLPH, Robert Decan 9
RANDOLPH, Robert Isham 3
RANDOLPH, Robert Lee 1
RANDOLPH, Sarah Nicholas 1
RANDOLPH, Theodore Fitz H
RANDOLPH, Thomas Jefferson H
RANDOLPH, Thomas Mann H
RANDOLPH, Tom 1
RANDOLPH, Vance 9
RANDOLPH, Wallace F. 1
RANDOLPH, William H
RANDOLPH, William Mann 2
RANDOLPH, Woodruff 4
RANE, Frank William 1
RANEY, George Pettus 1
RANEY, McKendree Llewellyn 5
RANEY, Richard Beverly 1
RANEY, William Eugene 4
RANGELER, William Francis 2
RANGER, Henry Ward 1
RANGER, Richard H. 4
RANGER, Walter Eugene 1
RANK, Joseph Arthur 5
RANK, Otto 4
RANKIN, B. Kirk 1
RANKIN, Carroll Watson 3
RANKIN, Christopher H
RANKIN, David 1
RANKIN, Egbert Guernsey 4
RANKIN, Emmet Woollen 3
RANKIN, Fred Wharton 3
RANKIN, George Clark 1
RANKIN, Henry Bascom 1
RANKIN, Isaac Ogden 1
RANKIN, James Doig 2
RANKIN, Jeannette 5
RANKIN, Jeremiah Eames 1
RANKIN, John H
RANKIN, John Chambers 1
RANKIN, John Elliott 4
RANKIN, John Hall 3
RANKIN, John Mercer 2
RANKIN, John Watkins 5
RANKIN, Joseph H
RANKIN, Karl Lott 10
RANKIN, Milledge Theron 3
RANKIN, Raymond Coile 10
RANKIN, Rebecca Browning 4
RANKIN, Robert Stanley 7
RANKIN, Rolfe M(ontgomery) 9
RANKIN, Rufus Grady 9
RANKIN, Thomas Ernest 3
RANKIN, Walter Mead 2
RANKIN, Watson Smith 6
RANKIN, Wellington Duncan 4
RANKIN, William Bradshaw 1
RANKIN, William Durham 2
RANKIN, William Thomasson 4
RANNELLS, Will 8
RANNEY, Ambrose Arnold 1
RANNEY, Ambrose Loomis 1
RANNEY, George Alfred 2
RANNEY, Henry Clay 1
RANNEY, Henry Joseph H
RANNEY, Leo 3
RANNEY, Rufus Percival H
RANNEY, William Tylee H
RANNEY, Winthrop Rodgers 3
RANNIGER, Klaus 7
RANNO, Frederick Sebastian 4
RANOUS, Dora Knowlton 1
RANOW, George R. 3
RANSDELL, Daniel Moore 1
RANSDELL, Joseph Eugene 3
RANSEEN, Mattis C. 1
RANSFORD, Charles Orrin 5
RANSIER, Alonzo Jacob H
RANSLEY, Harry C. 1
RANSOHOFF, Joseph 1
RANSOM, Brayton Howard 1
RANSOM, Caroline L. Ormes H
RANSOM, Caroline L. Ormes 4
RANSOM, Elmer 3
RANSOM, Frank Leslie 2
RANSOM, George Brinkerhoff 1
RANSOM, Harry Huntt 7
RANSOM, John Crowe 6
RANSOM, Marion 4
RANSOM, Mathew Whitaker 1
RANSOM, Rastus Seneca 1
RANSOM, Ronald 2
RANSOM, Thomas Edward Greenfield H
RANSOM, William Lynn 3
RANSOME, Frederick Leslie 1
RANSON, Arthur Jones 5
RANSON, Charles Wesley 9
RANSON, Stephen Walter 2
RANSONE, Coleman Bernard, Jr. 9
RANTA, Hugo Armas 9
RANTOUL, Augustus Neal 4
RANTOUL, Neal 3
RANTOUL, Robert* H
RANTOUL, Robert Samuel 1
RANTOUL, William Gibbons 2
RANTZ, Lowell Addison 4
RANUM, Arthur 1
RAO, K. Kirshna 5
RAO, Paul Peter 9
RAOUL, Gaston C. 4
RAOUL, William P(errin) 8
RAPACKI, Adam 5
RAPAPORT, Walter 10
RAPEE, Erno 2
RAPEE, Leon Andre 5
RAPEER, Louis Win 7
RAPELYE, Harry Andrew 7
RAPER, Arthur Franklin 7
RAPER, Charles L. 3
RAPER, Charles Lee 4
RAPER, John Robert 6
RAPER, John Robert 7
RAPHAELSON, Samson 8
RAPHALL, Morris Jacob H

RAPHEL, Arnold Lewis 9
RAPIER, James Thomas H
RAPIER, Thomas Gwynn 5
RAPKIN, Joseph E. 8
RAPORTE, Arthur James 9
RAPOSO, Joseph Guilherme 9
RAPP, George H
RAPP, John Cyril 7
RAPP, Wilhelm 1
RAPP, William Jourdan 2
RAPPAPORT, Max Edward 4
RAPPAPORT, Percy 5
RAPPAPORT, Sydney Charles 9
RAPPARD, William Emmanuel 3
RAPPE, Louis Amadeus H
RAPPLEYE, Willard Cole 7
RAPPOLD, Marie 3
RAPPOLO, Joseph Leon 4
RAPPORT, David 5
RAPUANO, Michael 6
RAREY, John Solomon H
RARICK, Clarence Edmund 2
RARICK, Joseph Francis, Sr. 10
RARIDEN, James H
RARIG, Frank M. R. 4
RARIG, Frederick John 10
RARIG, Howard R. 8
RASBACH, Oscar* 6
RASCH, Albertina 4
RASCHE, William Frank 8
RASCHEN, John Frederick Louis 3
RASCHIG, Frank Elmer 3
RASCHKE, Kenneth Edward 8
RASCO, Richmond Austin 1
RASCOE, Burton 3
RASELY, Hiram Newton 3
RASH, Frank Dillman 6
RASH, Jesse Keogh 8
RASHEVSKY, Nicolas 6
RASHKIND, William Jacobson 9
RASKIN, Ellen 9
RASKIN, Judith 8
RASKOB, John J. 3
RASMUS, Henry Irving, Jr. 10
RASMUSEN, Bertil Mathias 4
RASMUSEN, Edward A. 2
RASMUSSEM, Aaron Frederick 9
RASMUSSEN, Albert Terrill 5
RASMUSSEN, Andrew Theodore 7
RASMUSSEN, Carl Christian 8
RASMUSSEN, Frederik 1
RASMUSSEN, Marius Peter 5
RASMUSSEN, Otho Mills 3
RASMUSSEN, Phipps Louis 8
RASMUSSEN, Robert Vernon 9
RASOR, Samuel Eugene 3
RASSENFOSS, John Christopher 7
RASSIEUR, Leo 1
RASSMAN, Emil Charles 8
RASSMAN, Emil Charles 9
RATCHFORD, Michael D. 4
RATCLIFF, John Moses 3
RATCLIFFE, John H
RATCLIFFE, Myron Fenwick 10
RATH, Edwin R(oscoe) 10
RATH, Howard Harbin 5
RATH, Ruben A. 3
RATH, Theodore August 10
RATH, W. John 3
RATHBONE, Albert 2
RATHBONE, Alfred Day, IV 2
RATHBONE, Henry Bailey 2
RATHBONE, Henry Riggs 1
RATHBONE, Jared Lawrence 1
RATHBONE, John Finley 1
RATHBONE, Josephine Adams 1
RATHBONE, Justus Henry H
RATHBONE, Monroe Jackson 7
RATHBONE, Philip St John Basil 4
RATHBONE, St George Henry 1
RATHBORNE, J. Cornelius 3
RATHBUN, Edward Harris 2

RATHBUN, Elmer Jeremiah 3
RATHBUN, George Oscar H
RATHBUN, George St. John 7
RATHBUN, H. H. 2
RATHBUN, John Campbell 6
RATHBUN, John Charles 7
RATHBUN, Mary Jane 4
RATHBUN, Richard 3
RATHER, Howard C. 3
RATHER, John Thomas, Jr. 5
RATHJE, Frank C. 4
RATHMANN, Carl Gustav 1
RATHMANN, Walter Lincoln 3
RATHOM, John Revelstoke 1
RATHVON, Nathaniel Peter 5
RATHVON, William Roedel 1
RATIGAN, William 9
RATLIFF, Alexander L. 2
RATNER, Bret 3
RATNER, Irving Maurice 9
RATNER, Milton Dunne 10
RATOFF, Gregory 4
RATSHESKY, Abraham C. 2
RATTELMAN, William Adam 3
RATTI, Gino Arturo 7
RATTIGAN, Charles F. 4
RATTNER, Abraham 7
RATTNER, Herbert 4
RATZLAFF, Carl Johann 3
RAU, Albert George 2
RAU, Sir Benegal Rama 5
RAU, Charles H
RAU, Roscoe Russel 4
RAUB, Edward B. 5
RAUB, Kenneth Charles 4
RAUB, William Longstreth 4
RAUBENHEIMER, Albert Sydney 9
RAUCH, Basil 9
RAUCH, Frederick Augustus H
RAUCH, George W. 5
RAUCH, Harry Ernest 7
RAUCH, Harry Lee 3
RAUCH, John George 7
RAUCH, John Henry H
RAUCH, Rudolph Stewart 5
RAUDENBUSH, David Webb 5
RAUDENBUSH, George King 3
RAUE, Charles Gottlieb H
RAUH, Bertha Floersheim (Mrs. Enoch Rauh) 5
RAUH, Joseph L., Jr. 10
RAUL, Minnie Louise 3
RAULT, Clemens V. 10
RAULT, Joseph Matthew 4
RAUM, Green Berry 1
RAUNBORG, John Dee 5
RAUNIKAR, Robert 10
RAUP, Robert Bruce 4
RAUSCH, Emil Henry 1
RAUSCH, James Steven 8
RAUSCHENBUSCH, Augustus 9
RAUSCHENBUSCH, Walter 1
RAUSCHNING, Hermann 8
RAUSHENBUSH, Esther (Mrs. Carl Raushenbush) 7
RAUSHENBUSH, Stephen Walter 10
RAUTENSTRAUCH, Walter 3
RAVAGE, Marcus Eli (Name Americanized From Revici To Ravage) 7
RAVALLI, Antonio 5
RAVDIN, Isidor Schwaner 5
RAVDIN, Robert Glenn 6
RAVEL, Vincent Marvin 5
RAVEN, Anton Adolph 3
RAVEN, John Howard 2
RAVENEL, Beatrice Witte 3
RAVENEL, Edmund 4
RAVENEL, Gaillard Fitz Simons 7
RAVENEL, Harriott Harry 4
RAVENEL, Henry William H
RAVENEL, Mazyck Porcher 4
RAVENEL, St Julien H
RAVENEL, William de Chastignier 4
RAVENSCROFT, Edward Hawks 3
RAVENSCROFT, John Stark H
RAVER, Leonard 10

RAVESON, Sherman Harold 6
RAVICH, Abraham 9
RAVIN, Arnold Warren 7
RAVIN, Arnold Warren 8
RAVIOLA, d'Elia Giuseppina 10
RAVIOLO, Victor Gino 8
RAVITCH, Mark Mitchell 10
RAVLIN, Grace 3
RAVNDAL, Gabriel Bie 2
RAVOGLI, Augustus 4
RAWIDOWICZ, Simon 3
RAWL, Bernard Hazelius 1
RAWLE, Francis H
RAWLE, Francis 1
RAWLE, James 1
RAWLE, William H
RAWLE, William Henry H
RAWLEIGH, William Thomas 5
RAWLES, Jacob Beekman 1
RAWLES, William A. 1
RAWLEY, Joseph Pearson 1
RAWLINGS, Calvin W(illiam) 10
RAWLINGS, Eugene Hubbard 1
RAWLINGS, Majorie Kinnan 3
RAWLINGS, Norborne L. 10
RAWLINGS, Norborne L. 5
RAWLINS, George Herndon 4
RAWLINS, John Aaron H
RAWLINS, Joseph Lafayette 1
RAWLINS, Lester 9
RAWLINS, William Thomas 1
RAWLINSON, Frank Joseph 1
RAWLS, Fletcher Hooks 8
RAWLS, Flora Hayes 5
RAWLS, Joseph Leonard, Jr. 8
RAWLS, Nancy Vivian 8
RAWN, A. M. 8
RAWN, Arnold Edward 6
RAWN, Ira Griffith 1
RAWSON, Albert Leighton 1
RAWSON, Carl Wendell 5
RAWSON, Charles A. 1
RAWSON, Edward Kirk 4
RAWSON, Frederick Holbrook 1
RAWSON, Kennett Longley 10
RAWSON, Ralph William 10
RAY, Anna Chapin 2
RAY, Arthur Benning 3
RAY, Charles Andrew 1
RAY, Charles Bennett H
RAY, Charles Henry H
RAY, Charles Wayne 1
RAY, Charlotte Elizabeth 7
RAY, David Heydorn 4
RAY, E. Lansing 3
RAY, Edward Chittenden 1
RAY, Franklin Arnold 1
RAY, Frederick Augustus, Jr. 5
RAY, G. J. 4
RAY, George Washington 1
RAY, George Washington, Jr. 7
RAY, Gordon Norton 9
RAY, Guy W. 3
RAY, Herbert James 5
RAY, Hoyt Everett 8
RAY, Isaac H
RAY, Jefferson Davis 3
RAY, John Arthur 6
RAY, John Edwin 1
RAY, John Henry 6
RAY, Joseph H
RAY, Joseph R., Sr. 4
RAY, Louise Crenshaw 3
RAY, Marle Beynon 5
RAY, Milton S. 2
RAY, Ossian H
RAY, P. Henry 1
RAY, P(erley) Orman 5
RAY, Philip Alexander 5
RAY, Philip Lacey 9
RAY, Randolph 4
RAY, Robert Frederick 8
RAY, Royal Henderson 8
RAY, Ruth (Mrs. John R. Graham) 7
RAY, Satyajit 10
RAY, S(ilvey) J(ackson) 5
RAY, T. Bronson* 1
RAY, Ward Lowe 7
RAY, William Henry H
RAY, William Wallace 6
RAYBOLD, Walter James 1

RAYBURN, Sam 4
RAYCORFT, Joseph Edward 3
RAYFIEL, Leo F. 8
RAYMER, Albert Reesor 1
RAYMOND, Alexander Gillespie 3
RAYMOND, Anan 6
RAYMOND, Anan 7
RAYMOND, Andrew Van Vranken 1
RAYMOND, Anna Almy 4
RAYMOND, Antonin 7
RAYMOND, Benjamin Wright 1
RAYMOND, Bradford Paul 1
RAYMOND, C. Rexford 3
RAYMOND, Charles Beebe 2
RAYMOND, Charles Walker 1
RAYMOND, Clifford Samuel 3
RAYMOND, Daniel H
RAYMOND, Donat 4
RAYMOND, Mrs. Dora Neill 4
RAYMOND, Eleanor 9
RAYMOND, Ernest 6
RAYMOND, Evelyn Hunt 1
RAYMOND, Fred Morton 2
RAYMOND, Frederick Wingate 1
RAYMOND, George Lansing 1
RAYMOND, Harry Howard 1
RAYMOND, Henry Ingle 4
RAYMOND, Henry Jarvis H
RAYMOND, Henry Warren 1
RAYMOND, Howard Monre 2
RAYMOND, Jerome Hall 1
RAYMOND, John Baldwin H
RAYMOND, John Howard H
RAYMOND, John T. H
RAYMOND, Jonathan Stone 4
RAYMOND, Joseph Howard 1
RAYMOND, Josephine Hunt (Mrs. Jerome Hall Raymond) 5
RAYMOND, Mary Elizabeth 3
RAYMOND, Maud Mary Wotring 4
RAYMOND, Miner H
RAYMOND, Nell C. 4
RAYMOND, Percy Edward 6
RAYMOND, Reginald Irving 1
RAYMOND, Robert Fulton 1
RAYMOND, Rossiter Worthington 1
RAYMOND, Thomas Lynch 1
RAYMOND, William Galt 1
RAYMOND, William Lee 1
RAYNER, Charles 7
RAYNER, Emma 1
RAYNER, Ernest Adolphus 6
RAYNER, Isidor 1
RAYNER, Kenneth H
RAYNER, William Ward 7
RAYNOLDS, Herbert F. 5
RAYNOLDS, John Madison 6
RAYNOLDS, Joshua Saxton 1
RAYNOLDS, Robert 4
RAYNOR, Hayden 4
RAYSOR, Thomas Middleton 3
RAZMARA, Ali 3
RAZRAN, Gregory 6
REA, Gardner 4
REA, George Bronson 4
REA, Mrs. Henry R. 5
REA, James C(hilds) 1
REA, John H
REA, John Andrew 1
REA, John Dougan 1
REA, John Patterson 5
REA, Paul Marshall 1
REA, Robert 5
REA, Samuel 1
READ, Albert Cushing 4
READ, Albert Cushing H
READ, Almon Heath H
READ, Benjamin Stalker 1
READ, Cecil Byron 5
READ, Charles H
READ, Charles Francis 3
READ, Charles O. 1
READ, Charles William H

READ, Clark Phares 6
READ, Conyers 3
READ, Daniel* H
READ, Florence Matilda 6
READ, Florence Matilda 7
READ, George H
READ, George Campbell H
READ, George Windle 1
READ, George Windle H
READ, Granville M. 4
READ, Harlan Eugene 4
READ, Harold D. 2
READ, Harold E. 10
READ, Helen Appleton 6
READ, Helen Appleton 7
READ, Herbert 5
READ, Herbert Harold 6
READ, Horace Emerson 6
READ, Jacob H
READ, James Morgan 8
READ, John* H
READ, John Elliot 4
READ, John Joseph 1
READ, John Meredith* H
READ, John Royall 5
READ, Leonard Edward 8
READ, Mary Lillian 6
READ, Maurice Gallison 4
READ, Melbourne Stuart 1
READ, Nathan H
READ, Norman 7
READ, Oliver Middleton 5
READ, Oliver Middleton 8
READ, Opie 1
READ, Thomas H
READ, Thomas 4
READ, Thomas Albert 4
READ, Thomas Buchanan H
READ, Thomas Thornton 2
READ, Waldemer Pickett 6
READ, William Augustus 1
READ, William Augustus 7
READ, William Brown 4
READ, William Lewis 1
READ, William Merritt 8
READ, William Thackara 4
READ, William Thornton, Sr. 7
READE, Edwin Godwin H
READE, John Moore 1
READE, Philip 1
READER, Francis Smith 4
READING, Arthur Kenneth 8
READING, John Roberts H
READING, Richard William 3
READIO, Wilfred Allen 4
READY, Charles H
READY, Frank A. 4
READY, Joseph Louis 3
READY, Lester Seward 2
READY, Michael Joseph 3
REAGAN, Frank J. 3
REAGAN, John Henninger 1
REAGAN, Lewis M. 4
REAGAN, William J. 7
REALF, Richard H
REALS, Willis H. 4
REALS, Willis H(oward) 5
REAM, Louis Marshall 8
REAM, Norman Bruce 1
REAM, Norman Jacob 10
REAMES, Alfred Evan 2
REAMEY, George Spottswood 10
REAMS, Frazier 5
REAMY, Thaddeus Asbury 1
REANEY, George Humes 2
REARDON, James G. 7
REARDON, John 9
REARDON, John Edward 10
REARDON, Paul Cashman 9
REARICK, Allan Chamberlain 1
REASER, Matthew Howell 4
REASER, Wilbur Aaron 4
REASONER, Harold Carlton 7
REASONER, Harry 10
REATH, Theodore Wood 4
REATH, Thomas 6
REAVES, Samuel Watson 3
REAVIS, Charles Frank 1
REAVIS, James Bradly 1
REAVIS, James Overton 5
REAVIS, John Wallace 9
REAVIS, William Claude 4
REAVLEY, Lester S. 3
REBADOW, Richard F. 8
REBASZ, Eurith Trabue Pattison 4
REBEC, George 3
REBER, John 3
REBER, John U. 2
REBER, Louis Ehrhart 2

REBER, Samuel 1
REBER, Samuel 5
REBERT, Gordon Nevin 2
REBMANN, Godfrey Ruhland, Jr. 8
REBOLLO, Anthony Ernest 9
REBORI, Andrew Nicholas 4
REBSCHER, J. M. 4
RECCORD, Augustus Phineas 2
RECHT, Charles 4
RECINOS, Adrian 7
RECK, Franklin Mering 4
RECKLING, William Joseph 4
RECKMEYER, Luella 4
RECKNAGEL, Arthur Bernard 4
RECKNAGEL, Richard Otto 10
RECKORD, Milton A. 6
RECORD, James Lucius 2
RECORD, James Robert 6
RECORD, James Robert 7
RECORD, Samuel James 2
RECORDS, Edward 4
RECORDS, Ralph Lafayette 4
RECTOR, Edward 1
RECTOR, Elbridge Lee 1
RECTOR, Frank 1
RECTOR, Henry Massey H
RECTOR, John B. 4
RECTOR, Lizzie E. 3
RECTOR, Thomas M. 3
RECTOR, Walter Whiting 3
RECTOR, William George 7
RED CLOUD H
RED CLOUD 4
REDDALL, Frederic 4
REDDALL, H(enry) Hastings 10
REDDICK, Dewitt Carter 7
REDDICK, Donald 3
REDDIG, Edward Sterling 7
REDDING, Charles Summerfield 3
REDDING, John Mac Lean 4
REDDING, Joseph Deighn 1
REDDING, Leo L. 1
REDDING, Otis 4
REDDING, Robert Jordan 1
REDDISH, George Fults 4
REDDIX, Jacob L. 6
REDDY, William John 7
REDE, Wyllys 4
RED EAGLE H
REDEFER, Frederick Lovatt 7
REDEKE, Ernest William 4
REDER, Bernard 10
REDER, Bernard 4
REDFEARN, Daniel Huntley 4
REDFERN, Donald Verne 4
REDFERN, Frank James 7
REDFERN, Frank James 8
REDFERN, John Joseph, Jr. 9
REDFERN, Merrill F. 3
REDFIELD, Alfred Clarence 9
REDFIELD, Alfred Guillou 8
REDFIELD, Amasa Angell 1
REDFIELD, Casper Lavater 2
REDFIELD, Edward Willis 4
REDFIELD, Emanuel 9
REDFIELD, Henry Stephen 1
REDFIELD, Isaac Fletcher H
REDFIELD, Justus Starr H
REDFIELD, Robert 3
REDFIELD, William C. H
REDFIELD, William C. 1
REDGRAVE, Michael Scudamore 8
REDHEAD, Edwin Richard 1
REDHEAD, Hugh M. 7
REDIGER, Michel Jon 5
REDING, John Randall H
REDINGTON, Paul Goodwin 1
REDINGTON, Paul Goodwin 2
RED JACKET H
REDMAN, Ben Ray 4
REDMAN, Harry Newton 5
REDMAN, John H
REDMAN, Joseph Reasor 5
REDMAN, Lawrence V. 2
REDMOND, Daniel George 3
REDMOND, Daniel Walter 1
REDMOND, Granville 1
REDMOND, John Harris 6
REDMOND, Kenneth H 6
REDMOND, Paul Alonzo 7
REDMOND, Roland Livingston 8
REDPATH, James H
REDPATH, Robert Upjohn, Jr. 9
REDPATH, William Stanley 9
REDSTONE, Edward H. 3
REDWAY, Jacques Wardlaw 2
RED WING H
REDWOOD, Abraham H
REEB, James Joseph 4
REECE, B. Carroll 4
REECE, Mrs. Carroll (Louise Goff) 5
REECE, Ernest James 6
REECE, Richard H. 3
REED, A. F. 4
REED, Alan, Sr. 7
REED, Albert Augustus 5
REED, Albert Granberry 1
REED, Alexander Preston 7
REED, Alfred 1
REED, Alfred C(ummings) 7
REED, Alfred Zantzinger 2
REED, Allen E. 7
REED, Allen Visscher 1
REED, Amy Louise 2
REED, Anna Yeomans (Mrs. Joseph Ambrose Reed) 5
REED, Boardman 1
REED, Burleigh 7
REED, Sir Carol 7
REED, Carroll Edward 8
REED, Carroll Roscoe 3
REED, Cass Arthur 3
REED, Charles Alfred Lee 1
REED, Charles Bert 1
REED, Charles Dana 2
REED, Charles Hancock 7
REED, Charles John 4
REED, Charles Manning H
REED, Chauncey William 3
REED, Chester Allyn 4
REED, Clare Osborne (Mrs. Charles B. Reed) 5
REED, Clarence C. 9
REED, Clyde Martin 2
REED, Daniel Alden 3
REED, David H
REED, David Aiken 3
REED, Donald Ross 5
REED, Donna 9
REED, Earl F. 4
REED, Earl Howell 1
REED, Earl Howell 4
REED, Edward Bliss 1
REED, Edward Cambridge H
REED, Edward U(rbane) 7
REED, Edwin 1
REED, Edwin Clarence 5
REED, Elizabeth Armstrong 1
REED, Elmer Ellsworth 1
REED, Ernest 8
REED, Florence 4
REED, Florence 7
REED, Forrest Francis 6
REED, Francis Cables 6
REED, Frank Fremont 1
REED, Frank Hynes 3
REED, Frank Lefevre 5
REED, Frank Otheman 8
REED, Frank Otis 2
REED, Frank Walker 6
REED, Franklin Hancock 1
REED, George Edward 1
REED, George Franklin 10
REED, George Henry 6
REED, George Letchworth 5
REED, George Matthew 6
REED, George William 3
REED, Guy Euclid 3
REED, Harlow John 5
REED, Harold Lyle 8
REED, Harry Bertram 1
REED, Harry E. 4
REED, Harry James 4
REED, Harry Lathrop 4
REED, Helen Leah 5
REED, Henry Albert 1
REED, Henry Clay 5
REED, Henry Hope H
REED, Henry Morrison 2
REED, Henry Thomas 1
REED, Herbert 5
REED, Horace 5
REED, Howard Sprague 3
REED, Hugh Daniel 1
REED, Isaac H
REED, Ivy Kellerman* 5
REED, James H
REED, James 4
REED, James A. 2
REED, James A. 8
REED, James Byron 1
REED, James Calvin 3
REED, James Hay 1
REED, John* H
REED, John 1
REED, John 4
REED, John Alton 4
REED, John C. 3
REED, John Calvin 1
REED, John Oren 1
REED, Joseph H
REED, Joseph Rea 1
REED, Joseph Verner 6
REED, Lowell Jacob 4
REED, Luman H
REED, Luther Dotterer 5
REED, M(alcolm) W(illard) 6
REED, Mark 8
REED, Marshall Russell 9
REED, Martin M., Jr. 4
REED, Mary Dean (Mrs. Verner Z. Reed) 5
REED, Mary Williams (Kate Carew) 5
REED, Merle Roland 7
REED, Milton 1
REED, Ollie Ezekiel 7
REED, Perley Isaac 5
REED, Philip H
REED, Philip Dunham 10
REED, Philip Loring 4
REED, Phillip Allen 6
REED, Ralph John 1
REED, Ralph Thomas 4
REED, Richard Clark 1
REED, Richard Forman 1
REED, Robert Bowman 2
REED, Robert Cameron 1
REED, Robert Findley 8
REED, Robert Rentoul H
REED, Robert Rentoul 2
REED, Rodman Smith, Jr. 4
REED, Roland 1
REED, Sampson H
REED, Samuel Macon 6
REED, Sarah A. 1
REED, Simeon Gannett H
REED, Stanley Forman 7
REED, Stuart F. 1
REED, Stuart R. 4
REED, Sylvanus Albert 1
REED, Thomas Brackett 1
REED, Thomas Buck H
REED, Thomas Harrison 5
REED, Thomas Milburne 1
REED, Thomas Selden 7
REED, Vergil Daniel 9
REED, Verner Zevola 1
REED, Victor Joseph 5
REED, Walter H
REED, Walter Lawrence 3
REED, Warren Augustus 1
REED, Washington 3
REED, Wayne Otis 6
REED, Willard 2
REED, William H
REED, William Bradford H
REED, William Doyle 10
REED, William Hale 3
REED, William M. 3
REED, William Reynolds 5
REED, William Thomas, Jr. 4
REED, William Vernon 9
REEDER, Andrew Horatio H
REEDER, Charles L. 4
REEDER, Charles Leonard 5
REEDER, Edwin Hewett 3
REEDER, Edwin Thorley 4
REEDER, Frank 1
REEDER, Glezen Asbury, Jr. 5
REEDER, Grace Amelia 4
REEDER, Howard Chandler 7
REEDER, Lee 9
REEDER, Leo Glenn 7
REEDER, Ward Glen 4
REEDER, William Augustus 4
REEDER, William Herron 1
REED-HILL, Ellis 8
REEDY, J. Martin 3
REEDY, John Louis 8
REEDY, Rose Stroman (Mrs. F. C. Reedy) 5
REEDY, Thomas Albert 8
REEDY, William Marion 1
REEMAN, Edmund Henry 3
REEMELIN, Oscar Ben 6
REEP, Samuel Austen 5
REES, Albert (Everett) 10
REES, Albert William 5
REES, Alfred Cornelius 1
REES, Byron Johnson 1
REES, Charles Herbert 7
REES, Corwin Pottenger 1
REES, Edward H. 5
REES, Edwin Henry 6
REES, George E. 4
REES, James H
REES, John Krom 1
REES, Maurice Holmes 2
REES, Robert Irwin 1
REES, Rollin R. 4
REES, Thomas 1
REES, Thomas Henry 2
REES, William Henry 3
REESE, Addison Hardcastle 7
REESE, Albert Moore 4
REESE, Algernon Beverly 8
REESE, Benjamin Harrison 6
REESE, Charles H. 5
REESE, Charles Lee 1
REESE, Charles Lee, Jr. 10
REESE, Curtis Williford 4
REESE, Dale F. 3
REESE, David Addison H
REESE, Frederick Focke 1
REESE, George Lee 5
REESE, Gilbert A. 2
REESE, Hans H. F. 9
REESE, Harry Browne 10
REESE, Herbert Meredith 3
REESE, J. Allen 4
REESE, Jim Eanes 7
REESE, John D. 6
REESE, John James H
REESE, Joseph Hammond 5
REESE, Kenneth Wendell 10
REESE, Lizette Woodworth 1
REESE, Lizette Woodworth 2
REESE, Lowell Otus 3
REESE, Manoah Bostic 1
REESE, Millard 3
REESE, Raymond Castle 7
REESE, Scott Charles 5
REESE, T. T. 3
REESE, Theodore Irving 1
REESE, Thomas Whelan 8
REESE, Webster Paul 6
REESE, Wilbur Ford 5
REESE, Willis Livingston Mesier 10
REESER, Edwin B. 5
REESIDE, John Bernard, Jr. 3
REESING, John Palmer, Jr. 10
REESMAN, Budd Aaron 5
REEVE, Arthur Benjamin 1
REEVE, Arthur Benjamin 6
REEVE, Charles McCormick 4
REEVE, Felix Alexander 1
REEVE, James Knapp 1
REEVE, Sidney Armor 1
REEVE, Tapping H
REEVE, William David 4
REEVE, William Foster, III 5
REEVERTS, Emma (Marie) 6
REEVES, Albert Lee 9
REEVES, Alec Harley 5
REEVES, Alfred Gandy 1
REEVES, Archie R. 5
REEVES, Arthur Middleton H
REEVES, Charles Francis 4
REEVES, Daniel F. 5
REEVES, Floyd Wesley 7
REEVES, Francis Brewster 1
REEVES, Frank Daniel 5
REEVES, George Curtis 5
REEVES, Herbert James 4
REEVES, Ira Louis 1
REEVES, Isaac Stockton Keith 1
REEVES, James Aloysius Wallace 2
REEVES, James Haynes 5
REEVES, Jeremiah Bascom 2
REEVES, Jesse Siddall 2
REEVES, John Dudley, Jr. 4
REEVES, John Mercer 7
REEVES, John Richard Thomas, Jr. 5
REEVES, John Ruel 3
REEVES, John Walter, Jr. 4
REEVES, Joseph Mason 2
REEVES, Norman Pennington 7
REEVES, Norman Pennington 8
REEVES, Owen Thornton 4
REEVES, Perry Willard 2
REEVES, Robert James 4
REEVES, Rosser 8
REEVES, Russell Henry 6
REEVES, Ruth 4
REEVES, Thomas Rosser 3
REEVES, Walter 1
REEVES, Walter Perkins 3
REEVES, William Harvey 6
REEVES, William Peters 2
REEVES, Winona Evans 5
REFREGIER, Anton 7
REGAN, Ben 5
REGAN, Frank Stewart 2
REGAN, Frank W. 4
REGAN, James Joseph 6
REGAN, James L. 1
REGAN, Louis John 3
REGAN, Purdy C. 10
REGAR, Robert Smith 3
REGENSBURGER, Richard William 3
REGER, David Bright 3
REGESTER, John Dickinson 10
REGISTER, Edward Chauncey 1
REGISTER, Francis Henry 1
REGISTER, George Scott 5
REGISTER, Henry Bartol 3
REGNIER, Raymond Cobington, Jr. 7
REH, Carl William 8
REHAN, Ada 1
REHBERGER, George Edward 6
REHDER, Alfred 2
REHDER, Helmut 7
REHERD, Herbert Ware 3
REHFUSS, Walter Guy 10
REHG, Norman Melchior 9
REHM, Theodore A. 6
REHN, Frank Knox Morton 1
REHNER, Herbert Adrian 8
REHRING, George John 7
REHSE, George Washington 4
REICH, Jacques 1
REICH, Johann Mathias H
REICH, John 9
REICH, Max Isaac 2
REICHARD, Gladys Amanda 3
REICHARD, John Davis 4
REICHARDT, Konstantin 6
REICHARDT, Konstantin 7
REICHBERG, David 9
REICHEL, Charles Gotthold H
REICHEL, Frank Hartranft 4
REICHEL, William Cornelius H
REICHELDERFER, F(rancis) W(ilton) 10
REICHELDERFER, Francis Wilton 8
REICHELDERFER, Luther Halsey 2
REICHER, Louis Joseph 8
REICHERT, Edward Tyson 1
REICHERT, Herbert William 7
REICHERT, Irving Frederick 4
REICHERT, Philip 9
REICHERT, Rudolph Edward 4
REICHERT, Mother Thomas 5
REICHHOLD, Henry 10
REICHLER, Oxie 9
REICHMANN, Carl 4
REICHMANN, Donald August 5
REICK, William Charles 1
REID, Albert Turner 3
REID, Alberta Bancroft (Mrs.) 5
REID, Alfred Sandlin 7
REID, Charles Chester 2
REID, Charles Simpson 2
REID, Charles Wesley 4
REID, Daniel Gray 1
REID, David Boswell H
REID, David Settle H
REID, Delafayette 5
REID, Duncan Earl 6
REID, E. C. 3
REID, E. Emmet 6
REID, Edwin Kitchen 8
REID, Edwy Borradaile 7
REID, Elliott Gray 5
REID, Ernest W. 4
REID, Fergus 2
REID, Frank A. 8
REID, Frank R. 2
REID, Frederick Horman 2
REID, George Croghan 1
REID, George T. 1
REID, Gilbert 1
REID, Harry Fielding 2
REID, Helen Dwight 4
REID, Helen Rogers (Mrs. Ogden Mills Reid) 5
REID, Helen Rogers (Mrs. Ogden Mills Reid) 7
REID, Henry John Edward 5
REID, Ira De Augustine 5

REID, James L. H
REID, James L. 4
REID, James Randolph H
REID, James Sims 8
REID, John 6
REID, John Edward 8
REID, John Morrison H
REID, John Simpson 4
REID, John Thomas 7
REID, John Turner 7
REID, John William H
REID, Kenneth 3
REID, Kenneth Alexander 3
REID, Loudon Corsan 5
REID, Mont Rogers 2
REID, O. L. 5
REID, Ogden Mills 2
REID, Paul Apperson 8
REID, Philip Joseph 1
REID, Richard 4
REID, Robert 1
REID, Robert Haley 5
REID, Robert Raymond H
REID, Ross 10
REID, Samuel Chester H
REID, Silas Hinkle 3
REID, Sydney 4
REID, T. Roy 5
REID, Thomas Mayne H
REID, Thorburn 3
REID, W. Max 1
REID, Walter Williamson 3
REID, Whitelaw 1
REID, Will J. 3
REID, Willard Malcolm 10
REID, William 4
REID, William Alfred 5
REID, William Clifford 2
REID, William Duncan 2
REID, William James 1
REID, William James, Jr. 2
REID, William R. 3
REID, William Shields H
REID, William Thomas 4
REIDY, Daniel Joseph 4
REIDY, Daniel Joseph 7
REIDY, E. T. 6
REIDY, Edward Michael 10
REIDY, Peter J. 5
REIF, Edward C. 4
REIF, Herbert R. 5
REIFEL, Ben 10
REIFENSTEIN, Edward Conrad* 6
REIFF, Cecil K. 3
REIFF, Evan Allard 4
REIFF, Robert Frank 4
REIFFEL, Charles 2
REIFSNIDER, Charles Shriver 3
REIFSNIDER, Lawrence Fairfax 3
REIGER, Siegfried Heinrich 5
REIGHARD, Jacob 2
REIGNER, Charles Gottshall 9
REIK, Henry Ottridge 1
REIK, Theodor 5
REILAND, Karl 5
REILLEY, Mrs. J. Eugene 1
REILLY, Charles Francis, Jr. 7
REILLY, Frank Joseph 4
REILLY, Frank Kennicott 1
REILLY, Henry Joseph 4
REILLY, James Aloysius 3
REILLY, James William 1
REILLY, John David 5
REILLY, John Liguori 2
REILLY, Joseph F. 6
REILLY, Joseph John 3
REILLY, Maurice T. 4
REILLY, Michael Kiernan 1
REILLY, Peter C. 3
REILLY, Thomas Daniel 1
REILLY, Thomas Lawrence 4
REILLY, Walter B. 4
REILLY, William John 5
REILLY, William Patrick 10
REILLY, Wilson 1
REILY, E. Mont 3
REILY, George W. 3
REILY, Luther H
REILY, William Boatner, Jr. 8
REIMANN, Stanley P. 4
REIMER, Marie 5
REIMERS, Carl 8
REIMERS, Frederick W. 5
REIMERT, William Daniel 1
REIMOLD, Orlando Schairer 4
REINAGLE, Alexander H
REINARTZ, Eugen Gottfried 4
REINARTZ, Leo F. 8
REINDAHL, Knute 1

REINDEL, Harold Frederick 7
REINECK, Walter S. 8
REINECKE, Jean Otis 9
REINEKE, Ernest Conrad 7
REINEKE, Harold George 10
REINER, Fritz 4
REINER, Irving 9
REINER, Joseph 1
REINERT, Carl M. 5
REINHARD, Adolph Earl 5
REINHARD, L. Andrew 4
REINHARDT, Aurelia Henry 2
REINHARDT, Charles William 4
REINHARDT, Django 4
REINHARDT, Emil Fred 5
REINHARDT, Emma 6
REINHARDT, G(eorge) Frederick 5
REINHARDT, George Frederick 1
REINHARDT, Guenther 5
REINHARDT, Gustav Adolph 6
REINHARDT, James Melvin 6
REINHARDT, Max 2
REINHARDT, Ralph 5
REINHARDT, Siegfried Gerhard 8
REINHART, Benjamin Franklin H
REINHART, Bruce Lloyd 9
REINHART, Charles Stanley H
REINHART, Earl F. 1
REINHART, Joseph W. 1
REINHAUS, Stanley Marx 3
REINHEIMER, Bartel Hilen 2
REINHOLD, Eli Spayd 1
REINHOLD, James P. 4
REINHOLDT, Julius William 1
REINHOLDT, Julius William 4
REINICKE, Frederick George 5
REINICKE, Frederick George 8
REINING, Henry, Jr. 9
REINKE, Edwin Eustace 2
REINKING, Otto August 4
REINSCH, James Leonard 10
REINSCH, Paul Samuel 1
REIRSEN, Johan Reinhart H
REIS, Arthur M. 2
REISCHAUER, Edwin Oldfather 10
REISENBERG, Nadia 8
REISENKONIG, Herman Frank 9
REISER, Armand Edouard 5
REISER, Oliver Leslie 4
REISINGER, Curt H. 4
REISINGER, Harold Carusi 2
REISINGER, Hugo 1
REISLER, Raymond, Sr. 5
REISMAN, Morton 1
REISNER, Christian Fichthorne 1
REISNER, Edward Hartman 3
REISNER, George Andrew 2
REISS, Eric 9
REISS, Jacob L. 3
REISS, Raymond Henry 10
REISSIG, Frederick E. 7
REISSNER, Albert 5
REIST, Henry Gerber 2
REISTRUP, Jeanne Moss 8
REITELL, Charles 5
REITEN, Palmer James 7
REITER, Bernard L. 5
REITER, George H. 8
REITER, Geroge Cook 1
REITER, Walter Anderson 4
REITH, Francis C. 4
REITHERMAN, Wolfgang 7
REITMAN, Frank H. 9
REITZ, Harold Axtel 3
REITZ, Walter R. 3
REITZEL, Albert Emmet 4
REITZEL, Marques E. 4
REITZEL, Robert 1
RELFE, James Hugh H
RELIN, Bernard 6
RELLER, Charles J. 4
RELLSTAB, John 1
RELYEA, Charles M. 2
REMAK, Gustavus, Jr. 2
REMANN, Frederick H

REMARQUE, Erich Maria 5
REMBAUGH, Bertha 3
REMBERT, Arthur Gaillard 4
REMBERT, George William Francis 6
REMBOLT, Raymond Ralph 8
REMEIKA, Joseph Peter 9
REMENSNYDER, John Paul 8
REMENSNYDER, Junius Benjamin 1
REMENYI, Joseph 3
REMER, Charles Frederick 5
REMER, Helen 1
REMEY, Charles Mason 1
REMEY, George Collier 1
REMEY, Gilbert Pryce 7
REMICK, Grace May 5
REMICK, J. Gould 4
REMICK, James Waldron 2
REMICK, Lee (William Rory Gowans)* 10
REMINGTON, Eliphalet H
REMINGTON, Franklin 3
REMINGTON, Frederic 1
REMINGTON, Harold 1
REMINGTON, Harvey Foote 2
REMINGTON, John Warner 8
REMINGTON, Joseph Price 1
REMINGTON, Paul Ellsworth 9
REMINGTON, Philo H
REMINGTON, Preston 3
REMINGTON, William Procter 4
REMLEY, Milton 1
REMMEL, Arthur Kizer 1
REMMEL, Ellen Cates 4
REMMEL, Harmon Liveright 1
REMMEL, Valentine 4
REMON, Cantera 6
REMON CANTERA, Jose Antonio 3
REMOND, Charles Lenox H
REMONDINO, Peter Charles 1
REMSBURG, John Eleazer 1
REMSEN, Charles Cornell, Jr. 8
REMSEN, Daniel Smith 1
REMSEN, Ira 1
REMSTER, Charles 1
REMY, Alfred 1
REMY, Charles Frederick 5
REMY, Henri H
RENALDO, Duncan 7
RENAUD, Abel Etlenne Bernardeau 6
RENAUD, Pierre Jean Marie 10
RENAUD, Ralph Edward 2
RENAULT, Mary (lit. pseudonym for Mary Challans) 8
RENCHER, Abraham H
REND, William Patrick 1
RENDALL, John Ballard 1
RENDER, Sylvia Lyons 9
RENDLEMAN, John Samuel 6
RENDLEMAN, John Samuel 7
RENDON, Cecil Paul 7
RENEKER, Robert William 7
RENEKER, Robert William 8
RENFRO, Harold Bell 6
RENFROW, William Cary 1
RENG, Carl R. 9
RENICK, Felix H
RENICK, Ralph Apperson 10
RENIER, Joseph Emile 4
RENISON, Robert John 3
RENKEN, Henry Algernon 9
RENNAY, Léon 6
RENNEBOHM, Oscar 5
RENNELSOM, Clara H. 4
RENNER, George Thomas, Jr. 3
RENNER, John Wilson 10
RENNER, Karl 3
RENNER, Otto 4
RENNERT, Hugo Albert 1
RENNIE, Joseph 2
RENNIE, Sylvester Wilding 5
RENNIE, Thomas A. C. 3
RENO, Claude Trexler 4
RENO, Conrad 1

RENO, Doris Smith (Mrs. Paul Halvor Reno) 5
RENO, Guy Benjamin 5
RENO, Itti Kinney 4
RENO, Jesse Lee H
RENO, Jesse Wilford 5
RENOIR, Jean 7
RENOUF, Edward 1
RENOUVIN, Pierre Eugene Georges 5
RENSHAW, Alfred Howard 1
RENSHAW, Paul 7
RENSHAW, Raemer Rex 1
RENTSCHLER, Calvin Balthaser 6
RENTSCHLER, Frederick B. 3
RENTSCHLER, George Adam 5
RENTSCHLER, Gordon S. 2
RENTSCHLER, Harvey Clayton 2
RENTZEL, Delos Wilson 10
RENWICK, Edward Sabine 1
RENWICK, Henry Brevoort H
RENWICK, James* H
RENWICK, William Walter 8
RENWICK, William Whetten 1
RENYX, Guy Worden 3
REPASS, Joseph Wharton 1
REPASS, William Carlyle 1
REPLOGLE, Jacob Leonard 2
REPPLIER, Agnes 3
REPPLIER, Theodore Silkman 7
REPPY, Alison 3
REPPY, Roy Valentine 4
REQUA, Earl Francis 5
REQUA, Eloise Gallup 10
REQUA, Mark Lawrence 1
REQUARDT, Gustav Jaeger 7
REQUIER, Augustus Julian H
RESA, Alexander John 8
RESE, Frederick H
RESNICK, Joseph Yale 5
RESNICK, Nathan 7
RESO, Sidney J(oseph) 10
RESOR, Stanley 4
RESSLER, Edwin Devore 1
RESTARICK, Henry Bond 1
RESTEMEYER, William Edward 10
RETHBERG, Elisabeth 7
RETHERS, Harry Frederick 1
RETI-FORBES, Jean 6
RETTGER, Benedict Vincent 8
RETTGER, Leo Frederick 5
RETTGER, Robert Ernest 10
RETTIG, H. Earl 5
REU, Johann Michael 2
REUBEN, Allan Herbert 10
REUBEN, Odell Richardson 4
REUBEN, Robert Ervin 4
REULING, George 1
REULING, James R. 1
REUSSER, Walter Christian 7
REUTER, Edward Byron 2
REUTER, Irving Jacob 5
REUTER, Rudolph Ernst 5
REUTERDAHL, Arvid 1
REUTERDAHL, Henry 1
REUTHER, Walter Philip 5
REUTLINGER, Harry F. 4
REVEL, Bernard 1
REVELL, Alexander Hamilton 1
REVELL, Fleming H., Jr. 7
REVELL, Fleming H., Jr. 5
REVELL, Fleming Hewitt 1
REVELLE, Roger Randall Dougan 10
REVELLE, Thomas P. 1
REVELS, Hiram Rhoades H
REVERCOMB, Chapman 5
REVERE, Anne 10
REVERE, Edward H. R. 3
REVERE, Joseph Warren H
REVERE, Paul H
REVERMAN, Theodore Henry 1
REVILL, Milton Kirtley 3
REVILLE, Eugene Thomas 10
REVSON, Charles Haskell 6
REVZIN, Marvin E. 9
REW, Irving 1
REX, Charles Henry 6
REXDALE, Robert 1
REXFORD, Eben Eugene 1
REXFORD, Frank A. 1

REXROTH, Kenneth 8
REY, Alejandro 9
REY, Anthony H
REYBOLD, Eugene 4
REYBURN, Harold Orbra 10
REYBURN, John Edgar 1
REYBURN, Laurens H. 4
REYBURN, Robert 1
REYBURN, Samuel Wallace 4
REYBURN, William Stuart 7
REYERSON, Lloyd Hilton 5
REYES, Alfonso 3
REYMERT, Martin 3
REYNAL, Eugene 5
REYNAL, Louis 4
REYNARD, Grant 5
REYNAUD, Paul 4
REYNDERS, John V. W. 2
REYNIERS, James A. 4
REYNOLDS, Alexander H
Welch
REYNOLDS, Alfred 1
REYNOLDS, Allen 1
Holbrook
REYNOLDS, Amesbury L. 4
REYNOLDS, Arthur 2
REYNOLDS, Bruce D. 3
REYNOLDS, Carl Vernon 5
REYNOLDS, Carroll 6
Foster
REYNOLDS, Charles H
Alexander
REYNOLDS, Charles 8
Augustus
REYNOLDS, Charles 1
Bingham
REYNOLDS, Charles Lee 5
REYNOLDS, Charles 8
Nathan
REYNOLDS, Charles 5
Ransom
REYNOLDS, Chester A. 3
REYNOLDS, Clarence 6
REYNOLDS, Conger 5
REYNOLDS, Cuyler 4
REYNOLDS, Dudley 1
Sharpe
REYNOLDS, Earle Hay 3
REYNOLDS, Edward 8
Storrs
REYNOLDS, Edwin 1
REYNOLDS, Edwin Louis 8
REYNOLDS, Elmer Lewis 4
REYNOLDS, Elmer Robert 1
REYNOLDS, Emily Simms 7
Bellinger
REYNOLDS, Ernest Shaw 4
REYNOLDS, Frank 8
REYNOLDS, Frank 1
Bernard
REYNOLDS, Frank James 3
REYNOLDS, Frank 5
William
REYNOLDS, Fred Curtis 9
REYNOLDS, Frederick 1
Jesse
REYNOLDS, George 1
Delachaumette
REYNOLDS, George 1
Greenwood
REYNOLDS, George 1
McClelland
REYNOLDS, George 9
Stanley
REYNOLDS, George 2
William
REYNOLDS, Gideon H
REYNOLDS, Grace Banta 7
Urbahns
REYNOLDS, Grace 3
Morrison
REYNOLDS, H. Walter 6
REYNOLDS, Henry Grady 4
REYNOLDS, Henry James 2
REYNOLDS, Herbert 5
Byron
REYNOLDS, Hewitt 8
REYNOLDS, Horace 7
(Mason)
REYNOLDS, Howard H. 7
REYNOLDS, Igantius H
Aloysius
REYNOLDS, Isham E. 2
REYNOLDS, Jackson Eli 5
REYNOLDS, James A. 10
REYNOLDS, James B. H
REYNOLDS, James 1
Bronson
REYNOLDS, James Burton 2
REYNOLDS, John* H
REYNOLDS, John Edwin 1
REYNOLDS, John Fulton H
REYNOLDS, John 4
Gilliford
REYNOLDS, John Hazard H
REYNOLDS, John Henry 5

REYNOLDS, John Hughes 1
REYNOLDS, John Lacey, Jr. 4
REYNOLDS, John Merriman 1
REYNOLDS, John Parker 1
REYNOLDS, John Todd 8
REYNOLDS, John Whitcome 3
REYNOLDS, Joseph 1
REYNOLDS, Joseph B. 1
REYNOLDS, Joseph Berchmans 10
REYNOLDS, Joseph Gardiner, Jr. 7
REYNOLDS, Joseph Gardiner, Jr. 9
REYNOLDS, Joseph Jones H
REYNOLDS, Joseph Jones 1
REYNOLDS, Joseph Smith 1
REYNOLDS, Julian Louis 8
REYNOLDS, Katharine (Mrs. Henry T. Reynolds) 1
REYNOLDS, Lawrence 4
REYNOLDS, Malvina 1
REYNOLDS, Milton 6
REYNOLDS, Myra 1
REYNOLDS, Myron Herbert 1
REYNOLDS, Oliver Charlick 6
REYNOLDS, Paul Revere 2
REYNOLDS, Paul Revere 9
REYNOLDS, Paul Russell Benton 1
REYNOLDS, Powell Benton 1
REYNOLDS, Quentin 4
REYNOLDS, Richard J. 4
REYNOLDS, Richard S., Jr. 1
REYNOLDS, Richard Samuel 3
REYNOLDS, Robert J. 1
REYNOLDS, Robert Rice 4
REYNOLDS, Rollo George 7
REYNOLDS, Royal 6
REYNOLDS, Russel Burton 10
REYNOLDS, Samuel Godfrey H
REYNOLDS, Samuel Guilford 4
REYNOLDS, Samuel Robert Means 8
REYNOLDS, Samuel Williams 9
REYNOLDS, Thomas F. 7
REYNOLDS, Thomas Harvey 2
REYNOLDS, Thomas James 9
REYNOLDS, Victor George Fassett 6
REYNOLDS, Mrs. Virginia 1
REYNOLDS, Walter Ford 2
REYNOLDS, Wellington Jarard 4
REYNOLDS, Wiley Richard 2
REYNOLDS, William H
REYNOLDS, William G. 7
REYNOLDS, William G. 8
REYNOLDS, William Glasgow 9
REYNOLDS, William Howard 5
REYNOLDS, William Neal 3
REZANOV, Nikolai Petrovich H
REZNIKOFF, Charles 1
REZNIKOFF, Charles 7
RFVERE, Clinton T. 2
RHAESA, William A. 1
RHAME, Frank Phipps 8
RHAWN, Heister Gule 1
RHEA, Claude Hiram, Jr. 10
RHEA, Hortense 1
RHEA, John H
RHEA, John S. 4
RHEA, William Edward 1
RHEA, William Francis 4
RHEAD, Louis John H
RHEAUME, Louis 3
RHEE, Syngman 4
RHEEM, Richard Scoffield H
RHEES, John Morgan H
RHEES, Rush 1
RHEES, William Jones 1
RHEINHARDT, Rudolph H. 5
RHEINSTEIN, Alfred 8
RHEINSTROM, Charles Albert 7
RHEINSTROM, Henry 4
RHETT, Andrew Burnet 2
RHETT, Robert Barnwell H
RHETT, Robert Goodwyn 1

RHETTS, Charles Edward 5
RHIND, Alexander Colden H
RHIND, Charles H
RHIND, J. Massey 1
RHINE, Abraham Benedict 1
RHINELANDER, Philip Hamilton 9
RHINELANDER, Philip Mercer 1
RHINELANDER, T. J. Oakley 4
RHINOCK, Joseph Lafayette 1
RHOAD, Albert Oliver 4
RHOADES, Cornelia Harsen 1
RHOADES, Edward Henry, Jr. 3
RHOADES, John Harsen 1
RHOADES, John Harsen 2
RHOADES, Lewis Addison 1
RHOADES, Lyman 4
RHOADES, Mabel Carter 5
RHOADES, Nelson Osgood 1
RHOADES, Otto L. 9
RHOADES, Ralph Omer 4
RHOADES, William Caldwell Plunkett 1
RHOADS, Carroll Brewster 7
RHOADS, Charles James 3
RHOADS, Cornelius Packard 3
RHOADS, Esther Biddle 10
RHOADS, James H
RHOADS, Joseph Edgar 7
RHOADS, Joseph J. 3
RHOADS, McHenry 2
RHOADS, Paul Spotswood 9
RHOADS, Samuel H
RHOADS, Samuel Nicholson 5
RHODE, Clarence J. 3
RHODE, Paul Peter 2
RHODEN, Elmer Carl 8
RHODES, Bradford 1
RHODES, Charles Dudley 3
RHODES, Donald Gene 6
RHODES, Edward Everett 3
RHODES, Elisha Hunt 4
RHODES, Eugene Manlove 1
RHODES, Foster Twichell 5
RHODES, Fred H(offman) 9
RHODES, Frederic Harrison 2
RHODES, Frederick Leland 1
RHODES, George Irving 7
RHODES, George Milton 10
RHODES, George Pearson 1
RHODES, Harrison 1
RHODES, Henry Abraham 3
RHODES, Irwin Seymour 9
RHODES, James Ford 1
RHODES, Jeremiah 1
RHODES, John Bower 4
RHODES, John Franklin 2
RHODES, Kent 10
RHODES, Marion Edward 4
RHODES, Mosheim 4
RHODES, Robert Clinton 2
RHODES, Rufus Napoleon 1
RHODES, Stephen Holbrook 1
RHODES, Willard 10
RHODES, Willard E. 5
RHODES, William Luther, Jr. 9
RHONE, Rosamond Dodson 4
RHYNE, Brice Wilson 5
RHYS, Noel Andrew 6
RIALE, Franklin Nelman 1
RIANO Y GAYANGOS, Don Juan 1
RIBAK, Louis Leon 7
RIBAR, Ivan 5
RIBAUT, Jean H
RIBBLE, Frederick D. G. 5
RIBNER, Irving 5
RIBOUD, Jean 9
RICARD, Jerome Sixtus 1
RICARDO, Harry Ralph 6
RICAUD, James Barroll H
RICCHIUTO, D. Edward 9
RICCI, Ulysses Anthony 4
RICCIARDI, Franc Mario 10
RICCIUS, Hermann Porter 1
RICCIUTO, Harry Adrian 6
RICE, Abigail Ruth Burton (Mrs. Carl V. Rice) 5
RICE, Albert E. 4
RICE, Albert White 4
RICE, Alexander Hamilton H
RICE, Alexander Hamilton 1
RICE, Alice Caldwell Hegan 1
RICE, Alonzo Leora 4
RICE, Arthur Henry 6

RICE, Arthur Louis 2
RICE, Arthur Wallace 1
RICE, Ben H., Jr. 4
RICE, Benjamin Franklin 1
RICE, Cale Young 2
RICE, Calvin Winsor 1
RICE, Charles H
RICE, Charles A. 5
RICE, Charles Allen Thorndike H
RICE, Charles Atwood 6
RICE, Charles Edmund 1
RICE, Charles Francis 1
RICE, Charles M. 3
RICE, Claton Silas 5
RICE, Craig 3
RICE, Dan H
RICE, David H
RICE, Devereux Dunlap 2
RICE, Donald Blair 8
RICE, Edmund H
RICE, Edmund 1
RICE, Edward Irving 1
RICE, Edward Loranus 3
RICE, Edward Young 1
RICE, Edwin Wilbur 1
RICE, Edwin Wilbur, Jr. 1
RICE, Elmer 4
RICE, Ernest 3
RICE, Eugene 4
RICE, Eugene Franklin 9
RICE, F. Willis 1
RICE, Fenelon Bird H
RICE, Francis Edgar 7
RICE, Francis Owen 8
RICE, Frank James 1
RICE, Franklin Pierce 1
RICE, Frederick Adolph 3
RICE, George Arthur 7
RICE, George Brackett 2
RICE, George Samuel 2
RICE, George Staples 1
RICE, Grantland 3
RICE, Greek Lent 3
RICE, Harmon Howard 5
RICE, Harry Lee 3
RICE, Heber Holbrook 3
RICE, Henry 1
RICE, Henry Izard Bacon 6
RICE, Henry Mower H
RICE, Herbert Ambrose 4
RICE, Herbert Howard 1
RICE, Herbert Leigh 1
RICE, Herbert Wayland 1
RICE, Howard Crosby 4
RICE, Isaac Leopold 1
RICE, Jack Horton 4
RICE, James Edward 5
RICE, James Henry, Jr. 1
RICE, John 1
RICE, John Andrew 1
RICE, John Andrew 4
RICE, John Birchard H
RICE, John Blake 1
RICE, John Campbell 1
RICE, John Hodgen 1
RICE, John Holt H
RICE, John Hovey 1
RICE, John McConnell 1
RICE, John Pierrepont 2
RICE, John Stanley 8
RICE, John Stanley 9
RICE, John Winter 5
RICE, Jonas Shearn 1
RICE, Joseph J. 1
RICE, Joseph Lee 1
RICE, Joseph Mayer 1
RICE, Kingsley Loring 1
RICE, Laban Lacy 5
RICE, Leonard William 9
RICE, Lewis Frederick 1
RICE, Lloyd Preston 3
RICE, Louis Albert 10
RICE, Louise (Louise Guest) 7
RICE, Luther H
RICE, M. Wilfred 5
RICE, Maurice Smythe 1
RICE, Merton Stacher 2
RICE, Nathan Lewis 1
RICE, Neil W. 9
RICE, Oscar Knefler 7
RICE, Paul Harper 3
RICE, Paul North 4
RICE, Philip Blair 1
RICE, Philip Joseph, Jr. 10
RICE, Philip Lavergne 9
RICE, Raymond Main 8
RICE, Richard Ashley 3
RICE, Richard Austin 1
RICE, Richard Henry 1
RICE, Robert 5
RICE, Stephen Ewing 3
RICE, Stephen Oswald 1
RICE, Stuart Arthur 5
RICE, Theron Hall 1
RICE, Theron Moses H

RICE, Thomas H
RICE, Thomas Dartmouth H
RICE, Thomas Stevens 2
RICE, Thurman Brooks 3
RICE, Victor Arthur 8
RICE, Victor Moreau H
RICE, W. North 1
RICE, Wallace 1
RICE, Willard Martin 1
RICE, William H
RICE, William Ball 1
RICE, William Gorham 4
RICE, William Marsh 1
RICE, William Morton Jackson 1
RICE, William Whitney H
RICH, Adelbert P. 1
RICH, Arnold Rice 5
RICH, Benjamin Leroy 6
RICH, Buddy (Bernard Rich) 9
RICH, Carl W. 5
RICH, Charles H
RICH, Charles Alonzo 2
RICH, Daniel Catton 7
RICH, Edgar Judson 2
RICH, Ednah Anne 5
RICH, Edson Prosper 4
RICH, Edward P. 1
RICH, Edwin Gile 6
RICH, Elmer 4
RICH, George R. 7
RICH, Giles Willard 2
RICH, Henry Arnold 8
RICH, Isaac H
RICH, John A. 4
RICH, John Fletcher 9
RICH, John Frederick 6
RICH, John Harrison 1
RICH, John Lyon 3
RICH, John T. 1
RICH, Lorimer 7
RICH, Obadiah H
RICH, Raymond Thomas 2
RICH, Richard H. 6
RICH, Sir Robert H
RICH, Robert Fleming 5
RICH, Ronald Emil 3
RICH, Samuel Heath 2
RICH, Thaddeus 5
RICH, Williston C. 3
RICHARD, Auguste 8
RICHARD, Charles 7
RICHARD, Donat Radolphe 7
RICHARD, Ernst D. 1
RICHARD, Gabriel H
RICHARD, Harold Charles 3
RICHARD, Irwin 6
RICHARD, James William 1
RICHARD, John H. H
RICHARD, Matthias 1
RICHARD, William Ralph, Jr. 10
RICHARDS, Alfred Ernest 2
RICHARDS, Alfred Newton 4
RICHARDS, Alice Haliburton 1
RICHARDS, Alvin 8
RICHARDS, Arthur Lincoln 10
RICHARDS, Atherton 10
RICHARDS, Aute 7
RICHARDS, Bernard Gerson 5
RICHARDS, Charles Brinckerhoff 1
RICHARDS, Charles Gorman 5
RICHARDS, Charles Herbert 1
RICHARDS, Charles Lenmore 5
RICHARDS, Charles Malone 5
RICHARDS, Charles Russ 1
RICHARDS, Charles Russell 1
RICHARDS, Charles Walter 5
RICHARDS, Cyril Fuller 3
RICHARDS, De Forest 1
RICHARDS, Dickinson W. 5
RICHARDS, Donald 3
RICHARDS, E. F. 4
RICHARDS, Eben 2
RICHARDS, Edgar 4
RICHARDS, Edward A. 3
RICHARDS, Ellen Henrietta 1
RICHARDS, Emerson Lewis 4
RICHARDS, Emily S. Tanner 1
RICHARDS, Erwin Hart 1

RICHARDS, Eugene Lamb 1
RICHARDS, Eugene Scott 4
RICHARDS, Fletcher D(oughitt) 9
RICHARDS, Frank Sells 8
RICHARDS, Frederick Thompson 1
RICHARDS, George* 1
RICHARDS, George Franklin 2
RICHARDS, George Handyside 3
RICHARDS, George Gill 3
RICHARDS, George Huntington 5
RICHARDS, George Huntington 7
RICHARDS, George Warren 3
RICHARDS, Gertrude Randolph Bramlette 7
RICHARDS, Harold Marshall Sylvester 8
RICHARDS, Harry Sanger 1
RICHARDS, Henry Melchior Muhlenberg 1
RICHARDS, Herbert Maule 1
RICHARDS, Herbert Montague 5
RICHARDS, Irving Trefethen 4
RICHARDS, Ivor Armstrong 7
RICHARDS, Jacob H
RICHARDS, James Austin 6
RICHARDS, James L. 3
RICHARDS, James McDowell 9
RICHARDS, James Prioleau 7
RICHARDS, Janet E. Hosmer 2
RICHARDS, Jean Marie 5
RICHARDS, John* H
RICHARDS, John E. 1
RICHARDS, John Gardiner 1
RICHARDS, John Kelvey 1
RICHARDS, John Noble 8
RICHARDS, John Stewart 9
RICHARDS, John Thomas 2
RICHARDS, Joseph H. 5
RICHARDS, Joseph Havens Cowles 1
RICHARDS, Joseph William 1
RICHARDS, Laura Elizabeth 2
RICHARDS, Legrand 7
RICHARDS, Lela Horn (Pseudonym Lee Neville) 5
RICHARDS, Lewis Loomis 1
RICHARDS, Louise 5
RICHARDS, Mark H
RICHARDS, Mary Anne Mitchell 6
RICHARDS, Nathan Charles 1
RICHARDS, Paul Rapier 9
RICHARDS, Paul Stanley 5
RICHARDS, Paul William 3
RICHARDS, Preston 3
RICHARDS, Ralph 7
RICHARDS, Ralph H(are) 2
RICHARDS, Ralph Strother 2
RICHARDS, Ralph Webster 6
RICHARDS, Ray 3
RICHARDS, Rezin Howard 4
RICHARDS, Richard Kohn 8
RICHARDS, Robert Hallowell 2
RICHARDS, Robert Haven 3
RICHARDS, Robert L(aurence) 10
RICHARDS, Robert Watt 4
RICHARDS, Roger G. 5
RICHARDS, Rosalind (Miss) 5
RICHARDS, Roy 8
RICHARDS, Samuel H. 3
RICHARDS, Stephen L. 3
RICHARDS, Stewart Watson 6
RICHARDS, T. Addison 1
RICHARDS, Theodore William 1
RICHARDS, Thomas Cole 1
RICHARDS, Mrs. Waldo 1
RICHARDS, William H
RICHARDS, William Alford 1
RICHARDS, William George 10

Name	
RICHARDS, William Henry	4
RICHARDS, William Joseph	4
RICHARDS, William Rogers	1
RICHARDS, William Trost	1
RICHARDS, Zalmon	H
RICHARDS-BRANDT, Mary Robinson	10
RICHARDSON, Abby Sage	1
RICHARDSON, Albert Deane	H
RICHARDSON, Alexander Henderson	5
RICHARDSON, Anna Euretta	1
RICHARDSON, Anna Steese	2
RICHARDSON, Arthur Berry	8
RICHARDSON, Basil	1
RICHARDSON, Carlos Albert	10
RICHARDSON, Charles	1
RICHARDSON, Charles Francis	1
RICHARDSON, Charles Freemont	1
RICHARDSON, Charles Henry	1
RICHARDSON, Charles Tiffany	6
RICHARDSON, Charles Williamson	1
RICHARDSON, Clarence H.	3
RICHARDSON, Clifford	1
RICHARDSON, Cyril Charles	7
RICHARDSON, David Crockett	4
RICHARDSON, Donovan MacNeely	4
RICHARDSON, Dorothy	3
RICHARDSON, Edgar Preston	8
RICHARDSON, Edmund	H
RICHARDSON, Edward Elliott	3
RICHARDSON, Edward H(enderson)	5
RICHARDSON, Edward Peirson	2
RICHARDSON, Edwin Sanders	3
RICHARDSON, Ellen A.	1
RICHARDSON, Elliott Verne	1
RICHARDSON, Ernest Cushing	1
RICHARDSON, Ernest Gladstone	2
RICHARDSON, Francis Asbury	1
RICHARDSON, Francis Harrie	6
RICHARDSON, Francis Henry	1
RICHARDSON, Frank Chase	1
RICHARDSON, Frank Howard	6
RICHARDSON, Frederick Albert	1
RICHARDSON, Frederick William	5
RICHARDSON, Friend	2
RICHARDSON, George Adams	3
RICHARDSON, George Burr	5
RICHARDSON, George James	7
RICHARDSON, George Lynde	1
RICHARDSON, George Tilton	5
RICHARDSON, Guy A.	5
RICHARDSON, H. George	5
RICHARDSON, Harry Alden	1
RICHARDSON, Henry Brown	1
RICHARDSON, Henry Hobson	H
RICHARDSON, Henry Smith	5
RICHARDSON, Hester Dorsey	1
RICHARDSON, Hilary Goode	1
RICHARDSON, Holden Chester	6
RICHARDSON, Hugh	5
RICHARDSON, Ira	3
RICHARDSON, Israel Bush	H
RICHARDSON, James Bailey	1
RICHARDSON, James Daniel	1
RICHARDSON, James Hugh	4
RICHARDSON, James Julius	1
RICHARDSON, James Milton	7
RICHARDSON, James Montgomery	4
RICHARDSON, James Otto	6
RICHARDSON, James Parmelee	2
RICHARDSON, John	7
RICHARDSON, John Hamilton	8
RICHARDSON, John Peter	H
RICHARDSON, John S(anford)	5
RICHARDSON, John Smythe	H
RICHARDSON, Joseph*	H
RICHARDSON, Joseph Priestley	7
RICHARDSON, Katharine Berry	1
RICHARDSON, L. Janette	9
RICHARDSON, Lawrence	8
RICHARDSON, Leon Josiah	4
RICHARDSON, Louise	9
RICHARDSON, Lunsford Norman	3
RICHARDSON, Lyon Norman	7
RICHARDSON, M. S.	5
RICHARDSON, Mark E(dwin)	5
RICHARDSON, Mark Wyman	4
RICHARDSON, Maurice Howe	1
RICHARDSON, Norman Egbert	2
RICHARDSON, Norval	1
RICHARDSON, Oliver Huntington	1
RICHARDSON, Sir Owen Willans	3
RICHARDSON, Philip	2
RICHARDSON, Ralph David	8
RICHARDSON, Robert	H
RICHARDSON, Robert Charlwood, Jr.	3
RICHARDSON, Robert Kimball	3
RICHARDSON, Robert Newton	3
RICHARDSON, Robert Price	5
RICHARDSON, Robert William	4
RICHARDSON, Roland George Dwight	2
RICHARDSON, Roy Mundy Davidson	5
RICHARDSON, Rufus Byam	1
RICHARDSON, Rupert Norval	9
RICHARDSON, Russell	6
RICHARDSON, Seth Whitley	3
RICHARDSON, Sid Williams	3
RICHARDSON, Sid Williams	4
RICHARDSON, Thomas Franklin	9
RICHARDSON, Tobias Gibson	H
RICHARDSON, Tony	10
RICHARDSON, W. Symmes	1
RICHARDSON, Warfield Creath	1
RICHARDSON, Wilds Preston	1
RICHARDSON, Willard	H
RICHARDSON, Willard Samuel	3
RICHARDSON, William	H
RICHARDSON, William Adams	7
RICHARDSON, William Alan	7
RICHARDSON, William Alan	8
RICHARDSON, William Alexander	1
RICHARDSON, William Cummings	1
RICHARDSON, William D.	1
RICHARDSON, William E.	2
RICHARDSON, William Eddy	1
RICHARDSON, William Edwin	5
RICHARDSON, William Franklin	1
RICHARDSON, W(illiam) Garland	7
RICHARDSON, William King	5
RICHARDSON, William Lambert	1
RICHARDSON, William Lloyd	5
RICHARDSON, William Merchant	H
RICHARDSON, William Samuel	4
RICHART, Duncan Grant	3
RICHART, Frank Erwin	3
RICHBERG, Donald Randall	4
RICHE, Charles Swift	1
RICHEL, George William	5
RICHESON, John Jacob	4
RICHESON, John Jacob	5
RICHEY, Albert Sutton	1
RICHEY, Frederick David	3
RICHEY, Herman G(lenn)	10
RICHEY, Lawrence	3
RICHEY, Mary Anne Reimann	9
RICHEY, Robert William	7
RICHEY, Thomas B.	2
RICHINGS, Peter	H
RICHLING, Don Jose	5
RICHMAN, Arthur	7
RICHMAN, Barry Martin	7
RICHMAN, Frank Nelson	4
RICHMAN, Irving Berdine	1
RICHMAN, Milton Saul	9
RICHMOND, Adam	3
RICHMOND, Carleton Rubira	8
RICHMOND, Charles Alexander	1
RICHMOND, Charles Blair	5
RICHMOND, Charles Wallace	1
RICHMOND, Dean	H
RICHMOND, Euphemia Johnson	1
RICHMOND, Frederic Courtis	1
RICHMOND, George Chalmers	5
RICHMOND, Grace S.	3
RICHMOND, Harold Bours	5
RICHMOND, Hiram Lawton	H
RICHMOND, Isidor	10
RICHMOND, James Howell	2
RICHMOND, John Lambert	H
RICHMOND, John Wilkes	H
RICHMOND, Jonathan	H
RICHMOND, Kenneth Calvin	5
RICHMOND, Lloyd Hemingway	8
RICHMOND, Mary Ellen	1
RICHTER, Charles Francis	9
RICHTER, Conrad Michael	5
RICHTER, Curt Paul	9
RICHTER, Emil Heinrich	5
RICHTER, Gisela Marie Augusta	5
RICHTER, Gisela Marie Augusta	7
RICHTER, Henry Joseph	1
RICHTER, John Frederick	3
RICHTER, Julius	6
RICHTER, Karl Felix Johannes	7
RICHTER, Paul E.	2
RICHTER, Richard Biddle	5
RICHTER, Richard Scott	8
RICHTMYER, F. K.	1
RICKARD, Brent Neville	3
RICKARD, Edgar	3
RICKARD, George Lewis	H
RICKARD, George Lewis	4
RICKARD, Richard Darke	2
RICKARD, Thomas Arthur	5
RICKARDS, George Collins	1
RICKARDS, James S.	2
RICKBEIL, Raymond Earl	5
RICKENBACKER, Edward Vernon (Eddie)	5
RICKER, Charles Herbert	8
RICKER, George Alfred Joy	1
RICKER, Marilla M.	1
RICKER, N. Clifford	1
RICKERBY, Arthur Burroughs	5
RICKERT, Edith	1
RICKERT, Thomas A.	1
RICKETSON, Daniel	H
RICKETSON, Frank Henry, Jr.	9
RICKETSON, Walton	1
RICKETTS, Claude Vernon	4
RICKETTS, Henry Tubbs	7
RICKETTS, James Brewerton	1
RICKETTS, James Brewerton	7
RICKETTS, Louis Davidson	1
RICKETTS, Palmer Chamberlaine	1
RICKETTS, Pierre de Peyster	1
RICKEY, Branch	4
RICKEY, James Walter	2
RICKOVER, Hyman George	9
RICKS, Augustus J.	1
RICKS, James B.	1
RICKS, Jesse Jay	2
RICKS, Victor E.	9
RICKS, William Benjamin	4
RICORD, Frederick William	H
RICORD, Philippe	H
RIDABOCK, Raymond Budd	5
RIDDEL, Joseph Neill	10
RIDDELL, Guy Crosby	4
RIDDELL, Herman Ellis	4
RIDDELL, John Leonard	4
RIDDELL, Robert Gerald	3
RIDDELL, William Hugh	3
RIDDELL, William Renwick	4
RIDDER, Bernard Herman	6
RIDDER, Herman	1
RIDDER, Herman Henry	6
RIDDER, Joseph E.	4
RIDDER, Victor Frank	4
RIDDER, Walter Thompson	10
RIDDICK, Carl W.	5
RIDDICK, James Edward	1
RIDDICK, Thomas Kader	4
RIDDICK, Wallace Carl	2
RIDDICK, Walter Garrett	3
RIDDLE, Albert Gallatin	1
RIDDLE, Carl Brown	8
RIDDLE, George	1
RIDDLE, George Read	H
RIDDLE, Haywood Yancey	H
RIDDLE, James Marion, Jr.	5
RIDDLE, Jesse Hale	H
RIDDLE, John Ingle	8
RIDDLE, John Paul	10
RIDDLE, John Wallace	1
RIDDLE, Lawrence Melville	7
RIDDLE, Lincoln Ware	1
RIDDLE, Matthew Brown	1
RIDDLE, Oscar	5
RIDDLE, Theodate Pope	2
RIDDLE, William	4
RIDDLEBERGER, Harrison Holt	H
RIDDLEBERGER, James W.	8
RIDEAL, Charles Frederick	4
RIDEAL, Eric Keightley	6
RIDEING, William Henry	1
RIDENOUR, Louis N., Jr.	3
RIDEOUT, Henry Milner	1
RIDER, Arthur William	4
RIDER, Charles R.	4
RIDER, Fremont	4
RIDER, Ira Edgar	4
RIDER, Paul Reece	9
RIDGAWAY, Henry Basom	H
RIDGE, Albert Alphonso	4
RIDGE, Frank Isaac	7
RIDGE, Major	H
RIDGELEY, Charles Goodwin	H
RIDGELEY, Daniel Bowly	H
RIDGELEY, Henry Moore	H
RIDGELEY, Nicholas	H
RIDGELEY, Richard	H
RIDGELY, Benjamin H.	1
RIDGELY, Henry	1
RIDGELY, Hilliard Samuel	5
RIDGELY, Reginald Heber, Jr.	7
RIDGELY, William Barret	1
RIDGES, Robert Paul	5
RIDGEWAY, George L.	5
RIDGLEY, Douglas Clay	3
RIDGON, Sidney	H
RIDGWAY, Amos Caryl	4
RIDGWAY, Arthur Osbourne	3
RIDGWAY, Erman Jesse	5
RIDGWAY, Grant	5
RIDGWAY, Howard Eugene	6
RIDGWAY, Joseph	H
RIDGWAY, Robert	H
RIDGWAY, Robert*	1
RIDGWAY, Thomas	4
RIDGWAY, William Hance	2
RIDINGS, Eugene Ware	5
RIDLEY, Clarence Self	5
RIDLON, John	1
RIDLON, Joseph Randall	6
RIDOUT, Godfrey	8
RIDPATH, John Clark	1
RIDPATH, Robert Ferguson	3
RIDSDALE, Percival Sheldon	3
RIEBEL, Frank A.	5
RIEBEN, Louis	9
RIEBER, Charles Henry	2
RIEBER, Torkild	5
RIECHMANN, Donald August	6
RIECKEN, William Emil	3
RIED, William Wharry	H
RIEDEL, Karl Heinrich	2
RIEFKOHL, Frederic Luis	8
RIEFLER, Winfield William	6
RIEFSTAHL, Rudolf M.	6
RIEGEL, Benjamin D.	1
RIEGEL, Byron	6
RIEGEL, Catherine Thirza	6
RIEGEL, John Lawrence	9
RIEGEL, Robert Edgar	10
RIEGER, Ernest W.	8
RIEGER, Johann Georg Joseph Anton	H
RIEGER, William Henry	4
RIEGGER, Wallingford	4
RIEHLE, Theodore Martin	2
RIEHLMAN, R(oy) Walter	7
RIEKE, Marcus Clarence	4
RIEL, Louis	H
RIELY, John William	1
RIELY, John William	9
RIEMAN, Charles Ellet	5
RIEMENSCHNEIDER, Albert	3
RIEMER, Guido Carl Leo	1
RIENHOFF, William Francis, Jr.	7
RIEPE, Carl Christoph	5
RIES, Edward J.	9
RIES, Elias Elkan	1
RIES, Heinrich	3
RIES, Herman Elkan, Jr.	10
RIESEN, Emil Richert	7
RIESENBERG, Felix	1
RIESENBERGER, Frank Ralph	10
RIESENFELD, Hugo	1
RIESER, Leonard Moos	3
RIESMAN, David	1
RIESMAN, John Penrose	6
RIETHMULLER, Richard Henri	2
RIETMULDER, James	5
RIETZ, Henry Lewis	2
RIEVE, Emil	6
RIFE, John Maynard	5
RIFFLE, Jack Burdette	9
RIFORD, Lloyd Stephen	9
RIGBY, Edmund	4
RIGBY, Harry	8
RIGBY, William Cattron	2
RIGBY, William Otto	3
RIGBY, William Titus	1
RIGDON, Charles Loammi	5
RIGDON, Jonathan	1
RIGG, Ephraim	4
RIGG, George Burton	6
RIGG, Horace Abram, Jr.	7
RIGG, Horace Abram, Jr.	8
RIGGE, William Francis	1
RIGGINS, H. McLeod	5
RIGGINS, John Alfred, Jr.	10
RIGGINS, Russell Myers	4
RIGGIO, Vincent	4
RIGGLEMAN, Leonard	8
RIGGS, Alexander Brown	1
RIGGS, Alfred Longley	1
RIGGS, Arthur Stanley	6
RIGGS, Austen Fox	1
RIGGS, Charles Edward	4
RIGGS, Edward	1
RIGGS, Edward Gridley	1
RIGGS, Elias	1
RIGGS, Ernest Wilson	3

ROEBLING, Washington Augustus 1
ROEBUCK, Arthur Wentworth 6
ROEBUCK, John Ransom 4
ROEBUCK, John Ransom 5
ROEDDER, Edwin Carl Lothar Clemens 2
ROEDEL, John W. 7
ROEDEL, Philip Morgan 9
ROEDER, Adolph 4
ROEDER, Arthur 7
ROEDER, Bernard Franklin 5
ROEDER, Fred Vincent 5
ROEDER, Geraldine Morgan 4
ROEDER, Ralph Leclercq 8
ROEHM, Alfred Isaac 2
ROEHR, Julius Edward 1
ROEHRIG, Frederic Louis Otto 1
ROELKER, Charles Rafael 1
ROELKER, William Greene 3
ROELOFS, Howard Dykema 6
ROEMER, Ferdinand H
ROEMER, Henry A. 5
ROEMER, John Lincoln 1
ROEMER, Joseph 3
ROEMERSHAUSER, Alvin E(arl) 5
ROENNE, Torben Henning 6
ROERICH, Nicholas Konstantin 2
ROESCH, Charles Edward 1
ROESCH, Karl Alexander 5
ROESCH, Raymond August 10
ROESCH, Walter Alfred 4
ROESCH, William Robert 8
ROESSLER, John Edward 4
ROESSNER, Elmer (Stirling) 5
ROETHKE, Theodore 4
ROETHKE, William A. C. 4
ROETHLISBERGER, Fritz Jules 6
ROETTER, Paulus H
ROETZEL, Cletus G. 8
ROEVER, William Henry 3
ROGALSKY, George Frederick 7
ROGAN, Fred Leon 3
ROGAN, James S. 3
ROGAN, Octavia Fry 7
ROGAN, Ralph Frederic 3
ROGERS, A. Robert 9
ROGERS, Agnes Low 7
ROGERS, Alfred Moore 4
ROGERS, Alfred Thomas 2
ROGERS, Allan Buttrick 4
ROGERS, Allen 1
ROGERS, Allen Hastings 1
ROGERS, Arthur 1
ROGERS, Arthur Amzi 6
ROGERS, Arthur Curtis 1
ROGERS, Arthur Kenyon 1
ROGERS, Arthur Small 4
ROGERS, Austin Flint 3
ROGERS, Austin Leonard 1
ROGERS, B. Talbot 1
ROGERS, Benjamin Franklin 7
ROGERS, Bernard 5
ROGERS, Bruce 3
ROGERS, Bryon Giles 8
ROGERS, Burton R(ay) 6
ROGERS, Carl Ransom 9
ROGERS, Cephas Brainerd 1
ROGERS, Charles H
ROGERS, Charles B. 10
ROGERS, Charles Butler 1
ROGERS, Charles Custis 1
ROGERS, Charles Darius 1
ROGERS, Charles Edwin 2
ROGERS, Charles Elkins 9
ROGERS, Charles Gardner 3
ROGERS, Charlotte Boardman 6
ROGERS, Clara Kathleen 1
ROGERS, Daisy Fiske 3
ROGERS, David Banks 4
ROGERS, David Barss 4
ROGERS, David Camp 4
ROGERS, David P. 9
ROGERS, Donald Aquilla 5
ROGERS, Donald G. 3
ROGERS, Donald Irwin 7
ROGERS, Donald Lee 9
ROGERS, Dorothy 9
ROGERS, Dwight L. 3
ROGERS, Edith Nourse 4
ROGERS, Edmund Burrell 9
ROGERS, Edmund James Armstrong 1
ROGERS, Edward H
ROGERS, Edward Sidney 2
ROGERS, Edward Standiford H
ROGERS, Ernest Albert 5
ROGERS, Ernest Andrew 3
ROGERS, Ernest Elias 2
ROGERS, Eustace Barron 1
ROGERS, Fairman 1
ROGERS, Floyd Sterling, Jr. 4
ROGERS, Francis 3
ROGERS, Frazier 3
ROGERS, Fred A. 3
ROGERS, Fred S. 2
ROGERS, Frederick Morris 5
ROGERS, Frederick Titsworth 4
ROGERS, George Alfred 1
ROGERS, George Bartlett 4
ROGERS, George Blake 4
ROGERS, George Edward 10
ROGERS, George F. 2
ROGERS, George McIntosh 3
ROGERS, George Vernor 4
ROGERS, Gordon B. 4
ROGERS, Haratio 1
ROGERS, Harlan Bethune 7
ROGERS, Harriet Burbank H
ROGERS, Harriet Burbank 4
ROGERS, Harry Clayton 5
ROGERS, Harry E(dward) 9
ROGERS, Harry H. 3
ROGERS, Harry Lovejoy 1
ROGERS, Harry Stanley 3
ROGERS, Henry Darwin H
ROGERS, Henry H. 1
ROGERS, Henry Huddleston 1
ROGERS, Henry J. H
ROGERS, Henry Munroe 1
ROGERS, Henry Treat 1
ROGERS, Henry Wade 1
ROGERS, Herbert Wesley 4
ROGERS, Hopewell Lindenberger 2
ROGERS, Howard J. 3
ROGERS, Howard Jason 1
ROGERS, Hubert E. 3
ROGERS, Hugo Edward 7
ROGERS, Irving Emerson 8
ROGERS, Isaiah H
ROGERS, J. Harris 1
ROGERS, J. Speed 3
ROGERS, James H
ROGERS, James Blythe H
ROGERS, James Cunningham 7
ROGERS, James Edward 7
ROGERS, James Frederick 4
ROGERS, James Gamble 2
ROGERS, James Grafton 5
ROGERS, James Harvey 1
ROGERS, James Hotchkiss 1
ROGERS, James Sterling 5
ROGERS, James Tracy 4
ROGERS, Jason 1
ROGERS, John* H
ROGERS, John* 1
ROGERS, John 7
ROGERS, John Edward 2
ROGERS, John Henry 1
ROGERS, John I. 4
ROGERS, John Jacob 1
ROGERS, John Lenzie 8
ROGERS, John Rankin 1
ROGERS, John Raphael 1
ROGERS, John William 4
ROGERS, Jonathan C(lark) 7
ROGERS, Joseph Egerton 3
ROGERS, Joseph Morgan 1
ROGERS, Joseph Patrick 8
ROGERS, Julia Ellen 4
ROGERS, Lebbeus Harding 4
ROGERS, Leon Winfield 7
ROGERS, Lester Burton 5
ROGERS, Lester Cushing 5
ROGERS, Lindsay 9
ROGERS, Lockhart Burgess 10
ROGERS, Lore Alford 5
ROGERS, Louis William 4
ROGERS, Malcolm Joseph 5
ROGERS, Marvin Carson 5
ROGERS, Mary Cochrane 5
ROGERS, Max 1
ROGERS, Max Tofield 9
ROGERS, May 4
ROGERS, McLain 3
ROGERS, Moses H
ROGERS, Nat Stewart 10
ROGERS, Oscar H. 1
ROGERS, Paul 7
ROGERS, Philip Fletcher 1
ROGERS, Pleas Blair 6
ROGERS, Ralph Knickerbacker 7
ROGERS, Randolph H
ROGERS, Robert H
ROGERS, Robert Cameron 1
ROGERS, Robert Emmons 1
ROGERS, Robert Empie H
ROGERS, Robert Francis 10
ROGERS, Robert Samuel 5
ROGERS, Robert Wentworth 10
ROGERS, Robert William 1
ROGERS, Roswell Wesley 7
ROGERS, Sampson, Jr. 5
ROGERS, Samuel H. 5
ROGERS, Samuel Lyle 4
ROGERS, Sherman S. 1
ROGERS, Sion Hart H
ROGERS, Stephen H
ROGERS, Thomas H
ROGERS, Thomas Jones H
ROGERS, Thomas Wesley 6
ROGERS, Tyler Stewart 4
ROGERS, Vance 4
ROGERS, Virgil Madison 10
ROGERS, Waldo Henry 4
ROGERS, Walter Alexander 2
ROGERS, Walter Stowell 4
ROGERS, Warren Lincoln 1
ROGERS, Weaver Henry 1
ROGERS, Will 1
ROGERS, Willard Benjamin 4
ROGERS, Willard Benjamin 8
ROGERS, William Allen 1
ROGERS, William Arthur 2
ROGERS, William Augustus H
ROGERS, William Banks 1
ROGERS, William Barton H
ROGERS, William Boddie 1
ROGERS, William Crowninshield H
ROGERS, William F. 4
ROGERS, William Harlow 4
ROGERS, William King 1
ROGERS, William Loveland 5
ROGERS, William Nathaniel 2
ROGERS, William Oscar 4
ROGERS, William Pennock 1
ROGERS, William Perry 1
ROGERS, Wynne Grey 2
ROGERSON, Charles Edward 1
ROGERSON, James Russell 8
ROGG, Nathaniel H. 7
ROGGE, Benjamin Arnold 7
ROGGE, O(etje) John 7
ROGLIANO, Francis Teobaldo 6
ROGOSIN, I. 5
ROHBACH, James Alexander 1
ROHDE, Max Spencer 6
ROHDE, Ruth Bryan 3
ROHE, Charles Henry 1
ROHE, George Henry 1
ROHLFING, Charles Carroll 3
ROHLFS, Anna Katharine Green 1
ROHLFS, Charles 1
ROHLICH, Gerard Addison 8
ROHLMAN, Henry P. 3
ROHN, Oscar 1
ROHNSTOCK, J. Henry 3
ROHR, Elizabeth 3
ROHR, Frederick Hilmer 4
ROHR, John T. 8
ROHRBACH, John Francis Deems 5
ROHRBACH, John J. 3
ROHRBAUGH, Lewis Guy 7
ROHRBOUGH, Edward G. 3
ROHRBOUGH, Ralph Virgil 4
ROHRER, Albert Lawrence 3
ROHRER, Karl 1
ROHRLICH, Chester 6
ROHWER, Henry 1
ROIG, Antonio A. 3
ROIG, Harold Joseph 5
ROISMAN, Joseph 6
ROIZIN, Leon 10
ROJANKOVSKY, Feodor 5
ROJAS, P. Ezequiel 1
ROJAS PINILLA, Gustavo 6
ROJTMAN, Marc B. 4
ROKAHR, Theodore 10
ROKAW, Daniel Roy 7
ROLAPP, Henry Hermann 1
ROLER, Edward Oscar Fitzalan 4
ROLETTE, Jean Joseph H
ROLFE, Alfred Grosvenor 2
ROLFE, Charles Wesley 1
ROLFE, Daniel Thomas 5
ROLFE, Franklin P. 9
ROLFE, George William 2
ROLFE, Henry Winchester 4
ROLFE, John H
ROLFE, John Carew 2
ROLFE, John Furman 1
ROLFE, Stanley Herbert 2
ROLFE, William James 1
ROLFING, R. C. 6
ROLFS, Fred Maas 5
ROLFS, Peter Henry 2
ROLL, Curtis W. 7
ROLL, Lyle Charles 8
ROLL, Marlin Henry 9
ROLLAND, Romaine 2
ROLLEFSON, Gerhard Krohn 3
ROLLER, Charles S., Jr. 4
ROLLER, Robert Douglas, Jr. 1
ROLLER, Thomas J. 3
ROLLERT, Edward Dumas 5
ROLLINS, Alice Marland Wellington H
ROLLINS, Carl Purington 4
ROLLINS, Charlemae 7
ROLLINS, Charles E., Jr. 3
ROLLINS, Charles Leonard 4
ROLLINS, Clara Sherwood (Mrs.) 5
ROLLINS, Edward D. E. 7
ROLLINS, Edward Henry H
ROLLINS, Edward Warren 1
ROLLINS, Frank West 1
ROLLINS, George Sherman 1
ROLLINS, Hyder Edward 3
ROLLINS, James Sidney H
ROLLINS, James Wingate 1
ROLLINS, John Fox 4
ROLLINS, Montgomery 1
ROLLINS, Thornton 1
ROLLINS, Wallace Eugene 3
ROLLINS, Walter Huntington 1
ROLLINSON, William H
ROLNICK, Harry 7
ROLPH, James, Jr. 1
ROLPH, John Gladwyn 3
ROLPH, Samuel Wyman 4
ROLSHOVEN, Julius 1
ROLT-WHEELER, Francis William 4
ROLVAAG, Karl Fritjof 10
ROLVAAG, Ole Edvart 1
ROLZ-BENNETT, Jose 5
ROMA, Caro 1
ROMA, Lisa (Lisa Roma Trompeter) 9
ROMAINS, Jules 5
ROMAN, Andre Bienvenu H
ROMAN, Frederick William 2
ROMAN, Herschel Lewis 10
ROMAN, James Dixon H
ROMAN, Stephen Boleslav 9
ROMAN, Victor M. Reyes Y. 3
ROMANACH, Mario Jose 8
ROMANI, Geroge Thomas 7
ROMANO, Umberto 8
ROMANOFF, Alexis Lawrence 9
ROMANOWITZ, Harry Alex 5
ROMANS, Bernard H
ROMANS, John Francis 6
ROMAYNE, Nicholas H
ROMBAUER, Roderick Emile 4
ROMBERG, Paul F(rederick) 8
ROMBERG, Sigmund 3
ROME, Charles A. 3
ROME, Edwin Phillips 9
ROME, Morton Phillips 8
ROMEIKE, Henry 1
ROMER, Alfred Sherwood 6
ROMER, Arthur C. 4
ROMERA-NAVARRO, Miguel 4
ROMFH, Edward Coleman 6
ROMIG, Edgar Franklin 4
ROMIG, John Samuel 1
ROMIG, Lleuellen DeWight 10
ROMINGER, Carl Ludwig 1
ROMMEL, George McCullough 2
ROMNES, H(aakon) I(ngolf) 6
ROMNEY, Junius Stowell 7
ROMNEY, Marion George 9
ROMNEY, Roxey Stowell 8
ROMNEY, Vernon 7
ROMODA, Joseph J. 4
ROMUALDEZ, Miguel 6
ROMUALDEZ, Norberto 5
ROMULO, Carlos P(ena) 9
RONAN, Daniel John 5
RONAN, James Joseph 4
RONAYNE, Maurice 1
RONDTHALER, Edward 1
RONDTHALER, Howard Edward 3
RONEY, Jay Louis 8
RONGY, Abraham Jacob 2
RONNE, Finn 7
RONNE, Torben 6
RONNEBECK, Arnold 2
RONNEBERG, Earl Fridthjov 5
RONNERMANN, Charles, Jr. 7
RONNING, Magnar 7
RONON, Gerald 4
ROOD, A. Edward 4
ROOD, Dorothy B. A. 4
ROOD, James Theron 1
ROOD, John 6
ROOD, Ogden Nicholas 1
ROOD, Paul 10
ROOD, Paul William 3
ROOK, Charles Alexander 2
ROOK, Edward Francis 4
ROOK, Gustav S. 5
ROOKER, Frederick Zadok 1
ROOKS, Lowell W(ard) 6
ROOKS, R(aymond) Newton 9
ROOME, Kenneth Andrew 5
ROON, Leo 9
ROONEY, Arthur Joseph 9
ROONEY, John J. 6
ROONEY, John Jerome 1
ROONEY, Marie Collins 2
ROOP, Hervin Ulysses 3
ROOP, James Clawson 5
ROOP, James Clawson 8
ROORBACH, George Byron 1
ROOS, Charles Frederick 3
ROOS, Delmar Gerle 3
ROOS, Edwin G. 5
ROOS, Frank John, Jr. 4
ROOS, Jean Carolyn 9
ROOS, Robert Achille 3
ROOS, Walter L. 5
ROOSA, Daniel Bennett St John 1
ROOSEVELT, Anna Eleanor 4
ROOSEVELT, Archibald Bulloch, Jr. 10
ROOSEVELT, Edith Kermit Carow 2
ROOSEVELT, Elliott 10
ROOSEVELT, Franklin Delano H
ROOSEVELT, Franklin Delano 2
ROOSEVELT, Franklin Delano 4
ROOSEVELT, Franklin Delano, Jr. 9
ROOSEVELT, George Emlen 4
ROOSEVELT, George Washington 1
ROOSEVELT, Henry Latrobe 1
ROOSEVELT, Hilborne Lewis H
ROOSEVELT, James 10
ROOSEVELT, James I. H
ROOSEVELT, John A. 7
ROOSEVELT, Julian Kean 9
ROOSEVELT, Kermit 2
ROOSEVELT, Nicholas 8
ROOSEVELT, Nicholas J. H
ROOSEVELT, Philip James 2
ROOSEVELT, Robert Barnwell 1
ROOSEVELT, S. Montgomery 1
ROOSEVELT, Mrs. Theodore 4
ROOSEVELT, Theodore H
ROOSEVELT, Theodore 1
ROOSEVELT, Theodore 4
ROOSEVELT, Theodore, Jr. 2
ROOSEVELT, W. Emlen 1
ROOT, Amos Ives 1
ROOT, Azariah Smith 1
ROOT, Blake Smith 10
ROOT, Chapman Jay 2
ROOT, Darrell Astor 7
ROOT, Edward Clary 5
ROOT, Edward Tallmadge 2
ROOT, Edwin Alvin 4
ROOT, Edwin Park 1

ROSSMANN, Kurt 7
ROSSO, Augusto 4
ROSSO, Augusto 7
ROST, Otto Fredrick 8
ROSTOCK, Frank Witte 4
ROSTOCK, Frank Witte 7
ROSTOVTZEFF, Michael Ivanovich 3
ROSZAK, Theodore 8
ROSZEL, Brantz Mayer 1
ROTCH, A. Lawrence 1
ROTCH, Arthur H
ROTCH, Thomas Morgan 1
ROTCH, William H
ROTCH, William 1
ROTCHFORD, Hugh Babb 1
ROTH, Almon E. 7
ROTH, Ben 3
ROTH, Edward Ulysses 7
ROTH, Feri 5
ROTH, Filibert 1
ROTH, Frederic Hull 9
ROTH, Frederick George Richard 2
ROTH, George Byron 6
ROTH, George Frederic, Jr. 10
ROTH, Henry Warren 1
ROTH, John Ernest 4
ROTH, Lloyd Joseph 9
ROTH, Paul Hoerlein 4
ROTH, Philip A. 10
ROTH, Robert 1
ROTH, Stanley 8
ROTH, Stephen Alan 9
ROTH, Stephen John 6
ROTH, Willard Lawrence 7
ROTH, William P. 4
ROTHAFEL, Samuel Lionel H
ROTHAFEL, Samuel Lionel 4
ROTHBART, Hyman 9
ROTHBERG, Maurice 6
ROTHBERG, Sidney 5
ROTHE, Guillermo 6
ROTHENBERG, Milton 5
ROTHENBERG, Morris 3
ROTHENBURGER, William Frederic 5
ROTHERMEL, Amos Cornelius 2
ROTHERMEL, John Goodhart 1
ROTHERMEL, John H. 1
ROTHERMEL, Peter Frederick H
ROTHERMICH, Norman Oliver 8
ROTHIER, Leon 5
ROTHKO, Mark 5
ROTHMAN, Fred Bernard 10
ROTHMAN, Stephen 4
ROTHROCK, Addison M(ay)
ROTHROCK, David Andrew 4
ROTHROCK, E(dgar) P(aul) 8
ROTHROCK, Edward Streicher 4
ROTHROCK, Joseph Trimble
ROTHROCK, Mary Utopia 7
ROTHSCHILD, Alonzo 1
ROTHSCHILD, Herbert M. 5
ROTHSCHILD, Jerome J. 7
ROTHSCHILD, Karl 5
ROTHSCHILD, Louis F. 3
ROTHSCHILD, Louis Samuel 9
ROTHSCHILD, Marcus A. 1
ROTHSCHILD, Maurice 2
ROTHSCHILD, V(ictor) Henry, II 10
ROTHSCHILD, Walter Nathan
ROTHSTEIN, Arthur 9
ROTHSTEIN, Irma 5
ROTHWELL, Bernard Joseph 2
ROTHWELL, Charles Easton 9
ROTHWELL, Gideon Frank H
ROTHWELL, Paul Taylor 9
ROTHWELL, Richard Pennefather 1
ROTHWELL, Will A.
ROTKO, Bernard Benjamin 10
ROTNEM, Ralph Arthur 5
ROTTGER, Curtis Hoopes 4
ROTTSCHAEFER, Henry 8
ROTUNNO, Noreda Anthony 7
ROTZELL, Willett Enos 1
ROUAULT, Georges 3

ROUCOLLE, Adrienne (Miss) 5
ROUDEBUSH, Alfred Holt 2
ROUDEBUSH, Francis Wilshira 6
ROUDEBUSH, George M. 10
ROUILLER, Charles 6
ROULAND, Orlando 2
ROULHAC, Thomas Ruffin 4
ROULSTON, Marjorie Hillis 5
ROULSTONE, George H
ROUND, Lester A(ngell) 8
ROUND, William Marshall Fitts 1
ROUNDS, Arthur Charles 1
ROUNDS, David 8
ROUNDS, Leslie Raymond 4
ROUNDS, Ralph Stowell 2
ROUNSEVILLE, Robert Field 6
ROUNTREE, George 2
ROUQUETTE, Adrien Emmanuel H
ROUQUETTE, Francois Dominique H
ROURA-PARELLA, Juan 8
ROURKE, Anthony J(ohn) J(oseph) 6
ROURKE, Constance Mayfield 1
ROURKE, Frank W. 4
ROUS, Francis Peyton 5
ROUSE, Adelaide Louise 1
ROUSE, Arthur B. 5
ROUSE, Henry Clark 1
ROUSE, John Delos 4
ROUSE, John Gould 4
ROUSE, Louis Austin 6
ROUSE, W. R. 8
ROUSH, Galen James 9
ROUSH, Gar A. 5
ROUSH, Oliver Eugene 5
ROUSMANIERE, Edmund Swett 1
ROUSS, Charles Broadway 4
ROUSSE, Thomas Andrew 4
ROUSSEAU, Harry Harwood 1
ROUSSEAU, Theodore 6
ROUSSEAU, Theodore 7
ROUSSELOT, Harold Anthony 9
ROUSSELOT, Louis M. 6
ROUSSEVE, Ferdinand Lucien 4
ROUSSO, Eli L. 10
ROUTH, Eugene Coke 5
ROUTH, James (Edward) 6
ROUTH, John Sylvester 8
ROUTH, Joseph P. 10
ROUTH, Porter Wroe 9
ROUTLEY, Thomas Clarence
ROUTT, John Long 1
ROUTTENBERG, Max Jonah 9
ROUTZAHN, Evart Grant 1
ROUTZOHN, Harry Nelson 3
ROUXEL, Gustave Augustin 1
ROUZER, E(nglar) McClure 9
ROVE, Olaf N(orberg) 10
ROVELSTAD, A(dolph) M(arius) 6
ROVENSKY, Joseph Charles 3
ROVENSTINE, E. A. 4
ROVER, Leo Aloysius 4
ROVERE, Richard Halworth 7
ROVERSI, Louis 1
ROW, Edgar Charles 6
ROW, Robert Keable 1
ROW, William Hamilton 4
ROW, William Stanley 9
ROWAN, Andrew Summers 4
ROWAN, Charles A. 1
ROWAN, Charles Joseph 4
ROWAN, Dan Hale 9
ROWAN, Hugh Williamson 9
ROWAN, Jan Christopher 9
ROWAN, John 1
ROWAN, Joseph 1
ROWAN, M. Edward 7
ROWAN, Pelham Agee 10
ROWAN, Richard Wilmer 4
ROWAN, Stephen Clegg H
ROWAN, Thomas Leslie 5
ROWAN, William A. 4
ROWBOTTOM, Harry E. 1
ROWCLIFF, Gilbert 5
ROWE, Albert Holmes 5
ROWE, Alfred S(tanley) 8
ROWE, Allan Winter 1

ROWE, Benjamin Ackley 1
ROWE, Clifford Paul 5
ROWE, Donald Edward 10
ROWE, Frederick William 2
ROWE, Gilbert Theodore 4
ROWE, Guy 5
ROWE, Guy I. 7
ROWE, Harry Willison 4
ROWE, Hartley 4
ROWE, Henrietta Gould 1
ROWE, Henry Clarke 4
ROWE, Henry Kalloch 1
ROWE, Howard Marshall 7
ROWE, James Henry, Jr. 8
ROWE, Jesse Perry 4
ROWE, John Jay 7
ROWE, John Leroy 6
ROWE, Joseph Eugene 1
ROWE, L. Earle 4
ROWE, Leo S. 2
ROWE, Paul Nicholas 9
ROWE, Peter H
ROWE, Peter Trimble 1
ROWE, R(aphael) Robinson 7
ROWE, Robert G. 5
ROWE, Stanley M., Sr. 8
ROWE, Stuart Henry 5
ROWE, Theodore Spurling 6
ROWE, Wallace Prescott 8
ROWE, Walter Ellsworth 3
ROWE, William Dennison 7
ROWE, William Stanhope 1
ROWELL, Chester Harvey 2
ROWELL, Frank Wheaton 5
ROWELL, George Presbury 1
ROWELL, George Smith 4
ROWELL, Henry Thompson 6
ROWELL, Hugh Grant 4
ROWELL, James G. 3
ROWELL, John W. 1
ROWELL, Jonathan Harvey 1
ROWELL, Joseph Cummings 1
ROWELL, Ross Erastus 2
ROWELL, Wilbur Everett 2
ROWELL, Wilfrid Asa 3
ROWLAND, Adoniram Judson 1
ROWLAND, Albert Lindsay 7
ROWLAND, Arthur John 1
ROWLAND, Benjamin, Jr. 4
ROWLAND, Charles H. 4
ROWLAND, Charles Leonard 1
ROWLAND, Clarence H. 5
ROWLAND, Donald 10
ROWLAND, Donald Winslow 1
ROWLAND, Dunbar 1
ROWLAND, Harry T. 3
ROWLAND, Henry Augustus 1
ROWLAND, Henry Cottrell 1
ROWLAND, James Marshall Hanna 3
ROWLAND, Joseph Medley 1
ROWLAND, Kate Mason 1
ROWLAND, Roger Whittaker 6
ROWLAND, Thomas Mifflin 8
ROWLAND, Thomas Mifflin, Jr. 8
ROWLAND, Vernon Cecil 4
ROWLAND, William Samuel 1
ROWLANDS, William H
ROWLANDSON, Mary White H
ROWLEE, Willard Winfield 1
ROWLETT, John Miles 7
ROWLETT, Robert 1
ROWLEY, Francis Harold 3
ROWLEY, Frank Benjamin 7
ROWLEY, Frank S. 3
ROWLEY, George 4
ROWLEY, John 1
ROWLEY, William C. 4
ROWLEY, Worth 10
ROWNTREE, Jennie 6
ROWNTREE, Leonard George 7
ROWSE, Samuel Worcester H
ROWSON, Susanna Haswell H
ROXAS, Manuel 2
ROY, Arthur Jay 2
ROY, Francis Albert 5
ROY, Gabrielle 8
ROY, James Evans 6
ROY, Lillian Elizabeth 1
ROY, Maurice Cardinal 9
ROY, Percy Albert 2
ROY, Philip Seddon 4
ROY, Reuben Finnell 1

ROY, Ross 8
ROY, Sharat Kumar 5
ROY, Victor Leander, Sr. 5
ROYAL, Forrest 2
ROYAL, George 1
ROYAL, John Francis 7
ROYAL, Ralph 1
ROYAL, William Carson 7
ROYALL, Anne Newport 4
ROYALL, Kenneth Claiborne 5
ROYALL, Ralph 3
ROYALL, Tucker 1
ROYALL, William Bailey 1
ROYALTY, Paul 4
ROYALTY, Robert Malcolm 10
ROYCE, Alexander Burgess 4
ROYCE, Asa Marshfield 1
ROYCE, Donald 5
ROYCE, Frederick Page 1
ROYCE, George Monroe 1
ROYCE, Homer Elihu H
ROYCE, Josiah 1
ROYCE, Luman Herbert 1
ROYCE, Ralph 8
ROYCE, Robert Russel 5
ROYCE, Sarah Eleanor Bayliss H
ROYCE, Stephen Wheeler 7
ROYE, Edward James 5
ROYER, Arnold Lennel 5
ROYER, J. E. E. 3
ROYLE, Edwin Milton 2
ROYSE, John Anthony 10
ROYSE, Samuel Durham 4
ROYSTER, Frank Sheppard, Jr. 8
ROYSTER, Hubert Ashley 5
ROYSTER, James Finch 4
ROYSTER, Lawrence Thomas 5
ROYSTER, Paul Freeman 7
ROYSTER, Salibelle 6
ROZMAREK, Charles 6
ROZMAREK, Charles 7
ROZSNYAI, Zoltan Frank 10
RUARK, Robert Chester 4
RUBATTEL, Rodolphe 4
RUBEL, A. C. 4
RUBEN, Barney 3
RUBEN, Samuel A. 8
RUBENDALL, Clarence 3
RUBENDALL, Howard Lane 10
RUBENS, Harry 1
RUBENS, Horatio Seymour 1
RUBEY, Harry 7
RUBEY, Thomas Lewis 1
RUBEY, William Walden 6
RUBICAM, Raymond 7
RUBIN, Aaron 9
RUBIN, Abe 10
RUBIN, Alvin Benjamin 10
RUBIN, Edward Perry 7
RUBIN, Edward Perry 8
RUBIN, J. Robert 3
RUBIN, Morris Harold 1
RUBIN, Morris Harold 8
RUBIN, Reuven 6
RUBIN, Samuel 1
RUBIN, William Benjamin 5
RUBIN, Wladyslaw 10
RUBIN DE LA BORBOLLA, Daniel Fernando 5
RUBINKAM, Nathaniel Irwin 1
RUBINOFF, David 9
RUBINOVITZ, George 5
RUBINOW, Isaac Max 1
RUBINOW, Sydney Godfrey 8
RUBINOWICZ, Wojciech 6
RUBINSTEIN, Artur 8
RUBINSTEIN, Beryl 5
RUBINSTEIN, David 7
RUBINSTEIN, Helena 4
RUBINSTEIN, Lucien Jules 10
RUBIO, Antonio 3
RUBIO, David 4
RUBLEE, George 3
RUBLEE, Horace 1
RUBLEE, William Alvah 1
RUBLOFF, Arthur 7
RUBSAMEN, Walter Howard 6
RUBY, Edward Ernest 5
RUBY, Harry 6
RUBY, Lionel 5
RUCCIUS, Frederick Edward, Jr. 10
RUCH, Giles Murrel 2
RUCHAMES, Louis 7
RUCKER, Allen Willis 4

RUCKER, Atterson Walden 2
RUCKER, Casper Bell 2
RUCKER, D. H. H
RUCKER, Daniel Henry 1
RUCKER, Elbert Marion 1
RUCKER, Louis H. 1
RUCKER, Marvin Pierce 4
RUCKER, Tinsley White, III 8
RUCKER, Tinsley White, IV 8
RUCKER, Truman Burris 7
RUCKER, William Colby 1
RUCKER, William Waller 1
RUCKMAN, John Wilson 1
RUCKMICK, Christian Alban 4
RUCKS, Joseph Gibson 10
RUCKSTULL, Fred Wellington 2
RUDD, Hughes Day 10
RUDD, Judson Archer 5
RUDD, Stephan A. 1
RUDD, Thomas Brown 3
RUDD, William Platt 1
RUDDER, James Earl 5
RUDDIMAN, Edsel Alexander 3
RUDDIMAN, Edsel Alexander 5
RUDDOCK, Albert Billings 7
RUDDOCK, John Carroll 4
RUDDOCK, Malcolm Irving 4
RUDDY, Edward Michael 5
RUDDY, Howard Shaw 1
RUDE, Arthur H. 8
RUDE, Chester A. 10
RUDE, Joe Christopher 6
RUDENBERG, Reinhold 4
RUDENKO, William Bernard 4
RUDER, William Ernst 4
RUDERMAN, James 6
RUDERSDORFF, Hermine H
RUDESILL, Cecil Logan 8
RUDGE, William Edwin 1
RUDHYAR, Dane 10
RUDICK, Harry J. 4
RUDIN, Jacob Philip 8
RUDINGER, Ellen Eckstein (Mrs. George Rudinger) 5
RUDISILL, Dorus Paul 7
RUDKIN, Frank H. 1
RUDKIN, Margaret Fogarty 4
RUDNER, Richard Samuel 7
RUDOLF, Leslie E. 10
RUDOLPH, Andrew D. 7
RUDOLPH, Charles 4
RUDOLPH, Cuna H. 1
RUDOLPH, Herbert Blaine 3
RUDOLPH, Herman Louis 6
RUDOLPH, Irving 4
RUDOLPH, Jacob H. 3
RUDOLPH, Robert Livingston 1
RUDWIN, Maximilien (Josef) 7
RUDY, Charles 9
RUE, Lars 4
RUE, Levi Lingo 1
RUE, Milton 5
RUE, Ralph H. 4
RUE, William M. 9
RUEBUSH, James Hott 3
RUEDEMANN, Albert Darwin 6
RUEDEMANN, Rudolf 3
RUEDIGER, Gustav F. 1
RUEDIGER, William Carl 2
RUEHE, Harrison August 3
RUETENIK, Herman Julius 4
RUFF, G. Elson 5
RUFF, Robert Hamric 2
RUFFIN, Edmund H
RUFFIN, Margaret Ellen Henry 5
RUFFIN, Sterling 2
RUFFIN, Thomas* H
RUFFINI, Elise Erna 5
RUFFNER, Charles Shumway 1
RUFFNER, Ernest Howard 4
RUFFNER, Henry H
RUFFNER, William Henry 1
RUFI, John 9
RUFUS, Will Carl 1
RUGEN, Myrtle Louise 6
RUGER, Thomas Howard 1
RUGG, Arthur Prentice 1
RUGG, Charles Belcher 4
RUGG, Frederic Waldo 1

RUGG, Harold 4
RUGG, Henry Warren 1
RUGG, Herbert Dean 4
RUGG, Robert Billings 2
RUGGIERI, George Daniel 9
RUGGLES, Arthur Hiler 4
RUGGLES, Benjamin H
RUGGLES, Carl 5
RUGGLES, Charles 5
RUGGLES, Charles H
Herman
RUGGLES, Clyde Orval 3
RUGGLES, Colden 1
L'Hommedieu
RUGGLES, E. Wood 4
RUGGLES, George David 4
RUGGLES, Henry Joseph 4
RUGGLES, John H
RUGGLES, Nathaniel H
RUGGLES, Oliver W. 1
RUGGLES, Samuel Bulkley H
RUGGLES, Timothy 4
RUGGLES, William Brush 9
RUGGLES, William 4
Burroughs
RUGH, Charles Edward 4
RUGH, Roberts 7
RUHE, Percy Bott 4
RUHEMANN, Helmut 5
RUHL, Arthur Brown 5
RUHL, Christian H. 4
RUHL, James Brough 3
RUHL, Robert Waldo 4
RUHLENDER, Henry 4
RUHOFF, John Richard 6
RUHRAH, John 1
RUITENBEEK, Hendrik 8
M.
RUIZ, Cortines Adolfo 6
RUIZ, Jose Martinez 4
RUIZ GUINAZO, Enrique 4
RUKEYSER, Merryle 9
Stanley
RUKEYSER, Muriel 7
RULAND, Lloyd Stanton 3
RULE, Arthur Richards 3
RULE, Elton H. 10
RULE, James Noble 1
RULE, William 1
RULON, Phillip Justin 1
RUMBERGER, Calvin Lee 10
RUMBLE, Douglas 6
RUMBOLD, Frank Meeker 4
RUMBOLD, Thomas 1
Frazier
RUMELY, Edward A. 4
RUMELY, Edward 7
Aloysius
RUMELY, V. P. 4
RUMELY, William 3
Nicholas
RUMFORD, Count H
RUML, Beardsley 3
RUMMEL, Charles Garmin 10
RUMMEL, Joseph F. 4
RUMPF, Arthur Newell 5
RUMPLE, J. N. W. 1
RUMSEY, Benjamin H
RUMSEY, Charles Cary 4
RUMSEY, David H
RUMSEY, Dexter Phelps 4
RUMSEY, Edward 4
RUMSEY, Israel Parsons 4
RUMSEY, James H
RUMSEY, Mary Harriman 1
RUMSEY, William 1
RUNALS, Clarence Rider 8
RUNCIE, Constance 1
Fauntleroy
RUNDALL, Charles O. 3
RUNDELL, Oliver Samuel 3
RUNDLE, George 4
Mortimer
RUNDQUIST, George E. 5
RUNES, Dagobert David 8
RUNGE, Edith Amelie 4
RUNGIUS, Carl 3
RUNK, John 4
RUNKLE, Benjamin Platt 1
RUNKLE, Delmer 4
RUNKLE, Erwin William 1
RUNKLE, Harry Godley 4
RUNKLE, Harry Maize 4
RUNKLE, John Daniel 1
RUNKLE, Lucia Isabella 4
RUNNELLS, Clive 1
RUNNELLS, John Sumner 4
RUNNELLS, Russell 9
A(lger)
RUNNELS, Harold Lowell 7
RUNNELS, Orange Scott 1
RUNNELS, Richard Stitt 6
RUNNELS, Richard Stitt 7
RUNNER, Harvey Evan 4
RUNNING, Theodore 5
Rudolph

RUNNSTROM, John Axel 8
Mauritz
RUNYAN, Elmer Gardner 4
RUNYAN, William B. 3
RUNYON, Alfred Damon 2
RUNYON, John William 4
RUNYON, W. Parker 1
RUNYON, William Nelson 4
RUOFF, Henry Woldmar 1
RUOPP, Harold 4
Washington
RUOTOLO, Onorio 4
RUPE, Dallas Gordon 5
RUPEL, I(saac) Walker 5
RUPERTUS, William 2
Henry
RUPLEY, Arthur Ringwalt 4
RUPLEY, Joseph William 5
RUPP, Adolph Frederick 7
RUPP, Charles, Jr. 5
RUPP, Israel Daniel H
RUPP, Lawrence Henry 1
RUPP, Otto Burton 4
RUPP, Werner Andrew 4
RUPP, William 1
RUPPEL, Louis 5
RUPPENTHAL, Jacob 4
Christian
RUPPERT, George E. 2
RUPPERT, Jacob, Jr. 1
RUPPERT, Max King 1
RUPPRECHT, Frederick 3
Kelsey
RUSBY, Henry Hurd 1
RUSCH, Harold Paul 9
RUSCH, William George 9
RUSH, Benjamin H
RUSH, Benjamin 2
RUSH, Charles Andrew 4
RUSH, Charles Everett 7
RUSH, Frank Neill 7
RUSH, Franklin Smithwick 1
RUSH, Guy Mansfield 4
RUSH, Jacob H
RUSH, James H
RUSH, John Andrew 2
RUSH, Madelon Reine 6
Francis (Mrs. Alan
Sydney Rush)
RUSH, Olive 4
RUSH, Richard H
RUSH, Sylvester R. 1
RUSH, Thomas E. 1
RUSH, William H
RUSHING, James Andrew 5
RUSHMORE, David 1
Barker
RUSHMORE, Edward 4
RUSHMORE, John 4
Dikeman
RUSHMORE, Stephen 5
RUSHTON, Herbert J. 2
RUSHTON, John Henry 8
RUSHTON, Ray 1
RUSHTON, Richard Holt 1
RUSK, Henry Perly 3
RUSK, Howard A. 10
RUSK, Jeremiah McLain 1
RUSK, John 4
RUSK, Ralph Leslie 4
RUSK, Rogers D. 9
RUSK, Thomas Jefferson H
RUSK, William Sener 8
RUSKA, Ernest August 9
Friedrich
RUSKIN, Jerrold Harold 5
RUSLING, James Fowler 1
RUSS, Hugh McMaster 5
RUSS, John H
RUSS, John Denison 4
RUSS, John Megginson 5
RUSS, John T. 3
RUSSEL, Edgar 1
RUSSEL, George Howard 1
RUSSEL, Henry 1
RUSSEL, Walter S. 1
RUSSELL, Pastor 1
RUSSELL, Addison Peale 1
RUSSELL, Albert Hyatt 4
RUSSELL, Albert Richard 10
RUSSELL, Alexander 3
RUSSELL, Alexander 1
Wilson
RUSSELL, Alfred 1
RUSSELL, Annie 1
RUSSELL, Arthur Joseph 4
RUSSELL, Arthur Perkins 2
RUSSELL, Benjamin* H
Russell
RUSSELL, Bertrand, Earl 5
RUSSELL, Bruce Alexander 4
RUSSELL, Charles 1
RUSSELL, Charles Addison 1
RUSSELL, Charles 4
Augustus
RUSSELL, Charles Edward 1
RUSSELL, Charles Frank 7

RUSSELL, Charles Hinton 10
RUSSELL, Charles 1
Howland
RUSSELL, Charles Marion 1
RUSSELL, Charles 4
Partridge
RUSSELL, Charles Taze 1
RUSSELL, Charles Tier 3
RUSSELL, Charles Wells 1
RUSSELL, Clinton Warden 2
RUSSELL, Daniel 2
RUSSELL, Daniel Lindsay 1
RUSSELL, David Abel H
RUSSELL, David Allen H
RUSSELL, Donald Joseph 9
RUSSELL, Doris Aurelia 4
RUSSELL, Edmund A. 4
RUSSELL, Edward Hutson 5
RUSSELL, Edward 1
Lafayette
RUSSELL, Elbert 3
RUSSELL, Elias Harlow 4
RUSSELL, Ernest John 3
RUSSELL, Faris R. 5
RUSSELL, Francis 10
RUSSELL, Francis Henry 10
RUSSELL, Francis Thayer 3
RUSSELL, Francis 5
Wayland
RUSSELL, Frank 1
RUSSELL, Frank F. 5
RUSSELL, Frank Marion 5
RUSSELL, Franklin Ferriss 7
RUSSELL, Frederic Arthur 9
RUSSELL, Frederick Fuller 4
RUSSELL, George 1
RUSSELL, George Edmond 3
RUSSELL, George Harvey 1
RUSSELL, George Louis, 2
Jr.
RUSSELL, Gordon 1
RUSSELL, H(arry) Earle 5
RUSSELL, Harry Luman 4
RUSSELL, Harry Newton 1
RUSSELL, Helen Crocker 4
RUSSELL, Helen Gertrude 1
RUSSELL, Henry 4
RUSSELL, Henry Benajah 2
RUSSELL, Henry Dozier 5
RUSSELL, Henry Eastin 4
RUSSELL, Henry Moore 1
RUSSELL, Henry Norris 1
RUSSELL, Herbert Edwin 1
RUSSELL, Herman 4
RUSSELL, Horace 1
RUSSELL, Horace 6
RUSSELL, Howard Hyde 2
RUSSELL, Irwin H
RUSSELL, Isaac Franklin 1
RUSSELL, Israel Cook 1
RUSSELL, J. Henry 4
RUSSELL, J. J. 3
RUSSELL, J. Stuart 4
RUSSELL, James Alvin 7
RUSSELL, James Earl 2
RUSSELL, James 4
McPherson
RUSSELL, James Solomon 1
RUSSELL, Jane Anne 4
RUSSELL, Jeremiah 1
RUSSELL, John H
RUSSELL, John 4
RUSSELL, John, Jr. 10
RUSSELL, John Andrew 1
RUSSELL, John Benjamin, 7
Jr.
RUSSELL, John Edward 1
RUSSELL, John Edward 9
RUSSELL, John Henry H
RUSSELL, John Henry 2
RUSSELL, John McFarlane 9
RUSSELL, Jonathan 1
RUSSELL, Joseph* H
RUSSELL, Joseph Ballister 1
RUSSELL, Joseph Holt 4
RUSSELL, Joshua Edward 3
RUSSELL, Kenneth 6
Sherman
RUSSELL, Lao (Walter 10
Russell)
RUSSELL, Lee Maurice 2
RUSSELL, Lillian 1
RUSSELL, Louis Arthur 1
RUSSELL, L(ulu) Case 5
RUSSELL, Manley Holland 5
RUSSELL, Martin J. 1
RUSSELL, Mother Mary H
Baptist
RUSSELL, Melvin Gray 6
RUSSELL, Nelson Vance 3
RUSSELL, Norman Felt 3
Shelton
RUSSELL, Osborne H
RUSSELL, Paul Farr 9
RUSSELL, Paul Lawrence 10
RUSSELL, Paul Snowden 2
RUSSELL, Percy Hickling 7

RUSSELL, Phillips 7
(Charles)
RUSSELL, R. Dana 10
RUSSELL, Richard Brevard 1
RUSSELL, Richard Brevard 5
RUSSELL, Richard Joel 5
RUSSELL, Robert 4
RUSSELL, Robert Lee 3
RUSSELL, Robert 1
McWatty
RUSSELL, Robert Watrous 4
RUSSELL, Rosalind 7
RUSSELL, Samuel, Jr. 5
RUSSELL, Samuel Lyon 8
RUSSELL, Samuel Morris 8
RUSSELL, Scott 3
RUSSELL, Sol Smith 1
RUSSELL, Stanley Addison 3
RUSSELL, Talcott 1
Huntington
RUSSELL, Thomas 8
Dameron
RUSSELL, Thomas Halbert 1
RUSSELL, Thomas Herbert 4
RUSSELL, Thomas Wright 6
RUSSELL, Walter 1
RUSSELL, Walter C. 3
RUSSELL, Walter Earle 2
RUSSELL, Willard Lorane 6
RUSSELL, William* H
RUSSELL, William Eustus 1
RUSSELL, William Fiero H
RUSSELL, William Fletcher 3
RUSSELL, William Henry 4
Hepburn
RUSSELL, William 1
Hepburn
RUSSELL, William Logie 3
RUSSELL, William Logie 4
RUSSELL, William 4
Loughlin
RUSSELL, William T. 1
RUSSELL, William 4
Worthington
RUSSO, Joseph Louis 7
RUSSUM, B. C. 4
RUSSUM, Sarah Elizabeth 5
RUSSWURM, John Brown 4
RUST, Adlai H. 6
RUST, Albert 1
RUST, Charles Herbert 3
RUST, Edward Barry 8
RUST, Henry Bedinger 1
RUST, John Daniel 3
RUST, Mack Donald 4
RUST, Richard Sutton 9
RUST, Walter L. 3
RUSTAD, Elmer Lewis 6
RUSTGARD, John 2
RUSTIN, Bayard 9
RUSTIN, Henry 4
RUSTON, John Edward 1
RUSTON, William Otis 1
RUSZNYAK, Istvan 6
RUTAN, Charles Hercules 4
RUTAN, Harold Duane 3
RUTGERS, Henry 1
RUTH, Carl Douglas 1
RUTH, Earl Baker 10
RUTH, George Herman 2
RUTH, Henry Swartley 4
RUTH, John A. 5
RUTH, John P(illing) 5
RUTHENBURG, Louis 8
RUTHERFORD, Albert 1
Greig
RUTHERFORD, 3
Alexander H.
RUTHERFORD, Charles 7
Hayes
RUTHERFORD, Charles 6
Henry
RUTHERFORD, 1
Clarendon
RUTHERFORD, Emery 7
Gaythor
RUTHERFORD, George 4
H.
RUTHERFORD, Harry K. 7
RUTHERFORD, James J. 8
RUTHERFORD, Margaret 5
Lewis
RUTHERFORD, Mildred 1
RUTHERFORD, Richard 7
James
RUTHERFORD, Robert H
RUTHERFORD, S. 1
Morton
RUTHERFORD, Samuel 1
RUTHERFURD, John H
RUTHERFURD, John 4
RUTHERFURD, Lewis H
Morris
RUTHRAUFF, John 1
Mosheim
RUTHRUFF, Clifford Neil 8

RUTHVEN, Alexander 5
G(rant)
RUTHVEN, Alexander 7
G(rant)
RUTLAND, James Richard 2
RUTLEDGE, Ann H
RUTLEDGE, Archibald 6
(Hamilton)
RUTLEDGE, Benjamin 4
Huger
RUTLEDGE, Carl P. 3
RUTLEDGE, Edward H
RUTLEDGE, George Perry 2
RUTLEDGE, John H
RUTLEDGE, John, Jr. H
RUTLEDGE, Philip 10
Casteen
RUTLEDGE, Thomas G. 4
RUTLEDGE, Wiley Blount 2
RUTLEY, Frederick George 8
RUTSTEIN, David Davis 9
RUTT, Christian Louis 1
RUTTENBER, Edward 1
Manning
RUTTENBERG, Joseph 8
RUTTER, Frank Roy 1
RUTTER, Henley Chapman 1
RUTTER, Josiah Baldwin 3
RUTTER, Robert Lewis 4
RUTZ, William Edward 10
RUUD, Martin Bronn 1
RUUTZ-REES, Caroline 3
RUWE, Lester Nicholas 10
RUYL, Beatrice Baxter 6
RUYLE, John Bryan 3
RUZICKA, Charles 3
RUZICKA, Leopold 7
RUZICKA, Rudolph 7
RYALL, Daniel Bailey H
RYALS, Thomas Edward 2
RYAN, Abram Joseph H
RYAN, Allan A. 8
RYAN, Archie Lowell 6
RYAN, Arthur 5
RYAN, Clement Daniel 2
RYAN, Clendenin J. 3
RYAN, Cornelius Edward 5
RYAN, Cornelius John 6
RYAN, Daniel Joseph 1
RYAN, Dennis H
RYAN, Edward Francis 3
RYAN, Edward George H
RYAN, Edward William 1
RYAN, Elmer James 3
RYAN, Evelyn Althea 3
Murphy
RYAN, Francis Joseph 4
RYAN, Franklin Winton 3
RYAN, Frederick Behrens 3
RYAN, George Joseph 2
RYAN, Harold Francis 7
RYAN, Harris Joseph 1
RYAN, Hewson Anthony 10
RYAN, J. Harold 4
RYAN, James 1
RYAN, James 3
RYAN, James 9
RYAN, James Augustine 3
RYAN, James Hugh 2
RYAN, James W. 4
RYAN, Jerome Randolph 10
RYAN, John Augustine 2
RYAN, John D. 1
RYAN, John Dale 8
RYAN, John J., Jr. 4
RYAN, John William 5
RYAN, Leo Joseph 7
RYAN, Lewis Cook 4
RYAN, Sister M. Paton 10
RYAN, Marah Ellis 1
RYAN, Marah Ellis 4
RYAN, Martin Francis 1
RYAN, Michael Allan 8
RYAN, Michael J. 2
RYAN, Michael Sylvester 1
RYAN, O'Neill 1
RYAN, Oswald 8
RYAN, Patrick James 7
RYAN, Patrick John 1
RYAN, Patrick John 4
RYAN, Patrick L. 5
RYAN, Raymond Richard 1
RYAN, Robert 5
RYAN, Stanley Martin 3
RYAN, Stephen Vincent H
RYAN, Sylvester James 7
RYAN, Thomas 1
RYAN, Thomas Curran 1
RYAN, Thomas Fortune 1
RYAN, Thomas Jefferson 8
RYAN, Timothy Edward 1
RYAN, Tubal Claude 10
RYAN, Vincent J. 3
RYAN, Will Carson 5
RYAN, William 1
RYAN, William Fitts 5
RYAN, William Francis 8

221

RYAN, William Henry 1
RYAN, William Patrick 1
RYAN, William Russell 8
RYAN, William Thomas 1
RYBNER, Martin Cornelius 1
RYBURN, Frank M. 4
RYCKMAN, Charles 4
Silcott
RYCKMANS, Pierre 3
RYDBERG, Per Axel
RYDEN, Ernest Edwin 7
RYDEN, George Herbert 1
RYDEN, Roy Warren 7
RYDER, Albert Pinkham 1
RYDER, Arthur Hilton 2
RYDER, Arthur William 1
RYDER, Charles Jackson 1
RYDER, Charles Wolcott 4
RYDER, Chauncey Foster 2
RYDER, Frederick 1
Milliachip
RYDER, George Hope 2
RYDER, Harry Osborne 1
RYDER, Loren Lincoln 8
RYDER, Melvin 7
RYDER, Oscar Baxter 1
RYDER, Paul Bernhard 9
RYDER, Robert Oliver 1
RYDER, Thomas Philander H
RYDER, William Henry 1
RYDSTROM, Arthur
Gordon
RYERSON, Edward Larned 1
RYERSON, Edward Larned 5
RYERSON, Edwin Warner 4
RYERSON, Joseph Turner 2
RYERSON, Knowles 9
Augustus
RYERSON, Margery 7
Austen
RYERSON, Margery 10
Austin
RYERSON, Martin Antoine 1
RYERSON, William 5
Newton
RYGEL, John 3
RYGG, Andrew Nilsen 3
RYGH, George Taylor 4
RYKEN, Theodore James H
RYKENS, Paul 4
RYLANCE, Joseph Hine 1
RYLAND, Edward 1
RYLAND, John Peter 6
RYLAND, Joseph R. 1
RYLAND, Robert H
RYLAND, Robert Knight 3
RYLAND, William Semple 1
RYLE, Gilbert 7
RYLE, Walter Harrington 10
RYLEE, William Jackson 4
RYMAN, James H. T. 1
RYNEARSON, Edward 1
RYNNING, Ole 1
RYON, Harrison 5
RYON, Thomas S(hipley) 9
RYONS, Joseph Leslie 1
RYS, Carl Friedrich 2
Wilhelm
RYSKAMP, Henry Jacob 7
RYSKIND, Morrie 8
RYTAND, David A. 10
RYTINA, Anton George 7
RYUS, Celeste Nellis 5
RZYMOWSKI, Wincenty 7

S

SAAL, Irving Randolph 6
SAALFIELD, Ada Louise 5
(Ada Louise Sutton)
SAALFIELD, Albert 3
George
SAAR, Louis Victor Franz 1
SAARINEN, Aline 5
Bernstein
SAARINEN, Eero 4
SAARINEN, Eliel 3
SABATH, Aldoph J. 3
SABATINI, Rafael
SABEN, Mowry 3
SABES, Harold 8
SABIN, Alvah H
SABIN, Alvah Horton 1
SABIN, Charles Hamilton 1
SABIN, Dwight May 1
SABIN, Edwin Legrand 1
SABIN, Elbridge Hosmer 1
SABIN, Ellen Clara 2
SABIN, Florence Rena 2
SABIN, Frances Ellis 2
SABIN, Henry 1
SABIN, Joseph H
SABIN, Louis Carlton 3
SABIN, Pauline Morton 8
(Mrs. Dwight F. Davis)
SABIN, Wallace Arthur 1
SABINE, George Holland 4

SABINE, Lorenzo H
SABINE, Wallace Clement 1
SABINE, Wallace Clement 2
SABINE, William Tufnell 1
SABINI, Dominic Joseph 7
SABRY, H. E. Aly 10
SACAGAWEA H
SACCO, Nicola 4
SACHAR, Edward Joel 8
SACHS, Alexander 6
SACHS, Allan Maxwell 10
SACHS, Bernard 2
SACHS, Curt 3
SACHS, Ernest 3
SACHS, Howard Joseph 5
SACHS, James Henry 3
SACHS, Joseph 2
SACHS, Julius 1
SACHS, Morris Bernard 3
SACHS, Nelly 5
SACHS, Paul Joseph 4
SACHS, Teviah 3
SACHS, Walter Edward 5
SACHSE, Helena V. (Mrs.
Sadtler)
SACHSE, Julius Friedrich 1
SACHSE, Richard 3
SACHSE, Victor A., Jr. 8
SACK, A. Albert, Jr. 8
SACK, Alexander Naoum 3
SACK, Henri S(amuel) 5
SACK, Leo R. 3
SACKETT, Arthur Johnson 6
SACKETT, Arthur Johnson 7
SACKETT, Carl Leroy 5
SACKETT, Earl L. 5
SACKETT, Frederick 1
Moseley, Jr.
SACKETT, Henry 1
Woodward
SACKETT, Robert Lemuel 2
SACKETT, Samuel 1
Jefferson
SACKETT, Sheldon F(red) 5
SACKETT, Walter George 6
SACKETT, Walter Wallace, 9
Jr.
SACKETT, William August 1
SACKETT, William Edgar 1
SACKHEIM, Maxwell 9
Byron
SACKLER, Howard 8
SACKS, Albert Martin 10
SACKS, Emanuel 3
SACKS, Sheldon 7
SACKVILLE, Lord H
SACKVILLE-WEST, Lionel H
SACKVILLE-WEST, Lionel 4
Victoria
SADACCA, Henri 5
SADAT, Anwar Es- 9
SADD, Walter Allen 4
SADDLER, Owen Leslie 9
SADLAK, Antoni Nicholas 1
SADLEIR, Michael 3
SADLER, Daniel K. 1
SADLER, Everit Jay 2
SADLER, Frank Howard 6
SADLER, George Marion 4
SADLER, Herbert Charles 2
SADLER, Lena Kellogg 1
SADLER, McGruder Ellis 4
SADLER, Reinhold 1
SADLER, Sylvester Baker 1
SADLER, Thomas William H
SADLER, Wilbur Fisk 1
SADLIER, Denis H
SADOW, Leonard Bernard 6
SADOWSKI, George G. 1
SADTLER, John Phillip 4
Benjamin
SADTLER, Samuel Philip 1
SADUSK, Joseph Francis, 7
Jr.
SAENDERL, Simon H
SAENGER, Oscar 1
SAERCHINGER, Cesar 5
(Victor Charles)
SAFANIE, Murray D. 4
SAFAY, Fred A. 3
SAFFIN, William H
SAFFIN, William 1
SAFFOLD, William Berney 2
SAFFORD, Agnes Mabel 1
SAFFORD, Harry 2
Robinson
SAFFORD, James Merrill 1
SAFFORD, Mary Augusta 4
SAFFORD, Truman Henry 1
SAFFORD, William Cullen 7
SAFFORD, William Edwin 1
SAFRAN, Hyman 8
SAGAZ, Angel 4
SAGE, Agnes Carolyn 4
SAGE, Bernard Janin H
SAGE, Charles Gurdon 4

SAGE, Charles H(enry) 6
SAGE, Dean 2
SAGE, Eben Charles 1
SAGE, Ebenezer H
SAGE, Evan Taylor 1
SAGE, Henry Williams H
SAGE, John Charles 1
SAGE, John Davis 1
SAGE, John Hall 1
SAGE, Kay 4
SAGE, Robert Floyd 9
SAGE, Mrs Russel 1
SAGE, Russell 1
SAGE, William 4
SAGE, William Hampden 1
SAGEBEER, Joseph Evans 1
SAGENDORPH, Kent 5
SAGENDORPH, Robb 5
SAGER, Edward Anton 4
SAGUE, James E. 4
SAGUE, Mary Louise 7
Landon
SAHA, Meghnad 4
SAHAKIAN, Mabel Marie 8
Lewis
SAHLER, Charles Oliver 1
SAHLER, Helen 3
SAHLGREN, G. F. Joran 5
SAHS, Adolph Louis 9
SAID, Maraghai 6
Mohammad
SAIDLA, Leo Erval 4
Alexander
SAILER, Joseph 1
SAILLY, Peter H
SAINER, Leonard 10
SAINSBURY, Noël 7
Everingham, Jr.
SAINSBURY, William 3
Charles
SAINT, Harry Young 6
SAINT, Lawrence 4
SAINT, Percy 5
ST. ANGE, Louis De H
Bellerive
SAINT-AULAIRE, Felix
Achille
ST. CLAIR, Arthur H
ST. CLAIR, Leonard 4
Pressley
ST. CLAIR-MOSS, Luella 4
W.
SAINT-COSME, Jean H
Francois Buisson de
ST. CYR, John Alexander 4
ST. DENIS, Louis H
Juchereau de
SAINT-DENIS, Michel 5
Jacques
ST. DENIS, Ruth 5
SAINT GAUDENS, 1
Augustus
SAINT-GAUDENS, Homer 3
Schiff
SAINT GAUDENS, Louis 1
ST. GEORGE, William 4
Sterne
ST. HUSSON, Sieur de H
ST. JACQUES, Raymond 10
ST. JOHN, Charles H
ST. JOHN, Charles Edward 1
ST. JOHN, Charles Elliott 1
ST. JOHN, Charles Griffin 1
ST. JOHN, Charles J. 4
ST. JOHN, Cynthia Morgan 1
ST. JOHN, Daniel Bennett 1
ST. JOHN, Edward Porter 1
ST. JOHN, Everitte 1
ST. JOHN, Fordyce Barker 6
ST. JOHN, Francis R. 5
ST. JOHN, George Clair 4
ST. JOHN, Guy Bascom 6
ST. JOHN, Harold 9
ST. JOHN, Henry H
ST. JOHN, Isaac Munroe H
ST. JOHN, J. Hector 1
ST. JOHN, James 8
H(amilton)
ST. JOHN, John Pierce 1
ST. JOHN, John Price H
ST. JOHN, John Price H
ST. JOHN, Samuel Benedict 1
ST. JOHN, Theodore 3
Raymond
ST. JOHN, Thomas 5
Raymond
ST. LAURENT, Louis 5
Stephen
ST. LAUSSON, Simon H
Francois Daumont
ST. LEGER, BARRY 1
ST. LEWIS, Roy 5
ST. MARTIN, Louis 4
SAINT-MEMIN, Charles H
Bathazar Julien Fevret de
ST. ONGE, William Leon 4

SAINT-PALAIS, Jacques H
Maurice Landes de
ST. PIERRE, Charles 7
SAINT-QUENTIN, 7
RenéDoynel Comte De
ST. SURE, Adolphus 2
Frederic
ST. VRAIN, Ceran De H
Hault De Lassus de
SAIT, Edward McChesney 2
SAITO, Hirosi 1
SAJOUS, Charles Euchariste 1
de' Medici
SAKEL, Manfred Joshua 3
SAKHAROV, Andrei 10
Dimitriyevich
SAKOLSKI, Aaron M. 3
SAKURAI, Jun John 8
SALA, Antoine 6
SALANT, Robert Stephen 7
SALANT, William 1
SALATHE, Albert 8
SALAZAR 5
SALAZAR, Ontonio De 5
Oliveira
SALAZAR, Ruben 5
SALAZAR ARGUMEDO, 5
Carlos
SALBER, Eva Juliet 10
SALE, Charles Partlow 1
SALE, George 1
SALE, Samuel 1
SALE, William M., Jr. 7
SALEM, Hermann R. 4
SALEMME, Antonio 9
SALERNO, George Fred 5
SALERNO, Vito Lorenzo 5
SALES, Murray W. 3
SALESKY, Bernard 4
Leonard
SALET, Eugene Albert 10
SALIERS, Earl Adolphus 3
SALINAS, Pedro 3
SALINGER, Benjamin I. 1
SALINGER, Harry 3
SALINGER, Herman 8
SALISBURY, Albert 1
SALISBURY, Edward H
Elbridge
SALISBURY, Eugene 9
Franklin
SALISBURY, George 4
Robert
SALISBURY, Harold 8
Preston
SALISBURY, James Henry 1
SALISBURY, Lucius A. 7
SALISBURY, Morse 1
SALISBURY, Richard 10
Frank
SALISBURY, Rollin D. 1
SALISBURY, Stanton W. 4
SALISBURY, Stuart 9
McFarland
SALIT, Norman 4
SALK, Lee 10
SALKO, Henry S. 10
SALLER, Sylvester John 10
SALLES, George Adolphe 3
SALLET, Dirse Wilkis 10
SALLEY, Alexander 5
Samuel, Jr.
SALLEY, Nathaniel Moss 5
SALLMON, William Henry 1
SALM, Peter 10
SALMAGGI, Alfredo 6
SALMAGGI, Alfredo 4
SALMANS, Levi Brimmer 4
SALMON, Alvah Glover 1
SALMON, Daniel Elmer 1
SALMON, David Alden 6
SALMON, Edwin Ashley 1
SALMON, Joshua S. 1
SALMON, Kurt 9
SALMON, Lucy Maynard 1
SALMON, Paul Blair 8
SALMON, Thomas William 1
SALMON, Udall J. 7
SALMON, William Charles 1
SALMON, Wilmer Wesley 5
SALM-SALM, Prince H
SALM-SALM, Princess H
SALM-SALM, Princess H
SALOMON, Erich 4
SALOMON, Fred Z. 4
SALOMON, Haym H
SALOMON, Herbert 5
SALOMON, Irving 7
SALOMON, Mardoqueo 9
Isaac
SALOMONE, A. William 9
SALOUTOS, Theodore 9
SALOUTOS, Theodore 9
SALPETER, Harry 5
SALPETER, High 5
SALPOINTE, John Baptist H
SALSBURG, Zevi Walter 5

SALSBURY, Lant King 1
SALSBURY, Nate 8
SALSGIVER, Paul L. 3
SALSICH, Leroy 3
SALSINGER, Harry 7
George
SALT, Albert Lincoln 2
SALT, Waldo 9
SALTEN, Felix 2
SALTER, Herbert William 10
SALTER, John Thomas 6
SALTER, Leslie Earnest 4
SALTER, Lewis Spencer 10
SALTER, Lewis Spencer 4
SALTER, Mary Turner 1
SALTER, Moses 4
Buckingham
SALTER, Richard Gene 5
SALTER, Robert 3
Mundhenk
SALTER, Sumner 2
SALTER, William 1
SALTER, William 1
MacKintire
SALTER, William Thomas 3
SALTIEL, William David 10
SALTONSTALL, Dudley H
SALTONSTALL, Gurdon H
SALTONSTALL, Leverett H
SALTONSTALL, Leverett 7
SALTONSTALL, Nathaniel 5
SALTONSTALL, Richard H
SALTONSTALL, Richard 8
SALTONSTALL, William 10
Gurdon
SALTUS, Edgar 1
SALTZBERG, Bernard 10
SALTZGABER, Gaylord 1
Miller
SALTZMAN, Charles 2
McKinley
SALTZMAN, Joel 4
SALTZSTEIN, Benjamin 7
F(ranklin)
SALTZSTEIN, Harry C. 8
SALVAGE, Sir Samuel 2
Agar
SALVANT, Robert Milton 3
SALVATIERRA, Juan H
Maria
SALVATORE, Victor 4
SALVATORRELLI, Luigi 6
SALVEMINI, Gaetano 3
SALZEDO, Carlos 4
SALZER, Felix 9
SALZMAN, Herbert 10
SALZMANN, Joseph H
SAMALMAN, Alexander 3
SAMAROFF, Olga 2
SAMES, Albert Morris 3
SAMFIELD, Max 1
SAMFORD, Frank Park 6
SAMFORD, Frank Park, 9
Jr.
SAMFORD, John A. 5
SAMFORD, Thomas Drake 2
SAMFORD, William 1
Hodges
SAMINSKY, Lazare 2
SAMMARCO, G. Mario 5
SAMMARTINO, Peter 10
SAMMET, G. Victor 3
SAMMIS, Arthur Maxwell 5
SAMMIS, Donald Stuart 9
SAMMIS, Walter Henry 10
SAMMOND, Frederic 4
SAMMOND, Herbert 4
Stavely
SAMMOND, Herbert 5
Stavely
SAMMONS, Charles A. 10
SAMMONS, Edward Curf 9
SAMMONS, F. Elmer 3
SAMMONS, Thomas H
SAMMONS, Thomas 1
SAMMONS, Wheeler 3
SAMMONS, William Henry 2
SAMPEY, John Richard 2
SAMPEY, John Richard, Jr. 5
SAMPLE, Glenn W. 7
SAMPLE, John Glen 5
SAMPLE, Paul Lindsay 3
SAMPLE, Paul Starrett 6
SAMPLE, Robert Fleming 1
SAMPLE, Samuel Caldwell H
SAMPLE, Samuel 4
Williamson
SAMPLE, William Devore 6
SAMPLE, William Dodge 2
SAMPLE, William Roderick 4
SAMPSELL, David 9
Sylvester
SAMPSELL, Marshall 5
Emmett
SAMPSELL, Marshall 6
Grosscup
SAMPSON, Alden 1

SAMPSON, Archibald J. 1
SAMPSON, Arthur Francis 9
SAMPSON, Charles Henry 7
SAMPSON, Edith Spurlock 7
SAMPSON, Emma Speed 2
SAMPSON, Ezekiel Silas H
SAMPSON, Flemon Davis 4
SAMPSON, Francis Asbury 1
SAMPSON, Henry Ellis 2
SAMPSON, Henry Thomas 4
SAMPSON, Herbert 8
Martin, Jr.
SAMPSON, Homer 7
Cleveland
SAMPSON, John Albertson 2
SAMPSON, John Pattrson 4
SAMPSON, Martin Wright 1
SAMPSON, Thornton 1
Rogers
SAMPSON, William H
SAMPSON, William James, 5
Jr.
SAMPSON, William 1
Thomas
SAMPSON, Zabdiel H
SAMS, Earl Corder 3
SAMS, Howard Waldemar 6
SAMS, James C. 9
SAMS, James Hagood, Jr. 5
SAMS, Oliver Newton 1
SAMS, Robert Shields 5
SAMSON, George Clement 1
SAMSON, George H
Whitefield
SAMSON, William Holland 1
SAMSTAG, Gordon 10
SAMUEL, Bernard 3
SAMUEL, Bunford 2
SAMUEL, Donald Carol 7
SAMUEL, Edmund William 1
SAMUEL, Henry Paul 1
SAMUEL, Herbert 4
SAMUEL, Maurice 5
SAMUEL, Ralph E. 4
SAMUELS, Arthur Hiram 1
SAMUELS, Benjamin 4
SAMUELS, Edward 1
Augustus
SAMUELS, Green Berry H
SAMUELS, J. Clifton 7
SAMUELS, Maurice Victor 2
SAMUELS, Samuel 1
SAMUELS, Seymour, Jr. 10
SAMUELSON, Agnes 4
SAMY, Mahmoud 4
SANBORN, Alvan Francis 4
SANBORN, Arthur Loomis 1
SANBORN, Benjamin H. 1
SANBORN, Bruce Walter 7
SANBORN, Charles Henry 3
SANBORN, Edwin David H
SANBORN, Elwin Roswell 2
SANBORN, Franklin 1
Benjamin
SANBORN, Frederic 6
Rockwell
SANBORN, Helen 1
Josephine
SANBORN, Henry Nichols 1
SANBORN, Herbert 4
Charles
SANBORN, J. Pitts 1
SANBORN, John Albert 1
SANBORN, John Bell 1
SANBORN, John Benjamin 1
SANBORN, John Carfield 5
SANBORN, Joseph Brown 1
SANBORN, Katherine 1
Abbott
SANBORN, Mary Farley 3
SANBORN, Richard Dyer 9
SANBORN, Walter Henry 1
SANBORNE, Henry 4
Kendall
SANCHEZ, Allan Juan 5
SANCHEZ, Jose Bernardo H
SANCHEZ, Nellie Van de 1
Grift
SANCHEZ-LATOUR, 1
Francisco
SANCHINI, Dominick 10
Joseph
SAND, Harold Eugene 9
SAND, Inge (Mrs. Hans J. 6
Christensen)
SAND, Paul Meinrad 8
SANDALL, Charles 5
Edward
SANDBERG, Adolph 10
Engelbrekt
SANDBURG, Carl 4
SANDEFER, Jefferson 1
Davis
SANDEFUR, Ray Harold 8
SANDELL, Ernest Birger 8
SANDELL, Perry James 4
SANDEMAN, Robert H

SANDER, John Ferdinand 5
SANDER, Ludwig 6
SANDER, Theodore, Jr. 7
SANDERS, Allison 9
SANDERS, Alvin Howard 1
SANDERS, Archie D. 1
SANDERS, Benjamin 10
Elbert
SANDERS, Bilington H
McCarter
SANDERS, Charles Finley 3
SANDERS, Charles Walton 1
SANDERS, Daniel Clarke H
SANDERS, Daniel Jackson 1
SANDERS, Daniel 10
Selvarajah
SANDERS, Dorsey Addren 10
Elkins
SANDERS, Elizabeth H
SANDERS, Euclid 4
SANDERS, Everett 3
SANDERS, Frank Knight 1
SANDERS, Frederic 4
William
SANDERS, George 5
SANDERS, George 1
Nicholas
SANDERS, Harland 7
SANDERS, Harold 3
Frederick
SANDERS, Henry Arthur 3
SANDERS, Henry Martin 1
SANDERS, Henry Nevill 5
SANDERS, James Harvey H
SANDERS, Jared Young 4
SANDERS, Jared Young, 2
Jr.
SANDERS, Jared Young, 4
Jr.
SANDERS, J(esse) 8
T(homas)
SANDERS, John Adams 4
SANDERS, John Oliver 6
SANDERS, Joseph M. 1
SANDERS, Lee Stanley 5
SANDERS, Louis Peck 1
SANDERS, Morgan Gurley 3
SANDERS, Murray 9
Jonathan
SANDERS, Newell 1
SANDERS, Robert David 3
SANDERS, Robert L. 6
SANDERS, Ronald 10
SANDERS, Samuel D. 4
SANDERS, Thomas Henry 3
SANDERS, Thomas 2
Jefferson
SANDERS, W. Burton 4
SANDERS, Walter 5
Benjamin
SANDERS, Walter 7
Benjamin
SANDERS, Wilbur Fisk 1
SANDERS, William 7
SANDERS, William 1
Brownell
SANDERS, William King 6
SANDERSON, Bennett 10
SANDERSON, Charles 3
Rupert
SANDERSON, Edward 5
Frederick
SANDERSON, Edwin Nash 1
SANDERSON, Eugene 4
Claremont
SANDERSON, Ezra 2
Dwight
SANDERSON, George H
Andrew
SANDERSON, George 1
Augustus
SANDERSON, Henry H
SANDERSON, Henry 1
SANDERSON, Henry 6
Stephen
SANDERSON, John H
SANDERSON, John 3
SANDERSON, Joseph 4
SANDERSON, Joseph 8
Monteith
SANDERSON, Julia 6
SANDERSON, Lewis R. 4
SANDERSON, Percy, Sir 4
SANDERSON, Robert 4
SANDERSON, Robert 4
Louis
SANDERSON, Samuel 5
Gilbert
SANDERSON, Sibyl 1
SANDERSON, Walter W. 5
SANDFORD, James T. H
SANDFORD, Thomas H
SANDIDGE, John Milton 5
SANDIDGE, Roy Preston 8
SANDIFER, Durward 7
Valdamir

SANDIFER, Joseph 3
Randolph
SANDISON, George Henry 4
SANDISON, Helen 7
Estabrook
SANDITEN, Julius 7
SANDLIN, John Nicholas 5
SANDLIN, Marlin Elijah 6
SANDLIN, Marlin Elijah 1
SANDMAIER, Philip 9
James, Jr.
SANDMAN, Charles W., 9
Jr.
SANDMEL, Samuel 7
SANDONA, Matteo 7
SANDOR, Mathias 1
SANDOR, Pal 5
SANDOVAL, Hilary Joseph 6
SANDOZ, Mari Susette 4
SANDROK, Edward 5
George
SANDS, Alexander H., Jr. 1
SANDS, Benjamin Aymar 1
SANDS, Benjamin Franklin H
SANDS, Comfort H
SANDS, David H
SANDS, Diana Patricia 6
SANDS, Frank 3
SANDS, George Lincoln 1
SANDS, Herbert Stead 2
SANDS, James Hoban 1
SANDS, Joshua H
SANDS, Joshua Ratoon H
SANDS, Lawrence Eyster 1
SANDS, Lester Burton 8
SANDS, Merill Burr 3
SANDS, Oliver Jackson 4
SANDS, Robert Charles 1
SANDS, Robert Kenneth 6
SANDS, Stafford Lofthouse 5
SANDS, Thomas Edmund 5
SANDS, William Franklin 2
SANDSTEN, Emil Peter 4
SANDSTROM, Emil 4
SANDT, George 1
Washington
SANDWEISS, David Jacob 4
SANDY, William Charles 5
SANDY, William Charles 6
SANDYS, Edwyn William 1
SANDYS, George H
SANDZEN, Sven Birger 3
SANER, John Crawford 2
SANER, Robert E. Lee 1
SANFORD, Albert Hart 3
SANFORD, Alfred Fanton 2
SANFORD, Allan Douglas 1
SANFORD, Arthur Hawley 5
SANFORD, Charles F. 1
SANFORD, Charles Wilson 7
SANFORD, Chester Milton 1
SANFORD, Conley Hall 3
SANFORD, Daniel Sammis 1
SANFORD, Edmund Clark 4
SANFORD, Edward Field, 1
Jr.
SANFORD, Edward Terry 1
SANFORD, Elias Benjamin 1
SANFORD, Fernando 2
SANFORD, Fillmore 4
Hargrave
SANFORD, Francis Baird 2
SANFORD, Frank 5
Goodwin
SANFORD, George Bliss 1
SANFORD, Giles H
SANFORD, Graham 2
SANFORD, Harold 4
Williams
SANFORD, Henry Lindsay 1
SANFORD, Henry Shelton H
SANFORD, Hugh Wheeler 4
SANFORD, James Clark 1
SANFORD, John H
SANFORD, John 1
SANFORD, John B. 5
SANFORD, John Berkshire, 1
Jr.
SANFORD, John Edgar 4
SANFORD, John W. A. H
SANFORD, Jonah 1
SANFORD, Joseph William 3
SANFORD, Louis Childs 2
SANFORD, Maria L. 1
SANFORD, Myron Reed 1
SANFORD, Nathan 4
SANFORD, Orin Grover 2
SANFORD, Rollin B. 2
SANFORD, Roscoe Frank 1
SANFORD, Steadman 2
Vincent
SANFORD, Thomas 6
Ryland
SANG, Philip David 6
SANGER, Alexander 1
SANGER, Charles Robert 1
SANGER, George Partridge H

SANGER, Henry H. 3
SANGER, John Pomeroy 3
SANGER, Joseph Prentice 1
SANGER, Margaret 4
SANGER, Paul Weldon 5
SANGER, Ralph 4
SANGER, Richard 7
Harlakenden
SANGER, William Cary 1
SANGER, William Thomas 6
SANGER, William Thomas 7
SANGER, Winnie 5
Monroney (Mrs. Fenton
M. Sanger)
SANGREN, Paul Vivian 4
SANGSTER, Margaret 1
Elizabeth
SANIAL, Lucien 4
SANKEY, Ira Allan 1
SANKEY, Ira David 1
SANN, Paul 9
SANNER, Sydney 5
SANNO, James Madison 1
Johnston
SANROMA, Jesus Maria 8
SANSBURY, Marvin 4
Orville
SANSOM, Sir George 4
SANSOM, Marion 1
SANSOM, William 7
SANSONE, Robert 10
SAN SOUCI, Emery John 1
SANSUM, William David 1
SANTA ANNA, Antonio H
Lopez de
SANTAYANA, George 3
SANTE, Christopher Alfred 5
SANTE, Hans Heinrich 5
SANTE, Le Roy 4
SANTEE, Ellis Monroe 1
SANTEE, Harris Ellett 1
SANTELLI, T(homas) 8
Robert
SANTELMAN, Elmar 6
William
SANTELMANN, William 2
Henry
SANTOS, Eduardo 6
SANTOS, Epifanio de los 1
SANTOS Y BASCO, Jose 7
Abad
SAPERSTON, Alfred 8
Morton
SAPHIER, A. S. 10
SAPHORE, Edwin Warren 2
SAPIR, Edward 1
SAPIRO, Aaron 3
SAPIRSTEIN, Jacob 7
SAPOSS, David Joseph 7
SAPP, Arthur Henry 2
SAPP, Claud Napoleon 1
SAPP, Henry Grady 9
SAPP, William Fletcher 1
SAPP, William Frederick 1
SAPP, William Robinson 1
SAPPINGTON, A. D. 7
SAPPINGTON, Clarence 2
Olds
SAPPINGTON, John H
Watkins
SAPPINGTON, Samuel 3
SAPPINGTON, Thomas 9
Asbury
SAR, Samuel Leib 4
SARAFIAN, Armen 10
SARBACHER, George 5
W(illiam), Jr.
SARCHET, Corbin 5
Marquand
SARD, Grange 1
SARDEAU, Helene (Mrs. 5
George Biddle)
SARDESON, Frederick 3
William
SARETT, Lew 3
SARG, Tony 2
SARGEANT, Frank 5
Wadleigh
SARGEANT, Gaston 6
SARGEANT, Howland H. 8
SARGEANT, Howland H. 1
SARGEANT, William H. 1
SARGEANT, Winthrop 9
SARGENT, Aaron H
Augustus
SARGENT, Amor Hartley 5
SARGENT, Archer 5
Downing
SARGENT, Charles 1
Sprague
SARGENT, Charles Wesley 4
SARGENT, Christopher 5
Gilbert
SARGENT, Dudley Allen 1
SARGENT, Edward 2
SARGENT, Epes H
SARGENT, Fitzwilliam H

SARGENT, Fitzwilliam 3
SARGENT, Frank Pierce 1
SARGENT, Franklin Haven 1
SARGENT, Fred Wesley 1
SARGENT, Frederick 1
SARGENT, Frederick, II 7
SARGENT, Frederick Le 1
Roy
SARGENT, George Henry 1
SARGENT, Henry H
SARGENT, Henry Barry 4
SARGENT, Henry 1
Bradford
SARGENT, Henry H
Winthrop
SARGENT, Herbert 1
Howland
SARGENT, James 1
SARGENT, James Clyde 3
SARGENT, John Garibaldi 1
SARGENT, John Osborne H
SARGENT, John Singer 1
SARGENT, Ledyard 1
Worthington
SARGENT, Lucius Manlius H
SARGENT, Murray 7
SARGENT, Nathan H
SARGENT, Nathan 1
SARGENT, Noel Gharrett 5
SARGENT, Paul Dudley 5
SARGENT, Porter 5
SARGENT, Porter E. 3
SARGENT, Samuel 7
S(tegall)
SARGENT, Walter 1
SARGENT, William 1
Durham
SARGENT, William 4
Edward
SARGENT, Winthrop* H
SARLES, Elmore Yocum 1
SARNOFF, David 5
SARNOFF, Stanley Jay 10
SARONY, Napoleon H
SAROYAN, William 7
SARPER, Selim 5
SARPY, Peter A. H
SARTAIN, Emily 1
SARTAIN, John H
SARTAIN, Paul Judd 2
SARTAIN, Samuel 1
SARTAIN, William* 1
SARTHER, John M. 3
SARTON, George 3
SARTORI, Joseph Francis 1
SARTORI, Louis Constant 1
SARTORIUS, Irving A. 3
SARTRE, Jean-paul 7
SARTWELL, Henry Parker H
SARTZ, Richard Sophus 1
Nielsen
SARVELLA, Patricia Ann 7
SARVIS, Arthur H. 9
SARVIS, Guy Walter 6
SASLAVSKY, Alexander 1
SASLOW, Daniel L. 8
SASS, George Herbert 1
SASS, Herbert Ravenel 3
SASSACUS H
SASSCER, Lansdale G. 4
SASSOON, Siegfried 4
Loraine
SASTROAMIDJOJO, Ali 6
SATENSTEIN, Edward 5
SATENSTEIN, Frank 9
SATENSTEIN, Sidney 4
SATER, John Elbert 1
SATER, Richard Francis 7
SATERLEE, Gerald Britton 3
SATHERLY, Arthur 9
Edward
SATHRE, Jacob Cornelius 1
SATHRE, Peter O. 6
SATO, Eisaku 6
SATO, Sho 10
SATTEE, Andrew L. 10
SATTER, Gustav H
SATTER, Mark J. 5
SATTERFIELD, Dave 2
Edward, Jr.
SATTERFIELD, David 9
Edward, III
SATTERFIELD, John 8
Creighton
SATTERFIELD, John 5
Vines, Jr.
SATTERFIELD, M. H. 3
SATTERFIELD, Robert 2
Samuel
SATTERLEE, Eugene 1
SATTERLEE, George 1
Reese
SATTERLEE, Henry Yates 1
SATTERLEE, Herbert 1
Livingston
SATTERLEE, Hugh 4

SCHNEEBELI, G. Adolph 4
SCHNEEBELI, Herman T. 8
SCHNEIDER, Adolph 2
  Benedict
SCHNEIDER, Alan 8
SCHNEIDER, Albert 1
SCHNEIDER, Alma 6
  Kittredge
SCHNEIDER, Benjamin H
SCHNEIDER, Carl E. 4
SCHNEIDER, Charles 1
  Conrad
SCHNEIDER, Clement 5
  Joseph
SCHNEIDER, Edward 5
  Alexander
SCHNEIDER, Edward 3
  Christian
SCHNEIDER, Elisabeth 10
  Wintersteen
SCHNEIDER, Erich 5
SCHNEIDER, Erwin Henry 9
SCHNEIDER, Franz 9
SCHNEIDER, Frederick H. 10
SCHNEIDER, Frederick 2
  William
SCHNEIDER, George 5
SCHNEIDER, George J. 1
SCHNEIDER, Harold K. 9
SCHNEIDER, Heinrich 8
SCHNEIDER, Herbert 8
  Wallace
SCHNEIDER, Herman 1
SCHNEIDER, Hubert 7
  August
SCHNEIDER, J(ohn) 7
  Thomas
SCHNEIDER, Joseph 1
SCHNEIDER, Louis 7
SCHNEIDER, Melvin 10
SCHNEIDER, Mischa 9
SCHNEIDER, Oscar Albert 4
SCHNEIDER, Ralph 4
  Edward
SCHNEIDER, Ralph 8
  Frederick
SCHNEIDER, Richard Coy 9
SCHNEIDER, Samuel 1
  Hiram
SCHNEIDER, Stanley 6
  Frederick
SCHNEIDER, Theodore H
SCHNEIDER, Walter 3
  Arthur
SCHNEIDER, William 9
  Albert
SCHNEIDER, William B. 4
SCHNEIDER, William 8
  Henry
SCHNEIDER, Wilmar 6
  Rufus
SCHNEIDERMAN, 10
  Howard Allen
SCHNEIDERS, Alexander 5
  A(loysius)
SCHNEIDEWIND, 5
  Richard
SCHNEIERSON, Sol 7
  Stanley
SCHNEIRLA, Theodore 5
  Christian
SCHNELLER, Frederic 4
  Andrew
SCHNELLER, George Otto H
SCHNERING, Otto 3
SCHNIEBS, Otto Eugen 9
SCHNITZER, Germaine 8
  Alice
SCHNITZLER, John 1
  William
SCHNUCK, Edward J. 9
SCHNUR, George Henry, 1
  Jr.
SCHNURPEL, Hans Karl 6
SCHNURR, Martin K. 4
SCHNUTE, William Jacob 6
SCHOB, Anthony John 10
SCHOBECK, Arthur 4
  Ellwyn
SCHOBINGER, George 7
SCHOCH, Eugene Paul 5
SCHOCKEN, Gershom 10
  Gustav
SCHOCKEN, Theodore 6
SCHODDE, George Henry 1
SCHODER, Ernest William 5
SCHOECH, William Alton 4
SCHOEFFLER, Oscar 7
  Edmund
SCHOELLKOPF, Alfred 2
  Hugo
SCHOELLKOPF, J. Fred, 5
  IV
SCHOELLKOPF, Jacob F. 2
SCHOELLKOPF, Paul 2
  Arthur

SCHOEMAKER, Daniel 3
  Martin
SCHOEMANN, Peter 7
  Theodore
SCHOEN, Charles T. 4
SCHOEN, Edward 6
SCHOEN, John Edmund 5
SCHOEN, Max 8
SCHOENBERG, Arnold 3
SCHOENBERG, Bruce 9
  Stuart
SCHOENBERGER, 8
  H(arold) W(illiam)
SCHOENBORN, Edward 7
  Martin, Jr.
SCHOENBRUN, David 9
  Franz
SCHOENE, William Jay 6
SCHOENECK, Edward 5
SCHOENEFELD, Henry 4
SCHOENEMAN, George J. 8
SCHOENEMANN, Oscar 6
  Paul
SCHOENFELD, H. F. 3
  Arthur
SCHOENFELD, Hermann 1
SCHOENFELD, Rudolf 7
  Emil
SCHOENFELD, William 3
  Alfred
SCHOENRICH, Otto 7
SCHOENSTEIN, Paul 6
SCHOENY, Leo John 7
SCHOEPF, W. Kesley 5
SCHOEPFLE, Chester S. 3
SCHOEPPEL, Andrew F. 4
SCHOEPPERLE, Victor 4
SCHOETZ, Max 4
SCHOFF, Hannah Kent 1
SCHOFF, Stephen Alonzo 1
SCHOFF, Wilfred Harvey 1
SCHOFIELD, Albert 5
  George
SCHOFIELD, Charles 3
  Edwin
SCHOFIELD, Frank 2
  Herman
SCHOFIELD, Frank Lee 1
SCHOFIELD, Harvey A. 1
SCHOFIELD, Henry 1
SCHOFIELD, John 1
  McAllister
SCHOFIELD, Mary Lyon 2
  Cheney
SCHOFIELD, William 1
SCHOFIELD, William 1
  Henry
SCHOLANDER, Per 7
  Fredrik
SCHOLER, Charles Henry 7
SCHOLER, Walter 5
SCHOLES, Charles Marcel 6
SCHOLES, Samuel Ray 6
SCHOLL, John William 3
SCHOLL, William M. 5
SCHOLLE, Hardinge 5
SCHOLTE, Hendrick Peter H
SCHOLTZ, Joseph D. 5
SCHOLZ, Emil Maurice 2
SCHOLZ, Karl William 4
  Henry
SCHOLZ, Richard 1
  Frederick
SCHOMBURG, August 7
SCHOMMER, John J. 4
SCHOMP, Albert L. 3
SCHONBERGER, 5
  E(manuel) D(eo)
SCHONFELD, William A. 5
SCHONHARDT, Henri 3
SCHONLAND, Herbert 8
  Emery
SCHOO, Clarence John 7
SCHOOLCARFT, Henry H
  Rowe
SCHOOLCRAFT, Arthur 4
  Allen
SCHOOLCRAFT, John H
  Lawrence
SCHOOLER, Lewis 4
SCHOOLEY, Allen Heaten 7
SCHOONHOVEN, Helen 3
  Butterfield
SCHOONHOVEN, John 1
  James
SCHOONMAKER, H
  Cornelius Corneliusen
SCHOONMAKER, Edwin 1
  Davies
SCHOONMAKER, 2
  Frederic Palen
SCHOONMAKER, George 8
  Nelson
SCHOONMAKER, Nancy 4
  M.
SCHOONOVER, Draper 3
  Talman

SCHOONOVER, Frank 5
  Earle
SCHOONOVER, Lawrence 7
  Lovell
SCHOOTEN, Sarah 6
  Schilling
SCHOPF, James Morton 7
SCHOPF, Johann David H
SCHOPFLIN, Jack 4
SCHORGER, Arlie William 5
SCHORGER, Arlie William 7
SCHORLING, Raleigh 3
SCHORSCH, Alexander 3
  Peter
SCHORTEMEIER, 4
  Frederick Edward
SCHOTT, Carl Peter 7
SCHOTT, Charles Anthony 1
SCHOTT, Henry 1
SCHOTT, Lawrence 4
  Frederick
SCHOTT, Max 3
SCHOTTE, Oscar Emil 10
SCHOTTENSTEIN, Jerome 10
  M.
SCHOTTERS, Bernard 9
  William
SCHOULER, James 1
SCHOULER, John 1
SCHOULER, William H
SCHOUR, Isaac 4
SCHOW, Robert Alwin 8
SCHOYER, Alfred McGill 4
SCHRADE, Leo Franz 5
SCHRADER, Charles E. 5
SCHRADER, Edward 7
  Albert
SCHRADER, Frank 2
  Charles
SCHRADER, Franz 4
SCHRADER, Fred L. 4
SCHRADER, Frederick 2
  Franklin
SCHRADER, George H. 5
SCHRADER, Robert Estes 4
SCHRADIECK, Henry 4
SCHRAER, Rosemary S. J. 10
SCHRAKAMP, Josepha 5
SCHRAM, Emil 9
SCHRAM, Jack Aron 4
SCHRAM, Lauren 9
SCHRAMM, E. Frank 4
SCHRAMM, James 8
  Siegmund
SCHRAMM, Wilbur Lang 9
SCHRANK, Harry Paul 7
SCHRANK, Raymond 6
  Edward
SCHRATCHLEY, Francis 4
  Arthur
SCHRECKENGAST, Isaac 1
  Butler
SCHRECKER, Paul 4
SCHREIBER, Carl 3
  Frederick
SCHREIBER, Flora Rheta 9
SCHREIBER, George 8
  Arthur
SCHREIBER, Ludwig 7
  David
SCHREIBER, Manuel 1
SCHREIBER, Walter 3
SCHREINER, George Abel 5
SCHREINER, Oswald 5
SCHREMBS, Joseph 2
SCHRENK, Hermann von 1
SCHREYVOGEL, Charles 1
SCHRIBER, Louis 3
SCHRICKER, Henry 4
  Frederick
SCHRIECK, Sister Louise H
  Van der
SCHRIER, Allan Martin 9
SCHRIEVER, William 3
SCHRIVER, Edmund H
SCHRIVER, Lester 9
  Osborne
SCHROCK, Robert D. 7
SCHRODER, William 5
  Henry
SCHRÖDINGER, Erwin 4
SCHROEDER, Albert 4
  William
SCHROEDER, Alwin 4
SCHROEDER, Bernard A. 3
SCHROEDER, Carl A. 4
SCHROEDER, Charles 10
  Robbins
SCHROEDER, Ernest 1
  Charles
SCHROEDER, Frederick 1
  A.
SCHROEDER, George 6
  William
SCHROEDER, Henry 6
  Alfred

SCHROEDER, John 3
  Charles
SCHROEDER, John H
  Frederick
SCHROEDER, Joseph 5
  Edwin
SCHROEDER, Joseph 7
  Jerome
SCHROEDER, Joseph 8
  Jerome
SCHROEDER, Luther H. 9
SCHROEDER, Paul Louis 4
SCHROEDER, Reginald 4
SCHROEDER, Rudolph 3
  William
SCHROEDER, Seaton 1
SCHROEDER, Walter 4
SCHROEDER, Werner 4
  William
SCHROEDER, William 1
  Edward
SCHROEPFER, George 8
  John
SCHROFF, Joseph 4
SCHROPP, Rutledge 6
  Clifton
SCHROTH, Frank D. 7
SCHROY, Lee D. 8
SCHRUNK, Terry Doyle 6
SCHRUTH, Peter E. 7
SCHUBERT, Leo 7
SCHUCHARDT, Rudolph 1
  Frederick
SCHUCHARDT, William 3
  Herbert
SCHUCHERT, Charles 2
SCHUCK, Arthur Aloys 4
SCHUCK, Arthur Frederick 5
SCHUELEIN, Hermann 5
SCHUERMAN, William 1
  Henry
SCHUETTE, Conrad 1
  Herman Louis
SCHUETTE, Curt Nicolaus 6
SCHUETTE, Henry August 1
  Francis
SCHUETTE, Oswald 7
SCHUETTE, Walter Erwin 3
SCHUETTE, William 4
  Herman
SCHUETZ, Leonard 2
  William
SCHUETZ, Robert David 7
SCHUH, Henry Frederick 4
SCHUHMANN, George 1
  William
SCHUIRMANN, Roscoe 5
  Ernest
SCHUIRMANN, Roscoe 8
  Ernest
SCHULE, James Raymond 1
SCHULER, Anthony J. 2
SCHULER, Donald Vern 6
SCHULER, Hans 3
SCHULER, Henry J. 9
SCHULER, Loring Ashley 5
SCHULGEN, George 3
  Francis
SCHULHOFF, Henry 5
  Bernard
SCHULL, Herman Walter 5
SCHULLIAN, Dorothy 10
  May
SCHULLINGER, Rudolph 5
  Nicholas
SCHULMAIER, A. 3
  Talmage
SCHULMAN, Jack Henry 4
SCHULMAN, Samuel 3
SCHULTE, David A. 4
SCHULTE, Edward J. 8
SCHULTE, Herman von 1
  Wechlinger
SCHULTE, John H. 6
SCHULTE, Paul Clarence 8
SCHULTE, William Henry 3
SCHULTHEISS, Carl Max 4
SCHULTZ, Adolph H(ans) 7
SCHULTZ, Alfred Paul 6
SCHULTZ, Alfred Reginald 2
SCHULTZ, Clifford Griffith 8
SCHULTZ, Clinton M. 4
SCHULTZ, Edward Waters 5
SCHULTZ, Edwin William 8
SCHULTZ, Ernst William 1
SCHULTZ, George F. 5
SCHULTZ, Henry H
SCHULTZ, Henry 4
SCHULTZ, Henry Edward 7
SCHULTZ, Howard Louis 6
SCHULTZ, James Willard 2
SCHULTZ, John Richie 2
SCHULTZ, Louis 5
SCHULTZ, Martin C. 6
SCHULTZ, Sigrid (Lillian) 7
SCHULTZ, William Eben 4
SCHULTZE, Arthur 4

SCHULTZE, Augustus 1
SCHULTZE, Carl Emil 1
SCHULTZE, Leonard 3
SCHULZ, Carl Gustav 4
SCHULZ, Edward Hugh 3
SCHULZ, Ernst (Bernherd) 10
SCHULZ, George J. 7
SCHULZ, Leo 2
SCHULZE, J(ohn) William 2
SCHULZE, Paul 2
SCHULZE, Paul, Jr. 3
SCHUMACHER, Anton 5
  Herbert
SCHUMACHER, Bowen 7
  Emerson
SCHUMACHER, 1
  Ferdinand
SCHUMACHER, Henry 7
SCHUMACHER, Henry 5
  Cyril
SCHUMACHER, Matthew 4
  Aloysius
SCHUMACHER, Robert 10
  Kent
SCHUMACHER, Thomas 2
  Milton
SCHUMAKER, Albert 7
  Jesse Ringer
SCHUMAN, Frederick 7
  Lewis
SCHUMAN, Robert 4
SCHUMAN, William 10
  Howard
SCHUMANN, Edward 5
  Armin
SCHUMANN, John Joseph, 4
  Jr.
SCHUMANN-HEINK, 1
  Ernestine
SCHUMM, Herman Charles 3
SCHUMPETER, Joseph 2
  Alois
SCHUNEMAN, Martin H
  Gerretsen
SCHUNK, Arthur John 5
SCHUPP, Otto 4
SCHUPP, Robert William 2
SCHUR, Milton Oscar 10
SCHUREMAN, James H
SCHURICHT, Carl 4
SCHURMAN, George 9
  Munro
SCHURMAN, George 1
  Wellington
SCHURMAN, Jacob Gould 2
SCHURMAN, Jacob Gould 6
SCHURZ, Carl 1
SCHURZ, Carl Lincoln 1
SCHURZ, Franklin D. 9
SCHURZ, William Lytle 4
SCHURZ, William Lytle 7
SCHUSSELE, Christian H
SCHUSTER, Franklin 10
  Phillip
SCHUSTER, George Lee 4
SCHUSTER, Max Lincoln 10
SCHUTT, Harold Smith 4
SCHUTT, Walter Turvin 8
SCHUTTE, Charles 10
  Frederick
SCHUTTE, Louis Henry 3
SCHUTTLER, Peter 1
SCHUTZ, Anton (Friedrich 7
  Joseph)
SCHUTZE, Martin 3
SCHUTZER, Paul George 5
SCHUTZMAN, Julius 1
SCHUYLER, Aaron 1
SCHUYLER, Daniel J. 3
SCHUYLER, Eugene H
SCHUYLER, Garret 7
  Lansing
SCHUYLER, George H
  Washington
SCHUYLER, Hamilton 1
SCHUYLER, James Dix 1
SCHUYLER, James Marcus 10
SCHUYLER, Karl 1
  Cortlandt
SCHUYLER, Livingston 1
  Rowe
SCHUYLER, Margurita H
SCHUYLER, Montgomery 1
SCHUYLER, Montgomery 3
SCHUYLER, Peter H
SCHUYLER, Philip H
  Jeremiah
SCHUYLER, Philip John H
SCHUYLER, Philippa 4
  Duke
SCHUYLER, Walter 1
  Scribner
SCHUYLER, William 1
SCHWAB, Charles M. 1
SCHWAB, Francis Xavier 1
SCHWAB, Gustav Henry 1
SCHWAB, Harvey A. 3

SCHWAB, John Christopher 1
SCHWAB, John George 2
SCHWAB, Joseph Jackson 9
SCHWAB, Martin Constan 2
SCHWAB, Paul Josiah 4
SCHWAB, Robert Sidney 5
SCHWAB, Roy Valentine 5
SCHWAB, Sidney Isaac 2
SCHWABACHER, Albert E. 4
SCHWABACHER, James Herbert 3
SCHWABE, George Blaine 3
SCHWABE, H. August 1
SCHWACHA, George 9
SCHWACKE, John Henry 2
SCHWADA, John 10
SCHWAIN, Frank Robert 4
SCHWALM, Earl George 4
SCHWALM, Vernon Franklin 5
SCHWAMB, Herbert H. 4
SCHWAMB, Peter 4
SCHWAMM, Harvey 3
SCHWAN, Theodore 5
SCHWANTES, Arthur (John) 10
SCHWARDT, Herbert Henry 4
SCHWARTZ, A. Charles 4
SCHWARTZ, Abba Philip 10
SCHWARTZ, Abraham 8
SCHWARTZ, Alvin 10
SCHWARTZ, Andrew Thomas 2
SCHWARTZ, Arthur 8
SCHWARTZ, Arthur Harry 10
SCHWARTZ, B. Davis 5
SCHWARTZ, Charles 5
SCHWARTZ, Charles K. 9
SCHWARTZ, David 10
SCHWARTZ, Delmore 4
SCHWARTZ, Donald Edward 10
SCHWARTZ, George Melvin 9
SCHWARTZ, Hans Jorgen 3
SCHWARTZ, Harold 10
SCHWARTZ, Harwood Muzzy 2
SCHWARTZ, Herbert J. 5
SCHWARTZ, Isaac Hillson 5
SCHWARTZ, Jack William 3
SCHWARTZ, John H
SCHWARTZ, Julia Augusta 5
SCHWARTZ, Karl 1
SCHWARTZ, Lew 5
SCHWARTZ, Louis 4
SCHWARTZ, Maurice 4
SCHWARTZ, Milton Henry 5
SCHWARTZ, Samuel D. 5
SCHWARTZ, Sidney L. 7
SCHWARTZ, Thomas D. 10
SCHWARTZ, Walter Marshal, Sr.
SCHWARTZ, William Samuel 7
SCHWARTZ, William Spencer 5
SCHWARTZMAN, Daniel 7
SCHWARZ, Berthold Theodore Dominic 5
SCHWARZ, Edward R. 4
SCHWARZ, Frank Henry 3
SCHWARZ, Frederick August Otto 6
SCHWARZ, George Frederick 1
SCHWARZ, Gerhart Steven 8
SCHWARZ, Guenter 6
SCHWARZ, Helen Geneva 4
SCHWARZ, Henry Frederick 5
SCHWARZ, Otto Henry 3
SCHWARZ, Ralph Joseph 10
SCHWARZ, William Tefft 4
SCHWARZBURGER, Carl 4
SCHWARZE, William Nathaniel 2
SCHWARZENBACH, Ernest Blackbrook 5
SCHWARZKOPF, Paul 9
SCHWARZMANN, Herman J. H
SCHWARZSCHILD, William Harry 3
SCHWATKA, Frederick H
SCHWATT, Isaac Joachim 1
SCHWEBACH, James 1
SCHWEDTMAN, F. Charles 3
SCHWEGLER, Raymond Alfred 3
SCHWEICKHARD, Dean M. 9

SCHWEIGARDT, Frederick William 2
SCHWEIGERT, Bernard Sylvester 10
SCHWEIKER, Malcolm Alderfer 10
SCHWEIKERT, Harry Christian 1
SCHWEINFURTH, Charles Frederick 1
SCHWEINFURTH, Julius Adolph 1
SCHWEINHAUT, Henry Albert 5
SCHWEINITZ, Edmund Alexander H
SCHWEINITZ, Emil Alexander de 1
SCHWEINITZ, George Edmund de 1
SCHWEITER, Leo Henry 5
SCHWEITZER, Albert 4
SCHWEITZER, Gertrude Honig 10
SCHWEITZER, Paul 1
SCHWEITZER, Paul Henry 7
SCHWEIZER, Albert Charles 3
SCHWEIZER, J. Otto 5
SCHWELLENBACH, Edgar Ward 3
SCHWELLENBACH, Lewis Baxter 2
SCHWENDEMAN, J(oseph) R(aymond) 10
SCHWENDLER, William Theodore 7
SCHWENGEL, Frank Rudolph 6
SCHWENK, Erwin 9
SCHWENNING, Gustav Theodor 8
SCHWENTKER, Francis Frederic 3
SCHWEPPE, Alfred John 9
SCHWEPPE, Charles Hodgdon 1
SCHWERT, Pius Louis 1
SCHWERTNER, August John 1
SCHWIDETZKY, Oscar O. R. 4
SCHWIEGER, John Henry 9
SCHWIERING, Conrad 9
SCHWIERING, Oscar Conrad 7
SCHWIETERT, Arthur Henry 4
SCHWINGEL, Vincent John 5
SCHWINN, Frederick Sievers 5
SCHWINN, Sidoine Jordon 4
SCHWITALLA, Alphonse Mary 4
SCHWOEBEL, William Sylvester 9
SCHWYZER, Arnold 2
SCIASCIA, Leonardo 10
SCIDMORE, Eliza Ruhamah 1
SCIDMORE, George Hawthorne 1
SCIPIO, Lynn A. 5
SCISM, Don 3
SCISSON, Sidney E. 10
SCLATER, John Robert Paterson 3
SCOBIE, James Ralston 8
SCOFIELD, Carl Schurz 4
SCOFIELD, Cyrus Ingerson 1
SCOFIELD, Edward 1
SCOFIELD, Glenni William H
SCOFIELD, Louis A. 4
SCOFIELD, Perry Lee 6
SCOFIELD, Walter Keeler 1
SCOFIELD, William Bacon 1
SCOGGIN, William Allen 8
SCOGGINS, Charles Elbert 1
SCOLLARD, Clinton 1
SCONCE, Harvey James 2
SCOON, Robert 5
SCOPES, John T. 5
SCORE, John Nelson 2
SCOTFORD, John Ryland 8
SCOTSON-CLARK, George Frederick 1
SCOTT, Albert Lyon 2
SCOTT, Albert Woodburn, Jr. 5
SCOTT, Alexander Armstrong 4
SCOTT, Alfred James, Jr. 1
SCOTT, Alfred Witherspoon 6
SCOTT, Angelo Cyrus 1
SCOTT, Annie Velna 8

SCOTT, Arthur Carroll 1
SCOTT, Arthur Curtis 5
SCOTT, Arthur Ferdinand 8
SCOTT, Austin 1
SCOTT, Austin Wakeman 7
SCOTT, Bruce 1
SCOTT, Buford 6
SCOTT, Carlyle MacRoberts 2
SCOTT, Carrie Emma 2
SCOTT, Charles H
SCOTT, Charles 1
SCOTT, Charles E. 8
SCOTT, Charles Felton 2
SCOTT, Charles Frederick 1
SCOTT, Charles Herrington 5
SCOTT, Charles L. 3
SCOTT, Charles Payson Gurley 4
SCOTT, Charles Ray 8
SCOTT, Charlotte Angas 1
SCOTT, Clyde F. 6
SCOTT, Colin Alexander 1
SCOTT, Cyril Meir 7
SCOTT, D. R. 3
SCOTT, David H
SCOTT, Donald 4
SCOTT, Donnell Everett 3
SCOTT, Dred H
SCOTT, Earl Francis 1
SCOTT, Eben Greenough 1
SCOTT, Edwin William 6
SCOTT, Ellen C. 1
SCOTT, Elmer 3
SCOTT, Elmon 4
SCOTT, Emily M. 4
SCOTT, Emmett Jay 3
SCOTT, Ernest 1
SCOTT, Ernest 6
SCOTT, Ernest Darius 5
SCOTT, Ernest Findlay 3
SCOTT, Eugene Crampton 5
SCOTT, Fitzhugh 3
SCOTT, Flora Murray 9
SCOTT, Francis Markoe 1
SCOTT, Frank 8
SCOTT, Frank Augustus 2
SCOTT, Frank Hall 1
SCOTT, Frank Hamline 1
SCOTT, Frank Jesup 4
SCOTT, Franklin William 2
SCOTT, Fred Newton 1
SCOTT, Frederic William 4
SCOTT, Frederick Andrew 4
SCOTT, Frederick Bartlett 10
SCOTT, Frederick Hossack 1
SCOTT, Garfield 3
SCOTT, George 1
SCOTT, George Cromwell 2
SCOTT, George Eaton 1
SCOTT, George Gilmore 5
SCOTT, George Taylor 9
SCOTT, George Winfield 2
SCOTT, Gordon Hatler 5
SCOTT, Gustavus H
SCOTT, Guy Charles 1
SCOTT, Hamilton Gray 4
SCOTT, Harold W(illiam) 9
SCOTT, Harold Wilson 5
SCOTT, Harriet Maria 1
SCOTT, Harvey David H
SCOTT, Harvey W. 1
SCOTT, Henri 2
SCOTT, Henry Clay 6
SCOTT, Henry Dickerson 2
SCOTT, Henry Edwards 2
SCOTT, Henry Tiffany 1
SCOTT, Henry Wilson 2
SCOTT, Herbert 5
SCOTT, Hermon Hosmer 6
SCOTT, Homer Verlyn 10
SCOTT, Hugh Briar 4
SCOTT, Hugh Lenox 1
SCOTT, Hugh McDonald 1
SCOTT, Irving Murray 1
SCOTT, Isaac MacBurney 1
SCOTT, Isaiah Benjamin 1
SCOTT, J. G. 6
SCOTT, Jack Garrett 3
SCOTT, James Brown 2
SCOTT, James Edward 5
SCOTT, James Hutchison 4
SCOTT, James Ralph 8
SCOTT, James T. 7
SCOTT, James Wilmot H
SCOTT, Jeannette 1
SCOTT, Jerome Hayes 8
SCOTT, Job H
SCOTT, John* H
SCOTT, John 1
SCOTT, John 7
SCOTT, John Adams 2
SCOTT, John Addison 3
SCOTT, John Alden 9
SCOTT, John Dilworth 7
SCOTT, John Guier H
SCOTT, John Hart 4

SCOTT, John Hull 7
SCOTT, John Irving Elias 7
SCOTT, John Loughran 4
SCOTT, John Marcy 5
SCOTT, John Morin H
SCOTT, John Prindle 1
SCOTT, John R. K. 2
SCOTT, John Randolph H
SCOTT, John Reed 5
SCOTT, John Virgil 8
SCOTT, John William 1
SCOTT, Jonathan French 2
SCOTT, Joseph 3
SCOTT, Joseph Welch 7
SCOTT, Julia Green 1
SCOTT, Julian 1
SCOTT, K. Frances 8
SCOTT, Leland Wakefield 10
SCOTT, Leroy 1
SCOTT, Leslie M. 6
SCOTT, Leslie Wright 9
SCOTT, Llewellyn Davis 1
SCOTT, Lon Allen 1
SCOTT, Louis Allen 6
SCOTT, Lucy Jameson 1
SCOTT, Martin J. 3
SCOTT, Mary Augusta 1
SCOTT, Miriam Finn 2
SCOTT, Nathan Bay 1
SCOTT, N(athan) Stone 8
SCOTT, Norman 3
SCOTT, Norman 5
SCOTT, Orange H
SCOTT, Oreon Earle 3
SCOTT, Paul Ryrie 4
SCOTT, Paul Whitten 3
SCOTT, Sir Peter (Markham) 10
SCOTT, Philip B. 4
SCOTT, Philip Drennen 4
SCOTT, Richard H. 1
SCOTT, Richard Hugh 2
SCOTT, Richard John Ernst 1
SCOTT, Robert 4
SCOTT, R(obert) D(ouglas) 6
SCOTT, Robert Kingston 1
SCOTT, Robert Lindsay 3
SCOTT, Robert Nicholson H
SCOTT, Roger Burdette 5
SCOTT, Roy Wesley 3
SCOTT, Russell B(urton) 5
SCOTT, S. Spencer 5
SCOTT, Samuel Parsons 1
SCOTT, Stuart Nash 10
SCOTT, Sutton Selwyn 1
SCOTT, Theodore P. 8
SCOTT, Thomas 3
SCOTT, Thomas Alexander H
SCOTT, Thomas Fielding 1
SCOTT, Thomas Morton 1
SCOTT, Tom 4
SCOTT, Tully 5
SCOTT, Walter H
SCOTT, Walter 1
SCOTT, Walter Canfield 3
SCOTT, Walter Dill 3
SCOTT, Walter E., Jr. 3
SCOTT, Walter Tandy 8
SCOTT, Wendell G(arrison) 5
SCOTT, Wilfred Welday 1
SCOTT, Will 1
SCOTT, Willard 4
SCOTT, William H
SCOTT, William 1
SCOTT, William Amasa 2
SCOTT, William Anderson H
SCOTT, William Berryman 2
SCOTT, William Earl Dodge 1
SCOTT, William Edouard 4
SCOTT, William Edouard 7
SCOTT, William Forse 1
SCOTT, William George 10
SCOTT, William Henry 1
SCOTT, William John 9
SCOTT, William Kerr 3
SCOTT, William Lawrence H
SCOTT, William R. 1
SCOTT, William Sherley 1
SCOTT, William Wilson 4
SCOTT, Willis Howard 4
SCOTT, Winfield H
SCOTT, Winfield Townley 5
SCOTTEN, Robert McGregor 5
SCOTTEN, Samuel Chatman 1
SCOTT-HUNTER, George 5
SCOTTI, Antonio 1
SCOULAR, Florence Isabelle 10
SCOULLER, James Brown 1
SCOULLER, John Crawford 1
SCOVEL, Sylvester 7
SCOVEL, Sylvester Fithian H
SCOVELL, Melville Amasa 1

SCOVIL, Samuel 3
SCOVILL, Hiram Thompson 7
SCOVILLE, Annie Beecher 5
SCOVILLE, Harold Ralph 6
SCOVILLE, Herbert, Jr. 8
SCOVILLE, Jonathan H
SCOVILLE, Joseph Alfred H
SCOVILLE, Robert 1
SCOVILLE, Samuel, Jr. 3
SCOVILLE, Wilbur Lincoln 4
SCOWDEN, Frank F. 7
SCRANTON, Cassius A. 5
SCRANTON, George Whitefield H
SCRANTON, Marion Margery Warren 4
SCRANTON, Worthington 3
SCREWS, William Preston 5
SCREWS, William Wallace 1
SCRIBNER, Allison Kenneth 10
SCRIBNER, Arthur Hawley 1
SCRIBNER, Charles H
SCRIBNER, Charles 1
SCRIBNER, Charles 3
SCRIBNER, Charles Ezra 1
SCRIBNER, Frank Jay 4
SCRIBNER, Frank Kimball 1
SCRIBNER, George Kline 4
SCRIBNER, Gilbert Hilton 1
SCRIBNER, Gilbert Hilton 4
SCRIBNER, Gilbert Hilton 5
SCRIBNER, Gilbert Hilton, Jr. 9
SCRIBNER, Harvey 1
SCRIBNER, Joseph M. 7
SCRIBNER, Mrs. Lucy Skidmore 1
SCRIMENTI, Adolph Robert 8
SCRIMSHAW, Stewart 7
SCRIPPS, Edward Wyllis 1
SCRIPPS, James Edmund 1
SCRIPPS, James G(eorge) 9
SCRIPPS, John Locke H
SCRIPPS, John P. 10
SCRIPPS, Robert Paine 1
SCRIPPS, William Edmund 3
SCRIPTURE, Edward Wheeler 4
SCRIPTURE, Elizabeth 7
SCRIPTURE, William Ellis 1
SCRIVEN, George Percival 1
SCROGGS, Joseph Whitefield 4
SCROGGS, William Oscar 3
SCRUGGS, Anderson M. 3
SCRUGGS, Loyd 5
SCRUGGS, William Lindsay 1
SCRUGGS, William Marvin 3
SCRUGHAM, James Graves 2
SCRUGHAM, William Warburton 2
SCRYMSER, James Alexander 1
SCUDDER, Charles Locke 2
SCUDDER, Doremus 2
SCUDDER, Edward Wallace 3
SCUDDER, Henry Joel H
SCUDDER, Horace Elisha 1
SCUDDER, Hubert B. 5
SCUDDER, Isaac Williamson H
SCUDDER, Janet 1
SCUDDER, John H
SCUDDER, John Anderson H
SCUDDER, John Milton H
SCUDDER, Moses Lewis 1
SCUDDER, Myron Tracy 1
SCUDDER, Nathaniel H
SCUDDER, Samuel Hubbard 1
SCUDDER, Townsend 3
SCUDDER, Townsend, III 9
SCUDDER, Tredwell 5
SCUDDER, Vida Dutton 1
SCUDDER, Wallace McIlvaine 3
SCUDDER, Zeno H
SCULL, John H
SCULLEN, Anthony James 1
SCULLY, C. Alison 3
SCULLY, Cornelius Decatur 6
SCULLY, Hugh Day 5
SCULLY, James Wall 1
SCULLY, Thomas J. 1
SCULLY, William A. 1
SCULLY, William Augustine 1
SCUPHAM, George William 5

SCUPIN, Carl Albert 5
SCURFIELD, Ralph 8
Thomas
SCURRY, Richardson H
SEABERRY, Virgil 4
Theodore
SEABROOK, C. F. 4
SEABROOK, William 2
Buehler
SEABROOKE, Thomas Q. 1
SEABURY, Charles Ward 4
SEABURY, David 4
SEABURY, David 4
SEABURY, Francis William 2
SEABURY, George Tilley 2
SEABURY, John Ward 9
SEABURY, Samuel* H
SEABURY, Samuel 3
SEABURY, William Jones 1
SEABURY, William 2
Marston
SEACHREST, Effie M. 3
SEACREST, Frederick 5
Snively
SEACREST, Joseph 2
Claggett
SEAGER, Allan 5
SEAGER, Charles Allen 2
SEAGER, Henry Rogers 1
SEAGER, Lawrence H. 1
SEAGLE, Oscar 2
SEAGLE, William 7
SEAGO, Erwin 5
SEAGRAM, Joseph 7
Edward Frowde
SEAGRAVE, Frank Evans 1
SEAGRAVE, Gordon 4
Stiffer
SEAGRAVE, Louis H. 4
SEAGROVE, Gordon Kay 4
SEAL, Charles R(yland) 9
SEAL, John Frederick 4
SEAL, John Ridley 9
SEAL, Leo W. 8
SEALOCK, William Elmer 1
SEALS, Carl H. 3
SEALS, John H. 5
SEALS, Woodrow 10
SEALSFIELD, Charles H
SEALY, Donald Farrington 10
SEALY, Frank L. 1
SEALY, Tom 10
SEAMAN, A(lbert) Owen 6
SEAMAN, Arthur Edmund 1
SEAMAN, Augusta Huiell 3
SEAMAN, Elizabeth 4
Cochrane
SEAMAN, Eugene Cecil 1
SEAMAN, George Milton 1
SEAMAN, Gilbert Edmund 1
SEAMAN, Henry Bowman 1
SEAMAN, Henry John H
SEAMAN, Irving 6
SEAMAN, John Thompson 3
SEAMAN, Louis Livingston 1
SEAMAN, William Grant 4
SEAMAN, William Henry* 1
SEAMANS, Clarence 1
Walker
SEAMANS, Frank L. 9
SEARBY, Edmund Wilson 2
SEARCH, Frederick 8
Preston
SEARCH, Preston Willis 1
SEARCH, Theodore Corson 1
SEARCY, Chesley Hunter 1
SEARCY, Mrs. Earle 5
Benjamin
SEARCY, Hubert Floyd 5
SEARCY, James Thomas 4
SEARER, Jay Charles 5
SEARER, R. Floyd 8
SEARES, Frederick Hanley 6
SEARING, Hudson Roy 1
SEARING, John Alexander H
SEARING, Laura Catherine 4
Redden
SEARLE, Alonzo T. 1
SEARLE, Arthur 1
SEARLE, Augustus Leach 1
SEARLE, Charles James 1
SEARLE, Charles Putnam 1
SEARLE, George Mary 1
SEARLE, Harriet 5
Richardson (Mrs. Wiliam
D. Searle)
SEARLE, James H
SEARLE, John Gideon 7
SEARLE, John Preston 1
SEARLE, Robert Wyckoff 5
SEARLE, Robert Wycroff 4
SEARLES, Colbert 1
SEARLES, John Ennis 1
SEARLES, John William 1
SEARLES, William Henry 1
SEARLS, Carroll 5
SEARLS, David Thomas 5

SEARS, Arthur, Jr. 8
SEARS, Barnabas Francis 8
SEARS, Barnas H
SEARS, Charles Brown 3
SEARS, Charles Hatch 2
SEARS, Clinton Brooks 1
SEARS, Edmund Hamilton H
SEARS, Edmund Hamilton 2
SEARS, Ernest Robert 10
SEARS, Francis Philip 5
SEARS, Francis W(eston) 6
SEARS, Frank Irving 3
SEARS, Fred Coleman 3
SEARS, Frederick W. 1
SEARS, Frederick William 1
SEARS, George Gray 1
SEARS, George Wallace 6
SEARS, Herbert Mason 2
SEARS, Hess Thatcher 5
SEARS, Isaac H
SEARS, James Hamilton 1
SEARS, Jesse Brundage 5
SEARS, John Van Der Zee 4
SEARS, Joseph Hamblen 2
SEARS, Julian D(ucker) 5
SEARS, Kenneth Craddock 4
SEARS, Laurence 3
SEARS, Lester Merriam 4
SEARS, Lorenzo 2
SEARS, Nathan Pratt 2
SEARS, Nathaniel Clinton 1
SEARS, Paul Bigelow 9
SEARS, Philip Mason 6
SEARS, Philip S. 3
SEARS, Richard Warren 1
SEARS, Robert H
SEARS, Robert Richardson 10
SEARS, Russell Adams 1
SEARS, Samuel Powers 4
SEARS, Sarah Choate 1
SEARS, Taber 3
SEARS, Walter Herbert 1
SEARS, Walter James 1
SEARS, Willard Thomas 1
SEARS, William Gray (Will 10
Sears)
SEARS, William Henry 1
SEARS, William Joseph 2
SEARS, Willis G. 5
SEARS, Zelda 1
SEARSON, James William 1
SEASHORE, August 1
Theodore
SEASHORE, Carl Emil 2
SEASHORE, Robert 3
Holmes
SEASONGOOD, Murray 7
SEASTONE, charles Victor 6
SEASTONE, Charles Victor 6
SEATH, John 7
SEATH, John 8
SEATH, William 7
SEATON, Frederick 6
Andrew
SEATON, George 7
SEATON, John Lawrence 4
SEATON, John Lawrence 5
SEATON, Roy Andrew 5
SEATON, William Winston H
SEATTLE H
SEAVER, Ebenezer H
SEAVER, Edwin Pliny 1
SEAVER, Frank Roger 4
SEAVER, Fred Jay 5
SEAVER, Henry Latimer 5
SEAVER, Jay John 7
SEAVER, Kenneth 1
SEAVERNS, Joel Herbert 4
SEAVEY, Clyde Leroy 2
SEAVEY, Warren Abner 4
SEAWELL, Aaron Ashley 3
Flowers
SEAWELL, Emmet 1
SEAWELL, Herbert Floyd 1
SEAWELL, Molly Elliott 1
SEAY, Abraham Jefferson 1
SEAY, Edward Tucker 2
SEAY, Edward Ward 8
SEAY, Frank 3
SEAY, George James 3
SEAY, Harry Lauderdale 5
SEAY, William Albert 5
SEBALD, Joseph Francis 8
SEBALD, Weber William 4
SEBALD, William Joseph 7
SEBAST, Frederick Martin 1
SEBASTIAN, Benjamin H
SEBASTIAN, Jerome D. 1
SEBASTIAN, John 8
SEBASTIAN, William King H
SEBELIUS, Keith George 9
SEBELIUS, Sven Johan 3
SEBENIUS, John Uno 5
SEBENTHALL, Elizabeth 7
Roberta
SEBREE, Edmund B. 4
SEBREE, Uriel 1

SEBRELL, William Henry, 10
Jr.
SEBRING, Harold Leon 5
SECCOMB, John H
SECHER, Samuel H
SECKENDORFF, Max 1
Gebhard
SECKLER-HUDSON, 4
Catheryn
SECONDARI, John 6
Hermes
SECOR, John Alstyne 4
SECORD, Arthur Wellesley 3
SECORD, Frederick 4
SECRIST, Horace 2
SECUNDA, Sholom 6
SEDDON, James H
SEDDON, William Little 1
SEDER, Arthur Raymond 5
SEDGWICK, Allan E. 2
SEDGWICK, Anne 1
Douglas
SEDGWICK, Arthur 1
George
SEDGWICK, Catharine H
Maria
SEDGWICK, Charles H
Baldwin
SEDGWICK, Ellery, Jr. 10
SEDGWICK, Francis 5
Minturn
SEDGWICK, Henry H
Dwight
SEDGWICK, Henry 1
Dwight
SEDGWICK, Henry 3
Dwight
SEDGWICK, John H
SEDGWICK, Julius Parker 1
SEDGWICK, Paul J(oseph) 6
SEDGWICK, Robert H
SEDGWICK, Samuel 1
Hopkins
SEDGWICK, Theodore* H
SEDGWICK, Theodore, 2d 2
SEDGWICK, William 1
Thompson
SEDITA, Frank Albert 6
SEDLANDER, Norman 1
Robert
SEDLAR, Sasa 6
SEDLEY, Henry 1
SEDWICK, Ellery 4
SEE, Elliot M. 4
SEE, Harold Philip 5
SEE, Horace 1
SEE, Thomas Jefferson 4
Jackson
SEEBIRT, Eli Fowler 3
SEED, Harry Bolton 10
SEED, Thomas Finis 9
SEEDS, Asa Elmore 7
SEEDS, Russel M. 4
SEEGAL, David 5
SEEGER, Alan 4
SEEGER, Charles Louis 2
SEEGER, Charles Louis 6
SEEGER, Edwin W. 3
SEEGER, Eugene 4
SEEGER, Stanley Joseph 3
SEEGER, Walter G. 5
SEEGERS, John Conrad 5
SEEGMILLER, Wilhelmina 1
SEEGRABER, Frank 9
Joseph
SEEL, George Augustus 8
SEELBACH, Louis 5
SEELE, Keith C(edric) 6
SEELER, Albert Otto 6
SEELER, Albert Otto 7
SEELER, Edgar Viguers 1
SEELEY, Elias P. H
SEELEY, Frank Barrows 3
SEELEY, John Edward H
SEELEY, Levi 1
SEELEY, Paul Stark 5
SEELEY, Walter James 6
SEELIG, M. G. 5
SEELOS, Francis X. H
SEELVE, Laurens Hickok 4
SEELY, Elizabeth Caven 7
SEELY, Fred B. 7
SEELY, Fred Loring 4
SEELY, Henry Martyn 1
SEELY, Herman Gastrell 3
SEELY, Walter Hoff 1
SEELYE, Elizabeth 3
Eggleston
SEELYE, Julius Hawley 1
SEELYE, L. Clark 1
SEELYE, Theodore Edward 4
SEEM, Ralph Berger 10
SEEMAN, Bernard 10
SEEMAN, Ernest 8
SEENER, Ralph Berger 8
SEERLEY, Frank Newell 4
SEERLEY, Homer Horatio 4

SEES, John Vincent 2
SEESTED, August 1
Frederick
SEEVER, William John 2
SEEVERS, Charles 4
Hamilton
SEEVERS, Maurice 7
Harrison
SEEVERS, William Henry H
SEFERIADES, George 9
SEFRIT, Frank Ira 3
SEGAL, Bernice G. 10
SEGAL, Harry Louis 10
SEGAL, Martin 8
SEGAL, Paul Moses 5
SEGAR, Joseph Eggleston H
SEGAR, Louis Harold 9
SEGEL, David 5
SEGEL, Ronald George 10
SEGER, Charles Bronson 1
SEGER, George N. 1
SEGER, Gerhart Henry 3
SEGER, Walter G. 7
SEGHERS, Anna 7
SEGHERS, Charles Jean H
SEGHERS, Paul d'Otrenge 10
SEGNI, Antonio 5
SEGOE, Ladislas 10
SEGOVIA, Andres 9
SEGRÈ, Emilio 10
SEGUIN, Edouard 1
SEGUIN, Edward Constant H
SEHRT, Edward Henry 8
SEIBEL, Clifford Winslow 8
SEIBEL, Frederick Otto 5
SEIBEL, George 3
SEIBELS, Edwin Granville 3
SEIBELS, George 5
Goldthwaite
SEIBERLING, Charles 2
Willard
SEIBERLING, Francis 1
SEIBERLING, Frank A. 3
SEIBERT, Florence Barbara 10
SEIBERT, James Walter 4
SEIBERT, John F. 1
SEIBERT, Walter R. 4
SEIBERT, William Adam 1
SEIBOLD, Louis 2
SEIBOLD, Myron James 5
SEID, Herman 9
SEIDEL, Emil 2
SEIDEL, Harry George 6
SEIDEL, John George 6
SEIDEL, Toscha 4
SEIDEMANN, Henry Peter 3
SEIDENBAUM, Art David 10
SEIDENBUSH, Rupert H
SEIDENSTICKER, Oswald H
SEIDERS, George Melville 1
SEIDL, Anton 1
SEIDL, Frank J(oseph) 6
SEIDLIN, Oskar 7
SEIDLITZ, Walter George 6
SEIDMAN, Jacob Stewart 9
SEIDNER, Howard Mayo 7
SEIF, William Henry 1
SEIFERHELD, David 10
Froehlich
SEIFERT, Elizabeth (Mrs. 8
John Gasparotti)
SEIFERT, Mathias Joseph 2
SEIFERT, Ralph Louis 9
(Edwin)
SEIFERTH, Solis 10
SEIFRIZ, William 3
SEIGFRED, Earl Covert 5
SEIGLE, John Sanders 6
SEIGNOBOSC, Francoise 4
SEILER, Alexander Walter 7
SEILER, Paul Waldo 8
SEIME, Reuben Ingmar 6
SEINSHEIMER, J. Fellman 3
SEIP, Theodore Lorenzo 1
SEISS, Joseph Augustus 1
SEITZ, Albert Blazier 5
SEITZ, Charles Edward 5
SEITZ, Don Carlos 1
SEITZ, Frank Noah 4
SEITZ, George Albert 2
SEITZ, Ira James 5
SEITZ, William Chapin 6
SEITZ, William Chapin 6
SEIVER, George Otto 4
SEIXAS, Frank Archibald 10
SEIXAS, Gershom Mendes H
SEJOUR, Victor H
SEKERA, Zdenek 5
SEKERS, Nicholas Thomas 5
SELBY, Augustine Dawson 1
SELBY, Charles Baxter 4
SELBY, Clarence Davey 6
SELBY, Howard Williams 6
SELBY, John Allen 7
SELBY, Mark Webster 5
SELBY, Paul Owen 7
SELBY, Roger A. 7

SELBY, Thomas Jefferson 4
SELBY, William H
SELDEN, Albert W. 9
SELDEN, Armistead Inge, 9
Jr.
SELDEN, Charles A(lbert) 5
SELDEN, Dudley 5
SELDEN, George Baldwin 4
SELDEN, Lynde 5
SELDERS, Gilbert Vivian 10
SELDES, Gilbert (Vivian) 5
SELDIS, Henry James 7
SELDOMRIDGE, Harry 4
Hunter
SELECMAN, Charles 3
Claude
SELEKMAN, Benjamin 4
Morris
SELEY, Jason 8
SELF, Sir Henry 8
SELF, James C. 5
SELF, Victor H(arrison) 8
SELF, William King 6
SELFE, Robert W. 10
SELFOGEL, Morris 5
Richard
SELFRIDGE, Calvin 7
Frederick
SELFRIDGE, Harry 2
Gordon
SELFRIDGE, Thomas 1
Oliver*
SELIG, Lester North 5
SELIG, William Nicholas 2
SELIGER, Robert V. 5
SELIGMAN, Albert Joseph 1
SELIGMAN, Arnold Max 7
SELIGMAN, Arthur 1
SELIGMAN, Ben B(aruch) 5
SELIGMAN, Edwin Robert 1
Anderson
SELIGMAN, Eustace 7
SELIGMAN, Germain 7
SELIGMAN, Henry 1
SELIGMAN, Isaac Newton 1
SELIGMAN, Jefferson 1
SELIGMAN, Jesse H
SELIGMAN, Joseph H
SELIGMAN, Selig Jacob 5
SELIGMANN, Kurt 4
SELIJNS, Henricus H
SELIKOFF, Irving John 10
SELINGER, Jean Paul 1
SELKE, George Albert 5
SELKE, W(ilhelm) Erich 5
(Christian)
SELL, Edward Herman 1
Miller
SELL, Edward Scott 8
SELL, Henry Blackman 6
SELL, Henry Thorne 1
SELL, Lewis L. 3
SELL, Stephen 10
SELLAR, Robert F. 3
SELLARDS, Elias Howard 5
SELLARS, Roy Woods 6
SELLARS, Walter Bailey 7
SELLECK, Clyde Andrew 8
SELLECK, Willard 2
Chamberlain
SELLECK, William Alson 2
SELLEN, Arthur Godfrey 1
SELLERS, Charles Wilbur 8
SELLERS, Coleman 1
SELLERS, Coleman, Jr. 1
SELLERS, David Foote 2
SELLERS, Edwin Jaquett 4
SELLERS, Henry Eugene 7
SELLERS, Horace Wells 4
SELLERS, Isaiah H
SELLERS, James Clark 6
SELLERS, James Freeman 1
SELLERS, James McBrayer 10
SELLERS, Kathryn 1
SELLERS, Mark Ashley 7
SELLERS, Matthew Bacon 1
SELLERS, Ovid Rogers 7
SELLERS, Peter 7
SELLERS, Richard Morgan 10
SELLERS, Robert Daniel 4
SELLERS, Robert Henry 4
SELLERS, Sandford 1
SELLERS, Sandford, Jr. 9
SELLERS, Walton Preston 6
SELLERS, William H
SELLERY, George Clarke 4
SELLEW, George Tucker 4
SELLEW, Walter Ashbel 1
SELLING, Laurence 7
SELLMAN, William Nelson 4
SELLS, Cato 5
SELLS, Elijah Watt 1
SELLS, John F(rancis) 8
SELLS, Saul B. 9
SELLSTEDT, Lars Gustaf 1
SELMER, Ernst Westerlund 5
SELTZER, Charles Alden 1

SELTZER, Leon Eugene 9
SELTZER, Louis Benson 7
SELTZER, Theodore 3
SELVAGE, Watson 5
SELVIDGE, Robert 2
Washington
SELVIG, Conrad George 3
SELWYN, Edgar 2
SELYE, Hans 8
SELYE, Lewis H
SELZ, Lawrence 4
Hochstadter
SELZER, Arthur 10
SELZER, Charles Louis 10
SELZNICK, David Oliver 4
SELZNICK, Irene Mayer 10
SEMAN, Philip Louis 3
SEMANS, Edwin Walker 5
SEMANS, Harry Merrick 5
SEMBACH, J. 6
SEMBOWER, Alta Brunt 5
SEMBOWER, Charles 5
Jacob
SEMBRICH, Marcella 1
SEMELROTH, William 4
James
SEMENENKO, Serge 7
SEMLER, George Herbert 3
SEMMANN, Liborius 5
SEMMES, Alexander H
Jenkins
SEMMES, Benedict Joseph 4
SEMMES, John Edward 4
SEMMES, Raphael H
SEMMES, Thomas Jenkins
SEMNACHER, Wiliam M. 4
SEMPLE, Ellen Churchill 1
SEMPLE, Florence Emma 8
SEMPLE, Henry Churchill 1
SEMPLE, James
SEMPLE, Robert Baylor 9
SEMPLE, William Tunstall 4
SEMRAD, Charles A. 7
SEMRAD, Elvin Vavrinec 7
SEMSCH, Otto Francis 4
SENAN, Jose Francisco de H
Paula
SENANAYAKE, Don 3
Stephen
SENANAYAKE, Dudley 5
Shelton
SENCENBAUGH, Charles 3
Wilbur
SENDER, Ramon José 8
SENDON, Andres 10
Rodriguez
SENEAR, Francis Eugene 3
SENEFF, Edward H. 1
SENER, James Beverley H
SENEY, George Ingraham H
SENEY, Henry William 4
SENEY, Joshua 1
SENFT, Craig T. 6
SENGIER, Edgar 4
SENGSTACK, John 5
F(rederick)
SENIOR, Clair Marcil 1
SENIOR, Clarence 6
SENIOR, Harold Dickinson 1
SENIOR, John Lawson 1
SENIOR, Joseph Howe 5
SENIOR, Samuel Palmer 4
SENN, Milton John Edward 10
SENN, Nicholas 1
SENN, Pettus Holmes 9
SENN, Thomas J. 2
SENNER, Joseph Henry 1
SENNET, George Burritt H
SENNETT, Mach 4
SENNETT, Mack H
SENNING, John Peter 3
SENOUR, Charles 1
SENSENBRENNER, Frank 3
Jacob
SENSENBRENNER, John 7
Stilp
SENSENBRENNER, John 6
Stilp
SENSENBRENNER, 10
Maynard E.
SENSENEY, George Eyster 2
SENSENICH, Roscoe 4
Lloyd
SENSENIG, David Martin 1
SENTELL, George 3
Washington
SENTELLE, Mark Edgar 3
SENTER, John Henry 4
SENTER, Leon B. 4
SENTER, Ralph Townsend 4
SENTER, William Tandy H
SENTNER, David 6
SENTNER, P. David 4
SENTNER, Richard 5
Faulkner
SENYSHYN, Ambrose 7
Andrew

SEPPELT, Ian Howe 6
SEQUOYAH H
SERAFIN, Tullio 4
SERAKOFF, Leonard 5
SERA Y SERRANO, Jose 9
Agustin
SERESS, Raoul 4
SERFASS, Earl James 8
SERGEANT, Elizabeth 4
Shepley
SERGEANT, John* H
SERGEANT, Jonathan H
Dickinson
SERGEANT, Thomas H
SERGEL, Charles Hubbard 1
SERKIN, Rudolf 10
SERLES, Earl R. 3
SERLIN, Oscar 5
SERLING, Rod 6
SERLIS, Harry George 8
SEROTA, Herman Michael 9
SEROTTA, Elliott Cecil 6
SERPELL, Susan Watkins 1
SERRA, Junipero H
SERRELL, Edward 1
Wellmann
SERRIES, Mavis McGrew 6
SERRILL, William Jones 3
SERT, Jose Luis 8
SERVAAS, Sandra Jean 7
SERVEN, Abram Ralph 2
SERVICE, Robert William 3
SERVISS, Frederick 3
Leverne
SERVISS, Garrett Putman 1
SERVOSS, Thomas Lowery H
SESKIS, I. J. 3
SESSA, Frank Bowman 9
SESSINGHAUS, Gustavus 1
SESSIONS, Charles H. 2
SESSIONS, Clarence 1
William
SESSIONS, Edson Oliver 9
SESSIONS, Kenosha 2
SESSIONS, Robert Evans 9
SESSIONS, Roger 8
Huntington
SESSIONS, Walter Loomis 1
SESSIONS, William Edwin 1
SESSUMS, Davis 1
SESTINI, Benedict H
SETCHELL, William Albert 2
SETE, Bola (Djalma de 9
Andrade)
SETH, Julien Orem 4
SETO, Yeb Jo 8
SETON, Anya 10
SETON, Elizabeth Ann H
Bayley
SETON, Ernest Thompson 2
SETON, Grace Thompson 3
SETON, Julia 4
SETON, Robert 1
SETTERBERG, Carl 8
SETTERFIELD, Hugh E. 3
SETTI, Giulio 2
SETTLE, Evan E. 1
SETTLE, George Thomas 1
SETTLE, Peverill Ozroe 8
SETTLE, Raymond W. 9
SETTLE, Thomas* H
SETTLE, Thomas 7
Greenhow Williams
SETTLE, Warner Ellmore 4
SETTLEMIRE, Claude 7
Laprell
SETTLEMYER, Claude 10
Harold
SETZE, Julius Adolphus 3
SETZER, Richard 5
Woodrow
SETZLER, Edwin Lake 7
SETZLER, Frank Maryl 6
SEUBERT, Edward George 2
SEULKE, Karl John 8
SEVER, George Francis 4
SEVERANCE, Caroline 1
Maria Seymour
SEVERANCE, Cordenio 1
Arnold
SEVERANCE, Frank 1
Hayward
SEVERANCE, Henry 2
Ormal
SEVERANCE, John Long 1
SEVERANCE, Luther H
SEVERANCE, Mark Sibley 4
SEVERENS, Henry 4
Franklin
SEVERINGHAUS, Aura 7
Edward
SEVERINGHAUS, John 9
Walter
SEVERN, Edmund 3
SEVERS, John Ward 4
SEVERSKY, Alexander P. 6
de

SEVERSON, Harold 6
Clifford
SEVERSON, Lewis Everett 4
SEVERY, Melvin Linwood 4
SEVEY, Robert 3
SEVIER, Ambrose Hundley H
SEVIER, Charles Edwin 4
SEVIER, Clara Driscoll 6
SEVIER, Henry Hulme 1
SEVIER, Henry Hulme 2
SEVIER, John H
SEVIER, Joseph Ramsey 5
SEVIER, Landers 3
SEVIER, Randolph 4
SEVIGNY, Albert 4
SEVITZKY, Fabien 4
SEWALL, Arthur 1
SEWALL, Arthur 1
Wollaston
SEWALL, Charles S. H
SEWALL, Edmund 1
Devereux
SEWALL, Frank 1
SEWALL, Harold Marsh 1
SEWALL, Harriet Winslow H
SEWALL, Henry 1
SEWALL, James Wingate 2
SEWALL, John Smith 1
SEWALL, Jonathan 1
SEWALL, Jonathan H
Mitchell
SEWALL, Lee Goodrich 5
SEWALL, May Wright 1
SEWALL, Rufus King 1
SEWALL, Samuel* H
SEWALL, Stephen H
SEWALL, Sydney 6
SEWARD, Allin Carey, Jr. 5
SEWARD, Coy Avon 1
SEWARD, Frederick 1
William
SEWARD, George 1
Frederick
SEWARD, George Winn 6
SEWARD, Herbert Lee 4
SEWARD, James Lindsay H
SEWARD, John Perry 1
SEWARD, Merritt Elmer 8
SEWARD, Samuel Swayze 1
SEWARD, Samuel Swayze, 1
Jr.
SEWARD, Theodore 1
Frelinghuysen
SEWARD, William H
SEWARD, William Henry H
SEWARD, William Henry 1
SEWELL, Albert Henry 1
SEWELL, Amanda 1
Brewster
SEWELL, Dan Roy 6
SEWELL, Frank Asa 5
SEWELL, Jesse Parker 5
SEWELL, John Stephen 1
SEWELL, Oscar Marion 1
SEWELL, Robert van Vorst 1
SEWELL, Warren Pelmer 6
SEWELL, William Joyce 1
SEXAUER, Elmer H. 8
SEXSON, John Amherst 6
SEXTON, Anne Harvey 6
SEXTON, George Samuel 1
SEXTON, Harold Eustace 5
SEXTON, John Chase 1
SEXTON, John Moody 5
SEXTON, Lawrence Eugene 1
SEXTON, Leonidas H
SEXTON, Lewis Albert 1
SEXTON, Pliny Titus 1
SEXTON, Sherman J. 4
SEXTON, Thomas 1
Lawrence
SEXTON, Thomas Scott 5
SEXTON, Walton Roswell 2
SEXTON, William Henry 3
SEXTON, William Thomas 3
SEYA, Charles Louis 1
SEYBERT, Adam H
SEYBERT, Henry H
SEYBERT, John H
SEYBOLD, Lawrence F. 10
SEYBOLD, Roscoe 7
SEYBOLD, Robert Francis 3
SEYDELL, Ernest Morris 7
SEYDOUX, Roger 8
SEYFARTH, Henry 10
Edward
SEYFERT, Carl Keenan 4
SEYFERTH, Otto Adolph 9
SEYFFARTH, Gustavus H
SEYFFERT, Leopold 3
SEYMORE, Truman H
SEYMOUR, Alexander 3
Duncan, Jr.
SEYMOUR, Anne 9
SEYMOUR, Arthur Bliss 1
SEYMOUR, Augustus 1
Theodore

SEYMOUR, Augustus 4
Theodore
SEYMOUR, Burge Miles 4
SEYMOUR, Charles 4
SEYMOUR, Charles, Jr. 7
SEYMOUR, Charles Kinne 7
SEYMOUR, Charles Milne 1
SEYMOUR, Dan 8
SEYMOUR, David Lowrey 6
SEYMOUR, Edward 8
Palmer
SEYMOUR, Edward H
Woodruff
SEYMOUR, Ernest Richard 10
SEYMOUR, Flora Warren 2
SEYMOUR, Forrest W. 8
SEYMOUR, Frank 7
Marcellous
SEYMOUR, Frederick 1
SEYMOUR, George Dudley 2
SEYMOUR, George 1
Franklin
SEYMOUR, George Steele 2
SEYMOUR, Gideon 3
SEYMOUR, Harold J. 5
SEYMOUR, Horatio* H
SEYMOUR, Horatio 1
Winslow
SEYMOUR, James Alward 2
SEYMOUR, James Owens 8
SEYMOUR, John Sammis 1
SEYMOUR, Mary Harrison 3
SEYMOUR, Morris 1
Woodruff
SEYMOUR, Origen Storrs H
SEYMOUR, Ralph Fletcher 4
SEYMOUR, Raymond 10
Benedict
SEYMOUR, Robert Gillin 1
SEYMOUR, Samuel H
SEYMOUR, Storrs Ozias 1
SEYMOUR, Thomas Day 1
SEYMOUR, Thomas Hart H
SEYMOUR, Walton 7
SEYMOUR, Whitney 8
North, Jr.
SEYMOUR, William H
SEYMOUR, William 1
SEYMOUR, William 1
Wolcott
SEYMOUR, William 1
Wotkyns
SEYRIG, Henri Arnold 6
SHAABER, Matthias Adam 10
SHAAD, George Carl 1
SHAARA, Michael Joseph, 9
Jr.
SHABONEE H
SHACK, Ferdinand 4
SHACKELFORD, Edward 2
Madison
SHACKELFORD, Francis 6
SHACKELFORD, James 1
M.
SHACKELFORD, John H
Williams
SHACKELFORD, 2
Virginius Randolph
SHACKFORD, John 6
Walter
SHACKFORD, Martha 5
Hale
SHACKLEFORD, Dorsey 4
W.
SHACKLEFORD, Robet 4
Wooten
SHACKLEFORD, Thomas 1
Mitchell
SHACKLEFORD, Thomas 5
Mitchell, Jr.
SHACKLETON, Robert 1
SHADEGG, Stephen 10
SHADID, Michael 4
Abraham
SHADLE, Charles Stricklen 3
SHAFER, Don Cameron 6
SHAFER, George F. 2
SHAFER, George H. 2
SHAFER, Helen Almira H
SHAFER, Jacob K. 1
SHAFER, John Douglas 1
SHAFER, Morris Luther 5
SHAFER, Paul W. 3
SHAFER, Robert 3
SHAFER, Sara Andrew 1
SHAFFER, Bertram 6
SHAFFER, Charles 4
Norman
SHAFFER, Clyde H(oover) 10
SHAFFER, Cornelius 1
Thadeus
SHAFFER, Edward H. 2
SHAFFER, Elmer 6
Ellsworth Dale
SHAFFER, Floyd Elmer 4
SHAFFER, James Grant 7
SHAFFER, James Travis 7

SHAFFER, John Charles 2
SHAFFER, John Charles 5
SHAFFER, Joseph Crockett 3
SHAFFER, Laurance 7
Frederic
SHAFFER, Lewis 5
SHAFFER, Newton 1
Melman
SHAFFER, Philip 4
Anderson
SHAFFER, Ray Osborn 4
SHAFFER, Roy Lee 6
SHAFFER, William 4
Frederick
SHAFFNER, Henry Fries 2
SHAFFNER, Taliaferro H
Preston
SHAFROTH, John 1
Franklin
SHAFROTH, John 4
Franklin
SHAFROTH, Morrison 7
SHAFROTH, Will 10
SHAFTER, William Rufus 1
SHAFTESBURY, Archie 4
D.
SHAHAN, Thomas Joseph 1
SHAHEEN, John Michael 9
SHAHN, Ben 5
SHAIKEN, Joseph 6
SHAILER, Frank Alton 8
SHAINMARK, Eliezer L. 6
SHAINWALD, Richard 3
Herman
SHAINWALD, Richard S. 3
SHAKE, Curtis Grover 7
SHAKESPEARE, William, 3
Jr.
SHAKLEE, Forest Clell, Sr. 9
SHAKMAN, James Glikauf 9
SHAKOW, David 7
SHALER, Alexander 1
SHALER, Charles 1
SHALER, Clarence 2
Addison
SHALER, Nathaniel 1
Southgate
SHALER, William H
SHALLBERG, Gustavus 3
Adolphus
SHALLCROSS, Cecil 2
Fleetwood
SHALLENBERGER, 1
Ashton C.
SHALLENBERGER, 3
Martin C.
SHALLENBERGER, 1
William Shadrach
SHALTER, Irwin Maurer 6
SHAMBAUGH, Benjamin 1
Franklin
SHAMBAUGH, Bertha M. 5
H. (Mrs. Benjamin F.
Shambaugh)
SHAMBAUGH, George 5
Elmer
SHAMBORA, William 6
E(dward)
SHAMBURGER, Carl 5
Shuford
SHAMEL, Archibald Dixon 6
SHAMROY, Leon 6
SHAMROY, Leon 7
SHANAFELT, Thomas M. 4
SHANAHAN, David 1
Edward
SHANAHAN, Edmund 1
Thomas
SHANAHAN, Elwill 9
Mattson
SHANAHAN, Foss 4
SHANAHAN, Jeremiah H
Francis
SHANAHAN, John Daniel 4
SHANAHAN, John W. 4
SHANAHAN, T. J. 4
SHAND, Robert Gordon 4
SHAND, S. James 3
SHANDS, Aurelius Rives 1
SHANDS, Courtney 5
SHANDS, Garvin Dugas 1
SHANDS, Harley Cecil 8
SHANDS, Joseph Walter 9
SHANDS, William 8
Augustine
SHANE, Charles Donald 8
SHANE, George (Walker) 5
SHANE, Joseph Brooks 6
SHANK, Corwin Sheridan 2
SHANK, Donald J. 4
SHANK, Samuel Herbert 5
SHANK, William Capen 8
SHANKLAND, Edward 1
Clapp
SHANKLAND, Robert 8
Sherwood

SHANKLAND, Sherwood Dodge 2
SHANKLIN, Arnold 4
SHANKLIN, George Sea H
SHANKLIN, J. Gordon 1
SHANKLIN, John Gilbert 1
SHANKLIN, William Arnold 1
SHANKLIN, William Charles 7
SHANKMAN, Jacob Kestin 9
SHANKS, Carrol Meteer 7
SHANKS, David Carey 1
SHANKS, Henry Thomas 3
SHANKS, Lewis Piaget 1
SHANKS, Royal E. 4
SHANKS, William Franklin Gore 1
SHANLEY, Bernard Michael 10
SHANLEY, George Patrick 6
SHANLEY, James Andrew 4
SHANLEY, John 1
SHANNAHAN, John Newton 1
SHANNON, David Allen 10
SHANNON, Edgar Finley 9
SHANNON, Effie 3
SHANNON, Fred Albert 4
SHANNON, Frederick Franklin 5
SHANNON, George Pope 4
SHANNON, Hall 9
SHANNON, J. J. 4
SHANNON, James Coughlin 7
SHANNON, Joseph B. 2
SHANNON, Larry Joseph 9
SHANNON, Nellie 1
SHANNON, Philip Francis 8
SHANNON, Richard Cutts 1
SHANNON, Robert Thomas 1
SHANNON, Spencer Sweet 4
SHANNON, Thomas H
SHANNON, Thomas Bowles H
SHANNON, Thomas Vincent 3
SHANNON, William Vincent 9
SHANNON, Wilson H
SHANTARAM, Vankudre 10
SHANTZ, Homer Leroy 7
SHAPELY, Fern Rusk 9
SHAPERO, Nate S. 7
SHAPIRO, Arthur 6
SHAPIRO, Harry 4
SHAPIRO, Harry Lionel 10
SHAPIRO, Joseph 4
SHAPIRO, Joseph George 7
SHAPIRO, Joseph M. 5
SHAPIRO, Moses 10
SHAPIRO, Samuel Harvey 9
SHAPLEIGH, A. Wessel 8
SHAPLEIGH, Alfred Lee 2
SHAPLEIGH, Bertram 2
SHAPLEIGH, Frank Henry 1
SHAPLEIGH, Waldron 1
SHAPLEN, Robert Modell 9
SHAPLEY, Alan 6
SHAPLEY, Harlow 5
SHAPLEY, John 8
SHAPLEY, Rufus Edmonds 4
SHAPORIN, Yuri 4
SHARETT, Moshe 4
SHARFMAN, Herbert 10
SHARKEY, Joseph Edward 1
SHARKEY, Joseph Thomas 10
SHARKEY, Thomas Clifford 6
SHARKEY, William Lewis 1
SHARMAN, Jackson Roger 3
SHARON, William H
SHARP, Alexander 6
SHARP, Benjamin 1
SHARP, Carl J. 5
SHARP, Clarence Bryan 6
SHARP, Clayton Halsey 1
SHARP, Dale E(lbert) 8
SHARP, Dallas Lore 1
SHARP, Daniel 1
SHARP, Dudley Crawford 9
SHARP, Eckley Grant 4
SHARP, Edgar A. 2
SHARP, Edward Preston 1
SHARP, Edward Raymond 4
SHARP, Edwin Rees 1
SHARP, Frank Chapman 2
SHARP, George Clough 5
SHARP, George Gillies 1
SHARP, George Matthews 1
SHARP, George Stevenson 9
SHARP, George Winters 3
SHARP, Harold Harris 8
SHARP, Henry Staats 5

SHARP, Hugh Rodney 6
SHARP, Hunter 1
SHARP, James H. 6
SHARP, John H
SHARP, Mrs. John C. 1
SHARP, John Fletcher 1
SHARP, John H. 5
SHARP, Joseph C. 2
SHARP, Joseph Lessil 5
SHARP, Katharine Lucinda 1
SHARP, Lester Whyland 8
SHARP, Lewis Inman 7
SHARP, Marlay Albert 3
SHARP, Morell Edward 7
SHARP, Morris Louis 8
SHARP, Raymond Neil 7
SHARP, Robert 1
SHARP, Robert Sherman 1
SHARP, Solomon P. H
SHARP, Thelma Parkinson 10
SHARP, Thomas Enoch 3
SHARP, Waldo Z. 1
SHARP, Walter Bedford 4
SHARP, William H
SHARP, William F. 2
SHARP, William Graves 1
SHARP, William Wilson 4
SHARPE, Alfred Clarence 1
SHARPE, Dores Robinson 7
SHARPE, Dores Robinson 8
SHARPE, Francis Robert 2
SHARPE, Henry Augustus 1
SHARPE, Henry Dexter 3
SHARPE, Henry Granville 2
SHARPE, Horatio H
SHARPE, John C. 2
SHARPE, Mary Elizabeth Evans (Mrs. Henry Dexter Sharpe) 7
SHARPE, Merrell Quentin 4
SHARPE, Nelson 1
SHARPE, Peter H
SHARPE, Philip Burdette 4
SHARPE, William 1
SHARPLES, James H
SHARPLES, Laurence Price 9
SHARPLES, Philip M. 4
SHARPLES, Philip T. 8
SHARPLES, Stephen Paschall 1
SHARPLESS, Frederic Cope 5
SHARPLESS, Frederick F. 3
SHARPLESS, Isaac 1
SHARPLEY, John Miles 7
SHARSWOOD, George H
SHARTEL, Burke Woods 9
SHARTS, Joseph William 5
SHASTID, Thomas Hall 2
SHASTRI, Lal Bahadur 4
SHATTUC, William B. 1
SHATTUCK, Aaron Draper 1
SHATTUCK, Arthur 3
SHATTUCK, Charles 10
Harlen
SHATTUCK, Charles Houston 1
SHATTUCK, Edward Stevens 1
SHATTUCK, Edwin Paul 4
SHATTUCK, Frederick Cheever 1
SHATTUCK, George Brune 1
SHATTUCK, George Burbank 1
SHATTUCK, George Cheever 5
SHATTUCK, George Cheyne* H
SHATTUCK, H. Morgan 4
SHATTUCK, Harriette Lucy Robinson 1
SHATTUCK, Henry Lee 5
SHATTUCK, Howard Francis 5
SHATTUCK, John Garrett 4
SHATTUCK, Lemuel H
SHATTUCK, Lemuel C. 1
SHATTUCK, Mayo Adams 3
SHATTUCK, Samuel Walker 1
SHATTUCK, Sidney Frank 6
SHATTUCK, William 3
SHATZER, Charles Gallatin 3
SHAUCK, John Allen 1
SHAUGHNESSY, Clark Daniel 5
SHAUGHNESSY, Gerald 3
SHAUGHNESSY, Sir Thomas George 1
SHAVER, Charles William 4
SHAVER, Clement Lawrence 3
SHAVER, Dorothy 3
SHAVER, Erwin Leander 9

SHAVER, George Frederick 4
SHAVER, Jesse Milton 4
SHAVER, Robert Ezekiel 6
SHAVITCH, Vladimir 8
SHAW, Aaron H
SHAW, Albert 2
SHAW, Albert Duane 1
SHAW, Albert Sidney Johnston 6
SHAW, Alfred O. 8
SHAW, Anna Howard 1
SHAW, Arch Wilkinson 4
SHAW, Arnold 10
SHAW, Avery Albert 2
SHAW, (Benjamin) Chandler 10
SHAW, Bruno 8
SHAW, Charles Bunsen 1
SHAW, Charles Frederick 1
SHAW, Charles Gray 2
SHAW, Charles Green 6
SHAW, Clarence Reginald 3
SHAW, Dexter Nichols 6
SHAW, Earl 4
SHAW, Edgar Dwight 1
SHAW, Edward Richard 1
SHAW, Edwin Adams 3
SHAW, Edwin Coupland 2
SHAW, Elijah H
SHAW, Elton Raymond 7
SHAW, Elwyn Riley 3
SHAW, Esmond 5
SHAW, Eugene 6
SHAW, Eugene Wesley 1
SHAW, Florence Sylvia Berlowitz 4
SHAW, Frances Wills 2
SHAW, Frank Holcomb 7
SHAW, Frank L. 2
SHAW, F(red) Alden 7
SHAW, Frederic Lonsdale 6
SHAW, Frederick Benjamin 5
SHAW, Frederick William 2
SHAW, G. Bernard 4
SHAW, Gardiner Howland 4
SHAW, George Bernard 6
SHAW, George Bullen 1
SHAW, George Elmer 1
SHAW, George Hamlin 6
SHAW, Guy Loren 6
SHAW, Harriett McCreary Jackson 1
SHAW, Henry* H
SHAW, Henry G(eorge) 6
SHAW, Henry Larned Keith 1
SHAW, Henry Marchmore H
SHAW, Henry Overstreet 9
SHAW, Henry Southworth 6
SHAW, Henry Wheeler 1
SHAW, Herbert Bell 7
SHAW, Hobart Doane 2
SHAW, Howard Burton 2
SHAW, Howard Van Doren 1
SHAW, Irwin 9
SHAW, J. W. 1
SHAW, James Byrnie 2
SHAW, James Edward 6
SHAW, James Howard 9
SHAW, Jay Sadler 10
SHAW, John* H
SHAW, John Balcom 4
SHAW, John Jacob 6
SHAW, John Stewart 3
SHAW, John William 4
SHAW, Joseph Alden 1
SHAW, Joseph Bradfield 7
SHAW, Joshua H
SHAW, Lemuel H
SHAW, Leo Nelson 4
SHAW, Leslie Mortier 1
SHAW, Lloyd 3
SHAW, Lucien 1
SHAW, Mary 1
SHAW, Nathaniel H
SHAW, Oliver H
SHAW, Oliver Abbott 2
SHAW, Patrick 6
SHAW, Phillips Bassett 2
SHAW, Quincy A. 3
SHAW, Quincy A. 5
SHAW, Ralph Martin 2
SHAW, Ralph Robert 5
SHAW, Reuben T. 3
SHAW, Richard 5
SHAW, Robert 5
SHAW, Robert 7
SHAW, Robert Alfred 4
SHAW, Robert Anderson 1
SHAW, Robert Gould H
SHAW, Robert Kendall 4
SHAW, Robert Nelson 9
SHAW, Robert Sidey 1
SHAW, Roger 3
SHAW, Samuel* H
SHAW, Samuel Gormley 4

SHAW, Silas Frederick 6
SHAW, Sterling Price 1
SHAW, Sydney Dale 6
SHAW, Thomas H
SHAW, Thomas 4
SHAW, Thomas Mott 4
SHAW, Tristram H
SHAW, Walter Adam 1
SHAW, Walter Carlyle 6
SHAW, Walter Keith 1
SHAW, Walter Rice 10
SHAW, Walter Russell 8
SHAW, Warren Choate 8
SHAW, William Bristol 2
SHAW, William Edward 6
SHAW, William Frederick 5
SHAW, William Henry 9
SHAW, William James 3
SHAW, William Smith H
SHAW, Woody Herman 10
SHAWHAN, Narcissa Tayloe Maupin (Mrs. Charles S.) 5
SHAWKEY, Morris Purdy 1
SHAWN, Edwin M. (Ted Shawn) 5
SHAWN, William 10
SHAY, Felix 7
SHAY, Frank 3
SHAY, Howell Lewis 7
SHAY, Junior Ralph 7
SHAYLER, Ernest Vincent 2
SHAYS, Daniel H
SHAZAR, Zalman 6
SHCHERBITSKY, Vladimir Vaiilyevich 10
SHEA, Andrew Bernard 5
SHEA, Daniel William 1
SHEA, Edmund Burke 5
SHEA, Edward Lane 1
SHEA, Francis Michael 10
SHEA, George E., Jr. 7
SHEA, James J. 7
SHEA, James R. 3
SHEA, John Dawson Gilmary H
SHEA, John J. 1
SHEA, John Joseph 5
SHEA, John Joseph 8
SHEA, Joseph Bernard 1
SHEA, Joseph Hooker 1
SHEA, Lewis Anthony 5
SHEA, William Alfred 10
SHEA, William Joseph 1
SHEAFE, James H
SHEAFER, Arthur Whitcomb 2
SHEAFFER, Craig Royer 4
SHEAFFER, Daniel Miller 1
SHEAFFER, Joseph Guy 9
SHEAFFER, Walter A. 1
SHEAHAN, Henry B(eston) 8
SHEAN, Charles M. 1
SHEAR, Cornelius Lott 4
SHEAR, John Knox 3
SHEAR, Murray J(acob) 8
SHEAR, Theodore Leslie 2
SHEARD, Charles 1
SHEARD, Titus 1
SHEARER, Allen Everett 8
SHEARER, Andrew 1
SHEARER, Augustus Hunt 1
SHEARER, George Lewis 1
SHEARER, Henry 4
SHEARER, J. Harry 4
SHEARER, John Bunyan 1
SHEARER, John Louis 1
SHEARER, John Sanford 1
SHEARER, Maurice Edwin 6
SHEARER, Norma 8
SHEARER, P(hineas) S(tevens) 8
SHEARER, Tom Ellas 4
SHEARER, Tom Ellas 9
SHEARIN, Hubert Gibson 1
SHEARMAN, Robert William 7
SHEARMAN, Thomas Broadus 9
SHEARMAN, Thomas Gaskell 1
SHEARN, Clarence John 2
SHEARON, Marjorie (Mrs. William Shearon) 8
SHEATS, Paul Henry 9
SHEATS, William Nicholas 1
SHEATSLEY, Clarence Valentine 2
SHEATSLEY, Jacob 1
SHEATSLEY, Paul Baker 10
SHECUT, John Linnaeus Edward Whitridge H
SHEDD, Clarence Prouty 6
SHEDD, Fred Fuller 1
SHEDD, George Clifford 1
SHEDD, J. Herbert 1
SHEDD, John Cutler 1

SHEDD, John Graves 1
SHEDD, Solon 2
SHEDD, Thomas Clark 3
SHEDD, William Alfred 4
SHEDD, William Edgar, Jr. 7
SHEDD, William Greenough Thayer H
SHEDDEN, Lucian Love 1
SHEDLOVSKY, Theodore 7
SHEEAN, James B. 3
SHEEAN, James Vincent 6
SHEEDY, Dennis 1
SHEEDY, Herman James 10
SHEEDY, Joseph Edward 1
SHEEDY, Morgan M. 1
SHEEHAN, Daniel Michael 4
SHEEHAN, Donal 4
SHEEHAN, Donald Henry 6
SHEEHAN, J. Eastman 3
SHEEHAN, John Charles 7
SHEEHAN, John Clark 10
SHEEHAN, Joseph Green 8
SHEEHAN, Joseph Raymond 1
SHEEHAN, Murray 1
SHEEHAN, Paul Vincent 7
SHEEHAN, Perley Poore 5
SHEEHAN, Robert Francis, Jr. 2
SHEEHAN, Robert John 6
SHEEHAN, Robert Wade 5
SHEEHAN, Timothy J. 1
SHEEHAN, William Francis H
SHEEHAN, William Mark 4
SHEEHAN, Winfield R. 2
SHEEHY, Joe Warren 4
SHEEHY, Joseph E. 10
SHEEHY, Maurice S(tephen) 5
SHEELER, Charles 4
SHEELY, William Clarence 5
SHEEN, Daniel Robinson 4
SHEEN, Fulton John 7
SHEEP, William L. 6
SHEERIN, Charles Wilford 2
SHEERIN, James 1
SHEETS, Earl Wooddell 7
SHEETS, Frank Thomas 3
SHEETS, Harold F. 5
SHEETS, Millard Owen 10
SHEETS, Millard Owen 4
SHEETZ, Walter Franklin 9
SHEFELMAN, Harold S. 10
SHEFFER, Daniel H
SHEFFER, Eugene J. 7
SHEFFER, Henry Maurice 4
SHEFFEY, Daniel H
SHEFFEY, Edward Fleming 1
SHEFFIELD, Alfred Dwight 4
SHEFFIELD, Devello Z. 1
SHEFFIELD, Frederick 5
SHEFFIELD, J. S. 4
SHEFFIELD, James Rockwell 1
SHEFFIELD, Joseph Earl H
SHEFFIELD, William Paine* 1
SHEFFY, L(ester) Fields 8
SHEHAN, Lawrence Joseph Cardinal 8
SHEIB, Simon 7
SHEIL, Bernard J(ames) 5
SHEIN, Harvey M. 6
SHEININ, John J(acobi) 7
SHEKERJIAN, Haig 7
SHELBOURNE, Roy Mahlon 8
SHELBURNE, James M. 3
SHELBURNE, Lord H
SHELBY, David Davie 1
SHELBY, Evan H
SHELBY, Gertrude Singleton Mathews 1
SHELBY, Isaac H
SHELBY, John Todd 1
SHELBY, Joseph Orville H
SHELBY, Robert Evart 3
SHELBY, Thomas Hall 6
SHELBY, William Read 1
SHELDEN, Carlos Douglas 1
SHELDEN, Miriam Aldridge 6
SHELDON, Addison Erwin 2
SHELDON, Archibald McDaniels 7
SHELDON, Arthur Frederick 1
SHELDON, Caroline M. 1
SHELDON, Charles 1
SHELDON, Charles Mills 1
SHELDON, Charles Monroe 1
SHELDON, Charles Stuart 1
SHELDON, David Newton H

SHEWMAKER, Russell Newton 9
SHEWMAN, Eben B. 3
SHIBER, Etta 2
SHIBLEY, Alice Smith Patterson 4
SHIDEHARA, Baron Kijuro 5
SHIDELER, Ernest Hugh 9
SHIDELER, W. H. 3
SHIDEMAN, Frederick Earl 9
SHIDY, Leland Perry 1
SHIEL, George Knox H
SHIELD, Lansing P. 3
SHIELD, Lansing P. 4
SHIELDS, A. C. 2
SHIELDS, Benjamin Glover H
SHIELDS, Charles R. 1
SHIELDS, Charles Woodruff 1
SHIELDS, Cornelius 8
SHIELDS, Currin Vance 8
SHIELDS, Ebenezer J. H
SHIELDS, Edmund Claude 2
SHIELDS, Edwin John 6
SHIELDS, Emily L. 4
SHIELDS, G. O. 5
SHIELDS, George Howell 1
SHIELDS, George Robert 2
SHIELDS, Gertrude M. 8
SHIELDS, James* H
SHIELDS, John Franklin 2
SHIELDS, John Knight 1
SHIELDS, Leighton 7
SHIELDS, Paul Vincent 4
SHIELDS, Roy Franklin 4
SHIELDS, Thomas Edward 6
SHIELDS, Thomas Todhunter 3
SHIELDS, William Maurice 10
SHIELDS, William S. 1
SHIELS, Albert 1
SHIELS, Archibald Williamson 7
SHIELS, George Franklin 2
SHIELS, James 1
SHIELY, Albert Raymond, Jr. 10
SHIELY, Vincent Robert 7
SHIENTAG, Bernard Lloyd 3
SHIER, Calrton S. 3
SHIFRIN, Seymour 7
SHIGEMITSU, Mamoru 5
SHIKELLAMY H
SHILENSKY, Morris 9
SHILLABER, Benjamin Penhallow H
SHILLADY, John R. 5
SHILLING, Alexander 1
SHILLINGLAW, Clifford Allen 2
SHILLINGLAW, David Lee 6
SHILOAH, Reuven 3
SHIMEK, Bohumil 1
SHIMER, Hervey Woodburn 4
SHIMER, Porter William 1
SHIMER, William Allison 10
SHIMKIN, Leon 9
SHIMKIN, Michael Boris 9
SHIMP, Herbert Gilby 2
SHINE, Francis Eppes 1
SHINGLER, Don Gilmore 4
SHINKLE, Edward Marsh 4
SHINKMAN, Paul Alfred 6
SHINKMAN, Paul Alfred 7
SHINN, Asa H
SHINN, Charles Howard 1
SHINN, Everett 3
SHINN, Florence Scovel 1
SHINN, George Wolfe 1
SHINN, Henry Arthur 2
SHINN, John Calvin 6
SHINN, Milicent Washburn 1
SHINN, William Norton H
SHINNER, Ernest G. 7
SHIP, Irwin 9
SHIPHERD, H(enry) Robinson 6
SHIPHERD, John Jay 1
SHIPHERD, Zebulon Rudd H
SHIPLE, George J. 3
SHIPLEY, Charles Raymond 4
SHIPLEY, Edward Ellis 4
SHIPLEY, Frederick William 2
SHIPLEY, George 2
SHIPLEY, James Ross 10
SHIPLEY, Joseph T. 9
SHIPLEY, Maynard 1
SHIPLEY, Richard Larkin 2
SHIPLEY, Samuel R. 1
SHIPLEY, Walter Penn 2
SHIPLEY, William Stewart 3

SHIPMAN, Arthur Leffingwell 1
SHIPMAN, Benjamin Jonson 4
SHIPMAN, Fred W. 7
SHIPMAN, Herbert 1
SHIPMAN, Louis Evan 1
SHIPMAN, Nathaniel 1
SHIPMAN, Samuel 1
SHIPMAN, William Rollin 1
SHIPP, Albert Micajah H
SHIPP, Barnard 4
SHIPP, Cameron 4
SHIPP, Frederic B. 1
SHIPP, Scott 1
SHIPP, Thomas Roerty 1
SHIPPEE, Lester Burrell 2
SHIPPEN, Edward* H
SHIPPEN, Edward 1
SHIPPEN, Eugene Rodman 3
SHIPPEN, Joseph 1
SHIPPEN, Rush Rhees 1
SHIPPEN, William* H
SHIPPEY, H(enry) Lee 5
SHIPSEY, Edward 3
SHIPSTEAD, Henrik 4
SHIPTON, A. W. 4
SHIPTON, Clifford Kenyon 4
SHIPTON, Clifford Kenyon 7
SHIPTON, James Ancil 1
SHIR, Martin M. 6
SHIRAS, George, III 2
SHIRAS, George, Jr. 1
SHIRAS, Oliver Perry 1
SHIRER, John Wesley 6
SHIRES, Henry Millis 7
SHIRK, George Henry 7
SHIRKY, Sam(uel) B(ryan) 10
SHIRLAW, Walter 4
SHIRLEY, Cassius Clay 4
SHIRLEY, David Allen 10
SHIRLEY, James Clifford 6
SHIRLEY, Robert Kirby 3
SHIRLEY, William H
SHISKIN, Julius 7
SHIVE, John W(esley) 5
SHIVELY, Benjamin Franklin 1
SHIVELY, Carlton Adamson 3
SHIVERICK, Asa 1
SHIVERS, Allan 8
SHIVERS, R. Kevin 4
SHLENKER, Irvin Morris 5
SHOAFF, Fred B. 4
SHOALS, George 1
SHOBER, Francis E. 4
SHOBER, Francis Edwin 4
SHOBER, John Bedford 4
SHOCH, David Eugene 10
SHOCK, Nathan Wetherill 10
SHOCK, Thomas Macy 4
SHOCK, William Henry 4
SHOCKLEY, Frank William 3
SHOCKLEY, M. Augustus Wroten 5
SHOCKLEY, William Bradford 10
SHOCKLEY, Woodland Gray 10
SHOCKNESSY, James W. 4
SHOEMAKER, Charles Chalmers 2
SHOEMAKER, Charles Frederick 1
SHOEMAKER, Daniel Naylor 5
SHOEMAKER, Floyd Calvin 9
SHOEMAKER, Francis Henry 8
SHOEMAKER, Harlan 1
SHOEMAKER, Henry Francis 1
SHOEMAKER, Henry Wharton 3
SHOEMAKER, John Vietch 1
SHOEMAKER, Joseph Addison 5
SHOEMAKER, Lazarus Denison H
SHOEMAKER, Michael Myers 1
SHOEMAKER, Myrl Howard 8
SHOEMAKER, Rachel Hinkle 1
SHOEMAKER, Raymond L. 4
SHOEMAKER, Richard Heston 5
SHOEMAKER, Robert H
SHOEMAKER, Samuel Moor 1
SHOEMAKER, Vaughn 10

SHOEMAKER, Waite Almon 1
SHOEMAKER, William Rawle 1
SHOENBERG, Sydney Melville 6
SHOFFSTALL, Arthur Scott 3
SHOFNER, Orman Eugene 6
SHOHAT, James Alexander 2
SHOHL, Walter Max 5
SHOLES, Christopher Latham H
SHOLES, Walter Henry 7
(Surname Changed From Schulz to Sholes)
SHOLLEY, Sidney Llewellyn 4
SHOLTZ, David 3
SHOMO, E. H. 5
SHONMAKER, Marius H
SHONNARD, Christy Fox 6
SHONTS, Theodore Perry 1
SHONTZ, Vernon Lloyd 3
SHOOK, Alfred M. 1
SHOOK, Charles Francis 4
SHOOK, Edgar 5
SHOOK, Glenn Alfred 3
SHOOK, Karel Francis Antony 8
SHOOP, Clarence Adelbert 4
SHOOP, Duke 3
SHOOP, John Daniel 1
SHOPE, Leslie Reed 10
SHOPE, Richard Edwin 4
SHOPE, Simeon P. 1
SHOR, Bernard (Toots) 7
SHOR, Franc Marion Luther 6
SHOR, George Gershon 5
SHORE, Clarence Albert 4
SHORE, Maurice J. 4
SHORE, Nathan Allen 9
SHORE, Sidney 8
SHORELL, Irving Daniel 10
SHORES, Louis 8
SHORES, Robert James 6
SHOREY, Clyde Everett 4
SHOREY, Paul 1
SHOREY, Winston Kinney 7
SHORIKI, Matsutaro 5
SHORT, Albert 5
SHORT, Charles H
SHORT, Charles Wilkins H
SHORT, Dewey 4
SHORT, Francis Burgette 1
SHORT, Frank Hamilton 4
SHORT, Joseph 3
SHORT, Joseph Hudson, Jr. 4
SHORT, Josephine Helena 1
SHORT, Livingston Lyman 4
SHORT, Lloyd Milton 10
SHORT, Maxwell Naylor 8
SHORT, Oliver Clark 7
SHORT, Robert Earl 8
SHORT, Sidney Howe H
SHORT, Wallace Mertin 5
SHORT, Walter Campbell 2
SHORT, William H
SHORT, William Harrison 1
SHORT, William Hosley 10
SHORT, Zuber Nathaniel 5
SHORTALL, John G. 1
SHORTALL, Thomas Francis 4
SHORTER, Eli Sims 4
SHORTER, John Gill H
SHORTLE, Abraham Given 4
SHORTLEY, George Hiram 7
SHORTLIDGE, Jonathan Chauncey 1
SHORTLIDGE, Raphael Johnson 7
SHORTRIDGE, Charles M. 4
SHORTRIDGE, N. Parker 4
SHORTRIDGE, Samuel Morgan 3
SHORTRIDGE, Wilson Peter 6
SHORTS, Bruce Carman 2
SHORTS, Robert Perry 6
SHORTT, Elster Clayton 4
SHOSTAKOVICH, Dmitri 6
SHOTT, Hugh Ike 3
SHOTWELL, Abel V. 3
SHOTWELL, James Thomson 4
SHOUDY, Loyal Ambrose 4
SHOUDY, William Allen 6
SHOULDERS, Harrison H. 4
SHOUP, Arthur Glendinning 2
SHOUP, David Monroe 8
SHOUP, Earl Leon 3
SHOUP, Eldon Campbell 3
SHOUP, Francis Asbury H
SHOUP, George Laird 1

SHOUP, Guy V. 5
SHOUP, Merrill Edgar 4
SHOUP, Oliver Henry 1
SHOUP, Paul 3
SHOUP, Robert John 9
SHOUSE, James D. 4
SHOUSE, Jouett 5
SHOVE, Benjamin 9
SHOVE, Eugene Percy 1
SHOW, Arley Barthlow 1
SHOW, Stuart Bevier 7
SHOWALTER, Anthony Johnson 1
SHOWALTER, Jackson Whipps 1
SHOWALTER, Joseph Baltzell 4
SHOWALTER, Noah David 1
SHOWALTER, William Joseph 1
SHOWER, George Theodore 1
SHOWER, Jacob H
SHOWERMAN, Grant 1
SHOWERS, J. Balmer 4
SHOWMAN, Harry Munson 2
SHRADY, Frederick Charles 10
SHRADY, George Frederick 1
SHRADY, Henry Merwin 1
SHREINER, Charles Wesley 7
SHREVE, Charles Everett 5
SHREVE, Earl Owen 6
SHREVE, Forrest 3
SHREVE, Henry Miller H
SHREVE, Milton William 4
SHREVE, Randolph Norris 7
SHREVE, Richmond Harold 4
SHREVE, Thomas Hopkins H
SHREVE, Wickliffe Winston 4
SHRINER, Charles Anthony 3
SHRINER, Herb 5
SHRIVER, Alfred 4
SHRIVER, Alfred Jenkins 1
SHRIVER, George McLean 2
SHRIVER, Harry Clair 9
SHRIVER, J. Nicholas, Jr. 7
SHRIVER, John Shultz 1
SHRIVER, William Payne 4
SHRODER, William Jacob 3
SHRODES, Caroline 10
SHROPSHIRE, Courtney William 4
SHROYER, Curtis Clinton 6
SHROYER, Frederick Benjamin 8
SHRUM, George Dixon 4
SHRUM, Gordon Merritt 10
SHRYOCK, Burnett Henry, Sr. 5
SHRYOCK, Gideon H
SHRYOCK, Henry William 1
SHRYOCK, Joseph Grundy 3
SHRYOCK, Richard Harrison 5
SHUBERT, Jacob J. 4
SHUBERT, Lee 3
SHUBRICK, John Templer H
SHUBRICK, William Branford H
SHUBSDA, Thaddeus A. 10
SHUCK, Jehu Lewis 4
SHUEY, Edwin Longstreet 1
SHUEY, Herbert Stanley 7
SHUEY, Lillian Hinman 4
SHUEY, William John 1
SHUFELDT, Robert Wilson H
SHUFELDT, Robert Wilson 1
SHUFF, Benjamin L. 7
SHUFF, John A. 5
SHUFORD, A. Alex, Jr. 5
SHUFORD, Alonzo Craig 4
SHUFORD, Forrest Herman 3
SHUFORD, George A. 4
SHUGART, Kenneth Laverne 10
SHUGERMAN, Abe Louis 4
SHUGERT, Stanley Pulliam 7
SHULER, Ellis W. 3
SHULER, Robert Pierce 1
(Bob Shuler)
SHULL, A. Franklin 4
SHULL, Charles Albert 6
SHULL, Charles Graves 3
SHULL, Deloss Carlton 1
SHULL, Deloss P. 4
SHULL, Frank Leslie 5

SHULL, George Harrison 3
SHULL, Henry Carlton 9
SHULL, James Marion 2
SHULL, Joseph H. 2
SHULLENBERGER, William Arthur 6
SHULMAN, Charles E. 5
SHULMAN, Harry 3
SHULMAN, Kenneth 7
SHULMAN, Max 9
SHULTERS, Hoyt Volney 1
SHULTZ, William John 5
SHULZ, Adolph Robert 4
SHULZE, John Andrew H
SHUMAKER, E. Ellsworth 4
SHUMAKER, Edward Seitz 1
SHUMAKER, Ross W. 4
SHUMAN, Abraham 1
SHUMAN, Davis 4
SHUMAN, Edwin Llewellyn 1
SHUMAN, John Franklin 4
SHUMAN, Ronald Buswell 7
SHUMATE, Roger V. 3
SHUMATE, Wade Hampton 6
SHUMBERGER, John Calvin 4
SHUMLIN, Herman 7
SHUMWAY, Adelina Ritter 6
SHUMWAY, Daniel Bussier 1
SHUMWAY, Edgar Solomon 1
SHUMWAY, Edward D. 4
SHUMWAY, Frank Ritter 10
SHUMWAY, Harry Irving 4
SHUMWAY, Lowell 10
SHUMWAY, Sherman N. 3
SHUMWAY, Waldo 3
SHUMWAY, Walter Bradley 3
SHUNK, Francis Rawn H
SHUNK, Joseph Lorain 1
SHUNK, William Alexander 1
SHUNK, William Findlay 1
SHUPE, Henry Fox 1
SHUPING, Clarence Leroy 5
SHURCLIFF, Arthur Asahel 3
SHURCLIFF, Sidney Nichols 7
SHURCLIFF, Sidney Nichols 8
SHURE, Ralph Deane 7
SHURLOCK, Geoffrey Manwaring 7
SHURLY, Burt Russell 5
SHURTER, Edwin Dubois 2
SHURTER, Robert LaFevre 6
SHURTLEFF, Charles Allerton 1
SHURTLEFF, Ernest Warburton 1
SHURTLEFF, Eugene 3
SHURTLEFF, Flavel 6
SHURTLEFF, Glen Kassimer 1
SHURTLEFF, Nathaniel Bradstreet H
SHURTLEFF, Roswell Morse 1
SHURTLEFF, Roy 8
SHURTLEFF, Roy Lothrop 8
SHUSTER, Carl Nathaniel 9
SHUSTER, George Nauman 7
SHUSTER, W. Morgan 4
SHUTE, Abraham Lincoln 2
SHUTE, Daniel Kerfoot 1
SHUTE, Emmett R. 4
SHUTE, Henry Augustus 2
SHUTE, Nevil 3
SHUTE, Nevil 4
SHUTE, Samuel H
SHUTE, Samuel Moore 1
SHUTTER, Marion Daniel 1
SHUTTLEWORTH, V. Craven 4
SHUTTS, Frank Barker 2
SHUTZ, Byron Theodore 10
SHUTZE, Philip Trammel 8
SHVERNIK, Nikola (Mikhallvich) 5
SHY, George Milton 4
SHYRE, Paul 10
SIAS, Azariah Boody 7
SIAS, Ernest J. 3
SIBELIUS, Jean Julius Christian 5
SIBERELL, Lloyd E. 5
SIBERT, Franklin Cummings 7
SIBERT, William Luther 1
SIBLEY, Bolling 2
SIBLEY, Clyde Lawson 5

SLOAN, Fergus Martin 4
SLOAN, George A. 3
SLOAN, George Beale 1
SLOAN, Gordon McGregor 4
SLOAN, Harold Paul 4
SLOAN, Harold Stephenson 9
SLOAN, Hubert John 6
SLOAN, James H
SLOAN, James Forman H
SLOAN, James Forman 4
SLOAN, John 3
SLOAN, John Elliot, Jr. 10
SLOAN, John Emmet 8
SLOAN, Laurence Henry 2
SLOAN, Lawrence Wells 9
SLOAN, Leroy Hendrick 4
SLOAN, Marianna 4
SLOAN, Mary Herron 6
SLOAN, Matthew Scott 2
SLOAN, Raymond Paton 8
SLOAN, Richard E. 1
SLOAN, Robert James 4
SLOAN, Samuel* 1
SLOAN, Thomas Wylie 3
SLOAN, William Boyd 10
SLOAN, William Franklin 3
SLOANE, Alfred Baldwin 1
SLOANE, Charles Swift 1
SLOANE, Eric 8
SLOANE, John 1
SLOANE, John 1
SLOANE, John 7
SLOANE, Jonathan H
SLOANE, Joseph Curtis 5
SLOANE, Rush Richard 5
SLOANE, T. O'Conor 1
SLOANE, Thomas Morrison
SLOANE, William 1
SLOANE, William 6 (Milligan, III)
SLOANE, William A. 1
SLOANE, William Milligan 1
SLOAT, John Drake 4
SLOBIN, Hermon Lester 3
SLOBODKIN, Louis 6
SLOCTEMEYER, Hugo Ferdinand 1
SLOCUM, Arthur Gaylord 1
SLOCUM, Charles Elihu 1
SLOCUM, Clarence Alfred 3
SLOCUM, Clarence Rice 1
SLOCUM, Francis H
SLOCUM, Frederick 2
SLOCUM, George Warren 4
SLOCUM, Henry Warner H
SLOCUM, Herbert Jermain 1
SLOCUM, Joseph H
SLOCUM, Joshua H
SLOCUM, Joshua 4
SLOCUM, Lorimer B. 3
SLOCUM, Richard William 1
SLOCUM, Samuel H
SLOCUM, Stephen Elmer 5
SLOCUM, Thomas Williams 1
SLOCUM, William Frederick 1
SLOCUMB, Jesse H
SLOMAN, Ernest Gaynor 3
SLONE, Dennis 8
SLONECKER, J. G. 4
SLONEKER, Howard L. 4
SLONIM, Marc 7
SLOPER, Andrew Jackson 1
SLOPER, Leslie Akers 2
SLOSBERG, Samuel Louis 10
SLOSS, James Withers H
SLOSS, Louis 4
SLOSS, Marcus Cauffman 4
SLOSSER, Gaius Jackson 4
SLOSSON, Annie Trumbull 1
SLOSSON, Edwin Emery 1
SLOSSON, Leonard Butler 2
SLOTKIN, Hugo 8
SLOTKIN, Samuel 4
SLOTNICK, Daniel Leonid 9
SLOTT, Mollie 1
SLOTTMAN, George Vincent 3
SLOVER, Samuel Leroy 4
SLOWINSKI, Walter Aloysius 9
SLUSS, Homer Oscar 1
SLUSS, John William 1
SLUSSER, Charles Edward 4
SLUTER, George 1
SLUTZ, Frank D. 3
SLY, John Fairfield 1
SLY, Wiliam James 1
SLYE, Maud 3
SMADEL, Joseph Edwin 4
SMAIL, Lloyd Leroy 8
SMALL, Albion Woodbury 1
SMALL, Alex 4
SMALL, Alvah Randall 7

SMALL, Alvan Edmond H
SMALL, Andrew Buchanan 4
SMALL, Benjamin Francis 5
SMALL, Burrell Leslie 7
SMALL, Charles C. 5
SMALL, Charles Hughey 7
SMALL, Edward 7
SMALL, Elden 1
SMALL, Ernest Gregor 2
SMALL, Francis Aloysius 6
SMALL, Frank 4
SMALL, Frederick Percival 3
SMALL, Harold Patten 2
SMALL, John Clay 5
SMALL, John D. 4
SMALL, John Humphrey 1
SMALL, John Kunkel 1
SMALL, Len 4
SMALL, Philip Lindsley 4
SMALL, Robert Oren 8
SMALL, Robert Scott 1
SMALL, Sam 1
SMALL, Sergine Anne 6
(Mrs. Donald David Small)
SMALL, Sidney Aylmer 5
SMALL, Stanton Harrison 9
SMALL, Sydney French 4
SMALL, Vivian Blanche 2
SMALL, Willard Stanton 2
SMALL, W(illiam) A(rden) 6
SMALL, William Bradbury 4
SMALLENS, Alexander 5
SMALLEY, Bradley Barlow 1
SMALLEY, Eugene Virgil 5
SMALLEY, Eugene Virgil 1
SMALLEY, Frank 1
SMALLEY, Frank Mather 3
SMALLEY, George Washburn 1
SMALLEY, Harrison Standish 1
SMALLEY, Ruth Elizabeth 7
SMALLEY, William Cameron 6
SMALLS, Charlie 9
SMALLS, Robert H
SMALLS, Robert 4
SMALLSREED, George A., Sr. 4
SMALLWOOD, Della Graeme 5
SMALLWOOD, John William 10
SMALLWOOD, Joseph Roberts 10
SMALLWOOD, Robert Bartly 6
SMALLWOOD, William Martin H
SMALLWOOD, William 2
SMART, Charles
SMART, Charles Allen 4
SMART, David A. 3
SMART, Edmund Hodgson 2
SMART, Elizabeth Allen 4
SMART, Ephraim Knight 1
SMART, Frank Leroy 1
SMART, George Thomas 1
SMART, Jackson Wyman 5
SMART, James D. 3
SMART, James Dick 3
SMART, James Henry 1
SMART, John Stuart, Jr. 5
SMART, Richard Addison 5
SMART, Walter Kay 5
SMART, Wyatt Aiken 7
SMATHERS, William H. 3
SMAY, Joseph Edgar 6
SMEAD, Edward Leon 7
SMEALLIE, John Morris 2
SMEDLEY, Agnes 3
SMEDLEY, Graham B. 3
SMEDLEY, M(artin) Harvey 5
SMEDLEY, William Thomas 1
SMELO, Leon Samuel 6
SMELSER, Marshall 7
SMELT, Dennis H
SMELTZ, George Washington 4
SMELTZER, Clarence Harry 5
SMELZER, Baxter Timothy 4
SMELZER, Donald Campbell 10
SMEMO, Johannes 6
SMERTENKO, Clara Millerd 5
SMET, Pierre-jean de H
SMIBERT, John H
SMIGEL, Erwin O. 6
SMILEY, Albert Keith 1
SMILEY, Charles Newton 2
SMILEY, Charles Wesley 1
SMILEY, Daniel 1

SMILEY, David Elmer 4
SMILEY, Dean Franklin 5
SMILEY, Elmer Ellsworth 1
SMILEY, Francis Edward 4
SMILEY, John Stanley 2
SMILEY, Joseph Royall 10
SMILEY, Lyda May 4
SMILEY, Malcolm Finlay 8
SMILEY, Sarah Frances 4
SMILEY, William Brownlee 1
SMILEY, William Henry 1
SMILEY, William Henry 2
SMILIE, John H
SMILLIE, George Frederick Cumming H
SMILLIE, George Henry 1
SMILLIE, Helen Sheldon Jacobs 1
SMILLIE, James H
SMILLIE, James David 1
SMILLIE, Thomas W. 4
SMILLIE, Wilson George 5
SMISER, James A. 1
SMISSMAN, Edward Ervin 6
SMITH, A. Alexander 1
SMITH, A. Donaldson 1
SMITH, A. Frank 4
SMITH, Abby Hadassah H
SMITH, Abiel Leonard 2
SMITH, Abraham E. 1
SMITH, Abraham Herr H
SMITH, Ada Beatrice Queen Victoria Louisa Virginia (Bricktop) 8
SMITH, Addison Romain 2
SMITH, Addison Taylor 3
SMITH, Adrian W. H
SMITH, Alan Kellogg 8
SMITH, Albert* H
SMITH, Albert (Albert Schmidt) 9
SMITH, Albert Barnes, Jr. 10
SMITH, Albert C. 6
SMITH, Albert Charles 5
SMITH, Albert Daniel 8
SMITH, Albert Edward 4
SMITH, Albert Edwin 1
SMITH, Albert Holmes H
SMITH, Albert William 1
SMITH, Albert William 2
SMITH, Albridge Clinton 3
SMITH, Alexander 1
SMITH, Alexander Coke 1
SMITH, Alexander Rogers 4
SMITH, Alexander Wyly 1
SMITH, Alfred Emanuel 2
SMITH, Alfred Forrest 7
SMITH, Alfred Franklin 5
SMITH, Alfred Glaze, Jr. 9
SMITH, Alfred H. 1
SMITH, Alfred H. 4
SMITH, Alfred Theodore 1
SMITH, Alice Ravenel Huger 5
SMITH, Allan Adlph 7
SMITH, Allard 1
SMITH, Allen 1
SMITH, Allen John 1
SMITH, Allen S. 4
SMITH, Alpheus 10
SMITH, Alphonse J. 1
SMITH, Alson Jesse 5
SMITH, Alva J. 1
SMITH, Alvin Augustine 2
SMITH, Andrew Heermance 1
SMITH, Andrew Jackson H
SMITH, Andrew Thomas 1
SMITH, Anna Tolman 1
SMITH, Annie Morrill 4
SMITH, Anthony Wayne 10
SMITH, Archibald Cary 1
SMITH, Arthur H
SMITH, Arthur A. 5
SMITH, Arthur Cosslett 1
SMITH, Arthur D(ouglas) Howden 8
SMITH, Arthur Edward 9
SMITH, Arthur George 1
SMITH, Arthur Henderson 1
SMITH, Arthur Henry 10
SMITH, Arthur James Marshall 7
SMITH, Arthur L. J. 2
SMITH, Arthur Mumford 5
SMITH, Arthur St Clair 2
SMITH, Asa Dodge H
SMITH, Ashbel 1
SMITH, Augustus Wardlaw 1
SMITH, Austin Wheeler 7
SMITH, Azariah H
SMITH, B. Holly 1
SMITH, Barry Congar 3
SMITH, Barton 1
SMITH, Benjamin Eli 1
SMITH, Benjamin M. 3
SMITH, Benjamin Mosby H

SMITH, Bernard H
SMITH, Bessie H
SMITH, Bessie 4
SMITH, Betty 1
SMITH, Beverly Waugh, Jr. 5
SMITH, Blaine Spray 3
SMITH, Blanche A(nnette) 1
SMITH, Bolton 1
SMITH, Boyd Milford 6
SMITH, Bradford 4
SMITH, Bradford, Jr. 9
SMITH, Bridges 1
SMITH, Bromley Keables 9
SMITH, Bruce 3
SMITH, Bruce D. 3
SMITH, Bryan 10
SMITH, Bryce Byram 4
SMITH, Buckingham H
SMITH, Budd Elmon 7
SMITH, Bunnie Othanel 10
SMITH, Burton 2
SMITH, Byron Caldwell 1
SMITH, Byron Laflin 1
SMITH, C. Alphonso 4
SMITH, C. H. Erskine 6
SMITH, C. Ray 9
SMITH, Caleb Blood H
SMITH, Cameron C. 1
SMITH, Carl T. 4
SMITH, Carleton 8
SMITH, Carroll Earll 4
SMITH, Cecil H. 4
SMITH, Cecil Michener 3
SMITH, Cecil Weldon 9
SMITH, Chard Powers 7
SMITH, Charles A. 4
SMITH, Charles Adelbert 7
SMITH, Charles Axel 1
SMITH, Charles Bennett 1
SMITH, Charles Blood 1
SMITH, Charles Bunyan 9
SMITH, Charles Card 1
SMITH, Charles Carman 5
SMITH, Charles Copeland 6
SMITH, Charles Dennison 1
SMITH, Charles Edward 4
SMITH, Charles Edward 5
SMITH, Charles Emory 1
SMITH, Charles Ernest 1
SMITH, Charles F. 10
SMITH, Charles Ferguson H
SMITH, Charles Foster 1
SMITH, Charles Frederick 7
SMITH, Charles G. 4
SMITH, Charles George Percy (Lord Delacourt-Smith) 6
SMITH, Charles Grover 5
SMITH, Charles Henry* 1
SMITH, Charles Howard 1
SMITH, Charles J. 4
SMITH, Charles Jacob 1
SMITH, Charles Lavens 3
SMITH, Charles Lavens 5
SMITH, Charles Lee 3
SMITH, Charles Lysle 5
SMITH, Charles Manley 1
SMITH, Charles Perley 2
SMITH, Charles Perrin 1
SMITH, Charles Shaler H
SMITH, Charles Sidney 1
SMITH, Charles Spencer 1
SMITH, Charles Sprague 1
SMITH, Charles Stephenson 4
SMITH, Charles Stewart 1
SMITH, Charles Sumner 1
SMITH, Charles Theodore 1
SMITH, Charles Wenham 1
SMITH, C(harles) Willard 6
SMITH, Charles William 7
SMITH, Charles William 1
SMITH, Chase McKenzie 8
SMITH, Chauncey Wayland 1
SMITH, Chauncy 1
SMITH, Chester Clinton 2
SMITH, Chester F. 1
SMITH, Clarence Beaman 5
SMITH, Clarence Edwin 1
SMITH, Clarence James 1
SMITH, Claude Earle 9
SMITH, Clay 1
SMITH, Clement Andrew 9
SMITH, Clement Lawrence 1
SMITH, Clifford Pabody 2
SMITH, Clinton De Witt 1
SMITH, Clustor Quentin 4
SMITH, Clyde Harold 1
SMITH, Courtland 1
SMITH, Courtney Craig 5
SMITH, Cyril James 6
SMITH, Cyrus Rowlett 10
SMITH, D. Nevin 4
SMITH, Dan Morgan 2
SMITH, Dan Throop 8
SMITH, Daniel H

SMITH, Daniel Appleton White 1
SMITH, Daniel B. H
SMITH, Daniel Fletcher, Jr. 5
SMITH, Daniel Malloy 7
SMITH, David 4
SMITH, David Beach 10
SMITH, David Eugene 2
SMITH, David H. 6
SMITH, David Highbaugh 4
SMITH, David Morton 1
SMITH, David Stanley 2
SMITH, David Thomas 1
SMITH, David V. 6
SMITH, Dean (Mrs. Warren R. Smith) 5
SMITH, Dean Tyler 1
SMITH, DeLancey C. 8
SMITH, Delavan 1
SMITH, Delazon H
SMITH, Delos Hamilton 4
SMITH, Delos Owen 6
SMITH, Denton Henry 9
SMITH, Dewitt C(linton) 9
SMITH, Dick 8
SMITH, Dilman M. K. 5
SMITH, Donald Borden 3
SMITH, Donald Jenckes 4
SMITH, Donald S(hoecraft) 9
SMITH, Dorman Henry 3
SMITH, Douglas Forrest 3
SMITH, Dudley Crofford 3
SMITH, E. C. E. 3
SMITH, E. Norman 3
SMITH, E. Otis 7
SMITH, E. Sumter 1
SMITH, Earl Baldwin 3
SMITH, Earl Baxter 6
SMITH, Earl E. T. 10
SMITH, Earl Edward 4
SMITH, Earl Hamilton 8
SMITH, Earl Jonas 7
SMITH, Earle Clement 4
SMITH, Earle Samuel 7
SMITH, Ed Sinclair 4
SMITH, Edgar 1
SMITH, Edgar Bronson 1
SMITH, Edgar Fahs 1
SMITH, Edgar Moncena 3
SMITH, Edgar Pichard 10
SMITH, Edgar Wadsworth 4
SMITH, Edgar William 8
SMITH, E(dmund) Howard 5
SMITH, Edmund Kirby H
SMITH, Edmund Kirby 4
SMITH, Edmund Munroe 4
SMITH, Edric Brooks 8
SMITH, Edward B. 1
SMITH, Edward Byron 8
SMITH, Edward Curtis 1
SMITH, Edward Delafield H
SMITH, Edward Devereux 4
SMITH, Edward Everett 5
SMITH, Edward G. 3
SMITH, Edward Grandison 2
SMITH, Edward Hanson 4
SMITH, Edward Henry H
SMITH, Edward J. 1
SMITH, Edward Laurence* 1
SMITH, Edward Lincoln 1
SMITH, Edward North 2
SMITH, Edward Parson 1
SMITH, Edward St. Clair 1
SMITH, Edward Warren 6
SMITH, Edward Willis 1
SMITH, Edwin 1
SMITH, Edwin Bert 6
SMITH, Edwin Bradbury 4
SMITH, Edwin Burritt 1
SMITH, Edwin E. 1
SMITH, Edwin Whittier 1
SMITH, Egbert Watson 2
SMITH, Elbert Luther 6
SMITH, Elbert Sidney 1
SMITH, Eli H
SMITH, Elias H
SMITH, Elias Anthon Cappelen 2
SMITH, Elihu Hubbard 1
SMITH, Elizabeth Howell 4
SMITH, Elizabeth Oakes Prince H
SMITH, Ellen M. Cyr 1
SMITH, Elliott 2
SMITH, Elliott Dunlap 9
SMITH, Ellison Durant 2
SMITH, Ellison Griffith 1
SMITH, E(lmer) Boyd 1
SMITH, Elmer Dennison 2
SMITH, Elmer William 2
SMITH, Elmo 5
SMITH, Elva Sophronia 1
SMITH, Elwyn L. 8
SMITH, Erasmus Darwin 1
SMITH, Erasmus Deshine H
SMITH, Erastus Gilbert 1

SMITH, Erminnie Adelle Platt H
SMITH, Ernest Ashton 1
SMITH, Ernest Charles 4
SMITH, Ernest Ellsworth 1
SMITH, Ernest Gray 2
SMITH, Erwin F. 1
SMITH, Erwin Fletcher 6
SMITH, Erwin Jesse 1
SMITH, Ethan Henry 1
SMITH, Ethan Henry 2
SMITH, Ethelbert Walton 3
SMITH, Eugene 1
SMITH, Eugene Allen 1
SMITH, Eugene Hanes 1
SMITH, Eugene M. 9
SMITH, Everett 4
SMITH, Everett William 4
SMITH, Ezekiel Ezra 3
SMITH, F. Berkeley 4
SMITH, F. Hopkinson 1
SMITH, F. Janney 5
SMITH, Ferdinand Conrad 3
SMITH, Ferris 3
SMITH, Fitz-henry, Jr. 5
SMITH, Forrest 4
SMITH, Frances Stanton 5
SMITH, Francis Alward 4
SMITH, Francis Asbury 1
SMITH, Francis Edward 6
SMITH, Francis Edwin 5
SMITH, Francis Henney H
SMITH, Francis Henry 1
SMITH, Francis Marion 1
SMITH, Francis Ormand Jonathan H
SMITH, Francis Palmer 8
SMITH, Frank 1
SMITH, Frank Austin 2
SMITH, Frank Bulkeley 1
SMITH, Frank C. 5
SMITH, Frank Channing, Jr. 3
SMITH, Frank Gerard 6
SMITH, Frank Grigsby 3
SMITH, Frank Leslie 3
SMITH, Frank Marshall 1
SMITH, Frank O. 1
SMITH, Frank Sullivan 1
SMITH, Frank Webster 2
SMITH, Frank Whitney 2
SMITH, Franklin G. 5
SMITH, Franklin Guest 1
SMITH, Franklin Orion 1
SMITH, Fred Andrew 5
SMITH, Fred B. 1
SMITH, Fred Emory 4
SMITH, Fred M. 2
SMITH, Fred Wildon 9
SMITH, Frederic William 6
SMITH, Frederick Appleton 1
SMITH, Frederick Arthur 5
SMITH, Frederick Augustus 1
SMITH, Frederick Buren 10
SMITH, Frederick C. 3
SMITH, Frederick Danesbury 9
SMITH, Frederick H. 1
SMITH, Frederick Madison 2
SMITH, Frederick Miller 5
SMITH, Frederick Reuben 8
SMITH, G. Wallace 3
SMITH, G. Williamson 1
SMITH, Geoffrey F. N. 7
SMITH, Geoffrey F. N. 8
SMITH, George H
SMITH, George (William) 9
SMITH, George Albert 1
SMITH, George Albert 3
SMITH, George Albert, Jr. 5
SMITH, George Carson 1
SMITH, George C(line) 6
SMITH, George D. 4
SMITH, George Edson Philip 5
SMITH, George Frederick 10
SMITH, George Frederick 6
SMITH, George Frederick 7
SMITH, George Gilbert 4
SMITH, George Harris 2
SMITH, George Hathorn 3
SMITH, George Henry 1
SMITH, George Hunter 3
SMITH, George Jay 4
SMITH, George Joseph 4
SMITH, George L. 3
SMITH, George Luke H
SMITH, George M. 1
SMITH, George M. 4
SMITH, George Milton 3
SMITH, George Otis 2
SMITH, George P. F. 4
SMITH, George Rodney 4
SMITH, George Ross 4
SMITH, George Theodore 1
SMITH, George W. 1
SMITH, George Walter Vincent 1
SMITH, George Weissinger 1
SMITH, Gerald Birney 1
SMITH, Gerald Hewitt 3
SMITH, Gerrit H
SMITH, Gerrit 1
SMITH, Gertrude 1
SMITH, Gilbert Morgan 3
SMITH, Giles Alexander H
SMITH, Glenn J. 7
SMITH, Goldwin 1
SMITH, Gordon Arthur 2
SMITH, Grafton Adrian 5
SMITH, Green Clay H
SMITH, Gregory 10
SMITH, Gregory L. 1
SMITH, Gretchen Hart 6
SMITH, Griffin 3
SMITH, Gustavus Woodson H
SMITH, Guy Chester 6
SMITH, Guy Lincoln 5
SMITH, Guy Lincoln, III 9
SMITH, Guy-harold 7
SMITH, H. A. A. 1
SMITH, H. Alexander 4
SMITH, H. Allen 6
SMITH, H. Augustine 3
SMITH, H. Dewitt 9
SMITH, H. Lester 3
SMITH, H. M., Jr. 1
SMITH, H. Shelton 10
SMITH, Hal Horace 2
SMITH, Hal Horace, Jr. 5
SMITH, Halsey 8
SMITH, Hamilton H
SMITH, Hamilton Lamphere 1
SMITH, Hariette Knight 4
SMITH, Harlan Ingersoll 1
SMITH, Harlan James 10
SMITH, Harmon 1
SMITH, Harold 7
SMITH, Harold Armstrong 9
SMITH, Harold Babbitt 1
SMITH, Harold Colby 10
SMITH, Harold Dewey 2
SMITH, Harold Leonard 5
SMITH, Harold Morrison 9
SMITH, Harold Stephen 5
SMITH, Harold Travis 3
SMITH, Harold Vincent 4
SMITH, Harold Wellington 3
SMITH, Harriet Lummis 2
SMITH, Harrison 5
SMITH, Harry Alexander* 1
SMITH, Harry Bache 1
SMITH, Harry De Forest 5
SMITH, Harry Eaton 1
SMITH, Harry James 1
SMITH, Harry Pearse 3
SMITH, Harry Worcester 2
SMITH, Haviland 5
SMITH, Hay Watson 1
SMITH, Helen Evertson 4
SMITH, Henry A. M. 1
SMITH, Henry Boynton H
SMITH, Henry Bradford 1
SMITH, Henry Cassorte 1
SMITH, Henry Cooper 4
SMITH, Henry Erskine 5
SMITH, Henry Garfield 7
SMITH, Henry Gerrish 3
SMITH, H(enry) Gordon 6
SMITH, Henry J. 9
SMITH, Henry Justin 1
SMITH, Henry Leavitt 1
SMITH, Henry Lee, Jr. 5
SMITH, Henry Lester 4
SMITH, Henry Louis 3
SMITH, Henry Michelet 3
SMITH, Henry Monmouth 3
SMITH, Henry Nash 9
SMITH, Henry Oliver 8
SMITH, Henry Preserved 1
SMITH, Henry Tomlinson 1
SMITH, Herbert Atwood 3
SMITH, Herbert Augustine 2
SMITH, Herbert Booth 4
SMITH, Herbert Burling 8
SMITH, Herbert Edward 5
SMITH, Herbert Eugene 1
SMITH, Herbert Huntington 1
SMITH, Herbert Knox 1
SMITH, Herbert Livingston, III 8
SMITH, Herbert Wilson 5
SMITH, Herman Lyle 3
SMITH, Hezekiah H
SMITH, Hezekiah Bradley H
SMITH, Hiram H
SMITH, Hiram Moore 2
SMITH, Hiram Ypsilanti H
SMITH, Hoke 1
SMITH, Holland McTyeire 4
SMITH, Holmes 1
SMITH, Homer 1
SMITH, Homer William 4
SMITH, Horace H
SMITH, Horace Boardman H
SMITH, Horace Herbert 4
SMITH, Horatio Elwin 2
SMITH, Howard 9
SMITH, Howard Anthony 4
SMITH, Howard Caswell 4
SMITH, Howard Dwight 3
SMITH, Howard Everett 7
SMITH, Howard F(ranklyn) 7
SMITH, Howard Godwin 8
SMITH, Howard Leland 6
SMITH, Howard Leslie 4
SMITH, Howard Remus 5
SMITH, Howard Wayne 3
SMITH, Howard Worth 7
SMITH, Hubert Winston 5
SMITH, Hugh Allison 5
SMITH, Hugh Carnes 2
SMITH, Hugh F., Jr. 2
SMITH, Hugh McCormick 1
SMITH, Huntington 4
SMITH, Hurlbut William 3
SMITH, Huron H. 1
SMITH, Ida B. Wise 3
SMITH, Ignatius 3
SMITH, Irving Gardner 4
SMITH, (Irving) Norman 9
SMITH, Isaac* H
SMITH, Isaac B. 2
SMITH, Isaac Townsend 4
SMITH, Isabel E. 1
SMITH, Isaiah Perley 4
SMITH, Israel H
SMITH, Israel A. 3
SMITH, J. Allen 1
SMITH, J. Burritt 1
SMITH, J. Emil 5
SMITH, J. Frank 1
SMITH, J. Joseph 7
SMITH, J. Joseph 8
SMITH, J. M. Powis 1
SMITH, J. Neil 5
SMITH, J. Paul 3
SMITH, J. Ritchie 1
SMITH, J. Stanford 8
SMITH, J. Waldo 1
SMITH, J. Warren 1
SMITH, Jacob Getlar 3
SMITH, Jacob Hurd 1
SMITH, Jacqueline Sarah 10
SMITH, James* H
SMITH, James, Jr. 1
SMITH, James Allwood 1
SMITH, James Argyle 4
SMITH, James Craig 7
SMITH, James D. 3
SMITH, James Dickinson 1
SMITH, James Ellwood 1
SMITH, James Francis 1
SMITH, James Gerald 2
SMITH, James Gerald 8
SMITH, James Henry 10
SMITH, James Henry Oliver 1
SMITH, James Hopkins, Jr. 8
SMITH, James Irwin 4
SMITH, James Kellum 4
SMITH, James McCune H
SMITH, James McLain 1
SMITH, James Monroe 8
SMITH, James Perrin 1
SMITH, James Porter 1
SMITH, James Power 4
SMITH, James Sheppard 1
SMITH, James Strudwick H
SMITH, James W. 3
SMITH, James Walter 2
SMITH, James Willison 2
SMITH, James Youngs H
SMITH, Jane Luella Dowd 4
SMITH, Jane Norman 3
SMITH, Jeanie Oliver Davidson 1
SMITH, Jedediah Kilburn H
SMITH, Jedediah Strong H
SMITH, Jeremiah H
SMITH, Jeremiah 1
SMITH, Jeremiah, Jr. 1
SMITH, Jesse Merrick 1
SMITH, Jesse Sherwood 9
SMITH, Jessica 10
SMITH, Jessie Willcox 1
SMITH, Jim Clifford 2
SMITH, Job Lewis H
SMITH, Joe Frazer 3
SMITH, Joe L. 4
SMITH, Joel Perry 6
SMITH, Joel West 1
SMITH, John* H
SMITH, John Addison Baxter 1
SMITH, John Ambler H
SMITH, John Armstrong H
SMITH, John Augustine H
SMITH, John Bernhardt 1
SMITH, John Blair H
SMITH, John Butler 1
SMITH, John Charles 4
SMITH, John Corson 1
SMITH, John Cotton* H
SMITH, John Day 1
SMITH, John Edwin 10
SMITH, John Elijah 5
SMITH, John Eugene H
SMITH, John Francis, Jr. 7
SMITH, John Frederick 3
SMITH, John Gregory H
SMITH, John Hammond 1
SMITH, John Henry, Jr. 3
SMITH, John Hyatt H
SMITH, John James 7
SMITH, John Jay H
SMITH, John Joseph 5
SMITH, John Lawrence H
SMITH, John Lawrence 3
SMITH, John Lewis 3
SMITH, John Lewis, Jr. 10
SMITH, John Lucian, Jr. 7
SMITH, John M. C. 1
SMITH, John P. 2
SMITH, John Rowson H
SMITH, John Rubens H
SMITH, John Sloan 5
SMITH, John Speed H
SMITH, John T. H
SMITH, John Talbot 1
SMITH, John Thomas 2
SMITH, John Walter 1
SMITH, John Walter 5
SMITH, John Wesley 1
SMITH, Jonathan Bayard H
SMITH, Joseph* H
SMITH, Joseph* 1
SMITH, Joseph Adams 1
SMITH, Joseph Brodie 2
SMITH, Joseph Earl 5
SMITH, Joseph Edward 7
SMITH, Joseph Fielding 1
SMITH, Joseph Fielding 4
SMITH, Joseph Fielding 5
SMITH, Joseph Francis 2
SMITH, Joseph Henry 8
SMITH, Joseph Lindon 3
SMITH, Joseph Mather H
SMITH, Joseph Newton 3
SMITH, Joseph P. 4
SMITH, Joseph Rowe 1
SMITH, J(oseph) Russell 6
SMITH, Joseph Showalter H
SMITH, Joseph Thomas 4
SMITH, Joseph Wilson 8
SMITH, Josephine Wernicke 3
SMITH, Josiah H
SMITH, Josiah Renick 1
SMITH, Judson 1
SMITH, Jules Andre 6
SMITH, Julia Evelina H
SMITH, Julia Holmes 1
SMITH, Julius Clarence 5
SMITH, June C. 2
SMITH, Junius H
SMITH, Justin Harvey 1
SMITH, K. Wesley 4
SMITH, Kate (Kathryn Elizabeth Smith) 9
SMITH, Kendrick 9
SMITH, Kenneth 10
SMITH, Kenneth Gladstone 2
SMITH, Kent Hale 7
SMITH, Kirby Flower 1
SMITH, Kirk 9
SMITH, Langdon 1
SMITH, Larkin 10
SMITH, Laura Rountree 1
SMITH, Lawrence 4
SMITH, Lawrence Breese 8
SMITH, Lawrence Henry 3
SMITH, Lawrence Meredith Clemson 6
SMITH, Lawrence Weld 6
SMITH, Lee Irvin 9
SMITH, Lee Thompson 4
SMITH, Leland Leslie 7
SMITH, Lemuel Augustus, Sr. 3
SMITH, Lemuel F. 3
SMITH, Leo R. 4
SMITH, Leon E. 4
SMITH, Leon Edgar 6
SMITH, Leon Perdue 1
SMITH, Leon Perdue 4
SMITH, Leona Jones (Mrs. Robert James Smith) 5
SMITH, Leonard Bacon 3
SMITH, Leonard Bacon 4
SMITH, Leonard Charles 10
SMITH, Leonard Minuse 2
SMITH, Leonidas D'Entrecasteaux 1
SMITH, Lester Sherald 7
SMITH, Levi Pease 5
SMITH, Levi Pease 7
SMITH, Lewis Elden 4
SMITH, Lewis Martin 3
SMITH, Lewis Wilbur 3
SMITH, Lewis Worthington 2
SMITH, Lillian 4
SMITH, Linn Charles 8
SMITH, Livingston 6
SMITH, Livingston Waddell 3
SMITH, Lloyd Dewitt 5
SMITH, Lloyd Gaston 3
SMITH, Lloyd L. 8
SMITH, Lloyd Pearsall H
SMITH, Lloyd Preston 9
SMITH, Lloyd Raymond 2
SMITH, Lloyd Waddell 5
SMITH, Lloyd Weir 3
SMITH, Logan Pearsall 2
SMITH, Lothrop 3
SMITH, Louie Henrie 5
SMITH, Louise Pettibone 8
SMITH, Lowell H. 2
SMITH, Lura Eugenie Brown 4
SMITH, Luther Andrew 7
SMITH, Luther Ely 3
SMITH, Luther Wesley 5
SMITH, Lybrand Palmer 2
SMITH, Lyman Cornelius 1
SMITH, Lyndon Ambrose 1
SMITH, Lynwood H. 3
SMITH, M. Ellwood 4
SMITH, Mabell Shippie Clarke 2
SMITH, Madison Roswell 4
SMITH, Marcus H
SMITH, Marcus Aurelius 1
SMITH, Margaret Bayard H
SMITH, Margaret Vowell 4
SMITH, Marion 2
SMITH, Marion Couthouy 1
SMITH, Marion Gertrude 3
SMITH, Marion Lofton 8
SMITH, Marjorie C. 5
SMITH, Mark H
SMITH, Mark A. 2
SMITH, Martha Rose Kapantaes (Mrs. Robert Clifford Smith) 5
SMITH, Martin F. 3
SMITH, Martin Luther H
SMITH, Marvin Boren 3
SMITH, Mary Cynthia 6
SMITH, Mary Elizabeth 1
SMITH, Mary Prudence Wells 1
SMITH, Mason 4
SMITH, Matthew 3
SMITH, Matthew Dinsdale 9
SMITH, Matthew F. 1
SMITH, Matthew Hale H
SMITH, Matthew John Wilfred 4
SMITH, Matthew Joseph 8
SMITH, May Riley 1
SMITH, McGregor 5
SMITH, Melancton H
SMITH, Melvin Montgomery 6
SMITH, Meriwether H
SMITH, Merle Negley 5
SMITH, Merriman 5
SMITH, Mildred Catharine 6
SMITH, Miles Woodward 8
SMITH, Milton H. 1
SMITH, Milton Truman 3
SMITH, Minna Caroline 1
SMITH, Monroe William 6
SMITH, Mordon 6
SMITH, Morgan Lewis H
SMITH, Mortimer Brewster 8
SMITH, Morton 10
SMITH, Moses 4
SMITH, Munroe 1
SMITH, Murray 3
SMITH, Myrtle Holm 3
SMITH, Nathan* H
SMITH, Nathan Ryno H
SMITH, Nathaniel H
SMITH, Nathaniel Waite 5
SMITH, Neal Austin 10
SMITH, Newman 4
SMITH, Nicholas 1
SMITH, Nicol Hamilton 5
SMITH, Nora Archibald 1
SMITH, Norman Kemp 5
SMITH, Norman Murray 5
SMITH, O. Warren 1
SMITH, Oberlin 1
SMITH, O'Brien H
SMITH, Oliver H
SMITH, Oliver Hampton H
SMITH, Oramandal 3
SMITH, Orlando Jay 1
SMITH, Orma Jacob 2
SMITH, Orma Rinehart 9
SMITH, Ormond Gerald 1

SMITH, Orrin Harold 6
SMITH, Orson 1
SMITH, Oscar 8
SMITH, Oscar Alpheus 7
SMITH, Otis David 1
SMITH, Otterbein Oscar 1
SMITH, Owen Lun West 4
SMITH, Parke Gillespie 9
SMITH, Paul, Jr. 8
SMITH, Paul Althaus 7
SMITH, Paul Davis 8
SMITH, Paul Edward 5
SMITH, Paul Francis 4
SMITH, Paul Glen 6
SMITH, Paul Jordan 5
SMITH, Paul Jordan 7
SMITH, Paul Kenneth 4
SMITH, Paul Kimbrell 10
SMITH, Paul Samuel 10
SMITH, Payson 1
SMITH, Percey Franklyn 3
SMITH, Percy William 4
SMITH, Perry H
SMITH, Perry Coke 6
SMITH, Perry Dunlap 4
SMITH, Persifor Frazer H
SMITH, Peter H
SMITH, Peter P. 3
SMITH, Philip E. 5
SMITH, Philip Sidney 3
SMITH, Phillips Waller 4
SMITH, Preserved 1
SMITH, Quintius 4
Cincinnatus
SMITH, R. Waverley 1
SMITH, Ralph Boyd 8
SMITH, Ralph Carlisle 10
SMITH, Ralph Chester 4
SMITH, Ralph Eliot 5
SMITH, Ralph M. 3
SMITH, Ralph Tyler 5
SMITH, Ralph Winfield 5
SMITH, Randle Jasper 4
SMITH, Ray L. 3
SMITH, Ray M. 8
SMITH, Ray Victor 9
SMITH, Ray Winfield 9
SMITH, Raymond Abner 5
SMITH, Raymond D(aniel) 9
SMITH, Raymond G. 9
SMITH, Raymond 3
Underwood
SMITH, Raymond William 8
SMITH, Red 8
SMITH, Reed 2
SMITH, Reginald Heber 4
SMITH, Reuben Robert 1
SMITH, Rex 3
SMITH, Richard H
SMITH, Richard Garbett 7
SMITH, Richard Hewlett 2
SMITH, Richard Paul 4
SMITH, Richard Penn H
SMITH, Richard R. 3
SMITH, Richard Root 1
SMITH, Richard Somers 4
SMITH, Robert* H
SMITH, Robert A. C. 1
SMITH, Robert Armstrong 4
SMITH, Robert Aura 3
SMITH, R(obert) Blackwell, 5
Jr.
SMITH, Robert Brandon 2
SMITH, Robert Burns 1
SMITH, Robert Chester 4
SMITH, Robert Dwight 7
SMITH, Robert Edwin 3
SMITH, Robert Edwin 6
SMITH, Robert Fitch 4
SMITH, Robert H. 4
SMITH, Robert Hardy H
SMITH, Robert Hays 5
SMITH, Robert Keating 4
SMITH, Robert Lee 4
SMITH, Robert M. 9
SMITH, Robert Metcalf 3
SMITH, Robert Nelson 8
SMITH, Robert P. 4
SMITH, Robert Paterson 1
SMITH, Robert Paul 7
SMITH, Robert Seneca 1
SMITH, Robert Shufeldt 1
SMITH, Robert Sidney H
SMITH, Robert Sidney 4
SMITH, Robert Sidney 5
SMITH, Robert William 6
SMITH, Robinson 5
SMITH, Rodney 1
SMITH, Rogert Haskell 1
SMITH, Roland Cotton 1
SMITH, Roland Kidder 1
SMITH, Rollin Coleman, Jr. 7
SMITH, Roswell H
SMITH, Roy Campbell 4
SMITH, Roy Harmon 4
SMITH, Roy Lemon 8
SMITH, Roy Leon 1

SMITH, Ruel Perley 1
SMITH, Rufus Burr 7
SMITH, Rufus D. 3
SMITH, Russell H
SMITH, Russell Evans 10
SMITH, Russell Hunt 8
SMITH, Russell P(aul) 7
SMITH, Ruth Ann Cook 5
SMITH, S. Archibald 3
SMITH, S. Calvin 1
SMITH, S. Jennie 1
SMITH, S. Stephenson 4
SMITH, Sadie Adams 4
SMITH, Samray 5
SMITH, Samuel* H
SMITH, Samuel 4
SMITH, Samuel A. H
SMITH, Samuel Abbot 10
SMITH, Samuel Axley H
SMITH, Samuel Edwin 1
SMITH, Samuel Francis H
SMITH, Samuel George 1
SMITH, Samuel Harrison H
SMITH, S(amuel) L(eonard) 5
SMITH, Samuel Stanhope H
SMITH, Samuel William 1
SMITH, Seba H
SMITH, Seth MacCuen 4
SMITH, Seymour Wemyss 1
SMITH, Sherman Everett 6
SMITH, Sherrill 3
SMITH, Shirley Wheeler 3
SMITH, Sidney 1
SMITH, Sidney 4
SMITH, Sidney Earle 3
SMITH, Sidney Irving 1
SMITH, Sidney Mason 1
SMITH, Sion Bass 3
SMITH, Soloman Franklin H
SMITH, Solomon Albert 4
SMITH, Solomon Byron 9
SMITH, Sophia H
SMITH, St. Clair 8
SMITH, Stephen 1
SMITH, Sterling Bishop 7
SMITH, Stevenson 3
SMITH, Stuart Farwell 7
SMITH, Stuart Robertson 1
SMITH, Susan T. 4
SMITH, Sydney 2
SMITH, Sylvester Clark 1
SMITH, Sylvester 8
Comstock, Jr.
SMITH, T. Guilford 1
SMITH, T. V. 4
SMITH, Theobald 1
SMITH, Theodore Clarke 4
SMITH, T(heodore) 7
Townsend
SMITH, Thomas* H
SMITH, Thomas* 4
SMITH, Thomas Adams H
SMITH, Thomas Arthur 4
SMITH, Thomas Berry 1
SMITH, Thomas F. 1
SMITH, Thomas Franklin 1
SMITH, Thomas Jefferson 5
SMITH, Thomas Kilby H
SMITH, Thomas Latham 7
SMITH, Thomas Max 5
SMITH, Thomas Newill 5
SMITH, Thomas Octavius 1
SMITH, Thomas R. 2
SMITH, Thomas William 5
SMITH, Thomas William 9
Macaulay
SMITH, Thurber 3
Montgomery
SMITH, Tom K. 7
SMITH, Tony 7
SMITH, Truman H
SMITH, Ulysses Simpson 2
SMITH, Uriah 1
SMITH, Vincent E. 5
SMITH, Vincent Weaver 4
SMITH, Vine Harold 5
SMITH, Vivian Thomas 3
SMITH, W. A. 4
SMITH, W. Angle 10
SMITH, W. H. B. 4
SMITH, Wade Cothran 5
SMITH, Walt Allen 5
SMITH, Walter 8
SMITH, Walter Bedell 4
SMITH, Walter Byron 1
SMITH, Walter Driscoll 3
SMITH, Walter F. 8
SMITH, Walter George 4
SMITH, Walter Henry 7
SMITH, Walter Inglewood 1
SMITH, Walter Irvine 8
SMITH, Walter Lloyd 1
SMITH, Walter McMynn 1
SMITH, Walter Robinson 1
SMITH, Walter Tenney 1
SMITH, Walter Tenney 2
SMITH, Walter Winfred 2

SMITH, Warren Du Pre 3
SMITH, Warren Lounsbury 5
SMITH, Warren Robert 3
SMITH, Wayne Carleton 4
SMITH, Wendell 5
SMITH, Weston 6
SMITH, Wilbert L. 1
SMITH, Wilbur Cleveland 3
SMITH, Wilbur Fisk 1
SMITH, Wilbur Moorehead 7
SMITH, Wilbur Stevenson 10
SMITH, Wilfrid Russell 7
SMITH, Willard Adelbert 1
SMITH, Willi Donnell 9
SMITH, William* H
SMITH, William 1
SMITH, William Alden 1
SMITH, William Alexander 4
SMITH, William Alexander 1
SMITH, William Andrew 6
SMITH, William Anton 6
SMITH, William Arthur 10
SMITH, William Austin 1
SMITH, William Benjamin 1
SMITH, William Clarke 1
SMITH, William Clarke 2
SMITH, William 2
Cunningham
SMITH, William Eason 2
SMITH, William Edward 2
SMITH, William Ephraim H
SMITH, William Ernest 9
SMITH, William Farrar 1
SMITH, William Francis 4
SMITH, William French 10
SMITH, William Griswold 2
SMITH, William Hall 4
SMITH, William Harrison 4
SMITH, William Hawley 1
SMITH, William Henry* H
SMITH, William Henry 1
SMITH, William Henry 4
SMITH, William Hinckle 2
SMITH, William Hopton 2
SMITH, William Howard 7
SMITH, William Jones 3
SMITH, William Loughton H
SMITH, William Mason 4
SMITH, William Nathan H
Harrell
SMITH, William Oliver 4
SMITH, William Orlando 6
SMITH, William Owen 1
SMITH, William Owen 2
SMITH, William Robert 1
SMITH, William Roy 5
SMITH, William Russell 4
SMITH, William Ruthven 1
SMITH, William Skeldon 3
Adamson
SMITH, William Sooy 1
SMITH, William Stephens 4
SMITH, William Stevenson 5
SMITH, William Strother 1
SMITH, William Thayer 1
SMITH, William Thomas 2
SMITH, William W., II 3
SMITH, William Walker 1
SMITH, William Wallace 10
SMITH, William Walter 2
SMITH, William Ward 4
SMITH, William Waugh 1
SMITH, William 2
Wilberforce
SMITH, Willis 3
SMITH, Willis, Jr. 5
SMITH, Wilmot M. 1
SMITH, Wilmot Mott 9
SMITH, Wilson George 1
SMITH, Winchell 1
SMITH, Winford Henry 4
SMITH, Winthrop Hiram 4
SMITH, Worthington 1
SMITH, Worthington Curtis H
SMITH, Young Berryman 1
SMITH, Zachariah 1
Frederick
SMITH, Zemro Augustus 1
SMITH, Zilpha Drew 1
SMITHEE, James Newton 1
SMITHER, Henry 1
Carpenter
SMITHERS, Ernest 1
Leonard
SMITHERS, Nathaniel H
Barrett
SMITHERS, William West 2
SMITHEY, Louis Philippe 4
SMITHEY, Royall Bascom 1
SMITHEY, William Royall 5
SMITHIES, Arthur 8
SMITHIES, Elsie May 8
SMITHIES, Frank 1
SMITH-PETERSEN, 3
Marius Nygaard
SMITHSON, James H
SMITHSON, Noble 1

SMITHSON, William 1
Walpole
SMITHWICK, John Harris 3
SMOCK, Harry Berdan 6
SMOCK, John Conover 1
SMOCK, P(eter) Monroe 5
SMOCK, Wendell Merritt 4
SMOHALLA H
SMOHALLA 4
SMOKER, Edward Heise 1
SMOLAR, Boris (Ber) 9
SMOLEY, Constantine 3
Kenneth
SMOOT, Charles Head 1
SMOOT, Reed 1
SMOOT, Thomas Arthur 1
SMOOT, William Clay 7
SMOTHERS, Frank 7
(Albert)
SMUCKLER, Edward 9
Aaron
SMULL, Jacob Barstow 4
SMULL, Thomas Jefferson, 4
Jr.
SMULSKI, John F. 1
SMUTNY, Rudolf 6
SMUTS, Jan Christiaan 3
SMYKAL, Richard 1
SMYSER, Martin L. 1
SMYSER, William Emory 1
SMYTH, Albert Henry 1
SMYTH, Alexander 1
SMYTH, Calvin Mason, Jr. 4
SMYTH, Charles Edward 7
SMYTH, Charles Edward 8
SMYTH, Charles Henry, Jr. 1
SMYTH, Charles Phelps 10
SMYTH, Clifford 4
SMYTH, Constantine 1
Joseph
SMYTH, Egbert Coffin 1
SMYTH, Ellison Adger 1
SMYTH, Ellison Adger 2
SMYTH, Francis Scott 5
SMYTH, George H
Washington
SMYTH, Henry Dewolf 9
SMYTH, Henry Field 3
SMYTH, Henry Lloyd 2
SMYTH, Herbert 2
SMYTH, Herbert Weir 1
SMYTH, James Adger 1
SMYTH, Julian Kennedy 1
SMYTH, Margarita 5
Pumpelly
SMYTH, Newman 1
SMYTH, S. Gordon 3
SMYTH, Thomas H
SMYTH, Timothy Clement H
SMYTH, William* H
SMYTH, William Henry 1
SMYTH, Wilma Louise 1
SMYTH, Winfield Scott 1
SMYTHE, Augustine 1
Thomas
SMYTHE, Chauncey B. 9
SMYTHE, George Franklin 1
SMYTHE, George Winfred 5
SMYTHE, Hugh Heyne 4
SMYTHE, J. Henry, Jr. 3
SMYTHE, Sidney Thomas 1
SMYTHE, William E. 1
SNADER, David L. 8
SNAITH, William Theodore 6
SNAPE, John 2
SNAPP, Henry H
SNAPP, Howard Malcolm 1
SNAPPER, Arthur 10
SNAPPER, Isidore 8
SNARE, Frederick 3
SNARR, Frederic Earle 1
SNARR, Otto Welton 4
SNAVELY, Guy Everett 6
SNAVELY, John Robert 4
SNEAD, Thomas Lowndes H
SNEATH, E. Hershey 1
SNEATH, George Mark 7
SNEATH, Mrs. Samuel B. 5
(Laura S. Sneath)
SNEDDEN, Charles Willis 10
SNEDDEN, David 5
SNEDECOR, George W. 6
SNEDECOR, James George 4
SNEDEKER, Caroline Dale 3
SNEDEKER, Charles 1
Dippolt
SNEED, Albert Lee 4
SNEED, Earl 7
SNEED, Frank Woolford 2
SNEED, James Russell 1
SNEED, John Louis Taylor 1
SNEED, M. Cannon 7
SNEED, William Henry H
SNEED, William Lent 2
SNEIDER, Richard Lee 9
SNELHAM, John Sydney 4

SNELL, Albert M. 3
SNELL, Bertrand H. 3
SNELL, C(larence) 8
E(astlake)
SNELL, Earl Wilcox 2
SNELL, George H
SNELL, Henry Bayley 2
SNELL, John Leslie 5
SNELL, Roy Judson 6
SNELL, Walter Henry 8
SNELL, Willis Byron 9
SNELLGROVE, Harold 9
Sinclair
SNELLING, Charles 1
Mercer
SNELLING, Henry Hunt H
SNELLING, Josiah H
SNELLING, Richard 10
Arkwright
SNELLING, Rodman Paul 4
SNELLING, Walter 1
Otheman
SNELLING, William H
Joseph
SNETHEN, Nicholas H
SNEVE, Haldor 1
SNEVILY, Henry Mansfield 1
SNIDECOR, John Clifton 8
SNIDER, Arthur J. 7
SNIDER, Clyde Frank 5
SNIDER, Denton Jaques 1
SNIDER, John Raywaldt 7
SNIDER, Joseph Lyons 3
SNIDER, Luther Crocker 2
SNIDER, Samuel Prather 4
SNIFF, Littleton M. 1
SNIFFEN, Culver Channing 1
SNIVELY, Samuel Frisby 4
SNIVELY, William Andrew 1
SNOBERGER, Rantz 1
SNODDY, Elmer Ellsworth 1
SNODDY, Leland Bradley 3
SNODGRASS, Charles 4
Edward
SNODGRASS, David E. 4
SNODGRASS, David La 1
Fayette
SNODGRASS, George 1
Merrill
SNODGRASS, John Fryall H
SNODGRASS, John Harold 1
SNODGRASS, Robert 1
SNODGRASS, Robert 5
Evans
SNODGRASS, Robert 5
Richard
SNODGRASS, Samuel 6
Robert
SNOKE, Harry Conwell 8
SNOOK, Homer Clyde 7
SNOOK, John Lloyd 7
SNOOK, John Orla 9
SNOOK, John S. 5
SNOOK, John Wilson 5
SNOOK, Thomas E. 8
SNOW, Albert Sydney 1
SNOW, Alpheus Henry 1
SNOW, Alva Edson 4
SNOW, Baron (Charles 7
Percy Snow)
SNOW, Benjamin Warner 1
SNOW, Carmel 4
SNOW, Chalres Ernest 4
SNOW, Charles Armstrong 1
SNOW, Charles Henry 3
SNOW, Chauncey Depew 4
SNOW, Conrad Edwin 7
SNOW, Donald Francis 1
SNOW, Edgar Parks 5
SNOW, Elbert Clay 4
SNOW, Elbridge Gerry 1
SNOW, Eliza Roxey H
SNOW, Ernest Albert 1
SNOW, Francis 5
SNOW, Francis Huntington 1
SNOW, Franklin Augustus 2
SNOW, Frederic 4
SNOW, Henry Sanger 4
SNOW, Herman Bernard 9
SNOW, J. Parker 3
SNOW, John Ben 5
SNOW, Leslie Perkins 1
SNOW, Leslie W. 3
SNOW, Lorenzo H
SNOW, Louis Franklin 1
SNOW, Marshall Solomon 1
SNOW, Sydney Bruce 2
SNOW, Walter Bradlee 4
SNOW, Warren Howland 4
SNOW, Wilbert (Charles) 7
SNOW, William Benham 6
SNOW, William Dunham 3
SNOW, William Freeman 3
SNOW, William Josiah 2
SNOW, William W. H
SNOWDEN, A. Loudon 1
SNOWDEN, James Henry 1

SNOWDEN, James Ross	H
SNOWDEN, Robert Bogardus	1
SNOWDEN, R(obert) Brinkley	5
SNOWDEN, Thomas	1
SNOWDEN, Yates	1
SNOWDON, John Colin	7
SNURE, John	1
SNYDER, A.Cecil	3
SNYDER, Adam Wilson	H
SNYDER, Addison Hogan	6
SNYDER, Alban Goshorn	5
SNYDER, Albert Whitcomb	1
SNYDER, Arthur	4
SNYDER, Asa Edward	8
SNYDER, Baird, III	2
SNYDER, Carl	2
SNYDER, Carl J.	3
SNYDER, Charles B. J.	4
SNYDER, Charles Edward	3
SNYDER, Charles Edwin	7
SNYDER, Charles McCoy	4
SNYDER, Charles Philip	4
SNYDER, Daniel J., Jr.	7
SNYDER, Daniel J., Jr.	8
SNYDER, Donald B(ertram)	10
SNYDER, Edgar Callender	1
SNYDER, Edward	1
SNYDER, Eldredge	4
SNYDER, Erwin Paul	6
SNYDER, Franklyn Bliss	3
SNYDER, Fred Beal	3
SNYDER, Frederic Sylvester	5
SNYDER, Frederick Edward	10
SNYDER, George Gordon	6
SNYDER, Harris Noble	8
SNYDER, Harry	1
SNYDER, Henry	1
SNYDER, Henry Burgess	7
SNYDER, Henry George	3
SNYDER, Henry Nelson	2
SNYDER, Henry Steinman	1
SNYDER, Homer P.	1
SNYDER, Howard Mcc.	5
SNYDER, J. Ralph	3
SNYDER, Jefferson	1
SNYDER, John	H
SNYDER, John Buell	2
SNYDER, John I., Jr.	4
SNYDER, John Otterbein	5
SNYDER, John Stewart	7
SNYDER, John Taylor	3
SNYDER, John Wesley	9
SNYDER, John William	7
SNYDER, Jonathan Le Moyne	1
SNYDER, Leon Carleton	9
SNYDER, Leroy Edwin	2
SNYDER, Melvin Harold	9
SNYDER, Meredith Pinxton	1
SNYDER, Mitch	10
SNYDER, Monroe B.	1
SNYDER, Murray	5
SNYDER, Nicholas R.	4
SNYDER, Norman	10
SNYDER, Oliver P.	H
SNYDER, Oscar John	2
SNYDER, Otto	7
SNYDER, Reginald Clare	1
SNYDER, Robert McClure	1
SNYDER, Simon	H
SNYDER, Simon	1
SNYDER, Valentine P.	1
SNYDER, Virgil	2
SNYDER, Wahl John	10
SNYDER, William Cordes, Jr.	9
SNYDER, William Edward	3
SNYDER, William Franklin	7
SNYDER, William Lamartine	4
SNYDER, William P., Jr.	4
SNYDER, Zachariah Xenophon	1
SOANS, Cyril Arthur	6
SOANS, Cyril Arthur	7
SOARES, Theodore Gerald	5
SOBEL, Bernard	4
SOBEL, Eli	9
SOBELOFF, Jonathan	7
SOBELOFF, Simon E.	6
SOBER, Herbert Alexander	6
SOBEY, Albert	7
SOBEY, William Macdonald	10
SOBIESKI, John	4
SOBILOFF, Hyman Jordan	5
SOBOL, Louis	2
SOBOL, Louis	9
SOBOLEV, Arkady A.	4
SOBOLEWSKI, J. Friedrich Edvard	H
SOBY, James Thrall	7
SOCKMAN, Ralph Washington	5
SODDY, Frederick	3
SODERBERG, Carl Richard	7
SODERHOLM, Lars Gustav	10
SODT, William George	3
SOERGEL, E. W.	3
SOFFEL, Joseph August	6
SOFFEL, Sara Mathilde	7
SOFIELD, Harold Augustus	10
SOGGE, Tillman M.	3
SOGLOW, Otto	6
SOGNNAES, Reidar Fauske	8
SOHN, Joseph	1
SOHON, Frederick Wyatt	5
SOILAND, Albert	2
SOINE, Taito Olaf	7
SOKOL, Anthony Eugene	8
SOKOL, Herman	8
SOKOL, Sidney S.	10
SOKOLNIKOFF, Ivan John Stephan	7
SOKOLOFF, Nikolai	4
SOKOLOFF, Ruth H. Ottaway	3
SOKOLOW, Alexander Theodore	1
SOKOLOW, Asa D.	10
SOKOLSKY, George Ephraim	4
SOLARI, Joseph G.	8
SOLBERG, Archie Norman	7
SOLBERG, Carl Edward	8
SOLBERG, Charles Orrin	2
SOLBERG, Thorvald	2
SOLBERT, Oscar Nathaniel	3
SOLER, Juan José	6
SOLES, Thomas Franklin	7
SOLETHER, Pliny Louis	3
SOLEY, James Russell	1
SOLEY, Mayo Hallton	3
SOLFISBURG, Roy John	10
SOLF Y MURO, Alfredo	5
SOLGER, Reinhold Ernst Friedrich Karl	H
SOLHEIM, Arthur Oliver	5
SOLIDAY, David Shriver	5
SOLIDAY, Joseph Henry	2
SOLINSKY, Robert S.	7
SOLIS, Isaac Nathan	4
SOLIS, Seiferth	9
SOLIS-COHEN, D. Hays	8
SOLIS-COREN, Solomon	2
SOLLENBERGER, Isaac Jacob	9
SOLLENBERGER, Richard Talbot	6
SOLLERS, Augustus Rhodes	H
SOLLITT, Sumner S.	4
SOLLMANN, Torald Hermann	4
SOLLOTT, Ralph Preston	3
SOLLY, Samuel Edwin	1
SOLOMON, Barbara Miller	10
SOLOMON, Edward Davis	4
SOLOMON, Gus J.	9
SOLOMON, Harry C(aesar)	8
SOLOMON, Hyde	8
SOLOMON, Joel W.	8
SOLOMON, Louis H.	4
SOLOMON, Samuel Joseph	7
SOLOMON, Sidney L.	6
SOLON, Faustin Johnson	4
SOLON, Harry	5
SOLON, Leon Victor	5
SOLOW, Herbert	4
SOLTERER, Josef	10
SOLTES, Mordecai	3
SOMERALL, James Bentley	6
SOMERDIKE, John Mason	1
SOMERS, Andrew L.	2
SOMERS, Carin Alma	10
SOMERS, Gerald George	7
SOMERS, Grover Thomas	8
SOMERS, Joseph Patrick	6
SOMERS, Orlando Allen	1
SOMERS, Richard H	6
SOMERVELL, Brehon Burke	3
SOMERVILLE, Frederick Howland	5
SOMERVILLE, Harry Philip	4
SOMERVILLE, Henderson Middleton	1
SOMERVILLE, James Alexander	1
SOMERVILLE, James Fownes	2
SOMERVILLE, Ormond	1
SOMERVILLE, Pearl Cliffe	3
SOMERVILLE, Randolph	3
SOMERVILLE, Thomas Hugh	4
SOMERVILLE, William Clark	H
SOMES, Daniel Eton	H
SOMMER, Alvin Henry	4
SOMMER, Charles G.	1
SOMMER, Daniel Philip	4
SOMMER, Ernst August	1
SOMMER, Frank Henry	3
SOMMER, Henry Getz	3
SOMMER, Luther Allen	2
SOMMER, Martin S.	5
SOMMER, Peter W.	1
SOMMER, Reuben E.	4
SOMMER, William H.	3
SOMMERBURG, Miriam	7
SOMMERICH, Otto Charles	4
SOMMERS, Charles Leissring	5
SOMMERS, Henry Cantine	4
SOMMERS, Martin	4
SOMMERS, Paul Bergen	3
SOMMERVILLE, Charles William	1
SOMMERVILLE, Maxwell	1
SOMMERVILLE, Walter Byers	1
SOMOGYL, Erwin George	10
SOMOZA, Anastasio	3
SOMOZA, Luis	4
SONDERGAARD, Gale	9
SONDERN, Frederic Ewald	5
SONDLEY, F. A.	3
SONES, Frank Mason, Jr.	9
SONES, Warren Wesley David	3
SONFIELD, Robert Leon	5
SONIAT, Leonce Martin	1
SONNABEND, Abraham M.	4
SONNAKOLB, Franklin Schuyler	4
SONNE, Fred Theodore	4
SONNE, Hans Christian	9
SONNEBORN, Rudolf Goldschmid	9
SONNEBORN, Tracy Morton	7
SONNEBORN, Tracy Morton	8
SONNECK, Oscar George Theodore	1
SONNEDECKER, Thomas Harry	4
SONNENBERG, Benjamin	7
SONNENBERG, Henry L.	3
SONNENSCHEIN, Hugo	3
SONNETT, John Francis	5
SONNEYSYN, H. O. (Sonny)	5
SONNICHSEN, Albert	1
SONNICHSEN, Charles Leland	10
SONNICHSEN, Yngvar	1
SONNTAG, Marcus S.	1
SONNTAG, William Louis	1
SONSTEBY, John J.	1
SONTAG, Raymond James	5
SOONG, T. V.	5
SOOY, Francis Adrian	9
SOOYSMITH, Charles	1
SOPER, Alexander Coburn	1
SOPER, Edmund Davison	4
SOPER, Erastus Burrows	1
SOPER, Fred Lowe	7
SOPER, George Albert	2
SOPER, Henry Marlin	1
SOPER, Horace Wendell	5
SOPER, John Harris	1
SOPER, Morris Ames	4
SOPER, Pliny Leland	4
SOPHIAN, Lawrence Henry	3
SOPHOCLES, Evangelinus Apostolides	H
SOPHOULIS, Themistocles	3
SOPWITH, Sir Thomas Octave Murdoch	8
SORDONI, Andrew John, Sr.	5
SORDONI, Andrew John, Jr.	5
SORENSEN, Charles E.	5
SORENSEN, Christian Abraham	8
SORENSEN, Clarence Woodrow	8
SORENSEN, John Hjelmhof	5
SORENSEN, Royal Milner	8
SORENSEN, Royal Wasson	4
SORENSEN, Royal Wasson	7
SORENSEN, Svend Oluf	7
SORENSEN, Virginia (Alec Waugh)	10
SORENSON, Charles J(ames)	7
SORENSON, Herbert	10
SORENSON, Lloyd Raymond	10
SORENSON, Roy	5
SORG, Herbert Peter	7
SORG, Paul John	1
SORG, Theodore	3
SORIA, Dario	7
SORIANO, Andres	4
SORIN, Edward Frederick	H
SORKIN, Leonard	9
SORLIE, Arthur Gustav	1
SOROKIN, Pitrim Alexandrovitch	4
SORRELL, Lewis Carlyle	4
SORRELLS, John Harvey	2
SORSBY, William Brooks	4
SOSIN, Abraham	7
SOSKIN, William	3
SOSMAN, Merrill C.	3
SOSMAN, Robert Browning	5
SOSTRIN, Morey	9
SOTHERAN, Alice Hyneman	4
SOTHERAN, Charles	1
SOTHERN, Edward Askew	H
SOTHERN, Edward Hugh	1
SOTO, Juan B(autista)	7
SOTTER, George William	3
SOTTILE, James	8
SOTTILE, James, III	9
SOTZIN, Heber Allen	3
SOUBY, A. Max	1
SOUBY, James Martin	7
SOUCEK, Apollo	3
SOUCHON, Edmond	1
SOUDER, Edwin Mills	2
SOUERS, Loren Eaton	8
SOUERS, Loren Edmunds	4
SOUERS, Sidney William	5
SOUERS, Warren Earl	6
SOULBURY, 1st Baron (Herwald Ramsbotham)	8
SOULE, Andrew MacNairn	1
SOULE, Arthur Bradley	9
SOULE, Asa Titus	H
SOULE, Caroline Gray	4
SOULE, Charles Carroll	1
SOULE, Edgar Clarke Huckabee	7
SOULE, Edward Lee	5
SOULE, Elizabeth Sterling	5
SOULE, Elizabeth Sterling	7
SOULE, Frank F(lint)	9
SOULE, George	1
SOULE, George	9
SOULE, George Henry, Jr.	8
SOULE, Henri Remy	4
SOULE, Joshua	H
SOULE, Malcolm Herman	3
SOULE, Nathan	H
SOULE, Phelps	7
SOULE, Pierre	H
SOULE, Robert Homer	3
SOULE, Roland P.	10
SOULE, Winsor	3
SOULES, Mary E. (Mrs. Powell J. Bing)	6
SOUPART, Pierre	7
SOUPART, Pierre	8
SOUPAULT, Philippe	10
SOUR, Robert Bandler	8
SOURDIS, Evarista	5
SOUSA, Carlos Martins Pereira	4
SOUSA, John Philip	1
SOUSER, Kenneth	5
SOUSER, Kenneth	7
SOUSTELLE, Jacques Emile	10
SOUTER, Clyde Douglas	7
SOUTH, Jerry C.	1
SOUTH, John Glover	1
SOUTH, Lillian H.	6
SOUTHACK, Cyprian	H
SOUTHALL, James Cocke	H
SOUTHALL, James Powell Cocke	4
SOUTHALL, Robert Goode	3
SOUTHAM, H. S.	3
SOUTHAM, J. D.	3
SOUTHARD, Addison E.	7
SOUTHARD, Cecil D.	8
SOUTHARD, Elmer Ernest	1
SOUTHARD, Frank Allan, Jr.	10
SOUTHARD, George Franklin	1
SOUTHARD, Harry Green	4
SOUTHARD, Henry	H
SOUTHARD, Isaac	H
SOUTHARD, James Harding	1
SOUTHARD, Louis Carver	1
SOUTHARD, Lucien	H
SOUTHARD, Samuel Lewis	H
SOUTHER, Henry	1
SOUTHERD, Lucien H.	H
SOUTHERLAND, Clarence Andrew	6
SOUTHERLAND, Clarence Andrew	8
SOUTHERLAND, J. Julien	3
SOUTHERLAND, William Henry Hudson	1
SOUTHERN, Allen Carriger	4
SOUTHERN, Samuel Donald	10
SOUTHERN, William Neil, Jr.	3
SOUTHGATE, George Thompson	2
SOUTHGATE, Harvey William	8
SOUTHGATE, Horatio	H
SOUTHGATE, James Haywood	1
SOUTHGATE, Richard	2
SOUTHGATE, Thomas Somerville	1
SOUTHGATE, William Wright	H
SOUTHWICK, Albert Plympton	4
SOUTHWICK, George N.	1
SOUTHWICK, George Rinaldo	1
SOUTHWICK, Henry Lawrence	1
SOUTHWICK, John Leonard	1
SOUTHWICK, Philip Lee	10
SOUTHWICK, Soloman	H
SOUTHWORTH, Emma Dorothy Eliza Nevitte	1
SOUTHWORTH, Franklin Chester	2
SOUTHWORTH, George Champlin Shepard	4
SOUTHWORTH, George Clark	5
SOUTHWORTH, Herman McDowell	8
SOUTHWORTH, Melvin Deane	4
SOUTHWORTH, Thomas Shepard	1
SOUTTER, William Henry	8
SOUZA, Edgar Milton	8
SOVIAK, Harry	8
SOWDEON, Arthur John Clark	1
SOWELL, Ashley B.	2
SOWELL, Ellis Mast	3
SOWELL, Ingram Cecil	2
SOWELL, Paul Dibrell	5
SOWER, Charles Gilbert, Sr.	1
SOWER, Christopher*	H
SOWERBY, Leo	5
SOWERS, Don Conger	2
SOWERS, Joseph Cullen	5
SOWERWINE, Elbert Orla	7
SOYER, Isaac	8
SOYER, Moses	6
SOYER, Raphael	9
SPAAK, Paul Henri	5
SPAATZ, Carl	6
SPACHMAN, Harold Burton	3
SPACHNER, John Victor	6
SPACKMAN, Cyril Saunders	4
SPAETH, Adolph	1
SPAETH, Bernard Anton	3
SPAETH, Carl Bernhardt	10
SPAETH, Edmund Benjamin	7
SPAETH, J. Duncan	3
SPAETH, Otto Lucien	4
SPAETH, Raymond Julius	8
SPAETH, Reynold Albrecht	1
SPAETH, Sigmund	4
SPAFFORD, Earle	8
SPAFFORD, Edward Elwell	2
SPAFFORD, Frederick Angier	1
SPAFFORD, George Catlin	2
SPAFFORD, Ivol	8
SPAFFORD, John Lester	8
SPAHR, Boyd Lee	5
SPAHR, Charles Barzillai	1
SPAHR, George W.	1
SPAHR, Herman Louis	3
SPAHR, Walter Earl	5

STEELE, Wilbur Fletcher	4	STEINBREDER, Harry John, Jr.	9	STENGEL, (Charles Dillon) Casey	6	STEPHENS, William Edwards	8	STERN, Harold P.	7

STEELE, Wilbur Fletcher 4
STEELE, Willard 7
STEELE, William Gaston H
STEELE, William La Barthe 2
STEELE, William Owen 7
STEELL, Willis 1
STEELL, Willis 2
STEEN, Fred E 6
STEEN, Marguerite 6
STEEN, Melvin Clifford 10
STEEN, Thomas Wilson 8
STEEN, William Brooks 9
STEENBERG, Richard Wilbur 4
STEENBOCK, Harry 4
STEENDAM, Jacob H
STEENE, William 4
STEENERSON, Halvor 1
STEENROD, Lewis H
STEENROD, Norman Earl 5
STEENSTRA, Peter Henry 1
STEENWYCK, Cornelis H
STEEP, Thomas 2
STEER, Charles Melvin 10
STEERE, David D. 9
STEERE, Joseph Beal 1
STEERE, Joseph Hall 1
STEERE, Kenneth David 4
STEERE, Lloyd Randol 4
STEERE, Lora Woodhead 8
STEERE, William Campbell 4
STEERS, George H
STEERS, William Edward 6
STEESE, Edward 8
STEESE, James Gordon 3
STEEVER, Edgar Zell, 3d 7
STEEVER, Miller Didama 7
STEEVES, Harrison Ross 7
STEEVES, Harrison Ross 8
STEFAN, Karl 3
STEFANINI, Francois Ange Antoine 2
STEFANSSON, Vilhjalmur 4
STEFFAN, Roger 3
STEFFEL, Victor Lawrence 7
STEFFEN, Rey John 10
STEFFENS, Cornelius M. 1
STEFFENS, Lincoln 1
STEFFENS, Theodore Henry 3
STEFFENSEN, Vernal R. 4
STEFFIAN, Edwin Theodore 6
STEGEMAN, Gebhard 2
STEGER, Christian Talbot 3
STEGER, Julius 3
STEGER, Peyton 1
STEHLE, Aurelius 1
STEICHEN, Edward 5
STEIDTMANN, Waldo E. 3
STEIGER, Ernst 1
STEIGER, Frederic 10
STEIGER, George 2
STEIGER, G(eorge) Nye 7
STEIGER, William Albert 4
STEIGERS, William Corbet 1
STEIGUER, Louis Rudolph de 2
STEIL, William Nicholas 5
STEIMLE, Edmund Augustus 9
STEIN, Aaron Marc 9
STEIN, Albert Harvey 5
STEIN, Clarence S. 7
STEIN, Edward Thomas 4
STEIN, Emanuel 8
STEIN, Evaleen 1
STEIN, Fred W., Sr. 5
STEIN, Gertrude 2
STEIN, Hannah 6
STEIN, Harold 4
STEIN, I. Melville 4
STEIN, Jack Madison 7
STEIN, James Rauch 5
STEIN, Jess 9
STEIN, John Philip 1
STEIN, Joseph Sigmund 8
STEIN, Jules 7
STEIN, Louis P. 3
STEIN, Richard George 10
STEIN, Robert 1
STEIN, Sydney, Jr. 10
STEIN, William Howard 7
STEINBACH, Everett Mark 5
STEINBACH, Henry Burr 8
STEINBACH, Milton 5
STEINBECK, John Ernest 5
STEINBERG, Martin Remez 8
STEINBERG, Milton 3
STEINBERG, Samuel Sidney
STEINBERG, William 7
STEINBERGER, Franklin Jennings 6
STEINBOCK, Max 6

STEINBREDER, Harry John, Jr. 9
STEINBRINK, Meier 4
STEINBRUGGE, Edward Donald 6
STEINCROHN, Peter Joseph 9
STEINDEL, Bruno 5
STEINDLER, Arthur 3
STEINDORFF, Georg 3
STEINEM, Pauline 4
STEINER, Bernard Christian
STEINER, Bernard Sigfried 6
STEINER, Celestin John 5
STEINER, Edward Alfred 3
STEINER, Jesse Frederick 4
STEINER, Leo K. 2
STEINER, Lewis Henry H
STEINER, Max 5
STEINER, Richard Lewis 10
STEINER, Robert Eugene 3
STEINER, Stan 9
STEINER, Walter Ralph 2
STEINER, William Howard 4
STEINER, Williams Kossuth 2
STEINERT, Alan 5
STEINERT, William Joseph 6
STEINETZ, Bernard G. 4
STEINFELD, Albert 1
STEINGRUBER-WILDG-ANS, Ilona 5
STEINGUT, Stanley 10
STEINHARDT, Laurence A. 2
STEINHART, Frank 1
STEINHART, Jesse H. 4
STEINHAUER, Ralph 9
STEINHAUS, Arthur H. 5
STEINHAUS, Edward A(rthur) 5
STEINHOFF, Dan 9
STEININGER, Fred H. 5
STEINITZ, William 1
STEINKE, Paul Karl Willi 10
STEINKRAUS, Herman W. 6
STEINKRAUS, Warren Edward 10
STEINLE, John Gerard 10
STEINLE, Roland Joseph 4
STEINLE, Roland Joseph 5
STEINMAN, Andrew Jackson 1
STEINMAN, David Barnard 4
STEINMAN, James Hale 4
STEINMAN, John Frederick 7
STEINMETZ, Charles Proteus 1
STEINMETZ, Ferdinand Henry 7
STEINMETZ, Joseph Allison 1
STEINMETZ, Maurice 5
STEINREICH, Kenneth Pease 4
STEINSAPIR, Saul P. 5
STEINWAY, Charles Herman 1
STEINWAY, Christian Friedrich Theodore H
STEINWAY, Henry Engelhard H
STEINWAY, Theodore E. 3
STEINWAY, William H
STEINWAY, William Richard 4
STEINWEG, William Louis 4
STEIWER, Frederick 1
STEJNEGER, Leonhard 2
STELLA, Antonio 1
STELLA, Joseph 2
STELLE, Charles Clarkson 4
STELLE, John 4
STELLHORN, Frederick William 1
STELLWAGEN, Edward James 1
STELLWAGEN, Seitorde Michael 2
STELOFF, Frances 8
STELTER, Benjamin F. 3
STELWAGON, Henry Weightman 1
STELZLE, Charles 1
STEMBEL, Roger Nelson 1
STEMLER, Otto Adolph 3
STEMMLER, Theodore Washington 6
STEMPEL, Guido Hermann 3
STEMPEL, John Emmert 8
STEMPF, Victor Herman 2
STEMPLE, Frank 4
STENBECK, Hugo Edvard 9
STENGEL, Alfred 1

STENGEL, (Charles Dillon) Casey 6
STENGEL, Erwin 6
STENGEL, Frederick William 5
STENGLE, Charles Irwin 3
STENHOUSE, Evangeline E. 10
STENSETH, Martinus 8
STENSIÖ, Erik Anderson 9
STENTZ, John Clyde 6
STENZEL, Lula Vinette 5
STEPAN, Alfred Charles, Jr. 9
STEPÁNEK, Bedrich (Frederick) 7
STEPELTON, Norman Allen 5
STEPHAN, Arthur Theodore 6
STEPHAN, Frank Lawrence 3
STEPHAN, Frederick Franklin 5
STEPHAN, George 2
STEPHAN, Robert Downs 10
STEPHEN, George 3
STEPHENS, A. E. S. 6
STEPHENS, Abraham P. H
STEPHENS, Albert Lee, Sr. 4
STEPHENS, Alexander Hamilton
STEPHENS, Alice Barber 1
STEPHENS, Ambrose E. B. 1
STEPHENS, Ann Sophia H
STEPHENS, Benjamin Hughl 5
STEPHENS, Charles Asbury 1
STEPHENS, Claude P. 4
STEPHENS, Clyde Harrison 4
STEPHENS, Dan Voorhees 1
STEPHENS, Daniel Mallory 4
STEPHENS, David Stubert 1
STEPHENS, Edwin Lewis 1
STEPHENS, Edwin William 1
STEPHENS, Ferris J. 5
STEPHENS, Frank 1
STEPHENS, Frank Fletcher 6
STEPHENS, George 2
STEPHENS, George Asbury 3
STEPHENS, George Ware 4
STEPHENS, Guy Frederic 4
STEPHENS, H. Morse 1
STEPHENS, Harley Clifford 3
STEPHENS, Harold Montelle 3
STEPHENS, Harry T. 2
STEPHENS, Herbert Taylor 7
STEPHENS, Howard V. 3
STEPHENS, Hubert Durrett 2
STEPHENS, James 3
STEPHENS, James C(ollins) 5
STEPHENS, John Allen 7
STEPHENS, John Calhoun, Jr. 9
STEPHENS, John Hall 4
STEPHENS, John Leonard 1
STEPHENS, John Lloyd H
STEPHENS, John Vant 1
STEPHENS, Kate 1
STEPHENS, Lawrence Vest 1
STEPHENS, Leroy 1
STEPHENS, Linton H
STEPHENS, Louis L. 4
STEPHENS, Martin Bates 1
STEPHENS, Oren Melson 5
STEPHENS, Percy Rector 2
STEPHENS, Philander 1
STEPHENS, Philip B(lanton) 5
STEPHENS, Redmond Davis 1
STEPHENS, Robert Allan 2
STEPHENS, Robert Neilson 1
STEPHENS, Roderick 7
STEPHENS, Roswell Powell 3
STEPHENS, Russell Stout 4
STEPHENS, Theodore Pierson 4
STEPHENS, Thomas Edwin 9
STEPHENS, Uriah Smith H
STEPHENS, Ward 1
STEPHENS, Will Beth Dodson 9
STEPHENS, W(illiam) Barclay 5
STEPHENS, William Dennison 1
STEPHENS, William Edwards 7

STEPHENS, William Edwards 8
STEPHENS, William Richmond 9
STEPHENSON, Benjamin Franklin H
STEPHENSON, Benjamin Franklin H
STEPHENSON, C. S. 4
STEPHENSON, Carl 3
STEPHENSON, Clarence Bruce 10
STEPHENSON, Edward Morris 1
STEPHENSON, Francis Marion 8
STEPHENSON, Franklin Bache 4
STEPHENSON, George Malcolm 3
STEPHENSON, Gilbert Thomas 5
STEPHENSON, Henry Thew 5
STEPHENSON, Herbert Roy 9
STEPHENSON, Isaac 1
STEPHENSON, James H
STEPHENSON, James Pomeroy 2
STEPHENSON, James 3
STEPHENSON, John H
STEPHENSON, Josph Maxwell 2
STEPHENSON, Nathaniel Wright 1
STEPHENSON, Orlistus Bell 4
STEPHENSON, Rome Charles 1
STEPHENSON, Roy L. 8
STEPHENSON, S. Town 4
STEPHENSON, Sam 2
STEPHENSON, Wendell Holmes 5
STEPHENSON, William 4
STEPHENSON, William B., Jr. 3
STEPHENSON, William Benjamin 4
STEPHENSON, William Lawrence 4
STEPHENSON, William Prettyman 5
STEPHENSON, William Worth 1
STEPPAT, Leo 4
STEPTOE, Philip Pendleton 2
STERETT, Andrew H
STERETT, Samuel H
STERIGERE, John Benton H
STERKI, Victor 1
STERLEY, William F. 4
STERLING, Ansel H
STERLING, Bruce F. 5
STERLING, Chandler Winfield 9
STERLING, Donald Justus 3
STERLING, Edward Canfield 1
STERLING, Ernest Albert 6
STERLING, Frederick Augustine 3
STERLING, George 1
STERLING, George Mathleson 5
STERLING, Gordon Donald 9
STERLING, Graham Lee 5
STERLING, Guy 1
STERLING, Henry Somers 9
STERLING, James H
STERLING, John A. 1
STERLING, John C. 4
STERLING, John Ewart Wallace 8
STERLING, John Whalen H
STERLING, John William 1
STERLING, Micah H
STERLING, Philip 8
STERLING, Ross N. 9
STERLING, Ross Shaw 2
STERLING, Theodore 1
STERLING, Thomas 1
STERLING, W. T. 3
STERN, Adolph 6
STERN, Alfred Whital 4
STERN, Arthur Cecil 10
STERN, Bernard Joseph 3
STERN, Bill 5
STERN, Charles Frank 6
STERN, Curt 8
STERN, David Becker 4
STERN, Edgar Bloom 4
STERN, Edith Mendel 6
STERN, Elizabeth 3
STERN, Ellis Eaby 7
STERN, Gladys Bertha 6

STERN, Harold P. 7
STERN, Henry 7
STERN, Henry Root 3
STERN, Horace 5
STERN, Isaac Farber 3
STERN, Jo Lane 1
STERN, Joseph Smith 5
STERN, Joseph William H
STERN, Joseph William 4
STERN, Julius David 5
STERN, Kurt Guenter 3
STERN, Laurence Marcus 7
STERN, Lawrence Fish 4
STERN, Leo 2
STERN, Leon Thomas (Lefevre) 7
STERN, Louis 1
STERN, Louis 5
STERN, Martin 8
STERN, Max 8
STERN, Milton H. 10
STERN, Nathan 2
STERN, Oscar David 6
STERN, Otto 9
STERN, Philip Maurice 10
STERN, Philip Van Doren 7
STERN, Sigmund 3
STERN, Simon Adler 1
STERN, William 7
STERN, William Bernhard 2
STERNBERG, Charles Hazellus
STERNBERG, Eli 9
STERNBERG, George Miller 1
STERNBERG, Vernon Arthur 7
STERNBERG, Walter 4
STERNBERGER, Mrs. Estelle Miller 5
STERNBURG, Herman von Speck 1
STERNE, Albert Eugene 1
STERNE, Augustus Herrington 9
STERNE, Emma Gelders 10
STERNE, Maurice 3
STERNE, Mervyn Hayden 9
STERNE, Niel Paul 5
STERNE, Simon 1
STERNE, Theodore Eugene 5
STERNER, Albert 2
STERNER, Ralf Leech 7
STERNFELD, Harry 9
STERNHAGEN, John 3
STERNHELL, Charles Max 5
STERRETT, Cliff 5
STERRETT, Frances Roberta 2
STERRETT, Frank William 7
STERRETT, Henry Hatch Dent 6
STERRETT, James MacBridge 1
STERRETT, James Ralston 1
STERRETT, John Robert Sitlington 1
STETEFELDT, Carl August H
STETSON, Augusta E. 1
STETSON, Caleb Rochford 1
STETSON, Chandler Alton, Jr. 7
STETSON, Charles Augustus H
STETSON, Charles Walter H
STETSON, Eugene William 3
STETSON, Harlan True 4
STETSON, Henry Crosby 3
STETSON, Henry Thomas 7
STETSON, Herbert Lee 4
STETSON, Isaiah Kidder
STETSON, John Batterson
STETSON, Lemuel H
STETSON, Paul Clifford 1
STETSON, Raymond Herbert 3
STETSON, Thomas Drew 4
STETSON, William Wallace 1
STETSON, Willis Kimball 1
STETTEN, Dewitt 3
STETTEN, DeWitt, Jr. 10
STETTINIUS, Edward R. 1
STETTINIUS, Edward R., Jr. 2
STETTNER, Ludwig Wilhelmin 4
STEUART, George Hume 1
STEUART, James Aloysius 1
STEUBEN, Friedrich Wilhelm Ludolf Gerhard Augustin, Von H
STEUDEL, Arthur William 9
STEUER, Max David H
STEUER, Max David 4

STREERUWITZ, William H. Ritter von 4
STREET, Alfred Billings H
STREET, Allen M. 7
STREET, Augustus Russell H
STREET, Charles Larrabee 9
STREET, Clarence Park 9
STREET, Edward Robert 10
STREET, Elwood Vickers 8
STREET, Ida Maria 4
STREET, J. Fletcher 2
STREET, Jabez Curry 10
STREET, Jacob Richard 1
STREET, James Harry 9
STREET, James Howell 3
STREET, John Northcott 4
STREET, Joseph Montfort H
STREET, Julian 2
STREET, Oliver Day 2
STREET, Randall S. H
STREET, Robert H
STREET, Robert Gould 1
STREET, Thomas Atkins 1
STREET, Webster 1
STREET, William Ezra 7
STREETER, Carroll Perry 6
STREETER, Daniel Denison 7
STREETER, Daniel Denison, Jr. 7
STREETER, Daniel Willard 7
STREETER, Edward 7
STREETER, Edward Clark 5
STREETER, Frank Sherwin 1
STREETER, George Linius 2
STREETER, George Wellington 4
STREETER, John Williams 1
STREETER, Ruth Cheney 10
STREETER, Thomas Winthrop 4
STREETT, David 1
STREETT, St. Clair 5
STREHLOW, Roger Albert 10
STREIBERT, Theodore Cuyler 9
STREIFER, William 10
STREIGHT, Whitney Willard 7
STREIGHTOFF, Frank Hatch 1
STREISINGER, George 9
STREIT, Clarence Kirshman 9
STREIT, Paul Henry 6
STREIT, Paul Henry 7
STREIT, Samuel Frederick 6
STREITHORST, Tom 7
STREITZ, Ruth 9
STRELSIN, Alfred A. 7
STRENCH, Donald Davis 6
STRENG, J. Truman 3
STRENG, Jesse F. 6
STRETCH, David Albert 5
STRETCH, Lorena B. 9
STRETCH, Olive Minerva (Mrs. Carl Henry Rathjen) 6
STRIBLING, Thomas Sigismund 4
STRICKER, Frederick David 5
STRICKER, Paul Frederick 4
STRICKLAND, Charles Hobart 4
STRICKLAND, Francis Lorette 3
STRICKLAND, Frederic Hastings 1
STRICKLAND, Frederick Guy 5
STRICKLAND, Lily 3
STRICKLAND, Randolph H
STRICKLAND, Robert Marion 2
STRICKLAND, Silas A. 5
STRICKLAND, William H
STRICKLER, Cyrus Warren, Sr. 5
STRICKLER, Earl T. 6
STRICKLER, George Arnold 7
STRICKLER, Givens Brown 1
STRICKLER, John 4
STRICKLER, Thomas Johnson 3
STRICKLER, Woodrow Mann 6
STRICKLIN, James Alvin 7
STRIDE, Joseph Burton 3
STRIEBY, William 1
STRIETMANN, A. P. 4
STRIGHT, Hayden Leroy 6
STRIJDOM, Johannes Gerhardus 3
STRIKE, Clifford John 2

STRIKE, Clifford Stewart 7
STRINGER, Arthur 3
STRINGER, George Alfred 1
STRINGER, Henry Delphos 6
STRINGER, Lawrence Beaumont 2
STRINGER, William Henry 7
STRINGFELLOW, Ervin Edward 7
STRINGFELLOW, George Edward 9
STRINGFELLOW, Henry Martyn 1
STRINGFIELD, Lamar 3
STRINGHAM, Edwin John 6
STRINGHAM, Irving 2
STRINGHAM, Silas Horton H
STRINGHAM, Warde Barlow 5
STRITCH, Samuel Alphonsus 3
STRITZINGER, Raymond K(neas) 8
STRNAT, Karl Josef 10
STROBEL, Charles Louis 1
STROBEL, Edward Henry 1
STROBOS, Robert Julius 9
STROBRIDGE, Idah Meacham 1
STROCK, Daniel 1
STROCK, John Roy 7
STRODACH, Paul Zeller 2
STRODE, George King 3
STRODE, Hudson 7
STROH, Donald Armpriester 3
STROHL, Everett Lee 6
STROHM, Adam Julius 4
STROHM, Gertrude 4
STROHM, John H
STROHM, John Louis 9
STROM, Carl Walther 5
STROMBERG, Gustaf 3
STROMBERG, Hunt 5
STRÖMGREN, Bengt Georg Daniel 9
STROMINGER, Donald B. 8
STROMME, Peer 1
STRONG, Albert L. 8
STRONG, Alden George 4
STRONG, Anna Louise 5
STRONG, Augustus Hopkins 1
STRONG, Austin 3
STRONG, Benjamin 1
STRONG, Benjamin 9
STRONG, Caleb H
STRONG, Charles Augustus 1
STRONG, Charles Hall 1
STRONG, Charles Henry 4
STRONG, Charles Howard 2
STRONG, Charles Lyman 1
STRONG, Charles Stanley 4
STRONG, Earl D. 7
STRONG, Edward Kellogg, Jr. 4
STRONG, Edward Trask 1
STRONG, Edward William 10
STRONG, Edwin Atson 4
STRONG, Elnathan Ellsworth 1
STRONG, Frank 1
STRONG, Frederick Finch 5
STRONG, Frederick Smith 1
STRONG, Frederick Smith, Jr. 9
STRONG, George Alexander 4
STRONG, George Crockett H
STRONG, George Franklin 7
STRONG, George Frederic 3
STRONG, George Veazey 4
STRONG, Harry Allen 3
STRONG, Harry Eugene 4
STRONG, Hattie Maria 3
STRONG, Henry A. 1
STRONG, James* H
STRONG, James George 1
STRONG, James Hooker H
STRONG, James Woodward 1
STRONG, Jedediah 1
STRONG, John Donovan 10
STRONG, John Henry 4
STRONG, Josiah 1
STRONG, Julius Levi H
STRONG, L. Corrin 4
STRONG, Lee A. 1
STRONG, Leonell C(larence) 10
STRONG, L(ester) Corrin 9
STRONG, Moses McCure 1
STRONG, Nathan L. 1
STRONG, Oliver Smith 8

STRONG, Ormand Butler 3
STRONG, Reuben Myron 4
STRONG, Richard Pearson 2
STRONG, Robert Alexander 1
STRONG, Robert William 8
STRONG, Samuel M. 3
STRONG, Selah Brewster H
STRONG, Selah Brewster 5
STRONG, Solomon H
STRONG, Stephen H
STRONG, Sterling Price 1
STRONG, Sydney Dix 1
STRONG, Sylvester Emory 1
STRONG, Theodore H
STRONG, Theron George 1
STRONG, Theron Rudd 1
STRONG, Thomas Nelson 4
STRONG, Tracy 8
STRONG, Walter Ansel 1
STRONG, Wayne F. 3
STRONG, Wendell Melville 2
STRONG, William* H
STRONG, William Augustus 7
STRONG, William Barstow 1
STRONG, William Duncan 4
STRONG, William Ellsworth 3
STRONG, William L. 1
STRONG, William Walker 3
STROOCK, Alan Maxwell 8
STROOCK, James E. 4
STROOCK, Solomon M. 4
STROSACKER, Charles John 4
STROTHER, Dan J(ames) F(rench) 5
STROTHER, David Hunter H
STROTHER, French 1
STROTHER, George French H
STROTHER, James French H
STROTHER, James French 1
STROTHER, James H. 4
STROUD, James Bart 10
STROUD, Morris Wistar 1
STROUD, William Daniel 3
STROUP, Russell Cartwright 7
STROUP, Thomas Andrew 2
STROUSE, D. J. 6
STROUSE, Myer H
STROUT, Charles Henry 4
STROUT, Edwin Albert 3
STROUT, Richard Lee 10
STROUT, Sewall Cushing 1
STROVER, Carl Bernhard Wittekind 1
STROZIER, Fred Lewis 5
STROZIER, Robert Manning 3
STRUB, Charles Henry 7
STRUB, Paul 5
STRUBBERG, Friedrich Armand H
STRUBE, Gustav 5
STRUBLE, George R. 4
STRUBLE, Mildred 2
STRUCK, Ferdinand Theodore 2
STRUDWICK, Edmund 1
STRUDWICK, Edmund Charles Fox H
STRUDWICK, Shepperd 8
STRUDWICK, William Francis H
STRUM, Justin 4
STRUM, Louie Willard 3
STRUNK, Oliver 7
STRUNK, William 2
STRUNSKY, Simeon 2
STRUTHER, Jan 3
STRUTHERS, G. H. 4
STRUTHERS, Joseph 1
STRUTHERS, P(arke) H(ardy) 9
STRUTHERS, Robert 3
STRUVE, Gustav H
STRUVE, Otto 4
STRUYE, Paul 6
STRYKER, Josiah 6
STRYKER, Lloyd Paul 3
STRYKER, Melancthon Woolsey 1
STRYKER, Samuel Stanhope 1
STRYKER, William Scudder 1
STUART, Albert Rhett 5
STUART, Alexander Hugh Holmes H
STUART, Alexander Tait 1
STUART, Ambrose Pascal Sevilon 1
STUART, Andrew H
STUART, Archibald* H

STUART, C. A. 4
STUART, Carl Kirk 4
STUART, Charles H
STUART, Charles Beebe H
STUART, Charles Duff 4
STUART, Charles Edward 1
STUART, Charles Edward 2
STUART, Charles Jenckes 4
STUART, Charles Barnes 1
STUART, Charles MacAulay 1
STUART, Charles T. 3
STUART, Charles W. T. 3
STUART, Daniel Delehanty Vincent 1
STUART, David H
STUART, Della Tovrea (Mrs. William P. Stuart) 5
STUART, Donald Clive 3
STUART, Duane Reed 4
STUART, Edward 3
STUART, Edwin Roy 1
STUART, Edwin Sydney 1
STUART, Elbridge Amos 2
STUART, Elbridge Hadley 7
STUART, Eleanor 1
STUART, Francis Hart 1
STUART, Francis Joseph 6
STUART, Francis Lee 1
STUART, George 2
STUART, George Rutledge 1
STUART, Gilbert H
STUART, Harold Coe 7
STUART, Harold Leonard 4
STUART, Harry Allen 3
STUART, Henry Carter 1
STUART, Henry Waldgrave 5
STUART, Holloway Ithamer 3
STUART, Ian 5
STUART, Isaac William 1
STUART, James Arthur 6
STUART, James Austin 1
STUART, James Edward 1
STUART, James Edwin 5
STUART, James Everett 1
STUART, James Ewell Brown H
STUART, James Lyall 7
STUART, James Merton 4
STUART, James Milton 10
STUART, James Reeve H
STUART, James Reeve 4
STUART, Jesse Hilton 8
STUART, John H
STUART, John 5
STUART, John Leighton 9
STUART, John Todd H
STUART, Milo H. 1
STUART, Milton C(aleb) 5
STUART, Montgomery Alexander 6
STUART, Moses H
STUART, Philip H
STUART, Robert H
STUART, Robert C. 1
STUART, Robert Douglas 6
STUART, Robert Lee 7
STUART, Robert Leighton 4
STUART, Robert Terry 3
STUART, Robert Young 1
STUART, Ruth McEnery 1
STUART, Theresa Crystal 4
STUART, William Alexander 7
STUART, William Hervey 5
STUART, William Moore 10
STUART, William Plato 4
STUB, Hans Gerhard 1
STUB, Jacob Aall Ottesen 2
STUBBEMAN, Frank Diedrich 7
STUBBERT, J. Edward 4
STUBBINS, Allan Linder 4
STUBBLEFIELD, Frances Ogden 3
STUBBLEFIELD, Frank Albert 7
STUBBLEFIELD, William Higgason 4
STUBBS, Henry Elbert 1
STUBBS, John C. 4
STUBBS, John Osmon 1
STUBBS, Joseph Edward 1
STUBBS, Mattie Wilma 3
STUBBS, Merrill 1
STUBBS, Ralph Sprengle 2
STUBBS, Truett Tristian 5
STUBBS, Walter Roscoe 1
STUBBS, William Carter 1
STUBENRAUCH, Arnold Valentine 1
STUBER, William G. 3
STUBNITZ, Maurice 8
STUCK, Hudson 1
STUCKENBERG, John Henry Wilburn 1

STUCKEY, Lorin 6
STUCKSLAGER, Willard Coldren 1
STUDEBAKER, Clement 1
STUDEBAKER, Clement, Jr. 1
STUDEBAKER, Ellis M. 3
STUDEBAKER, John Mohler 1
STUDEBAKER, John Ward 8
STUDENROTH, Carl Wilson 9
STUDENSKI, Paul 4
STUDER, Jacob Henry 1
STUDLEY, Elmer E. 2
STUDY, Guy 6
STUECK, Frederick 4
STUEMPFIG, Walter 7
STUHLMAN, Otto, Jr. 4
STUHLMAN, Otto, Jr. 4
STUHR, William S. 6
STUKES, Taylor Hudnall 4
STULBERG, Louis 7
STULL, Charles Henry 5
STULL, Ray Thomas 5
STULTS, Walter Allen 7
STUMM, Erwin C(harles) 5
STUMM, Richard A. 4
STUMP, Felix Budwell 10
STUMP, Felix Budwell 5
STUMP, Forest J. 10
STUMP, John Sutton 1
STUMP, Joseph 1
STUMP, Lawrence M. 10
STUMPH, Calowa William 6
STUNTZ, Arba L. 4
STUNTZ, Homer Clyde 1
STUNTZ, Stephen Conrad 1
STURANI, Giuseppe 1
STURC, Ernest 7
STURC, Ernest 8
STURDEVANT, Clarence L. 3
STURDEVANT, William Lommer 3
STURDIVANT, J(ames) Holmes 5
STURDY, Herbert Francis 5
STURGEON, Daniel H
STURGEON, Guy 3
STURGEON, Theodore Hamilton 8
STURGES, Charles Mathews 4
STURGES, Donald George 1
STURGES, Dwight Case 1
STURGES, John Eliot 10
STURGES, Jonathan H
STURGES, Lewis Burr H
STURGES, Preston 5
STURGES, Wesley A. 4
STURGES, William Spencer 4
STURGIS, Charles Inches 3
STURGIS, Clarence Eugene 1
STURGIS, Cyrus Cressey 1
STURGIS, Frank Knight 1
STURGIS, Frederic Russell 1
STURGIS, Guy Hayden 5
STURGIS, Henry Sprague 5
STURGIS, John Hubbard H
STURGIS, Julian 1
STURGIS, Lindell Wymore 5
STURGIS, R. Clipston 3
STURGIS, Russell* H
STURGIS, Samuel Davis H
STURGIS, Samuel Davis 4
STURGIS, Samuel Davis, Jr. 4
STURGIS, Somers Hayes 10
STURGIS, William H
STURGIS, William Codman 2
STURGISS, George Cookman 1
STURM, Ernest 1
STURM, Justin 4
STURMAN, Joseph Howard 10
STURTEVANT, Albert Morey 3
STURTEVANT, Alfred Henry 5
STURTEVANT, Benjamin Franklin H
STURTEVANT, Carleton William 4
STURTEVANT, Edgar Howard 5
STURTEVANT, Edward Lewis H
STURTEVANT, John Loomis 1
STURTEVANT, Julian Monson H
STURTEVANT, Sarah Martha 2
STURZENEGGER, Otto 10

STUTESMAN, James Flynn 1
STUTLER, Boyd Blynn 9
STUTSMAN, Jesse O. 1
STUTSMAN, Oscar T. 9
STUTZ, Harry C. 1
STUYVESANT, Petrus H
STYER, Henry Delp 2
STYER, Wilhelm D. 6
STYGALL, James Henry 3
STYKA, Tade 3
STYLER, William Francis 7
STYRI, Haakon 7
SUAREZ-MUJICA, Eduardo 4
SUBLETTE, Clifford MacClellan 8
SUBLETTE, William Lewis H
SUCKOW, Ruth 3
SUDDUTH, William Xavier 1
SUDJARWO, Tjondronegoro 5
SUDLER, Arthur Emory 5
SUDLER, Mervin Tubman 5
SUDLOW, Elizabeth Williams 3
SUDWORTH, George Bishop 1
SUFFERN, Arthur Elliott 6
SUFFREN, Charles Carroll 1
SUGARMAN, Nathan 10
SUGARMAN, Norman Alfred 9
SUGDEN, Walter S. 1
SUGG, Redding Stancil 3
SUGGS, John Thomas 8
SUGHRUE, Timothy George 4
SUGRUE, Edward D. 7
SUGRUE, Thomas 3
SUHR, Charles Louis 5
SUHR, Otto Ernst Heinrich Hermann 3
SUHR, Robert Carl 6
SUHRIE, Ambrose L. 3
SUITER, Grant 4
SUITS, Chauncey Guy 10
SUKARNO 5
SUKER, George Francis 1
SULERUD, Allen Christen 6
SULLAVAN, Margaret 3
SULLENS, Frederick 3
SULLIVAN, Alexander 4
SULLIVAN, Aloysius Michael 7
SULLIVAN, Arthur George 2
SULLIVAN, Arthur George 3
SULLIVAN, Bolton 10
SULLIVAN, C. M. 7
SULLIVAN, Carl Rollynn, Jr. 10
SULLIVAN, Charles Bruce 3
SULLIVAN, Christopher D. 2
SULLIVAN, Corliss Esmonde 1
SULLIVAN, Daniel Clifford 4
SULLIVAN, David 6
SULLIVAN, Dennis Edward 10
SULLIVAN, Dennis Francis 5
SULLIVAN, Donal Mark 5
SULLIVAN, Edward Dean 1
SULLIVAN, Edward Vincent 6
SULLIVAN, Eleanor Regis 10
SULLIVAN, Elizabeth Higgins (Elizabeth Higgins) 5
SULLIVAN, Eugene Cornelius 4
SULLIVAN, Florence David 3
SULLIVAN, Francis John 1
SULLIVAN, Francis Loftus 3
SULLIVAN, Francis Paul 3
SULLIVAN, Francis William 4
SULLIVAN, Francis William 8
SULLIVAN, Frank (Franics John Sullivan) 6
SULLIVAN, Gael 3
SULLIVAN, George H
SULLIVAN, George F. 2
SULLIVAN, George Hammond 3
SULLIVAN, George Leonard 7
SULLIVAN, Harold Joseph 7
SULLIVAN, Harry Stack H
SULLIVAN, Harry Stack 4
SULLIVAN, Henry J. 4
SULLIVAN, Isaac Newton 1
SULLIVAN, James H
SULLIVAN, James 1
SULLIVAN, James Edward 1
SULLIVAN, James F. 1
SULLIVAN, James Mark 1

SULLIVAN, James William 4
SULLIVAN, Jeremiah Francis 1
SULLIVAN, Jeremiah Francis, Jr. 5
SULLIVAN, Jeremiah J. 4
SULLIVAN, Jerry Bartholomew 2
SULLIVAN, John H
SULLIVAN, John A. 4
SULLIVAN, John Berchmans 3
SULLIVAN, John Francis 3
SULLIVAN, John J. 3
SULLIVAN, John Joseph 8
SULLIVAN, John L. H
SULLIVAN, John L. 3
SULLIVAN, John Lawrence 3
SULLIVAN, John Lawrence 8
SULLIVAN, Joseph Peter 4
SULLIVAN, Joseph Timothy Patrick 9
SULLIVAN, Joseph V. 8
SULLIVAN, Lawrence 5
SULLIVAN, Leo Dennis 5
SULLIVAN, Leonor Kretzer 9
SULLIVAN, Louis Henry 1
SULLIVAN, Margaret Frances 1
SULLIVAN, Margaret M. 1
SULLIVAN, Mark 3
SULLIVAN, Matthew Gerard 9
SULLIVAN, Maurice J.* 4
SULLIVAN, Max William 10
SULLIVAN, Michael Crowley 1
SULLIVAN, Michael Xavier 4
SULLIVAN, Oscar Matthias 3
SULLIVAN, Owen J. 3
SULLIVAN, Patrick 1
SULLIVAN, Patrick F. 1
SULLIVAN, Patrick J. 5
SULLIVAN, Patrick U. 2
SULLIVAN, Paul E. 3
SULLIVAN, Peter John H
SULLIVAN, Philip Leo 4
SULLIVAN, Raymond F. 5
SULLIVAN, Richard Howard 8
SULLIVAN, Richard Thomas 8
SULLIVAN, Roger C. 1
SULLIVAN, Russell 6
SULLIVAN, Thomas Crook Michael 1
SULLIVAN, Thomas 10
SULLIVAN, Thomas Russell 1
SULLIVAN, Timothy D. 5
SULLIVAN, Walter Edward 7
SULLIVAN, Walter H. 4
SULLIVAN, William H
SULLIVAN, William Cleary 1
SULLIVAN, William Francis 7
SULLIVAN, William Francis 8
SULLIVAN, William Laurence 4
SULLIVAN, William Lawrence 4
SULLIVAN, William Van Amberg 4
SULLIVANT, William Starling H
SULLOWAY, Alvah Woodbury 1
SULLOWAY, Cyrus Adams 1
SULLOWAY, Frank J. 7
SULLY, Alfred 1
SULLY, Alfred 1
SULLY, Daniel 1
SULLY, Daniel J. 1
SULLY, John Murchison 1
SULLY, Thomas H
SULTAN, Daniel Isom 2
SULZBACHER, Louis 1
SULZBERGER, Arthur Hays 5
SULZBERGER, Cyrus L. 1
SULZBERGER, Iphigene Ochs 9
SULZBERGER, Marion Baldur 8
SULZBERGER, Mayer 1
SULZBY, James Frederick, Jr. 10
SULZER, Albert Frederick 1
SULZER, Charles August 1
SULZER, Hans A. 3
SULZER, William 1
SUMAN, John Robert 9

SUMICHRAST, Frederick Caesar de 4
SUMMERALL, Charles Pelot 3
SUMMERBELL, Carlyle 1
SUMMERBELL, Martyn 1
SUMMERBELL, Robert Kerr 4
SUMMERFIELD, Arthur E(llsworth) 5
SUMMERFIELD, Charles H
SUMMERFIELD, Lester D. 4
SUMMERFIELD, Solon E. 2
SUMMERFORD, Dealva Clinton 5
SUMMERLIN, George Thomas 2
SUMMERS, Alex 1
SUMMERS, Andrew Rowan 5
SUMMERS, Augustus Neander 4
SUMMERS, Cleon Aubrey 6
SUMMERS, Festus Paul 5
SUMMERS, George William H
SUMMERS, Henry Elijah 4
SUMMERS, Hollis 9
SUMMERS, James Colling 1
SUMMERS, John Edward* 1
SUMMERS, John William 1
SUMMERS, Lane 8
SUMMERS, Leland Laflin 3
SUMMERS, Lewis Preston 3
SUMMERS, Lionel Morgan 6
SUMMERS, Maddin 1
SUMMERS, Owen 1
SUMMERS, Thomas Osmond H
SUMMERS, Walter G. 1
SUMMERS, Walter Lee 1
SUMMERS, William Henry 1
SUMMERSELL, Charles Grayson 9
SUMMERSKILL, William Hedley John 7
SUMMERSON, John Newenham 10
SUMMERVILLE, Amelia Shaw 1
SUMMEY, George 3
SUMNER, (Bertha) Cid Ricketts 4
SUMNER, Caroline Louise 5
SUMNER, Charles H
SUMNER, Charles Allen 1
SUMNER, Charles Burt 4
SUMNER, Charles Ralsey 1
SUMNER, Clarence 3
SUMNER, Edward Alleyne 2
SUMNER, Edwin Vose H
SUMNER, Edwin Vose 1
SUMNER, Francis Bertody 2
SUMNER, Frederick Azel 1
SUMNER, G. Lynn 3
SUMNER, George Watson 1
SUMNER, Guilford Herman 1
SUMNER, Increase H
SUMNER, James Batcheller 3
SUMNER, Jethro H
SUMNER, John D. 3
SUMNER, John Osborne 1
SUMNER, John Saxton 5
SUMNER, Samuel Storrow 1
SUMNER, Walter Taylor 1
SUMNER, William Graham 1
SUMNERS, Chester Lamar 4
SUMNERS, Hatton W. 4
SUMPTER, William David 5
SUMRALL, Franklin H. 8
SUMTER, Thomas H
SUMTER, Thomas Delage H
SUNBERG, Carl Andrew Lawrence 4
SUNDAY, William Ashley 1
SUNDBACK, G. 3
SUNDELIUS, Marie 3
SUNDERLAND, Edson Read 3
SUNDERLAND, Edwin Sherwood Stowell 4
SUNDERLAND, Eliza Read 1
SUNDERLAND, Jabez Thomas 1
SUNDERLAND, Leroy H
SUNDERLAND, Thomas Elbert 10
SUNDERLAND, Wilfred Wilt 5
SUNDERLIN, Charles Algernon 1
SUNDFOR, Zalia Harbaugh (Mrs. Guttorm Sundfor) 5

SUNDHEIM, Anders M. 2
SUNDHEIM, George Melchoir 10
SUNDHEIM, Trig 6
SUNDSTROM, Frank Leander 7
SUNDSTROM, Swan 3
SUNDT, Edwin Einar 1
SUNDWALL, John 3
SUNKIN, Irving Burton 7
SUNLEY, Emil McKee 7
SUNNY, Bernard Edward 2
SUNSTROM, Mark A. 4
SUOZZO, John 6
SUPER, Charles William 1
SUPER, Ovando Byron 4
SUPLEE, Henry Harrison 4
SUPPON, Charles Richard 10
SURAMARIT, Norodom King of Cambodia 4
SURE, Barnett 4
SURETTE, Thomas Whitney 1
SURFACE, Frank Macy 4
SURFACE, Harvey Adam 4
SURKAMP, Arthur 5
SURLES, Alexander Day 2
SURMANN, John Fred 5
SURRAN, Edna M. Walsh 6
SURRAT, Mary Eugenia Jenkins H
SURRATT, John H. 4
SURREY, Stanley Sterling 8
SURTEES, Robert Lee 8
SUSANN, Jacqueline 6
SUSENS, George 7
SUSSKIND, David Howard 4
SUSSKIND, Walter 7
SUSSMAN, Jerry 9
SUSSMAN, Morty 7
SUSSMAN, Otto 3
SUSSMAN, Sidney X. 8
SUTCLIFFE, Emerson Grant 8
SUTER, Charles Russell 1
SUTER, Francis L. 5
SUTER, Herbert Wallace, Jr. 4
SUTER, John Wallace 2
SUTHERLAND, Abby Ann 6
SUTHERLAND, Allan 5
SUTHERLAND, Allen Jennings 10
SUTHERLAND, Annie 1
SUTHERLAND, Arthur Eugene 5
SUTHERLAND, Dan A. 3
SUTHERLAND, Earl Wilbur 6
SUTHERLAND, Edward Alexander 3
SUTHERLAND, Edwin Hardin 3
SUTHERLAND, Evelyn Greenleaf 1
SUTHERLAND, George* Alexander 2
SUTHERLAND, Gordon 3
SUTHERLAND, Howard 2
SUTHERLAND, Howard Vigne 4
SUTHERLAND, Joel Barlow H
SUTHERLAND, John Bain 2
SUTHERLAND, John Preston 1
SUTHERLAND, Joseph Hooker 5
SUTHERLAND, Josiah H
SUTHERLAND, Louis W. 7
SUTHERLAND, Richard K. 3
SUTHERLAND, Robert Edward Lee 6
SUTHERLAND, Robert Lee 7
SUTHERLAND, Roderick Dhu 3
SUTHERLAND, Thomas Henry 6
SUTHERLAND, William A. 1
SUTHERLAND, William Alexander, Jr 8
SUTHERLAND, William James 1
SUTLEY, Melvin Lockett 9
SUTLIFF, Milo Joseph 4
SUTLIFF, Phebe Temperance 5
SUTLIFF, Vincent E. 5
SUTPHEN, Duncan Dunbar 3
SUTPHEN, Henry Randolph 3

SUTPHEN, William Gilbert Van Tassel 2
SUTPHIN, Samuel Reid 9
SUTPHIN, William Halstead 8
SUTRO, Adolph Heinrich Joseph H
SUTRO, Alfred 2
SUTRO, Florence Clinton 1
SUTRO, Oscar 1
SUTRO, Richard 1
SUTRO, Theodore 1
SUTTER, Charles Clyde 7
SUTTER, Donald E(vans) 8
SUTTER, Harry Blair 3
SUTTER, John Augustus H
SUTTIE, Roscoe H(enry) 7
SUTTLE, Andrew Dillard 4
SUTTON, Charles Edward 4
SUTTON, Charles R(euel) 5
SUTTON, Charles Wood 5
SUTTON, Claude William 3
SUTTON, Dallas Gilchrist 5
SUTTON, David Nelson 6
SUTTON, Don C. 4
SUTTON, Donn 4
SUTTON, Frank 4
SUTTON, Frank Spencer 6
SUTTON, Frederick I. 5
SUTTON, George Miksch 8
SUTTON, Horace Ashley 10
SUTTON, John Brannen 2
SUTTON, Joseph Lee 5
SUTTON, Joseph Wilson 6
SUTTON, Lee Edwards, Jr. 4
SUTTON, Louis Valvelle 5
SUTTON, Loyd Hall 2
SUTTON, Mary Wooster Munson 5
SUTTON, Ottis Alton 9
SUTTON, Ransome 1
SUTTON, Reginald Miller 10
SUTTON, Rhoades Stansbury 1
SUTTON, Richard Lightburn 3
SUTTON, W. Henry 1
SUTTON, Wilbur Ervin 2
SUTTON, William 4
SUTTON, William Seneca 4
SUYDAM, Charles Crooke 4
SUYDAM, Henry 3
SUYDAM, John Howard 1
SUYDAM, Vernon Andrew 3
SUYKER, Hector 5
SUZUKI, Daisetsu Teitaro 4
SUZZALLO, Henry 1
SVANHOLM, Set 5
SVARTZ, Nanna Charlotta 9
SVEDBERG, Theodor 5
SVEDELIUS, Nils Eberhard 4
SVENDSEN, (James) Kester (Olaf) 5
SVERDRUP, Georg 1
SVERDRUP, George 1
SVERDRUP, Harald Ulrik 3
SVERDRUP, Leif John 6
SVERDRUP, Leif John 7
SVIEN, Hendrik Julius 6
SVININ, Pavel Petrovitch H
SVOBODA, Ralph Edward 5
SWABEY, Marie Collins 4
SWACKER, Frank M. 3
SWADOS, Harvey 5
SWAIM, H. Nathan 3
SWAIM, Joseph Skinner 1
SWAIM, Loring Tiffany 7
SWAIN, Anna Spencer Canada 8
SWAIN, Carl C. 7
SWAIN, David Lowry H
SWAIN, George Fillmore 1
SWAIN, Henry Huntington 1
SWAIN, Henry Lawrence 1
SWAIN, James H
SWAIN, James Obed 9
SWAIN, James Ramsay 5
SWAIN, Joseph 1
SWAIN, Joseph Ward 5
SWAIN, O.E. 8
SWAIN, Philip William 3
SWAIN, Robert Cuthbertson 9
SWAIN, Robert Eckles 4
SWAIN, Robert Lee 8
SWAINE, Robert Taylor 2
SWAINSON, William H
SWALES, William Edward 10
SWALLOW, Alan 4
SWALLOW, George Clinton 1
SWALLOW, Silas C. 1
SWALM, Albert Winfield 1
SWALWELL, Joseph Arthur 5
SWAN, Clifford Melville 3
SWAN, Dana Merrill 7

SWAN, Frank Herbert 3
SWAN, Gustaf Nilsson 1
SWAN, Henry Harrison 1
SWAN, Herbert S. 8
SWAN, James H
SWAN, James Edward 6
SWAN, John H
SWAN, John Mumford 3
SWAN, John Nesbit 1
SWAN, Joseph Edwards Corson
SWAN, Joseph R. 4
SWAN, Joseph Rackwell 2
SWAN, Joseph Rockwell H
SWAN, Lowell Benjamin 5
SWAN, Marshall 7
SWAN, Nathalie Henderson 6
SWAN, Paul 5
SWAN, Samuel H
SWAN, Thomas Walter 5
SWAN, Timothy H
SWAN, Verne Sturges 5
SWANBERG, Harold 5
SWANBERG, William Andrew 10
SWANDER, John I. 4
SWANEBECK, Clarence W. 5
SWANEY, William Bentley 2
SWANISH, Peter Theodore 5
SWANK, Arthur Jackson 10
SWANK, Fletcher B. 5
SWANK, James Moore 5
SWANLUND, Lester Herman 5
SWANN, Edward 4
SWANN, Michael Meredith 10
SWANN, Ralph Clay 4
SWANN, Theodore 7
SWANN, Thomas 5
SWANN, William Francis Gray 4
SWANSEN, Sam T. 3
SWANSON, Albert E. 5
SWANSON, Albert Gustav 5
SWANSON, Carroll Arthur 10
SWANSON, Charles Edward 5
SWANSON, Clarence Emanuel 5
SWANSON, Claude Augustus 1
SWANSON, David Verner 8
SWANSON, Edgar Walfred 5
SWANSON, Frank 10
SWANSON, Gloria 8
SWANSON, H(arold) N(orling) 10
SWANSON, John A. 2
SWANSON, Paul Gustaf 3
SWANSON, Roy Paul 8
SWANSON, W. Clarke 4
SWANSON, W(illiam) F(redin) 9
SWANTEE, Paul Frederick 5
SWANTON, Gerald F. 3
SWANTON, John Reed 5
SWANTON, William T. 5
SWARR, David Whitmyer 8
SWART, Charles Robberts 5
SWART, Joseph 4
SWART, Peter H
SWART, Robert Emerson 2
SWART, Robert Lee 7
SWART, Walter Goodwin 4
SWARTHOUT, Donald Malcolm 4
SWARTHOUT, Elvin 1
SWARTHOUT, Gladys 5
SWARTHOUT, Glendon Fred 10
SWARTHOUT, Herbert Marion 10
SWARTHOUT, Max van Lewen 6
SWARTLEY, Stanley Simpson 7
SWARTS, Gardner Taber 4
SWARTSBERG, Jerome F. 4
SWARTSWELTER, Ernest E. 8
SWARTWOOD, Howard Albright 4
SWARTWOUT, Denton Kenyon 9
SWARTWOUT, Egerton 2
SWARTWOUT, Mary Cooke 5
SWARTWOUT, Richard Henry 1
SWARTWOUT, Samuel H
SWARTZ, Charles Benjamin 3
SWARTZ, Charles Kephart 2
SWARTZ, Edward James 1
SWARTZ, Edward M(itchell) 10

SWARTZ, Harold 7
SWARTZ, Harry Raymond 2
SWARTZ, Herman Frank 5
SWARTZ, Jacob Hyams 6
SWARTZ, Joel 4
SWARTZ, Joshua W. 4
SWARTZ, Katherine H. 4
SWARTZ, Mifflin Wyatt 4
SWARTZ, Osman Ellis 5
SWARTZ, Peter Winferd 6
SWARTZ, Philip Allen 4
SWARTZ, Samuel Jackson 4
SWARTZ, Willis George 4
SWARTZBAUGH, William Lamson 4
SWASEY, Albert Loring 3
SWASEY, Ambrose 1
SWATLAND, Donald Clinton 4
SWAVELY, Eli 5
SWAYNE, Alfred Harris 1
SWAYNE, Noah Haynes H
SWAYNE, Wager 1
SWAYZE, Francis Joseph 1
SWAYZE, George Banghart Henry 1
SWEARER, Howard Robert 10
SWEARINGEN, Embry L. 1
SWEARINGEN, Henry H
SWEARINGEN, Henry Chapman 1
SWEARINGEN, J(ames) I(saac) 7
SWEARINGEN, John Eldred 5
SWEARINGEN, Lloyd Edward 5
SWEARINGEN, Mack Buckley 5
SWEARINGEN, Van Cicero 5
SWEARINGEN, Victor Clarence 5
SWEAT, Herbert J. 7
SWEATT, Charles Baxter 7
SWEATT, Harold W. 9
SWEATT, William R. 1
SWEAZEY, George Edgar 10
SWEDENBERG, Hugh Thomas, Jr. 7
SWEDLOW, Jerold Lindsay 10
SWEENEY, Alvin Randolph 3
SWEENEY, Bo 1
SWEENEY, Edward C. 4
SWEENEY, George H
SWEENEY, George Clinton 5
SWEENEY, Henry Whitcomb 10
SWEENEY, James G. 5
SWEENEY, James J. 5
SWEENEY, James Johnson 9
SWEENEY, James P. 4
SWEENEY, James William 7
SWEENEY, John William 5
SWEENEY, Joseph 7
SWEENEY, Martin L. 4
SWEENEY, Martin L. 4
SWEENEY, Mildred I. McNeal 5
SWEENEY, Orland Russell 5
SWEENEY, Thomas Bell, Sr. 3
SWEENEY, Thomas William H
SWEENEY, Walter Campbell 4
SWEENEY, William Northcut H
SWEENEY, William R. 6
SWEENEY, Zachary Taylor 1
SWEENIE, Denis J. 5
SWEENY, Charles Amos 5
SWEENY, Donald N. 9
SWEENY, Peter Barr H
SWEENY, Peter Barr 4
SWEENY, William Montgomery 5
SWEET, Ada Celeste 3
SWEET, Ada Celeste 4
SWEET, Alexander Edwin 1
SWEET, Alfred Henry 3
SWEET, Arthur Jeremiah 7
SWEET, Carroll Fuller 3
SWEET, Cyrus Bardeen 4
SWEET, David Emery 9
SWEET, Edwin Forrest 1
SWEET, Ellingham Tracy 2
SWEET, Elnathan 1
SWEET, Frank Herbert 4
SWEET, Frederic E(lmore) 6
SWEET, George Sullivan 4
SWEET, Harold Edward 4
SWEET, John Edson 1

SWEET, John Henry Throop, Jr. 3
SWEET, John Howard 9
SWEET, John Hyde 4
SWEET, Joshua Edwin 3
SWEET, Louis Dennison 1
SWEET, Louis Matthews 3
SWEET, Marion Atwood (Mrs. Hamilton Howard Sweet) 5
SWEET, Oney Fred 7
SWEET, Owen Jay 1
SWEET, Sidney Edward 7
SWEET, Thaddeus C. 1
SWEET, Timothy Bailey 1
SWEET, William Ellery 2
SWEET, William Luther 4
SWEET, William Merrick 4
SWEET, William Warren 5
SWEETING, Orville John 7
SWEETLAND, Cornelius Sowle 1
SWEETLAND, Leon Hiram 6
SWEETLAND, William Howard 1
SWEETS, David Matthis 4
SWEETS, Henry Hayes 3
SWEETSER, Arthur 4
SWEETSER, Arthur 8
SWEETSER, Charles H
SWEETSER, Delight 1
SWEETSER, Edwin Chapin 1
SWEETSER, Edwin Frederic 7
SWEETSER, John Anderson 2
SWEETSER, Kate Dickinson 1
SWEIGERT, Ray Leslie 7
SWEIGERT, William T. 8
SWEITZER, Caesar 5
SWEITZER, J. Mearl 4
SWEM, Lee Allan 3
SWENEY, Joseph Henry 1
SWENGEL, Uriah Frantz 1
SWENK, Myron Harmon 1
SWENSON, Birger 10
SWENSON, David Ferdinand 1
SWENSON, Eric P. 2
SWENSON, Laurits Selmer 2
SWENSON, Lowell Harvey 4
SWENSON, May 10
SWENSON, Merrill G. 4
SWENSON, Rinehart John 8
SWENSON, Stanley Prescott 6
SWENSSON, Carl Aaron 1
SWENT, James Waterman 4
SWEPSTON, John E. 4
SWERDFEGER, Elbert Byron 1
SWERN, Daniel 8
SWERTFAGER, Walter Milton 4
SWETLAND, Roger Williams 1
SWETMAN, Ralph Waldo 7
SWETT, Frank Tracy 5
SWETT, John 1
SWETT, Louis William 1
SWETT, Sophia Miriam 1
SWETT, Susan Hartley 1
SWEZEY, Goodwin Deloss 1
SWEZEY, Robert Dwight 7
SWICK, J. Howard 6
SWIETLIK, F(rancis) X(avier) 8
SWIFT, Archie Dean 4
SWIFT, Benjamin H
SWIFT, Carl Brown 1
SWIFT, Charles Henry 1
SWIFT, Clarence Franklin 1
SWIFT, Douglas 2
SWIFT, Eben 1
SWIFT, Edgar James 1
SWIFT, Edward Foster 1
SWIFT, Edward Wellington 4
SWIFT, Elijah Kent 3
SWIFT, Emerson H(owland) 8
SWIFT, Ernest Fremont 5
SWIFT, Ernest John 1
SWIFT, Eugene Clinton 6
SWIFT, Fletcher Harper 1
SWIFT, Frederic Fay 10
SWIFT, George B. 4
SWIFT, George Hastings, Jr. 8
SWIFT, George Robinson 8
SWIFT, George Wilkins 1
SWIFT, Gustavus Franklin 1
SWIFT, Gustavus Franklin 2
SWIFT, Gustavus Franklin, Jr. 7
SWIFT, Harold Higgins 4
SWIFT, Harry Ladrew 3

SWIFT, Homer Fordyce 3
SWIFT, Innis Palmer 3
SWIFT, Ivan 2
SWIFT, James Carroll 1
SWIFT, James Marcus 2
SWIFT, Jireh, Jr. 2
SWIFT, John Edward 6
SWIFT, John Franklin H
SWIFT, John Trumbull 4
SWIFT, Jonathan Dean 7
SWIFT, Joseph Gardner H
SWIFT, Josiah Otis 2
SWIFT, Lewis 1
SWIFT, Lewis Burrie 7
SWIFT, Lindsay 1
SWIFT, Louis Franklin 1
SWIFT, Lucian 3
SWIFT, Nathan Butler 3
SWIFT, Oscar William 1
SWIFT, Polemus Hamilton 1
SWIFT, Raymond W(alter) 6
SWIFT, Samuel 1
SWIFT, Willard Everett 2
SWIFT, William 1
SWIFT, William Henry H
SWIFT, Zephaniah H
SWIG, Benjamin Harrison 7
SWIGART, Charles H. 4
SWIGART, Clyde Arthur 6
SWIGART, Edmund Kearsley 1
SWIGART, La Vern Lake 6
SWIGER, Wilbur Moore 1
SWIGERT, Ernest Goodnough 9
SWIGERT, John Leonard, Jr. 8
SWIGGART, William Harris 4
SWIGGETT, Douglas Worthington 2
SWIGGETT, Douglas Worthington 3
SWIGGETT, Glen Levin 4
SWIM, Chester Lawrence 5
SWIM, Dudley 5
SWINBURNE, John H
SWINBURNE, William Thomas 1
SWINDALL, Charles 4
SWINDEREN, Jonkheer Reneke de Marees van 4
SWINDLER, Mary Hamilton 4
SWINDLER, William Finley 8
SWINEFORD, Oscar, Jr. 4
SWINEHART, Gerry 4
SWINERTON, Alfred B. 4
SWINEY, Daniel 4
SWINFORD, Mac 6
SWING, Albert Temple 1
SWING, David H
SWING, Gael Duane 10
SWING, Joseph M. 8
SWING, Philip David 5
SWING, Raymond 5
SWINGLE, D. B. 2
SWINGLE, Frank Bell 4
SWINGLE, Walter T. 3
SWINGLE, Wilbur Willis 9
SWINGLE, William S. 6
SWINGLER, William S(herman) 4
SWINK, John Lewis 10
SWINNERTON, Frank Arthur 4
SWINNERTON, James Guilford 6
SWINNEY, Edward Fletcher 2
SWINT, John J. 4
SWINT, Samuel H. 4
SWINTON, John 1
SWINTON, Stanley Mitchell H
SWINTON, William H
SWIRBUL, Leon A. 4
SWIRE, Willard 10
SWIREN, Max 4
SWISHER, Benjamin Franklin 3
SWISHER, Charles Clinton 1
SWISHER, Charles F. 1
SWISHER, Walter Samuel 7
SWISSHELM, Jane Grey Cannon H
SWITZ, Theodore MacLean 5
SWITZER, George Washington 1
SWITZER, Mary Elizabeth 4
SWITZER, Maurice 1
SWITZER, Robert Mauck 1
SWOOPE, Jacob H
SWOOPE, William Irvin 1
SWOPE, Ammon 1
SWOPE, Charles Siegel 3

SWOPE, Gerard 3
SWOPE, Gerard, Jr. 7
SWOPE, Guy J. 5
SWOPE, Herbery Bayard 3
SWOPE, King 4
SWOPE, Samuel Franklin H
SWORAKOWSKI, Witold S. 7
SWORD, James Brade 1
SWORDS, Henry Cotheal 1
SWORDS, Raymond Joseph 8
SWORDS, Vincent Thomas 7
SWYGERT, Luther Merritt 9
SYDENSTRICKER, Edgar 1
SYDENSTRICKER, Virgil Preston 4
SYDNESS, Joseph Truman 5
SYDNOR, Charles Sackett 3
SYDNOR, Giles Granville 2
SYKES, Charles Henry 2
SYKES, Edward 5
SYKES, Edward Turner 2
SYKES, Eugene Octave 2
SYKES, Frederick Henry 1
SYKES, George* H
SYKES, Gerald 8
SYKES, Howard Calvin 4
SYKES, James H
SYKES, Jerome H. 1
SYKES, Mabel 1
SYKES, M'Cready 3
SYKES, Richard Eddy 2
SYKES, Roosevelt 8
SYKES, Weathers York 10
SYKES, Wilfred 1
SYLE, Louis du Pont 1
SYLLA, James R. 9
SYLVA, Marguerita 3
SYLVESTER, Albert Lenthall 6
SYLVESTER, Allie Lewis 4
SYLVESTER, Arthur 7
SYLVESTER, Emma 4
SYLVESTER, Evander Wallace
SYLVESTER, Frederick Oakes 1
SYLVESTER, Herbert Milton 4
SYLVESTER, James Joseph H
SYLVESTER, Richard Standish 7
SYLVESTER, Robert 6
SYLVIS, William H. H
SYME, Conrad Hunt 2
SYME, John P. 5
SYMES, George Gifford H
SYMES, J. Foster 3
SYMES, James Miller 7
SYMINGTON, Charles Julian
SYMINGTON, Donald 2
SYMINGTON, Lloyd 9
SYMINGTON, Stuart 9
SYMMERS, Douglas 3
SYMMES, Edwin Joseph 1
SYMMES, Frank Jameson 1
SYMMES, John Cleves H
SYMMES, Leslie Webb 6
SYMMONDS, Charles Jacobs 1
SYMONDS, Brandreth 1
SYMONDS, Frederick Martin
SYMONDS, Gardiner 5
SYMONDS, Joseph White 1
SYMONDS, Nathaniel Millberry 5
SYMONDS, Percival Mallon 4
SYMONDS, Walter Stout 3
SYMONS, Gardner 1
SYMONS, Noel S. 4
SYMONS, Thomas Baddeley
SYMONS, Thomas William 1
SYMS, Benjamin H
SYNAN, Joseph Alexander, Sr. 8
SYNDERGAARD, Parley Rex 7
SYNG, Philip H
SYNICK, Henry 7
SYNNOTT, Joseph J. 1
SYNNOTT, Thomas Whitney 1
SYPHER, Josiah Rhinehart 4
SYPHERD, Wilbur Owen 5
SYRETT, Harold Coffin 8
SYRKIN, Marie 9
SYVERSON, Aldrich 10
SYVERTON, Jerome T. 4
SYVERTSEN, Rolf Christian 4
SZABO, Gabor 8
SZE, Sao-ke Alfred 3
SZEFTEL, Marc M. 8

SZEKELY, Ernest 3
SZENT-GYORGYI, Albert 9
SZERYING, Henryk 9
SZIGETI, Joseph 5
SZILARD, Leo 4
SZINNYEY, Stephen Ivor 1
SZLADITS, Lola Leontin 10
SZLUPAS, John 4
SZOLD, Harold James 10
SZOLD, Henrietta 2
SZOLD, Robert 7
SZUMOWSKA, Antoinette 1
SZYK, Arthur 3

T

TABB, John Banister 1
TABELL, Edmund Weber 4
TABER, David Fairman 3
TABER, Erroll James Livingstone 2
TABER, Frederic Howland 7
TABER, George Hathaway, Jr. 3
TABER, Gladys 7
TABER, Gladys 8
TABER, Harry Persons 4
TABER, Henry 1
TABER, John 4
TABER, John Starr 8
TABER, Louis John 4
TABER, Louise Eddy 8
TABER, Mary Jane Howland 4
TABER, Norman Stephen 3
TABER, Ralph Graham 4
TABER, Stephen H
TABER, Stephen 7
TABER, Thomas, 2d H
TABER, William Ira 1
TABOADA, Diogenes 7
TABOR, Carl Henry 3
TABOR, Edward A. 4
TABOR, Frederick Alfred Merlin 8
TABOR, Horace Austin Warner H
TABORS, Robert Gustav 4
TACK, Augustus Vincent 2
TACKETT, John Robert 4
TACKETT, William Clarence 3
TADD, J. Liberty 1
TAEUBER, Irene Barnes (Mrs. Conrad Taeuber) 6
TAEUSCH, Carl Frederick 4
TAFEL, Gustav 1
TAFEL, Leonard Immanuel 7
TAFF, Joseph Alexander 2
TAFFE, John H
TAFFINDER, Sherwoode Ayerst 4
TAFT, Alphonso H
TAFT, Charles Phelps 1
TAFT, Charles Phelps 8
TAFT, David Gibson 4
TAFT, Edward Augustine 7
TAFT, Elihu Barber 4
TAFT, Frederick Lovett 8
TAFT, George Wheaton 1
TAFT, Harry Deward 3
TAFT, Henry Waters 2
TAFT, Horace Dutton 2
TAFT, Horace Dwight 8
TAFT, Hulbert 3
TAFT, Julia Jessie 7
TAFT, Kendall B(ernard) 5
TAFT, Kingsley A. 5
TAFT, Levi Rawson 4
TAFT, Lorado 1
TAFT, Lorado 4
TAFT, Philip 7
TAFT, Robert 3
TAFT, Robert Alphonso 3
TAFT, Robert Burbidge 3
TAFT, Robert Stephen 9
TAFT, Robert Wendell 1
TAFT, Royal Chapin 1
TAFT, Russell Smith 1
TAFT, William Howard 1
TAG, Casimir 1
TAGG, Francis Thomas 1
TAGGARD, Genevieve 2
TAGGART, Arthur Fay 3
TAGGART, David Alexander 5
TAGGART, David Arthur 1
TAGGART, Elmore Findlay 4
TAGGART, Eugene Francis 3
TAGGART, Frank Fulton 2
TAGGART, Joseph 4
TAGGART, Joseph Herman 8
TAGGART, Kenneth Dale 10
TAGGART, Marion Ames 5
TAGGART, Ralph Enos 3
TAGGART, Rush 1
TAGGART, Samuel H
TAGGART, Thomas 1
TAGGART, Thomas Douglas 2
TAGGART, Walter Thomas 1
TAGGART, William Gilbert 7
TAGLIABUE, Giuseppe H
TAGUE, Peter F. 1
TAINTER, Charles Sumner 1
TAINTOR, Henry Fox 1
TAINTOR, Jesse Fox 1
TAISHOFF, Sol Joseph* 8
TAIT, Arthur Fitzwilliam 1
TAIT, Charles H
TAIT, Edgar Wendell 7
TAIT, Frank Morrison 4
TAIT, George 3
TAIT, John Robinson 1
TAITT, Francis Marion 2
TAKACH, Basil 2
TAKAHIRA, Kogoro 4
TAKAMINE, Jokichi 1
TALARICO, Samuel Joseph 8
TALBERT, Ansel Edward McLaurine 9
TALBERT, Ernest William 9
TALBERT, Joseph Truitt 1
TALBERT, Samuel Stubbs 5
TALBERT, W. Jasper 4
TALBOT, Adolphus Robert 2
TALBOT, Arthur Newell 2
TALBOT, Edith Armstrong 5
TALBOT, Ellen Bliss 4
TALBOT, Ethelbert 1
TALBOT, Eugene Solomon 1
TALBOT, Francis Xavier 3
TALBOT, George Frederick 3
TALBOT, Guy Webster 5
TALBOT, Henry Paul 1
TALBOT, Howard 1
TALBOT, Isham H
TALBOT, Israel Tisdale 1
TALBOT, John H
TALBOT, John William 1
TALBOT, Marion 2
TALBOT, Mary White 3
TALBOT, M(urrell) W(illiams) 5
TALBOT, Ralph 7
TALBOT, Silas H
TALBOT, Timothy Ralph 10
TALBOT, Walter Lemar 2
TALBOT, William Howe McElwain 7
TALBOT, Winifred Luella Winter (Mrs. John E. Talbot) 5
TALBOTT, Albert Gallatin H
TALBOTT, Everett Guy 2
TALBOTT, Francis Leo 9
TALBOTT, George Harold 10
TALBOTT, Harold E. 3
TALBOTT, Harold E. 4
TALBOTT, Henry James 1
TALBOTT, J. Fred C. 1
TALBOTT, John Harold 10
TALBOTT, Nelson S. 3
TALBOTT, Philip Melville 10
TALBURT, Harold M. 4
TALCOTT, Andrew H
TALCOTT, Charles Andrew 1
TALCOTT, Edward N. Kirk 1
TALCOTT, James Frederick 2
TALCOTT, Joseph H
TALIAFERRO, Benjamin H
TALIAFERRO, Harry Monroe 5
TALIAFERRO, Henry Beckwith 4
TALIAFERRO, James Piper 2
TALIAFERRO, John H
TALIAFERRO, Lawrence H
TALIAFERRO, Mabel 8
TALIAFERRO, Nicholas Lloyd 4
TALIAFERRO, Sidney Fletcher 7
TALIAFERRO, Thomas Hardy 1
TALIAFERRO, Thomas Seddon, Jr. 1
TALIAFERRO, William Booth H
TALIAFERRO, William Hay 6
TALL, Lida Lee 2
TALLAMY, Bertram Dalley 10
TALLANT, Hugh 3
TALLCOTT, Rollo Anson 7
TALLE, Henry O(scar) 5
TALLERDAY, Howard G. 2
TALLEY, Bascom Destrehan, Jr. 5
TALLEY, Dyer Findley 2
TALLEY, Franz G. 7
TALLEY, Lee 7
TALLEY, Lynn Porter 2
TALLEYRAND-PERIGORD, Charles Maurice de H
TALLIAFERO, Richard H
TALLICHET, Jules Henri 1
TALLMADGE, Benjamin H
TALLMADGE, Frederick Augustus H
TALLMADGE, Guy Kasten 4
TALLMADGE, James, Jr. H
TALLMADGE, Nathaniel Pitcher H
TALLMADGE, Thomas Eddy 1
TALLMAN, Clay 5
TALLMAN, Peleg H
TALLY, Robert Emmet 1
TALLY, William F. 4
TALMADGE, Constance 6
TALMADGE, Eugene 2
TALMADGE, Norma 3
TALMAGE, James Edward 1
TALMAGE, John Van Nest H
TALMAGE, T. Dewitt 1
TALMAN, Charles Fitzhugh 1
TALMAN, E. Lee 4
TALON, Pierre H
TALVELA, Martti Olavi 10
TALYZIN, Nikolai Vladimirovich 10
TAM, Reuben 10
TAMARKIN, Jacob David 2
TAMARON, Pedro H
TAMIRIS, Helen 4
TAMIROFF, Akim 5
TAMM, Edward Allen 9
TAMM, Igor 6
TAMM, Igor Y. 5
TAMMANY H
TAMMEN, Agnes Reid 2
TAMMEN, Harry Heye H
TAMMEN, Harry Heye 4
TAMS, James Elmore Moffett 9
TANAKA, Jeffrey Scott 10
TANAKA, Kotaro 6
TANDY, Charles David 7
TANENBAUM, Marc Herman 10
TANEY, Roger Brooke H
TANG, Anthony Matthew 10
TANG, K. Y. 4
TANGEMAN, Robert Stone 4
TANGEMAN, Walter W. 4
TANGLEY, Edwin Savory (Baron Tangley of Blackheath) 6
TANGUY, Yves 3
TANI, Masayuki 4
TANIZAKI, Junichiro 4
TANKOOS, Samuel Joseph, Jr. 7
TANNAHILL, Samuel O. 1
TANNEBERGER, David H
TANNEHILL, Adamson H
TANNEHILL, Urban Roy 9
TANNENBAUM, Albert 7
TANNENBAUM, Samuel Aaron 2
TANNENBAUM, Samuel William 8
TANNER, Adolphus Hitchcock H
TANNER, Benjamin H
TANNER, Benjamin Tucker 1
TANNER, Champ Bean 10
TANNER, Edward Everett, 3d (Patrick Dennis, Virginia Rowans) 7
TANNER, Edwin Platt 1
TANNER, Eugene Simpson 5
TANNER, Fred Wilbur 3
TANNER, Frederick Chauncey 4
TANNER, George Clinton 4
TANNER, Harold Brooks 5
TANNER, Henry Ossawa 1
TANNER, Henry Schenck H
TANNER, Jacob 5
TANNER, James 1
TANNER, John Henry 1
TANNER, John Riley 1
TANNER, Kenneth Spencer 4
TANNER, Rollin Harvelle 5
TANNER, Sheldon C. 4
TANNER, Willard Brooks 4
TANNER, William Vaughn 3
TANNER, Wilson Pennell 7
TANNER, Zera Luther 1
TANNIAN, Joy 9
TANNRATH, John Joseph 1
TANSEY, Patrick Henry 6
TANSIL, John Bell 3
TANSILL, Charles Callan 4
TANSILL, Donald Bender 10
TANZER, Laurence Arnold 4
TAPLEY, Walter Moore, Jr. 5
TAPLIN, Charles Farrand 7
TAPLIN, Frank E. 1
TAPLINGER, Richard Jacques 5
TAPP, Ernest Marvin 6
TAPP, Jesse W. 4
TAPP, Sidney C. 5
TAPPAN, Anna Helen 8
TAPPAN, Arthur H
TAPPAN, Benjamin H
TAPPAN, Benjamin 1
TAPPAN, David Stanton 1
TAPPAN, Eli Todd H
TAPPAN, Eva March 1
TAPPAN, Frank Girard 4
TAPPAN, Henry Philip H
TAPPAN, Lewis H
TAPPAN, Mason Weare H
TAPPAN, William Bingham H
TAPPEN, Frederick D. 1
TAPPEN, Paul W. 4
TAPPER, Bertha Feiring 1
TAPPER, Thomas 3
TAPPERT, Theodore Gerhardt 6
TAPPIN, John Lindsley 4
TAPSCOTT, Ralph Henry 4
TAQUINO, George James 3
TARACOUZIO, Timothy Andrew 3
TARAS, Anthony F. 8
TARBELL, Arthur Wilson 2
TARBELL, Edmund C. 1
TARBELL, Frank Bigelow 1
TARBELL, Gage E. 1
TARBELL, Horace Sumner 1
TARBELL, Ida Minerva 2
TARBELL, Joseph H
TARBELL, Martha 2
TARBELL, Thomas Freeman 3
TARBOUX, Joseph G. 3
TARBOX, Increase Niles H
TARBOX, John Kemble H
TARBUTTON, Ben James 4
TARCHER, Jack David 4
TARCHIANI, Alberto 4
TARJAN, George 10
TARKINGTON, Grayson Emery 1
TARKINGTON, John Stevenson 1
TARKINGTON, Newton Booth 2
TARLER, George Cornell 2
TARPEY, Michael Francis 1
TARR, Christian H
TARR, Frederick Courtney 3
TARR, Frederick Hamilton 2
TARR, Leslie Riley 5
TARR, Ralph Stockman 1
TARR, William Arthur 1
TARRANT, John Edward 10
TARRANT, Warren Downes 1
TARRANT, William Theodore 5
TARRANT, William Theodore 7
TARSKI, Alfred 8
TARSNEY, John C. 4
TARTAKOFF, Joseph 6
TARUMIANZ, Mesrop A. 7
TARVER, Malcolm Connor 4
TARVER, William Allen 1
TASCA, Henry J. 7
TASHIRO, Shiro 7
TASHLIN, Frank 5
TASKER, Cyril 3
TASKEY, Harry Leroy 3
TASSIN, Algernon de Vivier 1
TASSIN, Wirt 1
TASTROM, Edward P(hillip) 7
TATE, Albert, Jr. 9
TATE, Allen (John Orley) 7
TATE, Benjamin Ethan 4
TATE, Farish Carter 4
TATE, Fred N. 4
TATE, H. Theodore 4
TATE, H. Theodore 5
TATE, Hugh McCall 1
TATE, Jack Bernard 5
TATE, James Alexander 3
TATE, James Hugh Joseph 8
TATE, Joe Tom 8
TATE, John Matthew, Jr. 5
TATE, John Torrence 3
TATE, Magnus H
TATE, Robert 4
TATE, Sam 1
TATE, William Knox 1
TATE, Willis McDonald 10
TATGENHORST, Charles 4
TATHAM, Arthur Edward 9
TATHAM, William H
TATLOCK, Henry 2
TATLOCK, John 1
TATLOCK, John S. P. 2
TATMAN, Charles Taylor 2
TATNALL, Henry 1
TATOM, Absalom H
TATSCH, J. Hugo 1
TATTNALL, Edward Fenwick H
TATTNALL, Josiah* H
TATUM, Arthur 4
TATUM, Arthur Lawrie 3
TATUM, Edward Lawrie 6
TAUB, Abraham 10
TAUB, Ben 8
TAUB, Edward Allen 5
TAUB, Sam 3
TAUBE, Mortimer 4
TAUBENHAUS, Jacob Joseph 1
TAUBENHAUS, Leon Jair 6
TAUBER, Maurice Falcolm 7
TAUBER, Oscar Ernst 8
TAUBER, Richard 2
TAUBES, Frederick 8
TAUBMAN, George Primrose 2
TAUBMAN, Tom 4
TAUCH, Waldine 9
TAUL, Micah H
TAULBEE, Orrin Edison 9
TAULBEE, William Preston H
TAURIELLO, Anthony F. 8
TAUROG, Norman 7
TAUSSIG, Albert Ernst 2
TAUSSIG, Charles William 2
TAUSSIG, Edward David 1
TAUSSIG, Edward Holmes 9
TAUSSIG, Frances 7
TAUSSIG, Francis Brewster 5
TAUSSIG, Frank William 1
TAUSSIG, Frederick Joseph 2
TAUSSIG, Garfield Joseph 7
TAUSSIG, Helen Brooke 9
TAUSSIG, James Edward 2
TAUSSIG, Joseph Knefler 2
TAUSSIG, Rudolph Julius 1
TAUSSIG, William 1
TAVARES, Cyrus Nils 7
TAVENNER, Clyde Howard 1
TAVENNER, Clyde Howard 2
TAVENNER, Frank Stacy, Jr. 4
TAVES, Brydon 2
TAWES, John Millard 7
TAWNEY, Guy Alan 2
TAWNEY, James A. 1
TAWRESEY, John Godwin 2
TAYBACK, Vic (Victor Tabback)* 10
TAYLER, Benjamin Walter Rogers 1
TAYLER, Joseph Henry 3
TAYLER, Lewis H
TAYLER, Robert Walker 1
TAYLOR, A. Starke 8
TAYLOR, Abner 4
TAYLOR, Alan Carey 6
TAYLOR, Alan John Percivale 10
TAYLOR, Albert Davis 3
TAYLOR, Albert Hoyt 4
TAYLOR, Albert Pierce 1
TAYLOR, Albert Reynolds 1
TAYLOR, Alexander Wilson H
TAYLOR, Alfred Alexander 1
TAYLOR, Alfred Simpson 2
TAYLOR, Alrutheus Ambush 3
TAYLOR, Alva Edwards 1
TAYLOR, Alva Park 8
TAYLOR, Amos Elias 5
TAYLOR, Amos Leavitt 4
TAYLOR, Archer 6
TAYLOR, Archer 8
TAYLOR, Archibald Wellington 3
TAYLOR, Arthur Nelson 4
TAYLOR, Asher Clayton 1
TAYLOR, Aubrey E. 2
TAYLOR, A(ustin) Starke 9
TAYLOR, Barnard Cook 1
TAYLOR, Bayard H
TAYLOR, Benjamin Brown 7

THOMAS, Frederick Folger, Jr. 7
THOMAS, Frederick Lionel 5
THOMAS, Frederick William H
THOMAS, George H
THOMAS, George C(arroll) 7
THOMAS, George Comyns, Jr. 8
THOMAS, George Henry H
THOMAS, George Henry 4
THOMAS, George Herbert 1
THOMAS, George Morgan 4
THOMAS, Gerald Burison 5
THOMAS, Gilbert Joshua 7
THOMAS, Glen Herbert 4
THOMAS, Griffith H
THOMAS, Gus 3
THOMAS, Guy Alfred 2
THOMAS, Harold Allen 7
THOMAS, Harold Rudolph 6
THOMAS, Henry Bascom 3
THOMAS, Henry M. 1
THOMAS, Henry M., Jr. 4
THOMAS, Henry Wilton 4
THOMAS, Hiram Washington 1
THOMAS, Horace Davis 4
THOMAS, Howard Dudley 5
THOMAS, Isaac H
THOMAS, Isaiah H
THOMAS, Jackson Mash 4
THOMAS, James 1
THOMAS, James Augustus 1
THOMAS, James Bishop 3
THOMAS, James Gladwyn 10
THOMAS, James Houston H
THOMAS, James John 5
THOMAS, James Shelby 6
THOMAS, James Shelby 7
THOMAS, Jesse Burgess H
THOMAS, Jesse Burgess 1
THOMAS, Jessie Beattie 1
THOMAS, John H
THOMAS, John Charles 4
THOMAS, John Chew H
THOMAS, John Hampden 1
THOMAS, John Jacobs H
THOMAS, John Jenks 1
THOMAS, John Lewis, Jr. H
THOMAS, John Lloyd 1
THOMAS, John Martin 3
THOMAS, John Montague 3
THOMAS, John Parnell 5
THOMAS, John Peyre, Jr. 2
THOMAS, John Robert 1
THOMAS, John Rochester 1
THOMAS, John S. Ladd 1
THOMAS, John W. 2
THOMAS, John W. 3
THOMAS, John Wilson, Jr. 1
THOMAS, Joseph H
THOMAS, Joseph Albert 7
THOMAS, Joseph Brown 3
THOMAS, Joseph Loren 5
THOMAS, Joseph Peter 2
THOMAS, J(ulian) B(aldwin) 9
THOMAS, Kirby 1
THOMAS, Lee Baldwin, Sr. 9
THOMAS, Lee Emmett 4
THOMAS, Lewis F. 3
THOMAS, Lewis Victor 4
THOMAS, Lorenzo H
THOMAS, Lot 1
THOMAS, Louis Godfrey Lee 10
THOMAS, Lowell 8
THOMAS, Lucien Irving 2
THOMAS, M. Carey 1
THOMAS, M. Louise 2
THOMAS, Martin Henry 1
THOMAS, Mason Blanchard 1
THOMAS, Maurice J. 4
THOMAS, M(ilton) Halsey 7
THOMAS, Nathaniel Seymour 1
THOMAS, Norman (Mattoon) 5
THOMAS, O. Pendleton 9
THOMAS, Orlando Pendleton 8
THOMAS, Paul Henwood 6
THOMAS, Paul Kirk Middlebrook 4
THOMAS, Percy Champion 5
THOMAS, Percy H. 3
THOMAS, Philemon H
THOMAS, Philip Evan H
THOMAS, Philip Francis H
THOMAS, P(urdom) C(lark) 5
THOMAS, Ralph 10
THOMAS, Ralph Llewellyn
THOMAS, Ralph W. 1
THOMAS, Reuen 1

THOMAS, Richard H
THOMAS, Richard Curd Pope 1
THOMAS, Richard Henry 1
THOMAS, Robert Bailey H
THOMAS, Robert David 6
THOMAS, Robert Ellis 5
THOMAS, Robert McK. 6
THOMAS, Robert Young, Jr. 1
THOMAS, Rolla L. 1
THOMAS, Rolland Jay 4
THOMAS, Roy Zachariah 6
THOMAS, Russell Brown 8
THOMAS, Samuel 1
THOMAS, Samuel 3
THOMAS, Samuel Morgan 5
THOMAS, Seth H
THOMAS, Seth Edward, Jr. 1
THOMAS, Stanley Judson 4
THOMAS, Stanley Powers Rowland 6
THOMAS, Stephen Seymour 3
THOMAS, T. Rowland 1
THOMAS, Thaddeus Peter 4
THOMAS, Theodore 1
THOMAS, Theodore Gaillard 1
THOMAS, Walter F. 9
THOMAS, Walter Horstmann 2
THOMAS, Walter Ivan 8
THOMAS, Warren H. 4
THOMAS, Washington Butcher 1
THOMAS, Wilbur Kelsey 3
THOMAS, William 1
THOMAS, William, Jr. 8
THOMAS, William Aubrey 3
THOMAS, William David 1
THOMAS, William Davy 4
THOMAS, William Henry Griffith 1
THOMAS, William Holcombe 2
THOMAS, William Isaac 2
THOMAS, William Matthews Merrick 7
THOMAS, William Nathaniel 5
THOMAS, William Preston 4
THOMAS, William S. 4
THOMAS, William Sturgis 1
THOMAS, William Widgery 1
THOMASON, Alan Mims 8
THOMASON, John William, Jr. 2
THOMASON, Robert Ewing 6
THOMASON, Samuel Emory 2
THOMASSON, William Poindexter 1
THOMEN, August A. 2
THOMES, William Henry H
THOMPKINS, Leonard Joseph 6
THOMPSON, Albert Clifton 1
THOMPSON, Albert F. 4
THOMPSON, Alexander Marshall 3
THOMPSON, Alfred Charles 4
THOMPSON, Alfred Clark 1
THOMPSON, Alfred Wordsworth H
THOMPSON, Almon Harris 1
THOMPSON, Amos Burt 4
THOMPSON, Arthur Scott 3
THOMPSON, Arthur Webster 1
THOMPSON, Augustus Charles 1
THOMPSON, Bard 9
THOMPSON, Basil 1
THOMPSON, Beach 1
THOMPSON, Benjamin* H
THOMPSON, Bruce Rutherford 10
THOMPSON, C. Seymour 3
THOMPSON, C. Woody 4
THOMPSON, Calvin Miles 2
THOMPSON, Carl Dean 2
THOMPSON, Carmi Alderman 1
THOMPSON, Cecil Vincent Raymond 3
THOMPSON, Cephas Giovanni H
THOMPSON, Charles Edwin 1
THOMPSON, Charles Fullington 3
THOMPSON, Charles H. 5

THOMPSON, Charles H(enry) 7
THOMPSON, Charles Impey 3
THOMPSON, Charles James 1
THOMPSON, Charles Lemuel 1
THOMPSON, Charles Manfred 4
THOMPSON, Charles Miner 2
THOMPSON, Charles Nebeker 3
THOMPSON, Charles Oliver H
THOMPSON, Charles Perkins H
THOMPSON, Charles Thaddeus 1
THOMPSON, Charles William 1
THOMPSON, Charles Willis 2
THOMPSON, Charles Winston 1
THOMPSON, Chester Charles 5
THOMPSON, Clara 3
THOMPSON, C(larence) Bertrand 5
THOMPSON, Clarence Elmer 2
THOMPSON, Clark Wallace 8
THOMPSON, Clary 4
THOMPSON, Clem Oren 3
THOMPSON, Clifford Griffeth 4
THOMPSON, Cyrus 1
THOMPSON, Dale Moore 10
THOMPSON, Daniel Pierce H
THOMPSON, Daniel Varney 1
THOMPSON, David H
THOMPSON, David Alphaeus 1
THOMPSON, David Decamp 1
THOMPSON, David E. 2
THOMPSON, David Newton 4
THOMPSON, David P. 1
THOMPSON, Denman 1
THOMPSON, Dorothy 4
THOMPSON, Dwinel French 1
THOMPSON, E. E. 5
THOMPSON, Earle Spaulding 7
THOMPSON, Eben Francis 1
THOMPSON, Edward Archibald 3
THOMPSON, Edward Herbert 1
THOMPSON, Egbert H
THOMPSON, Elbert-nevius Sebring 2
THOMPSON, Eliza Jane Trimble 3
THOMPSON, Elizabeth McArthur 3
THOMPSON, Era Bell 9
THOMPSON, Ernest 2
THOMPSON, Ernest Othmer 4
THOMPSON, Ernest Seton 2
THOMPSON, Ernest Thorne 10
THOMPSON, Ernest Trice 10
THOMPSON, Erwin W. 1
THOMPSON, Fayette Lathrop 1
THOMPSON, Floyd E. 4
THOMPSON, Frank Abner 1
THOMPSON, Frank Dutton 1
THOMPSON, Frank E. 2
THOMPSON, Frank Forrester 1
THOMPSON, Frank M. 1
THOMPSON, Frank Victor 1
THOMPSON, Fred Lawrence 5
THOMPSON, Frederic Diodati Count 1
THOMPSON, Frederic Lincoln 1
THOMPSON, Frederick Delos 9
THOMPSON, Frederick Gregg 5
THOMPSON, Frederick Henry 1
THOMPSON, Frederick Ingate 3

THOMPSON, Frederick Roeck 8
THOMPSON, George* 1
THOMPSON, George B. 1
THOMPSON, George David 4
THOMPSON, George Jarvis 4
THOMPSON, G(eorge) K(ing) 9
THOMPSON, George Robert 9
THOMPSON, George Victor 5
THOMPSON, George Wallace 1
THOMPSON, George Wesley 7
THOMPSON, George Western H
THOMPSON, George Williston 5
THOMPSON, Gershom Joseph 7
THOMPSON, Gilbert 1
THOMPSON, Grover Cleveland 7
THOMPSON, Gustave Whyte 2
THOMPSON, Guy A. 5
THOMPSON, Hal Charles 4
THOMPSON, Harold William 9
THOMPSON, Harry Arthur 4
THOMPSON, Harry Charles 7
THOMPSON, Harry Leroy 3
THOMPSON, Harry Pleasant, Jr. 9
THOMPSON, Heber Samuel 1
THOMPSON, Hedge H
THOMPSON, Helen Elizabeth 1
THOMPSON, Helen Mulford 6
THOMPSON, Henry Adams 1
THOMPSON, Henry Burling 1
THOMPSON, Henry Dallas 1
THOMPSON, Holland 1
THOMPSON, Hollis Ring 2
THOMPSON, Homer Columbus 7
THOMPSON, Hope Keachie 8
THOMPSON, Hugh Lindsay 2
THOMPSON, Hugh Miller 1
THOMPSON, Hugh Smith 1
THOMPSON, Huston 4
THOMPSON, Ira Francis 1
THOMPSON, J. Eric S. 6
THOMPSON, J. Milton 1
THOMPSON, Jacob H
THOMPSON, James H
THOMPSON, James Edwin 1
THOMPSON, James F. 3
THOMPSON, James Goodhart 6
THOMPSON, James Kidd 5
THOMPSON, James Livingston 4
THOMPSON, James Ralph 5
THOMPSON, James Scott 8
THOMPSON, James Stacy 9
THOMPSON, James Stratton 3
THOMPSON, James Voorhees 3
THOMPSON, James Westfall 1
THOMPSON, Jean M. 5
THOMPSON, Jeremiah H
THOMPSON, Jerome B. H
THOMPSON, Joel H
THOMPSON, John* H
THOMPSON, John 2
THOMPSON, John 3
THOMPSON, John B. 8
THOMPSON, John Bert 6
THOMPSON, John Burton H
THOMPSON, John Cameron 1
THOMPSON, John Charles 7
THOMPSON, John Fairfield 5
THOMPSON, John Fawdrey, Jr. 5
THOMPSON, John Gilbert 2
THOMPSON, John Graves 4
THOMPSON, John Irvin 7
THOMPSON, John Kerwin 6
THOMPSON, John Q. 1
THOMPSON, John R. 1
THOMPSON, John Reuben H

THOMPSON, John Taliaferro 1
THOMPSON, John Winter 3
THOMPSON, Joseph Addison 3
THOMPSON, Joseph B. 1
THOMPSON, Joseph H. 5
THOMPSON, Joseph Osgood 3
THOMPSON, Joseph Parrish H
THOMPSON, Joseph S(exton) 5
THOMPSON, Joseph Trueman 9
THOMPSON, Joseph Whitaker 2
THOMPSON, Josiah Van Kirk 1
THOMPSON, Laforrest Holman 1
THOMPSON, Laroy Bernard 9
THOMPSON, Launt H
THOMPSON, Lawrance Roger 5
THOMPSON, Lawrence Sidney 9
THOMPSON, Leslie Prince 4
THOMPSON, Lewis 5
THOMPSON, Lewis Eugene 5
THOMPSON, Lewis Ryers 3
THOMPSON, Llewellyn E., Jr. 5
THOMPSON, Louis Ten Eyck 7
THOMPSON, Loyd 7
THOMPSON, M. Gladys 6
THOMPSON, Marshall Putnam 5
THOMPSON, Martin E. H
THOMPSON, Mary Wolfe (Mrs. Charles D. Thompson) 7
THOMPSON, Maurice 1
THOMPSON, Maurice Wycliffe 3
THOMPSON, Melville Withington 1
THOMPSON, Merle Dow 5
THOMPSON, Mills 2
THOMPSON, Milo Milton 5
THOMPSON, Milton John 5
THOMPSON, Oscar 2
THOMPSON, Owen Pierce 4
THOMPSON, Paul 2
THOMPSON, Paul Bryan 10
THOMPSON, Paul Dean 8
THOMPSON, Paul Jennings 1
THOMPSON, Paul Lamont 8
THOMPSON, Percy Wallace 4
THOMPSON, Philip H
THOMPSON, Philip Rootes H
THOMPSON, Porter 9
THOMPSON, Ralph 5
THOMPSON, Ralph Leroy 5
THOMPSON, Ralph Seymour 4
THOMPSON, Randall 3
THOMPSON, Reuben Cyril Hill 3
THOMPSON, Richard Ryan 7
THOMPSON, Richard Wigginton 1
THOMPSON, Robert Andrew 1
THOMPSON, Robert Augustine H
THOMPSON, Robert Bruce 5
THOMPSON, Robert Ellis 1
THOMPSON, Robert Elmo 4
THOMPSON, Robert Foster 5
THOMPSON, Robert Harvey 1
THOMPSON, Robert John 1
THOMPSON, Robert Leroy 5
THOMPSON, Robert Long 4
THOMPSON, Robert Means 1
THOMPSON, Robert S. 5
THOMPSON, Roby Calvin 4
THOMPSON, Rollin W. 8
THOMPSON, Ronald Burdick 6
THOMPSON, Roy H(erbert) 10
THOMPSON, Roy Leland 5
THOMPSON, Rupert Campbell, Jr. 5
THOMPSON, Russell Irvin 3
THOMPSON, Ruth Plumly 7
THOMPSON, Sam H. 3
THOMPSON, Sam(uel) Evans 5

TRACY, James Grant 2
TRACY, James Madison 1
TRACY, John Clayton 3
TRACY, John Evarts 3
TRACY, Joseph H
TRACY, Joseph Powell 3
TRACY, Leo James
TRACY, Lyall 3
TRACY, Martha 2
TRACY, Merle Elliott 2
TRACY, Nathaniel H
TRACY, Osgood Vose 2
TRACY, Phineas Lyman H
TRACY, Robert M. 8
TRACY, Roger Sherman 1
TRACY, Roger Walker 4
TRACY, Russel Lord 2
TRACY, Samuel Mills 1
TRACY, Spencer 4
TRACY, Thomas Henry 4
TRACY, Uri H
TRACY, Uriah H
TRACY, (William) Lee 5
TRACY, William W. 1
TRAEGER, Cornelius Horace 5
TRAEGER, William Isham 1
TRAER, Charles Solberg 2
TRAER, Glenn W. 8
TRAFFORD, Bernard Walton 2
TRAFFORD, William Bradford 9
TRAFTON, Gilbert Haven 2
TRAFTON, Mark 1
TRAFTON, William Henry 1
TRAGER, Frank Newton 8
TRAHER, William Henry 8
TRAIN, Arthur 2
TRAIN, Charles J. 1
TRAIN, Charles Russell H
TRAIN, Charles Russell 4
TRAIN, Elizabeth Phipps
TRAIN, Enoch H
TRAIN, Ethel Kissam 1
TRAIN, George Francis 1
TRAIN, Harold Cecil 5
TRAIN, John Lambert 3
TRAINER, David Woolsey, Jr. 4
TRAINER, James Edward 10
TRAINER, Leonard R. 7
TRAINER, Maurice Newlin 5
TRAISMAN, Alfred Stanley 6
TRAJETTA, Philip H
TRALLE, Henry Edward 2
TRAMBURG, John William 4
TRAMMELL, Charles Monroe 9
TRAMMELL, Leander Newton 1
TRAMMELL, Niles 5
TRAMMELL, Park 1
TRAMWELL, Paul Barclay
TRANE, Reuben Nicholas 3
TRANER, Frederick W. 4
TRANER, Fredrick W.
TRANSEAU, Edgar Nelson 5
TRANT, James Buchanan 5
TRANTHAM, Henry 4
TRAP, William Martin 3
TRAPHAGEN, Frank Weiss 1
TRAPHAGEN, John Conselyea 7
TRAPIER, Paul H
TRAPNELL, Frederick Mackay 6
TRAPNELL, William Colston 6
TRAPNELL, William Holmes 6
TRAPP, Martin Edwin 3
TRAPP, William O(scar) 9
TRASK, John Ellingwood Donnell
TRASK, John Jacquelin 7
TRASK, John William 1
TRASK, Kate Nichols 1
TRASK, Ozell Miller
TRASK, Spencer 1
TRASK, William Blake 1
TRATMAN, Edward Ernest Russell 5
TRATTNER, Ernest Robert
TRAUB, Peter Edward 3
TRAUBE, Shepard 8
TRAUBEL, Helen 5
TRAUBEL, Horace
TRAUDT, Bernard G. 5
TRAUGOTT, Albert Maser 3
TRAUTMAN, George M. 4
TRAUTMAN, Ray L. 8

TRAUTMANN, William Emil 5
TRAUTWINE, John Cresson H
TRAUTWINE, John Cresson, Jr. 1
TRAVEN, B. 5
TRAVER, John Gideon 2
TRAVER, Lewis B(enzon) 8
TRAVER, W. Allen 7
TRAVERS, Edward Schofield 2
TRAVIS, Charles Mabbett 2
TRAVIS, Homer Lee 4
TRAVIS, Ira Dudley 4
TRAVIS, Judson Cooper 6
TRAVIS, Juluis Curtis 4
TRAVIS, Merle Robert 8
TRAVIS, Philip H. 3
TRAVIS, Robert Falligant 3
TRAVIS, Simeon Ezekiel 1
TRAVIS, Walter John H
TRAVIS, Walter John 4
TRAVIS, Wesley Elgin 5
TRAVIS, William Barret H
TRAWICK, Arcadius McSwain 5
TRAWICK, Henry 4
TRAWICK, Leonard M. 4
TRAYLOR, John H. 4
TRAYLOR, Melvin Alvah 4
TRAYLOR, Robert Lee 4
TRAYNELIS, Vincent John 7
TRAYNOR, Philip Andrew 5
TRAYNOR, Roger John 8
TRAYNOR, William Bernard 4
TRAYNOR, William James Henry 4
TRAYSER, Lewis W. 4
TRAYWICK, Leland Eldridge 8
TREACY, John P. 4
TREADWAY, Allen Towner 2
TREADWAY, Charles Terry 3
TREADWAY, Lauris Goldsmith 7
TREADWAY, Walter Lewis 6
TREADWAY, Walter Lewis 7
TREADWELL, Aaron Louis 2
TREADWELL, Carleton Raymond 10
TREADWELL, Daniel H
TREADWELL, Edward Francis 5
TREADWELL, George A. 1
TREADWELL, Grace 10
TREADWELL, John 5
TREADWELL, Nancy Claar 5
TREANOR, Arthur Ryan 3
TREANOR, James Aloysius, Jr. 4
TREANOR, John 1
TREANOR, Joseph Holland 4
TREANOR, Walter Emanuel 1
TREAT, Charles Gould 1
TREAT, Charles Henry 1
TREAT, Charles Payson 1
TREAT, Charles Watson 4
TREAT, George Winfield 3
TREAT, Jay Porter 4
TREAT, John Harvey 1
TREAT, Joseph Bradford 4
TREAT, Mary 1
TREAT, Payson Jackson 5
TREAT, Robert H
TREAT, Robert Byron 1
TREAT, Samuel 1
TREAT, Samuel Hubbel H
TREBILCOCK, Paul 7
TREBILCOCK, Paul 8
TRECKER, Joseph Leonard 2
TRECKER, Theodore 3
TREDER, Oscar F. R. 3
TREDTIN, Walter C. 6
TREDWAY, William Marshall H
TREDWELL, Daniel M. 1
TREDWELL, Roger Culver 7
TREDWELL, Thomas 1
TREE, Herbert Beerbohm 1
TREE, Lambert 1
TREE, Marietta Peabody 10
TREECE, Elbert Lee 4
TREES, Clyde C. 4
TREES, Harry A. 4
TREES, Joe Clifton 2

TREES, Merle Jay 3
TREFFLICH, Henry 7
TREFZGER, Emil Anton 4
TREGASKIS, Richard 6
TREGOE, James Harry 4
TREIDE, Henry E. 7
TREIMAN, Joyce Wahl 10
TRELEASE, Richard Mitchell 4
TRELEASE, Sam F. 3
TRELEASE, Sam Farlow 4
TRELEASE, William 3
TRELOGAN, Harry Chester 8
TREMAIN, Albert Wright 4
TREMAIN, Eloise Ruthven 2
TREMAIN, George Lee 5
TREMAIN, Henry Edwin 1
TREMAIN, Lyman H
TREMAINE, Burton Gad 2
TREMAINE, Charles Milton 5
TREMAINE, Frederick Orlin 3
TREMAINE, Henry Barnes 1
TREMAN, Charles Edward 1
TREMAN, Robert Henry 1
TREMBLAY, Rene 4
TREMPER, Edward Payson 10
TRENAM, John James 7
TRENARY, James Marshall 4
TRENCH, William Washington 7
TRENCHARD, Edward C. 4
TRENCHARD, Hugh Montague 3
TRENCHARD, Stephen Decatur H
TRENCHARD, Thomas Whitaker 1
TRENDLE, George Washington 4
TRENERY, Matthew John 5
TRENHOLM, George Alfred H
TRENHOLM, William Lee 1
TRENHOLME, Norman MacLaren 1
TRENT, Richard Henderson 4
TRENT, William H
TRENT, William Johnson 4
TRENT, William Peterfield 1
TRESCOT, William Henry H
TRESCOTT, Paul Henry 6
TRESEDER, Ross Clemo 9
TRESIDDER, Donald Bertrand 2
TRESOLINI, Rocco John 5
TRESSLER, Donald Kiteley 7
TRESSLER, Irving Dart 2
TRESSLER, Jacob Cloyd 3
TRESSLER, Victor George Augustine 1
TRETTIEN, Augustus William 1
TREUDLEY, Frederick 4
TREUHAFT, William Columbus 9
TREUTING, Waldo Louis 4
TREVELLICK, Richard F. H
TREVELYAN, George MacAulay 4
TREVER, Albert Augustus 1
TREVER, George Henry 1
TREVES, Norman 4
TREVETHAN, Percy John 7
TREVISAN, Vittorio 4
TREVOR, John Bond 1
TREVOR, Joseph Ellis 1
TREVORROW, Robert Johns 2
TREVOY, William Vivian 7
TREWIN, James Henry 1
TREXLER, Frank M. 2
TREXLER, Harrison Anthony 7
TREXLER, Harry C. 1
TREXLER, Samuel Geiss 2
TREZEVANT, John Gray 10
TREZVANT, James H
TRIBBLE, Harold Wayland 9
TRIBBLE, Hugh Wallace 7
TRIBBLE, Lewis Herndon 4
TRIBBLE, Samuel Joel 1
TRIBLE, George Barnett 7
TRIBLE, William MacLohon 9
TRIBUS, Louis Lincoln 1
TRICKETT, William 1
TRIEBEL, Frederick Ernst 4
TRIEBER, Jacob 1
TRIEM, Paul Ellsworth 4
TRIGG, Abram H

TRIGG, Ernest T. 3
TRIGG, John Johns H
TRIGGS, Flloyd Willding 1
TRIGGS, Oscar Lovell 4
TRILLEY, Joseph 1
TRILLING, Lionel 6
TRILLING, Lionel 7
TRIM, Gordon Mariner 7
TRIMBEY, Edward James 7
TRIMBLE, Allen H
TRIMBLE, Carey Allen H
TRIMBLE, David H
TRIMBLE, Ernest Greene 5
TRIMBLE, Gilbert Kohler 10
TRIMBLE, Harry Evans 7
TRIMBLE, Harvey Marion 4
TRIMBLE, Isaac Ridgeway H
TRIMBLE, James W. 5
TRIMBLE, John 1
TRIMBLE, Lester Albert 9
TRIMBLE, Richard 1
TRIMBLE, Robert H
TRIMBLE, Robert Maurice 4
TRIMBLE, Selden Y. 4
TRIMBLE, South 2
TRIMBLE, South 6
TRIMBLE, William Allen H
TRIMBLE, William Pitt 2
TRIMMER, John Dezendorf 8
TRINE, Charles Clarke 4
TRINE, Ralph Waldo 5
TRINKLE, Elbert Lee 1
TRINKS, Willibald 5
TRIPLER, Charles E. 1
TRIPLETT, Arthur Fairfax 3
TRIPLETT, Elijah Henry 4
TRIPLETT, John Edwin 2
TRIPLETT, Norman 1
TRIPLETT, Philip H
TRIPLETT, William Hansford 8
TRIPP, Bartlett 1
TRIPP, Chester Dudley 7
TRIPP, Frank Elihu 4
TRIPP, Guy Eastman 1
TRIPP, Lena Elvina Flack 6
TRIPP, Louis H. 4
TRIPP, William Henry, Jr. 5
TRIPPE, Andrew Cross 1
TRIPPE, James McConky 1
TRIPPE, John 5
TRIPPE, Juan Terry 7
TRIPPET, Byron Kightly 8
TRIPPET, Oscar A. 1
TRISCOTT, Samuel Peter Rolt 1
TRISSAL, John Meredith 6
TRIST, Nicholas Philip H
TRITLE, John Stewart 2
TRITSCHLER, Y Cordova Gullermo 7
TRIVELLI, Albert F. 4
TRIVERS, Howard 9
TROBEC, James H
TROCHE, Ernst Gunter 5
TROEGER, John Winthrop Thompson 1
TROLAND, Leonard 1
TROMBLY, Albert Edmund 8
TROOP, J. G. Carter 1
TROOST, George Wilbur 4
TROOST, Gerard H
TROPER, Morris C. 4
TROSTER, Oliver John 7
TROTT, Benjamin H
TROTT, Clement Augustus 5
TROTT, Nicholas H
TROTT, Norman Liebman 9
TROTT, Raymond Harris 9
TROTT, Stanley B. 3
TROTTER, Alfred Williams 1
TROTTER, Frank Butler 1
TROTTER, James Fisher H
TROTTER, John Ellis 9
TROTTER, Melvin E. 1
TROTTER, Newbold Hough H
TROTTER, Spencer 1
TROTTI, Lamar 3
TROTTI, Samuel Wilds H
TROTTMAN, James Franklin 4
TROTZ, J. O. Emmanuel 1
TROUBETZKOY, Amelie Rives 2
TROUBETZKOY, Prince Pierre 1
TROUP, Alexander 1
TROUP, George Michael H
TROUP, Robert H
TROUP, Ronald Morrison 7
TROUPE, Ralph Anderson 9
TROUT, Clement E. 4
TROUT, David McCamel 3
TROUT, Ethel Wendell 1

TROUT, Grace Wilbur 3
TROUT, Hugh Henry, Sr. 2
TROUT, Michael Carver H
TROUTMAN, Henry Battey 7
TROUTMAN, Robert Battey 8
TROUYET, Carlos 5
TROW, John Fowler H
TROWBRIDGE, Alexander Buel 4
TROWBRIDGE, Alvah 1
TROWBRIDGE, Arthur Carleton 5
TROWBRIDGE, Arthur Carleton 7
TROWBRIDGE, Augustus 1
TROWBRIDGE, Calvin D. 10
TROWBRIDGE, Carl Hoyt 5
TROWBRIDGE, Charles Christopher 1
TROWBRIDGE, Edmund H
TROWBRIDGE, Edward Dwight 1
TROWBRIDGE, John 1
TROWBRIDGE, John Townsend 1
TROWBRIDGE, Mary Elizabeth Day 1
TROWBRIDGE, Perry Fox 1
TROWBRIDGE, Philip Newton 7
TROWBRIDGE, Rowland Ebenezer H
TROWBRIDGE, S. Breck Parkman 1
TROWBRIDGE, Vaughan 5
TROWBRIDGE, William Pettit 5
TROWBRIDGE, William Sherman 1
TROWER, Harry Allan
TROXELL, Edward Leffingwell 5
TROXELL, Millard Francis 4
TROXELL, Thomas Franklin 5
TROY, Alexander 1
TROY, George Francis 5
TROY, John Henry 3
TROY, John Weir 2
TROY, Peter Henry 3
TROY, Thomas Francis 4
TROYE, Edward H
TRUANT, Aldo Peter 6
TRUAX, Arthur Harold 4
TRUAX, Charles Henry 1
TRUAX, Charles Vilas 1
TRUAX, Chauncey Shaffer 1
TRUBY, Albert Ernest 5
TRUCCO, Manuel 5
TRUDE, Alfred Samuel 1
TRUDEAU, Arthur Gilbert 10
TRUDEAU, Edward Livingston 1
TRUDGIAN, Andrew B. 6
TRUE, Alfred Charles 1
TRUE, Allen Tupper 1
TRUE, Frederick William 1
TRUE, Gordon Haines 4
TRUE, Hiram L. 4
TRUE, John Preston 1
TRUE, Lilian Crawford (Sarah) 5
TRUE, Rodney Howard 1
TRUE, Theodore Edmond 1
TRUEBLOOD, Benjamin Franklin 1
TRUEBLOOD, Dennis Lee 4
TRUEBLOOD, Ralph Waldo 1
TRUEBLOOD, Robert Martin 6
TRUEBLOOD, Thomas Clarkson 1
TRUELL, Rohn 5
TRUELSEN, Henry 4
TRUEMAN, Walter Harley 5
TRUEMAN, William H. 4
TRUESDAIL, Roger Williams 7
TRUESDALE, Mrs. Joseph R. 7
TRUESDALE, Philemon E. 2
TRUESDALE, William Haynes 1
TRUESDELL, Hobart George 1
TRUESDELL, Karl 3
TRUESDELL, Leon Edgar 7
TRUESWELL, Richard William 8
TRUETT, George W. 2
TRUETTE, Everett Ellsworth 1
TRUEX, George Robert, Jr. 10
TRUFFAUT, Francois 8

TRUITT, James Steele 5
TRUITT, Max O'Rell 3
TRUITT, Ralph Purnell 5
TRUITT, Warren 1
TRUJILLO MOLINA, 4
  Rafael Leonidas
TRULLINGER, R. W. 3
TRULY, Jefferson 4
TRUMAN, Benjamin 1
  Cummings
TRUMAN, Bess Wallace 8
  (Mrs. Harry S. Truman)
TRUMAN, Harry S. 5
TRUMAN, Herbert 7
  Frederic
TRUMAN, James 1
TRUMAN, Ralph Emerson 4
TRUMBAUER, Frank 4
TRUMBAUER, Horace H
TRUMBAUER, Horace 4
TRUMBO, Andrew H
TRUMBO, Arthur Cook 3
TRUMBO, Dalton 7
TRUMBOWER, Henry 7
  Roscoe
TRUMBULL, Annie Eliot 2
TRUMBULL, Benjamin H
TRUMBULL, Charles 1
  Gallaudet
TRUMBULL, Frank 1
TRUMBULL, Grover C. 7
TRUMBULL, Gurdon 1
TRUMBULL, Henry Clay 1
TRUMBULL, James H
  Hammond
TRUMBULL, John* H
TRUMBULL, John H. 4
TRUMBULL, Jonathan* H
TRUMBULL, Jonathan 1
TRUMBULL, Joseph* H
TRUMBULL, Levi R. 4
TRUMBULL, Lyman 8
TRUMP, Edward Needles 4
TRUMP, Guy Winston 8
TRUMP, John George* 8
TRUMPLER, Paul Robert 10
TRUMPLER, Robert Julius 3
TRUOG, Emil 7
TRUPPNER, William 7
  Charles
TRUSCOTT, Frederick 1
  Wilson
TRUSCOTT, Lucian King, 4
  Jr.
TRUSDELL, Charles 1
  Gregory
TRUSLER, Harry 7
  Raymond
TRUSLOW, Francis Adams 3
TRUSLOW, John Bacchus 8
TRUSSELL, C(harles) 5
  P(rescott)
TRUSTY, S(amuel) David 5
TRUTEAU, Jean Baptiste H
TRUXAL, Andrew Gehr 5
TRUXTUN, Thomas H
TRUXTUN, William Talbot H
TRYON, Clarence Archer 6
TRYON, Clarence Howard 7
TRYON, Dwight William 1
TRYON, Frederick Gale 1
TRYON, George H
  Washington
TRYON, Henry Harrington 8
TRYON, James Libby 1
TRYON, James Rufus 1
TRYON, Lawrence Edwin 5
TRYON, Lillian 5
  (Wainwright) Hart (Mrs.
  Winthrop Pitt Tryon)
TRYON, Rolla Milton 3
TRYON, Thomas 10
TRYON, William H
TRYON, Winthrop Pitt 5
TRYTTEN, Merriam 7
  Hartwick
TSALDARIS, Constantin 5
TSALDARIS, M. 5
  Constantine
TSANOFF, Radoslav 7
  Andrea
TSCHACBASOV, Nahum 8
TSCHAPPAT, William H. 5
TSCHIRKY, Oscar 3
TSCHUDY, Arnold Nord 3
TSCHUDY, Herbert Bolivar 2
TSEDENBAL, Yumjaagiin 10
TSIANG, Tingfu F. 4
TSUKIYAMA, Wilfred C. 4
TSUTSUI, Minoru 8
TUBB, Ernest Dale 8
TUBBS, Arthur Lewis 2
TUBBS, Edward 3
TUBBS, Eston Valentine 2
TUBBS, Frank Dean 1
TUBBS, Tallant 10
TUBBY, Roger Wellington 10

TUBBY, William Bunker 2
TUBERMAN, Walter H. 3
TUBMAN, Harriet H
TUBMAN, Harriet 4
TUBMAN, William 5
  V(acanarat) S(hadrach)
  Wertheim
TUCHMAN, Barbara 9
TUCHMAN, Joseph 8
TUCK, Amos H
TUCK, Clyde Edwin 6
TUCK, Edward 1
TUCK, Henry 1
TUCK, James Leslie 5
TUCK, James Leslie 8
TUCK, Somerville Pinkney 1
TUCK, Somerville Pinkney 4
TUCK, William Hallam 4
TUCK, William Munford 8
TUCKER, Allan 10
TUCKER, B. Fain 5
TUCKER, Benjamin Ferree 5
TUCKER, Benjamin H
  Ricketson
TUCKER, Benjamin 4
  Ricketson
TUCKER, Beverley H
TUCKER, Beverley 1
  Dandridge
TUCKER, Beverley 5
  Dandridge
TUCKER, Beverley 2
  Randolph
TUCKER, C. M. 3
TUCKER, Carlton Everett 5
TUCKER, Charles Cowles 5
TUCKER, Chester Everett 6
TUCKER, Clarence R. 5
TUCKER, Donald Skeele 7
TUCKER, Ebenezer 1
TUCKER, Everett Brackin 7
TUCKER, Forrest Meredith 9
TUCKER, Frank 2
TUCKER, Gabriel 9
  Frederick, Jr.
TUCKER, Gardiner 1
  Chylson
TUCKER, George H
TUCKER, George Fox 1
TUCKER, Gilbert Milligan 1
TUCKER, Glenn (Irving) 7
TUCKER, Harry 1
TUCKER, Henry Holcombe H
TUCKER, Henry St George 1
TUCKER, Henry St George 1
TUCKER, Henry St George 3
TUCKER, Hiram G. 1
TUCKER, Hugh Clarence 5
TUCKER, Irvin B. 2
TUCKER, Irwin St. John 5
TUCKER, John Francis 1
TUCKER, John Francis 5
TUCKER, John Hellums, 9
  Jr.
TUCKER, John Randolph* H
  Dickinson
TUCKER, Katharine 3
TUCKER, Lem (Lemuel 10
  Tucker)
TUCKER, Luther H
TUCKER, N. Beverley 4
TUCKER, Nathaniel H
  Beverley
TUCKER, Preston Thomas 9
TUCKER, Raymond 5
  R(oche)
TUCKER, Richard 6
TUCKER, Richard 3
  Blackburn
TUCKER, Richard Hawley 1
TUCKER, Robert Henry 6
TUCKER, Samuel 1
TUCKER, Samuel Marion 4
TUCKER, Sophie 4
TUCKER, St George H
TUCKER, Starling 1
TUCKER, Thomas Tudor H
TUCKER, Tilghman H
  Mayfield
TUCKER, W. Leon 1
TUCKER, William Clifford 4
TUCKER, William 4
  Conquest
TUCKER, William Earle 1
TUCKER, William Jewett 1
TUCKER, William Roscoe 8
TUCKER, Willis Gaylord 1
TUCKERMAN, Alfred 1
TUCKERMAN, Arthur 3
TUCKERMAN, Bayard 1
TUCKERMAN, Edward 8
TUCKERMAN, Frederick 1
TUCKERMAN, Frederick H
  Goddard
TUCKERMAN, Henry H
  Theodore

TUCKERMAN, Jacob 6
  Edward
TUCKERMAN, Joseph H
TUCKERMAN, L. B. 4
TUCKERMAN, Samuel
  Parkman
TUCKEY, John Sutton 9
TUCKEY, William H
TUCKNER, Howard 7
  Melvin
TUDOR, Anthony (William 9
  Cook)
TUDOR, Charles William 5
TUDOR, Frederic H
TUDOR, Ralph Arnold 4
TUDOR, William 1
TUECHTER, August 2
  Herman
TUEMMLER, William 10
  Bruce
TUFTE, E(ngebret) T. 7
TUFTS, Bowen 1
TUFTS, Charles H
TUFTS, C(larence) Albert 1
TUFTS, Cotton H
TUFTS, Edgar 1
TUFTS, Eleanor May 10
TUFTS, James Arthur 1
TUFTS, James Hayden 2
TUFTS, John 1
TUFTY, Esther Van 9
  Wagoner
TUFTY, Herbert Iver 5
TUGGLE, Charles Summey 6
TUGGLE, Kenneth 7
  Herndon
TUGMAN, Orin 7
TUGMAN, William Masten 4
TUGWELL, Rexford Guy 7
TUHOLSKE, Herman 1
TUIGG, John H
TUITE, John Francis 10
TUKEY, Harold Bradford 5
TULANE, Paul H
TULEY, Henry Enos 1
TULEY, Murray F. 1
TULEY, Philip Speed 1
TULL, E. Don 8
TULLAR, Charles E. 7
TULLER, Edward Pratt 1
TULLER, John Jay 4
TULLEY, David Henry 6
TULLIO, Louis Joseph 10
TULLIS, H. H. 3
TULLIS, Robert Lee 5
TULLOSS, Rees Edgar 3
TULLY, Jasper William 9
TULLY, Jim 2
TULLY, John Patrick 9
TULLY, Joseph Merit 4
TULLY, Pleasant Britton 1
TULLY, Richard Walton 2
TULLY, Richard William 7
TULLY, William 1
TULLY, William John 1
TULP, Arnold 6
TUMILTY, Howard 5
  T(insley)
TUMULTY, Joseph Patrick 3
TUMULTY, Philip 10
  Anthony
TUNG PI-WU 6
TUNICK, Stanley Bloch 9
TUNISON, Abram Vorhis 5
TUNISON, George 1
  McGregor
TUNISON, Joseph Salathiel 4
TUNKS, Lehan Kent 9
TUNKS, Walter F. 3
TUNNARD, Christopher 7
TUNNELL, Ebe Walter 1
TUNNELL, James Miller 7
TUNNEY, Gene (James 7
  Joseph)
TUNSTALL, Mrs. A(lfred) 6
  M(oore)
TUNSTALL, Richard 1
  Baylor
TUNSTALL, Robert Baylor 3
TUNSTALL, Robert 1
  Williamson
TUNSTILL, Clover Dell 6
  Hill (Mrs. Garland Albert
  Tunstill)
TUOHY, Edward Boyce 3
TUOHY, Edward Leo 1
TUOHY, John Joseph 7
TUOHY, Walter Joseph 4
TUOMEY, Michael H
TUOMIOJA, Sakari Severi 4
TUPOLEV, Andrei 7
  Nikolaevich
TUPPER, Benjamin H
TUPPER, Claude A. 1
TUPPER, Frederick 4
TUPPER, Henry Allen* 1
TUPPER, James Waddell 5

TUPPER, Kerr Boyce 1
TURCHIN, John Basil 1
TURCK, Charles Joseph 9
TURCK, Fenton Benedict 1
TURCK, Fenton Benedict 5
TURCK, Raymond Custer 6
TURCOTTE, Edmond 4
TURCOTTE, Lawson 10
  Phillipe
TUREK, Robert Joseph 7
TUREMAN, Horace Elder 7
TURIN, John Joseph 6
TURINI, Giovanni 1
TURK, Leonard Gerald 10
TURK, Milton Haight 2
TURK, Morris Howland 1
TURKEVICH, Leonty 4
TURKINGTON, Grace 6
  Alice
TURKLE, Alonzo John 1
TURLEY, Clarence Milton 1
TURLEY, Henry Clay 4
TURLEY, Jay 1
TURLEY, Thomas Battle 1
TURLINGTON, Edgar 3
TURNAGE, Allen Hal 5
TURNBULL, Andrew H
TURNBULL, Andrew Blair 4
TURNBULL, Andrew 5
  Winchester
TURNBULL, Barton P. 2
TURNBULL, Charles 1
  Smith
TURNBULL, Douglas 10
  Taylor
TURNBULL, Edwin 1
  Litchfield
TURNBULL, Francese 1
  Hubbard Litchfield
TURNBULL, George 7
  (Stanley)
TURNBULL, Henry 6
  Rutherford
TURNBULL, J. Gordon 3
TURNBULL, Laurence 1
TURNBULL, Margaret 2
TURNBULL, Martin 2
  Ryerson
TURNBULL, Phillips 6
  Roome
TURNBULL, Robert H
TURNBULL, Robert 4
TURNBULL, Robert James 1
TURNBULL, Walter 1
  Mason
TURNBULL, William H
TURNBULL, William 9
  Watson
TURNEAURE, Frederick 3
  Eugene
TURNER, Abe W. 2
TURNER, Albert 9
TURNER, Archelaus Ewing 1
TURNER, Arthur Gordon 7
TURNER, Arthur Henry 1
TURNER, Asa H
TURNER, Benjamin 7
  Dickinson, III
TURNER, Benjamin H
  Sterling
TURNER, Charles, Jr. H
TURNER, Charles Edward 1
TURNER, Charles Henry 4
  Black
TURNER, Charles Root 2
TURNER, Charles Willard 1
TURNER, Charles Yardley 1
TURNER, Clair Elsmere 6
TURNER, C(larence) 8
  L(ester)
TURNER, Clarence W. 1
TURNER, Claude Allen 3
  Porter
TURNER, Daniel* H
TURNER, Daniel Lawrence 5
TURNER, Daniel W(ebster) 1
TURNER, Darwin 10
  Theodore Troy
TURNER, Don Abbott 9
TURNER, Douglas Kellogg 1
TURNER, Edward H
TURNER, Edward 3
  Crawford
TURNER, Edward Lewis 3
TURNER, Edward 1
  Raymond
TURNER, Ethel Louise 7
  Totman (Mrs. Charles
  Flavel Turner)
TURNER, Farrant Lewis 3
TURNER, Fennell Parrish 1
TURNER, Fred Harold 4
TURNER, Fred J. 4
TURNER, Frederick 1
  Jackson
TURNER, Gardner Clyde 5
TURNER, George 1

TURNER, George Kibbe 5
TURNER, Harold 4
TURNER, Harold Rhoades 3
TURNER, Helen M. 3
TURNER, (Henry) Arlin 7
TURNER, Henry Chandlee 3
TURNER, Henry Chandlee, 5
  Jr.
TURNER, Henry H. 6
TURNER, Henry McNeal 1
TURNER, Henry Ward 1
TURNER, Herbert Beach 1
TURNER, Herman Lee 9
TURNER, Homer Griffield 8
TURNER, J. Walter 3
TURNER, James* H
TURNER, James 3
TURNER, James H. 1
TURNER, James Jewett 4
TURNER, James Patrick 1
TURNER, Janet E. 9
TURNER, John Clyde 7
TURNER, John Pickett 4
TURNER, John Roscoe 3
TURNER, John Wesley H
TURNER, Jonathan H
  Baldwin
TURNER, Joseph 1
  Augustine
TURNER, Josiah H
TURNER, Justin George 10
TURNER, Justin George 7
TURNER, Kenneth B. 3
TURNER, Laura Lemon 1
TURNER, Lawrence 4
  Emerson
TURNER, Lewis M. 4
TURNER, Mabel Bascom 7
TURNER, Martin Luther 1
TURNER, Maurice Clark 3
TURNER, Nancy Byrd 6
TURNER, Nat H
TURNER, Oscar 1
TURNER, Oscar 4
TURNER, Ralph Edmund 4
TURNER, Richard Lazear 9
TURNER, Richmond Kelly 7
TURNER, Robert Clemens 7
TURNER, Rodolphus 4
  Kibbe
TURNER, Roscoe 5
TURNER, Ross Sterling 1
TURNER, Roy Joseph 5
TURNER, Samuel Gilbert 3
  Hathaway
TURNER, Samuel Hulbeart H
TURNER, Scott 5
TURNER, Sol 7
TURNER, Thomas H
  Johnston
TURNER, Victor Witter 8
TURNER, W. B. 1
TURNER, Walter Victor 1
TURNER, Wilfred Dent 1
TURNER, William 1
TURNER, William De 4
  Garmo
TURNER, William Henry 1
TURNER, William Jay 2
TURNER, William Wirt 9
TURNER, William Wood 5
TURNEY, Daniel Braxton 1
TURNEY, Hopkins Lacy H
TURNEY, Jacob H
TURNEY, Peter 1
TURNEY, William Ward 1
TURNIPSEED, B(arnwell) 6
  Rhett
TURNLEY, Parmenas 1
  Taylor
TURPIE, David 1
TURPIN, Ben H
TURPIN, Ben 4
TURPIN, C. Murray 2
TURPIN, Edna Henry Lee 1
TURPIN, Rees 2
TURQUETIL, Arsene 5
TURRELL, Charles Alfred 4
TURRELL, Edgar Abel 4
TURRELL, Jane H
TURRENTINE, James 7
  Lewis
TURRENTINE, John 7
  William
TURRENTINE, Samuel 3
  Bryant
TURRILL, Charles Beebe 1
TURRILL, Joel H
TURTON, Franklin E. 3
TUSKA, Gustave Robisher 1
TUSLER, Wilbur H(enry) 8
TUSTIN, Ernest Leigh 1
TUTEN, J(ames) Russell 5
TUTHILL, Alexander 5
  MacKenzie
TUTHILL, Joseph H
  Hasbrouck

URBAN, Joseph	1	VAILE, Joel Frederick	1	VANAMEE, Grace Davis	2

URBAN, Joseph 1
URBAN, Percy Linwood 6
URBAN, Wilbur Marshall 6
URDANETA ARBELAEZ, 8
  Roberto
URDANG, George 4
URE, Mary 6
URELL, M. Emmet 4
UREN, Lester Charles 4
U'REN, William Simon 4
URETZ, Lester Robert 5
UREY, Harold Clayton 7
URICE, Jay Adams 3
URICH, Walter K. 3
URIELL, Frank (Francis) 5
  Harold
URION, Henry Kimball 4
URIS, Percy 5
URMY, Clarence 1
URNER, Hammond 2
URNER, Mabel Herbert 4
URQUHART, George 8
  Alexander
URQUHART, John E. 9
URQUHART, Leonard 3
  Church
URQUHART, Norman 5
  Currie
URRIOLAGOITIA, H. 6
  Mamerto
URSO, Camilla H
URY, Ralph Jay 5
USHER, Abbott Payson 4
USHER, Edward Preston 1
USHER, John Palmer 4
USHER, Nathaniel Reilly 1
USHER, Noble Luke 4
USHER, Robert James 2
USHER, Roland Greene 6
USINGER, Robert L(eslie) 5
USSACHEVSKY, Vladimir 10
USSHER, Brandram 1
  Boileau
UTASSY, George d' 3
UTERHART, Henry Ayres 2
UTLEY, Francis Lee 6
UTLEY, Freda 7
UTLEY, George Burwell 4
UTLEY, Henry Munson 2
UTLEY, Joseph Simeon 2
UTLEY, Nelson Monroe 10
UTLEY, Samuel 1
UTLEY, Stuart Wells 2
UTNE, John Arndt 5
UTRECHT, James C. 9
UTT, James Boyd 4
UTTER, David 4
UTTER, George Benjamin 3
UTTER, George Herbert 4
UTTER, Rebecca Palfrey 1
UTTER, Robert Palfrey 5
UTTERBACK, Hubert 2
UTTERBACK, John Gregg 5
UTTLEY, Clinton B. 4
UTUDJIAN, Edouard 6
UZZELL, Thomas H. 7

V

VACANO, Wolfgang 9
VACCARA, Beatrice 8
  Newman
VACCARO, Ernest Bedford 7
VACHON, Alexandre 3
VACHON, Joseph Peter 4
VACHON, Louis A., Jr. 5
VADAKIN, James Charles 8
VAGIS, Polygnotos 6
  G(eorge)
VAGNOZZI, Egidio 7
VAGTBORG, Harold 6
VAGTBORG, Harold 6
VAHEY, James Henry 2
VAIL, Aaron H
VAIL, Albert Ross 6
VAIL, Alfred Lewis H
VAIL, Charles Davis 2
VAIL, Charles Delamater 1
VAIL, Charles Henry 1
VAIL, Curtis Churchill 3
  Doughty
VAIL, David Jameson 6
VAIL, Derrick T., Sr. 1
VAIL, Derrick Tilton 5
VAIL, Eugene 4
VAIL, George H
VAIL, Henry H
VAIL, Henry Hobart 1
VAIL, Herman Lansing 8
VAIL, Richard B. 2
VAIL, Robert William 4
  Glenrole
VAIL, Stephen Montfort H
VAIL, Theodore Newton 1
VAIL, Thomas Hubbard 1
VAILE, Anna Louise 1
  Wolcott

VAILE, Joel Frederick 1
VAILE, Rawson 3
VAILE, Roland Snow 8
VAILE, William Newell 4
VAILLANCOURT, Cyrille 5
VAILLANT, George Clapp 2
VAILLANT, Louis David 2
VAILLANT DE GUESLIS, H
  Francois
VAJNA, George 5
VAKIL, Nusservanji 2
  Kavasji
VAKIL, Rustom Jal 6
VALASEK, Otakar 3
VALE, Clair Fremont 8
VALE, Roy Ewing 3
VALENCIA, Guillermo 5
  Leon
VALENSTEIN, Lawrence 8
VALENTA, Frank Louis 3
VALENTE, Frances Louis 4
VALENTE, Maurice Remo 4
VALENTIEN, Anna Marie 4
VALENTINE, Alan 7
VALENTINE, Byron 4
  Warren
VALENTINE, Caro Syron 4
VALENTINE, David H
  Thomas
VALENTINE, Edward 5
  Abram Uffington
VALENTINE, Edward 5
  Robinson
VALENTINE, Edward 1
  Virginius
VALENTINE, Itimous T. 9
VALENTINE, John J. 1
VALENTINE, John 5
  W(adsworth)
VALENTINE, J(oseph) 7
  Alfred
VALENTINE, Lewis 5
  Joseph
VALENTINE, Lila Meade 2
VALENTINE, Milton 1
VALENTINE, Milton 4
  Henry
VALENTINE, Patrick 1
  Anderson
VALENTINE, P(ercy) 7
  F(riars)
VALENTINE, Robert 1
  Grosvenor
VALENTINE, Willard Lee 2
VALENTINER, William 3
  Reinhold
VALENTINO, Rudolph 1
VALERY, Paul 4
VALEUR, Robert 5
VALK, Joseph Elihu 5
VALK, William Weightman H
VALLANCE, Harvard 3
  Forrest
VALLANCE, William Roy 4
VALLANDIGHAM, H
  Clement Laird
VALLARINO, Don 8
  Joaquin José
VALLEE, Hubert Prior 9
  Rudy
VALLEE, Paul 9
VALLEJO, Mariano H
  Guadalupe
VALLENTINE, Benjamin 2
  Bennaton
VALLENTINE, Benjamin 1
  Benton
VALLETTA, Vittorio 4
VALLIANT, Leroy Branch 1
VALLOTTON, William 9
  Wise
VALPEY, Frank Russell 8
VALUE, Beverly Reid 1
VALYI, Peter 6
VAN, Billy B. 3
VAN ACKER, Achille H. 6
VAN ACKEREN, Gerald 7
VAN AERNAM, Henry H
VAN ALEN, James Isaac H
VAN ALEN, John Evert H
VAN ALEN, William 3
VAN ALLEN, Daniel D. 1
VAN-ALLEN, John W. 3
VAN ALLEN, Maurice 9
  Wright
VAN ALLEN, William 5
  Harman
VAN ALSTYNE, Eleanor 2
  Van Ness
VAN ALSTYNE, Henry 5
  Arthur
VAN ALSTYNE, J. H. 2
VAN ALSTYNE, Thomas H
  Jefferson
VANAMAN, Arthur 9
  William
VAN AMBURGH, Fred D. 1

VANAMEE, Grace Davis 2
VAN AMRINGE, John 1
  Howard
VAN ANDA, Carr V. 2
VAN ANTWERP, Eugene 4
  Ignatius
VAN ANTWERP, William 1
  Clarkson
VAN ARSDALE, 4
  Nathaniel H.
VAN ARSDALE, Talman 7
  Walker, Jr.
VAN ATTA, Robert S. 5
VAN ATTEN, William 5
  Teunis
VANAUKEN, Charles S. 5
VAN AUKEN, Wilbur Rice 2
VAN AUKEN, Wilbur Rice 7
VAN BAALEN, Chase 9
VAN BARNEVELD, 2
  Charles Edwin
VAN BAUN, William Weed 1
VAN BEINUM, Eduard 3
VAN BENSCHOTEN, 1
  James Cooke
VAN BENSCHOTEN, 1
  William Henry
VAN BEUREN, Amedee J. 1
VAN BEUREN, Archbold 6
VAN BEUREN, Frederick 2
  Theodore, Jr.
VAN BEUREN, Johannes H
  George (Achille)
VAN BIESBROECK, 6
  A.
VAN BOMEL, Leroy 4
  Allison
VAN BOMEL, Leroy 7
  Allison
VAN BORTEL, Francis 9
  John
VAN BOSKERCK, Robert 1
  Ward
VAN BRUNT, Charles H. 1
VAN BRUNT, Henry 1
VAN BRUNT, Jeremiah 2
  Rutger
VAN BUREN, Albert 1
  Alexander
VAN BUREN, Albert 6
  William
VAN BUREN, Alicia 1
  Keisker
VAN BUREN, Evelyn 8
  Heartt
VAN BUREN, James 1
VAN BUREN, John* H
VAN BUREN, John Dash 4
VAN BUREN, Martin 6
VAN BUREN, Maud 3
VAN BUREN, Raeburn 10
VAN BUREN, Robert 3
VAN BUREN, William H
  Holme
VAN BUSKIRK, Arthur B. 5
VAN CAMPEN, Marion 9
  (Kelly)
VAN CAMPENHOUT, 8
  Jacques Louis
VANCE, Arthur Turner 1
VANCE, Burton 4
VANCE, Estil 3
VANCE, Harold Sines 3
VANCE, Harrell Taylor, Jr. 4
VANCE, Henry T(homas) 5
VANCE, Hiram Albert 1
VANCE, James Isaac 1
VANCE, James Milton 3
VANCE, Jessica Smith 1
VANCE, John Edward 6
VANCE, John Thomas 2
VANCE, Johnstone 3
VANCE, Joseph 1
VANCE, Joseph Anderson 3
VANCE, Joseph Anderson, 7
  Jr.
VANCE, Lawrence Lee 7
VANCE, Louis Joseph 1
VANCE, Marshall Mounts 8
VANCE, Robert Brank H
VANCE, Robert Cummings 3
VANCE, Robert Smith 10
VANCE, Rupert Bayless 6
VANCE, Selby Frame 5
VANCE, Vivian 9
VANCE, William Ford 6
VANCE, William Reynolds 1
VANCE, Wilson 1
VANCE, Zebulon Baird 2
VAN CLEAVE, Harley 3
  Jones
VAN CLEAVE, Harley 6
  William
VAN CLEAVE, James 1
  Wallace
VAN CLEEF, Eugene 6
VAN CLEEF, Frank C. 6
VAN CLEEF, Lee 10

VAN CLEEF, Mynderse 1
VAN CLEVE, Thomas 6
  Curtis
VAN CORTLANDT, Oloff H
  Stevenszen
VAN CORTLANDT, Philip H
VAN CORTLANDT, Pierre H
  Pierre, Jr.
VAN CORTLANDT, H
  Stephanus
VAN COTT, Cornelius 1
VAN COTT, Harrison 7
  Horton
VAN COTT, Waldemar 3
  Quayle
VANCOUVER, George H
VANCURA, Zdenek 6
VAN CURLER, Arent H
VAN DAM, Rip H
VANDE BOGART, Guy 4
  Hudson
VAN DE CARR, Charles 4
  Rutherford, Jr.
VAN DE GRAAFF, 5
  Robert Jemison
VAN DE GRAAFF, 4
  Robert Jemison
VANDEGRIFT, Alexander 6
  Archer
VANDEGRIFT, Margaret 1
VANDEGRIFT, Rolland 2
  A.
VANDELL, Robert Frank 10
VANDEMAN, Esther Boise 1
VAN DEMAN, Henry Elias 1
VAN DEMAN, John D. 4
VAN DEMAN, Ralph 5
  Henry
VAN DE MARK, William 4
  Slau
VAN DE MORTEL, J. B. 4
  V. M. J.
VANDENBERG, Arthur 4
  H., Jr.
VANDENBERG, Arthur 3
  Hendrick
VANDEN BERG, Henry 4
  John
VANDENBERG, Hoyt 3
  Sanford
VAN DEN BERG, 2
  Lawrence Hoffman
VANDENBOSCH, Amry 10
VAN DEN BOSCH, Robert 7
VAN DEN BROEK, Jan A. 3
VAN DEN BROEK, 4
  Thedore J.
VANDENHOFF, George H
VAN DEPOELE, Charles H
  Joseph
VANDERBILT, Aaron 4
VANDERBILT, Alfred 1
  Gwynne
VANDERBILT, Amy 6
VANDERBILT, Arthur T. 3
VANDERBILT, Cornelius H
VANDERBILT, Cornelius 1
VANDERBILT, Cornelius 6
VANDERBILT, Cornelius, 2
  III
VANDERBILT, Frederick 1
  William
VANDERBILT, George 1
  Washington
VANDERBILT, Harold 5
  Stirling
VANDERBILT, Harold 7
  Stirling
VANDERBILT, Merritt 5
  David
VANDERBILT, Newell 5
  Fitzgerald
VANDERBILT, O. Deg 3
VANDERBILT, Reginald 1
  Claypoole
VANDERBILT, William 4
  Henry
VANDERBILT, William 1
  Kissam
VANDERBILT, William 5
  Kissam
VANDERBLUE, Homer 4
  Bews
VANDERBURGH, William H
  Henry
VANDERCOOK, John W. 4
VAN DER DONCK, H
  Adriaen
VAN DER GRACHT, A. 4
  J. M. Van Waterschoot
VANDERGRIFT, Jacob 4
  Jay
VANDERGRIFT, John Jay 4
VANDERHOOF, Albert 5
  Whittier
VANDERHOOF, Douglas 4

VANDERHORST, Arie 7
VAN DER KEMP, Francis H
  Adrian
VANDERKLEED, Charles 4
  Edwin
VANDERLIP, Mrs. Frank 4
  A.
VANDERLIP, Frank 1
  Arthur
VAN DERLIP, John 1
  Russell
VANDERLIP, Kelvin Cox 5
VANDER LUGT, Gerrit T. 5
VANDERLYN, John H
VAN DER MERWE, 6
  Henderik Johannes Jan
  Matthys
VANDER MEULEN, John 1
  Marinus
VAN DER NAILLEN, 4
  Albert
VANDERPLOEG, Watson 3
  H.
VANDERPOEL, Aaron H
VANDERPOEL, Emily C. 1
  Noyes
VANDERPOEL, John 1
  Henry
VANDERPOEL, Robert P. 3
VANDERPOOL, Eugene 10
VANDERPOOL, Frederick 2
  William
VANDERPOOL, Wynant 2
  Davis
VANDER PYL, Mary 8
  Chamberlain
VANDERSALL, Stanley 7
  Byron
VANDER SLUIS, George 8
  Jacob
VANDER SLUIS, George 9
  Jacob
VAN DER STRATEN 6
  PONTHOZ, Count
  Robert
VANDERSTUCKEN, 7
  Emile Felix, Jr.
VAN DER STUCKEN, 1
  Frank V.
VANDERVEER, Abraham H
VANDER VEER, Albert 1
VANDERVEER, Harold C. 8
VAN DER VEER, 4
  McClellan
VANDER VEER, Milton 6
  T.
VANDERVELDE, Conrad 6
VANDER VELDE, Lewis 6
  George
VANDERVOORT, James 4
  W.
VAN DERVOORT, 1
  William H.
VAN DER VRIES, Bernice 9
  Taber
VANDER VRIES, John 1
  Nicholas
VANDERWARKER, 5
  Richard Dean
VANDER WEE, John H
  Baptist
VANDERWERF, Calvin 9
  Anthony
VANDER WERF, Lester 10
  Seth
VAN DER WEYDEN, 4
  Harry
VANDERZEE, Abram 4
VAN DERZEE, Gould 7
  W(hitney)
VAN DER ZEE, Jacob 7
VAN DERZEE, James 7
VAN DER ZEE, James 8
  Augustus Joseph
VAN DER ZIEL, Aldert 10
VAN DEUSEN, Edwin H. 4
VAN DEUSEN, George 7
  Lane
VAN DEUSEN, George 4
  William
VAN DEUSEN, Henry 5
  Reed
VAN DEUSEN, John 8
  George
VAN DEUSEN, Robert 5
  Hicks
VAN DEVANTER, Willis 1
VANDEVEER, Welzie 8
  Wellington
VAN DE VELDE, James H
  Oliver
VAN DE VEN, Cornelius 1
VANDEVENTER, Braden 2
VAN DEVENTER, John 9
  Francis
VAN DEVENTER, John 3
  Herbert

VAN WYCK, Augustus 1
VAN WYCK, Charles Henry H
VAN WYCK, Robert Anderson 1
VAN WYCK, William 3
VAN WYCK, William William H
VAN WYK, William P. 2
VAN ZANDT, Charles Collins H
VAN ZANDT, Clarence Duncan 1
VAN ZANDT, Clarence Elmer 1
VAN ZANDT, James Edward 9
VAN ZANDT, Khleber Miller 1
VAN ZANDT, Lydia 7
VAN ZANDT, Marie 1
VAN ZANDT, Richard Lipscomb 1
VANZETTI, Bartolomeo 4
VAN ZILE, Edward Sims 1
VAN ZILE, Philip Taylor 1
VARCOE, Frederick Percy 8
VARDAMAN, James Kimble 1
VARDAMAN, John Wesley 7
VARDELL, Charles Gildersleeve 4
VARDELL, Charles Graves 3
VARDEN, George 3
VARDILL, John H
VARE, William Scott
VARELA, Jacobo 5
VARELA Y MORALES, Felix Francisco Jose Maria de la Concepcion H
VARESE, Edgard 4
VARGAS, George Leland 9
VARGAS, Getulio 3
VARGAS, Lester Lambert 7
VARIAN, Bertram Stetson 1
VARIAN, Charles Stetson 1
VARIAN, Donald Cord 5
VARIAN, Elayne H. 9
VARIAN, George Edmund 1
VARIAN, Russell Harrison 1
VARICK, James H
VARICK, Richard 1
VARIELL, Arthur Davis 1
VARLEY, John Philip 1
VARNEY, Charles Edward 4
VARNEY, H(arry) R(oss) 7
VARNEY, William Frederick 4
VARNEY, William Henry 4
VARNEY, William Wesley 2
VARNUM, James M.
VARNUM, James Mitchell H
VARNUM, John H
VARNUM, Joseph Bradley H
VARNUM, William Harrison 2
VARRELMAN, Ferdinand Armin 8
VARSER, Lycurgus Rayner 4
VARTAN, Vartanig Garabed 9
VARVARESSOS, Kyriakos 7
VASCHE, Joseph Burton
VASEY, Frank Thomas
VASEY, George H
VASILIEFF, Nicholas Loanovich 5
VASILIEV, Alexander Alexandrovich 5
VASQUEZ, Francisco Leonte 4
VASS, Alonzo Frederick 4
VASS, Guy Boyd 8
VASSALIO, Edward Andrew 6
VASSALL, John H
VASSAR, Matthew H
VATH, Joseph G. 9
VATTEMARE, Nicolas Marie Alexandre H
VAUCLAIN, Samuel Matthews 1
VAUDREUIL-CAVAGNA-L, Pierre de Rigaud
VAUGHAN, Agnes Carr 8
VAUGHAN, Alfred Jefferson 1
VAUGHAN, Arthur Winn 2
VAUGHAN, Benjamin H
VAUGHAN, Bill
VAUGHAN, Charles H
VAUGHAN, Charles Parker
VAUGHAN, Daniel H
VAUGHAN, David Davies 5
VAUGHAN, David Lisle 10

VAUGHAN, Elmer E. 1
VAUGHAN, Floyd Lamar 3
VAUGHAN, George 2
VAUGHAN, George Tully 2
VAUGHAN, George William 4
VAUGHAN, Guy W. 4
VAUGHAN, H. Leland 7
VAUGHAN, Harold 5
VAUGHAN, Harry Briggs, Jr. 4
VAUGHAN, Henry Frieze 9
VAUGHAN, Herbert Hunter 2
VAUGHAN, Horace Worth 1
VAUGHAN, John Colin 1
VAUGHAN, John Gaines 1
VAUGHAN, John George 2
VAUGHAN, John Henry 1
VAUGHAN, John Russell 3
VAUGHAN, John Samuel 1
VAUGHAN, John Walter 2
VAUGHAN, Lawrence J. 1
VAUGHAN, L(illiam) L(ee) Henry 7
VAUGHAN, Richard 7
VAUGHAN, Richard Miner 3
VAUGHAN, Robert Charles 7
VAUGHAN, Sarah Lois 10
VAUGHAN, T. Wayland 3
VAUGHAN, Thomas Rae Clarence 5
VAUGHAN, Victor 1
VAUGHAN, Warren Taylor 2
VAUGHAN, Wayland Farries 4
VAUGHAN, William Addison 10
VAUGHAN, William Hutchinson
VAUGHAN, William Washington 7
VAUGHAN, William Wirt H
VAUGHAN WILLIAMS, Ralph 3
VAUGHN, Arkell M. 10
VAUGHN, Earnest Van Court 5
VAUGHN, Francis Arthur
VAUGHN, Robert Gallaway 3
VAUGHN, Samuel Jesse 5
VAUGHN, William James 1
VAUGHT, Edgar Sullins 3
VAUGHT, George Washington 8
VAUX, Calvert H
VAUX, George, Jr. 1
VAUX, Richard H
VAUX, Roberts H
VAVRUSKA, Frank
VAWTER, Charles Erastus 1
VAWTER, John William 1
VAWTER, Keith 1
VAWTER, William Arthur, II 7
VAYHINGER, Monroe 1
VAZQUEZ, Siro 10
VEACH, Robert Wells 5
VEAL, Frank Richard 5
VEASEY, Clarence Archibald 3
VEATCH, Arthur Clifford 1
VEATCH, Byron Elbert 1
VEATCH, John C(urrin) 1
VEATCH, Nathan Thomas 6
VEAZEY, George Ross 8
VEAZEY, I. Parker 4
VEAZEY, Thomas Ward H
VEAZIE, George Augustus 1
VEBLEN, Andrew Anderson
VEBLEN, Oswald 4
VEBLEN, Thorstein B.
VECKI, Victor G. 1
VEDDER, Beverly Blair 3
VEDDER, Charles Stuart
VEDDER, Edward Bright 3
VEDDER, Elihu
VEDDER, Henry Clay 1
VEDDER, Commodore Perry
VEDITZ, Charles William Augustus
VEECK, Bill, Jr. (William Louis) 9
VEEDER, Major Albert 1
VEEDER, Albert Henry
VEEDER, Borden Smith 7
VEEDER, Curtis Hussey
VEEDER, Henry 2
VEEDER, Van Vechten 2
VEENEMAN, William H. 5

VEGA, Juan Bautista 8
VEHE, Karl Leroy 8
VEIHMEYER, Frank J. 7
VEITCH, Fletcher Pearre 2
VEKSLER, Vladimir I. 4
VELARDE, Hernan
VELAZQUEZ, Hector
VELDE, Gail Patrick 7
VELDE, Gail Patrick 8
VELIKOVSKY, Immanuel 7
VELTFORT, Theodore Ernst 8
VELTIN, Louis de Launay 1
VELVIN, Ellen 1
VENABLE, Abraham Bedford H
VENABLE, Abraham Watkins H
VENABLE, Charles Scott 1
VENABLE, Edward Carrington 7
VENABLE, Emerson 6
VENABLE, Francis Preston 1
VENABLE, Joseph Glass 1
VENABLE, Richard Morton 1
VENABLE, William Henry 1
VENABLE, William Mayo 3
VENABLE, William Webb 1
VENEMANN, H. Gerald 3
VENEZIALE, Carlo Marcello 10
VENING MEINISZ, Felix 7
VENIOT, Clarence Joseph 7
VENN, Grant 7
VENNEMA, Ame 3
VENNEMA, John 3
VENTH, Carl 4
VENTING, Albert 4
VENTRIS, Michael George Francis 4
VENTURI, Lionello 7
VERBECK, Guido Fridolin 1
VERBECK, Guido Herman Fridolin H
VER BECK, Hanna 1
VERBECK, William 1
VER BECK, William Francis 1
VER BECK, William Francis 4
VERBEEK, Gustave 4
VERBEKE, Alexis O. 4
VERBRUGGE, Frank 4
VERBRUGGHEN, Henri 1
VERBRYCKE, J. Russell, Jr. 7
VERCORS, Jean Bruller 10
VERDAGUER, Peter 1
VERDELIN, Henry 4
VERDI, William Francis 1
VEREEN, William Jerome 3
VERENDRYE, Sieur de la H
VERGENNES, comte de H
VERHAEGEN, Peter Joseph H
VERHAGEN, Aloysius Alphonsus 1
VERHOEFF, Frederick Herman 5
VERHULST, Alfred 7
VERITY, Calvin 8
VERITY, George Matthew 2
VERKUYL, Gerrit 5
VERLENDEN, Jacob Serill 6
VERMEULEN, Cornelius W. 10
VERMEULEN, Theodore 8
VERMILION, Charles William
VERMILYA, Charles E. 5
VERMILYE, Mrs. Kate Jordan 1
VERMILYE, William Moorhead 2
VERMUELE, Cornelius Clarkson 2
VERNADSKY, George 1
VERNER, Elizabeth O'Neill 7
VERNER, Samuel Phillips 1
VERNEY, Gilbert 7
VERNIER, Chester Garfield 2
VERNON, Ambrose White 5
VERNON, Clarence Clark 7
VERNON, Glenn Morley 9
VERNON, James William 3
VERNON, Leroy Tudor 1
VERNON, Robert Orion 6
VERNON, Samuel 1
VERNON, Samuel Milton 1
VERNON, Weston, Jr. 7
VERNON, William H
VERNON, William Tecumseh 5
VERNOR, Richard Edward 3

VERON, Earl Ernest 10
VERONDA, Maurice 4
VEROT, Jean Marcel Pierre Auguste H
VERPLANCK, Daniel Crommelin 1
VERPLANCK, Gulian Crommelin H
VERRALL, Richard P. 3
VERRAZANO, Giovanni da H
VERREE, John Paul H
VERRILL, Addison Emery 1
VERRILL, Alpheus Hyatt 1
VERRILL, Charles Henry 1
VERRILL, Elmer Russell 6
VERRILL, Harold Everett 10
VERRILL, Harry Mighels 5
VERRILL, Robinson 5
VERSENYI, Laszlo Gaspar 9
VERSFELT, William H. 1
VERSON, David C. 5
VERSTEEG, John Marinus 7
VER STEEG, Karl 3
VERTES, Marcel 4
VERWEY, Willard Foster 7
VER WIEBE, Walter August 8
VERWOERD, Hendrik Frensch 4
VERY, Frank Washington 1
VERY, Jones H
VERY, Lydia Louisa Anna 1
VERY, Samuel Williams 1
VESAK, Norbert Franklin 10
VESEY, Denmark H
VESEY, William
VESIC, Aleksandar Sedmak 8
VESPUCCI, Amerigo H
VESSELLA, Oreste 5
VESSEY, Robert Scadden 4
VEST, George Graham 1
VEST, H. Grant 5
VEST, Samuel Alexander, Jr. 3
VEST, Walter Edward 4
VESTAL, Albert Henry 1
VESTAL, Allan Delker 8
VESTAL, Edgar Fred 8
VESTAL, Samuel Curtis 3
VESTIN, John 1
VESTINE, Ernest Harry 5
VESTLING, Axel Ebenezer 2
VETCH, Samuel H
VETH, Martin 5
VETHAKE, Henry H
VEY, Ebenezer 7
VEYRA, Mrs. Jaime C. De 5
VEYRA, Jaime Carlos De 5
VEZIN, Charles 2
VIA, Lemuel R. 5
VIALL, Ethan 3
VIALL, Richmond 6
VIAUT, André Jules Armand 6
VIBBARD, Chauncey H
VIBBERT, William H. 1
VICHERT, John Frederick 2
VICK, James 5
VICK, Robert Ellsworth 5
VICK, Walker Whiting 1
VICKERS, Alonzo Knox 1
VICKERS, Enoch Howard 5
VICKERS, George
VICKERS, George Morley 4
VICKERS, Harry Franklin 7
VICKERS, James Cator 5
VICKERY, Herman Frank 1
VICKERY, Howard Leroy 2
VICKERY, Katherine 10
VICKREY, Charles Vernon 4
VICTOR, Alexander F. 4
VICTOR, Frances Fuller H
VICTOR, John Harvey 3
VICTOR, Martin 10
VICTOR, Metta Victoria Fuller H
VICTOR, Orville James
VICTORY, John Francis 9
VICTORY, John Patrick 4
VIDAL, Eugene Luther 5
VIDAL, Michel H
VIDAL DE LA FUENTE, Jorge 9
VIDAVER, Sidney Joseph 5
VIDMER, George 5
VIDOR, King Wallis 8
VIEHOEVER, Arno 5
VIEL, Etienne Bernard Alexandre H
VIELE, Aernout Cornelissen H
VIELE, Charles Delavan 1
VIELE, Egbert Ludovickus 1
VIELE, Egbert Ludovicus 1
VIELE, Herman Knickerbocker 1

VIERECK, George Sylvester 4
VIERECK, Louis C. 5
VIERLING, Bernard Julius 8
VIESSELMAN, Percival William 2
VIESULAS, Romas 9
VIETH, Henry Alvin 5
VIETH, Paul Herman 10
VIETOR, George Frederick 1
VIETOR, Karl 3
VIETS, Henry Rouse 8
VIETS, Howard T(hompson) 7
VIETT, George Frederic 3
VIEWEG, Frederic 2
VIGDERMAN, Alfred Greenfield 7
VIGIER, Henri 7
VIGNAUD, Henry 1
VIGNEC, Alfred J. 4
VIGNESS, David Martell 8
VIGNESS, Lauritz Andreas 2
VIGO, Joseph Maria Francesco H
VIGRAN, Nathan 5
VIGUERS, Richard Thomson 5
VIGUERS, Ruth Hill 5
VIJITAVONGS, Phya 5
VILAS, Charles Harrison 1
VILAS, George Byron 5
VILAS, Homer Albon 9
VILAS, William Freeman 1
VILATTE, Joseph Rene 4
VILBRANDT, Frank Carl 4
VILES, Blaine Spooner 2
VILES, Jonas 2
VILJOEN, Benjamin Johannis 4
VILJOEN, Philip Rudolph 8
VILLA, Francisco H
VILLA, Francisco 4
VILLAGRA, Gaspar Perez de H
VILLA-LOBOS, Heitor 3
VILLAMOR, Ignacio 1
VILLANI, Ralph A. 6
VILLARD, Henry H
VILLARD, Henry Hilgard 8
VILLARD, Oswald Garrison 2
VILLA-REAL, Antonio 6
VILLAROEL, Gualberto 2
VILLEDA-MORALES, Ramon 5
VILLENEUVE, J. M. Rodrigue 2
VILLERE, Jacques Philippe H
VILLERS, Thomas Jefferson 1
VILLON, Jacques 4
VILSACK, Carl Gregory 8
VIMEUR, Jean Baptiste Donatien de H
VINAL, Albert 9
VINAL, Harold 4
VINAL, William Gould 6
VINAVER, Chemjo 5
VINCENNES, sieur de* H
VINCENT, Beverly M. 8
VINCENT, Bird J. 1
VINCENT, Boyd 1
VINCENT, Clarence Augustus 2
VINCENT, Clarence Cornelius
VINCENT, Clinton Dermott 3
VINCENT, Clive Belden 1
VINCENT, Earl W. 3
VINCENT, Edgar La Verne 4
VINCENT, Frank 1
VINCENT, George Clark 7
VINCENT, George Edgar 1
VINCENT, Harold S(ellew) 1
VINCENT, Harry Aiken 1
VINCENT, Henry Bethuel 1
VINCENT, Howard P(aton) 9
VINCENT, Jesse Gurney 4
VINCENT, John Carter 5
VINCENT, John Heyl
VINCENT, John Martin 1
VINCENT, John Nathaniel 7
VINCENT, Leon Henry 1
VINCENT, Marvin Richardson 1
VINCENT, Mary Ann Farlow H
VINCENT, Thomas MacCurdy 1
VINCENT, Walter B. 1
VINCENT, Wilber Ddwain 5
VINCENT, William David 1
VINCI, Henry 5
VINEBERG, Arthur Martin 9
VINEBERG, Philip Fischel 9

VINER, Jacob 5
VINES, Fred Daniel 4
VINES, John Finley 5
VINES, William Madison 5
VINEYARD, George 9
  Hoagland
VINING, Edward Payson 1
VINING, John H
VINJE, Aad John 1
VINOGRAD, Jerome 7
  Rubin
VINSON, Albert Earl 5
VINSON, Arthur Ferle 4
VINSON, Carl 7
VINSON, Fred Moore, Jr. 8
VINSON, Frederic Moore 5
VINSON, Robert Ernest 2
VINSON, Taylor 5
VINSON, William Ashton 3
VINSONHALER, Frank 2
VINTON, Alexander H
  Hamilton
VINTON, Alexander 1
  Hamilton
VINTON, Arthur Dudley 5
VINTON, Francis H
VINTON, Francis Laurens H
VINTON, Frederic H
VINTON, Frederic Porter 1
VINTON, John Adams H
VINTON, Samuel Finley H
VINTON, Warren Jay 5
VIOLETTE, Ebal E. 4
VIOLETTE, Willis Gordon 4
VIOSCA, René Adams 5
VIPOND, Jonathan 3
VIPOND, Kenneth 6
  C(linton)
VIR DEN, Ray 3
VIRGIL, Almon Kincaid 4
VIRGIL, Antha Minerva 1
VIRGIN, Edward Harmon 5
VIRGIN, Herbert Whiting 5
VIRKUS, Frederick Adams 5
VIRTANEN, Artturi Ilmari 4
VIRTUE, Charles Franklin 5
VIRTUE, George Olien 5
VIRTUE, William Dale 10
VISCONTI, Luchino 6
VISHER, Stephen Sargent 4
VISHER, Stephen Sargent 5
VISHNIAC, Roman 10
VISHNIAC, Wolf Vladimir 6
VISHNIAK, Mark 7
VISSCHER, J. Paul 3
VISSCHER, William 5
  Lightfoot
VITALE, Ferruccio 1
VITETTL, Leonardo 6
VITS, George 5
VITT, Bruno Ceaser 4
VITTUM, Edmund March 1
VITTUM, Edmund March 1
VITTUM, Harriet E. 3
VITZ, Carl (Peter Paul) 7
VIVIAN, Alfred 4
VIVIAN, Harold Acton 5
VIVIAN, John Charles 4
VIVIAN, John Frederick 5
VIVIAN, Robert Evans 8
VIVIAN, Thomas Jondrie 1
VIZCAINO, Sebastian H
VIZETELLY, Frank Horace 1
VLASTOS, Gregory 10
VLIET, Elmer B(ennett) 10
VODREY, Joseph Kelly 7
VODREY, William Henry 7
VOEGELI, Henry Edward 2
VOEGELIN, Eric (Herman 8
  Wilhelm)
VOEGELIN, Harold 10
  Stanley
VOEGTLIN, Carl 6
VOEHRINGER, John 5
  Kasper, Jr.
VOELKEL, Robert 9
  T(ownsend)
VOELKER, John 10
  Donaldson (Robert
  Traver)*
VOELKER, Paul Frederick 5
VOETTER, Thomas Wilson 5
VOGDES, Anthony Wayne 4
VOGE, Marietta 8
VOGEL, Augustus Hugo 5
VOGEL, Charles Joseph 8
VOGEL, Charles Pfister 5
VOGEL, Charles W. 3
VOGEL, Clayton Barney 4
VOGEL, Cyril J. 1
VOGEL, Cyril J. 8
VOGEL, Edwin Chester 5
VOGEL, F. A. 8
VOGEL, Frank 1
VOGEL, Fred, Jr. 4
VOGEL, Herbert Davis 8
VOGEL, Joseph Richard 5

VOGEL, Joshua Holmes 5
VOGEL, Leo E. 4
VOGEL, Orville Alvin 10
VOGEL, Robert Willis 5
VOGEL, Rudolph Emerson 5
VOGELBACK, William 3
  Edward
VOGELER, Rudolf 6
  Frederick
VOGELGESANG, Carl 1
  Theodore
VOGELGESANG, Shepard 5
VOGELSANG, Alexander 1
  Theodore
VOGELSTEIN, Hans 4
  Alfred
VOGELTANZ, Edward 5
  Louis
VOGLER, William L. 5
VOGT, Henry F. 6
VOGT, Paul Leroy 6
VOGT, V. Ogden 4
VOGT, William 5
VOIGT, Andrew George 1
VOIGT, Carl Emil 7
VOIGT, Charles Ogden 8
VOIGT, Edward 1
VOIGT, Edwin Edgar 9
VOIGT, Irma Elizabeth 3
VOISLAWSKY, Antonie 1
  Phineas
VOLAVY, Marguerite 7
VOLD, George Bryan 4
VOLD, Lawrence 7
VOLD, Robert Donald 7
VOLDENG, Mathew 1
  Nelson
VOLINI, Italo Frederick 3
VOLIVA, Wilbur Glenn 2
VOLK, Douglas 1
VOLK, Garth William 9
VOLK, Leonard Wells H
VOLK, Lester David 7
VOLKER, Joseph Francis 10
VOLKER, William 2
VOLKERT, Edward 1
  Charles
VOLKOV, Vladislav N. 5
VOLLAND, Roscoe Henry 5
VOLLMER, August 3
VOLLMER, Clement 8
VOLLMER, John Phillip 1
VOLLMER, Lula 3
VOLLMER, Philip 1
VOLLMER, William 7
  Auerbach
VOLLMER, William G. 9
VOLLMERS, Henry 7
  Edward
VOLLRATH, Edward 1
VOLLUM, Howard 9
VOLPE, Arnold 1
VOLPE, Paul Anthony 5
VOLSTEAD, Andrew J. 2
VOLWILER, Albert 3
  Tangeman
VOLZ, Edward J. 6
VON BECKERATH, 7
  Herbert
VON BEKESY, Georg 5
VON BERGEN, Herbert 7
VON BERTALANFFY, 5
  Ludwig
VON BONNEWITZ, 5
  Orlando R.
VON BRAUN, Wernher 7
VON BRENTANO, 4
  Heinrich
VON CANON, Fred 9
VON CHOLTITZ, Dietrich 4
VON DER AHE, Charles 9
  T.
VONDER HAAR, Edward 6
  P.
VON DER HEYDE, 6
  Matthew Jennings
VON DER LAURITZ, H
  Robert Eberhard Schmidt
VONDERLEHR, Raymond 5
  Aloysius
VON DEWALL, Hans 4
  Werner
VON EGLOFFSTEIN, H
  Frederick W.
VON ELM, Henry C. 5
VON ENDE, Carl Leopold 5
VON ENGELKEN, 6
  Friedrich Johannes Hugo
VON ENGELN, Oskar 6
  Deitrich
VON ERFFA, Helmut 7
  Hartmann
VON ESCHEN, Clarence 7
  Raymond
VONESH, Raymond James 10
VON EULER, Ulf Svante 8

VON EULER-CHELPIN, 4
  Hans
VON FABER DU FAUR, 4
  Curt
VON FERSEN, Count 4
VON FIELITZ, Alexander 4
VON FREMD, Charles 4
  Spencer
VON FRISCH, Karl 7
VON GLAHN, William 8
  Carson
VON GONTARD, 7
  Adalbert
VON GOTTSCHALCK, 4
  Oscar Hunt
VON GRAVE-JONAS, 5
  Elsa (Baroness)
VON GRUNEBAUM, 5
  Gustave E(dmund)
VON GUTTENBERG, 5
  Karl Theodore
VON HEIMBURG, Ernest 7
  H(erman)
VON HIPPEL, Arthur 10
  Robert
VON HOFFMANN, 2
  Bernard
VON HOLST, Hermann 1
  Eduard
VON HUTTEN, Baroness 3
  Bettina
VON KAHLER, Erich 5
  Gabriel
VON KARAJAN, Herbert 10
VON KARMAN, Theodore 4
VON KELER, Theodore M. 1
  R.
VON KIENBUSCH, Carl 7
  Otto
VON KLEINWAECHTER, 5
  Ludwig Paul Viktor
VON KLENZE, Camillo 2
VON KOCHERTHAL, H
  Josua
VON KOERBER, Hans 7
  Nordewin Freiherr
VON LACKUM, John 4
  Peter
VON LAUE, Max 4
VON MACH, Edmund 1
VON MINDEN, William 6
  John
VON MISES, Ludwig Edler 6
VON MISES, Richard 3
VON MOSCHZISKER, 1
  Robert
VON NEUMANN, John 3
VON NEUMANN, Robert 9
  Franz Albert
VONNOH, Bessie Potter 1
VONNOH, Robert 1
VON PAGENHARDT, 2
  Maximilian Hugo
VON PHUL, Anna Maria H
VON PHUL, William 2
VON PRITTWITZ UND 3
  GAFFRON, Friedrich
  Wilhelm
VON RUCK, Karl 1
VON SALLMANN, 6
  Ludwig
VON SALTZA, Charles 1
  Frederick
VON SCHIERBRAND, 4
  Wolf
VON SCHLEGELL, David 10
VON SCHLIEDER, Albert 1
VON SCHMIDT, Harold 8
VON SCHON, Hans 5
  August Evald Conrad
VON SCHRENK, Hermann 3
VON SCHWEINITZ, Lewis H
  David
VON STEUBEN, Friedrich H
  Wilhelm Ludolf Gerhard
  August
VON STIEGEL, Baron H
VON STORCH, Searle 7
  Henry
VON STROHEIM, Erich 4
VON STRUVE, Henry Clay 1
VON TEMPSKI, Armine 2
VON THADDEN- 4
  TRIEGLAFF, Reinold
VON TRESCKOW, 5
  Egmont Charles
VON TRESS, Edward 1
  Campbell
VON TUNGELN, George 3
  Henry
VON WALTHER, Eckert 4
VON WENING, Anthony 9
VON WENING, Eugene, 9
  Jr.
VON WICHT, John 5
VON WILLER, Harry 5
  Walter

VOORHEES, Boynton 6
  Stephen
VOORHEES, Clark 1
  Greenwood
VOORHEES, Daniel H
  Wolsey
VOORHEES, Donald 9
VOORHEES, Donald 10
  Shirley
VOORHEES, Edward 1
  Burnett
VOORHEES, Enders 7
  McClumpha
VOORHEES, Foster 1
  MacGowan
VOORHEES, Henry Beiln 4
VOORHEES, James D. 5
VOORHEES, John Howard 2
VOORHEES, Josephine 10
  Palmer
VOORHEES, Louis 2
  Augustus
VOORHEES, Melvin 6
  Harold
VOORHEES, Oscar 2
  McMurtrie
VOORHEES, Philip H
  Falkerson
VOORHEES, Samuel 1
  Stockton
VOORHEES, Stephen 4
  Francis
VOORHEES, Stephen 1
  Hegeman
VOORHEES, Theodore 1
VOORHEES, Tracy S. 6
VOORHEES, Tracy S. 7
VOORHEES, Willard 1
VOORHEES, William 9
  Delano, Jr.
VOORHIES, Frank Corey 5
VOORHIES, Paul Warren 3
VOORHIS, Charles Brown 5
VOORHIS, Charles Henry H
VOORHIS, Harold Oliver 9
VOORHIS, Harry Malcolm 8
VOORHIS, Horace Jerry 8
VOORHIS, Warren Rollin 3
VOORSANGER, Jacob 1
VOOYS, Daniel William 7
VOPICKA, Charles J. 1
VORBECK, Marie Ludmilla 9
VORBERG, Martin Philip 6
VORENBERG, F. Frank 9
VORENBERG, Felix 2
VORHAUER, John Cook 4
VORHIES, Charles Taylor 2
VORIS, Anna Maybelle 10
VORIS, Harold Cornelius 7
VORIS, John Ralph 4
VOROSHILOV, Mazshal 5
  Kliment Yefremovich
VORSE, Albert White 1
VORSE, Mary Heaton 4
VORSTER, Balthazar 8
  Johannes
VORWALD, Arthur John 6
VORWALD, Arthur John 7
VORYS, Arthur Isaiah 1
VORYS, John Martin 5
VORYS, Webb Isaiah 5
VOS, Bert John 2
VOS, Geerhardus 3
VOSBURGH, George 1
  Bedell
VOSE, Clement Ellery 8
VOSE, Edward Neville 2
VOSE, James Wilson 6
VOSE, Robert Churchill 8
VOSE, Roger H
VOSE, William Preston 1
VOSGURGH, William 4
  Wallace
VOSHELL, Allen Fiske 6
VOSS, Carl August 2
VOSS, Ernst Karl Johann 1
  Heinrich
VOSS, Fred James 4
VOTAW, Albert Hiatt 1
VOTAW, Clyde Weber 4
VOTAW, Heber Herbert 4
VOTER, Perley Conant 3
VOTEY, Edwin Scott 1
VOTEY, Josiah William 1
VOTH, Ben 5
VOTIPKA, Thelma 5
VOUGHT, Chance Milton H
VOUGHT, Chance Milton 4
VOUTÉ, William Joseph 10
VOX, Herman H(arold) 5
VOYE, Joseph James 8
VREDENBURGH, William 4
  Henry
VREELAND, Albert 6
  Lincoln
VREELAND, Diana Dalziel 10

VREELAND, Edward 1
  Butterfield
VREELAND, Hamilton, Jr. 5
VREELAND, Herbert 2
  Harold
VREELAND, T. Reed 4
VREELAND, Walter J. 1
VREELAND, Williamson 2
  Updike
VROOM, Garret Dorset 1
  Wall
VROOM, Peter Dumont H
VROOM, Peter Dumont 1
VROOM, Robert Allyn 4
VROOMAN, Carl 4
VROOMAN, Clare Martin 2
VROOMAN, John Wright 1
VROOMAN, Vernon A. 8
VRUWINK, Henry Andrew 7
VUILLEQUEZ, Jean 10
VUILLEUMIER, Ernest 3
  Albert
VULTEE, Howard Fleming 5
VURSELL, Charles W. 6
VU-VAN-MAU 4
VYSHINSKY, Andrei 3
  Yanuarievich

W

WAASDORP, Leonard 7
  A(drian)
WABASHA H
WACH, Joachim 3
WACHENFELD, William 5
  A.
WACHENHEIMER, J. 1
WACHSMUTH, Charles H
WACHTEL, Howard 9
  Richard
WACHTEL, William W. 9
WACHTER, Frank C. 1
WACK, Henry Wellington 3
WACK, Otis 3
WACKER, Charles Henry 1
WACKERNAGEL, 1
  William
WACKERNISTER, 6
  William
WACKMAN, Kenneth B. 6
WADDEL, James H
WADDEL, Louise 1
  Forsslund
WADDEL, Moses H
WADDELL, Alfred Moore 1
WADDELL, Charles Carey 1
WADDELL, Charles 2
  Edward
WADDELL, Charles Wilkin 5
WADDELL, Chauncey L. 4
WADDELL, Harold 8
  Newton
WADDELL, Hugh H
WADDELL, James Iredell H
WADDELL, John 1
  Alexander Low
WADDELL, John Newton H
WADDELL, Joseph 1
  Addison
WADDELL, St. John 10
WADDILL, Edmund, Jr. 1
WADDINGTON, Conrad 5
  Hal
WADDINGTON, Ralph 5
  Henry
WADE, Benjamin Franklin H
WADE, Cyrus U. 4
WADE, Edward H
WADE, Edwin Carter 7
WADE, Festus John 1
WADE, Frank Bertram 3
WADE, Frank Edward 1
WADE, George Garretson 3
WADE, Harold Hamilton 8
WADE, Harry Van Nuys 7
WADE, Harry Vincent 4
WADE, Herbert Treadwell 3
WADE, H(erbert) Windsor 8
WADE, Ira Owen 8
WADE, James Francis 1
WADE, James Franklin 1
WADE, James William 7
WADE, Jason Lloyd 5
WADE, Jeptha Homer H
WADE, John Donald 4
WADE, John E. 5
WADE, John William 10
WADE, Joseph Sanford 4
WADE, Lester A. 4
WADE, Martin Joseph 1
WADE, Mary Hazelton 1
WADE, Mary L. Hill 4
WADE, Preston Allen 8
WADE, William Ligon 8
WADE, W(illiam) Wallace 7
WADE-GERY, Henry 8
  Theodore

WALKER, Hobart Alexander 5
WALKER, Horatio 1
WALKER, Hudson Dean 7
WALKER, Hugh Kelso 2
WALKER, Irving Miller 5
WALKER, Irving Miller 7
WALKER, Irwin Nolan 6
WALKER, Isaac Pigeon H
WALKER, Ivan N. 1
WALKER, Jacob Allen 8
WALKER, Jacob Garrett 1
WALKER, James* H
WALKER, James Alexander 1
WALKER, James Barr H
WALKER, James Barrett 9
WALKER, James Baynes 1
WALKER, James Everett 4
WALKER, James French 8
WALKER, James Herbert 2
WALKER, James Herron 9
WALKER, James J. 2
WALKER, James Peter H
WALKER, James V. 4
WALKER, James Wilson Grimes 3
WALKER, Jay P. 4
WALKER, John H
WALKER, John Alexander 9
WALKER, John Baldwin 2
WALKER, John Brisben 1
WALKER, John Earl 3
WALKER, John Franklin 6
WALKER, John Grimes 1
WALKER, John Leonard 5
WALKER, John Luther 8
WALKER, John Moore 3
WALKER, John O 8
WALKER, J(ohn) Randall 5
WALKER, John Thomas 10
WALKER, John Williams H
WALKER, John Yates Gholson 1
WALKER, Jonathan Hoge H
WALKER, Joseph 2
WALKER, Joseph 7
WALKER, Joseph Albert 4
WALKER, J(oseph) Frederic 5
WALKER, Joseph Henry 1
WALKER, Joseph Reddeford H
WALKER, Kenneth N. 3
WALKER, Kenzie Wallace 3
WALKER, Lapsley Greene 1
WALKER, Laurence Albert 8
WALKER, Leroy Pope H
WALKER, Lewis, 3d 5
WALKER, Lewis B. 4
WALKER, Lewis Carter 2
WALKER, Louis Carlisle 4
WALKER, Mary H
WALKER, Mary Adelaide 2
WALKER, Mary E. 1
WALKER, Meriwether Lewis 2
WALKER, Myron Hamilton 1
WALKER, Nancy (Ann Myrtle Swoyer)* 10
WALKER, Nat Gaillard 2
WALKER, Nathan Wilson 1
WALKER, Nellie Verne 5
WALKER, Nelson Macy 2
WALKER, Newton Farmer 1
WALKER, Norman McFarlane 4
WALKER, Oliver M. 10
WALKER, Paul Atlee 4
WALKER, Percy H
WALKER, Perley F. 1
WALKER, Pinkney Houston H
WALKER, Platt Dickinson 1
WALKER, Ralph Curry 4
WALKER, Ralph Thomas 5
WALKER, Ramsay M. 3
WALKER, Raymond Bridgham 8
WALKER, Reuben Eugene 1
WALKER, Reuben Lindsay H
WALKER, Richard Wilde 1
WALKER, Robert 3
WALKER, Robert Barney 5
WALKER, Robert Coleman 3
WALKER, Robert E. 3
WALKER, Robert Franklin 1
WALKER, Robert James H
WALKER, Robert John H
WALKER, Robert Sparks 6
WALKER, Roberts 1
WALKER, Roger A. P. 3
WALKER, Rollin Hough 3
WALKER, Ross H. 5
WALKER, Russell T. 9
WALKER, Ruth Irene 4
WALKER, Ryan 1
WALKER, Samuel J. 4
WALKER, Samuel Sloan, Jr. 10
WALKER, Scott Wells 4
WALKER, Sears Cook H
WALKER, Stanley 4
WALKER, Stanton 5
WALKER, Stewart McCulloch 4
WALKER, Stuart 1
WALKER, Stuart Wilson 1
WALKER, Theodore C. 4
WALKER, Theodore Penfield 3
WALKER, Thomas H
WALKER, Thomas Barlow 1
WALKER, Thomas Joseph 2
WALKER, Timothy* H
WALKER, Tom P. 4
WALKER, Walter 3
WALKER, Walter 4
WALKER, Walton Harris 3
WALKER, William H
WALKER, William Adams H
WALKER, William Alexander 6
WALKER, William David 1
WALKER, William G(eorge) 6
WALKER, William Henry 1
WALKER, William Henry Talbot H
WALKER, William Hultz 1
WALKER, William Johnson H
WALKER, William Kemble 1
WALKER, William May 6
WALKER, William S. 3
WALKER, William W. 7
WALKER, Willis J. 2
WALKER, Williston 1
WALKINSHAW, Robert Boyd 4
WALKLEY, Raymond Lowery 4
WALKOWICZ, Thaddeus F. 8
WALKOWITZ, Abraham 4
WALL, Albert Chandler 2
WALL, Alexander James 2
WALL, Edward Clarence 1
WALL, Edward Everett 2
WALL, Edward John 1
WALL, Francis Lowry 4
WALL, Frank Jerome 2
WALL, Garret Dorset H
WALL, Garrett Buckner 1
WALL, George Willard 4
WALL, Harry Rutherford 6
WALL, Hubert Stanley 5
WALL, James Walter H
WALL, Nathan Sanders 7
WALL, Stuart S. 4
WALL, William H
WALL, William Guy H
WALL, William Guy 1
WALL, Zeno 7
WALLACE, Addison Alexander 3
WALLACE, Alexander Doniphan 9
WALLACE, Alexander Gilfillan 1
WALLACE, Alexander Stuart H
WALLACE, Anthony Edward 8
WALLACE, Austin Edward 1
WALLACE, Benjamin Bruce 2
WALLACE, Brenton Greene 9
WALLACE, Bruce Hinds 4
WALLACE, Carl S. 8
WALLACE, Charles Frederick 4
WALLACE, Charles Hodge 2
WALLACE, Charles Loring 7
WALLACE, Charles William 1
WALLACE, Charlton 2
WALLACE, Clarence 10
WALLACE, Daniel H
WALLACE, Daniel Alden 3
WALLACE, David H
WALLACE, David A. 5
WALLACE, David Duncan 3
WALLACE, David M. 5
WALLACE, Dewitt 7
WALLACE, Dillon 1
WALLACE, Donald H. 3
WALLACE, Dwane L. 10
WALLACE, Earle Sessions 8
WALLACE, Edwin Sherman 4
WALLACE, Elizabeth 3
WALLACE, Fred Clute 8
WALLACE, George Barclay 2
WALLACE, George MacDonald 3
WALLACE, George Roberts 8
WALLACE, George Selden 6
WALLACE, Grant 4
WALLACE, Harold Ayer 3
WALLACE, Harry Brookings 3
WALLACE, Henry 1
WALLACE, Henry Agard 4
WALLACE, Henry Cantwell 1
WALLACE, Horace Binney H
WALLACE, Howard T. 4
WALLACE, Hugh Campbell 1
WALLACE, Hugh D. 3
WALLACE, Ira 4
WALLACE, Irving 10
WALLACE, J. Sherman 1
WALLACE, James 1
WALLACE, James Brevard 8
WALLACE, James M. H
WALLACE, James Murray 7
WALLACE, John Findley 1
WALLACE, John H., Jr. 10
WALLACE, John J. 1
WALLACE, John McChrystal 10
WALLACE, John William H
WALLACE, John Winfield H
WALLACE, Jonathan Hasson H
WALLACE, Joseph 1
WALLACE, Karl Richards 6
WALLACE, Lawrence Wilkerson 6
WALLACE, Leon Harry 9
WALLACE, Lew 8
WALLACE, Lewis 1
WALLACE, Lila Acheson 8
WALLACE, Lurleen Burns 5
WALLACE, Margaret Adair 5
WALLACE, Martha Redfield 10
WALLACE, Mary Kent 6
WALLACE, Nathaniel Dick H
WALLACE, Oates Charles Symonds 2
WALLACE, R. James 4
WALLACE, Raymond McElwain 8
WALLACE, Robert Charles 3
WALLACE, Robert Dwight 4
WALLACE, Robert Francis 9
WALLACE, Robert George 8
WALLACE, Robert Minor 3
WALLACE, Robert Moore 1
WALLACE, Rothvin 1
WALLACE, Rush Richard 1
WALLACE, S(amuel) Mayner 6
WALLACE, Schuyler Crawford 5
WALLACE, Sebon Rains 6
WALLACE, Stuart Allen 4
WALLACE, Susan Elston 1
WALLACE, Thomas F. 5
WALLACE, Thomas Ross 3
WALLACE, Tom 4
WALLACE, Westel Bruce 9
WALLACE, William, Jr. 1
WALLACE, William Alexander Anderson H
WALLACE, William Andrew H
WALLACE, William Charles 5
WALLACE, William Henry 1
WALLACE, William Henry 3
WALLACE, William Henson H
WALLACE, William James 1
WALLACE, William Kay 7
WALLACE, William Lewis 7
WALLACE, William McLean 5
WALLACE, William Miller 1
WALLACE, William Robert 4
WALLACE, William Ross H
WALLACE, William Ross 7
WALLACE, William Swilling 7
WALLACH, Luitpold 9
WALLACH, Sidney 7
WALLACK, Henry John H
WALLACK, James William* H
WALLACK, John Johnstone Lester H
WALLAU, Herman L. 5
WALLEN, Saul 5
WALLEN, Theodore Clifford 1
WALLENBERG, Axel Fingal 5
WALLENBERG, Jacob 9
WALLENBERG, Marc, Jr. 5
WALLENBERG, Marcus 8
WALLENDER, Elmer Forrest 8
WALLENDORF, Paul E. 8
WALLENIUS, Carl Gideon 2
WALLENSTEIN, Alfred Franz 8
WALLENSTEIN, Merrill Bernard 5
WALLER, Alfred Ernest 8
WALLER, Allen George 4
WALLER, C(arl) Richard 7
WALLER, Cecile Howell 3
WALLER, Claude 1
WALLER, Clifford Ellison 7
WALLER, Curtis L. 3
WALLER, David Jewett, Jr. 1
WALLER, Edwin James 6
WALLER, Ellis J. 10
WALLER, Elwyn 1
WALLER, Emma H
WALLER, Frank 1
WALLER, George Platt 4
WALLER, Gilbert Johnson 4
WALLER, Helen Hiett 4
WALLER, Henry 4
WALLER, John Lightfoot H
WALLER, John Robert 4
WALLER, Lewis 1
WALLER, Littleton W. T. 4
WALLER, Littleton Waller Tazewell 1
WALLER, Mary Ella 1
WALLER, Osmar Lysander 1
WALLER, Peter August 1
WALLER, Rose 1
WALLER, Thomas 4
WALLER, Thomas McDonald 1
WALLER, Thomas Small 8
WALLER, Willard Walter 2
WALLER, Wilmer Joyce 5
WALLERSTEDT, Alvar Gustaf 9
WALLERSTEIN, Edward 5
WALLEY, Samuel Hurd 5
WALLGREN, Monrad C. 4
WALLICH, Henry Christopher 9
WALLICHS, Glenn Everett 5
WALLIHAN, Allen Grant 4
WALLIN, Alfred 1
WALLIN, J(ohn) E(dward) Wallace 5
WALLIN, Samuel 4
WALLIN, Van Arthur 2
WALLIN, William John 4
WALLING, Anna Strunsky 4
WALLING, Ansel Tracy H
WALLING, Emory A. 1
WALLING, William English 1
WALLING, William Henry 5
WALLING, Willoughby George 1
WALLINGFORD, John Duvall 1
WALLINGTON, Nellie Urner 4
WALLIS, Everett Stanley 4
WALLIS, Frederick Alfred 3
WALLIS, George Edward 5
WALLIS, Hal Brent 9
WALLIS, Jenny 1
WALLIS, Philip 4
WALLIS, Severn Teackle H
WALLIS, William Fisher 5
WALLNER, Woodruff 8
WALLS, David Crawford 3
WALLS, Frank Xavier 5
WALLS, William Jacob 6
WALLS, William L. 1
WALMSLEY, Walter Newbold, Jr. 5
WALN, Nicholas H
WALN, Nora 4
WALN, Robert* H
WALPOLE, Ronald Noel 9
WALRATH, Florence Dahl 3
WALRATH, John Henry 4
WALRATH, Laurence Kaye 7
WALSH, Allan B. 5
WALSH, Arthur 2
WALSH, Basil Sylvester 2
WALSH, Benjamin Dann H
WALSH, Blanche 1
WALSH, Catherine Shellew 2
WALSH, Charles Clinton 2
WALSH, Cornelius Richard 7
WALSH, Correa Moylan 3
WALSH, SIR Cyril Ambrose 6
WALSH, David Ignatius 2
WALSH, Edmund 3
WALSH, Edward Anthony 6
WALSH, Edward J. 2
WALSH, Ellard A. 8
WALSH, Emmet M. 4
WALSH, Sister Frances Marie 5
WALSH, Francis W. 8
WALSH, Frank P. 1
WALSH, Frederick Harper 4
WALSH, George Ethelbert 1
WALSH, Gerald Groveland 3
WALSH, Gerald Powers 4
WALSH, Harold Vandervoort 9
WALSH, Henry Collins 1
WALSH, James A. 4
WALSH, James Anthony 1
WALSH, James Augustine 10
WALSH, James Clement 9
WALSH, James Edward 8
WALSH, James Joseph 2
WALSH, James Lawrence 3
WALSH, John 2
WALSH, John Edward 5
WALSH, John Gaynor 3
WALSH, John Henry 1
WALSH, John Klaerr 4
WALSH, Joseph 2
WALSH, J(oseph) Hartt 6
WALSH, Joseph Leonard 6
WALSH, Joseph Patrick 5
WALSH, Julius Sylvester 1
WALSH, Lawrence Aloysius 5
WALSH, Leonard Patrick 7
WALSH, Louis Sebastian 1
WALSH, Matthew J. 7
WALSH, Matthew James 4
WALSH, Michael H
WALSH, Michael Patrick 8
WALSH, Philip F. 6
WALSH, Raycroft 3
WALSH, Raymond Arnold 1
WALSH, Raymond James 4
WALSH, Richard John 4
WALSH, Robert H
WALSH, Robert Douglas 1
WALSH, Roy Edward 5
WALSH, Theodore Edwin 5
WALSH, Thomas 1
WALSH, Thomas F. 1
WALSH, Thomas James 1
WALSH, Thomas Joseph 3
WALSH, Thomas W. H
WALSH, Thomas Yates H
WALSH, Travis Walter 7
WALSH, Warren Bartlett 7
WALSH, William H
WALSH, William Concannon 6
WALSH, William Edwin 6
WALSH, William Francis 2
WALSH, William Henry 1
WALSH, William Robert 7
WALSH, William Thomas 2
WALSON, Charles Moore 3
WALSTER, Harlow Leslie 3
WALSTON, Charles 1
WALSTON, Vernon C. 4
WALT, Lewis William 10
WALTEMYER, William Claude 8
WALTER, A. Henry 4
WALTER, Adolph Schinner 8
WALTER, Albert G. H
WALTER, Alfred 1
WALTER, Allan Wylie 4
WALTER, Bruno 4
WALTER, Ellery 1
WALTER, Elliot Vincent 5
WALTER, Erich Albert 7
WALTER, Eugene 1
WALTER, Francis Eugene 4
WALTER, Frank J. 4
WALTER, Frank Keller 2
WALTER, George William 1
WALTER, Herbert Eugene 2
WALTER, Howard Arnold 1
WALTER, Luther Mason 2
WALTER, M. E. 4
WALTER, Paul Alfred Francis 6
WALTER, Raymond F. 1
WALTER, Robert 1
WALTER, Thomas H
WALTER, Thomas Ustick H
WALTER, William Emley 5
WALTER, William Henry H
WALTERS, Alexander 1
WALTERS, Anderson Howel 1
WALTERS, Basil L. 6

WATKINS, Charles W. 1
WATKINS, Dale Baxter 5
WATKINS, David Ogden 1
WATKINS, David Wayne 8
WATKINS, Dwight Everett 6
WATKINS, Edgar 2
WATKINS, Elton, Sr. 3
WATKINS, Everett C. 3
WATKINS, Ferre C. 4
WATKINS, Frank Thomas 3
WATKINS, Franklin 3
  Chenault
WATKINS, Frederick 5
  Mundell
WATKINS, G. Robert 5
WATKINS, George H
  Claiborne
WATKINS, Harry Evans 4
WATKINS, Henry Hitt 5
WATKINS, Henry Vaughan 2
WATKINS, Jabez Bunting 1
WATKINS, James (Keir) 5
WATKINS, J(ames) 5
  Stephen
WATKINS, John Elfreth 1
WATKINS, John Elfreth 2
WATKINS, John Thomas 5
WATKINS, Joseph Conrad 5
WATKINS, Mark Hanna 6
WATKINS, Mary Fitch 8
WATKINS, Myron Webster 7
WATKINS, Ralph James 9
WATKINS, Raymond 2
  Edward
WATKINS, Robert Henry 4
WATKINS, Thomas 6
  Franklin
WATKINS, Thomas 7
  Franklin
WATKINS, Thomas 9
  Graham
WATKINS, Thomas H. 4
WATKINS, Thomas James 5
WATKINS, Thomas Webb 7
WATKINS, Vernon Phillips 5
WATKINS, Walter Kendall 4
WATKINS, William Turner 4
WATKINS, William
  Woodbury
WATLING, John Wright 3
WATMOUGH, James 1
  Horatio
WATMOUGH, John H
  Goddard
WATNER, Abraham 4
WATRES, Louis Arthur 1
WATROUS, Charles Leach 1
WATROUS, David Gapen 7
WATROUS, Elizabeth 1
  Snowden Nichols
WATROUS, George Ansel 1
WATROUS, George Dutton 1
WATROUS, Harry Willson 1
WATROUS, Richard 3
  Benedict
WATSON, Adolphus 2
  Eugene
WATSON, Albert 1
WATSON, Alfred Augustin 1
WATSON, Alfred Nelson 10
WATSON, Alonzo Richard 1
WATSON, Amelia 1
  Montague
WATSON, Andrew 1
WATSON, Archibald 3
  Robinson
WATSON, Arthur Clinton 6
WATSON, Arthur 6
  Kittredge
WATSON, Barbara M. 1
WATSON, Benjamin Frank 1
WATSON, Benjamin Philip 6
WATSON, Benjamin Philp 7
WATSON, Bruce Mervellon 2
WATSON, Burl Stevens 6
WATSON, Byron S. 2
WATSON, C. Hoyt 8
WATSON, Cecil James 8
WATSON, Charles G. 5
WATSON, Charles Henry 1
WATSON, Charles Roger 2
WATSON, Clarence
  Wayland
WATSON, Claude A. 7
WATSON, Conrad 7
  Ethelbert
WATSON, Cooper H
  Kinderdine
WATSON, David Emmett 1
WATSON, David Kemper 4
WATSON, David Robert 5
WATSON, David 1
  Thompson
WATSON, Donald 8
  Stevenson
WATSON, Drake 3
WATSON, Dudley Crafts 5

WATSON, Earnest Charles 5
WATSON, Ebbie Julian 1
WATSON, Edith Sarah 3
WATSON, Edward Hann 6
WATSON, Edward Minor 1
WATSON, Edward Minor 2
WATSON, Edward Willard 1
WATSON, Edwin Martin 2
WATSON, Elizabeth Lowe 4
WATSON, Elkanah H
WATSON, Emile Emdon 3
WATSON, Emory Olin 1
WATSON, Ernest Charles 9
WATSON, Ernest W(illiam) 5
WATSON, Eugene Payne 4
WATSON, Eugene Winslow 1
WATSON, F. B. 3
WATSON, Floyd Rowe 5
WATSON, Frank Dekker 3
WATSON, Frank Rushmore 1
WATSON, G. Clarke 4
WATSON, George D. 1
WATSON, George Henry 3
WATSON, Goodwin 7
  Barbour
WATSON, H. Sumner 1
WATSON, Harry Legare 3
WATSON, Henry Chapman 1
WATSON, Henry Clay H
WATSON, Henry Cood H
WATSON, Henry David 1
WATSON, Henry Winfield 1
WATSON, Herbert L. 7
WATSON, Hugh Hammond 2
WATSON, Irving Allison 1
WATSON, James H
WATSON, James 1
WATSON, James Craig H
WATSON, James D. 1
WATSON, James E. 2
WATSON, James 6
  Fraughtman
WATSON, James Gray 3
WATSON, James Madison 1
WATSON, James S., Jr. 8
WATSON, James Sibley 3
WATSON, James Webster 3
WATSON, Jesse Paul 10
WATSON, John B. 3
WATSON, John Brown 2
WATSON, John Crittenden 1
WATSON, John Fanning H
WATSON, John Franklin 5
WATSON, John H., Jr. 4
WATSON, John Henry 1
WATSON, John Jay 1
WATSON, John Jordan 1
  Crittenden
WATSON, John Thomas 3
WATSON, John William H
  Clark
WATSON, Joseph Franklin 1
WATSON, Kenneth Nicoll 5
WATSON, Leroy Hugh 6
WATSON, Lewis Findlay H
WATSON, Mark Skinner 4
WATSON, Martin Wallace 9
WATSON, Osborn Stone 8
WATSON, Paul Barron 2
WATSON, Ralph Hopkins 4
WATSON, Robert 1
WATSON, Robert Clement 9
WATSON, Robert Earl 8
WATSON, Robert Walker 2
WATSON, Russell 5
  Ellsworth
WATSON, Russell 7
  Ellsworth
WATSON, Samuel Newell 1
WATSON, Sereno H
WATSON, Thomas 1
  Augustus
WATSON, Thomas E. 1
WATSON, Thomas 8
  Gaylord, Jr.
WATSON, Thomas John 3
WATSON, Thomas Leonard 1
WATSON, Walter Allen 1
WATSON, Willard 5
  Oliphiant
WATSON, William 3
WATSON, William
  Franklin
WATSON, William Gorrell 1
WATSON, William Henry 1
WATSON, William Richard 1
WATSON-WATT, Sir 6
  Robert (Alexander)
WATT, Barbara Hall 5
WATT, Ben H. 4
WATT, David Alexander 1
WATT, George Willard 7
WATT, Homer Andrew 4
WATT, James Arthur 7
WATT, James Robert 1
WATT, Richard Morgan 1

WATT, Robert J. 2
WATT, Robert McDowell 4
WATT, Rolla Vernon 1
WATTERS, Henry Eugene 1
WATTERS, James I(saac) 9
WATTERS, Philip 1
  Melancthon
WATTERS, Rev. Philip 5
  Sidney
WATTERS, Thomas 1
WATTERS, William Henry 1
WATTERSON, Harvey H
  Magee
WATTERSON, Henry 1
WATTERSON, Joseph 6
WATTERSON, Joseph 7
WATTERSTON, George 1
WATTIE, James 6
WATTLES, Edmund Orson 1
  Wallace
WATTLES, Thomas Irvin 5
WATTLES, Willard Austin 3
WATTLEY, Donald Hubert 8
WATTS, Alan Wilson 6
WATTS, Albert Edward 5
WATTS, Amos Holston 9
WATTS, Arthur S. 5
WATTS, Arthur Thomas 4
WATTS, Charles Henry 3
WATTS, Clyde Jefferson 7
WATTS, David Alden 7
WATTS, Edward Everett, 9
  Jr.
WATTS, Edward Seabrook 1
WATTS, Ethelbert 1
WATTS, Frank Overton 2
WATTS, Franklin Mowry 1
WATTS, Frederick H
WATTS, George 1
  Washington
WATTS, H. Bascom 3
WATTS, Harry Dorsey 5
WATTS, Harvey Maitland 4
WATTS, Herbert Charles 5
WATTS, John H
WATTS, John Clarence 5
WATTS, John Sebrie 1
WATTS, Joseph Thomas 3
WATTS, Legh Richmond 1
WATTS, Lyle Ford 4
WATTS, Mary Stanbery 4
WATTS, May Petrea 10
  Theilgaard
WATTS, May Petrea 6
  Theilgaard
WATTS, Olin E(thredge) 10
WATTS, Otto O(live) 10
WATTS, Ralph L. 2
WATTS, Richard Cannon 1
WATTS, Ridley 1
WATTS, Ridley 6
WATTS, Roderick John 3
WATTS, Stanley Saul 5
WATTS, Thomas Hill H
WATTS, Thoi.as Joseph 3
WATTS, W(arren) S(mith) 9
WATTS, William Carleton 1
WATTS, William Lord 4
WAUCHOPE, George 2
  Armstrong
WAUCHOPE, Robert 7
WAUGH, Albert E(dmund) 8
WAUGH, Alex (Alexander 8
  Raban Waugh)
WAUGH, Alfred S. H
WAUGH, Beverly H
WAUGH, Coulton H
WAUGH, Evelyn Arthur St 4
  John
WAUGH, Frank Albert 2
WAUGH, Frederick Judd 1
WAUGH, Frederick Vail 10
WAUGH, George Morton, 9
  Jr.
WAUGH, Ida 1
WAUGH, John McMaster 1
WAUGH, Karl Tinsley 5
WAUGH, Richey Laughlin 8
WAUGH, Samuel Bell 5
WAUGH, Samuel Clark 5
WAUGH, Sidney 4
WAUGH, William Francis 1
WAUGH, William 5
  Hammond
WAUGH, William Jasper 5
WAUL, Thomas Neville 1
WAVELL, Archibald 3
  Percival
WAVERLEY, Viscount 3
WAWZONEK, Stanley 10
WAXMAN, Franz 4
WAXMAN, Percy 1
WAXMAN, Samuel 7
  Montefiore
WAY, Cassius 2
WAY, George Brevitt 4

WAY, Gordon L. 6
WAY, John 1
WAY, Joseph Howell 1
WAY, Luther B. 2
WAY, Royal Brunson 1
WAY, Sylvester Bedell 2
WAY, Warren Wade 2
WAY, William 5
WAYBURN, Ned 2
WAYLAND, Francis H
WAYLAND, Francis 1
WAYLAND, Julius 1
  Augustus
WAYLAND, W. R. 7
WAYLAND-SMITH, 4
  Robert
WAYMACK, William 4
  Wesley
WAYMAN, Alexander H
  Walker
WAYMAN, Dorothy C. 6
WAYMAN, Harry Clifford 6
WAYMOUTH, George 1
WAYNE, Anthony H
WAYNE, Arthur Trezevant 4
WAYNE, Charles Stokes 4
WAYNE, Isaac H
WAYNE, James Moore H
WAYNE, John (Marion 7
  Michael Morrison)
WAYNE, Joseph, Jr. 2
WAYNICK, Capus Miller 8
WAYS, Max 8
WAYSON, James Thomas 6
WAYSON, Newton Edward 7
WEAD, Charles Kasson 1
WEAD, (Mary) Eunice 6
WEADOCK, Bernard 2
  Francis
WEADOCK, Edward E. 4
WEADOCK, John C. 3
WEADOCK, Thomas Addis 1
  Emmet
WEAGANT, Roy 2
  Alexander
WEAGLY, Mrs. Roy C. F. 3
WEAKLEY, Charles 5
  Enright
WEAKLEY, Robert H
WEAKLEY, Samuel Davies 1
WEAKLY, Frank Ervin 9
WEAKLY, Hazel Barnett 7
WEAN, Raymond John 7
WEAR, D. Walker 4
WEAR, Frank Lucian 5
WEAR, James Smith 9
WEAR, Joseph W. 1
WEAR, Samuel McConnell 6
WEARE, Meshech H
WEARING, Thomas 4
WEARN, Joseph Treloar 8
WEARSTLER, Earl Ford 8
WEART, Douglas Lafayette 5
WEATHERBY, Charles 2
  Alfred
WEATHERBY, Leroy 2
  Samuel
WEATHERED, Roy 6
  Bishop
WEATHERFORD, 7
  Harrison Mark
WEATHERFORD, 8
  Harrison Mark
WEATHERFORD, William H
WEATHERFORD, Willis 5
  Duke
WEATHERFORD, Willis 1
  Duke
WEATHERHEAD, Albert 4
  J., Jr.
WEATHERHEAD, Arthur 8
  Clason
WEATHERLY, James 4
  Meriwether
WEATHERLY, Ulysses 1
  Grant
WEATHERLY, W(illiam) 1
  H.
WEATHERRED, Preston 5
  Alonzo
WEATHERSPOON, Walter 7
  Herbert
WEATHERWAX, Hazelett 1
  Paul
WEAVER, Aaron Ward 1
WEAVER, Andrew Thomas 4
WEAVER, Archibald Jerard H
WEAVER, Arthur J. 2
WEAVER, Bennett 5
WEAVER, Charles 4
  Blanchard
WEAVER, Charles Clinton 5
WEAVER, Charles Parsons 4
WEAVER, Clarence Eugene 1
WEAVER, Claude 3
WEAVER, Earl 10

WEAVER, Edward 1
  Ebenezer
WEAVER, Erasmus 1
  Morgan
WEAVER, Frank Lloyd 9
WEAVER, Frederic Nixon 8
WEAVER, Fred(erick) 5
  H(enry)
WEAVER, George Calvin 3
WEAVER, George Howitt 2
WEAVER, Gilbert Grimes 5
WEAVER, Harry Otis 1
WEAVER, Harry Sands 1
WEAVER, Henry Grady 2
WEAVER, James B. 1
WEAVER, James Bellamy 1
WEAVER, James Harvey 5
WEAVER, James R. N. 8
WEAVER, John 1
WEAVER, John Ernst 7
WEAVER, John Van 1
  Alstyn
WEAVER, Jonathan 1
WEAVER, Joseph B. 6
WEAVER, Junius Vaden 6
WEAVER, Martha Collins 4
WEAVER, Myron 4
  McDonald
WEAVER, Paul 7
WEAVER, Paul John 2
WEAVER, Philip H
WEAVER, Philip Johnson 5
WEAVER, Philip Tennant 6
WEAVER, Powell 3
WEAVER, R. C. 5
WEAVER, R(alph) 6
  H(older)
WEAVER, Robert 9
  Augustus
WEAVER, Rudolph 2
WEAVER, Rufus B. 1
WEAVER, Rufus 2
  Washington
WEAVER, Samuel Pool 4
WEAVER, Silas Matteson 1
WEAVER, Thomas Arthur 10
WEAVER, Walter L. 1
WEAVER, Walter Reed 2
WEAVER, Warren 7
WEAVER, William Dixon 1
WEAVER, William 8
  Gaulbert
WEAVER, Winston Odell 10
WEAVER, Zebulon 2
WEBB, Aileen Osborn 9
WEBB, Alexander Stewart 1
WEBB, Alexander Stewart 2
WEBB, Atticus 2
WEBB, Carl N. 3
WEBB, Charles Aurelius 2
WEBB, Charles Henry 1
WEBB, Charles M. 5
WEBB, Charles Wallace 2
WEBB, C(hauncey) Earl 9
WEBB, Clifton 4
WEBB, Sir Clifton 4
WEBB, Daniel H
WEBB, Daniel Clary 3
WEBB, Del E. 5
WEBB, Earle W. 4
WEBB, Edward Fleming 1
WEBB, Edwin Douglas 5
WEBB, Edwin Yates 1
WEBB, Ernest Clay 3
WEBB, Frank Elbridge 2
WEBB, Frank Rush 1
WEBB, George Arthur 8
WEBB, George H. 1
WEBB, George James H
WEBB, George Thomas 4
WEBB, Gerald Bertram 2
WEBB, Hanor A. 4
WEBB, Harold Vernon 7
WEBB, Henry Walter 1
WEBB, Herschel F. 8
WEBB, J. Burkitt 4
WEBB, Jack 8
WEBB, James Avery 3
WEBB, James Duncan 4
WEBB, James Edwin 10
WEBB, James Henry 1
WEBB, James Ruffin 6
WEBB, James Watson H
WEBB, John H(enry) 7
WEBB, John Maurice 1
WEBB, Joseph James 3
WEBB, Kenneth Seymour 4
WEBB, Leland D(otson) 9
WEBB, Louie Winfield 7
WEBB, Nathan 1
WEBB, Richard L. 4
WEBB, Robert 8
WEBB, Robert Alexander 1
WEBB, Robert H. 3
WEBB, Robert Thomas 1
WEBB, Robert Wallace 9
WEBB, Robert Williams 2

WEBB, Stuart Weston 5
WEBB, Stuart Weston 7
WEBB, Thomas H
WEBB, T(homas) Dwight 1
WEBB, Thomas Smith H
WEBB, Thompson 6
WEBB, Ulys Robert 3
WEBB, Ulysses Sigel 2
WEBB, Vanderbilt 3
WEBB, Vivian Howell (Mrs. 5
  Thompson Webb)
WEBB, Walter Loring 1
WEBB, Walter Prescott 4
WEBB, Willard Isaac, Jr. 5
WEBB, William Alexander 1
WEBB, William Alfred 2
WEBB, William Henry 1
WEBB, William Robert 1
WEBB, William Seward 4
WEBB, William Snyder 1
WEBB, William Walter 1
WEBBER, Albert G., Jr. 7
WEBBER, Amos Richard 2
WEBBER, Charles Wilkins H
WEBBER, Clyde Mayo 7
WEBBER, Everard Leland 10
WEBBER, George Harris 1
WEBBER, Henry William 1
WEBBER, Herbert John 2
WEBBER, Hugh E. 9
WEBBER, James Benson, 3
  Jr.
WEBBER, Lane D(avis) 7
WEBBER, Le Roy 1
WEBBER, Oscar 4
WEBBER, Richard Hudson 4
WEBBER, Robert 10
WEBBER, Samuel H
WEBBER, Samuel Gilbert 4
WEBBINK, Paul 5
WEBER, Adna Ferrin 5
WEBER, Albert H
WEBER, Albert J. 4
WEBER, Alfred 3
WEBER, Arthur William 5
WEBER, Bertram Anton 10
WEBER, Carl Jefferson 7
WEBER, Clements 7
WEBER, Edouard 5
WEBER, Francis John 7
WEBER, Frederick Clarence 6
WEBER, Frederick 3
  Theodore
WEBER, Gustav C. E. 4
WEBER, Gustave Frederick 6
WEBER, Gustavus 2
  Adolphus
WEBER, Harold Christian 8
WEBER, Harry M. 3
WEBER, Henri Carleton 1
WEBER, Henry Adam 4
WEBER, Henry George 10
WEBER, Herman Carl 1
WEBER, J. Sherwood 7
WEBER, Jessie Palmer 5
WEBER, Joe Nicholas 5
WEBER, John 4
WEBER, John B. 1
WEBER, John Langdon 1
WEBER, Joseph M. 1
WEBER, Lois 1
WEBER, Max 2
WEBER, Max 4
WEBER, Paul 3
WEBER, Randolph Henry 4
WEBER, Samuel Edwin 5
WEBER, Shirley Howard 7
WEBER, William A 6
WEBER, William Lander 4
WEBERN, Anton 4
WEBNER, Frank Erastus 4
WEBSTER, Archibald 10
  Wilson
WEBSTER, Arthur Gordon 1
WEBSTER, Benjamin 6
  Francis
WEBSTER, Bethuel 10
  Matthew
WEBSTER, Bruce Peck 6
WEBSTER, Bruce Peck 7
WEBSTER, Burnice Hoyle 10
WEBSTER, Clyde Irvin 5
WEBSTER, Cornelius 2
  Crosby
WEBSTER, Daniel H
WEBSTER, David 1
WEBSTER, David Locke 9
WEBSTER, Edward Harlan 1
WEBSTER, Edward Jerome 6
WEBSTER, Edward Mount 7
WEBSTER, Edwin Hanson H
WEBSTER, Edwin Harrison 5
WEBSTER, Edwin Sibley 3
WEBSTER, Edwin Sibley, 3
  Jr.
WEBSTER, Eugene Carroll 1
WEBSTER, Francis Marion 1

WEBSTER, Frank Daniel 1
WEBSTER, Frank G. 1
WEBSTER, Frederic Smith 4
WEBSTER, George Lewis 8
WEBSTER, George Sidney 1
WEBSTER, George 1
  Smedley
WEBSTER, George Van 1
  O'Linda
WEBSTER, George 1
  Washington
WEBSTER, Harold E. 4
WEBSTER, Harold Tucker 7
WEBSTER, Harrie 1
WEBSTER, Harvey Curtis 9
WEBSTER, Helen 1
  Livermore
WEBSTER, Henry Kitchell 1
WEBSTER, Hutton 3
WEBSTER, Hutton, Jr. 3
WEBSTER, J. Stanley 4
WEBSTER, James R. 1
WEBSTER, Jean 1
WEBSTER, Jerome Pierce 6
WEBSTER, John Clarence 2
WEBSTER, John Hunter 1
WEBSTER, John Lee 1
WEBSTER, John White H
WEBSTER, Joseph Dana 1
WEBSTER, Leslie Tillotson 2
WEBSTER, Lorin 1
WEBSTER, Luther Denver, 1
  Jr.
WEBSTER, Margaret 5
WEBSTER, Marjorie Fraser 4
WEBSTER, Nathan 1
  Burnham
WEBSTER, Noah H
WEBSTER, Paul Francis 8
WEBSTER, Paul Kimball 3
WEBSTER, Pelatiah H
WEBSTER, Ralph Waldo 1
WEBSTER, Reginald H. 4
WEBSTER, Reginald 10
  Howard
WEBSTER, Reginald 8
  Nathaniel
WEBSTER, Rex 10
WEBSTER, Robert Morris 5
WEBSTER, Sidney 1
WEBSTER, Taylor H
WEBSTER, Warren 1
WEBSTER, William 5
WEBSTER, William 5
  Clarence
WEBSTER, William 4
  Franklin
WEBSTER, William Grant 4
WEBSTER, William Reuben 1
WECHSBERG, Joseph 8
WECHSLER, David 7
WECHSLER, Isreal Spanier 4
WECHSLER, James Arthur 8
WECKER, Walter Andre 10
WECKLER, Herman L. 5
WECTER, Dixon 4
WEDD, Stanley Musgrave 8
WEDDELL, Alexander 2
  Wilbourne
WEDDELL, Donald J. 3
WEDDERBURN, Joseph 2
  Henry MacLagan
WEDDERSPOON, William 1
  Rhind
WEDDINGTON, Frank 4
  Ruel
WEDEL, Cynthia Clark 9
WEDEL, Paul John 5
WEDEL, Theodore Otto 5
WEDELL, Hugo Theodore 4
WEDEMEYER, Albert 10
  Coady
WEDEMEYER, William 1
  Walter
WEDER, Erwin Henry 10
WEDGE, George Anson 8
WEE, Mons O. 2
WEED, Alonzo Rogers 1
WEED, Charles Frederick 1
WEED, Clarence Moores 1
WEED, Clive 1
WEED, Clyde E. 6
WEED, Edwin Gardner 1
WEED, Frank Watkins 2
WEED, George Ludington 1
WEED, Herbert M. 10
WEED, Hugh Hourston 3
  Craigie
WEED, J. Spencer 5
WEED, Jefferson 4
WEED, Leroy Jefferson 4
WEED, Lewis Hill 3
WEED, Oliver Eugene 7
WEED, Samuel Richards 1
WEED, Smith Mead 1
WEED, Theodore Linus 5
WEED, Thurlow H

WEED, Walter Harvey 2
WEEDEN, Norman Dexter 10
WEEDEN, William 1
  Babcock
WEEDON, Leslie 1
  Washington
WEEG, Gerard Paul 7
WEEKLEY, William 1
  Marion
WEEKS, Alanson 2
WEEKS, Andrew Jackson 1
WEEKS, Arland Deyett 1
WEEKS, Bartow Sumter 1
WEEKS, Benjamin D. 3
WEEKS, Carl 4
WEEKS, Charles Carson 10
WEEKS, Charles Peter 1
WEEKS, David Fairchild 1
WEEKS, Edgar 1
WEEKS, Edward Augustus 10
WEEKS, Edwin Lord 1
WEEKS, Edwin Ruthven 1
WEEKS, Francis Darling 4
WEEKS, Frank Bentley 1
WEEKS, George H. 1
WEEKS, Grenville Mellen 1
WEEKS, H. Hobart 3
WEEKS, Harry Curtis 6
WEEKS, John A. 1
WEEKS, John Eliakim 2
WEEKS, John Elmer 2
WEEKS, John L. 3
WEEKS, John Wingate H
WEEKS, John Wingate 1
WEEKS, Joseph H
WEEKS, Joseph Dame H
WEEKS, Lawrence B. 8
WEEKS, Lewis George 7
WEEKS, Mary Harmon 1
WEEKS, Oliver Douglas 10
WEEKS, Ralph Emerson 1
WEEKS, Raymond 3
WEEKS, Robert Kelley 1
WEEKS, Rufus Wells 1
WEEKS, Ruth Mary 7
WEEKS, Sinclair 5
WEEKS, Solan William 8
WEEKS, Stephen 1
  Beauregard
WEEKS, Stephen Holmes 1
WEEKS, Walter Scott 2
WEEKS, William Raymond 4
WEEMS, Capell Lain 4
WEEMS, Frank Taylor 10
WEEMS, John Crompton H
WEEMS, Julius Buel 1
WEEMS, Katharine Lane 4
WEEMS, Mason Locke H
WEEMS, Philip V(an) 7
  H(orn)
WEEMS, Wharton Ewell 4
WEER, John Henry 1
WEESE, A. O. 3
WEET, Herbert Seeley 1
WEFALD, Knud 1
WEGEMANN, Carroll 1
  Harvey
WEGENER, Theodore H. 3
WEGER, George Stephen 1
WEGG, David Spencer 1
WEGLEIN, David Emrich 5
WEGLOSKI, Daniel Joseph 10
WEGMANN, Edward 1
WEGNER, Earl Edward 7
WEGNER, Nicholas H. 7
WEHE, Frank Rumrill 1
WEHLE, Louis Brandeis 3
WEHLER, Charles 4
  Emanuel
WEHLING, Louis Albert 6
WEHMEYER, Lewis 5
  E(dgar)
WEHR, Frederick Lewis 7
WEHR, Perry Neal, Jr. 7
WEHRHAN, Nelson W. 6
WEHRLE, Vincent 2
WEHRLE, William Otto 3
  Joseph
WEHRMANN, Henry 5
WEHRWEIN, George 2
  Simon
WEIB, Taylor Bladen 7
WEIBLE, Rillmond 5
  Fernando
WEIBLE, Walter Leo 7
WEIBY, Maxwell Oliver 4
WEICHEL, Alvin F. 4
WEICHER, John 5
WEICHLEIN, William 9
  Jesset
WEICHSEL, Christial 5
  C(arl)
WEICKER, Lowell Palmer 7
WEICKER, Theodore 1
WEICKER, Theodore 5
WEIDA, Frank Mark 7

WEIDENAAR, Reynold 9
  Henry
WEIDENMANN, Jacob H
WEIDENMILLER, Carl 8
  Reed
WEIDHOPF, J. S. 8
WEIDIG, Adolf 1
WEIDLEIN, Edward Ray 6
WEIDLER, Albert Greer 3
WEIDLER, Deleth Eber 4
WEIDLER, Victor 3
  Otterbein
WEIDMAN, Charles 6
WEIDMAN, Frederick 3
  Deforest
WEIDMAN, Samuel 2
WEIDNER, Carl A. 1
WEIDNER, Charles 10
  Kenneth
WEIDNER, Revere 1
  Franklin
WEIER, T. Elliott 10
WEIGAND, Hermann John 9
WEIGEL, Albert Charles 4
WEIGEL, Eugene John 6
WEIGEL, George Kibler 5
WEIGEL, John C. 7
WEIGEL, William 1
WEIGEL, William 10
  Frederick
WEIGER, Robert William 8
WEIGHARDT, Paul 10
WEIGHTMAN, Richard 1
  Coxe
WEIGHTMAN, Richard H
  Hanson
WEIGHTMAN, Richard 7
  Hanson
WEIGLE, Clifford Francis 7
WEIGLE, Edwin F. 8
WEIGLE, Luther Allan 7
WEIGLE, Luther Allen 6
WEIK, Jesse William 3
WEIK, Mary Hays 7
WEIKEL, Anna Hamlin 5
WEIKEL, Charles Henry 5
  Harrison
WEIL, A. Leo 1
WEIL, Adolph Leopold 3
WEIL, Ann Yezner 5
WEIL, Arthur 7
WEIL, Carl 1
WEIL, Ferdinand Theobald 8
WEIL, Frank L. 3
WEIL, Fred Alban 1
WEIL, Irving 1
WEIL, Kurt Hermann 10
WEIL, Lee Herman 5
WEIL, Louis A. 3
WEIL, Morris 9
WEIL, Oscar 4
WEIL, Reuben W. 7
WEIL, Richard, Jr. 3
WEIL, Robert T. 6
WEILAND, Christian 3
  Frederick van Leeuwen
WEILER, Emanuel 7
  Thornton
WEILER, Royal William 2
WEILL, Harold 8
WEILL, Kurt 3
WEILL, Michel David 7
WEILL, Milton 4
WEIMAN, Rita 3
WEIMAR, Karl Siegfried 9
WEIMER, Albert Barnes 1
WEIMER, Aloysius George 7
WEIMER, Arthur Martin 9
WEIMER, Bernal Robinson 5
WEIMER, Claud F. 3
WEIN, Samuel 8
WEINBERG, Abraham 7
  Joseph
WEINBERG, Arthur 9
WEINBERG, Benjamin 5
  Franklin
WEINBERG, Bernard 5
WEINBERG, Chester 9
WEINBERG, Elbert 10
WEINBERG, Jack 9
WEINBERG, Max Hess 9
WEINBERG, Robert 6
  Charles
WEINBERG, Sidney James 5
WEINBERG, Tobias 5
WEINBERGER, Aloplh 9
WEINBERGER, Bernhard 5
  Wolf
WEINBERGER, Jacob 6
WEINBERGER, Jacob 7
WEINER, Egon 6
WEINER, Joseph Lee 6
WEINERMAN, Edwin 5
  Richard
WEINERT, Albert 2
WEINERT, Hilda B. 9
WEINFELD, Edward 9

WEINFELD, Marsha 10
  Elaine
WEINGARTEN, Joe 4
WEINGARTEN, Joe 7
WEINGARTEN, Lawrence 6
  A.
WEINHANDL, Ferdinand 6
WEINIG, Arthur John 4
WEINMAN, Adolph 3
  Alexander
WEINMAN, Carl Andrew 7
WEINMANN, Joseph Peter 4
WEINMANN, Louis 7
  Randolph
WEINREICH, Uriel 4
WEINSTEIN, Alexander 2
WEINSTEIN, Boris 8
WEINSTEIN, Israel 10
WEINSTEIN, Jacob Joseph 6
WEINSTEIN, Joe 4
WEINSTOCK, Harris 1
WEINSTOCK, Herbert 5
WEINSTOCK, Max E. 8
WEINTAL, Edward 5
WEINTRAUB, Abraham 6
  Allen
WEINTRAUB, Eugene 10
WEINTRAUB, Joseph 7
WEINTRAUB, Louis 10
WEINTRAUB, Sidney 8
WEINTRAUB, Wiktor 9
WEINTROUB, Benjamin 9
WEINZIRL, Adolph 4
WEIR, Ernest Tener 3
WEIR, F. Roney 1
WEIR, Gordon Bruce 10
WEIR, Hugh C. 1
WEIR, Irene 2
WEIR, J. Alden 1
WEIR, James, Jr. 1
WEIR, John Ferguson 1
WEIR, John M. 2
WEIR, Levi Candee 1
WEIR, Milton Nelson 7
WEIR, Paul 5
WEIR, Robert Fulton 1
WEIR, Robert Walter H
WEIR, Samuel 2
WEIR, W. Victor 4
WEIR, Walter C. 8
WEIR, William Clarence 5
WEIR, William Figley 3
WEIS, Mrs. Charles 9
  William, Jr.
WEISBACH, Harry 7
WEISBERG, Harold 5
  Charles
WEISBERGER, David 4
WEISBLAT, David Irwin 10
WEISBORD, Sam 9
WEISBROD, Benjamin 9
  Harry
WEISE, Arthur James 4
WEISENBURG, Theodore 1
WEISENBURGER, Walter 2
  Bertheau
WEISER, Emilius James 1
WEISER, Harry Boyer 3
WEISER, Johann Conrad H
WEISER, Walter R. 1
WEISFIELD, Leo Herman 9
WEISGERBER, Charles 5
  August
WEISGERBER, William 3
  Edwin
WEISIGER, George Bates 7
WEISIGER, Kendall 6
WEISL, Edwin Louis 5
WEISMAN, Milton Charles 7
WEISMAN, Russell 2
WEISMANN, Walter W. 5
WEISS, Adolph A. 5
WEISS, Albert Paul 1
WEISS, Anton Charles 1
WEISS, Dudley Albert 10
WEISS, Edward Huhner 1
WEISS, George 5
WEISS, George 8
WEISS, Herman Leonard 7
WEISS, Jerome Sidney 7
WEISS, John H
WEISS, John Morris 5
WEISS, Joseph John 10
WEISS, Lawrence Robert 10
WEISS, Leo Abraham 10
WEISS, Lewis Allen 3
WEISS, Louis Stix 3
WEISS, Milton 8
WEISS, Morton N. 9
WEISS, Myron 10
WEISS, Paul Alfred 10
WEISS, Raymond Lee 10
WEISS, Richard Alexander 6
WEISS, Roger William 10
WEISS, Samuel 3
WEISS, Samuel 4
WEISS, Samuel Arthur 7

WEISS, Seymour 5
WEISS, Theodore S. 10
WEISS, William 3
WEISS, William Casper
WEISS, William Erhard 2
WEISSBERGER, L. Arnold
WEISSBLUTH, Mitchel 10
WEISSE, Charles H. 1
WEISSE, Faneuil Dunkin
WEISSERT, Augustus 4
Gordon
WEISSLER, Gerhard 10
Ludwig
WEISSMAN, Arthur 7
WEIST, Dwight Wilson 10
WEITMAN, Robert M. 5
WEITZ, Rudolph Wilson 6
WEITZEL, Edwin Anthony 9
WEITZEL, George Thomas
WEITZEL, Godfrey 4
WEITZEN, Edward H. 10
WEITZMAN, Elliot David 8
WEITZMAN, Ellis 5
WEIZMANN, Chaim 4
WEIZMANN, Chaim 3
WELBORN, Curtis R. 5
WELBORN, Ira Clinton 5
WELBORN, Jesse Floyd 5
WELBY, Amelia Ball H
Coppuck
WELCH, Adonijah Strong H
WELCH, Anthony 4
Cummings
WELCH, Archibald Ashley 1
WELCH, Ashbel H
WELCH, Betty Jo 10
WELCH, Charles Buckley 7
WELCH, Charles Edgar 1
WELCH, Charles Whitefield 2
WELCH, Dale Dennis 6
WELCH, Deshler 4
WELCH, Douglas 5
WELCH, Earl Ellis 10
WELCH, Edward Sohier 7
WELCH, Ernest Rivers 7
WELCH, Frank H
WELCH, George Martin 3
WELCH, Herbert 5
WELCH, Howard A. 3
WELCH, J. Leo 4
WELCH, James Monroe 10
WELCH, James Overman 8
WELCH, John H
WELCH, John Collins 4
WELCH, John David 8
WELCH, John Edgar 5
WELCH, John R. 4
WELCH, Joseph N. 4
WELCH, Kenneth Curtis 9
WELCH, Leo Dewey 7
WELCH, Livingston 6
WELCH, Norman A. 4
WELCH, Paul M. 5
WELCH, Paul R. 3
WELCH, Paul Smith 7
WELCH, Philip Henry H
WELCH, Richard Edwin, 10
Jr.
WELCH, Richard Enlow 10
WELCH, Richard J. 2
WELCH, Robert 8
WELCH, Roy Dickinson 3
WELCH, (Samuel) Earl 9
WELCH, Samuel Wallace 1
WELCH, Stewart Henry 2
WELCH, Thomas Anthony 3
WELCH, Vincent Bogan 8
WELCH, Vincent S. 3
WELCH, W. S. 3
WELCH, William 8
WELCH, William Addams 1
WELCH, William Henry* 1
WELCH, William McNair 5
WELCH, William Wickham H
WELCHER, Amy Ogden 4
WELD, Alfred Winsor 4
WELD, C. Minot 2
WELD, Francis Minot 2
WELD, Frank Augustine 4
WELD, J. Linzee 3
WELD, Laenas Gifford 1
WELD, LeRoy Dougherty 6
WELD, Louis Dwight 7
Harvell
WELD, Stephen Minot 1
WELD, Theodore Dwight H
WELD, Thomas H
WELD, William Ernest 3
WELD, William Ernest 4
WELDIN, John Chilcote 5
WELDON, Charles Dater 1
WELDON, Fredric Edward 7
WELDON, James Brewer 6
WELDON, Lawrence
WELDON, R. Laurence 5
WELFLE, Frederick Edgar 3
WELFLING, Weldon 7

WELFORD, Walter 5
WELKE, Edward Arthur 3
WELKER, George Ernest 8
WELKER, Herman 3
WELKER, Philip Albert 1
WELKER, William Henry 3
WELLBORN, Marshall H
Johnson
WELLBORN, Maximilian 4
Bethune
WELLBORN, Olin 1
WELLBORN, Olin, III 4
WELLDON, Samuel A. 4
WELLER, Augustus 10
Bookstaver
WELLER, Carl Vernon 3
WELLER, Charles 4
Frederick
WELLER, Charles Heald 1
WELLER, Edwin 10
Estabrook
WELLER, Frank I. 3
WELLER, Fred Warren 4
WELLER, George Emery 1
WELLER, Herman Gayle 9
WELLER, John B. H
WELLER, Leroy 5
WELLER, Michael Ignatius 1
WELLER, Ovington E. 2
WELLER, Reginald Heber 1
WELLER, Royal H. 1
WELLER, Stuart 1
WELLES, Charles F. H
WELLES, Donald Phelps 1
WELLES, Edgar Thaddeus 1
WELLES, Edward Kenneth 1
WELLES, Edward 10
Randolph
WELLES, George Denison 2
WELLES, Gideon H
WELLES, Henry Hunter, 2
Jr.
WELLES, James Bell 1
WELLES, Kenneth Brakeley 3
WELLES, Noah H
WELLES, Orson 9
WELLES, Roger 1
WELLES, Sumner 4
WELLESZ, Egon Joseph 6
WELLFORD, Edwin 3
Taliaferro
WELLHOUSE, Frederick 1
WELLING, James Clarke H
WELLING, John C. 4
WELLING, Milton Holmes 5
WELLING, Richard 2
WELLINGTON, Arthur H
Mellen
WELLINGTON, C. G. 3
WELLINGTON, Charles 1
WELLINGTON, Charles 3
Oliver
WELLINGTON, George 1
Brainerd
WELLINGTON, George 1
Louis
WELLINGTON, Herbert 4
Galbraith
WELLINGTON, Richard 6
WELLINGTON, William
H.
WELLIVER, Judson 2
Churchill
WELLIVER, Lester Allen 6
WELLMAN, Arthur 2
Holbrook
WELLMAN, Arthur Ogden 9
WELLMAN, Beth Lucy 3
WELLMAN, Charles Aaron 5
WELLMAN, Creighton 5
WELLMAN, Francis L. 2
WELLMAN, Guy 1
WELLMAN, Harvey
Russell
WELLMAN, Hiller Crowell 3
WELLMAN, Holley
Garfield
WELLMAN, Mabel 5
Thacher
WELLMAN, Paul Iselin 4
WELLMAN, Rita (Mrs. 8
Edgar F. Leo)
WELLMAN, Samuel 9
Knowlton
WELLMAN, Samuel 1
Thomas
WELLMAN, Sargent 4
Holbrook
WELLMAN, Walter 1
WELLMAN, William 6
Augustus
WELLONS, William Brock H
WELLS, Addison E. 1
WELLS, Agnes Ermina 3
WELLS, Alfred 4
WELLS, Almond Brown 1
WELLS, Amos Russel 1

WELLS, Arthur George 1
WELLS, Arthur Register 3
WELLS, Barbara Jane 7
WELLS, Benjamin Willis 1
WELLS, Brooks Hughes 1
WELLS, Bulkeley 1
WELLS, Calvin 1
WELLS, Card Ovrey 10
WELLS, Carolyn 2
WELLS, Carveth 3
WELLS, Catherine Boott
WELLS, Channing 5
McGregory
WELLS, Charles Arthur 7
WELLS, Charles Edwin 1
WELLS, Charles J(oseph) 6
WELLS, Charles Luke 1
WELLS, Charles Raymond 4
WELLS, Chester 2
WELLS, Daniel Halsey 1
WELLS, David Ames H
WELLS, David Collin 1
WELLS, David Dwight 1
WELLS, Donald A. 5
WELLS, Ebenezer Tracy 4
WELLS, Edgar Herbert 1
WELLS, Edgar Huidekoper 1
WELLS, Edward Curtis 9
WELLS, Edward D. 4
WELLS, Edward Hubbard 1
WELLS, Edward L. 4
WELLS, Edward P. 4
WELLS, Erastus H
WELLS, Everett F. 5
WELLS, Frank Oren 4
WELLS, Frederic De Witt 1
WELLS, Frederic Lyman 4
WELLS, Frederick Brown 3
WELLS, George Burnham 4
WELLS, George Fitch 1
WELLS, George Harlan 5
WELLS, George Miller 3
WELLS, George Ross 7
(Maurice)
WELLS, George 1
Washington
WELLS, George W(illiam) 9
WELLS, Harry Edward 2
WELLS, Harry Gideon 1
WELLS, Harry H. 4
WELLS, Harry Lumm 6
WELLS, Harry Lumm 8
WELLS, Heber Manning 1
WELLS, Henry H
WELLS, Henry Parkhurst 1
WELLS, Herbert George 2
WELLS, Herbert Johnson 1
WELLS, Herbert Wilson 7
WELLS, Hermon J. 3
WELLS, Horace H
WELLS, Horace Lemuel 1
WELLS, Ira Kent 1
WELLS, J. Brent 4
WELLS, James Earl 4
WELLS, James Madison H
WELLS, James Simpson 1
Chester
WELLS, Joel Cheney* 3
WELLS, Joel Reaves 5
WELLS, Joel Reaves, Jr. 10
WELLS, John* H
WELLS, John Ashley 7
WELLS, John Barnes 1
WELLS, John Daniel 1
WELLS, John Edwin 2
WELLS, John Mason 5
WELLS, John Miller 2
WELLS, John Sullivan 1
WELLS, John Walter 1
WELLS, Joseph M(erton) 10
WELLS, Kenneth Robert 3
WELLS, Lemuel Henry 1
WELLS, Linton 6
WELLS, Linton 7
WELLS, Marguerite Jo Van 5
Dalsem (Mrs. Thaddeus
R. Wells)
WELLS, Marguerite Milton 4
WELLS, Mary Evelyn 6
WELLS, Newell Woolsey 4
WELLS, Newton Alonzo 1
WELLS, Oris Vernon 10
WELLS, Orlando William 3
WELLS, Oscar 3
WELLS, Peter Boyd, Jr. 10
WELLS, Philip Patterson 1
WELLS, Ralph Gent 6
WELLS, Ralph Olney 2
WELLS, Richard Harris 9
WELLS, Robert Lomax 9
WELLS, Robert William
WELLS, Roger Clark 2
WELLS, Rolla 2
WELLS, Samuel Calvin
WELLS, Samuel Roberts H
WELLS, Stuart Wilder 5
WELLS, Theodore D(onald) 5

WELLS, Thomas Bucklin 2
WELLS, Thomas Tileston 2
WELLS, Walter Farrington 3
WELLS, Webster 1
WELLS, Wesley Raymond 8
WELLS, William Calvin 3
WELLS, William Charles H
WELLS, William Charles 1
WELLS, William Edwin 1
WELLS, William Firth 8
WELLS, William Harvey H
WELLS, William Hill H
WELLS, William Hughes 1
WELLS, William Vincent H
WELLS, William Widney 5
WELLSTOOD, William 1
WELS, Richard Hoffman 10
WELSH, Ashton Leroy 4
WELSH, Charles 1
WELSH, Edward Cristy 10
WELSH, George A. 6
WELSH, George A. 5
WELSH, George Wilson 6
WELSH, Harry Lambert 8
WELSH, Herbert 1
WELSH, James Leroy 9
WELSH, John H
WELSH, John Rushing 6
WELSH, Judson Perry 4
WELSH, Leslie Thomas 9
WELSH, Lilian 4
WELSH, Martin I. 7
WELSH, Robert James 5
WELSH, Robert Kaye 2
WELSH, Vernon M. 5
WELSH, William Peter 9
WELSHIMER, Helen 4
Louise
WELSHIMER, Pearl H. 3
WELT, Mrs. Joseph M. 8
(Mildred Goldsmith Welt)
WELTE, Carl Michael 3
WELTE, Herbert David 9
WELTMER, (Cyrus) Ernest 6
WELTMER, Sidney Abram 1
WELTNER, Charles 10
Longstreet
WELTNER, Philip 8
WELTON, Thurston Scott 7
WELTY, Benjamin Franklin 5
WEMPLE, William Lester 1
WEMPLE, William Yates 1
WEMYSS, Francis Courtney H
WEMYSS, William Hatch 5
WEN, Chin Yung 8
WENCHEL, John Philip 4
WENCKEBACH, Carla 1
WENDE, Ernest 1
WENDEL, Hugo Christian 2
Martin
WENDEL, William Hall 10
WENDELL, Arthur Rindge 3
WENDELL, Barrett 1
WENDELL, Edith 1
Greenough
WENDELL, George 1
Vincent
WENDELL, James Isaac 3
WENDELL, Oliver Clinton 1
WENDEN, Henry Edward 10
WENDEROTH, Oscar 5
WENDLAND, John 7
Prentice
WENDLING, George 1
Reuben
WENDOVER, Peter H
Hercules
WENDT, Edgar Forsyth 8
WENDT, Edwin Frederick 3
WENDT, George Richard 7
WENDT, Gerald (Louis) 6
WENDT, Henry W. 4
WENDT, Julia Bracken 2
WENDT, Kurt Frank 8
WENDT, William 2
WENDTE, Charles William 1
WENE, Elmer H. 3
WENG, Armin George 10
WENGENROTH, Stow 7
WENGER, Arthur Daniel 7
WENGER, Joseph Numa 5
WENGER, Oliver Clarence 3
WENGERT, Egbert 4
Semmann
WENIGER, Willibald 3
WENKE, Adolph E. 4
WENLEY, Archibald 4
Gibson
WENLEY, Robert Mark 1
WENNAGEL, Leonard 6
Alvin
WENNER, Frank 3
WENNER, George Unangst 1
WENNER, Howard
Theodore
WENNER, William Ervin 2
WENNERSTRUM, Charles 9

WENNERSTRUM, Charles 8
F.
WENNING, T. H. 4
WENNINGER, Francis 1
Joseph
WENRICH, Calvin 5
Naftzinger
WENSLEY, Robert Lytle 4
WENTE, Carl Frederick 5
WENTE, Edward 5
Christopher
WENTWORTH, Benning H
WENTWORTH, Catherine 2
Denkman
WENTWORTH, Cecile De 1
WENTWORTH, Edward 3
Norris
WENTWORTH, Edward 7
Tubbs
WENTWORTH, Franklin 3
Harcourt
WENTWORTH, Fred 2
Wesley
WENTWORTH, George 1
Albert
WENTWORTH, John* H
WENTWORTH, John 3
WENTWORTH, John, Jr. H
WENTWORTH, Marion 5
Craig
WENTWORTH, Paul H
WENTWORTH, Ralph 8
Strafford
WENTWORTH, Reginald 7
A.
WENTWORTH, Tappan H
WENTWORTH, Walter 5
Allerton
WENTWORTH, William H
Pitt
WENTZ, Abdel Ross 7
WENTZ, Daniel Bertsch, Jr. 4
WENTZ, George Elmore 4
WENTZ, Louis Haines 2
WENTZ, Peter Leland 6
WENTZEL, Gregor 7
WENTZELL, Cecil Rodney 8
WENZEL, Caroline 3
WENZEL, Lee Bey 10
WENZEL, Thomas Philip 6
WENZELL, Albert Beck 1
WENZELL, Henry Burleigh 4
WENZLAFF, Gustav 4
Gottlieb
WENZLICK, Roy 9
WEPPNER, Oliver A. 5
WERBE, Thomas Chandler, 3
Sr.
WERDEN, Reed H
WERDEN, Robert M. 5
WERDER, Xavier Oswald 1
WERFEL, Franz 2
WERKER, Henry Frederick 8
WERKMAN, Chester 4
Hamlin
WERLE, Edward C. 4
WERLEIN, Elizabeth 2
Thomas
WERMUTH, Burt 6
WERNAER, Robert 5
Maximilian
WERNER, Adolph 1
WERNER, Alfred 7
WERNER, Anthony 10
Matthias
WERNER, August 7
Anthony
WERNER, Edwin H. 6
WERNER, Heinz 3
WERNER, Henry Paul 3
WERNER, Henry Paul 4
WERNER, Joseph Gustave 6
WERNER, Max 3
WERNER, Oscar Emil 3
Wade
WERNER, (Robert) Mort 10
WERNER, Victor Davis 5
WERNER, Walter 9
WERNER, William E. 1
WERNER, William 7
G(eorge)
WERNER, William M. 3
WERNETTE, Nicodemus 1
D.
WERNTZ, William Welling 4
WERNWAG, Lewis H
WERRENRATH, Reinald 3
WERT, James Edwin 4
WERTENBAKER, Charles 3
Christian
WERTENBAKER, Charles 1
Poindexter
WERTENBAKER, Thomas 4
Jefferson
WERTH, Alexander 5
WERTHAM, Fredric 8
WERTHEIM, Edgar 9

269

WERTHEIM, Maurice 3
WERTIME, Theodore Allen 8
WERTMAN, Floyd Rollan 2
WERTMAN, Kenneth Franklin 4
WERTMULLER, Adolph Ulrich H
WERTS, George Theodore 1
WERTZ, Edwin Slusser 2
WERTZ, George M. 1
WERWATH, Karl Oscar 7
WESBROOK, Frank Fairchild 1
WESCOAT, L. S. 5
WESCOTT, Cassius Douglas 2
WESCOTT, Glenway 9
WESCOTT, James Barney 3
WESCOTT, John Wesley 1
WESCOTT, Orville De Witt 5
WESCOTT, Thurman Cary 8
WESEEN, Maurice Harley 1
WESLEY, Charles Harris 9
WESLEY, Charles Sumner 1
WESLEY, Clarence Newton 5
WESLEY, Edgar Bruce 7
WESSEL, Carl John 9
WESSEL, Harold Cosby 10
WESSEL, Milton R. 10
WESSELHOEFT, Conrad 1
WESSELHOEFT, Lily Foster 1
WESSELHOFT, Walter 4
WESSELINK, John 5
WESSELLS, Henry Walton, Jr. 1
WESSLINK, Gerritt William 4
WESSON, Charles Macon 3
WESSON, Daniel Baird 1
WESSON, David 1
WESSON, Miley Barton 6
WESSON, Robert G. 10
WEST, Allen Brown 1
WEST, Andrew Fleming 2
WEST, Anson 1
WEST, Anthony Panther 9
WEST, Archa Kelly 5
WEST, Arthur 5
WEST, Arthur Benjamin 5
WEST, Ben 6
WEST, Benjamin* H
WEST, Caleb Walton 1
WEST, Reverend Canon Edward Nason 10
WEST, Carl Joseph 7
WEST, Charles 5
WEST, Charles Cameron 3
WEST, Charles Edwin 1
WEST, Charles H. 1
WEST, Charles Tyrrell 5
WEST, Charles W. 10
WEST, Christopher 6
WEST, Clifford Hardy 10
WEST, Dottie (Dorothy Marie Marsh)* 10
WEST, Duval 3
WEST, E. Lovette 2
WEST, Eben Moreau 7
WEST, Edward Augustus 3
WEST, Edward Staunton 10
WEST, Egbert Watson 2
WEST, Elizabeth Howard 1
WEST, Erdman 4
WEST, Ernest Holley 5
WEST, Francis H
WEST, George H
WEST, George Henry 1
WEST, George N. 1
WEST, George V. 6
WEST, Hamilton Atchison 4
WEST, Helen Hunt 1
WEST, Henry Litchfield 4
WEST, Henry Sergeant H
WEST, Henry Skinner 1
WEST, Herbert Buell 10
WEST, Herbert Faulkner 6
WEST, Howard H(iram) 1
WEST, James Edward 2
WEST, James Harcourt 4
WEST, James Hartwell 4
WEST, James Samuel 5
WEST, Jessamyn 8
WEST, Jesse Felix 1
WEST, John Chester 4
WEST, John Dunham 10
WEST, Joseph H
WEST, Judson S. 3
WEST, Junius Edgar 2
WEST, Kenyon 4
WEST, Levon 5
WEST, Louis Caulton 7
WEST, Luther Shirley 9
WEST, Mae 4
WEST, Mary Brodie Crump 4
WEST, Max 1
WEST, Millard F. 1

WEST, Milton H. 2
WEST, Nathanael H
WEST, Nathanael 4
WEST, Olin 3
WEST, Oswald 5
WEST, Paul 1
WEST, Paul Brown 1
WEST, Preston C. 5
WEST, Raymond M. 1
WEST, Rebecca (Cicily Isabel Fairfield) 8
WEST, Rhea Horace, Jr. 10
WEST, Robert Hunter 10
WEST, Robert Nias 8
WEST, Robert Rout 4
WEST, Roger Blake 7
WEST, Roy Owen 3
WEST, Samuel H
WEST, Samuel H. 1
WEST, Samuel Wallens 5
WEST, Thomas H
WEST, Thomas Dyson 1
WEST, Thomas Franklin 1
WEST, Thomas Hector 6
WEST, Thomas Henry 1
WEST, Thomas Henry 4
WEST, Thomas Henry, Jr. 1
WEST, Victor J. 1
WEST, William Edward H
WEST, William Henry 1
WEST, William John 9
WEST, William Nelson 7
WEST, William Stanley 1
WEST, Willis Mason 5
WESTBROOK, Arthur E. 4
WESTBROOK, Elroy 1
WESTBROOK, Herman
WESTBROOK, James Seymour 8
WESTBROOK, John H
WESTBROOK, Lawrence 4
WESTBROOK, Patrick Alan de Lujan 10
WESTBROOK, Theodoric Romeyn H
WESTBY, Gerald Holinbeck 8
WESTCOTT, Allan Ferguson 3
WESTCOTT, Charles Drake 5
WESTCOTT, Edward Noyes H
WESTCOTT, Frank Nash 1
WESTCOTT, George Lamar 10
WESTCOTT, Harry R. 6
WESTCOTT, James Diament, Jr. H
WESTCOTT, John Howell 2
WESTCOTT, Linn Hanson 7
WESTCOTT, Ralph Merrill 8
WESTCOTT, Richard Nutter 6
WESTCOTT, Thompson H
WESTCOTT, Thompson Seiser 3
WESTENGARD, Jens Iverson 1
WESTENHAVER, David C. 1
WESTERFIELD, Ray Bert 4
WESTERFIELD, Samuel Zaza, Jr. 5
WESTERGAARD, Harald Malcolm 3
WESTERGAARD, Waldemar Christian 7
WESTERLO, Rensselaer H
WESTERMAN, Harry James 2
WESTERMANN, Horace Clifford 8
WESTERMANN, William Linn 3
WESTERMEYER, H(arry) E(dward) 6
WESTERN, Forrest 5
WESTERN, Lucille H
WESTERVELT, Emery Emmanuel 4
WESTERVELT, Esther Julia Manning 6
WESTERVELT, Jacob Aaron H
WESTERVELT, Marvin Zabriskie 1
WESTERVELT, William Irving 3
WESTERVELT, William Young 3
WESTFALL, Alfred R. 1
WESTFALL, Byron Lee 5
WESTFALL, Katherine Storey 1
WESTFALL, Othel D. 4
WESTFALL, W. D. A. 3
WESTFELDT, George G(ustaf) 6

WESTGATE, John Minton 1
WESTGATE, Lewis Gardner 2
WESTGREN, Arne Fredrik 9
WESTHAFER, William Rader 2
WESTHEIMER, Irvin Ferdinand 7
WESTHUES, Henry J. 5
WESTINGHOUSE, George 1
WESTINGHOUSE, Henry Herman 1
WESTINGHOUSE, Marguerite Erskine Walker 1
WESTLAKE, Emory H. 4
WESTLAKE, J. Willis 1
WESTLEY, George Hembert 1
WESTMEYER, Troy Rudolph 9
WESTMORE, George Bud 6
WESTON, Charles 9
WESTON, Charles H(artshorne) 1
WESTON, Charles Sidney 2
WESTON, Charles Valentine 1
WESTON, Edmund Brownell 1
WESTON, Edward 1
WESTON, Edward 3
WESTON, Edward F. 5
WESTON, Edward Payson 1
WESTON, Elizabeth Stewart 6
WESTON, Eugene, Jr. 5
WESTON, Francis Hopkins 4
WESTON, Frank Morey 5
WESTON, George 5
WESTON, Harold 5
WESTON, Harry Elisha 1
WESTON, Henry Griggs 1
WESTON, James Augustus 1
WESTON, James Francis 3
WESTON, John Burns 1
WESTON, John Francis 1
WESTON, Karl Ephraim 3
WESTON, Melvile Fuller 1
WESTON, Nathan Austin 1
WESTON, Robert Spurr 2
WESTON, S. Burns 1
WESTON, Sidney Adams 5
WESTON, Stephen Francis 1
WESTON, Theodore 1
WESTON, Thomas H
WESTON, Willard Garfield 7
WESTON, William 5
WESTON, William Henry, Jr. 8
WESTOVER, Harry Clay 8
WESTOVER, Myron F. 1
WESTOVER, Oscar 1
WESTOVER, Russell Channing 4
WESTOVER, Russell Channing 7
WESTOVER, Wendell 1
WESTPHAL, Everett August 10
WESTWELL, Arthur Evans 9
WESTWOOD, Horace 7
WESTWOOD, Richard W. 4
WETENHALL, J(ohn) Huber H
WETHERALD, Charles E. 5
WETHERBEE, Frank Irving 5
WETHERBEE, George 4
WETHERED, John H
WETHERELL, Carl Bradlee 1
WETHERELL, Elizabeth H
WETHERILL, Charles Mayer H
WETHERILL, Horace Greeley 4
WETHERILL, Samuel* 1
WETHERILL, Samuel Price 7
WETHEY, Harold Edwin 9
WETJEN, Albert Richard 2
WETMORE, Alexander 7
WETMORE, Claude Hazeltine 4
WETMORE, Edmund 1
WETMORE, Edward Ditmars 2
WETMORE, Elizabeth Bisland 1
WETMORE, Frank O. 1
WETMORE, Frank Orton, II 10
WETMORE, George 1
WETMORE, George Peabody 1
WETMORE, Horace Orton 7

WETMORE, James Alphonso 1
WETMORE, Maude A. K. 3
WETMORE, Monroe Nichols 3
WETMORE, Ralph Hartley 9
WETTACH, Robert Hasley 4
WETTEN, Albert Hayes 3
WETTEN, Emil C. 2
WETTERAU, Oliver George 6
WETTERAU, Theodore Carl, Jr. 5
WETTLING, Louis Eugene 1
WETZEL, Harry H. 1
WETZEL, John Wesley 2
WETZEL, Lewis H
WETZLER, Benjamin 7
WETZLER, Joseph 1
WEXLER, Harry 4
WEXLER, Jacob 6
WEXLER, Jerrold 10
WEXLER, Max Mendel 10
WEXLER, Solomon 1
WEYAND, Ruth 10
WEYANDT, Carl Stanley 4
WEYBRIGHT, Victor 7
WEYBURN, Lyon 4
WEYER, Edward Moffat 5
WEYER, Frank E(lmer) 9
WEYERBACHER, Arthur 7
WEYERBACHER, Ralph Downs 8
WEYERHAEUSER, Charles Augustus 1
WEYERHAEUSER, Frederick 1
WEYERHAEUSER, Frederick Edward 2
WEYERHAEUSER, John Philip 1
WEYERHAEUSER, John Philip, Jr. 3
WEYERHAEUSER, Rudolph Michael 2
WEYERHAEUSER, Vivian O'Gara (Mrs. Frederick K. Weyerhaeuser) 8
WEYGANDT, Carl Victor 4
WEYGANDT, Cornelius 1
WEYHE, Erhard 5
WEYL, Charles 5
WEYL, Hermann 3
WEYL, Max 1
WEYL, Walter Edward 1
WEYL, Woldemar Anatol 6
WEYL, Woldemar Anatol 7
WEYLAND, Louis Frederick 10
WEYLER, George Lester 5
WEYMOUTH, Aubrey 1
WEYMOUTH, Clarence Raymond 2
WEYMOUTH, Frank Elwin 1
WEYMOUTH, George Warren 1
WEYMOUTH, Thomas Rote 3
WEYRAUCH, Martin Henry 3
WEYSSE, Arthur Wisswald 5
WHALEN, Grover A. 4
WHALEN, John 1
WHALEN, Robert E. 3
WHALEN, Will Wilfrid 7
WHALEY, A. R. 4
WHALEY, George P. 1
WHALEY, James V. 4
WHALEY, Kellian Van Rensalear H
WHALEY, Percival Huntington 4
WHALEY, Randall McVay 10
WHALEY, Richard Smith 3
WHALEY, W(illiam) Gordon 8
WHALING, Horace Morland 6
WHALING, Thornton 4
WHALLEY, Edward H
WHALLEY, J. Irving 7
WHALLON, Edward Payson 1
WHALLON, Reuben H
WHALLON, Walter Lowrie 6
WHAM, Benjamin 5
WHAPLES, Meigs H. 1
WHAREY, James Blanton 2
WHARTON, Anne Hollingsworth 1
WHARTON, Arthur Orlando 5
WHARTON, Carol Forbes 3
WHARTON, Charles Henry H
WHARTON, Charles S. 5

WHARTON, Cyrus Richard 8
WHARTON, Edith 1
WHARTON, Elizabeth Austin 9
WHARTON, Francis H
WHARTON, Henry Marvin 1
WHARTON, Henry Redwood 1
WHARTON, Hunter Poisal 7
WHARTON, James E. 2
WHARTON, James Pearce 4
WHARTON, Jesse 1
WHARTON, John Franklin 7
WHARTON, Joseph 1
WHARTON, Lang 2
WHARTON, Morton Bryan 1
WHARTON, Richard H
WHARTON, Robert 1
WHARTON, Samuel H
WHARTON, Theodore Finley 2
WHARTON, Thomas H
WHARTON, Thomas Isaac H
WHARTON, Thomas Kelah H
WHARTON, Tilford Girard 10
WHARTON, Turner Ashby 1
WHARTON, Vernon Lane 4
WHARTON, William Fisher 1
WHARTON, William H. H
WHARTON, William P 6
WHATCOAT, Richard H
WHATLEY, Barney Lee 7
WHATLEY, Brown Lee 8
WHATMORE, Marvin Clement 8
WHATMOUGH, Joshua 4
WHAYNE, Alfred Trevor 9
WHEALON, John Francis 10
WHEAT, Alfred Adams 2
WHEAT, Carl Irving 4
WHEAT, George Seay 1
WHEAT, Harry G(rove) 6
WHEAT, Harry G(rove) 7
WHEAT, Renville 5
WHEAT, William Howard 2
WHEATLAND, Marcus Fitzherbert 1
WHEATLAND, Stephen 10
WHEATLEY, Archer 7
WHEATLEY, Phillis H
WHEATLEY, Richard 4
WHEATLEY, William H
WHEATLEY, William Alonzo 5
WHEATON, Frank 1
WHEATON, Harrison Hylas 7
WHEATON, Henry H
WHEATON, Horace H
WHEATON, Laban H
WHEATON, Loyd 1
WHEATON, Nathaniel Sheldon H
WHEATON, William Lindus Cody 7
WHEDON, Daniel Denison H
WHEDON, John Fielding 5
WHEELAN, Fairfax Henry 4
WHEELAN, James Nicholas 1
WHEELER, Albert Gallatin 1
WHEELER, Albert Harry 5
WHEELER, Alexander 8
WHEELER, Alvin Sawyer 1
WHEELER, Andrew Carpenter 1
WHEELER, Arthur Dana 1
WHEELER, Arthur Leslie 1
WHEELER, Arthur Martin 1
WHEELER, Benjamin Ide 1
WHEELER, Burr 4
WHEELER, Burton Kendall 6
WHEELER, C. Gilbert 1
WHEELER, Candace Thurber 1
WHEELER, Candace Thurber 2
WHEELER, Charles (Reginald) 6
WHEELER, Charles Barker 1
WHEELER, Charles Brewster 2
WHEELER, Charles Francis 6
WHEELER, Charles Gardner 3
WHEELER, Charles Kennedy 4
WHEELER, Charles Leigh 9
WHEELER, Charles Stetson 1
WHEELER, Dan Hubert 7
WHEELER, Daniel Davis 1

WHITE, J. Campbell 4
WHITE, J. Du Pratt 1
WHITE, J. Harrison 4
WHITE, J. Warren 4
WHITE, Jack Edward 9
WHITE, Jacob Lee 2
WHITE, James* H
WHITE, James A. 2
WHITE, James Andrew 1
WHITE, James Asa 7
WHITE, James Bain H
WHITE, James Barlow 4
WHITE, James Charles 5
WHITE, James Clarke 1
WHITE, James Clarke 7
WHITE, James Dempsey 4
WHITE, James Dugald 9
WHITE, James Gilbert 2
WHITE, James Halley 5
WHITE, James McLaren 1
WHITE, James Terry 1
WHITE, James Watson 2
WHITE, James William 1
WHITE, Jay 1
WHITE, Jerome Baker 7
WHITE, Jesse Hayes 5
WHITE, Joan Fulton 6
WHITE, John* H
WHITE, John Baker 4
WHITE, John Barber 1
WHITE, John Beaver 5
WHITE, John Blake H
WHITE, John Blake 4
WHITE, John Campbell 4
WHITE, John Chanler 3
WHITE, John Dehaven H
WHITE, John Ellington 1
WHITE, John Griswold 1
WHITE, John Hazen 1
WHITE, John Jamieson, Jr. 8
WHITE, John P. 5
WHITE, John Phillip 5
WHITE, John Roberts 4
WHITE, John Stuart 1
WHITE, John Turner 2
WHITE, John W. 3
WHITE, John William 7
WHITE, John Williams 1
WHITE, John Z. 4
WHITE, Joseph Augustus 4
WHITE, Joseph Hill 5
WHITE, Joseph Livingston H
WHITE, Joseph M. H
WHITE, Joseph H
Worthington
WHITE, Josh 5
WHITE, Joshua Warren 3
WHITE, Julius 9
WHITE, Katharine Elkus 8
WHITE, Katharine 9
S(ergeant)
WHITE, Kathleen Merell 6
WHITE, Keith Merrill 10
WHITE, Kemble 5
WHITE, Lawrence Grant 3
WHITE, Lazarus 3
WHITE, Lee A. 5
WHITE, Leland Marion 7
WHITE, Leonard H
WHITE, Leonard Dupee 3
WHITE, Leslie Alvin 6
WHITE, Lewis Charles 6
WHITE, Lewis Charles 7
WHITE, Llewellyn Brooke 3
WHITE, Lowell Smiley 10
WHITE, Lucien 6
WHITE, Lucien Wendell 7
WHITE, Lucius Read, Jr. 8
WHITE, Luke Matthews 3
WHITE, Lynn Townsend 3
WHITE, Lynne Loraine 4
WHITE, Marcus 9
WHITE, Marian Ainsworth 5
WHITE, Martin Marshall 7
WHITE, Mastin Gentry 9
WHITE, Matthew, Jr. 1
WHITE, Michael Alfred 4
Edwin
WHITE, Milton Grandison 7
WHITE, Minor Martin 9
WHITE, Nehemiah 1
WHITE, Nelia Gardner 9
WHITE, Newman Ivey 2
WHITE, Octavius Augustus 1
WHITE, Orland Emile 7
WHITE, Orrin Augustine 4
WHITE, Patrick 10
WHITE, Paul Dudley 6
WHITE, Paul W. 3
WHITE, Pearl H
WHITE, Pearl 4
WHITE, Percival 5
WHITE, Peter 1
WHITE, Philip (Rodney) 5
WHITE, Phillips H
WHITE, Phineas H
WHITE, Ray Bridwell 2

WHITE, Raymond Baird 8
WHITE, Richard Grant H
WHITE, Robe Carl 3
WHITE, Robert 1
WHITE, Robert Arthur 7
WHITE, Robert I. 10
WHITE, Robert James 8
WHITE, Robert Vose 4
WHITE, Rodney Douglas 4
WHITE, Rollie Howard, Jr. 4
WHITE, Rollin Henry 4
WHITE, Roy Barton 4
WHITE, Rufus Austin 1
WHITE, Russell Lawrence 9
WHITE, S. Etelka 6
WHITE, S. Marx 4
WHITE, Sallie Joy 1
WHITE, Samuel H
WHITE, Samuel Stockton 4
WHITE, Sebastian Harrison 2
WHITE, Stanford 1
WHITE, Stanley 1
WHITE, Stephen Mallory 1
WHITE, Stephen Van Culen 1
WHITE, Steven Virgil 9
WHITE, Stewart Edward 2
WHITE, Terence Hanbury 4
WHITE, Theo Ballou 7
WHITE, Theodore Harold 9
WHITE, Thomas Dresser 4
WHITE, Thomas Holden 3
WHITE, Thomas Justin 2
WHITE, Thomas P(atrick) 4
WHITE, Thomas Raeburn 3
WHITE, Thomas Willis H
WHITE, Trentwell Mason 5
WHITE, Trueman Clark 1
WHITE, Trumbull 1
WHITE, Trumbull 2
WHITE, W. Wilson 4
WHITE, Wallace 3
Humphrey, Jr.
WHITE, Walter 3
WHITE, Walter C. 1
WHITE, Walter Louis 4
WHITE, Walter Porter 2
WHITE, Walter W(illiam) 5
WHITE, Weldon Bailey 6
WHITE, Wendelyn Florence 6
WHITE, Wilbert Webster 2
WHITE, Wilbur Wallace 3
WHITE, William H
WHITE, William 4
WHITE, William Alanson 1
WHITE, William Alfred 5
WHITE, William Allen 2
WHITE, William Bew 8
WHITE, William Chapman 3
WHITE, William Charles 2
WHITE, William Crawford 4
WHITE, William E. 1
WHITE, William Henry 10
WHITE, William Henry 1
WHITE, William Henry 6
WHITE, William Henry 8
WHITE, William Lawrence 3
WHITE, William Lee 5
WHITE, William L(indsay) 5
WHITE, William Lindsay 3
WHITE, William Lindsay 7
WHITE, William Mathews 4
WHITE, William Monroe 2
WHITE, William Nathaniel H
WHITE, William Parker 2
WHITE, William Patterson 7
WHITE, William Pierrepont 1
WHITE, William Prescott 4
WHITE, William 7
Richardson
WHITE, William R(obert) 8
WHITE, William Wallace 2
WHITE, William Wurts 5
WHITE, Willye Anderson 7
(Mrs. Frederick Hall
White)
WHITE, Wilson Henry 6
Stout
WHITE, Windsor T. 3
WHITE, Winifred Demarest 10
(Mrs. Herbert A. White)
WHITEAKER, Robert O. 3
George
WHITEBROOK, Lloyd 4
George
WHITEBROOK, Robert 10
Ballard
WHITED, F(rank) T(hayer) 9
WHITE EYES H
WHITEFIELD, Edwin H
WHITEFIELD, George H
WHITEFORD, Gilbert 2
Hayes
WHITEFORD, Roger J. 4
WHITEFORD, William 5
Kepler
WHITEHAIR, Charles 1
Wesley

WHITEHAIR, Francis 7
Preston
WHITEHALL, Harold 9
WHITEHEAD, Alfred 2
North
WHITEHEAD, Asa Carter 6
WHITEHEAD, Barry 10
WHITEHEAD, Cabell 1
WHITEHEAD, Cecil Lee 9
WHITEHEAD, Charles 1
Nelson
WHITEHEAD, Cortlandt 1
WHITEHEAD, Don 7
WHITEHEAD, Donald 3
Strehle
WHITEHEAD, Edwin 1
Kirby
WHITEHEAD, Ennis 4
Clement
WHITEHEAD, Frank 8
WHITEHEAD, Harold 6
WHITEHEAD, Henry C. 5
WHITEHEAD, James 1
Thomas
WHITEHEAD, John 1
WHITEHEAD, John 3
Boswell
WHITEHEAD, John Meek 1
WHITEHEAD, Joseph 4
WHITEHEAD, Matthew 10
Jackson
WHITEHEAD, Ralph 1
Radcliffe
WHITEHEAD, Richard 1
Henry
WHITEHEAD, Richard 9
Henry
WHITEHEAD, Robert 5
Frederick
WHITEHEAD, Thomas 3
Hillyer
WHITEHEAD, T(homas) 5
North
WHITEHEAD, Wilbur H
Cherrier
WHITEHEAD, Wilbur 4
Cherrier
WHITEHEAD, William H
Adee
WHITEHEAD, William 9
Grant
WHITEHILL, Clarence 1
WHITEHILL, Henry David 9
WHITEHILL, Howard 4
Joseph
WHITEHILL, James H
WHITEHILL, John H
WHITEHILL, Robert H
WHITEHILL, Walter Muir 7
WHITEHORN, John Clare 10
WHITEHORNE, Earl 1
WHITEHOUSE, Brooks 5
WHITEHOUSE, F. Cope 1
WHITEHOUSE, Florence 5
Brooks
WHITEHOUSE, Harold 7
Clarence
WHITEHOUSE, Henry 4
Remsen
WHITEHOUSE, Horace 3
WHITEHOUSE, James 1
Horton
WHITEHOUSE, John H
Osborne
WHITEHOUSE, Robert 5
Treat
WHITEHOUSE, Sheldon 4
WHITEHOUSE, Sheldon 7
WHITEHOUSE, Vira 5
Boarman (Mrs. Norman
De R. Whitehouse)
WHITEHOUSE, Walter 9
MacIntire
WHITEHOUSE, William 1
Fitz Hugh
WHITEHOUSE, William 1
Penn
WHITEHOUSE, William 9
Whitcomb
WHITEHURST, Camelia 1
WHITEHURST, George W. 9
WHITEHURST, John 1
Leyburn
WHITEIS, William Robert 5
WHITELAW, John Bertram 5
WHITELAW, Jordan M. 8
WHITELEATHER, Melvin 7
Kerr
WHITELEY, Emily Stone 1
WHITELEY, George Henry 8
WHITELEY, Isabel Nixon 5
WHITELEY, James 5
Gustavus
WHITELEY, Richard H
Henry
WHITELEY, William H
Gustavus

WHITELEY, William 10
Richard, Sr.
WHITELOCK, George 1
WHITELOCK, Louis 1
Clarkson
WHITELOCK, Louise 4
Clarkson
WHITELOCK, William 1
Wallace
WHITEMAN, Paul 4
WHITEMAN, Samuel 5
Dickey
WHITENACK, Carolyn 8
Irene
WHITENER, Basil Lee 10
WHITENER, Paul A. W. 3
WHITENTON, William 1
Maynard
WHITER, Edward Tait 4
WHITESELL, Faris Daniel 10
WHITESELL, William M. 4
WHITESIDE, Arthur Dare 4
WHITESIDE, Frank Reed 1
WHITESIDE, George 4
Morris, II
WHITESIDE, George 4
Walter
WHITESIDE, Horace 3
Eugene
WHITESIDE, James 1
Leonard
WHITESIDE, Jenkin H
WHITESIDE, John H
WHITESIDE, Stansell 7
Eugene
WHITESIDE, Walker 2
WHITFIELD, Albert Hall 4
WHITFIELD, Allen 8
WHITFIELD, Henry 4
WHITFIELD, Henry Lewis 1
WHITFIELD, J. Edward 1
WHITFIELD, James 2
WHITFIELD, James Bryan 2
WHITFIELD, John Wilkins H
WHITFIELD, Robert 8
Joseph
WHITFIELD, Robert Parr 1
WHITFORD, Alfred 5
E(dward)
WHITFORD, Edward 3
Everett
WHITFORD, Greeley 1
Webster
WHITFORD, Oscar F. 1
WHITFORD, Robert 3
Naylor
WHITFORD, William 1
Calvin
WHITFORD, William 1
Clarke
WHITHORNE, Emerson 3
WHITIN, Ernest Stagg 2
WHITING, Almon Clark 6
WHITING, Arthur 1
WHITING, Borden Durfee 4
WHITING, Charles 1
Goodrich
WHITING, Charles Sumner 1
WHITING, Edward Clark 6
WHITING, Edward Elwell 3
WHITING, Fred 5
WHITING, Fred T. 3
WHITING, Frederic Allen 5
WHITING, George Elbrige 1
WHITING, Gertrude 3
WHITING, Harry Hayes 1
WHITING, Henry H
WHITING, Henry Hyer 1
WHITING, John Downes 7
WHITING, John Talman 1
WHITING, Justin Rice 1
WHITING, Justin Rice 1
WHITING, Lawrence 6
Harley
WHITING, Lilian 2
WHITING, Mary Gray 4
WHITING, Percy Hollister 6
WHITING, Phineas 8
Wescott
WHITING, Richard Henry H
WHITING, Robert Rudd 1
WHITING, Samuel H
WHITING, Sarah Frances 1
WHITING, Walter Rogers 5
WHITING, William H
WHITING, William Alonzo 3
WHITING, William 1
Fairfield
WHITING, William Henry H
WHITING, William Henry, 2
Jr.
WHITING, William Henry H
Chase
WHITINGER, Ralph 8
Judson
WHITLEY, Cora Call 1

WHITLEY, James Lucius 5
WHITLEY, Johnson 5
Decosta
WHITLEY, Joseph Efird 10
WHITLEY, Mary Theodora 6
WHITLEY, Samuel Henry 2
WHITLEY, Wyatt Carr 8
WHITLOCK, Albert 8
Newton
WHITLOCK, Brand 1
WHITLOCK, Eliza Kemble H
WHITLOCK, Elliott 5
Howland
WHITLOCK, E(rnest) 7
Clyde
WHITLOCK, Foster Brand 10
WHITLOCK, Herbert Percy 2
WHITLOCK, Paul 6
Cameron
WHITLOCK, William 1
Francis
WHITMAN, Alfred 3
Freeman
WHITMAN, Ann C. 10
WHITMAN, Armitage 4
WHITMAN, Arthur 3
Dudley
WHITMAN, Benaiah 1
Longley
WHITMAN, Charles 1
Huntington
WHITMAN, Charles Otis 1
WHITMAN, Charles 1
Seymour
WHITMAN, Edmund Allen 5
WHITMAN, Edward A. 2
WHITMAN, Eugene 4
Winfield
WHITMAN, Ezekiel H
WHITMAN, Ezra Bailey 4
WHITMAN, Frank Perkins 1
WHITMAN, Frank S. 1
WHITMAN, Frederic 10
Bennett
WHITMAN, Hendricks 3
Hallett
WHITMAN, Henry Harold 4
WHITMAN, Howard 6
WHITMAN, John Lorin 1
WHITMAN, John Munro 1
WHITMAN, Lemuel H
WHITMAN, Leroy 5
WHITMAN, Malcolm 1
Douglass
WHITMAN, Marcus H
WHITMAN, Narcissa H
Prentiss
WHITMAN, Ralph 2
WHITMAN, Roger B. 2
WHITMAN, Roswell 4
Hartson
WHITMAN, Royal 2
WHITMAN, Russell 2
WHITMAN, Russell Ripley 1
WHITMAN, Sarah Helen H
Power
WHITMAN, Stephen 6
F(rench)
WHITMAN, Walter H
WHITMAN, Walter 6
Gordon
WHITMAN, William 1
WHITMAN, William 1
Edward Seaver
WHITMAN, William R. 6
WHITMARSH, Francis 5
Leggett
WHITMARSH, Henry 1
Allen
WHITMARSH, Hubert 4
Phelps
WHITMARSH, Theodore 1
Francis
WHITMER, David H
WHITMER, Joseph 4
Rutledge
WHITMER, Robert Forster 4
WHITMORE, Annie 4
Goodell
WHITMORE, Benjamin 9
Arthur
WHITMORE, Carl 3
WHITMORE, Edward 10
Hugh
WHITMORE, Elias H
WHITMORE, Eugene 5
R(andolph)
WHITMORE, Frank 2
Clifford
WHITMORE, George 7
Dewey
WHITMORE, George H
Washington
WHITMORE, William 1
Henry
WHITMYER, Edward 1
Charles

WHITNALL, Harold Orville 2
WHITNER, Daniel Jay 4
WHITNER, Robert Lee 8
WHITNEY, Adeline Dutton Train 1
WHITNEY, Alexander Fell 2
WHITNEY, Alfred Rutgers 2
WHITNEY, Allen Banks 5
WHITNEY, Allen Sisson 3
WHITNEY, Anne 1
WHITNEY, Asa* H
WHITNEY, Carl Everett 1
WHITNEY, Carrie Westlake 5
WHITNEY, Caspar 1
WHITNEY, Charles Smith 3
WHITNEY, Cornelius Vanderbilt 10
WHITNEY, Courtney 5
WHITNEY, David Day 6
WHITNEY, David Rice 1
WHITNEY, Donald Walker 9
WHITNEY, Edward Baldwin 1
WHITNEY, Edwin Morse 3
WHITNEY, Eli H
WHITNEY, Eli 1
WHITNEY, Emily Henrietta 4
WHITNEY, Frank I. 5
WHITNEY, George 4
WHITNEY, George Kirkpatrick 7
WHITNEY, George Kirkpatrick 8
WHITNEY, Gertrude Capen 1
WHITNEY, Gertrude Vanderbilt 2
WHITNEY, Guilford Harrison 5
WHITNEY, Gwin Allison 1
WHITNEY, Harry 1
WHITNEY, Harry Edward 1
WHITNEY, Harry Payne 1
WHITNEY, Hassler 10
WHITNEY, Henry Clay 4
WHITNEY, Henry Howard 7
WHITNEY, Henry Melville 7
WHITNEY, Henry Mitchell 1
WHITNEY, Herbert Baker 4
WHITNEY, James Amaziah 1
WHITNEY, James Lyman 1
WHITNEY, Jason F(ranklin) 6
WHITNEY, John Dunning 1
WHITNEY, John Hay 8
WHITNEY, Joseph Lafeton 4
WHITNEY, Josiah Dwight H
WHITNEY, Leon Fradley 6
WHITNEY, Loren Harper 1
WHITNEY, Marian Parker 2
WHITNEY, Mary Watson 1
WHITNEY, Milton 1
WHITNEY, Myron W. 1
WHITNEY, Nathaniel Ruggles 4
WHITNEY, Nelson Oliver 1
WHITNEY, Paul Clinton 3
WHITNEY, Payne 1
WHITNEY, Richard 6
WHITNEY, Robert Bacon 3
WHITNEY, Samuel Brenton 1
WHITNEY, Simon Newcomb 8
WHITNEY, Thomas Richard H
WHITNEY, Wheelock 3
WHITNEY, William Channing 2
WHITNEY, William Collins 1
WHITNEY, William Dwight H
WHITNEY, William Fiske 1
WHITNEY, William Kuebler 10
WHITNEY, William Locke 1
WHITNEY, Willis Rodney 3
WHITON, Herman Frasch 4
WHITON, James Morris 1
WHITRIDGE, Arnold 9
WHITRIDGE, Frederick Wallingford 1
WHITRIDGE, Morris 1
WHITSETT, William Thornton 1
WHITSIDE, Samuel Marmaduke 1
WHITSITT, William Heth 1
WHITSON, Andrew Robeson 5
WHITSON, Edward 1
WHITSON, John Harvey 1
WHITT, Hugh 3

WHITTAKER, Alfred Heacock 10
WHITTAKER, Charles E(vans) 6
WHITTAKER, Douglas Arthur 8
WHITTAKER, Edmund Boyd 3
WHITTAKER, Hudson (Tampa Red) 7
WHITTAKER, James 4
WHITTAKER, James Thomas 1
WHITTAKER, Miller F. 3
WHITTAKER, Robert Harding 7
WHITTED, Elmer Ellsworth 1
WHITTEKER, John Edwin 1
WHITTELSEY, Abigail Goodrich H
WHITTELSEY, Stuart Gordon, Jr. 10
WHITTEMORE, Amos H
WHITTEMORE, Arthur Austin 8
WHITTEMORE, Arthur Easterbrook 5
WHITTEMORE, Benjamin Franklin H
WHITTEMORE, Charles Otto 4
WHITTEMORE, Clark McKinley 3
WHITTEMORE, Don Juan 1
WHITTEMORE, Edward Loder 1
WHITTEMORE, Edward William 9
WHITTEMORE, Eugene Beede 4
WHITTEMORE, Harris 1
WHITTEMORE, Henry 4
WHITTEMORE, Herbert Lucius 3
WHITTEMORE, James Madison 1
WHITTEMORE, John Weed 4
WHITTEMORE, Joseph Damon 7
WHITTEMORE, Laurence Frederick 4
WHITTEMORE, Lewis Bliss 7
WHITTEMORE, Luther Denny 4
WHITTEMORE, Manuel 8
WHITTEMORE, Robert Clifton 10
WHITTEMORE, Thomas H
WHITTEMORE, Thomas 3
WHITTEMORE, Wilfred Doiloff 7
WHITTEMORE, William John 3
WHITTEMORE, Wyman 3
WHITTEN, Guy Raymond 8
WHITTEN, John Charles 1
WHITTEN, Robert 1
WHITTHORNE, Washington Curran H
WHITTIER, Charles Comfort 5
WHITTIER, Charles Franklin 1
WHITTIER, Clarke Butler 2
WHITTIER, John Greenleaf H
WHITTIER, SaraJane 10
WHITTIER, Warren Faxon 8
WHITTIER, William Frank 1
WHITTINGHAM, William Rollinson 1
WHITTINGHILL, Dexter Gooch 5
WHITTINGTON, Harry Benjamin 10
WHITTINGTON, Verle Glenn 10
WHITTINGTON, William Madison 1
WHITTLE, Francis McNeece 1
WHITTLE, Kennon C(aithness) 9
WHITTLE, Stafford Gorman 1
WHITTLES, Thomas Davis 1
WHITTLESEY, Derwent 3
WHITTLESEY, Eliphalet 1
WHITTLESEY, Elisha H
WHITTLESEY, Frederick 1
WHITTLESEY, Henry De Witt, Sr. 4
WHITTLESEY, Thomas Tucker H

WHITTLESEY, William Augustus H
WHITTLOCK, Douglas 6
WHITTON, Charlotte 6
WHITTREDGE, Worthington 1
WHITTY, Dame May 2
WHITTY, James Howard 1
WHITWELL, Frederick Silsbee 1
WHITWELL, George Edward 9
WHITWORTH, George Gillatt 1
WHITWORTH, John Burton 8
WHITWORTH, Pegram 5
WHITZEL, Raymond Thomas 9
WHOLBERG, Gerald Walter 6
WHORF, John 3
WHORF, Richard 4
WHORTON, John Lacy 1
WHYBURN, Gordon Thomas 5
WHYBURN, William Marvin 5
WHYTE, Carl Barzellous 4
WHYTE, Frederick William Carrick 3
WHYTE, James Primrose 1
WHYTE, Jessel Stuart 3
WHYTE, John 3
WHYTE, Malcolm K. 4
WHYTE, William Pinckney 1
WIBBERLEY, Leonard Patrick O'Connor 8
WIBLISHAUSER, Elmer Hubert 10
WIBORG, Frank Bestow 1
WICHER, Edward Arthur 3
WICHERS, Edward 9
WICK, Charles J. 4
WICK, Gian Carlo 10
WICK, James L. 4
WICK, Myron Arms 7
WICK, Samuel 5
WICK, Warner Arms 8
WICK, William Watson H
WICKARD, Claude Raymond 4
WICKENDEN, Arthur Consaul 4
WICKENDEN, William Elgin 2
WICKENS, Aryness Joy 10
WICKER, Cassius Milton 1
WICKER, George Ray 1
WICKER, James Caldwell 10
WICKER, John Jordan 3
WICKER, Samuel Evaristus 9
WICKERSHAM, Cornelius Wendell 4
WICKERSHAM, Cornelius Wendell, Jr. 1
WICKERSHAM, Edward Dean 4
WICKERSHAM, George Woodward 1
WICKERSHAM, James Pyle H
WICKERSHAM, James H
WICKERSHAM, Victor 9
WICKES, Eliphalet H
WICKES, Forsyth 4
WICKES, Harvey Randall 6
WICKES, Lambert H
WICKES, Stephen H
WICKES, Thomas H. 1
WICKETT, Frederick Henry 1
WICKEY, Gould 9
WICKEY, Harry Herman 9
WICKHAM, Henry Frederick 1
WICKHAM, Henry Taylor 3
WICKHAM, John 4
WICKHEM, John Dunne 2
WICKLIFFE, Charles Anderson H
WICKLIFFE, Robert C. H
WICKLIFFE, Robert Charles H
WICKLOW, Norman Louis 6
WICKMAN, Carl Eric 3
WICKS, Frank Scott Corey 3
WICKS, Robert Russell 4
WICKSER, Philip John 2
WICKSON, Edward James 1
WICKSTROM, Jack Kenneth 8
WICKWARE, Francis Graham 1
WICKWIRE, Jere Raymond 7

WICKWIRE, Theodore Harry 6
WICOFF, John Van Buren 3
WIDDEMER, Mabel Cleland 4
WIDDEMER, Margaret 7
WIDDOES, Howard V(incent) 7
WIDEMAN, Francis James 3
WIDENER, George D. 5
WIDENER, Herbert Lloyd 10
WIDENER, Joseph E. 2
WIDENER, Joseph Early H
WIDENER, Joseph Early 4
WIDENER, Peter A. Brown 1
WIDENGREN, Ulf Nils Joel 10
WIDGERY, William H
WIDMAN, Paul Edward 9
WIDMANN, Bernard Pierre 5
WIDMANN, Bernard Pierre 9
WIDMARK, George Norman 9
WIDMER, John Max 9
WIDMOYER, Fred Bixler 10
WIDNALL, William Beck 8
WIDTMANN, Arthur Albert 6
WIDTSOE, John Andreas 3
WIDTSOE, Leah Dunford 5
WIDUTIS, Florence 10
WIEAND, Albert Cassel 3
WIEBOLDT, Elmer F. 5
WIEBOLDT, Raymond Carl 5
WIEBOLDT, Werner A. 6
WIECHMANN, Ferdinand Gerhard 1
WIECK, Fred Dernburg 6
WIECZOREK, Max 3
WIEDEFELD, Mary Theresa 7
WIEDEMAN, George Henkins 10
WIEDHOPF, J. S. 8
WIEDMANN, Francis Edward 4
WIEGAND, Charles Dudley 4
WIEGAND, Ernest Herman 4
WIEGAND, Gustave Adolph 3
WIEGAND, Karl McKay 2
WIEGAND, William Bryan 8
WIEGMAN, Fred Conrad 3
WIEHE, Theodore Charles 5
WIELAND, Arthur J. 3
WIELAND, G. R. 3
WIELAND, Heinrich Otto 4
WIELBOLDT, William A. 3
WIEMAN, Elton Ewart 5
WIEMAN, Henry Nelson 6
WIEMAN, Henry Nelson 7
WIENER, Alexander S. 7
WIENER, Leo 1
WIENER, Meyer 5
WIENER, Norbert 4
WIENER, Paul Lester 4
WIENER, Samuel G. 7
WIENPAHL, Paul 7
WIENS, Henry Warkentin 5
WIER, Jeanne Elizabeth 3
WIER, John 4
WIER, Robert Withrow 5
WIER, Roy W. 4
WIERINGA, Robert T. 9
WIERS, Edgar Swan 1
WIERSMA, Cornelis Adrianus Gerrit 7
WIESE, Augusto N. 7
WIESE, Claus 10
WIESE, Otis L. 5
WIESEN, David Stanley 8
WIESENBERGER, Arthur 5
WIESINGER, Frederick P. 7
WIESNER, Karel Frantisek 6
WIESS, Harry Carothers 2
WIEST, Edward 6
WIEST, Howard 2
WIESTLING, Helen Merwin 6
WIEWEL, Walter Hoelling 9
WIG, Rudolph James 7
WIGFALL, Louis Tresevant H
WIGGAM, Albert Edward 3
WIGGANS, Cleo Claude 5
WIGGER, Winand Michael 1
WIGGERS, Carl John 4
WIGGIN, Albert Henry 3
WIGGIN, Frank H. 1
WIGGIN, Frederick Alonzo 9
WIGGIN, Frederick Holme 9
WIGGIN, Frederick Holme 1
WIGGIN, Kate Douglas 1
WIGGIN, Twing Brooks 5
WIGGINS, Archibald Lee Manning 7

WIGGINS, Benjamin Lawton 1
WIGGINS, Carleton 1
WIGGINS, Charles, II 2
WIGGINS, Dossie Marion 8
WIGGINS, Frank 1
WIGGINS, Guy 4
WIGGINS, Horace Leland 1
WIGGINS, Ira Loren 9
WIGGINS, Sterling Pitts 2
WIGGINS, Wayne A. 9
WIGGINS, William D. 3
WIGGINTON, George Peter 1
WIGGINTON, Peter Dinwiddie H
WIGGINTON, Thomas Albert 4
WIGGLESWORTH, Edward* H
WIGGLESWORTH, Edward 2
WIGGLESWORTH, George 1
WIGGLESWORTH, Michael H
WIGGLESWORTH, Richard Bowditch 4
WIGHT, Charles Albert 5
WIGHT, E. Van Dyke 3
WIGHT, Francis Asa 2
WIGHT, Frank Clinton 1
WIGHT, Frederick S. 9
WIGHT, John Fitch 5
WIGHT, John Green 1
WIGHT, Oliver Wesley 8
WIGHT, Orlando Williams H
WIGHT, Pearl 1
WIGHT, Peter Bonnett 1
WIGHT, Thomas 2
WIGHT, William Drewin 1
WIGHT, William Ward 1
WIGHTMAN, Clair S(mith) 9
WIGMORE, John Henry 2
WIGNELL, Thomas H
WIHT, Thomas 3
WIJERATNE, Ranjan 10
WIKEL, Howard Henry 7
WIKOFF, Frank J. 4
WIKOFF, Henry H
WIKTOR, Tadeusz Jan 9
WILBAR, Charles Luther, Jr. 5
WILBER, Charles Parker 1
WILBER, David H
WILBER, David Forrest 1
WILBER, Edward Bacon 1
WILBER, Francis Allen 4
WILBER, George M. 1
WILBER, Herbert Wray 1
WILBOR, William Chambers 4
WILBOUR, Isaac H
WILBUR, Marcus 10
WILBUR, Charles Edgar 1
WILBUR, Charles Toppan 1
WILBUR, Cressy Livingston 1
WILBUR, Curtis Dwight 3
WILBUR, Elisha Packer 1
WILBUR, Henry W. 1
WILBUR, Hervey H
WILBUR, Hervey Backus 1
WILBUR, James Benjamin 1
WILBUR, John H
WILBUR, John Milnor 5
WILBUR, Ray Lyman 2
WILBUR, Rollin Henry 1
WILBUR, Samuel H
WILBUR, Sibyl 1
WILBUR, William Allen 2
WILBUR, William Hale 7
WILBY, Arthur Clyde 4
WILBY, Ernest 3
WILBY, Francis Bowditch 1
WILCE, John Woodworth 8
WILCOX, Alexander Martin 1
WILCOX, Ansley 1
WILCOX, Armour David 1
WILCOX, Cadmus H
WILCOX, Marcellus 1
WILCOX, Carl C(lifford) 6
WILCOX, Charles Bowser 1
WILCOX, Charles Saxton 7
WILCOX, Clair 5
WILCOX, Clarence E. 3
WILCOX, Clarence Rothwell 4
WILCOX, Delos Franklin 1
WILCOX, Dewitt Gilbert 5
WILCOX, Edward Byers 5
WILCOX, Edwin Mead 3
WILCOX, Elgin Roscoe 6
WILCOX, Elias Bunn 5
WILCOX, Ella Wheeler 1
WILCOX, Elmer Almy 1

WILCOX, Floyd Cleveland 7
WILCOX, Francis Orlando 8
WILCOX, Frank Langdon 4
WILCOX, Frederick Bernon 4
WILCOX, George C. 7
WILCOX, George Horace 1
WILCOX, George Milo 4
WILCOX, Grafton Stiles 6
WILCOX, Henry Buckley 1
WILCOX, Herbert 3
Budington
WILCOX, J. Mark 3
WILCOX, Jeduthun H
WILCOX, Jerome K. 4
WILCOX, John 8
WILCOX, John A. H
WILCOX, John C. 2
WILCOX, John Walter, Jr. 2
WILCOX, Leonard 4
WILCOX, Leroy T. 3
WILCOX, Lucius Merle 4
WILCOX, Marrion 1
WILCOX, Nelson James 3
WILCOX, Perley S. 3
WILCOX, Reynold Webb 1
WILCOX, Robert William 1
WILCOX, Roy C. 6
WILCOX, Roy Porter 1
WILCOX, Sheldon E. 4
WILCOX, Sidney Freeman 1
WILCOX, Stephen H
WILCOX, Timothy Erastus 1
WILCOX, Walter Dwight 3
WILCOX, Walter H. 9
WILCOX, Wayne Ayres 6
WILCOX, William Craig 1
WILCOX, William Walter 4
WILCZYNSKI, Ernest 1
Julius
WILD, Fred 4
WILD, Harrison Major 1
WILD, Henry Daniel 4
WILD, John Caspar H
WILD, John Daniel 5
WILD, Laura Hulda 5
WILD, Norman Russell 6
WILDE, Arthur Herbert 1
WILDE, Bertram Merbach 10
WILDE, Cornel Louis (Béla 10
Louis Wilde)
WILDE, George Francis 1
Faxon
WILDE, Louise Kathleen 7
WILDE, Norman 1
WILDE, Percival 3
WILDE, Richard Henry H
WILDENHAIN, Frans 7
WILDENSTEIN, Lazare 4
Georges
WILDENTHAL, Bryan 4
WILDER, Abel Carter H
WILDER, Alec 7
WILDER, Alec 8
WILDER, Alexander 1
WILDER, Amos Parker 1
WILDER, Arthur Ashford 1
WILDER, Burt Green 1
WILDER, Charles Wesley 5
WILDER, Charlotte 1
Frances
WILDER, Clinton 9
WILDER, Daniel Webster 1
WILDER, George Warren 1
WILDER, Gerald Gardner 2
WILDER, Gerrit Parmile 1
WILDER, Harris 1
Hawthorne
WILDER, Herbert 1
Augustus
WILDER, Herbert Merrill 1
WILDER, Inez Whipple 1
WILDER, John Emery 1
WILDER, John Thomas 2
WILDER, Laura Ingalls 1
WILDER, Laurence Russell 1
WILDER, Mrs. Louise 1
Beebe
WILDER, Marshall H
Pinckney
WILDER, Marshall 1
Pinckney
WILDER, Mitchell 7
Armitage
WILDER, Ralph Everett 1
WILDER, Raymond Louis 8
WILDER, Robert Ingersoll 6
WILDER, Robert Parmelee 1
WILDER, Russell Morse 3
WILDER, Salmon 5
Willoughby
WILDER, Sampson Uryling H
Stoddard
WILDER, T. Edward 1
WILDER, Thornton Niven 6
WILDER, Wilbur Elliott 4
WILDER, William Hamlin 1
WILDER, William Henry* 1

WILDERMUTH, Joe 6
Henry
WILDERMUTH, Ora 4
Leonard
WILDES, Frank 1
WILDHACK, William 8
August
WILDMAN, Clyde Everett 3
WILDMAN, Edwin 1
WILDMAN, Marian 5
Warner (Mrs. Jesse A.
Fenner)
WILDMAN, Murray 1
Shipley
WILDMAN, William 7
Cooper
WILDMAN, Zalmon H
WILDNER, Harry Charles 4
WILDRICK, Isaac H
WILDS, George James, Jr. 1
WILDS, John Law 7
WILDS, William Naylor 3
WILDT, Rupert 6
WILDT, Rupert 7
WILE, Frank Sloan 6
WILE, Frederic William 1
WILE, Frederic William, Jr. 1
WILE, Ira Solomon 2
WILE, Udo Julius 1
WILE, William Conrad 1
WILENTZ, David Theodore 9
WILES, Charles Peter 2
WILES, Eugene F. 10
WILES, Irving Ramsay 2
WILES, John Henry 1
WILES, Kimball 5
WILES, Lemuel Maynard 1
WILEY, Alexander 4
WILEY, Andrew J. 1
WILEY, Ariosto Appling 1
WILEY, Bell Irvin 7
WILEY, Calvin Henderson H
WILEY, David H
WILEY, Edwin 1
WILEY, Ephraim Emerson H
WILEY, Franklin Baldwin 1
WILEY, Harvey 1
Washington
WILEY, Henry Ariosto 2
WILEY, H(enry) Orton 5
WILEY, Herbert V. 3
WILEY, Hugh 5
WILEY, Isaac William H
WILEY, James Sullivan H
WILEY, John Alexander 1
WILEY, John Cooper 4
WILEY, Louis 1
WILEY, Paul Luzon 7
WILEY, Ralph Benjamin 7
WILEY, Robert Hopkins 3
WILEY, Samuel Ernest 5
WILEY, Samuel Hamilton 8
WILEY, Walter H. 1
WILEY, William Foust 2
WILEY, William Halsted 1
WILEY, William Ogden 3
WILFLEY, Lebbeus 1
Redman
WILFLEY, Xenophon 1
Pierce
WILFONG, Albert E. 7
WILFORD, Loran 5
Frederick
WILG, Edwin Odde 7
WILGRESS, L. Dana 5
WILGUS, A(lva) Curtis 1
WILGUS, Horace La 1
Fayette
WILGUS, Sidney Dean 1
WILGUS, William John 2
WILHELM, Donald 2
WILHELM, Richard 5
Herman
WILHELM, Ross Johnston 8
WILHELM, Stephen Roger 1
WILHELMINA, Helena 4
Pauline Maria
WILHELMJ, Charles 4
Martel
WILHELMSEN, Karl John 4
WILHOIT, Eugene Lovell 4
WILKE, Otto John 5
WILKE, Ulfert S. 9
WILKER, Arthur V. 3
WILKERSON, Albert 1
Wadsworth
WILKERSON, James 2
Herbert
WILKERSON, Marcus 3
Manley
WILKERSON, William 4
Wesley, Jr.
WILKES, Charles H
WILKES, Charles S. 6
WILKES, Eliza Tupper 4
WILKES, George H
WILKES, Jack Stauffer 5

WILKES, James Claiborne, 5
Sr.
WILKES, John 3
WILKES, John Summerfield 1
WILKESON, Frank 4
WILKESON, Samuel H
WILKIE, Franc Bangs 1
WILKIE, Harold McLean 3
WILKIE, Horace W. 7
WILKIE, John 10
WILKIE, John Elbert 1
WILKIN, Jacob W. 1
WILKIN, James Whitney H
WILKIN, Samuel Jones 1
WILKINS, Beriah 1
WILKINS, Edwin Stiles 7
WILKINS, Ernest Hatch 4
WILKINS, Frank Lemoyne 1
WILKINS, George Thomas 8
WILKINS, Harold Tom 4
WILKINS, Horace M. 3
WILKINS, Sir Hubert 3
WILKINS, J. Ernest 3
WILKINS, James Raymond 10
WILKINS, John A. 3
WILKINS, John Robinson 1
WILKINS, Lawrence 2
Augustus
WILKINS, Lawson 4
WILKINS, Milan William 1
WILKINS, Raymond 5
Sanger
WILKINS, Ross H
WILKINS, Roy 8
WILKINS, Thomas Russell 1
WILKINS, Thomas Russell 2
WILKINS, Vaughan 3
WILKINS, Walter 4
WILKINS, William H
WILKINS, William Glyde 1
WILKINS, William James 3
WILKINS, Zora Putnam 7
WILKINSON, Albert 6
WILKINSON, Alfred 5
Dickinson
WILKINSON, Alfred 1
Ernest
WILKINSON, Andrew 1
WILKINSON, Cecil J. 4
WILKINSON, Charles 1
Fore, Jr.
WILKINSON, David H
Hays
WILKINSON, Elizabeth 6
WILKINSON, Ford L., Jr. 3
WILKINSON, George 3
Lawrence
WILKINSON, Horace 1
Simpson
WILKINSON, Howard 2
Sargent
WILKINSON, Ignatius 3
Martin
WILKINSON, James H
WILKINSON, James 6
Cuthbert
WILKINSON, James 8
Richard
WILKINSON, Jasper 4
Newton
WILKINSON, Jemima H
WILKINSON, Jeremiah H
WILKINSON, John 6
WILKINSON, John 7
WILKINSON, Joseph A. 3
WILKINSON, Joseph 1
Biddle
WILKINSON, Joseph 1
Green
WILKINSON, Lawrence 7
WILKINSON, Marguerite 1
Ogden Bigelow
WILKINSON, Melville Le 1
Vaunt
WILKINSON, Morton H
Smith
WILKINSON, Peter Barr 10
WILKINSON, Robert 3
Johnson
WILKINSON, Robert Shaw 1
WILKINSON, Theodore S. 2
WILKINSON, Warring 1
WILKINSON, William 5
Albert
WILKINSON, William 1
Cleaver
WILKINSON, William 1
Cook
WILKINSON, William 5
Donald
WILKINSON, William 3
John
WILKINSON, William 10
Scott
WILKS, Dick Lloyd 10

WILKS, Samuel Stanley 4
WILL, Allen Sinclair 1
WILL, Arthur A. 2
WILL, Arthur Percival 3
WILL, John Mylin 7
WILL, Louis 1
WILL, Theodore St. Clair 2
WILL, Thomas Elmer 4
WILLARD, Archibald M. H
WILLARD, Archibald M. 4
WILLARD, Arthur Cutts 4
WILLARD, Arthur Lee 1
WILLARD, Ashton Rollins 1
WILLARD, Charles 1
Andrew
WILLARD, Charles J(ulius) 6
WILLARD, Charles Wesley H
WILLARD, Charlotte 7
WILLARD, Chester Ezra 4
WILLARD, Daniel 2
WILLARD, Daniel Everett 4
WILLARD, Deforest 1
WILLARD, Deforest P. 3
WILLARD, Edward 6
Lawrence
WILLARD, Edward Smith 1
WILLARD, Eleanor Withey 1
WILLARD, Emma Hart H
WILLARD, Ernest Russell 1
WILLARD, Frances H
Elizabeth Caroline
WILLARD, Frank H. 3
WILLARD, Frank Henry 4
WILLARD, Frederic 2
Wilson
WILLARD, Henry 1
Augustus
WILLARD, Hobart Hurd 6
WILLARD, Horace Mann 1
WILLARD, Ira Farnum 1
WILLARD, James Field 1
WILLARD, John H
WILLARD, John Artemas 4
WILLARD, Joseh Edward 4
WILLARD, Joseph* H
WILLARD, Joseph 1
Augustus
WILLARD, Josiah Flynt 1
WILLARD, Julius Terrass 3
WILLARD, Leigh 3
WILLARD, Lillian 5
Winifred
WILLARD, Monroe 4
Livingstone
WILLARD, Roy H(obson) 5
WILLARD, Samuel* H
WILLARD, Sidney H
WILLARD, Simon* H
WILLARD, Solomon 3
WILLARD, Sylvester David H
WILLARD, Theodore A. 2
WILLARD, Thomas Rigney 1
WILLARD, William 5
A(lbert)
WILLARD, William 1
Charles
WILLAUER, Arthur 7
Osborne
WILLAUER, Whiting 4
WILLCOX, Bertram 10
Francis
WILLCOX, Cornelis de 1
Witt
WILLCOX, David 1
WILLCOX, James M. 1
WILLCOX, Joseph Taney 7
WILLCOX, Julius Abner 1
WILLCOX, Louise Collier 1
WILLCOX, Mary Alice 3
WILLCOX, Orlando 1
Bolivar
WILLCOX, Walter Francis 4
WILLCOX, Walter Francis 1
WILLCOX, Walter Ross 2
Baumes
WILLCOX, Westmore 5
WILLCOX, William 9
Bradford
WILLCOX, William G. 1
WILLCOX, William Henry 1
WILLCOX, William Russell 1
WILLCUTTS, Morton D. 8
WILLE, Frank 9
WILLE, Frank Joseph 7
WILLEBRANDT, Mabel 4
Walker
WILLEMS, J. Daniel 9
WILLEMS, John Murphy 7
WILLEN, Joseph 3
WILLEN, Pearl Larner 5
(Mrs. Joseph Willen)
WILLENBUCHER, Franz 7
Otto
WILLENS, Rita Jacobs 10
WILLENSKY, Elliot 10
WILLET, Anne Lee 2
WILLET, Henry Lee 8

WILLETS, David Gifford 5
WILLETS, Gilson 5
WILLETT, George F. 5
WILLETT, Henry Irving 9
WILLETT, Herbert 2
Lockwood
WILLETT, Howard 4
Levansellaer, Sr.
WILLETT, Hugh Carey 7
WILLETT, Marinus H
WILLETT, Oscar Louis 2
WILLETT, William, Jr. 5
WILLETTS, Ernest Ward 6
WILLETTS, Herbert 5
WILLETTS, William 4
Prentice
WILLEVER, John Calvin 5
WILLEY, Calvin H
WILLEY, Charles Herbert 5
WILLEY, D. Allen 1
WILLEY, Earle D. 2
WILLEY, Henry 1
WILLEY, John Heston 2
WILLEY, Malcolm 6
Macdonald
WILLEY, Norman Bushnell 4
WILLEY, Norman Leroy 4
WILLEY, Samuel Hopkins 4
WILLFORD, Albert 3
Clinton
WILLGING, Eugene P. 4
WILLGING, Joseph C. 3
WILLHELM, Donald S. 10
WILLHITE, Frank Vanatta 2
WILLHITE, Winfield Lyle 9
WILLI, Albert B(ond) 5
WILLIAM III H
WILLIAM, James Thomas, 7
Jr.
WILLIAM, Maurice 6
WILLIAMS, A. J. 3
WILLIAMS, Abraham 1
Pease
WILLIAMS, Alan Meredith 6
WILLIAMS, Albert Calvin 7
WILLIAMS, Albert Frank 3
WILLIAMS, Albert J., Jr. 10
WILLIAMS, Albert Lynn 8
WILLIAMS, Albert 4
Nathaniel
WILLIAMS, Albert Rhys 4
WILLIAMS, Albert Rhys 7
WILLIAMS, Alexander 3
Elliot
WILLIAMS, Alexander 4
Scott
WILLIAMS, Alford Joseph, 3
Jr.
WILLIAMS, Alfred 1
Brockenbrough
WILLIAMS, Alfred Hector 6
WILLIAMS, Alfred Hicks 5
WILLIAMS, Alfred L. W. 7
WILLIAMS, Alfred Mason H
WILLIAMS, Alfred Melvin 5
WILLIAMS, Alpheus 5
Americus
WILLIAMS, Alpheus H
Starkey
WILLIAMS, Anna Bolles 4
WILLIAMS, Anna Wessels 5
WILLIAMS, Archibald 3
Hunter Arrington
WILLIAMS, Arnold K. 10
WILLIAMS, Arthur 10
WILLIAMS, Arthur 1
WILLIAMS, Arthur B. 1
WILLIAMS, Arthur 1
Llewellyn
WILLIAMS, Ashton 4
Hilliard
WILLIAMS, Aubrey Willis 4
WILLIAMS, B. Y. 3
WILLIAMS, Barney H
WILLIAMS, Beatty Bricker 6
WILLIAMS, Ben Ames 3
WILLIAMS, Ben J. 3
WILLIAMS, Ben T. 4
WILLIAMS, Benjamin H
WILLIAMS, Benjamin 6
Harrison
WILLIAMS, Berkeley 3
WILLIAMS, Bert 4
WILLIAMS, Bert C. 3
WILLIAMS, Birkett Livers 4
WILLIAMS, Blanche 2
Colton
WILLIAMS, Bradford 4
WILLIAMS, Brian David 10
WILLIAMS, C. Arthur 9
WILLIAMS, Carl 3
WILLIAMS, Carlos Grant 2
WILLIAMS, Carrington 8
WILLIAMS, Carroll Milton 10
WILLIAMS, Catharine H
Read Arnold
WILLIAMS, Cecil Brown 4

WILLIAMS, Channing Moore 1
WILLIAMS, Charl Ormond 7
WILLIAMS, Charles Bray 3
WILLIAMS, Charles Burgess 2
WILLIAMS, Charles David 1
WILLIAMS, Charles Finn 3
WILLIAMS, Charles Grandison H
WILLIAMS, Charles Hamilton 6
WILLIAMS, Charles Ira 6
WILLIAMS, Charles Laidlaw 7
WILLIAMS, Charles Luther 1
WILLIAMS, Charles Mallory 3
WILLIAMS, Charles McCay 4
WILLIAMS, Charles Page 3
WILLIAMS, Charles Parker 3
WILLIAMS, Charles Richard 1
WILLIAMS, Charles Richard 6
WILLIAMS, Charles Sneed 4
WILLIAMS, Charles Sumner 1
WILLIAMS, Charles Thomas 4
WILLIAMS, Charles Turner 1
WILLIAMS, Charles Urquhart 1
WILLIAMS, Charles Wesley 4
WILLIAMS, Charles Weston 4
WILLIAMS, Christopher Harris H
WILLIAMS, Clanton Ware 7
WILLIAMS, Clara Andrews 7
WILLIAMS, Clarence Russell 2
WILLIAMS, Clarence Stewart 3
WILLIAMS, Clarissa Smith 1
WILLIAMS, Clark 2
WILLIAMS, Clarke 8
WILLIAMS, Claude Allen 3
WILLIAMS, Clayton Epes 5
WILLIAMS, Clement Clarence 2
WILLIAMS, Clifford Leland 5
WILLIAMS, Clifton 7
WILLIAMS, Clifton Curtis, Jr. 4
WILLIAMS, Clifton Curtis, Jr. 5
WILLIAMS, Clyde 3
WILLIAMS, Clyde Elmer 10
WILLIAMS, Constant 1
WILLIAMS, Cora Lenore 1
WILLIAMS, Cratis Dearl 8
WILLIAMS, Curtis Chandler 2
WILLIAMS, Cyril 5
WILLIAMS, Cyrus Vance 2
WILLIAMS, D. B. 5
WILLIAMS, Dana Scott 1
WILLIAMS, Daniel Albert 5
WILLIAMS, Daniel Day 6
WILLIAMS, Daniel H. 1
WILLIAMS, Daniel Roderick 5
WILLIAMS, David* 1
WILLIAMS, David Evans 4
WILLIAMS, David Lee 10
WILLIAMS, David P., Jr. 5
WILLIAMS, David Reichard 4
WILLIAMS, David Rogerson H
WILLIAMS, David Willard 9
WILLIAMS, Dean 3
WILLIAMS, Dion 5
WILLIAMS, Dwight 1
WILLIAMS, E. Virginia 8
WILLIAMS, Edgar Irving 6
WILLIAMS, Edmund Randolph 3
WILLIAMS, Ednyfed H. 3
WILLIAMS, Edward Bennett 9
WILLIAMS, Edward Foster, Jr. 7
WILLIAMS, Edward Francis 8
WILLIAMS, Edward Franklin 1
WILLIAMS, Edward Higginson, Jr. 1
WILLIAMS, Edward Huntington 2
WILLIAMS, Edward Thomas 2
WILLIAMS, Edward Thomas Towson 4
WILLIAMS, Edwin H
WILLIAMS, Edwin Bucher 6
WILLIAMS, Egerton Ryerson, Jr. 5
WILLIAMS, Eleazar H
WILLIAMS, Elihu Stephen 1
WILLIAMS, Elisha* H
WILLIAMS, Elizabeth Sprague 1
WILLIAMS, Elkanah H
WILLIAMS, Emerson Milton 4
WILLIAMS, Emlyn 9
WILLIAMS, Emma Elizabeth Thomas 5
WILLIAMS, Emmons Levi 3
WILLIAMS, Ennion Gifford 1
WILLIAMS, Ennion Skelton 4
WILLIAMS, Ephraim H
WILLIAMS, Erastus Appleman 4
WILLIAMS, Eric Eustace 7
WILLIAMS, Ernest 1
WILLIAMS, Ernest Bland, Jr. 5
WILLIAMS, Ernest S. 2
WILLIAMS, Ernest Y. 10
WILLIAMS, Espy 1
WILLIAMS, Eugene E. 6
WILLIAMS, Eugene S. 9
WILLIAMS, Eustace Leroy 5
WILLIAMS, E(van) Clifford 9
WILLIAMS, Everard Mott 5
WILLIAMS, Ferd Elton 8
WILLIAMS, Fielding Lewis 9
WILLIAMS, Francis Bennett 1
WILLIAMS, Francis Churchill 2
WILLIAMS, Francis Henry 1
WILLIAMS, Francis Howard 1
WILLIAMS, Frank Alvan 4
WILLIAMS, Frank B. 1
WILLIAMS, Frank Bacus 3
WILLIAMS, Frank D 8
WILLIAMS, Frank Eugene 3
WILLIAMS, Frank French 1
WILLIAMS, Frank Henry 8
WILLIAMS, Frank L. 2
WILLIAMS, Frank Martin 1
WILLIAMS, Frank Starr 8
WILLIAMS, Franklin G. 4
WILLIAMS, Franklin Hall 10
WILLIAMS, Franklin P. 7
WILLIAMS, Frankwood Earl 1
WILLIAMS, Fred Lincoln 3
WILLIAMS, Frederic Arlington 3
WILLIAMS, Frederic M. 1
WILLIAMS, Frederick Ballard 3
WILLIAMS, Frederick Ballard 5
WILLIAMS, Frederick Crawford 3
WILLIAMS, Frederick Wells 1
WILLIAMS, Gardner Fred 1
WILLIAMS, Gardner Stewart 1
WILLIAMS, George 3
WILLIAMS, George Alfred 1
WILLIAMS, George Bassett 2
WILLIAMS, George Burchell 1
WILLIAMS, George C. 5
WILLIAMS, George Clinton Fairchild 1
WILLIAMS, George Forrester 1
WILLIAMS, George Fred 1
WILLIAMS, George Gilbert 1
WILLIAMS, George Henry 1
WILLIAMS, George Howard 5
WILLIAMS, George Huntington H
WILLIAMS, George Orchard 3
WILLIAMS, George Philip 1
WILLIAMS, George S. 3
WILLIAMS, George Van Siclen 2
WILLIAMS, George Walton 1
WILLIAMS, George Washington H
WILLIAMS, George Washington 1
WILLIAMS, G(erhard) Mennen, Sr. 9
WILLIAMS, Gershom Mott 1
WILLIAMS, Gladstone 5
WILLIAMS, Glenn Carber 10
WILLIAMS, Gluyas 9
WILLIAMS, Gorham Deane 1
WILLIAMS, Griff 3
WILLIAMS, Guinn 2
WILLIAMS, Guy Yandall 6
WILLIAMS, H. Evan 1
WILLIAMS, Harold 1
WILLIAMS, Harold E. 3
WILLIAMS, Harold E. 5
WILLIAMS, Harold McNeal 10
WILLIAMS, Harold Putnam 4
WILLIAMS, Harold Wesley 6
WILLIAMS, Harrison 3
WILLIAMS, Harvey Ladew 9
WILLIAMS, Helen Burton (Mrs. Edward J. Williams) 5
WILLIAMS, Henry H
WILLIAMS, Henry 6
WILLIAMS, Henry A. 3
WILLIAMS, Henry Davison 2
WILLIAMS, Henry Edison 2
WILLIAMS, Henry Eugene 1
WILLIAMS, Henry Francis 1
WILLIAMS, Henry Horace 1
WILLIAMS, Henry Morland 2
WILLIAMS, Henry Robert 1
WILLIAMS, Henry Shaler 1
WILLIAMS, Henry Smith 2
WILLIAMS, Henry Willard H
WILLIAMS, Henry Winslow 1
WILLIAMS, Herbert Hoover 10
WILLIAMS, Herbert Oswald 1
WILLIAMS, Herbert Owen 1
WILLIAMS, Herbert Pelham 5
WILLIAMS, Herbert Upham 1
WILLIAMS, Hermann Warner 6
WILLIAMS, Hermann Warner, Jr. 7
WILLIAMS, Herschel 1
WILLIAMS, Hezekiah H
WILLIAMS, Homer B. 4
WILLIAMS, Homer D. 1
WILLIAMS, Horatio Burt 3
WILLIAMS, Howard David 8
WILLIAMS, Howard Rees 6
WILLIAMS, Hugh 2
WILLIAMS, Ira Jewell 5
WILLIAMS, Irving 3
WILLIAMS, Isaac, Jr. H
WILLIAMS, Israel H
WILLIAMS, J. Harold 8
WILLIAMS, J. Nelson 4
WILLIAMS, J. Ross 4
WILLIAMS, J. Whitridge 1
WILLIAMS, Jack 3
WILLIAMS, Jack G. 7
WILLIAMS, Jack Kenny 8
WILLIAMS, James H
WILLIAMS, James Cranston 1
WILLIAMS, James Douglas H
WILLIAMS, James Leon 4
WILLIAMS, James Mickel 6
WILLIAMS, James Monroe 1
WILLIAMS, James Patrick 8
WILLIAMS, James Peter, Jr. 4
WILLIAMS, James Peter, Jr. 7
WILLIAMS, James Robert 1
WILLIAMS, James Robert 3
WILLIAMS, James Thomas, Jr. 5
WILLIAMS, James Wray H
WILLIAMS, Jared H
WILLIAMS, Jared Warner H
WILLIAMS, Jerome Oscar 3
WILLIAMS, Jesse Feiring 4
WILLIAMS, Jesse Feiring 7
WILLIAMS, Jesse Lynch H
WILLIAMS, Jesse Lynch 1
WILLIAMS, Jesse Raymond 6
WILLIAMS, Job 1
WILLIAMS, John* H
WILLIAMS, John 4
WILLIAMS, John Alonzo 3
WILLIAMS, John Bell 8
WILLIAMS, John Carl 10
WILLIAMS, John Castree 3
WILLIAMS, John Clark 2
WILLIAMS, John David 8
WILLIAMS, John Davis 8
WILLIAMS, John Edward 2
WILLIAMS, John Elias 1
WILLIAMS, John Fletcher H
WILLIAMS, John Foster H
WILLIAMS, John Fred 7
WILLIAMS, John H. 4
WILLIAMS, John Harvey 4
WILLIAMS, John Healy 4
WILLIAMS, John Henry 7
WILLIAMS, John Howard 3
WILLIAMS, John Insco H
WILLIAMS, John J. 9
WILLIAMS, John Joseph 1
WILLIAMS, John Joseph, Jr. 5
WILLIAMS, John Langbourne 1
WILLIAMS, John McKeown Snow H
WILLIAMS, John Paul 5
WILLIAMS, John Powell 3
WILLIAMS, John Ralston 4
WILLIAMS, John Rodney 9
WILLIAMS, John Scott 6
WILLIAMS, John Sharp 1
WILLIAMS, John Skelton 1
WILLIAMS, John Taylor 5
WILLIAMS, John Townsend 4
WILLIAMS, John Woodbridge 10
WILLIAMS, Jonathan H
WILLIAMS, Joseph Campbell 8
WILLIAMS, Joseph John 1
WILLIAMS, Joseph Judson, Jr. 5
WILLIAMS, Joseph Lanier H
WILLIAMS, Joseph Tuttle 6
WILLIAMS, Joseph Vincent 2
WILLIAMS, Joseph White 1
WILLIAMS, Juanita Hingst 10
WILLIAMS, Judith Blow 3
WILLIAMS, Karl C. 8
WILLIAMS, Kathleen Mary 6
WILLIAMS, Keith Shaw 3
WILLIAMS, Kenneth Powers 3
WILLIAMS, Kenneth Raynor 10
WILLIAMS, L. Judson 1
WILLIAMS, Lacey Kirk 2
WILLIAMS, Langbourne M. 1
WILLIAMS, Laurens 6
WILLIAMS, Ledru A. 4
WILLIAMS, Lemuel H
WILLIAMS, Leroy Blanchard 2
WILLIAMS, Leslie Benjamin 6
WILLIAMS, Lester Alonzo 6
WILLIAMS, Lewis H
WILLIAMS, Lewis Blair 4
WILLIAMS, Lewis Kemper 5
WILLIAMS, Linsly Rudd 1
WILLIAMS, Lloyd Thomas 6
WILLIAMS, Louis Coleman 3
WILLIAMS, Louis Laval 3
WILLIAMS, Louis Sheppard 4
WILLIAMS, Lynn Alfred, Jr. 8
WILLIAMS, Malcolm Demosthenes 10
WILLIAMS, Marmaduke H
WILLIAMS, Marshall Jay 1
WILLIAMS, Martha McCulloch 5
WILLIAMS, Martin Tudor 10
WILLIAMS, Mary Lou 7
WILLIAMS, Mary Wilhelmine 2
WILLIAMS, Maynard Owen 4
WILLIAMS, Merton Yarwood 7
WILLIAMS, Michael 3
WILLIAMS, Miles Evans 4
WILLIAMS, Milton Mathias 1
WILLIAMS, Mornay 1
WILLIAMS, Moseley Hooker 1
WILLIAMS, Moses* 1
WILLIAMS, Nathan H
WILLIAMS, Nathan Boone 5
WILLIAMS, Nathan Winslow 1
WILLIAMS, Nathaniel H
WILLIAMS, Neil Hooker 3
WILLIAMS, Newell Franklin 9
WILLIAMS, O. B. 3
WILLIAMS, Ora 5
WILLIAMS, Orva Gilson 1
WILLIAMS, Oscar Fitzalan 1
WILLIAMS, Othneil Glanville 3
WILLIAMS, Otho Holland H
WILLIAMS, Pardon Clarence 1
WILLIAMS, Parley Lycurgus 1
WILLIAMS, Paul Revere 7
WILLIAMS, Philip Francis 5
WILLIAMS, R. Lancaster 1
WILLIAMS, Ralph Chester 8
WILLIAMS, Ralph E. 1
WILLIAMS, Ralph Olmsted 1
WILLIAMS, Ransome Judson 5
WILLIAMS, Reuel H
WILLIAMS, Richard Eaton 10
WILLIAMS, Richard Lippincott 10
WILLIAMS, Richard Peters 2
WILLIAMS, Richard Richardson 1
WILLIAMS, Robert* H
WILLIAMS, Robert* 1
WILLIAMS, Robert 2
WILLIAMS, Robert 3
WILLIAMS, Robert Campbell 4
WILLIAMS, Robert Carlton 3
WILLIAMS, Robert Day 1
WILLIAMS, Robert E. 3
WILLIAMS, Robert Einion 1
WILLIAMS, Robert Gray 2
WILLIAMS, Robert Hope, Jr. 10
WILLIAMS, Robert Lee 2
WILLIAMS, Robert Maurice 4
WILLIAMS, Robert Parvin 5
WILLIAMS, Robert Purcell, Jr. 3
WILLIAMS, Robert R. 4
WILLIAMS, R(obert) R(oyce) 7
WILLIAMS, Robert Seaton 6
WILLIAMS, Robert White 2
WILLIAMS, Robert Willoughby 4
WILLIAMS, Robert Wood 9
WILLIAMS, Roger H
WILLIAMS, Roger 3
WILLIAMS, Roger 4
WILLIAMS, Roger Butler 1
WILLIAMS, Roger D. 1
WILLIAMS, Roger Henry 3
WILLIAMS, Roger John 9
WILLIAMS, Ronald 9
WILLIAMS, Roswell Carter, Jr. 5
WILLIAMS, Roy Hughes 2
WILLIAMS, Roy T. 2
WILLIAMS, Rufus Phillips 1
WILLIAMS, Russell Raymond, Jr. 4
WILLIAMS, Samuel Baker 8
WILLIAMS, Samuel Clay 2
WILLIAMS, Samuel Cole 2
WILLIAMS, Samuel Hubbard 3
WILLIAMS, Samuel Leonard 5
WILLIAMS, Samuel May H
WILLIAMS, Samuel Riley 10
WILLIAMS, Samuel Robinson 6
WILLIAMS, Samuel Wells H
WILLIAMS, Sarah 4
WILLIAMS, Selden Thornton 9
WILLIAMS, Seth 4
WILLIAMS, Seward Henry 5
WILLIAMS, Sherman 1
WILLIAMS, Sherrod H
WILLIAMS, Sidney Clark 3
WILLIAMS, Sidney James 3
WILLIAMS, Stanley Thomas 3
WILLIAMS, Stephen Riggs 5
WILLIAMS, Stephen West H
WILLIAMS, T. Harry 7
WILLIAMS, Talcott 1
WILLIAMS, Tennessee Thomas Lanier 8
WILLIAMS, Theodore Chickering 1
WILLIAMS, Theresa Amelia 4
WILLIAMS, Thomas H
WILLIAMS, Thomas 1

WOODRUFF, Marston True 6
WOODRUFF, Nathan H. 4
WOODRUFF, Olive 4
WOODRUFF, Robert Eastman 4
WOODRUFF, Robert Winship 8
WOODRUFF, Rollin Simmons 1
WOODRUFF, Roy Orchard 3
WOODRUFF, Theodore Tuttle H
WOODRUFF, Thomas Adams 1
WOODRUFF, Thomas M. H
WOODRUFF, Timothy Lester 1
WOODRUFF, Wilford H
WOODRUFF, William Edward H
WOODRUFF, William Wight 5
WOODRUM, Clifton Alexander 3
WOODS, Alan Churchill 4
WOODS, Albert Fred 2
WOODS, Alfred W. 3
WOODS, Alice (Miss) 5
WOODS, Alva 4
WOODS, Andrew Henry 5
WOODS, Arthur 2
WOODS, Baldwin Munger 3
WOODS, Bertha Gerneaux 3
WOODS, Bill Milton 6
WOODS, Charles Albert 1
WOODS, Charles Carroll 1
WOODS, Charles Dayton 1
WOODS, Charles Robert H
WOODS, Clifford Curtis 10
WOODS, Cyrus E. 1
WOODS, David Walker, Jr. 4
WOODS, Edgar Hall 3
WOODS, Edgar Lyons 4
WOODS, Edward Augustus 1
WOODS, Francis Marion 1
WOODS, Frank Henry 3
WOODS, Frank Henry 7
WOODS, Frank P. 4
WOODS, Frederick Adams 1
WOODS, Frederick Shenstone 3
WOODS, George Benjamin 3
WOODS, George David 8
WOODS, George Herbert 6
WOODS, Granville Cecil 6
WOODS, Harry Irwin 5
WOODS, Henry H
WOODS, Henry 1
WOODS, Henry Cochrane 5
WOODS, Henry Ernest 1
WOODS, Hiram 1
WOODS, Homer Boughner 2
WOODS, Howard Burrell 7
WOODS, J. Albert 1
WOODS, James Haughton 1
WOODS, James Pleasant 2
WOODS, John* H
WOODS, John Carter Brown 1
WOODS, Kate Tannatt 1
WOODS, Katharine Pearson 1
WOODS, Katherine Irvin 7
WOODS, Leonard* H
WOODS, Leslie Victor 10
WOODS, Littleton A. 4
WOODS, Louis Earnest 5
WOODS, Mark White 5
WOODS, Mark Winton 8
WOODS, Matthew 1
WOODS, Michael Leonard 4
WOODS, Neander Montgomery 1
WOODS, Paul Harlow 10
WOODS, Robert Archey 1
WOODS, Robert Patterson 3
WOODS, Rufus 3
WOODS, Sam Edison 3
WOODS, Samuel Van Horn 1
WOODS, Thomas Cochrane 3
WOODS, Thomas Cochrane, Jr. 10
WOODS, Thomas Francis 2
WOODS, Thomas Hall 1
WOODS, Thomas Smith 4
WOODS, Tighe Edward 6
WOODS, Virna 1
WOODS, Walter Leslie James 5
WOODS, Walter Orr 3
WOODS, William H
WOODS, William Allen H
WOODS, William Burnham H
WOODS, William George 3
WOODS, William Hervey 4
WOODS, William Johnson 8
WOODS, William Seaver 4

WOODS, William Sharpless Derrick 5
WOODS, William Sledge 7
WOODS, William Stone 1
WOODS, William Wells 1
WOODS, William Whitfield 1
WOOD-SEYS, Roland Alex 4
WOODSIDE, Edmund Rector 10
WOODSIDE, John Archibald H
WOODSIDE, John Thomas 2
WOODSIDE, John Thomas 3
WOODSIDE, John W. 4
WOODSIDE, Robert I. 3
WOODSMALL, Ruth Frances 4
WOODSMALL, Ruth Frances 7
WOODSON, Archelaus M. 1
WOODSON, Aytch P. 3
WOODSON, Carter Godwin 3
WOODSON, George Frederick 4
WOODSON, Mary Blake 1
WOODSON, Omer Lee 3
WOODSON, Robert Everard, Jr. 4
WOODSON, Samuel Hughes* H
WOODSON, Urey 1
WOODSON, Walter Browne 2
WOODSON, Walter Worsham 1
WOODUL, J(ames) R(ichmond) 7
WOODWARD, Allan Harvey 3
WOODWARD, Augustus Brevoort H
WOODWARD, Benjamin Duryea 2
WOODWARD, Calvin Milton 1
WOODWARD, Carl Raymond 6
WOODWARD, Charles Edgar 2
WOODWARD, Charles Namby Wynn 10
WOODWARD, Chester 1
WOODWARD, Clark Howell 4
WOODWARD, Cleveland Landon 9
WOODWARD, Clifford Dewey 2
WOODWARD, Comer McDonald 5
WOODWARD, Donald Bosley 6
WOODWARD, Dudley Kezer 6
WOODWARD, Edmund Lee 2
WOODWARD, Elizabeth Ash 6
WOODWARD, Ellen Sullivan 1
WOODWARD, Ellsworth Dewey 1
WOODWARD, Ernest 5
WOODWARD, Sir Ernest Llewellyn 5
WOODWARD, Fletcher D(rummond) 5
WOODWARD, Frank Lincoln 1
WOODWARD, Franklin Cowles 4
WOODWARD, Fred William 8
WOODWARD, Frederic 3
WOODWARD, George 3
WOODWARD, George A. 3
WOODWARD, George Washington H
WOODWARD, Harold Christopher 4
WOODWARD, Harper 7
WOODWARD, Harper 8
WOODWARD, Helen (Mrs. William E. Woodward) 7
WOODWARD, Henry H
WOODWARD, Hugh Beistle 5
WOODWARD, Hugh McCurdy 1
WOODWARD, J. B. 1
WOODWARD, Jack Edward 6
WOODWARD, James T. 1
WOODWARD, John Charles 1

WOODWARD, Joseph Addison H
WOODWARD, Joseph Hersey, II 4
WOODWARD, Joseph Hooker 1
WOODWARD, Joseph Janvier H
WOODWARD, Julius Hayden 1
WOODWARD, Karl Wilson 6
WOODWARD, Lester Armand 5
WOODWARD, Luther Ellis 4
WOODWARD, P. Henry 1
WOODWARD, Richard Lewis 9
WOODWARD, Robert B. 1
WOODWARD, Robert Burns 7
WOODWARD, Robert M. 7
WOODWARD, Robert Simpson 1
WOODWARD, Robert Strong 3
WOODWARD, Roland Beavan 3
WOODWARD, Samuel Bayard H
WOODWARD, Samuel Bayard 3
WOODWARD, Samuel Lippincott 1
WOODWARD, Samuel Walter 1
WOODWARD, Stanley 1
WOODWARD, Stanley 4
WOODWARD, Stanley W(ingate) 9
WOODWARD, Thomas Mullen 6
WOODWARD, Thomas Mullen 7
WOODWARD, Walter Carleton 2
WOODWARD, William H
WOODWARD, William 1
WOODWARD, William Creighton 2
WOODWARD, William E. 3
WOODWARD, William Finch 1
WOODWORTH, Clyde Melvin 4
WOODWORTH, Edward Knowlton 1
WOODWORTH, Frank Goodrich 1
WOODWORTH, G(eorge) Wallace 5
WOODWORTH, Herbert Grafton 3
WOODWORTH, James Grant 4
WOODWORTH, James Hutchinson H
WOODWORTH, Jay Backus 1
WOODWORTH, Kennard 3
WOODWORTH, Laurence Neal 7
WOODWORTH, Laurin Dewey H
WOODWORTH, Melvin J. 3
WOODWORTH, Newell Bertram 1
WOODWORTH, Philip Bell 1
WOODWORTH, Robert Sessions 4
WOODWORTH, Samuel 4
WOODWORTH, Stewart Campbell 4
WOODWORTH, William W. H
WOODY, Clifford 2
WOODY, Frank H. 4
WOODY, McIver 7
WOODY, McIver 7
WOODY, Walter Thomas 4
WOODY, Walton L. 3
WOODYARD, Harry Chapman 1
WOODYATT, James Blain 7
WOODYATT, Rollin Turner 3
WOOFTER, Thomas Jackson 1
WOOL, John Ellis H
WOOLARD, Warden 4
WOOLBERT, Charles Henry 1
WOOLDRIDGE, Charles William 1
WOOLDRIDGE, Edmund Tyler 5
WOOLEVER, Harry Earl 1

WOOLF, Albert Edward 1
WOOLF, Benjamin Edward H
WOOLF, Herbert M 6
WOOLF, Philip 1
WOOLF, Samuel Johnson 2
WOOLFOLK, William Gordon 3
WOOLLARD, George Prior 7
WOOLLARD, William Edward 1
WOOLLCOTT, Alexander 2
WOOLLEN, Evans 2
WOOLLEN, Evans, Jr. 3
WOOLLEN, Herbert Milton 7
WOOLLETT, G(uy) H(aines) 8
WOOLLETT, William L. 1
WOOLLETT, William M. H
WOOLLEY, Alice Stone 2
WOOLLEY, Mrs (Anna) Lazelle Thayer 5
WOOLLEY, Celia Parker 1
WOOLLEY, Charles H. 3
WOOLLEY, Clarence Mott 1
WOOLLEY, Clarence Nelson 8
WOOLLEY, D. Wayne 4
WOOLLEY, Edward Mott 2
WOOLLEY, Edwin Campbell 1
WOOLLEY, Helen Bradford Thompson 3
WOOLLEY, Herbert Codey 1
WOOLLEY, John Granville 1
WOOLLEY, Knight 8
WOOLLEY, Mary Emma 2
WOOLLEY, Monty 4
WOOLLEY, Paul Gerhardt 1
WOOLLEY, Robert Wickliffe 3
WOOLLEY, Victor Baynard 2
WOOLMAN, C. E. 4
WOOLMAN, C. E. 6
WOOLMAN, Henry Newbold 3
WOOLMAN, John H
WOOLMAN, Mary Schenck 4
WOOLNER, Adolph 4
WOOLRYCH, Francis Humphry William 2
WOOLSEY, Clarence Olin 9
WOOLSEY, George 5
WOOLSEY, John Munro H
WOOLSEY, John Munro 2
WOOLSEY, John Munro 4
WOOLSEY, Lester Hood 4
WOOLSEY, Melancthon Taylor H
WOOLSEY, Richard Hay 9
WOOLSEY, Ross Arlington 2
WOOLSEY, Sarah Chauncey 1
WOOLSEY, Theodore Dwight H
WOOLSEY, Theodore Salisbury* 1
WOOLSON, Abba Louisa Goold 3
WOOLSON, Constance Fenimore H
WOOLSON, Harry Thurber 5
WOOLSON, Ira Harvey 1
WOOLSON, Kenneth Hazen 10
WOOLSON, L. Irving 4
WOOLSTON, Howard Brown 5
WOOLWINE, Thomas Lee 1
WOOLWINE, William David 1
WOOLWORTH, Charles Sumner 2
WOOLWORTH, Frank W. 1
WOOLWORTH, James Mills 1
WOOMER, Ephraim Milton H
WOON, Basil (Dillon) 6
WOOSLEY, John Brooks 3
WOOSLEY, William Bryant 6
WOOSTER, Carl Gould 8
WOOSTER, Charles Whiting H
WOOSTER, David H
WOOSTER, Harvey Alden 7
WOOSTER, Lorraine Elizabeth 5
WOOSTER, Lyman Child 1
WOOSTER, Lyman Dwight 7
WOOSTER, Roy Donald 9
WOOTAN, James Blythe 1
WOOTAN, James K. 5
WOOTEN, Benjamin Allen 2
WOOTEN, Benjamin Harrison 5
WOOTEN, Horace Oliver 2

WOOTEN, June Price 3
WOOTEN, Ralph H. 5
WOOTEN, William Preston 3
WOOTON, Paul 4
WOOTTON, Bailey Peyton 2
WOOTTON, Richens Lacy H
WORCESTER, Alfred 3
WORCESTER, Charles Henry 3
WORCESTER, David 2
WORCESTER, Dean Amory 9
WORCESTER, Dean Conant 1
WORCESTER, Edward Strong 1
WORCESTER, Edwin Dean 1
WORCESTER, Elwood 1
WORCESTER, Franklin 1
WORCESTER, Harry Augustus 1
WORCESTER, Henry E. 5
WORCESTER, Joseph Emerson H
WORCESTER, Joseph Ruggles 2
WORCESTER, Noah H
WORCESTER, P(hilip) G(eorge) 5
WORCESTER, Samuel Austin 1
WORCESTER, Samuel H
WORCESTER, Samuel Thomas H
WORCESTER, Thomas H
WORCESTER, William Loring 1
WORCESTER, Willis George 5
WORD, Thomas Jefferson H
WORDEN, Beverly Lyon 1
WORDEN, Charles Beatty 5
WORDEN, Charles Howard 1
WORDEN, Edward Chauncey I. 1
WORDEN, J. Perry 2
WORDEN, James Avery 1
WORDEN, John Lorimer H
WORDEN, Ruth 7
WORDIN, Nathaniel Eugene 1
WORK, Edgar Whitaker 1
WORK, Harold Knowlton 7
WORK, Henry Clay H
WORK, Hubert 2
WORK, James 4
WORK, James Aiken 4
WORK, Jeremiah Boston 1
WORK, Milton C. 1
WORK, Monroe Nathan 2
WORK, Richard Nicholas 8
WORK, William Roth 2
WORKING, Daniel Webster 2
WORKMAN, Fanny Bullock 1
WORKMAN, James Mims 4
WORKMAN, Robert Dubois 7
WORKMAN, W. Hunter 4
WORKMAN, William Douglas, Jr. 10
WORKS, George A. 3
WORKS, John Downey 1
WORLEY, Clair L. 4
WORLEY, Francis Eugene 6
WORLEY, Henry William 1
WORLEY, James F(rancis) 7
WORLEY, John Stephen 3
WORMAN, Ben James 5
WORMAN, James Henry 1
WORMAN, Ludwig H
WORMELEY, Katharine Prescott 1
WORMLEY, James 1
WORMLEY, Theodore George H
WORMSER, I. Maurice 3
WORMSER, Leo F. 1
WORMSER, René Albert 8
WORMWOOD, Kenneth Mendum 1
WORNALL, Kearney 9
WORNER, Jno 3
WORNHAM, Thomas Andrews 8
WORRALL, Ambrose Alexander 5
WORRALL, David Elbridge 2
WORRALL, Joseph Howard 4
WORRELL, William Hoyt 3
WORRILOW, George Melville 6
WORRILOW, William Henry 6